MANAGERIAL FINANCE

Lawrence J. Gitman, *Wright State University*
Michael D. Joehnk, *Arizona State University*
George E. Pinches, *The University of Kansas*

WITH MULTINATIONAL DIMENSIONS SECTIONS
Prepared by ARTHUR I. STONEHILL, *Oregon State University*

1817

HARPER & ROW, PUBLISHERS, New York

Cambridge, Philadelphia, San Francisco,
London, Mexico City, São Paulo, Singapore, Sydney

The piece of art on the cover of this book, and reproduced here, was designed by Lloyd Atkins for Steuben Glass. Entitled *Tetron*, it consists of radiating lines engraved on one surface multiplied by reflection throughout the crystal. The sculpture was chosen because the radiating lines suggest the varied elements involved in making financial decisions, and the structure symbolizes the precise nature of the finance discipline.

Sponsoring Editor: John Greenman/
   David Forgione
Project Editor: Nora Helfgott
Text Design: Helen Iranyi
Cover Illustration: Lloyd Atkins for
   Steuben Glass; Courtesy,
   Steuben Glass

Text Art: Fineline Illustrations, Inc.
Production Manager: Jeanie Berke
Compositor: Black Dot, Inc.
Printer and Binder:
   R. R. Donnelley & Sons Company

Managerial Finance

Copyright © 1985 by Lawrence J. Gitman, Michael D. Joehnk, and George E. Pinches

Library of Congress Cataloging in Publication Data

Gitman, Lawrence J.
   Managerial finance.

   Includes bibliographies and index.
   1. Business enterprises—Finance. 2. Corporations—Finance. 3. International business enterprises—Finance. I. Joehnk, Michael D. II. Pinches, George E. III. Title.
HG4026.G62 1985   658.1'5   84-15647
ISBN 0-06-042336-6

84 85 86 87 9 8 7 6 5 4 3 2 1

MANAGERIAL
FINANCE

To Our Families

CONTENTS

PREFACE

Managerial finance is a fundamental business activity that is interesting and rewarding both to study and practice. In recent years, important and swift changes have taken place in its theories, applications, and decision-making environment that yield new challenges and opportunities for financial managers. The financial literature continues to grow rapidly; existing concepts are being questioned and refined, and new tools and techniques are emerging. New technologies and relaxed regulation are changing the institutional setting. Economic factors are continuing to affect interest rates and inflation, and modifications of the tax laws are occurring with great frequency. Our objective in writing this text was to capture a sense of the dynamic nature of managerial finance and to convey financial theories, practices, tools, and techniques in an interesting and pedagogically modern fashion.

Managerial Finance was developed over the past five years according to a carefully designed plan. Surveys of professors teaching the subject at the MBA level and in advanced undergraduate courses were conducted, and detailed text outlines based on survey findings were prepared and reviewed. Eventually, a basic structure that would accommodate logical and pedagogically effective coverage of both traditional and emerging issues in financial theory and practice was established, and chapters were written. Several drafts of the manuscript were reviewed by finance instructors and practitioners, and necessary revisions were made. In addition, the text was class-tested at three universities, and more refinements were undertaken in response to users' feedback. Simply stated, this text has been created with the help of a great many people to assure the currency and accuracy of its financial theory and to provide material that will be highly *teachable*.

Managerial Finance is specifically designed for use in the core MBA finance course. Its balanced approach to financial theory and practice may also be used in second-level undergraduate managerial finance courses, in case courses, in management-development programs, and in executive study courses. The text uses a *decision-making approach* throughout to shape up-to-date factual and theoretical material into accurate and easily comprehensible form. Examples are used liberally to demonstrate theories and concepts in action.

ORGANIZATION

The text's organization conceptually links the decisions of the financial manager with the firm's value as it is determined in the financial market place. That is, we employ a valuation approach that constantly stresses risk, return, and the consequences of actions by financial managers on the value of the firm. This approach allows us to focus consistently on achievement of the financial manager's goal of owner wealth maximization. Each major decision area is presented both in terms of risk and return factors *and* their potential impact on the owner's wealth as reflected by share value.

Managerial Finance is divided into seven parts:

- Part One   The Financial Environment
- Part Two   Financial Analysis and Planning
- Part Three   Fundamental Valuation Concepts
- Part Four   Working Capital Management
- Part Five   Long-Term Asset Acquisition, Management, and Abandonment
- Part Six   Financial Structure Decisions
- Part Seven   Sources of Long-Term Financing

This part structure was adopted to group related topics together and, more importantly, to offer maximum flexibility in the ordering of parts or chapters to meet individual teaching needs and preferences. The book has 23 chapters. In addition, 14 chapter appendixes provide further detail on particular topics such as "Regression Analysis" (4A), "Capital Rationing: The Multiperiod Case" (13A), and "Hedging Financial Strategies with Interest Rate Futures" (21A).

In organizing each chapter, we have adhered to a managerial decision-making perspective. We do not merely describe a concept such as capital budgeting or financial leverage, we relate it to the financial manager's overall goal of owner wealth maximization. Once a particular concept has been explained, its applications are explored so that the reader truly senses the decision-making considerations and consequences of each financial action. New terms are always defined on first use, and a comprehensive glossary at the back of the text makes terms and definitions accessible in another way.

CONTENT FEATURES

An important feature of this text is its coverage of multinational aspects of finance. Rather than segregating international finance materials in a chapter or two at the end of the book, as has been customary in this field, we invited a well-known international finance expert, Arthur I. Stonehill of Oregon State University, to develop multinational materials that could be fully integrated with domestic discussions in appropriate chapters, in line with A.A.C.S.B. recommendations. As a result, readers will understand the multinational ramifications of a finance topic right after examining its domestic dimensions.

Other notable features of *Managerial Finance* are:

1. Complete and up-to-date treatment in Chapter 2 of the changes brought about by the Economic Recovery Tax Act of 1981, the Tax Equity and Fiscal Responsibility Act of 1982, and the Tax Reform Act of 1984. The accelerated cost recovery system (ACRS) of asset depreciation is clearly explained here and used throughout the text. In addition, recent changes in the investment tax credit (ITC) are discussed, and the most straightforward option is used thereafter.

2. Chapters 3 and 4 offer an extended treatment of financial analysis and forecasting that provides a firm foundation for anyone who has to analyze a firm and/or develop financial forecasts.

3. The key concepts of time value, risk and return, and valuation are presented early so that they may be used throughout the text. Chapter 6, "Risk and Return," is augmented with an extensive appendix that develops utility theory, portfolio theory, and the capital asset pricing model (CAPM) in greater detail.

4. Part Four, a strong section on working capital management, provides balance between short-term and long-term financial management.

5. A separate appendix (9A) on the mathematics of the money market develops important mathematical properties in detail.

6. Part Five, the long-term asset section on capital budgeting, presents the first integrated treatment of all major long-term acquisition and abandonment decisions, including mergers and acquisitions, as well as failure and liquidation.

7. An extended treatment of risk in capital budgeting (Chapter 14) delineates a practical way to effectively incorporate risk into the decision process. Appendix 14B, "Risk Analysis with PI and IRR Techniques," carries this treatment even further by illustrating how risk may be dealt with when employing the profitability index or internal rate of return instead of the net present value.

8. Chapter 15, "Evaluation of External Growth: Mergers and Acquisitions," and Chapter 16, "Abandonment, Divestiture, and Failure," are placed in the long-term asset section, since they are directly linked, both conceptually and practically, to the rest of the firm's capital budgeting process. Both chapters use a cash-flow decision-making orientation based on valuation, as opposed to the legalistic/descriptive approach still found in many texts.

9. The thorough, integrated cost of capital chapter (Chapter 17) is

supplemented by Appendix 17A, which illustrates how to find the cost of term loans, convertible securities, and leases.

10. A balanced approach to capital structure decisions, stressing both theory and practice, is included in Chapter 18, and capital structure theory is developed in detail in Appendix 18A.

11. The treatment of long-term debt financing in Chapter 21 provides the most complete and detailed coverage of the topic available. This is further extended by Appendix 21A, which describes how financial managers can hedge with interest rate futures.

12. The coverage of leasing in Chapter 22 is supported by Appendix 22A, which describes procedures for making simultaneous capital budgeting-lease evaluation decisions.

13. Appendix 23A, following Chapter 23 on convertibles, warrants, and options, describes and discusses the option pricing model.

PEDAGOGICAL FEATURES

Managerial Finance includes a number of real-world examples that illustrate concepts and assist in providing a balance between theory and practice. A detailed summary appears at the end of each chapter to assist readers in reviewing the material.

Questions and Problems

We are strong believers in the use of probing questions and many practice problems when teaching managerial finance. Therefore numerous questions and problems at the ends of chapters enable students to test their understanding of the chapters' coverage. More than one problem is provided for each major concept to assure multiple self-testing opportunities and provide a wide variety of assignable materials. As an instructional convenience, each problem begins with a brief title that identifies the concept that the problem is meant to test. Answers to selected end-of-chapter problems appear in Appendix B; these check figures help students evaluate their progress in preparing detailed problem solutions.

Support Items

A complete set of financial tables for rates between 1 and 50 percent is included in Appendix A. In addition, there is a normal distribution table, a table for the simplified use of ACRS present-value interest factors, and a table of the ACRS normal recovery year percentages. Also included are present-value tables on a removable, laminated card for use in working problems or taking tests.

SUPPLEMENTAL MATERIALS

Several ancillary items supplement this text to help facilitate the teaching-learning process.

Instructor's Manual

A comprehensive instructor's manual prepared by the authors, with additional material by Dennis T. Officer of Arizona State University, includes detailed solutions to all questions and problems in the text and offers chapter overviews and lecture notes.

Study Guide A study guide to accompany *Managerial Finance* by Eugene F. Drzycimski of the University of Wisconsin, Oshkosh, contains reviews of the major concepts and models in each chapter; four-to-six additional problems per chapter, with solutions shown; and a wealth of multiple-choice questions and answers for self-testing.

Test Bank An extensive test bank containing about 100 essay questions with representative answers, 100 additional problems with representative solutions, and over 500 multiple-choice questions with answers has been developed by Dennis T. Officer of Arizona State University and is available to adopters.

Transparency Masters A pack of about 100 transparency masters of figures, tables, and data from the text is also available to adopters.

ACKNOWLEDGMENTS

Numerous people have made significant contributions to *Managerial Finance*. Arthur I. Stonehill (Oregon State University) created the "multinational dimension" sections that so effectively address important international concerns of managerial finance and extend chapter discussions of domestic issues. Eugene F. Drzycimski (University of Wisconsin, Oshkosh) was a detailed reviewer of the manuscript and wrote an outstanding study guide to accompany the text; we are especially grateful for his help. Our special thanks also go to Dennis T. Officer (Arizona State University) for his contributions to the *Instructor's Manual* and *Test Bank* and to Laura I. Hoisington, Hyong J. Lee (Texas Tech University), and Michael T. York for their extensive work with the authors on the solutions to text questions and problems included in the *Instructor's Manual*.

While writing the text we received very useful reviews, suggested inclusions, or suggested revisions from a number of people. We would particularly like to thank:

- Peter W. Bacon, Wright State University
- Ernest Bloch, New York University
- John A. Boquist, Indiana University
- Richard C. Burgess, University of Tulsa
- Gary G. Chandler, Georgia State University
- Peter A. DeVito, Bell Laboratories
- Frank Fabozzi, Fordham University
- H. Stephen Grace, Century Corporation
- Ronald E. Hutchins, Eastern Michigan University
- Surendra Mansinghka, San Francisco State University

- Dileep Mehta, Georgia State University
- Roger A. Morin, Georgia State University
- Garnet Olive, Northern Illinois University
- John Percival, University of Pennsylvania
- William L. Sartoris, Indiana University
- Michael E. Solt, University of Cincinnati
- Roger D. Stover, Iowa State University
- Gary L. Trennepohl, University of Missouri, Columbia
- Pieter A. Vandenberg, San Diego State University

Also, numerous comments from our students helped us to clarify text discussions and problems; we greatly appreciate their help and encouragement. We are also grateful to the individuals who typed and retyped parts of the text and to Tammy Johns for her work on the *Instructor's Manual* and *Test Bank*. The editorial, development, and marketing staffs at Harper & Row, particularly John Greenman, Nora Helfgott, Lauren Bahr, and Jim Brennan, deserve special thanks for their professional expertise, creativity, enthusiasm, and continuing commitment to the text.

Finally, our families have played a most important part in patiently providing the support and understanding needed during the development of this book. To them we will be forever grateful.

Our goal in developing *Managerial Finance* has been to create a teachable, up-to-date, balanced approach to the subject that meets the challenges of the remainder of the 1980s. Your input remains important to us. We invite you to contact us directly with any comments, suggestions, or criticisms you have; we welcome opportunities to make further improvements in the text and its adjuncts.

Lawrence J. Gitman
Michael D. Joehnk
George E. Pinches

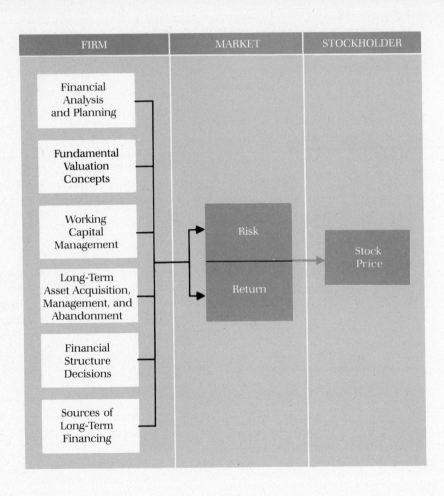

PART ONE

THE FINANCIAL ENVIRONMENT

The two chapters in this part of the text present an overview of managerial finance and describe the economic and operating environment in which a firm makes decisions. The first chapter discusses the evolution of managerial finance, describes financial viewpoints and objectives as well as the finance function, and presents an overview of the text. The second chapter describes the environment in which most firms operate: the financial system, international dimensions of money and capital markets, key aspects of the firm's accounting environment, basic features of the corporate tax structure, and the impact of inflation on corporate profits. Together, the two chapters provide the background for the study of the theory and practice of managerial finance.

1

An Overview of Managerial Finance

The study of managerial finance centers on understanding the theories and procedures for managing the firm in a fashion that will best benefit its owners. Today, inflation/disinflation, volatile interest rates, an unpredictable economy, and increased competition from abroad have increased the complexities as well as the responsibilities of the managerial finance function. At the same time, many new theories and research findings—providing both normative (how the firm ought to behave) and positive (how the firm does behave) information—have been reported in the financial literature. Knowledge of all these developments and their impact is necessary for the effective management and financial vitality of the modern business firm. This book provides an up-to-date look at the key theories and techniques of managerial finance; we begin with a discussion of the evolution of managerial finance. This discussion will be followed by a review of financial objectives and the multinational dimensions of finance, a brief examination of the finance function, and finally, an overview of the text.

The Evolution of Managerial Finance

The field of managerial finance as we know it today began in the early 1900s. The three key phases in its evolution were the descriptive-legalistic period, the internal decision-making period, and the investments-managerial finance period.[1]

Descriptive-Legalistic Period (1900–1950)

Managerial finance as a separate business function emerged in the early 1900s with emphasis on legal matters, such as the formation of firms, consolidations, securities, and the institutional aspects of the financial

---

[1]For an in-depth discussion of the evolution of managerial finance, see Ezra Solomon, "What Should We Teach in a Course in Business Finance?" *Journal of Finance* 21 (May 1966), pp. 411–415; and J. Fred Weston, *The Scope and Methodology of Finance* (Englewood Cliffs, N.J.: Prentice-Hall, 1966), chap. 2.

marketplace. Financial markets were just developing, and detailed accounting data and financial records were not available. The lack of reliable financial information, along with stock trading by insiders and manipulators, resulted in an extreme reluctance by many investors to purchase securities. Through the 1920s, managerial finance focused primarily on descriptive and legalistic issues concerned with expansion. The Depression of the 1930s caused attention to shift toward the preservation of liquidity as well as toward issues of bankruptcy, liquidation, and reorganization procedures. Abuses of debt—particularly by public utilities—were brought to light when many companies collapsed. Such failures, along with the associated losses suffered by many investors, led to passage of the Federal Securities Act of 1933 and the Securities Exchange Act of 1934. These laws helped stop abuses by controlling the amount and form of disclosure of financial data by publicly held firms and by requiring the monthly reporting of security transactions by corporate "insiders." Although the field of managerial finance remained largely descriptive and legalistic through the 1940s, the emphasis had shifted from expansion to survival.[2]

Internal Decision-Making Period (1950–1964)

Things began to change again in the early 1950s as capital budgeting—techniques for making fixed-asset investment decisions—began to receive substantial attention. A book by Joel Dean called *Capital Budgeting*, published in 1951, was influential in shifting the focus of managerial finance to internal decision making.[3] In 1958, a controversial article concerned with the firm's cost and mix of financing appeared. It was written by Franco Modigliani and Merton H. Miller,[4] and was the forerunner to a wealth of scholarly work related to capital budgeting, cost of capital, and financial structure. In fact, a recent survey[5] of a large sample of finance professors ranked Modigliani and Miller's 1958 article as the most significant contribution to the finance literature.

Investments-Managerial Finance Period (1964–Present)

At about the same time Dean's book was published, Harry Markowitz (1952) introduced the basic concepts of portfolio theory.[6] Markowitz's work was followed by that of William F. Sharpe (1964) and John Lintner (1965), among others. Their efforts resulted in an asset pricing theory

---

[2]The culmination of this trend is presented in the classic work of Arthur Stone Dewing, *Financial Policy of Corporations*, 5th ed., vols. 1 and 2 (New York: Ronald Press, 1953).

[3]Joel Dean, *Capital Budgeting* (New York: Columbia University Press, 1951).

[4]Franco Modigliani and Merton H. Miller, "The Cost of Capital, Corporation Finance, and the Theory of Investment," *American Economic Review* 48 (June 1958), pp. 261–297.

[5]See Philip L. Cooley and J. Louis Heck, "Significant Contributions to Finance Literature," *Financial Management*, Tenth Anniversary Issue (1981), pp. 23–33.

[6]Harry M. Markowitz, "Portfolio Selection," *Journal of Finance* 7 (March 1952), pp. 77–91; and Markowitz, *Portfolio Selection: Efficient Diversification of Investments* (New Haven, Conn.: Yale University Press, 1959).

that provided the link between expected risk and expected return.[7] Along with these developments came considerable theoretical and empirical research on the functioning of the financial marketplace. In conjunction with asset pricing theory, the concept of an efficient market for securities was developed. As a result of the link between risk and return and the pricing of assets in financial markets, a merger between what had been viewed as somewhat independent areas of finance— investments and managerial finance—has been taking place. Refinements in the links among risk, return, and value were stimulated by the work of Fischer Black and Myron Scholes[8] in the early 1970s (the option pricing model) and of Stephen A. Ross[9] in 1976 (the arbitrage pricing theory). These ideas provided a basis for valuing a variety of financial claims, thereby strengthening the links between the firm and the marketplace.

Today, financial decision making centers on the evaluation of risk and return and its expected impact on the value of the firm as reflected in the financial marketplace. Clearly, managerial finance is no longer primarily a descriptive discipline; instead, it relies heavily on economic theories as well as a variety of mathematical and statistical techniques.

Financial Objectives of the Firm

The objective of the firm, and therefore of the financial manager, is to provide maximum benefits for the owners. As we will see in subsequent chapters, operationally this objective involves *maximizing owners' wealth through share-price maximization*. Because confusion often surrounds this goal, it is important to establish a clear perspective on issues such as accruals versus cash flow, profit versus wealth maximization, and managers versus owners.

Accruals Versus Cash Flow

Accountants typically assemble data for the firm on an accrual basis, but the financial manager tends to be concerned primarily with cash flows. Under the *accrual system*, revenues and expenses are recognized when transactions involving the exchange of goods and services occur; revenues are recognized at the point of sale and expenses are recognized when incurred, regardless of whether any cash actually changes hands. With a *cash flow system*, primary attention is given to the timing of the actual receipt of revenues and the actual payment of expenses. The

[7]William F. Sharpe, "Capital Asset Prices: A Theory of Market Equilibrium Under Conditions of Risk," *Journal of Finance* 19 (September 1964), pp. 425–442; and John Lintner, "Security Prices, Risk, and Maximal Gains from Diversification," *Journal of Finance* 20 (December 1965), pp. 587–616.

[8]Fischer Black and Myron Scholes, "The Pricing of Options and Corporate Liabilities," *Journal of Political Economy* 81 (May–June 1973), pp. 637–654.

[9]Stephen A. Ross, "The Arbitrage Theory of Capital Asset Pricing," *Journal of Economic Theory* (December 1976), pp. 341–360.

Accrual Results		Cash Flow Results	
Sales revenue	$1,000,000	Cash receipts	$400,000
− Total expenses	900,000	− Cash disbursements	900,000
Profit	$ 100,000	Net cash flow	($500,000)

financial manager must understand accrual concepts, since they are utilized in the preparation of basic financial statements, but must give greater attention to cash flows.

Adequate cash flows are required to meet the firm's obligations, to acquire current and fixed assets, and for distribution of dividends to owners. In spite of having an acceptable level of profit, a firm that is not properly managed can fail as a result of having inadequate cash flow. This can be illustrated by comparing the accrual and cash flow outcomes of Aksen Enterprises for the year just ended. During the year, the firm sold $1 million worth of merchandise, which it had purchased at a total cost of $900,000. Aksen had paid in full for the merchandise, but had collected only $400,000 of the $1 million in sales; the other $600,000 remained outstanding as accounts receivable. The accrual and cash flow views of the firm are summarized in Table 1.1. It should be clear that although the firm earned a profit of $100,000 during the year, it had a net cash *outflow* of $500,000. Without other sources of cash inflow to meet this shortage, the firm would fail.

Cash flow is the lifeblood of the firm; accrual-based accounting in contrast, does not fully describe this important financial dimension. As such, the financial manager must routinely look beyond financial statements. *By concentrating on cash flow, the financial manager should be able to maintain solvency while achieving the long-run objective of wealth maximization.*

Profit Versus Wealth Maximization

The profitability of the firm is not necessarily maximized as a result of the same decisions that would maximize the wealth of owners, as measured by the stock price. The objective of the financial manager must be to maximize benefit to the firm's owners—an objective that translates into the maximization of wealth, rather than profit. The key differences between wealth and profit maximization concern the time horizon, the timing of returns, the distribution of returns, and risk. Profits in this case should be evaluated on a *per share basis,* since aggregate profits can be increased by simply selling more shares and using the proceeds to increase total profits.

Time Horizon. Profit maximization tends to be a short-run approach, whereas wealth maximization considers the long run. For example, a firm wishing to maximize profits could purchase inexpensive, low-quality machinery; perform maintenance on the machinery only when absolutely necessary; use low-grade raw materials; and use unskilled labor, while making a strong sales effort to market its products at a price that yields a high profit per unit. This strategy would result in high profits in the current year, but in subsequent years profits would decline due to (1) the realization by purchasers that the product is of low quality, and/or (2) the higher cost associated with frequent machine replacement. Another example of the short-run nature of profit maximization centers on research and development expenditures. Because research and development outlays must be treated as an expense in the year they are incurred, firms making sizable R & D outlays will have lower profits. But in the long run the firm should be better off, since current R & D outlays would be expected to result in the successful development and sale of new products that will increase profits. The use of wealth-maximization criteria considers—as will be demonstrated in Chapter 7—the returns expected over the long run, which for simplicity is typically viewed as an infinite time horizon.

Timing of Returns. Profit maximization, in addition to being a short-run strategy, generally ignores the timing of returns. Wealth maximization gives explicit consideration to their timing. For example, assume a firm is confronted with two alternative investments, A and B. Alternative A will return $0 in years 1 through 4 and at the end of the fifth year returns $11; alternative B is expected to return $2 at the end of each of the next 5 years. Alternative A therefore returns $11 over the 5 years, and alternative B returns $10 (5 years × $2 per year). The profit maximizer would prefer alternative A, since it provides higher total returns; the wealth maximizer, recognizing that money has a time value, would prefer alternative B, since 80 percent of its returns occur prior to the end of year 5. If we assume the firm can earn 10 percent annual interest on its investments, using certain financial calculations, discussed in detail in Chapter 5, the value of alternative B's returns measured today ($7.58) would exceed that of alternative A ($6.83).[10] Because earnings opportunities always exist (even a short-term government security, such as a Treasury bill, will at times earn in excess of 10 percent annual interest), the timing of returns must be considered. Wealth maximization gives explicit consideration to the timing of returns, and is therefore preferred over the use of a strict profit maximization approach.

---

[10]The present values of alternatives A and B were found using the appropriate present-value interest factors as follows:

Alternative	Return (1)	Present-Value Interest Factor (2)	Present Value (1) × (2) (3)
A	$11.00	$PVIF_{10\%, 5\,yr} = .621$	$6.83
B	$ 2.00	$PVIFA_{10\%, 5\,yr} = 3.791$	$7.58

A complete discussion of these techniques is presented in Chapter 5.

Distribution of Returns.   The profit-maximization goal ignores the fact that owners may wish to receive a portion of earnings in the form of periodic dividends. In the absence of any preference by owners for dividends, the firm could maximize profits from period to period by retaining all earnings and using them to acquire assets that would boost future returns. The wealth-maximization process considers expected dividends, which are actual cash flows, and not accrual-based profits, that are expected to be eventually distributed to owners. Many owners value the receipt of a regular dividend regardless of its size. This "clientele effect" is often used to explain the impact of dividend policy on the market value of stock. Many experts believe that by giving stockholders the dividends they expect, the stock price will be favorably affected.[11] While the level of earnings does affect the level of dividends, the key is the dividend, since it represents the cash flow to the owner. As will be shown in Chapter 7, expected dividend cash flows, coupled with risk, are the key determinants of share value—the owner's wealth in the firm.

Risk.   Finally, profit maximization does not consider risk, whereas the wealth-maximization approach gives risk explicit consideration. Risk and return are related; the higher the risk, the higher should be the expected return, and vice versa. This tradeoff between risk and return is a fundamental premise underlying nearly all aspects of modern financial theory. The importance of risk considerations can be illustrated with a simple example. Imagine that a firm can invest in either of two alternatives, C and D. Alternative C will generate returns of $3 per year at the end of each of the next 4 years, while alternative D will yield $3.10 at the end of each of the next 4 years. Ignoring any differences in risk and assuming the firm can earn 10 percent per year on its investments, the value of alternatives C and D measured today would be $9.51 and $9.83, respectively.[12] It is not surprising that alternative D would be preferred in the absence of any difference in risk because it has a higher present value. If, however, alternative D is assumed to be more risky than alternative C, then it may no longer be preferred. Assume that because of

---

[11]A school of thought exists which suggests that the payment of cash dividends has no effect on the stock price. A discussion of this and other arguments surrounding dividend policy is included in Chapter 19.

[12]These values were found using present-value techniques (described in Chapter 5) as follows:

Alternative	Return (1)	Present-Value Interest Factor (2)	Present Value (1) × (2) (3)
C	$3.00	$PVIFA_{10\%,\,4\,yr} = 3.170$	$9.51
D	$3.10	$PVIFA_{10\%,\,4\,yr} = 3.170$	$9.83

its higher risk, the firm must be compensated with a 14 percent return on alternative D, while the 10 percent return is adequate compensation for the lower-risk alternative C. Using 14 percent to recalculate the present value of alternative D yields $9.03.[13] By considering the need to earn a higher return for greater risk, alternative C is now preferred, since it has a higher present value ($9.51 for C versus $9.03 for D). Attention to risk is an important part of financial decision making. It is the combination of risk and return that determines share value and therefore owners' wealth. Because wealth maximization considers both risk and return while profit maximization is a return-oriented approach, wealth maximization is preferred.

Managers Versus Owners

Since shareholders may exert little or no control in the modern corporation, it is not always clear that management operates in a fashion consistent with owner wealth maximization. Some people feel that when control of the company is separate from ownership, management may not always act in the best interests of shareholders.[14] Managers might be primarily concerned with their own welfare (job security and remuneration), rather than that of the owners. Such managers are sometimes felt to be "satisfiers" rather than "maximizers," since they concern themselves with the achievement of acceptable results instead of attempting to maximize the wealth of the owners.[15] The primary goal of management in this environment may be survival. As a result, a manager may be unwilling to take more than a moderate financial risk for fear of making a mistake.[16] Because they may lose their jobs while shareholders may only lose a small percentage of their wealth, managers may tend to display satisficing behavior once risk is introduced.

Managers can be viewed as agents of the owners, hired to operate the

---

[13]Repeating the calculation of the present value for alternative D illustrated in footnote 12, this time using a 14 percent present-value interest factor, yields:

Alternative	Return (1)	Present-Value Interest Factor (2)	Present Value (1) × (2) (3)
D	$3.10	$PVIFA_{14\%,\,4\,yr} = 2.914$	$9.03

[14]See, for example, Gordon Donaldson, "Financial Goals: Management vs. Stockholders," *Harvard Business Review* 41 (May–June 1963), pp. 116–129; and M. Chapman Findlay III and G. A. Whitmore, "Beyond Shareholder Wealth Maximization," *Financial Management* 3 (winter 1974), pp. 25–35.

[15]Herbert A. Simon, "Theories of Decision Making in Economics and Behavioral Science," *American Economic Review* 49 (June 1959), pp. 253–283.

[16]J. W. Elliott, "Control, Size, Growth, and Financial Performance of the Firm," *Journal of Financial and Quantitative Analysis* 7 (January 1972), pp. 1309–1320, found a high propensity in nonowner-managed firms for high levels of liquidity. This could be indicative of greater risk aversion of nonowner managers.

firm for the owners' benefit.[17] If the firm is completely owned and managed by the same person, there is no possible conflict in objectives. More often, though, management has a less than 100 percent ownership interest in the firm and is to some degree an agent of the owner. In this case the private and individual consumption of the firm's wealth by the managers will cost them only in proportion to their fraction of ownership; the remainder of the cost—the agency costs—are borne by the nonmanager owners. These *agency costs* include (1) the monitoring expenditures made by other owners to try to prevent satisficing behavior by managers, (2) any bonding assurances made by the manager as agent that he or she will not pursue self-interest at the expense of the other owners, and (3) any residual losses that cannot be eliminated through monitoring or bonding actions. Agency costs therefore result when managers' incentives differ from those of the firm as a whole; in effect, the owners' losses are the costs of the agency relationship. Since agency costs tend to reduce the overall value of the firm, stockholders should try to minimize them.

Are such agency costs large? The answer is unclear at present, but theoretically these costs are quite small in a frictionless environment where information flows freely and is costless. In a not so perfect environment, agency costs appear to be larger. However, even in practice, it appears the assumption that managers operate to maximize shareholder wealth is fairly reasonable. Evidence suggests that the goals of managers and shareholders may not deviate too widely. This may be the result of the fact that more firms are tying management compensation to the firm's performance, and research suggests this incentive motivates managers to operate in a manner reasonably consistent with stock price maximization.[18] To further assure the congruence of management and owner objectives, many firms incur additional agency costs. These costs include the cost of bonding the managers, and audit and control procedures for assessing and limiting managerial behavior to those actions that would tend to be in the best interest of owners. Unconstrained, managers may have other goals in addition to share price maximization, but much of the evidence suggests that share price maximization is the primary goal of most firms.

Share price maximization, which is consistent with owner wealth maximization, connotes to some an image of managers continually

[17]Michael C. Jensen and William H. Meckling, "Theory of the Firm: Managerial Behavior, Agency Costs and Ownership Structure," *Journal of Financial Economics* 3 (October 1976), pp. 305–360.

[18]Wilbur G. Lewellen, "Management and Ownership in the Large Firm," *Journal of Finance* 24 (May 1969), pp. 299–322; and Robert T. Masson, "Executive Motivation, Earnings, and Consequent Equity Performance," *Journal of Political Economy* 79 (November–December 1971), pp. 1278–1292. Lewellen concludes that managers appear to make decisions that are largely consistent with share price maximization. Masson found that firms whose executives' compensation was closely tied to the performance of the firm's stock tended to outperform other firms in terms of stock returns.

following each movement in the firm's stock price for signs of how it is doing or what to do next. It also seems to suggest that managers should somehow be less interested in running the firm effectively than in manipulating the firm's stock price. Neither image is correct. In fact, the maximization of share price can best be viewed as a shorthand description of a much richer qualitative process. As will become clear in later chapters, we could express much the same objective if we simply stated that the firm is interested in taking only those actions that add to its value. It is the job of the financial manager to direct the firm's activities in such a way as to provide maximum benefit to owners; the fulfillment of this objective should also reap great rewards for the manager. Of course, this goal is important even if the firm does not maximize owners' wealth, since it provides a standard of comparison that can be used to assess the cost of not pursuing such a strategy.

The Goal of the Firm

Financial decisions must be made with some objective in mind. *Throughout this book, we assume that management's primary goal is to develop and allocate resources efficiently over the long run so as to maximize the value of the firm and thereby owners' wealth.* Implementation of this goal translates into the maximization of stock prices, since at any point in time, they reflect the value of the firm. From the owners' point of view, the only action that can be taken directly to display satisfaction or dissatisfaction with the firm is to buy or sell the firm's stock.[19] When the firm's actions are believed favorable to stockholders, the stock price will rise as more shares are demanded; when unfavorable actions have occurred, a decline in share prices would be expected. Because existing and prospective owners can buy or sell shares only at the market price, the value of their ownership interest in the firm at any point in time is directly related to the share price.

The basic economic premise that individuals prefer more consumption to less and therefore prefer more wealth to less can be used to illustrate the importance of share price maximization.[20] First, let us define an individual's total wealth, W, as consisting of two components —the value of nonstock income and investments, V_{NS}, and the value of stock investments, V_S.

$$W = V_{NS} + V_S \tag{1.1}$$

---

[19]While owners are given a voice in management (via a vote on certain managerial matters), the fact that the management tends to be able to perpetuate itself makes it difficult for owners to affect corporate management. Instead the marketplace tends to act as the mechanism through which owners at their own discretion are able to respond to the actions of management.

[20]For a more detailed theoretical treatment, see, for instance, Charles W. Haley and Lawrence D. Schall, *The Theory of Financial Decisions*, 2d ed. (New York: McGraw-Hill, 1979), chap. 2; Thomas E. Copeland and J. Fred Weston, *Financial Theory and Corporate Policy*, 2d ed. (Reading, Mass.: Addison-Wesley, 1983), chap. 1; and Eugene F. Fama and Merton H. Miller, *The Theory of Finance* (New York: Holt, Rinehart and Winston, 1972), chaps. 1 and 2.

Expressing the value of stock investment, V_S, as the sum of the product of the number of shares, n_j, and price per share, P_j, of each of the m stocks held, results in Equation 1.2:

$$W = V_{NS} + \sum_{j=1}^{m} n_j P_j \tag{1.2}$$

If we hold the wealth from nonstock investments, V_{NS}, and the number of shares of each stock, n_j, constant, it can be seen from Equation 1.2 that shareholder wealth, W, would be maximized by maximizing the price of each stock, P_j. In other words, the financial manager of any firm can help each investor achieve a wealth-maximization objective by taking actions aimed at maximizing share price, P_j. Only if firms operate in this manner will individuals be able to maximize their total wealth.

MULTINATIONAL DIMENSIONS

Financial Objectives Abroad

Although maximizing shareholder wealth is in accord with both the value system and the legal concept of the firm in the United States, it is not widely accepted as the prime goal of the firm by many other societies. In Japan and nearly all European countries (with the exception of the United Kingdom), as well as most developing countries, the firm is regarded as a vehicle that should be managed to maximize benefits and minimize risk from the perspectives of *each* of the firm's interest groups, rather than shareholders alone.[21] This goal is consistent with the behavioral theory of the firm as expressed by Cyert and March, among others.[22] The behavioral theory suggests that a firm does not have a single goal per se, but that each interest group has goals. In return for providing their services, the interest groups bargain with one another over the distribution of benefits. The shareholders demand dividends and capital gains; labor demands higher wages and more job security; creditors demand adequate liquidity and protection against excessive leverage; the local community demands a clean environment; and foreign host governments demand technology transfer and joint ownership.

Anglo-American finance theory assumes that shareholder wealth maximization should be the dominant goal but that the firm must

---

[21]For a comparative study of financial goals in an international context, see Arthur Stonehill, Theo Beekhuisen, Richard Wright, Lee Remmers, Norman Toy, Antonio Parés, Alan Shapiro, Douglas Egan, and Thomas Bates, "Financial Goals and Debt Ratio Determinants: A Survey of Practice in Five Countries," *Financial Management* 4 (autumn 1975), pp. 27–41.

[22]For a discussion of the behavioral theory of the firm, see Richard Cyert and James March, *A Behavioral Theory of the Firm* (Englewood Cliffs, N.J.: Prentice-Hall, 1963).

also treat demands by other interest groups as *constraints*. A large part of what has been introduced as agency costs may actually be due to management giving in to particularly strong demands by one or more interest groups. The Anglo-American legal tradition places shareholders in the controlling position, since shareholders elect the board of directors. In many other countries, the board is composed of members elected by each interest group. For example, in West Germany, The Netherlands, Denmark, Norway, and Sweden, industrial democracy has taken root. Members of the board of directors are elected not only by shareholders, but also by the employees and government. In addition, other types of control groups, such as workers' councils, often have a veto over certain types of decisions made by the board of directors, such as shutting down a factory. Given the legal status of nonshareholder groups, it is not surprising that firms in these countries do not overtly claim that maximizing shareholder wealth is their goal.

From a purely practical standpoint, equity markets are so thin in many countries that they are not able to provide firms with new capital. Instead, the banking system, supplemented sometimes by government, provides new external capital to finance growth. Since the firm does not expect to appeal to stockholders for capital, it is not under the same pressure as a U.S. firm might be to maintain a high share price. Furthermore, a low share price does not usually result in the firm being acquired by another firm. Most of the shares are typically held for the long term by financial institutions and other firms that also enjoy business relationships with the firm.

An outstanding example of these interrelationships can be found in Japan. Many of the most successful firms in Japan belong to business groups that include a bank, a trading company, and a number of manufacturing firms. Members of the group own a significant proportion of one another's ownership shares, which they intend to hold for the long run. Holding the shares is part of the price for membership in the group. The prime benefit of belonging comes from supplying one another with goods and services. Although shares in these firms are also owned by the public, the firms are not managed with a view to maximizing share price. On the other hand, public stockholders usually receive a relatively certain dividend commensurate with the perceived risk. Needless to say, Japanese firms have very high debt ratios, since they have been unable to attract significant new equity capital. (This may be changing now, however, as the Japanese open up their equity markets to foreign investors.)

Even if shareholder wealth maximization is not the single goal, firms do attempt to maximize earnings and cash flow while minimizing wide fluctuations in these variables. This is consistent with the preferences of all interest groups. The larger and less variable the "pot," the more benefits at less risk are potentially available for each interest group. The actual distribution of benefits is determined by bargaining among the groups. If the environment is favorable, the pot will be large and relatively certain. Under these conditions, the interest groups are "satisficed" and the coalition of groups is stable. The firm survives. If the environment is unfavorable, the pot may be too small and uncertain to satisfy all groups. Under these conditions, the coalition may be unstable and one or more interest groups may fall out (a strike, loans are called, or whatever). The firm fails or is merged into another firm.

Although this text is primarily concerned with financial management under conditions where shareholder wealth maximization is an accepted norm, we should note that most of the largest U.S. firms are multinational. They have important operating subsidiaries abroad which often account for a significant share of earnings. Examples can be found in most manufacturing, extraction, and service industries, such as automobiles, oil, and banking. The prominent role of multinational operations on the nation's leading firms can be seen in Table 1.2, which depicts foreign revenue and operating profit as a percentage of total revenue and operating profit, respectively, for the 40 largest U.S. multinationals. If these multinational firms are managed exclusively for the benefit of their shareholders in the United States, they will surely encounter severe resistance from host country governments and foreign joint venture partners. They may even have problems with their own local managers, who hold different norms concerning what should be maximized and from whose viewpoint risk should be minimized. This potential conflict can be particularly acute in those cases where a U.S. firm has acquired an existing foreign firm that has previously operated in accord with local norms.

The Finance Function

The role and importance of the finance function has grown considerably during recent years primarily as a result of the need to adapt to extremely volatile economic conditions. In the past, the marketing manager would make sales projections, the engineering and production staffs would estimate the level of assets needed to meet demand, and the financial manager would estimate and arrange adequate financing to implement these plans. Today, these decisions are made in a coordinated manner, with the chief financial officer having primary responsibility for much of the process, including the planning and control activity.

TABLE 1.2
Foreign Revenue and
Operating Profit
Percentages for the 40
Largest U.S.
Multinationals

Rank	Company	Foreign Revenue as % of Total	Foreign Operating Profit as % of Total
1	Exxon	71.4%	50.8%
2	Mobil	62.0	63.8
3	Texaco	66.2	65.0
4	Standard Oil Calif	49.3	29.3
5	Phibro-Salomon	62.2	64.7
6	Ford Motor	44.6	P/D[a]
7	IBM	44.6	37.3
8	General Motors	23.9	D/P[b]
9	Gulf Oil	40.5	33.3
10	E. I. DuPont de Nemours	33.3	32.7
11	Citicorp	61.0	62.0
12	Intl Tel & Tel	44.8	71.3
13	BankAmerica	53.8	65.0
14	Chase Manhattan	61.0	70.0
15	Dow Chemical	52.2	40.2
16	General Electric	20.2	21.7
17	Sun Company	31.1	7.7
18	Standard Oil Indiana	17.1	33.8
19	Occidental Petroleum	25.4	63.0
20	Safeway Stores	24.8	52.5
21	J. P. Morgan	62.0	71.8
22	Eastman Kodak	38.7	16.2
23	Manufacturers Hanover	51.4	49.8
24	Proctor & Gamble	31.2	11.3
25	Xerox	42.9	35.6
26	Goodyear	38.4	29.4
27	Phillips Petroleum	19.4	52.3
28	Union Carbide	33.2	41.9
29	United Technologies	21.5	26.7
30	Colgate-Palmolive	58.5	56.6
31	Dart & Kraft	28.5	35.0
32	Coca-Cola	42.7	60.4
33	CPC International	65.2	64.5
34	Pan Am World Airways	70.6	15.6
35	Tenneco	17.3	19.0
36	Bankers Trust New York	55.3	50.7
37	Minn Mining & Mfg	38.3	33.7
38	R. J. Reynolds Industries	22.8	9.7
39	Johnson & Johnson	42.6	52.2
40	Chemical New York	44.0	38.7

[a]Profit over deficit.
[b]Deficit over profit.
SOURCE: "The 100 Largest U.S. Multinationals," *Forbes*, July 4, 1983, pp. 114 and 118.
Reprinted by permission of *Forbes* Magazine, © Forbes Inc., 1982.

After examining the organization of the finance function and key activities of the financial manager, attention is given to two special considerations that can significantly affect the finance function: inflation/disinflation and social responsibilities.

Organizational Aspects

The size and importance of the finance function depends on the size of the business. In small firms, the finance function is commonly performed as part of the accounting activity. Its primary concern is with credit procedures, which involve evaluating, selecting, and following up on customers to whom credit is extended. Little attention is given to investment decisions and financing matters. As the firm grows, however, the importance of the finance function expands. In time, it evolves into a separate department, an autonomous organizational unit linked directly to the company president through a vice-president of finance. The responsibilities of the finance activity would include financial analysis and planning activities, management of current and fixed assets, and management of both short-term and long-term financing, including dividend decisions.

Organizational structures vary from firm to firm, but Figure 1.1 provides a fairly typical picture of the role of finance within a large business firm. The chief financial officer, who has a title something like vice-president—finance, reports directly to the president or chief executive officer (CEO) of the firm. Reporting to the vice-president of finance are the treasurer and the controller. The treasurer normally has direct responsibility for overseeing activities related to financial planning and fundraising, the management of cash, capital expenditure decisions, credit decisions, and the management of the investment portfolio. The controller tends to concentrate on accounting activities related to taxes, data processing, and cost and financial accounting. The emphasis in this text will center on the activities of the treasurer or financial manager. Because manufacturing and marketing activities are closely related to the finance function, there has been a trend toward greater interaction between financial decision makers and their counterparts in these areas of the firm.

Most firms have a finance committee made up of top executives from different functional areas and selected members of the board of directors. The purpose of the committee is to analyze and make recommendations to the board on major capital expenditure and financing proposals.

Key Activities of the Financial Manager

In attempting to maximize share price, the financial manager must undertake a variety of activities. Two key areas are the investment and financing decisions. As part of these activities, the financial manager must continuously monitor and make plans consistent with the achievement of the firm's short- and long-run objectives. This involves the use of

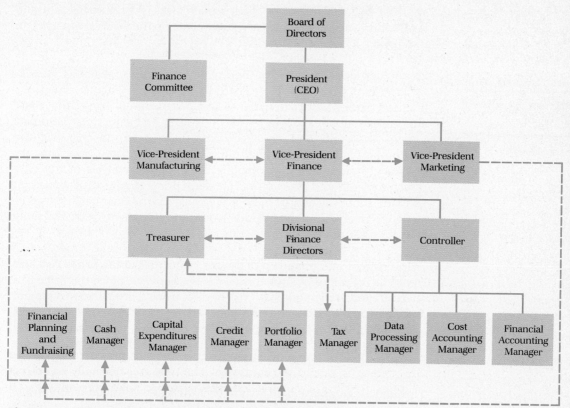

Figure 1.1   The Finance Function in a Typical Business Firm.

ratios and various other measures to assess the firm's financial condition and operating results; financial management is also concerned with the development of plans and budgets for funding and controlling the firm's expenditures, both in the short and the long run. Proper implementation of the financial analysis and planning activities is an important prerequisite to carrying out the two primary financial decisions of the firm—investment and financing—effectively.

Investment Decisions.   The financial manager, often with approval of the board, must make investment decisions that determine the portfolio —both mix and type—of assets held by the firm. The mix refers to the number of dollars of current versus fixed assets. Once the desired mix has been established, the financial manager must determine and attempt to maintain optimal levels of each type of current asset. The manager must also recommend which are the best fixed assets to acquire and know when existing fixed assets are economically obsolete and need to be replaced or modified. The decision process is a complex one; the financial manager must isolate risk and return factors and assess them in light of their potential impact on the firm's share price in the market.

Financing Decisions.   The second major area of responsibility is making decisions that affect the right side of the firm's balance sheet—its financial structure. Two major areas are involved. First, the most appropriate mix of short-term and long-term financing must be determined. A second and equally important concern is choosing the appropriate form of financing. Although some of these decisions are dictated by necessity, most require an in-depth analysis of the risk-return tradeoffs and their impact on share price. Finally, decisions must be made about dividends; these are also viewed as financing decisions, since the retention of such funds would provide a source of internally generated financing.

Investment and financing decisions in turn affect the firm's risk and return as perceived by investors in the marketplace. Since the price of a share of stock is dependent on risk and return, it follows that investment and financing decisions directly affect share price. By assessing the risk and return impact of these decisions on share price, the financial manager should be able to make decisions consistent with the firm's overall goal.

The Impact of Inflation/ Disinflation on Financial Decisions   Throughout the 1970s and in the early 1980s, worldwide *inflation* has become the norm; in some years, such as 1974, 1979, 1980, and 1981, inflation reached the double-digit levels in the United States. These high rates of inflation as well as *disinflation*—a slowing in the rate of inflation as experienced in 1983—can cause problems not only for consumers, but for business firms as well. The high rates of inflation and disinflation experienced in recent years have made it more difficult for financial managers to achieve the goal of owner wealth maximization. Figure 1.2 shows the annual percentage change in the consumer price index and the annual percentage change in the Standard & Poor's 500 Stock Composite Index for year-end 1971 through 1983. It appears that during periods of high inflation, a significant negative effect on stock prices results.[23] Clearly, the financial manager must learn to cope with inflation and disinflation in order to achieve the owners' objectives.

The planning problems created by inflation are also plentiful. Key among them is the tendency of the firm's operating, investment, and financing costs to rise with inflation. The cost of raw materials, labor,

---

[23]It is interesting to note that these data indicate that during the period year-end 1971–1983 common stock outperformed inflation in only 5 of 13 years. Clearly, common stock does not appear to have provided the hedge against inflation that many people often expect.

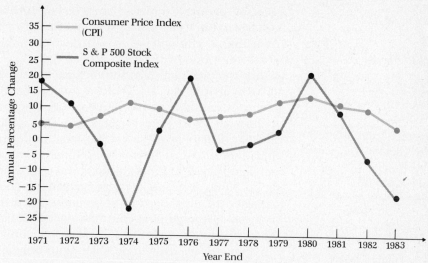

Figure 1.2   Annual Percentage Changes in the CPI and S & P's 500 Stock Composite Index (Year-end 1971–1983).
Source: Year-end data used to calculate the annual percentage changes were drawn from the *Federal Reserve Bulletin,* selected issues.

capital equipment, and the financing—debt or equity—used to acquire them tend to rise with inflation. By considering the impact of expected inflation on these factors, managers can attempt to adjust prices and time outlays and fundraising actions to allow the firm to achieve its objectives. Anticipated inflation also affects the choice of investments and financing. During periods of very high inflation firms are less likely to make capital expenditures because of high financing costs; instead, they tend to hold more short-term assets. They also use more short-term financing unless they feel that the high rate of inflation will continue for a number of years. In addition to these strictly financial considerations, inflation may distort profits due to its effect on inventory and the rising replacement cost of assets that are being depreciated on a strictly historical basis. On the other hand, disinflation also introduces planning problems requiring special attention by the manager, by slowing the rate of increase in the firm's operating, investment, and financing costs. Inflation and disinflation will be further discussed as they relate to each of the financial manager's activities presented throughout this text.

The Social Responsibility of Financial Managers

Much of the concern about shareholder wealth maximization arises because of the question of social responsibility. That is, should firms operate solely in the stockholders' interests, or should they also respond to concerns related to the welfare of society at large? It should be obvious that if two firms are equally profitable, but one devotes more of its profits to socially beneficial projects, the long-run profits of the two firms will probably diverge. Unless the socially beneficial projects result in increased sales for the socially oriented firm, it will have lower profits in the future. This will occur because the firm has less funds to reinvest in the business. An investor considering these two firms is likely to choose the profit-oriented rather than the socially oriented firm. After all, why should the stockholders of one firm subsidize society to a greater extent than the stockholders of other firms?

Although most firms engage in some socially oriented projects, virtually all of them are somewhat constrained in terms of the amount of funds they invest. At annual stockholder meetings, many firms in recent years have faced probing questions and even formal resolutions attempting to limit their dollar commitment to social projects. Typically, management's response to these questions or resolutions has been to justify social programs as contributing to long-run wealth maximization. The cost-increasing nature of most socially oriented programs suggests why they are typically undertaken with only a limited commitment of funds, or undertaken only after they have been mandated. Thus, fair hiring practices, product safety, pollution control, proper working conditions, and the like are typically undertaken by most firms only after they have been mandated by the government.

If firms attempt to maximize share prices, is that good or bad for society in general? Basically, it is good because aside from certain illegal actions that are typically constrained by the government, the same actions that maximize share prices also benefit society. Share-price maximization requires efficient, low-cost operations that get the most value out of a given set of resources. Share-price maximization requires the development of new products that consumers want or need, so the wealth-maximization motive leads to new products, new technology, and new jobs. Finally, share-price maximization requires efficient service, adequate stocks of merchandise, and well-designed and located operations. Therefore, in general, the actions a firm undertakes to maximize its share price are directly beneficial to society at large. This is why profit-motivated economic systems have generally been more successful than other types of economic systems.

An Overview of the Text

This text was developed to convey the theories, concepts, tools, and techniques of managerial finance in the most pedagogically efficient manner. We have been guided by three fundamental precepts. First, the book stresses both theory and practice in a balanced fashion. Second, the focus is on the idea of financial decision making. Third, the major influences of recent developments in the area of finance are reflected as they relate to the theory and practice of financial decision making. The text is divided into seven parts, each addressing an important aspect of the financial manager's duties.

- Part One: The Financial Environment
- Part Two: Financial Analysis and Planning
- Part Three: Fundamental Valuation Concepts
- Part Four: Working Capital Management
- Part Five: Long-Term Asset Acquisition, Management, and Abandonment
- Part Six: Financial Structure Decisions
- Part Seven: Sources of Long-Term Financing

The unifying link for each part of the text is wealth maximization, which is tied to the various financial decisions through the risk-return mechanism. Figure 1.3 relates each part of the text to this framework. Part One includes a discussion of the evolution, viewpoint, objectives, and function of managerial finance and describes the economic and operating environment (including the financial marketplace, taxes, and accounting considerations) of the firm. In Part Two, the practical aspects of analyzing financial statements, budgeting, and forecasting are presented. Part Three presents the concepts of the time value of money

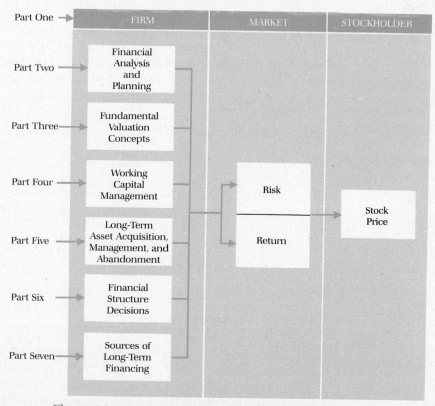

Figure 1.3 An Overview of Major Parts of the Text.

followed by discussions of risk and return and valuation. These concepts and techniques lie at the core of financial theory and are employed throughout the balance of the text.

Part Four focuses on short-term financial management. It examines current, ongoing operations—first the role of finance in ensuring that cash, accounts receivable, and inventory are used effectively, and then how short-term funds can be utilized effectively. Part Five is concerned with long-term asset acquisition, management, and abandonment, commonly known as capital budgeting. The capital budgeting process is described, along with procedures to determine the proper cash flow stream under conditions of both certainty and risk. Also included is a discussion of some special types of capital budgeting decisions related to external growth, divestiture, and failure.

Part Six focuses on financial structure decisions. The procedures for determining and using the firm's cost of capital in decision making are discussed, along with the impact of the capital structure on the value of the firm. The tendency of firms to adopt target capital structures is examined, along with the key aspects of dividend policy, which can have a significant impact on the firm's value. Finally, in Part Seven, specific sources of long-term financing are discussed. These include common stock, long-term debt and preferred stock, leasing, and convertible securities, warrants, and options. Discussion of the multinational dimensions of financial topics is included where appropriate throughout.

SUMMARY

Managerial finance has evolved over the last 80 years from a legalistic, descriptive, and external orientation to an orientation that is conceptual and concentrated on internal financial decision making. Today, with the merging of managerial finance and investment theory, financial decisions are viewed in light of their potential impact on share price.

Managerial finance tends to concentrate on cash flow rather than the accrual concepts typically used by accountants. Financial managers are primarily concerned with maximization of wealth rather than profits. Wealth maximization is a long-run concept that explicitly considers the timing of returns, the distribution of returns, and risk; profit maximization is a short-run concept that ignores these factors. Certain agency costs may be incurred in providing incentives as well as for monitoring managers' actions. Throughout this book, the goal of management is viewed as maximizing the value of the firm, which should contribute to maximization of owners' wealth.

Organizational structure varies depending on firm size, but the finance function is generally under control of the vice-president of finance, who reports to the president. The treasurer and controller commonly report to the vice-president of finance. The treasurer normally handles the finance activities, while the controller is in charge of accounting and data processing. Many firms have finance committees made up of top executives from different functional areas within the firm. In addition to monitoring and planning the firm's performance, the financial manager's key functions are making investment and financing decisions. In each of these areas, the financial manager must assess the risk and return factors and their impact on share price. In recent years, high rates of inflation as well as disinflation have complicated the financial decision process. The financial manager must plan for and aggressively deal with anticipated inflation/disinflation when making investment and financing decisions. He or she must also consider the social responsibility of the firm and undertake nonmandated programs when an increase in share price is expected to result.

QUESTIONS

1.1. Describe the evolution of managerial finance. Explain the impetus for, as well as the implications of, the merging of managerial finance and investments.

1.2. Can a firm go broke in a strict financial sense while it is making a profit? In answering this question, be sure to discuss the differing views and activities of finance and accounting.

1.3. Explain the conceptual differences between profit maximization and wealth maximization as they relate to: (a) the time horizon, (b) the timing of returns, (c) the distribution of returns, and (d) risk.

1.4. Given their nonowner status, why might financial managers tend to be "satisfiers" rather than "maximizers"? Explain how agency costs relate to the behavior of managers who own less than 100 percent of a firm.

1.5. Describe and justify the use of a share-price maximization goal to guide the financial manager's activities. Be sure to relate this goal to that of the owners, who are assumed to prefer more wealth, rather than less.

1.6. Describe the organizational aspects of the finance function within a large corporation. Differentiate between the role of the treasurer and controller and discuss the role of the finance committee.

1.7. In addition to monitoring and planning the firm's activities, describe the two key areas of financial decision making. Relate the financial decision process in each of these areas to the balance sheet, risk and return, and share price.

1.8. What impact, if any, do high rates of inflation have on the financial decision process? What general strategies might the financial manager who anticipates high levels of inflation undertake today? Explain.

1.9. Some critics of the financial theory of the firm have argued that the assumption of shareholder wealth maximization is not descriptive of financial practice. In attacking this objective, they stress that firms do things that are not necessarily oriented to shareholder wealth maximization, such as making philanthropic contributions, providing recreational facilities for employees, and maintaining pollution control standards. How would you defend the shareholder wealth-maximization goal against these social responsibility critics?

SELECTED REFERENCES

Beck, Paul J., and Thomas S. Zorn. "Managerial Incentives in a Stock Market Economy." *Journal of Finance* 37 (December 1982), pp. 1151–1167.

Black, Fischer, and Myron Scholes. "The Pricing of Options and Corporate Liabilities." *Journal of Political Economy* 81 (May–June 1973), pp. 637–654.

Branch, Ben. "Corporate Objectives and Market Performance." *Financial Management* 2 (summer 1973), pp. 24–29.

Cooley, Philip L., and Charles E. Edwards. "Ownership Effects of Managerial Salaries in Small Business." *Financial Management* 11 (winter 1982), pp. 5–9.

Cooley, Philip L., and J. Louis Heck. "Significant Contributions to Finance Literature." *Financial Management*, Tenth Anniversary Issue, 1981, pp. 23–33.

Copeland, Thomas E., and J. Fred Weston. *Financial Theory and Corporate Policy*, 2d ed. Reading, Mass.: Addison-Wesley, 1983.

Cyert, Richard, and James March. *A Behavioral Theory of the Firm.* Englewood Cliffs, N.J.: Prentice-Hall, 1963.

Davis, Keith. "Social Responsibility Is Inevitable." *California Management Review* 19 (fall 1976), pp. 14–20.

Dean, Joel. *Capital Budgeting.* New York: Columbia University Press, 1951.

Dewing, Arthur Stone. *Financial Policy of Corporations*, 5th ed., vols. 1 and 2., New York: Ronald Press, 1953.

Donaldson, Gordon. "Financial Goals: Management versus Stockholders." *Harvard Business Review* 41 (May–June 1963), pp. 116–129.

Eiteman, David K., and Arthur I. Stonehill. *Multinational Business Finance*, 3d ed. Reading, Mass.: Addison-Wesley, 1982.

Elliott, J. W. "Control, Size, Growth, and Financial Performance of the Firm." *Journal of Financial and Quantitative Analysis* 7 (January 1972), pp. 1309–1320.

Fama, Eugene F., and Merton H. Miller. *The Theory of Finance.* New York: Holt, Rinehart and Winston, 1972.

Findlay, M. Chapman III, and G. A. Whitmore. "Beyond Shareholder Wealth Maximization." *Financial Management* 3 (winter 1974), pp. 25–35.

Gerstner, Louis V., and Helen M. Anderson. "The Chief Financial Officer as Activist." *Harvard Business Review* 54 (September–October 1976), pp. 100–106.

Grossman, S. J., and J. E. Stiglitz. "On Value Maximization and Alternative Objectives of the Firm." *Journal of Finance* 32 (May 1977), pp. 389–402.

Haley, Charles W., and Lawrence D. Schall. *The Theory of Financial Decisions*, 2d ed. New York: McGraw-Hill, 1979.

Hill, Lawrence W. "The Growth of the Corporate Finance Function." *Financial Executive* 44 (July 1976), pp. 38–43.

Jensen, Michael C., and William H. Meckling. "Theory of the Firm: Managerial Behavior, Agency Costs and Ownership Structure." *Journal of Financial Economics* 3 (October 1976), pp. 305–360.

Levy, Haim, and Marshall Sarnat. "A Pedagogic Note on Alternative Formulations of the Goal of the Firm." *Journal of Business* 50 (October 1977), pp. 526–528.

Lewellen, Wilbur G. "Management and Ownership in the Large Firm." *Journal of Finance* 24 (May 1969), pp. 299–322.

Lintner, John. "Security Prices, Risk, and Maximal Gains from Diversification." *Journal of Finance* 20 (December 1965), pp. 587–616.

Markowitz, Harry M. "Portfolio Selection." *Journal of Finance* 7 (March 1952), pp. 77–91.

———. *Portfolio Selection: Efficient Diversification of Investments.* New Haven, Conn.: Yale University Press, 1959.

Masson, Robert T. "Executive Motivation, Earnings, and Consequent Equity Performance." *Journal of Political Economy* 79 (November–December 1981), pp. 1278–1292.

Modigliani, Franco, and Merton H. Miller. "The Cost of Capital, Corporation Finance, and the Theory of Investment." *American Economic Review* 48 (June 1958), pp. 261–297.

Ross, Stephen A. "The Arbitrage Theory of Capital Asset Pricing." *Journal of Economic Theory* (December 1976), pp. 341–360.

Schwert, G. William. "The Adjustment of Stock Prices to Information About Inflation." *Journal of Finance* 36 (March 1981), pp. 15–29.

Sharpe, William F. "Capital Asset Prices: A Theory of Market Equilibrium Under Conditions of Risk." *Journal of Finance* 19 (September 1964), pp. 425–442.

Simon, Herbert A. "Theories of Decision Making in Economics and Behavioral Science." *American Economic Review* 49 (June 1959), pp. 253–283.

Solomon, Ezra. "What Should We Teach in a Course in Business Finance?" *Journal of Finance* 21 (May 1966), pp. 411–415.

Stern, Joel. "Earnings per Share Doesn't Count." *Financial Analysts Journal* 30 (July–August 1974), pp. 39–43.

Stonehill, Arthur, Theo Beekhuisen, Richard Wright, Lee Remmers, Norman Toy, Antonio Parés, Alan Shapiro, Douglas Egan, and Thomas Bates. "Financial Goals and Debt Ratio Determinants: A Survey of Practice in Five Countries." *Financial Management* 4 (autumn 1975), pp. 27–41.

Weimer, George A. "Finance Favored as Key to Executive Boardroom." *Iron Age,* April 16, 1979, pp. 36–38.

Weston, J. Fred. "Developments in Finance Theory." *Financial Management,* Tenth Anniversary Issue, 1981, pp. 5–22.

———. "New Themes in Finance." *Journal of Finance* 24 (March 1974), pp. 237–243.

———. *The Scope and Methodology of Finance.* Englewood Cliffs, N.J.: Prentice-Hall, 1966.

2

The Operating Environment of the Firm

Maximizing shareholder wealth is the overriding objective of financial management. Among other things, it means that the firm must constantly interact with financial institutions and markets to invest any idle funds and to raise the capital needed for investment opportunities. The more efficiently the firm interacts with its environment, the greater the likelihood that it will achieve its goal. An understanding of the impact of accounting procedures, taxes, and inflation is also important to financial management, since the value being maximized in most financial decisions is linked to the firm's profitability. The first section of this chapter describes the financial system; it emphasizes both the interaction of firms with financial institutions and markets and the potential impact of the financial system on the decisions and well-being of the firm. The second section discusses the international dimensions of the money and capital markets, followed by a brief discussion of the corporation and the key aspects of the firm's accounting and tax environment. The final section discusses the impact of inflation on corporate profits.

The Financial System

For many years, the attention of corporate management was centered almost exclusively on finding the best investment opportunities for the firm; this was prompted in large part by the fact that money was cheap and financing was readily available. Things changed abruptly in the late 1960s, however, as interest rates soared and money became more expensive. Suddenly, financing decisions took on new importance and began to have a significant impact on the long-run well-being of the firm. To a large extent, success in financing the firm is a function of the financial manager's ability to deal with financial institutions and to participate in the money and capital markets; a basic understanding of the role of these institutions and markets is essential to raising funds in the needed quantities and in the most efficient way.

Functions of the Financial System

Savings and investing are essential to a well-developed financial system. These activities go together, since a significant and sustained flow of savings must be generated and transferred into productive investments (like plant and equipment, and inventory) if an acceptable standard of living is to be attained. Capital formation relies on a steady flow of funds from savers—those economic units whose consumption is less than their income. These units have money to lend and as a result provide a supply of funds. Those who use the funds for productive purposes are the investors; these economic units (business firms and others) have consumption that is greater than income and therefore create a demand for funds. The financial system, which consists of both institutions and markets, evolved over time to bring these two parties together and to facilitate the flow of funds between them.[1] Specifically, the role of the financial system is to collect savings and to allocate them efficiently to the ultimate user for investment in productive assets and/or current consumption. The larger the flow and the more efficiently funds are allocated, the greater the output and welfare of the economy. Consider, for example, a manufacturer who wants to modernize a plant by investing in new, more efficient equipment, or a company that wants to introduce a new product line, or a retailer that wants to increase volume by building a new store: In all these cases, while some of the required funds may be available internally, a major portion of the needed monies will probably have to be obtained externally, either directly from a financial institution or publicly in the financial markets.

Structure of the Financial System

A schematic overview of how our financial system fits together is provided in Figure 2.1. As seen, households and other savers look to the financial institutions and markets as a way to channel excess funds to attractive investment opportunities. They deal with institutions such as banks, savings and loans, and credit unions, or make transactions in the money or capital markets in order to acquire financial assets (such as savings accounts, notes, stocks, and bonds). Business firms and other investing units in need of funds participate by obtaining funds through financial institutions such as banks, insurance companies, and pension funds, as well as the money and capital markets. In exchange for the

---

[1]We will only briefly review some of the key dimensions of the financial system in this book; for an excellent and far more complete discussion of the financial system, see James C. Van Horne, *Financial Market Rates and Flows*, 2d ed. (Englewood Cliffs, N.J.: Prentice-Hall, 1984); and Herbert E. Dougall and Jack E. Gaumnitz, *Capital Markets and Institutions*, 4th ed. (Englewood Cliffs, N.J.: Prentice-Hall, 1980).

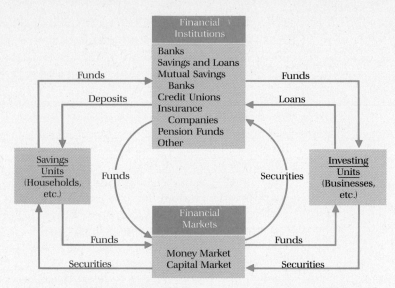

Figure 2.1   The Financial System.

money they receive, these firms issue promissory notes, bonds, or stock certificates. The funds received are invested by the firm with the expectation of generating increased returns which, in turn, are used to pay interest and dividends as well as to retire debt.

Throughout this text we will assume that the financial system is *efficient*—that it allocates funds from savers to investors at a price commensurate with the risk involved.[2] The higher the risk, the higher the return (or cost), and vice versa.[3] In equilibrium, the supply of funds equals the demand for funds. When there is an imbalance in the supply of or demand for funds, a disequilibrium occurs, and the level of return or cost adjusts in order to achieve a new equilibrium. For example, with a shortfall in the supply of funds, rates would increase, making savings more attractive and reducing the economic incentive to invest. Efficiency not only provides for proper rewards, but helps to allocate funds to those investing units that have the most attractive opportunities and the best capacity to meet their obligations.

Financial Institutions.   Financial institutions, such as banks, savings and loans, mutual savings banks, credit unions, insurance companies, and pension funds act as intermediaries in the financial system. They

---

[2] The concept of market efficiency as it relates to the capital markets will be discussed in much greater detail in Chapter 6 and Appendix 6A.

[3] This presumes, of course, that the financial system is not burdened by excessive government interference and regulation, and/or a nonproductive tax structure.

accept deposits or provide contractual services for a large number of savers, and after meeting operating expenses, pool these resources and channel them to various investment outlets. As shown in Figure 2.1, these outlets make loans directly to investing units and execute security transactions in the financial markets. The returns earned on the investments made by financial institutions are passed on (in part at least) to their savers/depositors.

Financial institutions are important in providing a profitable outlet for the funds of savings units and by making those funds available at reasonable costs to investing units. All firms regularly and actively interact with various financial institutions. Firms maintain checking accounts, receive other processing services, and borrow from banks; they purchase various forms of insurance including life insurance on key executives and obtain loans from insurance companies; and they direct funds to pension plans as well as obtain loans from them.

Financial Markets.   The financial markets facilitate corporate and economic growth by permitting savings and investing units to make direct transactions. These transactions are commonly facilitated by stockbrokers and investment bankers—firms hired by issuers to help distribute securities.[4] Of course, as can be seen in Figure 2.1, financial institutions may act as issuers, sellers, or purchasers of securities in the financial markets. The two key financial markets are the money market and the capital market. Short-term debt securities (those with maturities of 1 year or less) are issued and traded in the *money market*. In contrast, long-term debt and equity securities are traded in the *capital market*. All securities, whether they belong in the money or capital markets, are initially issued in the *primary market*. This is the only market in which the corporation is directly involved in the transaction and receives direct benefit from the issue—that is, the company actually receives the proceeds from the sale of the securities. Once the securities begin to trade between individual and/or institutional savers and investors, they become part of the *secondary market*. A closer look at money and capital markets will provide a better understanding of their role in business financing.

The Money Market   The money market is the economic arena in which short-term debt instruments are bought and sold. A vital part of the U.S. financial system, it is the market in which commercial banks and other businesses adjust their liquidity positions, the federal reserve conducts its monetary policy, and the federal government sells its debt to finance day-to-day

---

[4]A detailed discussion of the role, activities, and procedures used by the investment banker to assist firms in the design and sale of securities is included in Chapter 20.

operations. In the money market, businesses, governments, and sometimes individuals borrow or lend funds for short periods—usually less than 270 days. The money market actually consists of a collection of markets, each trading distinctly different financial instruments. There is no formal organization, such as the New York Stock Exchange. Central to the activity of the money market are the dealers and brokers who specialize in one or more money market instruments; such dealers buy securities for their own position and sell from their security inventories when a trade takes place.

Generally speaking, money market instruments are financial claims that have low default risk, short (less than 1-year) maturities, and high marketability. These short-term debt instruments are commonly called *marketable securities.* Key money market instruments include Treasury bills, tax anticipation bills, federal agency issues, short-term municipals, negotiable certificates of deposit (CDs), commercial paper, banker's acceptances, money market funds, and repurchase agreements. These marketable securities, which are issued by government, business, and financial institutions, are described in detail in Chapter 9. One characteristic common to this class of securities is that they are quite liquid; they can be sold quickly at little or no variation from current market price. The return or yield on these securities directly reflects the "tightness" or "looseness" of money. The financial manager is often an active participant in the money market, primarily as a purchaser of marketable securities (a savings unit), but also as an issuer of *commercial paper* (an investing unit).

The Capital
Market

The capital market provides a forum in which savers and investors can make transactions in long-term (greater than 1-year maturity) securities. Included are transactions in the debt and equity issues of businesses and the debt issues of federal, state, and local governments. Key securities are all types of bonds and common stocks, preferred stocks, and convertible issues. The capital markets are vital to the long-run growth and prosperity of business, since they provide the channel through which needed funds can be raised.[5] In essence, capital markets facilitate the transfer of funds from savers to investors, and in so doing enhance the economic development and vitality of the country. Because of the lengthy maturities of the securities, the existence of a secondary market is especially important as it allows investors and financial institutions to alter the liquidity, composition, and risk of their portfolios

---

[5]While our discussion will center mostly on corporate securities, it should be understood that other issuers (most notably the U.S. Treasury, agencies of the U.S. government, and state and local governments) are also a part of the financial market network and play an important role in affecting the demand for loanable funds and the market rate of interest.

in response to new information and/or changes in general market conditions. Security exchanges—both organized and over-the-counter— form the backbone of our capital market system by providing the framework and procedures needed to permit savers and investors to achieve their goals.

Functions of Security Exchanges.   One of the primary functions of security exchanges is to create a continuous market for securities, at a price that does not significantly deviate from transaction to transaction. The continuity of these markets provides securities with the liquidity necessary to attract funds. In addition, a continuous market also reduces the volatility of security prices, further enhancing their liquidity. An efficient securities market is also instrumental in allocating scarce funds; that is, by requiring the disclosure of certain corporate financial data, an efficient market system allows prospective and existing investors to assess the risk-return tradeoff involved in a transaction and to move the funds into the most promising investment. Finally, security markets help determine and publicize security prices. The price of an individual security is largely determined by what is bought and sold—the demand for and supply of the security. Most important from the corporate perspective, in fulfilling these functions, security markets provide firms with an ongoing and efficient method of obtaining new financing. Of course, smaller firms are often unable to raise funds in these markets, but the presence of organized and over-the-counter markets does give many firms direct access to the savings of individuals, other firms, and financial institutions in order to finance new capital investments. Without these markets, new capital could be obtained only through direct negotiations with holders of large amounts of money.

Organized Security Exchanges.   *Organized security exchanges* are organizations on whose physical premises securities are traded. The key exchanges are the New York Stock Exchange (NYSE) and the American Stock Exchange (AMEX), both located in New York City and accounting for better than 90 percent of the total annual dollar volume of equity shares traded (the NYSE alone accounts for about 80 percent of all equity security transactions on organized security exchanges). Regional exchanges, such as the Midwest Stock Exchange, Pacific Stock Exchange, Boston Stock Exchange, and eleven others, account for the balance of share volume, although most of the transactions on these exchanges are in securities with regional or local appeal. The New York Stock Exchange is typical of most exchanges, so a brief review of its membership policies will provide an indication of the standards employed by these exchanges.

Membership on the New York Stock Exchange is open to individual and institutional investors, as well as brokerage firms; in order to become a member, an individual or firm must own a "seat" on the exchange. There are a total of 1,366 seats on the New York Stock Exchange, and these seats have sold for as much as $515,000 and as little as $4,000—although most recently they have gone for about $300,000. Most seats are owned by brokerage firms, and many brokerage firms own more than one seat. Only seat holders or those designated by them are permitted to make transactions on the floor of the exchange. The membership is often divided into broad classes based on the members' activities. Thus, membership is made up of institutions and individuals who trade the securities listed on the exchange for themselves or for third parties. Corporations that issue securities are not members of the exchange; rather, their securities are listed on the exchanges.

The Over-the-Counter Market.   In contrast to the organized security exchanges, the *over-the-counter (OTC)* market is not a specific institution; instead it is a nationwide network of brokers and dealers who execute transactions in securities that are not listed on one of the organized exchanges. It is estimated that 30,000 to 40,000 different common stocks are traded in the over-the-counter market; the vast majority of these are shares of regional interest, and most are fairly small firms. However, several thousand firms traded on the OTC market are *not* small regional companies. For example, most banks and insurance companies are traded on OTC markets, and a number of major industrial firms continue to be traded on the OTC. Active traders in this market are linked by a telecommunications network. The prices at which securities are traded over-the-counter are determined by competitive bids and through negotiation; the actual process depends on the general activity of the security in question. A major part of the OTC market is the National Association of Security Dealers Automated Quotation System (NASDAQ), an automated system that provides up-to-date bid and ask prices on several thousand securities. Common and preferred stocks are included on NASDAQ on the basis of investor interest and share volume; as such, NASDAQ has provided a great deal of continuity to the OTC market. In addition, the OTC plays a vital role in the initial distribution of new issues of common stock and is important in transactions involving large blocks of securities, known as *secondary distributions*.

Cost of Funds   In an efficient market, capital is allocated on the basis of rates of return. To lenders, these returns are compensation for the temporary use of their money and take the form of interest payments; to equity investors, such compensation comes as dividends and capital gains. For bondholders, the compensation is a fixed contractual amount; for stockholders, it is an expected—not guaranteed—return. While these rates of return represent a payoff to savers, they also are indicative of the cost of funds to business firms and other investing units.

In general, the cost of funds, k, to issuers can be viewed as a function of economic forces and issue characteristics; that is:

$$k = f \text{(economic forces + issue characteristics)} \qquad (2.1)$$

Economic forces include numerous variables that affect the supply and demand for loanable funds, such as the supply of money, the government's taxation and expenditure policies, institutional investment plans, and corporate profits. Inflation has also had a significant effect on the cost of funds, k, during the past decade: the higher the expected rate of inflation, the higher k must be in order to allow savers to protect their purchasing power. Equally important is the impact of inflation on the volatility of k; the wide swings in interest rates that have occurred since the late 1960s can be attributed, in large part, to swings in real or perceived inflation. (A recent exception occurred in 1982 when interest rates remained relatively high even though substantial disinflation took place.)

The second key determinant of the cost of funds is issue characteristics. In essence, this "risk premium" component of k is directly related to the characteristics of the security and the issuer. Key characteristics include marketability, the reputation of the issuer (default risk), tax treatment, the term to maturity of the security, and to a lesser extent, the various contractual provisions of the security, such as coupon and call feature. The subtle differences in the cost of funds resulting from these features become important in the financing decision process. Especially important is the risk-return tradeoff, which is reflected in the capital markets. Capital market theory holds that a close relationship exists between the return offered on a class of securities and its exposure to risk; the greater the risk, the greater the return necessary to compensate investors.[6] Figure 2.2 illustrates the typical relationship between risk and return for several popular securities; clearly, higher returns (costs to the issuer) are expected with greater risk. Financial managers must attempt to keep financing costs down, but they must also consider the risks associated with each financing alternative; as noted in Chapter 1, the decision will ultimately rest on an analysis of the combined effect of risk and return on share price.

---

[6]See, for example, William F. Sharpe, "Capital Asset Prices: A Theory of Market Equilibrium Under Conditions of Risk," *Journal of Finance* 19 (September 1964), pp. 425–442; and Michael Jensen, "Capital Markets: Theory and Evidence," *Bell Journal of Economics and Management Science* 3 (autumn 1972), pp. 357–398. This topic will be discussed in detail in Chapter 6 and Appendix 6A.

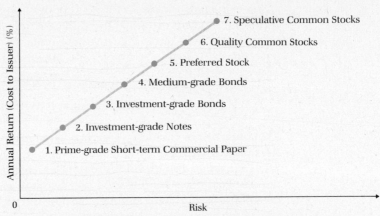

Figure 2.2   The Risk-Return Profile of Alternative Securities.

MULTINATIONAL DIMENSIONS

Money and Capital Markets Abroad
The Foreign Exchange Market

Money and capital markets are linked internationally through the interplay of inflation, interest rates, and foreign exchange rates. Financial managers must be familiar with economic conditions in other countries, since they can affect domestic money and capital markets. Furthermore, government monetary and fiscal policies are often a direct reaction to international economic pressures.

In order to understand these linkages, it is useful to review briefly the nature of the foreign exchange market, the vehicle through which one country's currency is exchanged for another's. The *foreign exchange market* is actually an international communications network linking banks, firms, brokers, government agencies, and individuals who need to trade in foreign currencies. There is no single physical location such as a stock exchange.

Foreign exchange is traded in both "spot" and "forward" markets. A *spot transaction* means that the buyer will take possession of the foreign currency at once. A *forward transaction* means that the buyer will take possession of the foreign currency at some date in the future, but the rate of exchange is agreed upon now. For example, a firm that has a commitment one year from now to pay 1 million German Deutsche marks could purchase the marks from its bank for delivery now or for delivery in one year. If delivered now, the bank would charge the spot rate, say $.50 per Deutsche mark. If delivery is one year from now, the bank would charge the one-year forward rate, say $.53. In this case, the Deutsche mark is selling forward at a 6 percent premium, calculated as follows:

$$\text{Premium (or discount)} = \frac{\text{forward rate} - \text{spot rate}}{\text{spot rate}} \times \frac{12}{\text{number of months}} \times 100$$

$$\text{Premium} = \frac{\$.53 - \$.50}{\$.50} \times \frac{12}{12} \times 100 = 6\%$$

If the forward rate on Deutsche marks had been $.47, it would have been selling at a 6 percent discount calculated with the same formula.

The International Equilibrium Model

Figure 2.3 illustrates the theoretical relationship among inflation rates, interest rates, and foreign exchange rates using a simplified two-country model. In this example, forecasted inflation in Germany is 6 percent lower than in the United States. Interest rates are also 6 percent lower in Germany. By the end of 1 year the Deutsche mark is expected to increase in value relative to the dollar by 6 percent. The 1-year forward rate on Deutsche marks is at a 6 percent premium.

Each of the relationships depicted in Figure 2.3 is explained by an economic theory. Moreover, there is a tendency for these relationships to remain in equilibrium over the long run. Therefore, if expected inflation in Germany should increase, there would be corresponding adjustments in interest rates and the foreign exchange rate in both Germany and the United States. In other words, U.S. interest rates are affected by seemingly distant economic events in Germany.

Purchasing Power Parity

The theory of purchasing power parity holds that differences in expected rates of inflation between two countries should be offset in

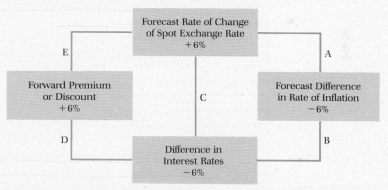

Figure 2.3 Theoretical Relationships Among Inflation Rates, Interest Rates, and Foreign Exchange Rates.
Assumptions: Spot exchange rate, 1 Deutsche mark, $.50; 1-year forward premium on the Deutsche mark, +6%; forecast rate of inflation, 1 year—U.S., 11%; Germany, 5%; interest rates 1-year maturities—U.S., 14%; Germany, 8%; forecast spot exchange rate in 1 year, 1 Deutsche mark, $.53.

the long run by an equal but opposite change in the exchange rate. Thus, a 6 percent lower rate of inflation in Germany is offset by an upward revaluation of the Deutsche mark (relationship A in Figure 2.3). The rationale behind this theory is that if Germany consistently maintains a relatively lower rate of inflation than the United States, German goods and services will become more and more price-competitive in Germany, in the United States, and in third markets. The German balance of payments will run a surplus and the U.S. balance of payments a deficit. This will put pressure on the exchange rate to change enough so that the price of similar goods and services is once again the same in both Germany and the United States. A 6 percent devaluation of the dollar (or a 6 percent revaluation of the Deutsche mark) would cause that to occur. The dollar price of goods and services would continue to inflate at the expected 6 percent higher rate than in Germany (11 percent versus 5 percent) but buyers in third countries would only experience a 5 percent increase in price in terms of their own currency due to the 6 percent devaluation of the dollar. Given the fact of floating exchange rates since 1973, this adjustment in exchange rates to inflation differentials takes place every day rather than accumulating for a big devaluation as it did under fixed exchange rates prior to 1973. On the other hand, there are lags in the adjustment process which prevent purchasing power parity from always holding true in the short run. Furthermore, foreign exchange rates are influenced by factors other than just differential prices. These include shifts in relative productivity, new discoveries such as oil, and rapid shifts in monetary policies.

The Fisher Effect

The *Fisher effect* postulates that nominal interest rates in each country are equal to the required real rate of return to the investor plus the expected rate of inflation. Thus in Figure 2.3 investors in the United States require a real rate of return of 3 percent plus compensation for the 11 percent expected rate of inflation, or a nominal interest rate of 14 percent. German investors also require a real rate of return of 3 percent, plus 5 percent for expected inflation, or a nominal interest rate of 8 percent. Therefore the interest rate differential between the two countries should just equal their differential expected inflation rate (relationship B in Figure 2.3).

The *international Fisher effect* states that the expected change in the spot exchange rate should be in an equal but opposite direction to the differential interest rate between two countries. Hence the 6 percent interest differential between Germany and the United States is matched by an expected 6 percent revaluation upward of the Deutsche mark (relationship C in Figure 2.3). The reason this theory is believed valid is that German investors in U.S. securities must receive a 6 percent higher interest rate in order to compensate them for the expected 6 percent foreign exchange loss when they later convert the security's dollar proceeds back to Deutsche marks.

Interest Rate Parity

The theory of *interest rate parity* postulates that the forward exchange rate discount or premium should be equal but opposite in sign to the difference in national interest rates for similar securities. Thus the Deutsche mark is at a 6 percent premium in the 1-year forward market, which reflects the difference in interest rates between Germany and the United States on similar securities of 1-year maturity (relationship D in Figure 2.3). Except for transaction costs or exchange controls, this relationship should always hold because of covered interest arbitrage activity by international bankers and others.

Covered interest arbitrage is a technique whereby an investor can make a profit almost without risk, provided the forward premium or discount does not equal the interest rate differential. For example, suppose the forward rate on the Deutsche mark rises to $.54. In that case, the forward premium on the mark rises to 8 percent in Figure 2.3. The covered interest arbitrager would take the following action:

Step 1. Day 1. Borrow $1,000,000 for 1 year at 14 percent per year.
Step 2. Convert to 2,000,000 Deutsche marks at 1 Deutsche mark = $.50.
Step 3. Buy Deutsche mark securities worth 2,000,000 Deutsche marks and yielding 8 percent per year.
Step 4. Sell the Deutsche mark principal and interest forward for delivery in 1 year at an 8 percent premium. The forward contract would be for 1.08(2,000,000) = 2,160,000 Deutsche marks and the receipt in dollars would be $.54(2,160,000) = $1,166,400.

Step 5. One Year Later. Receive 2,160,000 Deutsche marks principal and interest.
Step 6. Deliver 2,160,000 Deutsche marks on the forward contract and receive $1,166,400.
Step 7. Repay the $1,000,000 loan plus 14 percent interest, or a total of $1,140,000.
Step 8. Pay transaction costs, which we assume to be $200.

The net profit on this transaction is as follows:

$$
\begin{array}{lr}
\text{Receipt from forward contract} = & \$1,166,400 \\
\text{Less: Repayment of dollar loan} = & -1,140,000 \\
\text{Transaction cost} = & -200 \\
\hline
\text{Net profit} & \$26,200 \\
\end{array}
$$

Since this profit is certain as long as the bank lives up to its forward contract and the securities do not default, covered interest arbitragers would move immense sums of money to Germany from the United States. This would tend to restore interest rate parity as interest rates in Germany declined under the increased demand for German securities, and the forward premium on the Deutsche mark was reduced by the increased sale of Deutsche marks forward. Thus each country's interest rates can be affected very quickly by events in the foreign exchange market. Financial managers must be aware that we are not an island, but part of an integrated world money and capital market.

Forward Rate as an Unbiased Predictor of Future Spot Rate

Relationship E in Figure 2.3 suggests that the forward rate is an unbiased predictor of the future spot rate. This is based on the assumption that the foreign exchange markets are efficient. All relevant information is already reflected in both the spot and forward rates. Since the forward rate represents the market's best guess as to the future spot rate, there is no reason to believe that sellers or buyers can consistently outguess the market with respect to the future spot rate. This is the foreign exchange equivalent of trying to outguess the stock market in individual securities. We will return to this particular relationship later when we discuss foreign exchange risk management.

The Corporation

The three major forms of business organization are the sole proprietorship, the partnership, and the corporation. A _sole proprietorship_ is generally a small firm owned by one person and operating in a wholesale, retail, or service industry. A _partnership_ involves two or more people doing business together, commonly in a service-oriented business such as finance, insurance, or real estate. The _corporation_ is a legal entity given the statutory powers of an individual and owned by stockholders. Corporations are found in all sectors of the economy and are especially important in manufacturing and other types of industrial and financial activities. The relative dominance of the corporation is reflected in Table 2.1, which indicates that although corporations represent only 16 percent of all businesses, they account for 88 percent of all business receipts and 78 percent of net profits. Because of its dominant role, the organization under study throughout this text will be the corporation.[7]

---

[7]This business form is used not for simplicity, but rather because the self-contained nature of these organizations provides an almost laboratorylike condition for the study of managerial finance. Nevertheless, other forms of business organization will be mentioned from time to time.

TABLE 2.1
Number, Receipts, and
Profits of Alternative
Forms of
Nonagricultural
Business Firms

Form of Business Organization	Percentage of Total			Average Operating Results in Dollars	
	Number of Firms	Business Receipts	Net Profits	Business Receipts	Net Profits
Sole proprietorships	76.0%	7.8%	17.5%	$ 39,828	$ 4,366
Partnerships	7.8	3.7	4.8	186,715	11,701
Corporations	16.2	88.5	77.7	2,114,568	90,978
	100.0%	100.0%	100.0%		

SOURCE: The data for sole proprietorships and partnerships were obtained from U.S. Department of the Treasury, Internal Revenue Service, *Statistics of Income, 1976 Business Income Tax Returns* (Washington, D.C.: U.S. Government Printing Office, 1979), pp. 16, 240. The data for corporations were obtained from U.S. Department of the Treasury, Internal Revenue Service, *Statistics of Income, 1975 Corporation Income Tax Returns* (Washington, D.C.: U.S. Government Printing Office, 1979), p. 13.

MULTINATIONAL
DIMENSIONS

Joint Ventures

A *joint venture* is a hybrid organization form often used to conduct foreign operations, but sometimes also used domestically. A typical joint venture would be a corporation owned by two or more other corporations. It could also be a partnership formed by two or more other partnerships, or even some mix of partnerships, individuals, corporations, and government agencies. Joint ventures are more common abroad than in the United States because of federal antitrust legislation. The purpose of a joint venture is usually to undertake a project that is either too big or too complicated for any one firm. The joint venture enables each partner to contribute expertise, capital, or both. For example, North Sea Oil projects are typically undertaken by joint ventures composed of firms from the oil industry, shipping firms, and government agencies.

Apart from size and expertise, joint ventures are also motivated by the desire of countries to maintain some degree of ownership of their firms in national hands. Thus, Japan, Mexico, India, Nigeria, and many others require that firms located in their countries have a majority of shares owned by local nationals. There are sometimes exceptions for foreign firms with expertise that is particularly desired, but on the whole, it would be difficult today for a foreign firm to establish or acquire majority control of a firm in these countries. A number of other countries require majority local ownership only in certain industries, such as Canada is now doing with the energy sector. Still other countries merely require some minority participation by local nationals. Legal liabilities and the method by which the joint venture or its partners will be taxed are spelled out in a separate agreement that usually must be agreed to by the governments involved. For example, the joint venture members might form a corporation in the United Kingdom as the legal entity under which it does business. This would subject it to British tax and liability laws. However, the definitions of taxable income, transfer prices, and operating policies are subject to joint agreement. It is not possible to generalize about the effective tax or legal liabilities of joint ventures without being familiar with the joint venture agreement in each case.

The Accounting and Tax Environments of the Firm

While the value of the firm is a function of risk and expected return, the firm's activities are commonly assessed in terms of cash flow and profits. In essence, the financial manager contributes to the value of the firm when he or she makes decisions that improve the firm's expected cash flow without affecting its risk. Since profit often affects cash flow, it is important to understand the basic techniques used to calculate it. We will examine next the concepts and components of corporate income, noting especially the effects of depreciation and taxes on reported profits.

The Income Statement and Cash Flow

Profits are vital to the American economic system—they create jobs, finance growth, generate tax revenues, and pay dividends to millions of Americans. In 1982, corporate profit after taxes amounted to $115.1 billion. This was the amount remaining after deducting various expenses and taxes from revenues and which was used to pay dividends and/or, if retained in the firm, to pay off debt and finance corporate growth. A general format for the corporate income statement is shown in Table 2.2. Although not shown, any nonoperating income and losses (like interest income and realized capital gains and losses) are also included on the income statement. For the most part, profits are directly affected by the level of sales and indirectly by the control of various costs and expendi-

TABLE 2.2
General Income
Statement Format

Sales
Less: Cost of goods sold
    Depreciation
    Operating expenses
Operating profit (earnings before interest and taxes, EBIT)
Less: Interest expense
Profit before taxes (earnings before taxes)
Less: Taxes
Profit after taxes (earnings after taxes)
Less: Preferred stock dividends
Earnings available to common stockholders
Less: Common stock dividends
Addition to retained earnings

tures. It is also important to observe that before common stockholders can receive dividends, preferred stockholders' claims must be satisfied. A large portion of corporate profit before taxes go toward meeting corporate tax liabilities; in 1982 corporations paid $59.1 billion on pretax profits of $174.2 billion, or about 34 percent of profit before taxes. About 60 percent of the profits that remained was distributed as dividends, and the balance was retained.

Accounting Ambiguity.   Income statements and other financial reports are prepared under *generally accepted accounting principles (GAAP),* a series of statements of acceptable accounting practices and procedures. The major rule-setting body of the accounting profession responsible for GAAP is the Financial Accounting Standards Board (FASB), which in 1973 replaced the Accounting Principles Board (APB). A part of the American Institute of Certified Public Accountants (AICPA), the paid, full-time members of the FASB periodically issue authoritative statements that constitute the generally accepted accounting principles (GAAP). Unfortunately, while GAAP are an outgrowth of admirable intentions (to provide viable financial information about the economic resources and obligations of a business enterprise), they have led to serious problems with regard to ambiguity in reported income.[8] Specifically, the basic theme of matching historic cost with future revenues under GAAP has resulted in wide differences in reported income of similar operations and prompted a lack of confidence in reported accounting data. As a result, firms that are similar—same products, revenue functions, and costs—can indeed report *totally different after-tax profits.*

Some of the important reasons for differences in after-tax profits include accounting for inventories, depreciation methods, research expenses, accounting for mergers and acquisitions, pension costs, income of subsidiaries, and the investment tax credit. Especially important are the alternative accounting treatments allowed for inventories and depreciation; the choice of procedures is left largely to the judgment of management. An extensive review of alternative accounting practices is beyond the scope of this text,[9] but we can say that such alternatives can significantly affect the level of after-tax profits reflected on the income statement. Studies have shown that while the value of common shares is affected by reported accounting data, market value is not affected by

---

[8]For a more thorough discussion of the issues surrounding the ambiguity in reported income, see James Lorie and Mary Hamilton, *The Stock Market: Theories and Evidence* (Homewood, Ill.: Irwin, 1973), chap. 8; Anthony Curley and Robert Bear, *Investment Analysis and Management* (New York: Harper & Row, 1979), chap. 7; and Abraham Briloff, *Unaccountable Accounting* (New York: Harper & Row, 1972).

[9]See, instead, David Hawkins, *Corporate Financial Reporting—Text and Cases* (Homewood, Ill.: Irwin, 1977).

faulty or misleading information.[10] It is therefore in the best interests of the owners for the financial manager to select accounting procedures that fairly and accurately report the operating results of the firm.

Operating Cash Flow. As noted in Chapter 1, the profits of a firm generally have little relation to the firm's cash flow; in fact, it's quite possible for a firm to show a profit, and at the same time generate a negative cash flow, or vice versa. Profits are differences in revenues and expenses and are calculated on an accrual basis as a way to reflect the operating results of a firm over a specific period of time (usually 1 year). In contrast, cash flow is concerned with the actual cash receipts and expenditures that occurred during the same time period; specifically, net cash flow equals cash inflows minus cash outflows.[11] Profit is an accounting concept; cash flow is an economic concept that is more reflective of the true value of a real or financial asset.

A company's cash flow from operations is really an extension of its profits. A *rough estimate* can be made by adjusting the firm's after-tax profit for any noncash expenditures such as depreciation, amortization, or depletion made during the period.[12]

$$\begin{matrix} \text{Cash flow from} \\ \text{operations} \end{matrix} = \begin{matrix} \text{profit after} \\ \text{taxes} \end{matrix} + \begin{matrix} \text{noncash} \\ \text{expenditures} \end{matrix} \qquad (2.2)$$

It can be seen from Equation 2.2 that cash flow from operations will differ from profit after taxes by the amount of noncash charges—the dominant source being depreciation. If a company has a considerable amount of depreciation for tax purposes (as would be the case for a highly capital-intensive firm), it could report a modest after-tax profit, or even a loss, and still have sizable operating cash flows. For example, a firm with a $2 million operating loss and $7 million of depreciation would have a cash flow from operations of $5 million.

Depreciation Methods

Firms regularly acquire various types of capital assets to carry out their activities. Such assets include plant, machinery, equipment, and motorized vehicles, all having relatively long useful lives. An asset depreciation system exists to permit the allocation of the cost—not the value—of capital assets to the periods in which they provide benefits. Thus, while

---

[10]Nicholas Dopouch, "Discussion of an Empirical Test of the Relevance of Accounting Information for Investment Decisions," supplement to *Journal of Accounting Research*, 1971, pp. 32–40; and W. Beaver, P. Kettler, and M. Scholes, "The Association Between Market Determined and Accounting Determined Risk Measures," *Accounting Review* (October 1970), pp. 654–682.

[11]Various aspects of the "net cash flow" concept are discussed in Chapters 3, 4, and 12.

[12]It is important to recognize that the firm's cash flow is affected by many factors in addition to profits and noncash expenditures. In subsequent chapters attention will be given to the effect of various balance sheet accounts on the firm's cash flow.

TABLE 2.3
Comparative Income
Statements

	With Straight-Line Depreciation		With Accelerated Depreciation
Sales	$1,000,000		$1,000,000
Less: Cost of goods sold	350,000		350,000
Depreciation	100,000	<	200,000
Operating expenses	100,000		100,000
Operating profit	$ 450,000		$ 350,000
Less: Interest expense	50,000		50,000
Profit before taxes	$ 400,000	>	$ 300,000
Less: Taxes (40%)	160,000	>	120,000
Profit after taxes	$ 240,000	>	$ 180,000
Plus: Depreciation	100,000		200,000
Cash flow from operations	$ 340,000	<	$ 380,000

the asset is acquired at a point in time, its cost is charged to income over a period of years in order to match the costs with the revenues they help to generate.[13] Since depreciation does not involve an outflow of cash each time it is charged to the firm's books, it is commonly viewed as a noncash expenditure. Because the objectives of the firm in reporting income differ depending upon whether it is reporting to the owners or the IRS, most firms maintain at least[14] two sets of books. One set, in conformance with generally accepted accounting principles, would be used to report to owners; the other set would be used to report the firm's tax liability to the IRS and other taxing agencies. The firm's objective in reporting to owners would be to show high and reasonably stable levels of earnings; when reporting to the IRS, the firm would attempt to lower earnings in order to minimize tax liability and thereby increase cash inflows.

The choice of method of depreciation used to write off the cost of capital assets can have a profound effect on reported profits, taxes, and cash flow from operations. Consider, for example, the two income statements given in Table 2.3. The only difference between the two statements lies in the depreciation charge. In the first case, straight-line depreciation is used, while in the second case, accelerated depreciation is employed. With accelerated depreciation, the firm would have more tax-deductible expenses, less taxable income, less taxes, and less profits. However, the "tax shield" (lower tax liability) provided by the added depreciation results in higher cash flows from operations. Since the

---

[13]Two other cost systems that are similar in many respects to depreciation are depletion (cost allocations for natural resources such as oil and mineral deposits) and amortization (cost allocations for intangible assets such as patents and leaseholds); they too are noncash expenditures and have much the same effect as depreciation on profits, taxes, and cash flow.

[14]Many firms will in addition maintain their financial records and prepare financial statements for use in internal decision making. In the event a firm is performing work under a government contract, a special set of books and statements may be required as well.

financial manager is primarily concerned with cash flows, accelerated depreciation is routinely used in computing the firm's actual tax liability. Such an approach will result in greater economic value for the firm, since cash inflows are increased and real out-of-pocket tax payments are correspondingly reduced. In contrast, published financial statements reported to the shareholders often reflect the use of straight-line depreciation in order to enhance profits.[15]

In a fashion consistent with a cash flow orientation, the financial manager is primarily concerned with tax depreciation, rather than the methods used to depreciate assets for financial reporting. For tax purposes, depreciation is based on the rules and guidelines established by the Internal Revenue Code, which underwent sweeping modifications with passage of the Economic Recovery Tax Act of 1981 (ERTA) as modified by the Tax Equity and Fiscal Responsibility Act of 1982 (TEFRA) and the Tax Reform Act of 1984. These rules state how certain assets can be depreciated and establish guidelines for the depreciable value and depreciable life of most fixed assets.[16] Depreciation for tax purposes is determined using the *Accelerated Cost Recovery System (ACRS or "Acres,"* as it is more popularly called) set down by the tax code, while for financial reporting purposes a variety of methods are available.

Depreciable Life of an Asset.   The life over which an asset is depreciated can significantly affect the pattern of cash flows. The shorter the depreciable life, the quicker the cash flow created by the depreciation tax shield will be received. Given the financial manager's preference for faster cash flows, a shorter depreciable life is preferred to a longer one. The firm must abide by certain Internal Revenue Service regulations

---

[15]To reconcile the fact that straight-line depreciation is reflected in published statements, while the taxes shown are based on the use of accelerated depreciation, a liability denoted as "deferred taxes" is included on the balance sheet. This liability reflects the amount by which the taxes are understated as a result of the use of accelerated depreciation. The use of accelerated depreciation for the firm in Table 2.3 would result in $40,000 ($160,000 − $120,000) of deferred taxes. Theoretically, if absolutely everything remained the same, the taxes would eventually come due, since the total amount of depreciation that can be taken is the same regardless of whether straight-line or accelerated depreciation is employed. In a real sense, however, as we will see later, deferred taxes do *not* represent an actual liability or obligation on the part of the company. Accelerated depreciation causes early-year taxes to be lower and later-year taxes to be higher than they would be in the event straight-line depreciation were utilized. In the event that the same method of depreciation was used for both reporting and tax purposes, the firm would not have deferred taxes resulting from depreciation. Note that deferred taxes are further discussed in Chapter 3. For more detailed discussion of deferred taxes, see Kirkland A. Wilcox and Joseph C. San Miguel, *Introduction to Financial Accounting*, 2d ed. (New York: Harper & Row, 1984), pp. 358–363.

[16]Certain minimum requirements must be met in order for an asset to qualify for depreciation; specifically, (1) the asset must be used in the business for the purpose of producing a stream of income; (2) the asset must have a limited useful life (land has an unlimited life and therefore is not depreciable even though it is classified as a fixed asset); and (3) the firm must have an ownership interest in the asset.

TABLE 2.4
Property Classes
(excluding real
property) and Normal
and Optional Extended
Recovery Periods
under ACRS

Property Class	Normal Recovery Period	Optional Extended Recovery Periods
Autos, light-duty trucks, research and experiment equipment, and certain special tools	3 yr	5 or 12 yr
All other machinery and equipment	5 yr	12 or 25 yr
Certain public utility property, railroad tank cars, and residential manufactured homes	10 yr	25 or 35 yr
All other public utility property	15 yr	35 or 45 yr

when determining depreciable lives for tax purposes. These accelerated cost recovery system (ACRS) standards, which apply to both new and used assets, permit the taxpayer to use the normal ACRS recovery periods, or to elect to take an extended recovery period. Table 2.4 briefly describes the four property classes (excluding real property) under ACRS for normal recovery periods and shows the optional extended recovery periods associated with each. Since for tax purposes the shorter normal recovery periods would be preferred, primary emphasis is given them throughout the text.[17] The four property classes under ACRS are referred to by their normal recovery periods—3-year, 5-year, 10-year, and 15-year property.

Alternatives.   There are two alternatives for depreciating assets under ACRS: (1) using the specified accelerated depreciation percentages over the normal recovery period, or (2) using straight-line depreciation over the same or an extended period.[18] For tax purposes, using the normal recovery periods, assets are depreciated using the accelerated percentages shown in Table 2.5. Special tables of depreciation percentages for real property are available.[19] The firm can also choose to depreciate the asset using straight-line depreciation over the normal or optional extended recovery periods. When using either accelerated or straight-line methods, the amount depreciated (the depreciable value of an asset) is its *full cost*—no adjustment is required for salvage value.

---

[17]The optional extended recovery periods would be attractive only to those firms anticipating negative predepreciation income in the near term. In such a case, deferring depreciation to later years when predepreciation income would be available would prove beneficial.

[18]The Economic Recovery Tax Act of 1981, as modified by the Tax Reform Act of 1984, permits firms to elect to expense rather than capitalize and depreciate up to a total of $5,000 per year in 1984, 1985, 1986, and 1987 for certain depreciable business assets. This amount is scheduled to increase to $7,500 per year in 1988 and 1989, and to $10,000 in 1990 and thereafter.

[19]Rather than becoming involved in the intricacies of the tax laws, the decisions throughout this and subsequent chapters will tend to concentrate on the strict use of normal recovery periods and the percentages given in Table 2.5.

Recovery Year	Percentage by Recovery Year			
	3-Year	5-Year	10-Year	15-Year Public Utility
1[a]	25%	15%	8%	5%
2	38	22	14	10
3	37	21	12	9
4		21	10	8
5		21	10	7
6			10	7
7 to 10			9	6
11 to 15				6

[a]The fact that the first-year depreciation percentage is lower than in subsequent years stems from the fact that a half-year convention applies to the year in which the asset was first placed in service—regardless of when during the year this occurs.

While from a financial standpoint, primary concern is given to tax depreciation, recall that for financial reporting purposes, a variety of other depreciation methods are available—straight-line, double declining balance, sum-of-the-year's-digits, and units of production.[20] Since primary concern in managerial finance centers on cash flows, only tax depreciation methods will be utilized throughout this text. The application of the tax depreciation percentages given in Table 2.5 can be demonstrated by a simple example. The GJP Company just acquired for $40,000 a machine having a normal recovery period of 5 years. Applying the appropriate depreciation percentages from Table 2.5 to the full cost of the machine, the depreciation in each year is calculated below. It should be clear from column 3 that the total cost of the asset—its depreciable value—is written off over the 5-year recovery period.

Year	Cost (1)	Percentages (from Table 2.5) (2)	Depreciation (1) × (2) (3)
1	$40,000	15%	$ 6,000
2	40,000	22	8,800
3	40,000	21	8,400
4	40,000	21	8,400
5	40,000	21	8,400
Total		100%	$40,000

Corporate Income Taxes

The value of the firm and therefore the shareholders' wealth is largely dependent on the firm's risk and return. The financial manager's actions

[20]For a review of these depreciation methods, as well as other aspects of financial reporting, see Donald E. Keiso and Jerry J. Weygandt, *Intermediate Accounting*, 4th ed. (New York: Wiley, 1983).

in making investment and financing decisions directly affect these two key parameters. Since after-tax profits are a vital part of the commonly used measures of return, the level of taxes paid has considerable bearing on the valuation process. In order to understand the financial decision-making process, it is essential to have at least a general understanding of the manner in which corporate income is taxed. Taxes are an important fact of life, and they simply cannot be ignored by financial managers. But taxes are complicated and ever-changing and as a result, only the highlights of the latest version of the corporate tax structure are covered here. Such exposure should provide a working knowledge of the tax system and needed insight with respect to the impact of federal taxes on corporate financial decisions.[21]

Corporations may earn two types of income—ordinary income and capital gains—each subject to a different tax rate. By the same token, corporations can experience two types of tax losses—operating and capital losses—which may be carried back or forward and applied against income in other years. The amount of taxes paid can be significantly impacted by the investment tax credit. It is also important to recognize that interest and dividend payments are treated differently for tax purposes.

Ordinary Income.   The ordinary or operating income of a corporation is taxed at the following rates:

- 15 percent on first $25,000
- 18 percent on next $25,000
- 30 percent on next $25,000
- 40 percent on next $25,000
- 46 percent on greater than $100,000

Corporations with taxable income in excess of $1,000,000 must, in addition, increase the tax calculated using the above rate schedule by the lesser of $20,250 or 5 percent of taxable income in excess of $1,000,000.

For example, if Jessie Manufacturing has before-tax earnings of $1,200,000, the tax on these earnings can be found by taking:

.15 × $25,000	= $ 3,750
.18 × 25,000	= 4,500

[21]Noncorporate organizations, like sole proprietorships and partnerships, are subject to individual federal income taxes; what's more, certain small corporations (those organized as Subchapter S corporations) may also be taxed as individuals. For a review of individual federal income taxes and more detail on federal corporate taxes, see *Federal Tax Course* (New York: Commerce Clearing House) or *Federal Tax Course* (Englewood Cliffs, N.J.: Prentice-Hall), both published annually. Corporations are subject to a variety of state and local taxes levied primarily against income and property; these other sources of taxation are not discussed here.

$$.30 \times 25,000 = 7,500$$
$$.40 \times 25,000 = 10,000$$
$$.46 \times (1,200,000 - 100,000) = \underline{506,000}$$

Total $531,750

Plus lesser of:
$$\begin{bmatrix} \$20,250 \\ \text{or} \\ .05(\$1,200,000 - \$1,000,000) \\ = .05(\$200,000) = \$10,000 \end{bmatrix} = \underline{10,000}$$

Total taxes due $541,750

The firm's total taxes on earnings are therefore $541,750. If the firm had earned only $20,000 before taxes, its total tax liability would have been .15 × $20,000, or $3,000.

The *average tax rate* paid on the firm's ordinary income can be found by dividing its taxes by its taxable income. Average tax rates range from 15 to 46 percent (the average tax rate reaches 46 percent when taxable income equals or exceeds $1,405,000 (($20,250 ÷ .05) + $1,000,000 = $405,000 + $1,000,000 = $1,405,000). The average tax rate paid by Jessie Manufacturing in the preceding example was 45.1 percent ($541,750 ÷ $1,200,000). The *marginal tax rate*, in contrast, represents the rate at which additional income is taxed. The marginal tax rate on income up to $25,000 is 15 percent; from $25,000 to $50,000 it is 18 percent; from $50,000 to $75,000 it is 30 percent; from $75,000 to $100,000 it is 40 percent; for income between $100,000 and $1,000,000 it is 46 percent; for income between $1,000,000 and $1,405,000 it is in excess of 46 percent due to the scheduled adjustment; and for income in excess of $1,405,000 it is 46 percent. For example, if Jessie Manufacturing's earnings go up to $1,300,000, the marginal tax rate on the additional $100,000 of income will become 51 percent (46-percent rate + 5 percent adjustment). In order to simplify the explanation of certain tax concepts in this text, a 40 percent tax rate is assumed for ordinary corporate income. This rate is not far out of line with the marginal tax rate of 46 percent and makes the calculations in the various examples much easier to follow.

Most corporations are required to make estimated tax payments. These are generally made in four equal instalments, payable on April 15, June 15, September 15, and December 15. Any tax refunds or additional tax payments that may be due (resulting from an over- or underpayment of estimated taxes) must be settled by March 15 of the following year; in order to discourage the obvious urge to underestimate taxable income intentionally, the IRS may levy penalties on corporations that "significantly" underestimate their tax liability.

Capital Gains.   The other major form of income a corporation may earn is capital gains. If a firm sells certain capital assets for more than their *original purchase price,* the difference between the sale price and the purchase price is called a *capital gain.*[22] A short-term capital gain occurs when an asset held for 6 months or less is sold for more than its original purchase price; a long-term capital gain occurs when the asset has been held for more than 6 months. For corporations as well as individuals, only long-term capital gains receive special tax treatment; short-term gains are taxed as ordinary income.

The federal tax code provides for a rate of 28 percent or the ordinary rate, whichever is lower, on long-term corporate capital gains. Taxation of long-term capital gains at the ordinary rate is advisable only when a firm's operating income is below $50,000, since the marginal tax rate for earnings over $50,000 is equal to or greater than 30 percent. When a firm sells a depreciable asset[23] for more than its book value but less than its initial purchase price, the gain, which represents recaptured depreciation, is taxed as ordinary income. The 28 percent rate applies only to gains above the initial purchase price on assets held for longer than 6 months (long-term capital gains). If a gain above the purchase price is made on an asset held for 6 months or less—a short-term capital gain—the total gain is taxed as ordinary income.

To illustrate, assume the Commodore Company has operating earnings of $100,000 and has just sold for $40,000 a machine initially purchased 2 years ago for $36,000. The machine was being depreciated over a 5-year normal recovery period according to the ACRS percentages (see Table 2.5). Because it was purchased 2 years ago, its current book value is $22,680, that is, $36,000 − [(.15 + .22) × $36,000]. The firm thus makes a capital gain of $4,000 ($40,000 − $36,000) and recaptures depreciation of $13,320 ($36,000 − $22,680) on the sale. The ordinary income represents the amount of recaptured depreciation the firm obtains as a result of the sale. The total gain over book value of the asset is therefore $17,320 ($40,000 − $22,680). Of this gain, $4,000 will be taxed at 28 percent, since the asset has been held for more than 6 months, while the remaining $13,320 will be taxed as ordinary income. The firm's total tax liability from its operating earnings and the sale of the machine is calculated as follows:

---

[22]The tax code specifically defines the types of assets eligible for this treatment. See William H. Hoffman, ed., *West's Federal Taxation: Corporations Partnerships, Estates and Trusts* (St. Paul, Minn.: West Publishing Company), published annually, for an excellent discussion of capital assets and capital gains.

[23]The tax on the recapture of depreciation on real property—real estate—differs significantly from that on personal property because the amount of depreciation eligible for recapture depends on a variety of factors, such as method of depreciation used and type of property involved.

Taxable income	
Operations	$100,000
Sale of asset	17,320
Total	$117,320
Less: Capital gain (long term)	4,000
Total ordinary income	$113,320
Taxes	
Ordinary income: .15($25,000) + .18($25,000) + .30($25,000) + .40($25,000) + .46($113,320 − $100,000), or $3,750 + $4,500 + $7,500 + $10,000 + $6,127	$31,877
Capital gain (long term): .28($4,000)	1,120
Total tax liability	$32,997

If a firm sells certain assets for less than their original purchase price but more than book value, the gain above book value is taxed as ordinary income. For example, if the Commodore Company sells the machine described in the preceding example for $30,000, no capital gain will result. But the firm would recapture depreciation of $7,320 ($30,000 − $22,680, the book value). It would therefore have a total taxable income of $107,320 ($100,000 + $7,320), on which the tax liability would be $29,117 [.15($25,000) + .18($25,000) + .30($25,000) + .40($25,000) + .46($107,320 − $100,000)]. If the company sells the machine for its exact book value of $22,680, no gain of any type will result and the firm's only taxable income would be $100,000 of operating income. Its taxes would then be $25,750 [.15($25,000) + .18($25,000) + .30($25,000) + .40($25,000)].

Tax Losses.   While the discussion thus far has concentrated on taxable income, companies sometimes experience losses. Three different types of tax-loss situations may confront the firm; a corporation may experience (1) an operating loss, (2) a capital loss on personal or real property used in the business, or (3) a capital loss on nonbusiness assets such as securities held for speculation.

The first type of loss occurs whenever a firm has negative before-tax profits—costs and expenses in excess of revenues. In contrast, when a company sells personal or real property used in the business for less than its book value, a capital loss occurs. The amount of the capital loss is equal to the difference between the asset's book value and its sale price; such losses may be deducted from ordinary operating income and act to reduce the taxable income of the firm. For financial decision-making purposes, these savings accrue at the firm's prevailing marginal tax rate. For example, if a firm sells an asset used in the business and having a book value of $30,000 for $20,000, a capital loss of $10,000 can be applied against ordinary income. If the firm's marginal tax rate is 46 percent, the loss will result in a tax savings of $4,600 (.46 × $10,000). Finally, a special kind of capital loss occurs when assets not used in the business are sold at a loss. For example, when $1 million of marketable securities are sold for $900,000, the $100,000 short- or long-term capital loss can be used to offset a corresponding short- or long-term capital gain.

In the event that there is not sufficient operating income or capital gains in a given year to absorb the respective operating or capital loss, a firm is allowed to carry such losses backward or forward for tax purposes. This feature is included in the tax code to provide equitable treatment for corporations that experience volatile patterns of income, as is customary in cyclical industries such as construction. The tax code requires that a firm first net all losses against current income (or capital gains) and then carry losses back, applying them to the earliest (most distant) year allowable and then progressively moving forward until the loss has been fully applied or the carryforward period has expired. All three types of losses described above can be carried back 3 years; operating losses can be carried forward for another 15 years, while capital losses are only allowed a 5-year carryforward.[24] Carrying losses back and then forward means using the losses to offset past and/or future income, and therefore, recomputing the firm's taxes based on the reduced income; in essence, the firm will receive either a tax refund (on carrybacks) or incur reduced future tax liabilities (on carryforwards).[25]

Investment Tax Credit (ITC).   A firm may be eligible for an *investment tax credit (ITC)* whenever it acquires certain types of depreciable capital assets.[26] This credit has more impact than a tax-deductible expense, since it is applied directly to the firm's tax liability and acts to reduce the firm's taxes on a dollar-for-dollar basis. Congress intended the investment tax credit to encourage business to invest in machinery and equipment. First enacted in 1962 during the Kennedy administration, the ITC was on and off the books until 1971, when it was reinstated. It has remained in force ever since—in fact, it was made a permanent part of the tax laws in 1979.

Under the latest version of the investment tax credit,[27] property that

---

[24]A corporation can elect to give up the 3-year carryback for losses if such an election is made by the due date for filing the return in the year of the loss. See *Federal Tax Course* (Englewood Cliffs, N.J.: Prentice-Hall), published annually, for an in-depth discussion of tax loss carrybacks and carryforwards.

[25]While the carryback-carryforward feature can have significant impact on cash flows, it is ignored in this text in order to provide for the straightforward presentation of concepts and theories.

[26]Property that qualifies includes, with certain exceptions, only depreciable or amortizable property with lives of at least three years.

[27]Like many parts of the tax code, this provision has been changed repeatedly in the past; our discussion in this book is based on the version enacted in the Tax Equity and Fiscal Responsibility Act of 1982 as modified by the Tax Reform Act of 1984; for more detailed discussion of ITC, see Prentice-Hall, *Federal Tax Course*, latest annual edition.

has a normal recovery period of 3 years is eligible for a 6 percent credit, while all other classes (5-year, 10-year, and 15-year) of qualified property are eligible for a 10 percent credit. As a result of the Tax Equity and Fiscal Responsibility Act of 1982 (TEFRA), firms taking these credits must reduce the cost basis of the asset by an amount equal to 50 percent of the credit for depreciation purposes. This means that firms taking the 6 percent credit on 3-year assets can depreciate only 97 percent of the cost of the asset for tax purposes while those taking the 10 percent credit on longer-lived assets can depreciate only 95 percent of their cost. As an alternative, a firm *may elect* not to make this reduction in basis by instead reducing the investment tax credit by 2 percent. In other words, the firm may take the full depreciation allowance if it takes a 4 percent ITC (instead of 6 percent) on 3-year lived assets and an 8 percent ITC (instead of 10 percent) on all other classes. For example, a firm that purchases an asset having a 5-year normal recovery period and costing $50,000 can either (1) take the full 10 percent credit of $5,000 and depreciate $47,500 (i.e., 95% × $50,000) over the 5-year normal recovery period or (2) take an 8 percent credit of $4,000 and depreciate $50,000 (i.e., 100% × $50,000) over the 5-year normal recovery period. While the firm will choose the alternative it believes would prove most economically advantageous in view of its tax situation, for purposes of expositive simplicity we will use the alternative of the reduced credit and the full cost for depreciation throughout this text.

All qualifying new property purchased during the year plus a limit of $125,000[28] in used property is eligible for the credit. The amount of the credit cannot exceed a firm's tax liability in a given year. Under TEFRA the maximum credit limit is $25,000 plus 85 percent of the tax liability in excess of $25,000. When the investment tax credit cannot be fully applied in a given year because of the maximum-credit limitation, a 3-year carryback and 15-year carryforward are permitted. These carrybacks and carryforwards are similar to those for operating and capital losses.

As an example of how the ITC works, suppose the Precision Milling Company's tax liability from operations for 1984 was $80,000. During 1984, the firm purchased two depreciable assets. One was a new machine having a 5-year normal recovery period and costing $900,000; the other was a used machine having a 3-year normal recovery period and costing $200,000. The total investment tax credit available can be calculated with respect to each machine, A and B, assuming the firm chooses to take the reduced credit and thereby depreciate 100 percent of the asset's cost.

---

[28]The Economic Recovery Tax Act of 1981 as modified by the Tax Reform Act of 1984 includes a scheduled increase to a limit of $150,000 in eligible used property which is to take effect for taxable years beginning after 1987.

Machine A: 8% × $900,000 = $72,000
Machine B: 4% × $125,000 =   5,000
        Total credit $77,000

The $5,000 figure for machine B is found by multiplying the $125,000 maximum for used property by the 4 percent alternative rate applicable to eligible property having a normal recovery period of 3 years. The maximum credit that can be applied to the current year's tax liability is $71,750 [$25,000 + .85($80,000 − $25,000)]. Since the firm is eligible for a credit of $77,000, the remaining credit of $5,250 ($77,000 − $71,750) can be carried back 3 years and then forward for as many as 15 years.

A few important points relative to the investment tax credit require amplification.

1. Depending upon the election made, a firm may change the depreciable value of the asset. For example, the original cost of machine A above (of $900,000) would be used to determine its depreciable value without regard to the ITC, but had the firm elected to take the full 10 percent credit, only $855,000 (i.e. 95% × $900,000) would be depreciable.

2. The ITC does not apply to buildings; it applies only to machinery and equipment.

3. A firm that takes the investment tax credit but does not hold the asset long enough to earn the credit must recapture the ITC when the asset is sold. This recapture represents a reversing process, in which the amount of the unearned ITC is returned to the government in the form of a tax payment.[29]

Interest and Dividends.   Although both interest and dividend payments represent compensation for the use of capital, they are treated differently for tax purposes. The interest paid by a corporation on bank loans and debt securities is considered to be a tax-deductible expense, but the dividends paid to stockholders are not (nor is the repayment of principal on loans which, like dividends, is paid from the firm's after-tax cash flow). As might be expected, this has a notable effect on the comparative cost of funds. Other things being equal, it encourages debt financing over the use of equity. For example, at a marginal tax rate of 40 percent, it

---

[29]Because the rules relative to the recapture of an unearned ITC are complicated by the alternative ITC election introduced by TEFRA, detailed discussion of them is beyond the scope of this text. For detailed discussion of these procedures, see the most recent editions of *Federal Tax Course* (New York: Commerce Clearing House) or *Federal Tax Course* (Englewood Cliffs, N.J.: Prentice-Hall).

takes only $100,000 to service $1 million of 10 percent debt, but $166,667 ($100,000 ÷ 0.60) is required (in pre-tax earnings) to pay the same $100,000 in the form of dividends.

The situation is equally inconsistent when corporations are on the receiving end. Unless derived from tax-exempt municipal issues, the interest income received by a company is treated as ordinary income and taxed at regular rates. However, 85 percent of the dividends received by one domestic corporation from another are exempt from taxes; the remaining 15 percent is taxed as ordinary income. Thus, for a firm at the 40 percent marginal tax rate, the receipt of $50,000 in dividends would mean taxes of:

$$\$50,000 \ (1 - .85) \ (.40) = \$3,000$$

This translates into a marginal tax rate on dividend receipts of only 6 percent ($3,000 ÷ $50,000) and yields $47,000 in after-tax cash flow. These numbers compare quite favorably to the $30,000 that would be left after paying taxes on $50,000 worth of interest income, and explain in large part why some corporate money managers are looking to stocks as a way to increase the returns on their investment portfolios.[30]

It would seem to be a simple matter for closely held corporations to refrain from paying dividends so that their well-to-do stockholders could avoid personal income taxes on dividends. But the IRS expressly prohibits this type of activity. If the IRS can determine that a firm has accumulated an excess amount of earnings in order to avoid ordinary income taxes, it may levy an excess earnings accumulation tax on any retained earnings above $250,000—the amount currently exempt from this tax for all firms, except personal corporations. In order to avoid penalty, everything over $250,000 should be retained for some legitimate business purpose (to pay off debt, finance growth, and/or provide the company with a cushion for when times are rough). There is no limit on the amount of earnings that a company can retain, so long as the corporation is not using retained earnings as a tax shelter.

MULTINATIONAL DIMENSIONS

Taxation of Foreign Income

The U.S. government taxes U.S. firms on their worldwide income. The purpose is to neutralize tax incentives that might favor or impede U.S. direct investment in developed countries. This principle is called *domestic tax neutrality*. One dollar earned domestically is taxed at the same rate as one equivalent dollar earned abroad. In order to prevent double taxation of the same income, most countries, including the United States, grant foreign tax credit for income taxes

---

[30]The strategy is known as a "dividend roll" and will be fully explored in Chapter 9.

paid to the host country. For example, if a U.S. firm earns the dollar equivalent of $1 million in Japan, it would typically pay $400,000 in income taxes to Japan at the Japanese income tax rate of 40 percent. The U.S. tax due on that income would be reduced by a $400,000 foreign credit.

The actual payment of the net U.S. tax liability may be deferred until the foreign income is actually remitted as a dividend from a U.S. affiliate incorporated abroad. If the affiliate is an unincorporated branch, however, payment of U.S. taxes cannot be deferred. In both cases, the foreign tax credit may be claimed only when the U.S. tax is due. Despite the loss of tax deferral, there are valid reasons for some kinds of firms to organize abroad as branches. Firms in the oil and mining industries do so because they are able to claim the depletion allowance on foreign as well as domestic operations. This is worth more in tax deferral than could be gained from incorporation abroad. New foreign affiliates often generate losses during the first few years until they get established. These might be started as branches in order to deduct their losses against other corporate income. When the affiliates become profitable, they are then incorporated in order to start the deferral privilege. It should be noted that affiliates incorporated abroad cannot be consolidated with the parent for U.S. tax purposes, although they are consolidated for financial reporting purposes.

Corporate Profits in Times of Inflation

Inflation was a serious problem in this country from the latter part of the 1960s through 1981—and the jury is still out as to whether inflation has been finally brought under control. While it affects some groups more than others, it is clear that inflation is just as hard on the economic well-being of most business concerns as it is on most wage earners and consumers. The alleged causes of inflation are well known and include excessive government regulation, significant and continued deficit spending, declining rates of worker productivity, the increased cost of energy, a tax structure that encourages consumption and discourages savings, and changing monetary conditions. Whatever the cause, the impact is always the same: pressure on the cost of production and rising prices. The discussion thus far has dealt with corporate profits as if inflation can simply be ignored. But inflation, as we will see, cannot be ignored.

The Problem

Because of the serious distortions high inflation causes in traditionally reported income, the accounting profession has studied the merits of adjusting financial statements for price-level changes. The major problem with inflation is, of course, that it severely overstates real income. By some estimates, a gap of as much as 30 to 40 percent has existed between the profits reported by companies and what economists consider real earnings. There are two major reasons for this: depreciation and inventory.

On a historical cost basis, depreciation is normally viewed as a way of systematically costing out a long-lived expenditure; in a going concern sense, however, and particularly when serious inflation is prevalent, depreciation is seen as providing funds for the replacement of fixed assets. In this latter view, it's clear that depreciation allowances have been seriously inadequate and create an illusion of profits when companies are actually using up their fixed assets without adequately providing for replacement at current (or future) costs. Inventory is important because of the effect it has on the firm's cost of goods sold. For one reason or another, many firms still use FIFO (first in–first out) as an inventory valuation method; unfortunately, such a system in times of inflation usually results in measuring cost of goods sold in terms of the oldest and cheapest items in inventory, and as a result understates this important expense in terms of current costs.[31]

Accounting Remedies

After years of debate, the Financial Accounting Standards Board (FASB) is beginning to come to grips with the problem and establish new guidelines for inflation accounting. Essentially, both depreciation charges and inventory expenses (cost of goods sold) will be adjusted upward to reflect replacement requirements at current cost levels. Thus, as these two important costs increase, inflation-adjusted profits will decline. Hardest hit will be the capital-intensive firms—particularly those like the steel industry, that are using dated plant and equipment—and those that have high inventory costs and insist on using FIFO. The new guidelines became effective with the 1979 annual reports and for the time being at least, apply only to the largest corporations—specifically, to those firms with gross fixed assets and inventory of at least $125 million and/or total assets of $1 billion or more. Undoubtedly, if the guidelines are successful, they will spread to a wider range of firms.

The firms covered by the guidelines are required to produce three sets of figures: the traditional historical cost statement remains and is supplemented by a constant-dollar statement (which makes the necessary inflation adjustments by using a general price level index) and a current-cost statement (which determines replacement-cost adjust-

---

[31]For more discussion of this important accounting matter, see Hawkins, *Corporate Financial Reporting*, chap. 15, AICPA, "Reporting the Financial Effects of Price Level Changes," *Accounting Research Study No. 6*, New York, 1963; FASB, *Summary Statement of Financial Accounting Standard No. 33: Financial Reporting & Changing Prices*, September 1979; and S. Davidson and R. L. Weil, "Inflation Accounting: What Will General Price-Level Adjusted Income Statements Show," *Financial Analysts Journal* 31 (January–February 1975), pp. 27–31.

ments for specific fixed assets and inventory lines). An example of the new reporting system as it relates to the income statement is reproduced in Table 2.6; note its effects on reported costs and profit. Such a scheme, it is hoped, will provide users not only with traditionally derived figures, but also with an indication of the undesirable effects inflation has on reported profits. It is interesting to note, however, that the new standards still have not made traditional accounting statements more useful.

Financial Strategies

Generally speaking, pricing is the key defense mechanism of the firm in periods of inflation, and is used to combat spiraling costs and/or excessive demand for goods and services. Increased prices, with or without greater output, will lead to more revenues for business. But when the cost of production rises, the firm may not necessarily experience a corresponding increase in profits. In fact, many firms probably cannot raise prices in line with their increased costs because of the elasticity of demand for their products or because their price structure is subject to the actions of regulatory bodies (as is the case, for example, with public utilities). But even if prices do rise and profits keep pace, the purchasing power of the dollar will have declined, so the firm may not be that well off in real terms after all. Many observers refer to this phenomenon as a crisis in the quality of earnings. That is, while reported profits are rising, sometimes at record rates, they are not as "obscene" as some political and social commentators would have us believe when they are viewed in terms of real earnings, adjusted for inflation and inadequate depreciation.

Financial managers, of course, must adapt to this and other inflation-derived problems. They can generally do this by minimizing their

TABLE 2.6
Statement of Annual Income from Continuing Operations, Adjusted for Changing Prices (Dollars in Thousands)

	As Reported in Primary Statements	Adjusted for General Inflation	Adjusted for Changes in Specific Prices (Current Costs)
Net sales and other operating revenues	$253,000	$253,000	$253,000
Cost of goods sold	$197,000	$204,384	$205,408
Depreciation and amortization expense	10,000	14,130	19,500
Other operating expense	20,835	20,835	20,835
Interest expense	7,165	7,165	7,165
Provision for income taxes	9,000	9,000	9,000
Total costs and expenses	$244,000	$255,514	$261,908
Profit (loss) from continuing operations	$ 9,000	$ (2,514)	$ (8,908)

SOURCE: Financial Accounting Standards Board, *Summary Statement of Financial Accounting Standard No. 33: Financial Reporting and Changing Prices.* New York, September 1979, p. 5.

company's purchasing power losses and maximizing purchasing power gains so as to at least maintain the purchasing power equivalent of their stockholders' equity. Cash, accounts receivable, and other monetary assets are all exposed to purchasing power losses during inflationary periods; in contrast, accounts payable, long-term debt, and similar monetary liabilities are subject to purchasing power gains to the extent that these liabilities are repaid with "cheaper" funds than those borrowed. Consequently, in inflationary times, most businesses are well advised to try to maintain a net monetary liability balance (monetary liabilities greater than monetary assets).

A caveat is in order, however. For as some firms learned in 1981 and 1982, when the rate of inflation slows down (disinflation) or disappears, a net monetary liability position can cause *serious* debt-service problems since the firm may no longer be able to generate ever-increasing levels of revenues and cash flows.

While it is not always possible to reduce monetary assets (especially accounts receivable) to as low a level as desired, one way to do so is to shift resources from monetary to physical assets (like inventory, plant, and equipment). The premise is that inventories will be protected against inflation so long as the price of raw materials and finished goods keep pace with the rate of inflation; similarly, fixed assets will be protected to the extent that their resale value rises with inflation and their rising cost of replacement is recovered, not through depreciation, but through increases in the prices of the goods and services produced with these assets (increased profits). The risk of this strategy is, of course, being caught with costly excess inventory and capacity when business slows down.

SUMMARY	

Financial institutions, by making the deposits received from savers available to investors, act as intermediaries in the financial system. The financial markets provide a mechanism that allows saving units to make direct transactions with investing units—often with the assistance of a stockbroker and/or investment banker. The financial market is made up of the money market—a short-term securities market—and the capital market—a long-term securities market. The capital markets contain organized security exchanges as well as the over-the-counter market. The returns on securities traded in the capital market tend to be related to economic forces and issue characteristics. With higher risk, of course, higher returns are expected.

Profits—and especially cash flow—along with risk, are important determinants of the value of a firm. By adding back any noncash expenditures such as depreciation to profits after taxes, a rough estimate of cash flow from operations can be made. Most firms maintain at least two sets of books. When reporting to owners, straight-line depreciation is commonly used to show high and stable profits. In reporting to the IRS, accelerated depreciation is used to minimize tax payments and increase operating cash flows. Under the Economic Recovery Tax Act of 1981 as modified by the Tax Equity and Fiscal Responsibility Act of 1982 and the Tax Reform Act of 1984, assets are depreciated for tax purposes using the accelerated cost recovery system (ACRS).

Corporate tax rates on ordinary operating income range from 15 to 46 percent; long-term capital gains are subject to a maximum rate of 28 percent. Firms can carry operating and capital losses backward 3 years and forward 5 to 15 years. An investment tax credit of as much as 10 percent of cost is available to firms acquiring certain assets. Interest paid is tax deductible, while dividend and principal payments must come from after-tax cash flows. All interest earned by a corporation is included as income, but 85 percent of dividends received on stock of domestic corporations is exempt for tax purposes. Accounting (or accounting-derived) values are measured at historical (original) dollar costs and, as a result, do not reflect many of the serious distortions caused by prolonged periods of inflation.

QUESTIONS

2.1. Describe the function, structure, and importance of the financial system.
   a. What role do financial institutions play in this system?
   b. What role do financial markets play in the financial system? Who are the active participants in these markets?

2.2. For each of the following financial markets, describe (1) its function; (2) the major participants; and (3) the key securities traded.
   a. Money market.
   b. Capital market.

2.3. Briefly describe the function of security exchanges and compare and contrast organized security exchanges and the over-the-counter market.

2.4. What relationship, if any, do economic forces and issue characteristics have with the rate of return on a given security? Why might speculative common stock be a more costly form of financing than prime-grade short-term commercial paper?

2.5. Is there a relationship between corporate profits and corporate cash flow? Explain. Which is more significant to the financial decisions of the firm?

2.6. Briefly discuss the "accounting ambiguity" that often exists in published financial statements. Why do firms commonly maintain two sets of books—one for financial reporting and another for tax purposes?

2.7. Contrast accelerated with straight-line depreciation. Explain why accelerated depreciation is normally preferred over straight-line for tax purposes, and why the choice of a depreciation method is an important corporate decision.

2.8. What is the accelerated cost recovery system (ACRS)? Describe the key property classes under this system and the recovery periods and depreciation percentages associated with each.

2.9. Compare and contrast the corporate tax structure for ordinary income with that applicable to capital gains. Discuss and differentiate between short-term and long-term capital gains. Is it possible for a firm to sell an asset and be subject to both ordinary income and long-term capital gains taxes? Explain.

2.10. Describe the investment tax credit (ITC) and explain the broad economic objective it is intended to fulfill. What happens in the event a firm takes the ITC, but does not fully earn it?

2.11. Can the corporate tax structure per se have an influence on the choice of a financing vehicle used by the firm? On certain types of corporate investment decisions?

2.12. Explain the impact of prolonged inflation on reported profits. What kind of distortions does it cause? What course of action should financial managers adopt in the face of prolonged inflation?

PROBLEMS

2.1. *INCOME STATEMENT AND CASH FLOW.* Adams Enterprises wishes to assess the potential impact of its choice of depreciation method on both profits and cash flow. It can select either an accelerated depreciation method that would provide $40,000 in depreciation in the current year or straight-line depreciation that will provide $15,000 in depreciation writeoffs. Other financial data for the year are given below:

Common dividends (cash)	$ 15,000
Total assets	600,000
Tax rate	40%
Sales revenue	400,000
Interest expense	40,000
Cost of goods sold	200,000
Total liabilities	420,000
Preferred dividends	4,000
Operating expenses	80,000
Stockholders' equity	180,000

With the applicable information given above:

a. Using total depreciation during the year of $40,000, calculate (1) profits after taxes, (2) additions to retained earnings, and (3) cash flow from operations.

b. Using total depreciation during the year of $15,000, calculate (1) profits after taxes, (2) additions to retained earnings, and (3) cash flow from operations.

c. In light of your findings in (a) and (b), explain why many firms prefer to maintain two sets of books—one for reporting to stockholders and another for tax purposes. Which choice of depreciation would be used in each instance? Explain.

2.2.   *DEPRECIATION OPTIONS—ACRS.*   Matt Benz and Company recently acquired an asset costing $200,000 and having a normal recovery period of 5 years. The president of the company has called upon you to develop the alternative depreciation schedules that could be used for tax purposes. Using Tables 2.4 and 2.5:

a.   Develop each of the *four* alternative depreciation schedules (includes straight-line over the normal recovery period) that could be used under ACRS to depreciate the asset for tax purposes. [*Note*: When straight-line depreciation is used under ACRS, only half of the first-year depreciation can be taken in that year; the other half-year of depreciation must be taken in the year immediately following the last year of the recovery period over which the straight-line depreciation was calculated.]

b.   If the firm anticipates high levels of profits in the coming years, which depreciation schedule from (a) would you recommend for tax purposes? Explain why.

c.   If, on the other hand, the firm anticipates losses in the coming years, which depreciation schedule from (a) would you recommend for tax purposes? Explain why.

d.   From your findings in (b) and (c), explain the impact of expected pretax profits on the choice of depreciation method used for tax purposes.

2.3.   *DEPRECIATION—ACRS.*   Martin Industries acquired three assets during the year. Each is described below.

Asset	Type of Property	Cost
A	General purpose milling machine	$300,000
B	Research microscope	60,000
C	Chain hoist	120,000

a.   Calculate the annual depreciation on each of the new assets, assuming the firm uses the normal ACRS recovery periods.

b.   If the firm chose to use straight-line depreciation over the longest optional extended recovery period under ACRS, find the annual depreciation for each of the assets in each year. [*Note*: Under this method, only half of the first-year depreciation can be taken in that year; the other half-year of depreciation must be taken in the year following the last year of the optional recovery period.]

c.   Compare and contrast your findings in (a) and (b) and explain under what circumstances a firm might choose to use the optional extended recovery period rather than the normal recovery period to depreciate an asset.

2.4. **DEPRECIATION AND CASH FLOWS.**   A firm expects to have earnings before depreciation and taxes of $160,000 in each of the next five years. It is considering the purchase of a fixed asset costing $150,000 and having a normal recovery period of 5 years.

    a. Calculate the annual depreciation for the asset purchase using the ACRS depreciation percentages given in Table 2.5.

    b. Calculate the annual cash flow from operations for each of the 5 years. Assume a 40 percent ordinary tax rate.

    c. Compare and discuss your findings in (a) and (b).

2.5. **CORPORATE TAXES.**   Interstate Bull Shippers, Inc., is a major livestock trucking firm that operates out of Kansas City. The financial vice-president of the firm, Ernie Shotts, has prepared the following information about the operating results for 1984.

Total revenues	$4,500,000
Depreciation charges	350,000
Interest expense	250,000
All other operating expenses	2,900,000
Preferred dividends	100,000
Common dividends (cash)	250,000
Principal repaid on loans	150,000
Capital asset acquired (new piece of equipment with a 5-year normal recovery period) at a cost of	1,000,000
Capital asset sold (original cost, $400,000; age, 2 years; current book value, $252,000) at a price of	350,000
Long-term capital gains realized during 1984	250,000

Using the information above, along with the actual corporate tax rates and assuming the firm uses ACRS normal recovery periods to depreciate assets, compute the firm's:

    a. Total tax liability.

    b. Net profit after tax.

    c. After-tax operating cash flow.

    d. Earnings available to common stockholders,

    e. Additions to retained earnings.

2.6. **TAX ON SALE OF ASSETS.**   Waters Manufacturing purchased a new machine 3 years ago for $80,000. It is being depreciated under ACRS over its normal 5-year recovery period using the percentages given in Table 2.5. Assume a 40 percent ordinary tax rate and a 28 percent tax rate on long-term capital gains.

a. What is the current book value of the machine?
b. Calculate the firm's tax liability (assuming it is profitable) if it sells the machine for the following: $100,000, $56,000, $33,600, $25,000.

2.7.   ORDINARY AND CAPITAL GAINS TAXES: TOTAL TAX LIABILITY.   The Lionel Corporation just sold a two-year-old machine that originally cost $500,000 and was being depreciated using the normal ACRS 5-year recovery period and the applicable percentages given in Table 2.5. Assume that the firm has a 40 percent tax rate on ordinary income and 28 percent on long-term capital gains. The firm has before-tax operating earnings of $195,000.

a. Calculate the *total* tax liability from ordinary and capital gains income assuming the firm sells the machine for $550,000.
b. Recalculate the *total* tax liability assuming a sale for $450,000.
c. Calculate the firm's *total* tax liability if the machine is sold for $250,000.

2.8.   LOSS CARRYBACK–CARRYFORWARD.   The accountants have some bad news for Fields Haberdashery, Inc.: the firm had a big loss in 1984. The firm's historical (1981–1984) and estimated (1985–1991) operating incomes (we will presume the company has operating income only and therefore no capital gains or losses) and taxes appear as follows:

Year	Operating Income	Income Taxes
1981	$300,000	$117,750
1982	450,000	186,750
1983	350,000	140,750
1984	loss	—
1985	200,000	71,750
1986	400,000	163,750
1987	500,000	209,750
1988	750,000	324,750
1989	900,000	393,750
1990	1,000,000	439,750
1991	1,100,000	490,750

Using the corporate tax rates given in the text, recompute the historical and estimated income and determine the amount of tax refund due and future accrued tax relief (a) assuming the 1984 operating loss amounted to $1,000,000, and (b) using a 1984 operating loss of $2,500,000.

2.9.   INVESTMENT TAX CREDIT.   Zachary, Inc., just purchased two assets—X and Y. Asset X is a new piece of equipment costing $600,000 and having a 5-year normal recovery period. Asset Y is a used piece of research equipment costing $200,000 and having a 3-year normal recovery period. The firm has decided to use the alternative reduced investment tax credits so that it can depreciate 100 percent of the cost of each asset.

a. Calculate the total tax credit the firm would be eligible to receive as a result of acquiring the two assets.

b. If after 2 years the firm sells asset X, discuss, but do not work out, tax consequences.

2.10. *INTEREST AND DIVIDENDS.* The well-known XYZ Company recently bought 10,000 shares of Timely Calendar, a stock that pays $2 per share in annual dividends. XYZ pays taxes at a 40 percent marginal rate.

a. Compute the annual tax liability and after-tax cash flow from this investment.

b. XYZ's investment manager is considering selling the Timely stock and investing the proceeds in a bond that pays $20,000 a year in interest; based only on comparative returns, would you recommend the switch?

2.11. *AFTER-TAX COST OF FUNDS.* The Weaver Manufacturing Company needs to raise $1 million; its investment bankers advise that it can do this by issuing either 7 percent preferred stock or 11 percent bonds. The company is in the 40 percent marginal tax bracket and turns to you for help. Which procedure would be least costly? Based on cost alone, which procedure would you recommend?

SELECTED REFERENCES	

American Institute of Certified Public Accountants. "Reporting the Financial Effects of Price Level Changes." *Accounting Research Study No. 6.* New York: American Institute of Certified Public Accountants, 1963.

Beaver, W., P. Kettler, and M. Scholes. "The Association Between Market Determined and Accounting Determined Risk Measures." *Accounting Review* (October 1970), pp. 654–682.

Briloff, Abraham. *Unaccountable Accounting.* New York: Harper & Row, 1972.

Commerce Clearing House. *Federal Tax Course,* annual edition. New York: Commerce Clearing House.

Curley, Anthony, and Robert Bear. *Investment Analysis and Management.* New York: Harper & Row, 1979.

Davidson, S. and R. L. Weil. "Inflation Accounting: What Will General Price-Level Adjusted Income Statements Show." *Financial Analysts Journal* 31 (January–February 1975), pp. 27–31.

Dopouch, Nicholas. "Discussion of an Empirical Test of the Relevance of Accounting Information for Investment Decisions." Supplement to *Journal of Accounting Research,* 1971, pp. 32–40.

Dougall, Herbert E., and Jack E. Gaumnitz. *Capital Markets and Institutions*, 4th ed. Englewood Cliffs, N.J.: Prentice-Hall, 1980.

Dufey, Gunter, and S. L. Srinivasulu. "The Case for Corporate Management of Foreign Exchange Risk." *Financial Management* 12 (winter 1983), pp. 54–62.

Financial Accounting Standards Board. *Summary Statement of Financial Accounting Standard No. 33: Financial Reporting and Changing Prices*. New York, September 1979.

Gandolfi, Arthur E. "Inflation, Taxation, and Interest Rates." *Journal of Finance* 37 (June 1982), pp. 797–807.

Geske, Robert, and Richard Roll. "The Fiscal and Monetary Linkage Between Stock Returns and Inflation." *Journal of Finance* 38 (March 1983), pp. 1–33.

Gup, Benton E. *Financial Intermediaries: An Introduction*, 2d ed. Boston: Houghton Mifflin, 1980.

Hamilton, James L. "Marketplace Organization and Marketability: NASDAQ, The Stock Exchange, and the National Market System." *Journal of Finance* 33 (May 1978), pp. 487–503.

Hawkins, David. *Corporate Financial Reporting—Text and Cases*. Homewood, Ill.: Irwin, 1977.

Hoffman, William H., ed. *West's Federal Taxation: Corporations, Partnerships, Estates and Trusts*, annual edition. St. Paul, Minn.: West Publishing.

Jensen, Michael. "Capital Markets: Theory and Evidence." *Bell Journal of Economics and Management Science* (autumn 1972), pp. 357–398.

Kaufman, George G. *Money, the Financial System, and the Economy*, 3rd ed. Boston: Houghton Mifflin, 1981.

Keiso, Donald E., and Jerry J. Weygandt. *Intermediate Accounting*, 4th ed. New York: Wiley, 1983.

Kidwell, David S., and Richard L. Peterson. *Financial Institutions, Markets, and Money*, 2d ed. Hinsdale, Ill. Dryden, 1984.

Lorie, James, and Mary Hamilton. *The Stock Market: Theories and Evidence*. Homewood, Ill. Irwin, 1973.

McFarland, James W., R. Richardson Pettit, and Sam K. Sung. "The Distribution of Foreign Exchange Price Changes: Trading Day Effects and Risk Measurement." *Journal of Finance* 37 (June 1982), pp. 693–715.

Peek, Joe, and James A. Wilcox. "The Postwar Stability of the Fisher Effect." *Journal of Finance* 38 (September 1983), pp. 1111–1124.

Prentice-Hall, Inc. *Federal Tax Course*, annual edition. Englewood Cliffs, N.J.: Prentice-Hall.

Protopapadakis, Aris, and Hans R. Stoll. "Spot and Futures Prices and the Law of One Price." *Journal of Finance* 38 (December 1983), pp. 1431–1455.

Sharpe, William F. "Capital Asset Prices: A Theory of Market Equilibrium Under Conditions of Risk." *Journal of Finance* 19 (September 1964), pp. 425–442.

Van Horne, James C. *Financial Market Rates and Flows*, 2d ed. Englewood Cliffs, N.J.: Prentice-Hall, 1978.

Wilcox, Kirkland A., and Joseph C. San Miguel. *Introduction to Financial Accounting*, 2d ed. New York: Harper & Row, 1984.

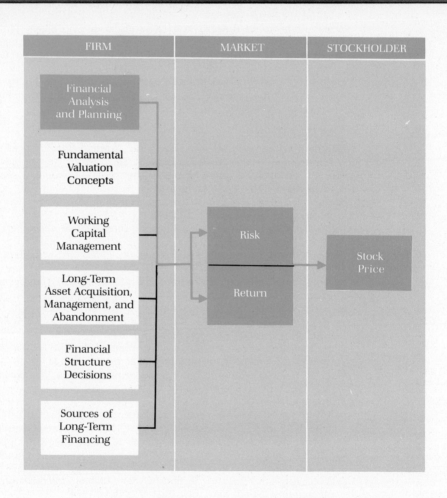

PART TWO

FINANCIAL ANALYSIS AND PLANNING

During the normal course of business, the level and composition of a firm's assets and liabilities will vary as sales change and other variables—like competitive pressures—affect the firm. It is obviously in management's best interest not only to monitor the operating results and financial condition of the firm, but also to plan for the future course of business. This part of the book deals with financial analysis and planning. Financial analysis, which is concerned with the historical performance of the firm, is the topic of Chapter 3. As an analytical tool, it addresses the financial relationships that exist at a given point in time and the trends in these relationships over time. The liquidity and composition of resources, financial leverage, and the profitability of the firm are all studied not simply for their historical significance, but for the clues they provide in formulating the firm's future courses of action. In Chapter 4, our attention is centered directly on the future as we take up the practice of budgeting and financial forecasting. Budgets and forecasts provide management with a summary statement of the potential financial consequences of present-day decisions; as such, they give direction to the firm and help management obtain the most productive and profitable use of the firm's limited resources.

3

Analysis
of Financial
Statements

A business acquires assets in order to provide needed support for its operations; in a like manner, the financial structure exists as a way to support assets. Defining the amount and composition of assets according to the operating needs of the firm, and the volume and structure of financing by the liquidity of the assets employed, are sound financial principles that contribute to the value of the firm. But just how does management know whether the firm is, in fact, carrying enough inventory to support a desired level of sales? And how can it tell if operating results are improving, or that the company will have an adequate cash flow to service its debt? These questions, and others like them, are recurring problems that can be addressed through *financial analysis*—a widely used analytical system that involves the in-depth study of a firm's financial statements. In this chapter we will examine the principles and techniques of financial analysis, and demonstrate how it can be used by management in making decisions that affect the operations and asset-financing mix of the firm.

| Financial Analysis | The value of the firm and shareholder wealth depends on how well the company can maintain or improve its profitability, the manner in which the firm allocates the scarce resources it has at its disposal, the amount of leverage being used, and in general, on the level and certainty of projected cash flows. We noted in Chapter 1 that maximizing the value of the firm, and therefore shareholder wealth, is the ultimate goal of financial management. Financial analysis can help in this regard as it (1) enables management to periodically assess the extent to which the operating results and financial condition of the firm are contributing to |

share price maximization, and (2) assists management in developing plans that will keep the company on course toward its long-run goals. Financial analysis is used not just to increase profits and rate of return, but more important, to enhance corporate cash flow. Granted, other things being equal, reducing the supply of inventory (without affecting sales) promotes profitability, but it also improves the cash flow of the firm. And it is the cash flow which is of major economic consequence to the firm since it affects the long-run value of the company.

The process of financial analysis can be broadly summarized as follows:

1. A series of comparative annual[1] financial statements is obtained (at the minimum, this would include balance sheets and income statements); these are studied for general content and to assure comparability of accounting procedures.
2. Various measures are then computed for each year in the analysis —such measures include common size statements, flow of funds, profit margins, and a number of other financial ratios.
3. The ratios and schedules are then studied and evaluated.
4. Based on the insights obtained through evaluation and diagnosis, recommendations are made regarding future actions.

Financial analysis is normally conducted over a 2- to 5-year period, including the results and financial condition of the most recent fiscal year. This time frame is needed to identify emerging developments, and study the thrust and implications of any trends. The evaluation and diagnosis stage has traditionally been concerned with the study of operating relationships that exist at a given point in time, and with trends in these relationships over time; the analysis is thus both cross-sectional and time-series in nature. It should be clear, however, that the historical performance of the firm is evaluated only because of the insight it provides with regard to assessing future behavior.

The basic managerial objective of financial analysis is to obtain information that can be used for decision-making purposes. Such information, for example, can be used to judge individual performances and managerial talent; it is also useful in assessing divisional perform-ance and in maintaining a coordinated perspective on activities. The most important use of financial analysis, however, is in corporate planning and control. For financial analysis enables management to monitor the firm's performance from period to period and uncover information that will be helpful in planning the future direction of the firm. Deficiencies and weaknesses can be identified and corrective

---

[1] Financial analysis can just as easily be conducted on interim (monthly or quarterly) statements; except for some obvious time frame or seasonal adjustments, the underlying principles and analytical procedures are the same as those used when annual statements are analyzed.

actions set into motion; too, by better understanding the more intricate dimensions and requirements of the firm, management can evaluate the possible implications of alternative courses of action and more precisely pinpoint the type of action necessary to bring about desired results.

Financial Statements

A complete set of financial statements[2] is made up of four parts: (1) a balance sheet, (2) an income statement, (3) a statement of changes in stockholders' equity, and (4) a flow of funds statement. Because they represent the raw materials of financial analysis and because of their importance in the analytical process, we will briefly review each of the major accounting statements. The statements are those of the Mid-America Corporation and are obtained from the 1984 Annual Report of this hypothetical energy firm.[3] The company transports natural gas to markets in the central United States through a network of over 7000 miles of pipeline; it is also a major producer of coal, and is actively engaged in the exploration, production, and marketing of oil, gas, and natural gas liquids.

Balance Sheet

The *balance sheet* is a statement of the company's assets, liabilities, and stockholders' equity; it may be thought of as a summary of the firm's resources balanced against its debt and ownership positions at a single point in time (e.g., the last day of the calendar or fiscal year). Mid-America's balance sheets for 1983–1984 are illustrated in Table 3.1. The company's assets are listed in the top half of the report, and are broken into two parts: current and long-term assets. Current assets consist of cash and other assets that will be converted into cash (or in the case of "prepaid expenses," consumed) in 1 year or less.[4] These assets represent the firm's working capital and provide support for day-to-day operations. The long-term assets of the firm are made up primarily of land and facilities. Note the "Accumulated depreciation and depletion allowance"

---

[2]For an excellent in-depth discussion of the information content of financial statements, see S. Davidson, C. Stickney, and R. Weil, *Accouting: The Language of Business*, 5th ed. (Sun Lakes, AZ: Thomas Horton and Daughters, Inc., 1982), pp. 66–91. The authors reproduce GE's 1981 annual report and provide extensive explanatory comments about the various accounting entries that appear in the statements and accompanying notes.

[3]In addition to the annual report, financial statement information may also be obtained from the company's 10-K Report (a document filed annually with the SEC which contains detailed financial and operating data), and/or from unpublished internal financial sources. Both sources will provide more financial information than an annual report; even so, their impact on financial analysis is largely limited to the amount of detail that can be worked into the analytical process. That is, except for being able to provide more detailed or segmented information about such things as turnover ratios and product line profit margins, the mechanical and diagnostic stages of financial analysis are much the same as presented here with the use of annual report data.

[4]Some firms (like airframe manufacturers, for instance) have production cycles which often exceed one calendar year; as a result, their current assets are defined to include assets (like inventory) that will be converted to cash within a single production cycle.

TABLE 3.1.
Mid-America's
Balance Sheets
(For Fiscal Years
Ending December 31;
Dollars in Thousands)

	1984	1983
ASSETS		
Current assets		
Cash and short-term marketable securities	$ 10,230	$ 56,792
Accounts receivable, less allowance for doubtful accounts (1984—$1,349; 1983—$1,048)	259,336	186,412
Inventories	151,582	65,932
Prepaid expenses	38,882	18,869
Total current assets	$ 460,030	$ 328,005
Long-term assets		
Pipeline	$ 362,902	$ 259,600
Mining	314,386	285,229
Oil and gas	235,917	195,980
Refining	168,826	109,741
Marketing and other	180,977	137,288
Gross fixed assets	$1,263,008	$ 987,838
Less: Accumulated depreciation and depletion allowance	(313,079)	(268,240)
Net fixed assets	$ 949,929	$ 719,598
Investments and other long-term assets	62,778	44,169
Goodwill	5,719	5,811
Total assets	$1,478,456	$1,097,583
LIABILITIES AND STOCKHOLDERS' EQUITY		
Current liabilities		
Accounts payable	$ 210,828	$ 128,639
Accrued income taxes	5,170	15,310
Other accrued expenses	40,139	37,004
Long-term debt and capitalized lease obligations maturing within 1 year	26,185	36,340
Other current liabilities	29,098	33,345
Total current liabilities	$ 311,420	$ 250,638
Long-term obligations		
Long-term debt and lease obligations due beyond 1 year	$ 509,185	$ 323,979
Deferred income taxes	136,966	109,464
Other deferred credits	19,171	5,893
Stockholders' equity		
Common stock; $1 par value (shares authorized: 1984—50,000,000; 1983—35,000,000; shares issued: 1984—27,271,165; 1983—25,463,487)	$ 27,271	$ 25,463
Capital in excess of par value	108,134	75,719
Retained earnings	366,421	307,204
	501,826	408,386
Less: Common shares held in treasury, at cost (1984—3,351; 1983—23,227)	(112)	(777)
Total equity	$ 501,714	$ 407,609
Total liabilities and stockholders' equity	$1,478,456	$1,097,583

account; this is the total of past depreciation that has been charged against properties still on the books, and of depletion allowances taken against holdings of natural resource deposits. It is strictly an accounting entry and does not represent a pool of cash. The "goodwill" account represents an intangible asset that arises when a company acquires another firm (through a "purchase" rather than "pooling" type of transaction) for a price in excess of the net book value of its assets. It is a rather insignificant item for Mid-America, but even so, since the custom is to exclude goodwill from financial ratios, we will use net tangible assets in our computations: *net tangible assets* = total assets − goodwill.

Mid-America's financial structure appears in the lower half of the table, where liabilities and stockholders' equity are listed. This portion of the balance sheet is divided into three parts: (1) current liabilities, (2) long-term obligations, and (3) stockholders' equity. Current liabilities are the debts owed to suppliers (accounts payable), employees and taxing authorities (accruals), and lenders, and like their counterparts on the asset side of the balance sheet, are due and payable within a period of 1 year or less. The long-term obligations have maturities that extend beyond a year (often as far as 30 to 40 years). The capital leases of the company are also reported; in accordance with established accounting standards, these leases are capitalized and included on both the asset and liability sides of the balance sheet. For example, included as part of Mid-America's 1984 "gross fixed assets" were over $11 million of "lease rights"—assets held (but not owned) under capital leases. The capitalized value of the lease obligations is shown as a liability, which amount is equal to the present value of all future payments due under the lease arrangement. Such reporting practices provide a truer picture of the firm's financing activities, and more accurately reflect leverage and debt service positions. Finally, we should note the deferred items listed as a part of long-term obligations. These include deferred credits and deferred taxes, and are mostly bookkeeping entries used to account for unearned revenues or deferred profits. Deferred income tax is usually the biggest and most important type of deferred credit; it reflects the amount of a company's potential income tax obligation that has been deferred to future periods as a result of using different accounting practices for book and tax purposes (as noted in Chapter 2, straight-line depreciation is commonly used for book purposes, while accelerated depreciation is used for tax purposes). Deferred taxes (and many other deferred credits) are not legal obligations like most long-term debt; as such, they tend to overstate the leverage position of the company.

In addition to the money the company owes, another type of claim against assets is that of the firm's owners or stockholders. This is represented by the stockholders' equity (or net worth) accounts on the balance sheet, the major components of which are the common stock account, capital surplus ("capital in excess of par value"), and retained earnings. The first two represent paid-in capital and are equal to the proceeds from the sale of stock. Retained earnings are used to account for the accumulation of prior earnings that have been retained in the company—they are the earnings left after dividends have been paid and which have been used to pay off debt, acquire facilities, and invest in receivables, inventories, and the like. Retained earnings do not represent cash or a pool of untapped financing, but instead are resources that have been previously allocated to various areas of the firm. Finally, note that Mid-America lists a small amount in the treasury stock account, an entry which reflects a reduction in equity equal to the amount that has been spent to buy back the company's own shares.

Income Statement

The second important financial statement is the *income statement*; it provides a financial summary of the operating results of the firm. Unlike the balance sheet, the income statement covers activities that have occurred over time. Table 3.2 shows Mid-America's income statements for the years 1983 and 1984; they cover operations over the 12-month period ending December 31. The income statement provides a summary of the amount of revenues (sales and income) generated over the period, the costs and expenses incurred, and the company's profits. The reported profit of the company is not to be confused with the firm's cash flow. For the cash flow is a function not only of the operating results of the firm, but as we'll see, is also influenced by the company's investment and financing decisions. Profit is an accounting concept that attempts to relate costs to revenues in a given time period, whereas cash flow is an

TABLE 3.2
Mid-America's
Income Statement
(For Fiscal Years
Ending December 31;
Dollars in Thousands)

	1984	1983
Net sales	$1,769,740	$1,261,443
Outside purchases of raw materials, crude oil, and other products	1,107,962	734,423
Gross profit	661,778	527,020
Operating expenses	299,148	230,652
Selling, general, and administrative expenses	82,282	60,117
Depreciation and depletion	54,037	51,592
Exploration, dry hole, and lease expenses	17,715	9,651
Operating profit	$ 208,596	$ 175,008
Other income and (expense)—*net*[a]	14,818	5,930
Earnings before interest and taxes	$ 223,414	$ 180,938
Interest expense	37,272	31,134
Profit before tax	$ 186,142	$ 149,804
Provision for income tax	63,882	61,204
Net profit after tax	$ 122,260	$ 88,600
Cash dividends	$ 38,283	$ 31,636

[a]According to customary accounting practices, these amounts are shown as *additions* to operating profits since other income, in this case, was apparently larger than other expenses; if the reverse were true the numbers would be shown in parentheses—for example, (14,818)—and *subtracted* from operating profits.

economic concept that captures the movement of a single resource—cash—through the firm. Because the income statement and the whole reporting process is based on accrual accounting it contains some serious short-term timing problems. That is why throughout this book we emphasize the use of *cash flow* as the proper vehicle for evaluating the risk and return of corporate investment and financing decisions.

Statement of Changes in Stockholders' Equity

A company's balance sheet and its income statement are linked together, accounting wise, in a number of ways; one of them is the tie between net profits and retained earnings. *A statement of changes in stockholders' equity* shows how profits, dividends, and other transactions affect retained earnings and other components of the stockholders' position. Table 3.3 depicts the 1983–1984 statements for Mid-America Corporation. It shows in considerable detail the causes of any changes in paid-in capital, retained earnings, and treasury stock. The purpose of this statement is to reconcile changes in stockholders' equity from one period to the next. It is intended primarily to provide additional accounting detail and to demonstrate the amount of accounting integrity imbedded in the statements, and as such, they have very limited use in financial analysis.

Flow of Funds Statement

The *flow of funds statement* (or the statement of changes in financial position, as it is also known) summarizes significant financial changes which have occurred over a given accounting period. It provides insight on how the activities of the firm have been financed (its sources of funds) and how financial resources have been used (its uses or applications of funds). The flow of funds statement does this by integrating the balance sheet (or more specifically, changes in balance sheet accounts over time) with key summary figures from the income statement. Although it is normally included as part of a complete set of audited financial statements, a firm's flow of funds can easily be constructed by using a company's annual income statement and two of its balance sheets (one that is dated at the beginning and the other at the end of the accounting period covered in the income statement).

Basic sources of funds include the following:

1. A decrease in an asset account.
2. An increase in a liability or equity account.
3. Net profits after taxes.
4. Depreciation and other noncash expenditures.

Note that all these items have one thing in common: They all involve a potential inflow of funds to the firm. For example, when accounts receivable are collected or some of the fixed assets are liquidated, money becomes available to the firm as these assets are converted to cash; in like manner, money flows into the company when it borrows funds from the bank or sells stock. Obviously, profits provide funds, and we include depreciation (and similar charges) as a source of funds, since they are

TABLE 3.3

Mid-America's Statement of Changes in Stockholders' Equity (For Fiscal Years Ending December 31; Dollars in Thousands)

	Common Stock $1 Par Value		Capital in Excess of Par Value	Retained Earnings	Common Stock in Treasury at Cost	
	Shares	Amount			Shares	Amount
BALANCE, DECEMBER 31, 1982	25,405,752	$25,406	$75,041	$250,240	(10,489)	($351)
Net profit after tax				88,600		
Dividends ($1.40 per share)				(26,374)		
Difference between fair market value and cost of treasury shares issued to officers and employees under incentive compensation plan			(48)		7,411	248
Purchases					(20,149)	(674)
Equity transactions by pooled company prior to combination:						
Dividends ($1 per share)				(5,262)		
Stock options exercised	26,538	26	253			
Stock purchase plan	11,691	12	143			
Dividend reinvestment plan	19,506	19	279			
Other			51			
BALANCE, DECEMBER 31, 1983	25,463,487	$25,463	$75,719	$307,204	(23,227)	($777)
Change in fiscal year by pooled company	40,942	41	752	3,187		
Net profit after tax				122,260		
Dividends ($1.65 per share)				(31,084)		
Difference between fair market value and cost of treasury shares issued to officers and employees under incentive compensation plan				282	19,876	665
Equity transactions by pooled company prior to combination:						
Dividends ($1.50 per share)				(7,199)		
Stock options exercised	118,376	118	1,933			
Stock purchase plan			7			
Dividend reinvestment plan	4,991	5	123			
Stock dividend (20%)	1,344,578	1,345	26,602	(27,947)		
Warrants exercised	300,000	300	2,500			
Other	(1,209)	(1)	216			
BALANCE, DECEMBER 31, 1984	27,271,165	$27,271	$108,134	$366,421	(3,351)	($112)

noncash expenditures which are treated as adjustments (additions) to reported profits.

The sum of these sources represents the net amount of funds that were available to management for dividends, investments, and other purposes. The uses (or applications) side of the flow of funds statement provides a summary of what management actually did with the resources at its disposal. The basic uses of funds include these:

1. An increase in an asset account.
2. A decrease in a liability or equity account.
3. A net loss from operations.
4. The payment of dividends.

The order is reversed with the uses of funds, although the same type of logic can be employed to explain the nature of funds uses; that is, these resources are used for investment purposes (to acquire assets), or to service the firm's financial structure (by retiring debt and/or paying dividends).

After obtaining the necessary financial statements, the first step in the preparation of a flow of funds statement is to determine the amount and direction of changes in the asset, liability, and equity accounts of the balance sheet. This is done below for 1984 using the 1983 and 1984 Mid-America statements (dollars in thousands):

	1983	1984	Change
Cash and marketable securities	$ 56,792	$ 10,230	−$ 46,562
Accounts receivable	186,412	259,336	+ 72,924
Inventories	65,932	151,582	+ 85,650
Prepaid expenses	18,869	38,882	+ 20,013
Current assets	$ 328,005	$ 460,030	+$132,025
Net fixed assets	719,598	949,929	+ 230,331
Other assets	49,980	68,497	+ 18,517
Total assets	$1,097,583	$1,478,456	+$380,873
Accounts payable	$ 128,639	$ 210,828	+$ 82,189
Accrued income taxes	15,310	5,170	− 10,140
Other accrued expenses	37,004	40,139	+ 3,135
Current maturities	36,340	26,185	− 10,155
Other current liabilities	33,345	29,098	− 4,247
Current liabilities	$ 250,638	$ 311,420	+$ 60,782
Long-term debt and leases	323,979	509,185	+ 185,206
Deferred taxes	109,464	136,966	+ 27,502
Other deferred credits	5,893	19,171	+ 13,278
Common stock	25,463	27,271	+ 1,808
Capital surplus	75,719	108,134	+ 32,415
Retained earnings	307,204	366,421	+ 59,217
Treasury stock	(777)	(112)	+ 665
Total liabilities and stockholders' equity	$1,097,583	$1,478,456	+$380,873

Preparing the flow of funds statement involves combining most of the values from the balance sheet *change* column with several items from the income statement; chiefly, these are net profits after tax, dividends paid, depreciation charges, depletion charges, and other noncash expenditures. Mid-America's 1984 income statement is summarized below (dollars in thousands):

Summarized Income Statement	1984
Net sales	$1,769,740
Less: Outside purchases	1,107,962
Operating, selling and exploration	399,145
Depreciation and depletion[a]	54,037
Other income—*net*	(14,818)
Interest expense	37,272
Income taxes	63,882
Net profit after tax	$ 122,260
Cash dividends	$ 38,283

[a]Depreciation charges included in the depreciation and depletion figure are $42,155.

Net profits and dividends are used in place of the change in retained earnings figure as they (along, perhaps, with any surplus adjustments[5]) will account for the retained earnings changes that have occurred over the period in question. Also, in order to capture the effects of depreciation on fixed-asset liquidations and acquisitions, the net amount spent on facilities and other fixed assets is computed according to the following formula:

$$\Delta FA_t = \Delta NFA_t + Dep_t \tag{3.1}$$

where ΔFA_t = change in fixed assets for period t
ΔNFA_t = change in net fixed assets for period t (obtained from the balance sheet change column)
Dep_t = depreciation charges for period t (obtained from the income statement)

The change in fixed asset figure (ΔFA_t) will often differ from recorded changes in gross fixed assets as the latter will *understate* additions to fixed assets whenever fixed asset liquidations occur. The procedure in Equation 3.1 at least partially compensates for this and as such, more fully accounts for the sale and write-off of assets, as well as replacements and new acquisitions. Applying Equation 3.1 to Mid-America data, we see that over $270 million was spent on facilities in 1984 (with dollars in thousands, $230,331 + $42,155 = $272,486).

---

[5]A *surplus adjustment* is any unexplained change in retained earnings; they are not unusual when dealing with the company-prepared statements of small and medium-sized firms (with CPA-prepared statements, all changes to retained earnings are explained in the statement of changes in stockholders' equity). Any surplus adjustments to retained earnings should, of course, be treated as a source or use of funds, whichever is appropriate.

TABLE 3.4

Mid-America's 1984
All-Inclusive Funds
Flow Statement
(Dollars in Thousands)

SOURCES OF FUNDS		
Net profit after tax		$122,260
Depreciation and depletion charges		54,037
Provision for deferred taxes		27,502
From operations		$203,799
From working capital:		
Cash and marketable securities	$46,562	
Accounts payable	82,189	
Accrued expenses	3,135	131,886
Increase in long-term debt and leases		185,206
Increase in other deferred credits		13,278
Total sources		$534,169
USES OF FUNDS		
Cash dividends paid		$ 38,283
To working capital:		
Accounts receivable	$72,924	
Inventories	85,650	
Prepaid expenses	20,013	
Accrued taxes	10,140	
Current maturities	10,155	
Other current liabilities	4,247	203,129
Facilities[a]		272,486
Other assets acquired		18,517
Changes in stockholders' equity due to prior year adjustments, exercise of stock options, and dividend reinvestment plans—net of stock dividend[b]		1,754
Total uses		$534,169

[a]Funds used to acquire facilities = change in net fixed assets + depreciation charges = $230,331 + $42,155 = $272,486.

[b]A stock dividend was distributed in 1984, which reduced retained earnings by $27,947, increased the common stock account by $1,345, and raised capital surplus by $26,602—a net effect on flow of funds of zero (see Table 3.3 for details).

The input data are now complete; at this point, it is only a matter of categorizing the balance sheet changes and income statement items as sources or uses of funds, and then preparing the actual flow of funds statement. Two formats are widely used: the "all-inclusive" funds flow statement and the statement of changes in working capital. The accounting authorities officially "encourage" the use of the first type, which defines funds as all types of financial resources.[6] Everything from cash to fixed assets and accounts payable to common stock is included directly on this form of the flow of funds statement. This version provides more detailed insight into the sources and uses of funds. Table 3.4 contains Mid-America's 1984 all-inclusive funds flow statement. The format used

---

[6]J. A. Mauriello, *Accounting for the Financial Analyst,* rev. ed. (Homewood, Ill.: Irwin, 1971), p. 91.

is a fairly standard one that lists operating (income statement) items first, followed by working capital entries, and then long-term changes. It is a convenient and logical sequence that works equally well for both sources and uses of funds. The alternative form of the flow of funds, the statement of changes in working capital, defines the funds concept more narrowly because it is concerned with how investment and financing decisions affect the working capital position. Table 3.5 depicts this version of the 1984 flow of funds statement for Mid-America Corporation. Clearly, it contains substantially less information, since only noncurrent assets and financing are used. This version would probably have its greatest use in situations where the level, rather than the composition, of working capital is a particular problem.

A look at the flow of funds statement reveals that Mid-America obtained most of its funds from operations ($203.8 million) and by taking on more long-term debt and leases (which provided some $185.2 million); these funds, in turn, were used chiefly to build up working capital and acquire $272 million in facilities. When such insight is used with other financial ratios and measures, it is possible to determine whether there are any patterns developing that might be in conflict with (or beneficial to) the firm's established financial policies. It could be that using cash as a major source of funds has had an ill effect on the company's liquidity. Whatever its form, a flow of funds statement is intended to shed light on investment, financing, and dividend decisions, and the possible risk-return implications such decisions hold.

Cash Flow Versus Funds Flow

Many people have the idea that the funds flow statement is indicative of the firm's cash flow. Not so. Not even the "all-inclusive" format captures the flow of cash; rather, it merely summarizes the net impact of the

---

TABLE 3.5

An Alternative Flow of Funds Statement for Mid-America Corporation—The 1984 Statement of Changes in Working Capital (Dollars in Thousands)

SOURCES OF FUNDS	
Net profit after tax	$122,260
Depreciation and depletion charges	54,037
Provision for deferred taxes	27,502
From operations	$203,799
Increase in long-term debt and leases	185,206
Increase in other deferred credits	13,278
Total sources	$402,283
USES OF FUNDS	
Cash dividends paid	$ 38,283
Facilities	272,486
Other assets acquired	18,517
Other changes in stockholders' equity	1,754
Increase in net working capital[a]	71,243
Total uses	$402,283

[a]Increase in current assets	$132,025
Less: Funds raised by increase in current liabilities	(60,782)
Change in net working capital	$ 71,243

company's investment and financing decisions on its cash (or working capital) position. Cash flow deals with *receipts and expenditures,* and shows the net amount of cash received and spent by the firm over a given period of time. Table 3.6 illustrates the 1984 cash flow statement for Mid-America; it provides a viable measure of the actual flow of cash through the firm and reconciles changes in the cash accounts from one period to the next.

Like the flow of funds, the *cash flow statement* is constructed by combining data from the income statement (in this case, both revenue and cost figures are used in place of profits and depreciation) with changes in the balance sheet. The only difference is that the changes in balance sheet items are not categorized simply as sources or uses of funds, but instead are added to or subtracted from receipts and expenditures, depending upon their effects on cash flow. For example, the increase in accounts receivable is shown as a reduction in operating

TABLE 3.6 Mid-America's 1984 Cash Flow Statement (Dollars in Thousands)			
OPERATING RECEIPTS			
Net sales	$1,769,740		
Less: Change in accounts receivable	(72,924)		
Total operating receipts		$1,696,816	
OPERATING EXPENDITURES			
Outside purchases	$1,107,962		
Operating, selling, and exploration expenses	399,145[a]		
Plus: Change in inventories	85,650		
Less: Increase in accounts payable and accrued expenses	(85,324)		
Total operating expenditures		$1,507,433	
Net operating cash flow			$189,383
FACILITIES			
Additions to fixed assets		$ 272,486	
FINANCIAL, TAXES, AND OTHER			
Interest paid	$ 37,272		
Taxes paid	63,882		
Less: Changes in accrued and deferred taxes	(17,362)		
Additional debt and leases incurred (net of current maturities)	(175,051)		
Cash dividends paid	38,283		
Change in prepaids, deferred credits, and other current liabilities (net)	10,982		
Additions to other assets	18,517		
Other income (net)	(14,818)		
Changes in stockholders' equity (net)	1,754		
Total financial, taxes, and other		($ 36,541)	
Total outflow to facilities, financial, etc.			$235,945
Net cash flow			($ 46,562)

[a]This figure does *not* include depreciation and depletion charges, since the cash flow is concerned only with expenses that involve an actual outflow of cash.

receipts, since it reflects a net increase in sales that were not collected; likewise, the increase in accounts payable and accrued expenses is recorded as a reduction in operating expenditures to the extent that it reflects operating costs paid for with outside financing. Also, note in Table 3.6 that current depreciation charges (from the income statement) are netted out of operating expenses since the cash flow statement is concerned only with expenses that actually involve an outflow of cash. Measuring cash flow much like the procedure shown in Table 3.6 is often used to arrive at a cash flow figure for capital budgeting purposes, and as we will see in the following chapter, a variation of this statement is also used in cash budgeting and financial forecasting. In contrast to the flow of funds (see, for example, Table 3.4), the cash flow statement in Table 3.6 shows that Mid-America generated a cash inflow of nearly $1.7 billion in 1984, spent $1.5 billion for operating costs and expenses, and another $236 million on facilities, interest, taxes, and other nonoperating items. This resulted in a net cash outflow of nearly $47 million and explains why the cash account went down by this amount.

Ratio Analysis

Ratio analysis is the study of the relationships that exist among and between various financial statement accounts at a given point in time and over time. It provides a different perspective of the operating results and financial condition of the firm, and as a result, expands the information content of financial statements. In essence, the financial statements are recast into more usable information so that a better understanding can be obtained about the company. Ratio analysis is carried out by computing and studying the behavior over time of a variety of financial ratios, each of which emphasizes a particular dimension of the balance sheet and/or income statement. Each measure relates one item on the balance sheet (or income statement) with another; or as is more often the case, a balance sheet account is related to an operating (income statement) element. In this way, attention is directed *not* toward the absolute magnitude of the financial statement accounts, per se, but to the liquidity, turnover, leverage, and profitability of the resources, financial structure, and operating results of the firm.

In addition to the firm's management, there are many parties interested in a company's financial affairs, including labor unions, regulatory agencies, and most importantly, current and prospective stockholders and lenders. These groups use ratio analysis in different ways and for different purposes. For example, labor unions use financial analysis to establish an economic basis for collective bargaining; government regulatory agencies use it for rate setting. Current and prospective stockholders tend to center their attention on the firm's present and projected level of earnings. When undertaken by (or for) the benefit of stockholders, this process is known as *security analysis* and is aimed at assessing the potential risk and return from common stock investments and ultimately for making portfolio decisions. *Credit analysis* is the term used to describe the same process when it is applied by creditors to lending situations. The major interest here is the ability of the firm to service its debt in a prompt and timely fashion and as such, liquidity and leverage measures are important. Credit analysts are concerned with the working capital position of the firm, its debt structure, cash flow, and profits—all of which are reviewed to evaluate the borrower's creditworthiness, structure the credit, and price the loan.

Financial Ratios

The mechanics of ratio analysis are actually quite simple: Selected information is obtained from annual financial statements and used to compute a set of ratios,[7] which are then compared to historical and/or industry standards to evaluate the financial developments of the firm. *Financial ratios* can be divided into five groups: (1) liquidity, (2) activity, (3) leverage, (4) profitability, and (5) market. The various ratios that fall into each group are, of course, distinguished by the fact that they tend to emphasize certain dimensions of the balance sheet and/or income statement. We will now identify and briefly discuss some of the more popular measures in each of these five categories, and then examine the information content of such ratios.

Measures of Liquidity. A firm's liquidity is measured by its ability to satisfy short-term obligations as they come due. Of major concern is whether or not the firm has adequate short-term resources—cash and other liquid assets—to service debts in a prompt and timely fashion. Several measures provide insight into a company's liquidity position; these include the current ratio, net working capital, and quick ratio. Such ratios are intended to provide an overview of the firm's liquidity position, but they do not supply information about the size and timing of a company's cash flow.[8] At best, the measures can provide only an overall

---

[7]While we use single point (end-of-year) balance sheet data in the ratios we demonstrate here, average (beginning and ending) values could have been used instead. So long as the information content of the ratios (the trends and insights they provide) are not seriously affected by the type of input, it makes little difference whether single-point or average values are employed; however, because large intraperiod changes can have a dramatic impact on reported ratios, use of average balance sheet data is recommended whenever there is a significant difference in the asset or liability and net worth accounts from one statement date to the next.

Moreover, it should be kept in mind that in our discussion of ratio analysis, we presume that accurately prepared financial statements are used throughout; in addition, we assume that statements are truly comparable from one period to the next—that there are no unusual corporate developments and/or that similar accounting procedures are used throughout the period of analysis. Major discrepancies in accounting statements can lead to serious distortions in reported income and balance sheet entries, and in themselves, destroy intra- and/or interyear comparisons.

[8]Kenneth W. Lemke, "The Evaluation of Liquidity: An Analytical Study," *Journal of Accounting Research* 8 (spring 1970), pp. 47–77.

TABLE 3.7
Liquidity Ratios

Measure	Function	Interpretation
CURRENT RATIO (CR) $$CR = \frac{\text{current assets}}{\text{current liabilities}}$$ $$\text{Mid-America's} \atop \text{1984 CR} = \frac{\$460,030}{\$311,420} = 1.48$$	Shows the amount of short-term resources available to service every dollar of current debt; assumes that firm's cash flow is highly predictable, and that current assets can be converted to cash in a timely and orderly fashion.	Other things being equal, the higher the current ratio, the better (as a frame of reference, the average current ratio of American corporations is approximately 1.50).
NET WORKING CAPITAL (NWC) $$NWC = \text{current assets}$$ $$- \text{current liabilities}$$ $$\text{Mid-America's} = \$460,030 - \$311,420$$ $$\text{1984 NWC} = \$148,610$$	An absolute measure of a firm's liquidity, it indicates the dollar amount of equity (and possibly long-term debt) in the working capital position and, as such, provides a measure of the margin of safety offered to short-term lenders.	Measured in dollars, a relatively high net working capital is desirable (a net working capital of zero is equal to a current ratio of 1.0).
QUICK RATIO (QR) $$QR = \frac{\substack{\text{cash} + \text{marketable securities} \\ + \text{ accounts receivable}}}{\text{current liabilities}}$$ $$\text{Mid-America's} \atop \text{1984 QR} = \frac{\$10,230 + \$259,336}{\$311,420}$$ $$= 0.87$$	Also known as the "acid test" ratio, it measures the ability of the firm to meet current liabilities by using only its more liquid current assets (note that the two least liquid current assets—inventories and prepaids—are not included in the computation); provides an indication of the "staying power" of the firm. The quick ratio is most useful when there are liquidity problems with inventory.	Quick ratios of less than 1 are not uncommon and should not (by themselves) be a cause for alarm; however, other things being equal, a high quick ratio is better than a low one.

"handle" on the firm's basic liquidity position; to be useful, they should be supplemented with a more thorough study of the composition and character of current assets and liabilities. Table 3.7 presents the computational procedures and brief remarks about each of the three liquidity measures; in addition, using figures from Mid-America Corporation's financial statements (Tables 3.1 and 3.2), we also provide the 1984 ratios.

Activity Ratios. Measuring the general liquidity of a firm also requires that the composition and underlying liquidity of key current assets be assessed. This can be done with activity ratios, which measure the use of corporate assets by evaluating how effectively the firm is managing its resources. These ratios relate important asset accounts to operating results and indicate the payoff from each dollar invested in the various assets. A glance at most financial statements will reveal that the asset side of the balance sheet is dominated by just a few asset accounts, which make up 80 to 90 percent, or perhaps even more, of total resources. The popular activity ratios concentrate on these assets. Table 3.8 provides a computational and interpretative summary of four widely used activity ratios that deal with accounts receivable, inventory, fixed assets, and total assets.

Leverage Ratios. The leverage position of the firm indicates the amount of debt that is being used to support the resources and operations of the company. With leverage measures, attention is centered on the firm's financial structure, the degree of indebtedness, and the ability of the firm to service its debt. The amount of debt a company employs in its financial structure has a bearing on its financial risk exposure, since debt represents fixed-payment obligations that must be serviced regardless of how successful the firm has been in generating sales and profits; the more debt the firm incurs, the greater the exposure to risk of default. However, stability of sales and other operating characteristics are also important in defining financial risk exposure; as a result, industry standards are important in assessing leverage ratios. Three of the most widely used leverage ratios are (1) the debt-equity ratio; (2) times interest earned; and (3) debt service margin. These ratios are presented and briefly discussed in Table 3.9.

Profitability Ratios. Unlike profits, which are measured in absolute (or dollar) terms, profitability is a relative measure of success—that is, profitability measures relate the returns (profits) of the firm to its sales, assets, or equity. As a group, these measures enable management to evaluate the firm's earnings with respect to the amount of sales necessary to generate the profits, the level of assets required to support operations, and the owners' contribution. Profits provide the vehicle through which the firm can grow and continue to attract outside capital. Creditors, owners, and management pay close attention to boosting profits because of the great importance placed on earnings in the marketplace. However, care should be taken not to lose sight of the long-range goals of the firm, for the use of various return and profitability

TABLE 3.8

Activity Ratios

Measure	Function	Interpretation
ACCOUNTS RECEIVABLE TURNOVER (ART) $$ART = \frac{annual\ sales}{net\ accounts\ receivable}$$ $$\frac{Mid\text{-}America's}{1984\ ART} = \frac{\$1,769,740}{\$259,336}$$ $$= 6.82$$	A measure of how well these resources are being managed, this ratio provides an indication of the quality of receivables and how successful the firm is in collecting them; shows the amount of sales support provided by each dollar invested in accounts receivable. If information on credit sales is available, it can be used in place of annual sales (in the equation numerator).	Generally. high (or increasing) turnover figures are more desirable than low ratios; however, excessively high turnovers may be a source of concern as they may be signaling credit policies that are too restrictive. In Mid-America's case, they were turning receivables about 6.8 times per year during 1984.
INVENTORY TURNOVER (IT) $$IT = \frac{cost\ of\ goods\ sold}{inventory}$$ $$\frac{Mid\text{-}America's}{1984\ IT} = \frac{\$1,107,962}{\$151,582}$$ $$= 7.31$$	Provides an indication of the amount of resources required to support a given level of operations; this ratio is a measure of how well the investment in inventory is being controlled and provides insight into the possibility of inventory obsolescence.	Other things being equal, the higher the turnover, the better the control management has over inventory; however, caution should be exercised with excessively high turnovers as they could be indicative of low inventories and frequent stockouts.
FIXED ASSET TURNOVER (FAT) $$FAT = \frac{annual\ sales}{net\ fixed\ assets}$$ $$\frac{Mid\text{-}America's}{1984\ FAT} = \frac{\$1,769,740}{\$949,929}$$ $$= 1.86$$	A measure that reveals capacity utilization, the fixed asset turnover shows the extent to which the company is using its plant and equipment. The measure does not take into account the impact of inflation on the market value of capital assets, and as such overstates turnover in real terms.	A high or increasing turnover figure reveals a greater payoff from capital investments; in the case of Mid-America Corporation, it was able to generate about $1.86 in revenues for every $1.00 invested in fixed assets during 1984.
TOTAL ASSET TURNOVER (TAT) $$TAT = \frac{annual\ sales}{net\ tangible\ assets}$$ $$\frac{Mid\text{-}America's}{1984\ TAT} = \frac{\$1,769,740}{\$1,472,737}$$ $$= 1.20$$	Also called the "capital intensity ratio," it provides an indication of the efficiency with which the firm is able to use its assets to support sales; it reveals the control management has been able to exhibit over its investments in assets.	A high or increasing turnover figure is desirable, as it indicates an increased volume of sales is being supported from a given level of assets—which has a direct and significant bearing on the profitability of the firm.

Note: A popular variation of accounts receivable turnover is the *average collection period*, which measures the age of a firm's accounts receivable by indicating how long it takes to convert a typical receivable to cash; it is found by dividing a 360-day year by the previously computed accounts receivable turnover figure (for Mid-America: 360/6.82 = 52.8 days). A similar measure can be obtained for inventory—i.e., *days supply of inventory*, which indicates how long an item is held (on average) in inventory, is found as: 360/IT; for Mid-America, it equals 360/7.31 = 49.2 days.

TABLE 3.9
Leverage Ratios

Measure	Function	Interpretation
DEBT EQUITY RATIO (DER) $$DER = \frac{\text{total debt}}{\text{tangible net worth}}$$ Mid-America's 1984 DER $$= \frac{\$311,420 + \$509,185}{\$501,714 - \$5,719} = 1.65$$	A measure of the relative amount of funds provided by lenders and owners, the debt-equity ratio is an important measure of solvency that indicates the extent to which the firm is "trading on the equity"—the amount of financial leverage it is using.	A ratio of less than 1 indicates more resources have been provided by owners than creditors; an increasing number reveals greater use of financial leverage and therefore increased exposure to financial risk. Note the total debt figure *excludes* deferred items, and the tangible net worth equals total stockholders' equity less intangibles (e.g., goodwill).
TIMES INTEREST EARNED (TIE) $$TIE = \frac{\text{earning before interest and taxes}}{\text{annual interest expense}}$$ Mid-America's 1984 TIE $$= \frac{\$223,414}{\$37,272}$$ $$= 5.99$$ *Coverage ratio* $$= \frac{\begin{array}{c}\text{earnings before lease}\\\text{payments, interest}\\\text{and taxes}\end{array}}{\begin{array}{c}\text{interest expense}\\+ \text{ lease payments}\\+ \text{ preferred dividends}\\\times [1/(1-T)]\end{array}}$$ Mid-America's 1984 coverage ratio $$= \frac{\$223,414 + \$2,024^{a}}{\$37,272 + \$2,024^{a}} = 5.74$$	Indicates how well the firm can handle its debt; times interest earned measures the ability of the firm to meet fixed interest payments. Shows how far income can decline before the firm has trouble servicing its obligations. A variation of this measure is known as the *coverage ratio* (shown at left) and is used whenever the firm has a significant amount of preferred stock outstanding and/or does a significant amount of leasing.	An important bond/loan covenant ratio; the higher the ratio, the better. In Mid-America's case, the company generated almost \$6 in earnings for every dollar of interest due in 1984. The coverage ratio is of interest to investors and lenders as an indication of the firm's ability to service all the nonequity components of its capital structure; the T in the ratio equals the company's tax rate on income and is used to adjust preferred dividends to a pretax amount. As a point of reference, the average coverage ratio for large corporations stood at 4.2 times at year-end 1981.
DEBT SERVICE MARGIN (DSM) $$DSM = \frac{\begin{array}{c}\text{net profit after tax}\\+ \text{ depreciation}\\\& \text{ depletion expenses}\end{array}}{\text{current maturities}}$$ Mid-America's 1984 DSM $$= \frac{\$122,260 + \$54,037}{\$26,185} = 6.73$$	Shows the ability of the firm to service the *principal* portion of its long-term debt and lease obligations; these "current maturities" (defined as long-term debt and capitalized lease obligations maturing within 1 year) must be met in a timely and orderly fashion to avoid default.	A high or increasing debt service margin is considered desirable; the measure shows the amount of cushion provided to lenders by indicating how far operations would have to fall before the margin approaches 1.0 and potentially serious problems occur.

[a]Lease expense is obtained from detailed financial statements; preferred dividends are ignored since the company has no preferred stock.

measures like those we will examine below can often lead to an undesirable emphasis on short-term results.[9] For example, in order to maintain an increasing return measure, management may become reluctant to incur near-term costs in exchange for future gains, actions that could well be detrimental to the long-run goal of maximizing shareholder wealth. Table 3.10 provides summary commentary about four widely used profitability measures: (1) net profit margin, (2) operating ratio, (3) return on investment, and (4) return on equity.

Market Ratios.   There are several common stock ratios that are important to publicly traded firms because of their use in the stock valuation process. These include (1) earnings per share,[10] (2) dividends per share, (3) dividend payout ratio, (4) book value per share, (5) price/earnings ratio, and (6) dividend yield. These market ratios are monitored on the assumption that the financial condition and operating results of the firm are reflected in the market price of the company's shares, a condition that has generally been shown to exist even in an efficient market.[11] Certainly, the behavior of these ratios over time depends on the performance of key corporate financial variables like liquidity, leverage, and profitability.[12] As such, these ratios convey information about the ability of the company to convert aggregate operating results into maximum (optimum) per share performance. Table 3.11 on pp. 91–92 provides a brief overview of six market ratios; in it, we presume Mid-America's stock was trading for $65 per share at year-end 1984.

Other
Assessment
Measures

Common Size Income Statement.   The income statement is usually converted to common size figures for analytical purposes to gain insight into the comparative behavior of a firm's cost structure and profit

---

[9]See Ben Branch, "The Impact of Operating Decisions on ROI Dynamics," *Financial Management* 7 (winter 1978), pp. 54–60.

[10]For a more complete coverage of the accounting for earnings per share, including the derivation and computation of "primary earnings per share" and "fully diluted earnings per share," see David F. Hawkins, *Corporate Financial Reporting*, rev. ed. (Homewood, Ill.: Irwin, 1977), chap. 11. In addition, to see how (high) EPS and price-earnings multiples can yield misleading signals regarding the use of equity financing in certain investment and capital structure decisions, refer to John J. Pringle, "Price Earnings Ratios, Earnings-Per-Share, and Financial Management," *Financial Management* 2 (spring 1973), pp. 34–39.

[11]For an excellent review of the literature and the line of reasoning underlying this proposition, see James H. Lorie and Mary T. Hamilton, *The Stock Market: Theories & Evidence* (Homewood, Ill.: Irwin, 1973), pp. 113–167.

[12]See, for example, Gary P. Spraakman, "The Sensitivity of Earnings Per Share Growth to Some of Its Financial Components," *Financial Management* 9 (winter 1979), pp. 41–46.

TABLE 3.10
Profitability Ratios

Measure	Function	Interpretation
NET PROFIT MARGIN (NPM) $\text{NPM} = \dfrac{\text{net profit after tax}}{\text{net sales}}$ $\begin{aligned}\text{Mid-America's} \\ \text{1984 NPM}\end{aligned} = \dfrac{\$122,260}{\$1,769,740}$ $= 6.91\%$	The net profit margin is among the most widely followed financial ratios; it shows the rate of return the company is earning on its sales. Also known as the "net profit rate," it has a substantial impact on a company's growth prospects and long-run competitive posture.	Mid-America's net profit margin indicates it is generating about 7 cents in earnings for each dollar of sales. Profit margins can also be obtained for gross and operating profits by simply changing the numerator in NPM—*gross profit margin* = gross profit/ sales, and *operating profit margin* = operating profit/ sales.
OPERATING RATIO (OR) $\text{OR} = \dfrac{\text{total operating expenses}}{\text{net sales}}$ $\begin{aligned}\text{Mid-America's} \\ \text{1984 OR}\end{aligned} = \dfrac{\$1,561,144^{a}}{\$1,769,740}$ $= 88.2\%$	Provides an indication of the managerial control of the firm's cost structure; the operating ratio indicates the relative amount of operating expenses used to generate sales and provides a measure of the operating efficiency of the firm.	A low or decreasing ratio is desirable, as it translates into a higher profit rate for the firm. Another, more detailed, perspective of the cost structure can be obtained through breakeven analysis.[b]
RETURN ON INVESTMENT (ROI) $\text{ROI} = \dfrac{\text{net profit after tax}}{\text{net tangible assets}}$ $\begin{aligned}\text{Mid-America's} \\ \text{1984 ROI}\end{aligned} = \dfrac{\$122,260}{\$1,472,737}$ $= 8.30\%$	Also known as "return on total assets," this profitability measure looks at the amount of resources used by the firm to support the current level of operations; a key measure in assessing the overall effectiveness of management in generating profits from available resources. Shows payoff from investments and assets, and reveals overall liquidity and profitability of resource allocation and investment decisions.	The higher this measure, the better; ROI is an important ratio because of the underlying implications it holds for the growth prospects of the firm and its ability to attract capital.
RETURN ON EQUITY (ROE) $\text{ROE} = \dfrac{\text{net profit after tax}}{\text{tangible net worth}}$ $\begin{aligned}\text{Mid-America's} \\ \text{1984 ROE}\end{aligned} = \dfrac{\$122,260}{\$501,714 - \$5,719}$ $= 24.65\%$	ROE introduces corporate financing decisions into the assessment of profitability, and relative to return on investment, indicates the extent to which leverage can increase return to stockholders.	As a measure of the return to stockholders, it follows that the higher the return on equity figure, the better; ROE shows annual payoff to investors, which in the case of Mid-America, amounted to almost 25 cents for every dollar of equity in 1984.

[a]Total operating expenses include everything from outside purchases through lease expenses—that is, from Table 3.2: $1,107,962 + $299,148 + $82,282 + $54,037 + $17,715.

[b]Breakeven analysis considers the fixed and variable components of a firm's cost structure, and evaluates the extent to which fixed costs affect operating profit; breakeven analysis is discussed in detail in the appendix to this chapter (Appendix 3A).

margin. Common size statements neutralize the effects that size, or level of sales, have on operating results. They are often used when the profitability position of the firm is being assessed. In a common size statement, each item on the income statement is expressed as a percentage of net sales. In essence, the income statement is reconstructed by using a series of ratios, all of which have net sales as a common denominator. The common size statement is prepared in the same format as a standard income statement, and it adds up (algebraically) like any income statement. Table 3.12 on p. 93 provides Mid-America Corporation's common size statement for 1984; the standard dollar-based statement is also provided for comparative purposes. Note that net sales always equal 100 percent in a common size statement,[13] and that nonoperating forms of income (like interest and investment earnings) are not included in the sales figure. Common size statements concentrate on the structure of costs and profits, and are especially useful in comparing operating results from one year to the next. Costs and profits are evaluated from a relative perspective, but sales and revenues are also examined in an absolute context, particularly with regard to their level and growth patterns over time.

The DuPont System.   The DuPont system was developed over a half a century ago as a way to assess a company's earning power. The system concentrates on earning power by breaking return on investment (ROI) into its major component parts. This enables financial managers to gain greater insight into the firm's operating efficiency and profitability, and

---

[13]If sales and/or gross profits are available by product line (or some other similar corporate grouping), such information should be included in the common size statement, as it provides insight on the marketing and pricing decisions of the firm. This is done by relating sales from the various product lines to total sales, and the product line gross profits to *their respective product line sales;* total gross profit and all other income and expense entries below it are handled like any common size statement and related to total sales. For example:

Sales—product group A	$ 650	44.8%
Sales—product group B	800	55.2
Total sales	$ 1,450	100.0%
Gross profit—product group A	250	38.5
Gross profit—product group B	275	34.4
Total gross profit	$ 525	36.2%
Selling expenses	100	6.9
General and administrative expenses	250	17.2
Operating profit	$ 175	12.1%
Interest, taxes, etc.	100	6.9
Net profit	$ 75	5.2%

TABLE 3.11
Market Ratios

Measure	Function	Interpretation
EARNINGS PER SHARE (EPS) $$EPS = \frac{\text{net income} - \text{preferred dividends}}{\text{number of common shares outstanding}}$$ Mid-America's 1984 EPS $$= \frac{\$122,260}{27,271^a}$$ $$= \$4.48$$	EPS translates total corporate profits into profits on a per-share basis and provides a convenient measure of the amount of earnings available to common stockholders; the measure is indicative of potential growth in stockholders' equity, and, hopefully, will eventually translate into capital gains to common stockholders.	Because of its positive effect on the market price of a share of stock, financial management can be expected to attempt to maximize earnings per share (so long as such behavior does not interfere with long-run wealth maximization goals).
DIVIDENDS PER SHARE (DPS) $$DPS = \frac{\text{cash dividends to common stock}}{\text{number of common shares outstanding}}$$ Mid-America's 1984 DPS $$= \frac{\$38,283}{27,271^a}$$ $$= \$1.40$$	Another popular market measure, it shows the total aggregate dividends paid by the company on a per-share basis; reflects the amount of current income paid to stockholders, and is an important component of valuation and stockholder returns.	The amount of dividends paid per share is dependent on the type of stock: growth stocks can be expected to pay less than non-growth-income shares.
DIVIDEND PAYOUT RATIO (DPR) $$DPR = \frac{\text{dividends per share}}{\text{earnings per share}}$$ Mid-America's 1984 DPR $$= \frac{\$1.40}{\$4.48}$$ $$= 31.25\%$$	An important dividend measure, it provides an indication of the amount of earnings paid out to stockholders in the form of cash dividends; this measure has a bearing on the firm's growth and financial leverage, since it indirectly affects the amount of earnings retained for internal purposes. The payout ratio is useful in assessing the cash dividend policy of a firm.	The size of the ratio is a function of the type of company (growth vs. nongrowth) and the amount that needs to be retained internally; the higher the ratio, the greater the annual payoff to stockholders, but the less that is available to the company for internal growth purposes. As a benchmark, most companies that pay dividends tend to pay out 40 to 60% of earnings.

TABLE 3.11 continued

BOOK VALUE PER SHARE (BVS)

$$BVS = \frac{\text{tangible net worth}^b}{\text{number of common shares outstanding}}$$

Mid-America's 1984 BVS

$$= \frac{\$501,714 - \$5,719}{27,271^a}$$

$$= \$18.19$$

Book value per share is an indication of the amount of stockholders' equity embedded in each share of stock.

Presumably, a stock should sell for more than its book value, *at least over the long-run;* however, because BVS is an accounting-based measure, it should not be viewed as representative of the true economic value of the firm. In late 1983, the stocks of major U.S. corporations were selling at prices that averaged about 150% of book value.

PRICE/EARNINGS RATIO (P/E)

$$P/E = \frac{\text{market price of a share}}{\text{earnings per share}}$$

Mid-America's 1984 PE

$$= \frac{\$65.00}{\$4.48}$$

$$= 14.50$$

The P/E ratio relates the firm's earnings to its share price behavior and, as such, is an important measure of market capitalization (since it is the reciprocal of the capitalization rate used with perpetuities, the P/E ratio establishes a market price by effectively capitalizing the firm's EPS as though it were a perpetual stream); price/earnings multiples are an essential part of many stock valuation models, as they indicate how much investors are willing to pay for a dollar of earnings.

Given Mid-America had a year-end market price of \$65/share, it was trading at 14½ times earnings. Other things being equal, high multiples suggest the market has confidence in the growth and future prospects of the firm. As a matter of interest, the average P/E ratio for the 500 stocks in the S & P Composite Index *dropped* by over 50% between 1971 & 1981 (to an average of 8.5 times in 1981); although much of that drop was erased, as the average multiple rose to 13.2 times earnings by the fall of 1983.

DIVIDEND YIELD (DY)

$$DY = \frac{\text{dividends per share}}{\text{market price of a share}}$$

Mid-America's 1984 DY

$$= \frac{\$1.40}{\$65.00}$$

$$= 2.15\%$$

Also known as a stock's "current yield," it is an indication of the rate of current (annual) income earned by investors; it shows the payoff to stockholders in the form of annual dividends and represents one important source of return (the other being capital gains). Dividend yield is a vital element in the stock valuation process.

Other things equal, share price is inversely related to dividend yield, and, as a result, an increase in dividend yield will lead to a decrease in the price of the stock; generally speaking, dividend yield tends to move with competitive bond rates and the level of actual and anticipated inflation.

[a]Number of shares outstanding obtained directly from financial statements; number of shares in thousands.
[b]Tangible net worth is found by subtracting goodwill from total common stock equity.

TABLE 3.12
Mid-America's
Common Size Income
Statement (For the
Fiscal Year Ending
December 31, 1984)

	1984	
	Dollar-based ($ Thousands)	Common Size
Net sales	$1,769,740	100.0%
Outside purchases of raw materials, crude oil, and other products	1,107,962	62.6
Gross profit	$ 661,778	37.4%
Operating expenses	299,148	16.9
Selling, general, and administrative expenses	82,282	4.6
Depreciation and depletion	54,037	3.1
Exploration, dry hole, and lease expenses	17,715	1.0
Operating profit	$ 208,596	11.8%
Other income and (expense)—*net*	14,818	0.8
Earnings before interest and taxes	$ 223,414	12.6%
Interest expense	37,272	2.1
Profit before tax	$ 186,142	10.5%
Provision for income tax	63,882	3.6
Net profit after tax	$ 122,260	6.9%

to more accurately pinpoint differences in earning power over time. The DuPont system defines ROI as follows:

$$\text{ROI} = \text{(total asset turnover)(net profit margin)} \qquad (3.2)$$

Viewed in this way, ROI is seen to be a product of the asset utilization of the firm (total asset turnover) and its operating efficiency (net profit margin). The 1984 ROI figure for Mid-America can be restated using Equation 3.2 as:

$$\text{ROI} = \frac{\$1,769,740}{\$1,472,737} \times \frac{\$ 122,260}{\$1,769,740}$$

$$= 1.2017 \times .0691 = 8.3\%$$

The DuPont system shows that the more sales the company is able to generate from every dollar of resources, and/or the more profit it is able to earn from every dollar of sales, the greater will be the return on investment. Thus, if profit margin is a problem, management can review the common size income statement to see where cost control may be breaking down; if it is a matter of asset utilization, the various activity ratios can be examined for possible inefficiencies in the allocation and use of resources.

The DuPont system can be extended to return on equity (ROE) by introducing financial leverage; that is:

$$\text{ROE} = \frac{\text{ROI}}{\text{tangible net worth/net tangible assets}} \qquad (3.3)$$

For Mid-America in 1984, the figures are as follows:

$$\text{ROE} = \frac{.083}{\$495,995/\$1.472,737}$$

$$= \frac{.083}{.337} = 24.6\%$$

Now profit margin, asset utilization, and leverage are all directly included in the analysis. In fact, as Figure 3.1 shows, the total financial condition and operating results of the firm are brought into focus in the ROE–DuPont framework.[14]

Performance Benchmarks

By themselves, financial ratios have little meaning other than reflecting the mathematical relationships between two accounting values at a given point in time. To be meaningful, financial ratios need to be compared to certain types of performance benchmarks that provide standards against which developing trends can be assessed, and corporate strengths and weaknesses identified. There are two basic types of performance standards: historical and industry. Nearly all analytical reports involve the use of historical standards, which are simply internally derived financial ratios that measure a firm's performance over time. It is a time-series approach that evaluates current performance in relation to the past; this is usually done on a fiscal or calendar year basis, and normally includes 3 to 5 years of analysis (including the latest current year). Historical standards are most effective in uncovering developing trends and in assessing actual performance.

Industry standards represent a cross-sectional approach to financial analysis; their use involves comparing the firm's latest ratios with industry averages at the same point in time. The idea is to compare the performance of the company to that of its competitors in order to isolate corporate strengths and weaknesses. Industry figures are available from such sources as *Dun & Bradstreet's Key Business Ratios, Robert Morris Associates Statement Studies, Leo Troy's Almanac of Business and Financial Ratios, FTC Quarterly Reports,* and various other credit agencies and trade associations. Moreover, the widespread availability of Standard &

---

[14]Note that Figure 3.1 uses an "equity multiplier" to relate ROI to ROE; the equity multiplier is simply the reciprocal of the net worth ratio which appears in the denominator of Equation 3.3.

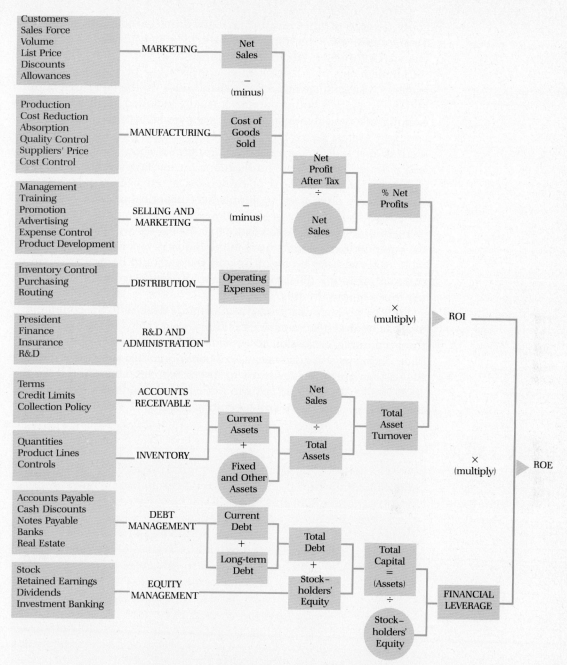

Figure 3.1   The Dimensions of ROI and ROE: the DuPont System as an Analytical Framework.

Poor's *Compustat* tapes means that many firms (particularly the publicly traded ones) have convenient access to a considerable amount of financial information about their competitors.

Complete sets of financial ratios are prepared periodically by these agencies, using either mean or median values (in the latter case, upper and lower quartile bounds are also usually included in the reports). An example of a typical industry report is contained in Table 3.13. When the company's latest figures are compared to industry standards, management is able to isolate areas where the firm is above or below average, and evaluate the possible implications on the firm's valuation and its access to external sources of capital. As a practical matter, industry standards are often used to supplement historical analysis because of the added insights they provide. However, care should be taken when using industry standards to ensure that the figures are *truly comparable;* the computation methods used in the industry reports must be comparable to those used by the firm, and there should be no corporate or regional operating differences that could have a significant impact on the firm's financial ratios.

Another problem of increasing magnitude deals with the comparative analysis of diversified companies. Even though steps are being taken in the accounting profession to provide a greater amount of segmented data, problems still arise because of behavioral differences over time in the various operating segments of diversified companies and from the need to allocate common costs to the various subsidiaries. Thus, even if the financial condition and operating results of each of the major

MULTINATIONAL DIMENSIONS

International Standards

In some industries, the main competitors are based abroad and thus should logically be included in the ratio comparisons. However, it is possible that the foreign ratios will not be comparable. Not only are there great differences in accounting principles abroad, but industry norms differ as well. For example, debt-equity ratios in Japan are often very high, so ratios of 4.0 or more are not uncommon. Other ratios of liquidity and leverage would suggest, by American standards at least, that Japanese firms are extremely risky. This is likely to be a misleading conclusion, however, to the extent that it ignores the Japanese system of support from the government, labor unions, and other members of the industry. In fact, without a deep understanding of the Japanese business environment, it would be impossible to come to any rational conclusions through international ratio comparisons. The same can be said about firms in most countries, each of which has unique business, environmental, and accounting systems.

TABLE 3.13

Industry Standards for Key Business Ratios (Soft Drink Bottling Companies and Record Companies)

RATIOS	SIC 2086 Btl, Can Soft Drinks (No Breakdown) 1984 (302 Estab)			SIC 2086 Btl, Can Soft Drinks Industry Assets Under $100,000 1984 (12 Estab)			SIC 2086 Btl, Can Soft Drinks Industry Assets $100,000 – $1,000,000 1984 (107 Estab)		
	UQ	MED	LQ	UQ	MED	LQ	UQ	MED	LQ
Solvency									
Quick ratio (times)	1.9	1.0	0.6	86.0	6.8	1.3	2.0	1.0	0.4
Current ratio (times)	3.3	2.0	1.3	4.1	2.3	1.4	3.8	2.1	1.2
Curr liab to nw (%)	18.6	42.5	71.0	3.6	26.9	58.0	16.4	42.1	71.0
Curr liab to inv (%)	74.8	127.1	237.0	14.1	100.0	291.0	62.1	107.0	195.5
Total liab to nw (%)	29.1	71.0	135.0	21.5	48.0	63.0	20.1	45.0	96.7
Fixed assets to nw (%)	37.5	56.8	95.0	15.4	30.0	34.2	30.4	56.7	91.3
Efficiency									
Coll period (days)	16.4	22.6	28.8	14.2	16.0	21.5	12.7	18.9	25.5
Sales to inv (times)	22.8	16.1	11.3	18.4	11.3	8.1	21.2	14.7	9.3
Assets to sales (%)	31.1	40.8	52.2	20.6	27.9	50.3	27.5	34.9	47.0
Sales to nwc (%)	16.3	10.3	7.4	24.6	8.5	7.1	15.7	10.1	6.5
Acct pay to sales (%)	1.9	4.1	6.2	0.4	1.3	4.7	1.3	2.9	6.2
Profitability									
Return on sales (%)	6.5	4.4	2.1	7.9	2.1	(0.8)	6.8	3.6	1.6
Return on assets (%)	14.5	10.1	5.5	38.0	25.4	2.1	16.1	11.5	5.4
Return on nw (%)	23.4	15.9	9.9	44.9	32.2	3.4	28.2	15.9	7.1

RATIOS	SIC 3652 Phonograph Records (No Breakdown) 1984 (117 Estab)			SIC 3652 Phonograph Records Industry Assets Under $100,000 1984 (22 Estab)			SIC 3652 Phonograph Records Industry Assets $100,000— $1,000,000 1984 (65 Estab)		
	UQ	MED	LQ	UQ	MED	LQ	UQ	MED	LQ
Solvency									
Quick ratio (times)	1.4	1.0	0.6	1.4	1.2	0.7	1.9	1.0	0.6
Current ratio (times)	3.2	1.6	1.1	2.3	1.6	0.7	2.6	1.4	1.0
Curr liab to nw (%)	19.6	51.5	128.3	15.9	44.6	71.1	19.6	51.5	144.0
Curr liab to inv (%)	128.3	234.9	435.7	96.0	340.1	999.9	138.1	229.5	513.9
Total liab to nw (%)	31.3	72.2	183.1	16.5	50.8	71.1	40.0	77.6	183.8
Fixed assets to nw (%)	29.4	76.7	130.3	72.7	104.6	495.3	53.7	82.4	141.5
Efficiency									
Coll period (days)	31.7	56.9	86.8	13.5	31.0	81.7	39.4	56.9	91.6
Sales to inv (times)	22.6	11.6	7.0	31.0	22.6	20.7	38.8	12.2	6.5
Assets to sales (%)	40.7	66.8	105.1	33.8	44.5	61.7	46.9	69.6	106.7
Sales to nwc (%)	12.1	5.3	3.5	14.7	9.3	3.7	12.1	6.3	3.5
Acct pay to sales (%)	3.3	7.0	12.3	1.2	4.4	6.9	2.1	7.0	13.0
Profitability									
Return on sales (%)	13.7	7.6	2.2	30.7	16.6	0.3	13.1	7.6	2.2
Return on assets (%)	18.2	8.4	4.1	64.1	23.9	1.0	18.2	9.1	9.4
Return on nw (%)	37.6	15.3	9.7	148.8	66.4	14.4	30.4	15.2	10.0

SOURCE: Adapted from Dun & Bradstreet, *Key Business Ratios.*

divisions of the company can be partially isolated, the segmentation is never complete. As a result, discrepancies and distortions can occur in the interfirm analysis of diversified companies.[15]

Managerial Uses

After the various financial ratios have been computed and standards of performance obtained, the analysis moves into the evaluation and diagnostic stage. At this point, concern shifts from accounting and computational matters to the task of interpreting the ratios for purposes of finding out just what the accounting statements have to say about the financial condition and operating results of the firm. In essence, the "bottom line" of financial analysis is to use the historical information to uncover significant strengths, weaknesses, and developing trends, and to determine appropriate courses of action which the firm might follow to correct any deficiencies and/or to enhance any areas of particular strength. In this phase of the analysis, attention is centered on relating the ratios to one another *horizontally*—comparing the same ratio historically and to industry standards—and *vertically*—seeking cause and effect relationships by comparing different ratios at a given point in time. Often what one ratio fails to reveal, another will. What's more, a condition that is vaguely suggested by one ratio may be corroborated by another; or the information so obtained may act as a trigger to the extent that it might reveal areas that warrant more detailed analysis.

This type of diagnosis and interpretation can be (and, in fact, usually is) conducted on a fairly informal basis that depends in large part on the skills of the individual analyst. However, there is a small but growing group of researchers who have had varying degrees of success in applying more sophisticated procedures to the practice of financial analysis. These procedures are heavily computerized (on the grounds that financial analysis is essentially an information-processing system) and involve the extensive adaptation of various statistical techniques to the data derived from financial ratios; at the same time, most such approaches attempt formally to integrate various theories and models of finance directly into the decision-making process. For example, these techniques might involve the application of regression models to the estimation of such variables as profits, rates of return, or earnings per share.[16] From an internal, financial management perspective, the objective of such an approach is basically the same as the more informal procedure: to obtain information that can be used to provide direction for the future course of business.

---

[15]For a more thorough discussion of the analytical problems encountered with diversified companies, see Baruch Lev, *Financial Statement Analysis: A New Approach*, (Englewood Cliffs, N.J.: Prentice-Hall, 1974), pp. 44–45.

[16]For an excellent discussion of this more sophisticated approach to financial analysis, see Lev, op. cit., and George Foster, *Financial Statement Analysis* (Englewood Cliffs, N.J.: Prentice-Hall, 1978).

	Historical		1984 Industry Averages
	1983	1984	
Liquidity measures			
Current ratio	1.31	1.48	1.60
Quick ratio	0.97	0.87	0.90
Activity measures			
Accounts receivable turnover	6.77	6.82	8.75
Inventory turnover	11.14	7.31	7.50
Fixed asset turnover	1.75	1.86	1.60
Total asset turnover	1.16	1.20	1.05
Leverage measures			
Debt-equity ratio	1.43	1.65	0.66
Times interest earned	5.81	5.74	8.83
Debt service margin	5.86	6.73	9.71
Profitability measures			
Net profit margin	7.02%	6.91%	7.20%
Return on investment	8.12%	8.30%	7.60%
Return on equity	22.01%	24.65%	15.60%
ABBREVIATED COMMON SIZE INCOME STATEMENT			
Sales	100.0%	100.0%	100.0%
Outside purchases	58.2	62.6	64.2
Gross profit	41.8	37.4	35.8
Total operating expenses	27.9	25.6	27.1
Operating profit	13.9	11.8	8.7
Other income and (expenses)	(2.0)	(1.3)	(.2)
Taxes	4.9	3.6	3.9
Net profit	7.0%	6.9%	4.6%
Market measures			
Dividend payout ratio	35.70%	31.25%	44.00%

Table 3.14 provides a summary of historical and industry figures for most of the Mid-America ratios discussed before. It shows that the liquidity and activity ratios are generally well maintained, though there does appear to be a problem with accounts receivable. In particular, the receivables turnover figure shows that this area remains considerably below the industry average. The magnitude of this shortfall can be seen by converting the receivable turnover measure to an average collection period; for 1984 we see that Mid-America had an average collection period of nearly 53 days (360/6.82 = 52.8), while the average in the industry was only 41 days (360/8.75 = 41.1). Viewed in this light, the accounts receivable position is seen to be about 12 days (or almost 30 percent) above normal. To the extent that the industry figures are valid, and the product mix and/or the composition of customers are not distorting the comparisons, it seems credit management may be having problems controlling the receivables portfolio. In this case, the 12-day excess supply of receivables is absorbing a whopping $58.9 million in

corporate resources, which, given the firm's net profit rate, has an after-tax opportunity cost of some $4 million.[17]

Likewise, the firm's leverage position also appears substandard, as Mid-America's debt-equity ratio reveals a growing and much higher level of debt than one would normally expect to find in a firm of this type. In fact, we can see that Mid-America is carrying about $1.65 in debt for every dollar of equity, as compared to the industry average of only 66 cents per dollar of equity. While the greater level of debt is probably being used to finance rapid growth, it is nonetheless adversely affecting the firm's exposure to financial risk; note the considerably substandard performance of times interest earned and debt service margin. Finally, the profitability measures show a fairly stable net profit margin, which remains slightly below average. Note that while the difference amounts to only 29/100 of 1 percent, it is not insignificant; for an improvement in the net profit rate of this magnitude would have added *over $5 million* to Mid-America's 1984 net profit.[18] Some insight on corporate profitability can be obtained by referring to the common size income statement; it shows that a likely cause of the company's below-average net income is the hefty amount of nonoperating expenses it incurred, a major portion of which is (probably) made up of the interest charges that accompany the firm's high level of financial leverage. Even so, Mid-America's ROI continues to improve and remains well above average as its substandard net profit margin was more than offset by an above-average total asset turnover. This performance, when combined with the company's high financial leverage, yields an ROE figure that also remains well above the industry average.

The Information Content of Financial Ratios

Financial analysis is predicated on the assumption that financial ratios provide information about the firm. If this is not the case, then financial analysis simply becomes a matter of reviewing the past—which might be useful in assessing the actions and skills of managers and profit centers, but is of little help in financial planning. Fortunately, a number of empirical studies have documented the predictive powers and information content of financial ratios, and offer strong support for their use as a planning tool. One study, for example, showed that accounting numbers

---

[17]To find the dollar value of excess receivables or inventory (or any asset account for that matter), simply multiply one day's supply by the number of days that the firm's current position exceeds the industry standard or desired level; for example, one day's supply of accounts receivable equals $4,911.7 (total receivables/average collection period = $259,336/52.8) which, when multiplied by the 12-day excess supply of receivables, yields an average of $58,940,400 ($4911.70 × 12). Given this figure and the firm's net profit rate (of 6.9 percent), the opportunity cost of the excess investment can be found as $58,940,400 × .069 = $4,066,900.

[18]An addition of 29 basis points (i.e., 29/100 of 1 percent) to Mid-America's net profit margin will increase earnings as follows: change in profit margin × sales = .0029 × $1,769,740,000 = $5,132,246.

and financial ratios do have an impact on the market for common stocks and can affect the stock valuation process.[19] However, this merely confirms the fact that financial information about the company is reflected in the current market price of the stock; it does not mean that financial ratios can be used to predict the future price behavior of the stock. In fact, the vast body of literature dealing with efficient markets shows conclusively that simple extrapolation models based on past financial data will usually be ineffective as predictors of future earnings and prices. In a market valuation context, we can conclude therefore that while the information content of financial ratios is potent (other things being equal, we can expect firms with consistently high liquidity and profitability measures to be priced higher than firms with low measures), their predictive powers are limited, at best.

On a more positive note, financial ratios have been shown to be useful in discriminating financially sound firms from weak ones; this has been verified in studies of the ability of financial ratios to predict corporate failure and to determine the quality of bonds and loans.[20] Researchers like Altman, Beaver, and Moyer used regression models and multiple discriminant analysis to show that certain financial ratios (like total asset turnover, ROI, and coverage ratios) are highly effective in predicting corporate failure.[21] More recently, Largay and Stickney[22] applied ratio analysis to a single company, W. T. Grant. Their study served to reinforce the predictive powers of financial ratios by showing that the traditional liquidity, activity, and profitability ratios had established a definite downward trend for several years prior to the massive collapse of this company; in fact, with the benefit of hindsight, they demonstrate that the company's deteriorating cash flow gave signals of impending doom long before its actual failure.

With regard to bond quality, an early study by Lawrence Fisher found that earnings variability and leverage variables, among others, played an important role in defining the size of risk premiums on corporate bonds.[23] Other studies addressed the issue of bond ratings more directly

---

[19]W. H. Beaver, P. Kettler, and M. Scholes, "The Association Between Market Determined and Accounting Determined Risk Measures," *Accounting Review* 45 (October 1970), pp. 654–682.

[20]William H. Beaver, "Financial Ratios as Predictors of Failure," *Journal of Accounting Research* 6 (1966), pp. 71–111; J. O. Horrigan, "The Determination of Long-Term Credit Standing with Financial Ratios," *Journal of Accounting Research* 6 (1966), pp. 44–62; and Y. E. Orgler, "A Credit Scoring Model for Commercial Loans," *Journal of Money, Credit and Banking* 2 (November 1970), pp. 435–445.

[21]Edward I. Altman, "Financial Ratios, Discriminant Analysis and the Prediction of Corporate Bankruptcy," *Journal of Finance* 23 (September 1968), pp. 589–609; Beaver, "Financial Ratios as Predictors of Failure"; and R. Charles Moyer, "Forecasting Financial Failure: A Re-examination," *Financial Management* 6 (spring 1977), pp. 11–17.

[22]James A. Largay and Clyde P. Stickney, "Cash Flows, Ratio Analysis, and the W. T. Grant Company Bankruptcy," *Financial Analysis Journal* 36 (July–August 1980), pp. 51–54.

[23]Lawrence Fisher, "Determinants of Risk Premiums on Corporate Bonds," *Journal of Political Economy* 67(June 1959), pp. 217–237.

and were able to show that financial ratios, along with other market and issue characteristics, are embedded in agency ratings and therefore are useful in predicting (with 60 to 70 percent accuracy) which rating is likely to be assigned to a company's bond.[24] Finally, still other studies have shown that financial ratios can be successful in differentiating good from bad commercial loans.[25] Using multiple discriminant analysis, some success has been achieved in developing and applying credit scoring models to a bank's commercial lending activities. Like bond rating models, such developments hold promise for corporate financial managers, since they reveal the financial variables that are important to rating agencies and commercial loan officers.

Financial Analysis in an Inflationary Environment

The previous comments are strongly supportive of financial analysis as a technique that provides valuable information about the firm, but it is important to remember that inflation (and especially high levels of inflation) can distort results. To the extent that this is true, it is possible that at least part of the financial performance of a company can be attributed to exogenous forces over which management has no control. To be sure, not all companies are adversely affected by inflation—in fact, a 1980 study by one of the Big Eight accounting firms, Ernst & Whinney, found that less than half (40 percent) of the 695 companies in their survey reported inflation-adjusted income that was less than the earnings reported on the traditional historical cost basis. The effects of inflation vary widely, with the most detrimental impact experienced by older, capital-intensive companies, and companies that do not use the LIFO (last in, first out) method of inventory accounting.

For those companies that are hurt by inflation, the biggest change will come in reported profits and probably dividend payout; in addition, fixed assets are likely to be understated on historical cost balance sheets, since price appreciation is ignored in such statements. Also, the extent to which a firm is a net debtor (or creditor) will determine whether it gains (or loses) from inflation: business firms are presumed to gain from inflation if they are net debtors (since the debt is repaid in cheaper dollars). As a result of all this, various financial ratios (particularly those dealing with profitability) are likely to be distorted as well. In fact, a study by Smith and Reilly showed that the following ratios of nonfinancial corporations could be substantially altered if the impact of inflation were fully considered: current ratio, inventory turnover, total asset turnover, debt-equity ratio, net profit margin, earnings per share, divi-

---

[24]George E. Pinches and Kent A. Mingo, "A Multivariate Analysis of Industrial Bond Ratings," *Journal of Finance* 28 (March 1973), pp. 1–18; and Richard R. West, "An Alternative Approach to Predicting Corporate Bond Ratings," *Journal of Accounting Research* 10 (spring 1970), pp. 118–125.

[25]See, for example, J. A. Haslem and W. A. Longbrake, "A Credit Scoring Model for Commercial Loans," *Journal of Money, Credit and Banking* 4 (August 1972), pp. 733–744.

dend payout ratio, ROI, and ROE.[26] Not all these ratios will be affected in every case, and the extent of any distortions will, of course, vary on a firm-by-firm basis. Overall, the information content of financial ratios remains strong for most firms, even in the face of inflation; but for firms that are heavily influenced by inflation, management should exercise caution when evaluating financial ratios and, if need be, make adjustments to reflect its impact.

SUMMARY

Financial analysis is an effective and widely used process whereby various dimensions of past and current financial statements are evaluated to obtain insights about the firm. The liquidity and composition of resources, financial leverage, profitability, and market measures of performance are all matters of concern to management and are studied not simply for their historical significance, but for the direction they provide in formulating a future course of action. Financial analysis deals with relationships that exist within a set of financial statements at a given point in time and with trends in these relationships over time. Financial analysis is usually conducted over a 2- to 5-year period and normally involves annual (fiscal or calendar year) figures. One of the important preliminary steps is to make sure that the financial statements being used in the analysis are truly comparable—that there have been no significant corporate developments or accounting changes that would distort reported results.

Ratio analysis is an important ingredient of financial analysis and is at the heart of the whole analytical process. Ratio analysis expands the perspective and information content of financial statements through the study of relationships that exist among and between various financial statement accounts. It is implemented by computing and studying the behavior over time of a variety of ratios, each of which emphasizes a particular dimension of the balance sheet and/or income statement. Financial ratios can be divided into liquidity, activity, leverage, profitability, and market measures of performance. Regardless of the type, these ratios are useful only when they can be compared to other ratio values; in essence, performance benchmarks are necessary to provide standards against which strengths, weaknesses, and developing trends can be evaluated. There are two types of performance standards: historical (which show a firm's performance over time) and industry averages (which involve comparing the firm's ratios to that of its competitors). When ratios and other measures are assessed relative to performance standards, valuable information about the operations and financial condition of the firm can be obtained. In fact, empirical studies have supported the information content and usefulness of financial ratios in

---

[26]Ralph E. Smith and Frank K. Reilly, "Price-Level Accounting and Financial Analysis," *Financial Management* 4 (summer 1975), pp. 21–26.

such areas as predicting corporate failure, distinguishing good from bad loans, and developing credit scoring models.

QUESTIONS	

3.1 What is the purpose and objective of financial analysis?

3.2 How can financial analysis be useful when its ratios and measures are derived from historical information?

3.3 Homes TV & Appliances has had 3 consecutive years of expanding sales and improved profits; even so, the company remains strapped for cash and is having difficulty servicing its debt. Arnie Homes, one of the three principals in the firm, feels that this is due in large part to the higher and higher dividends that are being paid out to the owners. Would the preparation of flow of funds statements give Homes the proof he is looking for? Explain. What other type of information (financial ratios, etc.) might be helpful in pinpointing the source(s) of Homes' problems?

3.4 Contrast the all-inclusive funds flow statement with the statement of changes in working capital; note the conditions that might encourage the use of the latter type of statement.

3.5 Butterfield Paper recently completed a major corporate acquisition; the acquired company produces a product line similar to its own, but operates in a different geographical region. Explain how such an acquisition could affect the interyear comparability of Butterfield's financial statements; can financial analysis still be used with Butterfield's financial statements?

3.6 Identify and briefly discuss the five major categories of financial ratios; note and briefly discuss two or three important measures in each ratio category. Explain the DuPont system and note its importance as a financial analysis concept.

3.7 Taskmaster Oil was having trouble maintaining what management felt was an acceptable ROI measure; some key people in the firm felt insufficient and deteriorating profitability was at the heart of the problem. Explain how the common size income statement could be used in conjunction with the DuPont system to determine if profitability was, in fact, the cause of Taskmaster Oil's ROI problems.

3.8 Why are performance benchmarks so important to ratio analysis? Distinguish between the two major types of performance standards.

3.9 Contrast the mechanical (or computational) aspect of financial analysis with the analytical/diagnostic phase. Is it safe to say that the mechanical part has little bearing on the success or failure of financial analysis? Explain.

PROBLEMS		

3.1 FLOW-OF FUNDS. Given the following financial statements:

Balance Sheets, December 31

	1983	1984
Cash	$ 2,510	$ 3,167
Marketable securities	475	625
Accounts receivable	8,635	9,420
Notes receivable	100	—
Inventories	15,210	13,520
Total current assets	$26,930	$26,732
Plant and equipment	$54,312	$63,478
Less: Accumulated depreciation	22,560	26,913
Net fixed assets	$31,752	$36,565
Prepaid items	25	20
Total assets	$58,707	$63,317
Accounts payable	$ 3,312	$ 4,498
Notes payable	1,500	1,000
Accrued expenses	45	18
Accrued federal income tax	2,174	2,827
Current portion of long-term debt	3,000	3,000
Total current liabilities	$10,031	$11,343
Long-term debt	25,000	24,500
Common stock	5,000	5,000
Retained earnings	18,676	22,474
Total liabilities and stockholders' equity	$58,707	$63,317

Income Statement For the Year Ended December 31, 1984

Sales (net)	$88,432
Cost of goods sold	53,976
Gross profit	$34,456
Selling and administrative expense[a]	22,394
Operating profit	$12,062
Interest expense	650
Other income	312
Profit before taxes	$11,724
Provision for federal income tax	6,176
Net profit after tax	$ 5,548
Dividends paid	1,750
Addition to retained earnings	$ 3,798

[a]Includes depreciation for the period of $4,625.

a. Prepare the all-inclusive funds flow statement for 1984.

b. What do you know about this company from its flow of funds statement? Does your evaluation suggest areas that warrant further analysis? If so, what analytical tools would you use?

c. Prepare the company's 1984 cash flow statement; contrast it to the flow of funds statement. (Hint: follow the procedure exactly as it is illustrated in Table 3.6.)

3.2 *FINANCIAL RATIOS.* Using the financial statements in Problem 3.1:

a. Prepare the 1984 ratios listed in the box below, and compare the results to the 1984 industry averages.

	1984 Company Figures	1984 Industry Averages
Current ratio		1.95
Quick ratio		1.30
Inventory turnover		6.5 times
Average collection period		35 days
Total asset turnover		1.55 times
Debt-equity ratio		0.70
Debt service margin		4.25 times
Operating ratio		86.0%
Net profit margin		7.5%
Return on investment		11.6%
Return on equity		19.5%

b. Interpret the results and discuss your findings.

3.3 *RATIO ANALYSIS.* The Fred Bates Company is a regional household products manufacturer; it has just finished its annual review, and selected financial data for the latest period are provided below:

Present sales level	$1,850,000
Sales	100.0%
Cost of goods sold	63.7
Gross profit margin	36.3%
Operating expenses	21.5
Operating profit margin	14.8%
Other income (expenses)—*net*	(3.2)
Taxes	5.0
Net profit	6.6%
Current ratio	1.75
Accounts receivable turnover	4.50 times
Total asset turnover	0.95 times
Owners' equity ratio (tangible net worth/net tangible assets)	34.4%

Financial analysis has uncovered three areas of concern: a deteriorating net profit margin, a slow turnover rate, and an excessive use of leverage. Management obviously would like to correct these problems, but before it initiates any action, it feels it needs answers to the following questions:

a. How far would receivables have to drop to achieve a 60-day supply?

b. Would that bring the total asset turnover up to 1.5 times?

c. If not, by how much would sales have to increase (given the drop in receivables can be achieved) to achieve the desired turnover of 1.5 times?

d. Given that this new level of sales is within reach, what kind of profits and profit rate could be expected if the operating ratio can be lowered to 82.5 percent (assume other income and expenses, and tax rates remain unchanged)?

e. Given the asset level derived above in (b), how much new equity will be required to reduce leverage to 50 percent of total assets? If the profit level above in (d) can be attained, will it be sufficient to meet the equity requirements of the firm? What will be the new owners' equity ratio if all these earnings are plowed back into the company?

3.4 *CREDIT ANALYSIS.* The Second National Bank of Jenks is presently conducting an evaluation of Beezer Products, Inc., which has requested a $1.5 million term loan; the loan proceeds will be used to finance a major capital expansion program and would be repaid in five annual instalments. Beezer's financial statements for 1984, its historical ratios for 1982 and 1983, and appropriate industry averages for 1984 are presented below:

Balance Sheet
Beezer Products, Inc.
December 31, 1984

ASSETS		
Current assets		
Cash		$ 200,000
Marketable securities		50,000
Accounts receivable		800,000
Inventories		950,000
Total current assets		$ 2,000,000
Gross fixed assets	$12,000,000	
Less: Accumulated depreciation	3,000,000	
Net fixed assets		9,000,000
Other assets		1,000,000
Total assets		$12,000,000
LIABILITIES AND STOCKHOLDERS' EQUITY		
Current liabilities		
Accrued liabilities		$ 100,000
Notes payable		200,000
Accounts payable		900,000
Total current liabilities		$ 1,200,000
Long-term debts[a]		3,000,000
Stockholders' equity		
Preferred stock[b]		1,000,000
Common stock (40,000 shares at $75 par)		3,000,000
Paid-in capital in excess of par value		2,800,000
Retained earnings		1,000,000
Total stockholders' equity		$ 7,800,000
Total liabilities and stockholders' equity		$12,000,000

[a]The annual principal payment on the long-term debt is $100,000.
[b]The firm has 25,000 shares of $2 preferred stock outstanding.

Income Statement
Beezer Products, Inc.
For the Year Ended
December 31, 1984

Net sales:		
Cash		$ 300,000
Credit		9,700,000
Total		$10,000,000
Less: Cost of goods sold		7,500,000
Gross profit		$ 2,500,000
Less Operating expenses:		
Selling	$300,000	
General and administrative	700,000	
Depreciation	200,000	$ 1,200,000
Operating profits		$ 1,300,000
Less: Interest expense		200,000
Profits before taxes		$ 1,100,000
Less: Taxes		440,000
Profit after taxes		$ 660,000
Less: Preferred stock dividends		50,000
Earnings available for common		$ 610,000
Less: Common stock dividends		200,000
To retained earnings		$ 410,000

Historical and Industry
Data—Beezer
Products, Inc.

Data	1982	1983	Industry Average 1984
Current ratio	1.40	1.55	1.85
Net working capital	$760,000	$720,000	$1,600,000
Quick ratio	1.00	.92	1.05
Average collection period (days)	45.0	36.4	35.0
Inventory turnover	9.52	9.21	8.60
Total asset turnover	.74	.80	.74
Debt-equity ratio	.25	.27	.39
Times interest earned	8.2	7.3	8.0
Debt service margin	4.8	4.5	4.5
Operating ratio	.88	.88	.90
Net profit margin	.067	.067	.058
Return on investment	.049	.054	.043
Return on equity	.078	.085	.084
Earnings per share	$12.75	$14.00	$13.50
Dividend payout ratio	.45	.38	.48
Book value per share	$135.00	$150.00	$150.00

a. Compute the necessary liquidity, activity, leverage, profitability, and market ratios for 1984.
b. Using historical and industry standards, analyze the company and evaluate the creditworthiness of Beezer Products, Inc.
c. Should the Second National Bank extend the credit requested? Explain.

3.5 *THE DuPONT SYSTEM.* Rockford Mining & Manufacturing has the following comparative balance sheets and income statements:

	1983	1984
BALANCE SHEETS		
Cash	$ 450,000	$ 520,000
Accounts receivable	400,000	700,000
Inventory	750,000	1,280,000
Fixed assets	1,400,000	2,160,000
Other assets	250,000	290,000
Total	$3,250,000	$4,950,000
Current liabilities	$ 525,000	$ 750,000
Long-term debt	925,000	1,850,000
Stockholders' equity	1,800,000	2,350,000
Total	$3,250,000	$4,950,000
INCOME STATEMENTS		
Sales	$4,100,000	$4,750,000
Cost of goods sold	2,665,000	3,135,000
Operating expenses	943,000	1,075,000
Operating profit	$ 492,000	$ 540,000
Interest, taxes and other expenses	207,000	240,000
Net profit	$ 285,000	$ 300,000

a. Using margin, turnover, and financial leverage ratios, compute the return on investment (ROI) and return on equity (ROE) measures for 1983 and 1984.

b. Now prepare comparative common size income statements and compute various turnover ratios to explain how margin and turnover affected the decline in ROI. Be specific. Did a change in financial leverage contribute to the drop in ROE? Explain.

3.6 *A COMPLETE FINANCIAL ANALYSIS.* Many companies rely on periodic financial analysis reports as a way to identify emerging financial problems. As a senior financial analyst, presume you are given the following comparative financial statements and asked to conduct a complete analysis of the firm's financial condition and operating results. (Dollars are in thousands, rounded to hundreds.)

	12-31-82	12-31-83	12-31-84
BALANCE SHEETS			
Cash	$ 47.8	$ 51.2	$ 65.4
Accounts receivable	60.3	60.1	49.0
Machinery inventory	401.7	303.0	312.6
Equipment inventory	93.9	122.9	92.4
Current assets	603.7	537.2	519.4
Fixed assets (at cost)	37.4	50.2	550.1
Accumulated depreciation	(20.4)	(26.9)	(35.2)
Prepaid expenses	42.5	28.7	46.9
Other assets	—	—	44.1
Total assets	$ 663.2	$ 589.2	$1,125.3
Accounts payable	$ 29.2	$ 34.3	$ 52.5
Notes payable—banks	396.1	322.4	313.0
Miscellaneous accruals	39.1	33.5	38.6
Current maturities	—	—	60.0
Current liabilities	464.4	390.2	464.1
Term debt	28.4	12.7	445.0
Capital stock	40.0	40.0	40.0
Retained earnings	130.4	146.3	176.2
Total liabilities and net worth	$ 663.2	$ 589.2	$1,125.3
INCOME STATEMENTS			
Machinery sales	$1,884.9	$1,240.6	$1,137.8
Equipment sales	1,538.4	1,490.3	1,468.1
Total sales	$3,423.3	$2,730.9	$2,605.9
Machinery gross profit	209.2	134.8	110.3
Equipment gross profit	378.3	382.7	384.6
Total gross profit	$ 587.5	$ 517.5	$ 494.9
Operating expense:			
Selling	90.8	57.7	61.7
General and admin.	404.6	404.4	386.9
Operating profit	$ 92.1	$ 55.4	$ 46.3
Net other income or (expense)	33.7	9.7	3.0
Executive bonuses	63.9	39.3	—
Income tax	23.0	10.8	19.4
Net profit after tax	$ 38.9	$ 15.0	$ 29.9
Depreciation charges	$ 5.5	$ 7.2	$ 9.3

a. For *each* of the 3 years in the period of analysis, compute as many financial ratios as you can, and prepare comparative flow of funds and common size income statements.

b. Analyze your findings and comment on any developing trends, as well as the firm's strengths and weaknesses.

c. Does your analysis indicate any areas that are in need of improvement? If so, what are they? How serious are the problems (cite figures expressing the extent or magnitude of the problems)? Based on your analysis of the firm, what recommendations would you propose as possible ways to rectify the problems? Be specific.

3.7 *FINANCIAL ANALYSIS.*   The following data are taken from the financial report of Cole Drug Stores, Inc. In addition, relevant industry data are provided.

a. Compute the ratios for Cole corresponding to the industry ratios.

b. What are its strengths (weaknesses) compared to the retail drug industry?

Balance Sheet as of January 31, 1984 (Thousands of Dollars)

Cash	$ 8,143
Receivables	5,596
Inventories	148,554
Other current	11,608
Net fixed assets	132,609
Total	$306,510
Accounts payable	$ 54,449
Notes payable	7,711
Accrued expenses	28,823
Deferred income taxes	20,347
Long-term debt and leases	103,662
Net worth	91,518
Total	$306,510

Income Statement for Year Ended January 31, 1984

Sales		$761,734
Cost of goods sold		550,930
Gross profit		210,804
Operating, general, and administrative expenses	$156,070	
Depreciation	10,784	166,854
EBIT		43,950
Interest		15,245
EBT		28,705
Taxes		12,056
Net Income		$ 16,649

Retail Drug Industry Ratios

Current	2.00 times
Quick	0.50 times
Collection period (365-day year)	12 days
Inventory turnover	4.00 times
Fixed asset turnover	8.00 times
Total asset turnover	3.20 times
Total debt/total assets	0.43
Times interest earned	3.00 times
Net profit margin	3.33%
Return on total assets	10.60%
Return on equity	18.40%

**SELECTED
REFERENCES**

Altman, Edward I. "Financial Ratios, Discriminant Analysis and the Prediction of Corporate Bankruptcy." *Journal of Finance* 23 (September 1968), pp. 589–609.

Backer, Morton, and Martin L. Gosman. "The Use of Financial Ratios in Credit Downgrade Decisions." *Financial Management* 9 (spring 1980), pp. 53–56.

Basu, Sanjoy. "The Information Content of Price-Earnings Ratios." *Financial Management* 4 (summer 1975), p. 53–61.

Beaver, William H., "Financial Ratios as Predictors of Failure." *Journal of Accounting Research* 6 (1966), pp. 71–111.

———, P. Kettler, and M. Scholes. "The Association Between Market Determined and Accounting Determined Risk Measures." *Accounting Review* 45 (October 1970), pp. 654–682.

Branch, Ben. "The Impact of Operating Decisions on ROI Dynamics." *Financial Management* 7 (winter 1978), pp. 54–60.

Chen, Kung H., and Thomas A. Shimerda. "An Empirical Analysis of Useful Financial Ratios." *Financial Management* 10 (spring 1981), pp. 51–60.

Davidson, S., C. Stickney, and R. Weil, *Accounting: The Language of Business*, 5th ed. Sun Lakes, AZ: Thomas Horton and Daughters, Inc., 1982.

Deakin, Edward B. "A Discriminant Analysis of Predictors of Business Failure." *Journal of Accounting Research* 10 (spring 1972), pp. 167–179.

Elam, Rick. "The Effects of Lease Data on the Predictive Ability of Financial Ratios." *Accounting Review* 50 (January 1975), pp. 25–43.

Fisher, L. "Determinants of Risk Premiums on Corporate Bonds." *Journal of Political Economy* 67 (June 1959), pp. 217–237.

Foster, George. *Financial Statement Analysis*. Englewood Cliffs, N.J.: Prentice-Hall, 1978.

Haslem, J. A., and W. A. Longbrake. "A Credit Scoring Model for Commercial Loans." *Journal of Money, Credit and Banking* 4 (August 1972), p. 733–744.

Horrigan, James C. "A Short History of Financial Ratio Analysis." *Accounting Review* 43 (April 1968), pp. 284–294.

Johnson, W. Bruce. "The Cross-Sectional Stability of Financial Ratio Patterns." *Journal of Financial and Quantitative Analysis* 14 (December 1979), pp. 1035–1048.

Largay, James A., and Clyde P. Stickney. "Cash Flows, Ratio Analysis, and the W.T. Grant Company Bankruptcy." *Financial Analysts Journal* 36 (July–August 1980), pp. 51–54.

Laurent, C. R. "Improving the Efficiency and Effectiveness of Financial Ratio Analysis." *Journal of Business, Finance and Accounting* 3 (autumn 1979), pp. 401–413.

Lemke, Kenneth W. "The Evaluation of Liquidity: An Analytical Study." *Journal of Accounting Research* 8 (spring 1970), pp. 47–77.

Lev, Baruch. *Financial Statement Analysis: A New Approach*. Englewood Cliffs, N.J.: Prentice-Hall, 1974.

———. "Decomposition Measures for Financial Analysis." *Financial Management* 2 (spring 1973), pp. 56–63.

Libby, Robert. "Accounting Ratios and the Prediction of Failure: Some Behavioral Evidence." *Journal of Accounting Research* 13 (spring 1975), pp. 150–161.

Mauriello, J. A. *Accounting for the Financial Analyst*, rev. ed. Homewood, Ill.: Irwin, 1971.

Moyer, R. Charles. "Forecasting Financial Failure: A Re-examination." *Financial Management* 6 (spring 1977), pp. 11–17.

O'Connor, Melvin C. "On the Usefulness of Financial Ratios to Investors in Common Stock." *Accounting Review* 48 (April 1973), pp. 339–352.

Orgler, Y. E. "A Credit Scoring Model for Commercial Loans." *Journal of Money,*

Credit and Banking 2 (November 1970), pp. 435–445.

Pinches, George E., and Kent A. Mingo. "A Multivariate Analysis of Industrial Bond Ratings." *Journal of Finance* 28 (March 1973), pp. 1–18.

———, ———, and J. Kent Caruthers. "The Hierarchical Classification of Financial Ratios." *Journal of Business Research* 5 (October 1975), pp. 295–310.

———, J. Clay Singleton, and Ali Jahankhani. "Fixed Coverage as a Determinant of Electric Utility Bond Ratings." *Financial Management* 7 (summer 1978), pp. 44–55.

Pringle, John J. "Price Earnings Ratios, Earnings-Per-Share, and Financial Management." *Financial Management* 2 (spring 1973), pp. 34–39.

Richards, Verlyn D., and Eugene J. Laughlin. "A Cash Conversion Cycle Approach to Liquidity Analysis." *Financial Management* 9 (spring 1980), pp. 32–38.

Smith, Ralph E., and Frank K. Reilly. "Price-Level Accounting and Financial Analysis." *Financial Management* 4 (summer 1975), pp. 21–26.

Spraakman, Gary P. "The Sensitivity of Earnings Per Share Growth to Some of Its Financial Components." *Financial Management* 8 (winter 1979), pp. 41–46.

Theil, Henri. "On the Use of Information Theory Concepts in the Analysis of Financial Statements." *Management Science* 15 (May 1969), pp. 459–480.

West, Richard R. "An Alternative Approach to Predicting Corporate Bond Ratings." *Journal of Accounting Research* 10 (spring 1970), pp. 118–125.

Appendix 3A

Breakeven Analysis

Breakeven analysis is used in evaluating corporate profitability. It enables management to study current operations—specifically, the amount of operating leverage a firm employs—and formulate ideas that can be used as part of a profit plan. Also, because breakeven analysis considers the interrelationships between sales, fixed costs, and variable expenses, it is useful in making certain strategic decisions that are likely to have a significant bearing on corporate profits, like changing the firm's price structure, or deciding whether or not to build a capital-intensive rather than labor-intensive plant.

Operating Leverage

Operating leverage pertains to the amount of fixed costs a company employs in its cost structure. Other things being equal, increasing leverage increases the sensitivity of possible returns; as such, it also increases the uncertainty of returns and the likelihood of a loss. The amount of operating leverage being used by a firm, therefore, will influence its exposure to business risk. Operating leverage evolves from the existence of fixed operating costs; by definition, these fixed operating costs do not vary with sales, and therefore must be paid regardless of the amount of revenue available. Business risk, in essence, is a reflection of the probability that the firm will be unable to generate the sales volume necessary to cover these fixed expenses.

As shown below, total leverage is made up of two parts—operating leverage and financial leverage:

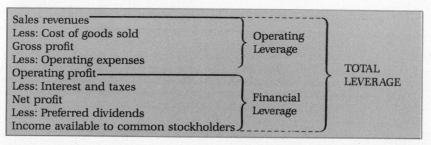

Operating leverage is concerned with a company's cost structure and deals with the relationship between sales and operating profit; financial leverage, in contrast, is concerned with the effects financing decisions have on returns to owners, and involves the relationship between the firm's operating profit and earnings available to common stockholders (financial leverage is examined in Chapter 18).

While in the long run, all costs are variable, in the short run, operating costs can be broken into fixed and variable components.[1] It makes no difference whether they are categorized as cost of goods sold, selling expenses, general and administrative expenses, or some other operating expense;[2] what is important is whether these costs are *fixed* (a level of costs that exists in a given accounting period regardless of the volume of sales), or *variable* (costs that vary in direct proportion to the firm's sales). Fixed costs do not change with sales, so any increase in sales will contribute directly to changes in profits; likewise, the greater the amount of fixed costs in the operating cost structure, other things being equal, the greater will be the impact on profits from a given change in sales. This principle is illustrated below:

	Alpha Products		Zebra Sales	
	Initially	With a 50% Increase in Sales	Initially	With a 50% Increase in Sales
Sales	$100,000	$150,000	$100,000	$150,000
Less: Fixed operating costs	40,000	40,000	5,000	5,000
	$ 60,000	$110,000	$ 95,000	$145,000
Less: Variable operating costs	40,000	60,000	75,000	112,500
Operating profit	$ 20,000	$ 50,000	$ 20,000	$ 32,500
Percent increase in profits	—	150%	—	62%

Alpha Products uses more fixed operating costs and less variable operating costs than Zebra Sales; as a result, it is able to enjoy more fully the benefits of operating leverage. That is, while both firms started with the same amount of operating profit, a given change in sales resulted in a greater change in profits for Alpha.

---

[1]Costs can sometimes be "semivariable" (or "semifixed") to the extent that they remain fixed over a given range of sales but tend to increase (in a step fashion) to higher levels as sales move to new volume levels; only a relatively small percentage of total costs fall into such a category, and they are generally included as a part of variable costs in most breakeven analyses.

[2]Note that the several categories of nonoperating expenses are specifically excluded from operating leverage and breakeven analysis.

Determining the Breakeven Point

Breakeven analysis, or as it is sometimes called, *cost-volume-profit analysis,* involves finding the point at which the level of sales will just equal total operating costs (or to put it another way, where operating profit equals zero). Recasting cost of goods sold and other operating expenses into fixed and variable costs—in the absence of more precise information, a general guideline is to define cost of goods sold and selling expenses as variable operating costs, and general and administrative expenses (e.g., executive salaries, insurance, utilities, rent, and other "overhead" expenses) as fixed costs—we can specify the breakeven point as:

$$\text{Operating costs} = \text{operating revenues} \tag{3A.1}$$

$$F + vX = pX$$

where F = fixed operating costs
v = variable operating cost per unit
p = price per unit
X = unit volume

Rearranging and solving for X, we can find the breakeven point in units of production as:

$$X = F/(p - v) \tag{3A.2}$$

As an example, consider a company that sells its only product at $5 a unit, has a variable cost of $2 per unit (a variable cost rate of 40 percent), and fixed costs of $40,000. It must sell 13,333 units just to break even:

$$X = \$40,000/(\$5 - \$2)$$
$$= \$40,000/\$3 = 13,333 \text{ units}$$

The operating leverage and breakeven concept can also be captured graphically, as in Figure 3A.1, which illustrates the cost structure and revenues of a hypothetical firm with sales of $82,100 per year (from a current volume of roughly 22,500 units), fixed costs of $20,000 per year, a variable cost rate of about 55 percent ($2 per unit), and a product sales price of $3.65 per unit (all of which adds up to an operating profit of some $17,000). It has a breakeven point of 12,100 units: the point where the total cost line intersects the total revenue line. Observe that up to the breakeven point, every dollar of sales is allocated to variable and fixed costs (55 cents to variable operating costs and 45 cents to fixed). After the breakeven point, profits begin to accrue as every dollar of sales is then allocated to variable costs and profits (in the same ratio as above).

It should be evident that, other things being equal, profits can be

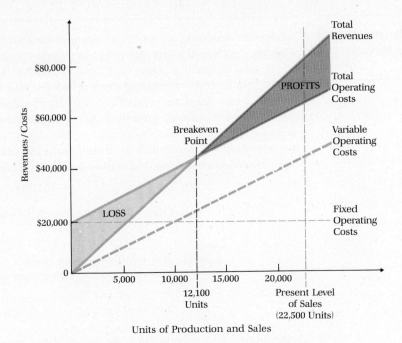

Figure 3A.1   Graphic Illustration of the Breakeven Concept.

increased by increasing the slope of the revenue line and/or decreasing the slope of the total operating cost line. But as we will see, these actions have conflicting effects on operating leverage and the breakeven point. Three variables can be altered to bring about desired changes in the revenue and cost lines: the revenue line can be changed by increasing or decreasing the unit sales price (note that changing only unit volume will result simply in moving up or down an existing revenue line), and the total cost line can be changed by substituting fixed costs for variable costs or vice versa. Figure 3A.2(a) shows what happens to our hypothetical firm when we increase the selling price to $4 per unit. This action would lead to the desirable result of a drop in the breakeven point. And if sales can be maintained at 22,500 units, operating earnings will increase to $25,000. However, the risk in this approach is that the firm will not be able to maintain its unit volume at the higher price—at the least, the sales volume must equal 18,550 units just to match the profits generated under the old pricing system. Thus, management must assess the tradeoff it is willing to tolerate between an increased sales price and a likely reduction in sales volume (in the example, a drop in the unit volume of more than 17.6 percent will result in decreased operating income).

Figure 3A.2(b) shows what happens when the fixed operating costs are increased; note that the results are undesirable. Not only does the

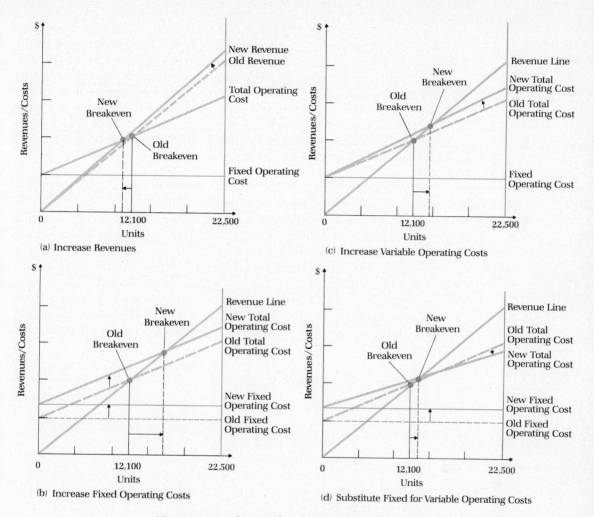

Figure 3A.2 Altering the Breakeven Point.

breakeven point increase, but operating profits (at the current level of 22,500 units) drop as well. Such behavior is due to the fact that an increase in fixed costs results only in an upward shift of the total cost line, without a corresponding change in its slope. Only when variable costs are changed will the slope of the cost line change. This is depicted in Figure 3A.2(c), which shows what happens when the variable cost rate of the firm is increased. However, note that the net results are still unattractive; the breakeven point once again rises, while the operating profits decline.

These results should not be altogether surprising as increased costs, regardless of whether they are fixed or variable, normally do result in reduced profits. The situation is considerably different, however, when one type of cost can be substituted for another. Then the slope and location of the total cost line can be altered enough to bring about positive effects on profits. For example, increasing fixed costs so that the variable cost rate may be reduced (via substituting capital for labor) might have the sought-after effects (so long as the absolute drop in the latter $\geq$ the rise in the former). Such a condition is portrayed in Figure 3A.2(d); as we can see, the breakeven point also increases under these circumstances, so management must be willing to accept the increased operating risk in exchange for the improved profit potential.[3]

Sales Breakeven

Normally a firm has more than one product line and/or unit volume activity is not available. Under such circumstances, the breakeven point can be calculated in terms of dollars—by finding the sales level at which the breakeven point will occur. The sales breakeven point is simply a variation of the basic breakeven formula that uses contribution margin (1 − variable cost rate) in place of the dollar contribution to fixed costs and profits $(p - v)$. The *contribution margin* is the percentage of each sales dollar that remains after satisfying the variable costs; it reflects the per dollar (or rate of) contribution toward meeting fixed costs and profits:

$$\text{Contribution margin} = 1 - \text{variable cost rate} \qquad (3A.3)$$
$$= 1 - \frac{VC}{S}$$

where VC = total variable operating costs at a given (prevailing) level of sales

S = total sales revenue in dollars

Used in the breakeven formula, the sales breakeven point (X^*) is determined as follows:

$$X^* = \frac{F}{1 - \dfrac{VC}{S}} \qquad (3A.4)$$

The similarity between the sales breakeven point and the unit breakeven equation should be obvious. Except for breaking operating expenses into fixed and variable costs, the income statement provides

---

[3]Breakeven analysis, unfortunately, is not without its shortcomings. Specifically, the assumption of linearity is considered a weakness of this analytical tool. What's more, the cost classification system is difficult to apply in practice and the concept has only limited application to multiproduct firms. Finally, because it is primarily a short-term concept, breakeven analysis also has limited multiperiod applications. Such limitations notwithstanding, breakeven analysis can still prove to be a useful decision-making tool so long as it is carefully applied and the implications of its shortcomings are understood.

the basic input to the solution of X^*. Consider, for example, the case of Frontier Chemical, which in 1984 had sales of $900,000, variable operating costs of $350,000, and fixed operating costs of $400,000 (leaving it an operating profit of $150,000). Based on such information, we can see that Frontier's sales breakeven in 1984 equaled:

$$X^* = \frac{\$400,000}{1 - \dfrac{\$350,000}{\$900,000}}$$

$$= \frac{\$400,000}{1 - .389} = \$654,664$$

In essence, at a sales level of $654,664 the company will have an operating profit that just equals zero.

Breakeven Margin

Instead of working in absolute values, the *breakeven margin* can be used to assess operating leverage and the breakeven point in relative terms. This measure relates the breakeven point (in units or sales dollars) to prevailing or anticipated sales volume as a way to determine the "margin of safety" for a given level of operations. It is computed as follows:

$$B/E \text{ margin} = \frac{S - B/E}{S} \tag{3A.5}$$

where S = actual or anticipated sales volume
B/E = the previously determined breakeven point—use either the sales breakeven point (X^*), or convert the unit breakeven point (X) to a dollar value, $X \times p$

In the previous example, we see that Frontier Chemical has a breakeven margin of:

$$B/E \text{ margin} = \frac{\$900,000 - \$654,664}{\$900,000} = 27\%$$

That is how far sales would have to drop before the firm hits its breakeven point and encounters difficulties in meeting normal operating expenses. The breakeven margin is especially useful in evaluating operating risk. It is an indication of the amount of operating cushion embedded in a firm's sales level; other things being equal, the higher the breakeven margin of safety, the greater the drop in sales that must occur before the firm shows a loss (and therefore, the lower the firm's exposure to business risk).

Cash Breakeven

Because most firms report costs on an accrual rather than a cash basis, it is often useful to perform a *cash breakeven analysis* in place of or in addition to determining the unit or sales breakeven point. This type of analysis recognizes that the firm's cash receipts and expenditures do not correspond exactly with the accounting recognition of income and expense. Although a variety of differences may occur, the key items requiring attention in the cash breakeven are noncash charges like depreciation. These noncash expenditures are normally included as part of fixed operating costs and therefore must be netted out in the preparation of the cash breakeven point. The presence of such noncash charges in fixed costs tends to overstate the customary breakeven point. Defining depreciation and other noncash expenditures as N, we can easily adjust the unit and sales breakeven equations to determine the cash breakeven point:

$$\text{Cash breakeven point} = \frac{F - N}{p - v} \quad \text{or} \quad \frac{F - N}{1 - (VC/S)} \quad \text{(3A.6)}$$

Consider once more the case of Frontier Chemical; this time assume it has $100,000 of noncash expenditures included in fixed operating costs. Given that all other conditions remain the same, its cash breakeven point would be as follows:

$$\text{Cash breakeven} = \frac{\$400,000 - \$100,000}{1 - \dfrac{\$350,000}{\$900,000}}$$

$$= \frac{\$300,000}{1 - .389} = \$491,000$$

This measure is well below the customary sales breakeven point (the presence of noncash expenses in fixed operating costs will always result in higher unit or sales breakeven points), and represents the level of sales necessary to meet the cash operating needs of the company.

PROBLEMS

3A.1. *BREAKEVEN POINT.* The Phoenix Press, Inc., publishes the *Annual Arizona Review & Almanac*. Last year, the book sold for $8 a copy, with variable costs per book of $6; the company has fixed costs of $40,000. How many books will it have to sell this year to achieve its breakeven point?

a. What if fixed costs should rise to $44,000 (and all other figures remain unchanged)?

b. What if the selling price of the book rises to $8.50 a copy (again assume all other figures remain unchanged)?

c. What if variable costs per book rise to $6.50 (and all else remains the same)?

d. What conclusions about the firm's breakeven point can be drawn from your answers?

3A.2. *BREAKEVEN ANALYSIS.* Given the following income statement:

	Year Ending 12/31/84
Sales	$30,000,000
Cost of goods sold	21,000,000
Gross profit	$ 9,000,000
Selling expenses	3,000,000
General and administrative expenses	2,000,000
Depreciation expenses	1,000,000
Operating profit	$ 3,000,000
Interest expense	1,000,000
Taxes	800,000
Net profits	$ 1,200,000

Assume cost of goods sold and selling expenses are variable operating costs, and general and administrative expenses and depreciation are fixed.

a. Compute the firm's sales breakeven point.
b. Determine the company's breakeven margin of safety.
c. Calculate its cash breakeven.

4

Budgeting and Forecasting

Financial analysis, examined in the preceding chapter, was shown to be useful because it provides insights that help managers make decisions about the future course of the firm. Budgeting and financial forecasting are managerial techniques that also deal with the future, but in a more direct fashion. Budgets and forecasts provide management with a summary statement of the potential financial consequences of present-day decisions, and are used, in one form or another, in a wide array of decision-making situations. After reviewing essential general concepts, this chapter will examine the preparation and use of budgets and forecasts. Sales forecasts, various types of financial budgets, pro forma statements, and variance analysis will all be studied, with due consideration given to their information content and to the role they play in the decision-making process.

Managerial and Organizational Dimensions of Budgeting

To find out how much profit a company made last year, one need only look at the firm's income statement; likewise, we can refer to the balance sheet to see its asset mix or the kind of financing it has been using. But what happens if we look at the future and raise such questions as these: How profitable will the firm be next year? What will sales be, and what kind of resources will be required to support operations? Managers can use budgets to assess these and other similar concerns; the information obtained can then be employed to establish full-fledged profit plans, to administer the firm's marketable securities portfolio, to define future resource requirements and financing needs, and to attend to other matters that affect the competitiveness and future well-being of the company. The budget concept, in effect, provides management with a systematic process for translating operating plans into a coordinated accounting model of financial operations. If effectively used, budgets can make significant contributions to the basic financial goal of maximizing shareholder wealth because they can reduce operating uncertainties and assist management in more efficiently utilizing the resources at its command.

From a strictly managerial perspective, budgets are used for planning, coordination, and control. A company can decide, for one reason or another, to take whatever comes along—indeed, many firms (especially smaller ones) do just that. Others, however, attempt to actively influence the future and do so by formulating operating and financial plans. Such plans provide guidelines that help management establish effective:

- Marketing and promotion efforts
- Manpower planning
- Research and development expenditures
- Facilities and capital budgets
- Working capital investments
- Financing and dividend policies
- General profit planning

The coordination of corporate activities is also achieved through budgeting. This is especially so in firms with numerous divisions, groups, and/or operating units that require a comprehensive set of guidelines to ensure that the various parts of the company are working toward the same goal. Such coordination furnishes a link between actual day-to-day operations and corresponding financial plans. Finally, budgets provide a means for controlling the operations of the firm. In essence, a budget establishes a standard of performance, against which actual operating results can be judged.

Information Flow

To be effective, budgets require input from each of the major operating units of the company. Each of the major product lines should be considered, as should input from marketing and production and the various regional offices. Relying on the operating segments for input not only yields useful information for developing budgets, but it also establishes credibility and enhances adherence to the budgets by the various parts of the company. A whole series of budgetary inputs is shown in Figure 4.1. The depicted information flow, which was adapted from a procedure actually used by a major corporation, is typical of that used by many large companies. In this case, various ground rules and forecasting schedules are established by the division planning group, which provides the cost- and revenue-producing segments of the company with guidelines that they, in turn, can use in generating estimates and forecasts. The resulting reports and schedules are then channeled to the financial forecasting group, where they are verified, revised (as necessary), correlated, and assembled into budget reports that are distributed to various levels of management. Such a system

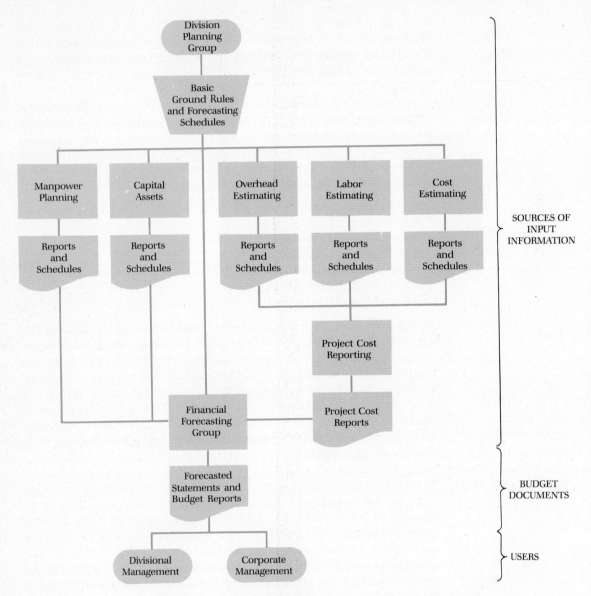

Figure 4.1   The Flow of Information in a Financial Forecast.

generates data input that reflects corporate, financial, manufacturing, and marketing policies.

Budget Reports   The data input denoted above results in a network of budget reports and forecasted statements, a complete set of which would likely include the following:

- Sales forecasts
- Cash budgets (or long-range financial forecasts)
- Pro forma income statements (profit plans)
- Pro forma balance sheets

The sales forecast is prepared first; information from it is then used to develop a cash budget (and/or long-range financial forecast). The pro forma income statement, or profit plan, is produced concurrently with the cash budget, since it is needed to identify a major disbursement item: taxes paid. Preparation of the pro forma balance sheet is the final step in the budgeting process as it relies on the other budget reports for much of its information.[1] These budget documents are prepared in detail at least once a year and then revised periodically (usually on a monthly or quarterly basis) in accordance with an established budget cycle.

The *sales forecast* is the key element in the budget system, since the projected level of sales defines the level of production and operating needs of the firm and therefore has a direct bearing on future cash flow, profitability, level and composition of assets, and financing mix. The *cash budget*, usually prepared on a monthly basis and covering a period of 1 year or less, summarizes the estimated cash receipts and expenditures of the firm (as opposed to accounting-derived revenues and costs). It reveals the amount and timing of expected cash flows and enables the financial manager to determine borrowing needs and lending opportunities. The cash budget provides information management can use to determine the future financing needs of the company, map out the direction of the firm's portfolio of marketable securities, and exercise control over the company's cash and liquidity position. An extension of the cash budget is the *long-range financial forecast*, which employs basically the same format (perhaps in less detail), but deals with expected receipts and expenditures that extend further into the future— usually 3 to 7 years, sometimes longer. These forecasts focus on projected multiyear capital expenditures and other long-term programs such as research and development outlays, marketing and product development, and major sources of financing.

Profit plans are also prepared over both short- and long-term budget horizons.[2] These plans are basically forecasted income statements that summarize revenues and costs, and reflect the potential impact of cash

---

[1]There are a variety of budgetary techniques used in practice; the procedure presented here is one of the more popular as it provides for relatively easy sequential development of a comprehensive budget document. A slight variation of this procedure, and one that is also widely found in practice, is where the sales forecast is developed first, followed by the pro forma income statement and then the cash budget and pro forma balance sheet.

[2]Normally, a short-term budget horizon is defined as 1 year or less, whereas a long-term horizon covers more than a year.

budgets and long-range financial forecasts on operating results. They show how and to what extent earnings will accrue to the company, and assist management in assessing ways of improving profitability. *Pro forma balance sheets*, in contrast, demonstrate the effects of budgets and forecasts on the company's asset and financing mix. They provide an indication of the resource requirements and financing needs that can be expected at various levels of operations; they help management identify operating capabilities and shortfalls, and establish plans and programs to meet them.[3]

The Sales Forecast

Regardless of the type of projected financial report being prepared, the basic starting point is always the same: the sales forecast. A sales forecast evaluates the probable future economic and industry environment and attempts to specify what sales are expected to be under such conditions. The marketing area obviously plays an important role in this regard, as a crucial element in the sales forecast is the projected level of demand for the company product(s). In addition to projected unit volume, it is also important that future price per unit be specified. While many firms deal in forecasted unit volumes and prices, other companies, for a variety of reasons, may find it more useful to project final sales figures directly. The basic forecasting principles (and most important, the final results) should be the same regardless of which procedure is used. For purposes of simplicity, we will use total sales to describe sales forecasts. The three most popular ways of projecting sales are: (1) trend line forecasts; (2) single- or multivariable regression analysis; and (3) judgmental forecasting.[4]

Trend Line Forecasts

The principle behind the trend line forecast is that the forces which produced the observed historical performance in sales will continue to behave in the same manner in the future. The procedure is admittedly naive, but it may be perfectly acceptable for many firms—particularly those that are experiencing an obvious trend in revenues. A time series is a set of observations, on the same variable (sales), ordered in time; time

---

[3]While the discussion in this chapter purposely avoids extensive mathematical modeling, there is an abundance of literature dealing with mathematically based planning procedures; see, for example, Roy L. Crum, Darwin Klingman, and Lee A. Tavis, "Implementation of Large-Scale Financial Planning Models: Solution Efficient Transformations," *Journal of Financial and Quantitative Analysis* 14 (March 1979), pp. 137–152; James L. Pappas and George P. Huber, "Probabilistic Short-Term Financial Planning," *Financial Management* 2 (autumn 1973), pp. 36–44; Gerald A. Pogue and Ralph N. Bussard, "A Linear Programming Model for Short-Term Financial Planning Under Uncertainty," *Sloan Management Review* (spring 1972), pp. 69–98; and James M. Warren and John P. Shelton, "A Simultaneous Equation Approach to Financial Planning," *Journal of Finance* 26 (December 1971), pp. 1123–1142.

[4]For a discussion of forecasting techniques actually used in practice, see Judy Pan, Donald R. Nichols, and O. Maurice Joy, "Sales Forecasting Practices of Large U.S. Industrial Firms," *Financial Management* 6 (fall 1977), pp. 72–77.

series forecasts, in turn, are performed by projecting established trends into the future.

Trend line forecasts are performed by using a least squares technique —a statistical procedure that yields a mathematical expression of a straight line that best describes the relationship between an observed variable (sales) and time.[5] The computed line describes the trend in revenues, which is used, along with the least squares equatiōn, to forecast (extrapolate) sales into the future. As an illustration, consider the case of Specialty Automotive, Inc.—a small manufacturer of high-performance auto parts. As shown by the following data, the company has experienced a steady growth in sales over the years:

Year	Sales	Year	Sales
1973	$ 884,000	1979	$1,545,000
1974	964,000	1980	1,634,000
1975	1,031,000	1981	1,769,000
1976	1,086,000	1982	1,983,000
1977	1,233,000	1983	2,248,000
1978	1,468,000	1984	2,303,000

Assume management wants to forecast sales for each of the next 5 years (1985–1989); using the least squares technique, this can be done by calculating the coefficients of the following linear equation:

$$Y = a + bX \qquad (4.1)$$

where a is a constant and b is the slope of the line (see Appendix 4A for computational details). This equation depicts the variable under study (Y = sales) as a function of time (X). The resulting trend line is illustrated in Figure 4.2, which shows both actual and forecasted sales. The equation for Specialty Automotive turns out to be:

$$Y = 771.5 + 134.7X$$

It shows that sales are increasing at the rate of about $135,000 a year, and from their present level of $2.3 million, sales are expected to grow to nearly $3 million by the end of the 5-year forecast horizon.[6] Note that, at

---

[5]Basically, least squares is little more than a variation of the linear regression technique, wherein the independent (X) values are represented by equal units of time. Regression analysis is discussed in detail in the appendix to this chapter; for more discussion of trend analysis, see, for example, Clark A. Hawkins and Jean E. Weber, *Statistical Analysis: Applications to Business and Economics* (New York: Harper & Row, 1980), chaps. 13, 14.

[6]The selection of a base year is a crucial element in the forecasting procedure. If 1976 (rather than 1973) were used as the first year in the analysis, the slope of the trend line would increase by almost 15 percent and the 1989 forecast would change by about $150,000. Care should be exercised in choosing the base year to assure that it (and the ensuing historical data) is as compatible as possible to the conditions expected to prevail over the forecast period.

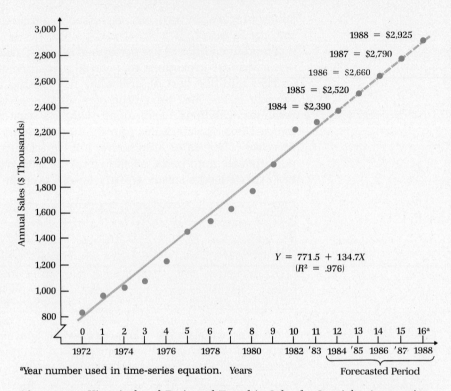

Figure 4.2   Historical and Projected Trend in Sales for Specialty Automotive.

this point, there is no further forecasting required, since all we have to do to obtain, say, the 1985 forecasted sales figure is define the value for X in the equation. That is, counting from our base year of 1973 (where $X = 0$), it can be seen that 1985 would be the twelfth year in our series of observations. Defining X as 12, we have:

$$\text{Estimated 1985 sales} = 771.5 + 134.7(12)$$
$$= 771.5 + 1616.4$$
$$= 2387.9 \approx \$2390$$

The same procedure was repeated in estimating 1986 and subsequent years' sales.

Because these forecasts are historically derived, they are subject to error to the extent that residual forces can influence the future behavior of the dependent variable (sales). From a historical perspective, it is possible to check the line's "fit" by calculating the coefficient of determination (R^2), which denotes how close to the estimated straight line the data points lie, and therefore the extent to which sales have been related to time. In this particular situation, the coefficient of determination, R^2, is .976. Since this suggests an almost perfect correlation, we can conclude, in the absence of any evidence to the contrary, that it is reasonable to use the trend line forecasts.

Regression Analysis

Another way to forecast sales is to analyze the causative forces operating on sales, and to base the forecast on the disclosed relationships and on any anticipated changes in these forces. Regression analysis (which is described in greater detail in Appendix 4A) is helpful in this regard, as it can be used to determine those exogenous forces that have a significant effect on the level of corporate sales. The objective is to develop a mathematical model of the behavior of sales; if we can determine why sales behave the way they do, we can concentrate our forecasting attention on those factors which have a pronounced impact on sales. For example, new car sales may be a function of GNP, the number of cars registered in the previous year, and the number of people in the 18 to 25 age bracket. On the basis of available empirical evidence, regression analysis can be used to test this relationship and produce a mathematical model that combines all these factors into an equation, which can then be employed for estimating annual sales.

An example will help demonstrate this procedure. Consider once again the case of Specialty Automotive, but this time assume that we are viewing company sales as a function of industrial production—an index of commercial and economic activity. This problem is much like that addressed with trend line analysis, even to the extent that the same regression equation is used:[7]

$$Y = a + bX$$

Determining the coefficients of this equation will yield a model that can be used to estimate values of the dependent variable (Y = sales) from given (projected) values of the independent variable (X = industrial production). In this procedure, the historical evidence is examined in order to identify key predictive variables that can be used to develop a forecasting model. Assume the historical record of behavior in the independent variable is as follows:

---

[7]Many times, multivariable regression analysis is needed to explain the behavior of the dependent variable, Y. When more than one independent variable is used, the regression equation will take on the following general form:

$$Y = a + b_1 X_1 + b_2 X_2 + \ldots + b_n X_n$$

In any event, the mechanical aspects and interpretation of multivariable analysis are much the same as the single-variable case. See, for example, Morris Hamburg, *Statistical Analysis for Decision Making*, 2d ed. (New York: Harcourt Brace Jovanovich, 1977), pp. 410–431, for a more extensive discussion of regression analysis, and some of the problems that must be dealt with when using this procedure.

Year	Industrial Production	Year	Industrial Production
1973	258.1	1979	397.5
1974	284.6	1980	419.2
1975	329.0	1981	442.8
1976	347.0	1982	444.5
1977	365.4	1983	482.7
1978	363.1	1984	503.4

Such empirical observations are combined with company sales data and plotted on a scatter diagram, as in Figure 4.3. The joint sales and industrial production data yield the following regression equation:

$$Y = -910.27 + 6.27X$$

and produce the depicted regression line. The reported coefficient of determination (R^2) suggests a highly viable estimation model, as it indicates that almost 94 percent of the variation in company sales was accounted for by changes in industrial production.

At this point, estimates of the future behavior of the industrial production index must be prepared or obtained. *Given such projections,* the regression model can then be used to predict the future sales of Specialty Automotive. That is:

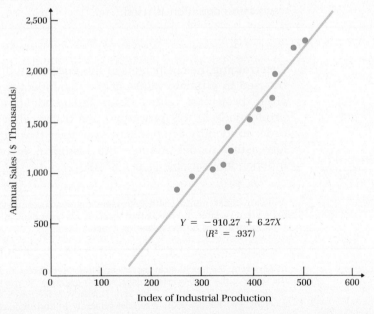

$$Y = -910.27 + 6.27X$$
$$(R^2 = .937)$$

Figure 4.3   Scatter Diagram of Company Sales and the Index of Industrial Production.

Year	Projections of Industrial Production (X)	Computed Future Company Sales (Y) (in $ Thousands)
1985	525	$2,380
1986	545	2,510
1987	570	2,665
1988	595	2,820
1989	630	3,040

Note that sales are estimated from projections of the independent variable (X), and by solving the computed regression model for Y; for 1985 estimated sales, $Y = -910.27 + 6.27(525) = 2381.5 \approx \$2,380$. While this forecasting technique is based on established cause-and-effect relationships and therefore may be a more rational and intuitively more appealing approach than the trend line procedure, it is predicated on projections of the independent variable and as such, subject to obvious forecasting errors. (Note that from a technical standpoint, the validity of the model is predicated on the assumption that the independent variable—industrial production—is not serially correlated with time; if it is, then the time series approach should be used directly to forecast sales.)

Judgmental Forecasting

Trend line forecasts and regression analysis provide concise mathematical expressions of possible future sales activity, but the importance of subjective input from key personnel cannot be overlooked. Although their numbers are rapidly declining, there are companies that still base sales forecasts exclusively on the judgment of experienced, knowledgeable personnel. Inputs are obtained from the people in the field regarding sales potential by product line and/or customer; this is combined with inputs from other knowledgeable or dependable sources and provides the data on product demand, sales potential, and so on that is worked into a sales forecast. For example, a major airframe manufacturer prepares its sales forecasts by developing detailed delivery schedules for each of its customers around the world. Many firms use judgmental input in combination with trend line or regression models. A common practice (especially among larger firms) is to generate the major elements of a sales estimate from a regimented forecast model (like trend line or regression analysis), and then make modest adjustments based on an analysis of conditions and recommendations by knowledgeable company personnel.

Cash Budgets

Once the sales forecast has been produced, attention can shift to preparation of the cash budget and other forecast documents. We will look next at the mechanics involved in developing a short-range cash

TABLE 4.1
A Format for a
Cash Budget Report

OPERATING RECEIPTS
Cash sales and accounts receivable
   collected in month of transaction . . . .
Collection of accounts receivable:
    1-month lag. . . . .
    2-month lag. . . . .
      Total operating receipts . . . .

OPERATING EXPENDITURES
Payment on raw material purchases:
    Month of transaction . . . .
    1-month lag. . . . .
Direct labor. . . . .
Overhead (excludes depreciation charges) . . . .
Operating (selling and
   administrative) expenses. . . . .
      Total operating expenditures . . . .

       Net operating cash flow. . . . .

FACILITIES, TAXES, AND OTHER
Plant and equipment expenditures . . . .
Taxes paid. . . . .
Interest paid . . . .
Principal payments on debt. . . . .
Dividends paid . . . .
Other nonoperating expenses . . . .
Other nonoperating income[a] . . . .
     Total other expenditures. . . . .

      Net cash flow . . . .

CASH RECONCILIATION
Beginning cash balance . . . .
Net cash flow (per above) . . . .
Ending cash balance . . . .
Minimum cash balance . . . .
Cash excess (or shortfall) . . . .

[a]Other nonoperating income is entered as a negative value, since it will result in a net reduction in "other expenditures."

budget.[8] A budget format like the one in Table 4.1 will be used to demonstrate cash budgeting. It is typical of a fairly standard budget format that captures all the essential operating and nonoperating cash flow elements.

Estimation
Procedures

When cash budgets are prepared, attention is usually centered on major receipt and expenditure items, like the collection of accounts receivable and inventory transactions. These elements normally account for the

[8]Note that the same principles and procedures used with cash budgets are equally applicable (with obvious modest modifications) to the preparation of long-range financial forecasts.

largest portion of the firm's total cash flow and as a result require more attention. Often the minor receipt and expenditure items will simply be extrapolated into the future at some constant (albeit representative) rate or level. In contrast, major receipt and expenditure values are normally based on forecasted sales and derived from either statistical procedures or historical standards.

The same statistical procedures that were used with the sales forecast (trend line or regression analysis) can be adopted to the estimation of key receipt and expenditure items. For example, a regression model could be developed to determine the estimated level of accounts receivable or probable inventory payment patterns. More likely, however, a series of historical standards will be developed and applied to forecasted sales (or some derivation thereof) to provide the projections. To do this, an analyst would examine the company's historical records and/or financial statements to develop a series of ratios and measures that are typical of corporate operating behavior and expected to hold in the foreseeable future. If inventory purchases, for instance, are closely related to sales, a ratio can be developed and used in conjunction with forecasted sales to project expected inventory transactions.

The historical standards attempt to capture the firm's important behavioral patterns so that they can be used in projecting future cash flows. So-called ground rules, which are budget assumptions based on historical measures or standards of performance, are often established as a way to expedite the cash budgeting process. The ground rules stipulate how the receipt and expenditure items will be forecasted into the future—in effect, they are procedural guidelines. Assume that the following ground rules have been established for Specialty Automotive:

1. Twenty percent of forecasted sales are on a cash basis or collected in the month of sale—there is no cash discount for prompt payment.[9]

2. Of the remaining sales, 60 percent is collected 1 month after sale and the balance in the following month.[10]

3. Purchases of raw materials inventory are based on projected sales 3 months hence; they equal 37.5 percent of such sales; half of this amount is paid in the month of transaction, the balance 1 month later.

4. Likewise, expenditures for direct labor amount to 19.5 percent of the level of sales 3 months in the future, all of which is paid in the month in which it is incurred.

---

[9]If cash discounts were offered and a significant portion of sales were on such terms, then such discounts should be reflected in the budget; the portion of total sales transacted on a cash discount basis should be indicated and receipt figures reduced by the amount of these discounts.

[10]We ignore bad debts in our ground rules, but they can be worked into the forecast by reducing accounts receivable collections accordingly—in essence, the percentage of accounts receivable collections would fall short of credit sales by the amount of bad debts.

5. The same sales base is also used to determine factory overhead—specifically, these expenditures are projected at the rate of 13 percent of such sales, and they too are paid in full in the month in which they are incurred; in addition, current and projected depreciation schedules[11] reveal that depreciation charges will amount to $40,000 in each of the next two years and then jump to $70,000 per year thereafter.

6. Operating expenses equal $20,000 per month plus 8 percent of the current month's sales.

7. The capital expenditure plan (prepared separately) contains details on forecasted plant and equipment expenditures.

8. Quarterly taxes will be paid in March, June, September, and December at customary corporate rates.[12]

9. The long-range financing plan (prepared separately) shows that all debt service and dividend requirements are to be paid quarterly in March, June, September, and December—specifically, interest expenses should amount to about $20,000 per year, annual dividend payments will hold at $20,000 per year, and existing current maturities are scheduled at $18,000 for each of the next 3 years and $35,000 per year thereafter.

Preparing the Cash Budget

For purposes of simplicity, assume that Specialty Automotive constructs its cash budget by using monthly figures for the first half of the year and quarterly data for the second half. While a full year's cash budget will often appear on a single comparative statement, the March figures will be isolated below in order to illustrate the budgeting process in action. Using the 1985 projected sales of $2,390,000 from Figure 4.2, the first step is to break revenues down according to monthly and quarterly sales. Assume that Specialty Automotive experiences a pronounced seasonal pattern in their level of sales; in particular:

Period	Percentage of Annual Sales
First quarter sales	16%
Second quarter sales	35
Third quarter sales	28
Fourth quarter sales	21

---

[11]Depreciation schedules are worked up separately from the cash budget and reflect actual depreciation charges for existing facilities as well as those expected to come on line during the course of the budget horizon.

[12]Tax figures are computed in conjunction with the profit plan (see Chapter 2 for appropriate tax rates). Note that while we assume taxes are paid as they accrue, the situation is actually much more complicated in practice; for a more complete discussion of income tax accounting, see David F. Hawkins, *Corporate Financial Reporting: Text and Cases*, rev. ed. (Homewood, Ill.: Irwin, 1977), chap. 12.

In order to reflect such behavior in the budget, annual sales estimates are converted to monthly or quarterly figures, as follows:

Period	1985
January	$105,000
February	125,000
March	150,000
April	210,000
May	345,000
June	285,000
Third quarter	670,000
Fourth quarter	500,000
Total	$2,390,000

Operating Receipts.   Table 4.2 provides the March 1985 budget figures. Given that March revenues are expected to equal $150,000, and starting with cash sales, we see that (according to ground rule 1) these transactions account for 20 percent of current period revenues—$150,000 × .20 = $30,000. Ground rule 2 indicates how receivables will be collected: 48 percent (.60 × .80) of *February* sales will be collected in March, one month after they were incurred, and 32 percent (.40 × .80) of *January* sales will also be collected in March, to reflect a 2-month lag. Thus, collection of accounts receivable are $60,000 ($125,000 × .48), and $33,600 ($105,000 × .32), respectively. Total operating receipts for March, therefore, should amount to $123,600.

Operating Expenditures.   Ground rules 3 through 5 indicate how raw material purchases, direct labor, and factory overhead will be handled. In all three cases, these expenditures are derived from sales projected to occur 3 months in the future. These March disbursements, in effect, are based on June sales of $285,000. Raw material purchases for March are $106,800, representing 37.5 percent of June sales. Given the payment pattern denoted in ground rule 3, only half of this amount ($53,400) appears as an expenditure in March; the balance goes to accounts payable and will be paid next month. Such a payment pattern explains the amount shown as a one-month lag ($64,700), as it represents disbursements on May purchases—$345,000 × .375 × .50. The expenditures for direct labor and overhead, as well as operating expenses, are clear from the ground rules; observe that depreciation charges are not included in the cash budget, since they do not require an outflow of cash. With total operating expenditures equaling $242,800, the net operating cash flow for the month will amount to a negative $119,200.

TABLE 4.2
A Completed
Cash Budget for
Specialty Automotive,
March 1985
($ Thousands)

OPERATING RECEIPTS	March, 1985
Cash sales and accounts receivable	
collected in month of transaction	$ 30.0
Collection of accounts receivable:	
1-month lag	60.0
2-month lag	33.6
Total operating receipts	$123.6
OPERATING EXPENDITURES	
Payment on raw material purchases:	
Month of transaction	$ 53.4
1-month lag	64.7
Direct labor	55.6
Overhead (excludes depreciation charges)	37.1
Operating (selling and	
administrative) expenses	32.0
Total operating expenditures	$242.8
Net operating cash flow	($119.2)
FACILITIES, TAXES, AND OTHER	
Plant and equipment expenditures	$ 40.0
Taxes paid	3.4
Interest paid	5.0
Principal payments on debt	4.5
Dividends paid	5.0
Other nonoperating expenses	0.0
Other nonoperating income	−0.0
Total other expenditures	$ 57.9
Net cash flow	($177.1)
CASH RECONCILIATION	
Beginning cash balance	$198.0
Net cash flow (per above)	($177.1)
Ending cash balance	$ 20.9
Minimum cash balance	50.0
Cash excess (or shortfall)	($ 29.1)

Facilities, Taxes, and Other. Facilities, taxes and other nonoperating expenditures are also important, even though they are not directly related to the production of revenues. According to ground rule 7, assume that details of the capital expenditures plan reveal that the second instalment of $40,000 will be made in March for the purchase of a new fleet of trucks; no other capital expenditures are anticipated. Likewise, debt service and dividend requirements are given in ground rule 9. With estimated taxes for the quarter of $3,400 (obtained from the profit plan, to be developed below), we see that nonoperating cash outflows total $57,900, and that total cash flow for March 1985 will amount to a shortfall of $177,100.

Cash Reconciliation. This, the final portion of the cash budget, relates the net cash flow expected to develop over the budget period to the cash on hand at the beginning of the period. It shows what the ending cash balance is likely to be (in the absence of any other action on the part of management), as opposed to what the company would like it to be, as defined by the desired minimum cash balance. A cash excess or shortfall is shown as the last entry in the budget. If sufficiently large, it indicates that some sort of action may be necessary to bring the cash balance to a more desirable level. For example, a company can eliminate an excess cash position by adding to its portfolio of marketable securities or reducing its line of credit; in contrast, a cash shortfall would suggest that the company may have to increase its borrowing, sell off some marketable securities, or possibly even alter its level of operations in order to eliminate a potential cash deficiency.

Expected Values

The budget formats, ground rules, and procedures presented above represent single-point estimates that largely ignore the possibility of other outcomes occurring. One way of dealing with the uncertainty imbedded in a cash budget is to use expected values for sales and other key estimators. While almost any variable can be developed on an expected value basis, such an approach is usually confined to a few of the more important cash flow items. Applying probability concepts to the forecasting process can be done by generating *probability distributions* for key variables like sales, which represent potential outcomes for a variety of different economic and operating conditions (probability and expected value concepts are reviewed in Chapter 6).

The procedure can be demonstrated with the Specialty Automotive sales forecast. Suppose the regression technique is used to derive the model defined in Figure 4.3 ($Y = -910.27 + 6.27X$, where X = projected industrial production). Although the model itself may be completely valid, it should be clear that the outcome is dependent upon the predictability of the index of industrial production. Thus, rather than using a single-point estimate of the index of industrial production to project sales, we can develop a probability distribution of the index. Using 1985 as a basis of discussion, assume that a thorough economic analysis uncovers the following possibilities:

Estimated 1985 Index of Industrial Production (X)	Probability of Occurrence
504	.30
520	.40
544	.20
556	.10

This information is then used, along with the regression equation, to generate the following probability distribution of estimated 1984 sales:

Estimated 1985 Sales Outcome ($ Thousands)	Probability of Occurence
$2,250	.30
2,350	.40
2,500	.20
2,575	.10

The sales levels are derived from the different assumptions about the economic outlook; each sales figure in the probability distribution is determined by solving the regression equation for an associated probability estimate of the index of economic activity, X. For example, the first sales estimate (of $2,250) was found by using an index of industrial production of 504 (see the preceding probability distribution) and solving for the regression equation as follows:

$$1985 \text{ estimated sales, } Y = -910.27 + 6.27(504) = 2,249.8 \approx \$2,250$$

The probability distribution above yields a mean sales value of approximately $2,370,000 and a standard deviation, σ, of $110,000. If this were the only variable subject to expected value computations, this expected sales figure could be used to develop a cash budget. At this point, a possible range of cash flow activity could be produced to show the impact of the uncertain economic outlook on the cash budget. One way of doing this would be to prepare two additional (albeit abbreviated) sets of budgets based on the low and high sales projections (of $2,250,000, and $2,575,000 respectively). This would show the best and worst that management can expect to happen.

An alternative is to establish statistical confidence intervals around the mean sales estimate. Given that the sales estimates are normally distributed (technically they are not, but we can relax that condition for our purposes here), a range of outcomes can be determined within stipulated confidence levels. This is easily done with the following equation:

$$\hat{y} = \mu \pm Z\sigma \tag{4.2}$$

where $\hat{y}$ = estimated sales outcomes, μ = expected sales value ($2,370,000), σ = standard deviation ($110,000), and Z = the standard normal deviate, as obtained from a normal distribution table (see Table A.5 in Appendix A).

Using this procedure, if Specialty Automotive wanted to find the range of possible sales outcomes at, say, the 90 percent confidence level, it would use the appropriate Z value (1.64) to complete Equation 4.2 as follows:

$$\hat{y} = \$2,370,000 \pm 1.64(\$110,000)$$

$$\text{low sales} = \$2,370,000 - 1.64(\$110,000)$$
$$\text{high sales} = \$2,370,000 + 1.64(\$110,000)$$

Thus, management can be 90 percent certain that sales in 1985 will fall between $2,190,000 and $2,550,000; such information can then be used to prepare the two additional sets of abbreviated budgets. This approach allows the financial manager to assess the riskiness of the cash budget and the range of cash flow outcomes that can occur under different economic conditions. Equally important, the implications of such a range of behavior on the firm's asset and financing requirements can be carefully studied, and contingency plans devised as needed.

Pro Forma Statements

Pro forma figures are projected financial statements that show expected revenues and costs, and the company's expected financial position at the end of a forecast period. They are not only useful in the internal financial planning process, but are often required by current and prospective lenders. Pro forma income statements and balance sheets are an integral part of the cash budgeting process; they are both extensions of the cash budget. The pro forma statements employ many of the same ground rules as the cash budget and rely on the finished budget as a basic source of input.

Pro Forma Income Statement

While pro forma figures are sometimes prepared on a monthly basis to correspond with monthly cash flow data, it is equally common to find such statements being produced on a quarterly basis as a way to summarize operating results. Assume that such is the case with Specialty Automotive. Thus, the problem is to produce a profit plan (pro forma income statement) for the first quarter of 1985; Table 4.3 contains such figures. Given the monthly sales forecasts denoted earlier, it can be seen that revenues for the quarter should amount to $380,000. The company's cost structure is spelled out in detail in the ground rules for the cash budget (see especially items 3 through 6, and 8 and 9). More specifically, estimated raw materials, direct labor, and overhead expenses are obtained by applying their respective cost rates (37.5, 19.5, and 13 percent) to projected sales for the period. For example, raw material expenses amount to $380,000 × .375 = $142,500. Following ground rule 5, the projected depreciation schedule (prepared separately) contains information on estimated depreciation charges. Ground rule 6 provides detailed information on operating expenses. Using this ground rule, we see that operating expenses for the quarter amount to: ($20,000 × 3) + ($380,000 × .08) = $90,400. Finally, interest expenses are obtained from the cash budget, and taxes are computed by applying the company's

TABLE 4.3
A Profit Plan for
Specialty Automotive:
First Quarter, 1985
(For 3 Months'
Operations Ending
March 31, 1985;
$ Thousands)

	Projected Figures QI, 1985
Sales	$380.0
Less: Cost of sales	
Raw materials	$142.5
Direct labor	74.1
Overhead	49.4
Depreciation	10.0
Total costs	$276.0
Gross profit	$104.0
Operating expenses	90.4
Operating profit	$ 13.6
Interest expense	5.0
Taxes	3.4
Net profit after tax	$ 5.2
Less: Quarterly dividends paid	$ 5.0
Amount to retained earnings	$ .2

marginal tax rate (of 40 percent) to estimated pretax earnings: .40 × $8,600 = $3,400.

We can see in Table 4.3 that if expectations are realized, Specialty Automotive should generate a profit of about $5200, which after meeting normal quarterly dividends will leave internally generated funds of only about $200. As noted earlier, because of the company's seasonal sales pattern, the first quarter is the worst time of the year for revenues. That fact is clearly reflected not only in the cash budget, but in the profit plan as well.

Pro Forma Balance Sheet

The cash budget provides information about various corporate assets and liabilities, and the profit plan contains estimates of earnings, depreciation charges, and dividends, all of which are important to the preparation of a pro forma balance sheet. Also vital is the preceding period's balance sheet (either the latest actuals or, if farther into the forecast period, the latest or prior period's pro forma figures). These data are necessary in order to obtain the initial values against which to measure changes in various balance sheet accounts, such as fixed assets, certain current liabilities, common stock, and retained earnings. Other balance sheet items—like estimated cash, accounts receivable, inventory, and accounts payable—are determined directly from the budget ground rules and/or the cash budget. Table 4.4 illustrates the pro forma balance sheet for Specialty Automotive as of the end of the first quarter, 1985.

Procedurally, the projected cash position can be obtained directly from the cash budget (see the "ending cash balance" from the March

TABLE 4.4
A Pro Forma Balance
Sheet for Specialty
Automotive: First
Quarter, 1985
(Projected Position as
of March 31, 1985; $
Thousands)

	Projected Figures (March 31, 1985)	Latest Actual Figures (December 31, 1984)
Cash	$ 20.9	$ 257
Accounts receivable	160.0	172
Inventories	588.0	262
Current assets	$ 768.9	$ 691
Fixed assets: Gross	2,118.0	2,038
Less: Accumulated depreciation	927.0	917
Net fixed assets	$1,191.0	$1,121
Other assets	38.0	38
Total Assets	$1,997.9	$1,850
Accounts payable	$ 53.4	$ 168
Accrued expenses	74.0	74
Notes payable	59.0	59
Current maturities	18.0	18
Current liabilities	$ 204.4	$ 319
Long-term debt	222.5	227
Common stock	120.0	120
Retained earnings	1,184.2	1,184
Total	$1,731.1	$1,850
Additional financing required	$ 266.8[a]	$ 0
Total debt and equity	$1,997.9	$1,850

[a]Financing required will increase by $29,100 (to $295,900) if the firm wants to maintain a minimum cash balance of $50,000 (see "cash reconciliation" section of cash budget, Table 4.2).

budget, Table 4.2). Receivables, however, are a bit more difficult to compute. Specifically, the ground rules state that sales revenues are collected over a 3-month period; therefore, accounts receivable should behave in the following manner:

Month	Estimated Sales ($ Thousands)	Less Cash Sales and Accounts Receivable Collected in Month of Transaction	End-of-Month Receivables Outstanding			
			Jan.	Feb.	Mar.	Apr. ...
Jan.	$105	$21.0	$ 84.0	$ 33.6		
Feb.	125	25.0		100.0	$ 40.0	
Mar.	150	30.0			120.0	$ 48.0
Apr.	210	42.0				168.0
.	.	.				
.	.	.				
.	.	.				
Accounts receivable balances			$157.4	$133.6	$160.0	$216.0 ...

Note: The accounts receivable position at the end of January ($157.4) includes receivables incurred during December, 1984.

The above matrix shows how receivables will be collected; for the month of March, in addition to the $30,000 in "cash sales," the company will collect the balance of January receivables ($33,600), and $60,000 in February sales (note that the February receivables balance changes from $100,000 to $40,000 in March). Thus, what is left in March is the balance of February receivables ($40,000) plus the new receivables incurred in March ($120,000); this is shown as total end-of-month receivables outstanding of $160,000.

Inventory—which is made up of raw materials, work in process, and finished goods—is computed in a similar fashion. The following matrix provides a summary of Specialty Automotive's inventory position:

Month	Estimated Sales ($ Thousands)	Cost of Sales[a]	End-of-Month Inventory Position		
			Jan.	Feb.	Mar
Jan.	$105	$ 73.5			
Feb.	125	87.5	$ 87.5		
Mar.	150	105.0	105.0	$105.0	
Apr.	210	147.0	147.0	147.0	$147.0
May	345	241.5		241.5	241.5
June	285	199.5			199.5
.	.	.			
.	.	.			
.	.	.			
Inventory balances:			$339.5	$493.5	$588.0

[a]Cost of sales is computed at 70 percent (37.5% purchases + 19.5% labor + 13.0% overhead) of sales; this figure includes raw material purchases, direct labor, and factory overhead, and *excludes* depreciation charges.

Inventory is maintained at a 3-month supply and as a result, the position for March is projected to be $588,000.

With regard to fixed assets, according to ground rule 7, the capital expenditures plan contains the specifics on plant and equipment investments. Specialty Automotive's major investment plans for 1985 involve additions to their fleet of trucks. Let us assume that through the first quarter of the year, it expects to take delivery on some $80,000 worth of equipment. This is reflected in gross fixed assets by adding that amount to the latest 12/31/84 position; in addition, depreciation charges of $10,000 (obtained from the first quarter profit plan) are added to the accumulated depreciation of 12/31/84 to reflect activity in this area. Given that other assets are assumed to remain unchanged, total assets will grow to almost $2 million—much of it due to the buildup of inventory.

Financing requirements are also spelled out in Table 4.4, starting with accounts payable (which, for projection purposes, are simply the unpaid portion of raw materials purchases—June sales of $285,000 × .375 × .5 = $53,400). Accrued expenses and notes payable are given (no changes are anticipated), and since no new long-term financing is anticipated in 1985, current maturities will remain at their present level. Long-term debt, on the other hand, will decline from the December 31 level by the amount of principal payments made in the first quarter of the year: $4,500 (as noted on the cash budget). There will be no new common stock issued in 1985, so that balance sheet item also remains unchanged. Finally, retained earnings will increase by $200 over the 12/31/84 amount (obtained from the pro forma profit plan, this is the amount of net profit left after dividends are paid). The net effect of the increase in assets and the built-in changes in financing is a capital *shortfall* of some $266,800— shown as "additional financing required." Clearly, management will have to develop a plan for dealing with this deficiency, or else curtail operations and/or the buildup in assets.

Managerial Uses of Budgets and Forecasts

Budgets and financial forecasts are useful to management in several ways: (1) in the administration of the cash and marketable securities portfolio; (2) in defining the firm's resource requirements and financing needs; and (3) in profit planning. The budgeted figures produce "signals" (like a buildup in receivables, a financing shortfall, or a negative cash flow) that are used to make decisions about future behavior. Generally, at this point, given the uncertainty embedded in the forecasts, management is more concerned with the extent and kinds of activity that will be necessary than with administrative details.[13] Let us look now at some of the managerial uses of budgets and forecasts.

Managing the Cash and Marketable Securities Portfolio

An important element of the cash budget is the periodic net cash flow that can be expected to occur from a given level of operations. When combined with beginning and desired minimum cash balances, such net cash flow figures translate into a continuous set of signals regarding when to borrow and when to invest. Borrowing (or security sales) would be in order when the projected cash balance falls *below* the desired minimum amount, and security purchases (or debt repayment) would be indicated when estimated cash on hand rises *above* minimum standards.

The liquidity position of a firm is made up of three parts: the company's cash, its marketable securities holdings, and a line of credit (short-term borrowed funds). These resources are administered simultaneously, and cash budget information is a vital ingredient in the decision-making process. For example, consider the following set of

---

[13]It should be clear, for example, that monthly (or quarterly) cash budgets provide information that is inadequate for assuring solvency; instead, the financial manager must look closely at the projected pattern of *daily* cash receipts and disbursements to make sure that adequate cash will be available for meeting payments as they come due.

projected monthly cash flow figures, obtained in part from the "cash reconciliation" section of a cash budget:

Month	Projected Monthly Net Cash Flow	Month-End Liquidity Position
Dec.	$ —	$200[a]
Jan.	131	331
Feb.	85	416
Mar.	54	470
Apr.	5	475
May	(98)	377
June	(115)	262
July	(263)	(1)
Aug.	(126)	(127)
Sept.	(34)	(161)
Oct.	(28)	(189)
Nov.	152	(37)
Dec.	247	210

[a]$200 = beginning cash balance ($50) + marketable securities holdings ($150).

A tabulation of the projected monthly liquidity position, like the one above, provides information that, when combined with the firm's marketable securities holdings and revolving lines of credit, is helpful in effectively administering the company's cash position. Essentially, the firm wants to keep just enough cash on hand to meet liquidity demands and at the same time, employ any excess funds in as profitable a manner as possible. Achieving such goals is the purpose of cash planning.

The month-end liquidity position is like a "running total" that combines the latest liquidity position with projected net cash flow. For example, the company started the year with a liquidity position of $200, to which was added the January projected net cash flow of $131, resulting in a liquidity position at the end of January of $331. Positive values in the month-end liquidity position column indicate funds are expected to be available to meet minimum cash balance requirements, for marketable security holdings, and/or to reduce borrowings from the company's line of credit. When the month-end position becomes sufficiently low or turns negative, it means the company will have to tap its line of credit (increase the amount of borrowed funds it has outstanding) and/or sell off some marketable securities in order to maintain a desired cash balance. Thus, the projected month-end liquidity position acts as a signal to management with respect to the kind of investment transactions and/or borrowing activity that will be necessary to maintain desired liquidity and cash holdings.

To see how this works, let's continue with the situation developed above. Given the projected month-end liquidity positions, decisions can be made with regard to the *composition* of these liquidity resources. That is:

Month	Month-End Liquidity Position	Makeup of Month-End Liquidity Position		
		Minimum Cash Balance	Marketable Securities Holdings	Line of Credit
Dec.	$200	$50	$150	$ 0
Jan.	331	50	281	0
Feb.	416	50	366	0
Mar.	470	50	420	0
Apr.	475	50	425	0
May	377	50	327	0
June	262	50	212	0
July	(1)	50	0	51
Aug.	(127)	50	0	177
Sept.	(161)	50	0	211
Oct.	(189)	50	0	239
Nov.	(37)	50	0	87
Dec.	210	50	160	0

The month-end liquidity positions depicted above lead to certain levels of cash, marketable securities, and borrowed funds (as specified in the last three columns); that is, month-end liquidity position = minimum cash balance + marketable securities holdings − funds obtained from line of credit. Clearly, investing and borrowing—that is, decisions affecting the firm's marketable securities holdings and the amount of borrowed funds from its line of credit—are done in response to projected liquidity positions, given the constraint of maintaining a minimum cash balance. More specifically, defining C^* as a cash excess (or shortfall), we have:

$$C^* = \text{month-end liquidity position} - \text{minimum cash balance} \qquad (4.3)$$

If C^* is greater than zero, funds are available for marketable security investments (or debt repayment), and if C^* is less than zero, funds must be borrowed (or marketable securities sold).[14] Applying Equation 4.3 to the March liquidity position, we see that:

$$C^* = \$470 - \$50 = \$420$$

---

[14] If, in order to meet unexpected emergencies, a firm has a policy of carrying a minimum securities position of something greater than zero, then that amount (X) should be reflected in the decision rule; if $C^* > X$, then invest; if $C^* < X$, then borrow.

Thus, the firm has an excess cash position of $420 and because it has nothing outstanding against its line of credit, it can use all these funds in its marketable securities portfolio. When the cash flow starts acting as a drain on liquid resources, marketable securities holdings are worked down to some predetermined minimum level (in this case, zero) before management begins using its line of credit.

Clearly, the budget helps management coordinate and plan activities in the cash, marketable securities, and short-term borrowing areas. With respect to marketable securities, the illustrated cash flow shows a build up in security holdings and then a rapid work off as net cash flow turns negative; such information is helpful to management in structuring the liquidity and maturity dimensions of the portfolio. Likewise, management has ample notice that the firm will be in need of borrowed funds during the second half of the year and they can take steps now to obtain a financing package that offers attractive terms and conditions.

Defining Future Resource and Funding Requirements

In addition to liquid assets, other resource requirements must be met in order to achieve stated operating objectives. To the extent that capital expenditures are controlled via the capital budget and liquid resources are addressed separately (per above), the major areas of concern at this point are accounts receivable and inventory—two important and often highly volatile assets. The pro forma balance sheet, along with the cash budget, provides the financial manager with details of expected changes in receivable and inventory positions, and assists management in assessing possible actions that can be taken to meet likely needs. As shown by the study of financial ratios, a close relationship usually exists between a given level of operations and the amount of assets needed to support it. As a result, growth in operations normally portends a buildup in accounts receivable and inventory. The exact magnitude of the buildup, however, is a function of how faithful management is to the cash budget, and whether or not some of the resource requirements can be met by tightening up control standards. It may be possible, for example, to reduce a projected buildup in inventory by employing tighter purchasing standards.

The financing needs of the firm will also be closely related to operations and projected resource requirements. For example, given a buildup in assets is expected to accompany a projected growth in operations, it follows that the firm will also be facing the need for additional financing. Part of this need will be spelled out in the long-range financing plan, though such funding is intended primarily to meet capital expenditure and capital structure requirements. Even after these needs have been fulfilled, however, it is likely that the firm will still have major financing requirements that must be taken care of if the company is to attain stated objectives. Some of these needs can be met internally, by plowing back earnings; additional amounts can be covered with spontaneous financing, like accounts payable and accrued expenses. Any balance that remains will have to be obtained externally. The amount can be stated algebraically as:

$$F^* = \Delta A - \Delta SF - \Delta LTF - \Delta RE \qquad (4.4)$$

where F^* = External financing requirements
   ΔA = Change in assets
   ΔSF = Change in the amount of spontaneous financing used
   ΔLTF = Funds obtained from long-term financing
   ΔRE = Increase in retained earnings (internally generated funds)

For example, assume that a firm has an asset turnover of 0.8 times; thus, if sales are expected to increase next year by $10 million (and if this turnover figure holds), the assets of the company should grow by $10 million/0.8 = $12.5 million. Management can use Equation 4.4 to assess ways of financing this buildup and to determine the amount of additional external financing required. If, for example, 20 percent of the buildup can be handled with spontaneous forms of financing and if $4.25 million is expected to be added to retained earnings next year, then in the absence of any new planned long-term financing (ΔLTF = $0), the company will have to raise externally the following amount of money:

$$F^* = \$12.5 \text{ million} - \$2.5 \text{ million} - \$0 - \$4.25 \text{ million}$$
$$= \$5.75 \text{ million}$$

The decision on how to divide F^* among short- and long-term financing is a function of the firm's target capital structure, the current ratio the firm wants to maintain, as well as the competitive cost and availability of funds (also important in such a financing plan is the proposed borrowing activity that emanates from the cash management area).

Profit Planning   A key concern of management centers around corporate profitability and the achievement of a satisfactory level of earnings. Pro forma income statements are used for profit planning purposes. They enable management to evaluate product mix and alternative pricing strategies. Break-even analysis and other analytical techniques can be applied early in the planning and evaluation process to examine the benefits and costs of various product mix and pricing options open to management. The profit plan also specifies production levels that must be achieved in order to lend required support to sales, and cost standards that must be met if targeted earnings are to be realized. With such information, each of the major operating units of the firm know what is expected of them and what action will be necessary to reach the forecasted goals.

Budget Variances

The budget cycle starts with input obtained from various elements of the firm. Such information is worked up into preliminary forecast figures, revised, and reworked until cash budgets and pro forma statements are prepared that are compatible with the long-run goals of the firm. The forecasted information is then used for a variety of purposes, including corporate planning and control. The final step in the process is the completion of a *budget variance report*—a statement that reconciles actual performance with forecasted behavior. Such reports as cash budgets, profit plans, and pro forma balance sheets are subject to error simply because they are made up of forecasted figures. Whether or not actuals end up as predicted will depend on the actions of management, the type of prevailing operating and economic environment, and the validity of the forecasted figures.

A budget variance report is illustrated for Specialty Automotive in Table 4.5; it shows variances for the March 1985 cash budget, first quarter profit plan, and first quarter pro forma balance sheet. A brief perusal of the table indicates that, overall, the company's actual cash flow ended up remarkably close to projections; that is, actual net cash flow is within 5 percent of the forecasted figure. It appears that most of the discrepancies are caused by higher than expected sales activity (though the profit plan suggests that operating results seemed to have benefited from the increase, as costs were well controlled and profit margins were much better than forecasted). The variance in receivables was probably also due in large part to sales activity, although the cash budget does show a slight slowdown in collections even in the face of increased revenues. The big variances in current liabilities are due to the fact that the plug figure ("additional financing required") has been replaced with actual financing procedures. Clearly, if sales are expected to continue to grow at an accelerated rate, such expectations should be reflected in the next round of budgets. What is more, it appears from the budget variance report that receivable collections should be closely examined and action taken in the upcoming budget cycle to bring inventory back up to a more acceptable level.

The payoffs from comparing actuals to forecasts are that such comparisons let management know where it went wrong, what caused the error, and the extent to which such discrepancies affect budgets and forecasts currently outstanding and under preparation. The objective of variance analysis is not punitive, nor should it be viewed as a vehicle through which blame can be laid for perceived shortfalls. Rather, it should be used for the information it provides about improving the budgeting process, the planning procedures, and the effectiveness of control standards.

TABLE 4.5
A Budget Variance Report for Specialty Automotive ($ Thousands)

Cash Budget	Forecasted March 1985	Actuals March 1985	Cash Flow Variances
OPERATING RECEIPTS			
Cash sales and accounts receivable			
collected in month of transaction	$ 30.0	$ 35.3	+$ 5.3
Collection of accounts receivable:			
1-month lag	60.0	52.7	− 7.3
2-month lag	33.6	31.8	− 1.8
Total operating receipts	$123.6	$119.8	−$ 3.8
OPERATING EXPENDITURES			
Payments on raw material purchases:			
Month of transaction	$ 53.4	$ 46.7	−$ 6.7
1-month lag	64.7	58.3	− 6.4
Direct labor	55.6	59.4	+ 3.8
Overhead (excludes depreciation charges)	37.1	43.2	+ 6.1
Operating (selling and administrative) expenses	32.0	39.5	+ 7.5
Total operating expenditures	$242.8	$247.1	+$ 4.3
Net operating cash flow	($119.2)	($127.3)	− 8.1
FACILITIES, TAXES, AND OTHER			
Plant and equipment expenditures	$ 40.0	$ 40.0	—
Taxes paid	3.4	4.5	+ 1.1
Interest paid	5.0	4.8	− .2
Principal payments on debt	4.5	4.5	—
Dividends paid	5.0	5.0	—
Other nonoperating expenses	0.0	0.0	—
Other nonoperating income	−0.0	−0.0	—
Total other expenditures	$ 57.9	$ 58.8	+$ .9
Net cash flow	($177.1)	($186.1)	−$ 9.0
CASH RECONCILIATION			
Beginning cash balance	$198.0	$263.7	+$65.7
Ending cash balance	20.9	77.6	+ 56.7

TABLE 4.5 continued

PROFIT PLAN	Forecasted 3 Months Ending 3/31/85	Actuals 3 Months Ending 3/31/85	Profit Plan Variances
Sales	$380.0	$442.1	+$62.1
Less: Cost of sales			
Raw materials	$142.5	$167.4	+ 24.9
Direct labor	74.1	84.3	+ 10.2
Overhead	49.4	56.3	+ 6.9
Depreciation	10.0	10.0	—
Total costs	$276.0	$318.0	+$42.0
Gross profit	$104.0	$124.1	+$20.1
Operating expenses	90.4	92.5	+ 2.1
Operating profit	$ 13.6	$ 31.6	+$18.0
Interest expenses	5.0	5.0	—
Taxes	3.4	4.5	+ 1.1
Net profit	$ 5.2	$ 22.1	+$16.9
Less: Quarterly dividends paid	$ 5.0	$ 5.0	—
Amount to retained earnings	$ 0.2	$ 17.1	+$16.9

PRO FORMA BALANCE SHEET	Forecasted 3/31/85	Actuals 3/31/85	Balance Sheet Variances
Cash	$ 20.9	$ 77.6	+$56.7
Accounts receivable	160.0	187.2	+ 27.2
Inventories	588.0	502.4	− 85.6
Current assets	$ 768.9	$ 767.2	−$ 1.7
Fixed Assets: Gross	2,118.0	2,118.0	
Less: Accumulated depreciation	927.0	926.4	− 0.6
Net fixed assets	$1,191.0	$1,191.6	+$ 0.6
Other assets	38.0	5.7	− 32.3
Total assets	$1,997.9	$1,964.5	−$33.4
Accounts payable	$ 53.4	$ 84.3	+$30.9
Accrued expenses	74.0	96.0	+ 22.0
Notes payable	59.0	222.6	+163.6
Current maturities	18.0	18.0	—
Current liabilities	$ 204.4	$ 420.9	+$216.5
Long-term debt	222.5	222.5	—
Common stock	120.0	120.0	—
Retained earnings	1,184.2	1,201.1	+ 16.9
Total	$1,731.1	$1,964.5	+$233.4
Additional financing required	266.8	0	−$266.8
Total debt and equity	$1,997.9	$1,964.5	−$33.4

SUMMARY

Budgets and forecasts are financial plans that enable management to assess the future. They give direction to the firm and assist management in obtaining the most productive and profitable use of the company's limited resources. Budgets and forecasts are used to plan operations, coordinate activities, and establish "standards of performance" that can be used to control operations and assess actual behavior.

The budgeting process begins with the preparation of a sales forecast, a document that projects revenues over the budget period. Popular methods of forecasting include trend line forecasts, single- or multivariable regression analysis, and judgmental forecasting. At the heart of every sound budgeting system is the statement of projected cash flow. Known as the cash budget (or long-range financial forecast), this report shows the projected impact of operations on corporate receipts and expenditures; it is also the basis for establishing resource needs and financing requirements. The profit plan is another vital element of the budget system; actually a pro forma income statement, it provides a summary of what is expected to happen to revenues and expenses if the behavior depicted in the cash budget materializes. Finally, the pro forma balance sheet is prepared; this statement projects the firm's financial condition (its asset mix and financing structure) at the end of various forecast periods.

Budgets and other forecasted statements are useful to management in a variety of ways. They provide insight, for example, that can be used in administering the firm's cash and marketable securities portfolio. Budgets and forecasts are also helpful in defining future resource requirements and planning the financing needs of the firm, and of course, they are an indispensable profit planning tool, since they not only provide cost control standards, but also enable management to evaluate product mix and pricing strategies. The budget cycle, however, is not complete until a budget variance report is prepared—until actual performance is reconciled with forecasted behavior and resulting variances noted. Variance analysis is used to improve the budgeting process and to achieve more accurate and effective control.

QUESTIONS

4.1. Given that the future is uncertain, why should firms even bother to prepare budgets and financial forecasts? Can budgets and forecasts eliminate the uncertainty inherent in operations? Explain.

4.2. Southwest Manufacturing Company is experiencing serious problems in trying to keep an adequate supply of finished inventory on hand; specifically, it tends to let the level of finished inventory run low and then experiences high overtime costs in building the supply back up to acceptable amounts. Explain how budgeting could be used to deal with this problem.

4.3. Coordination of activities and standards of performance are two important products of the budgeting process; what do you see as the major benefit(s) of each? Briefly note how each could be useful in the following situations:

    a. The firm's operating expenses are increasing at an alarming rate.

    b. A company is experiencing difficulties in maintaining a positive net cash flow.

    c. Receivables are building up and approaching excessive levels.

4.4. Why should the budget process begin with the sales forecast? Note how each of the following events and conditions might affect a company's forecasted sales:

    a. Industry sales are expected to move up sharply.

    b. There will be more foreign imports than ever.

    c. The firm's market penetration is expected to improve.

    d. Reduced demand will cause unit volume to drop, but inflation will prompt higher prices.

4.5. Contrast the trend line technique with single- or multivariable regression analysis as ways to forecast sales; which would be best for companies with highly volatile sales?

4.6. What are ground rules and why are they important to the preparation of cash budgets and other forecast documents? Why are pro forma statements often treated as an extension of the cash budget?

4.7. Explain the likely effects of the following actions on the cash budget *and* pro forma financial statements:

    a. The firm experiences a slowdown in the rate at which accounts receivables are collected.

    b. The firm decides to speed up payment on deliveries in order to take advantage of the cash discounts that are offered.

    c. Management decides to prepay a large portion of its long-term debt.

    d. At the last minute, the company decides to lease rather than buy an expensive piece of equipment.

    e. The company's profit rate has eroded because of increased operating costs.

    f. Management decides to forego a cash dividend.

4.8. Discuss in some detail several of the managerial uses of budgets and forecasts. Give an example of how budgets and forecasts are useful to management in these situations.

    a. Allocating resources.

    b. Improving corporate profitability.

    c. Reducing the cost of financing.

4.9. What are budget variances; how do they come about; and what purpose(s) do they serve?

PROBLEMS

4.1.   *FORECASTING SALES.*   Travis Enterprises is made up of two operating divisions. One division uses the trend line technique to
forecast sales, and the other uses regression analysis for such
purposes. Assume you have just been handed a computer printout
containing the following information:

- Division One, results from least-squares trend line:
    $Y = 128.6 + 759.9X$
    $R^2 = .586$
    Time period used: 1965 ($X = 0$) through 1984 ($X = 19$)
    Annual sales (Y) in thousands of dollars
- Division Two, results from regression model:
    $Y = 1603.2 + 102.5X$
    $R^2 = .855$
    $X =$ gas drilling rigs in place
    Annual sales (Y) in thousands of dollars

Given the above information:

a.   Forecast Division One sales for the next 3 years (1985–1987).
b.   Assume the following projections for the independent variable
have been obtained:

Year	Estimates of Future Rig Activity (Gas Drilling Rigs in Place)
1985	416
1986	492
1987	535

Use this information to forecast Division Two sales for the next
3 years (1985–1987).

c.   How much confidence would you place in each of the
respective forecasts? Is there any room for judgmental input
to either (or both) the Division One or Division Two forecasts?
Explain.
d.   Given the sales figure you projected for Division Two, and
using the historical data provided below, determine the *1985*
sales on a quarterly basis.

Year	1st Q Sales	2nd Q Sales	3rd Q Sales	4th Q Sales
1982	$6,560,000	$5,135,000	$ 9,698,000	$7,132,000
1983	8,721,000	6,137,000	10,013,000	7,429,000
1984	9,962,000	6,775,000	14,346,000	8,767,000

4.2. *EXPECTED VALUE FORECASTING.* As part of its normal budget preparation routine, Northeastern Pipe develops a probability distribution of expected annual sales volume and uses this information, along with other estimates, to prepare several budgetary statements. The following probability distribution has been prepared for the first year of the forecast horizon:

Probability	Annual sales
.10	$ 7,450,000
.10	7,900,000
.20	8,500,000
.30	9,000,000
.20	10,000,000
.10	10,500,000

a. Use the information above to compute the mean sales volume.
b. Assume the distribution has a standard deviation (σ) of $914,300; using the mean sales value you computed above, along with the given σ, determine a high and low range of sales outcomes using a 75 percent confidence level (*Hint: Z = 1.15*).

4.3. *SALES FORECASTING.* It has been determined through extensive statistical analysis that the following regression model does an excellent job of defining the sales behavior of Atlas Manufacturing Company:

Sales = 318.20 + 42.38X

where: X = consumer price index (1967 = 100)
          Sales = dollars in thousands

The firm uses the model to project corporate sales and obtains estimates of the consumer price index from an economic forecasting service. Recently, the company received the following projections about the behavior of the consumer price index for next year:

Projected Consumer Price Index	Probability of Occurrence
347.6	.30
351.5	.40
355.0	.20
360.4	.10

a. Given the information above, compute next year's expected sales for Atlas.
b. Given an 80 percent confidence level, what is the *minimum* sales level the company can expect?

4.4. *CASH BUDGETING.*   Fried Painting is a major Midwest paint contractor; the company regularly prepares a monthly cash budget, which it uses for planning and control purposes. Actual sales for the last quarter of 1984, along with forecasted sales for the first 7 months of 1985, are provided below:

Month	Sales
Actuals:	
Oct.	$ 852,000
Nov.	965,000
Dec.	695,000
Forecasts:	
Jan.	750,000
Feb.	800,000
Mar.	900,000
Apr.	950,000
May	850,000
June	1,000,000
July	1,250,000

Fried Painting uses the following ground rules to produce its budgets:

1. 10 percent of sales are collected in the month of sale, 40 percent are collected a month later, 30 percent are collected in the second month after sale, and the balance have a 3-month lag.
2. Cost of sales is made up of paint products (this element equals 20 percent of sales, is purchased the month before it is used, and paid for the month after the sale), and labor (which accounts for 50 percent of sales, the disbursement of which occurs in the month of sale).
3. $5,500 rent payments for the office and warehouse are made monthly; other G&A (general and administrative) expenses amount to $50,000 per month plus 12.5 percent of monthly sales (all disbursed in the month in which they occur); and depreciation charges equal $6,500 per month.

4. The company plans to purchase some new mixing and spray equipment, and partially replace its fleet of vans and pickup trucks during the month of May, at a total estimated cost of $85,000; of this amount, $70,000 will be obtained from a new long-term note with the bank; no other capital expenditures are planned by the company during the first half of the year.

5. Income taxes for the first half of the year are estimated at $250,000 and will be paid in June.

6. The company makes loan instalment payments of $3,500 per month.

7. The company pays dividends quarterly (on the last day of March, June, etc.) at the rate of $50,000 per quarter.

Assume that the figures have been prepared for January, February, and March. Your task is to complete the process for April, May, and June.

a. Determine monthly operating receipts for April, May, and June.

b. Determine monthly operating expenditures for the same period.

c. Now complete the cash budget by determining the monthly net cash flow and preparing a cash reconciliation. (*Note*: Assume the March 31, 1985, cash balance is $350,000, and the company likes to maintain a minimum cash balance of $175,000).

4.5. *CASH BUDGETING.* Petersen Beverage Company's actual sales and purchases for May and June, along with its forecasted sales and purchases for the second half of the year, are presented below:

Month	Sales	Purchases
Actuals:		
May	$360,000	$260,000
June	400,000	290,000
Forecasts:		
July	320,000	280,000
Aug.	310,000	240,000
Sept.	290,000	220,000
Oct.	330,000	250,000
Nov.	350,000	240,000
Dec.	400,000	230,000

The company makes 20 percent of all sales for cash and collects on 40 percent of its sales in each of the 2 months following the sales. Other monthly cash inflows are expected to be $18,000 in July and September; $20,000 in November; and $26,000 in August, October, and December. The firm pays cash for 10 percent of its purchases; of the balance 50 percent is paid the month after purchase and the rest 2 months later. Salaries and wages amount to 20 percent of the preceding month's sales; rent of $25,000 per month must be paid; and interest payments of $15,000 are due in September and December. A principal payment of $35,000 is also due in December and the firm expects to pay cash dividends of $20,000 in August and again in November; taxes of $100,000 are due in December and the firm plans to make a capital outlay of $50,000 in October.

a. Assume the firm starts the month of July with a cash balance of $26,000; determine the end-of-month cash balances for July through December.

b. Determine the monthly borrowing requirement (or excess cash position) given the firm wants to maintain a minimum cash balance of $25,000.

c. If the company were requesting a line of credit to cover its borrowing requirements for the balance of the year, how large would this line have to be? Explain.

4.6. *DEALING WITH CASH EXCESSES AND SHORTFALLS.* As part of the short-range planning activities of the company, the cash manager of Henderson Tool & Die periodically prepares a forecast of the firm's cash position over time. These forecasts are worked up from projected cash flow figures, and of particular concern to the cash manager are excess cash positions and cash short-falls. Assume the company presently holds $40,000 in cash and $110,000 in marketable securities; it has a projected net cash flow for each of the next 12 months as follows:

Jan.	$ 85,000		July	$ 30,000
Feb.	32,000		Aug.	40,000
Mar.	(64,000)		Sept.	25,000
Apr.	(108,000)		Oct.	(15,000)
May	(115,000)		Nov.	50,000
June	(25,000)		Dec.	65,000

Given this information and the fact that management likes to hold a minimum cash balance of $40,000 and a minimum marketable securities position of $50,000, determine the firm's month-end cash balances, marketable securities holdings, and line of credit positions for the upcoming year.

4.7. ***BUDGETS AND PRO FORMA STATEMENTS.*** Return to the Specialty Automotive situation developed in this chapter and work up: (1) the June 1985 cash budget; (2) the second quarter 1985 profit plan; and (3) the pro forma balance sheet for the end of the second quarter of 1985. Use all the groundrules presented in the text, as well as the financial statements and forecasted data through March (first quarter) 1985. Also, add the following monthly sales figures (in place of the third and fourth quarter forecasts) to those already available for the first half of the year.

July	$255,000
Aug.	215,000
Sept.	200,000
Oct.	200,000
Nov.	175,000
Dec.	125,000

Finally, assume the company starts the month of June with a cash position of $105,000, that it anticipates no capital expenditures during the second quarter of the year, and that the procedure for projecting the financial structure will remain the same as that used in forecasting first quarter data. Critically analyze the reports you prepare, and comment on your findings. Note any major implications for future resource requirements, financing needs, and profitability patterns.

4.8. ***MEASURING FINANCING NEEDS.*** The following historical standards have been developed with respect to the Barker Drilling Company:

Total asset turnover	0.667 times
Cost of goods sold as a percent of sales	62.5%
Operating expense as a percent of sales	17.2%
After-tax profit margin	8.5%
Dividend payout ratio	25.0%
Change in spontaneous financing	+$600,000

Determine Barker's external financing requirements (F^*) given that sales are expected to grow next year by $2.5 million to $15 million, and the firm is planning for a $1 million preferred stock issue.

4.9. *PRO FORMA STATEMENTS.* Assume that on December 31, 1984 the Roto Ruler Company had a balance sheet which appeared as follows (dollars in thousands):

	12/31/84
Cash	$ 200
Accounts receivable	300
Inventory	300
Fixed assets	1,000
Less: Accumulated depreciation	(400)
Other assets	100
Total assets	$1,500
Accounts payable	$ 200
Notes payable	200
Long-term debt	600
Common stock	100
Retained earnings	400
Total liabilities and equity	$1,500

Assume further that the following forecasted quarterly cash budgets have been prepared for 1985 (dollars in thousands):

	First Quarter	Second Quarter	Third Quarter	Fourth Quarter
OPERATING RECEIPTS				
Sales	$1,000	$1,400	$1,700	$1,500
Change in accounts receivable	100	100	(500)	200
Total operating receipts	$1,100	$1,500	$1,200	$1,700
OPERATING EXPENDITURES				
Cost of sales	$ 800	$1,100	$1,500	$1,200
Less: Depreciation	(25)	(25)	(25)	(25)
Operating expenses	100	150	150	190
Change in inventory	(75)	300	(200)	(100)
Change in accounts payable	—	—	(150)	100
Total operating expenditures	$ 800	$1,525	$1,275	$1,275
FACILITIES, TAXES, AND OTHER				
Additions to fixed assets	$ 100	$ 100	$ 300	$ 0
Payment on notes	50	(150)	(200)	150
Payment on long-term debt	50	50	(200)	50
Interest paid	10	10	10	10
Taxes paid	60	60	60	60
Dividends paid	25	25	25	25
Total other expenditures	$ 295	$ 95	$ (5)	$ 295
Net cash flow	$ 5	$ (120)	$ (70)	$ 130

Given the above balance sheet and forecasted quarterly cash budgets, prepare a pro forma income statement for the year 1985, and a 12/31/85 pro forma balance sheet.

4.10. *VARIANCE ANALYSIS.* Charlene Weaver is director of budgets and forecasts for the Chris-Terr Corporation, a medium-sized conglomerate with operations in the energy exploration, chemicals, and motion picture fields. Budgets and pro forma statements are prepared for each subsidiary on a monthly basis and variance reports are worked up when the actuals become available. The October statements for one of the subsidiaries has just come in from the accounting department, so Weaver worked up an abbreviated cash flow statement which will be used, along with the latest balance sheet and income statement, to prepare a budget variance report (dollars in thousands):

a. Given the information below, prepare the October budget variance report; include the cash flow, profit plan, and balance sheet in your report.
b. Comment on your findings, and develop some managerial recommendations from your variance analysis.

	October Forecasted Figures	October Actuals
ABBREVIATED CASH FLOW		
Cash sales	$ 120.0	$ 148.5
Collection of receivables	1,895.0	1,729.0
Total operating receipts	$ 2,015.0	$ 1,877.5
Payments on inventory purchases	$ 1,434.0	$ 1,486.3
Direct labor	254.0	322.9
Operating expenses	195.0	207.0
Total operating expenditures	$ 1,883.0	$ 2,016.2
Net operating cash flow	$ 132.0	($ 138.7)
Capital expenditures	$ 74.0	$ 85.7
Taxes paid	28.0	42.6
Interest and principal payments on debt	105.0	105.0
Total other expenditures	$ 207.0	$ 233.3
Net cash flow	($ 75.0)	($ 372.0)
ABBREVIATED INCOME STATEMENT		
Sales	$ 2,125.0	$ 2,507.6
Cost of goods sold	1,594.5	1,977.3
Operating expenses	195.0	207.0
Operating profit	$ 335.5	$ 323.3
Interest expense	42.5	42.5
Taxes paid	28.0	42.6
Net profit after tax	$ 265.0	$ 238.2

	October Forecasted Figures	October Actuals
ABBREVIATED BALANCE SHEET		
Cash and short-term securities	$ 725.0	$ 420.0
Accounts receivable	3,460.0	3,995.6
Inventory	4,625.0	5,035.8
Current assets	$ 8,810.0	$ 9,451.4
Net fixed assets	11,250.0	11,302.6
Other assets	3,121.0	3,115.0
Total assets	$23,181.0	$23,869.0
Accounts payable	$ 2,625.0	$ 2,964.0
Notes payable	3,000.0	3,225.0
Accrued expenses	892.5	1,046.5
Current maturities	62.5	62.5
Current liabilities	$ 6,580.0	$ 7,298.0
Long-term debt	4,980.0	4,980.0
Stockholders' equity	11,621.0	11,591.0
Total debt and stockholders' equity	$23,181.0	$23,869.0

SELECTED REFERENCES

Barrett, M. E., and L. B. Fraser. "Conflicting Roles in Budgeting for Operations." *Harvard Business Review* 55 (July–August 1977), pp. 137–146.

Chambers, John C., Satinder K. Mullick, and Donald D. Smith. "How to Choose the Right Forecasting Technique." *Harvard Business Review* 49 (July–August 1971), pp. 45–74.

Clarke, D. G. "Corporate Forecasting: Promise and Reality." *Harvard Business Review* 54 (November–December 1976), pp. 40–42.

Crum, Roy L., Darwin Klingman, and Lee A. Tavis. "Implementation of Large-Scale Financial Planning Models: Solution Efficient Transformations." *Journal of Financial and Quantitative Analysis* 14 (March 1979), pp. 137–152.

Francis, J. C., and D. R. Rowell. "Simultaneous Equation Model of the Firm for Financial Analysis and Planning." *Financial Management* 7 (spring 1978), pp. 29–44.

Gattis, D. R., and T. H. Naylor. "Corporate Planning Models." *California Management Review* 18 (summer 1976), pp. 69–78.

Higgins, Robert C. "How Much Growth Can a Firm Afford?" *Financial Management* 6 (fall 1977), pp. 7–16.

———. "Sustainable Growth Under Inflation." *Financial Management* 10 (autumn 1981), pp. 36–40.

Lin, W. T. "Corporate Planning and Budgeting: An Integrated Approach." *Managerial Planning* 27 (May 1979), pp. 29–33.

Lindsey, B. A. "Forecasting for Control." *Management Accounting* 18 (September 1976), pp. 41–43.

Merville, Larry J., and Lee A. Tavis. "Long-Range Financial Planning." *Financial Management* 3 (summer 1974), pp. 56–63.

———, and ———. "Financial Planning in a Decentralized Firm Under Conditions of Competitive Capital Markets." *Financial Management* 6 (fall 1977), pp. 17–23.

Mohn, N. C., and others. "Input-Output Modeling: New Sales Forecasting Tool." *University of Michigan Business Review* (July 1976), pp. 7–15.

Pan, Judy, Donald R. Nichols, and O. Maurice Joy. "Sales Forecasting Practices of Large U.S. Industrial Firms." *Financial Management* 6 (fall 1977), pp. 72–77.

Pappas, James L., and George P. Huber. "Probabilistic Short-Term Financial Planning." *Financial Management* 2 (autumn 1973), pp. 36–44.

Parker, George G. C., and E. L. Segura. "How to Get a Better Forecast." *Harvard Business Review* 51 (March–April 1973), pp. 99–109.

Pogue, Gerald A., and Ralph N. Bussard. "A Linear Programming Model for Short-Term Financial Planning Under Uncertainty." *Sloan Management Review* 13 (spring 1972), pp. 69–98.

Rappaport, Alfred. "Measuring Company Growth Capacity During Inflation." *Harvard Business Review* 57 (January–February 1979), pp. 91–100.

Spivey, W. Allen. "Forecasting: A Perspective for Managers." *Journal of Contemporary Business* 18 (July–September 1979), pp. 61–78.

Taggart, R. A. "A Model of Corporate Financing Decisions." *Journal of Finance* 26 (December 1971), pp. 1467–1484.

Appendix 4A

Regression Analysis

Numerous business and financial problems necessitate specification of functional relationships between different variables. These relationships are established by one form or another of regression analysis, and are used to (1) interpolate between data points, (2) extrapolate beyond a sequence of data, (3) ascertain the existence of trends, or (4) estimate other characteristics that are important for decision making. For example, in this chapter we saw how the use of regression analysis was helpful in formulating various types of forecasted financial data; in later chapters, we will see that the technique can also be used in assessing risk and return, in firm valuation, in capital budgeting, and in credit management. This appendix will briefly examine the underlying concepts and basic mathematics of regression analysis, including two popular variations of this statistical procedure: linear regression and time series models.[1]

Linear Regression

In linear regression, a straight-line relationship between one variable and another is assumed. The variable under examination is called the dependent, or regressed, variable—usually designated as Y. An independent, or regressor, variable (indicated by X) is used to establish the functional relationship:

$$Y = f(X) \qquad (4A.1)$$

---

[1]For a more complete discussion of regression and time series analysis, see Morris Hamburg, *Statistical Analysis for Decision Making*, 2d ed. (New York: Harcourt Brace Jovanovich, 1977), chaps. 9, 10.

Since a perfect relationship between X and Y is seldom obtained, a regression equation of Y on X is normally written as follows:

$$Y = f(X) + \epsilon \tag{4A.2}$$

where the term ϵ is the residual error. Residual errors are due to measurement errors in the data or because the functional specification, $f(X)$, does not capture all the possible influences on the dependent variable. A general equation for the single variable regression model can be obtained by rewriting Equation 4A.2 as follows:

$$Y_i = \alpha + \beta X_i + \epsilon_i \tag{4A.3}$$

The procedure requires that the constant (α) and the slope (β) coefficient be computed (estimated) from the data. Once this is done, a working version of the regression model (which ignores the residual error term, ϵ) can be developed as follows:

$$Y_i = \alpha + \beta X_i \tag{4A.4}$$

The most common statistical method of estimating the parameters, α and β, in Equation 4A.4 is a procedure known as ordinary least-squares regression. Using the least-squares technique, the line constructed from the observed relationship between the X and Y variables is that which minimizes the squared vertical deviations from the fitted line. Minimizing such discrepancies defines a "best fit line"; that is, minimize:

$$\sigma_\epsilon^2 = \sum_{i=1}^{n} (Y_i - \hat{\alpha} - \hat{\beta} X_i)^2 \tag{4A.5}$$

where $\hat{\alpha}$ and $\hat{\beta}$ are estimates of the α and β coefficients in Equation 4A.4, and n is the number of observations.

Using differential calculus and Equation 4A.5, it is possible to find the α and β coefficients that minimize the variability in the "best fit line" as defined by σ_ϵ^2 in 4A.5. Without going through the details, suffice it to say that the derivatives of σ_ϵ^2 will yield two important estimates:

$$\overline{Y} = \hat{\alpha} + \hat{\beta}\overline{X} \tag{4A.6}$$

and

$$\sum_{i=1}^{n} Y_i X_i = \hat{\alpha}\sum_{i=1}^{n} X_i + \hat{\beta}\sum_{i=1}^{n} X_i^2 \tag{4A.7}$$

where the overbars in Equations 4A.6 indicate the arithmetic mean of the given variable.

Equations 4A.6 and 4A.7 are defined as "normal equations," and the least squares estimator for α falls directly out of 4A.6 when we solve for α:

$$\alpha = \overline{Y} - \beta\overline{X} \qquad (4A.8)$$

In contrast, the least squares estimator of β is obtained by substituting Equation 4A.8 for Equation 4A.7; when this is done we have:

$$\beta = \frac{\sum\limits_{i=1}^{n} Y_iX_i - n(\overline{Y})(\overline{X})}{\sum\limits_{i=1}^{n} X_i^2 - n(\overline{X})^2} \qquad (4A.9)$$

Another aspect of interest in linear regression analysis is the variation of the dependent variable, Y. Three terms are defined which express variation in Y. First, the total sum of the squares, $\sum\limits_{i=1}^{n}(Y_i - \overline{Y})^2$, gives the total variation of the dependent variable. The total variation, in turn, can be further divided into two additional parts; the variation explained due to regression, $\sum\limits_{i=1}^{n}(\hat{Y}_i - \overline{Y})^2$, and the leftover (or residual) variation, $\sum\limits_{i=1}^{n}(\hat{Y}_i - Y_i)^2$. The relationships between the explained variation and the total variation determines the goodness-of-fit of the regression line to the data points. This measure, called the *coefficient of determination*, is defined as:

$$R^2 = \frac{\sum\limits_{i=1}^{n} (\hat{Y}_i - \overline{Y})^2}{\sum\limits_{i=1}^{n} (Y_i - \overline{Y})^2} \qquad (4A.10)$$

The coefficient of determination (R^2) indicates the percentage of total variation in the dependent variable that is explained by the regression line equation. Equation 4A.10 can be restated as:

$$R^2 = \left[\frac{\sum\limits_{i=1}^{n} Y_iX_i - n(\overline{Y})\,(\overline{X})}{(n)\sqrt{\dfrac{\sum\limits_{i=1}^{n} X_i^2}{n} - (\overline{X})^2}\ \sqrt{\dfrac{\sum\limits_{i=1}^{n} Y_i^2}{n} - (\overline{Y})^2}} \right]^2 \qquad (4A.11)$$

Equation 4A.11 uses the same numerator as that found in Equation 4A.9, and though it looks more threatening than 4A.10, it is computationally simpler and should therefore be used when the calculations are performed manually.

The following example will illustrate the mechanics and use of the linear regression technique:

Assume that the Z-Car Corporation is concerned with the effects of increasing gas prices on revenues from car sales. It has collected the data shown in Table 4A.1 with respect to the price per gallon of gasoline and the seasonally adjusted number of cars sold during the corresponding month. Z-Car is currently gathering gasoline price forecasts for the coming year and needs to estimate the relationship between car sales and gasoline prices. Management feels the most recent year is indicative of the upcoming year.

TABLE 4A.1
Sales Forecast Data
for the Z-Car
Corporation

Month	Average Retail Gas Price/Gallon (X variable)	Number of Cars Sold[a] (Y variable)
Jan.	.80	70
Feb.	.83	67
Mar.	.85	69
Apr.	.90	60
May	.91	58
June	.93	59
July	.95	58
Aug.	1.00	56
Sept.	1.03	52
Oct.	1.10	47
Nov.	1.12	48
Dec.	1.18	41

[a]Unit sales in thousands.

A regression worksheet is illustrated in Table 4A.2 (see p. 170); the columns are all self-explanatory. The computation is relatively simple, as it requires nothing more than a summation of the columns and a determination of mean values for X and Y; this information is then used (as defined in Equations 4A.8, 4A.9, and 4A.11) to determine α, β, and R^2. The estimated regression line for this example turns out to be:

$$Y_i = 128.03 - 73.39X_i$$

This model can now be used to forecast the number of cars sold, given the estimated price of one gallon of gas. For example, if gas goes up to $1.20 per gallon, monthly car sales will drop to about 40,000 units: 128.03 − 73.39(1.20) = 39.96. The regression line has an R^2 of .9684, meaning that the equation explains about 96.8 percent of the variation in the number of cars sold.

Time Series Models

The least squares linear regression model is an econometric model that predicts future movements in a dependent variable by relating it to one or more independent variables. Time series (or trend line) models, on the other hand, base predictions solely on the historical behavior of the variable being considered. In essence, they examine past movements in the selected variable, and use the information or pattern of behavior obtained to predict future movements in the variable.

However desirable it may be to build a structural model, it may be impossible or impractical to develop a viable regression model based on sound a priori economic relationships. For instance, if a lagged relationship does not exist, forecasting the independent variable in the model can be as difficult, or more difficult, than the prediction of the dependent variable itself. Time series models can be used under such circumstances, whenever relatively long periods of historical data are available. The time series model employs the basic regression equation as defined in Equation 4A.4, except in this case, the independent variable (X_i) becomes time, where years (or other time periods) are measured ordinally. For the period 1981 through 1985, the base year, 1981, would equal 0, 1982 would equal 1, 1983 would equal 2, and so on. Once the coefficients in Equation 4A.4 are defined, the estimated equation can be used for forecasting by setting the independent variable, X_i, equal to the desired future time period. For example, if we wanted to estimate the 1986 value of the dependent variable in the illustration above, we would let $X_i = 5$, and solve 4A.4 for Y_i. There is no need to forecast the independent variable when using this version of the time series model, as the procedure basically extrapolates the data into the future.

PROBLEMS

4A.1. *FORECASTING SALES.* Linch-Industries, Inc, is preparing its annual sales forecast. The following historical figures have been obtained:

Year	Annual Sales ($ Thousands)	Economic Index of Activity (1965 = 100.0)
1973	$ 478	127.9
1974	571	138.3
1975	754	144.8
1976	841	147.5
1977	757	156.1
1978	863	152.8
1979	1,337	191.3
1980	1,163	283.4
1981	962	278.6
1982	1,170	246.9
1983	1,338	268.9
1984	1,751	297.6

The company wants to forecast annual sales for 1985 and 1986.

a. Use the least squares time series (trend line) approach to estimate sales for each of the next 2 years; also compute the coefficient of determination for the resulting forecast equation—comment on the R^2 you computed.

TABLE 4A.2
Linear Regression Worksheet (Z-Car Corp. Data)

Month	Y_i	X_i	Y_iX_i	X_i^2	Y_i^2
Jan.	70	.80	56.00	.6400	4,900
Feb.	67	.83	55.61	.6889	4,489
Mar.	69	.85	58.65	.7225	4,761
Apr.	60	.90	54.00	.8100	3,600
May	58	.91	52.78	.8281	3,364
June	59	.93	54.87	.8649	3,481
July	58	.95	55.10	.9025	3,364
Aug.	56	1.00	56.00	1.0000	3,136
Sept.	52	1.03	53.56	1.0609	2,704
Oct.	47	1.10	51.70	1.2100	2,209
Nov.	48	1.12	53.76	1.2544	2,304
Dec.	41	1.18	48.38	1.3924	1,681
Sums:	685	11.60	650.41	11.3746	39,993

Means: $\overline{Y} = 57.0833$, $\overline{X} = .9667$

Eq. 4A.9: $\beta = \dfrac{\sum\limits_{i=1}^{n} Y_iX_i - n(\overline{Y})(\overline{X})}{\sum\limits_{i=1}^{n} X_i^2 - n(\overline{X})^2} = \dfrac{650.410 - (12)(57.0833)(.9667)}{11.3746 - (12)(.9667)^2} = \dfrac{650.410 - 662.1891}{11.3746 - 11.2141} = \dfrac{-11.7791}{.1605} = -73.39$

Eq. 4A.8: $\alpha = \overline{Y} - \beta\overline{X} = 57.0833 - (-73.39)(.9667) = 57.0833 + 70.9461 = 128.03$

Thus $Y_i = 128.03 - 73.39X_i$

Eq. 4A.11: $R^2 = \left[\dfrac{\sum\limits_{i=1}^{n} Y_iX_i - n(\overline{Y})(\overline{X})}{(n)\sqrt{\dfrac{\sum\limits_{i=1}^{n} X_i^2}{n} - (\overline{X})^2}\sqrt{\dfrac{\sum\limits_{i=1}^{n} Y_i^2}{n} - (\overline{Y})^2}}\right]^2 = \left[\dfrac{650.410 - (12)(57.0833)(.9667)}{(12)\sqrt{\dfrac{11.3746}{12} - (.9667)^2}\sqrt{\dfrac{39993}{12} - (57.0833)^2}}\right]^2$

$= \left[\dfrac{-11.7791}{(12)\sqrt{.0134}\ \sqrt{74.2469}}\right]^2 = \left[\dfrac{-11.7791}{11.9695}\right]^2 = .9684$

Thus $R^2 = 96.84\%$

b. Presume Linch-Industries employs the economic index of activity above as the independent variable used to derive forecasted sales; use regression analysis to produce a forecast model based on the information provided above. Then:

(1) Compute the coefficient of determination (R^2) and comment on your findings.

(2) Given the economic index is expected to equal 340.0 in 1985 and 380.0 in 1986, use the regression equation you computed above to project sales for each of the next two years.

SELECTED REFERENCES

Box, G. E. P., and G. M. Jenkins. *Time-Series Analysis: Forecasting and Control*, rev. ed. San Francisco: Holden-Day, 1976.

Fogler, H. Russell, and S. Ganapathy. *Financial Econometrics*. Englewood Cliffs, N.J.: Prentice-Hall, 1982. Chaps. 2, 4, 5.

Foster, George. *Financial Statement Analysis*. Englewood Cliffs, NJ.: Prentice-Hall, 1978. Chap. 4

Hawkins, Clark A., and J. E. Weber. *Statistical Analysis: Applications to Business and Economics*. New York: Harper & Row, 1980.

Hamburg, Morris. *Statistical Analysis for Decision Making*, 2d ed. New York: Harcourt Brace Jovanovich, 1977.

Valentine, Jerome L., and E. A. Mennis. *Quantitative Techniques for Financial Analysis*, rev. ed. Homewood, Ill.: Irwin, 1980. Chaps. 6, 7, 12.

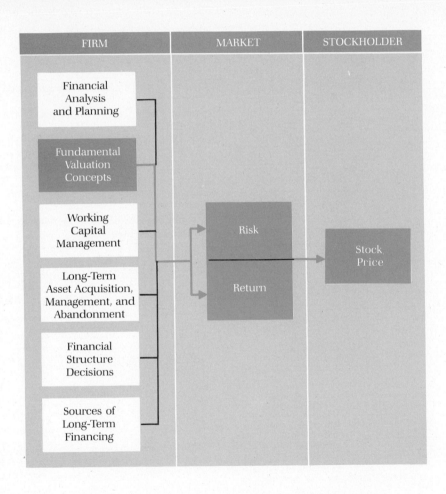

FIRM	MARKET	STOCKHOLDER

Financial Analysis and Planning

Fundamental Valuation Concepts

Working Capital Management

Long-Term Asset Acquisition, Management, and Abandonment

Financial Structure Decisions

Sources of Long-Term Financing

Risk

Return

Stock Price

PART THREE

FUNDAMENTAL VALUATION CONCEPTS

The three chapters in this part of the text present fundamental concepts that provide the link between financial decisions and share price. An understanding of the time value of money, risk and return, and the valuation process is the foundation for making decisions consistent with the goal of maximizing owners' wealth. The first chapter—Chapter 5—describes key aspects of the time value of money, with emphasis on future and present values and their use in financial decisions. Chapter 6 develops the concepts of risk and return, describes the interrelationships between them, and discusses their implications for financial decisions. Chapter 7 then presents valuation concepts for securities. It shows how risk and return factors are linked in determining the value of bonds and stocks and thus owners' wealth. Together, the techniques and concepts presented in these three chapters form a yardstick against which the decisions of financial managers can be assessed.

5

Time Value of Money

Financial managers are continuously making decisions about investment opportunities and methods of financing. Rates of return are computed and potential risk exposure is assessed in order to find investment outlets that will most effectively use the resources at the firm's disposal. Likewise, the cost and risk exposure of various financing alternatives are assessed to select the best sources of financing. Present-value-based decision models provide managers with a rational, systematic way of evaluating alternative investment and financing opportunities. Such procedures are widely used in valuation, capital budgeting, mergers and acquisitions, capital structure, bond refunding, leasing, and other asset-mix and financial structure decisions. Although present value is applied mostly to long-term investment and financing decisions, the risk-return concepts used with many short-term working capital decisions are actually little more than variations of present value. As a result, this concept underlies many short-term decision-making models as well.

In this chapter we examine the concept and mathematics of present value. However, because of the importance of compound interest to present value, our discussion begins with a look at the concept of future value. We then turn to present value, including the time value of money concept and the various mathematical dimensions of present value. The chapter concludes with illustrations of some special applications of time value ideas.

Future Value

The concept of *future value* deals with the accumulation of funds to some date in the future. Money is placed in an interest-earning investment vehicle, and depending on the rate of return, the investment increases in value over time as interest earnings accrue. For our

175

purposes, the concept of future value, (or *compound value* as it is also known), is important, in large part, because of its relationship to the properties of present value. Although most financial decision-making models are based on present value, the concept of present value itself is derived from (is a reciprocal of) the notion of future value. Let us now briefly examine the future value concept, review the basic mathematics of compound interest, and look at other compounding periods.

The Concept: Growth in Value

Consider the following situation: A financial manager is evaluating a proposed capital expenditure that would require a substantial investment on the part of the firm. How does the manager value this investment opportunity—or, put another way, on what basis should this investment be valued? The answer, of course, is that the investment has value to the firm to the extent that it provides a future value greater than the amount originally invested. The amount of cash inflow needed to make the proposal sufficiently attractive depends on such conditions as risk exposure, required rate of return, and other variables that we will examine in detail later in the book. But the underlying notion of future value is *growth*—growth in the original principal value of the investment, given the compound rate of return earned thereon.

The future value concept can be displayed graphically as follows:

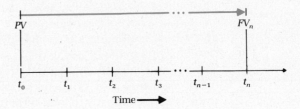

In this case, we see that the original principal value, PV, placed in the investment today, t_0, will grow over time to some future value, FV_n, n periods later. The amount of growth is, of course, a function of the compound rate of return, k, earned on the investment and the amount of time, n, that the money is tied up. All the essential parts of future value appear in the time continuum, except for the rate of interest. Clearly, this variable is crucial to the definition of FV to the extent that the higher the rate of interest, the faster the rate of growth—a condition that can be seen in Figure 5.1. Given an equal time frame, FV increases as k increases except when $k = 0$, in which case the "investment" offers no rate of return and therefore no growth in value.

With a compound rate of return, part of the growth in an investment is derived from the fact that the earnings are *compounding*—that is, the investment earns interest on interest so that at the end of each period, the earnings base (invested funds) increases according to the rate of return, k, earned on the investment. In essence, because future value

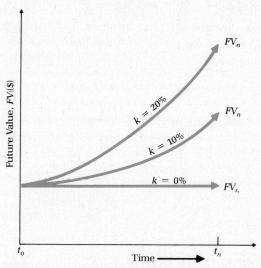

Figure 5.1 Alternative Compound Interest Rates and the Growth in Future Value.

Note: This graph assumes interest is compounded continuously.

results from earning interest on interest, a higher earnings base during the investment period means even greater return than if this base did not change over time. Thus, if a firm can invest $1000 for a year at 15 percent, it should expect the future value of that investment at the end of the year to amount to $1150 [$1000 + ($1000 × .15)]; keeping this sum invested for another year at 15 percent will yield a future value of $1322.50 [$1150 + ($1150 × .15)]; and so forth.

The Mathematics of Future Value

Savings institutions often advertise that they pay "compound interest at k percent" or "k percent interest compounded quarterly." Interest is compounded when the amount earned on the initial deposit (PV) becomes part of the earnings base. The concept of compounding is best explained in terms of a single cash flow.

The Future Value of a Single Cash Flow.

Suppose you place $1000 in an investment that pays 10 percent interest compounded annually. How much would you have at the end of one year? If we let the initial amount of the investment equal PV and the rate of interest on the investment equal k, then:

$$FV_1 = PV + [PV(k)] \qquad (5.1)$$
$$= \$1000 + [\$1000\,(.10)]$$
$$= \$1000 + \$100$$
$$= \$1100$$

In this case, we see that the future value is actually a function of the original investment plus the earnings on the investment $[PV(k)]$. The equation can, of course, be simplified:

$$FV_1 = PV + PV(k) \qquad (5.2)$$
$$= PV(1 + k)$$

Now, what happens if the investment is left on deposit for another year, and the rate of interest remains at 10 percent? As seen below, the earnings in the second year are a function of the investment base that existed at the beginning of the period (FV_1):

$$FV_2 = FV_1 + [FV_1(k)] \qquad (5.3)$$
$$= \$1100 + [\$1100 \,(.10)]$$
$$= \$1210$$

Simplifying, as we did with Equation 5.2, we have:

$$FV_2 = FV_1 \,(1 + k) \qquad (5.4)$$

Now, substituting Equation 5.2 for FV_1 in Equation 5.4, we see that:

$$FV_2 = PV \,(1 + k) \,(1 + k) \qquad (5.5)$$
$$= PV \,(1 + k)^2$$
$$= \$1000 \,(1.10)^2$$
$$= \$1210$$

The series of basic algebraic simplifications and substitutions above yielded the ending equation, 5.5, which results in a future value at the end of period 2 of $1210. A similar process would take place for each subsequent period in the investment horizon. Viewed in this light, it is clear that the future value in any period is a function of the amount invested at the beginning of the period and the rate of return earned on these funds. The basic relationship depicted in Equation 5.5 can be generalized to reflect this, as noted below:

$$FV_n = PV(1 + k)^n \qquad (5.6)$$

For example, if we want to find the future value of the $1000 investment (with $k = 10$ percent) at the end of 10 years, we could substitute into Equation 5.6, which results in a future value of nearly $2600:

$$FV_{10} = \$1000 \,(1.10)^{10}$$
$$= \$1000 \,(2.5937)$$
$$= \$2593.70$$

Solving Equation 5.6 can be time-consuming whenever n is large. To simplify the calculations, future-value interest tables have been compiled; such tables appear in Appendix Table A.1, a portion of which is reproduced in Table 5.1. The table provides a series of values for the interest factor portion of Equation 5.6—values for $(1 + k)^n$:

$$\text{Future-value interest factor} = FVIF_{k,n} = (1 + k)^n$$

The appropriate value for $FVIF_{k,n}$ can be obtained by defining the subscripts k and n, and by accessing the future-value table according to the defined annual rate of return (k) and number of years in the investment horizon (n). When factors from future-value interest tables are used to compute future value, Equation 5.6 can be written as follows:

$$FV_n = PV \times FVIF_{k,n} \tag{5.7}$$

The same three pieces of information are still needed to find future value $(PV, k, \text{and } n)$; the only difference is that Equation 5.7 simplifies the mechanical aspects of the computation. For example, to find the future value of $1000 invested at 10 percent for 5 years, we can use Equation 5.7 and Table 5.1 (or Appendix Table A.1) to find the appropriate factor for $FVIF_{10\%, 5\,yr}$; using this factor (note from Table 5.1 that it equals 1.611), we can arrive at a future value in year 5 (FV_5) of $1000 (PV): i.e., $1000 (1.611) = $1611.

Table 5.1 reveals certain characteristics of future-value interest factors. First, the factors in the table represent the future values of $1 realized at the end of a given year. Second, note that as the rate of return increases for any given year, the future value interest factor also increases. Thus, the higher the rate of return, the greater the future value. The third point is that for a given interest rate, the future value of a dollar increases with the passage of time. These characteristics underlie the concept of future value and are inherent in the mechanics of compound interest.

TABLE 5.1
Future-Value Interest Factors for a One-Dollar Single Cash Flow, $FVIF_{k,n}$

| Period (n) | \multicolumn{6}{c}{Rate of Return (k)} |
	5.00%	6.00%	7.00%	8.00%	9.00%	10.00%
1	1.050	1.060	1.070	1.080	1.090	1.100
2	1.102	1.124	1.145	1.166	1.188	1.210
3	1.158	1.191	1.225	1.260	1.295	1.331
4	1.216	1.262	1.311	1.360	1.412	1.464
5	1.276	1.338	1.403	1.469	1.539	1.611
6	1.340	1.419	1.501	1.587	1.677	1.772
7	1.407	1.504	1.606	1.714	1.828	1.949
8	1.477	1.594	1.718	1.851	1.993	2.144
9	1.551	1.689	1.838	1.999	2.172	2.358
10	1.629	1.791	1.967	2.159	2.367	2.594

$(FVIF_{10\%, 5\,yr})$

The Future Value of an Annuity.   An *annuity* is a stream or series of equal cash flows that occur at regular time intervals over a specified period of time. For example, an annuity might consist of annual end-of-year deposits of $1000 for each of the next five years. When deposits occur at the end of each year, the annuity is called an *ordinary annuity;* when beginning-of-year deposits are made, it is an *annuity due.*[1] The future value of an *n*-year ordinary annuity, FVA_n, can be depicted as follows:

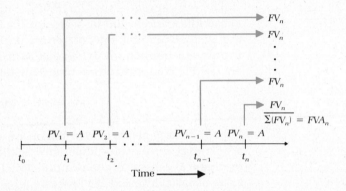

Each of the cash flows (noted $PV_1, PV_2, \cdots PV_n$) received at the end of each period $t_0, t_1 \cdots t_n$ is compounded to the end of year n and summed in order to find the future value of the annuity. Table 5.2 illustrates the future value calculation for a 5-year, $1000 ordinary annuity, using a 7 percent rate of return.

A variation of Equation 5.6 can be used to specify the future value of an ordinary annuity at the end of year n, FVA_n:

$$FVA_n = PV_1(1 + k)^{n-1} + PV_2(1 + k)^{n-2} \qquad (5.8)$$
$$+ \cdots + PV_{n-1}(1 + k)^1 + PV_n$$

Since $PV_1 = PV_2 = \cdots = PV_{n-1} = PV_n$, for an annuity, by letting $A = PV_1 = PV_2 = \cdots = PV_{n-1} = PV_n$, Equation 5.8 can be simplified as follows:

$$FVA_n = A(1 + k)^{n-1} + A(1 + k)^{n-2} + \cdots + A(1 + k)^1 + A \qquad (5.9)$$
$$= A[(1 + k)^{n-1} + (1 + k)^{n-2} + \cdots + (1 + k)^1 + 1]$$

$$= A\left[\sum_{t=1}^{n}(1 + k)^{t-1}\right] \qquad (5.10)$$

To make the computation of the future value of an ordinary annuity easier, tables of future-value interest factors for annuities, $FVIFA_{k,n}$, are available. These tables give the value of the bracketed portion of Equation

---

[1]The discussions of annuities included throughout this text concentrate on the more common form of annuity—the ordinary annuity.

	TABLE 5.2

TABLE 5.2
Future Value of a
5-Year, $1000 Ordinary
Annuity Compounded
at 7 Percent

End of Year	Amount Deposited (1)	Number of Years Compounded (2)	Future-Value Interest Factor from Table 5.1 (3)	Future Value at End of Year 5 [(1) × (3)] (4)
1	$1000	4	1.311	$1311
2	1000	3	1.225	1225
3	1000	2	1.145	1145
4	1000	1	1.070	1070
5	1000	0	1.000	1000
			Future value of annuity at end of year 5	$5751

5.10 for various combinations of periods, n, and interest rates, k. Appendix Table A.2 contains a detailed table of future-value interest factors for (ordinary) annuities. An excerpt from this table is given in Table 5.3. Note that the annuity factors actually represent the sum of 1.000 plus the first $n - 1$ future-value interest factors (from Table 5.1).[2]

The future-value interest factor table reduces the calculation to:

$$FVA_n = A \times FVIFA_{k,n} \tag{5.11}$$

Use of the table can be illustrated with the 5-year, $1000 ordinary annuity earning 7 percent presented previously. Using $FVIFA_{7\%, 5 \text{ yr}}$, Equation 5.11 can be applied as follows:

$$FVA_5 = \$1000(5.751)$$
$$= \$5751$$

In this case, total receipts over the life of the annuity amount to $5000, but using compound interest at 7 percent for 5 years causes the annuity to have a future value of $5751—the same value calculated in Table 5.2.

---

[2]With an ordinary annuity, each deposit begins earning in the following rather than the current period, and the last deposit earns zero; therefore, the value 1.000 reflects the lack of earnings on the final deposit. For an annuity due, the future-value interest factor would be equal to the sum of the first n future-value interest factors, since the deposits occur at the beginning of the period:

$$FVIFA_{k,n} = \sum_{t=1}^{n} (1 + k)^t \text{ for an annuity due}$$

To convert an ordinary annuity factor, $FVIFA_{k,n}$, into an annuity due factor, we would use the $FVIFA$ factor for $n + 1$ periods and subtract 1.000.

$$FVIFA_{k,n} \text{ for an annuity due} = FVIFA_{k,n+1} \text{ for an ordinary annuity} - 1.000$$

For example, while the $FVIFA$ for a 5-year ordinary annuity at 7 percent is 5.751, the appropriate factor for a 5-year annuity due at 7 percent is 6.153 ($FVIFA_{7\%,6 \text{ yr}} - 1.000 = 7.153 - 1.000$).

TABLE 5.3
Future-Value Interest
Factors for a
One-Dollar (Ordinary)
Annuity, $FVIFA_{k,n}$

($FVIFA_{7\%, \, 5 \, yr}$)

Period (n)	Rate of Return (k)					
	5.00%	6.00%	7.00%	8.00%	9.00%	10.00%
1	1.000	1.000	1.000	1.000	1.000	1.000
2	2.050	2.060	2.070	2.080	2.090	2.100
3	3.152	3.184	3.215	3.246	3.278	3.310
4	4.310	4.375	4.440	4.506	4.573	4.641
5	5.526	5.637	5.751	5.867	5.985	6.105
6	6.802	6.975	7.153	7.336	7.523	7.716
7	8.142	8.394	8.654	8.923	9.200	9.487
8	9.549	9.897	10.260	10.637	11.028	11.436
9	11.027	11.491	11.978	12.488	13.021	13.579
10	12.578	13.181	13.816	14.487	15.193	15.937

Other Compounding Periods

The discussion thus far has been couched in terms of annual compounding; sometimes, however, it is necessary to compound more often than annually. Interest can be compounded monthly, daily, or continuously. While the conceptual underpinnings of future value are not affected by the compounding period, more frequent compounding raises the future value of a single cash flow or annuity. In effect, *the more often compounding occurs, the larger the future value.*

A general equation for intrayear compounding can be developed using the basic future value formula, Equation 5.6, and defining m as the number of times per year interest is compounded.[3]

$$FV_n = PV(1 + k/m)^{m \times n} \qquad (5.12)$$

Note that in Equation 5.12, more frequent compounding is handled by the interest factor expression. Thus, whether a single cash flow, an annuity, or an uneven cash flow stream is being compounded, the process involves nothing more than two simple adjustments to the interest-factor expression. The interest rate, k, is reduced according to the number of compounding periods in the year, and the time element, n, is increased to reflect the greater number of compounding periods in the investment horizon. It is possible to use the future-value interest factor tables for many intrayear compounding situations; that is, instead of accessing the table for k percent and n years, as we do when interest is compounded annually, we would obtain the appropriate interest factor

---

[3] When m equals ∞, interest is said to be compounded continuously—over the smallest time interval imaginable. Mathematically,

$$\lim_{m \to \infty} \left[(1 + k/m)^{n \times m} \right] = e^{k \times h}$$

Continuous compounding is sometimes used by savings institutions to calculate the interest on savings accounts. Both continuous compounding and discounting are discussed in greater detail in Appendix 5A.

for k/m percent and $m \times n$ periods. Consider a deposit of $2000 earning interest over the next 5 years; if we wanted to find the future value of this deposit using an interest rate of 10 percent compounded semiannually ($m = 2$), we would have to apply an interest factor for 5 percent ($k/m = 10\%/2 = 5\%$) and 10 semiannual periods (2 semiannual periods per year $\times$ 5 years) to determine the future value of this cash flow.

$$FV_5 = PV \times FVIF_{k/m, m \times n} = PV \times FVIF_{5\%, 10 \text{ periods}}$$
$$= \$2000 \times 1.629$$
$$= \$3258$$

All else remaining unchanged, the more frequently interest is compounded, the greater the resulting future value. Had interest been compounded annually in the preceding example, the future value of the deposit would have been $3222 ($2000 $\times$ $FVIF_{10\%, 5\text{yr}}$ = $2000 $\times$ 1.611), which is $36 less than the $3258 that results from using semiannual compounding.

Present Value

The concept of future value has rather limited applications in finance; its usefulness is confined to such things as finding the terminal value of an investment, computing amortization and sinking fund payments on debt, and the like. Not so with present value, however; this concept has wide application in financial decision making and is routinely used in a variety of financial decision-making models. The concept of present value, like the concept of future value, is based on the premise that the value of money is affected by when it is received. The axiom underlying this precept is that a dollar today is worth more than a dollar received at some future date. In other words, the *present value* of a dollar that will be received in the future is less than the value of a dollar in hand today. The actual present value of a dollar depends on the earnings opportunities of the recipient and the point in time when the money is to be received.

The Present Value Concept: Discounting

Finding present value involves "discounting" future cash flows; this process is actually the inverse of compounding. Present value is concerned with answering the question: "If I can earn k percent on my money, what is the most I would be willing to pay today for an opportunity to receive a future dollar amount, FV, n years from now?" *Discounting* is the process used to determine the present value (normally at time t_0) of a future amount. The rate of return, k, used in the discounting process represents the time value of money. The time value of money, in turn, results from its *opportunity cost*—money always has an alternative use that will yield a positive rate of return to the investor (or firm). The earning capacity of money provides the theoretical underpinning for the notion that the present value (*PV*) of a future cash flow (*FV*) is less than the amount of the cash flow itself.

The time value of money, in fact, provides the link between present and future values. Present value is the inverse of future value, and the whole discounting process is based on the notion that the discount rate, *k*, captures the opportunity cost of the funds employed. A dollar received today, in effect, is worth the same as some larger amount to be received in the future because a positive return can be generated on the money received at the earlier date, thereby causing its future value to be greater than its present value. That is:

$$PV < FV_n \text{ for } k > 0$$
$$PV = FV_n \text{ for } k = 0$$

The magnitude of the difference between present and future values is a function of the rate of return that can be earned. If it takes a *k* percent rate of return to move from *PV* to *FV* some *n* periods into the future, and if the investor feels that he or she can earn that rate of return on the money (opportunity cost), then the investor should, in fact, be indifferent as to receiving either of the two sums, even though they are not of equal size.

Role in Financial Decision Making.   Present value is one of the most powerful tools in the arsenal of the financial manager, and is at the very heart of many decision models not only in managerial finance, but also in other areas of finance, including investments, portfolio management banking, real estate, and insurance. Present value is also used by public and not-for-profit institutions, such as state and local governments and hospitals.[4] The concept is crucial because it captures the essence of the resource allocation problem—in particular, present-value-based decision models view the resource allocation decision in a theoretically correct manner by introducing and considering the opportunity cost of each decision. A firm has only a limited amount of resources to allocate to the various parts of the company, and the question of how they are to be allocated should be based, in large part, on the contribution they make to the firm's value. One of the corporate facts of life today is that firms do not enjoy access to an unlimited amount of resources. As a result, when decisions are made regarding the use of scarce financial resources, they should be made so that the investment can at least

---

[4]For a review of some of the noncorporate applications of present value, see, for example, Lennox L. Moak and Albert M. Hillhouse, *Concepts and Practices in Local Government Finance* (Chicago: Municipal Finance Officers Association, 1975), chap. 16, and J. Richard Aronson and Eli Schwartz, ed., *Management Policies in Local Government Finance*, 2d ed. (Washington, D.C.: International City Management Association, 1981), chap. 19.

provide a rate of return equal to or greater than that which can be earned in some other similar-risk investment.

The Basic Discounting Process.   As a rule, the present value of a sum of money due *n* years in the future is equivalent to the amount which, if it were on hand today, would grow to equal the future sum. For example, given that $283 will grow to $300 in a year if it is invested at 6 percent, we can define the $283 as the present value of $300 due one year from now, given that our money can earn a fully compounded rate of return of 6 percent. In this case, it should be clear that as long as 6 percent represents a viable opportunity cost, an individual or firm should be indifferent to receiving either $283 today or $300 one year from now. Discounting reduces the future value of an investment to its present value in a manner that reflects the opportunity cost of funds, *k*. Present value, in effect, looks at the cash payoffs from an investment (FV_n) and discounts these to their present value (PV). Such cash payoffs come in a variety of forms, including single cash flows, annuities, and uneven cash flow streams. As will become clear, present value provides management with a way to assess expected cash payoffs in relation to the amount of initial investment required to generate them.

In the simple numerical illustration above, the future value concept would convert the present sum of $283 to its future value of $300. This process would be reversed with present value, as it would discount the $300 future value back to its present sum of $283. Present value and the notion of discounting are captured graphically below:

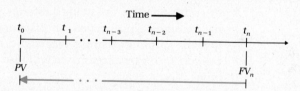

With present value, it is not a matter of finding the value to which an investment will grow over time; rather, present value is concerned with discounting a future sum in order to determine its value in terms of present dollars.

Figure 5.2 depicts the basic discounting process and shows that as the discount rate increases, the resulting present value decreases, other things being equal. It shows that a higher discount rate implies a higher opportunity cost of funds and, therefore, that a smaller sum will be required at the start of the period to generate the same given future value (FV_n). In essence, the more the investment can earn, the lower will be the required present value needed to obtain a given future value. Clearly, if an investor has a zero percent opportunity cost, it will take $1000 to generate a future value of $1000 in, say, five periods from now; however, if

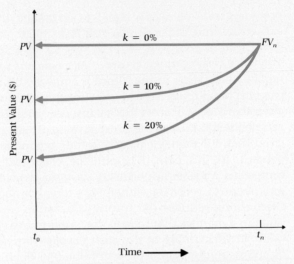

Figure 5.2   Alternative Discount Rates and the Behavior of Present Value.
Note: This graph assumes continuous discounting.

an investor has a 10 percent opportunity cost and the same 5-year investment horizon, then only $621 will be required to generate the same $1000 future value.

The Mathematics of Present Value

Present value arithmetic is much like that performed with future value except, as noted before, the process is reversed from compounding to discounting. The following material will deal with some of the basic mathematical properties of discounting, including determining the present value of a single cash flow, an annuity, a perpetuity, and an uneven cash flow stream; we will also look at using discounting periods other than a year.

The Present Value of a Single Cash Flow.   As the term implies, a single cash flow is simply a future value that is expected to occur only once, at some given time in the future; we have previously labeled this type of cash flow as FV_n. Nowhere else is the link between future value and present value more evident than in the mathematical expression for the present value of a single cash flow. Recall from Equation 5.6 that the future value of an investment is defined as follows:

$$FV_n = PV(1 + k)^n$$

Because present value is the inverse of future value, we can solve the above equation for PV and derive the general equation for the present value of a single cash flow:

$$PV = \frac{FV_n}{(1 + k)^n} = FV_n \left[\frac{1}{(1 + k)^n} \right] \qquad (5.13)$$

Because Equation 5.13 involves finding the reciprocal of the future-value interest factor, the calculation can become a bit cumbersome as n increases. Tables of present-value interest factors have been prepared to simplify the operation. The present-value interest factor for $1, $PVIF_{k,n}$, represents the interest-factor expression $[1/(1 + k)^n]$ for a variety of rates of return, k, and numbers of years in the investment horizon, n. Appendix Table A.3 contains present-value interest factors for various rates of return and periods, a portion of which is re-created in Table 5.4. Using the notation for the present-value interest factor, Equation 5.13 can be rewritten as follows:

$$PV = FV_n \times PVIF_{k,n} \qquad (5.14)$$

As this expression indicates, in order to find the present value, PV, of an amount to be received in the future, we need only multiply the future amount, FV_n, by the appropriate present-value interest factor. To appreciate the simplicity of Equation 5.14, consider the following illustration: Assume that a financial manager wants to find the present value of $2500 to be received 7 years from now, given that the firm has an opportunity cost of 9 percent. Defining k as 9 percent and n as 7 years, we see from Table 5.4 that the correct interest factor, $PVIF_{9\%,\,7\,yr}$, is .547; substituting appropriate values in Equation 5.14, therefore, yields:

$$PV = \$2500 \,(.547)$$
$$= \$1367.50$$

This amount ($1367.50) represents the present value (at time zero) of a single cash flow ($2500) to be received in 7 years, when that future value

TABLE 5.4
Present-Value Interest Factors for a One-Dollar Single Cash Flow, $PVIF_{k,n}$

Period (n)	Rate of Return (k)					
	5.00%	6.00%	7.00%	8.00%	9.00%	10.00%
1	.952	.943	.935	.926	.917	.909
2	.907	.890	.873	.857	.842	.826
3	.864	.840	.816	.794	.772	.751
4	.823	.792	.763	.735	.708	.683
5	.784	.747	.713	.681	.650	.621
6	.746	.705	.666	.630	.596	.564
7	.711	.665	.623	.583	.547	.513
8	.677	.627	.582	.540	.502	.467
9	.645	.592	.544	.500	.460	.424
10	.614	.558	.508	.463	.422	.386

($PVIF_{9\%,\,7\,yr}$)

is discounted at a 9 percent opportunity cost. Put another way, it is the amount of money that must be invested today (at 9 percent interest compounded annually) in order to have $2500 in 7 years.

Several characteristics of present-value interest factors are evident in Table 5.4. First, observe that the present-value interest factor for a single cash flow is always less than 1; in fact, only if the opportunity cost was zero would this factor equal 1. Second, Table 5.4 shows that the higher the opportunity cost for a given year, the smaller the present-value interest factor. As noted earlier, this results from the fact that the higher the opportunity cost, the greater the earning capacity of the dollar and, therefore, the less money it will take today to generate a given future value. Finally, note that, for a given discount rate, the farther into the future a sum is to be received, the less it is worth today (in other words, the *PVIFs* decline as time to receipt increases). Again this results from the power of compounding: The longer the period of time money has to work, the greater is the return that can be generated, and in an inverse sense, the less that will be required today to generate a given FV_n. Clearly, other things being equal, an investment will grow to a larger value over a period of 10 years than it would over a period of 5 years; reversing this principle for the purposes of present value, we see that the increased earning power results in a lower amount being needed at present if the investment horizon is 10 years as opposed to 5.

The Present Value of an Annuity.   In a fashion similar to that used to depict the future value of an annuity, the present value of an annuity (PVA_n) can be depicted as follows:[5]

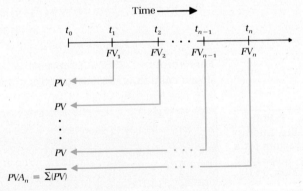

Each of the future cash flows in an annuity is discounted to its respective present value, and then summed to find the present value of the entire annuity.

---

[5]Again we are concentrating on ordinary annuities since—especially when finding present value—they are the rule rather than the exception. The assumption that cash flows occur at the end of the period is standard in financial computations and therefore will be used throughout this text, except when otherwise noted.

A variation of Equation 5.13 can be used to find the present value of an annuity, PVA_n. That is, restating the equation to deal with a series of future cash flows rather than a single cash flow, we have:

$$PVA_n = FV_1 \left[\frac{1}{(1 + k)^1} \right] + FV_2 \left[\frac{1}{(1 + k)^2} \right] + \cdots \qquad (5.15)$$

$$+ FV_{n-1} \left[\frac{1}{(1 + k)^{n-1}} \right] + FV_n \left[\frac{1}{(1 + k)^n} \right]$$

Since each of the periodic cash payoffs in an annuity is equal ($FV_1 = FV_2 = \cdots = FV_{n-1} = FV_n$), the mathematics of finding the present value of an annuity can be simplified. If we define the constant periodic cash flow in an annuity as A, where $A = FV_1 = FV_2 = \cdots = FV_{n-1} = FV_n$, then:

$$PVA_n = A \left[\frac{1}{(1 + k)^1} \right] + A \left[\frac{1}{(1 + k)^2} \right] + \cdots \qquad (5.16)$$

$$+ A \left[\frac{1}{(1 + k)^{n-1}} \right] + A \left[\frac{1}{(1 + k)^n} \right]$$

$$= A \left[\frac{1}{(1 + k)^1} + \frac{1}{(1 + k)^2} + \cdots \right.$$

$$\left. + \frac{1}{(1 + k)^{n-1}} + \frac{1}{(1 + k)^n} \right]$$

$$= A \left[\sum_{t=1}^{n} \frac{1}{(1 + k)^t} \right] \qquad (5.17)$$

Clearly, Equation 5.17 is far simpler than the cash flow computations noted above, since once the value of the interest factor has been determined, only a single multiplication is required to find the present value of the annuity.

Fortunately, because the interest-factor expression can be determined independently, present-value tables are useful in finding the present value of an annuity. Appendix Table A.4 contains detailed present-value interest factors for a one-dollar annuity, $PVIFA_{k,n}$, for specified rates and periods—excerpts of which are contained in Table 5.5. Note that the present-value interest factor is represented by the bracketed portion of Equation 5.17—$PVIFA_{k,n} = \sum_{t=1}^{n} \frac{1}{(1 + k)^t}$. It should be clear that the present-value interest factor for an annuity actually represents the sum of the first n present-value interest factors from the single cash flow table for a given discount rate: $PVIFA_{5\%, 3 \text{ yr}} = PVIF_{5\%, 1 \text{ yr}} + PVIF_{5\%, 2 \text{ yr}} + PVIF_{5\%, 3 \text{ yr}} = .952 + .907 + .864 = 2.723$. Stated in a general form, $PVIFA_{k,n} = \sum_{t=1}^{n} PVIF_{k,n}$.

TABLE 5.5
Present-Value Interest
Factors for a
One-Dollar Annuity,
$PVIFA_{k,n}$

$PVIFA_{10\%, 5\,yr}$

Period	Rate of Return (k)					
(n)	5.00%	6.00%	7.00%	8.00%	9.00%	10.00%
1	.952	.943	.935	.926	.917	.909
2	1.859	1.833	1.808	1.783	1.759	1.736
3	2.723	2.673	2.624	2.577	2.531	2.487
4	3.546	3.465	3.387	3.312	3.240	3.170
5	4.329	4.212	4.100	3.993	3.890	3.791
6	5.076	4.917	4.767	4.623	4.486	4.355
7	5.786	5.582	5.389	5.206	5.033	4.868
8	6.463	6.210	5.971	5.747	5.535	5.335
9	7.108	6.802	6.515	6.247	5.995	5.759
10	7.722	7.360	7.024	6.710	6.418	6.145

Such tables simplify the computations immensely; the mathematics of finding the present value of any annuity reduces to:

$$PVA_n = A \times PVIFA_{k,n} \tag{5.18}$$

To illustrate, consider a 5-year, $1000 annuity that is to be discounted to its present value at a rate of 10 percent. This can be done using Equation 5.18 as follows:

$$PVA_5 = \$1000\,(3.791)$$
$$= \$3791$$

The total receipts from this annuity will amount to $5000 over its full life. When discounted at 10 percent, it yields a present value of $3791, which represents the required investment that must be made initially (at time zero) earning a 10 percent compound annual rate of return to generate a 5-year annuity of $1000 per year.

The Present Value of a Perpetuity. A *perpetuity* is an infinite-lived annuity, or an annuity that never stops providing its holder with A dollars per period. The present-value interest factor for a perpetuity discounted at k percent, $PVIFA_{k,\infty}$, can be represented by:

$$PVIFA_{k,\infty} = \lim_{n \to \infty} \sum_{t=1}^{n} \frac{1}{(1+k)^t} = \frac{1}{k} \tag{5.19}$$

In other words, the appropriate factor is found by merely dividing the discount rate (stated as a decimal) into 1. For example, imagine you wished to determine the present value of a $1,000 (per year) perpetuity discounted at 10 percent. Substituting $k = .10$ into Equation 5.19 yields an interest factor, $PVIFA_{10\%,\infty}$ of $1/.10 = 10.0$. Substituting $A = \$1,000$ and the computed $PVIFA$ factor into Equation 5.18 yields a present value of:

$$PVA_\infty = \$1{,}000 \left(\frac{1}{.10}\right)$$

$$= \$1{,}000 \ (10.0) = \$10{,}000$$

The present value of the perpetuity is therefore $10,000. Intuitively this result has appeal, since the annual interest at 10 percent would provide an annual cash flow of $1,000 without damaging the $10,000 of principal, thereby providing for an annuity of infinite life.

The Present Value of an Uneven Cash Flow Stream. Quite often in managerial decision-making situations, there is a need to find the present value of an uneven stream of cash flows. That is, unlike an annuity, there is no particular pattern to the cash flows over time; rather, the receipts differ from year to year. For example, management may want to use a 5 percent discount rate to find the present value of the following stream of future cash flows:

Year	Cash Flow Amount
1	$1500
2	2000
3	0
4	3000
5	5000

This can be solved by applying Equation 5.15 (using *PVIF* notations) and finding the sum of a series of present values—one for each annual cash flow in the stream. In effect, the discounting process reverts to the use of single cash flows:

$$
\begin{aligned}
PV &= \$1500 \ (PVIF_{5\%,\ 1\ yr}) + \$2000 \ (PVIF_{5\%,\ 2\ yr}) + \$0 \ (PVIF_{5\%,\ 3\ yr}) \\
&\quad + \$3000 \ (PVIF_{5\%,\ 4\ yr}) + \$5000 \ (PVIF_{5\%,\ 5\ yr}) \\
&= \$1500 \ (.952) + \$2000 \ (.907) + \$0 \ (.864) \\
&\quad + \$3000 \ (.823) + \$5000 \ (.784) \\
&= \$1428 + \$1814 + 0 + \$2469 + \$3920 \\
&= \$9631
\end{aligned}
$$

After obtaining the present-value interest factors ($PVIF_{kn}$) from the single cash flow table (Table 5.4), the present value of each future cash flow is determined and then summed to a total present-value figure. Observe throughout that *the integrity of the timing of the cash flows is main-tained*, since the timing of the present-value interest factors utilized must always be compatible with the timing of the cash flow itself. Also, this computed present-value figure is like any other to the extent that it represents the investment required, at a 5 percent compound rate of return (opportunity cost), to generate annual cash flows of $1500, $2000, $0, $3000, and $5000 over years 1 through 5, respectively.

An interesting variation of the uneven cash flow involves the combination of different annuities:

Year	Cash Flow Amount
1	$1000
2	1000
3	1000
4	1000
5	1500
6	1500
7	1500
8	1500
9	1500
10	2000

In this case, a 4-year annuity of $1000 in years 1 through 4 is followed by a 5-year annuity of $1500 in years 5 through 9 and then capped off with a single cash flow of $2000 in year 10. The *PVIFA* for the first annuity can be obtained directly from Table 5.5, just as the interest factor for the single cash flow in year 10 can be obtained directly from Table 5.4. The problem comes with respect to the 5-year $1500 annuity that occurs in years 5 through 9. It can be handled in one of two ways. First, the annuity can be viewed as a stream of single cash flows, in which case the calculations would involve finding the present value of a series of single cash flows, much like what was done previously. Alternatively, the stream can be treated as an annuity and the present value can be determined as denoted in Equation 5.18, except that the present-value interest factor for the annuity will be a computed number rather than one obtained directly from the *PVIFA* table. The appropriate *PVIFA* can be determined by either (1) summing the present-value interest factors, *PVIF*, from Appendix Table A.3 for periods 5 through 9 inclusive, or (2) by using the *PVIFA* table (Appendix Table A.4) and taking the difference in the annuity interest factors (for period 9 less period 4). For example, using a 9 percent discount rate:

$$PVIFA_{9\%, \, 5 \, to \, 9 \, yr} = PVIF_{9\%, \, 5 \, yr} + PVIF_{9\% \, 6 \, yr} + \cdots + PVIF_{9\%, \, 9 \, yr}$$
$$= .650 + .596 + .547 + .502 + .460 = 2.755$$
$$\text{or} \quad PVIFA_{9\%, \, 5 \, to \, 9 \, yr} = PVIFA_{9\%, \, 9 \, yr} - PVIFA_{9\%, \, 4 \, yr}$$
$$= 5.995 - 3.240 = 2.755$$

The present value of this uneven stream can now be computed by combining the two annuities with the single cash flow as follows:

$$PV = \$1000 \ (PVIFA_{9\%, \ 4 \ yr}) \ + \ \$1500 \ (PVIFA_{9\%, \ 5 \ to \ 9 \ yr}) \ + \ \$2000 \ (PVIF_{9\%, \ 10 \ yr})$$
$$= \$1000 \ (3.240) \ + \ \$1500 \ (2.755) \ + \ \$2000 \ (.422)$$
$$= \$8216.50$$

Other Discounting Periods   Occasionally, it is necessary to discount cash flows more frequently than once a year. This would occur, for example, if management were attempting to value a bond that pays interest semiannually (as is customary), or if the firm were considering an investment proposal where interest is compounded quarterly. Like intrayear compounding discussed earlier, cash flows can be discounted over any period of time—semiannually, quarterly, daily, or even continuously (as discussed in the appendix to this chapter). All the conceptual underpinnings of present value exist for shorter discounting periods; the key point, however, is that the shorter the discounting period, the lower the present value of a single cash flow or stream of cash flows. More frequent discounting, in effect, results in a lower present value—the more work compounding does, the less money required today to generate a given future value.

The general equation for intrayear discounting can be developed using the basic formula for present value—Equation 5.13—and again, as in intrayear compounding, letting m equal the number of times per year interest is discounted:

$$PV = FV_n \left[\frac{1}{(1 + k/m)^{m \times n}} \right] \tag{5.20}$$

Like intrayear compounding, intrayear discounting requires the use of a discount rate of k/m percent and $m \times n$ periods; present-value interest factor tables can often be used in intrayear discounting situations. To demonstrate, consider a cash flow of $2000 to be received at the end of 5 years ($n = 5$); if we wanted to find the present value of this cash flow using a discount rate of 10 percent ($k = 10$ percent) discounted semiannually ($m = 2$), the present value of the cash flow would be determined as follows:

$$PV = FV_n \times PVIF_{k/m, m \times n}$$
$$= \$2000 \times PVIF_{5\%, \ 10 \ periods}$$
$$= \$2000 \times .614$$
$$= \$1228$$

Had the cash flow of $2000 been discounted at the annual interest rate of 10 percent over 5 years, the present value of the cash flow would have been $1242 ($2000 $\times PVIF_{10\%, \ 5 \ yr}$ = $2000 $\times$ .621), which is $14 greater than the $1228 that results from semiannual discounting.

Some Applications of Time Value Concepts

Present value is applied in one form or another to a wide variety of financial decisions. The question of whether or not a long-term corporate bond should be refunded, or whether a firm should lease a piece of equipment or buy it, are examples of areas where present-value decision models have been developed. In all cases, the approach involves the assessment of the resources required to execute a transaction as compared to its potential benefits or profitability.[6] We will encounter present value repeatedly throughout the remainder of this book, but it is helpful at this point to illustrate its application to some typical financial decision-making situations; two excellent examples are the computation of growth rates and calculating instalment loan payments and interest rates.

Growth Rates

Sometimes it is necessary to calculate the compound annual rate of growth associated with a particular benefit stream. For example, management might want to determine how fast the firm is growing, or the rate of growth in its earnings per share. This can be done by using either compound-interest or present-value tables; we will use present value to demonstrate the process below. Assume the annual sales of a company have grown over time according to the following pattern:

Year		Annual Sales
1977		$1,460,000
1978	1	1,700,000
1979	2	1,950,000
1980	3	2,200,000
1981	4	2,500,000
1982	5	2,750,000
1983	6	3,100,000
1984	7	3,650,000

The discount rate that would cause annual sales in 1984 ($3,650,000) to have a present value equal to that which prevailed in 1977 ($1,460,000) would be the growth rate associated with the data. This present-value problem deals with a single cash flow (the 1984 sales level as it relates to the 1977 level), and as a result, Equation 5.14 can be used to determine the rate of growth in sales.[7]

---

[6]In fact, not only has present value been used in many areas of managerial finance, but it is also widely used in other areas as well—for example, in banking, underwriting, securities analysis, and portfolio management. Present value is truly one of the major finance techniques and enjoys virtually universal application within the discipline.

[7]Other techniques for finding growth or interest rates are available; some of them use all the data rather than only the earliest and most recent value. For example, the rate of growth can also be determined via the geometric mean of the annual rates of growth in sales.

Defining PV as the 1977 sales level and FV_n as the 1984 sales volume, the only unknown in Equation 5.14 is the present-value interest factor:

$$PV = FV_n \times PVIF_{k,n}$$
$$\$1{,}460{,}000 = \$3{,}650{,}000 \times PVIF_{k,\,7\,yr}$$

Solving for the present-value interest factor we have:

$$PVIF_{k,\,7\,yr} = \$1{,}460{,}000/\$3{,}650{,}000$$
$$= .400$$

Note that $n = 7$, since that is the number of years of growth in the period from 1977 to 1984; thus, the only unknown left is the discount rate, k. Using the present-value interest factor table for a single cash flow, and looking across the 7-year row, we find that an interest factor of .400 is associated with a discount rate of 14 percent (observe that under the 14 percent, 7-year column, the $PVIF$ equals .400). We can conclude, therefore, that the annual compound rate of growth of this particular cash flow is 14 percent. Note that in this case a simple variation of the basic present-value model was used to find the growth rate: Instead of finding the present value of a future cash flow, we solved for the present-value interest factor, $PVIF$, to determine the compound annual rate of growth.[8]

Instalment Loan Payments and Interest Rates

Often long-term business loans are retired by making equal loan payments over time. Such periodic instalments are known as *loan amortization payments*, each of which provides the lender with a specified interest return, or yield, on unrepaid capital and the partial recovery of loan principal. In the absence of a *balloon payment*, which is a final payment considerably larger than earlier payments, the total amount of principal will be recovered through the equal payments by the loan's maturity. The loan amortization process involves finding an annuity of future payments whose present value, at the loan interest rate, just equals the amount of initial principal borrowed. Another variation of the basic present-value model can be used for such purposes. That is, the annuity form of the present-value model, Equation

---

[8]The interest rate on a single-payment loan can be found in the same way as the growth rate. Dividing the initial principal by the amount to be repaid (principal and interest) at maturity yields $PVIF_{k,n}$; since n is known, the interest rate, k, can be found using the present-value interest factors. For example, for a \$10,000 5-year loan to be repaid in a single payment of \$15,400, the interest rate would be estimated as

$$\frac{\$10{,}000}{\$15{,}400} = .649 = PVIF_{k,5}$$

Using Appendix Table A.3, the present-value interest factor, $PVIF$, closest to .649 for 5 years is .650, which is associated with 9 percent. Hence the interest rate, k, is 9 percent.

5.18, is used. Defining PVA_n as the size of the loan and A as the size of the equal periodic loan payments, we would solve for A in Equation 5.18 to determine the size of the payments required to pay off the loan over a stipulated time horizon, n. For example, if a company borrowed $50,000 at 10 percent and agreed to make equal annual payments over a period of 6 years, we could determine the size of the payments as follows:

$$PVA_n = A \times PVIFA_{k,n}$$
$$\$50,000 = A \times PVIFA_{10\%,\,6\,yr}$$
$$\$50,000 = A \times 4.355$$

Solving for the size of the annuity, A, we have:

$$A = \$50,000/4.355 = \$11,481.06$$

In this case, the loan can be paid off in six years by making annual payments of $11,481.06; such a loan repayment would enable the bank to recover its $50,000 and at the same time earn a fully compounded rate of return of 10 percent on the outstanding loan balance over the term of the loan.[9]

Sometimes, instead of finding the size of loan payments, it is necessary to determine the rate of interest or yield on a loan. This would be the case if both the size of the loan and the size of the periodic payments were known and the company wanted to find its cost of funds. To find the annual interest rate on an amortized loan, a procedure similar to that employed with growth rates is used, except that we would be dealing with annuity interest factors rather than single cash flow interest factors. For example, if the $50,000 loan required annual payments of $11,817.54 over a 6-year term, then:

$$PVA_n = A \times PVIFA_{k,n}$$
$$\$50,000.00 = \$11,817.54 \times PVIFA_{k,\,6\,yr}$$
$$PVIFA_{k,\,6\,yr} = \$50,000.00/\$11,817.54$$
$$= 4.231$$

Looking at the present-value interest factor table for an annuity for $n = 6$ years, we see that a $PVIFA$ of 4.231 is associated with an 11 percent rate of interest. Thus, amortizing this $50,000 loan at $11,817.54 per year will result in an annual cost to the firm of 11 percent.

---

[9]It should be obvious that if loan payments are to be made more often (on a semiannual, quarterly, or monthly basis), the present-value model will have to be adjusted according to procedures outlined earlier in the chapter to reflect the shorter compounding periods.

SUMMARY

One of the key mathematical concepts of managerial finance is present value. Present-value procedures are widely used in valuation, capital budgeting, mergers and acquisitions, capital structure, bond refunding, leasing, and a number of other asset-mix and financial structure decisions. The concept of present value is based on the notion that money has a time value—that money has an opportunity cost to the extent that if not used for one purpose, it can always be employed profitably somewhere else.

The time value of money rests, in large part, on compound interest, a concept that deals with determining the future value of an investment or deposit. Interest can be compounded annually, semiannually, quarterly, or over even shorter periods; more frequent compounding increases the future value of an investment. Present value rests on the time value of money and is the reciprocal of future value. The basic idea of present value is that a dollar today is worth more than a dollar to be received at some date in the future, the actual difference being a function of the earnings opportunities of the recipient. Present value, in effect, looks at the future cash payoffs from an investment and discounts these back to their present value. Such cash flows come in a variety of forms, including single cash flows, annuities, perpetuities, and uneven streams. Like compounding, discounting can be done on a more frequent than annual basis; the more frequently interest is discounted, the lower the present value of a future sum.

Present value is an important managerial tool for making resource-allocation and fundraising decisions. In addition, variations in the basic present-value model can be made in order to find the fully compounded growth rate imbedded in a cash flow, the size of loan amortization payments, or the interest rate being charged on a loan. These and other applications testify to the importance and universality of the present-value concept, which is used repeatedly throughout the remainder of the book.

QUESTIONS

5.1. Briefly describe the compounding process and explain the impact of (a) increasing interest rates, and (b) increasing time on the future value of a given deposit.

5.2. Differentiate between an ordinary annuity and an annuity due. Give the formula for the future value of an ordinary annuity, A, at an interest rate, k, at the end of n years.

5.3. What impact, if any, does the fact that interest is compounded more frequently than annually have on future value? What, if any, impact would the fact that interest is discounted more frequently than annually have on the present value of a future cash flow?

5.4. Contrast the concept of future value with that of present value.

Discuss the conceptual and mathematical linkage of present value to compound interest.

5.5. Why is the time value of money important to the present-value concept? Could the concept of present value exist if money did not have a time value? Explain.

5.6. Explain the effects of rate of return, k, and holding period, n, on the present value of (a) a single sum, and (b) an annuity.

5.7. Present value looks at the cash payoffs from an investment and discounts these to the present; explain how an annuity is simply one form of a cash payoff.

5.8. Use any stream of cash flow to explain the notion that present value represents the minimum investment required to generate the cash payoffs in question.

5.9. Define a perpetuity and explain the procedure used to find the present value of a perpetuity.

5.10. Explain why present value plays such an important role in financial decision making. What kind of information does it provide the decision maker?

5.11. The Lighthouse Electric Company had earnings of $5 million in 1978; some 5 years later, the company reported earnings had grown to $10 million. Therefore, we can conclude: Since earnings grew by 100 percent over a period of 5 years, it follows that the compound annual rate of growth was 20 percent per year (100%/5 years). Discuss the logic or fallacy of this statement.

PROBLEMS

5.1. *FUTURE VALUE.* Compute the future value of each of the following deposits, given interest is compounded annually:

Case	Initial Deposit	Interest Rate	Period (in years)
A	$ 500	6%	10
B	4,000	12	6
C	15,555	8	12

5.2. *THE COMPOUND INTEREST ON A LOAN.* Alpha Marine & Sail recently took out a $10,000 loan with interest payable at the rate of 12 percent, compounded annually; the loan is to be paid off in a single lump sum (there will be no instalment or amortization payments) and any interest due will be paid at the same time.

a. What amount will be due if the loan is paid off after 6 months?

b. If it is repaid at the end of a year?

c. What is the amount if repayment is at the end of year 3? At the end of year 5?

d. Explain the role of compounding in determining the size of the payment required to retire the loan.

5.3. *FUTURE VALUE OF AN ANNUITY.*   Charles Schmidt plans to place $3000 at the *end* of each of the next 4 years into an investment paying 12 percent annual interest. He does not plan to withdraw any funds during the period.

a. How much will be available to Charles at the *end* of the fourth year?

b. If Charles were to place the funds into an investment at the *beginning* of each year, how much would be available at the *end* of the fourth year?

c. Contrast and discuss your findings in (a) and (b).

5.4. *DEPOSITS TO ACCUMULATE A FUTURE SUM.*   Carol Williams has estimated that she needs to accumulate $14,000 by the end of 6 years in order to make the down payment on her dream home. She wishes to accomplish this goal by making equal, annual end-of-year deposits into an account paying 8 percent annual interest. How much must Carol deposit at the end of each of the next 6 years to achieve her goal?

5.5. *INFLATION AND FUTURE VALUE.* A retirement home at Mel Webber's Sun Village now costs $45,000. Inflation is expected to cause this price to increase at the rate of 8 percent per year over the 20 years before Ollie Packard retires. How much will Packard have to save at the end of each year at an annual interest rate of 12 percent in order to have the necessary cash to purchase the home upon retirement?

5.6. *COMPOUNDING PERIOD.* Dynamic Industries has $10,000 of idle funds it wishes to deposit in one of three savings accounts. The stated rate of interest on each account is 16 percent. Interest is compounded annually on account A, semiannually on account B, and quarterly on account C.

a. Calculate the future value if the money is left on deposit for 2 years for account A, account B, and account C.

b. In which account would you recommend the firm deposit its money? Explain the relationship between the compounding period and interest earnings illustrated by your findings in (a).

5.7. *PRESENT VALUE.* Find the present value of the following single cash flows, using annual discounting:

Case	Cash Flow	Received at End of Year	Discount Rate
A	$ 800	6	6%
B	2,950	15	10
C	25,458	9	14

a. Do likewise using semiannual discounting.
b. Explain the differences in your answers.

5.8. *PRESENT VALUE OF AN ANNUITY.* Three investments are currently under evaluation by Arizona Logging; they involve the following cash flows: (1) an annuity of $600 per year for 5 years; (2) an annuity of $3,500 per year for 12 years; and (3) an annuity of $20,000 per year for 15 years.
a. How much is each investment worth if Arizona Logging uses a 12 percent discount rate?
b. What happens to the value of each investment if the discount rate is increased to 18 percent? What accounts for the change?

5.9. *PRESENT VALUE OF A PERPETUITY.* For each of the following perpetuities

Perpetuity	Annual Amount	Discount Rate
A	$ 20,000	8%
B	100,000	10
C	3,000	6
D	60,000	5

a. Determine the appropriate present-value interest factor.
b. Determine the present value of the perpetuity.

5.10. *THE MATHEMATICS OF COMPOUNDING AND PRESENT VALUE.* Assume interest-factor tables do not exist; as a result, the arithmetic of compounding and present value is strictly a "do-it-yourself" proposition.
a. *Without using tables,* find the future value of $1000 deposited for 5 years at 10 percent interest, compounded annually.
b. *Without using tables,* find the present value of $5000 to be

received in 4 years, given an annual discount rate of 6 percent.

c. *Without using tables*, find the present value of $5000 to be received in 2 years, given a discount rate of 12 percent, discounting semiannually.

d. *Without using tables*, find the present value of an annuity of $5000 per year to be received for 4 years, given a 5 percent discount rate.

e. Now, use the appropriate interest-factor table to check your answers with each of the four problems above.

5.11. *THE PRESENT VALUE OF AN UNEVEN STREAM OF CASH FLOWS.* The Barker-Buchanan Company is examining three equally risky investment proposals, the cash flows of which are as follows:

Year	Investments		
	A	B	C
1	$ 1,000	$ 0	$ 650
2	1,500	0	900
3	2,000	0	1,500
4	3,000	2,000	2,000
5	0	2,000	−3,000
6	0	2,000	−5,000
7	5,000	2,000	−5,000
8	10,000	8,000	−5,000
9	0	8,000	15,000
10	0	8,000	25,000

a. Use a 10 percent discount rate to find the present value of each investment.

b. Which investment would you be willing to pay the most for? Why?

5.12. *VALUES OF CASH FLOWS.* Jane Brown-Smith is vice-president of investments at Black Fox Manufacturing. Recently she was trying to decide which of three cash flow situations to accept: (1) $1000 to be paid today; (2) $1974 to be paid as one lump sum in 6 years (at the end of year 6); or (3) an annuity of $177 per year for each of the next 10 years (to be paid at the end of each year). Assume that Black Fox has a 12 percent opportunity cost. Which of the options should she select? Why?

5.13. *DISCOUNTING PERIOD.* Using a 12 percent annual interest rate, calculate the present value of $8000 to be received 2 years from now if discounting takes place on: (1) an annual, (2) a quarterly, and (3) a monthly basis. What effect does the frequency of discounting have on present value?

5.14.   **BOND PRICE.**   The State of New York wants to issue a savings bond that can be converted to $100 at maturity, 5 years from purchase. In order to be competitive in the market, the state treasurer suggests that the issue carry an 8 percent yield, compounded annually. At what price should New York sell its bonds? (*Note*: Assume no cash payments are made prior to redemption.)

5.15.   **DETERMINING THE REQUIRED INVESTMENT.**   What initial sum would one have to deposit at 11 percent annual interest in order to be able to pay out $100 at the end of each of the next 12 years? How do your computations demonstrate the notion of present value?

5.16.   **GROWTH RATES.**   You are given the following series of cash flows:

Year	A	B	C
1972	$ 0	$1800	$ 0
1973	0	1850	0
1974	0	1900	0
1975	0	2000	0
1976	0	2100	2000
1977	0	2150	2100
1978	500	2500	2250
1979	560	2600	2400
1980	650	2750	2450
1981	750	3000	2600
1982	900	3100	2800
1983	950	3150	2900
1984	1000	3250	3000

Calculate the compound rate of growth (from the earliest year of cash flow to the later year of cash flow) for each of the three cash flow streams.

5.17.   **LOAN AMORTIZATION.**   The Romero Motor Company is in the process of negotiating a loan with its bank. The company wants to borrow $100,000 for 5 years at 10 percent interest, the loan to be amortized in five equal annual payments; in contrast, the bank is willing to lend the full $100,000, but only for 4 years and at 12 percent interest, with the loan to be amortized in equal semiannual payments.

a. Determine the size of the loan payments given Romero's loan request; do likewise using the bank's counteroffer.

b. What arguments can you make in support of Romero's loan request?

5.18.   *DETERMINING INTEREST RATES.* Financial Learning Systems, Inc., has been shopping around for a loan to finance a new venture. The company has found three possibilities that seem attractive and it wants to select the one having the lowest interest rate. The firm wants to borrow $50,000, and information about each of the three loan possibilities is as follows:

Loan	Principal	Annual Payment	Maturity
A	$50,000	$13,528	5 years
B	50,000	15,432	4 years
C	50,000	20,104	3 years

a. Determine the interest rate for each loan.

b. Which option should the company select? Why?

SELECTED REFERENCES

Aronson, J. Richard, and Eli Schwartz, eds. *Management Policies in Local Government Finance*, 2d ed. Washington, D.C.: International City Management Association, 1981.

Cissell, Robert, Helen Cissell, and David C. Flaspohler. *Mathematics of Finance*, 6th ed. Boston: Houghton Mifflin, 1982.

Clayton, Gary E., and Christopher B. Spivey. *The Time Value of Money*. Philadelphia: Saunders, 1978.

Hart, William L. *Mathematics of Investment*, 5th ed. Lexington, Mass.: D. C. Heath, 1975.

Moak, Lennox L., and Albert M. Hillhouse. *Concepts and Practices in Local Government Finance*. Chicago: Municipal Finance Officers Association, 1975.

Seitz, Neil. *Financial Analysis: A Programmed Approach*. Reston, Va.: Reston, 1976.

Shao, Stephen P. *Mathematics for Management and Finance*, 3d ed. Cincinnati: South-Western, 1974.

Vichas, Robert P. *Handbook of Financial Mathematics, Formulas, and Tables*. Englewood Cliffs, N.J.: Prentice-Hall, 1979.

Wright, M. G. *Discounted Cash Flow*, 2d ed. London: McGraw-Hill, 1973.

Appendix 5A

Continuous Compounding and Discounting

The assumption used in Chapter 5, and throughout this book, is that interest is compounded over discrete intervals that correspond to the cash flow patterns—usually annually, but sometimes semiannually or even quarterly. Rather than using discrete compounding or discounting periods, it may be more appropriate to use *continuous compounding* or *discounting*. This may be the case when the cash flows from an investment occur over a given time period, instead of at the end of it. For example, the benefits from an investment may come about in the form of reduced operating costs realized evenly over the years, rather than as a series of annual lump sums. In the following material we will briefly examine the concepts of continuous compounding and discounting; we will look first at the future value and present value of single cash flows and then annuities.

Continuous Compounding of a Future Value

Using Equation 5.12, we can state the general equation for intrayear compounding of a future value as follows:

$$FV_n = PV \, (1 \, + \, k/m)^{m \times n} \tag{5A.1}$$

Equation 5A.1 can be expressed in terms of natural logarithms when the number of intrayear compounding periods (m) approaches infinity. That is, rewriting 5A.1 by letting $X = m/k$ and substituting into Equation 5A.1, we have:

$$FV_n = PV \ (1 \ + \ 1/X)^{X \times k \times n} \qquad\qquad (5A.2)$$

$$= PV \ [(1 \ + \ 1/X)^X]^{k \times n}$$

Now, as $X \rightarrow \infty$, the expression within the brackets becomes:

$$\lim_{X \to \infty} (1 \ + \ 1/X)^X = e = 2.71828 \ . \ . \ .$$

Thus, the general equation for future value, using continuous compounding, is as follows:

$$FV_n = PV \times e^{k \times n} \qquad\qquad (5A.3)$$

where k = annual interest rate and n = number of years in the period. To illustrate, we would find the future value of $1000 deposited today for 5 years at 8 percent, compounded continuously, as follows:

$$FV_5 = \$1000 \times 2.71828^{.08 \times 5}$$
$$= \$1000 \times 1.49182$$
$$= \$1491.82$$

As a matter of interest, the same investment would grow in 5 years to a future value of only $1469.00 under conditions of annual compounding; the difference, of course, is attributable to the larger payoff that accrues from more frequent compounding.

Continuous Discounting of a Present Value

The present value of a future sum can also be converted from discrete to continuous discounting in a fashion similar to that used above with future value. The general equation for finding present value under conditions of continuous time discounting is this:

$$PV = FV_n \times e^{-k \times n} \qquad\qquad (5A.4)$$

For example, the present value of $10,000 to be received in 7 years, given a continuous time discount rate of 12 percent is as follows:

$$PV = \$10,000 \times 2.71828^{-.12 \times 7}$$
$$= \$10,000 \times .431711$$
$$= \$4317.11$$

In comparison, the same cash flow has a present value of $4520.00 when discounted annually; the higher value is, of course, not surprising, since with annual (rather than continuous) discounting, less of the future payoff accrues from compounding and more, has to come from the original investment (the computed present value). The major benefit of continuous discounting is slightly improved accuracy in the computed present-value figure. Even so, an annual or some other discrete discounting period is most widely used in practice not only since the notion (and mathematics) are more readily comprehensible, but because fine-tuned precision is obviously not needed at this point in the analysis, given the uncertain nature of the projected cash flows used in present-value-based models.

Annuities

Compounding and discounting functions are used to value streams of payments at any point in time. A special outcome occurs when an investment provides an annuity—equal periodic payments. Using discrete time, the future value, FVA_n, of an n period ordinary annuity, A, can be shown as the geometric series:

$$FVA_n = A(1 + k)^0 + A(1 + k)^1 + \ldots \qquad (5A.5)$$
$$+ A(1 + k)^{n-2} + A(1 + k)^{n-1}$$

This series can be simplified by the following steps:

Step 1.   Multiply both sides of Equation 5A.5 by $(1 + k)$:

$$FVA_n (1 + k) = A(1 + k)^1 + A(1 + k)^2 \qquad (5A.6)$$
$$+ \ldots + A(1 + k)^{n-1} + A(1 + k)^n$$

Step 2.   Subtract Equation 5A.5 from 5A.6 and rearrange:

$$FVA_n = A \left[\frac{(1 + k)^n - 1}{k} \right] \qquad (5A.7)$$

The term in brackets is the future-value interest factor for an annuity.

Continuous compounding for annuities is very similar, except we posit that cash payments are received at a continuous rate from the beginning to the end of the asset's life, rather than in discrete amounts at the end of specified time periods. To solve a problem involving continuous annuity flows, introductory integral calculus is necessary. The discrete payment annuity implied in Equation 5A.5 is illustrated in Figure 5A.1(a); the future value of the discrete payment annuity is equal to the area under the steplike function. If the annuity had been received continuously, its future value would be equal to the area under the continuous curve in Figure 5A.1(b). Each point N on the curve can be evaluated as:

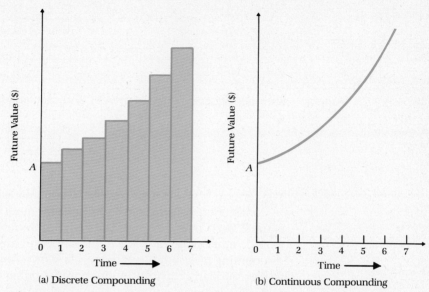

Figure 5A.1   Future Value of an Annuity Using Discrete and Continuous Compounding.

$$A_N = Ae^{k \times N} \qquad (5A.8)$$

The area under the curve in Figure 5A.1(b) represents the future value of the continuous annuity at the end of any year n and can be written as:

$$FVA_n = \int_{N=0}^{n} Ae^{k \times N}\, dN \qquad (5A.9)$$

$$= A \left[\frac{e^{k \times N}}{k} \right]_0^n$$

$$= A \left[\frac{e^{k \times n}}{k} - \frac{e^0}{k} \right]$$

$$= A \left[\frac{e^{k \times n} - 1}{k} \right] \qquad (5A.10)$$

The continuous time equation for the sum of an annuity given in Equation 5A.10 parallels the discrete future value of an annuity formula given in Equation 5A.7.

In a fashion similar to that used for discrete compounding, Equation 5.16 for the present value of an n period annuity can be simplified, using the following steps:

Step 1.   Multiply both sides of Equation 5.16 by $(1 + k)$:

$$PVA_n (1 + k) = A + A \left[\frac{1}{(1 + k)^1} \right] + \ldots \quad (5A.11)$$

$$+ A \left[\frac{1}{(1 + k)^{n-2}} \right] + A \left[\frac{1}{(1 + k)^{n-1}} \right]$$

Step 2.   Subtract Equation 5.16 from 5A.11 and rearrange:

$$PVA_n = A \frac{\left[1 - \dfrac{1}{(1 + k)^n} \right]}{k} \quad (5A.12)$$

The term in brackets is the present-value interest factor for an annuity.

Continuous discounting for annuities is quite similar, except that we assume cash flows are received at a continuous rate throughout the period rather than as discrete end-of-period amounts. For continuous discounting of an annuity, an approach involving integral calculus in a fashion similar to the continuous compounding case is applied. Mathematically, letting N equal any point in time:

$$PVA_n = \int_{N=0}^{n} Ae^{-k \times N} \, dN \quad (5A.13)$$

which reduces to

$$= A \left[\frac{1 - e^{-k \times n}}{k} \right] \quad (5A.14)$$

The similarity between the continuous discounting equation given in Equation 5A.14 and the discrete discounting equation given in 5A.12 should be clear.

6

Risk
and Return

The two key factors affecting the firm's value, and therefore the wealth of its owners, are risk and return. The financial manager operates in an environment of risk (or uncertainty), which means that the manager expects a given level of return but cannot be certain ahead of time as to its actual value. Investors must be compensated for both: (1) postponing present consumption for future consumption, and (2) accepting risk. With adequate compensation, individuals and firms will consider investing in risky assets like bonds, common stocks, or plant and equipment. Because of their preference for higher rather than lower returns and lower rather than higher risk, both investors and financial managers seek investment opportunities offering the highest return for the least risk. Such a strategy is consistent with the firm's goal of owner wealth maximization. The concepts of risk and return are relatively easy to understand; it is their quantification and the link between them that are a bit more difficult to grasp. In this chapter we develop the concepts of risk and return, discuss risk in a portfolio context, and then describe the relationship between risk and return using the capital asset pricing model (CAPM). The impact of changes in key economic variables on the risk-return tradeoff, as well as comments on empirical risk-return relationships, are also presented. The emphasis here is on the technical dimensions of risk and return; their application is taken up in subsequent chapters.

Risk and Return Concepts

Risk and return can be viewed in relation to a single asset or as they relate to a portfolio of assets. Before we discuss risk and return in a portfolio context, we need to understand them as they relate to a single asset held in isolation. In addition, we need to understand correlation, an important statistical concept related to portfolio theory.

Return Defined

The *return* from an investment is the realizable cash flow earned on behalf of its owner during a specified period of time. It is commonly stated as a percentage of the beginning-of-period investment value. For simplicity, common stock will be used here to illustrate the return measurement process.

For a holding period of length t, the benefits from ownership of common stock include the cash dividend paid during the period, together with any appreciation or loss in the market price (capital gain or loss) realized at the end of the period. Thus, the return on the investment is equal to:

$$k = \frac{P_t - P_{t-1} + D_t}{P_{t-1}} \qquad (6.1)$$

where k = the actual, expected, or required rate of return[1]
P_t = price of the stock at time t
P_{t-1} = price of the stock at time $t - 1$
D_t = cash dividends paid on the stock during the time period from $t - 1$ to t.

Suppose an individual purchased a share of stock for $60 and the firm was expected to pay $2 per share in dividends during the year; if the market price at the end of the year (after payment of the dividend) was estimated to be $64, then the expected return on the common stock for the year is:

$$k = \frac{\$64 - \$60 + \$2}{\$60} = \frac{\$6}{\$60} = 10\%$$

This same approach can be employed to determine the expected rate of return on any asset, with t being as short as one day or less, or as long as 10 years or more. However, t is typically defined on a yearly basis so that the frame of reference is the rate of return per year.[2] As we will see later, while multiyear returns can be measured using Equation 6.1, it is not the preferred procedure since it fails to consider the time value of money. Of

---

[1] Throughout this text, the terms *expected return* and *required return* are used interchangeably. The rationale underlying this treatment is described in some detail in Chapter 7.

[2] Much of the empirical research concerning common stock returns has been done with monthly returns. The selection of this time period apparently was due to the availability of Center for Research in Security Prices (CRSP) data from the Graduate School of Business, University of Chicago. The CRSP tape provides monthly returns for all securities ever listed on the New York Stock Exchange (NYSE) from January 1926 to the present. More recently, weekly, daily, and even intradaily returns have increasingly been used in research. For expository purposes and consistency, we have used yearly returns throughout the book.

course, return is only one side of the coin; the risk associated with each level of return must also be considered in the decision-making process.

Risk and Uncertainty Defined

The difference between risk and uncertainty as defined by the statistician is related to the knowledge of the probabilities, or chances, of certain outcomes occurring. *Risk* refers to situations where we know or can estimate, using historic data, the probabilities associated with various outcomes; we can make a probability distribution. *Uncertainty* exists where we do not know all the probabilities and often have no historical data from which to develop a probability distribution. In such a situation, often the best one can do is make educated guesses. Most financial decisions are made under conditions of uncertainty, although decision-making techniques are based on the assumption that conditions of risk exist. There is a growing tendency to use these terms interchangeably in finance, and we will follow this practice here.

Two points relative to risk and uncertainty should be emphasized. First, some risk is present in almost every decision that investors or financial managers make. Suppose an investor buys $50,000 of short-term government bonds that will mature in one month. In this case, the return or yield of 10 percent can be estimated with a good deal of certainty in terms of the amount to be received, its timing, and the certainty of the return. This is probably as close as we can get to a risk-free security, so the yield on U.S. Treasury bills is often used as the risk-free rate of return, R_F. On the other hand, the $50,000 could have been invested in the stock of General Motors. Although we may have substantial historical data to guide us, it is still difficult to forecast with reasonable accuracy the rate of return, especially that component of return due to appreciation or loss in market price. Hence, because actual outcomes are not known in advance, it is safe to conclude that risk characterizes almost all investment and managerial finance decisions. The second point is that since risk cannot be avoided, one must understand it, measure it, and make choices using rules that specifically consider it.

Probability

An event's *probability* is defined as the chance, or odds, that it will occur. Suppose, for example, an investor says there is a 3 to 2 chance that the market price of a particular stock will increase during the next month. This statement is equivalent to saying there is a 60 percent chance that the stock will increase in price from its current level, while there is a 40 percent chance that the price will remain constant or decline in value during the next month. This information could be presented as follows:

Possible Outcome (i)	Probability (Pr_i)
Stock price will rise	.60 = 60%
Stock price will not rise	.40 = 40
Total	1.00 = 100%

TABLE 6.1
Rates of Return and
Associated Probabilities
for Allen Paper and
Collins Glass

State of the Economy	Probability of State Occurring	Rate of Return, k (%)	
		Allen Paper	Collins Glass
Boom	0.20	40%	70%
Normal	0.60	20	20
Recession	0.20	0	−30

Note two important properties of all probabilities from this example. First, all probabilities, Pr_i, fall between zero and one, or $0 \le Pr_i \le 1$. Second, the sum of all the probabilities over all possible outcomes is equal to one; $\sum_{i=1}^{n} Pr_i = 1.00$, where n is equal to the number of possible outcomes.

As another example of probabilities, consider two possible common stock investments. The first stock, Allen Paper, has three expected rates of return for next year, with associated probabilities of occurrence based on the state of the economy during this period; this information is shown in Table 6.1. The second stock, Collins Glass, also has three expected rates of return and associated probabilities of occurrence, as shown in Table 6.1. The probabilities of occurrence indicate that there is a 20 percent possibility of a boom next year, a 60 percent possibility of a normal year, and a 20 percent possibility of a recession. Note that the rates of return—each of which represents an expected rate of return, k, as computed from Equation 6.1—are expected to vary considerably more for Collins Glass than for Allen Paper. This is intuitively reasonable when we consider that Allen Paper makes newsprint for newspapers, and the demand for newspapers is rather insensitive to economic conditions. Collins Glass, on the other hand, supplies plate glass for windows; since construction activity is very susceptible to fluctuations in the state of the economy, the sales, and hence rates of return of Collins Glass, are more sensitive to changing economic conditions.

Expected Return: The Mean

Earlier we defined return as the realizable cash flow earned from an investment during a specified period of time. At this point, the measurement of return is reintroduced to show how it can be measured in the context of risk. Rather than deal with an entire probability distribution, it is often simpler and sufficiently accurate to assess return using a measure of central tendency, such as the *expected value* or *mean*.[3] The expected rate of return is defined as:

---

[3]Several other measures of central tendency are often used for special purposes in finance. The foremost of these include the geometric mean, the median, and the mode. The arithmetic mean (or expected value) is especially useful in measuring central tendency if the distribution of returns is reasonably symmetrical about the mean. If the distribution is skewed, other measures may prove more useful.

$$\text{Expected rate of return} = \bar{k} = \sum_{i=1}^{n} k_i Pr_i \qquad (6.2)$$

where $\bar{k}$ = the expected rate of return
k_i = the ith possible outcome
Pr_i = the probability associated with the ith outcome
n = the number of possible outcomes

Thus $\bar{k}$ is a weighted average of all possible outcomes, with each outcome being weighted by its probability of occurrence. For Allen Paper, the expected rate of return is:

$$\bar{k}_A = (k_1)\,(Pr_1) + (k_2)\,(Pr_2) + (k_3)\,(Pr_3)$$
$$= (40\%)\,(0.20) + (20\%)\,(0.60) + (0\%)\,(0.20)$$
$$= 20\%$$

Likewise, the expected rate of return on Collins Glass is:

$$\bar{k}_C = (70\%)\,(.20) + (20\%)\,(0.60) + (-30\%)\,(.20)$$
$$= 20\%$$

Other things being equal, investors are presumed to prefer investments that have large expected returns, $\bar{k}$. In the example above, the mean or expected rate of return is the same for both securities; hence, if other things were equal, the investor would be indifferent between the two securities. However, as we know, other things are not equal: We can determine by inspection that there is more dispersion in the rates of return for Collins Glass than for Allen Paper.

Probability Distributions
A *probability distribution* provides a complete description of the possible outcomes of an event and their associated probabilities. Table 6.1 presented the probability distribution for the rates of return of the two common stocks introduced above, Allen Paper and Collins Glass. Often it is easier to get a "feel" for the information by graphing the possible outcomes and associated probabilities. Figure 6.1 provides an example of a *discrete* probability distribution, which is one showing the probabilities associated with a finite number of returns. A comparison indicates that although both Allen Paper and Collins Glass have a probability of .60 of having an expected return of 20 percent, the dispersion of rates of return is greater for Collins Glass.

Thus far, we have considered only three states of the economy: boom, normal, or recession. Actually, the state of the economy can vary from a fantastic boom to a severe recession, i.e., depression. If we knew all the possible expected rates of return and associated probabilities, a *continuous* probability distribution, which shows all possible outcomes and

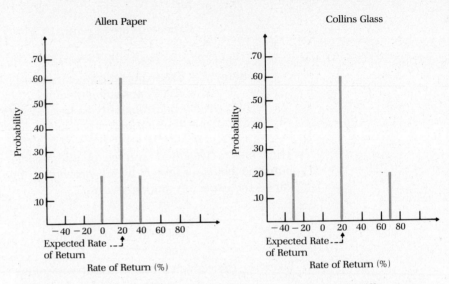

Figure 6.1 Discrete Probability Distribution: Rates of Return for Allen Paper and Collins Glass.

associated probabilities, could be developed. Figure 6.2 presents a graph of continuous probability distributions for Allen Paper and Collins Glass. The total area under the continuous curve is equal to 100 percent, since it describes all possible outcomes. Continuous probability distributions are extremely useful for displaying information and for assisting decision makers in measuring risk.

Risk Measures The risk in a probability distribution is measured by its degree of dispersion: How much, on average, do the individual outcomes deviate from the expected value? A basic method for measuring dispersion is the use of the *range* of outcomes, which is the difference between the highest and lowest outcomes. Using the return data in Table 6.1 for both Allen Paper and Collins Glass, their ranges are found to be 40 percent and 100 percent, respectively. Clearly, as depicted in Figures 6.1 and 6.2, and as reflected by the range, Collins Glass' return is more risky than that of Allen Paper. Two more sophisticated measures of dispersion—the standard deviation and the coefficient of variation—are commonly used to measure the risk associated with the probability distribution of returns.[4]

---

[4]Several other measures of dispersion are employed in finance. These include the interquartile range and semivariance. The standard deviation and coefficient of variation are appropriate for measuring the dispersion of expected returns when the distribution of expected returns is reasonably symmetrical about the mean. If the distribution of expected returns is skewed, the standard deviation and coefficient of variation may not be the appropriate measures.

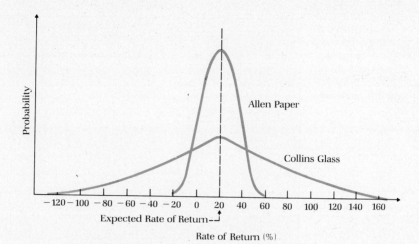

Figure 6.2 Continuous Probability Distribution: Rates of Return for Allen Paper and Collins Glass.

Note: The probabilities in this figure do not appear to be exactly the same as those in Figure 6.1 because many more possible outcomes are considered. Continuous probability distributions are often shown as cumulative distributions in which the probability of a given outcome or less is plotted against the outcome. These distributions are useful in analyzing the likelihood of the actual outcome occurring over a given range of values.

Standard Deviation.   The *standard deviation,* which measures the average deviation about the expected return, is calculated as follows:

$$\text{Standard deviation} = \sigma = \sqrt{\sum_{i=1}^{n} (k_i - \bar{k})^2 \times Pr_i} \tag{6.3}$$

where σ = the standard deviation about the expected rate of return
   $\bar{k}$ = the expected rate of return
   k_i = the *i*th possible outcome
   Pr_i = the probability associated with the *i*th outcome
   n = the number of possible outcomes

As can be seen by examining Equation 6.3, the standard deviation is the square root of the sum of the product of each deviation from the expected value, $(k_i - \bar{k})^2$, weighted by the associated probability of occurrence. Table 6.2 presents the calculation of the standard deviation for Allen Paper and Collins Glass. Since the units of measure for the standard deviation are the same as both the original data and the mean, standard deviations can be employed to determine the dispersion about the distribution. In light of the fact that Allen Paper and Collins Glass both have the same expected rate of return (20 percent), we see that Allen Paper has less dispersion, since its standard deviation of 12.65 percent is

TABLE 6.2
The Standard Deviation About the Expected Rate of Return for Allen Paper and Collins Glass

Allen Paper

i	State	k_i	$\bar{k}$	$k_i - \bar{k}$	$(k_i - \bar{k})^2$	Pr_i	$(k_i - \bar{k})^2 \times Pr_i$
1	Boom	40%	20%	20	400	0.20	80
2	Normal	20	20	0	0	0.60	0
3	Recession	0	20	−20	400	0.20	80

$$\sum_{i=1}^{3} (k_i - \bar{k})^2 \times Pr_i = 160$$

$$\sigma_{\text{Allen Paper}} = \sqrt{\sum_{i=1}^{3} (k_i - \bar{k})^2 \times Pr_i} = \sqrt{160} \approx 12.65\%$$

Collins Glass

i	State	k_i	$\bar{k}$	$k_i - \bar{k}$	$(k_i - \bar{k})^2$	Pr_i	$(k_i - \bar{k})^2 \, Pr_i$
1	Boom	70%	20%	50	2500	0.20	500
2	Normal	20	20	0	0	0.60	0
3	Recession	−30	20	−50	2500	0.20	500

$$\sum_{i=1}^{3} (k_i - \bar{k})^2 \times Pr_i = 1000$$

$$\sigma_{\text{Collins Glass}} = \sqrt{\sum_{i=1}^{3} (k_i - \bar{k})^2 \times Pr_i} = \sqrt{1000} \approx 31.62\%$$

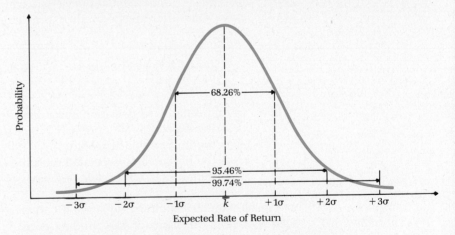

Figure 6.3   Probability Ranges for a Normal Distribution.

Note: The area under the normal curve equals 1.00 or 100 percent. The curve is symmetrical, indicating that 50 percent of the area lies below the mean, $\bar{k}$, and 50 percent lies above the mean. The equation for the normal curve is

$$f(x) = \frac{1}{\sqrt{2\pi\sigma^2}} e^{-(x-u)^2/2\sigma^2}$$

where π and e are mathematical constants, u is the mean of the distribution, σ is the standard deviation of the distribution, and x is any outcome.

smaller than that of Collins Glass, which is 31.62 percent. Given its greater dispersion, we can conclude that Collins Glass is the riskier common stock investment.

If the distribution is normal, the probability of an event occurring can be easily estimated using its mean and standard deviation. For any normal distribution, such as that shown in Figure 6.3, there is a 68.26 percent chance that the actual outcome will be within ±1 standard deviation of the expected outcome; there is a 95.46 percent chance the actual outcome will be within ±2 standard deviations of the expected outcome; and there is a 99.74 percent chance the actual outcome will be within ±3 standard deviations of the expected outcome. The probabilities associated with normal continuous distributions can be found by calculating the area under the curve between various points of interest.[5] Using Allen Paper's mean ($\overline{k}$ = 20%) and standard deviation (σ = 12.65%), you can be 68.3 percent certain that the actual return will be between ±1 standard deviation of its mean; that is, between 7.35 percent (20% − 12.65%) and 32.65 percent (20% + 12.65%). For Collins Glass, which has a mean return of 20 percent and a standard deviation of 31.62 percent, the range of outcomes at the 68.3 percent level of certainty would be between −11.62 percent and 51.62 percent. Clearly, the stock of Allen Paper is significantly less risky than that of Collins Glass.

Coefficient of Variation.   When comparing the risk of stocks (or other assets) with different rates of return, the use of the standard deviation

---

[5] The area under a continuous probability curve can be determined by integrating the curve over the appropriate interval, or if the distribution is assumed normal, by referring to a standard normal curve table (Appendix Table A.5). To use the table, it is necessary to know the mean and standard deviation of the probability distribution in question and then standardize them. To standardize the distribution, use the following equation:

$$Z = \left| \frac{x - \mu}{\sigma} \right|$$

where Z = the standardized variable
x = the outcome of interest
μ = the mean of the distribution
σ = the standard deviation of the distribution

If we wanted to know the probability of Allen Paper's rate of return being equal to or greater than 15 percent, Z would be calculated as:

$$Z = \left| \frac{15 - 20}{12.65} \right| = .395$$

The area associated with this Z value, as found in Appendix Table A.5, is .1536. This is the probability that the rate of return outcome for Allen Paper will be between 15 percent and the mean of 20 percent. Since the distribution is symmetrical, we add this probability to .5000, which is the probability that the actual rate of return will be greater than the mean of 20 percent, to determine the total probability of .6536 (.1536 + .5000, or 65.36 percent). Thus, the probability that the actual rate of return for Allen Paper will be equal to or greater than 15 percent is 65.36 percent.

can be enhanced by converting it into a coefficient of variation. The *coefficient of variation, CV,* is a relative measure of risk calculated by dividing the standard deviation, σ, by its respective expected value, $\bar{k}$. Thus, the coefficient of variation is:

$$CV = \frac{\sigma}{\bar{k}} \qquad (6.4)$$

For Allen Paper, the *CV* is .633 (12.65% ÷ 20%), while it is 1.581 (31.62% ÷ 20%) for Collins Glass. The higher the coefficient of variation, the greater the relative dispersion about the expected rate of return. Hence, we conclude again that Collins Glass has more relative dispersion about its expected rate of return than Allen Paper—all of which simply confirms what we have said above: Collins Glass is the riskier of the two securities.

In the example above there was no need to calculate the coefficient of variation because the two expected rates of return were equal, but consider the following situation. Suppose the standard deviations for Allen Paper and Collins Glass remain at 12.65 and 31.62 percent, respectively, but the expected rates of return are now 15 percent for Allen Paper and 40 percent for Collins Glass. Which stock has the most dispersion about its expected value? If we examine the standard deviations, Collins Glass appears to have more dispersion, but it also has the higher return. Given that the standard deviation does not account for the differences in the expected rates of return, what is needed is a measure of relative dispersion (relative to the mean)—the coefficient of variation.

The coefficient of variation for Allen Paper is .843 (12.65% ÷ 15%), whereas it is .791 (31.62% ÷ 40%) for Collins Glass. Since the higher the coefficient of variation, the greater the relative dispersion about an expected return, we see that Allen Paper now has wider dispersion about its expected rate of return than does Collins Glass, and therefore is subject to a greater relative amount of risk. Clearly, an objective comparison of risk for assets having differing expected returns can be achieved by using the coefficient of variation.

Correlation   The preceding discussion of expected returns and standard deviations focused on a single common stock. But to understand the concept of investment risk, we must understand how two variables co-vary, or move together. Co-movement can be measured in many different ways; the most common method (and the one we will use) is to consider the linear relationship between the two variables. The *correlation coefficient* is a standardized statistic that describes how much linear co-movement exists between two random variables. By "standardized" we mean it is always expressed in terms of values that range between −1 (perfect negative correlation) and +1 (perfect positive correlation), regardless of the units of measure of either of the original variables. The correlation between two variables, x and y, is expressed by a correlation coefficient, noted ρ_{xy}.

The correlation coefficient indicates the degree to which two variables move together; it may be positive ($\rho_{xy} > 0$), negative ($\rho_{xy} < 0$), or zero ($\rho_{xy} = 0$). If the correlation is positive, it means that as one variable increases, the other also tends to increase. The closer the correlation coefficient gets to +1.0, the more closely the two variables tend to move together; the more closely the correlation coefficient is to zero, the less the two variables tend to move together. A negative correlation means that the two variables move in opposite directions. In Figure 6.4, six different possible relationships between two variables, x and y, are indicated. Figures 6.4(a) and (b) indicate positive correlation between the two variables; 6.4(c) and (d) are examples of negative correlation; and 6.4(e) and (f) indicate no linear relationship—zero correlation. Note that in Figures 6.4(b) and (d) there is *perfect correlation*; that is, for every increase in one variable, there is a corresponding increase (or decrease) in the other. Rates of return on common stocks are good examples of variables that are generally positively, but not perfectly, correlated. The

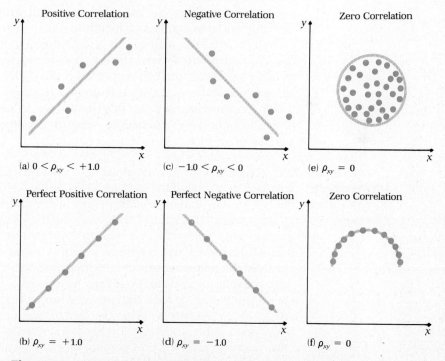

Figure 6.4   Graphic Depiction of Basic Correlation Relationships.

reason for the positive correlation is that nearly all stocks tend to fluctuate in the same general direction, but not the same magnitude, as the economy fluctuates from boom to recession and back again. We will discuss this phenomenon in greater detail as we delve into portfolio considerations and the capital asset pricing model

Risk in a Portfolio Context

The financial manager must use basic risk and return concepts in order to measure these key dimensions as they relate to financial decision making. Since the firm can be viewed as a portfolio of both assets and financing sources, attention must be given to the relationship between the decision alternative's risk and return and that of the firm. Particularly in the case of risk, the degree and direction of correlation of returns between the decision alternative and the firm's existing portfolio of assets (or financing) can significantly affect the risk of a proposed investment (or financing) decision. The financial manager must therefore understand risk in a portfolio context.

Most investors (both individuals and institutions) hold securities (or assets) in portfolios. As we will see, the risk of a security held in a well-diversified portfolio is less than the risk of that same security held in isolation. One important assumption underlies the discussion that follows: *Investors are risk-averse*. Given a choice between two investments, one that has an expected return of $1000 with 100 percent certainty and one that has an expected return of $1000 with a 50 percent probability that the return will be $2000 and a 50 percent probability that the return will be zero, the risk-averse investor will choose the first. In other words, given equal expected returns, the rational investor will always choose the least risky investment. This topic is discussed in more detail in Appendix 6A. At this point, we focus on the concept of diversification, the use of beta to measure nondiversifiable risk, and the calculation of beta.

Risk: Diversifiable and Nondiversifiable

For securities held in a portfolio, the relevant risk measure is not the standard deviation of the individual securities' return as we defined it in the last section. Rather, it is the degree of nondiversifiable risk possessed by the security. Because of the risk-reducing benefits of diversification, the nondiversifiable risk of a security held in a well-diversified portfolio is less than its risk when held in isolation. To understand this concept, consider the following example. Suppose you had $20,000 to invest and were considering two stocks—Frank Industries and Sampson Company. Let's assume that, at least initially, you are willing to project the future returns from the two securities as being equal to their returns over the last 4 years. Table 6.3 shows the historical rates of return for both firms (mean rates of return are 15 percent for both securities). Hence, on your investment of $20,000 you would expect to earn $3000 per year (15% ×

TABLE 6.3
Security and Portfolio
Returns and Standard
Deviations for Frank
Industries and
Sampson Company

Year	Frank Industries	Sampson Company	Portfolio: 50% Frank, 50% Sampson
1981	10%	25%	17.5%
1982	35	5	20
1983	−10	30	10
1984	25	0	12.5
STATISTICS[a]			
Mean Return ($\bar{k}$)	15%	15%	15%
Standard Deviation (σ)	19.58%	14.72%	4.56%

[a]Since historical return data rather than the probability distributions of returns are given, the formulas used to calculate the mean return and its standard deviation differ from those given by Equations 6.2 and 6.3, respectively. The mean return is calculated as:

$$\bar{k} = \left[\sum_{t=1}^{n} k_t \right] / n$$

and the standard deviation about the mean historical return is calculated by:

$$\sigma = \sqrt{\frac{\sum_{t=1}^{n} (k_t - \bar{k})^2}{n - 1}}$$

These formulas should be used whenever historical return data are being analyzed.

$20,000) on either security individually, or from a portfolio composed of equal amounts of both. Examining the standard deviation about each security's return, we see that it is 19.58 percent for Frank Industries and 14.72 percent for Sampson.[6] Given that you, as an investor, are risk-averse, if you had to choose between Frank Industries or Sampson, you would invest in Sampson because it provides the same return as Frank Industries, but has less risk.

Now let's see what happens to the standard deviation of a portfolio composed of 50 percent Frank Industries and 50 percent Sampson Company. The expected return on the portfolio is the same as either company individually, 15 percent, but the portfolio standard deviation of 4.56 percent is *much lower* than the standard deviation of either security individually. Individual security and portfolio rates of return in Figure 6.5 show that the fluctuations (or dispersions) in the portfolio rates of return are much less than the fluctuations in the individual security

---

[6]Since the means, or expected rates of return, are equal, the standard deviation is the relevant measure of dispersion. If the means had been unequal, then the coefficient of variation would have been the appropriate measure. Note that the formulas used to determine the means and standard deviations in Table 6.3 differ from those presented earlier in the chapter. Previously we employed probability distributions; in this example we calculate the mean and standard deviation from their historical outcomes.

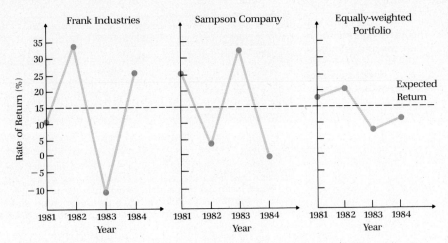

Figure 6.5　Rates of Return for Frank Industries, Sampson Company, and an Equally-weighted Portfolio Consisting of Both Securities.

rates of return. Why is the standard deviation on the portfolio return so much less than either of the individual security standard deviations? To answer this, we must use the correlation coefficient. If the correlation between the individual security's rates of return is less than perfectly positive, then there are benefits in the form of risk reduction to be gained by diversification.[7] When securities are held in portfolios, the relevant

---

[7]In the preceding example, the returns not only are not perfectly positively correlated, they are negatively correlated. In order to calculate the correlation between two securities, we need

$$\rho_{xy} = \frac{COV(x,y)}{\sigma_x \sigma_y}$$

$$\text{and}\quad COV(x,y) = \sum_{i=1}^{n} \frac{(x_i - \bar{x})(y_i - \bar{y})}{n-1}$$

where　ρ_{xy} = the correlation between two variables, x and y
$COV(x,y)$ = the covariance between variables x and y
σ_x = the standard deviation of variable x
σ_y = the standard deviation of variable y
n = the number of observations
x_i, y_i = the individual observations for x and y
$\bar{x}, \bar{y}$ = the means for variables x and y

To calculate the correlation between the rates of return of Frank Industries and Sampson Company, we proceed in the following steps:

Step 1.　Calculate the means and standard deviations for both variables. As shown in Table 6.3, the mean and standard deviation for Frank Industries are 15 and 19.58 percent and for Sampson Company the mean is 15 percent and the standard deviation is 14.72 percent.

Step 2.　Calculate the covariance between the rates of return for Frank Industries and Sampson Company.

measure of risk is not the standard deviation of the individual security's returns; instead, it is a measure of the security's nondiversifiable risk, or contribution to portfolio risk.

To better see how diversification affects portfolio risk, consider Figure 6.6.[8] With a single security in a portfolio, the standard deviation of the security is equal to the standard deviation of the portfolio. As we start adding securities to the portfolio, the portfolio's standard deviation decreases and approaches a limit.[9] Research indicates the majority of the benefits of diversification, in terms of risk reduction, can be gained by

| Year | Frank Industries (x) | | | Sampson Company (y) | | | Product of the Deviations $[(3) \times (6)]$ (7) |
	Return (1)	Mean Return (2)	Deviation $[(1) - (2)]$ (3)	Return (4)	Mean Return (5)	Deviation $[(4) - (5)]$ (6)	
1981	10%	15%	− 5%	25%	15%	10%	− 50
1982	35	15	20	5	15	−10	−200
1983	−10	15	−25	30	15	15	−375
1984	25	15	10	0	15	−15	−150
							−775

$$COV(x,y) = \sum_{i=1}^{n} \frac{(x_i - \bar{x})(y_i + \dot{y})}{n - 1} = \frac{-775}{3} = -258.333$$

Step 3. Calculate the correlation.

$$\text{Correlation} = \frac{COV(x,y)}{\sigma_x \sigma_y} = \frac{-258.333}{(19.58)(14.72)} = -.8963 \approx -.90$$

Thus, in this example, the two securities have a negative correlation of − .90; this means the security returns move almost in opposite directions. Hence, as the returns on one security tend to increase, the returns on the second security tend to decrease. This type of extreme relationship is not typical for all securities, but was employed to better illustrate the effects of diversification. The portfolio standard deviation is reduced, although not by the same magnitude, as long as the correlation between the individual security rates of return is less than perfectly positive, $\rho \neq +1.0$. Many small calculators have functions for calculating correlation coefficients directly.

[8]See Jack Evans and Stephen H. Archer, "Diversification and the Reduction of Dispersion: An Empirical Analysis," *Journal of Finance* 23 (December 1968), pp. 761–767; Wayne H. Wagner and Sheila Lau, "The Effect of Diversification on Risk," *Financial Analysts Journal* 26 (November–December 1971), pp. 48–53; K. H. Johnson and D. S. Shannon, "A Note on Diversification and the Reduction of Dispersion," *Journal of Financial Economics* 1 (December 1974), pp. 365–372; and Michael J. Brennan, "The Optimal Number of Securities in a Risky Asset Portfolio When There Are Fixed Costs of Transacting: Theory and Empirical Results," *Journal of Financial and Quantitative Analysis* 10 (September 1975), pp. 483–495 for empirical support of the relationship depicted in Figure 6.6.

[9]All the research has been conducted on portfolios where each security has an equal weight. If there are five securities in the portfolio, each comprises 20 percent of the portfolio. This limits the generalizability of the results somewhat, since other weights are possible and perhaps preferable. An infinite number of other weighting schemes might be employed. These results appear to be reasonably representative of the impact on risk as additional securities are added to portfolios; in a strict sense, however, the results apply only to equally weighted portfolios.

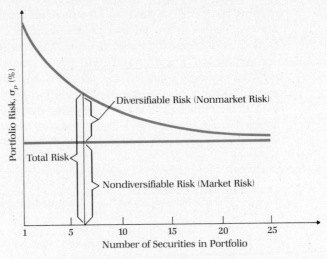

Figure 6.6   The Reduction in Portfolio Risk Due to Diversification.

forming portfolios of 10 to 20 securities. The *total risk* of a security in effect consists of two parts:

Total security risk = nondiversifiable risk + diversifiable risk

Diversifiable risk, or as it is sometimes called, nonmarket or unsystematic risk, can be eliminated by including uncorrelated securities in a portfolio. Nondiversifiable risk, or market or systematic risk, cannot be eliminated no matter how many securities are included in a portfolio. If we assume, as is customary, that investors are risk-averse and hence form portfolios to eliminate risk, it is nondiversifiable risk that is the appropriate measure of financial risk for individual assets. *Diversifiable risk* is that risk which is unique to the firm and can be diversified away in a portfolio. It results from factors such as vulnerability to new competition, lawsuits, and other events unique to a specific firm. Any events that have their primary effect on a specific firm without affecting the returns on firms in general result in unique or diversifiable risk for that firm. Since diversifiable risk is essentially random, its impact can be eliminated by diversification. An undesirable event that causes a reduction in the rate of return for one firm will be offset by the good fortunes of another firm. *Nondiversifiable risk* stems from factors that influence all returns—inflation, oil embargos, recessions, interest rates, and political attitudes toward profits and free enterprise—and tends to affect rates of return on all firms simultaneously. Since these factors affect all firms, investors are always subject to nondiversifiable or market risk.

MULTINATIONAL
DIMENSIONS

International
Diversification

Although nondiversifiable risk cannot be eliminated, the inclusion of foreign securities should reduce the size of the nondiversifiable risk in a portfolio. The reason is that returns on foreign securities are usually dependent on economic and political influences different from those in the United States. If these foreign influences are not closely correlated with events in the United States, it follows that returns on foreign securities will not be closely correlated with returns on U.S. securities. Sometimes there are barriers to holding some desirable foreign securities, but normally sufficient opportunities exist to build a good internationally diversified portfolio. This should reduce but not eliminate nondiversifiable risk; in other words, the horizontal line in Figure 6.6 would be a little bit lower than otherwise if the portfolio includes some foreign securities.

**Beta
as a Measure
of Nondiversifiable
Risk**

Given that nondiversifiable, or market, risk is the relevant measure of investment risk, two questions must be answered. First, do all stocks have the same degree of nondiversifiable risk? No, they do not. An easy way to assess nondiversifiable risk is to determine the variability of the security's returns in relation to market returns. Consider Figure 6.7, where k_M is the return on the market over time and k_C and k_R represent the returns on a conservative stock (k_C) and a risky stock (k_R). As market returns fluctuate, some stocks experience much wider volatility in returns than others. In Figure 6.7, the returns on k_C vary considerably less than the returns on the market, whereas the returns on the risky stock (k_R) vary much more widely than the market.

Second, how do we measure nondiversifiable risk? We can do so by

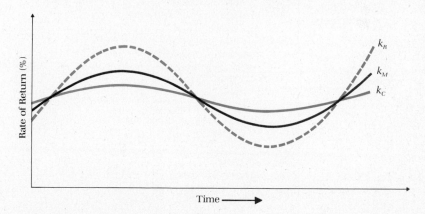

Figure 6.7   Returns for the Market (k_M), a Conservative Stock (k_C), and a Risky Stock (k_R) over Time.

using a measure known as *beta*; although not perfect, beta provides an indication of the extent to which the return on a financial asset varies with the market. Betas can be positive or negative, though rarely are there negative betas for common stocks. The beta for the market, β_M, is by definition equal to 1.0. A security that has a beta equal to 1.0 would exactly follow the movements in the market. (In Figure 6.7, a security with a beta of 1.0 could be plotted *on top* of the line for the market returns, k_M). A security that has a beta of 1.5 fluctuates more than the market. If the market return is expected to increase by 20 percent, the return on a security with a beta of 1.5 would be expected to increase by 30 percent (1.5 × 20%). In contrast, the return on a security with a beta of .80 would be expected to increase by only 16 percent (.80 × 20%) as the market return increases by 20 percent. On the other hand, when the market return is expected to decrease, securities with betas greater than 1.0 would fall more than the market, whereas securities with betas less than 1.0 would fall by less than the market.

Betas for common stocks are calculated and published by Value Line, Wells Fargo Bank, and numerous brokerage firms such as Merrill Lynch Pierce Fenner & Smith. The beta coefficients for some selected firms (in 1984) are presented in Table 6.4. The highest beta, which is the one most responsive to the volatility of the market, is Paine Webber, followed by Financial Corp. of America and Mohawk Data Sciences; the least responsive is Opelika Manufacturing; closely followed by Banc One. Both International Business Machines and U.S. Steel respond exactly like the market—they have betas of 1.00.

TABLE 6.4		
List of Selected Beta Coefficients	**Firm**	**Beta**
	Avon Products	.95
	Banc One	.55
	Caesars World	1.15
	Campbell Soup	.65
	Exxon Corporation	.85
	Federal Express	1.45
	Financial Corp. of America	1.80
	General Motors	1.05
	Honda Motor	.90
	Mohawk Data Sciences	1.65
	Opelika Manufacturing	.35
	Paine Webber	2.00
	Texaco	.95
	Unilever	.60
	U.S. Steel	1.00
	Wisconsin Public Service	.70
	Zale Corp.	.95

SOURCE: *Value Line Investment Survey;* April 20, 1984. Reprinted by permission of the publisher. Copyright Value Line, Inc.

As a rule, betas for individual firms are rarely negative and tend to fall between .60 and 1.70. Note that the betas of foreign securities (Hondo Motor and Unilever) are commonly less than 1.00 because their returns are not closely correlated to events in the United States.

Calculation of Beta

Although financial managers may not have to calculate beta themselves, they should understand the procedures involved. The market model developed by William F. Sharpe[10] provides the appropriate means of measuring nondiversifiable risk, as calculated by beta, β. The model is based on a linear relationship between the returns of any security j, k_j, and the returns on the market, k_M:

$$k_j = \alpha_j + \beta_j k_M + e_j \tag{6.5}$$

where k_j = the rate of return on the jth security
α_j = an intercept, alpha
β_j = a regression coefficient, beta, which is the slope of a fitted regression line
k_M = the rate of return on the market portfolio
e_j = a random error term

Beta is the measure of nondiversifiable risk that we are seeking, as it reflects the volatility of returns of the jth security relative to the market. It should be noted for later use that β_j is:

$$\beta_j = \frac{COV(k_j,k_M)}{\sigma_M^2} = \frac{\rho_{jM}\sigma_j\sigma_M}{\sigma_M^2} = \frac{\rho_{jM}\sigma_j}{\sigma_M} \tag{6.6}$$

where $COV(k_j,k_M)$ = the covariance between the returns on the jth security and the returns on the market portfolio, M

$$= \frac{\sum\limits_{t=1}^{n} (k_{j,t}-\overline{k}_j)\ (k_{M,t}-\overline{k}_M)}{n-1}$$

σ_M^2 = the variance of returns on the market portfolio
σ_j = the standard deviation of returns on the jth security
σ_M = the standard deviation of returns on the market portfolio
ρ_{jM} = the correlation coefficient between the returns on the jth security and the returns on the market portfolio

[10]William F. Sharpe, "A Simplified Model for Portfolio Analysis," *Management Science* 9 (January 1963), pp. 277–293.

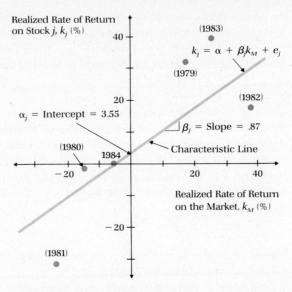

Figure 6.8   Realized Rates of Return for Stock j and the Market M, 1979–1984.
Note: Each dot on the scatter diagram represents the market return–stock return coordinate for the year indicated in parens.

Beta is calculated by dividing (1) the covariance between the returns on the jth security and the returns on the market portfolio by (2) the variance of returns on the market portfolio, σ_M^2. Given that covariance and correlation are related by $COV(k_j, k_M) = \rho_{jM}\sigma_j\sigma_M$, we can also express β_j as a function of the correlation coefficient, ρ_{jM}, so that $\beta_j = \frac{\rho_{jM}\sigma_j\sigma_M}{\sigma_M^2}$. Note from the above expression that the calculated beta largely depends on the strength of the correlation between the security's and the market returns.

An example will help us understand what β_j is and how to calculate it. Figure 6.8 and Table 6.5 present the returns for stock j and the market (M) for the years 1979–1984.[11] The returns were calculated in the manner indicated by Equation 6.1. In Figure 6.8, we see there is a tendency for the returns on stock j to be positive when the returns on the market are positive, and for the returns on the stock to be negative when the returns on the market are negative. Without any calculation, inspection of Figure 6.8 should suggest two points:

1. Stock j appears to exhibit some nondiversifiable risk to the extent that the returns on the stock tend to move with the market.

---

[11]Betas are generally estimated using monthly or weekly data with, normally, 50 to 75 observations. We use yearly data and only 6 observations for simplicity in order to illustrate the calculations.

Year	k_j (Stock j)	k_M (Market)	$k_j \times k_M$	$k_M{}^2$
1979	29.96%	17.69%	529.9924	312.9361
1980	− 1.36	−15.62	21.2432	243.9844
1981	−32.71	−25.12	821.6752	631.0144
1982	17.10	38.45	657.4950	1478.4025
1983	39.44	26.35	1039.2440	694.3225
1984	0.55	− 5.21	− 2.8655	27.1441
Totals	52.98%	36.54%	3066.7843	3387.8040

Mean: $\bar{k}_j = 8.83$ $\bar{k}_M = 6.09$

Beta: $\beta_j = \dfrac{COV(k_j, k_M)}{\sigma_M{}^2} = \dfrac{\displaystyle\sum_{i=1}^{n} k_j k_M - n(\bar{k}_j)(\bar{k}_M)}{\displaystyle\sum_{i=1}^{n} k_M{}^2 - n(\bar{k}_M)^2} = \dfrac{3066.7843 - (6)(8.83)(6.09)}{3387.8040 - 6(6.09)^2}$

$= \dfrac{3066.7843 - 322.6482}{3387.8040 - 222.5286} = \dfrac{2744.1361}{3165.2754} = .86695 \approx .87.$

Alpha: $\alpha_j = \bar{k}_j - \beta_j \bar{k}_M = 8.83\% - (.86695)(6.09\%) = 8.83\% - 5.28\% = 3.55\%$

Note: Many small calculators have functions for use in calculating the regression coefficients, β_j and α_j, directly.

2. This co-movement with the market indicates a positive correlation between the returns for the stock and the returns for the market. However, since all the dots in Figure 6.8 cannot be joined by a single straight line, we know the correlation between the two rates of return has to be less than perfect.

To calculate β_j, we must solve a least squares regression equation (see Appendix 4A for technical details of regression analysis). As identified in Figure 6.8, the graphic depiction of the least squares line is commonly called the *characteristic line*. Equation 6.6 specified that in order to calculate the slope, β_j, of the characteristic or regression line, we must calculate the covariance between the returns for stock j and for the market, and the variance ($\sigma_M{}^2$) of the market portfolio returns. In Table 6.5, using the computational procedure presented in Appendix 4A, the measure of nondiversifiable risk of .87 for stock j is calculated.[12] Since stock j has a beta of .87, we can conclude it has slightly less volatility that the market. If the market return goes up 10 percent, stock j's returns would be expected to increase 8.7 percent (10% × .87). If the returns on

---

[12]Other formulas are available for use in calculating beta, but the formula applied in Table 6.5 and presented in Appendix 4A is the most straightforward and is therefore emphasized throughout this text.

the market fall by 15 percent, stock j's returns would be expected to decrease by 13.05 percent (15% × .87).

For completeness, we also compute the value for the intercept term, α_j, in Table 6.5. As shown, the intercept is equal to 3.55 percent; it represents stock j's return when the market return, k_M, is zero. Note on the characteristic line relating the rate of return of stock j to the rate of return on the market, shown in Figure 6.8, the intercept on the vertical axis of 3.55 percent is α_j and the slope of the line, β_j, is .87.[13] The financial manager's primary concern would of course center on beta, since it measures the nondiversifiable (relevant) risk.

The Relationship Between Risk and Return: CAPM

Once a manager has measured the nondiversifiable risk and the expected level of return associated with a decision alternative, he or she must assess the expected return relative to the risk. If the expected return is inadequate given the risk, the proposal should be rejected; if the return is equal to or greater than that required for the given level of risk, it may be accepted. By using beta as the appropriate measure of nondiversifiable risk, we can evaluate its relationship with return. The capital asset pricing model (CAPM) enables us to specify the risk-return relationship using the measures presented earlier in the chapter.

The Capital Asset Pricing Model (CAPM)

The *capital asset pricing model, CAPM*, allows us to specify the relationship between risk and return, when rates of return are measured as noted earlier and the relevant measure of nondiversifiable risk is beta. The CAPM is the fundamental financial theory specifying the relationship that is expected to hold between rates of return and risk.[14] It is important to the financial manager, since it provides a mechanism for assessing expected returns relative to the return required for (or appropriate to) a given level of risk. The financial manager should take only those actions that are expected to provide returns equal to or greater than those required for a given level of risk. The capital asset pricing

---

[13]The beta specified by Equation 6.6 and computed in Table 6.5 is the "market model" beta. Betas can also be estimated by regressing the risk premium, or "excess returns," of a given stock against the "excess returns" of the market. Beta calculated by employing excess returns may differ from the market model beta if the risk-free rate of return, R_F, has shifted during the period.

[14]Other theories on the relationship between risk and return are emerging and have been given a great deal of attention in the financial literature. Two key ones are the option pricing model (OPM) and the arbitrage pricing theory (APT). The original work on OPM was presented by Fischer Black and Myron Scholes, "The Pricing of Options and Corporate Liabilities," *Journal of Political Economy* 81 (May–June 1973), pp. 637–654. A discussion of OPM is presented in Appendix 23A of this text. The newer APT was formulated by Stephen A. Ross, "The Arbitrage Theory of Capital Asset Pricing," *Journal of Economic Theory* 13 (December 1976), pp. 341–360, and empirically investigated by Richard Roll and Stephen A. Ross, "Empirical Investigation of the Arbitrage Pricing Theory," *Journal of Finance* 35 (December 1980), pp. 1073–1103.

model specifies a linear relationship between expected risk and expected return:

$$k_j = R_F + \beta_j \times (k_M - R_F) \qquad (6.7)$$

where k_j = the required or expected rate of return on the jth security

R_F = the risk-free rate, generally measured by the rate on 90-day U.S. Treasury bills

β_j = the beta coefficient for the jth security

k_M = the required or expected rate of return on the market portfolio

$(k_M - R_F)$ = the market risk premium, or the risk premium required for the average stock by investors

$\beta_j \times (k_M - R_F)$ = the risk premium for the jth security

The linear relationship specified in the CAPM (Equation 6.7) implies that the required return on any security is equal to the sum of the risk-free rate (the price of time) and a risk premium (the price of risk). Thus, for a risky stock Q, if R_F is 7 percent, β_Q is 1.5, and k_M is 11 percent, the required rate of return is:

$$
\begin{aligned}
k_Q &= R_F + \beta_Q \times (k_M - R_F) \\
&= 7\% + 1.5 \times (11\% - 7\%) \\
&= 7\% + 6\% \\
&= 13\%
\end{aligned}
$$

It should be clear that, other things being equal, the higher the beta, the greater the required return, and vice versa.

The Security Market Line (SML)

Graphically, the CAPM is called the *security market line (SML)*,[15] which shows the required returns, k_j, associated with various degrees of nondiversifiable risk as measured by β_j. Figure 6.9 depicts the SML associated with the basic data presented above. It can be seen that the risk-free rate (7 percent) is associated with a beta of zero; at a beta of 1.0, we get the market return of 11 percent and a market risk premium of 4 percent $(k_M - R_F = 11\% - 7\%)$; and stock Q, with a beta of 1.5, has a risk premium of 6 percent $[1.5 \times (11\% - 7\%)]$ and a required return of 13 percent. The security market line is a straight line reflecting a direct

---

[15]Although the security market line was developed as a single time period model, it is frequently applied to multiperiod settings under certain assumptions. See Eugene F. Fama, "Multiperiod Consumption-Investment Decisions," *American Economic Review* 60 (March 1970), pp. 163–174; and Eugene F. Fama, "Risk-Adjusted Discount Rates and Capital Budgeting Under Uncertainty," *Journal of Financial Economics* 5 (August 1977), pp. 3–24.

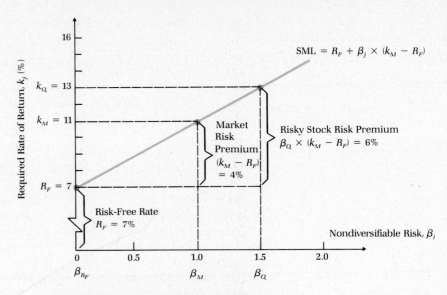

Figure 6.9 The Security Market Line (SML).

relationship between risk and return. It can be utilized to illustrate the potential impact of changes in risk aversion, changes in inflation expectations, and changes in beta on the risk-return structure specified by the CAPM.

Changes in Risk Aversion. The slope of the security market line reflects the extent to which investors are averse to risk. The steeper the slope of the SML, the greater the risk aversion. Another way to state this relationship is to say that the more risk-averse investors are, the greater the risk premium required. If investors in general were not risk-averse, the SML would be horizontal and all risky assets would provide the same return as R_F. However, since most investors are risk-averse, the security market line generally slopes upward, as shown in Figures 6.9 and 6.10.

The SML does not always maintain the same slope. As the economy begins to boom, as interest rates fall, and so on, investors become, at the margin, less risk-averse. Figure 6.10 illustrates a situation where risk aversion has decreased. The market risk premium, $k_M - R_F$, had been equal to 4 percent; however, because of events that caused investors to become less risk-averse, the SML shifts downward from SML_1 to SML_2. The increased willingness of investors to invest in risky assets reduces the rate of return required as compensation for a given level of risk. This reduction results from the fact that the price of these assets rises due to their increased demand. A rising price without a change in expected earnings will, of course, result in a lower rate of return.

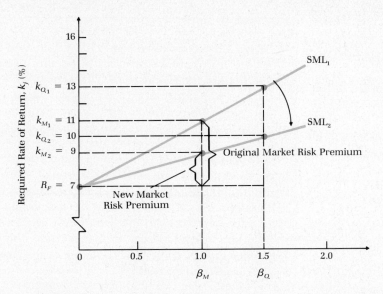

Figure 6.10 Shift in the Security Market Line (SML) Caused by a Decrease in Risk Aversion.

In Figure 6.10, it can be seen that at a beta of 1.0, the market risk premium associated with SML_1 had been 4 percent ($k_M - R_F = 11\% - 7\% = 4\%$); the reduction in risk aversion to SML_2 decreased the market risk premium to 2 percent. Likewise, the required rate of return for a risky stock with a beta of 1.5 had been 13 percent (7% R_F + 6% risk premium) prior to the decrease in risk aversion; because of the shift in SML caused by decreased risk aversion, the required rate of return fell to 10 percent:

$$
\begin{aligned}
k_Q &= R_F + \beta_Q \times (k_M - R_F) \\
&= 7\% + 1.5 \times (9\% - 7\%) \\
&= 7\% + 3\% \\
&= 10\%
\end{aligned}
$$

Changes in Inflation Expectations.   Changing inflationary expectations can also cause the SML to shift. However, it may maintain its slope while shifting up or down parallel to the original SML as a result of changes in R_F. The value of R_F reflects the price of money (or the price of time) to the riskless borrower, based on certain expectations about interest rates. As expectations of increased (decreased) inflation develop, the value of R_F will rise (fall), causing an upward (downward) shift in the SML.

The risk-free rate can be viewed as consisting of two components—(1) the real or inflation-free rate of return, and (2) the anticipated rate of inflation. Thus, if the inflation-free rate of return is 3 percent and the anticipated rate of inflation is 4 percent, the initial risk-free rate is 7

**MULTINATIONAL
DIMENSIONS**

*Exchange Rates
and Risk Aversion*

In recent years foreign investors have increased their trading in U.S. securities and have become an important class of investor. Their perceptions of the riskiness of U.S. securities are determined in part by factors not important to domestic investors. In particular, the relative desirability of holding U.S. securities varies over time with investors' perception of foreign exchange rate risk, as expressed by the international Fisher effect (see Chapter 2). From the perspective of foreign investors, the expected rate of return on U.S. securities depends not only on the dollar rate of return as seen by U.S. investors, but also on the rate of exchange that will exist when they sell their U.S. securities and convert the dollar proceeds into their local currency. Thus, to the extent that foreign investors shift their perceptions about foreign exchange risk, and thereby shift their portfolios of U.S. securities, the slope of the security market line in Figure 6.10 will also change.

percent. If, as a result of various economic developments, the anticipated rate of inflation rose to 7 percent, the new risk-free rate would rise to 10 percent (3% inflation-free rate + 7% anticipated rate of inflation). Assuming that the risk disposition of investors is not affected by the new data, an upward and parallel shift in the SML would result from the increased inflationary expectation.

The shift in the SML (from SML_1 to SML_2) resulting from the increased inflation expectation is depicted graphically in Figure 6.11. Careful examination of the figure indicates that changes in R_F do not affect market or security risk premiums, since the required return on the market portfolio, k_M, changes by an amount equal to the change in R_F. For example, in Figure 6.11, as R_F goes from 7 percent to 10 percent, k_M goes from 11 percent to 14 percent. The net effect is that the market risk premium, $k_M - R_F$, remains at 4 percent. Likewise, for a security with a beta of 1.5, the risk premium would remain at its original level, while the required return will increase from 13 percent to 16 percent. The increase in the risk-free rate of 3 percent causes the required return to increase by 3 percent.

Changes in Beta. Not only may the SML shift over time, but the nondiversifiable risk of the firm as measured by beta may also change. Beta may change due to management decisions to expand into a new market, to restructure debt, or to merge with another firm. In addition, beta may change as a result of some action that is not entirely under the control of the firm. Accidents, such as the blowout at General Public

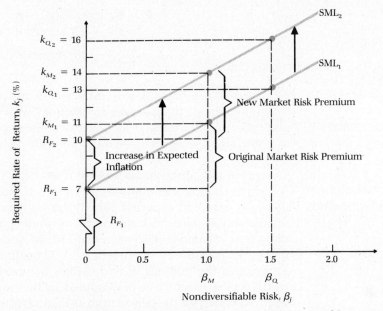

Figure 6.11 Shift in the Security Market Line (SML) Caused by an Increase in Expected Inflation.

Utilities' Three Mile Island nuclear plant, or the crash of a McDonnell Douglas DC-10 that caused the FAA temporarily to revoke the plane's certification, may affect the firm's beta. Also, increased competition in the industry, the expiration of patents, or changes in management personnel may cause investors to reassess the riskiness of a firm. If, as a result of collective action by investors, beta for the firm changes, the required rate of return will also change. Suppose, for example, that because of increased competition in the computer industry spearheaded by International Business Machines (IBM) Corporation, the riskiness of Plug-In Computers, Inc., a small computer hardware manufacturer, is perceived by investors to have increased. Its previous beta had been 1.75; because of the increased competition, investors now believe the appropriate beta is 2.5. With R_F at 7 percent and k_M at 11 percent, the original required rate of return demanded by investors for Plug-In was:

$$k_1 = R_F + \beta_1 \times (k_M - R_F)$$
$$= 7\% + 1.75 \times (11\% - 7\%)$$
$$= 7\% + 7\%$$
$$= 14\%$$

Because of investors' revised expectations, the revised beta of 2.5 leads to an increase in the required rate of return to 17 percent:

$$k_2 = R_F + \beta_2 \times (k_M - R_F)$$
$$= 7\% + 2.5 \times (11\% - 7\%)$$
$$= 7\% + 10\%$$
$$= 17\%$$

The increased competition is expected to cause the required rate of return to increase by 3 percent. In Chapter 7 we will demonstrate that all else remaining unchanged, an increase in the required return will result in a decline in share price—clearly an undesirable outcome.

Empirical Risk-Return Relationships

The preceding discussions suggest that expected risk, β, should be linearly related to the required rate of return. However, since the entire theory is based on expected conditions, we need to assess the *historic* relationship between risk and return to validate the theory. Obviously, if there is no relationship between realized risk and return, our confidence in β as the measure of investment risk will be diminished. Tables 6.6 and 6.7 present the findings of two studies in which historical betas and realized rates of return were examined. In Table 6.6, individual securities were examined for the period from 1945 to 1970. In virtually all cases, the actual risk-return relationship makes sense. Consumer product companies like Swift, Bayside Cigars, and American Snuff were all less risky than the market portfolio (represented by the NYSE index). On the other hand, steel, automobiles, and electronics were riskier. The linearity of the relationship (if the data are plotted) appears reasonable, and there is a clear positive tradeoff between risk and return.

In Table 6.7, the risk-return results for portfolio deciles (where a decile is equal to one-tenth of the total securities in the study) are presented. Again, the relationships make sense. More risky portfolios tended to have higher returns than less risky portfolios. As was the case for individual securities, the relationship (if plotted) is approximately linear, and the

---

TABLE 6.6
Rates of Return and Betas for Selected Companies (1945–1970)

Company	Average Annual Rate of Return (%)	Standard Deviation of Return (%)	Beta
City Investing	17.4%	11.09%	1.67
Radio Corporation of America	11.4	8.30	1.35
Chrysler Corporation	7.0	7.73	1.21
Continental Steel	11.9	7.50	1.12
NYSE Index	8.3	3.73	1.00
Swift	5.7	5.89	.81
Bayside Cigars	5.4	7.26	.71
American Snuff	6.5	4.77	.54
Homestake Mining	4.0	6.55	.24

SOURCE: Franco Modigliani and Gerald A. Pogue, "An Introduction to Risk and Return," *Financial Analysts Journal* 30 (March–April 1974), pp. 68–80.

TABLE 6.7
Rates of Return and
Betas for New York
Stock Exchange
Companies (1931–1967)

Risk Level	Decile	Average Annual Rate of Return (%)	Beta
Highest	10	22.67%	1.42
	9	20.45	1.18
	8	20.26	1.14
	7	21.77	1.24
Middle	6	18.49	1.06
	5	19.13	.98
	4	18.88	1.00
	3	14.99	.76
	2	14.63	.65
Lowest	1	11.58	.58

SOURCE: William F. Sharpe and Guy M. Cooper, "Risk-Return Classes of New York Stock Exchange Common Stocks," *Financial Analysts Journal* 28 (March–April 1972), pp. 46–54.

risk-return tradeoff is positive. We can conclude, therefore, that realized risk and return behavior are approximately as indicated by the security market line (SML), and as such, beta is a relevant measure of investment risk.

A Word
of Caution

A word of caution about betas and the capital asset pricing model (CAPM) is in order. First, beta is generally calculated from historical data, whereas the theory is stated in terms of required (or expected) returns. There is an approximately linear relationship between historic betas and realized returns, but it should be obvious that betas derived from past data are not necessarily exact estimates of expected betas. Analysts and other users of betas commonly make subjective adjustments to historically determined betas to reflect their expectations of the future when such expectations differ from the actual risk-return behavior of the past. Also, empirical evidence indicates that betas for individual securities are not stable from one time period to the next, although betas for portfolios of 10 to 20 securities or more tend to be relatively stable from period to period. Finally, empirical evidence suggests that, in addition to beta, the standard deviation of historic returns is also related to realized rates of return. The implication of these caveats is clear; i.e., the SML relationship is not as precise as suggested by theory. Managers must exercise care and understand the strengths and weaknesses of employing beta as a measure of investment risk.

SUMMARY

The return on an investment is the actual cash flow, often stated as an annual rate of return, received by the investor over a specified period of time. Because some risk, or uncertainty, is present in nearly all financial decisions, the financial manager must attempt to measure and consider risk when making decisions. Measures of risk and return can be derived from probability distributions. Risk is related to the variability of expected returns and for a single asset can be measured using the range, standard deviation, or coefficient of variation.

The linear relationship between two variables can be measured statistically using the correlation coefficient, which ranges between -1.0 for perfect negative correlation and $+1.0$ for perfect positive correlation. Portfolios of securities having less than perfect positive return correlation will provide for reduced risk—often without significantly affecting the level of return. The total risk of a portfolio is made up of nondiversifiable and diversifiable risk. Diversifiable risk can be eliminated through diversification; therefore it is the nondiversifiable risk that is of major concern to the financial manager. Nondiversifiable risk for a given security j is measured by its beta, β_j, which is an index of the volatility of the security's return relative to the market. Stocks can have positive or negative betas; in absolute terms, stocks with betas of greater than 1.0 are more volatile than the market, and stocks with betas of less than 1.0 are less volatile than the market.

The capital asset pricing model (CAPM), using beta as a measure of risk, links risk and return. For each beta, a unique required return exists such that a linear relationship between risk and return results. Graphically, this relationship is called the security market line (SML). An understanding of the direct relationship between risk and return, as well as the potential impact of changes in risk aversion, changes in inflation expectations, and changes in beta on the required return, are necessary for effective decision making.

QUESTIONS	

6.1. Define the following terms; use graphs or equations where appropriate:
  a. Return.
  b. Probability distribution.
  c. Expected value or mean.
  d. Standard deviation.
  e. Coefficient of variation.
  f. Normal distribution.
  g. Correlation coefficient.
  h. Risk aversion.
  i. Total security risk.
  j. Nondiversifiable (market) risk.
  k. Diversifiable (nonmarket) risk.
  l. Beta coefficient.
  m. Capital asset pricing model (CAPM).
  n. Security market line (SML).
  o. Risk premium.
  p. Risk-return tradeoff.

6.2. Probability distributions indicate the spread or riskiness of expected security returns. What would be the shape of the probability distribution for a security having:

    a. Completely certain returns?

    b. Completely uncertain returns?

6.3. An investor is considering the purchase of one security. (*Note:* the security will be held in isolation, not as part of a portfolio.) Security A has an expected return of 15 percent and a standard deviation of 10 percent; security B has an expected return of 25 percent and a standard deviation of 17 percent. If the investor is risk-averse, which security should he or she choose?

6.4. Investments whose returns are less than perfectly positively correlated $(\rho_{xy} \neq +1.0)$ are, other things being equal, desirable investments. Explain this idea.

6.5. Differentiate between nondiversifiable and diversifiable risk. In answering, be sure to explain:

    a. What factors cause the two types of risk.

    b. Whether or not and how each type of risk can be eliminated.

    c. How to measure nondiversifiable risk.

    d. Why the returns on securities are generally positively correlated.

6.6. Explain in detail how beta is calculated and the relationship of correlation to covariance.

6.7. Under what condition would the standard deviation of an individual asset's rate of return be an appropriate measure of its risk?

6.8. Other things being equal, what would be the effect on beta for the Carter Clothes Company if:

    a. The correlation between the rate of return on Carter and the market returns decreased?

    b. The standard deviation of the market returns increased?

    c. The standard deviation of the rate of return on Carter Clothes Company's stock increased?

6.9. Briefly describe the capital asset pricing model (CAPM) and explain how it provides a link between nondiversifiable risk and the expected return on a security. Differentiate between the market risk premium and a security's risk premium.

6.10. Draw the security market line on the appropriate set of axes; label R_F, β_M, k_M, and the market risk premium.

    a. Discuss the relationship reflected by the SML and explain its link to CAPM.

    b. Depict security A with beta, β_A, less than 1.0, on the security market line, and note its required return, k_A, on the graph.

    c. Compare the risk-return behavior of security A to the risk and return of the market and describe the basic tradeoff reflected in these data.

6.11. Other things being equal, what would be the effect on the required rate of return and the risk premium for a company whose stock has a beta less than 1.0 if:

 a. Investors in general decide that they have become more risk-averse.

 b. Investors in general increase their expectations concerning future rates of inflation.

 c. Investors decide that nondiversifiable risk, β, has increased.

6.12. Briefly discuss the empirical findings on the relationship between risk and return. In spite of these findings, what difficulties arise when we use historic betas on an *expected* basis? Explain.

PROBLEMS

6.1. *HISTORICAL RETURNS AND RISK.* Nordic Industries common stock has had the following prices and dividends:

Time Period	Common Stock Price	Dividends Paid per Share
0	$40	$—
1	42	1
2	46	1
3	41	1
4	38	2
5	36	2
6	40	2

 a. Find the individual rates of return for each of the six periods.

 b. Calculate the mean (or expected) return, the standard deviation, and the coefficient of variation using the six return figures computed in (a).

6.2. *PROBABILITY DISTRIBUTIONS.* Stocks A, B, and C have the following probability distributions of expected returns:

	A		B		C	
i	Pr_i	k_i	Pr_i	k_i	Pr_i	k_i
1	.1	40%	.1	40%	.4	35%
2	.2	20	.2	10	.3	10
3	.4	10	.4	0	.3	−20
4	.2	0	.2	− 5		
5	.1	−20	.1	−10		

 a. Calculate the expected rate of return, $\bar{k}$, for each of the three stocks. Which provides the largest expected return?

b. Find the standard deviation and coefficient of variation of the expected returns for stocks A, B, and C.

c. Which stock is most risky when held in isolation—not in a portfolio? Explain your answer.

6.3. *AREA UNDER A PROBABILITY DISTRIBUTION.* Helen Parker is considering investing in one of two stocks, X or Y. She has estimated the expected return to be 24 percent for X and 14 percent for Y. The standard deviation for X is 20 percent; it is 10 percent for Y. She has concluded that the probability distribution of expected returns is approximately normal. (*Hint:* A review of footnote 5 would be helpful in working this problem.)

a. What is the probability that the expected returns for stock X and for stock Y are below zero?

b. What is the probability that the expected returns for each stock are equal to or greater than 20 percent?

c. Between 10 percent and 30 percent?

6.4. *RETURNS, STANDARD DEVIATION, AND BETA.* The following probabilities and associated returns for stock R and the market have been estimated as follows:

		Rate of Return	
i	Pr_i	Stock R	Market
1	.4	35%	20%
2	.2	25	15
3	.2	15	10
4	.2	5	0

a. Determine the expected return and standard deviation of returns for stock R and the market.

b. If the expected correlation between the returns from R and the market returns is +.46, what is stock R's beta? What can we say about the riskiness of stock R?

6.5. *MEASUREMENT OF RISK.* Karen Mann is considering investing in one of three securities—A, B, or C. She has estimated the returns under the assumptions of "good," "normal," and "bad" economic climates. A summary of her estimates, along with estimated correlation coefficients, ρ, indicating how the returns on the three securities are correlated with the market returns, follows:

		Rate of Return		
Economic Climate	Probability (Pr_i)	A	B	C
Good	.2	40%	50%	55%
Normal	.5	0	5	25
Bad	.3	− 10	− 5	− 15
Correlation coefficient, ρ		+.70	+.55	+.80

  a. Calculate the expected rate of return for each of the three securities and rank them according to expected returns.

  b. Calculate the standard deviation, σ, and coefficient of variation, CV, for each security and rank them using each of these measures.

  c. Rank the securities in terms of nondiversifiable risk by calculating their beta coefficients. (*Hint:* Even though σ_M is not given, remember that it will be the same for all three securities and hence does not affect their ranking.)

  d. On the basis of the information on expected return and risk, which security should Karen select? What assumption(s) do you have to make in arriving at this decision?

6.6. *EQUIVALENCE OF NONDIVERSIFIABLE RISK.* You are given the following information on two securities, R and S.

	Security R		Security S	
i	Pr_i	k_i	Pr_i	k_i
1	.4	40%	.3	65%
2	.4	10	.4	15
3	.2	−10	.3	−15
	$\rho_{RM} = +.50$			

  a. Calculate the expected return and standard deviation of returns for each security.

  b. What must the value of ρ_{SM} be to make the two securities equally risky in terms of their beta coefficients?

6.7. *BETA AND THE MARKET'S RISK.* New England Tire Company has a beta coefficient of 1.65, and the correlation between its returns and the market is +.60. The distribution of rates of return for New England Tire is:

i	Pr_i	Returns for New England Tire
1	.1	30%
2	.4	15
3	.3	0
4	.2	−5

a. What is the expected rate of return and the standard deviation of returns for New England Tire?

b. What standard deviation of the market rate of return is implied by the data for New England Tire?

6.8. **BETA AND REQUIRED RETURN.** Charles Hartman wishes to use the capital asset pricing model to estimate the required return associated with each of five investment alternatives. The key data needed to perform the analysis are given below.

Investment Alternative	Expected Rate of Return (%)	Beta Value
Risk-free asset	9	0
Market portfolio	14	1.00
A	—	1.50
B	—	.75
C	—	2.00
D	—	− .50
E	—	0

a. Calculate the required return associated with each of the alternatives.

b. Draw the security market line (SML) and locate each of the alternatives on it.

c. Discuss the risk-return tradeoff associated with each alternative, relative to the risk-free asset and the market portfolio.

6.9. **PORTFOLIO BETA AND SML.** The Spartan Mutual Fund has all its assets invested in six stocks, as follows:

Stock	Investment ($ Millions)	Stock Beta Coefficient
A	$10	.8
B	20	1.1
C	30	1.5
D	10	.9
E	20	.7
F	10	1.2

The current risk-free rate is 7 percent, and the expected market return, k_M, for the next period has the following probability distribution:

i	Pr_i	Market Return (k_M)
1	.1	17%
2	.3	16
3	.3	12
4	.2	10
5	.1	9

a. What is the beta coefficient for the Spartan Mutual Fund? (*Hint:* Take the weighted average of the individual security beta coefficients.)

b. What is the expected return on the market, $\bar{k}_M$?

c. Calculate the security market line that specifies the tradeoff between expected risk and expected return. What is the expected return for the Spartan Mutual Fund?

d. Spartan Mutual is considering adding $20 million of one of two new stocks to the portfolio. One security, G, has a beta coefficient of .5; the other security, H, has a beta of 1.7.

   (1) If both securities' returns are depicted by the security market line calculated in (c), what is the expected return on both G and H?

   (2) What is the portfolio beta and expected portfolio return if security G or H (but not *both*) is added to the Spartan Mutual Fund? (*Hint:* The portfolio beta is 1.0 if stock G is added.)

6.10. *GRAPHIC DETERMINATION OF BETA AND ALPHA.* Gary Furniture and the market earned the following returns during the period 1978–1984:

Year	Returns on Gary Furniture (k_j)	Returns on the Market (k_M)
1978	14.5%	7.4%
1979	− 2.7	1.3
1980	5.2	3.9
1981	19.4	12.4
1982	16.1	21.7
1983	−25.1	−14.6
1984	20.9	6.4

a. Calculate the mean rate of return for Gary Furniture and the market over the 7-year period.

b. Graphically estimate the beta and alpha for the characteristic line relating the returns of Gary Furniture to the returns on the market.

6.11. **CALCULATION OF BETA AND ALPHA.** You are given the following information about the returns on Sharon Industries stock, k_S, and the market, k_M.

Year	Returns on Sharon (k_S)	Returns on the Market (k_M)
1979	7%	2%
1980	10	8
1981	19	16
1982	16	10
1983	12	11
1984	20	13

a. Calculate the mean and standard deviation of returns for Sharon Industries and the market and the covariance between them. (*Hint:* $\sigma_M = 5.1768$ and $COV(k_S,k_M) = 22.0$.)

b. What are beta and alpha for the characteristic line relating the returns of Sharon Industries to the returns on the market? Is Sharon Industries more or less risky than the market?

c. Suppose the regression line calculated in (b) had been downward sloping and the beta coefficient had been negative. What would this imply about (1) the relative riskiness of Sharon Industries, (2) its correlation with k_M, and (3) its probable risk premium?

6.12. **CHANGES IN THE SML OR BETA.** Suppose $R_F = 8$ percent, $k_M = 12$ percent, and the beta for stock G, β_G, = 1.3.

a. What is k_G, the required return on stock G?

b. Now assume R_F remains constant at 8 percent, but k_M (1) increases to 14 percent, or (2) falls to 10 percent. How will this affect k_G? (*Note:* The slope of the SML does not remain constant.)

c. Now suppose R_F (1) increases to 9 percent, or (2) decreases to 6 percent. How does this affect k_M and k_G? (*Note:* The slope of the SML remains constant.)

d. Now assume that R_F remains at 8 percent and k_M is 12 percent, but β_G (1) increases to 1.6, or (2) falls to .8. How does this affect k_G?

SELECTED REFERENCES

Alexander, Gordon J., and P. George Benson. "More on Beta as a Random Coefficient." *Journal of Financial and Quantitative Analysis* 17 (March 1982), pp. 27–36.

Ayres, Herbert F., and John Y. Barry. "Prologue to a Unified Portfolio Theory." *Journal of Finance* 37 (May 1982), pp. 625–635.

Black, Fischer, Michael C. Jensen, and Myron S. Scholes. "The Capital Asset Pricing Model: Some Empirical Tests." In *Studies in the Theory of Capital Markets*, Michael C. Jensen, ed. New York: Praeger, 1972.

———, and Myron Scholes. "The Pricing of Options and Corporate Liabilities." *Journal of Political Economy* 81 (May–June 1973), pp. 637–654.

Blume, Marshall E. "Betas and Their Regression Tendencies." *Journal of Finance* 30 (June 1975), pp. 785–796.

———, and Irwin Friend. "A New Look at the Capital Asset Pricing Model." *Journal of Finance* 28 (March 1973), pp. 19–33.

Brennan, Michael J. "The Optimal Number of Securities in a Risky Asset Portfolio When There Are Fixed Costs of Transacting: Theory and Empirical Results." *Journal of Financial and Quantitiative Analysis* 10 (September 1975), pp. 483–495.

Chen, Son-Nan. "An Examination of Risk-Return Relationship in Bull and Bear Markets Using Time-Varying Betas." *Journal of Financial and Quantitative Analysis* 17 (June 1982), pp. 265–286.

Dybvig, Philip H., and Jonathan E. Ingersoll, Jr. "Mean-Variance Theory in Complete Markets." *Journal of Business* 55 (April 1982), pp. 233–251.

Evans, Jack, and Stephen H. Archer. "Diversification and the Reduction of Dispersion: An Empirical Analysis." *Journal of Finance* 23 (December 1968), pp. 761–767.

Fama, Eugene F. "Efficient Capital Markets: A Review of Theory and Empirical Work." *Journal of Finance* 25 (May 1970), pp. 383–417.

———, "Multiperiod Consumption-Investment Decisions," *American Economic Review* 60 (March 1970), pp. 163–174.

———. "Risk-Adjusted Discount Rates and Capital Budgeting Under Uncertainty." *Journal of Financial Economics* 5 (August 1977), pp. 3–24.

———, and James D. MacBeth. "Risk, Return, and Equilibrium: Empirical Tests." *Journal of Political Economy* 81 (May–June 1973), pp. 607–636.

———, and Merton H. Miller. *The Theory of Finance*. New York: Holt, Rinehart and Winston, 1972.

Firth, Michael. "The Relationship Between Stock Market Returns and Rates of Inflation." *Journal of Finance* 34 (June 1979), pp. 743–749.

Foster, George. "Asset Pricing Models: Further Tests." *Journal of Financial and Quantitative Analysis* 13 (March 1978), pp. 39–54.

Gehr, Adam K., Jr. "Risk and Return." *Journal of Finance* 34 (September 1979), pp. 1027–1030.

Gilster, John E., Jr. "Capital Market Equilibrium with Divergent Investment Horizon Length Assumptions." *Journal of Financial and Quantitative Analysis* 18 (June 1983), pp. 257–268.

Haugen, Robert A., and James A. Heins. "Risk and the Rate of Return on Financial Assets." *Journal of Financial and Quantitative Analysis* 10 (December 1975), pp. 775–784.

Jensen, Michael C. "Capital Markets: Theory and Evidence." *Bell Journal of Economics and Management Science* 3 (autumn 1972), pp. 357–398.

Johnson, K. H., and D. S. Shannon. "A Note on Diversification and the Reduction of Dispersion." *Journal of Financial Economics* 1 (December 1974), pp. 365–372.

Klemkosky, Robert C., and Kwang W. Jun. "The Monetary Impact of Return Variability and Market Risk Premia." *Journal of Financial and Quantitative*

Analysis 17 (December 1982), pp. 663–681.

Klemkosky, Robert C., and John D. Martin. "The Adjustment of Beta Forecasts." *Journal of Finance* 30 (September 1975), pp. 1123–1128.

Kroll, Yoram, Haim Levy, and Harry M. Markowitz. "Mean-Variance Versus Direct Utility Maximization." *Journal of Finance* 39 (March 1984), pp. 47–61.

Lintner, John. "The Market Price of Risk, Size of Market and Investor's Risk Aversion." *Review of Economics and Statistics* 52 (February 1970), pp. 87–99.

———. "Security Prices, Risk and Maximal Gains from Diversification." *Journal of Finance* 20 (December 1965), pp. 587–616.

———. "The Valuation of Risk Assets and the Selection of Risky Investments in Stock Portfolios and Capital Budgets." *Review of Economics and Statistics* 47 (February 1965), pp. 13–37.

Markowitz, Harry M. *Portfolio Selection: Efficient Diversification of Investments.* New York: Wiley, 1959.

———. "Nonnegative or Not Nonnegative: A Question about CAPMs." *Journal of Finance* 38 (May 1983), pp. 283–295.

Modigliani, Franco, and Gerald A. Pogue. "An Introduction to Risk and Return." *Financial Analysts Journal* 30 (March–April 1974), pp. 68–80.

Morgan, I. G. "Dividends and Capital Asset Prices." *Journal of Finance* 37 (September 1982), pp. 1071–1086.

Pettit, R. Richardson, and Randolph Westerfield. "Using the Capital Asset Pricing Model and the Market Model to Predict Security Returns." *Journal of Financial and Quantitative Analysis* 9 (September 1974), pp. 579–606.

Robichek, Alexander A., and Richard A. Cohn. "The Economic Determinants of Systematic Risk." *Journal of Finance* 29 (May 1974), pp. 439–447.

Rogalski, Richard J., and Seha M. Tinic. "Risk-Premium Curve vs. Capital Market Line: A Re-examination." *Financial Management* 7 (spring 1978), pp. 73–84.

Roll, Richard. "A Critique of the Asset Pricing Theory's Tests. Part I, On the Past and Potential Testability of the Theory." *Journal of Financial Economics* 4 (March 1977), pp. 129–176.

———, and Stephen A. Ross. "Empirical Investigation of the Arbitrage Pricing Theory." *Journal of Finance* 35 (December 1980), pp. 1073–1103.

Rosenberg, Barr, and James Guy. "Beta and Investment Fundamentals." *Financial Analysts Journal* 32 (May–June 1976), pp. 60–72.

Ross, Stephen A. "The Arbitrage Theory of Capital Asset Pricing." *Journal of Economic Theory* 13 (December 1976), pp. 341–360.

———. "The Current Status of the Capital Asset Pricing Model (CAPM)." *Journal of Finance* 33 (June 1978), pp. 885–901.

Sharpe, William F. "Capital Asset Prices: A Theory of Market Equilibrium under Conditions of Risk." *Journal of Finance* 19 (September 1964), pp. 425–442.

———. *Portfolio Theory and Capital Markets.* New York: McGraw-Hill, 1970.

———. "A Simplified Model for Portfolio Analysis." *Management Science* 9 (January 1963), pp. 277–293.

———, and Guy M. Cooper. "Risk-Return Classes of New York Stock Exchange Common Stocks." *Financial Analysts Journal* 28 (March–April 1972), pp. 46–54.

Stapleton, R. C., and M. G. Subrahmanyam. "The Market Model and Capital Asset Pricing Theory: A Note." *Journal of Finance* 38 (December 1983), pp. 1637–1642.

Thompson, Donald J. II. "Sources of Systematic Risk in Common Stocks." *Journal of Business* 49 (April 1976), pp. 173–188.

Tobin, James. "Liquidity Preference as Behavior Towards Risk." *Review of Economic Studies* 25 (February 1958), pp. 65–86.

Wagner, Wayne H., and Sheila Lau. "The Effect of Diversification on Risk." *Financial Analysts Journal* 26 (November–December 1971), pp. 48–53.

Appendix 6A

Utility Theory, Portfolio Theory, and the Capital Asset Pricing Model (CAPM)

In Chapter 6 we discussed various measures of risk and then intuitively related nondiversifiable risk, β_j, to rates of return. This appendix presents a more systematic approach to the theoretical highlights of the relationship between risk and return. First we examine utility theory, which underlies all the major financial theories. Understanding utility theory is important because it provides insight into: (1) risk aversion, (2) why expected rate of return and standard deviation are employed, and (3) the goals of investors. Next we turn to portfolio theory and consider: (1) how to form efficient portfolios of risky securities and (2) why standard deviation is not an adequate measure of individual security risk when the securities are in an efficient portfolio. This discussion leads directly to the final topic—the capital asset pricing model (CAPM) which, by merging the risk-free asset, R_F, and portfolio theory, provides us with a specification of the relationship between expected return and risk. The CAPM indicates that risk-averse investors will incur additional risk only if they expect to be compensated by sufficient additional return. The effects of relaxing the assumptions of the CAPM are also discussed.

Utility Theory

The expected utility model presented here is widely used and allows us to describe how individual investment decisions are made under conditions of uncertainty. *Utility* (measured in units called *utils*) is a measure of psychic gain. Investment in a project that goes bankrupt, for example, will decrease most investors' level of utility; it yields disutility. On the other hand, receipt of a positive return on investment will be viewed by most investors as increasing their utility. The basic reason most people make investments is to maximize their personal happiness, or utility. They hope to maximize their utility by investing in risky assets that will increase their wealth.

Marginal and Expected Utility

A utility of wealth function can be graphed as shown in Figure 6A.1. At the heart of utility theory is the idea of *marginal utility*, which may be defined as the additional utility an investor receives from a change in wealth. Graphically, marginal utility can be viewed as the change in total utility per unit change in wealth. In Figure 6A.1, the marginal utility derived by going from 0 to $5,000 is 8 utils; from $5,000 to $10,000 the marginal utility is 5 (13 − 8) utils; from $10,000 to $15,000 it is 3 (16 − 13) utils; and the marginal utility of the last increment from $15,000 to $20,000 is 2 (18 − 16) utils. Marginal utility is a measure of the increase or decrease in utility derived by increasing or decreasing total wealth by one unit. In financial theory it is generally assumed that investors make decisions consistent with the concept of *diminishing marginal utility*. In other words, investors derive less and less incremental utility from each additional increment in total wealth. Such investors are called risk-averse investors. Figure 6A.1, which was constructed assuming diminishing marginal utility, is representative of the utility of wealth function for a risk-averse investor.[1]

In an uncertain world, investors cannot know in advance which investments will yield the highest returns. So, under conditions of uncertainty, investors make decisions that maximize expected utility, which is determined by expected return and risk:

$$\text{Maximize } E(U) = f[\text{expected return, risk}] \qquad (6A.1)$$
$$= f[\bar{k}, \sigma]$$

where $E(U)$ = the expected utility (note that E is the symbol for "expected")
f = some mathematical function
$\bar{k}$ = the mean or expected rate of return[2]
σ = the standard deviation of the return

---

[1]For a much more extensive discussion of utility theory, see James Tobin, "Liquidity Preference as Behavior Towards Risk," *Review of Economic Studies* 25 (February 1958), pp. 65–86; Ralph O. Swalm, "Utility Theory—Insights into Risk Taking," *Harvard Business Review* 44 (November–December 1966), pp. 124–136; Eugene F. Fama and Merton H. Miller, *The Theory of Finance* (New York: Holt, Rinehart and Winston, 1972), or David P. Baron, "On the Utility Theoretical Foundation of Mean-Variance Analysis," *Journal of Finance* 32 (December 1977), pp. 1683–1698.

[2]In keeping with our practice throughout the book, for mathematical and expositional simplicity we do not use the symbol for expectation, E, with rates of return.

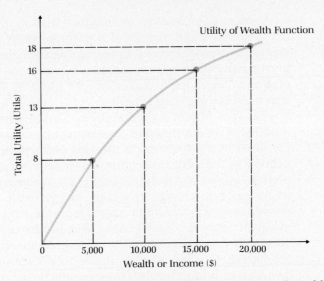

Figure 6A.1   The Relationship Between Utility and Wealth.

Theoretically investors should maximize utility in an uncertain world, but in an operational sense they try to maximize expected utility, as defined by Equation 6A.1. An increase in expected returns will increase the investor's expected utility if risk does not increase; likewise, a decrease in the standard deviation of returns will increase expected utility if the expected return does not decrease simultaneously.

An Illustration   To understand the concepts of maximization of expected utility and risk aversion, let's consider an example of two investments available to a risk-averse investor. Investment F has a 50 percent probability of an outcome of $5,000, and a 50 percent probability of $15,000. The expected return, $\bar{k}_F$, is $10,000. Investment G has a 50 percent probability of an outcome of zero, and a 50 percent probability of an outcome of $20,000. The expected return, $\bar{k}_G$, is $10,000. On the basis of expected return alone, the investor is indifferent between the two, since their expected returns are both $10,000. However, that indifference does not take into account: (1) that the investor is risk-averse; (2) that risk is measured by the standard deviation of the returns; and (3) that investment G has a wider dispersion in returns and hence a larger standard deviation than investment F. Once investors consider this information, they are in a position to make a decision on the basis of maximization of expected utility.

To see how this works, we need to examine the investors' utility of

Wealth or Income ($)	Total Utility (Utils)	Marginal Utility (Utils)
0	0	0
5,000	8	8
10,000	13	5
15,000	16	3
20,000	18	2

wealth function. As shown in Figure 6A.1 and Table 6A.1, the investors' utility for zero wealth or income is zero; it is 8 utils for $5,000, 13 utils for $10,000, 16 utils for $15,000, and 18 utils for $20,000. Notice that since marginal utility decreases with each increment in wealth or income, the investor is risk-averse. Using this information, it is possible to derive the expected utility to the investor of both investments—F and G. As shown in Table 6A.2, the expected utility of investment F is calculated to be 12 utils, while the expected utility of investment G is 9 utils; hence, the risk-averse investor has a lower expected utility from investment G than from investment F. The lower expected utility for investment G is directly attributable to the fact that it has a wider dispersion or standard deviation of returns. Thus, all else being equal, the larger the standard deviation, the less attractive an investment to the risk-averse investor. What does our investor do? Since he or she makes decisions based on expected utility and since both investments have the same expected return, the investor will choose the one with the least risk or the greatest expected utility. Our risk-averse investor chooses investment F.

Closing Comments

Some additional topics require brief comment. In a strict sense, the expected value and standard deviation describe only normal, symmetrical distributions. It should be obvious that the risk of an investment is not dispersion, but the possibility of downside deviations from the expected rate of return. Some progress has been made in measuring downside risk using measures such as semivariance; however, we will not pursue those measures here.[3] There is also some evidence that security returns are, in fact, not completely symmetrical—they often appear to be skewed because they are bounded on the lower side but have unlimited upside potential.[4] Because of the difficulty of dealing mathematically with moments of probability distributions higher than

---

[3]For more on semivariance as a measure of risk, see Harry M. Markowitz, *Portfolio Selection: Efficient Diversification of Investments* (New York: Wiley, 1959), and Bernell K. Stone, "A Certain Class of Three-Parameter Risk Measures," *Journal of Finance* 28 (June 1973), pp. 675–686.

[4]See Eugene F. Fama, *Foundations of Finance* (New York: Basic Books, 1976); Richard W. McEnally, "A Note on the Return Behavior of High Risk Common Stocks," *Journal of Finance* 29 (March 1974), pp. 199–202; and Fred D. Arditti and Haim Levy, "Portfolio Efficiency Analysis in Three Moments: The Multiperiod Case," *Journal of Finance* 30 (June 1975), pp. 797–809.

TABLE 6A.2
Calculation of
Expected Utility for
Investments F and G

Investment F				Investment G			
Probability (1)	Outcome (2)	Utils (3)	Weighted Utility [(1) × (3)] (4)	Probability (1)	Outcome (2)	Utils (3)	Weighted Utility [(1) × (3)] (4)
.50	$ 5,000	8	4 utils	.50	$ 0	0	0 utils
.50	15,000	16	8	.50	20,000	18	9
Expected utility			12 utils	Expected utility			9 utils

the second, our analysis is confined to the first two moments—the expected rate of return and standard deviation. For distributions that are reasonably symmetrical, this approach should closely approximate investor attitudes toward risk.

Portfolio Theory

To understand the major premise that underlies the theory of why investors diversify, we reviewed utility theory, which suggests investors are, in general, risk-averse as they attempt to maximize wealth. In arriving at decisions about investments, investors begin the process by projecting for individual securities the states of nature, associated probabilities of occurrence, and rates of return associated with the states of nature. This leads directly, as we saw in Chapter 6, to the expected rate of return and standard deviation of returns for individual securities. To understand why it is in the investor's best interest to diversify, we need to investigate *portfolio theory*. Portfolio theory is often called Markowitz portfolio theory after its originator, Harry M. Markowitz; it is also called two-parameter portfolio theory or mean-variance portfolio theory. The latter two names refer to the fact that it is based on the assumption that all the relevant information can be obtained by considering two parameters of distributions, the mean or expected value, and variance or standard deviation.

A *portfolio* is simply a combination of assets. Our interest is in a subset of all portfolios called efficient portfolios. Efficient portfolios have two specific properties: (1) They provide the highest possible return for any specific degree of risk; or (2) they have the lowest degree of risk for any specific rate of return. Throughout this section we assume all assets are risky; $\sigma_j > 0$. After discussing portfolio theory, we will introduce the risk-free asset, R_F.

The Two-Asset Case

Consider two assets available to an investor represented by the shares of stock of Albert Brothers and Baker Publishing. The investor has derived the mean rate of return and standard deviation for both securities (Albert is called security A and Baker is called security B), so that:

Security A	Security B

$$\bar{k}_A = \sum_{i=1}^{n} k_i Pr_i \qquad\qquad \bar{k}_B = \sum_{i=1}^{n} k_i Pr_i$$

$$\sigma_A = \sqrt{\sum_{i=1}^{n} (k_i - \bar{k}_A)^2 \times Pr_i} \qquad \sigma_B = \sqrt{\sum_{i=1}^{n} (k_i - \bar{k}_B)^2 \times Pr_i}$$

Portfolio Rate of Return. To form a portfolio of these two securities, one immediate question must be answered: How much will be invested in security A and how much in security B? Any proportion of the investor's funds, from zero to 100 percent, could be placed in security A or in security B; alternatively, some fraction could be placed in both. We denote the percentage of total funds (where the total is 1.0 or 100 percent) devoted to security A as W_A; the proportion devoted to security B is denoted as W_B. Note that the sum of W_A and W_B must equal 1.0. The expected rate of return on a two-security portfolio is:

$$k_P = W_A\bar{k}_A + W_B\bar{k}_B \qquad\qquad (6A.2)$$

where k_P = the portfolio rate of return[5]
W_A and W_B = the proportion of the total funds devoted
                  to security A and security B
        $\bar{k}_A$ = the mean rate of return on security A
        $\bar{k}_B$ = the mean rate of return on security B

If the one-period expected return is 5 percent on Albert (security A) and 10 percent on Baker (security B), the expected portfolio rate of return, with weights of W_A = 75 percent and W_B = 25 percent, is:

$$\begin{aligned} k_P &= W_A\bar{k}_A + W_B\bar{k}_B \\ &= (0.75)(5\%) + (0.25)(10\%) = 3.75\% + 2.50\% = 6.25\% \end{aligned}$$

Alternatively, if the investor had elected to place 100 percent of the funds in security A and none in security B, the portfolio rate of return (with W_A = 1.00 and W_B = 0.0) is:

$$k_P = (1.0)(5\%) + (0)(10\%) = 5\% + 0\% = 5\%$$

As the proportions invested in one security or another change, the expected portfolio rate of return will vary. The minimum it can be is 5

---

[5]For simplicity, the symbol k_P will represent the mean of the portfolio rate of return instead of the more technically correct symbol of $\bar{k}_P$.

percent (when everything is invested in Albert), while the maximum the rate of return can be is 10 percent (when everything is invested in Baker).

Portfolio Standard Deviation.   The standard deviation is more complicated, since it depends, in part, on the covariance or correlation between the expected rates of return. The standard deviation for the two-security case is:

$$\sigma_P = \sqrt{W_A^2\sigma_A^2 + W_B^2\sigma_B^2 + 2W_AW_B COV(k_A,k_B)} \qquad (6A.3)$$

$$= \sqrt{W_A^2\sigma_A^2 + W_B^2\sigma_B^2 + 2W_AW_B\rho_{AB}\sigma_A\sigma_B}$$

where σ_P = the standard deviation of the portfolio returns
W_A and W_B = the proportion of the total funds devoted
  to security A and security B
σ_A^2 = the variance (standard deviation squared) for security A
σ_B^2 = the variance (standard deviation squared) for security B
$COV(k_A,k_B)$ = the covariance between the rates of return of
  securities A and B
ρ_{AB} = the correlation between the rates of return of
  securities A and B

Thus, the standard deviation about the portfolio rate of return is equal to the square root of the sum of the weighted variances and twice the weighted covariance between returns, as in Equation 6A.3. Since we know the covariance between the returns on securities A and B, $COV(k_A,k_B)$, is equal to the correlation between securities A and B times the respective standard deviations, $COV(k_A,k_B) = \rho_{AB}\sigma_A\sigma_B$, we can also express the standard deviation about the portfolio expected rate of return as noted below Equation 6A.3.

For Albert, the standard deviation, σ_A, is equal to 4 percent, while for Baker, the standard deviation, σ_B, is equal to 8 percent. If the correlation coefficient between the two security rates of return is equal to +1.0 (perfect positive correlation) and half the funds are invested in each of the securities, the portfolio standard deviation (case 1 in Table 6A.3) is equal to 6 percent with a portfolio rate of return equal to 7.5 percent. On the other hand, if only 25 percent of the portfolio is composed of Albert and 75 percent is composed of Baker and the correlation coefficient, ρ_{AB}, is −.50, the portfolio standard deviation is 5.57 percent, with a portfolio rate of return of 8.75 percent (case 2 in Table 6A.3).

Comparing Return and Risk.   The important aspects of the preceding discussion can be summarized by examining Table 6A.4, where portfolio rates of return and standard deviations for four different cases are presented. In the table, note the following points:

TABLE 6A.3
Portfolio Rate of
Return and Standard
Deviation for Two
Combinations of
Security Weights
and Correlation
Coefficients

	Security Returns			
	$\overline{k}$	σ	Case 1	Case 2
Albert Brothers (security A)	5%	4%	$W_A = 0.50$	$W_A = 0.25$
Baker Publishing (security B)	10	8	$W_B = 0.50$	$W_B = 0.75$
			$\rho_{AB} = +1.0$	$\rho_{AB} = -.50$

$$k_P = W_A\overline{k}_A + W_B\overline{k}_B$$

$$\sigma_P = \sqrt{W_A^2\sigma_A^2 + W_B^2\sigma_B^2 + 2W_AW_B\rho_{AB}\sigma_A\sigma_B}$$

Case 1: $k_P = (0.50)(5\%) + (0.50)(10\%) = 2.5\% + 5\% = 7.5\%$

$\sigma_P = \sqrt{(0.50)^2(4\%)^2 + (0.50)^2(8\%)^2 + 2(0.50)(0.50)(1.0)(4\%)(8\%)}$

$= \sqrt{4\% + 16\% + 16\%} = \sqrt{36\%} = 6\%$

Case 2: $k_P = (0.25)(5\%) + (.75)(10\%) = 1.25\% + 7.5\% = 8.75\%$

$\sigma_P = \sqrt{(0.25)^2(4\%)^2 + (0.75)^2(8\%)^2 + 2(0.25)(0.75)(-.50)(4\%)(8\%)}$

$= \sqrt{1\% + 36\% + (-6)} = \sqrt{31\%} = 5.57\%$

1. The portfolio rates of return increase as we increase the percentage of the portfolio invested in security B (to a maximum of 10 percent), and decrease as we reduce the percentage of the portfolio invested in security B (to a minimum return of 5 percent).
2. The portfolio standard deviation is a function of three items: (a) the security weights, W_A and W_B; (b) the individual security standard deviations, σ_A and σ_B; and (c) the correlation between the security returns, ρ_{AB}.

In fact, diversification among securities (unless they are perfectly positively correlated) enables the risk-averse investor to reduce the dispersion of the probability distribution of possible returns relative to the expected portfolio rate of return. To understand why this is so, it is necessary to investigate in more detail the impact of correlation on the portfolio standard deviation.

The Effect of Correlation on Portfolio Risk

Correlations between security rates of return can be positive, negative, or zero. They are typically positive because the returns on most stocks tend to fluctuate to a greater or lesser degree as the economy fluctuates. Because the correlations between security returns are rarely, if ever, perfectly positive, combining securities to form portfolios will usually

TABLE 6A.4
Portfolio Rates of
Return and Standard
Deviations for
Four Cases

	100% in Security A (ρ_{AB} not relevant)	Case 1 50% in Security A, 50% in Security B ($\rho_{AB} = +1.0$)	Case 2 25% in Security A, 75% in Security B ($\rho_{AB} = -.50$)	100% in Security B (ρ_{AB} not relevant)
k_P	5%	7.5%	8.75%	10%
σ_P	4	6	5.57	8

result in some reduction of risk. Further, the lower the degree of correlation between the security returns, the greater the benefits of diversification.

To examine the impact of correlation on portfolio standard deviations, consider Table 6A.5, which presents the expected portfolio return, k_P, and standard deviation, σ_P, for various weights (W) and correlation coefficients (ρ_{AB}) for Albert Brothers and Baker Publishing. This same information is graphed in Figure 6A.2. Reviewing the risk-return combination graphs in column (c) of Figure 6A.2, it should be clear that the less positive the correlation between the returns of securities A and B, ρ_{AB}, the greater the risk-reduction that can be achieved by combining the two securities into a portfolio. The risk-return tradeoff reflected in these data can be further illustrated by Figure 6A.3, which shows the tradeoffs for five different correlations between securities A and B. The most interesting aspect of this graph is the clear demonstration that the lower the value of ρ_{AB}, the "better" the portfolio of risky assets that can be constructed. We will consider how investors proceed to make decisions concerning portfolios of risky assets after we examine portfolio theory with more than two securities.

The Three-Asset and n-Asset Case   In the previous section we developed and explored the concepts of portfolio returns and standard deviations with two risky assets. Obviously, most investors own more than two assets, so we need to expand our definitions of k_P and σ_P to account for this. Unfortunately, the equations get rather cumbersome for more assets. In the three-security case (A, B, and C), the portfolio return and standard deviation are defined as:

$$k_P = W_A\overline{k}_A + W_B\overline{k}_B + W_C\overline{k}_C \tag{6A.4}$$

$$\sigma_P = \sqrt{W_A^2\sigma_A^2 + W_B^2\sigma_B^2 + W_C^2\sigma_C^2 + 2W_AW_B COV(k_A,k_B) + 2W_AW_C COV(k_A,k_C) + 2W_BW_C COV(k_B,k_C)} \tag{6A.5}$$

where all the symbols are as defined previously, and the sum of $W_A + W_B + W_C$ is 1.0 or 100 percent. The expected portfolio return, k_P, is now the weighted average of the expected returns of the three securities, A, B, and

			TABLE 6A.5	Security Weight in Portfolio		Expected Portfolio Rate of Return	Portfolio Standard Deviation, σ_P, if the Correlation Coefficient Is		
				W_A	W_B	k_P	$\rho_{AB} = +1.0$	$\rho_{AB} = 0$	$\rho_{AB} = -1.0$

TABLE 6A.5

The Effect of Changing Weights and Correlation Coefficients on the Standard Deviation of a Two-Security Portfolio

Security Weight in Portfolio		Expected Portfolio Rate of Return	Portfolio Standard Deviation, σ_P, if the Correlation Coefficient Is		
W_A	W_B	k_P	$\rho_{AB} = +1.0$	$\rho_{AB} = 0$	$\rho_{AB} = -1.0$
100%	0%	5.00	4.00	4.00	4.00
75	25	6.25	5.00	3.61	1.00
$66\frac{2}{3}$	$33\frac{1}{3}$	6.67	5.33	3.77	0
50	50	7.50	6.00	4.47	2.00
$33\frac{1}{3}$	$66\frac{2}{3}$	8.33	6.67	5.50	4.00
25	75	8.75	7.00	6.08	5.00
0	100	10.00	8.00	8.00	8.00

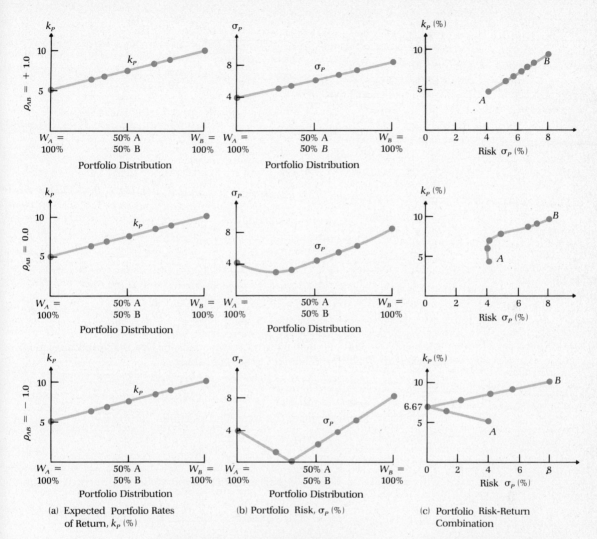

Figure 6A.2 Expected Portfolio Returns (k_p) and Standard Deviations (σ_p) for Different Combinations of Weights (W) and Correlation Coefficients (ρ_{AB}), Albert Brothers and Baker Publishing.

C. The portfolio standard deviation, σ_P, is the square root of the sum of the weighted variances and covariances of the three securities. Since there are three securities, there are three covariances, one for each *pair* of assets. Equation 6A.5 may be rewritten in terms of the correlations so that:

$$\sigma_P = \sqrt{W_A^2\sigma_A^2 + W_B^2\sigma_B^2 + W_C^2\sigma_C^2 + 2W_AW_B\rho_{AB}\sigma_A\sigma_B + 2W_AW_C\rho_{AC}\sigma_A\sigma_C + 2W_BW_C\rho_{BC}\sigma_B\sigma_C}$$

where all the symbols are as defined previously.

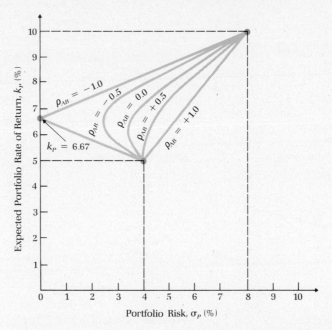

Figure 6A.3 Portfolio Risk-Return Combinations for Five Different Correlation Coefficients, Albert Brothers and Baker Publishing.

For the n-security case, the expected portfolio return is:

$$k_P = \sum_{i=1}^{n} W_i \bar{k}_i \qquad (6A.6)$$

where $\sum_{i=1}^{n} W_i = 1.0$ or 100 percent and the portfolio standard deviation is:

$$\sigma_P = \sqrt{\sum_{i=1}^{n} W_i^2 \sigma_i^2 + 2 \sum_{i=1}^{n} \sum_{j=i+1}^{n} W_i W_j COV(k_i, k_j)} \qquad (6A.7)$$

$$= \sqrt{\sum_{i=1}^{n} W_i^2 \sigma_i^2 + 2 \sum_{i=1}^{n} \sum_{j=i+1}^{n} W_i W_j \rho_{ij} \sigma_i \sigma_j}$$

Since Equations 6A.6 and 6A.7 have n securities, there are n standard deviations and $n(n - 1)/2$ covariances or correlations Since the number of terms increases rapidly as the number of assets increases, the expanded equation becomes quite complex if n is large. Computer programs are available to handle portfolios of 100 securities or more, but the usual procedure is to simplify the process by using the single-index model developed by William F. Sharpe.[6]

Diversification with Many Securities

The Efficient Frontier. When there are many assets, opportunities for diversification abound. Individuals may hold hundreds of different securities; by forming portfolios, some risk (standard deviation) can be eliminated as long as returns are not perfectly positively correlated. Suppose we have n risky securities, where n is greater than two.[7] These securities can be combined into a large number of different portfolios by changing the weights, W_i, as long as the sum of the weights equals 1.0:

$$\sum_{i=1}^{n} W_i = 1.0 \text{ or } 100\%$$

Each portfolio will have an expected return, k_P, and a standard deviation, σ_P. The set of all possible portfolios is defined as the feasible or attainable set and is shown as the shaded area in Figure 6A.4. (The area bounded by ABYZCDEF is the feasible set.) Every point in the attainable set represents an individual portfolio with a specific portfolio return and standard deviation.

Given the full set, which portfolio should the investor select? The choice involves two separate decisions: (1) determining the efficient set of portfolios, and (2) choosing from the efficient set the single portfolio of risky assets that is optimum for the investor. An *efficient portfolio*, one of the efficient set, is defined as a portfolio that provides the highest expected return for a given degree of risk, or the lowest risk for a given expected return. In Figure 6A.4, the boundary BYZC defines the set of efficient portfolios; it is often called the *efficient frontier*. Portfolios to the left of the efficient frontier are not available for investment, since they lie outside the attainable set; portfolios that lie on the right of the efficient frontier are not desirable because they are dominated by portfolios on the efficient frontier.

The Optimal Portfolio. In the absence of a risk-free asset, the best combination of expected rate of return and standard deviation depends on the investor's utility function. If an investor is risk-averse and associates risk with standard deviation, that investor's utility function (or risk-return indifference curves) can be depicted graphically, as in

---

[6]See William F. Sharpe, "A Simplified Model for Portfolio Analysis," *Management Science 9*, (January 1963), pp. 277–293; or William F. Sharpe, *Portfolio Theory and Capital Markets* (New York: McGraw-Hill, 1970).

[7]The reason for requiring that n be greater than two is because in the two-security case, all possible risk-return combinations of portfolios fall on a single (but generally not straight) line. In the more general case of $n > 2$ securities, not all risk-return combinations fall on a single line.

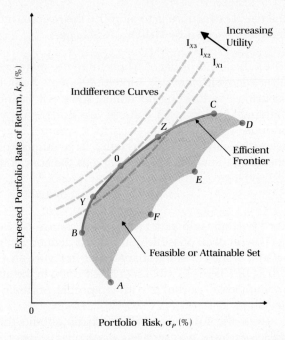

Figure 6A.4   The Feasible (or Attainable) Set and Efficient Frontier.

Figure 6A.4. These curves, known as indifference curves, indicate that the investor is indifferent between any combination of expected rate of return and standard deviation on a particular curve. In other words, the curve is defined by those combinations of expected return and standard deviation that result in a constant level of utility. For a single investor, investor X, a family of indifference curves exists. Figure 6A.4 shows three curves from this family. The higher the indifference curve, the greater the level of utility or satisfaction.

The investor will want to hold that portfolio of securities which places him or her on the highest possible indifference curve. This can be illustrated with the three indifference curves for investor X along with the set of efficient portfolios shown in Figure 6A.4. Investor X will not employ indifference curve I_{X1} because utility can be increased by shifting to curve I_{X2}. The optimal portfolio, O, is at the point of tangency of the highest possible indifference curve, I_{X2}, and the efficient frontier. This portfolio represents the highest level of satisfaction the investor can achieve. Although another indifference curve is shown, I_{X3}, the investor cannot reach it given the efficient frontier.

The investor will maximize utility by investing in portfolio O of risky assets. It should be emphasized that this portfolio is composed of some set (but not necessarily all) of the n risky securities available, weighted by appropriate weights, W_i. Hence, in the absence of a risk-free asset, we see how the individual investors determine the portfolio (and hence the securities) in which to invest. In the following section, the introduction of the risk-free asset will result in a change in the way investors choose optimal portfolios.

The Capital Asset Pricing Model (CAPM)

In the preceding section, we developed the concepts of portfolio theory to understand how investors decide on an optimum portfolio of risky assets—assets that have positive standard deviations for every level of expected return. Now we proceed to add one more element to our model and assume not only risky assets, but also the risk-free asset, R_F. This addition, which enables us to determine the required return for individual securities or other assets, is embodied in the capital asset pricing model (CAPM). The CAPM specifies risk-return tradeoffs for assets. As such, it is important not only for investors, but more significantly from our standpoint, for financial managers.

Basic Assumptions of the CAPM

Since the CAPM is a complex financial/economic theory, it is necessary to make some simplifying assumptions in order to reduce its complexity while still maintaining its essential elements. The assumptions of the CAPM are:

1. All investors are single-period, expected utility of terminal wealth maximizers who evaluate alternative portfolios on the basis of means and standard deviations of portfolio returns.
2. All investors can borrow or lend an unlimited amount at a given risk-free rate of interest, R_F, and there are no restrictions on the short sales of any assets.
3. All investors have homogeneous expectations; that is, they have identical subjective estimates of the means, standard deviations, and covariances of returns among all assets.
4. There are no transactions costs, and all assets are perfectly divisible and liquid (marketable at the going price).
5. There are no taxes.
6. All investors are price takers and cannot, based on their buying or selling, influence the market price.
7. The quantities of all assets are known and finite.

Although these assumptions may appear to be limiting, many of them can be relaxed without destroying the basic conclusions derived from the model. In addition, substantial empirical testing has produced results that are, in general, consistent with the CAPM. So it appears both feasible and desirable to employ the model to enhance our understanding of the various components of risk and to determine a relevant measure of risk for individual assets.

The Capital
Market Line (CML)

When a risk-free asset $(R_F$ with $\sigma = 0)$ is introduced, the investor's decision changes from that shown in Figure 6A.4, where we concluded that the optimum portfolio was determined by the point of tangency between the investor's highest indifference curve and the efficient frontier. Now the investor is faced with a different two-step procedure for decision making that involves: (1) determination of the capital market line (CML) depicting the attainable combinations of portfolios comprised of the risk-free asset, R_F, and the market portfolio of risky assets, M; and (2) choosing from this set of attainable combinations the best portfolio.

The important first point to understand is that when a risk-free asset is introduced, the choice becomes one of allocating funds between R_F and M; previously in discussing portfolio theory we were concerned only about investing all our funds in a specific portfolio comprised solely of risky assets that lay on the efficient frontier. With the introduction of R_F, the sum of our funds must be split between R_F and M.

The new situation is presented graphically in Figure 6A.5 where the feasible set is the same as presented in Figure 6A.4,[8] R_F is the expected return on the risk-free asset where $\sigma_{RF} = 0$. The line drawn from R_F tangent to the efficient frontier at M and continuing to T is the *capital market line (CML)*. This line describes the tradeoff between the expected rate of return and risk for various holdings of R_F and M. The slope of the CML represents the market price of risk. It tells us the amount of added expected return required for an increase in standard deviation, or total portfolio risk.[9]

The capital market line, R_FMT in Figure 6A.5, depicts the various combinations of R_F and M that are available to all investors. Note that the CML dominates (lies above) the efficient frontier at every point except M. A rational investor will always choose some combination of R_F and M that lies on the CML. Thus, if investors are given the choice between a portfolio of risky assets that lies on the efficient frontier, $BYZC$, or a portfolio of equal risk lying on the CML, they will always choose the total portfolio of R_F and M lying on the capital market line. Such a situation is shown in Figure 6A.5, where risky portfolio Y lies on the efficient frontier and portfolio Y', which is directly above Y and hence has the same risk, lies on the capital market line. Rational investors will always chose Y' over Y because they can increase their expected rate of return without

---

[8]Theoretically this feasible set includes all types of risky assets, not just stocks or bonds. Included in the set are such assets as real estate, livestock, commodities, paintings, and even human capital. See David Mayers, "Nonmarketable Assets and the Determination of Capital Asset Prices in the Absence of a Riskless Asset," *Journal of Business* 46 (April 1973), pp. 258–267; and Eugene F. Fama and G. William Schwert, "Human Capital and Capital Market Equilibrium," *Journal of Financial Economics* 5 (1977), pp. 95–125. In the past the market portfolio of risky assets, M, was often approximated by employing only common stocks; more recently combinations of common stocks, corporate bonds, and government bonds have been employed in some empirical tests.

[9]For the capital market to be in equilibrium, M must be a portfolio that contains every asset in exact proportion to that asset's fraction of the total market value of all assets. In other words, M must be a value-weighted portfolio of all risky assets.

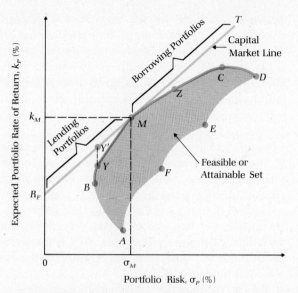

Figure 6A.5   The Capital Market Line: Combining the Risk-Free Asset (R_F) and the Market Portfolio of Risky Assets (M).

increasing their risk and thereby achieve a higher possible indifference curve than attainable in Figure 6A.4.

The set of total portfolios on the CML between R_F and M represent lending portfolios, in that they consist of M and R_F where the investor has lent money to others at the rate R_F (see Figure 6A.5). The portion of the CML above M (the segment M to T) are leveraged or borrowing portfolios. They are constructed by borrowing at the rate R_F and investing the proceeds in the market portfolio M, thereby increasing the total portfolio expected rate of return and risk, as shown on the upper portion of the CML.

The capital market line has an intercept of R_F and a slope of ($k_M - R_F)/\sigma_M$. Mathematically, the relationship between the expected rate of return and standard deviation for a portfolio is:

$$k_P = R_F + \left(\frac{k_M - R_F}{\sigma_M} \right) \sigma_P \tag{6A.8}$$

where k_P = the expected rate of return on the portfolio
R_F = the risk-free rate of interest
k_M = the expected rate of return on the market portfolio
σ_M = the standard deviation of the market portfolio returns
σ_P = the standard deviation of the portfolio returns

Equation 6A.8 states that the expected return on a portfolio in equilibrium is equal to the risk-free rate of return, plus the market price of risk [($k_M - R_F)/\sigma_M$] multiplied by the standard deviation of the portfolio's returns. As we have stated previously, portfolio M is the market portfolio. At first, it may appear that the assumption that all investors hold every security in the market as a portion of their portfolio is unreasonable. Yet in reality every investor does not have to be so well diversified. For the relationship to be a reasonable description of reality, it only need be true that financial markets are dominated by investors who are well diversified.

Measuring Risk for Individual Securities; The Security Market Line (SML)

Investors holding the market portfolio, M, or some combination of M and R_F, have eliminated part of the risk because they have invested in the efficient portfolio, M. However, they cannot eliminate all risk, since the market portfolio (or any efficient portfolio) still has some risk, as measured by the portfolio standard deviation, σ_P. Consequently, for any individual security, the only risk that is relevant is that portion of the variability of the individual security's returns that cannot be diversified away, but is attributable to the variation in the overall return and risk for the total market portfolio.

We can think of the total risk (all variability) of an individual security as being composed of two parts:

Total security risk = nondiversifiable risk + diversifiable risk

Nondiversifiable (market) risk is that part of an individual security's risk that cannot be diversified away. Diversifiable (nonmarket) risk is unique to the particular company and is independent of economic, political, and other factors that affect all securities in a systematic manner. By efficient diversification, diversifiable risk can be reduced and even eliminated. The expected return on individual securities can be related to nondiversifiable or market risk by the following equation:[10]

$$k_j = R_F + \left[\frac{k_M - R_F}{\sigma_M^2}\right] COV(k_j, k_M) \qquad (6A.9)$$

$$= R_F + \left[\frac{k_M - R_F}{\sigma_M^2}\right] \rho_{jM} \sigma_j \sigma_M$$

where k_j = the expected return on the jth asset
R_F = the risk-free rate of interest
k_M = the expected return on the market portfolio
σ_M^2 = the variance of the market portfolio
$COV(k_j, k_M)$ = the nondiversifiable risk, the covariance between the

---

[10]The proof is contained in many places; see Sharpe, *Portfolio Theory and Capital Markets,* or Fama, *Foundations of Finance.* Also the $COV(k_j, k_M)$ is strictly speaking only a proxy for risk. This point is in addition discussed by Sharpe.

returns on the jth security and the returns on the market portfolio

ρ_{jM} = the correlation coefficient between the returns on the jth security and the returns on the market portfolio

σ_j = the standard deviation of the jth asset

σ_M = the standard deviation of the market portfolio

The nondiversifiable risk of the security, $COV(k_j,k_M)$, is that portion of the total security risk that cannot be diversified away in efficient portfolios.

The market measure of risk $COV(k_j,k_M)$ is often divided by the variance of the market returns, σ_M^2 (*Note:* This is the denominator of the term in brackets in Equation 6A.9.), to obtain a relative measure of nondiversifiable or market risk called beta. Thus, beta, β_j, is equal to

$$\beta_j = \frac{COV(k_j,k_M)}{\sigma_M^2} = \frac{\rho_{jM}\sigma_j\sigma_M}{\sigma_M^2} = \frac{\rho_{jM}\sigma_j}{\sigma_M} \tag{6A.10}$$

where all symbols are as defined before (see Equation 6.6). Beta as a measure of relative risk can also be described as a measure of the sensitivity or responsiveness of the rates of return on individual securities to movements in the market. Equation 6A.9 can be rewritten in the form most often used for the capital asset pricing model, Equation 6.7, so that

$$k_j = R_F + \beta_j \times (k_M - R_F) \tag{6A.11}$$
$$= \text{price of time} + \text{risk premium}$$

Using this information, it is easy to see that the required or expected rate of return on individual securities is composed of two parts. The first is compensation for the time value of money, R_F; the second part of the required return is a risk premium that varies by asset depending on the relative market risk, β_j, of each asset. Equation 6A.11 is the fundamental equation specifying the relationship between risk and return for securities and other risky assets.

The relationship between the required return for a security, k_J, and relative nondiversifiable risk, β_j, can be shown as in Figure 6A.6, where the relationship between individual security returns and nondiversifiable risk is called the security market line (SML). By definition, beta for the market portfolio, β_M, is equal to 1.0. Those assets that have betas less than 1.0 have less relative nondiversifiable or market risk than securities in general. Hence, the returns on assets with low betas will fluctuate proportionately less than the market portfolio. Likewise, assets with high beta values have more relative nondiversifiable risk and will, other things being equal, have returns that fluctuate more than the returns on the market portfolio.

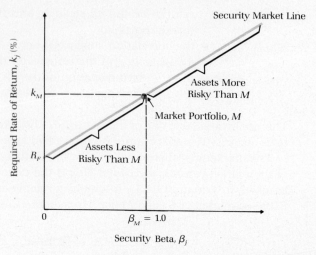

Figure 6A.6   The Security Market Line (SML) for Individual Securities.

The SML differs from the CML in two respects. First, for individual securities the appropriate measure of nondiversifiable or market risk is the covariance instead of the standard deviation. For convenience, we have substituted beta, a measure of relative nondiversifiable risk, for the covariance. This is an important conceptual difference, because it recognizes that the risk of an individual security is measured by its contribution to the risk of the portfolio in which it is placed. Second, note that the covariance of the market with itself is:

$$COV(k_M, k_M) = \rho_{M,M}\sigma_M\sigma_M = (1.0)\ \sigma_M^2 = \sigma_M^2$$

By dividing the covariance, $COV(k_j, k_M)$ by the variance of the market returns, σ_M^2, we obtain the relative measure of nondiversifiable risk, β_j. This changes the scale of the SML when compared with the CML.

Relaxing the Assumptions

At the start of our discussion of the capital asset pricing model, we stated the assumptions underlying the model. Now we briefly examine the effect of relaxing some of these assumptions.

The first is assumption 2, that investors can both borrow and lend at the risk-free rate, R_F. Obviously an investor can lend at this rate; however, there is considerable doubt whether, in general, investors can borrow at R_F. If the borrowing rate is higher than the lending rate, the capital market line is no longer linear. As shown in Figure 6A.7, the CML is straight from R_L to the market portfolio M_L. This segment represents combinations of the risk-free asset (for lending) and the portfolio M_L. Because the borrowing rate is higher, another tangency portfolio is necessary, M_B. The relevant portion of this segment of the CML is from

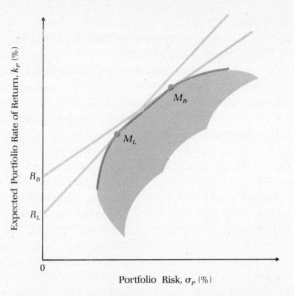

Figure 6A.7 The Capital Market Line (CML) When Borrowing (R_B) and Lending (R_L) Rates Differ.

portfolio M_B to the right; it represents borrowing to invest in the market portfolio M_B. The segment of the CML from M_L to M_B is curved and follows the efficient frontier of risky portfolios. Obviously, the greater the difference between the lending rate (R_L) and the borrowing rate (R_B), the greater the curved portion of the CML. The impact of these different rates is that equilibrium prices are not possible for all securities.[11]

Relaxation of assumption 3, that all investors have homogeneous expectations, complicates the problem in a different way. With heterogeneous expectations, a complex blending of expectations, wealth, and utility preferences emerges in the equilibrating process. The effect of this is that the CML becomes "fuzzy." The more expectations differ, the "fuzzier" the CML becomes. In effect, they become bands. With only moderate heterogeneity in expectations, however, the basic tenets of the CAPM still hold, and rough estimates of the expected risk-return tradeoffs are still possible.

Relaxation of assumption 4, to recognize the existence of transactions costs, also affects market equilibrium. The greater the transaction costs, the less likely investors will undertake transactions to make their portfolios truly efficient. Rather than all portfolios lying on the CML, some will lie to one side or the other because transaction costs offset the advantages of being right on the line. Thus, there would be bands on

---

[11]The impact of relaxing the assumptions could also be traced through to the security market line. For further discussion see Jack Clark Francis, *Investments: Analysis and Management,* 3d ed. (New York: McGraw-Hill, 1980), ch. 19.

both sides of the CML within which portfolios would lie. Obviously, the greater the transactions costs, the wider the bands.

Finally, let's relax assumption 5 to recognize both ordinary income taxes and the capital gains taxes. This imperfection causes the after-tax return to differ between investors, depending on their tax bracket and whether the return is taxed as ordinary income or long-term capital gains. The impact is that each investor would see a slightly different CML, depending on his or her particular tax status.

It should be clear that the introduction of capital market imperfections and the relaxation of other assumptions complicates the generalizations possible from the CAPM. The conclusion is that the relationship between expected return and risk, the security market line (SML), still holds, but this relationship is not as clear or exact as described previously. The greater the imperfections, the more important the diversifiable (nonmarket) risk of the firm. The CAPM assumes the diversifiable risk can be diversified away through an efficient portfolio. However, in the presence of capital market imperfections and relaxation of assumptions, the diversifiable risk becomes more important for investors, while the importance of nondiversifiable risk, as measured by beta, becomes less important. This has obvious implications for the reliance investors and managers can place on the precise relationships suggested by the CAPM.[12] This probably explains why empirical studies have found that both σ and β are relevant measures of risk for individual firms.

PROBLEMS

6A.1.   EXPECTED UTILITY.   An investor has the following utility function:

Wealth or Income ($)	Total Utility (Utiles)
0	0
100	20
200	39
300	55
400	69
500	80
600	86
700	90

---

[12]Considerable recent theoretical developments have extended or modified the single-period capital asset pricing model described in this appendix. Two of the most important developments are the intertemporal or multiperiod CAPM developed by Robert C. Merton in "An Intertemporal Capital Asset Pricing Model," *Econometrica* 41 (September 1973), pp. 867–887; and the zero beta portfolio developed by Fischer Black in "Capital Market Equilibrium with Restricted Borrowing," *Journal of Business* 45 (July 1972), pp. 444–454.

The investor faces the following investment decision: An asset can be purchased for $350 that has a 50 percent probability of returning $700 and a 50 percent probability of returning $100.

a. Graph the investor's utility function. Does the investor's utility of wealth curve indicate decreasing marginal utility of wealth? Calculate the investor's marginal utility. Does this agree with your conclusion?

b. Calculate the expected return on the proposed investment. What is the expected utility associated with the investment?

c. Should the investor accept the proposed investment? If so, why? If not, what would the purchase price have to be before the investor should purchase the investment?

6A.2. ***PORTFOLIO RETURN AND RISK.*** Allan Rhodes has a portfolio that has a return (k_p) of 15 percent and a standard deviation (σ_p) of 14 percent. He is investigating the possibility of adding one of three new securities to the portfolio, as follows:

Security (j)	Expected Return (k_j)	Expected Risk (σ_j)	Correlation Between Security j and Portfolio p (ρ_{jp})
X	10%	10%	+.75
Y	18	50	+.90
Z	12	25	+.80

Allan intends to invest 20 percent of his wealth in one of these three securities, keeping 80 percent in his current, well-diversified portfolio.

a. Calculate the expected portfolio rate of return and standard deviation for each of the three alternatives.

b. Which prospective portfolio: (1) maximizes expected return; (2) minimizes risk? Is there any obvious choice as to which alternative security Allan should add to his portfolio? Why or why not?

c. If Allan had not wanted to calculate total portfolio risk, how else could he have determined the riskiness of the prospective investments? (*Hint:* Calculate the security beta coefficients assuming $\sigma_M = 14\%$.)

6A.3. ***PORTFOLIO RISK AS CORRELATION CHANGES.*** Grant Investment Advisors is evaluating a portfolio composed of two securities, N and O. The expected return on security N is 10 percent and the standard deviation is 20 percent. For security O, the expected return is 20 percent and the standard deviation is 50 percent.

Assume that the correlation coefficients, ρ_{NO}, are +1.0, +.50, 0.0, −.50, and −1.0. For each of the correlation coefficients what are the expected portfolio return and standard deviation if W_N is 40 percent and W_O is 60 percent?

6A.4.   *PORTFOLIO RISK AND RETURN: DIFFERENT CORRELATIONS AND SE-CURITY WEIGHTS.*   You plan to invest in some combination of two stocks, A and B. The expected return on security A is 5 percent and its standard deviation is 4 percent. For security B, the expected return is 10 percent and the standard deviation is 12 percent. For each of the three different correlations, ρ_{AB}, of +1.0, 0.0, and −1.0:

a.   What is the expected portfolio return and standard deviation for weights of 100 percent, 75 percent, 50 percent, 25 percent, and 0 percent invested in security A?

b.   Graph the results obtained in (a). Highlight the efficient frontier.

6A.5.   *PORTFOLIO RISK AND RETURN WITH DIFFERENT SECURITY WEIGHTS.* You are planning to invest $20,000. Two securities, C and D, are available and you can invest in either or both. You have estimated the following probability distribution of returns for the securities:

Security C		Security D	
Pr_i	k_i	Pr_i	k_i
.2	28%	.2	10%
.3	14	.3	6
.3	2	.3	2
.2	− 2	.2	− 2

a.   What is the expected rate of return and standard deviation for both securities? (*Hint:* $\bar{k}_C$ = 10% and σ_D = 4.10%).

b.   If ρ_{CD} = −.40, calculate the expected portfolio return and standard deviation for portfolios containing 100 percent, 75 percent, 50 percent, 25 percent, and 0 percent of security C.

c.   Plot the attainable portfolios. Which lie on the efficient frontier?

d.   Which of these portfolios should you invest in (assuming there is no risk-free asset)?

6A.6.   *EFFICIENT FRONTIER.*   The following portfolios are available:

Portfolio	Return (k_P)	Risk (σ_P)
A	9%	8%
B	3	3
C	14	10
D	12	14
E	7	11
F	11	6
G	10	12
H	16	16
I	5	7
J	8	4

You cannot mix portfolios.

a. Which of these portfolios lie on the efficient frontier? (*Hint:* It may help to plot the data.)

b. In the absence of a risk-free asset, R_F, which of these portfolios would you favor? Why?

c. Assume now that a risk-free borrowing and lending rate, R_F, of 5 percent exists. Which portfolio of risky assets do you now prefer? Why?

SELECTED REFERENCES

Arditti, Fred D., and Haim Levy. "Portfolio Efficiency Analysis in Three Moments: The Multiperiod Case." *Journal of Finance* 30 (June 1975), pp. 797–809.

Baron, David P. "On the Utility Theoretical Foundation of Mean-Variance Analysis." *Journal of Finance* 32 (December 1977), pp. 1683–1698.

Black, Fischer. "Capital Market Equilibrium with Restricted Borrowing." *Journal of Business* 45 (July 1972), pp. 444–454.

Blume, Marshall E. "On the Assessment of Risk." *Journal of Finance* 26 (March 1971), pp. 1–10.

Fama, Eugene F. *Foundations of Finance.* New York: Basic Books, 1976.

———, and G. William Schwert. "Human Capital and Capital Market Equilibrium." *Journal of Financial Economics* 5 (January 1977), pp. 95–125.

Francis, Jack Clark. *Investments: Analysis and Management*, 3d ed. New York: McGraw-Hill, 1980.

Levy, Robert A. "On the Short-Term Stationarity of Beta Coefficients." *Financial Analysts Journal* 27 (November–December 1971), pp. 55–62.

Mayers, David. "Nonmarketable Assets and the Determination of Capital Asset Prices in the Absence of a Riskless Asset." *Journal of Business* 46 (April 1973), pp. 258–267.

McEnally, Richard W. "A Note on the Return Behavior of High-Risk Common Stocks." *Journal of Finance* 29 (March 1974), pp. 199–202.

Merton, Robert C. "An Intertemporal Capital Asset Pricing Model." *Econometrica* 41 (September 1973), pp. 867–887.

Stone, Bernell K. "A Certain Class of Three-Parameter Risk Measures." *Journal of Finance* 28 (June 1973), pp. 675–686.

Swalm, Ralph O. "Utility Theory—Insights into Risk Taking." *Harvard Business Review* 44 (November–December 1966), pp. 123–136.

7

Valuation and Financial Decision Making

As noted in Chapter 1, the goal of the firm and therefore its financial manager is owner wealth maximization—or for the publicly traded corporation the goal may be restated as share price maximization. In order to maximize stock prices, the financial manager must fully understand the concept of *valuation*—the process used to determine the worth or value of a financial or real asset. Valuation relies on the use of the time value of money (presented in Chapter 5), coupled with risk and return concepts (presented in Chapter 6). This chapter links these concepts in a framework that can be used to determine the value of any asset. Applications of these techniques to key financial assets—bonds, preferred stocks, and common stocks—are presented in this chapter; subsequent chapters describe the procedures used to determine the value of real corporate assets such as plant and equipment. We begin with a discussion of basic valuation concepts and then present the techniques used in bond and stock valuation; we conclude with a discussion that relates the decisions of the financial manager to common stock valuation.[1]

Valuation Concepts

From a financial standpoint, the basis for determining the value of any asset is the expected future cash flow it will provide over its life. Theory suggests that the amount one should pay for an asset depends on the level and certainty of return it is expected to provide. Generally the

---

[1]For convenience, corporations are emphasized throughout this text, but the concepts can be applied equally well to all firms, regardless of their legal form of organization.

return one expects includes both the recapture of the original investment and some positive earnings on the investment over time. The valuation process involves estimating the future cash flows expected from an asset and then discounting them at an appropriate rate (or opportunity cost) in order to determine its present value. This relatively simple process can be applied to expected cash flows from bonds, stocks, rental properties, oil wells, and so on in order to determine their worth at a given point in time.

The Basic Valuation Equation

Simply stated, the value of any asset is equal to the present value of all the future benefits it is expected to provide. The value of an asset is therefore determined by discounting the benefits, which take the form of expected cash flows, back to their present value—using a discount rate that is commensurate with the asset's exposure to risk. Employing the present value techniques presented in Chapter 5, the value of any asset at time zero, V_0, can be expressed as:

$$V_0 = \frac{C_1}{(1 + k)^1} + \frac{C_2}{(1 + k)^2} + \cdots + \frac{C_n}{(1 + k)^n} \qquad (7.1)$$

$$= \sum_{t=1}^{n} \frac{C_t}{(1 + k)^t}$$

where V_0 = value of an asset at time zero
C_t = expected cash flow in period t
k = the appropriate discount rate
n = the expected life of the asset

If, for example, an investor expects an investment to provide annual cash inflows of $80 per year for each of the next 5 years and the appropriate discount rate is 12 percent, the value of this investment can be found by substituting C_t (for t = 1 to n) = $80, k = 12%, and n = 5 into Equation 7.1.

$$V_0 = \sum_{t=1}^{5} \frac{\$80}{(1 + .12)^t} = \$80 \ (PVIFA_{12\%, \, 5 \, yr})$$

$$= \$80(3.605) = \$288.40$$

The rational, wealth-maximizing investor would therefore pay no more than $288.40 for the investment. Paying more than that would result in a return of less than 12 percent.

Market Efficiency

Before discussing the application of valuation to bonds and stocks, a few comments on the efficiency of the securities markets are necessary. Typically (or perhaps, ideally) prospective buyers and sellers will estimate an asset's cash flows and then discount them at the appropriate rate to determine value. To the buyer, this value represents the maximum price that will be paid to acquire the asset, while to the seller it is the minimum sale price. In well-established markets, such as the New York Stock Exchange, the interaction of many buyers and sellers results in a consensus price or *market value* for each security. This price occurs at the intersection of the supply and demand schedules for the given security. The market value is, in effect, the price at which transactions take place between marginally satisfied buyers and sellers.

For financial assets like bonds and stocks, there normally are a large number of competing buyers and sellers such that any single buyer or seller has little influence on the asset's price. In this situation, the buyers or sellers are "price takers"; that is, they buy or sell at the market price without having any impact (individually) on the market value of the security. However, buyers or sellers acting collectively *may* influence the market value of an asset. This could happen if, due to something that many investors evaluated in the same manner, they all (individually) acted in such a way that the demand or supply schedule for the asset changed, resulting in a new market value for the security.

Based on their own preferences for risk and return, prospective investors will arrive at different appropriate (or required) rates of return for securities. These different rates of return, in combination with the individual investor's assessment of the amount and timing of future cash flows, will cause them to buy or sell securities at certain times. However, at the market level, given some consensus of expected future cash flows, it is possible to simplify this process and refer to "the" required rate of return for the market. This is the rate required for the marginally satisfied buyer or seller. The required return is not the same for all investors; however, a necessary simplification is to assume the existence of a consensus. Thus, market values stem from a continuous process in which individual investors estimate future cash flows and discount them at their required rates of return. In the aggregate, we call these individual investors "the market"; we call the interaction of their aggregate supply and demand schedules the "market value"; and we call the consensus rate of return "the required rate of return."

In recent years, a great deal of attention has been given to the concept of *market efficiency.* An efficient market is made up of many rational investors who react quickly and in an unbiased fashion to new information. In an efficient market, if new information concerning the future prospects of a firm becomes available (and it is perceived as influencing the value of the firm), individual investors can be expected to make buy-or-sell decisions that will cause the market value of the firm's securities to adjust to a new equilibrium price. The efficient market hypothesis states:

1. Securities are typically in equilibrium, meaning that they are fairly priced based upon their expected returns and the risks involved.

2.   At any point in time, security prices fully reflect the public information available about the firm and its securities, and such prices react swiftly to new information.
3.   Since stocks are fairly and fully priced, it follows that investors should not waste their time trying to find undervalued or bargain securities.

In effect, if stock prices reflect all available information and are fairly priced, and investors cannot consistently "beat the market," the market is efficient. It is generally agreed that the stock market is reasonably efficient.[2] In an efficient market, the market price at any point in time is the best estimate of value. This is the assumption on which we will work.

Return, Risk, and Market Equilibrium

As noted in Equation 6.1 in the preceding chapter, the return to an investor is the realizable cash flow earned during a specified period of time. It is customary in finance to measure such returns as an annual percentage rate in relation to the initial investment. For example, if an investor purchased a security for $100 at the beginning of the year, received a cash flow of $8 from the security during the year, and sold the security for $105 at the end of the year, substituting into Equation 6.1 yields an annual rate of return of:

$$k = \frac{\$105 - \$100 + \$8}{\$100} = \frac{\$5 + \$8}{\$100} = \frac{\$13}{\$100} = 13\%$$

It is common in finance to refer to returns as realized, expected, and required. Because of the potential ambiguity associated with use of these terms, it is important to understand their differences. *Realized return* is a historic return that could have been received by an investor who actually owned the given security during the period in question. In the preceding example, the investor would have had a realized return of 13 percent (before any brokerage fees and taxes).[3] An *expected return* is a future return one expects to receive from owning a given investment vehicle. For example, an investor may expect a share of common stock costing $60 per share today to pay $5 in cash dividends during the coming year and to be worth $62.50 at the end of the year. The investor expects to earn $5 in dividend income and $2.50 in capital appreciation, resulting

---

[2]There is an impressive body of recent research on various aspects of market efficiency. While there are some indications of market inefficiency, the literature suggests that the major securities markets are reasonably efficient. The selected references at the end of this chapter include some of the key literature on market efficiency.

[3]Note that throughout this and the following discussions, the payment of brokerage fees and taxes as a result of purchasing and selling financial assets is ignored, although these factors can significantly affect an investor's return.

in a cash flow of $7.50 from the $60 investment. The expected return therefore would be 12.5 percent ($7.50 ÷ $60).

Finally, the *required return* is the minimum return an investor would like to receive from an investment; it is largely dependent on the level of risk involved in the investment and the investor's general disposition toward risk. As noted in Chapter 6, the capital asset pricing model is used to determine the level of return required:

$$k_j = R_F + \beta_j \times (k_M - R_F) \tag{7.2}$$

The expected risk is measured by beta, the index of nondiversifiable risk. The degree of risk aversion of market participants is reflected in the market risk premium, $k_M - R_F$ (the required or expected rate of return on the market portfolio minus the risk-free rate). For example, an investor considering a stock having a beta of 1.25 when the risk-free rate is 10 percent and the market return is 14 percent would have a required return of

$$k = 10\% + 1.25 \times (14\% - 10\%) = 10\% + 5\% = 15\%$$

In actual practice, investors often subjectively estimate the required return to be the rate of return available on what are viewed as similar-risk investments. The use of such a proxy has appeal, since it bypasses the need to make the calculations required by the theoretically preferred CAPM approach.

Equilibrium will exist in an efficient market since suppliers and demanders through their interaction agree on a price and therefore expect a level of return equal to that required. Since efficient security markets are assumed throughout this text, the terms *expected return* and *required return* are used interchangeably when discussing security returns.

Bond Valuation

Corporate *bonds* are financial assets that indicate that a corporation has borrowed a certain amount of money which it has promised to repay in the future. Most corporate bonds pay interest semiannually (every 6 months), have an initial maturity of 10 to 30 years,[4] and have a *par (or face) value* of $1000 that must be repaid at maturity.[5] The *coupon interest*

---

[4]There are, in fact, a few examples of bonds that are perpetual in nature, since no maturity date is attached to the issue. During the Napoleonic Wars (1814) England sold an issue of perpetual bonds called Consols (because they were issued to consolidate past debts). In more recent times, the Canadian government raised $55 million by issuing perpetual bonds at a 3 percent annual interest rate. Valuation of perpetuities is illustrated in a subsequent section of this chapter.

[5]Bonds often have other features that allow them to be retired by the issuer prior to maturity; these call and conversion features are presented in Chapters 21 and 23. For the purpose of the current discussion, these features are ignored.

rate indicates the amount of interest to be paid each year and is expressed as a percentage of the bond's par value. Since bond interest is typically paid semiannually, the bond would pay half the stated coupon every 6 months.

Basic Bond Valuation

Consistent with Equation 7.1, the value of a bond at any time is the present value of the contractual payments its issuer is obligated to make until the day it matures. The basic equation for the value of a bond, B_0, that pays annual interest of I dollars, has n years to maturity, has an M dollar par value, and for which the required return is k_b, is given by Equation 7.3. This equation is a straightforward application of the present value techniques presented in Chapter 5.

$$B_0 = \frac{I}{(1 + k_b)^1} + \frac{I}{(1 + k_b)^2} + \cdots + \frac{I}{(1 + k_b)^n} + \frac{M}{(1 + k_b)^n} \tag{7.3}$$

$$= I \sum_{t=1}^{n} \left[\frac{1}{(1 + k_b)^t} \right] + M \left[\frac{1}{(1 + k_b)^n} \right] \tag{7.3a}$$

$$= I(PVIFA_{k_b,n}) + M(PVIF_{k_b,n}) \tag{7.3b}$$

Suppose we wish to find the value of a $1000, 10 percent coupon, 20-year bond issued by the Boston Manufacturing Company. Assuming that the interest is paid annually, $I = .10 \times \$1000 = \$100$, and the required return is equal to the bond's stated rate of interest, we see that by substituting the appropriate values into Equation 7.3:

$$B_0 = \$100 \ (PVIFA_{10\%, 20 \text{ yr}}) + \$1000 \ (PVIF_{10\%, 20 \text{ yr}})$$
$$= \$100(8.514) + \$1000(.149)$$
$$= \$851.40 + \$149.00 = \$1000.40$$

The bond has a value of approximately $1000.[6] Note that the value calculated above is equal to par value; this will always be the case when the coupon rate of interest is equal to the required return.

Required Returns and Bond Values. Whenever the required return on a bond differs from the bond's coupon rate, its value will differ from par. The required return on a bond is likely to differ from the coupon rate for either of two reasons:

1. *Shift in the supply and demand relationship for money.* This will cause the basic cost of money—the interest rate—to rise or fall, depending on whether there is a reduction in supply relative to

---

[6]Note that a slight rounding error ($.40) results here due to the use of the table factors, which are rounded to the nearest one-thousandth.

demand or an increase in supply relative to demand, respectively. Shifts in the supply-demand relationship result from a variety of economic forces.

2. *Change in risk.* This will affect the required return such that if the risk of the firm's bonds as perceived by market participants increases, the required return on them will rise, and vice versa.

Regardless of the exact cause, the important point is that when the required return is greater than the coupon rate, the bond value, B_0, will be less than its par value, M. In this case the bond is said to sell at a discount, which equals $M - B_0$. On the other hand, when the required rate of return falls below the coupon rate of interest, the bond value will be greater than par. In this situation, the bond is said to sell at a premium, which equals $B_0 - M$.

The Boston Manufacturing Company bond can be used to illustrate this point. Imagine that although the coupon rate on the bond is 10 percent, its required return is 12 percent; in this case the bond's value would be:

$$B_0 = \$100 \ (PVIFA_{12\%, \ 20 \ yr}) + \$1000 \ (PVIF_{12\%, \ 20 \ yr})$$
$$= \$100 \ (7.469) + \$1000 \ (.104) = \$850.90$$

The bond would therefore sell at a discount of $149.10 ($1,000 par value — $850.90 value). If, on the other hand, the required return fell to, say, 8 percent, the bond's value would be:

$$B_0 = \$100 \ (PVIFA_{8\%, \ 20 \ yr}) + \$1000 \ (PVIF_{8\%, \ 20 \ yr})$$
$$= \$100 \ (9.818) + \$1000 \ (.215) = \$1196.80$$

The bond in this case would sell at a premium of $196.80 ($1,196.80 value — $1,000 par value). These results are summarized in Table 7.1, where it can be seen that when the required return is above the coupon rate, the bond sells at a discount; and when it is below the coupon rate, it sells at a premium.

Bond values are also affected by the number of years to maturity. If the required return differs from the coupon rate, a bond's value will change as the bond approaches maturity, no matter what happens to market rates. The actual change in

	Required Return, k_b	Bond Value, B_0	Status
TABLE 7.1 Boston Manufacturing's Bond Values for Various Required Returns	12%	$ 850.90	Discount Bond
	10	1000.00	Par Bond
	8	1196.80	Premium Bond

value depends on whether or not the required return is greater or less than the coupon rate.

1. *Required Return Greater Than Coupon Rate.* If the required return is greater than the coupon rate, the bond will sell at a discount. As the bond approaches maturity, the discount will decline and the bond will *increase* in value. In other words, the closer the bond is to maturity, the higher its value. For example, at a 12 percent required return, the Boston Manufacturing Company bond at 18 years to maturity would have a value of:

$$B_0 = \$100 \ (PVIFA_{12\%, \ 18 \ yr}) + \$1000 \ (PVIF_{12\%, \ 18 \ yr})$$
$$= \$100 \ (7.250) + \$1000 \ (.130) = \$855.00$$

Comparing this figure to the $850.90 for the 20-year bond in Table 7.1, we can see that the bond increases in value as it approaches maturity. Given the 12 percent required return, the bond will increase in value each year until it matures, when its value will equal its $1000 par value.[7] The bottom portion of Figure 7.1 depicts the bond value as a function of time to maturity when the bond is selling at a discount.

2. *Required Return Less Than Coupon Rate.* If the required return is less than the coupon rate, the bond will sell at a premium. As the bond approaches maturity, the premium will decline and the bond value will *decrease*. In other words, the closer the bond is to maturity, the lower its value. For example, at an 8 percent required return and with 18 years to maturity, the Boston Manufacturing Company bond would have a value of:

$$B_0 = \$100 \ (PVIFA_{8\%, \ 18 \ yr}) + \$1000 \ (PVIF_{8\%, \ 18 \ yr})$$
$$= \$100 \ (9.372) + \$1000 \ (.250) = \$1187.20$$

Comparing this value to the $1196.80 for the 20-year bond in Table 7.1, we see that the bond decreases in value as it approaches maturity. As noted in the top portion of Figure 7.1, at an 8 percent required return, the bond value will decrease each year until it equals its face value.

Bond values are not stationary over time; they fluctuate inversely with changes in the required return. A bond's value will fluctuate more in response to a change in interest rates the longer the time to maturity. This property can be observed in Figure 7.1. For example, if with 18 years

---

[7]This increase in market value assumes that the required return remains constant at 12 percent until maturity.

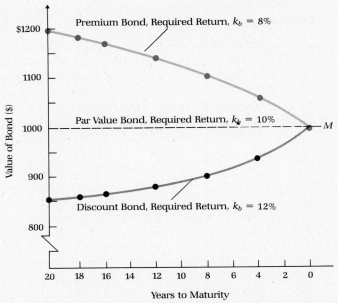

Figure 7.1 Time Path of the Value of a 10 Percent Coupon Bond, $1000 Par Value, 20-Year Maturity, when Required Returns are 8 Percent, 10 Percent, and 12 Percent.

to maturity, the required return declines from 10 percent to 8 percent, the bond's value goes from $1000 to $1187.20—an 18.72 percent increase. If the same change in required return had occurred with only 4 years to maturity, the bond value would have risen to just $1066.20—only a 6.6 percent rise.

Yield to Maturity   Bonds generally trade on the basis of *yield to maturity (YTM)*: that is, the rate investors earn if they buy the bond at a specific price (B_0) and hold it until maturity. Suppose you were offered a 12 percent coupon, 15-year, $1000 par bond selling at $1050. Clearly, you would be paying more than par for the bond, but what would be your return if you held it to maturity? Assuming interest is paid annually, the yield to maturity on the bond can be determined by solving Equation 7.3 for k_b:

$$B_0 = \$1050 = \left[\frac{\$120}{(1 + k_b)^1} + \frac{\$120}{(1 + k_b)^2} + \cdots + \frac{\$120}{(1 + k_b)^{15}} \right] + \frac{\$1000}{(1 + k_b)^{15}}$$

$$= \$1050 = \$120 \sum_{t=1}^{15} \left[\frac{1}{(1 + k_b)^t} \right] + \frac{\$1000}{(1 + k_b)^{15}}$$

$$= \$1050 = \$120 \, (PVIFA_{k_b, \, 15 \, yr}) + \$1000 \, (PVIF_{k_b, \, 15 \, yr})$$

In order to solve for YTM, a trial and error procedure is necessary.[8] By examining the equation, we see that the initial value, $B_0 = \$1050$, is greater than the maturity value. Hence, the discount rate (or YTM) that equates the present value of the cash inflows with B_0 must be *less* than 12 percent. By trying 11 percent, we see that the present value of the annual interest payments and maturity value equals $1071.92:

$$\$120 \ (PVIFA_{11\%, \ 15 \ yr}) \ + \ \$1000 \ (PVIF_{11\%, \ 15 \ yr}) = \$120 \ (7.191) + \$1000 \ (.209)$$
$$= \$862.92 + \$209 = \$1071.92$$

Since our discounted present value is greater than the purchase price of $1050, the 11 percent rate is too low. Interpolation allows us to determine that the YTM on this bond is 11.31 percent.[9] The yield to

---

[8]Bond traders do not generally employ this trial-and-error approach; instead, they rely on specialized tables called bond tables that give yields on bonds of different maturities selling at different premiums and discounts. In addition, many of the specialized small calculators have functions that make finding the YTM on a bond an easy matter. Instead of finding the yield to maturity by the trial-and-error approach, a formula can be employed to find the *approximate* YTM on a bond:

$$k_b = \frac{I + (M - B_0)/n}{(M + B_0)/2}$$

In the situation where $I = \$120$, $M = \$1000$, $B_0 = \$1050$, and $n = 15$ years, the approximate yield to maturity is 11.38 percent:

$$k_b = \frac{\$120 + (\$1000 - \$1050)/15}{(\$1000 + \$1050)/2} = \frac{\$120 - \$3.33}{\$1025} = \frac{\$116.67}{\$1025} = 11.38\%$$

This value is close to the YTM of 11.31 percent determined by the more precise present-value approach.

In addition, many bonds have a provision that makes them *callable*—the issuer has the option to buy them back at a specified price. A typical provision is that a bond may not be called for the first 5 or 10 years from the date of issue. To account for this possibility, the *yield to call*, in addition to the YTM, is often calculated. The yield to call is calculated in the same manner as the YTM, but employs the shorter time period based on the earliest call date for the bond.

[9]To determine the yield to maturity by trial and error, interpolation must be employed. The necessary steps required to calculate the YTM are these:

a. Find the present value of the outflows at the two consecutive rates that cause the initial amount, B_0, to be straddled. In this case the present value at 12 percent (found using the present-value interest factors in Table A.3) is $1000.32; at 11 percent it is $1071.92. B_0 is $1050, which is between these values.
b. Find the difference between the present value of the two flows, which in this case is $71.60 ($1071.92 − $1000.32).
c. Find the difference between the present value of the outflows at the *lower* rate ($1071.92 at 11 percent) and the desired value, $1050, which in this case is $21.92 ($1071.92 − $1050).
d. Divide the result from (c), which is $21.92, by the result from (b), which is $71.60. This results in a value rounded to the nearest one-hundredth of 0.31.
e. Add the fraction from (d) to the lower of the two rates developed in (a), 11 percent. This results in a yield to maturity of 11.31 percent (0.31 + 11.00).

maturity for a bond selling at par is exactly equal to its coupon rate. If the bond sells at a premium, the YTM will be less than the coupon rate; if it sells at a discount, the YTM will be greater than the coupon rate. The YTM indicates the return one would receive if the bond is held to maturity; however, YTMs do change over time as economic conditions and interest rates in general change.

Semiannual Interest and Bond Values

The procedure used to value bonds paying interest semiannually is similar to that illustrated in Chapter 5 (see the discussion on the use of other discounting periods when finding present value). The process involves these steps:

Step 1. Convert annual interest, I, to semiannual interest by dividing it by 2.

Step 2. Convert the number of years to maturity, n, to the number of 6-month periods to maturity by multiplying n by 2.

Step 3. Convert the required return from an annual rate, k_b, to a semiannual rate by dividing it by 2.

Substituting these changes into Equation 7.3 yields[10]

$$B_0 = \frac{I}{2} \sum_{t=1}^{2n} \left[\frac{1}{(1 + k_b/2)^t} \right] + M \left[\frac{1}{(1 + k_b/2)2n} \right] \tag{7.4}$$

$$= \frac{I}{2} \ (PVIFA \ k_b/2, \ 2n) + M \ (PVIF \ k_b/2, \ 2n) \tag{7.4a}$$

The Boston Manufacturing Company bond can be used to illustrate the application of Equation 7.4 to find the value of a bond paying semiannual interest when the required rate is 12 percent; that is:

$$B_0 = \frac{\$100}{2} \ (PVIFA_{12\%/2, \ 2 \times 20 \text{ yr}}) + \$1000 \ (PVIF_{12\%/2, \ 2 \times 20 \text{ yr}})$$

$$= \$50 \ (PVIFA_{6\%, \ 40 \text{ periods}}) + \$1000 \ (PVIF_{6\%, \ 40 \text{ periods}})$$

$$= \$50 \ (15.046) + \$1000 \ (.097) = \$849.30$$

This figure is slightly less than the $850.90 value found earlier using annual compounding, a condition which will always result when bonds sell at a discount; for bonds selling at a premium the opposite will occur.

---

[10]Although it may appear inappropriate to use the semiannual discounting procedure on the maturity value, M (second term to the right of the equal sign), this technique is necessary in order to find the bond value correctly. One way to confirm the accuracy of this approach is to calculate the bond value in the case where the required return and stated rate of interest are equal; in order for B to equal M, as would be expected in such a case, the maturity value must be discounted on a semiannual basis.

Perpetual Bonds and Preferred Stock Valuation

A *perpetual bond* is one that pays a stated amount of interest periodically (annually or semiannually) over an infinite time horizon; in other words, its par value, M, is never repaid. Preferred stock, while a form of equity, is like a perpetual bond in that it never matures.[11] It pays a fixed dividend amount, stated on an annual basis, usually in equal quarterly instalments. Because it is a fixed-income security with preference over common stock, both in terms of receipt of income and liquidation, it is grouped with debt rather than equity for purposes of comparison.

Assuming for simplicity that a perpetual bond or preferred stock makes an annual payment of interest or dividends, I, and that the required return is k_b, the value of either of these vehicles can be defined as:

$$B_0 = \frac{I}{k_b} = I\left(\frac{1}{k_b}\right) \qquad (7.5)$$

Recall from Chapter 5 that the present-value interest factor for a perpetuity is $PVIFA_{k_b,\infty} = 1/k_b$; this factor is the righthand term in Equation 7.5. To illustrate, assume the Globe Tool Company has an issue of preferred stock outstanding that has a stated annual dividend of $5 and a required return of 13 percent. Substituting $I = \$5$ and $k_b = 13\%$ into Equation 7.5 yields a preferred stock value of $38.46. Note that the same calculation would have been used to value a perpetual bond or, for that matter, *any* perpetuity with an annual return of $5 and having a required return of 13 percent.

Common Stock Valuation

Common stockholders are the owners of the company; as such they are the last to receive any return from their investment and are considered the "residual" owners. In exchange for purchasing common stock, these owners expect to be rewarded through the receipt of periodic cash dividends and, hopefully, an increasing—or at least nondeclining—share value. It is not only existing owners who are concerned with share value; prospective owners and security analysts are involved in the valuation process as well. They choose to purchase the stock when they believe it to be undervalued (computed value greater than market price) and to sell when they feel it is overvalued (market price greater than computed value).[12] We will look now at some of the ratio approaches for estimating share value.

---

[11]Technically a firm may be able to retire preferred stock in a number of ways; a discussion of these and other features of preferred stocks appears in Chapters 21 and 23.

[12]As noted earlier, a growing body of financial data suggests that widely held stocks that are actively traded are always properly valued in the marketplace. In other words, the market is efficient—the market price equals intrinsic value. Such a conclusion tends to make obsolete much of what security analysts do. But a great deal of controversy surrounds this conclusion.

Ratio
Approaches

Book Value.   Book value per share is simply the value of the firm's ownership per share in the event that all assets are liquidated for their exact book (accounting) value, and the proceeds remaining after paying all liabilities (including preferred stock) are divided among the common stockholders. This method lacks sophistication and can be criticized on the basis of its reliance on historical balance sheet data; it ignores the firm's expected earnings potential. Let us look at an example. Sunshine Industries currently (December 31, 1984) has total assets of $6 million, total liabilities (including preferred stock) of $4.5 million, and 100,000 shares of common stock outstanding. Its book value per share, therefore, would be:

$$\frac{\$6,000,000 - \$4,500,000}{100,000 \text{ shares}} = \$15 \text{ per share}$$

Since this value assumes that assets are liquidated for their book value, it is in no way indicative of the firm's going concern value. As a matter of fact, although most stocks sell above book value (at least over the long run), it is not unusual to find some stocks selling below book value.

Liquidation Value.   Liquidation value is the amount each common stockholder would receive if the firm's assets are sold "on the auction block," creditors and preferred stockholders are paid, and any remaining money is divided among the common stockholders.[13] This measure may be more realistic than book value, but it still fails to consider the earning power of the firm's assets. To illustrate, assume Sunshine Industries estimated that it would obtain only $5,250,000 if it liquidated its assets today. The firm's liquidation value per share therefore would be:

$$\frac{\$5,250,000 - \$4,500,000}{100,000 \text{ shares}} = \$7.50 \text{ per share}$$

Ignoring any expenses of liquidation, this would be the firm's minimum value.

Price/Earnings Multiples.   The average price/earnings (P/E) ratio in an *industry* can be used as a guide to a firm's value if it is assumed that investors value the earnings of a given firm in the same way as they do the earnings of the average firm in the industry. The average P/E for an industry can be obtained from a source such as Standard & Poors

---

[13]In the event of liquidation, creditors' claims must be satisfied first, then those of the preferred stockholders. Anything left goes to common stockholders. A more detailed discussion of liquidation procedures is presented in Chapter 16.

Industrial Ratios. Multiplying the forecasted annual earnings per share of a firm by this ratio gives an estimate of the value of the firm's shares.

This measure of value, like the preceding ones, lacks any deep theoretical roots. It is best looked on as a tool for estimating a firm's share price. The accuracy of the estimate depends on how "average" the company is. This technique is commonly used to value firms that are not publicly traded; the use of market price may be preferable in the case of a publicly traded firm. But in any case, the price/earnings multiple approach is believed to be superior to the use of book or liquidation values when estimating going concern values, since it implicitly considers expected earnings. Consider the following example of how price/earnings multiples are used to value stock. Assume Sunshine Industries is expected to earn $2.60 per share next year (1985); this expectation is based on an analysis of the firm's historical earnings trend and certain industry factors expected to be operating in the coming year. The average price/earnings ratio for the industry is 6.67. Multiplying Sunshine's expected earnings per share of $2.60 by this ratio gives us a value for the shares of $17.34, assuming that investors consider the firm to be "average."[14]

Common Stock Valuation: The Single-Period Time Horizon

The value of common stock can be assessed using a single-period time horizon—typically 1 year—or a multiperiod time horizon. The multiperiod horizon is most common, but the single-period approach is a logical prerequisite to a thorough understanding of the more popular multiperiod model. Ownership of common stock entitles the holder to participate in financial gains or losses through dividends declared and paid by the firm, and capital gains (or losses). The following terminology is used in our discussion of stock valuation:

P_t = price of the stock at the end of the year t;[15] P_0 is the price of the stock today.

D_t = dividend the shareholder expects to receive at the end of year t. D_0 is the dividend paid today; D_1 is the dividend expected to be received one year from today; and so on.

---

[14]The actual rate at which an investor is assumed to discount earnings is found by taking the inverse of the price/earnings ratio (1/6.67, or .150). Dividing this value into the firm's expected earnings of $2.60 would once again yield approximately $17.34. The price/earnings multiple approach to valuation, when viewed in this manner, does have a theoretical explanation. If we view 1 divided by the price/earnings ratio, or the earnings/price ratio, as the rate at which investors discount the firm's earnings, and if we assume that the projected earnings per share will be earned indefinitely, the price/earnings multiple approach can be looked on as a method of finding the present value of a perpetuity of projected earnings per share at a required rate of return equal to the earnings/price ratio.

[15]In common stock valuation it is typical to use annual data. While data on some other basis could be employed, the associated problems appear to outweigh any benefits in terms of greater precision.

g = expected growth rate in dividends (and earnings and market price) per share over time.

k_s = expected or required rate of return on the stock.

The value of a stock to an investor is, as with any other asset, a function of the cash flows the investor expects to receive. The investor is particularly interested in three items that affect these cash flows—dividends paid per share, expected growth rate in dividends, and the period of growth in dividends—all of which have a bearing on annual income and capital gains. In addition, an investor is also interested in the expected or required rate of return on common stock (which is a function of general economic conditions and firm-specific factors expected to influence risk and return). Since common stocks do not have contractual or "promised" payment streams and have a claim on income and assets secondary to that of bonds, there is more risk for a firm's stockholders in comparison to its bondholders. Therefore, the required rate of return on a firm's stock will be greater than the required rate of return on a firm's bonds.

If an investor buys a stock today which she intends to hold for only one year, how much would the investor be willing to pay for the stock? The price today, P_0, is simply equal to the discounted present value of the dividend to be received at the end of the year plus the discounted present value of the expected market price in one year:

$$P_0 = \frac{D_1}{(1 + k_s)^1} + \frac{P_1}{(1 + k_s)^1} = \frac{D_1 + P_1}{(1 + k_s)^1} \qquad (7.6)$$

If, for example, Sunshine Industries has estimated dividends of $1.50 per share in 1985, an expected market price of $19.85 at the end of 1985, and a required rate of return of 15 percent, the value of one share of Sunshine Industries would equal:

$$P_0 = \frac{\$1.50 + \$19.85}{(1 + .15)^1}$$
$$= (\$1.50 + \$19.85) \, (PVIF_{15\%, 1yr})$$
$$= \$21.35 \, (.870) = \$18.57$$

If the investor purchases Sunshine for $18.57, receives the dividend of $1.50, and is able to sell the stock for $19.85 in 1 year, she will earn 15 percent return on her investment. In other words, in the single-period case, the value of a share of stock is merely the present value of any dividends expected during the period plus the present value of the estimated end-of-period share price (we will see below how the end-of-period share price, P_1, is determined). But many investors have horizons that extend beyond a single period; they require multiperiod valuation models.

Common Stock
Valuation:
Multiperiod Time
Horizons

In moving from a single-period valuation model to the more complicated multiperiod model, all we need do is add one more term for each year's dividends to Equation 7.6 until the equation is expanded to a general stock valuation model, as specified below:

$$P_0 = \frac{D_1}{(1 + k_s)^1} + \frac{D_2}{(1 + k_s)^2} + \cdots + \frac{D_\infty}{(1 + k_s)^\infty} \tag{7.7}$$
$$= \sum_{t=1}^{\infty} \frac{D_t}{(1 + k_s)^t}$$

where P, D, and k_s are as previously defined. In this form, the company is expected to exist forever and the value of the stock is simply the present value of all future dividends. Although this model has considerable theoretical appeal, it does have obvious problems in terms of practical application. The most obvious is what to do when the investment horizon is finite (less than infinite). This problem is easy to resolve. To determine the value of a stock, based upon expected dividends and an expected market price over an n-year time horizon, Equation 7.7 can be rewritten as:

$$P_0 = \frac{D_1}{(1 + k_s)^1} + \frac{D_2}{(1 + k_s)^2} + \cdots + \frac{D_n}{(1 + k_s)^n} + \frac{P_n}{(1 + k_s)^n} \tag{7.8}$$
$$= \sum_{t=1}^{n} \left[\frac{D_t}{(1 + k_s)^t} \right] + \frac{P_n}{(1 + k_s)^n}$$

This is exactly the same approach we used to value bonds (see Equation 7.3). In comparing Equations 7.7 and 7.8, it is important to recognize that the price at the end of period n, P_n, equals the present value of all future dividends expected from the end of period $n + 1$ to ∞; that is,

$$P_n = \sum_{t=n+1}^{\infty} \left[\frac{D_t}{(1 + k_s)^t} \right]$$

Suppose Sunshine Industries had an expected dividend stream of $D_1 = D_{1985} = \$1.50$, $D_2 = D_{1986} = \$1.55$, and $D_3 = D_{1987} = \$1.60$; also, its future price P_{1987}, is expected to be \$25, and k_s is (once again) 15 percent. Applying Equation 7.8, the stock value today, $P_0 = P_{1984}$, would be:

$$
\begin{aligned}
P_{1984} &= D_{1985}(PVIF_{15\%,\,1\,yr}) + D_{1986}(PVIF_{15\%,\,2\,yr}) + D_{1987}(PVIF_{15\%,\,3\,yr}) \\
&\quad + P_{1987}(PVIF_{15\%,\,3\,yr}) \\
&= \$1.50\,(.870) + \$1.55\,(.756) + \$1.60\,(.658) + \$25\,(.658) \\
&= \$1.31 + \$1.17 + \$1.05 + \$16.45 = \$19.98
\end{aligned}
$$

While the result seems no more difficult to obtain than bond values, the expected dividends, D_t, in stock valuation are not necessarily constant, as are the interest payments, I, in bond valuation. In addition, the values of D_t and P_n in Equation 7.8 are not known with certainty, whereas in bond valuation, the amount of the interest payments, I, and maturity value, M, are known with certainty. Stock valuation is a bit more challenging than bond valuation, but certain refinements can be used to simplify the operation without significantly affecting the accuracy of the results.

The Role of Dividends

We have seen above that a stock's price is determined by the present value of the stream of future cash flows. These cash flows have been stated in terms of expected cash dividends (or in Equations 7.6 and 7.8 as both cash dividends and future market prices). One question that should be raised here is, why aren't earnings important? In fact, they are important, since it is the stream of earnings that enables the dividends to be paid.[16] Many valuation models allow the flows related to equity valuation to be stated in alternative forms. The three most common approaches to equity valuation involve capitalizing (1) the stream of dividends, (2) the stream of earnings, or (3) the current earnings plus flows resulting from future investment opportunities. Miller and Modigliani have demonstrated that these different approaches are equivalent and yield the same valuation.[17] Since multiperiod common stock valuation models are inherently complicated, we will illustrate the model using the least complicated approach—dividend valuation.

Another point that needs to be addressed is what happens when the firm pays no current dividends? Is the value of the firm zero? The answer is no, because the present market price depends on *all* future expected dividends. Even if dividends for, say, the next 10 years are expected to be zero, the current price, P_0, will not be zero, since the underlying assumption is that sooner or later the company will start paying dividends. Only if the stock is *never* expected to pay any cash dividends and no other prospect of value (in any form) is available would we be safe in assigning a value of zero to the current share price.

We can use Equations 7.7 or 7.8 for stock valuation purposes when dividends are rising, falling, or even fluctuating randomly. However, because it is useful to develop simplified versions of these equations for

---

[16]Due to the accounting ambiguity that often results from the multiplicity of techniques available for measuring earnings, the use of dividends, which are real cash flows distributed to owners, is most consistent with the cash flow viewpoint generally accepted by financial managers as well as investors. It is cash received as dividends—not earnings—that provides a spendable return on one's investment and therefore is the key source of value.

[17]See Merton Miller and Franco Modigliani, "Dividend Policy, Growth, and the Valuation of Shares," *Journal of Business* 34 (October 1961), pp. 411–433.

such purposes, we will now consider three special cases: zero dividend growth, constant dividend growth, and variable dividend growth.

Zero Dividend Growth.   In the simplest of these three cases, suppose a firm is expected to pay constant (nongrowing) dividends over the foreseeable future. In terms of the notations already introduced,

$$D_1 = D_2 = \cdots = D_\infty$$

Letting D_1 equal the amount of the annual dividend, Equation 7.7 would reduce to[18]

$$P_0 = D_1 \left[\sum_{t=1}^{\infty} \frac{1}{(1 + k_s)^t} \right] = D_1 (PVIFA_{k_s,\infty})$$

$$= \frac{D_1}{k_s} \tag{7.9}$$

The equation shows that with zero growth, the value of a share of stock is equal to the present value of a perpetuity of D_1 dollars, discounted at a

---

[18]This is another perpetuity—their valuation was considered in Chapter 5. The derivation of Equation 7.9 from Equation 7.7 is as follows:

$$P_0 = \frac{D_1}{(1 + k_s)^1} + \frac{D_2}{(1 + k_s)^2} + \cdots + \frac{D_\infty}{(1 + k_s)^\infty}$$

Since $D_1 = D_2 = \cdots = D_\infty$, Equation 7.7 may be rewritten as follows, letting $D = D_1 = D_2 = \cdots = D_\infty$:

$$P_0 = D \left[\frac{1}{(1 + k_s)^1} + \frac{1}{(1 + k_s)^2} + \cdots + \frac{1}{(1 + k_s)^n} \right]$$

Multiplying both sides by $(1 + k_s)$ yields:

$$P_0 (1 + k_s) = D \left[1 + \frac{1}{(1 + k_s)^1} + \frac{1}{(1 + k_s)^2} + \cdots + \frac{1}{(1 + k_s)^{n-1}} \right]$$

Subtracting the preceding equation from the most recent equation results in:

$$P_0 (1 + k_s - 1) = D \left[1 - \frac{1}{(1 + k_s)^n} \right]$$

As $n \rightarrow \infty$, $\frac{1}{(1 + k_s)^n} = 0$, so:

$$P_0 (k_s) = D$$

and $P_0 = D/k_s$; since $D = D_1$; $P_0 = D_1/k_s$.

rate k_s.[19] It should be clear that the form of this equation is identical to that of Equation 7.5, which is used to value perpetual bonds and preferred stock. To illustrate, suppose Sunshine Industries expects its dividends to remain constant and equal to its $2.60 per share earnings indefinitely. If the required return on the stock is 15 percent, the stocks' value, using Equation 7.9, would be approximately $17.34 ($2.60 ÷ .15).

Constant Dividend Growth.   Many firms have dividend streams that can be described as growing at a constant (or reasonably steady) rate for the foreseeable future. Letting D_0 represent the most recent dividend, and g equal the constant rate of growth in dividends, Equation 7.7 can be rewritten as follows:

$$P_0 = \frac{D_0(1 + g)^1}{(1 + k_s)^1} + \frac{D_0(1 + g)^2}{(1 + k_s)^2} + \cdots + \frac{D_0(1 + g)^\infty}{(1 + k_s)^\infty} \qquad (7.10)$$

If we simplify Equation 7.10, it can be rewritten as follows:[20]

---

[19]Since to achieve zero growth the firm must pay out all earnings as dividends, the earnings in each period, E_0, would equal each period's dividend, D_0. Equation 7.9 could therefore be rewritten as

$$P_0 = \frac{E_0}{k_s}$$

In comparing this equation to the approach for finding value using price/earnings multiples presented earlier, it should be clear the approaches are similar; each determines the value of an infinite stream of earnings, E_0. The value for k_s when using the price/earnings multiple approach is the inverse of the industry price/earnings multiple:

$$P_0 = \frac{E_0}{E/P}$$

where E/P is the industry earnings/price multiple. In other words, the use of the price/earnings multiple approach to estimate value is consistent with the zero-growth stock valuation model.

[20]Since $D_t = D_0(1 + g)^t$, Equation 7.7 can be rewritten as:

$$P_0 = \frac{D_0(1 + g)^1}{(1 + k_s)^1} + \frac{D_0(1 + g)^2}{(1 + k_s)^2} + \cdots + \frac{D_0(1 + g)^\infty}{(1 + k_s)^\infty}$$

for the case where g is the expected constant growth rate. Multiplying both sides of this equation by $(1 + k_s)/(1 + g)$ and subtracting this equation from the product, we obtain

$$\frac{P_0(1 + k_s)}{(1 + g)} - P_0 = D_0 - \frac{D_0(1 + g)^\infty}{(1 + k_s)^\infty}$$

Since k_s is assumed to be greater than g, the second term on the right side of this equation should be zero. Thus,

$$P_0 \left(\frac{1 + k_s}{1 + g} - 1 \right) = D_0$$

$$P_0 = \frac{D_1}{k_s - g} \qquad (7.11)$$

where D_1 represents the dividend expected to be paid at the end of the coming year.

This is probably the most widely cited dividend valuation model.[21] To illustrate the application of Equation 7.11, assume that Sunshine Industries, which has a required return, k_s, of 15 percent, has paid the dividends shown below during the period 1979 through 1984.

Year		Dividend
1979		$1.00
1980		1.05
1981		1.12
1982		1.20
1983		1.29
1984	$D_0 = D_{1984} =$	1.40

Using the table of present-value interest factors, Table A.3, in conjunction with the technique described in Chapter 5 for finding growth rates, we find that g, the annual growth rate of dividends, equals 7 percent,[22] and note that this rate is expected to remain constant for the foreseeable

---

Simplifying, we have:

$$P_0 \left(\frac{(1 + k_s) - (1 + g)}{1 + g} \right) = D_0$$

$$P_0(k_s - g) = D_0(1 + g)$$

$$P_0 = \frac{D_1}{k_s - g}$$

If k_s were less than g, the market price of the stock would be infinite. See David Durand, "Growth Stocks and the Petersburg Paradox," *Journal of Finance* 12 (September 1957), pp. 348–363.

[21]One of the assumptions of the constant growth model as presented is that earnings and dividends grow at the same rate. This assumption is true only in cases where a firm pays out a fixed percentage of its earnings each year (has a fixed payout ratio).

[22]The technique involves two basic steps. First, dividing the earliest dividend ($1) by the most recent dividend ($1.40), a factor for the present value of one dollar of .714 results. Although six dividends are shown, they reflect only 5 years of growth. Looking across the table for the present-value interest factors, *PVIF*, for 5 years, the factor closest to .714 occurs at 7 percent (.713). Therefore, the growth rate of the dividends rounded to the nearest whole percentage is 7 percent. It is important to recognize that while this approach is easy, it does not consider any dividends other than in the first and last year; hence it may suggest a pattern of constant growth when, in fact, there has not been a constant rate of growth in the stream of dividends.

future. In order to find D_1, 1984 dividends (D_0) must be multiplied by $(1 + g)$: that is, $D_1 = D_0(1 + g)^1$. Therefore, $D_{1985} = D_{1984}(1 + g)^1$. If $D_{1984} = \$1.40$, $g = 7\%$, and $k_s = 15\%$, substituting into Equation 7.11 results in a current share price of:

$$P_{1984} = \frac{\$1.40(1 + .07)}{.15 - .07} = \frac{\$1.50}{.08} = \$18.75$$

The constant growth model in Equation 7.11 is often called the *Gordon model* for its developer, Myron Gordon. The main assumptions embedded in Equation 7.11 are that growth is constant, that it continues to infinity, and that the required return, k_s, is greater than the growth rate, g. Although all these assumptions may not be strictly met in application, Equation 7.11 is a very useful device for approximating share price. Probably the most important (and difficult) aspect of common stock valuation is the assessment of future growth prospects. Other things being equal, the higher the growth rate, the higher the value of common stock.[23]

Variable Dividend Growth.   Common stock valuation models like those presented in Equations 7.9 and 7.11 are extremely simple to use, but they do not allow for any shift in expected growth rates. The range of models one might develop is limited only by the imagination, but becoming overly concerned about all possible shifts in growth is unlikely to yield much more accuracy than a simpler model. However, it would be helpful to develop a model that allows for one or two shifts in growth rates. For example, assume that Sunshine Industries is in a growth industry and expects to grow at 13 percent for 3 years, followed by a slowdown to a "normal" growth rate of 7 percent for the foreseeable future. Given $D_0 = D_{1984} = \$1.40$, assume the time pattern of dividends over the next 6 years is as shown in Figure 7.2. (Dividends are expected to continue to grow at a 7 percent annual rate beyond the sixth year.)

To determine the value of the Sunshine stock given a single shift in growth rates (occurring at the end of year N), we proceed in three steps:

Step 1.   Find the present value of the dividends expected during the initial

---

[23]Alternatively, the firm could be declining and dividends might be decreasing at a constant rate. For Sunshine Industries, we can illustrate this using $D_0 = \$1.40$, $g = -3\%$, and $k_s = 15\%$:

$$P_0 = \frac{\$1.40\ (1 - .03)}{.15 - (-.03)} = \frac{\$1.36}{.18}$$
$$= \$7.56$$

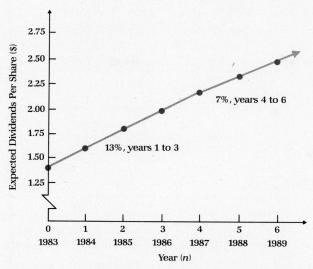

Figure 7.2 Variable Dividend Growth Rate for Sunshine Industries (13 Percent Growth in Years 1 to 3 and 7 Percent Growth in Years 4 to 6).

growth period. Using the notation presented earlier, this sum can be represented by:

$$\sum_{t=1}^{N} \frac{D_t}{(1 + k_s)^t}$$

Step 2. Find the price of the stock at the end of the initial growth period, $P_N = \dfrac{D_{N+1}}{k_s - g}$, which is a function of all dividends from year $N + 1$ to infinity, and discount it back to present value. This value can be represented by:

$$\left[\frac{1}{(1 + k_s)^N}\right] \times \left[\frac{D_{N+1}}{k_s - g}\right]$$

Step 3. Add the two present-value components to find the value of the stock, P_0, which is given in Equation 7.12.

$$P_0 = \underbrace{\sum_{t=1}^{N} \left[\frac{D_t}{(1 + k_s)^t}\right]}_{\substack{\text{Present value of} \\ \text{dividends during} \\ \text{initial growth} \\ \text{period}}} + \underbrace{\left[\left[\frac{1}{(1 + k_s)^N}\right] \times \left[\frac{D_{N+1}}{k_s - g}\right]\right]}_{\substack{\text{Present value of price of} \\ \text{stock at the end of initial} \\ \text{growth period}}} \qquad (7.12)$$

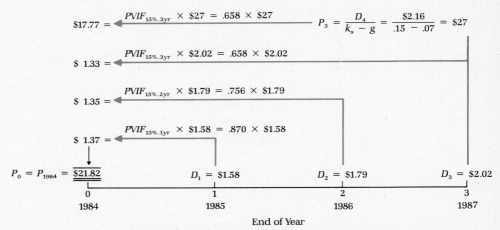

Figure 7.3   Finding Value For Sunshine Industries with Variable Growth.

The application of these steps can be illustrated using the Sunshine Industries data already presented. A diagram of this process is given in Figure 7.3.

Step 1.   Determine the amount of dividends at the end of years 1 through 3 using the most recent dividend, $D_0 = D_{1984}$, of $1.40 per share and the 13 percent growth rate; then find the sum of the present value of these dividends using the 15 percent required return, k_s. Application of this step is illustrated in Table 7.2, where it can be seen that the present value of the dividends totals $4.05.

Step 2.   Find the price of the stock at the end of year 3 using the constant growth formula given in Equation 7.11 and employing the 7 percent growth rate applicable for years 4 through infinity. Then, discount this price back to year zero at the 15 percent required return.

					Present Value of Dividends
		$D_0 = D_{1984}$	$FVIF_{13\%, t}$	D_t [(1) × (2)]	$PVIF_{15\%, t}$	[(3) × (4)]
t	Year	(1)	(2)	(3)	(4)	(5)
1	1985	$1.40	1.130	$1.58	.870	$1.37
2	1986	1.40	1.277	1.79	.756	1.35
3	1987	1.40	1.443	2.02	.658	1.33

TABLE 7.2

Calculation of the Present Value of Dividends for Sunshine Industries (1985–1987)

$$\text{Sum of present value of dividends} = \sum_{t=1}^{3} \frac{D_t}{(1 + k_s)^t} = \$4.05$$

$$P_3 = P_{1987} = \frac{D_4}{k_s - g} = \frac{D_3\,(1 + .07)}{.15 - .07} = \frac{\$2.02\,(1 + .07)}{.08} = \frac{\$2.16}{.08} = \$27.00$$

$$\text{Present value of } P_3 = \$27.00\,(PVIF_{15\%,\,3\,yr}) = \$27\,(.658) = \$17.77$$

Step 3. Add the sum of the present value of dividends to the present value of the market value at the end of year 3 to obtain the current price, P_0.

$$P_0 = P_{1984} = \$4.05 + \$17.77 = \$21.82$$

Thus, the market value of Sunshine Industries stock is $21.82. The most difficult aspects of the variable growth model are (1) specifying the proper growth rates, g, for the proper years; and (2) correctly estimating the future share value. Even so, using the step-by-step approach above, we can solve any variable rate valuation problem—even those with *no dividends* in the early (or initial) years of the investment horizon. The market values for Sunshine Industries obtained using the various models are summarized in Table 7.3. Examination of these results indicates the importance of the magnitude of the expected growth rate in dividends. Other things being equal, the higher the growth rate in dividends, the higher the market price of common stock, and vice versa.

The Impact of Growth on Price, Returns, and P/E Multiples

The preceding discussion of growth rates and market value provides a basis for evaluating how investors assess firms with different growth prospects. To make such comparisons, it is helpful to use measures of the two key components of the total return—dividends and capital gains. Each of these returns can be measured by its respective yield; that is, these yields in period t can be measured by the following formulas:[24]

TABLE 7.3
Summary of Market Values for Sunshine Industries with Different Growth Rates (15% Required Return Assumed)

Type of Growth	Initial Dividend $D_0 = D_{1984}$	Growth Rate and Period g	Market Value $P_0 = P_{1984}$
Zero growth	$D_0 = E_0 = \$2.60$	0%, forever	$17.34
Constant growth	1.40	7%, forever	18.75
Variable growth	1.40	13%, 3 years, followed by 7% forever	21.82

---

[24]By adding the dividend and capital gain yield in period t, we get the total return in period t:

$$\frac{D_t}{P_{t-1}} + \frac{P_t - P_{t-1}}{P_{t-1}} = \frac{D_t + P_t - P_{t-1}}{P_{t-1}}$$

which is identical to the formula for total return given in Equation 6.1 and applied earlier in this chapter.

$$\text{Dividend yield in period } t = \frac{D_t}{P_{t-1}}$$

$$\text{Capital gain yield in period } t = \frac{P_t - P_{t-1}}{P_{t-1}}$$

To illustrate the application of these two formulas, consider the first 5 years of the Sunshine Industries example where growth is expected to equal 13 percent in years 1 to 3 and 7 percent thereafter. In order to determine these yields, we need to calculate the value of the stock at the end of each year, as illustrated in Table 7.4. The calculations reflect the application of Equation 7.12 at the end of each year.

Using the dividend data from column 3 of Table 7.2, along with the end-of-year share value data developed in Table 7.4, the dividend yield, capital gain yield, and total yield for Sunshine Industries over the first 5 years, 1985 through 1989, are calculated in Table 7.5. An examination of these results discloses two key points: (1) The total yield is 15 percent in each case (this result is expected, since the 15 percent required return was used as the discount rate for determining value); and (2) the dividend yield is lower and the capital gain yield higher during the first couple of years due to the higher prevailing growth rate (13 versus 7 percent).

Table 7.6, page 298, summarizes price, return, and price/earnings multiple data for year 1 only for Sunshine Industries under each of the growth rate assumptions illustrated earlier. (Note that Sunshine's present earnings per share are $2.60; $E_0 = \$2.60$.) The table clearly shows that the required rate of return in each growth case is 15 percent. In the zero growth case, this return consists solely of the expected dividend yield; in

---

TABLE 7.4

Calculation of Share Value at End of Years 1 Through 5 for Sunshine Industries

t	End of Year	Calculation	Share Value
0	1984	$P_0 = $ (calculated earlier)	$21.82
1	1985	$P_1 = \$1.79 \ (PVIF_{15\%, 1\,yr}) + \$2.02 \ (PVIF_{15\%, 2\,yr}) + \$27.00 \ (PVIF_{15\%, 2\,yr})$	
		$= \$1.79(.870) + \$2.02(.756) + \$27.00(.756)$	
		$= \$1.56 + \$1.53 + \$20.41$	$23.50
2	1986	$P_2 = \$2.02 \ (PVIF_{15\%, 1\,yr}) + \$27.00 \ (PVIF_{15\%, 1\,yr})$	
		$= \$2.02(.870) + \$27.00(.870) = \$1.76 + \$23.49$	$25.25
3	1987	$P_3 = $ (calculated earlier)	$27.00
4	1988	$P_4 = \dfrac{D_5}{k_s - g} = \dfrac{D_4(1 + g)}{.15 - .07} = \dfrac{\$2.16(1 + .07)}{.08} = \dfrac{\$2.31}{.08}$	$28.88
5	1989	$P_5 = \dfrac{D_6}{k_s - g} = \dfrac{D_5(1 + g)}{.15 - .07} = \dfrac{\$2.31(1 + .07)}{.08} = \dfrac{\$2.47}{.08}$	$30.88

TABLE 7.5
Dividend, Capital Gain,
and Total Yield for
Sunshine Industries

t	Year	D_t	P_t	Dividend Yield $[D_t/P_{t-1}]$	Capital Gain Yield $[(P_t - P_{t-1})/P_{t-1}]$	Total Yield (Dividend Yield + Capital Gain Yield)	
0	1984	$1.40	$21.82				
1	1985	1.58	23.50	7.24%	7.70%	14.94%	$\simeq$ 15%
2	1986	1.79	25.25	7.62	7.45	15.07	$\simeq$ 15
3	1987	2.02	27.00	8.00	6.93	14.93	$\simeq$ 15
4	1988	2.16	28.88	8.00	6.96	14.96	$\simeq$ 15
5	1989	2.31	30.88	8.00	6.93	14.93	$\simeq$ 15

all other cases, it consists of both the dividend yield and expected capital gain yield. The results in Table 7.6 indicate two important points:

1. As more growth in dividends is expected, other things being equal, the expected returns are more dependent on capital gains and less dependent on the dividend yield.
2. The higher the expected growth rate in dividends, other things being equal, the higher the P/E ratio.[25]

The second point indicates that investors are willing to pay more for current earnings if the expected growth rate is higher—because they are basing their estimates primarily on future earnings and dividends, not on present earnings and dividends. This finding illustrates how firms are often viewed by investors. Other things being equal, firms with high dividend yields and low P/E ratios are generally viewed by investors as having few growth opportunities. Likewise, firms that have low dividend yields and high P/E ratios are viewed as having above-average growth prospects. Hence, "growth" firms are typified by low dividend yields and high P/E ratios, while mature or declining firms are typified by high dividend yields and low P/E ratios.

Decision Making and Common Stock Valuation

The efficiency of the stock market is important because it means that as financial decisions are made, new information is transmitted to investors who react to it quickly. With the reaction to new information, investors at the margin will revise their evaluations of the dividend stream and/or appropriate discount rate, and market value will rise or fall to a new equilibrium price. The process by which financial decisions affect stock prices is depicted in Figure 7.4, page 299. An understanding of this process is clearly important. Although our attention is devoted primarily

---

[25]Differences in P/E ratios among firms may also arise from differences in the required rate of return which investors employ in capitalizing future dividend streams. Hence, a higher P/E ratio may be caused by a higher growth rate, a lower required return, or some combination of these two factors.

TABLE 7.6

Price, Return, and P/E Multiples for Year 1 (1985) for Sunshine Industries, Using Various Growth Rate Assumptions

Type of Growth	g	Price $P_0 = P_{1984}$	Year 1 Yields			
			Dividend	Capital Gain (15% − Dividend Yield)	Total (Dividend Yield + Capital Gain Yield)	P/E Ratio[a]
Zero growth	0%	$17.34	15 %	0 %	15%	6.67
Constant growth	7	18.75	8	7	15	7.21
Variable growth	13% yrs 1–3, 7% thereafter	21.82	7.24	7.76	15	8.39

[a]Calculated by dividing price, P_0, by the earnings per share, E_0, which equals $2.60.

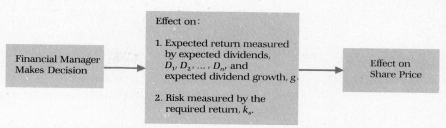

Figure 7.4   The Effect of Financial Decisions on Share Price.

to the impact of financial decisions on share value, a brief comment on earnings is in order here.

Impact
of Managerial
Decisions
on Value

Since the goal of the financial manager is to maximize shareholder wealth by maximizing share price, a key consideration in financial decision making is return (as measured by D_t and g) and risk (as measured by the required return, k_s). Using the constant growth valuation model, we can see that expected return and risk combine to create share value. Since the actions of the financial manager can cause the value of the firm to change, it is important to look more closely at these variables.

Changes in Expected Return.   Assuming that economic conditions remain stable, any management action that would cause existing and prospective stockholders to raise their dividend expectations should increase the firm's value as long as the required return does not increase. In Equation 7.11 we can see that P_0 will increase for any increase in D_1 or g. Any action the financial manager can take that will increase the level of expected returns without changing the required return (risk) will positively affect owners' wealth. Imagine that Sunshine Industries, which was found to have a share value of $18.75 in the 7 percent constant growth example presented earlier, on the following day announced a major technological breakthrough that would revolutionize its industry. Current and prospective shareholders are not expected to adjust their required return of 15 percent (that is, risk does not change), but they expect that future dividends will be increased. Specifically, they feel that although the dividend next year, D_1, will remain at $1.50, the expected rate of growth will increase to 9 percent. Substituting $D_1 = \$1.50$, $k_s = .15$, and $g = .09$ into Equation 7.11, the resulting value is found to equal $25. The increased value therefore resulted from the higher expected future dividends reflected in the increase in the growth rate, g.

An increase in the dividend expected in the coming year, D_1, without any change in the expected rate of growth in dividends, g, would also result in an increased share price. For instance, if for some reason the dividend expected in the coming year increased to, say, $1.80 and the growth rate remains at 7 percent, all else remaining unchanged, the resulting share value would increase to $22.50. In this case, the increased value resulted from the higher expected future dividends resulting from an increased dividend expectation in 1984, $D_1 = D_{1984} = 1.80.

Changes in Risk.   Although k_s is defined as the required return, it is, as pointed out in Chapter 6, directly related to nondiversifiable risk, which can be measured by beta. Specifically, using Equation 6.7,

$$k_s = R_F + \beta \times (k_M - R_F) \tag{7.13}$$

With the risk-free rate, R_F, and the required return on the market, k_M, held constant, the required return, k_s, depends directly on beta, β. In other words, any action of the financial manager that increases risk will increase required return. In Equation 7.11 it can be seen that with all else constant, an increase in the required return will reduce share value, and vice versa. Thus, any action of the financial manager that increases risk contributes toward a reduction in value, and vice versa. An example will illustrate this.

Assume that Sunshine Industries' 15 percent required return resulted from a risk-free rate of 9 percent, a market return of 13 percent, and a beta of 1.50. Substituting into the capital asset pricing model, Equation 7.13, the 15 percent required return results:

$$k_s = 9\% + 1.50 \times (13\% - 9\%) = 15\%$$

Using this return, the value of the firm, P_0, was calculated to be $18.75 in an earlier illustration of the constant growth model.

Now imagine the financial manager makes a decision that, without changing expected dividends, increases the firm's beta to 1.75. Assuming that R_F and k_M remain at 9 and 13 percent, respectively, the required return will increase to 16 percent to compensate stockholders for the increased risk. Substituting $D_1 = 1.50, $k_s = .16$, and $g = .07$ into the valuation equation, Equation 7.11, results in a share value of $16.67. As expected, the owners, by raising the required return to compensate for increased risk (without any corresponding increase in expected return), cause the firm's share value to decline. Clearly the financial manager's action was not in the owners' best interest.

Combined Effect.   A financial decision rarely affects return and risk independently; most decisions affect both factors. In accordance with the risk-return tradeoff, with increased return generally comes increased risk, and vice versa. Or, in terms of the measures presented, with an increase in beta one would expect an increase in D_1 or g, or both, assuming k_M and R_F remain unchanged. Depending on the relative magnitude of the changes in these variables, the net effect on value can be difficult to assess. Table 7.7 summarizes the effect on price expected from a change in each of the key variables discussed in this chapter. (The effect reported for each variable is based on the assumption that all other variables remain unchanged, which in reality will likely not be the case.) Note that general shifts in economic and market conditions, which have been ignored here, would in fact be introduced into the process through the risk-free rate, R_F, or the market return, k_M, or both. An example shows why.

If we assume that the two changes (g increased to 9 percent and k_s increased to 16 percent) illustrated for Sunshine Industries in the preceding examples occur simultaneously as a result of an action of a financial decision maker, key variable values would be $D_1 = \$1.50$, $k_s = .16$, and $g = .09$. Substituting into the valuation model, a price of $21.43 is obtained. The net result of the decision, which increased return (g from 7 to 9 percent) as well as risk (β from 1.50 to 1.75 and therefore k_s from 15 to 16 percent) is positive, since the share price increased from $18.75 to $21.43. Assuming that the key variables are accurately measured, the decision appears to be in the best interest of the firm's owners, since it increases their wealth.

The key point to remember from this discussion is that return and risk are important dimensions of value. Most financial decisions affect both variables, and it is their combined effect on value that must be assessed by the financial manager.

A Comment on Earnings Maximization

We have indicated that the goal of maximizing shareholder wealth can be accomplished by maximizing the market price of a firm's stock. This still leaves unanswered the question of how, operationally, a firm can proceed to maximize stock price. Does this mean that it should attempt to maximize total earnings or earnings per share? As noted earlier, maximization of stock price does not necessarily mean maximizing

---

TABLE 7.7

Effect of Increases[a] in Key Valuation Variables on Price (Assuming All Other Variables Remain Unchanged)

Increase in Variable	Change in Price: Increase (I) or Decrease (D)
R_F	D for $\beta < 1$; I for $\beta > 1$
k_M	D
β	D
k_s	D
D_1	I
g	I

[a]Decreases in each of the variables shown would have the opposite effect from that shown on P_0.

TABLE 7.8
Average Price/Earnings
(P/E) Ratios for
Standard & Poor's
Composite 500 Stock
Price Index, 1970–1983

Year	Average P/E Ratio[a]
1970	15.87
1971	17.10
1972	17.20
1973	13.02
1974	9.12
1975	10.41
1976	10.03
1977	9.08
1978	7.87
1979	6.98
1980	8.06
1981	8.17
1982	9.70
1983	12.44

[a]These "averages" represent the midpoint of the "High" and "Low" values given for each year.

SOURCES: Standard & Poor's Corporation, *Analyst's Handbook*, 1983 annual edition (New York: Standard & Poor's Corporation, 1983), p. 181; and Standard & Poor's Corporation, *Statistical Survey: Current Statistics* (New York: Standard & Poor's Corporation), March 1984, p. 30.

earnings. Unfortunately, many executives seek to operationalize the goal of maximizing share price by stating their financial objectives in terms of earnings per share or earnings growth, a practice that often leads to inappropriate financial decisions.

The use of earnings for stating corporate financial objectives appears to rest on the perception that there is a direct relationship between earnings per share and stock price. Many executives reason that any decision which increases earnings per share automatically increases the market price of the firm's stock. Formally, this identity assumes that $P_0 = cE_0$, where c is assumed to be a constant of proportionality and E_0 represents the most recent earnings per share. The constant, c, is equivalent to the price/earnings multiple. It is a key element, in that if c, the P/E ratio, were indeed constant and independent of changes in the firm's financial policies, then maximization of E_0, earnings per share, would lead to maximization of stock price, P_0. However, as we know, the valuation of a firm's shares depends on both risk and return. Like the required return, k_s, the P/E ratio is dependent upon the risk perceived by investors in the marketplace. As investors change their expectations relative to risk, they adjust the required return or P/E ratio; higher risk results in higher required returns and lower P/E ratios, and vice versa.[26]

To show that P/E ratios do not remain constant over time, consider Table 7.8, which presents the average P/E ratios for Standard & Poor's

---

[26]As noted earlier, when the P/E ratio is used in estimating share value, its inverse, the E/P ratio, or earnings yield, can be viewed as the required rate of return, k_s. Therefore, with higher risk comes a higher k_s equaling higher E/P, which results in a lower P/E ratio.

Composite 500 Stock Price Index for the period 1970 through 1983. During this 12½-year period, the average P/E ratio ranged from a high of 17.20 in 1972 to a low of 6.98 in 1979. When one considers that this is the *average* P/E ratio, it is easy to see that individual firm's ratios might fluctuate even more widely. To the extent that the P/E ratio is not constant, it follows that the maximization of earnings or earnings per share will not necessarily lead to maximization of stock price. It is the combined impact of return (earnings) and risk (P/E ratio) that causes share value; level of earnings is important, but it must be considered in view of the associated risk.

SUMMARY

The basic valuation equation applicable to any asset is based on the fact that the value of any asset is equal to the present value of all its future cash flows, discounted at the appropriate rate, over its expected life, *n*. Because bonds and stocks are assumed to be traded in efficient markets, the required return on an asset will equal its expected return. The value of a corporate bond is the present value of its contractual payments, which include annual interest paid over its life, and its par value paid at maturity, discounted at the required rate of return, which depends on the prevailing supply-demand relationship and risk. When the required return is above the coupon rate, the bond sells at a discount; when the required return is less than the coupon rate, the bond sells at a premium. The closer to maturity, the smaller the discount or premium associated with a given interest rate. Bonds commonly trade on the basis of yield to maturity.

Ratio approaches to common stock valuation include the use of book value, liquidation value, and price/earnings multiples, but the theoretically preferred approach defines the share value as the present value of all future dividends expected to be received over an infinite time horizon. The most popular dividend valuation model is one that assumes constant dividend growth; other approaches assume a zero or a variable rate of growth. The return an investor earns from common stock can be dividends or capital gains. In general, the higher the growth rate, the more dependent the total yield will be on capital gains. Also, the higher the expected growth rate, the greater the P/E ratio.

Managerial decisions are made on the basis of expected return measured by dividends, and expected risk measured by the required return. It is their combined effect on share price that governs financial decisions. Independently, any action that would increase the next dividend or the expected rate of dividend growth would increase share price, whereas actions that increase risk would tend to reduce share price. In spite of the common notion, maximization of earnings or earnings per share will *not* necessarily result in maximization of a firm's stock price or shareholder wealth.

7.1. According to basic valuation theory, what general factors determine security value? Describe the basic valuation equation and explain the role return and risk play in this model.

7.2. Describe what is meant by market efficiency and explain the implication of efficient markets on the valuation process. Why, in an efficient market, are the expected and required returns on an asset commonly assumed to be equal?

7.3. Bond prices vary inversely with the required returns on similar-risk bonds, leading to bond discounts or bond premiums. Explain how this process works. Why do required returns often differ from bond coupon rates? What effect does the amount of time to maturity have on the size of bond discounts and/or premiums? Explain.

7.4. Bonds generally trade on the basis of their yield to maturity (YTM). Explain what is meant by YTM and how one would calculate it. If market interest rates on similar-risk bonds differ from the coupon rates, what will happen to YTM? Explain.

7.5. Describe the approach for determining the value of a perpetual bond or preferred stock. How is this process similar to that used to value a zero-growth stock? Explain.

7.6. Briefly describe each of the following ratio approaches to common stock valuation. Point out any strengths or weaknesses of each.

  a. Book value.

  b. Liquidation value.

  c. Price/earnings multiples.

7.7. Explain the underlying assumptions of each of the following common stock valuation models and indicate under what general conditions each would be applicable.

  a. Zero growth: $P_0 = D_1/k_s$

  b. Constant growth: $P_0 = \dfrac{D_1}{k_s - g}$

  c. Variable growth: $P_0 = \sum_{t=1}^{N} \left[\dfrac{D_t}{(1 + k_s)^t} \right] + \left[\left[\dfrac{1}{(1 + k_s)^N} \right] \times \left[\dfrac{D_{N+1}}{k_s - g} \right] \right]$

7.8. A buyer of common stock typically expects to receive a return in the form of a dividend yield and a capital gain yield.

  a. Define and discuss what is meant by dividend yield and capital gain yield.

  b. How would you expect the distribution between dividend yield and capital gain yield to be influenced by a firm's decision to pay more dividends rather than to retain and reinvest earnings? What might this decision indicate about the future prospects of the firm for growth above a "normal" rate?

  c. Under what conditions does one expect to receive a return in the form of either a dividend yield or capital gain yield, but not both?

7.9. Suppose an investor possessed "inside information" (information the general public does not have) about new investments made by a firm that will dramatically increase earnings. Using a common stock valuation model, explain how such knowledge could prove valuable to the investor.

7.10. Assume you own stock in a privately held firm that has no public market and hence no readily observable market value. Explain how you might go about determining the value of this stock.

7.11. In light of the firm's goal of shareholder wealth maximization, explain the process through which the actions of the financial decision maker can affect shareholder wealth. Be sure to discuss the role of return and risk in this process.

7.12. Imagine that while visiting with a corporate executive, he tells you his firm has operationalized the goal of maximizing share price by attempting to maximize earnings per share. Explain how you might convince the executive this may not lead to share price maximization.

PROBLEMS

7.1. *BOND VALUATION.* Imagine you can purchase a $1000 par value bond with a 13 percent coupon rate, paying annual interest and having 20 years to maturity.
   a. How much would you be willing to pay for the bond if you could earn the following on similar-risk bond investments? (1) 10 percent; (2) 13 percent; (3) 16 percent.
   b. Using your findings in (a), explain the relationship between coupon rate, required return, and bond value.

7.2. *BOND YIELD TO MATURITY.* The Jones Company's bonds have 4 years remaining to maturity. Interest is paid annually, the bonds have a maturity value of $1000, and the coupon rate is 12 percent.
   a. What is the yield to maturity if the current market price is (1) $969.88? (2) $1063.40?
   b. Using the findings in (a), discuss the general relationship between yield to maturity, coupon rate, and market price.

7.3. *BOND VALUATION AND MATURITY.* Each of the following bonds pay interest annually.

Bond	Par Value	Coupon Interest Rate	Market Interest Rate
X	$1000	12%	16%
Y	1000	12	12
Z	1000	12	8

a. Calculate the value of each bond, using the following maturities: (1) 2 years; (2) 8 years; (3) 20 years.
b. Graphically depict your findings in (a) on a set of years to maturity (X axis), and value of bond (Y axis) axes in a fashion similar to Figure 7.1.
c. What conclusions can be drawn from your findings (above) about coupon interest rate, market interest rate, time to maturity, and bond value?

7.4. **BOND VALUE AND INTEREST FREQUENCY.** Given the following information:

Bond	Par Value	Coupon Interest Rate	Maturity	Required Rate of Return
A	$ 100	12%	10 yr	10%
B	500	14	15	14
C	1000	16	20	12

a. Determine the value of the bond, assuming interest is paid annually.
b. Determine the value of the bond, assuming interest is paid semiannually.
c. Compare and contrast your findings in (a) and (b). What effect does interest frequency have on bond value?

7.5. **BOND VALUES.**   Below is information about three $1000 bonds that trade in the marketplace All pay interest semiannually.

Bond	Coupon Interest Rate	Maturity
A	8%	10 yr
B	10	15
C	12	20

Given current market conditions, all bonds have the same required rate of return of 10 percent.
a. Without any computations, what can you say about the market value relative to each bond's $1000 par value?
b. Compute the market value of each.
c. Are your answers consistent with what you expected?

7.6. **PERPETUAL VALUATION AND BETA.**   You have observed two different financial instruments that sell in a financial market. One is a bond issued in perpetuity, which promises to pay 10 percent of its $100 par value once every year. The second is a share of preferred stock, which promises a $10 annual dividend. The beta of the bond is .8 and the beta of the stock is .9. Given that the risk-free rate is 8 percent and the market portfolio's return is 12 percent, compute the following:

a. The value of the perpetual bond.
b. The value of the preferred stock.
c. Assume that the preferred stock's beta is equal to .8. What is its value?

7.7. BOOK AND LIQUIDATION VALUE. The balance sheet for Imperial Mill Company follows:

Balance Sheet
Imperial Mill
Company
Year Ending
December 31

Assets		Liabilities and Stockholder's Equity	
Cash	$ 40,000	Accounts payable	$100,000
Marketable securities	60,000	Notes payable	30,000
Accounts receivable	120,000	Accrued wages	30,000
Inventory	160,000	Total current liabilities	$160,000
Total current assets	$380,000	Long-term debt	$180,000
Fixed assets	$400,000	Preferred stock	$ 80,000
Total assets	$780,000	Common stock (1000 shares)	360,000
		Total liabilities and stockholder's equity	$780,000

The following additional information with respect to the firm is available:

1. Cash and marketable securities can be liquidated at book value.
2. Accounts receivable and inventory can be liquidated at 90 percent of book value.
3. Fixed assets can be liquidated at 70 percent of book value.
4. Preferred stock can be liquidated for its book value.
5. All interest and dividends are currently paid up.

Given this information, answer the following:

a. How large is Imperial Mill's book value per share?
b. How large is its liquidation value per share?
c. Compare, contrast, and discuss the values found in (a) and (b).

7.8. PRICE/EARNINGS MULTIPLES AND VALUATION. Given the forecast earnings per share (eps) for each of five companies in the same industry, estimate their values using price/earnings multiples, assuming that the average price/earnings ratio for the industry is 12.

Company	Forecast eps
A	$3.00
B	4.50
C	1.80
D	2.40
E	5.10

7.9. *COMMON STOCK VALUE.* A common stock is expected to pay a constant dividend of $3, and the market discounts these expected dividends at a 13 percent required rate of return.

a. What is the market value of the stock?

b. What will the market value be if: (1) The dividends change to a constant $2 per year and nothing else changes? (2) The dividends change to a constant $2 per year and the market's required rate of return falls to 11 percent? (3) The required rate of return remains at 13 percent, but dividends will be eliminated for 2 years? [Assume in (3) that the dividends for year 3 and thereafter are constant at $3 per year.]

7.10. *COMMON STOCK VALUE—CONSTANT GROWTH.* The Baxter Boiler Company has paid the following dividends over the past 6 years:

Year	Dividend per share
1979	$2.25
1980	2.37
1981	2.46
1982	2.60
1983	2.76
1984	2.87

The firm's dividend per share next year (1984) is expected to be $3.02. If you can earn 13 percent on similar-risk investments, what is the most you would pay per share for this firm? Explain your answer.

7.11. *COMMON STOCK VALUE—CONSTANT GROWTH.* The investors of the Addison Company require a rate of return of 12 percent (k_s = 12%). At what price will the stock sell if dividends at present are $1 ($D_0$ = $1) and the growth in dividends is expected to be:

a. 3 percent?

b. 6 percent?

c. 9 percent?

d. 0 percent?

e. −3 percent?

7.12. *COMMON STOCK VALUE—VARIABLE GROWTH.* The dividends for a firm are currently $2 ($D_0$ = $2) and the required rate of return for this firm is 10 percent. What is the market price if:

   a. Dividends are expected to grow at 9 percent per year for each of 3 years, followed by a constant growth rate thereafter of 6 percent to infinity?

   b. Dividends are expected to grow at 9 percent per year for each of 3 years, followed by zero growth thereafter to infinity?

   c. Dividends are expected to grow at 9 percent per year for each of 3 years, followed by an expected growth of 6 percent for the next 3 years (years 4, 5, and 6), after which the expected growth rate is constant at 1 percent to infinity?

7.13. *EQUITY VALUATION.* Mr. Last Chance is contemplating the purchase of a funeral home that has current earnings after taxes of $25,000 per year ($D_0$ = $25,000). He requires a 20 percent return on the after-tax earnings if he decides to purchase the funeral home. How much is the maximum price he should pay, if he estimates the future growth in earnings after taxes to be:

   a. 0 percent per year to infinity?

   b. 5 percent per year to infinity?

   c. 10 percent per year for each of 2 years, followed by 5 percent per year for the next 2 years (years 3 and 4), followed by 2 percent per year to infinity?

7.14. *IMPLIED GROWTH RATE.* The common stock of Mission Investment Company is expected to pay a dividend next year of $3.30 and currently sells for $44. What is the implied growth rate for Mission if the required rate of return expected by investors is 18 percent?

7.15. *EQUITY VALUE—VARIABLE GROWTH.* General Industries, Inc., is contemplating the purchase of the Winn Company. During the most recent year, Winn had earnings of $5 million and paid dividends of $2 million. The earnings and dividends of Winn are expected to grow at 25 percent per year for 5 years, after which they are expected to grow at 10 percent per year to infinity. What is the maximum General Industries should pay for Winn if it has a required rate of return of 15 percent on investments with risk characteristics similar to those of Winn Company?

7.16. *VALUE, DIVIDEND YIELD, CAPITAL GAIN YIELD, AND TOTAL YIELD.* Favorate Foods, Inc., is expected to experience dividend growth of 12 percent per year for the next 3 years, followed by 6 percent per year thereafter. D_0 = $4 and the rate of return required by investors (at the margin) is 10 percent.

a. Determine the expected dividends in years 1 through 4. (Remember that the growth rate changes after year 3.)

b. Determine the market value of Favorate Foods stock, at t_1, t_2, t_3, and t_4 (as in Table 7.4).

c. Calculate the dividend yield, capital gain yield, and total yield for years 1 and 3. These yields for years 2 and 4 are as follows:

Year (t)	Dividend Yield D_t/P_{t-1}	+	Capital Gain Yield $(P_t - P_{t-1})/P_{t-1}$	=	Total Yield, 10%
1					
2	3.79		6.25		10.04
3					
4	4.00		6.00		10.00

d. Explain why the dividend yield changes over the years and then stabilizes at 4 percent.

7.17. *MANAGERIAL ACTION AND VALUE.* The Sierra Company has the following characteristics: $D_0 = \$2$, $g = 3\%$, and $k_s = 8\%$. Because of a recent management shakeup, a new team of executives is contemplating alternative financial actions that would have the results listed below. For each possible course of action, determine the anticipated effect on the firm's stock price and identify the best one.

a. Invest in several projects that will increase the expected dividend growth rate to 5 percent and increase the required rate of return to 12 percent.

b. Eliminate some unprofitable investments that will increase the expected dividend growth rate to 4 percent and increase the required rate of return to 11 percent.

c. Merge with Safe Products Company, which will increase to $3 the dividend in the coming year, increase the expected dividend growth rate to 9 percent, and increase the required rate of return to 16 percent.

d. Liquidate part of the firm, which will have the effect of reducing the dividend in the coming year to $1.50, leave the growth rate at 3 percent, and reduce the required rate of return to 7 percent.

7.18. *COMMON STOCK VALUE—CAPM.* Jackson Steel Company wishes to determine the value of Acme Foundry, a firm it is considering acquiring for cash. Jackson wishes to use the capital asset pricing model to determine the applicable discount rate to use as an input to the constant growth valuation model. Because Acme's stock is not publicly traded, Jackson, after studying the betas of similar firms that are publicly traded, believes that an appropriate beta for Acme's stock would be 1.25. The risk-free rate is currently 9 percent and the market return is 13 percent. Acme's historic dividend per share for each of the past 6 years is:

Year	Dividend per Share
1979	$2.45
1980	2.75
1981	2.90
1982	3.15
1983	3.28
1984	3.44

a.   Given that Acme is expected to pay a dividend of $3.68 per share next year (1985), determine the maximum cash price Jackson should pay for each share of Acme.

b.   Discuss the use of CAPM for estimating the value of common stock and describe the effect on the resulting value (of Acme) of: (1) an increase in the risk-free rate to 10 percent (with $k_M =$ 13%); (2) a decrease in the beta to 1; (3) an increase in the market return to 14 percent; (4) all these changes occurring simultaneously.

7.19.   **CHANGE IN SML OR BETA AND INFLUENCE ON STOCK PRICE.**   The Illinois Transit Company has a beta coefficient of 0.75, the risk-free rate is 6 percent, and the expected return on the market is 14 percent.

a.   What is the expected return on Illinois Transit?

b.   If $D_1 = 2 and the expected dividend growth for Illinois Transit is 6 percent, what is the price at which it should sell? (*Hint*: Assume a constant dividend growth, g.)

c.   Now assume that the Federal Reserve Board decreases the money supply, causing the risk-free rate to increase to 9 percent and the market return to drop to 11 percent. Other things being equal, what will this change do to the security market line (SML)? What is the new price at which Illinois Transit should sell?

d.   Independent of (c), now assume that investor's risk aversion declines, which causes the expected return on the market to drop to 10%. Other things being equal, what will this change do to the SML? What is the new implied equilibrium price for Illinois Transit?

e.   Independent of (c) and (d), now assume that Illinois Transit has decided to purchase another company. This action has the following effects: Illinois Transit's beta coefficient increases to 1.5, D_1 is now \$2.25, and the expected rate of dividend growth is 10 percent. Other things being equal, what is the new implied price for Illinois Transit?

7.20. *CHANGES IN BETA AND PRICE.* Capital Industries, Inc., has three major divisions—commercial aircraft manufacturing, data services, and financial services. The $R_F = 7\%$, beta for Capital Industries = 1.33, $k_M = 13\%$, $D_1 = \$5$, and $g = 10\%$.

a. What is the equilibrium price for Capital Industries?

b. Because of a recent crash of one of the planes Capital Industries produces, investors felt Capital was more risky, causing beta to become 1.67. In addition, because of the cancellation of orders for planes, the expected dividend growth rate for Capital has fallen to 8 percent. If there is no change in D_1, what is the implied price for Capital Industries?

c. What is the implied price as a result of the crash if beta moves to 1.67, D_1 falls to \$4, and g falls to 8 percent?

d. Independent of (b) and (c), assume management has recommended that Capital Industries expand by emphasizing financial services. Because this division is less risky than the other two, Capital's beta falls to 1.0 and the expected dividend growth rate falls to 9 percent. Other things being equal, what is the market price for Capital Industries?

e. After expanding into the financial services area in (d), Capital finds that it will have the long-run effect of reducing dividend growth to 7 percent. Other things being equal, what is the market price?

SELECTED REFERENCES

Baker, H. Kent, and John A. Haslem. "Toward the Development of Client-Specified Valuation Models." *Journal of Finance* 29 (September 1974), pp. 1255–1263.

Basu, Sanjoy. "The Information Content of Price-Earnings Ratios." *Financial Management* 4 (summer 1975), pp. 53–64.

Bauman, W. Scott. "Investment Returns and Present Value." *Financial Analysts Journal* 27 (November –December 1969), pp. 107–120.

Block, Frank E. "The Place of Book Value in Common Stock Evaluation." *Financial Analysts Journal* 22 (March–April 1964), pp. 29–33.

Bower, Richard S., and Dorothy M. Bower. "Risk and the Valuation of Common Stock." *Journal of Political Economy* 77 (May–June 1969), pp. 349–362.

————, Keith B. Johnson, Walter J. Lutz, and T. Craig Topley, "Investment Opportunities and Stock Valuation," *Journal of Business Research* 5 (March 1977), pp. 39–61.

Brigham, Eugene F., and James L. Pappas. "Duration of Growth, Changes in Growth Rates, and Corporate Share Prices." *Financial Analysts Journal* 24 (May–June 1966), pp. 157–162.

Brennan, Michael J. "Note on Dividend Irrelevance and the Gordon Valuation Model." *Journal of Finance* 26 (December 1971), pp. 1115–1123.

Durand, David. "Growth Stocks and the Petersburg Paradox." *Journal of Finance* 12 (September 1957), pp. 348–363.

Fama, Eugene F. "Components of Investment Performance." *Journal of Finance* 27 (June 1972), pp. 551–567.

Fewings, David R. "The Impact of Growth on the Risk of Common Stocks." *Journal of Finance* 30 (May 1975), pp. 525–531.

Finnerty, Joseph E. "Insiders and Market Efficiency." *Journal of Finance* 31 (September 1976), pp. 1141–1148.

Gordon, Myron J. *The Investment, Financing, and Valuation of the Corporation.* Homewood, Ill.: Irwin, 1962.

Haugen, Robert A. "Expected Growth, Required Return, and the Variability of Stock Prices." *Journal of Financial and Quantitative Analysis* 5 (September 1970), pp. 297–308.

Hawawini, Gabriel A., and Ashok Vora. "Yield Approximations: A Historical Perspective." *Journal of Finance* 37 (March 1982), pp. 145–156.

Holt, Charles C. "The Influence of Growth Duration on Share Prices." *Journal of Finance* 17 (September 1962), pp. 465–475.

Hubbard, Charles L., and Clark A. Hawkins. *Theory of Valuation.* Scranton, Pa.: International Textbook, 1969.

Jaffe, Jeffery J. "Special Information on Insider Trading." *Journal of Business* 47 (July 1974), pp. 410–428.

Kraft, John, and Arthur Kraft. "Determinants of Common Stock Prices: A Time Series Analysis." *Journal of Finance* 33 (May 1977), pp. 417–425.

Lewellen, Wilbur G., and John J. McConnell. "Tax Reform, Firm Valuation, and Capital Costs." *Financial Management* 6 (winter 1977), pp. 59–66.

Long, John B. Jr. "The Market Valuation of Cash Dividends: A Case to Consider." *Journal of Financial Economics* 6 (June–September 1978), pp. 235–264.

Malkiel, Burton G. "Equity Yields, Growth and the Structure of Share Prices." *American Economic Review* 53 (December 1963), pp. 467–494.

Mao, James C. T. "The Valuation of Growth Stocks: The Investment Opportunities Approach." *Journal of Finance* 21 (March 1966), pp. 95–102.

Michaud, Richard O., and Paul L. Davis. "Valuation Model Bias and the Scale Structure of Dividend Discount Returns." *Journal of Finance* 37 (May 1982), pp. 563–573.

Miller, Merton, and Franco Modigliani. "Dividend Policy, Growth, and the Valuation of Shares." *Journal of Business* 34 (October 1961), pp. 411–433.

Olsen, I. J. "Valuation of a Closely Held Corporation." *Journal of Accountancy* 128 (August 1969), pp. 35–47.

Pringle, John J. "Price/Earnings Ratios, Earnings per Share, and Financial Management." *Financial Management* 2 (spring 1973), pp. 34–40.

Reilly, Frank K., and Thomas J. Zeller. "An Analysis of Relative Industry Price-Earnings Ratios." *The Financial Review*, 1974, pp. 17–33.

Robichek, Alexander A. "Risk and the Value of Securities." *Journal of Financial and Quantitative Analysis* 4 (December 1969), pp. 513–538.

————, and Marcus C. Bogue. "A Note on the Behavior of Expected Price/Earnings Ratios over Time." *Journal of Finance* 26 (June 1971), pp. 731–736.

Sharpe, William F. *Investments*, 2d ed. Englewood Cliffs, N.J.: Prentice-Hall, 1981.

Stone, Bernell K. "The Conformity of Stock Values Based on Discounted Dividends to a Fair Return Process." *Bell Journal of Economics* 6 (autumn 1975), pp. 698–702.

Turnbull, Stuart M. "Market Value and Systematic Risk." *Journal of Finance* 32 (September 1977), pp. 1125–1142.

Umstead, David A. "Forecasting Stock Market Prices." *Journal of Finance* 32 (May 1977), pp. 427–441.

Van Horne, James C., and William F. Glassmire, Jr. "The Impact of Unanticipated Changes in Inflation on the Value of Common Stocks." *Journal of Finance* 27 (December 1972), pp. 1081–1092.

Walter, James B. *Dividend Policy and Enterprise Valuation*. Belmont, Calif.: Wadsworth, 1967.

Warren, James M. "An Operational Model for Security Analysis and Valuation." *Journal of Financial and Quantitative Analysis* 9 (June 1974), pp. 395–422.

Wendt, Paul F. "Current Growth Stock Valuation Methods." *Financial Analysts Journal* 23 (March–April 1965), pp. 3–15.

Williams, Alex O., and Phillip E. Pfeifer. "Estimating Security Price Risk Using Duration and Price Elasticity." *Journal of Finance* 37 (May 1982), pp. 399–411.

Williams, John Burr. *The Theory of Investment Value*. Cambridge, Mass.: Harvard University Press, 1938.

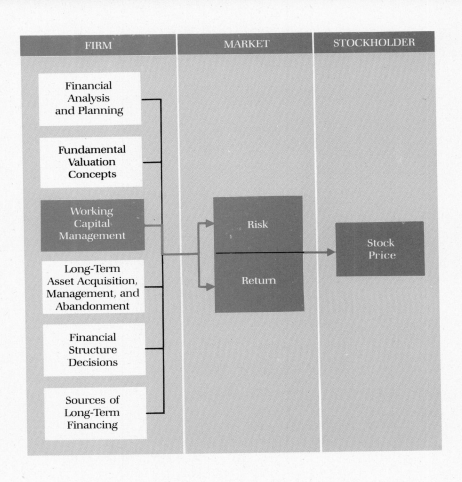

PART FOUR

WORKING
CAPITAL
MANAGEMENT

This part of the text is devoted to the management of working capital—that area that deals with the management of current assets and current liabilities. An understanding of the financial decisions surrounding the management of working capital is particularly important, since short-run viability is an obvious prerequisite to the long-run survival of the firm. Four chapters are included in this part; the first, Chapter 8, presents an overview of working capital management, including a comprehensive discussion of its multinational dimensions. Chapter 9 then describes the key aspects of managing the firm's cash and marketable securities position. Chapter 10 is devoted to the management of accounts receivable—credit policies, credit terms, and collection policies—and some basic inventory considerations. Finally, Chapter 11 looks at the management of current liabilities. Major sources of unsecured and secured short-term financing are covered, along with their appropriate managerial implications.

8

The Management of Working Capital

The management of working capital centers on the routine day-to-day administration of current assets and current liabilities. While this activity may lack the glamour of long-term financial decision making, it does involve a considerable amount of the financial manager's time and is fundamental to the firm's success. The ultimate goal of working capital management is, of course, to manage each of the firm's current assets and current liabilities in such a way as to achieve risk-return tradeoffs that maximize the value of the firm. Current assets must be available on a continuous basis to provide needed support for the operations of the firm; likewise, current liabilities must be obtained and used in ways that minimize costs and provide adequate operating flexibility. Working capital management is the topic of this chapter; individual current assets and current liabilities are discussed in the following three chapters. First we will examine the basic concepts and institutional dimensions of working capital, and then the risk-return tradeoff of several working capital strategies. Analysis of these strategies will reveal that working capital decisions can indeed have a dramatic impact on profits, cash flow, and risk. In the next section of the chapter we continue this theme by addressing the impact of working capital management on the risk and value of the firm. The final section provides a comprehensive discussion of the management of working capital on an international scale.

Basic Working Capital Concepts

In the broadest sense, the management of working capital pertains to the administration of both current assets and current liabilities. Customarily, these assets and liabilities are defined as having lives or maturities of 1 year or less. The major current assets include cash, marketable securities, accounts receivable, and inventory; major current liabilities include short-term loans and notes, accounts payable, accrued expenses (like wages), and accrued taxes. Working capital management is not an episodic, one-time event; rather, it is a continuous, day-to-day activity that occupies a large part of the financial manager's time. Especially in small firms, working capital management may be *the* factor that decides success or failure; in larger firms, efficient working capital management can significantly affect the firm's risk, return, and share price.

Because a substantial portion of total assets are allocated to short-term uses, corporate returns as well as risk are quite sensitive to working capital management. Firms that maintain excessive levels of cash, accounts receivable, and inventory will find that return on total investment is probably substandard, and that risk is low as well. Firms that operate with too little current assets, in contrast, will continually be affected by shortages and difficulties in maintaining smooth operations. Similarly, improper current liability management may result in a high cost of credit, problems with suppliers of materials, and perhaps even corporate failure should liabilities not be met. Careful management of working capital is therefore essential to the growth and long-run success of the firm.

Net Working Capital

Table 8.1 provides an abbreviated balance sheet for a hypothetical firm, Walker Manufacturing Company. It highlights Walker's working capital position and shows that the firm holds $725,000 in current assets and

TABLE 8.1
Balance Sheet and Working Capital Position of Walker Manufacturing Company

ASSETS

Cash	$ 25,000
Marketable securities	50,000
Accounts receivable	200,000
Inventories	450,000
Total current assets	$ 725,000
Fixed and other assets	775,000
Total assets	$1,500,000

LIABILITIES AND STOCKHOLDERS' EQUITY

Notes payable	$ 100,000
Accounts payable	125,000
Accruals	75,000
Current maturities	50,000
Total current liabilities	$ 350,000
Long-term debt and stockholders' equity	1,150,000
Total liabilities and stockholders' equity	$1,500,000

WORKING CAPITAL POSITION

Net working capital = $725,000 − $350,000
= $375,000

$$\text{Current ratio} = \frac{\$725,000}{\$350,000} = 2.07$$

owes $350,000 in current liabilities. Perhaps the most common definition of working capital is that of *net working capital*, the difference between a firm's current assets and its current liabilities. In the case of Walker, we see that it has a net working capital position of some $375,000 ($725,000 − $350,000). Net working capital enables the firm to operate in the face of nonsynchronous and uncertain cash flows. That is, because receipts and disbursements can neither be predicted nor matched with precision, net working capital is required to fill cash flow gaps, guard against uncertainty, and provide liquidity for ongoing operations. Net working capital provides a cushion to creditors and represents the portion of current assets that is financed with long-term debt and/or equity. The amount of cushion in a firm's working capital position can also be captured by its current ratio; as we saw in Chapter 3, the current ratio is an alternative (or complementary) measure of net working capital that shows the working capital position in relative, rather than absolute, terms. Walker's current ratio, also shown in Table 8.1, is 2.07 ($725,000 ÷ $350,000). Because current assets represent sources of cash receipts and current liabilities represent a potential drain on cash resources, the higher the net working capital (or current ratio), the better able the firm is to meet obligations as they come due.[1]

Working capital, and particularly its current asset segment, can also be viewed in terms of its permanence. As Figure 8.1 shows, a portion of total current assets is in fact "permanent," since the minimum amount of current assets on hand tends to grow with the firm. The temporary portion of current assets is represented by the part that fluctuates with the firm's seasonal and operating needs. Examining the behavior of current assets over the period of time shown in Figure 8.1, we see that the buildup in total current assets has resulted in a substantial amount of temporary current assets; in addition, note that at a point in time (t_x) all the temporary and a portion of the permanent current assets are financed with current liabilities. The balance, of course, represents net working capital—the amount financed with long-term debt and/or equity. Presumably, as the level of current assets varies, the level of current liabilities will vary accordingly.

Historic Behavior of Working Capital

As a rule, current assets represent nearly half of the total assets of manufacturing firms. In fact, available statistics[2] indicate that in 1983 manufacturing firms devoted an average of over 41 percent of total resources to current assets. Likewise, their current liabilities represent-

---

[1]This statement generally holds *unless*, of course, all (or most) of these cash resources are tied up in delinquent accounts receivable and/or obsolete inventory.

[2]Federal Trade Commission, *Quarterly Financial Report: Manufacturing, Mining and Trade Corporations* (Washington, D.C.: U.S. Government Printing Office 3d quarter, 1983).

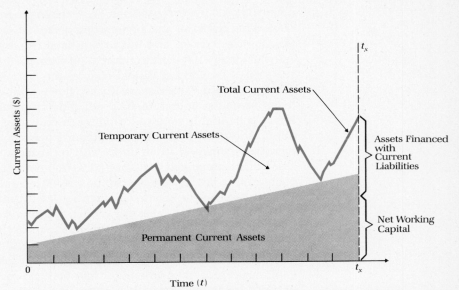

Figure 8.1 The Behavior of Temporary and Permanent Working Capital.

ed, on average, over 25 percent of total debt and equity financing. Measured as a percentage of total assets (or total financing), the composition of working capital for U.S. manufacturing firms in 1983 averaged as follows:

Cash	2.7%	Notes payable and	
Marketable securities	3.0	current maturities	3.4%
Accounts receivable	15.5	Accounts payable	8.5
Inventories	17.1	Accrued taxes	1.6
Prepaids and other	3.1	Accrued expenses	
Total current assets	41.4%	and other	12.0
		Total current liabilities	25.5%

Note: Items expressed as a percentage of total assets.

Clearly, current assets represent a significant investment on the part of most firms; moreover, this investment, as well as the level and composition of short-term financing, tends to be relatively volatile. Figure 8.2 shows the behavior of current assets and current liabilities over the past two decades. Part (a) shows that the level of current assets, relative to total assets, has actually *declined* over time; from a high of almost 55 percent of total assets, current assets declined to just over 41 percent in 1983. Most of this decline has been due to significantly

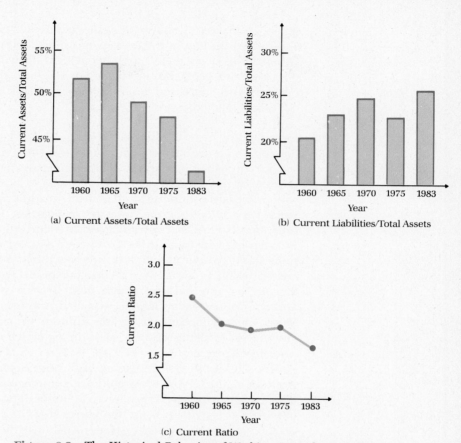

Figure 8.2   The Historical Behavior of Working Capital: 1960–1983.
Source: Federal Trade Commission, *Quarterly Financial Report: Manufacturing, Mining and Trade Corporations* (Washington, D.C.: U.S. Government Printing Office, 3d quarter, 1983).

reduced holdings of cash and marketable securities, and to some reductions in the level of inventory. One of the major forces behind the decrease in current assets has undoubtedly been the increased opportunity cost of holding these resources; high interest rates have provided a real incentive for reducing holdings. Note in Figure 8.2(b) that as firms reduced their investments in short-term resources, current liabilities *increased* to over 25 percent of total assets by 1983; and with the exception of accrued taxes (which actually went down in importance), this growth was fairly evenly shared by notes payable and current maturities, accounts payable, and accrued expenses. Such behavior was probably prompted by the fact that current liability financing is normally less expensive than long-term debt and equity financing—an especially important feature in periods of relatively high interest rates. Not surprisingly, Figure 8.2(c) shows that the net result of all this has been a substantial decline in the average current ratio of manufacturing firms. Other things being equal, such behavior is likely to have positive effects on corporate profitability, but as we will see, the reduced operating cushion and increased leverage also suggests a general increase in corporate risk exposure.

Industry and Size Variations.   The optimum level of working capital depends on a number of factors, including the size of the firm and the industry in which it operates. As the firm grows in terms of total assets, a portion of this growth occurs in the area of current assets; projected sales increases produce a similar effect. In addition, operating characteristics vary widely across industry categories, producing substantial differences in levels of current assets and current liabilities, as is evident in Table 8.2. Note that the level of current assets varies from 19 percent of total assets to over 66 percent. Note also that most of the variations in current asset holdings are accounted for by accounts receivable and inventories, the levels of which tend to vary according to operating and/or production cycles. As expected, the level of current liabilities tends to vary according to the amount of current asset holdings, although as evidenced by the variation in current ratios, this relationship is far from perfect.

The size of the firm is also an important determinant of the level of working capital. Table 8.3 provides a summary of the levels of current assets and current liabilities for a variety of different-sized manufacturing firms. It is evident from the figures that the relative level of current assets required to support operations declines directly with increases in the size of the firm, and this tends to hold for all the major types of current assets except marketable securities. Given the purported benefits of economies of scale, such behavior is not surprising. Nor is it surprising that larger firms tend to rely less on current liabilities as a source of financing. Clearly, the greater access to public capital markets that larger firms enjoy opens up options many smaller companies simply do not have.

Impact of Inflation/Disinflation.   Inflation—and most recently *disinflation*, which involves a positive but declining rate of growth in prices—has become a central concern to business. Although general price increases affect the entire asset-liability structure of the firm, major impact is felt in the current asset and liability accounts. Among current assets, cash, accounts receivable, and inventories are all affected as high opportunity costs and declining real values place a premium on keeping cash and accounts receivable levels to an absolute minimum. What is worse, rising prices distort inventory values and produce artificially inflated profit and tax levels. Of course, the opposite effects result during periods of disinflation.

TABLE 8.2
Industry Variations in Current Assets and Current Liabilities: 1981 Averages
(Figures Reported as Percentage of Total Assets or Total Financing)

	Drugs	Nondurable Manufacturing	Petroleum and Coal Products	Nonferrous Metals	Electrical Equipment	Aircraft and Aerospace Manufacturing	Mining	Wholesale Trade
				Industry Group				
CURRENT ASSETS								
Cash	1.5%	2.1%	.8%	2.5%	3.8%	2.0%	2.4%	3.5%
Marketable securities	2.6	2.6	2.1	.9	4.1	1.8	2.2	4.2
Accounts receivable	14.2	13.7	8.4	14.4	20.7	12.4	8.5	25.3
Inventories	14.0	13.0	6.0	15.2	24.0	49.5	4.1	27.9
Prepaids and other	4.1	3.0	1.9	1.9	4.5	1.1	2.0	4.1
Total current assets	36.4%	34.4%	19.2%	34.9%	57.1%	66.8%	19.2%	65.0%
CURRENT LIABILITIES								
Notes payable and current maturities	6.1%	3.0%	1.3%	3.8%	4.2%	1.6%	2.7%	17.6%
Accounts payable	4.0	8.6	8.7	7.4	8.5	8.4	5.7	20.4
Accrued taxes	2.8	1.8	1.9	1.3	1.5	5.2	.3	.6
Accruals and other	9.9	8.4	5.8	7.4	20.3	38.5	6.8	8.5
Total current liabilities	22.8%	21.8%	17.7%	19.9%	34.5%	53.7%	15.5%	47.1%
Current ratio	1.59	1.58	1.08	1.76	1.66	1.24	1.24	1.38

SOURCE: Federal Trade Commission, Quarterly Financial Report: Manufacturing, Mining and Trade Corporations (Washington, D.C.: U.S. Government Printing Office, 3d quarter, 1983).

TABLE 8.3

Effects of Firm Size on Current Assets and Current Liabilities: 1983 Averages for All Manufacturing Companies (Figures Reported as Percentage of Total Assets or Total Financing)

	Asset Size ($ Millions)				
	Under $5	$10 to $25	$50 to $100	$250 to $1000	Over $1000
CURRENT ASSETS					
Cash	7.6%	6.3%	7.1%	3.5%	1.8%
Marketable securities	3.8	3.8	4.4	3.1	2.0
Accounts receivable	26.0	24.7	21.9	18.7	11.9
Inventories	25.1	25.7	23.8	19.0	14.5
Prepaids and other	2.9	3.4	2.6	2.6	3.1
Total current assets	65.4%	63.9%	59.8%	46.9%	33.3%
CURRENT LIABILITIES					
Notes payable and current maturities	8.3%	7.4%	4.8%	3.6%	4.5%
Accounts payable	13.1	12.2	9.9	8.3	7.3
Accrued taxes	1.5	1.5	1.4	.9	1.8
Accruals and other	8.9	10.6	9.8	10.5	10.7
Total current liabilities	31.8%	31.7%	25.9%	23.3%	24.3%
Current ratio	2.06	2.01	2.31	2.00	1.37

SOURCE: Federal Trade Commission, *Quarterly Financial Report: Manufacturing, Mining and Trade Corporations* (Washington D.C.: U.S. Government Printing Office, 3d quarter, 1983).

Inflation also affects current liability management. High interest rate levels cause suppliers of capital to restrict their lending activities, and credit terms become increasingly unattractive, putting pressure on firms to reduce purchases and speed up payments. At the same time, bank lenders become more reluctant to roll over short-term notes and require higher interest rates at each renewal. Most important, additional uncertainty about the availability of short-term funds makes the task of liability management even more difficult. An inflationary environment, therefore, increases both the costs and the risks associated with the firm's working capital management policies. Disinflation, such as that which occurred in 1982, likewise poses problems and risks for the financial manager to consider in managing the firm's working capital.

Working Capital Strategies

Working capital strategies range from the aggressive to the conservative; between these two extremes are many subtle variations that produce marked differences in the firm's profitability and risk exposure. Within a risk-return context, an aggressive policy sacrifices safety in the hope of increasing profits. A conservative policy, in contrast, takes a safety-first approach, with profitability as a secondary concern. The financial manager may alter the level and composition of current assets and current liabilities to change the profitability of the firm and its exposure to risk. The tradeoff between these two variables is such that the manipulation of working capital to increase profitability will result in a corresponding increase in risk.

The Risk-Return Tradeoff

There is a direct tradeoff between a firm's profitability and its exposure to risk. In this context, profitability is measured as profits after expenses, and is related to the total asset investment of the firm. Risk is measured by the probability that a firm will become *technically insolvent* and be unable to pay bills as they come due; additional risk also results from the probability of stockouts, production interruptions, and other difficulties that may lead to lost sales and profits. A firm's profits can be increased in one of two ways: by increasing revenues or by decreasing costs. Costs, for example, can be reduced by paying less for an item or a service, or by using existing resources more efficiently. Profits can also be increased by investing in assets that are capable of producing higher levels of revenues, such as plant and equipment, as opposed to marketable securities—or by using less costly forms of financing, such as current liabilities. The risk of becoming technically insolvent is commonly assessed by measuring the firm's net working capital or its current ratio; both will be used in the following discussions to capture the firm's exposure to insolvency. In effect, it is assumed that the greater the firm's current ratio, the less risky the firm. Presumably, risk can be reduced by investing more heavily in current assets (which are more liquid than fixed assets), or by using more long-term financing (which typically carries smaller and less frequent debt repayment burdens).

The Profitability of Assets. Generally speaking, a company would expect to earn more on fixed assets than on current assets. Fixed assets represent the true earning assets of the firm and include such things as plant, machinery, equipment, and rolling stock—all of which enable the firm to produce goods and services that can ultimately be sold for a profit. The firm's current assets, except for marketable securities, do not *directly* earn any type of return. Rather, they provide a buffer that allows the firm to smooth out their production cycle, make sales, and extend credit. Current assets are essential for the effective operation of the firm. At the same time, without fixed assets to produce the finished products that generate the cash, marketable securities, accounts receivable, and inventories, the firm could not operate at all. In effect, if the firm cannot earn more on its fixed assets than on its current assets, it should sell all its fixed assets and use the proceeds to purchase current assets.

The Cost of Financing.   A firm can obtain financing from either current liabilities or long-term funds, such as long-term debt, preferred stock, and equity. Current liabilities normally are considered less expensive than long-term financing. Of all the different types of current liabilities, only notes payable have a stated (explicit) financing cost. This is because notes payable represent the only negotiated form of short-term borrowing. Accounts payable and accruals are less expensive sources of funds because they do not normally carry direct interest charges—although as we will see in Chapter 11, there is an implicit cost in foregoing any cash discounts offered on accounts payable. In addition, even the short-term funds that carry an explicit cost have done so in the majority of the last 20 years at a lower rate than is normally charged for long-term money.[3]

Asset Mix Decisions

Assuming that total assets and short-term financing remain constant, it follows that an increase in current assets at the expense of fixed assets will increase net working capital and, as a result, reduce not only the firm's risk, but also its productive capacity. The opposite is true when the firm increases fixed assets at the expense of working capital. When fixed assets are compared to current assets, the former are normally expected to produce the product, whereas the latter are expected to facilitate the process. For this reason, the explicit return on current assets is lower than that on fixed assets. To maximize returns, therefore, the firm should limit current asset investments and allocate capital to the more productive fixed assets. In an ideal world of perfectly synchronized and certain cash flows, almost no current assets would be required; instead, investments could be allocated almost exclusively to the highly productive fixed assets. In reality, of course, the firm faces a tradeoff: For as it reduces current assets to invest in the more profitable fixed assets, the risk of cash shortages, stockouts, shipping delays, and lost sales increases accordingly. An appropriate balance between short-term and long-term asset investments is thus an important goal of working capital management.

The current ratio can be used to illustrate this risk-return tradeoff. When the ratio increases, both the firm's returns and its risk exposure decrease as a larger portion of assets is allocated to the less profitable current assets. At the same time, the increase in net working capital results in greater liquidity and therefore less risk of insolvency. This principle can be seen by referring once again to the working capital position of Walker Manufacturing. Recall from Table 8.1 that the firm had total current assets of $725,000 and total assets of $1.5 million; let us assume for discussion purposes that current assets earn 6 percent, on average, and that fixed assets generate a more respectable 20 percent rate of return. Assume further that management feels the current working capital position is too conservative and wants the firm to take a more aggressive stance by reducing current assets by some $225,000. This could be done by eliminating marketable securities, reducing receivables by about $75,000, and reducing inventory by approximately $100,000; such released funds would then be invested in fixed assets. (We

---

[3]There have, of course, been times in the past (such as in 1981) when short-term money actually cost more than long-term debt; such events usually occur when both short- and long-term interest rates are relatively high.

TABLE 8.4
Effects on Risk and Return from Changes in Working Capital Policy: Altering the Asset Mix

ASSUMPTIONS

Current assets earn 6%
Fixed assets earn 20%
No change in amount of total assets
Total current liabilities, $350,000
No change in financing mix
Cost of total financing, $152,000

	Walker Manufacturing Company		
	Conservative (Current Position)		**Aggressive (Proposed Change)**
ASSET MIX			
Current assets	$ 725,000	−$225,000	$ 500,000
Fixed assets	775,000	+$225,000	1,000,000
Total assets	$1,500,000		$1,500,000
NET PROFITS			
Current assets	.06($725,000) = $ 43,500		.06($ 500,000) = $ 30,000
Fixed assets	.20($775,000) = 155,000		.20($1,000,000) = 200,000
Profits on total assets	$198,500		$230,000
−Cost of total financing	152,000		152,000
Net profits	$ 46,500		$ 78,000
RATIOS			
Current assets/total assets	48.3%		33.3%
Return on investment[a]	3.1%		5.2%
Net working capital	$375,000		$150,000
Current ratio	2.07		1.43

[a]Net profits/total assets.

assume no change in the financing mix—$350,000 in current liabilities and $1,150,000 in long-term funds.)

The impact of this suggested policy change is depicted in Table 8.4, which shows that the proposed working capital change will reduce the relative level of current assets from about 48 percent of total assets to slightly more than 33 percent. This will mean a pronounced improvement in corporate profitability (return on investment increases from 3.1 to 5.2 percent), but it will also increase the risk of insolvency, as suggested by the changes in net working capital and current ratio. Clearly, aggressive management of the asset mix results in high profit and high risk, while a more conservative approach results in lower profits and risk.

Financing Mix Decisions

Like the asset mix, the mix of financing also affects the risk and return of the firm. The effect of short-term versus long-term financing can be captured in the ratio of current liabilities to total financing. An increase in this ratio should lead to an increase in profitability; that is, profitability will improve as a result of the greater use of lower-cost short-term financing. At the same time, assuming the level of current assets remains unchanged, an increase in the level of current liabilities will result in a decrease in the net working capital position, thus increasing the risk of insolvency. Again we can look to Walker Manufacturing to see how this works. In this case, we assume that current liabilities cost 4 percent, whereas long-term funds carry a 12 percent cost. Note that the very low current liability cost is due to the fact that a large portion of short-term financing (such as accounts payable and accruals) has no explicit cost. The 4 percent figure represents an *average* for all current liabilities, and not necessarily the cost of such items as negotiated bank loans, which will carry a much higher interest rate.

In this case, management is considering a more aggressive posture for the company by increasing the reliance on current liabilities and reducing the reliance on long-term funds. The details of this proposed change are worked out in Table 8.5. (*Note*: We assume no change in the asset mix—$725,000 in current assets and $775,000 in fixed assets.) The values in Table 8.5 reveal performance remarkably similar to that which accrues from a decrease in the relative level of current assets. That is, although net working capital does decline substantially, the rate of profitability increases as the firm uses more current liabilities in its financial structure. Note the ratio of current liabilities to total financing rose from about 23 to slightly more than 33 percent. Also note that a policy change which moves the firm from a conservative to an aggressive working capital position results in both increased profitability (return on investment increases from 3.1 to 3.9 percent) and increased risk, as suggested by the changes in net working capital and current ratio.

bank the £1 million for delivery in 6 months through a forward contract[5] at the existing 6-month forward rate. Dallas Electronics would then lose $40,000 on this foreign exchange transaction. In this case, however, it cannot lose more than $40,000, nor will it benefit if the pound strengthens in value. Dallas has traded the risk of a foreign exchange gain or loss of uncertain size for the certainty of a $40,000 loss. The money market hedge would accomplish the same purpose at about the same cost. Dallas Electronics could borrow just enough pounds at an interest cost of 8 percent for 6 months (16 percent per year) so that its principal plus interest payment would equal £1 million. The interest cost would be 2 percent higher than for the same amount borrowed in dollars at 6 percent for 6 months. Thus the opportunity cost of the 6-month money market hedge would be approximately $2,000,000 × .02 = $40,000.[6] Once again, uncertainty about the future exchange rate is eliminated at a price.

Of course, Dallas Electronics could have eliminated its foreign exchange risk altogether by bidding the semiconductor devices in dollars. On the other hand, since London Computers would then assume the exchange risk, it would probably have tried to bargain the price down to $1.96 rather than $2 million in order to leave room to cover the foreign exchange risk. London Computers would have purchased the dollars forward or made a dollar loan, both of which would have cost it about $40,000 for 6 months.

The fact that each strategy leads to the same $40,000 loss is simply an example of the international equilibrium model described in Chapter 2. Is there any strategy Dallas Electronics could use to avoid a $40,000 loss? The answer lies not in finance, but in marketing. At the time Dallas Electronics bid the semiconductor devices to London Computers, the marketing manager should have included the cost of a forward contract in the cost of the project. The cost of covering a bid with a forward contract is just like any other insurance policy, or for that matter any other cost. If the sale to London Computers at £1 million, after deducting all costs including the forward contract,

---

[5]Dallas Electronics could have just as well sold a *currency futures contract* in the currency futures market rather than arranging a forward contract with its bank. However, such a transaction would be much more speculative than the forward contract due to the many uncertainties existing in the futures market. More detailed discussion of futures contracts can be found in Appendix 21A, which is concerned with hedging strategies with interest rate futures.

[6]The actual loan amount would be £1,000,000 ÷ 1.08 = £925,926. When this is converted to dollars at £1 = $2, it would provide $1,851,852 in financing. The opportunity cost at 2 percent would be $37,037 instead of $40,000, but the remaining $148,148 would still need to be financed by a dollar loan.

provided the desired contribution margin, then there really was no loss of $40,000, even though it will show up in the accounting books as a foreign exchange loss.

Translation Exposure. A firm is subject to *translation exposure* to the extent that certain of its assets, liabilities, revenues, or expenses are originally denominated in a foreign currency. A firm must prepare its financial statements on a worldwide consolidated basis, using its home currency as the ultimate reporting currency. When foreign-currency-denominated accounts are consolidated into a U.S. parent's financial statement, an exchange rate must be chosen to "translate" from the foreign currency to its U.S. dollar equivalent. Sometimes the current exchange rate is used; other times, the historical exchange rate in effect when the foreign currency account was originally booked is used. This choice is determined by accounting principles, which for U.S. firms are presently embodied in Financial Accounting Standards Board Statement 52 (FASB 52).

According to FASB 52, all foreign-currency-denominated balance sheet accounts, except net worth, are translated at the current exchange rate in effect on the date of the balance sheet. Net worth accounts are translated at historical rates. Income statement accounts are translated at average exchange rates for the reporting period. Foreign exchange translation gains and losses are not included in the income statement but are accumulated in an equity adjustment account on the balance sheet.

Unlike transaction exposure, which results in cash gains or losses, translation exposure results only in book gains or losses. For example, if a U.S. firm's assets denominated in Mexican pesos are greater than its liabilities denominated in Mexican pesos, and the peso is devalued, the firm will suffer a translation loss. This loss will reduce the firm's accounting net worth through the equity adjustment account, but no cash loss occurs. If the Mexican peso should strengthen during the next reporting period, a translation gain would be recorded in the equity adjustment account. Translation gains and losses do not affect taxable income or worldwide taxes.

Does translation exposure influence a firm's stock price? Although empirical tests of this question have produced inconclusive results, some financial managers believe the answer is yes. In order to eliminate translation exposure, these managers often attempt to maintain a rough equality between exposed assets and liabilities in each foreign currency. In such a case any change in the foreign exchange rate would cause offsetting translation gains and losses.

In practice, it is almost impossible to maintain a perfect balance in each currency. The easiest way to balance is by adjusting local currency debt to equal local currency assets. However, it is often impossible to borrow in some of the more exotic local currencies, nor are forward contracts or other instruments always available to offset translation exposure. On the other hand, multinational firms are usually naturally diversified by currency, which means that losses on one currency may be offset by gains on another.

Economic Exposure.   *Economic exposure* is the possibility that the market value of a firm will be affected by a change in long-run cash flows due to an *unexpected* change in exchange rates. In an efficient stock market, the impact on future cash flows of an *expected* change in an exchange rate should be reflected in the price of a firm's common stock. If the international equilibrium model is working, differential inflation rates, differential interest rates, and the forward rate should all point to the same forecasted change in the spot exchange rate. For example, under equilibirum conditions if these variables forecast that the Italian lira is going to devalue by 6 percent, then U.S. firms exporting to Italy have probably already calculated this 6 percent devaluation cost into their Italian lira prices, or if billed in dollars, the Italian importers have probably calculated in the 6 percent dollar appreciation cost.

The problem of economic exposure arises because the international equilibrium model does not always work. For example, in the first half of 1981, the U.S. dollar appreciated far more than expected against the Deutsche mark and other European currencies. This was due to unexpectedly high interest rates in the United States and perhaps a sign of confidence that the Reagan administration would succeed in reducing U.S. inflation. The dollar appreciation was undoubtedly stronger than could have been predicted by expected differential national rates of inflation. Indeed, the forward rate on the dollar throughout its appreciation was generally at a discount with respect to most other European currencies, rather than at a premium. (Remember that the forward rate is supposed to be an unbiased predictor of the future spot rate, or at least the market's best guess.)

Unexpected changes in the exchange rate can lead to windfall gains and losses on existing and maturing contracts and obligations. These would show up as transaction and translation gains or losses. More important, however, is the potential effect on a firm's long-run competitive position. For example, as a result of the appreciation of the dollar in early 1981, U.S. firms that exported to Europe found their dollar-based prices uncompetitive with prices based on European currencies during late 1981. The European importer must pay more in local currency for the same U.S. goods and services that previously were equal in local currency price to comparable local goods. European goods and services will look more attractive in price to U.S. importers, who will pay fewer dollars for goods maintaining the same local currency prices. In the longer run, appreciation of the dollar can affect future cash flows in a number of ways. If U.S. exporters reduce their prices to maintain parity with local currency prices, their profit margins on sales will suffer, but sales volume may stay the same. On the other hand, if they maintain their dollar prices, their sales margins will stay the same, but volume will probably suffer. The best pricing strategy depends on the price elasticity of demand for a particular good or service in each country.

The impact of the appreciation of the dollar on the cost side might adversely affect the cash flow of firms that produce in the United States compared to firms that produce in Europe. For example, a U.S. firm that previously produced its sales to Europeans in the United States would find the dollar cost of its labor unchanged, but the cost of competing European labor, expressed in dollars, would be lower than before. Thus a U.S. firm might need to shift labor-intensive production to Europe if the new exchange rates were expected to continue into the future. Naturally, the U.S. multinational that already has comparable production facilities in both the United States and Europe would have the big advantage of being able to shift production very quickly if there is excess capacity in its European facilities. In fact, it might even pay to produce a portion of its sales to the U.S. market and elsewhere from a European facility. Apart from labor costs, dollar appreciation will also change the cost of raw materials and other factors of production. Some factors, such as oil, will become more expensive for European-based production, because the price of oil is based on dollars. This could offset the relative improvement in European labor costs. In general, firms that produce in the United States will usually find imported raw materials are either less expensive or cost the same in dollar terms. Domestic factors, of course, will have unchanged dollar costs.

This analysis of the potential impact of an unexpected change in the dollar exchange rate on future cash flows, and thus the market value of a firm, is too simplistic. As firms in the United States and the rest of the world react to the dollar appreciation, employment and national incomes will be affected. In addition, relative rates of inflation can be affected by "imported inflation" as the rest of the world pays more for dollar-based goods. In the long run, these macroeconomic developments will influence the relative competitiveness of firms throughout the world. Predicting the ultimate impact on a firm's long-run cash flow, and designing strategies to react to long-run economic exposure, is still one of the less well understood areas of international finance in particular and management in general. Any successful long-run strategy must be based on inputs from marketing, production, and personnel, as well as finance. It is a top management problem and one of critical importance to the competitive survival of many firms, as well as to the immediate market value of their common stock.

Political Risks

Political risks affect working capital management in subtle ways. Most of us associate political risk with a government expropriating foreign-owned firms, or even privately owned firms. But this is actually rare, although when it happens it makes headlines. Apart from such aberrations, however, less dramatic forms of political intrusion can affect the way a firm positions its funds internationally. For example, some countries limit the size of dividends to a fixed percentage of a firm's book net worth. License fees and other payments for knowhow are also closely monitored, both for size and for appropriateness. In extreme cases, countries that are experiencing severe balance of payments problems and a resulting shortage of foreign exchange reserves may block any movement of funds abroad (such as was done in Mexico in 1982).

It is very difficult for an individual firm to react to political risk, since a sovereign state is "always right." Most firms try to avoid direct confrontation by *unbundling transfers* of funds. A parent firm will structure its financial relationships with foreign affiliates in such a way that repatriation of funds to the parent need not be only in the form of politically sensitive dividends. For example, an affiliate might be required to pay the parent a license fee for the right to use technology and management expertise provided by the parent or other affiliates. This form of payment has the additional advantage of being a legitimate expense and thus deductible from taxable income of the paying affiliate. A dividend would, of course, have to be paid in after-tax income. It is also common for a country to "withhold" taxes on dividends to compensate it for not being able to tax foreign recipients in the same manner as domestic recipients. The amount of withholding is usually decided through bilateral agreements often incorporated in bilateral tax treaties, which also try to eliminate other problems of double taxation.

Another technique that can be used to unbundle fund transfers is to weight the financial structure of a foreign affiliate more heavily with debt from the parent or related affiliates. Now funds can be repatriated in the form of regularly scheduled amortization payments, rather than irregularly declared dividends.

Transfer Pricing

Transfer pricing refers to the price at which goods or services are purchased or sold to related affiliates. Because in some cases it may be possible to transfer both income and funds from one affiliate to another, host country authorities are careful to monitor all transfer prices. In the United States, it is the duty of the Department of the Treasury to scrutinize transfer prices under Section 482 of the Internal Revenue Code. The objective is to make sure that the United States tax base is not eroded through artificial transfer prices to related firms abroad. The usual rule in the United States and other countries is that transfer prices should be at market value, as determined by completely objective, or "arms length," bargaining. Despite close monitoring, however, gray areas do exist. Such areas include the transfer of parts, subassemblies, used equipment, and intangibles (like technical and managerial expertise).

In order to illustrate transfer pricing, assume that a U.S. firm owns a profitable affiliate in Brazil that is accumulating partially blocked excess funds. That is, the affiliate cannot return as much cash to the U.S. firm as it desires. The U.S. parent might be tempted to sell the Brazilian affiliate parts or subassemblies that are normally used in the manufacturing process. The transfer price would be set relatively high, so that cash flow and profits would be reduced in Brazil but increased in the United States. The Brazilian authorities might question the transfer price but lack evidence on what an arms length price should be. Presumably the transferred items would have little value in the external market because they are specifically made for the firm's own differentiated products. Manipulation of transfer prices, of course, involves the danger of actually increasing political risk. If the host country suspects consistent bias in transfer prices but cannot prove it, other areas of government relationships might be utilized by the host country to "recapture" suspected lost profits.

Transaction Costs

The transaction cost of positioning funds in multinational corporations could be relatively high compared to that for a domestic firm because of the need to pass through the foreign exchange market. To minimize foreign exchange transaction costs, multinational firms usually utilize a worldwide cash management system. Some of the best systems are offered to these firms as a service by large international banks. Worldwide cash management systems feature not only basic working capital techniques that are used to minimize idle cash, but also sophisticated reporting systems that allow a firm to net payments between related affiliates. Netting greatly reduces transaction costs, since fewer funds are transferred through the foreign exchange market.

To illustrate a multinational netting system, assume that a U.S. parent has affiliates in The Netherlands (Dutch), France, and Denmark (Danish). Figure 8.4 shows a simplified set of financial relationships within this group. The Dutch affiliate owes $1 million worth of guilders to the French affiliate. The French affiliate owes $1 million worth of francs to the Danish affiliate. The Danish affiliate owes $1 million worth of kroner to the U.S. parent. Finally, the U.S. parent owes the Dutch affiliate $1 million. Each unit owes as much as it is owed, and all belong to the same firm. *Netting* would entail each unit dropping its claim against other units, thus eliminating all transfer of funds. Such a procedure could be implemented by a central coordinator who simply sends an accounting memorandum to each unit. As a result, the firm saves the transaction cost of going to the foreign exchange market four times for $1 million. A few countries do not permit netting, but enough do so that the practice is widely used.

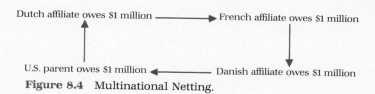

Figure 8.4   Multinational Netting.

SUMMARY

The management of working capital is an important and time-consuming aspect of managerial finance. Inadequate levels of working capital can result in serious financial difficulties, and even bankruptcy; excessive levels are likely to reduce corporate profitability and ultimately cause the firm's effectiveness and market value to decline. When determining the appropriate working capital policy, the firm always faces a tradeoff between profitability and risk; policies that reduce risk typically also reduce profits, and vice versa. It is possible, for instance, for aggressive firms to pursue higher profitability (at the cost of increased risk exposure) by reducing current asset investments in relation to fixed assets and/or using more current liabilities in place of long-term sources of financing.

Because the management of working capital affects corporate risk and return, it has an important bearing on the value of the firm. Using the capital asset pricing model, a firm's value can be shown to increase whenever additional expected returns more than compensate for additional nondiversifiable risk. Working capital policies that increase the correlation between profits and economic activity increase nondiversifiable risk and must provide increased returns in order to be economically justified. When the firm has risk-return opportunities not available to individual investors, its value is increased by policies that exploit such opportunities.

For firms operating in the international environment, foreign exchange risks, political risks, transfer pricing, and transaction costs all complicate the working capital management process. The three types of foreign exchange risk exposure are transaction exposure, translation exposure, and economic exposure. Political risk is concerned with the limits placed by the host government on the firm's movement of funds out of the host country. Transfer pricing is concerned with the price at which goods or services are purchased or sold to related affiliates. Transaction cost is concerned with the positioning of funds in subsidiaries to minimize transaction costs. All these international exposures must be managed to allow for the free flow of funds at minimum cost from and between foreign subsidiaries and the parent company.

QUESTIONS

8.1. Why is working capital management so important to stockholders, creditors, and the firm's financial managers?

    a. What relationship would you expect to exist between the predictability of a firm's cash flows and its required level of net working capital?

    b. How are net working capital, liquidity, technical insolvency, and risk related?

8.2.   **a.** Explain how an excessive investment in current assets can be detrimental to the firm; is it possible that such a condition could have any benefits?

    b. Discuss the detrimental effects of using an excessive amount of current liabilities; note the benefits of such action.

8.3. Contrast temporary current assets with permanent current assets; show why it may be appropriate to use long-term funds to finance at least a portion of the "permanent" current assets.

    a. Do you think it would be appropriate to finance a firm's current assets with long-term funds, even though all its current assets were temporary (it had no permanent current assets)? Explain.

    b. Would you expect the seasonal nature of a firm's sales to influence its short-term financing decisions? Explain.

8.4. The management of American International Metals is presently assessing its investment in current assets to determine whether or not it would be in the best interests of the firm to adopt a new working capital strategy. The company is considering several changes, any one of which will involve *shifting* current asset resources to fixed assets, or vice versa. With respect to each recommendation listed below, briefly explain the probable net result on the firm's overall risk and return position:

   a. American International increases its investment in inventory.

   b. American International eliminates its marketable securities and substantially reduces its cash position.

   c. American International decides to let its investment in accounts receivable rise by liberalizing credit policies.

8.5. Briefly explain how working capital decisions can affect the value of the firm.

   a. Would it be possible for working capital decisions to have an effect on corporate risk and return and yet not have an impact on the value of the firm?

   b. What use would working capital management serve if decisions in this area did not affect the value of the firm?

8.6. Using the capital asset pricing model (CAPM) as a framework, discuss how working capital management can affect the value of the firm.

8.7. Briefly describe the key issues and managerial strategies used to deal with each of the following complications resulting from the management of working capital in a *multinational environment*.

   a. Foreign exchange risks.

   b. Political risks.

   c. Transfer pricing.

   d. Transaction costs.

PROBLEMS

8.1. *COMPARATIVE PROFITABILITY OF CURRENT AND FIXED ASSETS.* Mid-Continent Asphalt wants to modernize part of its mixing plant; the problem is the firm is somewhat strapped for money at present. Management is now evaluating a proposal to fund this addition to fixed assets by working down current assets—and shifting these resources to fixed assets. The new equipment and facilities will cost $250,000. Mid-Continent estimates that it earns an average of 7.5 percent on current assets, and 18 percent on fixed assets (preliminary figures suggest the proposed investment should generate a similar rate of return). The firm's current liabilities cost 4.5 percent and its long-term financing carries a 12.5 percent cost; its latest year-end balance sheet appears as follows:

Current assets	$ 700,000	Current liabilities	$ 350,000
Fixed assets	1,000,000	Long-term financing	1,350,000
Total assets	$1,700,000	Total financing	$1,700,000

a. Compute the firm's current net profits and return on investment (ROI); contrast these with the net profits and ROI that would prevail if the proposed investment and shift from current to fixed assets is carried out.

b. Do you think the proposal has any merit? What potential pitfalls do you see?

c. As an alternative, assume the company could raise all the needed funds by issuing a new 12 percent long-term bond; what effect would this course of action have on the net profits and ROI of the firm? (*Note:* Ignore any tax considerations.)

d. All things considered, do you think the approach in (c) is superior to the proposal to shift funds from current to fixed assets? Explain.

8.2. *RISK AND RETURN OF SHORT-TERM FINANCING.* The Smokehaus Sausage Company is going to require the following amounts of new financing in each of the next 3 months. (*Note:* The $7500 in September is required *in addition* to the $12,000 in August. The same applies to the $21,500 in October.)

Month	Amount
August	$12,000
September	7,500
October	21,500

In addition, the company currently has a balance sheet that looks like this:

Current assets	$140,000	Current liabilities	$ 80,000
Fixed assets	375,000	Long-term financing	435,000
Total assets	$515,000	Total financing	$515,000

Assume current liabilities cost an average of 5 percent, and long-term financing costs 15 percent.

a. What would the firm's total financing cost be in August, September, and October if it met its needs by increasing current liabilities? What if all the funds were raised in the form of long-term financing?

b. Compute the net working capital and current ratio under both options.

c. Which option would be most desirable from the point of view of company profitability? Explain.

8.3. *CHANGING WORKING CAPITAL POLICY.* New England Oil & Gas has the following balance sheet:

Current assets	$ 3,000,000	Current liabilities	$ 1,500,000
Fixed assets	9,000,000	Long-term financing	10,500,000
Total assets	$12,000,000	Total financing	$12,000,000

Assume the firm can earn 3 percent on its current assets and 20 percent on fixed assets (after taxes, but before financing costs), and that current liabilities cost the firm 5 percent and long-term financing costs 12 percent.

a. Calculate the profits earned on total assets, total financing costs, net profits, current ratio, and return on investment (ROI).

b. Do the same, assuming the firm can earn 10 percent on current assets and 20 percent on fixed, and that current liabilities cost 8 percent and long-term financing costs 10 percent. All other assumptions remain the same.

c. Contrast your results in (b) with those obtained in (a) and comment on your findings. What caused the changes, and what implications do they hold for management?

d. Assume the company wants to increase net working capital by $1,000,000 *without changing the level of total assets or total financing.* This can be done by (1) increasing current assets while decreasing fixed assets; (2) decreasing current liabilities while increasing long-term financing; or (3) a combination of the two (increase current assets by $500,000 and decrease current liabilities by $500,000). Using the original asset earning rates and cost of financing assumptions, compute profits earned on total assets, total financing costs, net profits, current ratio, and ROI.

e. Using your findings in (d), and based on comparative risk and return, which action would you recommend? Explain.

SELECTED REFERENCES

Caldwin-Russell, Jorge A. "Covering Foreign Exchange Risks of Single Transactions." *Financial Management* 8 (autumn 1979), pp. 78–85.

Cohen, Allen M. "Treasury Terminal Systems and Cash Management Information Support." *Journal of Cash Management* 3 (August/September 1983), pp. 9–18.

Gitman, Lawrence J., and Kanwal S. Sachdeva. "A Framework for Estimating the Required Working Capital Investment." *Review of Business and Economic Research* 17 (spring 1982), pp. 36–44.

Kallberg, Jarl G., and Kenneth Parkinson. *Current Asset Management: Cash, Credit and Inventory.* New York: Wiley, 1984.

Lambrix, R. J., and S. S. Singhvi. "Managing the Working Capital Cycle." *Financial Executive* 47 (June 1979), pp. 32–41.

Merville, Larry J., and Lee A. Tavis. "Optimal Working Capital Policies: A

Chance-Constrained Programming Approach." *Journal of Financial and Quantitative Analysis* 8 (January 1973), pp. 47–59.

Petty, J. William II, and Ernest W. Walker. "Optimal Transfer Pricing for the Multinational Firm." *Financial Management* 1 (winter 1972), pp. 74–87.

Richards, Verlyn D., and Eugene J. Laughlin. "A Cash Conversion Cycle Approach to Liquidity Analysis." *Financial Management* 9 (spring 1980), pp. 32–38.

Sartoris, William L., and M. L. Spruill. "Goal Programming and Working Capital Management." *Financial Management* 3 (spring 1974), pp. 67–74.

Sartoris, William L., and Ned C. Hill. "A Generalized Cash Flow Approach to Short-Term Financial Decisions." *Journal of Finance* 38 (May 1983), pp. 349–360.

Schwab, Bernhard, and Peter Lusztig. "Apportioning Foreign Exchange Risk Through the Use of Third Currencies: Some Questions on Efficiency." *Financial Management* 7 (autumn 1978), pp. 25–30.

Severn, Alan K., and David R. Meinster. "The Use of Multicurrency Financing by the Financial Manager." *Financial Management* 7 (winter 1978), pp. 45–53.

Smith, Keith V. *Guide to Working Capital Management*. New York: McGraw-Hill, 1979.

————. "An Overview of Working Capital Management." In *Readings on the Management of Working Capital*, 2d ed., Keith V. Smith. St. Paul, Minn.: West, 1980.

————, ed. *Readings on the Management of Working Capital*, 2d ed. St. Paul, Minn.: West, 1980.

————, and Shirley Blake Sell. "Working Capital Management in Practice." In *Readings on the Management of Working Capital*, 2d ed., ed. Keith V. Smith. St. Paul, Minn.: West, 1980.

Stobaugh, Robert B., and Sidney M. Robbins. "Financing Foreign Affiliates." *Financial Management* 1 (winter 1972), pp. 56–65.

Van Horne, James C. "A Risk-Return Analysis of a Firm's Working Capital Position." *Engineering Economist* 14 (winter 1969), pp. 71–88.

Walker, Ernest W. "Toward a Theory of Working Capital." *Engineering Economist* 10 (winter 1964), pp. 21–35.

Yardini, Edward E. "A Portfolio-Balance Model of Corporate Working Capital." *Journal of Finance* 33 (May 1978), pp. 535–552.

9

The Management of Cash and Marketable Securities

The management of cash and marketable securities is an important area of working capital management, since by effectively managing these liquid resources, the financial manager can maintain desired levels of liquidity and at the same time generate a return on temporarily idle funds. The amount of cash and marketable securities held by major companies has at times reached staggering heights—for example, at year-end 1982, IBM had $3.3 *billion* worth of cash and short-term securities, American Express had $3.2 billion, General Motors had over $3.1 billion, and Texaco had over $2.3 billion. With this kind of money at stake, it is easy to see why companies are encouraged to spend time and money managing cash and marketable securities. By carefully balancing the risk of insolvency against the rewards of earning returns on cash balances, the financial manager can positively affect the value of the firm. This chapter presents the key concepts, tools, and techniques of cash and marketable securities management. The first section presents a general description of the management of liquid resources. Next, we describe and illustrate basic concepts and techniques for managing the firm's cash flow and then the procedures used to establish and maintain an optimum cash balance. In the final section, we consider the process, outlets, and strategies involved in the management of the marketable securities portfolio.

Managing the Firm's Liquid Resources

At the very minimum, a business needs enough cash on hand to pay debts as they come due and to meet emergencies; in addition, cash is sometimes held as a way to take advantage of unforeseen investment opportunities. A number of developments since the mid-1960s have stirred a greater interest in cash management and increased the desire of corporate treasurers to minimize the level of cash balances.

A primary factor in the concern over the efficient use of cash resources has been the sharp rise in interest rates over the last two decades (see Figure 9.1). For example, the rate on short-term Treasury bills averaged about ½ of 1 percent in the 1940s, 2 percent in the 1950s, almost 4 percent during the 1960s, nearly 6 percent during the 1970s, and over 17 percent in the early months of 1982. On the other hand, borrowing costs have also increased: the rate on 4- to 6-month commercial paper, which averaged less than 1 percent in the 1940s, rose to an average of near 7 percent during the 1970s, and reached over 20 percent in 1980! Today, due to the many attractive short-term investment opportunities, there is a substantial opportunity cost to holding cash in the form of barren demand deposits.[1] At the same time, the cost of borrowing to cover cash shortfalls is equally high.

A second factor affecting attitudes toward cash management is the increasingly sophisticated financial markets that have developed since the mid-1960s. Not only have advanced technology and communications improved the ability to market securities, but there is also a much wider variety of securities available for investment. Traditionally, U.S. Treasury bills were the primary short-term investment vehicle for corporations with excess cash. These securities could be sold easily, with little risk of loss. In the mid-1960s, commercial banks, short of loanable funds because of credit restraints imposed by the Federal Reserve, began issuing negotiable certificates of deposit to attract excess corporate funds. Since that time, a host of investment vehicles have developed in the bid for idle business funds, and today the corporate treasurer can choose investments tailored specifically to the amounts and maturities needed, even if the investment period is as short as one day. Technological advances have enabled firms to monitor widespread holdings of cash and to influence the timing of receipts and disbursements. Banking relationships have greatly encouraged this trend, as banks have played

---

[1]The Depository Institutions Deregulation and Monetary Control Act of 1980 provides for payment of interest on demand deposits. Of course, since business firms have for years been compensated for the "balances" they hold in commercial banks by receiving reduced activity fees or lower interest rates on loans, or both, this legislation has not significantly affected corporate banking relationships. Because the interest paid or earnings credit given on corporate demand deposits is low in comparison to short-term investment opportunities, the cost of holding excess demand deposits remains high. For a detailed description of this act, see "The Depository Institutions Deregulation and Monetary Control Act of 1980," *Federal Reserve Bulletin*, June 1980, pp. 444–453.

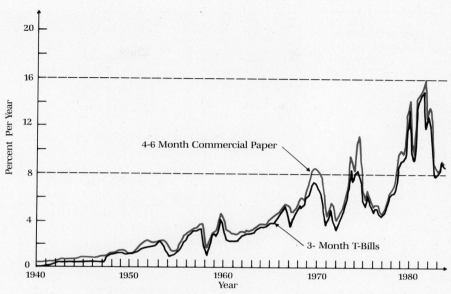

Figure 9.1   The Behavior of Selected Short-Term Interest Rates over Time.
Source: Federal Reserve Bulletin, selected issues.

an important role in helping corporations determine their cash needs and in altering their cash flows to maximize potential investment earnings.

The Historic Behavior of Liquid Resources

Table 9.1 presents some interesting comparisons between the proportion of total assets held in cash and in marketable securities. An especially noteworthy trend has been the reduction in liquid assets relative to total assets. In 1960, corporations were holding 10.8 percent of their assets in a liquid form; that position had dropped to 5.7 percent by the end of 1983. In a similar fashion, the ratio of liquid assets to current liabilities has also dropped markedly. This significant reduction in the proportion of liquid assets may at first seem alarming, but the drop is in large part due to greater sophistication in liquidity management. The computer, for example, enhanced the financial manager's ability to better utilize liquid assets by providing up-to-the-minute information regarding bank balances and cash inflows and outflows.

The Cash Management Activity

Corporations hold cash in the form of currency or in demand deposits at commercial banks. Checks are used for most payments, while currency is held primarily for transactions with consumers or for purchases out of a petty cash fund. The demand deposit balances held in banks must be adequate to meet the firm's working capital needs and to compensate the bank for its services. An important function of the cash manager, therefore, is to determine the level of balances necessary to meet those

TABLE 9.1
Corporate Holdings of
Liquid Assets (In
Percentages)

ALL MANUFACTURING CORPORATIONS	Year					
	1960	1965	1970	1975	1980	1983
Cash[a]	6.0%	6.1%	4.3%	3.9%	3.3%	2.7%
Marketable securities[a]	4.8	2.7	0.7	3.3	2.1	3.0
Total liquid assets[a]	10.8%	8.8%	5.0%	7.2%	5.4%	5.7%
Total liquid assets as % of current liabilities	51.9%	37.6%	20.3%	31.0%	20.0%	13.7%

LIQUIDITY BEHAVIOR (1983)	Industry			
	Nonferrous Metals	Aircraft	Petroleum and Coal	Mining
Cash[a]	2.5%	2.0%	0.8%	2.4%
Marketable securities[a]	0.9	1.8	2.1	2.2
Total liquid assets[a]	3.4%	3.8%	2.9%	4.6%
Total liquid assets as % of current liabilities	9.7%	5.7%	14.8%	24.1%

[a]Cash, marketable securities, and total liquid assets are listed as a percentage of total assets.

SOURCE: Federal Trade Commission, *Quarterly Financial Report: Manufacturing, Mining and Trade Corporations*, (Washington D.C.: U.S. Government Printing Office, various issues).

two criteria; in addition to, or as part of this function, the cash manager predicts expected cash inflows and outflows over various periods of time, decides how to finance shortfalls or invest excess funds, and weighs the costs of altering the cash flow against the costs of borrowing or the opportunity cost of not investing.

Figure 9.2 shows the basic cash management model. As seen, cash management is actually made up of several distinct, yet interrelated, functions. First, the financial manager must be concerned about cash flow management, which involves speeding up cash receipts, slowing down disbursements, and maintaining sound banking relationships. In addition, the financial manager must estimate cash requirements by preparing a cash budget (using the techniques and procedures described in Chapter 4). This statement is of key importance, since it allows the manager to plan, coordinate, and control the actual flow of cash through the firm. The operating expectations reflected in the cash budget help the manager maintain desired cash balances, establish effective borrowing strategies, and properly structure the portfolio of marketable securities. Once the level of cash flow has been estimated, the optimal cash balance can be established. Finally, given this desired balance, the financial manager can develop a short-term financing strategy and a marketable security investment strategy.

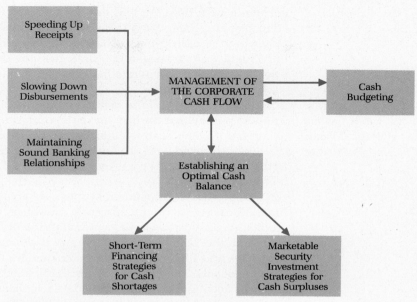

Figure 9.2   The Cash Management Activity.

The Goal of Cash Management

The management of cash and marketable securities plays a vital role in defining the overall performance of the company and its exposure to risk; as such, it contributes to (or affects) shareholder wealth. The goal of cash management, quite simply, is to minimize the level of these current assets while providing adequate liquidity. If too much is invested in cash and marketable securities, the firm's asset base will increase unnecessarily and its asset turnover will fall, reducing return on investment. If too little liquidity is maintained, the firm will have to borrow more; therefore, the firm's profitability, and its return on investment, will decline due to rising financial costs. If the firm is continually late with cash disbursements, it may also be faced with increasingly reluctant suppliers of raw materials. So, effective cash management is critical to the goals of financial management. Too much liquidity reduces returns, whereas too little increases risk exposure.

Managing the Cash Flow

In Figure 9.2 we identified the management of the firm's actual cash flow as one of the key elements of corporate cash management. This involves the ongoing planning and administration of cash receipts and disbursements, as well as maintaining sound banking relationships. The success of this aspect of cash management centers on anticipating future needs through effective cash forecasting. Each of these functions is, of course, interrelated, and all play an important role in management of the corporate cash flow. We will now look first at basic cash management concepts, and then, using these concepts, illustrate basic strategies for managing the cash cycle. Next, specific techniques commonly used to implement cash management strategies are described, followed by a brief discussion of corporate banking relationships.

Basic Concepts: Cash Cycles and Cash Turnover

The *cash cycle* of a firm is defined as the amount of time that elapses from the point when the firm makes an outlay to purchase raw materials to the point when cash is collected from the sale of the finished good that was produced with the raw material. The term *cash turnover* refers to the number of times each year the firm's cash is actually turned over; it indicates cash velocity. The concepts of cash cycles and cash turnovers can perhaps best be illustrated by means of an example. Assume that the Buffalo Bearing Company currently purchases all its raw materials on credit and, likewise, sells all its merchandise on credit.[2] The credit terms extended the firm currently require payment within 30 days of a purchase, and the firm requires its customers to pay within 60 days of the date of sale. The firm calculates that it is taking, on average, 35 days to pay its accounts payable and 70 days to collect its accounts receivable. Further calculations reveal that, on average, 85 days elapse between the time a raw material is purchased and the finished good is sold. In other words, the average age of the firm's inventory is 85 days.

Cash Cycle.   The firm's cash cycle can be shown by a graph, as in Figure 9.3. Note that the firm's money is tied up for 120 days between the cash outflow to pay the account payable (on day 35) and the cash inflow from the collection of the account receivable (on day 155). When the firm initially purchased the raw materials (on day 0), an account payable was established. It remained on the firm's books until it was paid, 35 days later. It was at this point that a cash outflow occurred. After the sale of the finished good (on day 85), the firm established an account receivable. This account receivable remained on the books until it was collected some 70 days later. It was therefore on day 155 (70 days beyond the day of sale) that a cash inflow occurred. A firm's cash cycle is calculated by finding the average number of days that elapse between the cash outflows associated with paying accounts payable and the cash inflows associated with collecting accounts receivable. The cash cycle for the Buffalo Bearing Company is 120 days (155 days − 35 days).

Cash Turnover.   A firm's cash turnover can be calculated by dividing the cash cycle into 360, the assumed number of days in a year; Buffalo's

---

[2]This assumption of all credit purchases and credit sales simplifies the cash management model. Although purchases and sales for cash could easily be incorporated into it, they have not been in order to convey the key cash management strategies with a minimum of complexity.

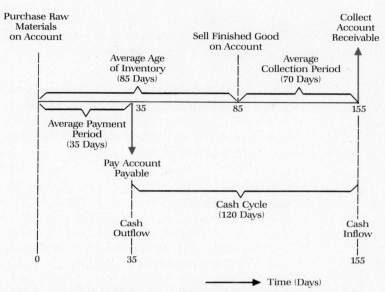

Figure 9.3   The Buffalo Bearing Company's Cash Cycle.

cash turnover is currently 3.0 times (360/120). The higher a firm's cash turnover, the less cash the firm requires. Cash turnover, like accounts receivable or inventory turnover, should be maximized, but not to such an extent that the firm runs out of cash. The firm's goal in managing liquidity should be to minimize the cash cycle and maximize cash turnover, subject to prudent managerial decisions regarding ability to stretch payables and tighten receivables collection practices. The end result of managing the firm's cash cycle effectively is to utilize the firm's assets fully and thereby reduce the firm's reliance on costly external financing. Effective management of the cash cycle also reduces the liquidity risk of the company and increases returns by increasing asset turnover and profit margin.

Basic Strategies for Managing the Cash Cycle

The cash cycle is made up of three basic elements: payables, inventories, and receivables. Several strategies can be used to affect the length of the cash cycle. For the most part, such strategies are highly effective in getting as much mileage from corporate cash resources as possible. The strategies are as follows:

1. *Pay accounts payable as late as possible* without damaging the firm's credit rating, and also take advantage of any favorable cash discounts.
2. *Turn over inventory as quickly as possible,* but avoid stockouts that might result in shutting down the production line or a loss of sales.

3. *Collect accounts receivable as quickly as possible* without losing future sales because of high-pressure collection techniques. Cash discounts, if they are economically justifiable, may be used to accomplish this objective.

The underlying objective of each strategy is to free up as much cash as possible without endangering the operating capability and productivity of the firm. The rationale is that cash has a high opportunity cost and is therefore better used in profitable investment outlets than to finance receivables or inventories.

Stretching Accounts Payable.   One strategy available to Buffalo Bearing is to stretch its accounts payable; that is, to pay its bills as late as possible without damaging its credit rating. (Specific techniques for stretching payables are described later in this chapter.) For example, if Buffalo Bearing can stretch its payables from 35 days to an average of 45 days, its cash cycle will be reduced to 110 days and it will be able to increase its cash turnover rate from 3.0 to 3.27 times (360 ÷ 110). More important, such a shift will enable the firm to get by with less cash and liquid resources. Thus, other things being equal, increasing the turnover rate from 3.0 to 3.27 times means the firm can reduce its cash holdings to 91.7 percent (110 ÷ 120) of the previous level. If Buffalo is operating with an average cash and marketable securities position of, say, $5 million, it will be able to reduce that amount to $4,585,000. Such action will free up over $400,000 in liquid assets, which, given a 10 percent incremental[3] opportunity cost, will result in annual (recurring) returns to the firm of some $41,500 [($5,000,000 − $4,585,000) × .10].

The payoff from stretching accounts payable for Buffalo Bearing should be clear. However, firms are quite often limited in the amount of stretching they can do. For example, firms that regularly stretch payments and therefore always pay late run the risk of damaging their credit reputation; such damage could increase the difficulty and cost of obtaining future credit. Firms must carefully assess the potential impact of stretching on both risk and return to assure that their actions are consistent with the goal of maximization of shareholder wealth.

Efficient Inventory-Production Management.[4]   Another way of minimizing required cash is to increase the inventory turnover rate. This can be achieved in any one of three ways:

---

[3]The *incremental* opportunity cost represents the difference in average returns from other (operating) investments of the firm versus returns on liquid assets.

[4]Although the actual management and control of inventory typically lies within the manufacturing manager's responsibilities, due to the sizable inventory investment required by most firms, the financial manager must act as a watchdog over inventory, as described in Chapter 10.

1. *Increasing the raw materials turnover.* By using more efficient inventory control techniques, the firm may be able to increase its raw materials turnover.
2. *Decreasing the production cycle.* By initiating better production planning, scheduling, and control techniques, the firm can reduce the length of the production cycle; shortening the production cycle will cause the work-in-process inventory turnover to increase.
3. *Increasing the finished goods turnover.* The firm can increase its finished goods turnover by better forecasting of product demand and by better planning of production to coincide with these forecasts; more efficient control of the finished goods inventory will contribute to a faster finished goods inventory turnover rate.

Regardless of which aspect of the firm's overall inventory turnover is adjusted, the result will be a reduction in the amount of operating cash required. If the Buffalo Bearing Company could manage to reduce its inventory from the current level of 85 days to 70 days, there would be a reduction in the cash cycle from 120 days to 105 days. In effect, the firm would be able to get the product to the customer quicker and thereby reduce the amount of time that cash is tied up in inventory. The decreased average age of inventory for Buffalo Bearing increases the annual cash turnover rate from the initial level of 3.0 to 3.43 times (360 ÷ 105), and reduces cash holdings from $5 million to $4,375,000. The increased cash velocity in this case frees $625,000 and, with the 10 percent incremental opportunity cost, generates annual returns of $62,500 to the firm. So long as the action does not have a perceptible impact on exposure to risk, such increased profitability is indicative of the effect efficient inventory control has on cash management and the value of the firm.

Speeding Up the Collection of Accounts Receivable.   Another way of reducing the firm's operating cash requirement is to speed up the collection of accounts receivable. (Specific techniques for speeding up accounts receivable collection are described later in this chapter.) Accounts receivable, like inventory, tie up dollars that could be invested in other earning assets. Accounts receivable are a necessary investment, since the extension of credit normally allows the firm to achieve higher levels of sales than would be possible by operating on a strictly cash basis. The actual credit terms extended by a firm are normally dictated by the industry in which it operates.[5] These credit terms affect not only the pattern of collections, but also credit and collection policies.

---

[5] A discussion of various types of credit terms is presented in Chapter 10; credit terms state when payment is due and whether or not, and under what conditions, a cash discount is offered.

Credit policies are the firm's criteria for determining to whom and under what conditions credit will be extended; collection policies define the effort put forth to collect tardy accounts receivable. Changes in credit terms, credit policies, and collection policies can all be used to decrease the average collection period. Typically, the initiation of a cash discount for early payment, the use of more restrictive credit policies, or the initiation of more aggressive collection policies will decrease the average collection period. It is, of course, important that the firm fully consider beforehand the consequences of these actions on sales and profits.

An example will clarify the effects of faster collections on the required operating cash holdings. If Buffalo Bearing, by changing its credit terms, can reduce the average collection period from 70 to 50 days, it will be able to reduce its cash cycle by 20 days and raise the firm's annual cash turnover rate from 3.0 to 3.60 times. This action will reduce the firm's operating cash requirement from $5 million to about $4,150,000 and improve annual corporate profitability by about $85,000 per year.

Cash Management Techniques

In addition to effectively managing (and altering) the firm's current assets and current liabilities, financial managers have at their disposal a variety of techniques that have a direct impact on the cash and liquid asset holdings of the firm. The objective is to affect the inflow and outflow of cash in such a way that management is able to reduce the amount of cash required for operations. In general, this can be done by speeding up collections and/or slowing down disbursements. If we assume that the firm has done all it can in terms of credit policy, credit terms, and collection policy to stimulate customers to pay promptly and that it has carefully selected vendors to receive the most attractive and flexible credit terms, it still can take advantage of certain imperfections in the payment system. Given that a customer is going to make a payment on a given day, our main concern is what can be done to get those funds into spendable form as quickly as possible? On the other hand, in the case of payments, the key question is: What can be done by the firm to delay the withdrawal of its funds for as long as possible? Before describing some of these procedures, we will briefly discuss the concept of float.

Float.   In the broadest sense, *float* refers to those funds that have been dispatched by a payor to a payee but which are not yet in a form that can be spent by the payee. Float exists in the collection-payment system as a result of time delays caused by environmental as well as institutional imperfections. Business firms as well as individuals can experience both collection and disbursement float as part of the process of making financial transactions. *Collection float* results from the time delay between when a customer deducts a payment from its checking account ledger and when the vendor actually receives these funds in a spendable

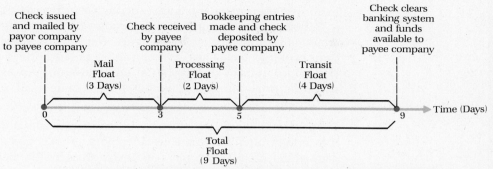

Figure 9.4   Float Resulting from a Check Issued and Mailed by the Payor Company to the Payee Company.

form. *Disbursement float* results from the time lapse between when a firm deducts a payment from its checking account ledger and when funds are actually withdrawn from its account. Collection float is experienced by a payee and is a delay in receipt of funds; disbursement float is experienced by the payor and results in a delay in the actual withdrawal of funds.

Regardless of which view we take, float has three basic components:

1. *Mail float.* The amount of time that elapses between when a payment is placed in the mail and when it is received by the payee.
2. *Processing float.* The amount of time that elapses between the receipt of a check by the payee and the actual deposit of it in the firm's account.
3. *Transit float.* The amount of time that elapses between the deposit of a check by the payee and the actual availability of the funds to it. This component of float is attributable to the time required for a check to clear the banking system.[6]

Figure 9.4 illustrates the key components of float resulting from the issuance and mailing of a check by the Payor Company to the Payee Company on day zero. It can be seen that a total float of 9 days resulted; it consisted of 3 days mail float, 2 days processing float, and 4 days transit float. To the Payor Company, the delay is disbursement float; to the Payee Company, the delay is collection float.

Collection Procedures.   The firm's objective relative to accounts receivable is not only to stimulate customers to pay as promptly as possible, but

---

[6]On checks cleared through the Federal Reserve banking system, clearing time of less than two days is guaranteed to the collecting bank; but of course this does not assure the depositor (payee) that the bank will make the money available within two days.

to convert their payments into a spendable form as quickly as possible—in other words, *to minimize collection float.* A variety of procedures aimed at reducing collection float are available; they include concentration banking, lockboxes, direct sends, preauthorized checks (PACs), depository transfer checks (DTCs), and wire transfers. As we will see, all of these procedures are aimed at the same goal of speeding up collections.

Concentration Banking.   Firms with numerous sales outlets throughout the country often designate certain offices as collection centers for given geographic areas. Customers in these areas remit their payments to these sales offices, which in turn deposit the receipts in local banks. At certain times, or on a "when needed" basis, funds are transferred by wire from these regional banks to a concentration, or disbursing, bank, from which bill payments are dispatched.[7]

Concentration banking is used to reduce collection float by shortening the mail and transit float components. Mail float is reduced because regionally dispersed collection centers bring the collection point closer to the point from which the check is sent. Transit float should also be reduced, since the payee's bank is likely to be in the same Federal Reserve district or the same city as the bank on which the check is drawn; it may even be the same bank. A reduction in transit float will, of course, make funds available to the firm more quickly.

Reducing collection float, and therefore speeding up the receipt of funds, reduces the firm's operating cash requirements and operating costs. A savings of only a few days in the collection process may provide significant dollar savings to the firm. Such benefits are not without their costs, however; for in return for this service, firms are often asked to maintain a certain level of compensating balances with the various regional banks, or a company might be charged a fee by the bank for providing the transfer service. The decision of whether or not to switch to (or expand the use of) concentration banking rests on the amount of net benefits and costs. For instance, suppose a firm could go to concentration banking and reduce its collection period by 3 days; if the company normally carried $10 million in receivables and that level equaled a 30-day supply, then cutting 3 days from the collection process would result in a $1 million drop in receivables [(3 ÷ 30) × $10 million]. Given a 12 percent opportunity cost, the gross annual benefits (profits) of concentration banking would amount to $1 million × .12 = $120,000. Clearly, assuming no change in risk, so long as total annual costs—*incremental* administrative costs and bank service fees, and/or the opportunity cost of holding compensating balances—are less than the

---

expected annual benefits of $120,000, the recommended program of concentration banking should be implemented.

Lockboxes. Another method used to reduce collection float is the *lockbox system.* Like concentration banking, the use of a lockbox system reduces the level of accounts receivable, but it is different in several important ways. The payor, instead of mailing payment to a collection center, sends it to a post office box that is emptied by the firm's bank. The bank will normally empty the box one or more times each business day. The bank opens the payment envelopes, deposits the checks in the firm's account, and sends a deposit slip (or under certain arrangements, a computer tape) indicating the payments received, along with any enclosures, to the collecting firm. Lockboxes are normally geographically dispersed, and the funds, when collected, are wired from each lockbox bank to the firm's disbursing bank.[8]

The lockbox system is superior to concentration banking because it reduces processing float as well as mail and transit float. The receipts are immediately deposited in the firm's account by the bank, so processing occurs after, rather than before, funds are deposited in the firm's account. This allows the firm to use the funds almost immediately for disbursing payments. Additional reductions in mail float may also result, since payments do not have to be delivered. Instead, the bank picks them up at the post office. Of course, the cost of geographically dispersed lockboxes must be considered. Each lockbox bank charges the firm a fee and/or requires the firm to maintain a specified minimum balance. As with concentration banking, these costs must be carefully evaluated against the volume of checks received and the benefits derived in order to determine the economic feasibility of a lockbox system. Such systems are prevalent among large retailers such as oil companies, which bill large numbers of customers throughout the country.

Direct Sends. To reduce transit float, firms that have received large checks drawn on distant banks, or a large number of checks drawn on banks in a given city, may arrange to directly present these checks for payment by the bank on which they are drawn; such a procedure is called a *direct send.* Rather than depositing these checks in its collection account, the firm may be able to reduce transit float by 3 or 4 days or more by arranging to present the checks to the bank on which they are

---

[8]Quantitative models for determining where and what number of lockboxes a firm should have, given its typical receipt distribution, have been developed. See Ferdinand K. Levy, "An Application of Heuristic Problem Solving to Accounts Receivable Management," *Management Science* 12 (February 1966), pp. 236–244, for the original model. Two more practical articles are Steven F. Maier and James H. Vander Weide, "The Lock-Box Location Problem: A Practical Reformulation," *Journal of Bank Research* 5 (summer 1974), pp. 92–95; and Robert M. Nauss and Robert E. Markland, "Solving Lock Box Location Problems," *Financial Management* 8 (spring 1979), pp. 21–31.

drawn and receiving immediate payment. A variety of methods are used for direct sends. The firm can use Express Mail, Federal Express, Purolator, or other services to get the checks into a bank in the same city or to a sales office where an employee can take the check to the bank and present it for payment. In most cases, the funds will be transferred via wire into the firm's disbursement account.

Deciding whether or not to use direct sends is relatively straightforward; if the benefits from the reduced transit time are greater than the cost, the check(s) should be sent directly for payment rather than cleared through normal banking channels. For example, if a firm with an opportunity to earn 12 percent on its idle balances can, through a direct send, make available $1 million 3 days earlier than otherwise would be the case, the benefit of this direct send would be $1,000 [.12 × (3 days/360 days) × $1,000,000]. If the cost of achieving this 3-day reduction in float is less than $1,000, the direct send would be recommended.

Preauthorized Checks (PACs), Depository Transfer Checks (DTCs), and Wire Transfers.   A number of other instruments can be used to mobilize cash receipts to reduce collection float. One method commonly used by firms such as insurance companies, savings and loans, and lessors (all of whom collect a fixed amount from customers on a regular basis) is the preauthorized check. A *preauthorized check (PAC)* is a check written for an agreed-upon amount by the firm and drawn on the given customer's checking account at a scheduled future date. The firm deposits the PAC in its account, and the check clears through the banking system just like a check written by the customer and received and deposited by the firm. In addition to the elimination of mail float and possible reductions in processing float, the use of PACs enhances the predictability of the firm's cash flows and provides clerical cost savings to both firm and customer.

Another method commonly used by firms with multiple collection points is the depository transfer check. A *depository transfer check (DTC)* is an unsigned check drawn on one of the firm's bank accounts and deposited into its account at another bank—typically a concentration or major disbursing bank. Once the DTC has cleared the bank on which it is drawn, the actual transfer of funds is completed. Traditionally, DTCs have been mailed from the bank of deposit to the firm's concentration bank, thereby providing little if any reduction in collection float; today, more and more firms are transmitting deposit information via telephone to their concentration banks, which prepare and deposit DTCs into the firms' accounts. One major company, the National Data Corporation, can be hired to collect deposit information from a firm's collection centers, accumulate these data, and transmit them to the firm's concentration bank. Whether or not the firm uses its own telecommunications capability or hires a firm to act as an intermediary, the use of automated DTCs can eliminate mail float and reduce processing float. Of course, any savings resulting from use of DTCs must be measured and compared to the costs of using this system.

Many firms use wire transfers to reduce collection float by quickly transferring funds from one bank account to another. *Wire transfers* are telegraphic communications that, via bookkeeping entries, remove funds from the payor bank and deposit them in an account of the payee bank. Wire transfers are typically made via bank wire, which is a cooperative wire network among major banks, or through the Federal Reserve Wire System, which is operated by the Fed for use by member banks. Wire transfers typically cost $4 to $10 and can easily be justified for large transfers. They are commonly used to mobilize funds into key disbursing accounts in lieu of the DTC in concentration banking, lockbox, and direct send programs. Wire transfers can eliminate mail and transit float and may provide processing float reductions as well. Like other mobilization techniques, the economics of using wire transfers can be easily analyzed by comparing the benefits in terms of float reduction to the associated costs.

Disbursement Procedures. The firm's objective relative to accounts payable is not only to pay as late as possible, but to slow down the availability of funds to suppliers and employees once the payment has been dispatched—in other words, *to maximize disbursement float.* A variety of procedures aimed at slowing down disbursements and thereby increasing disbursement float are available. They tend to focus on lengthening mail and transit float—the opposite aim of the procedures designed to minimize collection float. The key techniques used to maximize disbursement float include controlled disbursing, playing the float, overdraft systems, and zero-balance accounts.

Controlled Disbursing. Firms can use controlled disbursing procedures to increase mail and transit float. When the date of postmark is considered the effective date of payment by the supplier, the firm may be able to lengthen the mail time associated with disbursements. *Controlled disbursing,* which can be defined as the strategic use of mailing points and bank accounts to lengthen mail and transit floats, respectively, involves placing payments in the mail at locations from which it is known it will take a great deal of time to get the payment to the supplier. Typically, small towns that are not close to major highways and cities provide excellent opportunities to increase mail float. It is not unusual for large firms to mail batches of payments from a variety of locations, each chosen to provide the longest mail time to the addressees. Another approach sometimes suggested for lengthening processing float is to mail payments to the supplier's corporate headquarters address rather than the post office box or collection center specified by the supplier. If the firm can do this without violating the terms of sale specified by the supplier,[9] the mail time may not be directly increased, but because most corporate headquarters cannot process receipts, the entire collection process for the supplier is slowed down, lengthening the paying firm's disbursement float.

In recent years, with the widespread availability of computers and data on the clearing time between and among various banks, many firms have been using disbursement schemes that tend to maximize transit float on their payments. These schemes involve assigning payments going to vendors in certain geographic areas to be drawn on the firm's bank account at a bank from which maximum transit float will result. Data on transit time among banks located in various cities can be developed by the firm itself; it can be obtained from a major bank's cash management service department; or it can be purchased from a firm such as Phoenix Hecht Cash Management Services, a Chicago-based firm which sells information to banks and other firms. Firms attempting to assign checks to be drawn on banks providing maximum float to the vendor city typically will run a computer program each payment cycle; the program will draw on the transit-time data base and assign the checks to be drawn on the bank account providing maximum transit float to each vendor.[10] The number of potential bank accounts considered will depend on the economics of the system. Once the computer has assigned payments to banks, the computer will print the checks on blank check forms, and the checks will then be sorted and mailed from remote points, as mentioned earlier. Although such controlled disbursement systems are commonly used today, their cost must be justified by the additional earnings achieved by the firm on the disbursement float created.

Playing the Float.   When firms "play the float," they try to maximize disbursement float. Because of the presence of float in the payment system, many firms play the float by writing checks against money not currently in their checking accounts. Firms are able to play the float because they know a delay is likely between the receipt and the deposit of checks by suppliers and the actual withdrawal of funds from their checking accounts. In spite of the fact that their suppliers' banks may be

---

[9]A supplier's credit terms as well as any penalties associated with late payment are typically stated in the invoice that accompanies the shipment of merchandise. Of course, depending upon the supplier, the terms of the invoice may or may not be enforced. Knowledge of the strictness of suppliers' credit terms is often useful for developing the firm's accounts payable strategies.

[10]For descriptions of quantitative approaches to the controlled disbursement technique, see Lawrence J. Gitman, D. Keith Forrester, and John R. Forrester, Jr., "Maximizing Cash Disbursement Float," *Financial Management* 5 (summer 1976), pp. 15–24; Steven F. Maier and James H. Vander Weide, "A Unified Location Model for Cash Disbursements and Lock-Box Collections," *Journal of Bank Research* 7 (summer 1976), pp. 166–172; and Roy J. Shanker and Andris A. Zoltners, "The Corporate Payment Problem," *Journal of Bank Research* 3 (spring 1972), pp. 47–53.

reimbursed within a few days, it is likely that the firm's bank account will not be drawn down by the amount of the payments for a few additional days. *Playing the float* is a method of consciously anticipating the resulting float associated with the payment process. Although ineffective use of this practice may result in certain legal problems, many firms use float to stretch out their accounts payable.[11]

Firms can play the float in a variety of ways. Firms often write checks on a bank that is slow in clearing checks deposited in their suppliers' bank in the hope that it will take longer for the checks to clear the Federal Reserve system. This strategy allows the firm to keep its money longer. In many cases, the firm will keep this money in some interest-earning form, such as a marketable security, and not transfer it into its checking account until several days later. Even if a firm does not pay bills from a distant bank, it may play the float for a few days. However, it should be cautious in using this strategy, since "bouncing" checks is not favorably looked on by banks, businesses, or the government.

Another way of playing the float is to deposit a certain proportion of a payroll or payment in the firm's checking account each day *after* the actual issuance of a group of checks. For example, if a firm can determine from historical data that only 25 percent of its payroll checks are cashed on the day immediately following the issuance of the checks, then only 25 percent of the value of the payroll needs to be in its checking account one day later. The number of checks cashed on each succeeding day can also be calculated, until the entire payroll is accounted for. Normally, to protect itself against any irregularities, a firm will place slightly more money in its account than is needed to cover the expected check cashings.

Another way of playing the float is to use payable-through drafts, rather than checks, to pay large sums of money like the payroll. A *payable-through draft* is similar to a check in that it is drawn on the payor's checking account and payable to a given payee; unlike a check, however, it is not payable on demand: Approval of the draft by the issuer is required before the bank pays the draft. The advantage of these drafts to the issuer is that money does not have to be kept on deposit until the draft clears the bank; instead of keeping the money on deposit, the firm can invest it in short-term money market instruments. As the drafts are cleared for payment by the issuer, the investments can be liquidated and the funds used to cover the drafts. Banks may charge a modest fee for processing the drafts, but this technique enables the firm to keep its

---

[11]Issuing checks against nonexistent funds can be prosecuted only if the check is drawn on insufficient funds. The fact that a check bounces is viewed as prima facie—but not irrefutable—evidence of fraud. The burden of proof that the act causing insufficient funds was not willful is placed on the issuer. If such proof cannot be given, the issuer will be convicted of fraud. Prosecution rarely results, since the issuer usually obtains sufficient funds to satisfy the obligation prior to the filing of any criminal charges.

money more fully invested for a longer period of time. For example, the use of payable-through drafts in place of checks to meet a payroll might increase disbursement float by as much as 5 days; for a firm with a monthly payroll of, say, $10 million, such an increase in float will translate into profits of $200,000 per year given an opportunity cost (money market investment rate) of 12 percent. That is the amount of profit the firm would realize by keeping $10 million invested at 12 percent (per year) for 5 additional days each month for an entire year [.12 × (5 days/360 days) × $10,000,000 × (12 months/year) = $200,000]. But many vendors will not accept payable-through drafts as payment for the goods or services provided, and in some states the use of these drafts is prohibited by law. Before initiating the use of drafts, it is therefore important that the financial manager investigate the potential impact of these two factors on the effectiveness of their use.

Overdraft Systems and Zero-Balance Accounts.   Firms that aggressively manage their cash disbursements will often arrange for some type of overdraft system or zero-balance account. Under an *overdraft system*, if the firm's checking account balance is insufficient to cover all checks presented against the account, the bank will automatically lend the firm enough money to cover the amount of the overdraft. The bank, of course, will charge the firm interest on the funds lent and will probably provide only some specified maximum amount of overdraft coverage. Such an arrangement is important for a firm that actively plays the float to keep its funds fully invested for as long as possible. A second technique that is especially useful for large firms with multiple disbursing operations is the *zero-balance account*, which is a checking account in which a zero balance is maintained. Each day the bank will total the amount of checks presented against the account, and the firm—typically from a master account or through liquidation of a portion of its marketable securities portfolio—will transfer that amount of funds into the account, causing the account balance to remain at zero. The use of a zero-balance account allows the firm to maintain better control over its cash, while allowing idle balances to earn for as long as possible. Of course, the bank will charge a fee or require that balances be maintained in other accounts as compensation for this service. As long as the benefits of control as well as additional earnings are greater than the cost of such a system, its use is recommended.

Corporate Banking Relationships

Establishing and maintaining strong bank relations is one of the most important elements in an effective cash management system. Banks have become keenly aware of the profitability of corporate accounts, and in recent years have developed a number of innovative services and packages designed to attract various types of businesses. No longer are banks simply a place to establish demand deposit accounts and/or secure loans; instead, they have become the source of a wide variety of cash management services. For example, in addition to providing advice and assistance with government securities portfolios, banks are selling sophisticated information-processing packages to commercial clients; these packages deal with everything from basic accounting and budgeting to complex multinational disbursement and centralized cash control. All are designed to help financial managers maximize day-to-day cash availability and facilitate short-term investing.

A number of bank services are offered to corporations on a direct fee basis, but most of the depository functions are still paid for with compensating balances rather than direct charges. Banks prefer the compensating balance approach, since it fosters deposit growth and provides a foundation for the future growth of bank earnings. Bank services available to cash managers should be used only so long as the benefits derived from their use are greater than their costs.

Consider, for example, a firm that has been offered a cash management service that should result not only in eliminating "excess" cash on deposit, but also in actually reducing some administrative and clerical costs now absorbed by the firm. Assume the service, which costs $50,000 per year, involves the collection, movement, and reporting of corporate cash. The purported benefits are these: (1) the firm should be able to reduce the cash required to support operations by some $500,000 (as a result of tighter control over the cash flow); and (2) clerical and administrative costs should drop by about $1,000 per month (since the bank will be taking on clerical-administrative duties as part of the service). Using a 12 percent opportunity cost, the benefits and costs would be as follows:

Benefits (annual)	
Extra returns from reduced cash on hand ($500,000 × .12)	$60,000
Reduced administrative-clerical costs	12,000
Total benefits	$72,000
Less: Costs (annual)	
Bank service charges	$50,000
Net benefits (annual)	$22,000

From a benefit-cost perspective, the proposal looks promising; the major risk, of course, is that the purported benefits will fall far short of the mark. Management, however, can at least get a handle on the risk of this occurring via probability estimates or sensitivity analysis. Sensitivity analysis, for example, would indicate the minimum drop in cash and/or opportunity cost required to generate a sufficient level of total benefits. On the other hand, some positive risk reductions may result from adoption of the bank's program, such as less exposure to volatile interest rates, and these should obviously also be considered.

Maintaining an Optimum Cash Balance

A firm's net cash flow is constantly changing; as a result, it is not uncommon for a company's cash balance to build up to excessive levels, or to decline to dangerously low levels. Because of unhealthy risk-return implications, neither condition is desirable. Rather, cash managers normally establish an optimum cash balance that they strive to maintain on an ongoing basis.[12] Actual cash inflows and outflows continuously interact with cash on hand to raise or lower the cash balance. When cash surpluses begin to develop, resources are shifted from cash to interest-bearing short-term marketable securities; when cash shortages develop, the marketable securities are sold to provide cash, or short-term financing is obtained from lenders. As a rule, securities will be liquidated before negotiated short-term loans are used, since the yield on these securities is normally less than the cost of short-term bank loans. In this section, we take a broader view of cash as a liquid resource that can be divided between cash on hand and marketable securities holdings. Such a division of liquid resources lies at the heart of maintaining a minimum cash balance. Not surprisingly, it is closely related to other cash management functions, like cash forecasting and the management of actual cash flows.

The first step in defining a minimum cash balance is to obtain a forecast of the cash flows. A corporation typically projects cash flows over three time horizons—the capital period, the annual budget period, and the short-term budget period. The capital period forecast is used to project the permanent financing needs of the firm in periods beyond a year. The annual budget period forecast includes monthly or quarterly projections of cash needs; among other things, the purpose of this forecast is to plan the amount of cash required to support the company during the year and to determine when excess cash is expected to build up and when cash shortfalls are expected. Cash managers use the annual budgets to plan short-term investing and borrowing. The short-term budget is used to forecast daily and weekly cash receipts and disbursements. Cash managers are the primary users of these forecasts because they directly assist management in seeing to it that obligations are paid on time, that bank balances are adjusted, and that excess funds are invested. The short-term forecast is used to analyze cash receipt and

---

[12]As noted earlier, firms can arrange to have zero-balance accounts in which the minimum as well as average cash balance is by design maintained at zero. Of course, the firm must compensate the bank for providing this service.

disbursement patterns and is relied on in determining the optimal minimum cash balance.

We have already discussed the use of cash budgets to forecast cash requirements (see Chapter 4). In addition, we have noted several methods by which the financial manager may either speed up cash inflow or slow down cash disbursements. However, we have not really addressed the question of just how much cash should be maintained in cash balances versus the dollar level of cash transferred into marketable securities. A number of theoretical and practical models have been developed for use in managing the firm's cash balances, and these are briefly examined below.

An Early Inventory Approach: Baumol's Model

Early cash flow models were derived from economic theories of the demand for money. Most of the early models treated cash balances as an inventory item; the *Baumol model* was one of the first to use the inventory approach to maintaining appropriate cash balances.[13] It assumed that corporations disburse funds in a steady (certain) stream, and that cash is obtained by borrowing it or withdrawing it from an investment (and that surplus cash is used to repay loans or increase investments). The objective of the model was to determine how many dollars of marketable securities should be liquidated to increase cash balances (or purchased to reduce cash balances) in order to minimize total cost—the sum of transaction cost and opportunity cost—while still providing adequate cash.

The equation for the total cost of managing cash in Baumol's model can be given as follows:

$$\text{Total cost} = b\left[\frac{T}{C}\right] + i\left[\frac{C}{2}\right] \tag{9.1}$$

where b = the fixed cost of making a transaction, which includes brokerage fees, taxes, and other administrative costs

T = the total amount of cash needed over the given period of concern

C = the optimum cash conversion quantity— the amount of cash accumulated before converting to marketable securities and vice versa

i = the opportunity cost rate, which can be measured by the interest rate earned on short-term marketable security investments

---

[13]William J. Baumol, "The Transactions Demand for Cash: An Inventory Theoretic Approach," *The Quarterly Journal of Economics* 65 (November 1952), pp. 545–556.

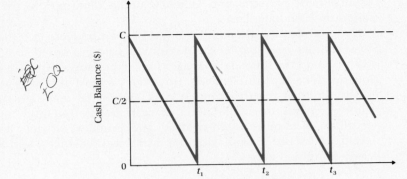

Figure 9.5 Cash Balances Under Baumol's Model.

In Equation 9.1 T/C represents the number of transactions made over the planning period, and $C/2$ represents the firm's average cash balance. Since the model assumes that cash is used or accumulated at a constant rate and that security transactions are made instantaneously when needed, the cash balance can be represented over time as shown in Figure 9.5.[14] Note that the cash balance is restored on a regular basis (points t_1, t_2, t_3, . . .) by acquiring cash in an amount equal to C.

Graphically, the transaction cost, $b[T/C]$, the opportunity cost, $i[C/2]$, and the total cost equation can be depicted as shown in Figure 9.6. The optimal cash conversion quantity, C, is shown as the quantity that minimizes total cost. Algebraically, the optimal value of C, which represents the value of C for which Equation 9.1 is minimized, can be calculated by:

$$C = \sqrt{\frac{2bT}{i}} \qquad (9.2)$$

The optimal cash balance, $C/2$, can be derived from Equation 9.2; the resulting value is:

$$\text{Optimal cash balance} = C/2 = \sqrt{\frac{bT}{2i}} \qquad (9.3)$$

From Equation 9.3, it should be clear that the optimal cash balance

---

[14]An alternative but similar model based on a steady receipt of cash with periodic cash disbursements was presented by Beranek; see William Beranek, *Analysis for Financial Decisions* (Homewood, Ill.: Irwin, 1963), chap. 11. Beranek's rationale for this approach rests on the fact that the financial manager has more control over cash disbursements than cash receipts. While theoretically appealing, Beranek's model has not been given the attention devoted to Baumol's model in the financial literature.

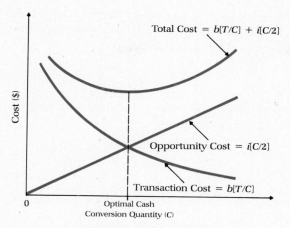

Figure 9.6   Cost Functions and Optimal Cash Conversion Quantity Under Baumol's Model.

represents the average amount of cash maintained over time. As might be expected, Equation 9.3 is most sensitive to the opportunity cost rate, i; that is, a decrease in i will prompt a much larger increase in C than a corresponding increase in b. The most significant contribution of the Baumol model is not its adaptability to reality (indeed, few firms could apply the approach), but rather the insight it offers with respect to the cost structure of cash management.

A Probabilistic Approach: Miller and Orr's Model

Subsequent cash balance models have relaxed some of the rigid assumptions of the Baumol approach. The *Miller and Orr (M&O) model,* for example, assumes that net cash flows fluctuate in a completely random fashion, rather than being certain and constant.[15] This model assumes there are two assets, cash and a securities portfolio; and it requires estimates of both the maximum cash balance and the minimal acceptable cash level. When the cash balance reaches the upper boundary of the range, funds are transferred to the securities portfolio (securities are purchased); when balances drop to zero (or an assumed lower limit), securities are sold to return the cash balance to its optimum level. The optimal return balance, z, is determined by the following equation:

$$z = \sqrt[3]{\frac{3b\,\sigma^2}{4(i/360)}} \qquad (9.4)$$

---

[15]Merton H. Miller and Daniel Orr, "A Model of the Demand for Money by Firms," *The Quarterly Journal of Economics* 80 (August 1966), pp. 413–435.

where b and i are as defined earlier, and σ is the standard deviation of daily changes in the cash balance. The maximum cash balance level h, is determined by the equation:

$$h = 3z \tag{9.5}$$

In addition, the average cash balance, m, held by the firm is derived from the following equation:

$$m = \frac{(h + z)}{3} \tag{9.6}$$

A graph of the behavior of a firm's cash balance over time is shown in Figure 9.7.

As Figure 9.7 shows, the daily cash balance is allowed to drift until it reaches either (1) the upper limit, h, at which time cash in the amount of $h - z$ is used to purchase marketable securities; or (2) some lower limit (for our purposes, zero), at which time marketable securities in the amount of z are sold to return the cash balance to its optimum level, z. As long as the cash balance level fluctuates between the upper and lower bounds, h and zero, marketable securities are neither bought nor sold.

To see how this approach works, consider a firm with an average daily net cash flow of \$125,000 and a standard deviation, σ, of \$95,000 (therefore, $\sigma^2 = \$9.025$ billion); in addition, the company experiences a transaction cost, b, of \$50 every time it buys or sells securities, and has determined that the current yield on marketable securities, i, stands at 9.5 percent. Note that all the data required for the M&O model is

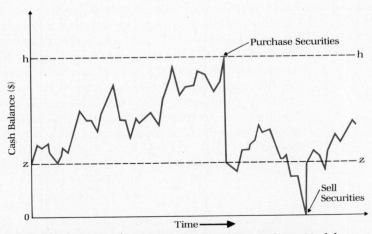

Figure 9.7   Cash Balances Under the Miller and Orr Model.

conveniently obtained either historically (as in the case of σ^2), or by observation (both b and i). Using Equation 9.4, we can find the optimum cash balance, z, as:

$$z = \sqrt[3]{\frac{3(\$50)(\$9.025 \text{ billion})}{4(.095/360)}} = \sqrt[3]{\frac{\$1353.75 \text{ billion}}{.00105556}}$$

$$= \sqrt[3]{\$1,282,500 \text{ billion}} = \$108,647$$

From this, we can find the upper cash balance boundary, h, as follows:

$$h = 3z$$
$$= 3(\$108,647)$$
$$= \$325,941$$

So long as the firm's cash balance remains between \$325,941 and zero, no action is necessary on the part of the cash manager; when it hits \$325,941, securities are bought to bring the cash balance back to its optimum level of \$108,647; likewise, when cash on hand hits zero, securities are sold and the proceeds used to bring cash on hand back up to the optimum level of \$108,647.

The objective of this model is, again, to minimize the total cost of holding cash—to minimize both transaction and opportunity costs over time—and as might be expected, it is most sensitive to the variability in the firm's cash flow. That is, the greater the variability of a company's daily net cash flow, σ^2, the wider the spread between the upper and lower cash balance boundaries. Under this approach, the cash manager will continue to hold cash between the computed values of h and zero until conditions (especially σ^2 and i) change sufficiently so that a new z (and therefore h) has to be determined.

A Practical Approach: Stone's Model

The two models presented above represent extreme boundary points along the risk continuum. The Baumol model assumes complete *certainty* about future cash needs, while the Miller and Orr model assumes complete *uncertainty*. Obviously, neither polar viewpoint is correct. Rather, most financial managers are aware that a portion of their future cash needs is predictable, and a portion is unpredictable. Bernell Stone has developed a cash balance model which recognizes that future cash balances, to a certain degree, are predictable.[16]

Basically, the *Stone model* develops an algorithm that provides flexible control limits which can be adjusted as experience requires. More important, as current cash balances reach the control limits,

---

[16]Bernell K. Stone, "The Use of Forecasts and Smoothing in Control-Limit Models for Cash Management," *Financial Management* 1 (spring 1972), pp. 72–84.

instead of an automatic transaction occurring, the model allows the cash manager to refer to recent forecasted cash flow data to better estimate corporate cash needs. If the forecast suggests additional cash will be needed, the appropriate type of transaction is made; if the cash is not needed, a different course of action will be followed. For example, if it is determined that additional cash will be needed, then even though the company may now have excess cash, it may decide to retain the excess to meet near-term needs. The Stone model smooths out the transactions associated with cash management by not only considering the current status of the firm's cash balance, but also by recognizing the existence of fairly accurate near-term cash balance forecasts and incorporating these into the cash management decision-making process.

The Miller and Orr model is a good one, and it is workable in practice; the Stone model, however, makes some improvements to M&O to the extent that it reduces some of the model's rigidity. So long as cash on hand stays within the limits established by either of these models, the money manager has a guide that enables him or her to monitor cash on a daily basis; the manager can then devote more time to the management of the actual cash flow (control of receipts and disbursements) and the firm's portfolio of marketable securities.

Managing the Marketable Securities Portfolio

Although the use of various decision models is helpful in establishing optimum cash balances, the actual management of the firm's liquid resources (cash and marketable securities) remains a separate and distinct function. The cash management process described in Figure 9.2 indicates that in addition to managing the firm's actual flow of cash, the money manager also has to obtain short-term financing when cash deficits occur, and structure the marketable securities portfolio to absorb any cash surpluses. The question of short-term financing will be addressed in detail in Chapter 11; for now, our attention will shift to another aspect of cash management, the management of the firm's marketable securities.

The Portfolio Selection Process

A firm's investment in marketable securities is designed basically to act as a shock absorber; the investment is necessary because it is impossible to predict future cash balances with complete accuracy. Moreover, the existence of a liquid balance of surplus funds held in the form of marketable securities smooths out the firm's demand for external sources of financing. Marketable securities are short-term money market instruments that can be easily converted into cash—in effect, they represent a storehouse of liquidity. As cash balances dwindle, a certain stock of marketable securities is sold. As cash balances become excessive, the excess can be invested in marketable securities. Remember, however, that nonfinancial corporations are not in the business of managing a portfolio of liquid assets; rather, the primary purpose of such a company is to produce and sell a product or service. Thus, an underlying precept of portfolio management in the nonfinancial firm is that the portfolio of securities fulfills a support function, although it also has an attractive by-product: Not only does the portfolio lend desired support for the operating needs of the firm, it also enables management to earn a return on temporarily idle funds.

Segmenting the Portfolio.   Over a short-term planning horizon, a firm may expect to face several different types of cash needs. For example, over its operating cycle there will be periods when cash inflows exceed cash outflows, and vice versa. In addition, over this same cycle there will be controllable and predictable expenditures, such as tax payments, dividend distributions, and capital expenditures. These different cash needs call for different short-term investment vehicles. Toward this end, it is often helpful to visualize a portfolio of marketable securities in segments, according to the need for cash. Three segments can be identified:

1.   *Ready cash segment (RCS)*. In this segment the major requirement is instant liquidity, since RCS securities are intended to provide the first line of defense against the unknown operating needs of the firm; these securities may have to be liquidated on very short notice.

2.   *Controllable cash segment (CCS)*. Securities in this segment can be more precisely specified than for RCS, since the disbursement dates and amounts (such as an estimated tax payment or a dividend payment) are known with greater certainty.

3.   *Free cash segment (FCS)*. Securities in this segment tend to be held for speculative purposes, and therefore the emphasis is on yield rather than liquidity. Often the motive for holding FCS securities is to maintain excess liquidity in order to enable the firm to participate in currently unforeseen lucrative opportunities. Unless the firm is in the business of holding and trading marketable securities, the financial manager should view these securities as redundant.

Together, the three segments—ready cash, controllable cash, and free cash—make up the total portfolio of short-term investments. Managers who do not recognize the different reasons for holding short-term investments may well be sacrificing a significant yield differential if they consistently invest in the most highly liquid alternatives.

Selection Criteria.   In addition to these cash need constraints, other criteria play a role in the security selection process. These include (1) exposure to risk of default and capital loss, (2) marketability, and (3) yield. Primary concern in selecting securities is normally given to minimizing risk exposure. Then, depending on the portfolio segment into which the issue falls, attention is given to maximizing issue marketability—or at least, to seeing that the security possesses a level of marketability compatible with the portfolio segment in which it will be placed. This follows logically from the fact that the primary purpose of a corporate marketable securities portfolio is to employ temporarily idle cash so that it provides maximum support for the unexpected and the known operating needs of the firm. Only after risk and marketability have been considered does attention shift to yield. Thus, after the first two criteria have been satisfied, the firm's money manager presumably selects securities with an eye toward obtaining as generous a rate of return as possible.

Yield Curves.   It is helpful when making marketable security investments to understand the relationship between the rates of return on short- and long-term securities. At any point in time, this relationship can be assessed by comparing the yield to maturity (the annual rate of interest a buyer would earn on a security if it were purchased on the given day and held to its maturity) of securities having differing terms to maturity. The comparison is commonly made graphically by plotting yields against maturities for similar-risk securities; the resulting graph is called a *yield curve*. Figure 9.8 depicts two yield curves. (See Appendix 9A for detailed discussions of the mathematics of the money market used to calculate various yields.)

The yield curve reflects (1) general supply and demand conditions for money, (2) the general preference of fund suppliers toward more liquid

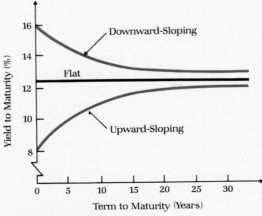

Figure 9.8   Yield Curves.

short-term securities, and (3) the general expectations of investors for the future level of interest rates. The effect of interest rate expectations results from the fact that although short-term interest rates reflect current behavior, long-term interest rates embody a consensus of expected future short-term interest rates. In Figure 9.8, it can be seen that the bottom yield curve is upward-sloping, reflecting higher expected future interest rates. The top yield curve, on the other hand, is downward-sloping, reflecting an expectation of generally lower future interest rates. The center yield curve is flat, indicating a stable expectation. The financial manager needs to consider the yield curve when making a variety of decisions, since it provides information on current as well as future expectations for interest rates.

Alternative Investment Outlets

A wide range of potential marketable securities is available. (Note that although some of these short-term investments do not actually involve a security transaction, for convenience they are referred to as marketable securities.) Each marketable security has certain unique characteristics —liquidity, risk, and return—that allow it to fulfill the firm's objectives. Tables 9.2 and 9.3 summarize these characteristics for the most popular marketable securities. They are broken into two groups: (1) the government issues shown in Table 9.2, including Treasury bills (T-bills), Treasury notes, federal agency issues, and short-term municipals; and (2) the nongovernment issues shown in Table 9.3 on pp. 380–381, including negotiable certificates of deposit (CDs), commercial paper, banker's acceptances, money market mutual funds, repurchase agreements, and Eurodollar deposits. Primary emphasis is on marketable securities held in the ready cash segment (RCS) or the controllable cash segment (CCS) of the firm's portfolio. The segment most often filled by each type of security is noted in Tables 9.2 and 9.3 as well. To provide a sense of the relative returns of these securities, Table 9.4 on p. 383 presents some recent yield data. Although it gives yields for only selected securities, the differences can be seen from these data.

Alternative Investment Strategies

We have described a variety of short-term marketable securities that are widely used in corporate portfolios, not only because of their attractive liquidity and risk features, but also because of the yields they offer. Through these vehicles, corporate money managers can earn a return on temporarily idle cash; in fact, at times (like the 1980-1982 period), the market may be such that investors can actually generate very high yields without altering their basic investment approach. Corporate investors can, of course, use the various marketable securities in a number of different ways and in so doing affect the realized yield from a portfolio. Not only can conditions in the market affect prevailing yield and

TABLE 9.2
Popular Marketable Securities: Government Issues

Marketable Security	General Description	Relative Liquidity	Relative Risk	Relative Return	Typical Portfolio Segment[a]
Treasury bills (T-bills)	Obligations of the U.S. Treasury, issued weekly on an auction basis. The most common maturities are 91 and 182 days, although bills with 9-month and 1-year maturities are also sold, though less frequently and in smaller amounts. Treasury bills are sold by competitive bidding, with a portion of each issue reserved for distribution on a noncompetitive basis. They are sold at a discount, the face value being received at maturity. The smallest denomination is $10,000. Since they are issues of the U.S. government, they are considered virtually risk-free.	Strong secondary market	Lowest	Low	RCS, CCS
Treasury notes	Obligations of the U.S. Treasury having initial maturities anywhere from 1 to 7 years. Because of the strong secondary market, they are often held in the marketable securities portfolio. A firm that purchases a Treasury note with less than 1 year to maturity is in the same position as if it had purchased a marketable security with an initial maturity of less than 1 year.	Strong secondary market	Lowest	Low, but slightly above T-bills	RCS, CCS

Federal agency issues	Obligations of certain *agencies* of the federal government. These issues are not part of the public debt and are not a legal obligation of the U.S. Treasury; most are not even guaranteed by the U.S. Treasury. Regardless of their lack of direct government backing, the issues of government agencies are readily accepted as low-risk securities, since most purchasers feel they are implicitly guaranteed by the federal government. Agencies commonly issuing short-term securities are these: 1. The Federal Home Loan Bank (FHLB) 2. The Federal Intermediate Credit Bank (FICB) 3. The Federal Land Banks (FLB) 4. The Bank for Cooperatives (BCs) 5. The Federal National Mortgage Association (FNMA)	Strong secondary market	Low	Low, but higher than Treasury issues	RCS, CCS
Short-term municipals	Obligations regularly sold by various cities and states. They generally have maturities of 3 to 6 months and their yields (which are exempt from federal taxes and in many cases from state taxes as well) will vary according to the quality of the issuer. Such issues are especially attractive to firms with considerable tax exposure. Because of their tax-exempt feature, the yields on these obligations tend to be much lower than the yields on taxable securities; however, the after-tax returns may be greater. For a taxable security to have a higher yield than a tax-exempt security, the following must hold: $$\left[\begin{pmatrix}\text{Yield on} \\ \text{taxable} \\ \text{security}\end{pmatrix} \times \begin{pmatrix}1 - \text{tax} \\ \text{rate}\end{pmatrix}\right] > \begin{pmatrix}\text{Yield on} \\ \text{tax-exempt} \\ \text{security}\end{pmatrix}$$ For a corporation with a 40% tax rate, the yield on a taxable security must be 1.67 times that on a tax-exempt security to be more profitable.	Weak secondary market	Low to moderate	Low but tax exempt, which may generate a high yield	CCS

[a]RCS, ready cash segment; CCS, controllable cash segment.

TABLE 9.3
Popular Marketable Securities: Nongovernment Issues

Marketable Security	General Description	Relative Liquidity	Relative Risk	Relative Return	Typical Portfolio Segment[a]
Negotiable certificates of deposit (CDs)	Negotiable instruments evidencing the deposit of a certain number of dollars in a commercial bank. The amount and the maturity are normally tailored to the investor's needs. Minimum maturities of 30 days are quite common. A good secondary market for negotiable CDs exists. The interest rate paid on CDs is set on the basis of size and maturity. Normally, the smallest denomination for a negotiable CD is $100,000.	Strong secondary market	Moderate; depends on bank	High	RCS, CCS
Commercial paper	Short-term, unsecured promissory notes issued by a corporation with a very high credit standing. Notes are issued by all types of firms and have maturities ranging from 3 to 270 days; because the Securities and Exchange Commission requires formal registration of corporate issues having maturities greater than 270 days, 270-day maximum maturities typically exist. Commercial paper can be sold directly by the issuer or to dealers who resell the paper to investors.	Weak secondary market	Moderate; depends on issuer	High, but slightly less than CDs	CCS
Banker's acceptances	"Notes" that result from a short-term credit arrangement used by businesses to finance transactions, especially those involving firms in foreign countries and/or firms with unknown credit capacities. The purchaser, in order to assure payment to the seller with the approval of its bank, issues a *draft*, a check on which payment is contingent on some event or action rather than on demand, to the seller in the amount of the purchase. The draft guarantees payment by the purchaser's bank at a specific point in time. The seller who holds such an acceptance may choose to sell it at a discount in order to obtain immediate funds. As a result of such a sale, the banker's acceptance becomes a marketable security that can be traded in the marketplace. The maturities of banker's acceptances are typically between 30 and 180 days. Banker's acceptances are moderate-risk securities, since as many as three parties may be liable for payment at maturity.	Strong secondary market	Moderate; as many as three parties liable	High, similar to commercial paper yields	RCS, CCS

Security	Description				
Money market mutual funds	Money market mutual funds, often called "money funds," are portfolios of marketable securities such as those described above and in Table 9.2. Shares or interests in these funds can be easily acquired, often without paying any brokerage commissions. They provide instant liquidity in much the same fashion as a checking or savings account. In exchange for investing in these funds, investors earn returns that during periods of high interest rates are generally higher than those obtainable from most other marketable securities. Because of the high liquidity, competitive yields, and often low transaction costs, these funds have achieved phenomenal growth in size and popularity in recent years.	Strong	High; often invest in high-risk foreign securities	High during period of generally high interest rates, but lower than most other marketable securities when interest rates are low	RCS, CCS
Repurchase agreement	Not a specific security, but an arrangement whereby a bank or security dealer sells specific marketable securities to a firm and at the same time agrees to repurchase the securities at a specific price at a specified later point in time. In exchange for the tailor-made maturity date, the bank or security dealer provides the purchaser with a return slightly below that obtainable through outright purchase of similar marketable securities. The benefit to the purchaser is the guaranteed repurchase; the repurchase date effectively eliminates marketability risk, as it assures the purchaser that the firm will have cash at a specified point in time. The actual securities involved may be government or nongovernment issues. And although the issues used in these agreements are generally short term, money managers have been showing increased interest in the past several years in using long-term bonds as a way to obtain increased returns, without violating the integrity of the repurchase concept.	Does not exist since maturities are custom made	Moderate; slightly below that obtained on the underlying securities	Varies, depending on the securities	CCS

TABLE 9.3 continued

Popular Marketable Securities: Nongovernment Issues

Marketable Security	General Description	Relative Liquidity	Relative Risk	Relative Return	Typical Portfolio Segment[a]
Multinational dimensions: Eurodollar deposits	A Eurodollar is a U.S. dollar deposited in a bank located outside the United States. The nationality of the bank makes no difference; it might be a foreign bank or the foreign branch of a U.S. bank. The deposit is always a time deposit or negotiable CD in large denominations, typically in units of $1 million. Although London is the center of the Eurodollar market, other important centers are in Paris, Frankfurt, Zurich, Nassau (the Bahamas), Singapore, and Hong Kong. Deposits in Singapore and Hong Kong are called "Asiadollars" but are virtually identical to Eurodollars in yield, maturity, and other characteristics. In addition to Eurodollars, other Eurocurrencies exist in the same centers. For example, there are Eurodeutschemarks, which are German Deutsche marks on deposit outside Germany. Although the Eurocurrency market is huge, the absolute numbers hide one important characteristic: It is very much an "interbank market." Over 85% of the Eurodollar liabilities and 90% of the other Eurocurrency liabilities are interbank deposits. Eurodollar deposit yields closely follow the yields available on large-denomination domestic dollar deposits.	Strong secondary market	Moderate; depends on bank	High	RCS, CCS

[a]RCS, ready cash segment; CCS, controllable cash segment.

TABLE 9.4
Yields on Selected
Marketable Securities,
February 1984

Security	Maturity	Yield
Treasury bill	3 mo	9.09%
Treasury notes	5 yr	11.54
Negotiable CDs	3 mo	9.54
Commerical paper	3 mo	9.32
Banker's acceptances	3 mo	9.38
Money market mutual funds	Instant liquidity	8.50
Eurodollar deposits	3 mo	9.91

SOURCE: All data except for money market mutual funds obtained from Board of Governors of the Federal Reserve System, *Federal Reserve Bulletin*, March 1984, p. A26. Money market mutual fund data are from *Wall Street Journal*, March 1, 1984, p. 47.

therefore return to investors, but perhaps equally important, the money manager can have a pronounced effect on portfolio yield through the portfolio strategies he or she adopts.[17]

Different strategies, of course, affect risk and return in different ways; as a result, corporate money managers should always consider risk-return tradeoffs when altering portfolio strategies or structures. Even though the marketable securities widely used in corporate portfolios have very short lives (generally 180 days or less), there is a surprising variety of strategies that can be used to enhance return. Several of the more popular investment strategies will be briefly examined next; these include buy-and-hold, riding the yield curve, money spreads, and preferred dividend rolls.

Buy-and-Hold.   This is the simplest and, as a result, the most widely practiced money market investment strategy. As the name implies, the object of this approach is to buy securities that carry maturities which closely correspond to the expected cash and investment needs of the firm. If a firm has idle cash it does not anticipate needing for the next 60 days (this might be the case, for instance, with the controllable cash segment of the portfolio), the portfolio manager who adheres to a buy-and-hold approach would purchase a 60-day instrument and hold it to maturity. Since this strategy minimizes subsequent portfolio trading, it results in correspondingly low risk of capital loss—that is, having to sell a security when the market has moved against the investor and the issue is trading at or below its original purchase price.

A *buy-and-hold* portfolio can be aggressively managed by altering the portfolio's structure and composition. In effect, the corporate money manager can affect portfolio return by investing in higher-yielding

---

[17]Hedging strategies that employ interest rate futures contracts can, under the proper conditions, be used profitably to lock in high rates of return on marketable security investments; interest rate futures hedging is a sophisticated, but quite effective, way of improving the return on portfolios. Hedging strategies with interest rate futures are described in detail in Appendix 21A.

securities. For instance, in February 1984, the average spread between high-yield negotiable CDs (9.54 percent) and lower-yielding Treasury bills (9.09 percent) was about .45 percent—and when market rates were much higher, the spread was about 1.70 percent (negotiable CDs were 13.80 percent and Treasury bills were 12.09 percent in May 1982). Clearly, a whole structure of interest rates exists in the market at any given point in time; such yield spreads, of course, lead to differential investment opportunities for the alert money manager. The aggressively managed buy-and-hold portfolio will have to assume slightly greater risk of default and some marketability problems, but it is clear that the money manager can increase return by shopping around for high-yield securities.

Riding the Yield Curve.   Instead of seeking out the yield differentials between one type of security and another, riding the yield curve involves taking advantage of yield spreads that exist because of maturity differences. As noted earlier, a yield curve relates yield to maturity to term to maturity for similar-risk securities. Although yield curves can change in shape over time, a prevalent form historically has been an upward-sloping curve. In this case, the yield to maturity increases as the issue's term to maturity lengthens; such a term structure is considered a necessary condition for riding the yield curve.

Riding the yield curve works like this: Suppose a money manager has funds to invest for a 90-day period. The manager has two options—she can buy a 90-day issue and hold it to maturity, or she can buy a longer issue and sell it in the open market after 90 days (for example, the manager buys a 6-month instrument and sells it 3 months later, when the issue still has 90 days remaining to maturity). The latter approach is known as *riding the yield curve*. The objective is to invest in the higher-yielding end of the yield curve. Figure 9.9 can be used to illustrate this strategy. In the figure, the buy-and-hold approach (point A) involves investing at a market rate of return of 10.60 percent. Riding the yield curve (point B) involves an issue offering a much higher return of 11.50 percent. But there is more, for if things work out as expected, riding the yield curve will result in a realized return even higher than the 11.50 percent. This is so since the money manager expects to generate a modest amount of "capital gains" by selling the issue (at point A) at a rate lower than that which existed when the issue was purchased.

The expected return—$E(R_{yc})$—from riding the yield curve can be approximated by using the following equation:[18]

---

[18]For a more complete discussion of the benefits and risks of riding the yield curve, see Edward A. Dyl and Michael D. Joehnk, "Riding the Yield Curve—Does It Work?" *Journal of Portfolio Management* 7 (spring 1981), pp. 13–17.

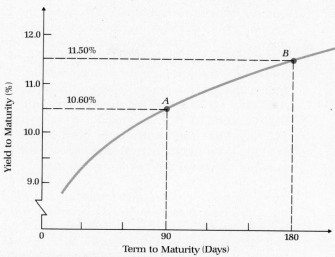

Figure 9.9   Riding the Yield Curve.

$$E(R_{yc}) = R_o + [[(R_o - E(R_s))\,(n - h)]/h] \qquad (9.7)$$

where R_o = original yield to maturity on the security
at the time of purchase
$E(R_s)$ = expected yield on the security
when it is sold
n = number of days to maturity when the
issue is purchased
h = number of days the issue will be held
before it is sold (the holding period)

Continuing our illustration, if the portfolio manager chooses to ride the
yield curve for 90 days, she could buy the 6-month (180-day) bills at a
yield to maturity of 11.50 percent and liquidate them after 90 days, at
which time, if interest rates and the yield curve have not changed, the
bills should sell at a yield to maturity of 10.60 percent. Given these
conditions, the approximate rate of return from riding the yield curve
will be:

$$\begin{aligned}
E(R_{yc}) &= 11.50\% + [[(11.50\% - 10.60\%)\,(180 - 90)]/90]\\
&= 12.40\%
\end{aligned}$$

Not only does this 12.40 percent rate of return exceed the 11.50 percent
promised by a wide margin, but more important, it is also much more
generous than the 10.60 percent rate available from buying a bill and

holding it to maturity (point A). Of course, the 12.40 percent return is not certain, since bill rates can change over time and as a result, the portfolio manager may not be able to sell the bills at the expected 10.60 percent yield. Thus, although riding the yield curve is an exciting way of increasing the return from investments in Treasury bills and similar money market investment vehicles, the tactic does result in substantially increased exposure to risk. It may not be appropriate for some segments of the portfolio—this is especially true for the ready cash segment and possibly even the controllable cash segment. Having to liquidate a position prior to maturity always exposes the investment to interest rate risk and therefore the risk of capital loss.

Money Spreads.   In addition to riding the yield curve, other investment strategies have been developed to increase the return from a portfolio of money market securities. One of the most fascinating is a technique called a *money spread.* Also known as an interest rate arbitrage, the tactic can be used whenever the yield differential between two types of money market securities is abnormally wide. Under such conditions, a portfolio manager would short sell[19] the lower-yielding (higher-priced) issue, and use the proceeds to invest in the higher-yielding (lower-priced) security. The short sale, in effect, represents a way of "borrowing" money that is then used for investing in the higher-yielding issue.

Say, for example, that a low yield in the T-bill market exists relative to certificates of deposit. If the distortion becomes pronounced, the spread between bill rates and CD returns will become abnormally wide, thus providing an opportunity to short sell the more expensive item (the T-bill) and buy the cheaper one (the CD). This situation might present itself if T-bills were yielding 11 percent at a time when the return on CDs equaled 12.5 percent. Little or no corporate cash is required to execute the transaction through established dealer channels. The objective is simply to reap the yield differential between the two types of securities. A major part of the return from the high-yielding issue (the CD in the example) is used to "service" the interest requirement on the short sale—that is, interest in the amount of 11 percent must be paid to the lender of the T-bills, in addition to a slight "borrowing fee" that normally accompanies short sale transactions. Thus, in our example, the yield differential equals 1.5 percent (12.5 percent on the CD less the 11 percent on the T-bill), which is the maximum amount the investor stands to net

---

[19]A short sale is a common investment strategy in both the money and the capital markets. Essentially, it represents the sale of borrowed securities, which in time have to be returned to the lender in the form of a comparable number of securities, or if they have matured, an equivalent amount of cash. The dealer firm holds all the cash and securities as collateral, and the lender's position is always fully protected; also, as long as the short sale is outstanding, the short seller is obligated to make payments to the lender of the securities for earnings that would accrue from the securities.

out (after all expenses and fees) on the amount invested in the certificates of deposit. Over a 90-day period, and using a $5 million transaction for illustration purposes, a 1.5 percent differential will generate nearly $19,000 in income to the firm[20]—all obtained without the use of any company money. And the technique has an attractive by-product: There is *no* additional risk in the arbitrage transaction, since it is always executed with a "positive carry" (in other words, the cost of "borrowing" the money through a short sale is less than the income earned on the borrowed money).

Preferred Dividend Rolls.   Today an increasing number of corporate money managers are investing a portion of their temporarily idle cash in preferred stocks. They do this to take advantage of the attractive returns that are made possible, in large part, by the preferential tax treatment afforded these issues. Corporations enjoy an income-tax exemption of 85 percent of the dividends received from other domestic corporations. These portfolio managers, though, are adding an unusual twist; for rather than investing in preferreds for the long term and collecting the customary 4 dividends per year, they are actively trading in and out of preferreds to collect as many as 8 to 12 dividends a year. Such a trading strategy is called a *preferred dividend roll.*

The tactic is actually quite simple in concept and in execution. In a typical preferred dividend roll, a company will buy an issue (usually an A-rated or better utility obligation) some 15 to 45 days before its ex-dividend date. A few days after it qualifies to receive the dividend, the firm "rolls out of" (sells) its holding and invests the proceeds either in another preferred issue whose ex-dividend date is several weeks away, or in an alternative (money market) investment vehicle. Although even shorter holding periods may seem more appealing, there is an important legal constraint: Treasury statutes hold that in order to qualify for the 85 percent tax exclusion, the stock must be held for a period of not less than 16 days. A single preferred roll will often involve between 5,000 and 15,000 shares of preferred stock, and upwards of half a million dollars or more.

On average, the after-tax return from preferred dividend rolls amounts to better than 10 percent;[21] keep in mind this represents a return of more than 18 percent on a before-tax basis for firms with 46 percent marginal tax rates. As might be expected, this attractive rate of return carries with it significant risk exposure. One obvious risk is that

---

[20]Borrowing fees were ignored in the illustration; they normally amount to anywhere from ¼ to ½ of 1 percent and would reduce gross earnings accordingly.

[21]See Michael D. Joehnk, Oswald D. Bowlin, and J. William Petty, "Preferred Dividend Rolls: A Viable Strategy for Corporate Money Managers?" *Financial Management* 9 (summer 1980), pp. 78–87.

the issuing corporation may pass its dividend. Such occurrences are rare, however, and can be fairly well hedged by confining transactions to the higher-rated preferreds. The biggest risk in a preferred dividend roll accrues from another, far less controllable source: the marketplace. Unfortunately, this exposure is often double edged! For not only can the market unexpectedly move against the investor (as when interest rates increase), but since preferreds do not trade on an accrual basis, their price tends to rise in anticipation of an upcoming dividend and then drop after the ex-dividend date. Because of the extensive risk exposure embedded in preferred dividend rolls, as well as the generally reduced marketability of preferred shares, the tactic is normally confined to securities in the free cash segment of the portfolio.

SUMMARY

The management of cash and marketable securities in a typical nonfinancial firm involves management of the cash flow, cash forecasting using the cash budget, determining an optimal cash balance, and developing short-term financing and investment strategies. The goal of cash management is to minimize the level of current assets while providing adequate liquidity. Several strategies can be followed in this regard, including paying bills as late as possible, managing the inventory-production cycle efficiently, and collecting accounts receivable quickly. Certain constraints are placed on each of these strategies, but by maximizing its cash turnover, the firm will be able to minimize the level of operating cash required and add to its profitability.

The financial manager should attempt to minimize collection float and maximize disbursement float; both forms of float are made up of mail float, processing float, and transit float. Techniques used to reduce collection float include concentration banking, the lockbox system, direct sends, preauthorized checks (PACs), depository transfer checks (DTCs), and wire transfers; techniques for slowing disbursements include controlled disbursing, playing the float, and overdraft systems and zero-balance accounts. In addition, the financial manager must establish and maintain strong bank relationships.

It is the financial manager's job to establish an optimum cash balance and temporarily divert excess cash to appropriate short-term investment vehicles, or to arrange for appropriate short-term financing over those periods when cash deficits occur. The division of the firm's liquid resources between cash and marketable securities is a crucial cash management function that can usually be performed by using one of the available cash management models. These models attempt to find the optimum cash balance by minimizing the total cost, which consists of a fixed transaction cost and a variable opportunity cost. The models developed by Baumol, Miller and Orr, and Stone are most popular.

Firms hold marketable securities to earn a return on temporarily idle funds. The selection criteria are applied differently to different segments of the portfolio—the ready cash segment (RCS), the controllable cash segment (CCS), and the free cash segment (FCS). An understanding of yield curves is helpful when making marketable security investments. The most commonly held marketable securities include U.S. Treasury bills (T-bills), Treasury notes, federal agency issues, short-term municipals, negotiable certificates of deposit (CDs), commercial paper, banker's acceptances, money market mutual funds, repurchase agreements, and Eurodollar deposits. Corporate portfolio managers, in addition to carefully structuring their portfolios by investing in higher-yielding securities, can adopt a variety of sophisticated investment strategies, including buy-and-hold, riding the yield curve, money spreads, and preferred dividend rolls.

QUESTIONS

9.1.   What is the goal of cash management? What is a firm's cash cycle? How are the cash cycle and cash turnover of a firm related? What should the firm's objective be with respect to its cash cycle and cash turnover?

9.2.   The management of Albany Auto Parts is concerned about a problem it is having with cash; specifically, the firm seems to be experiencing continued cash shortfalls. The company has turned to your management consulting firm for help. After extensive evaluation, you conclude that the problem can best be handled by tighter internal control of accounts receivable, inventory, and accounts payable.

a.   Trace the impact of each of the following actions, and comment on the benefits and costs of each: (1) The average collection period and average age of inventory are brought down by a total of 12 days (4 days from the former and 8 from the latter). (2) The average payment period is "stretched" by 5 days.

b.   Given that all other things remain unchanged, does the reduction of an asset like accounts receivable really free up cash that can become available, on a permanent basis, to meet the cash needs of the firm?

9.3.   Would a lockbox system be helpful to a firm experiencing cash flow difficulties? Explain.

a.   Why is geographical dispersion normally a necessary prerequisite to establishing a lockbox system?

b.   What is the major benefit of a lockbox system to the firm?

c.   What is the major cost?

d.   Does establishing a lockbox system affect a firm's exposure to risk?

9.4.   Describe each of the following techniques for speeding up collections (note which aspects of float tend to be affected by each of these techniques).

a. Direct sends.
b. Preauthorized checks (PACs).
c. Depository transfer checks (DTCs).
d. Wire transfers.

9.5. Briefly explain how each of the following can be used to slow down disbursements:

a. Using controlled disbursing.
b. Playing the float.
c. Overdraft systems and zero-balance accounts.

9.6. Explain how the establishment of an optimum cash balance involves dividing the firm's liquid resources between cash and marketable securities.

a. Once an optimum cash balance has been established, management need only monitor the daily cash flow to make sure cash on hand remains within established limits; but what happens if (1) a cash surplus occurs, or (2) a cash shortfall occurs?
b. Under what conditions is it necessary to establish a new (revised) optimum cash balance?

9.7. Because of the seasonal nature of its business, the Packard Packing Company will often maintain a substantial marketable securities portfolio. Not surprisingly, the composition of the portfolio tends to change over the course of the year as the demands of the portfolio change. Assuming the portfolio is made up of a ready cash segment (RCS) and a controllable cash segment (CCS), note which type of security (RCS or CCS) would likely dominate under each of the following conditions (briefly explain your answer):

a. It is now the peak season, and the securities portfolio has been worked down to a low level.
b. It is now the slow time of the year, when the portfolio is at or near its maximum size.
c. Would your answer to (a) and (b) change if Packard normally used short-term financing to meet increased cash and working capital demands during the peak season? Explain.

9.8. Briefly describe each of the following types of investment vehicles:

a. Treasury bills.
b. Federal agency issues.
c. Banker's acceptances.
d. Money market mutual funds.
e. Repurchase agreements.
f. Eurodollar deposits.

9.9. Answer each of the following questions related to short-term investment strategies.

a. Contrast the risk and return of riding the yield curve with that of the buy-and-hold approach.

b. What is a money spread? Does it involve more risk than a buy-and-hold strategy?

c. What segment of the portfolio would preferred dividend rolls be most adaptable to? Explain.

PROBLEMS

9.1. *MANAGING THE CASH CYCLE.* The Mid-Central Auto Distribution Company is currently encountering some problems in maintaining an adequate supply of cash. An extensive analysis of the firm reveals that, on average, its receivables are collected in 40 days; it holds inventory an average of 62 days; and accounts payable are paid approximately 30 days after they are incurred. The company's annual spending amounts to about $40 million (assume it spends at a constant rate over a 360-day year).

a. How long is Mid-Central's cash cycle?

b. What is its current required level of cash holdings?

c. The firm currently carries an average daily cash balance of about $7.5 million; is this supply of cash adequate? Explain.

d. Management feels that by instituting new policies and tightening up internal controls, it should be able to bring the level of receivables down to about 35 days and reduce the amount of inventory carried to about a 50-day supply; at the same time, management feels it could safely "stretch" payables by about 10 days. If all these things can, in fact, be accomplished, then:

1. What would be the firm's new cash cycle and its new required level of cash holdings?

2. If the firm has a 12 percent opportunity cost, what annual savings can be realized by achieving the indicated reduction in the required level of cash holdings?

3. Will the plan solve the firm's cash problems? Do you see other types of problems arising once the stated goals are achieved?

9.2. *CONCENTRATION BANKING.* Cal-Man Industrial Products Company sells to a national market and bills all its credit customers out of its Los Angeles office. The customers, in turn, are instructed to remit payments on invoices directly to the L.A. office; Cal-Man currently has collections that average about $2.5 million per day. Management has under consideration a proposal to establish a concentration banking system that would have customers mail payments to a designated regional office (the one nearest the customer) where upon receipt, the staff would post the necessary entries and deposit the payments in a local bank. It is estimated that such a system will reduce the accounts receivable collection period by about 2 days; however, it is also estimated that the cost (bank fees, additional administrative expenses, and so on) of implementing the program will amount to $225,000 per year. Given that Cal-Man has an 11 percent opportunity cost, would you recommend the change to the proposed system of concentration banking? Explain.

9.3.   *LOCKBOX SYSTEMS.*   The financial administrator of the Maness Supply Company is unhappy with the amount of time it takes the company to collect and process checks received from credit customers. The firm presently utilizes two lockboxes that together run an average daily volume (based on a 360-day year) of $1 million. The banks, as compensation for their services, require $2 million in compensating balances (that is, $1 million for each bank). Due to the growing geographical dispersion of Maness customers, management feels a considerable savings in float (2 days to be exact) can be achieved by establishing 6 lockboxes, dispersed around the country. The financial package Maness would offer the banks includes a total compensating balance of $1.8 million ($300,000 for each bank), plus $.05 per check processed (the average check is for $500). Assume that the firm has an opportunity cost of 9 percent.

a.   Should the firm switch from the old lockbox plan to the new lockbox plan?

b.   Would your answer change if management felt it could get by with as little as $750,000 (in checking accounts balances) were it not necessary to meet the compensating balance requirements of the lockbox plans?

9.4.   *SLOWING DOWN DISBURSEMENTS.*   A large Miami, Florida, manufacturing firm has annual cash disbursements of approximately $600 million, made continuously over the (360-day) year. A cash management consulting firm recently suggested that the firm could increase its total disbursement float by about 2 days if it were to write checks on a remote bank location. The company has located a reputable, financially sound bank in Laramie, Wyoming, and has decided to pursue the possibility of using this bank as its major disbursement bank. The firm estimates it will cost about $150,000 per year (mostly in additional administrative expenses) to administer the program; if the firm has a 10 percent opportunity cost, should it move the disbursement account to the Laramie bank?

9.5.   *DIVIDING UP THE FIRM'S LIQUID RESOURCES.*   Assume that as a recent graduate, one of the first tasks you have been asked to undertake for your new employer (a Fortune 500 firm) involves the determination of a desirable cash balance level. Since the firm carries marketable securities in addition to its cash, you decide to apply the Miller and Orr approach to the problem, and go about gathering the necessary information. A phone call to the firm's government securities dealer reveals that the cost of buying and selling round lots of securities amounts to $50 per transaction; an analysis of money market conditions indicates that short-term government securities are presently yielding about 9.5 percent. Finally, extensive review of the firm's records provides daily cash flow figures for the past 18 months, which are used to determine that the standard deviation of the daily changes in net cash flow over this period has been $285,000. Given this information:

a. What is the optimum cash balance this firm should carry?

b. What is its maximum cash balance level?

c. Would your answers to (a) and (b) change if the variability of daily changes in net cash flow (σ) increased by 50 percent to $427,500, and all other variables remained the same? Explain.

d. What effect would result if the yield on securities fell by 50 percent to 4.75 percent, while all other variables remained unchanged?

e. Is the Miller and Orr derived optimum cash balance more sensitive to the variability of daily net cash flow changes, or to the yield on short-term securities? Is such relative sensitivity rational? Explain.

9.6. *MANAGING THE FIRM'S OPTIMUM CASH BALANCE.* The cash management team at Worldwide Products recently determined that the variance (σ^2) of its daily net cash flow changes amounted to $10,280. Using the Miller and Orr model, and letting b = $10 and i = 18%:

a. Compute the firm's optimal return point (z) and its maximum cash balance level (h).

b. Assuming a lower cash balance boundary of zero, and using your answers from (a), complete the following table. Assume the firm starts (on day 0) with a cash balance of $1500 and a securities balance of $2500, and that marketable securities can be bought and sold in any dollar amount:

Day	Daily Net Cash Flow	Optimal Marketable Securities Transactions	Revised Cash Balance	Revised Marketable Securities Balance
1	+$295			
2	+ 110			
3	− 55			
4	− 270			
5	− 285			
6	− 340			
7	+ 290			
8	+ 345			
9	+ 350			
10	+ 595			

c. Now calculate the actual average cash balance (over days 1 through 10) using the Miller and Orr model. Also, calculate the average cash balance (m) using the formula in the text (Equation 9.6). How do you explain the difference?

d. Ignoring the marketable securities position and given that cash is totally unmanaged (cash can go to any balance—there are no upper and lower boundaries), use the beginning cash balance and daily cash flow information that was given in (b) to determine the average cash balance over the 10-day period.

1. How does this compare to the average cash balance that can be achieved by using the Miller and Orr model?

2. For the average unmanaged cash balance, use the average cash balance derived from the Miller and Orr procedure and a 15 percent opportunity cost (of holding cash) to determine the benefits, if any, of using the Miller and Orr model.

9.7. *ALTERNATIVE INVESTMENT STRATEGIES.*   The portfolio manager at Pacific Northwest Utilities has approximately $1 million to invest for a period of 60 days. After extensive analysis of the current money market, the portfolio manager concludes that there are two options: (1) buy some prime-grade 60-day commercial paper currently yielding 8.75 percent; or (2) buy 150-day T-bills at a yield of 9 percent and then sell them 60 days later at a yield of 8.5 percent.

a. What is the expected return from buying and holding the commercial paper?

b. What is the expected return from riding the yield curve with T-bills?

c. What would happen to the return from riding the yield curve if the T-bills had to be sold (after 60 days) at a yield of 10 percent? How does this return compare to the commercial paper option?

d. To what level can the expected yield at sale $[E(R_s)]$ rise before riding the yield curve is no longer the superior alternative? (*Hint:* The change is less than ¼ of 1 percent). Which option would you recommend? Why?

9.8. *MONEY SPREADS.*   C. Maxwell and Company has $3 million in the controllable cash segment (CCS) of its marketable securities portfolio. The cash has been earmarked for use in paying the firm's quarterly tax estimate, due in 60 days. Currently, T-bills are selling at a yield of 12.25 percent, while the best-quality commercial paper can be purchased to yield 13.75 percent. The company's cash manager is contemplating using a money spread to increase the return on the portfolio. Ignorning any borrowing or brokerage fees that might apply to this transaction:

a. Explain how the cash manager would go about creating the money spread in order to benefit from the differential interest rates between the T-bills and the commercial paper.

b. Over the 60-day period, how much income will the firm generate from this transaction?

c. Could a preferred dividend roll have been used to accomplish the same objective? Explain why or why not.

SELECTED REFERENCES

Arnold, Jasper H. "Banker's Acceptance: A Low-Cost Financing Choice." *Financial Executive* 48 (July 1980), pp. 14–19.

Batlin, Carl Alan, and Susan Hinko. "A Game Theoretic Approach to Cash Management." *Journal of Business* 55 (July 1982), pp. 367–381.

Baumol, William J. "The Transactions Demand for Cash: An Inventory Theoretic Approach." *The Quarterly Journal of Economics* 65 (November 1952), pp. 545–556.

Beranek, William. *Analysis for Financial Decisions.* Homewood, Ill.: Irwin, 1963.

Board of Governors of the Federal Reserve System. "The Depository Institutions Deregulation and Monetary Control Act of 1980." *Federal Reserve Bulletin,* June 1980, pp. 444–453.

Bokos, William J., and Anne P. Clinkard. "Multilateral Netting." *Journal of Cash Management* 3 (June–July 1983), pp. 24–34.

Bonocore, Joseph J. "Getting a Picture of Cash Management." *Financial Executive* 48 (May 1980), pp. 30–33.

Carleton, Willard T., and Ian A. Cooper. "Estimation and Uses of the Term Structure of Interest Rates." *Journal of Finance* 31 (September 1976), pp. 1067–1083.

Daellenbach, Hans G. "Are Cash Management Optimization Models Worthwhile?" *Journal of Financial and Quantitative Analysis* 9 (September 1974), pp. 607–626.

Driscoll, Mary C. *Cash Management: Corporate Strategies for Profit.* New York: Wiley, 1983.

Dyl, Edward A., and Michael D. Joehnk. "Riding the Yield Curve—Does it Work?" *Journal of Portfolio Management* 7 (spring 1981), pp. 13–17.

Gitman, Lawrence J., and Mark D. Goodwin. "An Assessment of Marketable Securities Management Practices", *Journal of Financial Research* 2 (fall 1979), pp. 161–169.

———, D. Keith Forrester, and John R. Forrester, Jr. "Maximizing Cash Disbursement Float." *Financial Management* 5 (summer 1976), pp. 15–24.

———, Edward A. Moses, and Thomas I. White. "An Assessment of Corporate Cash Management Practices." *Financial Management* 8 (spring 1979), pp. 32–41.

Hill, Ned C., William L. Sartoris, and Sue L. Visscher. "The Components of Credit Line Borrowing Costs." *Journal of Cash Management* 3 (October–November 1983), pp. 47–56.

Joehnk, Michael D., Oswald D. Bowlin, and J. William Petty. "Preferred Dividend Rolls: A Viable Strategy for Corporate Money Managers?" *Financial Management* 9 (summer 1980), pp. 78–87.

Levy, Ferdinand K. "An Application of Heuristic Problem Solving to Accounts Receivable Management." *Management Science* 12 (February 1966), pp. 236–244.

Liss, Ronald E. "The ANSI X12 Committee: A Status Report on Standards for Cash Cycle Management." *Journal of Cash Management* 3 (August–September 1983), pp. 39–48.

Lordan, James F. "Cash Management: The Corporation-Bank Relationship." *The Magazine of Bank Administration* 48 (January 1975), pp. 14–19.

Maier, Steven F., and James H. Vander Weide. "The Lock-Box Location Problem: A Practical Reformulation." *Journal of Bank Research* 5 (summer 1974), pp. 92–95.

————, and ————. "A Unified Location Model for Cash Disbursements and Lock-Box Collections." *Journal of Bank Research* 7 (summer 1976), pp. 166–172.

————, and ————. "What Lockbox and Disbursement Models Really Do." *Journal of Finance* 38 (May 1983), pp. 361–371.

————, David W. Robinson, and James H. Vander Weide. "A Short-Term Disbursement Forecasting Model." *Financial Management* 10 (spring 1981), pp. 9–20.

Mathur, Ike, and David Loy. "Corporate-Banking Cash Management Relationships: Survey Results." *Journal of Cash Management* 3 (October–November 1983), pp. 35–46.

Miller, Merton H., and Daniel Orr. "An Application of Control-Limit Models to the Management of Corporate Cash Balances." In *Financial Research and Financial Decisions*, ed. Alexander A. Robichek. New York: Wiley, 1967.

————, and ————. "A Model for the Demand for Money by Firms." *The Quarterly Journal of Economics* 80 (August 1966), pp. 413–435.

Morris, James R. "The Role of Cash Balances in Firm Valuation." *Journal of Financial and Quantitative Analysis* 18 (December 1983), pp. 533–545.

Nauss, Robert M., and Robert E. Markland. "Solving Lock Box Location Problems." *Financial Management* 8 (spring 1979), pp. 21–31.

Osteryoung, Jerome S., Gordon S. Roberts, and Daniel E. McCarty. "Ride the Yield Curve When Investing Idle Funds in Treasury Bills?" *Financial Executive* 47 (April 1979), pp. 10–15.

Parkinson, Kenneth L. "Dealing with the Problems of International Cash Management." *Journal of Cash Management* 3 (February–March 1983), pp. 16–25.

Shanker, Roy J., and Andris A. Zoltners. "The Corporate Payment Problem." *Journal of Bank Research* 3 (spring 1972), pp. 47–53.

————, and ————. "An Extension of the Lock-Box Location Problem." *Journal of Bank Research* 3 (winter 1972), p. 62.

Smith, Keith V. *Guide to Working Capital Management.* New York: McGraw-Hill, 1979.

————, ed. *Readings on the Management of Working Capital*, 2d ed. St. Paul, Minn.: West, 1980.

Stone, Bernell K. "The Use of Forecasts and Smoothing in Control-Limit Models for Cash Management." *Financial Management* 1 (spring 1972), pp. 72–84.

————, and Ned C. Hill. "Cash Transfer Scheduling for Efficient Cash Concentration." *Financial Management* 9 (autumn 1980), pp. 35–43.

————, and Tom W. Miller. "Daily Cash Forecasting: A Structuring Framework." *Journal of Cash Management* 1 (October 1981), pp. 35–50.

————, and Robert A. Wood. "Daily Cash Forecasting: A Simple Method for Implementing the Distribution Approach." *Financial Management* 6 (fall 1977), pp. 40–50.

Appendix 9A

Mathematics of the Money Market

Most money market investments—such as Treasury bills, commercial paper, and banker's acceptances—are quoted and traded on a *discount* basis. That is, the securities are issued and traded at less than par, and the difference between the discount price paid for the issue and its par value represents interest income. Other securities (like negotiable certificates of deposit) are initially issued for a stipulated principal amount and at a given rate of return; at maturity, the holder receives the principal plus the interest income earned on the certificate. However, because issuing banks can neither repurchase their own certificates nor redeem them prior to maturity (except under conditions which would be costly and inconvenient to holders), there is an active secondary market for negotiable CDs, and in this market, negotiable CDs are also quoted and traded on the same discount basis as other money market securities. Because of the widespread use of discounts, portfolio managers must convert such quotes to dollar prices and equivalent bond yields.

Determining Issue Prices

For securities that are initially issued on a discount basis, the dollar price can be found according to the following equation:

$$P = \left[1 - \frac{d \times n}{360}\right] \times M \qquad (9A.1)$$

where P = dollar price of a discounted security
d = the stated or quoted (ask) discount rate (6.5% = .065)
n = days remaining to maturity
M = par (or maturity) value of the security

Equation 9A.1 is used to find either the purchase or the selling price of a discounted security. A perusal of the equation reveals that within the bracketed portion of the model, the amount of the discount $[(d \times n)/360]$ is subtracted from 1.0 to yield the price of the security on a percentage of par basis; multiplying this percentage of par figure by the issue's par value provides the dollar price of the security. For example, to see how Equation 9A.1 works, consider a $1 million T-bill that has 70 days remaining to maturity and that is being quoted at a discount of 8.47 percent:

$$P = \left[1 - \frac{.0847 \times 70}{360}\right] \times \$1,000,000$$
$$= [1 - .01647] \times \$1,000,000 = \$983,530$$

The price of this million-dollar T-bill is $983,530; the difference between this dollar price and its par value is the interest ($16,470) that will be earned on the investment over its 70-day holding period.

A different price model is used with interest-bearing securities like CDs; specifically, the dollar price of these securities when they trade at quoted discounts in the secondary market is determined as follows:

$$P_c = \left[\frac{[(d^* \times M)\,(r/360)] + M}{[(d \times M)\,(n/360)] + M}\right] \times M \tag{9A.2}$$

where P_c = dollar price of an interest-bearing security
d^* = stated interest rate on the security
r = original days to maturity
$d, n,$ and M = as defined in Equation 9A.1

To illustrate, assume an investor finds it necessary to sell a $1 million, 6 percent, 180-day certificate at a discount of 5.75 percent while it still has 45 days remaining to maturity. The price of the money market instrument would be:

$$P_c = \left[\frac{[(.06 \times \$1,000,000)\,(180/360)] + \$1,000,000}{[(.0575 \times \$1,000,000)\,(45/360)] + \$1,000,000}\right] \times \$1,000,000$$
$$= \left[\frac{\$1,030,000}{\$1,007,188}\right] \times \$1,000,000$$
$$= \$1,022,649$$

Note that the numerator of the bracketed portion of the equation represents the total maturity value of the security—the original principal plus interest at 6 percent for half a year = $1,030,000. The price of $1,022,649 includes both the *accrued interest* earned by the original owner (for holding the security for its first 135 days), and a modest amount of *capital gains*, which is generated because the CD is sold at a rate *less* than that stated on the issue.[1] Thus, the new owner can expect to earn $7,351 in interest ($1,030,000 − $1,022,649) by holding this CD to maturity, 45 days hence.

Equivalent Bond Yields and Holding Period Returns

All discounts in the money market, including those for CDs, are computed on the basis of a 360-day year. As a result, the quoted (discount) return is an understatement of the true (effective) annualized yield on the investment. It is possible to convert a discount to its corresponding effective yield, Y (known in the money market as an *equivalent bond yield*) by using the following equation:

$$Y = \left[\frac{365 \times d}{360 - (d \times n)} \right] \times 100 \qquad (9A.3)$$

Where d and n are as previously defined. For example, the equivalent bond yield, Y, of a security with 90 days to maturity trading at a discount of 8.75 percent is:

$$Y = \left[\frac{365 \times .0875}{360 - (.0875 \times 90)} \right] \times 100$$
$$= 9.07\%$$

This yield of 9.07 percent is obviously well above its stated discount rate, and represents the effective return to an investor assuming the security is held to its maturity date.

Frequently, Treasury bills and other money market securities are sold prior to maturity at a rate basis *different* from that at which they were purchased; for example, this was shown to be an essential ingredient of riding the yield curve. Under such conditions, money managers may want to compute the actual *holding period return*—the return realized from the investment over a specified period of time. Recall from our discussion of riding the yield curve that a model (Equation 9.7) was developed for measuring *expected* return; that is:

$$E(R_{yc}) = R_o + \left[\frac{[R_o - E(R_s)](n - h)}{h} \right]$$

A variation of this model can be used to measure the *actual* holding period return (HPR):

$$HPR = \left(d_o \pm \left[\frac{|d_o - d_s|(n - h)}{h} \right] \right) \times 100 \qquad (9A.4)$$

---

[1]Whenever an interest-bearing issue is traded at a rate *less* than the stated rate (or coupon) on the security $(d < d^*)$, a capital gain will accrue to the seller; in contrast, whenever the reverse occurs $(d > d^*)$, the seller incurs a capital loss.

where d_o = discount rate at purchase
d_s = discount rate at sale
n = as defined previously
h = number of days in the holding period

In this form of the model, the bracketed portion of 9A.4 is *added* to d_o whenever the discount rate drops over the holding period, and it is *subtracted* from d_o when the rate increases; note also that it is the *absolute* difference in the sale and purchase discount that is used. To demonstrate, assume a money manager bought a 90-day security at a discount of 7.5 percent and then sold it 40 days later at a rate of 8.25 percent:

$$HPR = \left(.0750 - \left[\frac{|.0750 - .0825|\ (90 - 40)}{40} \right] \right) \times 100$$

$$= \left(.0750 - \left[\frac{.0075(50)}{40} \right] \right) \times 100 = 6.56\%$$

In this case, the investor realized a holding period return of 6.56 percent. It dropped relative to that promised at the time of purchase since rates rose over the holding period, and as a result the investor incurred a modest capital loss. This holding period return, however, is on a discount basis and must be converted to find the effective yield of the transaction. Fortunately, HPR can be readily converted to an equivalent bond yield by using Equation 9A.3 and defining HPR as d and the length of the holding period as n; with respect to the above example, the effective realized yield, Y, of this investment would be:

$$Y = \left[\frac{365 \times d}{360 - (d \times n)} \right] \times 100$$

$$= \left[\frac{365 \times .0656}{360 - (.0656 \times 40)} \right] \times 100$$

$$= 6.70\%$$

As expected, the effective realized yield of this investment is greater than the return shown on a discounted basis.

PROBLEMS

9A.1.   *DOLLAR PRICES AND EQUIVALENT BOND YIELDS.*   Determine the purchase price and equivalent bond yield of the following T-bills:

T-bill[a]	Days to Maturity	Discount at Purchase
A	60	6.00%
B	185	6.75

[a]Assume par value = $1 million.

9A.2. *HOLDING PERIOD RETURN.* Using the same two bills as in Problem 9A.1, assume that the respective holding periods and discounts at sale are as follows:

T-bill	Days Held	Discount at Sale
A	45	6.50%
B	120	6.25

a. Find the dollar profit (or loss) for each transaction.
b. Determine holding period return for both T-bills.
c. Calculate the effective realized yield of each T-bill.

9A.3. *PRICING A CD.* A money manager recently purchased a 6.5 percent, 180-day CD, with 90 days remaining to maturity, at a discount of 8 percent; 30 days later, she sold the issue at a discount of 7.5 percent.

a. Given that the CD had a principal value of $1 million, determine the price paid for the security.
b. Find the equivalent bond yield that existed at the time of purchase; contrast this with the effective yield actually realized from this transaction. How do you account for the differences?

10

The Management of Accounts Receivable and Inventory

Accounts receivable and inventories represent two of the most important assets held by many firms. They act as a buffer that allows the production and sale process to operate with a minimum of disturbance. Accounts receivable result from the firm's decision to extend credit to customers; they are created and exist until a cash payment is received. The firm's investment in accounts receivable should be viewed as a portfolio of accounts, each having certain risk-return characteristics that affect the firm's overall risk and return. Inventories, on the other hand, act to smooth the production process and reduce the chance of lost sales due to stockouts. The ability to control inventories is also important to the firm's overall risk-return behavior. For the average manufacturer, accounts receivable and inventory account for over 80 percent of *current* assets. Table 10.1 presents data on the level of accounts receivable and inventory held by a selected sample of manufacturing firms in late 1983. Together they account for more than 32 percent of the *total* assets of manufacturing corporations. Although there are industry differences in the relative size of the accounts, these two current assets consume considerable amounts of capital. This chapter is concerned with the management of accounts receivable and inventories. We begin by describing the key characteristics of accounts receivable, and then take up the routine management of the receivables portfolio. In the third section of the chapter we present certain analytical procedures that can be used to make credit policy decisions. The final section deals with the role of the financial manager in the inventory management process.

TABLE 10.1
Accounts Receivable
and Inventory as a
Percentage of Total
Assets for Selected
Industries, Third
Quarter, 1983

Industry Group	Percentage of Total Assets		
	Accounts Receivable	Inventory	Total Accounts Receivable and Inventory
All Manufacturers	15.5%	17.1%	32.6%
Drugs	14.2	14.0	28.2
Nondurable manufacturers	13.7	13.0	26.7
Petroleum and coal products	8.4	6.0	14.4
Nonferrous metals	14.4	15.2	29.6
Electrical equipment	20.7	24.0	44.7
Aircraft and aerospace manufacturing	12.4	49.5	61.9
Mining	8.5	4.1	12.6
Wholesale trade	25.3	27.9	53.2

SOURCE: Federal Trade Commission, *Quarterly Financial Report: Manufacturing, Mining and Trade Corporations* (Washington, D.C.: U.S. Government Printing Office, 3d quarter, 1983).

Key Characteristics of Accounts Receivable

Accounts receivable arise when a firm makes a sale on credit. Most commercial sales and many sales to the ultimate consumer are made on credit. To the firm extending credit, the resulting account receivable represents a short-term investment of funds. The size of this investment is related to the level of sales and is affected by the type of credit customer accepted, the credit terms extended by the firm, and the firm's collection policies. The establishment and implementation of credit and collection policies is a key element of working capital management. In managing accounts receivable, the financial manager must analyze marginal revenues and costs to make decisions. Establishing and administering credit standards, credit terms, and collection policies that strike an appropriate balance between revenues and costs (while recognizing any risk effects) is fundamental to effective accounts receivable management.

Credit Policy

The activities encountered in accounts receivable management can be categorized as part of the firm's overall *credit policy*. The three key components of credit policy are credit standards, credit terms, and collection activities.[1] *Credit standards* provide the basis for specifying acceptable levels of credit risk and determining who will receive credit. Such decisions rely on the use of analytical tools and credit investigation. *Credit terms* establish the conditions under which credit will be

---

[1] These three components are representative of the traditional divisions of credit policy. They are employed here to provide a clear exposition of decision-making criteria and results. Clearly, interactive effects among the three components are quite important in a final, general policy decision.

extended, including cash discount policies, the length of time for which credit will be extended, and in some cases, the finance charges levied when accounts are not paid on time. *Collection activities* are the firm's basis for action when established credit terms are violated.[2]

The Role and Cost of Credit Policy

In a sense, credit sales are a convenience for all parties concerned. Through established credit procedures, sales and shipments can be handled in a smooth and orderly fashion without unnecessary delays in the operating cycle of either party.[3] Providing credit can also be viewed as a service to the customer. Unlike a bank, a business firm generally extends credit not for interest income, but for the purpose of attracting sales. From a marketing perspective, competitive pressures and industry tradition may strongly influence credit policy. In special situations, firms may deviate from their stated credit policy to assist a longstanding customer through difficult times. The marketing considerations associated with credit policy must be given careful consideration by the financial manager.

On the other hand, credit policies must also be established with an eye toward the costs associated with accounts receivable. These costs include: (1) the earnings foregone on alternative investment opportunities (opportunity costs), (2) administrative costs associated with managing and collecting accounts receivable, and (3) bad debt losses. Funds invested in receivables could be used, for example, to increase cash and marketable securities, thereby providing both improved liquidity and interest income for the firm. Similarly, the resources allocated to accounts receivable might be used to purchase additional inventories for use in increasing output. Regardless of the specific situation, the cost of foregone opportunities significantly affects credit policy. As we will see, this cost, along with administrative and bad debt costs, must be viewed in relation to the marginal revenues and profits that are obtained from the receivables portfolio when making credit policy decisions.

The Accounts Receivable Investment

The firm's investment in accounts receivable is sometimes called its *receivables portfolio*, since it contains a collection of accounts receivable, each possessing certain risk-return characteristics. This portfolio must generate revenues that compensate for the cost of the resources em-

---

[2]Follow-up action on overdue accounts is perhaps one of the credit manager's most difficult jobs. Regardless of stated credit terms, some firms will habitually "ride" suppliers beyond payment dates. Careful judgment must be employed in valuing an important customer's goodwill and considering it in light of the costs associated with past due accounts.

[3]A smoothly functioning credit system also allows various operating functions of the firm (such as purchasing, production, and marketing) to be carried out independently of the billing and collection procedures. With established credit policies, for example, an outside salesperson may concentrate entirely on the marketing aspects of the firm's operation, rather than also worrying about credit and collection activities.

ployed. An implicit return in the form of additional profits is weighed against the carrying, administrative, and bad debt costs associated with receivables, and against the firm's exposure to risk. If the receivables investment becomes too large, creditors of the firm may view long collection periods and slow receivables turnover as danger signals in the firm's overall working capital policy. If the investment is too small, however, sales and competitive status within the industry may be lost. Investment in the receivables portfolio therefore must be carefully monitored to maintain an appropriate balance and, ultimately, to increase the value of the firm.

The balance established reflects the firm's managerial objectives. Firms that have strong production and marketing orientations tend to offer more liberal credit terms than firms with more direct concerns for credit costs and close financial control. Either approach may produce successful results so long as the tradeoffs involved are recognized and are suitable to the firm's managerial objectives. Shifts in managerial objectives may also affect receivables management. When a firm attempts to penetrate a new market, it may use favorable credit terms as a vehicle for attaining an increased market share. In times of financial stress, a firm may reduce its receivable investment to generate additional cash or to reduce short-term debt obligations.

In many cases, direct competitive pressure may also be an important determinant of the credit policy. Although industry tradition may establish minimum credit terms, the individual firm must react to competitive pressures in the market. During periods of tight money, customers may demand more favorable credit terms. As is often the case during such periods, markets soften, and the maintenance of sales levels may require concessions to buyers. The firm may view additional receivables investment as a favorable alternative to lost sales and increased inventory levels. Especially in seasonal or faddish markets, the firm may wish to avoid inventory buildups by offering liberal credit terms rather than risk obsolescence.

The final and perhaps most important consideration in receivables policy is its impact on profits. A firm behaving rationally will not intentionally extend credit to customers who cannot or will not eventually pay for the merchandise shipped. Such a policy would result in bad debt writeoffs and lost profits. The impact on profits must be considered relative to the probability of nonpayment on the additional sales that are expected to be generated. Profits are generally increased so long as the expected value of collections exceeds the expected costs associated with the particular credit policy. For example, from among a number of marginal credit risks, the firm must estimate the level of bad debt losses in relation to additional revenues generated by such customers. If management is willing to accept the risks involved, credit should be extended to the point where expected marginal revenue meets expected marginal costs. At this point, profits are maximized. We will explore a specific credit policy model incorporating this concept later in the chapter.

Routine Management of the Receivables Portfolio

The management of accounts receivable, like most areas of managerial finance, involves both nonroutine as well as routine activities. Nonroutine activities center on policy decision making in regard to credit standards, credit terms, and collection activities. These decisions, which are discussed later in the chapter, tend to be episodic; they are made only when conditions warrant. Routine activities, in contrast, are concerned primarily with the day-to-day management of the receivables portfolio. These activities include selection of credit customers and establishing of credit limits, controlling credit terms, and collecting receivables. Careful attention to routine activities can mean the difference between a smoothly functioning credit system and one that detracts from the firm's objectives. Managed properly, receivables are an important marketing tool and a valuable short-term investment. Improper management, however, can result in lost sales, collection difficulties, and a severe drain on the firm's resources. We will look now at the key routine activities in the management of the accounts receivable portfolio.

Selecting Credit Customers and Establishing Credit Limits

Once the firm's credit standards have been established, they must be routinely applied to screen potential credit customers. In addition, the amount of credit extended to each customer must be determined, and credit limits set, when appropriate.[4] Credit standards are applied through the collection and analysis of credit information, and through the evaluation of expected returns, costs, and risks associated with a given account. These standards are important since they can significantly affect the level of sales, the size of the investment in accounts receivable, the level of bad debts, and the level of administrative and collection costs.

The size and frequency of credit purchases expected from a given customer will impact the type of information gathered as well as the formality of the analysis performed. For example, the firm clearly does not want to spend much time and money making a credit decision for a customer requesting credit for a one-time purchase of a $50 item. On the other hand, the firm will be justified in spending both time and money to carefully investigate a customer wishing to make credit purchases of $20,000 a month over the coming year. The decision relative to the formality and cost of the analysis performed on a given credit applicant must therefore be viewed in light of the anticipated payoffs. The

---

[4]Objective standards are vital to applying consistent criteria to credit decisions and evaluating credit policies over time. Implementation, however, is also very important, and the judgment of an experienced credit manager is essential to success.

discussions which follow describe information sources and analytical techniques that would be most appropriate in analyzing larger credit customers, where the benefits of credit analysis are assumed to exceed the associated costs.

Gathering Credit Information.   The first step in evaluating credit customers is the collection, analysis, and maintenance of credit information. Numerous sources of information are available. The applicant's financial statements are a basic source; in addition, credit-granting firms commonly rely on professional credit investigation agencies to summarize financial information and evaluate past payment records. Dun & Bradstreet (D&B), the largest mercantile credit-reporting agency, as well as local credit bureaus and credit interchanges are popular sources of such credit information. Figure 10.1 is an example of the information available to D&B subscribers. The lower portion of Figure 10.1 is D&B's Key to Ratings; these ratings can be used to categorize customers in terms of financial strength and credit appraisal. If more detailed information is required, a D&B Business Information Report, as illustrated in Figure 10.2 on p. 409, can be obtained. The report provides summary information about the firm and its D&B rating, and information on payments, finances, banking, history, operations, and any other special events.

In addition to credit reporting agencies, the firm may obtain credit information from other sources. Its commercial bank may be able to obtain account information as well as the loan payment history of a potential credit customer. Another important source is other suppliers who have made credit sales to the customer and are willing to share information with the firm. In many industries where the suppliers make credit sales to numerous mutual customers, an active exchange of payment data is often standard practice. And, of course, the firm's own experience with the customer is an important source of information for use in an ongoing evaluation of credit customers.

Credit Analysis.   Once the necessary data on a given credit customer have been gathered, they must be carefully analyzed to make the credit decision. A variety of analytical procedures are available for this task; they range from simple ratio analysis to sophisticated multivariate techniques and large, computer-based systems. Regardless of which technique is employed, these tools do not replace, they merely supplement, the credit manager's judgment. Ratio analysis, described in Chapter 3, allows the analyst to assess the applicant's credit worthiness in light of historic financial results. It is also useful in establishing credit limits; for example, some firms as a rule limit credit to an amount equal to no more than a specified percentage of the customer's net worth.

Risk Classification.   Because of the difficulty associated with quantifying credit risk, many firms base their credit standards and associated

Industry Code

Town Name

Population (1980)

County Name **Rating**

Branch reference to headquarters in a different state (rating shown)

Names of local banks, officers, and capital

Reference to headquarters in the same state or to a primary style in the same town. In these instances no rating is shown

* **Symbol after business name indicates a corporation when 'Corp' or 'Inc.' is not a part of the name**

Town without Post Office, with reference to Post Office town

51 81	Fairbury Sales Co		
51 91	Farmers Union Coop Elev Assn*		
55 41	Farmers Union Coop Oil Assn*		
55 41	Fitzgerald Charles L & Mrs OL		
	Br of Jansen Neb		
57 22	Flowers TV & Appliance		
54 11	Fuller Thriftway		
76 41	Furniture Fix It Shoppe	2	
32 72	G & M Sand & Gravel	6	
53 99	Gamble Skogmo Inc		
	Br of Minneapolis Minn		
52 51	Gamble Store 4371	9	
55 71	Garbers Honda Sales		
51 98	Gaugenbaugh Frank		
17 11	Gibson Plumbing & Heating Co		
53 99	Gibsons of Fairbury Inc	7	
59 12	Globe Rexall Drug Store Inc		
17 11	Goeking Plumbing & Heating		
C 48 32	Great Plains Broadcasting Inc	6	
51 72	Griess Oil Co		
55 41	H & H Sinclair Oil Co		
	Br of Beatrice Wis		

	17 31 Williams Clyde Electric		DC2 2
	51 91 Williams Feed Co		
BEAVER CREEK 13,118 DODGE 32			
	FAIRFIELD STATE BANK		$128M
	D Enger Pr, J Voorhess Cas		
C 07 51	Bauman Lockers AnimalSV 0		FF3
76 99	Dales Bros	5	SG2
15 21	Drudik Construction		FF2
C 50 83	Fairfield Implement Inc		CC2
51 91	Fairfield Non Stk Cp Fert Assn		RA1
C 55 41	Fairfield Oil Co		DD2
51 53	Farmers Union Coop Assn*		BB2
C 54 11	Stephens Market		EE2
BEAVER FALLS (SEE NORTHPORT)			
BEDENVILLE PIERCE 87			
	FARMERS STATE BANK		$253M
	H Wilkins Pr, F Tous Cas		
53 11	Beavers Department Store		CC2
17 91	Block Construction & Farm Sup	7	DD3

Key to Ratings

ESTIMATED FINANCIAL STRENGTH		COMPOSITE CREDIT APPRAISAL			
		HIGH	GOOD	FAIR	LIMITED
5A	$50,000,000 and over	1	2	3	4
4A	$10,000,000 to 49,999,999	1	2	3	4
3A	1,000,000 to 9,999,999	1	2	3	4
2A	750,000 to 999,999	1	2	3	4
1A	500,000 to 749,999	1	2	3	4
BA	300,000 to 499,999	1	2	3	4
BB	200,000 to 299,999	1	2	3	4
CB	125,000 to 199,999	1	2	3	4
CC	75,000 to 124,999	1	2	3	4
DC	50,000 to 74,999	1	2	3	4
DD	35,000 to 49,999	1	2	3	4
EE	20,000 to 34,999	1	2	3	4
FF	10,000 to 19,999	1	2	3	4
GG	5,000 to 9,999	1	2	3	4
HH	Up to 4,999	1	2	3	4

GENERAL CLASSIFICATION

ESTIMATED FINANCIAL STRENGTH		COMPOSITE CREDIT APPRAISAL		
		GOOD	FAIR	LIMITED
1R	$125,000 and over	2	3	4
2R	$ 50,000 to $124,999	2	3	4

EXPLANATION

When the designation "1R" or "2R" appears, followed by a 2, 3 or 4, it is an indication that the Estimated Financial Strength, while not definitely classified, is presumed to be in the range of the ($) figures in the corresponding bracket, and while the Composite Credit Appraisal cannot be judged precisely, it is believed to fall in the general category indicated.

"INV." shown in place of a rating indicates that the report was under investigation at the time of going to press. It has no other significance.

"FB" (Foreign Branch). Indicates that the headquarters of this company is located in a foreign country (including Canada). The written report contains the location of the headquarters.

ABSENCE OF RATING, expressed by two hyphens (- -), is not to be construed as unfavorable but signifies circumstances difficult to classify within condensed rating symbols. It suggests the advisability of obtaining a report for additional information.

EMPLOYEE RANGE DESIGNATIONS IN REPORTS ON NAMES NOT LISTED IN THE REFERENCE BOOK

Certain business do not lend themselves to a Dun & Bradstreet rating and are not listed in the Reference Book. Information on these names, however, continues to be stored and updated in the D&B Business Information File. Reports are available on such businesses and instead of a rating they carry an Employee Range Designation (ER) which is indicative of size in terms of number of employees. No other significance should be attached.

KEY TO EMPLOYEE RANGE DESIGNATIONS		
ER 1	1000 or more	Employees
ER 2	500 - 999	Employees
ER 3	100 - 499	Employees
ER 4	50 - 99	Employees
ER 5	20 - 49	Employees
ER 6	10 - 19	Employees
ER 7	5 - 9	Employees
ER 8	1 - 4	Employees
ER N		Not Available

Figure 10.1 An Excerpt from the Dun & Bradstreet Reference Book and a Key to Ratings.

Source: Dun & Bradstreet, Inc., New York. By permission of Dun & Bradstreet Credit Services, a company of the Dun & Bradstreet Corporation.

❶ SUMMARY

— digests important facts detailed in the Report
— business name and address
— chief executive
— product and function
— D&B Rating, reflecting estimated financial strength and composite credit appraisal
— plus the concise facts that back up that rating

❷ PAYMENTS

How a business pays its bills as reported by suppliers . . . millions of trade experiences, both computerized and manual

❸ FINANCE

Financial condition, trend of sales and profits

❹ BANKING

Relations with bank, balances, loans and amounts owing

❺ HISTORY

When business started, background of the principals including specific dates

❻ OPERATIONS

What a business does . . . where it's located . . . premises

Dun & Bradstreet, Inc.

BE SURE NAME, BUSINESS AND ADDRESS MATCH YOUR FILE

ANSWERING INQUIRY

This report has been prepared for:

SUBSCRIBER: 008-001042

THIS REPORT MAY NOT BE REPRODUCED IN WHOLE OR IN PART IN ANY MANNER WHATEVER.

| CONSOLIDATED REPORT | | {FULL REVISION} |

DUNS: 06-647-3261
RETTINGER PAINT CORP.

727 WHITMAN WAY
BENSON, MI 48232
TEL 313 961-0720

CARL RETTINGER, PRES.

DATE PRINTED
AUG 13, 198-

WHOL PAINTS & VARNISHES

SIC NO.
51 98

SUMMARY

	RATING	CC2
①	STARTED	1950
	PAYMENTS	DISC-PPT
	SALES	$ 424,612
	WORTH	$ 101,867
	EMPLOYS	5
	HISTORY	CLEAR
	CONDITION	GOOD
	TREND	STEADY

SPECIAL EVENTS Business burglarized July 3 but $18,000 loss is fully insured.

② PAYMENTS REPORTED {Amounts may be rounded to nearest figure in prescribed ranges}

PAYING RECORD	HIGH CREDIT	NOW OWES	PAST DUE	SELLING TERMS	LAST SALE WITHIN
07/8-					
Disc	30000	17000	-0-	2 10 30	1-2 mos.
Disc	27000	14000	-0-	1 10 30	2-3 mos.
Disc-Ppt	12000	4400	200	2 10 30	1 mo.
Ppt	9000	8000	-0-	30	1 mo.
06/8- Disc	16000	7500	-0-	2 10 30	2-3 mos.
05/8- Disc	9000	3800	-0-	2 10 30	1 mo.
Ppt	1500	-0-	-0-	30	1-2 mos.

③ FINANCE
06/22/8-

Fiscal statement dated May 31, 198-

Cash	$ 20,623	Acts Payable	$47,246
Accts Rec	55,777	Owing Bank	34,000
Merchandise	92,103	Notes Pay {Trucks}	7,020
Current	168,503	Current	88,266
Fixts. & Equip.	13,630	Common Stock	35,000
Trucks	8,000	Earned Surplus	66,867
Total Assets	$ 190,133	Total	$ 190,133

SALES {Yr}: $424,612. Net profit $17,105. Fire ins. mdse $95,000; equipt $20,000. Mo. rent: $3500. Prepared by Steige Co., CPAs, Detroit, MI.

—0—

06/22/8- Lawson defined monthly payments.* $3000 to bank, $400 on notes. Admitted collections slow but losses insignificant. Said inventory will drop to $60,000 by December. Expects 5% sales increase this year.

PUBLIC FILINGS
03/25/8-

March 17, 198- financing statement H741170 named subject as debtor and NCR Corp., Dayton, O. as secured party. Collateral: equipment.

05/28/8-

May 21, 198- suit for $200 entered by Henry Assoc., Atlanta, Ga. Docket H27519. Involves merchandise which Lawson says was defective.

④ BANKING
06/25/8-

Account, long maintained, carries average balances low to moderate five figures. Unsecured loans to moderate five extended and now open.

⑤ HISTORY
06/22/8-

CARL RETTINGER, PRES.   JOHN J. LAWSON, V. PRES.
DIRECTORS: The Officers
Incorporated Michigan February 2, 1950. Authorized capital 3500 shares, no par common. Paid in capital $35,000, officers sharing equally.
RETTINGER, born 1920, married. Employed by E-Z Paints, Detroit 12 yrs, five as manager until starting subject early 1950.
LAWSON, born 1925, married. Obtained accounting degree 1946 and then employed by Union Carbide, Chicago until joining Rettinger at inception.

⑥ OPERATION
06/22/8-

Wholesales paints and varnishes {85%}, wallpaper and supplies. 500 local accounts include retailers {75%} and contractors. Terms: 2 10 30. Peak season spring thru summer.
EMPLOYEES: Officers active with three others. LOCATION: Rents 7500 sq ft. one-story block structure, good repair.

THIS REPORT, FURNISHED PURSUANT TO CONTRACT FOR THE EXCLUSIVE USE OF THE SUBSCRIBER AS ONE FACTOR TO CONSIDER IN CONNECTION WITH CREDIT, INSURANCE, MARKETING OR OTHER BUSINESS DECISIONS, CONTAINS INFORMATION COMPILED FROM SOURCES WHICH DUN & BRADSTREET, INC. DOES NOT CONTROL AND WHOSE INFORMATION, UNLESS OTHERWISE INDICATED IN THE REPORT, HAS NOT BEEN VERIFIED. IN FURNISHING THIS REPORT, DUN & BRADSTREET, INC. IN NO WAY ASSUMES ANY PART OF THE USER'S BUSINESS RISK, DOES NOT GUARANTEE THE ACCURACY, COMPLETENESS, OR TIMELINESS OF THE INFORMATION PROVIDED, AND SHALL NOT BE LIABLE FOR ANY LOSS OR INJURY WHATEVER RESULTING FROM CONTINGENCIES BEYOND ITS CONTROL OR FROM NEGLIGENCE.

9 R2-25(750320)

Figure 10.2 A Dun & Bradstreet Business Information Report.

Source: Dun & Bradstreet, Inc., New York. By permission of Dun & Bradstreet Credit Services, a company of the Dun & Bradstreet Corporation.

TABLE 10.2
Risk Classes and
Expected Bad Debt
Experience

Risk Class	Expected Bad Debt Experience as a Percentage of Sales
A1–A3	0.0– 0.5%
B1–B3	0.5– 2.0
C1–C3	2.0– 5.0
D1–D3	5.0–10.0
F	Over 10

analysis on some type of risk classification scheme. These schemes center on placing customers in risk classes based on expected bad debt experience, such as those illustrated in Table 10.2. Credit classifications (A, B, C, D, F) can be subdivided by customer size and financial strength characteristics (1, 2, 3) in a fashion similar to the rating system used by Dun & Bradstreet.[5] Acceptable categories can be specified as part of the firm's credit policy; and once a customer's classification has been determined, the credit decision can be made. In addition, this scheme can be used to establish credit limits. One rule of thumb is that the maximum line of credit should not exceed 10 percent of D&B's estimated financial strength for the firm.

Credit Scoring.   While categorizing customers into risk classes should be tempered by judgment and experience, a strictly objective initial classification scheme is quite useful, especially for a firm dealing with a large number of new credit accounts. One such method is *credit scoring,* a quantitative procedure that results in a score representing the applicant's overall credit strength, and which is derived as a weighted average of the scores obtained on a variety of key financial and credit characteristics. The use of credit scoring is most prevalent when making consumer credit decisions in large credit card operations such as MasterCard, Sears, and Shell Oil, but the method can also be applied to mercantile credit decisions. Based on selected financial ratios, credit ratings, credit references, and so on, the credit scoring model assigns a quality rating to each applicant in the following way:

$$Y_i = a_1 X_{1i} + a_2 X_{2i} + \cdots + a_n X_{ni} \tag{10.1}$$

where Y_i = quality rating score for applicant i

a_j = predetermined weight attached to each financial and credit characteristic j $(j = 1, 2, \ldots n)$

$$\left(\sum_{j=1}^{n} a_j = 1.00 \right)$$

---

[5]The rating system used here is a simplified example of one any firm might develop for its own use. The Dun & Bradstreet ratings in Figure 10.1 are perhaps the most widely employed in actual credit decisions.

TABLE 10.3
Credit-Scoring Analysis
of Lowston Enterprises

Financial and Credit Characteristic	Value (1)	Score (0 to 100) (2)	Predetermined Weight (3)	Weighted Score [(2) × (3)] (4)
Current ratio	1.82	90	.15	13.50
Times interest earned	4.60×	80	.05	4.00
Net profit margin	3.32%	80	.05	4.00
D&B rating	3A3	70	.20	14.00
Payment history	Fair	75	.20	15.00
Credit references	Good	85	.25	21.25
Future business possibilities	Fair	75	.05	3.75
Other factors	Good	85	.05	4.25
Total			1.00	Credit score 79.75

SOURCES: Column 1: Obtained from credit information and the analyst's appraisal of it. Column 2: Scores assigned by the analyst using company guidelines on the basis of the values of each financial and credit characteristic given in column 1. As is customary, the scores range from 0 (the lowest) to 100 (the highest). Column 3: These weights are based on the company's analysis of the relative importance of each financial and credit characteristic in predicting whether or not a credit customer will pay its account. These weights must sum to 1.00.

$$X_{ji} = \text{financial and credit characteristic score}$$
$$\text{for } j \text{ received by applicant } i$$

To apply the credit scoring model, the analyst must provide scores for each of the applicant's financial and credit characteristics. The values for the weights are typically predetermined using discriminant analysis—a statistical technique that can be applied to historical data to determine the importance of various characteristics in predicting a given behavior.[6] (See Appendix 10A for a discussion of discriminant analysis.) Table 10.3 illustrates the application of credit scoring to data for Lowston Enterprises. Note that the credit analyst must calculate and/or obtain values for each financial and credit characteristic (column 1) and score these values (column 2). Then, by multiplying the scores by the predetermined weights indicating the relative importance of each characteristic to the credit decision (column 3), the weighted values are determined for each characteristic and summed to find the applicant's credit score (column 4). It should be clear from a comparison of Equation 10.1 and the calculation of Lowston Enterprises' credit score in Table 10.3 that Y_i is the resulting credit score of 79.75, the a_j coefficients in Equation 10.1 are the predetermined weights in column 3, and the X_{ji}s are the financial and credit characteristic scores in column 2.

By comparing the credit score to the firm's predetermined cutoff score, the credit decision can be made. For example, assume that the

[6]Discriminant analysis has become a widely recognized tool for evaluating credit and default risk. See Edward I. Altman, "Financial Ratios, Discriminant Analysis and the Prediction of Corporate Bankruptcy," *Journal of Finance* 23 (September 1968), pp. 589–609.

company evaluating Lowston Enterprises' financial data has a cutoff score of 75. This means any applicant with a score greater than 75 would be deemed an acceptable credit risk, whereas those with scores below 75 would be rejected. Sometimes a gray area will exist; for example, firms with scores of 65 to 75 might be further analyzed or extended a limited amount of credit. Clearly Lowston Enterprises would be an acceptable credit risk, since its score of 79.75 is above the cutoff rate. Of course, credit scores should be evaluated in light of some type of credit analysis to develop and establish credit limits. The judgment of the credit manager should come into play not only in scoring the applicant's financial and credit characteristics (see column 2 of Table 10.3), but also in making the ultimate credit decision.

Controlling Credit Terms

Credit terms specify the length of time for which credit will be extended and the amount of any cash discounts the firm may offer for early payment. A typical example is the 2/10 net 30 policy, which indicates that a 2 percent discount is given for payments made within 10 days and that the full invoice amount must be paid within 30 days. Credit terms may be very important in marketing the firm's products; certainly such terms affect the size of investment in the accounts receivable portfolio. Terms that shorten the collection period and increase the accounts receivable turnover tend to reduce both the firm's commitment of resources and level of sales; more liberal terms, in contrast, increase sales, slow the receivables turnover, and require an increased investment. A look at the turnover and aging of accounts receivable will give us a better sense of the routine management activities associated with controlling credit terms.

Accounts Receivable Turnover. For a given level of sales, the level of accounts receivable investment is directly related to the rate of receivables turnover. As noted in Chapter 3, the receivables turnover ratio is calculated by dividing annual sales by net accounts receivable. This ratio is influenced by credit standards, credit terms, and collection activities. The more restrictive the credit standards, the shorter the credit terms, and the more aggressive the collection activities, the slower the receivables turnover, and vice versa.

If all accounts were paid on time, a policy of net 30 days would imply that receivables are converted into cash on a monthly basis and that the receivables turnover ratio is 12 (360 days ÷ 30 days). Under such circumstances, the firm's average investment in receivables would be one-twelfth of annual credit sales. Although the actual amount of time required to convert receivables into cash is also a function of credit standards and collection activities, the stated credit terms do affect accounts receivable investment. Altering credit terms can affect the level of investment. For example, if a stated policy of net 30 days results in average collections running 40 days, the firm might evaluate offering a cash discount to encourage prompt payment. The decision would hinge on whether the cost of the discount is offset by the savings from the reduced receivables investment. Assume credit terms are changed from net 30 days to 2/10 net 30, and as a result the actual collection period is reduced from 40 to 30 days. The decision to make such a change would depend on the cost of funds for receivables investment compared to the cost of the cash discount.[7] Although it is important for the credit manager to understand these facets of behavior, routine activities concerned with credit terms tend to center on making sure that existing terms are correctly offered to all qualified credit customers.

Aging Accounts Receivable.   Even the best credit policies result in some bad debts, as well as slow payments from certain customers. These results tend to lead to slower than expected turnover and increased levels of accounts receivable investment. By analyzing past experiences in the collection of accounts receivable, the firm can assess all aspects of its credit policy in light of its credit terms and take any appropriate action. Accounts found to be long past due create more serious problems. Without careful analysis, the behavior of these "problem" accounts may be hidden in the average values used to calculate the accounts receivable turnover. In the aggregate, good accounts and early payments when discounts are offered may produce satisfactory turnover rates even though delinquent accounts exist. An *aging schedule*, which provides the analyst with a sense of the composition of accounts by showing the proportion of the accounts receivable balance[8] that has been outstanding for a given period of time, is the appropriate tool for investigating this possibility.

An example of an aging schedule for Alpert, Inc., a company with credit terms of 2/10 net 30, is shown in Table 10.4.[9] It can be seen that about 74 percent (46% + 28%) of its accounts are current (less than 30 days), with most of these less than 10 days old. Another 17 percent are zero to 30 days overdue, 6 percent are 31 to 60 days late, and the final 3 percent are more than 60 days overdue. In spite of the fact that the calculated average collection period is about 23 days, it should be clear

---

[7]Other factors, such as bad debt expenses and collection costs, might also be affected by a change in credit terms. These combination effects are considered in detail later in the chapter.

[8]Aging schedules can also be based on the percentage of the number of accounts, rather than account balances, outstanding for a given period of time. Like accounts receivable, an aging schedule can also be prepared for accounts payable.

[9]A more detailed breakdown of account age could easily be established if required. Also, where credit terms vary among product lines, aging schedules reflecting this factor are required to evaluate the age of the various accounts.

TABLE 10.4
Aging Schedule for
Alpert, Inc.

Aging Range	Dollar Amount in Accounts Receivable	Percentage of Total Accounts Receivable
10 days or less	$161,000	46%
11 to 30 days	98,000	28
31 to 60 days	59,500	17
61 to 90 days	21,000	6
Over 90 days	10,500	3
Totals	$350,000	100%

from the aging schedule that a number of slow-paying accounts exist. As a result, the firm should investigate the slower accounts to make sure that its credit policy is being correctly administered. Clearly, the use of an aging schedule adds to the knowledge gained from the accounts receivable turnover or average collection period data.

Collecting
Receivables

The firm's collection activity involves the application of certain routine procedures to collect past due accounts. The effectiveness of the collection operation is commonly evaluated by looking at the level of bad debt losses. This level depends not only on collection policies, but on the credit standards on which the extension of credit is based. If we assume the level of bad debts attributable to credit standards is relatively constant, increasing levels of collection expenditure would be expected to reduce the bad debts. This relationship between collection expenditures and bad debt losses is depicted in Figure 10.3. As the figure indicates, beyond point A additional collection expenditures will not reduce the firm's bad debt losses enough to justify the outlay of funds. The firm must therefore develop collection procedures that are cost effective.

Regardless of the level of collection activity, some bad debts are inevitable. Occasionally a customer will actually go into bankruptcy, and the firm will recover only a small part or none of the amount due. In such cases, a review of credit standards may be in order, but obviously no amount of additional collection effort will improve the situation. In other instances, the firm may choose to write off an uncollectible account by deducting (as an expense) the amount of the loss when calculating its taxable income.[10] By writing off the loss, the firm can avoid the costs as well as the problems associated with further collection

[10]The actual accounting treatment of bad debts involves the establishment of a reserve for bad debts against which actual bad debts are written off. The reserve is established by charging a prespecified "allowance for bad debts" against revenue each period; the amount of the allowance is based on the expected level of bad debts in the coming period. Technically, when a bad debt is actually recognized, it is charged against the reserve, not revenue; but since the reserve was established by making charges against revenue, the bad debt ultimately is treated as an expense.

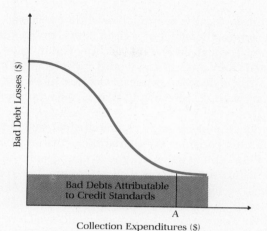

Figure 10.3   Collection Expenditures and Bad Debt Losses.

action. Especially in smaller firms, a direct writeoff is often preferred to pursuing collection activities that would force the customer into bankruptcy. The decision depends on the size of the account in relation to the additional costs associated with collection. Further evaluation and quantification of the tradeoffs involved when making collection decisions are presented later in the chapter.

Credit Policy Decision Making

In addition to the routine aspects of accounts receivable management, the financial manager must periodically make major credit policy decisions on the basis of an evaluation of the revenues and costs associated with a proposed action. Regardless of whether the decision involves credit standards, credit terms, or collection activities, the proposed action must provide benefits in excess of the additional costs incurred. When making these periodic policy decisions, management's objective should be to increase profits and control risks, and thus to enhance the value of the firm. Within this broad objective, the firm has considerable leeway in defining alternatives and actions. An analytical framework is needed to evaluate specific policy changes with respect to their impact on profits and risk exposure.

An Analytical Framework

The analytical model for making credit policy decisions must isolate the key revenue and cost variables, which include changes in sales contribution, changes in the cost of accounts receivable investment, changes in bad debt costs, and any changes in administrative costs.[11] By combining

---

[11]Estimating future sales, costs, and bad debt experience introduces the need for forecasting techniques and methods of dealing with uncertainty. These tools are discussed in Chapter 4.

and comparing the marginal revenue and cost resulting from a given policy action, the effect of a given action on profitability and risk can be assessed. For a given level of risk, any action increasing profits would be accepted, and any others would be rejected. Of course, if risk is not constant, the decision process becomes more complex. The judgment of the financial manager would play a major role in such a case.

Demand Considerations.   An analytical accounts receivable decision model must consider the demand elasticities (the degree of responsiveness of changes in sales volume to changes in the cost to the demander) of the firm's products, as well as competitive reaction to credit policy changes. A tightening of credit policy may increase the cost of the product to the customer, while a relaxation in credit policy may reduce this cost. For example, revenues could well increase by offering more attractive credit terms on a product with a relatively elastic demand; for a product with an inelastic demand, more attractive terms may not have much of an impact on sales revenues.

When evaluating credit policy decisions, the financial manager must consider the potential response of sales to the effective changes in cost. In addition, the manager must consider the response of competitors to the firm's actions. Potential benefits anticipated from a given credit policy change, such as relaxation of credit standards or offering more attractive credit terms, may not result if other suppliers alter their credit policies in response to the firm's actions. Careful examination of potential competitive responses is therefore important when analyzing credit policy changes.

Basic Tradeoffs.   The basic financial tradeoffs expected from key credit policy changes are summarized in Table 10.5. Comparing the two sides of each major area of credit policy in Table 10.5, we can see that clear-cut tradeoffs exist for sales, the level of accounts receivable investment, bad debts, various administrative costs, and risk exposure. Generally, more stringent policies reduce sales, costs, and risk exposure. In the case of certain administrative costs (such as investigation and collection costs) more aggressive policies may actually reduce sales and at the same time increase these costs.[12]

Basic Decision Model.   The basic decision criterion used to evaluate proposed credit policy actions involves the use of marginal analysis. By quantifying the basic tradeoffs, the marginal benefits and marginal costs associated with a proposed change in some aspect of credit policy can

---

[12]More stringent customer screening and tough collection policies may prevent some customers from being extended credit and drive away others in the collection process. The intended result, of course, is to reduce bad debt losses by more than the cost of lost sales and additional collection costs.

TABLE 10.5
Basic Financial
Tradeoffs for Key
Credit Policy Changes

Credit Standards	
Stringent	Lax
Reduced sales volume	Increased sales volume
Reduced receivables investment	Increased receivables investment
Reduced bad debts	Increased bad debts
Increased investigation costs	Reduced investigation costs
Reduced collection costs	Increased collection costs
Reduced risk exposure	Increased risk exposure
Credit Terms	
Severe	Liberal
Reduced sales volume	Increased sales volume
Reduced discount costs	Increased discount costs
Reduced receivables investment	Increased receivables investment
Reduced bad debts	Increased bad debts
Reduced risk exposure	Increased risk exposure
Collection Activities	
Aggressive	Passive
Reduced sales volume	Increased sales volume
Reduced receivables investment	Increased receivables investment
Reduced bad debts	Increased bad debts
Increased collection costs	Reduced collection costs
Reduced risk exposure	Increased risk exposure

be determined. After comparing marginal benefits and costs, the analyst would recommend a given action only if the marginal benefits exceed the marginal costs. In terms of the tradeoffs mentioned above, accounts receivable decisions can be made by answering either of the following two questions: (1) Are foregone sales and increased costs more than offset by the savings derived from more stringent policies? (2) Do increased sales and profits more than offset the costs and problems associated with less stringent policies? A yes answer to either question, assuming risk and other qualitative factors are favorable, suggests that the proposed action be undertaken, since the marginal benefits would exceed marginal costs.

Although the basic decision model is conceptually quite simple, its actual application is often difficult, for a variety of reasons. First of all, a large number of forecasted as well as historical variable values are required; the financial manager must therefore estimate the expected outcomes of proposed actions. Second, the equations differ depending on the specific policy action being evaluated—credit standards, credit terms, or collection activities. Finally, the analysis is generally not symmetrical; the equation used to evaluate a proposed action that results in the relaxation of credit policy differs from that used to evaluate the opposite action resulting in a tightening of credit policy. The

S_0 = Sales revenues under existing policies	\$10,000,000
A_0 = Accounts receivable under existing policies	\$ 1,250,000
$\overline{C}_0$ = Average collection period under existing policies	45 days
P_0 = Profit before taxes	\$ 1,000,000
D_0 = Cash discount percentage	0%
r = Opportunity cost of funds	15%
V = Variable cost as percentage of sales	80%
B_0 = Bad debt percentage for marginal customers	10%
$\overline{B}_0$ = Average bad debt percentage	4%
Stated credit terms	Net 30 days

nonsymmetrical nature of the equation tends to result from the fact that the responses of old and new customers to a given action must be treated individually.

Basic Illustrative Data.   Throughout the remainder of this section, we present the basic equations used to evaluate various credit policy decisions, using data for Bacon Machine, Inc. The key decisions illustrated concern credit standards, credit terms, and collection activities. Basic data for Bacon Machine are presented in Table 10.6.[13] The company is assumed to be operating under what its management considers a "moderate" credit policy. We will do a detailed analysis of more stringent and less stringent credit standards, as well as summarize the analysis of more stringent and more relaxed credit terms and collection activities.

Credit Standards   As a result of discussions with the marketing department, Bacon Machine's credit manager gathered the data on changes in credit standards summarized in Table 10.7. It was expected that switching from the present standard of accepting marginal customers with a 10 percent expected default rate (as specified by B_0 in Table 10.6) to standard A, with a 5 percent default rate for marginal customers, would reduce sales by \$1 million. Standard B, with a 15 percent expected default rate for marginal customers, should increase sales by \$1.5 million.

To evaluate the two policy alternatives, Bacon Machine needs to estimate the expected change in profits that would result from each. Given that Bacon currently operates above the breakeven point (\$1 million profit before taxes) and assuming there is excess capacity, only variable costs are relevant to the analysis.[14] The three areas that affect

[13]Some controversy exists regarding the exact nature of inputs into the accounts receivable decision model. In each policy area, the reader should keep in mind the marginal analysis procedure: The difference between an existing situation and the situation expected to exist after a policy change provides the relevant data for analysis. For an excellent discussion of the basic framework, see Edward A. Dyl, "Another Look at the Investment in Accounts Receivable," *Financial Management* 6 (winter 1977), pp. 67–70.

[14]Dyl, "Another Look," also provides an excellent discussion of cost factors relevant to the receivables decision.

TABLE 10.7
Proposed Credit
Standard Changes for
Bacon Machine

Standard A (More Stringent Standards)	Standard B (Less Stringent Standards)
Standard: Extend credit only to customers in risk classes with a 5% or lower expected default rate.	Standard: Extend credit to customers in risk classes with up to a 15% expected default rate.
S_m = Lost sales from eliminating marginal customers, − $1 million	S_n = New sales from extending credit to additional risk class, $1.5 million
C_m = Collection period for eliminated marginal customers, 60 days	C_n = Collection period for new customers, 75 days
B_m = Bad debt percentage for remaining marginal customers, 5%	B_n = Bad debt percentage for new customers, 15%

Bacon's profit in this case are these: (1) the level of sales and gross contribution margin, (2) the change in the receivables investment and the associated carrying costs, and (3) the change in bad debt costs. (Other factors such as collection expenditures might also change, but they are assumed to be constant for the moment.)

More Stringent Standards.   For the more stringent standard A:

Change in gross contribution margin, $S_m (1 - V)$:

$$= -\$1,000,000(1 - .80)$$
$$= -\$200,000$$

Change in receivables investment, I_m:

$$I_m = (C_m/360)(V)(S_m)$$
$$= (60/360)(.80)(-\$1,000,000)$$
$$= -\$133,333$$

Change in carrying costs, rI_m:[15]

$$= .15(-\$133,333)$$
$$= -\$20,000$$

---

[15]Because various credit policy decisions tend to commit the firm to long-run behaviors, a number of authors have suggested that credit policy decisions should be made using a present-value framework. (See Yong H. Kim and Joseph C. Atkins, "Evaluating Investments in Accounts Receivable: A Maximizing Framework," *Journal of Finance* 33 (May 1978), pp. 402–412.) While their suggestions are valid, a more recent article by Kanwal S. Sachdeva and Lawrence J. Gitman, "Accounts Receivable Decisions in a Capital Budgeting Framework," *Financial Management* 10 (winter 1981), pp. 45–49, has shown that the single-period decision rules presented by Dyl and applied throughout this chapter will provide correct accept-reject decisions without the computational rigor of the present-value approach.

Change in bad debt costs, $B_0 S_m$:

$$= .10(-\$1,000,000)$$
$$= -\$100,000$$

Combining the impact on all three areas, the net impact on profits, P_m, is:

$$P_m = S_m(1 - V) - r[(C_m/360)(V)(S_m)] - B_0 S_m \qquad (10.2)$$
$$= -\$200,000 - (-\$20,000) - (-\$100,000)$$
$$= -\$80,000$$

This result indicates that a shift to standard A would reduce profits by $80,000, and obviously should not be undertaken.

Less Stringent Standards.   The more relaxed standard B can be evaluated in a fashion similar to that used for standard A.

Change in gross contribution margin, $S_n(1 - V)$:

$$= \$1,500,000(1 - .80)$$
$$= \$300,000$$

Change in carrying costs, $r I_n$:

$$= r[(C_n/360)(V)(S_n)]$$
$$= .15[(75/360)(.80)(\$1,500,000)]$$
$$= \$37,500$$

Change in bad debt costs, $B_n S_n$:

$$= .15(\$1,500,000)$$
$$= \$225,000$$

Combining the three effects from standard B, the net impact on profits, P_n, is:

$$P_n = S_n(1 - V) - r[(C_n/360)(V)(S_n)] - B_n S_n \qquad (10.3)$$
$$= \$300,000 - \$37,500 - \$225,000$$
$$= \$37,500$$

Standard B, relaxing credit standards, appears to be worthwhile, since profits are increased by $37,500.

Credit Terms   Credit terms can be evaluated using the same type of analytical framework as that presented for credit standards. The key inputs as well as the basic behavioral assumptions are, however, somewhat

TABLE 10.8
Proposed Credit Period
Changes for Bacon
Machine

Credit Period A (Tighter Credit Terms)	Credit Period B (More Relaxed Credit Terms)
Policy: Net 20 days S_m = Lost sales, −$500,000 $\overline{C_m}$ = Average collection period, 30 days B_m = Bad debt percentage on lost sales, 10%	Policy: Net 45 days S_n = New sales, $500,000 $\overline{C_n}$ = Average collection period, 60 days B_n = Bad debt percentage on new sales, 12%

different. Changes in credit terms might involve both the length of the credit period and the magnitude of any cash discounts offered for early payment. Only changes in the credit period are illustrated here.[16] To demonstrate the impact of changing credit terms, we will again assume that Bacon Machine's current position is as reflected in Table 10.6, and that the company now wishes to evaluate the feasibility of tightening credit terms (credit period A) or offering more relaxed credit terms (credit period B). Unlike the marginal analysis utilized in the credit standards decision, an evaluation of credit terms must be based on the use of average values, since all customers are assumed to take full advantage of available terms; when more liberal terms are allowed, they are obviously available to existing as well as new customers.

The data in Table 10.8 represent the anticipated results of implementing tighter credit terms under credit period A or more relaxed credit terms under credit period B. In a fashion similar to the credit standards case, changes in credit terms may affect: (1) the level of sales and gross contribution margin, (2) the change in the receivables investment and the associated carrying costs, and (3) the change in bad debt costs. Several differences must be incorporated into the analysis, however; tightening credit terms is not analyzed using exactly the inverse of the procedures used to analyze relaxing credit terms. The key equations and results of analyzing the Bacon Machine data are summarized in Table 10.9. The results in Table 10.9 indicate that the firm's expected profits would be enhanced by shortening (credit period A) rather than lengthening (credit period B) the credit period. If the analysis had considered the possible inclusion of cash discounts for early payment, the discount cost would have been treated as an additional element in the analytical scheme illustrated here.

Collection
Activities

Changes in the level of collection activity may affect sales, investment in receivables, and level of bad debts. Direct costs associated with collections are incorporated into the firm's total variable cost percentage. If a

---

[16]For a thorough analysis of cash discount decisions, the interested reader should see Ned C. Hill and Kenneth D. Riener, "Determining the Cash Discount in the Firm's Credit Policy," *Financial Management* 8 (spring 1979), pp. 68–73.

TABLE 10.9
Analysis of Credit
Term Changes for
Bacon Machine

TIGHTER CREDIT TERMS (CREDIT PERIOD A)
Change in gross contribution margin:

$$S_m(1 - V) = -\$500,000 \ (1 - .80) = -\$100,000$$

Change in receivables investment:

$$I_m = [(\overline{C_m} - \overline{C_0})/360](S_0 + S_m) + [(\overline{C_0}/360)(V)(S_m)]$$
$$= [(30 - 45)/360](\$10,000,000 - \$500,000) + [(45/360)(.80)(-\$500,000)]$$
$$= -\$395,833 - \$50,000 = -\$445,833$$

Change in carrying costs:

$$rI_m = .15 \ (-\$445,833) = -\$66,875$$

Change in bad debt costs:

$$B_m S_m = .10 \ (-\$500,000) = -\$50,000$$

Net impact on profits, P_m:

$$P_m = S_m(1 - V) - rI_m - B_m S_m \qquad (10.4)$$
$$= -\$100,000 - (-\$66,875) - (-\$50,000) = \$16,875$$

MORE RELAXED CREDIT TERMS (CREDIT PERIOD B)
Change in gross contribution margin:

$$S_n \ (1 - V) = \$500,000 \ (1 - .80) = \$100,000$$

Change in receivables investment:

$$I_n = [(\overline{C_n} - \overline{C_0})/360]S_0 + [(\overline{C_n}/360)(V)(S_n)]$$
$$= [(60 - 45)/360] \ \$10,000,000 + [(60/360)(.80)(\$500,000)]$$
$$= \$416,667 + \$66,667 = \$483,334$$

Change in carrying costs:

$$rI_n = .15(\$483,334) = \$72,500$$

Change in bad debt costs:

$$B_n S_n = .12 \ (\$500,000) = \$60,000$$

Net impact on profits, P_n:

$$P_n = S_n(1 - V) - rI_n - B_n S_n \qquad (10.5)$$
$$= \$100,000 - \$72,500 - \$60,000 = -\$32,500$$

particular collection program (such as hiring new collectors) substantially changes costs, the variable cost percentage would change. Alternatively, for computational purposes, incremental costs can be incorporated directly into the analytical model. Such a model would be identical to the one for credit standard decisions, except that it would include a collection cost term. Letting A equal the change in collection cost, the additional profit from increased collection activity, P_m, can be expressed by subtracting A from Equation 10.2 for the profit from more stringent standards:

$$P_m = S_m (1 - V) - r[(C_m/360)(V)(S_m)] - B_0 S_m - A \qquad (10.6)$$

In a similar fashion, the additional profit from a reduction in collection activity, P_n, can be expressed by subtracting A from Equation 10.3 for the profit from less stringent standards:

$$P_n = S_n (1 - V) - r[(C_n/360)(V)(S_n)] - B_n S_n - A \qquad (10.7)$$

Using the same basic variable definitions presented in earlier discussions, these equations, by considering additional revenues and costs, provide an efficient and effective means for evaluating proposed changes in collection activity.

Combined Credit Policy Decisions

The preceding discussion has shown that individual credit policy decisions can be evaluated using straightforward analytical procedures that compare marginal revenue with marginal cost. Unfortunately, policy decisions involving a combination of credit standard, credit term, and collection activity changes are more difficult to analyze quantitatively. The added difficulty stems from the need to estimate the combined effect of the proposed actions on each financial variable—level of sales and gross contribution margin, cost of accounts receivable investment, and bad debt costs and collection expenditures. Using estimates of these variables, the decision rule, of course, continues to be as follows: Accept all proposals for which marginal benefits exceed marginal costs. The important point to recognize is that because of the uncertainties surrounding actual outcomes as well as combined effects, credit policy decisions require a great deal of managerial judgment and expertise.

Inventory Management

Inventories are made up of the firm's stock of raw materials, work in process, and finished goods. They provide the basis for increased production and sales. As Table 10.1 shows, inventory, like accounts receivable, represents a significant investment on the part of most firms. In Chapter 9, we noted the importance of turning inventory over quickly to minimize investment. This financial objective often conflicts with that of carrying sufficient inventories to satisfy production demands and minimize stockouts. The firm must determine the "optimal" level of inventories that reconciles these conflicting objectives. Also, because obsolescence can severely reduce the value of inventories in many business areas, careful control of inventory is needed to avoid potential major losses in asset values. This aspect is crucial for small firms, since an inability to convert inventories to cash can result in bank loan defaults and possibly bankruptcy. The financial manager, however, does not control inventory directly and therefore tends to have only indirect input into inventory management. Here we will look at the aspects of inventory that concern the financial manager: that is, at the amount invested in inventory, the relationship between inventory and accounts receivable management, and several popular techniques for controlling inventory.

Investing in Inventory

As in all other areas of the firm, inventory management is directed toward enhancing returns and controlling risks, and thus increasing owners' wealth. Like accounts receivable, the investment in inventory must be evaluated in terms of associated revenues and costs—additional investment must be justified by additional profits. From a financial point of view, constraining inventory levels enhances profitability by releasing funds to be used in more profitable investments. From production and marketing perspectives, however, expanding inventories provides for smooth production runs, good product selection, and prompt delivery schedules. These often conflicting objectives must be properly balanced when implementing a successful inventory management system.

Basic Tradeoffs. Firms that operate with low levels of inventory risk losing sales due to stockouts and production delays. Firms that hold large inventories can provide prompt shipment of orders and can often take advantage of quantity shipments when unexpectedly large product demand arises. The tradeoff is that large inventories result in sizable carrying costs in the form of bank interest, foregone earnings in other areas of the firm, storage and insurance fees, and potential obsolescence. Costs associated with minimal inventories include potential stockouts and production interruptions, and high administrative costs associated with frequent replacement of inventory supplies.[17]

The financial manager should consider several specific factors in designing an inventory management system. On the asset side of the balance sheet, inventories represent an important short-term investment. At a given level of sales and profit margin, smaller inventory levels increase overall asset turnover, which in turn increases return on investment (ROI). More rapid inventory turnover also reduces the potential for obsolescence and the attendant price reductions that reduce profit margins. On the liability side of the balance sheet, sources of financing inventories must be considered. The firm's basic raw materials are often financed with accounts payable having no explicit

---

[17]Although costs associated with inventories will be divided into these two specific categories, some costs and benefits, such as in the production and marketing areas, are considered only subjectively in the remainder of the chapter.

interest cost. For manufactured and purchased finished goods, however, short-term bank loans are a typical source of funds for at least a portion of the operating cycle. In either case, better control of inventories and more rapid conversion into cash reduces financial costs, either by providing funds to take advantage of cash discounts offered by suppliers, or by directly reducing bank interest costs.

The basic financial tradeoff associated with inventory investment can be illustrated with an example. Hartman Manufacturing is contemplating making larger production runs to reduce the high setup costs associated with production of its only product. The total annual savings in setup costs is estimated at $20,000. Currently inventory is turning over six times a year; with the proposed larger production runs, the inventory turnover is expected to drop to four times. If the cost of goods sold of $1.2 million is unaffected by this proposal, and assuming the firm's required return on equal-risk investments is 25 percent, the analysis would be performed as shown in Table 10.10. It can be seen that an additional $100,000 will have to be invested in inventory, which will cost the firm $25,000 per year. Clearly, the proposed system should be rejected, since the $25,000 annual cost is greater than the $20,000 annual savings. This illustration should make it clear that the higher the average level of inventory, the larger the dollar investment required, and vice versa. Only when the savings exceed the costs of additional inventory investment (assuming no change in risk) should a proposed action be undertaken.

Accounting for Inventory Investment. The actual investment in inventory as reflected on the firm's balance sheet is affected by the method used to account for inventory. The two extreme methods are first-in,

TABLE 10.10		
Analysis of Inventory Investment for Hartman Manufacturing		

ANALYSIS

Average investment in inventory[a]

Proposed system	$\dfrac{\$1,200,000}{4} =$	$300,000
Present system	$\dfrac{\$1,200,000}{6} =$	200,000
Increased inventory investment		$100,000
× required return		.25
Annual cost of increased inventory investment		$ 25,000

DECISION

Since this annual cost ($25,000) is greater than the annual savings in setup costs ($20,000), the proposed system should be rejected.

[a]The average investment in inventory is calculated using the following formula:

$$\frac{\text{Average inventory}}{\text{investment}} = \frac{\text{cost of goods sold}}{\text{inventory turnover}}$$

The formula is derived from the formula for inventory turnover, cost of goods sold/inventory, given in Chapter 3.

first-out, and last-in, first-out; a third method, which reflects a compromise between the two, is the average cost method. Under *first-in, first-out (FIFO)*, the earliest costs of inventory are assigned to the cost of goods sold, while under *last-in, first-out (LIFO)*, the costs of the most recently purchased items are assigned to the cost of goods sold. Under the *average cost method*, a weighted cost per unit is computed and used to determine the cost of goods sold. Assume a firm had two items of inventory—one purchased January 1 for $5 and the other purchased on March 1 for $7. Under FIFO, when the first of these items is charged to sales it will be charged at $5; under LIFO, $7 would be charged to sales; and under the average cost method, $6 [or ($5 + $7)/2] would be charged to sales.

The key points to recognize for each of these inventory costing methods are that in an inflationary economy (rising prices and costs):

1. FIFO results in the highest ending inventory value and the lowest cost of goods sold. Therefore, FIFO results in the highest net income.
2. LIFO results in the lowest ending inventory value and the highest cost of goods sold. LIFO therefore results in the lowest net income.
3. The average cost method results in ending inventory values and cost of goods sold that are always somewhere between FIFO and LIFO.

Of course, in a period of declining prices and costs, the opposite impact would result in each case. Because in the recent past increasing prices tended to be the norm, LIFO has been preferred since it raises costs, lowers profits, and thereby reduces the firm's tax payments. LIFO also keeps the firm's inventory investment to a minimum during inflationary periods, since as much of these costs as possible are charged to income and are thereby recovered by the firm through a reduced level of cash outflow for taxes.

The Relationship Between Inventory and Accounts Receivable Management

The level and management of inventory and accounts receivable are closely related. In the case of manufacturing firms, when an item is sold, it generally moves from inventory to accounts receivable and ultimately to cash. Because of the close relationship between these current assets, the inventory management and accounts receivable management functions should not be viewed as independent of each other. For example, the decision to extend credit to a customer can result in an increased level of sales, which can be supported only by higher levels of inventory and accounts receivable. The credit terms extended will also affect the investment in inventory and receivables, since longer credit terms may allow a firm to move items from inventory to accounts receivable. Generally there is an advantage to such a strategy, since the cost of carrying an item in inventory is greater than the cost of carrying an account receivable. This is true because the cost of carrying inventory includes, in addition to the required return on the invested funds, costs such as storage and insurance.

The basic relationship between inventory and accounts receivable can be illustrated with a simple example. The Maxwell Company estimates the annual cost of carrying $1 of merchandise in inventory for a 1-year period is $.25, while the annual cost of carrying $1 of receivables is $.15. The firm currently maintains average inventories of $300,000 and an average investment in accounts receivable of $200,000. Maxwell believes that by altering credit terms, it can cause its customers to purchase in larger quantities on the average, thereby reducing its average inventories to $150,000 and increasing the average investment in accounts receivable to $350,000. The altered credit terms are not expected to generate new business; they result only in a shift in purchasing and payment patterns. The costs of the present and proposed systems, calculated in Table 10.11, indicate that by shifting $150,000 of inventory cost to accounts receivable investment, Maxwell is able to lower the cost of carrying inventory and accounts receivable from $105,000 to $90,000—a $15,000 addition to profits. This profit is achieved without changing the $500,000 total level of average inventory and accounts receivable investment. Rather, the profit is attributed to a shift in the mix of these current assets so that a larger portion is held in the form of accounts receivable, which are less costly to hold than inventory.

Inventory—especially finished goods—and accounts receivable are therefore closely related. The relationship is affected by decisions made in all areas of the firm—finance, marketing, manufacturing, and purchasing. The financial manager should consider the interactions between inventory and accounts receivable when developing strategies for and making decisions about the production-sales process. Recognition of this interaction is especially important in credit decisions, since the required as well as the actual levels of inventory will be directly affected.

Techniques for Controlling Inventory

A variety of techniques, such as the ABC system, the basic economic order quantity (EOQ) model, and reorder points and safety stock, are commonly used for controlling inventory. Although these techniques are

TABLE 10.11
Analysis of
Inventory–Accounts
Receivable Systems for
the Maxwell Company

Account	Cost Per Dollar (1)	Present		Proposed	
		Average Balance (2)	Cost [(1) × (2)] (3)	Average Balance (4)	Cost [(1) × (4)] (5)
Average inventories investment	.25	$300,000	$ 75,000	$150,000	$37,500
Average receivables investment	.15	200,000	30,000	350,000	52,500
Total		$500,000	$105,000	$500,000	$90,000

not aimed at strictly financial matters, it is helpful for the financial manager to understand them.

The ABC System.   A firm using the *ABC system* segregates its inventory into three groups, A, B, and C. The A items are those in which it has the largest dollar investment. In Figure 10.4, which depicts a typical distribution of inventory items, this group consists of 20 percent of the inventory items but account for 90 percent of the firm's dollar investment. These are the most costly items of inventory. The B group consists of the items accounting for the next largest investment. In Figure 10.4, the B group consists of 30 percent of the items accounting for about 8 percent of the firm's dollar investment. The C group typically consists of a large number of items accounting for a small dollar investment. In Figure 10.4, the C group consists of approximately 50 percent of all items of inventory, but accounts for only about 2 percent of the firm's dollar investment. Such items as screws, nails, and washers would be in this group.

Dividing its inventory into A, B, and C groups allows the firm to determine the level and types of inventory control procedures needed. Control of the A items should be most intensive due to the high dollar investments involved, whereas the B and C items would be subject to correspondingly less sophisticated procedures.

The Basic Economic Order Quantity (EOQ) Model.   One of the most commonly mentioned tools for determining the optimal order quantity for an item of inventory is the *economic order quantity (EOQ) model*. This model could be used to control the firm's high ticket inventory items (like those mentioned in Group A above). It takes into account various operating and financial costs and determines the order quantity that

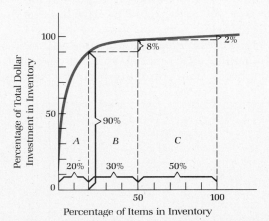

Figure 10.4   Applying the ABC System to a Typical Distribution of Inventory Items.

minimizes overall inventory costs. Our discussion of the economic order quantity model will cover basic costs, a graphic approach, and a mathematical approach.

Basic Costs.   Excluding the actual cost of the merchandise, the costs associated with inventory can be divided into three broad groups— order costs, carrying costs, and total cost. Each has certain key components and characteristics.

Order Costs.   Order costs include the fixed clerical costs of placing and receiving an order—the cost of writing a purchase order, of processing the resulting paperwork, and of receiving an order and checking it against the invoice. Order costs are normally stated as dollars per order.

Carrying Costs.   Carrying costs are the variable costs per unit of holding an item in inventory for a specified time period. These costs are typically stated as dollars per unit per period. Carrying costs have a number of components, such as storage costs, insurance costs, the cost of deterioration and obsolescence, and most important, the opportunity cost of tying up funds in inventory. The opportunity cost is the financial cost component; it is the value of the returns that have been foregone (in equal-risk investments) in order to have the current investment in inventory. A commonly cited rule of thumb suggests that the cost of carrying an item in inventory for 1 year represents approximately 20 percent to 25 percent—and even as much as 30 percent—of the cost (value) of the item.

Total Cost.   The total cost of inventory is defined as the sum of the order and carrying costs. Total cost is important in the EOQ model, since the model's objective is to determine the order quantity that minimizes it.

A Graphic Approach.   The stated objective of the EOQ model is to find the order quantity that minimizes total inventory cost.[18] The economic order quantity can be found graphically by plotting order quantities on the X axis and costs on the Y axis. Figure 10.5 shows the general behavior of these costs. The minimum total cost occurs at the point labeled *EOQ.* The EOQ occurs at the point where the order cost line and the carrying cost line intersect; since this is always true for this model when the costs are defined as strictly fixed and strictly variable,[19] the mathematical calculations required to determine the EOQ are quite simple.

---

[18]The EOQ method is applied to other situations where the firm wishes to minimize a total cost with fixed and variable components. It is commonly used to determine optimal production quantities when there is a fixed setup cost and a variable operating cost. The EOQ model is the same as Baumol's model, demonstrated in Chapter 9, for determining the optimum cash conversion quantity in the cash–marketable security decision process.

[19]In situations where one or more of the component costs has both fixed and variable elements, the EOQ will likely not occur at the point of intersection of the order cost and carrying cost lines. To simplify this presentation, only the situation where order cost is strictly fixed and carrying cost is strictly variable is considered.

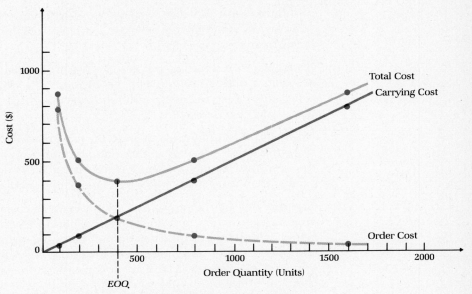

Figure 10.5   A Graphic Presentation of an EOQ.

It is important to recognize the nature of the cost functions in Figure 10.5. The order cost function varies inversely with the order quantity. In other words, as order quantity increases, the order cost for the period decreases. This can be explained by the fact that, since the annual usage is fixed, if larger amounts are ordered, fewer orders and therefore lower order costs per unit are incurred. Carrying costs are directly related to order quantities. The larger the order quantity, the larger the average inventory and therefore the higher the firm's carrying cost. The total cost function exhibits a U shape, which means that a minimum value for the function exists. The total cost line represents the sum of the order costs and carrying costs for each order quantity. Within a range of plus or minus 20 percent of the EOQ, the total cost function is quite flat, indicating that total cost is relatively insensitive to small shifts away from the EOQ.

A Mathematical Approach.   A formula can be developed for determining the firm's EOQ for a given inventory item. By letting

$$S = \text{usage in units per period}$$
$$O = \text{order cost per order}$$
$$C = \text{carrying cost per unit per period}$$
$$Q = \text{order quantity in units}$$

the firm's total cost equation can be developed. The first step in deriving the total cost equation is to develop an expression for the order cost function and the carrying cost function. The order cost can be expressed as the product of the cost per order and the number of orders. Since the number of orders equals the usage during the period divided by the order quantity (S/Q), the order cost can be expressed as follows:

$$\text{Order cost} = O \times S/Q \qquad (10.8)$$

The carrying cost is defined as the cost of carrying a unit per period multiplied by the firm's average inventory $(Q/2)$. The average inventory is defined as the order quantity divided by 2, since inventory is assumed to be depleted at a constant rate. Thus, the carrying cost can be expressed as follows:

$$\text{Carrying cost} = C \times Q/2 \qquad (10.9)$$

Analyzing Equations 10.8 and 10.9 shows that as the order quantity, Q, increases, the order cost will decrease while the carrying cost increases proportionately.

The total cost equation is obtained by combining the order cost and carrying cost expressions in Equations 10.8 and 10.9, as follows:

$$\text{Total cost} = (O \times S/Q) + (C \times Q/2) \qquad (10.10)$$

Since the EOQ is defined as the order quantity that minimizes the total cost function, Equation 10.10 must be solved for the EOQ.[20] The following formula results:

$$EOQ = \sqrt{\frac{2SO}{C}} \qquad (10.11)$$

---

[20]The solution can be found by taking the first derivative of Equation 10.10 with respect to Q and setting it equal to zero and solving for Q, the EOQ, or by setting the order cost equal to the carrying cost and solving for Q, as demonstrated below. See note 19 for further clarification.

$$O \times \frac{S}{Q} = C \times \frac{Q}{2}$$

(1) Multiply both sides by Q $\qquad O \times S = C \times \frac{Q^2}{2}$

(2) Multiply both sides by 2 $\qquad 2OS = C \times Q^2$

(3) Divide both sides by C $\qquad \dfrac{2OS}{C} = Q^2$

(4) Take the square root of both sides $\qquad \sqrt{\dfrac{2SO}{C}} = Q = EOQ$

For a firm that annually uses 1600 units of an item, has order costs of $50 per order, and has carrying costs of $1 per unit per year, substituting $S = 1600$, $O = \$50$, and $C = \$1$ into Equation 10.11 yields an EOQ of 400 units:

$$EOQ = \sqrt{\frac{2 \times 1600 \times \$50}{\$1}} = \sqrt{160,000} = 400 \text{ units}$$

If the firm orders in quantities of 400 units, it will minimize its total inventory cost. A review of Equation 10.11 should make it clear that the economic order quantity is an increasing function of sales and ordering costs and a decreasing function of carrying costs.

Reorder Points and Safety Stock.   The EOQ model assumes that inventory usage follows the "sawtooth" pattern shown in Figure 10.6(a). It can be seen that the firm orders 400 units (its assumed EOQ) and uses them at a constant rate of 20 per day (400 units ÷ 20 days) and instantaneously on day 20, when the stock is exhausted, a new order of 400 additional units is received. This approach implies perfect certainty for both product usage and delivery from suppliers.

To allow for uncertainty of demand and shipment time from suppliers, reorder points and safety stocks are typically established. Figure 10.6(b) illustrates the modifications produced by these adjustments to the model. Assuming a constant rate of inventory usage, a reorder point is simple to compute, using the following equation:

$$\text{Reorder point} = \text{lead time in days} \times \text{daily usage} \qquad (10.12)$$

With the usage of 20 units per day in Figure 10.6 and assuming that typical delivery time averages 3 days, a reorder point of 60 units should be maintained. If the firm's demand for the product could double or the delivery time could double, the firm must maintain a safety stock, as shown in Figure 10.6(b), to provide for these contingencies. In the illustration, the safety stock was set at 100 units, which represents 5 days of inventory at the normal usage rate. This value would be determined by an analysis of the probabilities of increased usage rates and delivery delays, coupled with a comparison of the cost of carrying the safety stock versus the cost of lost sales resulting from potential stockouts of inventory.[21]

---

[21]For in-depth discussions of inventory models, see Frank S. Budnick, Richard Mojena, and Thomas E. Vollmann, *Principles of Operations Research for Management* (Homewood, Ill.: Irwin, 1977), chap. 11; G. Hadley and T. M. Whitin, *Analysis of Inventory Systems* (Englewood Cliffs, N.J.: Prentice-Hall, 1963); and Harvey M. Wagner, *Principles of Operations Research—with Applications for Managerial Decisions* (Englewood Cliffs, N.J.: Prentice-Hall, 1975).

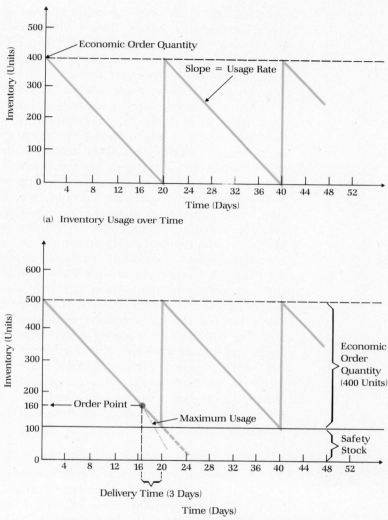

(a) Inventory Usage over Time

(b) Inventory Usage over Time with Order Points and Safety Stock

Figure 10.6   Inventory Usage, Order Point, and Safety Stock.

SUMMARY

The two dominant current assets—accounts receivable and inventory—represent sizable investments by the firm and therefore should be quickly turned into cash while maintaining an adequate level of service. Credit policy involves routine management as well as periodic decision making. It includes credit standards, credit terms, and collection activity, and requires a balancing of returns from additional sales against the cost of accounts receivable investment, bad debt losses, and administration, as well as the risks associated with a given action. Credit standard decisions center on selecting credit customers—often with the aid of credit scoring—and establishing credit limits using information gathered from a variety of sources. Credit terms influence the marketability of a firm's products by establishing the repayment requirements for credit customers. In general, liberal credit terms improve sales while increasing receivables investment, bad debts, and risk, and vice versa. Accounts receivable turnover as well as aging accounts receivable are often used to evaluate the effectiveness of the firm's credit terms. Collection activities, which involve the type and degree of effort expended to collect overdue accounts, likewise involve tradeoffs between revenues and costs. Of course, any uncollectible account can be written off by charging the amount of the loss to the reserve for bad debts.

The financial manager, who has only a watchdog role in the management of inventory, must make sure that the amount of money tied up in inventory—raw materials, work in process, and finished goods—is justified by the returns generated from such investment. Of course, the actual investment in inventory is affected by the accounting procedures —FIFO, LIFO, or average cost—used. The relationship between inventory and accounts receivable must also be considered when making production-sale decisions, since it is less expensive to carry accounts receivable than inventory. Several techniques are used to control inventory. The ABC system is aimed at determining which inventory items require the most attention. One of the most popular techniques for determining optimal order quantities is the economic order quantity (EOQ) model. Once the optimal order quantity has been determined, the reorder point and level of safety stock can be set to allow for the uncertainty associated with usage rates and the lead times required to fill orders.

QUESTIONS

10.1. Compare and contrast credit standards and credit terms. How can credit standards and credit terms affect the amount invested in receivables and the return on such investments?

10.2. The management of receivables involves both routine and episodic activities. Contrast and discuss the nature of these activities as they relate to each aspect of credit policy: (1) credit standards, (2) credit terms, and (3) collection activities.

10.3. Explain why it is important to perform credit analysis on prospective customers even though a firm has well-established credit standards.
    a. What role could credit scoring play in this process? Explain.
    b. Is it necessary to perform credit analysis on existing customers? Explain.

10.4. Contrast aging accounts receivable with the accounts receivable turnover or average collection period. Are they perfect substitutes for each other? Explain.

10.5. What key variables should be considered when evaluating possible changes in the firm's credit policy? Briefly explain the possible effects of a more restrictive credit policy on:

a. Sales volume.

b. Average collection period.

c. Investment in receivables.

d. Cost of receivables investment.

e. Bad debt costs.

10.6. What role does the firm's required return on investment play in the analytical scheme used to evaluate credit policy decisions?

10.7. Why must demand elasticities and the possible actions of competitors be considered when evaluating changes in credit policy? Use an increase in the cash discount to illustrate how these two variables can affect the benefits and costs of a pending credit policy change.

10.8. The LaBonte Manufacturing Company is presently conducting an in-depth evaluation of its receivables portfolio. (The firm's credit terms currently are 2/10 net 30). It is considering a number of actions to improve its return from the funds invested in receivables. Briefly describe the probable impact on the level of receivables and on the firm's profits from each of the following actions:

a. All accounts not paid within a 45-day period will be placed on a cash on delivery (COD) basis.

b. Eliminate all customers having low (or unsatisfactory) credit scores.

c. Improve the appeal of the cash discount by changing the credit terms to 3/15 net 30.

d. Begin offering extended credit terms to large-volume customers.

10.9. What is the financial manager's primary role with respect to the management of inventory? Why is it important for the financial manager to understand production-oriented inventory control techniques? Explain how controlling the investment in inventory can affect the profitability of the firm.

10.10. What tradeoff confronts the financial manager in relation to inventory turnover, inventory cost, and stockouts?

a. In what sense can inventory be viewed as an investment?

b. What effect does the inventory accounting method—FIFO, LIFO, or average cost—have on the level of inventory investment? Explain.

10.11. Briefly describe the relationship between inventory and accounts receivable. What impact would an easing of credit standards and a lengthening of credit terms have on the levels of inventory and receivables? Explain.

10.12. Describe the objective as well as basic assumptions of the EOQ model.

    a. Explain how the model works and to what group of inventory items it is most applicable.

    b. Explain how and why the firm must establish a reorder point and safety stock once the EOQ has been determined.

PROBLEMS

10.1. *INVESTING IN RECEIVABLES.* Murray Machine Products has annual credit sales of $3.6 million, and an average collection period of about 45 days (assume a 360-day year).

    a. What is the firm's average accounts receivable balance?

    b. If the cost of products is 85 percent of sales, what is the average investment in receivables?

    c. Using an 18 percent interest rate, find the opportunity cost of the firm's average investment in accounts receivable.

10.2. *CREDIT SCORING.* The credit manager for Eiteman and Sons is trying to decide whether or not to extend credit to two new applicants—Frankfort Company and Traverse Enterprises. An analysis of the credit information gathered on each of the companies resulted in the credit scores (on a scale of 0 to 100) for key financial and credit characteristics given below.

	Credit Scores	
Financial and Credit Characteristic	Frankfort	Traverse
Credit references	70	85
Current ratio	90	90
D&B rating	80	95
Fixed payment coverage	75	90
Growth potential	70	50
Net working capital	90	85
Payment history	75	90
Profitability	90	80
Other	80	85

Based on a detailed analysis of the financial and credit characteristics and payment behavior of their credit customers over the past 10 years, Eiteman and Sons feels the following weights reflect the importance of each characteristic in predicting whether a credit applicant is an acceptable risk.

    a. Using the data given, determine the credit score for Frankfort Company and Traverse Enterprises.

    b. If Eiteman and Sons credit standards provide for extending

Financial Characteristic	Weight
Credit references	.20
Current ratio	.10
D&B rating	.10
Fixed payment coverage	.10
Growth potential	.05
Net working capital	.05
Payment history	.25
Profitability	.05
Other	.10
Total	1.00

credit only to those firms having credit scores of 80 or more, what recommendation would you make relative to the two applicants?

c. Describe the pros and cons of using credit scoring to make accept-reject credit decisions. How might Eiteman and Sons modify or supplement this procedure to make better credit decisions? Explain.

10.3. *AGING OF RECEIVABLES.* Southwest Consolidated generates sales of $100 million per year. Recently, the credit manager, Julie Hall, was evaluating the firm's accounts receivable position; she received the latest (month-end) aging of accounts receivable, which appeared as follows:

Aging Range	Dollar Amount in Accounts Receivable	Percentage of Total Accounts Receivable
Current (0–30 days)	$ 7,000,000	50%
1 month late (31–60 days)	3,500,000	25
2 months late (61–90 days)	2,100,000	15
Past due 3 months or more (91 days or more)	1,400,000	10
Total	$14,000,000	100%

a. Use the aging report to find the average collection period. (*Hint:* Use distribution midpoints and 100 days for accounts that are past due 3 months or more.)

b. Now use the total accounts receivable balance (of $14 million) and the average collection period formula (see Chapter 3) to compute the average collection period. Is this value different from (a)?

c. Which average collection period measure is better? Explain.

d. From a managerial perspective, is it the composition (aging) of receivables, or the level of receivables that matters? Explain.

e. Using a 15 percent opportunity cost rate, and assuming no change in the level of sales, what benefits (if any) would accrue to the firm if it could move toward the following aging schedule?

Aging Range	Dollar Amount in Accounts Receivable
Current	$ 8,400,000
1 month late	3,500,000
2 months late	1,400,000
Past due 3 months or more	700,000
Total	$14,000,000

10.4. *CHANGING CREDIT STANDARDS.* The Cleary Company currently sells $180 million of its finished product; its variable costs represent 90 percent of sales. Its average collection period is 40 days, and its bad debt percentage for the marginal customer is 8 percent of sales. The firm, which has a required return on investment of 20 percent, wishes to evaluate two credit standard policy proposals:

Credit Standard Policy 1: This policy involves tightening credit standards by extending credit to only the most creditworthy customers. As a result of this policy, sales would decline by $10 million; the average collection period on eliminated customers would be 72 days; and the bad debts for remaining marginal customers would be 4 percent of sales.

Credit Standard Policy 2: This policy involves a relaxation of credit standards resulting in an increase in sales by $12 million, an average collection period on new customers of 80 days, and a bad debt percentage of 10 percent of sales for new customers.

a. Calculate the net profit (loss) expected to result from implementation of credit standard policy 1.

b. Calculate the net profit (loss) expected to result from implementation of credit standard policy 2.

c. Which, if either, of the proposed credit policies would you recommend Cleary implement? Explain.

d. Rework (a) through (c), assuming the variable cost rate is 75 percent of sales and all other values remain unchanged. Describe and explain the effect, if any, of this change on your earlier analysis.

10.5. *CHANGING CREDIT TERMS.* The Bell-Aire Company is considering lengthening its credit period from net 30 to net 45 days. All accounts pay on the net date. The firm currently bills $450,000 in sales, has $345,000 in variable costs, and $45,000 in fixed costs. The proposed credit period change is expected to increase sales to $510,000. Bad debt expenses on old customers will remain at 1 percent; for the new customers, it will be 1.5 percent. The firm has a required rate of return on investments of 15 percent.

a. What change in gross contribution margin is expected to result from the proposed change?

b. What change in the cost of financing the investment in accounts receivable and bad debt costs will result from the proposal?

c. Would you recommend that Bell-Aire implement the proposed lengthening of its credit period? Why or why not?

10.6. *DROPPING A CASH DISCOUNT.* Ben Gentle is the financial manager for a large industrial products firm. His analysis of accounts receivable has disclosed that while the firm offers a 3 percent discount for payment within 10 days, the average collection period is 28 days. It is Ben's contention that the discount should be dropped. Based on his estimates, the average collection period would increase to only 30 days, and the firm would save 3 percent on all accounts taking the discount (30 percent of the firm's customers currently take the discount). The marketing manager informed him that as a result, sales will probably drop from 21,000 to 20,000 units per year. The firm has a 20 percent required rate of return on investments. If the selling price is $22 per unit, average cost per unit is $20 at the current sales volume, and variable cost is $17 per unit, should the firm discontinue the discount? Why or why not?

10.7. *RELAXING COLLECTION ACTIVITY.* The East Indian Rug Company is trying to decide whether to relax its collection activities. The firm currently sells 72,000 rugs per year at an average price of $32 each. With the relaxing of collection activities, sales are expected to increase to 75,000 rugs per year. Bad debt expenses are currently 1 percent of sales, and annual collection expenditures total $60,000. Bad debt expense for the new customers is expected to be 20 percent of sales. The average collection period is currently 40 days; for new customers it is expected to be 60 days. The average cost per unit is $29 at the current sales level, and the variable cost per unit is $28. By relaxing its collection activity, East Indian expects to save $20,000 per year in collection expense. If the firm's required rate of return is 24 percent, what recommendation would you give regarding the proposed relaxation in collection activity?

10.8. **TIGHTENING CREDIT POLICY.** Binker Company is contemplating a general tightening of its credit policy as a result of the currently high opportunity cost of funds. The tightening is expected to be accomplished by tightening credit standards, shortening credit terms, and increasing collection activity. The key data required to analyze the firm's plan are summarized below

Current Data

- Variable cost rate, 65%
- Required rate of return, 25%
- Average collection period, 60 days
- Sales revenue, $30,000,000
- Bad debt percentage for marginal customers, 10%
- Average bad debt percentage, 8%

Proposed Data

- Change in sales, −$4,000,000
  Due to elimination of marginal customers, −$2,500,000
  Due to shorter credit terms and increased collection activity, −$1,500,000
- Average collection period for eliminated marginal customers, 80 days
- Average collection period, 45 days
- Average bad debt percentage on remaining customers, 5%
- Change in collection cost, +$40,000

a. Using the data given, analyze and make a recommendation to Binker on the proposed tightening of credit policy.

b. If the required rate of return were 10 percent and the change in collection cost attributable to the proposed tightening were +$25,000, what, if any, effect would this have on your conclusions above? Reassess the proposal using these data, and discuss your results in light of the analysis in (a).

10.9. **INVESTING IN INVENTORIES.** Determine the average investment in inventory for each of the following cases (assume a 360-day year):

a. A company has sales of $18 million, a gross profit margin of 32 percent, and a supply of inventory that averages 45 days.

b. Another company has annual cost of goods sold of $1.2 million and an inventory turnover ratio of 8.0 times.

10.10.   *COST OF CARRYING INVENTORY AND RECEIVABLES.*   The management of Connecticut Wholesale Distributors estimates the annual cost of carrying a dollar of inventory is $.27, while the carrying cost of an equal investment in accounts receivable is $.17. The firm's current balance sheet reflects its average inventory of $400,000 and average investment in accounts receivable of $100,000. If the firm can convince its customers to purchase in larger quantities, the level of average inventory can be reduced by $200,000, and the average investment in receivables increased by the same amount. Assuming no change in annual sales, what addition to profits will be generated from this shift? Explain your answer.

10.11.   *INVENTORY MODELS.*   The Matt Boone Ski Company uses 800 units of a product per year on a continuous basis. The product has order costs of $50 per order and carrying costs of $2 per unit per year. It takes 5 days to receive a shipment after an order is placed, and the firm wishes to hold in inventory 10 days' usage as a safety stock.

   a.   Calculate the EOQ.

   b.   Determine the average level of inventory.

   c.   Determine the reorder print.

   d.   Which of the following variables change in the event the firm does not hold a safety stock: (1) order costs, (2) carrying costs, (3) total inventory cost, (4) average level of inventory, (5) number of orders per year, (6) economic order quantity, or (7) reorder point? Explain.

SELECTED REFERENCES

Atkins, Joseph C., and Yong H. Kim. "Comment and Correction: Opportunity Cost in the Evaluation of Investment in Accounts Receivable." *Financial Management* 6 (winter 1977), pp. 71–74.

Ben-Horim, Moshe and Haim Levy. "Management of Accounts Receivable Under Inflation." *Financial Management* 12 (spring 1983), pp. 42–48.

Beranek, William. "Financial Implications of Lot-Size Inventory Models." *Management Science* 13 (April 1967), pp. B401–B408.

Boggess, William P. "Screen-Test Your Credit Risks." *Harvard Business Review* 45 (November–December 1967), pp. 113–122.

Budnick, Frank S, Richard Mojena, and Thomas E. Vollmann. *Principles of Operations Research for Management.* Homewood, Ill.: Irwin, 1977.

Carpenter, Michael D., and Jack E. Miller. "A Reliable Framework for Monitoring Accounts Receivable." *Financial Management* 8 (winter 1979), pp. 37–40.

Celec, Stephen, and Joe D. Icerman. "A Comprehensive Approach to Accounts Receivable Management." *The Financial Review* 15 (spring 1980), pp. 23–34.

Christie, George N., and Albert E. Bracuti. *Credit Management.* Lake Success, NY: Credit Research Foundation, 1981.

Dyl, Edward A. "Another Look at the Investment in Accounts Receivable." *Financial Management* 6 (winter 1977), pp. 67–70.

Greer, Carl C. "The Optimal Credit Acceptance Policy." *Journal of Financial and Quantitative Analysis* 2 (December 1967), pp. 399–415.

Hadley, G., and T. M. Whitin. *Analysis of Inventory Systems*. Englewood Cliffs, N.J.: Prentice-Hall, 1963.

Haley, Charles W., and Robert C. Higgins. "Inventory Control Theory and Trade Credit Financing." *Management Science* 20 (December 1973), pp. 464–471.

Halloran, John A., and Howard P. Lanser. "The Credit Policy Decision in an Inflationary Environment." *Financial Management* 10 (winter 1981), pp. 31–38.

Herbst, Anthony F. "Some Empirical Evidence on the Determinants of Trade Credit at the Industry Level of Aggregation." *Journal of Financial and Quantitative Analysis* 9 (June 1974), pp. 377–394.

Hill, Ned C., and Kenneth D. Riener. "Determining the Cash Discount in a Firm's Credit Policy." *Financial Management* 8 (spring 1979), pp. 68–73.

———, Robert A. Wood, and Dale R. Sorensen. "Factors Influencing Corporate Credit Policy: A Survey." *Journal of Cash Management* 1 (December 1981), pp. 38–47.

Kallberg, Jarl G., and Anthony Saunders. "Markov Chain Approaches to the Analysis of Payment Behavior of Retail Credit Customers." *Financial Management* 12 (summer 1983), pp. 5–14.

Kim, Yong H., and Joseph C. Atkins. "Evaluating Investments in Accounts Receivable: A Maximizing Framework." *Journal of Finance* 33 (May 1978), pp. 402–412.

Lewellen, Wilbur G., and Robert O. Edmister. "A General Model for Accounts Receivable Analysis and Control." *Journal of Financial and Quantitative Analysis* 8 (March 1973), pp. 195–206.

———, and Robert W. Johnson. "Better Way to Monitor Accounts Receivable." *Harvard Business Review* 50 (May–June 1972), pp. 101–109.

Long, Michael S. "Credit Screening System Selection." *Journal of Financial and Quantitative Analysis* 11 (June 1976), pp. 313–328.

Magee, John F., and Harlan C. Meal. "Inventory Management and Standards." In *The Treasurers Handbook*, J. Fred Weston and Maurice B. Goudzwaard, eds. Homewood, Ill.: Dow Jones-Irwin, 1976.

Mao, James C. T. "Controlling Risk in Accounts Receivable Management." *Journal of Business Finance and Accounting* 1 (autumn 1974), pp. 395–403.

Mehta, Dileep. "The Formulation of Credit Policy Models." *Management Science* 15 (October 1968), pp. 30–50.

———. "Optimal Credit Policy Selection: A Dynamic Approach." *Journal of Financial and Quantitative Analysis* 5 (December 1970), pp. 421–444.

Myers, James H., and Edward W. Foray. "The Development of Numerical Credit Evaluation Systems." *Journal of the American Statistical Association* 58 (September 1963), pp. 799–806.

Oh, John S. "Opportunity Cost in the Evaluation of Investment in Accounts Receivable." *Financial Management* 5 (summer 1976), pp. 32–36.

Sachdeva, Kanwal S., and Lawrence J. Gitman. "Accounts Receivable Decisions in a Capital Budgeting Framework." *Financial Management* 10 (winter 1981), pp. 45–49.

Schiff, Michael. "Credit and Inventory Management: Separate or Together?" *Financial Executive* 40 (November 1972), pp. 28–33.

———, and Zvi Lieber. "A Model for the Integration of Credit and Inventory Management." *Journal of Finance* 29 (March 1974), pp. 133–140.

Shapiro, Alan. "Optimal Inventory and Credit-Granting Strategies under Inflation and Devaluation." *Journal of Financial and Quantitative Analysis* 8 (January 1973), pp. 37–46.

Smith, Keith V. *Guide to Working Capital Management*. New York: McGraw-Hill, 1979.

Snyder, Arthur. "Principles of Inventory Management." *Financial Executive* 32 (April 1964), pp. 16–19.

Stone, Berrell K. "The Payments-Pattern Approach to the Forecasting and Control of Accounts Receivable." *Financial Management* 5 (autumn 1976), pp. 65–82.

Wagner, Harvey M. *Principles of Operations Research—with Applications to Managerial Decisions*, 2d ed. Englewood Cliffs, N.J.: Prentice Hall, 1975.

Walia, Tirlochan S. "Explicit and Implicit Cost of Changes in the Level of Accounts Receivable and the Credit Policy Decision of the Firm." *Financial Management* 6 (winter 1977), pp. 75–78.

Weston, J. Fred, and Pham D. Tuan. "Comment on Analysis of Credit Policy Changes." *Financial Management* 9 (winter 1980), pp. 59–63.

Wilcox, Kirkland A., and Joseph C. San Miguel. *Introduction to Financial Accounting*, 2d ed. New York: Harper & Row, 1984.

Appendix 10A

Discriminant Analysis

Financial data provide the corporate decision maker with an abundance of information. To make optimal use of this data, firms must have established procedures to organize and analyze information that pertains to specific problems. Discriminant analysis can be viewed as a variation of regression analysis (see Appendix 4A); it provides an analytical technique that can be employed when the problem involves the classification of objects into groups, based on a set of given characteristics. For instance, a firm may be concerned with establishing a procedure to determine which credit applicants are "good" or "bad" risks. Discriminant analysis is the appropriate technique, as it develops a classification model for "good" and "bad" credit risks by reviewing historical data on past and current credit customers of the firm. Since the past and current customers can be easily segregated into "good" and "bad" credit risks, the actual group constituency is predetermined.

Discriminant analysis then derives the linear combination of the customers' characteristics that best separates the two defined groups. In the case of credit risk, perhaps an analysis of the current ratio and net profit margin shown in Table 10A.1 would permit an initial analysis. This problem is a simple dichotomous classification ("good" or "bad"), whereas other examples of more complex problems involve more than two predetermined groups (such as bond quality classification).

Simple Linear Discriminant Analysis

The following discussion concerns a simple linear discriminant function that transforms an original set of two measurement variables into a single discriminant score.[1] The discriminant function is defined as:

---

[1]Several assumptions are needed for the application of discriminant analysis, such as two or more discrete groups having at least the same number of descriptive variables. The descriptive variables must also have multivariate normal distributions and equal variance-covariance matrices. For more information on these constraints, see O. Maurice Joy and John O. Tollefson, "On the Financial Applications of Discriminant Analysis," *Journal of Financial and Quantitative Analysis* 10 (December 1975), pp. 723–739, as well as George E. Pinches, "Factors Influencing Classification Results from Multiple Discriminant Analysis," *Journal of Business Research* 8 (December 1980), pp. 429–456.

TABLE 10A.1
Data on "Good" and
"Bad" Credit
Customers

Customer (i)	Current Ratio (X_1)	Net Profit Margin (X_2)	Credit Risk	Z_i Score
1	3.75	6.08%	Good	1.233
2	2.27	5.72	Good	.138
3	2.10	5.91	Good	.204
4	4.96	5.88	Good	1.720
5	5.61	5.94	Good	2.120
6	3.19	5.38	Good	.352
7	2.50	4.94	Good	− .382
8	3.00	7.00	Good	1.589
9	2.87	4.50	Good	− .546
10	3.27	6.21	Good	1.082
11	2.46	4.03	Good	−1.155
12	4.41	3.07	Good	− .897
13	4.31	4.73	Good	.420
14	7.01	2.74	Good	.232
15	1.80	8.72	Good	2.363
16	4.53	2.10	Bad	−1.633
17	1.93	4.34	Bad	−1.185
18	6.10	1.02	Bad	−1.680
19	1.63	4.51	Bad	−1.206
20	.83	3.21	Bad	−2.711
$\bar{X}_{Total}$ =	3.43	4.80		
$\bar{X}_{Good}$ =	3.57	5.39		
$\bar{X}_{Bad}$ =	3.00	3.04		
$\bar{D} = \bar{X}_{Good} - \bar{X}_{Bad}$ =	.57	2.35		

$$Z_i = a + b_1X_1 + b_2X_2 \qquad (10A.1)$$

where Z_i = discriminant score for customer i

a = constant term

X_1 = variable for current ratio

X_2 = variable for net profit margin

b_1, b_2 = weighting coefficients[2]

The graph in Figure 10A.1 shows the position of each customer in two-dimensional space.

Each discriminant score Z_i represents the position of that particular case on the line Z defined by the linear discriminant function. Therefore, discriminant analysis reduces this multivariate problem to a problem that can be analyzed along one dimension. The best discriminant function is determined by finding the equation that minimizes the ratio

[2]The mathematical solution to finding the weighting coefficients can be found in many texts on multivariate analysis, including Paul E. Green and Donald S. Tull, *Research for Marketing Decisions*, 4th ed. (Englewood Cliffs, N.J.: Prentice-Hall, 1978), pp. 382–402; Robert A. Eisenbeis and Robert B. Avery, *Discriminant Analysis and Classification Procedures* (Lexington, Mass.: Heath, 1972); and William W. Cooley and Paul R. Lohnes, *Multivariate Data Analysis* (New York: Wiley, 1971), chaps. 9, 10.

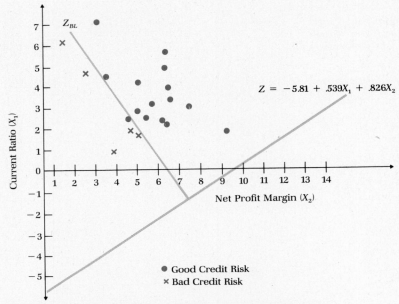

Figure 10A.1   Discriminant Analysis of Credit Customers.

of the difference in group multivariate means $(\overline{D})$ to the multivariate variance within the two groups. Viewing customers in these two groups as points in multivariate space, we search for the discriminant function or reference axis Z that provides the greatest separation between the two groups, as illustrated in Figure 10A.1.

In Figure 10A.1, Z represents the discriminant function and the line perpendicular to Z (labeled Z_{BL}) is defined as the discriminant boundary line between "good" and "bad" credit risks. The discriminant equation for this example is:

$$Z = -5.81 + .539X_1 + .826X_2$$

Notice the signs of the coefficients are as expected, indicating that better credit risks have higher current ratios and higher net profit margins. The value of Z_i for each customer is found by substituting their X_1 and X_2 values into the discriminant equation, Z: the calculated Z_i values are given in the final column of Table 10A.1.

Group	Number of Customers	Score
Good	$N_G = 15$	$\overline{Z}_G = \quad .562$
Bad	$N_B = 5$	$\overline{Z}_B = -1.686$

TABLE 10A.2
Group Mean
Discriminant Scores

Group	Number of Customers	Predicted Group Membership	
		Good	Bad
Good	15	14	1
Bad	5	0	5
Correct classification, 95%			

The mean Z scores for the "good" and "bad" credit groups are given in Table 10A.2. The mean Z scores can be used to find the discriminant boundary line that separates "good" and "bad" credit risks. This boundary line Z score (Z_{BL}) is calculated as follows:

$$Z_{BL} = \frac{N_B \overline{Z}_G + N_G \overline{Z}_B}{N_G + N_B} \tag{10A.2}$$

where $\overline{Z}_G$ = mean Z score for good credit risks

$\overline{Z}_B$ = mean Z score for bad credit risks

N_G = number of customers in "good" group

N_B = number of customers in "bad" group

$$Z_{BL} = \frac{5(.563) + 15(-1.683)}{20} = -1.121$$

Notice that boundary line changes depend on the relative size of the groups under consideration. More sophisticated boundary lines can also be calculated that consider misclassification costs.[3]

Assessing the Effectiveness of the Discriminant Function

Discriminant analysis is meaningful only if the percentage of correct classifications is larger than the percentage expected by chance. In this example, if future credit customers have the same probability of being bad credit risks, we could achieve 75 percent correct classifications by accepting all credit customers. Therefore, to be beneficial, the discriminant analysis must classify more than 75 percent correctly. The classification matrix for the original data is given in Table 10A.3. Only one case (customer 11) is misclassified by the discriminant function, giving the function 95 percent accuracy.[4] If the new credit applicants are similar to

---

[3]For more detail on misclassification, see Joy and Tollefson, "On the Financial Applications of Discriminant Analysis," pp. 735–737.

[4]The 95 percent accuracy figure may be upwardly biased due to the same data being used to form the discriminant function as well as to test its accuracy. This problem can be reduced by reclassifying a randomly chosen holdout sample or employing a one object at a time holdout technique as described by P. A. Lachenbruch and M. Mickey, "Estimation of Error Rates in Discriminant Analysis," *Technometrics* 10 (February 1968), pp. 1–11.

past and current credit customers, the derived discriminant function should perform reasonably well for classification of new applicants.

Quantitative techniques do not do away with the task of credit analysis or the financial analyst. However, they allow the analyst to review greater amounts of data by performing a computerized screening process. The analyst can then spend time performing an intense review of the marginal credit applicants selected by the discriminant analysis algorithm.

SELECTED REFERENCES

Altman, Edward I. "Financial Ratios, Discriminant Analysis and the Prediction of Corporate Bankruptcy." *Journal of Finance* 23 (September 1968), pp. 589–609.
———, and Robert A. Eisenbeis. "Financial Applications of Discriminant Analysis: A Clarification." *Journal of Financial and Quantitative Analysis* 13 (March 1978), pp. 185–195.
Ball, Michael. "Z Factor: Rescue by the Numbers." *INC.*, December 1980, pp. 45–48.
Cooley, William W., and Paul R. Lohnes. *Multivariate Data Analysis.* New York: Wiley, 1971.
Eisenbeis, Robert A. "Pitfalls in the Application of Discriminant Analysis in Business, Finance, and Economics." *Journal of Finance* 32 (June 1977), pp. 875–900.
———, and Robert B. Avery. *Discriminant Analysis and Classification Procedures.* Lexington, Mass.: Heath, 1972.
Green, Paul E., and Donald S. Tull. *Research for Marketing Decisions*, 4th ed. Englewood Cliffs, N.J.: Prentice-Hall, 1978.
Joy, O. Maurice, and John O. Tollefson. "On the Financial Applications of Discriminant Analysis." *Journal of Financial and Quantitative Analysis* 10 (December 1975), pp. 723–739.
Lachenbruch, Peter A. *Discriminant Analysis.* New York: Hafer Press, 1972.
———, and M. Mickey. "Estimation of Error Rates in Discriminant Analysis." *Technometrics* 10 (February 1968), pp. 1–11.
Lang, Sylvia. "Submarginal Credit Risk Classification." *Journal of Financial and Quantitative Analysis* 7 (January 1972), pp. 1379–1385.
Perreault, William D., Douglas N. Behrman, and Gary M. Armstrong. "Alternative Approaches for Interpretation of Multiple Discriminant Analysis in Marketing Research." *Journal of Business Research* 7 (1979), pp. 151–173.
Pinches, George E. "Factors Influencing Classification Results from Multiple Discriminant Analysis." *Journal of Business Research* 8 (December 1980), pp. 429–456.
Scott, Elton. "On the Financial Application of Discriminant Analysis: Comment." *Journal of Financial and Quantitative Analysis* 13 (March 1978), pp. 201–205.
Tollefson, John O., and O. Maurice Joy. "Some Clarifying Comments on Discriminant Analysis." *Journal of Financial and Quantitative Analysis* 13 (March 1978), pp. 197–200.

11

The Management of Current Liabilities

Maintaining an appropriate level of current liabilities is an important managerial function, and one that has considerable impact on the long-run well-being of the firm. The amount and composition of short-term debt is important not only because it provides required support to the firm's current assets, but also because it complements the liquidity and operating needs of the company. Just as assets have to be managed effectively if the firm is to realize an attractive rate of return, it is equally important to obtain and manage short-term financing in an efficient manner, especially in light of the high interest rates that have existed over much of the recent past. Clearly, when the days of cheap money disappeared, the rewards of efficient debt management increased accordingly; in periods when financing costs are high, more efficient debt management translates into greater profits to the firm and increased rates of return. This chapter is devoted to managing the firm's current liabilities. After examining key aspects of short-term credit as a source of funds, we shift our attention to alternative short-term financing methods —spontaneous forms of credit, like accounts payable and accruals, will be considered as will unsecured bank loans, secured loans, factoring accounts receivable, commercial paper, and Eurodollar loans. We will also explore alternative financing strategies, hedging with interest rate futures, and the managerial dimensions of current liabilities.

Short-Term Credit as a Source of Funds

Although closely linked to some of the activities in the cash management area, the management of short-term credit is, nonetheless, a separate and unique function in itself. In fulfilling this function, the financial manager must see to it that: (1) the cash and liquidity needs of the firm are being met; (2) the structure of current liabilities (type of loan, maturity, etc.) is compatible with the operating and cash flow characteristics of the firm; (3) the liabilities are serviced in a prompt and orderly fashion; and (4) the financing is obtained in a manner that minimizes the cost of funds to the firm.

Role and Importance to the Firm

Normally, the current portion of a firm's financial structure will contain one or more of the following: accounts payable, accruals, notes payable, and current maturities. For the most part, accounts payable are made up of the debt owed to suppliers; accruals represent the amount of money owed to employees and the government; notes payable reflect the amounts due to banks and other financial institutions; and current maturities are the portion of any long-term debt due within a year. There are a variety of different types of loans and financing arrangements within the accounts and notes payable categories and, along with accruals, they will be explored in this chapter; however, because of their link to long-term debt, discussion of current maturities will be deferred to Chapter 21, which deals with long-term sources of debt financing.

The amount and composition of current liabilities is a function of the size of the firm and the industry in which it operates. The statistics below provide an indication of the extent to which American manufacturers relied on short-term funds as a source of financing in 1983:

	Industry Group (% of Total Assets)		
Current Liability	Manufacturing	Mining	Wholesale Trade
Accounts payable	8.5%	5.7%	20.4%
Loans and current maturities	3.4	2.7	17.6
Accruals and other	13.6	7.1	9.1
Total	25.5%	15.5%	47.1%

SOURCE: Federal Trade Commission, *Quarterly Financial Report: Manufacturing, Mining and Trade Corporations* (Washington, D.C.: U.S. Government Printing Office, 3d Quarter, 1983).

Use of Short-Term Credit. With the exception of current maturities, short-term credit is used predominantly to finance the temporary and permanent working capital needs of the company; it is used to support the ongoing operations of the firm and its cash position, receivables, and inventory.[1] On one hand, short-term credit is used to meet the temporary (seasonal or cyclical) working capital needs of the firm. Such financing is also used to support some of the permanent portion of working capital. Finally, short-term debt is sometimes used as a form of "stopgap" financing when interest rates become excessively high. That is,

---

[1]So long as a firm's net working capital (NWC) exceeds zero, it should be clear that some portion of current assets is supported by long-term debt and/or equity. As we saw in Chapter 8, this condition must follow, for if NWC > 0, then current liabilities < current assets, and the difference (as defined by the level of NWC) must be financed with a long-term source of funds.

rather than locking the firm into high interest rates over the long run, some financial managers will use short-term financing to meet immediate capital needs and then, when long-term rates decline, the interim short-term loans will be converted to reasonably priced long-term loans and bonds. This practice is fairly common during periods of economic expansion, when corporations accumulate short-term debt not only to finance increased working capital activity, but also to avoid financing their capital needs with high coupon long-term bonds.[2]

Advantages and Disadvantages.   From a managerial perspective, short-term credit has several attributes that typically make it an attractive financing vehicle. Historically, one advantage of borrowing short has been *cost;* the prevailing yield curve[3] over the past 50 or so years has been upward-sloping, indicating that short-term funds are less expensive than long-term money. Under such conditions, there is a cost advantage to short-term borrowing. Unfortunately, over the recent past periods of tight money, the yield curve has been downward-sloping, reflecting high short-term borrowing costs. Another advantage is *flexibility*. Short-term debt is excellent for meeting seasonal or cyclical funds requirements; when demand slackens and investments in receivables, inventories, and so on are worked down, current liabilities can be paid off. Not only can long-term commitments be avoided, but since most short-term loans do not carry prepayment penalties, the debt can be paid off early should the firm's cash flow turn out to be stronger than expected.

The flexibility afforded short-term borrowers is not without its problems, however; for short-term borrowing normally exposes the firm to greater *risk* than long-term debt. Such behavior reflects traditional risk-return relationships to the extent that lower borrowing costs translate into higher return to the firm, and therefore we should expect risk to increase commensurately. The increased risk exposure is derived from the fact that short-term rates are fairly volatile, so the firm is continuously exposed to the possibility of higher borrowing rates in the future. By not locking in the rates today (via long-term borrowing), the firm is facing the possibility of higher financing costs in the future. Consider, for example, the events that occurred in June 1980; at that time, companies could borrow short-term (in the commercial paper market) at rates of about 8.0 percent, versus obtaining funds in the long-term bond market at a cost of about 11.4 percent. There was an obvious advantage to the short-term loans, but it disappeared as short-term funds quickly became more expensive. Just fourteen months later, short-term money was at the astronomical rate of 16 to 17 percent.

---

[2]The idea of converting short-term debt into long-term bonds (a practice known as *funding*) is reviewed in "Pressure Builds for More Bond Financing," *Dun's Review*, March 1980, pp. 76–80.

[3]See Chapter 9 for discussion of yield curves.

Another reason for the greater risk of short-term debt is the demands it places on the firm's cash flow. That is, shorter maturities mean more frequent debt service requirements and as such, the company may sometimes find that its financial condition and cash flow, for one reason or another, are inadequate to repay the loan and that the lender is unwilling to roll the debt over. Such circumstances, of course, pose serious solvency problems and might even lead to bankruptcy.

Key Sources of Short-Term Credit

Short-term financing is available from a variety of different sources. Some are actively in the business of lending, and others provide financing indirectly by selling goods and services on credit. One of the most important sources of credit is other business firms. In fact, it is customary in most industries for one company to sell its goods and services to another on credit; such transactions, of course, lead to the creation of accounts payable. To many firms, trade credit is often the single most important source of funds. This is especially true in most wholesale and retail trade, where such debt is used to finance inventory and often dominates the short-term portion of the financial structure, and for younger and/or smaller companies that lack access to alternative financing vehicles.

Another, closely related, source of short-term financing is the employees of the firm. They supply credit in the form of accruals by putting in time on the job without getting paid for it at the end of each day. As might be expected, accrued wages and salaries are particularly important to manufacturing firms and other operations that are highly labor-intensive. Various levels of government provide a similar form of credit—accrued taxes. A firm's own estimated income taxes, social security and income taxes withheld from employees, and sales tax collections are paid periodically (monthly or quarterly), and are all forms of accrued taxes. Like accrued wages, to the extent that they do not have to be paid as incurred (or collected), they represent a source of financing to the firm.[4]

In addition to the credit available in the normal course of a firm's operations, short-term funds can also be obtained from various financial institutions. Banks are undoubtedly the best known of these lenders, but the list also includes commercial finance companies and factors. Rather than goods and services, these institutions supply needed cash to the firm in the form of unsecured and secured loans, lines of credit, and advances. Finally, there are the investors who supply funds to the money market and who deal in commercial paper. Various types of financial institutions (like money market mutual funds and insurance companies)

---

[4]The federal government also makes loans and lines of credit available to businesses through programs sponsored by such agencies as the Small Business Administration; these and other government-sponsored lending activities will be explored in Chapter 21.

regularly invest in commercial paper and therefore provide financing to the issuing firms. In addition, other nonfinancial business concerns that are in an excess cash position will often add commercial paper to their marketable securities portfolio, and in so doing provide direct cash support to the issuing firm.

Cost
of Short-Term
Credit

The cost of short-term business credit can be categorized as follows: (1) There is no explicit cost of financing associated with accrued wages and taxes (in essence, the credit is free). (2) There is an implicit cost of missing cash discounts on trade credit (i.e., there is a very real financing cost to using trade credit beyond its cash discount date). (3) There is an explicit cost (stated interest rate) associated with commercial paper, factoring, and other forms of negotiated loans and lines of credit. Regardless of whether the costs are implicit or explicit, the impact on corporate profitability is the same to the extent that both cash discounts lost and interest paid reduce the firm's returns. From a historical perspective, the cost of short-term funds to business firms has fluctuated widely over time and has generally been drifting upward. Figure 11.1 provides a look at the behavior of several key interest rates over the 33-year period from 1951 through 1983. The behavior of short-term rates in comparison to long-term rates is shown in Figure 11.1; we can see that corporate bond yields normally exceed short-term borrowing rates, but there are times (particularly when rates increase rapidly and the market becomes unsettled) when this cost differential reverses itself—short-term rates exceed long-term yields.

Although the market rates contained in Figure 11.1 are important economic indicators and generally reflect the supply and demand for funds in the marketplace, most firms do not actually borrow at these rates. Table 11.1 provides some statistics on actual lending terms at commercial banks; although the best customers can sometimes borrow at less than prime, the data show that companies usually borrow at rates above the prime rate, and loan size does have an effect on borrowing costs. Also evident in the table (and the figure) is the impact inflation has had on interest rates, both long and short: As inflation has ravaged the economy, the compensation to lenders has had to be adjusted accordingly. And rightly so; for if we conceptually define interest rates, i, as:

$$i = R_F + I + P \qquad\qquad (11.1)$$

where R_F = risk-free rate
 I = perceived or expected inflation rate
 P = risk premium associated with the loan or bond

it follows that, other things being equal, changes in the *perceived* inflation rate will prompt corresponding changes in the rate of interest, given that lenders want to maintain their real rates of return. The

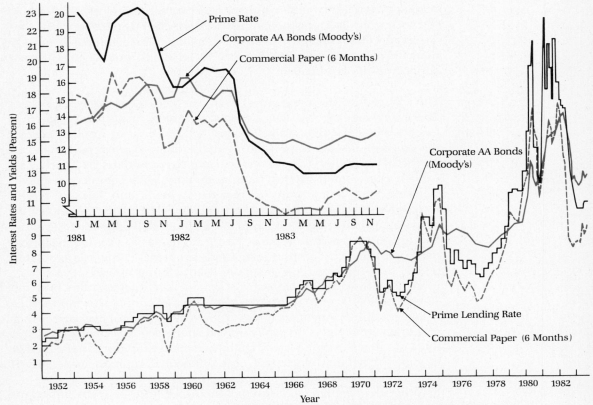

Figure 11.1   The Behavior of Corporate Interest Rates, 1951–1983.
Sources: Federal Bulletins and Surveys of Current Business.

conceptual model stipulated in Equation 11.1 is a widely accepted statement of general interest rate behavior; its inflation component explains, in large part, why rates have been drifting upward over the past decade and a half. Exceptions sometimes occur, such as was the case in early 1982 when rates, did *not* drop as sharply as inflation. At that time

TABLE 11.1
Survey of Lending
Rates at Major
Commercial Banks

Loan Size ($ thousands)	November 1978	November 1980	November 1981	November 1982	November 1983
$ 1–99	10.67%	16.13%	19.60%	15.07%	13.64%
100–499	11.53	15.52	21.22	13.85	12.34
500–999	11.19	15.87	18.52	12.93	11.82
Over 999	11.37	15.68	17.55	10.79	10.59
Average—all sizes	11.44	15.71	18.94	11.26	10.95
Prime rate	10.44	14.93	17.65	11.85	11.00

SOURCE: *Federal Reserve Bulletins*, 1979 to 1984.

many lenders did *not* believe there was going to be a lasting drop in inflation—thus Equation 11.1 is still valid when we keep in mind that it is *perceived* inflation that counts.

Alternative Short-Term Financing Methods

Having examined some of the basic attributes of short-term credit, we now examine some alternative short-term financing vehicles. Short-term financing can be broadly classified as either spontaneous or nonspontaneous. *Spontaneous financing* results from the normal operations of the business and is used to acquire the goods and services the firm uses in its operations; accounts payable and accruals are the two major sources of such short-term financing. *Nonspontaneous financing*, in contrast, represents funds obtained through negotiating directly with banks and other financial institutions. Such debt is incurred to obtain cash that can be used to meet the firm's operating and financing needs—for instance, the money may be needed to finance a buildup in inventory, or to pay off trade credit so that the firm can take advantage of a cash discount. Unsecured bank loans, secured loans, factoring accounts receivable, commercial paper, and Eurodollar loans are all examples of nonspontaneous financing vehicles.

Accounts Payable and Accruals

Two of the most important types of credit are spontaneous forms of financing—accounts payable and accruals. As a method of financing, they are just as important as negotiated loans. Clearly, any portion of the firm's resources financed with these forms of spontaneous credit means that much less that has to be financed with costly negotiated loans.

Accounts Payable.   *Accounts payable* result when a firm purchases goods or services from other firms on credit; inventory, for example, is normally purchased "on open account," and as such, *trade credit* results. Trade credit is a form of spontaneous financing because it is tied to the operations of the firm; when operations increase, the level of inventory will also increase and therefore so will the amount of trade credit being used by the firm. Such open account purchases are the single most important source of short-term financing for business firms. They include all transactions in which merchandise or services are purchased, but no formal note is signed evidencing the purchaser's liability to the seller. The purchaser, by accepting the merchandise or service, in effect agrees to pay the supplier the amount required according to the supplier's terms of sale. The credit terms extended in such transactions are normally stated on the supplier's invoice, which often accompanies the goods or services provided.

Although the obligation of the purchaser to the supplier may not seem as legally binding as it would if the supplier had required the purchaser to sign a note, there is actually no legal difference between the two arrangements. If a firm were to go bankrupt, a creditor who sold it goods or services on open account would have as strong a legal claim on the firm's assets as a creditor who held a note. The only advantage of using a note is that it gives the holder stronger proof of merchandise (or services) sold to the bankrupt firm. The use of notes for purchases of raw materials is quite rare; normally, they are used only if a supplier has reason to believe that the creditworthiness of a customer is questionable.

Credit Terms.   Credit terms stipulate the conditions under which a sale is made and credit extended. The terms spell out how the liability is to be repaid, and if a cash discount is offered, the size of that discount, along with the length of time the customer has to take advantage of it. Each of these aspects of credit terms is concisely stated in expressions such as "2/10 net 30." In this case, the length of the credit period (30 days), the cash discount (2 percent), and the cash discount period (10 days) are all identified. The *credit period* is the length of time that can elapse before payment in full is required. The credit period is also known as the "net" period, and the prefix "net" indicates that the face amount of the purchase must be paid within the number of days indicated. The beginning of the credit period is implied by industry custom or stated specifically in the credit terms. It can be specified in a number of ways—such as the date of the invoice, the end of the month (EOM), the middle of the month (MOM), or on receipt of the goods (ROG).

Credit periods usually range from about 30 to 90 days, although in certain instances longer periods are provided. This would be the case, for example, with *seasonal dating*—a technique used by suppliers in seasonal businesses that provides customers with considerably longer credit periods than would normally be extended. The supplier would ship the finished goods to the purchaser in advance of the selling season, but would not require payment until after the actual demand for the seasonal items is expected. For shipments made during the season, the supplier will use normal credit terms. The use of seasonal dating enables the supplier to shift inventory management problems to the customer, and the customer benefits by having the inventory on hand when the season starts (yet does not have to pay for the goods until after sales have been generated). Using seasonal dating, the supplier can extend credit terms 4 to 6 months, without formally instituting the lengthier credit terms for all of the year.

The use of *cash discounts* is found in a wide variety of credit transactions; for the most part, cash discounts are a function of industry practice and are intended to speed up the collection of accounts. The cash discount normally ranges from about 1 percent to as much as 5 percent of the face amount of the invoice or statement; that is, it represents a percentage deduction that may be taken off the top of the invoiced amount so long as payment is made within the cash discount period. A 5 percent cash discount indicates that the purchaser of $100 worth of merchandise can reduce his or her payment by 5 percent and therefore need pay only $95 so long as payment is made within the cash discount period. If payment is made after the discount period, the purchaser must pay the full face amount of the invoice. The *cash discount period* indicates the maximum number of days after the beginning of the credit period that the cash discount can be taken; typically, the cash discount period is between 5 and 20 days. In some industries, more than one cash discount may be offered; for example, 3/10, 1/20 net 45. Under such conditions, if the customer pays within 10 days, he or she can take the 3 percent discount; but if payment is made between the 11th and the 20th day, then only a 1 percent discount can be taken. Often, large customers of smaller firms use their position as key customers as a form of leverage, and take cash discounts far beyond the end of the cash discount period. This financially attractive strategy raises an important ethical issue, since it may cause the firm to violate an agreement with a supplier. Clearly, a firm would not look kindly upon a customer that employs such a strategy.[5]

Cost of Trade Credit.   Although there is normally no explicit cost levied on trade credit, the firm incurs an implicit cost whenever it foregoes a cash discount. In order to delay paying its bills for an additional number of days, the firm must forego the opportunity to pay less for the items purchased. (Of course, if no cash discount is offered, there is no cost whatsoever to trade credit—like accruals, this form of financing is virtually cost-free.) Whenever a cash discount is offered on trade credit, the firm has the option of taking the cash discount and paying a lesser amount on the invoice, or foregoing the cash discount and paying in full for the merchandise. The cost of trade credit under these conditions is obvious—the amount of cash discount that can be realized by paying the account within the cash discount period.

When a firm foregoes a cash discount, it does so presumably because it wants to (or has to) delay paying the bill until the final net payment date. Thus, with credit terms of, say, 2/10 net 30, the firm enjoys an extra 20 days of financing by paying the trade credit on the 30th rather than the 10th day. In this instance, the cost of using the credit for the additional 20 days is the cash discount foregone. Normally, because the time period involved is so short, foregoing cash discounts becomes a

---

[5]This ethical issue is not further addressed in this text. Suffice it to say that although the use of various techniques to reduce or slow down payments is widespread due to their financial appeal, such use may not be justifiable on ethical grounds.

very costly form of financing. The following equation can be used to determine the implicit cost of such financing:

$$\text{Cost of financing} = \frac{CD}{1 - CD} \times \frac{360}{N} \qquad (11.2)$$

where CD = the cash discount percentage (in decimal terms)

N = number of days payment can be delayed by foregoing the cash discount (net date minus cash discount date)

Equation 11.2 relates the cash discount foregone to the number of days of additional financing obtained by paying the net rather than the discount price; in effect, it provides an annualized cost of financing. For example, foregoing the cash discount on credit terms of 2/10 net 30 translates into an effective annualized cost of financing of 36.73 percent:

$$\text{Cost of financing} = \frac{.02}{1 - .02} \times \frac{360}{(30 - 10)}$$

$$= \frac{.02}{.98} \times \frac{360}{20} = 36.73\%$$

This high annualized cost results from the fact that the full 2 percent discount is the price paid to use the trade credit for a period of only 20 days.[6] Like the interest on a loan, the net effect of passing up cash discounts is higher cost to the firm and therefore reduced profits.

Accruals.   *Accruals* are liabilities for services received by the firm for which payment has not yet been made; the most common items accrued are wages and taxes. Other examples of accrued expenses would be utility bills paid on the basis of actual use rather than on a prepayment basis; rental and lease expenses paid at the end of a period rather than at the beginning; and a variety of subcontract services (like janitorial, security, and so on) paid on an as-used basis. By deferring the actual payment, a liability is created and a form of spontaneous financing comes into existence.

Since there is no explicit or implicit cost associated with accruals, they represent a virtually cost-free source of financing. It follows that a firm can save money by accruing as many expenses as possible. In effect,

---

[6]A rough estimate of the annualized cost of trade credit can be found by using the following equation $CD \times (360/N)$, where the notations are as described above. For example, the cost of foregoing the cash discount on credit terms of 2/10 net 30 is $.02 \times (360/20) = 36\%$; this approach will always yield a slightly lower figure than its more precise counterpart, but it is a good approximation of the actual cost (36% versus 36.73%).

accruals have value to the firm, since they represent zero-cost substitute financing that can be used in place of costly negotiated loans. This is particularly so in periods of high interest rates. For example, consider a firm that carries an average of $1 million in accrued liabilities on its balance sheet; with interest rates at, say, 15 percent, this firm is able to save about $150,000 per year (before taxes) by using accruals rather than bank loans to carry the expenses, taxes, and services in question. However, since custom, statute, and/or industry practice dictate the frequency and timing of payments on most of these current liabilities, financial managers have little opportunity to manipulate the level of accruals.

Unsecured Bank Loans

Banks and other financial institutions, such as commercial finance companies, represent important sources of funds to all types and sizes of business firms; of the major types of financial institutions that regularly make loans to business concerns, the most important is, not surprisingly, commercial banks.[7] Banks do not like to tie their money up for extended periods of time, so the major type of loan made by banks is the *short-term self-liquidating loan*. These loans are made to provide the firm with sufficient financing to meet seasonal needs—for example, to cover increases in accounts receivable and/or inventories. Such loans are considered self-liquidating, since it is expected that as receivables and inventories are worked down and converted into cash, the funds needed to retire these loans will automatically be generated.

Forms of Unsecured Bank Borrowing.   Banks make loans to businesses on both secured and unsecured bases. A secured loan has some type of collateral behind it, whereas an unsecured loan does not. Various forms of secured debt will be explored later in this chapter; our attention here is directed exclusively to unsecured forms of financing. Known as *signature loans*, such unsecured credit is backed by nothing more than the full faith and credit of the borrowing firm. Often, guarantees from the key owners will be obtained, especially with smaller firms; this enables the lending institution to look to the assets of these owners in case the loan does go bad and collection problems develop. Irrespective of whether bank loans carry the guarantee of the owners, the financing arrangements will generally take one of two forms: (1) a single-payment note, or (2) a line of credit.

Single-Payment Note.   A *single-payment note* is a one-shot deal made when a borrower needs funds for a short period of time, but does not believe the need will recur. The instrument that results is the single-

---

[7]Although our discussion at this point will, for simplicity, be couched in terms of bank loans and commercial bank lenders, similar financing arrangements are also available from other types of financial institutions, like commercial finance companies.

payment note, which is signed by the borrower and states the terms of the loan, including the length of the loan and the interest rate being charged. Typically, these loans have maturities that range anywhere from 30 days to as much as 9 months or more.

Line of Credit. A *line of credit* is an agreement between a commercial bank and a business firm that states the amount of short-term borrowing the bank will make available to the firm over a given period of time. A line of credit is often established for a period of one year, although shorter lines are also available. Such lines, particularly if they are unsecured, are usually made only to established customers who have demonstrated outstanding performance records. The line of credit stipulates the maximum amount of money the firm can owe the bank through the line *at any given point in time*. Of course, it is possible for a firm to borrow more than the amount of its line over time, but at no single point can the loan balance exceed the amount of the line of credit; this principle is graphically demonstrated for a $1 million line of credit in Figure 11.2.

A major attraction of a line of credit is that it provides the company with needed financing flexibility, and in so doing eliminates the need to apply for and take out a single-payment note each time a need arises. Once a line of credit is set up, a company can borrow, virtually by phone, as much as it wants and as often as it wants—so long as the amount outstanding does not exceed the amount of the line and the outstanding loans remain current. A line of credit is applied for like any other loan, and the application process must usually be repeated each time a new

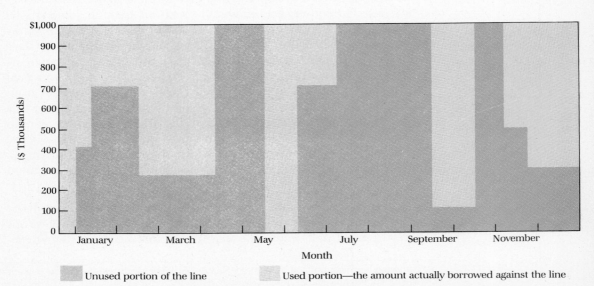

Unused portion of the line   Used portion—the amount actually borrowed against the line

Figure 11.2   The Used and Unused Portions of a Hypothetical Line of Credit.

line is established (or when the period of an existing line expires). Working with the borrower's financial statements and given the details of the loan request, the bank will decide if the line should be established; if it decides to establish the line, it will stipulate the amount, the period of time covered, the rate of interest being charged, and any other special conditions, such as annual cleanups, that might be required. (For obvious reasons, the credit analysis conducted by the bank on requested lines of credit is usually more extensive than that on comparable single-payment notes—this is necessary if for no other reason than the added risk exposure of a line of credit.) Of course, the firm is not obliged to actually take out any credit, although as we will see, it may be costly to set up a line and then not use it.

Cost of Unsecured Bank Loans. The interest charged on single-payment notes and lines of credit can be fixed or floating; The rate usually ranges between 0 and 4 percent above the prime rate. A *fixed percentage rate* establishes a given charge for the loan as long as the credit is outstanding (or until it is renewed). A *floating rate* is pegged at or near the bank's prime rate and varies over the life of the credit as the prime (or some other bench-mark) rate varies. In a floating rate arrangement, the bank will lend money to a business customer at its stated prime rate or at some rate pegged to its prime.

For example, if a bank is charging prime plus a point and a half on a loan, and if prime goes from 12 to 12.5 percent, the borrower's rate of interest will change from 13.5 to 14 percent on the same day the prime rate changes (with a floating rate the bank determines interest charges on a daily basis). The floating rate concept is further demonstrated in the following example, which shows the interest costs for a hypothetical $1 million, 6-month loan. In this case, the floating rate equals the prime rate plus three-quarters of 1 percent.

Time Period	Prime Rate	Rate on the Loan	Interest Charged on the Loan
day 1–30 (30 days)	12.00%	12.75%	$10,625[a]
day 31–90 (60 days)	12.25	13.00	21,667
day 91–120 (30 days)	12.40	13.15	10,958
day 121–180 (60 days)	11.50	12.25	20,417
		Total	$63,667

[a].1275 × 30/360 × $1 million = $10,625. The other values are calculated in a similar manner.

The question of when to use a fixed or a floating rate is an important one, and depends largely on the outlook for future interest rate behavior. The type of interest being charged on a loan is often a nonnegotiable point; when it is negotiable, however, it makes sense for the firm to use a fixed rate whenever it feels interest rates are about to rise, and to use floating rates whenever rates are expected to decline over the near term. Of course, the lending institution is going to want to take just the opposite position, and it is likely to be willing to offer such terms only at a premium. That is, if the bank also thought interest rates were going to rise, then rather than making a fixed-rate loan at, say, 12 percent, it might well make it at 12.5 or 13 percent. On the other hand, if it expected rates to fall, the floating rate might be as much as prime plus 2.5 percent or more, rather than their usual prime plus 1 percent. If possible, the best approach is to obtain both a fixed and a floating rate quotation from the bank and then use the firm's expectations to determine the expected cost under both alternatives. The choice would be the one that is perceived to be least costly. Obtaining accurate estimates of future interest rate behavior is extremely difficult,[8] but the firm could adopt some probabilistic procedure to assess future interest rates and their expected cost to the firm. Financial managers could also use sensitivity analysis to determine how far interest rates would have to rise (or fall) in order to make the fixed (or floating) rate arrangement unattractive. Regardless of the approach or the amount of sophistication used, the main issue is one of determining the financing method which is expected to be least costly.

Commitment Fees. In addition to the stated rate on the amount borrowed from a bank, there is another charge the firm must consider whenever a line of credit is being used—the commitment fee. A *commitment fee* is the fee charged for the *unused* portion of the line, and represents compensation to the bank for making the money available on a when-needed basis. As a rule, unless the bank charges a commitment fee on the unused portion of the line, the financial institution may be under no legal obligation to make the money available to the borrower, but will do so only so long as it has sufficient funds available to meet the requirements of the borrower. Normally, commitment fees average about half of 1 percent, although the actual rate tends to vary directly with the level of interest rates. The commitment rate is applied to the unused portion of the line of credit to determine the size of the fee. For example, if a company had a $1 million line and was using only say, $600,000, it would be paying a normal interest rate on the $600,000 actually outstanding, and a commitment fee on the $400,000 unused portion. If a firm is paying a one-half percent commitment fee and goes 30 days with $400,000 of unused credit, it would be liable for commitment fee charges of about $167 [.005 × (30/360) × $400,000].

---

[8]See, for example, Oswald D. Bowlin and John D. Martin, "Extrapolations of Yields over the Short Run: Forecast or Folly?" *Journal of Monetary Economics* 1(1975), pp. 275–288.

Interest Computations.   There are several different ways of computing the interest cost on a loan. Banks commonly use simple or discount interest. Simple interest is the most straightforward, least expensive, and fortunately, the most commonly used form of interest. *Simple interest* bases the amount of interest charged on the actual amount borrowed; that is, the interest is based on the amount of debt actually outstanding on a day-to-day basis. The effective rate of interest on a simple interest loan is determined according to the following formula:

$$\text{Effective rate of interest} = \frac{\text{interest paid}}{\text{amount borrowed}} \qquad (11.3)$$

To illustrate, consider a $100,000 one-year loan at 13 percent simple interest; the interest due on this loan would be $13,000. The effective rate of interest would be:

$$\text{Effective rate of interest} = \frac{\$13,000}{\$100,000} = 13\%$$

More often than not, short-term loans are made for periods of less than a year. Under these conditions, the amount of interest charged, and the effective rate of interest, must be adjusted according to the maturity of the loan. Normally, a 360-day year is assumed for such purposes. Given the terms of the loan, the bank will determine that portion of the year for which the loan is outstanding. The interest rate, adjusted to reflect the period covered by the loan, would then be applied to the amount borrowed. For example, a $50,000, 12 percent, 90-day loan would result in interest charges of $1,500 [.12 × (90/360) × $50,000 = $1,500]. In essence, interest of 3 percent [.12 × (90/360)] is being charged on the full $50,000 over the 90 days of the loan.

Banks sometimes compute interest by using the *discount method.* The amount of interest charged on a discount loan is determined in the same way as simple interest; however, the interest is deducted from the initial principal rather than being paid at the end of the loan. As a result, the effective rate of interest is increased. For example, in the $100,000, 13 percent, 1-year loan above, if the loan were discounted, the $13,000 interest would be deducted from the initial proceeds. The borrower would receive $87,000 at the time of the loan and be expected to repay the full $100,000. The borrowing firm is thus being charged a rate of interest based on the full face amount of the loan, but actually receives only a portion of that amount for its use. The net result is that the effective rate of interest is driven up. The following equation can be used to find the effective rate of interest on discount loans:

$$\text{Effective rate of interest} = \frac{\text{interest paid}}{\text{amount borrowed} - \text{interest paid}} \qquad (11.4)$$

Using Equation 11.4, we can see that the effective rate of interest actually being charged on this $100,000 discount loan is 14.94 percent, not the 13 percent simple interest:

$$\text{Effective rate of interest} = \frac{\$13,000}{\$100,000 - \$13,000}$$
$$= 14.94\%$$

As noted in Chapter 9, most money market securities are issued and/or traded on a discount basis.

Compensating Balances.   One of the conditions often attached to bank credit is the requirement for compensating balances. This requirement is typical for short-term, unsecured, single-payment notes and lines of credit. A *compensating balance* is a required minimum balance the firm must maintain in its demand deposit account over the term of the loan. Compensating balance requirements are commonly stated as a percentage of the amount borrowed, and normally range from about 10 to 20 percent of the face amount of the loan.[9] As might be expected, compensating balance requirements tend to vary with the level of interest rates, the mood of the market, and the availability and demand for funds. For instance, when money is readily available and interest rates are at fairly low levels, compensating balance requirement tends to decline substantially. Compensating balance requirements will raise the cost of funds to the borrowing firm if the firm normally does not carry such balances to begin with. The reason is that if the firm has to use part of the proceeds from the loan to meet the compensating balance requirement, this effectively reduces the amount of funds available, even though the interest being charged on the loan is based on the total amount borrowed.[10]

Compensating balance requirements not only affect the cost of borrowing, they also have an impact on the borrowing activities of the firm. That is, compensating balance requirements can affect the size of the loan as well as the cost of funds. The size of the loan actually taken out would be affected if the firm normally did not carry funds on deposit in an amount equal to or greater than the compensating balance requirement. This would clearly be the case if the firm normally kept

---

[9]Sometimes the compensating balance will be stated as a percentage of the amount of the line of credit rather than the amount borrowed. In other cases, the compensating balance will be linked to both the amount borrowed and the amount of the line.

[10]The borrowing firm should determine whether the compensating balance applies to the actual or average balance on deposit; obviously a compensating balance requirement tied to the average amount kept in the account is less costly and provides the firm with more flexibility than one which binds the company to an absolute minimum balance. To say that the actual balance may never fall below $100,000 is far more rigorous than saying the firm must maintain an average daily balance of $100,000 over the month.

very little on deposit, but was facing a sizable compensating balance in a particular borrowing arrangement. Given that a firm has certain needs for funds, the size of the loan that must be taken out to cover both the firm's needs and the compensating balance required by the bank can be determined according to the following equation:

$$\text{Size of the loan} = \frac{F - NDB}{1 - C} \qquad (11.5)$$

where F = funds required by the firm
    NDB = normal deposit balance—the amount of money the firm normally keeps on deposit at the bank
    C = compensating balance requirement on the loan

For example, if a firm needed $100,000 that its bank was willing to make available on terms of a 20 percent compensating balance, the amount of money it actually would have to borrow would be a function of the size of the demand deposit it normally kept on balance at the bank. Suppose the firm normally kept a minimum of about $8,000 on deposit. The amount that would have to be borrowed under these conditions would be:

$$\begin{aligned}
\text{Size of the loan} &= \frac{\$100,000 - \$8,000}{1 - .20} \\
&= \frac{\$92,000}{.80} \\
&= \$115,000
\end{aligned}$$

The firm would have to borrow $115,000 to meet the 20 percent compensating balance requirement and still have $100,000 available for expenditures.

The cost of funds obtained under these conditions is obviously higher than the stated rate, since the firm can use only a portion of the loan proceeds, even though the interest charges are based on the total amount of the loan. For example, if the stated rate on the $115,000 loan above was 12.5 percent, the firm would pay $14,375 for the use of the money over the period of 1 year. By relating this amount to the funds actually available to the firm, it is possible to determine the effective rate of interest on a compensating balance loan:

$$\begin{array}{l}
\text{Effective rate of} \\
\text{interest with} \\
\text{compensating} \\
\text{balance requirement}
\end{array} = \frac{\text{interest paid}}{\text{amount borrowed} - \text{funds required for}} \qquad (11.6)$$
$$\hspace{4cm}\text{compensating balance}$$

Using Equation 11.6, we can see that the effective rate of interest on the $115,000, 12.5 percent, 1-year loan would be:

$$\text{Effective rate of interest} = \frac{\$14,375}{\$115,000 - \$15,000}$$
$$= 14.38\%$$

Secured Loans

A firm normally has available only a limited amount of unsecured credit. Beyond that point, some type of security is required to obtain additional funds. Many firms are unable to obtain any unsecured, short-term money; secured financing is their only source of funds. These firms are typically small, growing companies that have yet to establish themselves as being financially mature enough to receive unsecured loans. Secured financing includes all those loans for which the lender requires collateral. *Collateral* commonly takes the form of a financial or physical asset such as accounts receivable or inventory, but can also include such items as equipment (which is popular for long-term secured credit, but also is used on occasion to secure short-term financing), stocks, bonds, and money market securities. For our purposes, we will confine the discussion to the most popular forms of short-term loan collateral: accounts receivable and inventory.

Secured financing is arranged by means of *security agreements*. These documents specify the property being pledged and provide the lender with an enforceable claim on the collateral. In addition, other conditions are spelled out, including the interest rate on the loan, repayment dates, compensating balance requirements, and the like. Although it is argued that holding collateral reduces the risk of a loan, lenders do not customarily view secured loans in such a fashion. Rather, lenders recognize that they may be able to use the pledged collateral to reduce or eliminate losses in those instances where the borrower actually defaults on the loan, but as far as actually changing the risk that the borrower will default, collateral is felt to have no effect. Lenders will often require collateral if they feel the loan is marginal and want to be able to cover their position in the event of default. But if the bank truly feels the credit risk is high, the use of collateral alone is not likely to be sufficient reason for it to enter into the loan. If the debt cannot be repaid through normal operating cash flows, the risk will probably be viewed as unacceptable. After all, the last thing the lender wants to do is to administer and liquidate collateral.

Pledging Accounts Receivable.

There are two ways of obtaining short-term financing through accounts receivable—pledging them and factoring them. Actually, only a *pledge of accounts receivable* creates a secured short-term loan; factoring really involves the sale of receivables at a discount. Although factoring is not a form of short-term borrowing, we discuss it below because it does involve the use of accounts receivable to obtain short-term funds. But first we consider the practice of pledging accounts receivable.

Both commercial banks and commercial finance companies extend loans against accounts receivable, because they normally view such assets as highly liquid and attractive collateral. Accounts receivable are normally pledged on a selective basis. The prospective lender analyzes the past payment records of the firm's accounts to determine which accounts are acceptable loan collateral. A lender will generally advance money only against those accounts determined to be acceptable credit risks, and the amount actually advanced will seldom exceed 90 percent of the face value of the selected receivables. An alternative is to use a *floating lien* that covers all the firm's receivables. This type of arrangement is normally used when a firm has many accounts that, on average, have only a small dollar value, and/or when the borrowing firm is so creditworthy that the collateral value of the pledged receivables is of lesser concern. Due to the difficulty of identifying each item of collateral and therefore of policing the pledged accounts, the percentage advanced against a pledge of accounts receivable under a floating lien is normally less than 50 percent of the book value of the accounts.

Procedures. Pledging accounts receivable generally involves four steps: (1) identification and selection of acceptable accounts, (2) adjustment of the acceptable accounts, (3) determination of the size of the advance against the pledged accounts, and (4) notification and collection of the pledged accounts. When a business firm approaches a prospective lender to request a loan against accounts receivable, the lender will first evaluate the firm's accounts to determine their desirability as collateral. One consideration is whether the accounts are of sufficient size to warrant being pledged. Assuming that the firm has accounts of sufficient size to warrant consideration, the lender will investigate the firm's accounts receivable to determine which are acceptable as collateral. This process is usually based on the past payment patterns of the various credit customers.

After selecting the acceptable accounts, the lender will normally "adjust" the dollar value of these accounts for expected returns and allowances. If a customer whose account has been pledged returns merchandise or receives some type of allowance, such as a cash discount for early payment, the amount of collateral is automatically reduced. For protection under such circumstances, the lender will normally reduce the value of the acceptable collateral by a fixed percentage—say 5 percent of the book value of the acceptable accounts. After the lender has determined the acceptable accounts and made the necessary adjustments, the percentage to be advanced against the "adjusted" collateral must be determined on the basis of the lender's overall evaluation of the quality of the acceptable receivables and the expected cost of their liquidation. For selected accounts receivable, this percentage will normally range between 50 and 90 percent of the adjusted collateral value. The more confident the lender is about the quality of the accounts, the larger the percentage advanced.

Normally, pledges of accounts receivable are made on a nonnotification basis; this means that the customers whose accounts have been pledged in a secured loan are not notified of the action. Rather, these customers continue to remit payments to the firm. If a pledge of accounts receivable is made on a notification basis, the customers are notified to remit payments directly to the lender. Nonnotification is, of course, preferred by borrowers, since the customers may construe the fact that their accounts have been pledged to mean that the firm is in financial difficulty. A notification arrangement may be safer from the lender's point of view, but lenders are normally willing to trust the borrower and lend on a nonnotification basis.

Under a notification arrangement, when the bank receives payment, it deducts the actual pledged portion of the receivable as partial payment on the loan. For instance, if a loan of $100,000 were made against a total receivables position of $150,000, the bank would use a ratio of two-thirds to one-third: two-thirds of anything collected would go to the bank and the balance would represent the unsecured portion of the receivable and be credited to the borrowing customer's account.[11] The borrowing firm is then responsible for any amounts still uncollected at the maturity date of the loan. If the loan is made on a nonnotification basis, the borrower is expected to remit payments on pledged accounts as received, or within a certain period of time after their receipt. To police nonnotification arrangements, the lender will verify the collateral by conducting unannounced audits of the borrower's records to see if the pledged accounts are still outstanding.

Cost.   The stated cost of pledging accounts receivable is normally 2 to 5 percentage points above the prime rate; in addition, a service charge of up to 3 percentage points may be levied to cover the administrative costs involved. The administrative costs result from the need to inspect the accounts, keep records of pledged accounts, make entries as accounts are collected, and generally police the lending arrangement. In exchange for the higher cost, however, the borrowing firm receives several advantages, the most noteworthy of which is the ability to obtain needed financing. In addition, the loan balance outstanding is constantly reduced as accounts receivable are collected. As a result, the cost of financing is kept lower than it would be if the full principal value of the loan were to remain outstanding to maturity.

---

[11]Often there is a modest reserve that is held back to cover the receipt of bad checks and similar collection problems.

The Use of Inventory as Collateral. Another current asset, inventory, is generally considered second to accounts receivable in desirability as short-term collateral. Inventory loans are generally made in one of three ways—on the basis of: (1) floating inventory liens, (2) flooring lines, or (3) warehouse receipt loans.

Floating Inventory Liens. *Floating inventory liens* are used when the firm has a fairly stable level of inventory that consists largely of a diversified group of merchandise, no single item of which has a high dollar value. Since it is difficult to verify the presence of the inventory, the bank will generally advance less than 50 percent of its book value. Inventories made up of such items as automobile tires, nuts and bolts, and shoes are candidates for floating liens. The interest charged on floating inventory liens is normally about 3 to 5 percentage points above the prime rate.

Flooring Lines. *Flooring lines* are another popular form of inventory loan. Also known as trust receipt loans or floor planning, these loans are regularly made to retailers that carry large amounts of relatively expensive merchandise which can be identified by serial number. For example, flooring lines are widely used by automobile dealers to finance their inventory of cars, by major equipment dealers (such as those selling trucks and construction equipment), and by retailers that sell TVs and appliances. Such financing is a routine form of credit and is available not only from banks and commercial finance companies, but also from many captive finance companies, such as GMAC, the financing subsidiary of General Motors. In this type of loan arrangement, the inventory remains in the hands of the borrower, and the lender advances often as much as 100 percent of the cost of the merchandise. The lender files a lien on each item financed (the items in inventory are identified according to serial number). When the items are sold from inventory, repayment is expected by the lender within a matter of days. The lender makes periodic unannounced checks on the borrower's inventory to make sure that all the required collateral is still in the hands of the borrower. Because of the high market value of the collateral and the low risk of liquidation losses, the interest rate charged to the borrower on flooring lines is normally only a percentage point or two (at most) above the prime rate.

Warehouse Receipt Loans. A third form of inventory financing is known as the *warehouse receipt loan,* and is an arrangement whereby the lender actually gains control of the pledged collateral. This device provides the lender with the ultimate degree of security; it is to inventory what notification is to accounts receivable loans. When a warehouse receipt loan is established, the lender selects the inventory that is acceptable for collateral and hires a warehousing company to take possession of it.

Either terminal warehouses or field warehouses are used. A terminal warehouse is one located in the geographical vicinity of the borrower; the borrower is required to move the collateralized merchandise from its premises to the terminal warehouse. When the goods arrive, the warehouse official checks the merchandise in, listing each item received on a warehouse receipt, and noting the quantity, serial or lot numbers, and estimated value. Once the merchandise has been checked in, the borrower takes the warehouse receipt to the bank, which then advances the firm a specified percentage of the collateral value and files a lien on all the items listed on the receipt. Under a field warehouse arrangement, the lender will hire a company to set up a warehouse on the borrower's premises. The procedures followed by the field warehouse personnel are similar to those used in terminal warehousing. A field warehouse may be nothing more than a fence around a stock of inventory, or it may be an actual warehouse constructed by the warehousing company on the borrower's premises.

Regardless of which type of warehouse is used, the warehousing company places a guard over the inventory. The guard or warehouse official is then not permitted to release any of the collateralized inventory without authorization from the lender. The actual lending agreement will state the requirements for the release of inventory. Normally, the bank will release items only after receipt of at least partial payment on the loan. As in the case of other secured loans, the lender generally loans against only a portion—typically 75 to 90 percent—of the collateral's value. The types of collateral normally most adaptable to warehouse receipt loans include such things as canned foods, lumber, refined products, and basic metal stocks.

The specific costs of warehouse receipt loans are generally higher than those of other forms of secured lending because of the need to hire and pay a third party to guard and attend to the collateral. The basic interest rate charged on warehouse receipt loans is 3 to 5 percentage points above the prime rate. In addition to the interest charge, the borrower must also absorb the cost of the warehousing agent or company, which generally amounts to about 1 to 3 percent of the amount of the loan, depending on the size of the loan and other factors (for instance, a firm's marginal warehousing costs may be small if it already has the warehouse to hold the inventory). Such service or warehousing fees, of course, add to the cost of funds and should be considered just as much a cost of financing as the interest rate charged on the loan.

Factoring Accounts Receivable

Factoring receivables involves the outright sale of accounts receivable to a third party. A handful of firms in the United States buy receivables and act primarily as factors, but other financial institutions, like commercial finance companies and banks, often engage in factoring as well. Most major commercial finance companies have a division or subsidiary devoted to the factoring of receivables, and the same is true for many commercial banks. Commercial banks, for instance, really act as factors when they buy instalment "paper" from automobile, appliance, and furniture dealers. While factoring receivables does not actually represent a short-term loan, it is in many respects similar to borrowing with accounts receivable as collateral.

Procedures.   When a factor purchases accounts receivable, it generally accepts all the credit risks associated with those receivables. The recourse of the factor, accounts receivable selection and notification procedures, and other conditions, charges, and procedures for factoring are set down in a factoring agreement. Typically, firms that factor receivables do so on a continuous basis, selling all their accounts to the factor. This type of arrangement is quite common in the textile and garment industries. Factoring is normally done on a notification basis. Since the factor is purchasing the accounts, it seems only reasonable that payments be made directly to it. The customers whose accounts have been factored may not be aware of this, however, as they may be advised simply to send their payments to a specified address or post office box that turns out to be the factor's. The degree of secrecy with respect to the arrangement depends largely on the firm's expectations of how its customers may react. Factors usually buy receivables on a nonrecourse basis. This means that the factor agrees to accept all credit risks; if purchased accounts turn out to be uncollectible, the factor must absorb the loss. Only on rare occasions are factoring agreements made with recourse that enables the factor to look to the firm for payment on uncollectible accounts.

The factoring agreement not only states the accounts to be factored and the criteria for continuous factoring, but also indicates the payment dates for the factored accounts. Typically, the factor is not required to pay the firm until the account is collected or the last day of the credit period arrives, whichever occurs first. As the receivables are collected, the factor will deduct the discount, withhold a stipulated reserve (normally about 5 to 10 percent of the amount being factored) as protection against bad checks, returned goods, and the like,[12] and disburse the balance of the collections to the firm as specified in the factoring agreement. The factor also stands behind any accounts that remain uncollected as of the net due date and will disburse the funds (net of the factor's discount or any reserves) to the firm at the end of the

---

[12]The reserve withheld by the factor is subject to limitations, of course; normally, a maximum amount will be stipulated, the attainment of which will trigger a payment (refund) to the firm, or certain dates will be established (quarterly, semi-annually), at which time the reserve will be drawn down to a predetermined level and a refund made to the firm.

credit period, just as though the account was actually paid. To expedite the payment process, a factor typically sets up an account (similar to a bank deposit account) for each customer. As the factor receives payment, or as the due date arrives, it simply deposits money into the firm's account, from which the firm is free to withdraw as needed. In many cases, if the firm leaves the money in the account, a surplus will exist on which the factor will pay interest of about one-half percent per month. If the firm needs more cash than is available in its account, the factor will make advances against the uncollected and not due accounts. The advances represent a negative balance in the firm's account, and interest is charged on any advances received from a factor.

Cost.   The interest on advances is just one cost of factoring; normally the interest charge levied on advances is about 2 to 4 percentage points above the prime rate. In addition, the interest on advances is normally charged on a discount basis, so the effective borrowing cost is actually much higher than the stated rate. Factors also charge commissions or discounts on the amount of receivables they purchase. Such commissions or discounts represent payment to the factor for the administrative costs of checking and collecting the receivables, and for taking the risk of purchasing the accounts without recourse. Commissions usually run from about 1 to 3 percent of the face value of the factored accounts receivable and are also charged on a discount basis. The total cost of using a factor to obtain needed financing can therefore, under certain conditions, become very expensive.

Advantages and Disadvantages.   Factoring does have certain advantages that make it quite attractive to many firms. One is the ability it gives the firm to turn accounts receivable into cash immediately without having to worry about repayment. Another advantage is that it ensures a known cash flow pattern. The firm that factors its accounts knows it will receive the cash (less the factoring fees) by a certain date; this clearly simplifies cash flow planning. Also, if factoring is undertaken on a continuous basis (which it commonly is), the firm benefits from the elimination of its credit and collection departments. The factor takes over the firm's credit analysis function when it determines which accounts are acceptable credit risks; it handles the collection functions by buying the receivables without recourse. The obvious disadvantage of factoring is the considerable cost sometimes associated with it; in addition, in certain situations it may carry with it a stigma of financial weakness.

Financing with Commercial Paper

Commercial paper is the short-term, unsecured promissory notes issued by firms having high credit standings. Generally, only large firms of unquestionable financial soundness are able to issue commercial paper.

Maturities range from 3 days to 9 months;[13] and although there is no set denomination, most commercial paper is issued in minimum amounts of $100,000. In recent years, the issuance of commercial paper has become an increasingly important source of short-term financing for many types of corporations, including utilities, industrial firms, finance companies, insurance companies, and bank holding companies. More and more, commercial paper is being used not only as a source of working capital, but also as a means of interim financing for major projects such as buildings, ships, pipelines, and plant expansions. Commercial paper is generally backed by unused bank credit lines that are available to refund the paper in the event of an adverse market.

The volume of commercial paper outstanding has expanded rapidly in the last two decades; from only $6 billion in December 1962, the amount grew to over $185 billion by the end of 1983. Most commercial paper is issued by various types of financial institutions; known as "finance paper," it accounts for about 75 percent of the market. Commercial (or finance) paper is issued in bearer form (i.e., the holder is considered the owner; the issuer keeps no record of ownership), but can be made payable to the order of a specific investor. It is sometimes issued on a discount basis, but more often than not it is issued as an interest-bearing security—it carries a stipulated coupon rate, and its maturity value is equal to the principal amount of the note plus accrued interest. Most paper is directly placed to the extent that it is issued directly to investors by the issuers. All other forms of commercial (or finance) paper are known as dealer placed because they are sold through commercial paper dealers on behalf of a diversified group of issuers.

The interest rate on commercial paper is closely tied to that of other money market investment vehicles like Treasury bills, large negotiable certificates of deposit, and banker's acceptances, and tends to move with them. As a rule, prime commercial paper usually yields anywhere from 1 to 3 percent below the prime rate. As such, it is also normally less costly than borrowing directly from the bank (however, cost comparisons with banks are often blurred by the fact that although commercial paper does not involve compensating balances, it does at times have to contend with commitment fees on unused lines of credit). Commercial paper, because of its attractive yield and high quality, is considered to be a prime investment outlet for the marketable securities portfolios of many business firms, as well as for insurance companies, pension funds, and other types of financial institutions. Although many purchasers hold commercial paper until maturity, an active secondary market exists and

---

[13]The maturities on commercial paper rarely exceed 270 days, since the Securities Act of 1933 specifically exempts from SEC registration all forms of corporate securities that have maturities at a time of issue of 9 months or less.

contributes to the liquidity of these investment vehicles. All trading in the secondary market is done on a discount basis; the calculations used to determine price, yield, and realized return are the same as those reviewed in Appendix 9A.

MULTINATIONAL DIMENSIONS
Eurodollar Loans

The immense Eurodollar market is an important source of bank loans for multinational and purely domestic U.S. firms. Access to the market is limited to the larger, better-known firms, since it is a wholesale market characterized by multimillion-dollar loans.

Eurodollar loans have most of the same characteristics as large domestic dollar loans. They can be negotiated under a straight loan agreement or as revolving loans under a line of credit. Although significant amounts of these loans are for short maturities, medium-term loans are also available. Since very large loans are typically syndicated to spread the risk, they are usually for average maturities of 8 to 10 years, with some stretching to 15 years.

Nearly all Eurodollar loans today carry variable interest rates that are adjusted every quarter. Until recently, the basic rate to which all other interest rates were tied was called *LIBOR (London Interbank Offered Rate)*. As the name suggests, this is the rate large banks charge one another for Eurodollars. Interest to nonbank borrowers is quoted as a certain percentage over LIBOR. For example, a firm might be charged one-half percent over LIBOR.

Since the Eurodollar market is a competitive wholesale market, spreads between deposit and loan rates are often less than 1 percent. This narrow spread has discouraged smaller regional U.S. banks from participating. To attract them, some of the recent syndicated loans have been negotiated with interest charged at a certain percentage over the U.S. prime rate rather than LIBOR. This makes the loans competitive with U.S. domestic loans for the regional banks.

Short- and medium-term loans can also be negotiated by U.S. firms in nondollar Eurocurrencies in the same way as for dollars. These loans, however, introduce foreign exchange risk. Although almost all Eurocurrencies have had lower interest rates than the dollar in recent years, a U.S. borrowing firm must anticipate foreign exchange transaction and translation gains and losses as exchange rates change. During 1978, it would have been a costly mistake for a U.S. firm to have borrowed most foreign currencies, because the dollar weakened sharply. During 1981, the opposite was true; the dollar strengthened dramatically and unexpectedly. For example, not only were Deutsche mark interest rates considerably lower than dollar interest rates, but the sharp decline in the value of the Deutsche mark in 1981 would have resulted in large transaction and translation gains for U.S. borrowers.

Over the long run, U.S. interest rates have not always been higher than those of its main trading partners. Figure 11.3 shows short-term rates for the United States and some of its competitors for the period 1979 through the end of 1982. The Eurocurrency rates for that period would have followed a path almost identical to the domestic rates depicted in Figure 11.3.

Managing the Firm's Current Liabilities

As is evident from the preceding review of alternative short-term financing vehicles, financial managers have at their disposal a wide variety of debt instruments. Their objective, of course, is to select the vehicles and techniques that contribute most to the continuity of operations and the value of the firm. Toward this end, the financial manager must develop formal or informal short-run financing strategies. A variety of issues must be addressed in developing a short-run financing strategy and successfully managing the current liabilities of the firm. We will look here at funding strategies, hedging with interest

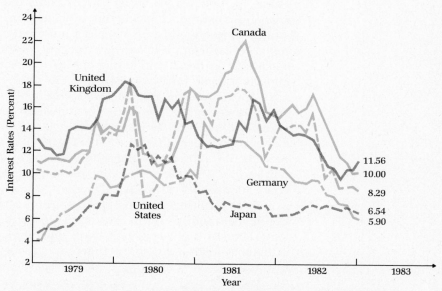

Figure 11.3   Short-Term Interest Rates for Selected Countries (1979–1982).
Source: Federal Reserve Bank of St. Louis, *International Economic Conditions,* April 21, 1983, p. 60.

rate futures, the special problem of managing accounts payable, and the factoring decision. The goal throughout is (assuming risk is unaffected) to minimize the cost of financing while maintaining needed financing support. Achieving this goal should contribute to the operating efficiency, profitability, and value of the firm. We begin with some basic managerial considerations.

Basic Considerations

In a general sense, the level and composition of current liabilities is a function of the type of financing support required and the competitive costs of financing. Given that effective debt management should contribute to the long-run well-being of the company and the value of the firm, it follows that in the area of short-term funding, financial managers should attempt to maximize support from the current liabilities, and at the same time, minimize the cost of financing and exposure to risk. This may seem a Herculean task, but certain management actions can move the firm closer to the attainment of these goals. To begin with, the financing package should be structured primarily to meet the operating needs and constraints of the firm. Clearly, since the firm is paying for the use of the money, liabilities should be structured so that they provide maximum support to the firm and interfere as little as possible with operations.

Several basic principles are paramount to effective debt management and are especially important when negotiating and managing loans.[14] These include: (1) carefully determining the amount and type of financing required; (2) giving due consideration to both the source and timing of repayment; and (3) making sure that a strong financial base is being constructed, with an eye toward the possible future financial needs of the firm. Pinpointing the amount of financing required is important in minimizing costs, especially during periods of high interest rates. For example, in August 1981, when the cost of short-term loans to business was in the 18 to 20 percent range, lowering the average amount of debt outstanding by just $500,000 would reduce interest costs (and increase pretax profits) by about $100,000 per year! By more precisely defining the amount of money required, and by determining the amount that can be generated internally (see the discussion in Chapter 4), the financial manager can keep the amount of costly external funds needed to operate the firm to a minimum. Determining the best type of financing to use is also important to debt management, as different kinds of debt (and different debt provisions) carry different costs, and different types of financial institutions charge different rates for their money. In essence, it often pays to shop around for the best financing package. What is more, some types of financing arrangements are often more compatible

---

[14]The managerial dimensions of spontaneous credit are discussed in a subsequent part of this section.

with the operating characteristics of the firm and/or cause less interference in the operations of the company, and should obviously be sought to fill certain financing needs; a good example of this is the use of flooring lines to finance certain types of inventory.

The question of loan repayment is an often overlooked but nonetheless essential ingredient of effective debt management; and it is an issue that should be addressed at the time the loan is taken out. For the debt to be truly supportive of the needs of the firm, repayment should not place undue strains on operations. Rather, management should assess projected cash flow to determine whether or not, and to what extent, the firm will have resources available to service the debt "comfortably"—that is, the firm should be able to repay the debt while maintaining a normal operating posture. If repayment places an onerous burden on the operations of the firm, the loan is hardly providing the support desired. Finally, because the firm will undoubtedly have additional financing needs in the future, it is best to structure current financing in such a way as to leave open as many options as possible with regard to future needs. Obviously, present requirements must be filled, but the more they can be filled with an eye toward the future, the better off the firm will be.

Funding Strategies

Managing current liabilities has a direct effect on the profitability and therefore the value of a firm in two ways: it can affect both the cost of financing and the amount of financing outstanding. Obviously, the higher the cost and/or the greater the amount of short-term debt being used, the more expensive this form of financing will be. Financing costs are nonoperating expenditures and as such, represent a direct drain on profits, especially in periods of high-cost financing. So long as the necessary financing can be arranged, the level of operations and the amount of operating profit should be independent of the financing decisions of the firm. On the other hand, controlling financing costs and the level of current liabilities is not solely a debt management function. The operating efficiency, the level of operating resources required to conduct the business, and the firm's cash flow all directly affect the amount (and possibly even the cost) of financing. Success in the management of current liabilities, therefore, is at least in part a function of the management of operations and assets.

We also saw above that successful debt management depends on the amount and type of financing being used, the timing of the debt, and the term (repayment date) of the loan. Each of these decision variables is clearly within the control of the financial manager, and each can have a direct impact on short-term funding activities. Financial managers can control the amount and maturity of nonspontaneous financing, as well as the type of lending arrangement set up; they also have an input as to when a loan will be taken out and when it will be repaid. Determining comparative effective interest rates can help management assess the cost of alternative financing vehicles and select the one with the competitive cost advantage, all other things being the same.

Hedging
with Interest Rate
Futures

The timing decision can significantly affect the cost of financing and therefore the level of profitability. Short-term rates are quite volatile, and altering the date that a loan is taken out by a week or two can often have a significant bearing on the total cost of funds. Financial managers have two options with respect to actively timing new loans: The firm can time the debt according to predicted interest rate behavior, or it can hedge the risk of interest rates moving against the firm by using interest rate futures. Hedging with interest rate futures is an effective, low-cost way of dealing with the timing problem. Predicting interest rates consistently and accurately, unless the forecasting time frame is very short, is difficult, if not impossible.[15]

Interest rate futures are a relatively recent development that have enabled debt managers to obtain a substantial amount of protection against interest rate risks. (Interest rate futures contracts and several hedging strategies are described in detail in Appendix 21A.) An *interest rate futures contract* is nothing more than a commodities contract written on a large quantity of an underlying debt instrument; T-bills, 90-day commercial paper, and bank CDs, for example, are traded as futures contracts in units of $1 million. *Hedging* involves taking a position in the futures market as a temporary substitute for the purchase or sale of an actual financial instrument (like a Treasury bill, commercial paper, or a bank CD). A hedge would be used, for example, when it is known that the firm will have to raise short-term money in the near future, but the debt manager is concerned that interest rates will undergo a measurable increase by the date of issue. Hedging under these conditions would provide a way of "locking in" a prevailing low rate on a loan well before the debt is actually taken out. Obviously, if the manager feels strongly that rates are about to move down, there would be no incentive to hedge, since the procedure would effectively "lock in" the current higher rate.

To illustrate, assume it is January 1984 and the treasurer of a firm knows he will have to issue $10 million worth of commercial paper in the middle of May to finance a seasonal buildup in receivables and inventory. Although the market rate of interest for commercial paper is 11.5 percent by mid-May. So the financial manager decides to sell 10 June commercial paper contracts, each with a face value of $1 million. Now, no matter what happens to the rate on commercial paper, the financial

---

[15]See, for example, Bowlin and Martin, "Extrapolations of Yields," and Michael J. Prell, "How Well Do the Experts Forecast Interest Rates?" Federal Reserve Bank of Kansas City, *Monthly Review*, September–October 1973.

manager is protected to the extent that he has locked in the prevailing 11 percent rate. In essence, any profit or loss from the 10 interest rate futures contracts is (approximately) offset by the increase or decrease in the final cost of actually issuing the commercial paper. In fact, the worst thing that can happen at this point is for rates to fall, since the hedge position will cause the firm to miss the lower rates. Given that the debt manager will issue $10 million worth of 90-day paper in May, the net cost of borrowing the money under different interest rate conditions is spelled out below:

	Interest Rates Drop to 10.5%	Interest Rates Stay at 11%	Interest Rates Rise to 11.5%
Interest cost on issue of 90-day, $10 million commercial paper in mid-May	$262,500	$275,000	$287,500
Less: Profit (or loss) from interest rate futures position[a]	(12,500)	—	12,500
Net cost	$275,000	$275,000	$275,000

[a]A 1 basis point (.0001) movement in a $1 million, 90-day commercial paper contract is worth $25 [.0001 × $1,000,000 × (90/360)]; therefore, a 50 basis point change for 10 contracts results in a profit (or loss) of 50 × 10 × $25 = $12,500.

In the case of interest rates rising to 11.5 percent, the debt manager sold the futures contracts in January, bought them back in May at a discount due to the higher interest rate, and then used the profit from the futures transaction to offset the added interest charges incurred when the commercial paper was actually issued in May. Although this tactic essentially locks in the interest rate that prevailed when the futures contracts were sold (the hedge initiated), it does work to the disadvantage of firms when rates drop. Note above that the hedge cost the company $12,500 when rates fell by half a point to 10.5 percent since the contract would have to be bought back at a premium due to the lower interest rate. Also note that this turned out to be a "perfect" hedge (to the extent that the loss in one transaction was offset precisely by a gain in the other), since both the futures contracts and the commercial paper issue had 90-day maturities. Hedging tactics can be helpful, since they enable treasurers to maintain or reduce borrowing costs and thus contribute to effective debt management.[16]

---

[16]For additional discussion on interest rate futures and corporate hedging strategies, see Appendix 21A, as well as Peter W. Bacon and Richard E. Williams, "Interest Rate Futures: New Tool for the Financial Manager," *Financial Management* 5 (spring 1976), pp. 32–38.

Managing
Accounts Payable

Since accounts payable are a form of spontaneous credit, there is no direct managerial discretion exercised with respect to whether or not the debt should be incurred; rather, that decision is made automatically when it is decided to acquire the inventory from the supplier. Managemént, however, does have considerable influence over deciding when such debt will be repaid. In fact, in most forms of trade credit, financial managers face two decisions: The first is whether or not the cash discount should be taken, and the second is that if the firm does not pay on the cash discount date (or if no cash discount is offered), deciding whether to repay the obligation on the net due date or to attempt to stretch the payable beyond the specified time.

The Cash Discount Decision.   Assume a firm is extended credit terms that include a cash discount provision for early payment—say, 2/10 net 30. The financial manager must determine whether it is advisable to take or forego the cash discount offered in this situation. This can be done by comparing the effective cost of the cash discount with the firm's opportunity cost (or competitive borrowing rate). For example, with credit terms of 2/10 net 30, the cost of foregoing the cash discount (as we saw from Equation 11.2) amounts to 36.73 percent. If the firm has an investment opportunity that offers an even greater rate of return ($r >$ 36.73%), and the probability of realizing that rate of return is virtually assured,[17] the firm should obviously forego the cash discount and use the money internally. This action will clearly improve the marginal return and long-run profitability of the firm.

Most firms, of course, do not regularly have such attractive (and risk-free) investment opportunities, and therefore the incentive is to take the cash discount and benefit from the resulting cost reduction. This is appropriate for firms that have the cash (or marketable securities) readily available for such purposes. But what about the company that is temporarily short of funds? Though management would like to take the cash discount, the money simply is not available. Under such conditions, the cost of the cash discount should be compared to competitive financing costs to determine whether or not it is appropriate to take the discount. For instance, if a firm buys $100,000 of inventory on terms of 2/10 net 30, and if it can borrow from its bank at 18 percent, it is obviously worthwhile to borrow the money to take the cash discount. The effective annual cost of the loan is much less than the benefits to be derived from taking the discount (18% $<$ 36.73%). This can be confirmed with dollar figures, as follows:

---

[17]A high probability of success is a necessary condition, since management knows with certainty that taking the cash discount will result in an effective interest savings of 36.73 percent.

Cash discount available for paying the credit 20 days early—on the 10th rather than the 30th day ($100,000 × .02)	$2,000
Less: Interest cost on a 20-day loan from the bank at 18% per year [$98,000 × .18 × (20/360)]	980
Net savings	$1,020

Note that the size of the loan amounts to only $98,000 because after the cash discount is deducted, the firm need pay its supplier only the net amount. Borrowing from the bank is clearly in the best interest of the firm; and keep in mind that the net savings are obtained in a span of only 20 days (it is assumed that since the trade credit would otherwise be repaid on the net due date, the bank loan will also be retired on the same date).

Stretching Payables.   Accounts payable that are not paid on the cash discount date are supposed to be retired no later than the stipulated net due date. In practice, however, it is not uncommon for firms to delay repayment beyond the net due date, especially during periods of tight money and/or high interest rates. The practice is known as *stretching payables*, and it is used as a way to reduce the implicit cost of using trade credit. The idea is really quite simple: To implement a stretching program, the firm need only be late in paying its accounts payable; that is, the firm makes its payments some 10 to 15 days after the net due date. The risk, of course, is that the supplier will lower the firm's credit rating and place the company on a cash basis. To see the effect on the cost of financing, consider the 2/10 net 30 terms we have been using. We saw from Equation 11.2 that these terms had an implied interest cost of 36.73 percent. By stretching payables just half a month (15 days), the effective cost of foregoing the cash discount (the cost of using trade credit as a financing vehicle) drops to 20.99 percent [(.02 ÷ .98) × (360 ÷ 35 days)]—a cost of financing that may be highly competitive with borrowing from a bank, when the prime rate is high.

The Factoring Decision

Generally, the decision whether or not to factor is more serious than most other debt management decisions. To begin with, it is normally an infrequent decision to the extent that the issue being raised is whether or not to use a factor on a continuous basis; in essence, the firm is making a decision about the company's manner of operations. Factors customarily are not used as temporary (seasonal) fundraising vehicles—the cost of such financing is simply prohibitive. Instead, the decision to use a factor normally implies that management has decided to use the factoring organization in place of the company's own credit and collection department.[18]

Evaluating the factoring decision involves consideration of the ongoing benefits and costs that are likely to accrue to the firm. Among the benefits are these: (1) the partial or complete elimination of credit and collection administrative expenses, (2) the eradication of bad debts (since such risks are assumed by the factor), and (3) the additional investment returns that will accrue from any speedup of cash flow to the firm. On the cost side, the firm will have to bear: (1) the cost of the discount, (2) the opportunity cost (or profit lost) from the hold-back reserve, and (3) the interest charges on any advances. As a practical matter, the decision to use a factor should be made independently from the decision to obtain an advance from the factor.

To see how the evaluation process works, consider the following situation. A company has annual credit sales of $10 million and carries an average 60-day supply of receivables; a factor has offered to buy all the company's accounts (on a continuous basis) at a 2 percent discount from the face value. The factor requires a 25 percent hold-back reserve on current average receivables outstanding, and once the reserve is built up, will automatically deposit collections in the firm's checking account on a daily basis; it will also make payment on any accounts still uncollected at the end of the firm's 30-day credit period and will make advances on uncollected receivables at the prime rate plus 2 percentage points. If the receivables are factored, the company estimates it will save $85,000 per year in credit and collection expenses, and another $50,000 in bad debt writeoffs (annual bad debts have been amounting to about one half of 1 percent of sales); the company has an 18 percent pretax opportunity cost. The first step in the process is to determine whether the firm should use the factor. The numerical analysis for this decision is shown in Table 11.2.

In this case, the benefits are expected to exceed the costs, and, as a result, the firm should give serious consideration to factoring. The major benefit is the reduced cost of investment in receivables. This results in a speedup in the cash flow to the firm, since the level of receivables will drop from the current 60 days to an estimated 20 days with the services of the factor. The lower level results primarily from a provision in the factoring agreement that sets a maximum 30-day limit on payment to the firm. Since that sets an outside limit on the collection of receivables and since some accounts pay early, receivables should amount to about a 20-day supply if the services of the factor are used. This acts as a net

---

[18]When factors are used on an occasional basis, the fundraising question is paramount and presumably the firm has no intention of dismantling its credit and collection department. Given that the cost of discounting the receivables plus the interest charge on advances would seldom, if ever, be competitive with more traditional forms of financing, it would seem that the use of factors as periodic sources of financing is done more out of necessity than by choice.

TABLE 11.2
Benefit-Cost Analysis of
the Factoring Decision

ANNUAL BENEFITS		
Cost savings—credit and collection expenses	$ 85,000	
Cost savings—bad debt expenses	50,000	
Reduced cost of investment in receivables—estimated 20-day level of receivables with a factor vs. 60-day without [$10 million ÷ (360/(60 − 20)) × .18]	200,000	
Total annual benefits		$335,000
ANNUAL COSTS		
Discount on receivables (.02 × $10 million)	$200,000	
Opportunity cost of holdback reserve [$10 million ÷ (360/60) × .25 × .18]	75,000	
Less: Total annual costs		275,000
Annual net gain (loss)		$ 60,000

reduction in receivables and essentially frees funds that the firm can use elsewhere (at an estimated 18 percent pretax rate of return).

If the firm wanted to consider using the factor as a source of financing for a temporary loan or line of credit, it could simply compare the cost of advances from the factor (prime plus 2 percent) with the cost of obtaining similar funds from some other form of nonspontaneous financing. One thing that would probably work in favor of the factor is that the mechanism is already in place to execute the loan (or line). Of course, there is a limit to this benefit; it would make a difference only in those cases where the cost of obtaining advances from the factor would be about equal to, or slightly more expensive than, alternative forms of financing.

SUMMARY

The management of current liabilities is important because of the direct bearing it has on the firm's cost of funds as well as the impact it has on the firm's liquidity, exposure to risk, continuity of operations, and value. Managing current liabilities involves meeting the cash and liquidity needs of the firm, structuring current liabilities in a fashion consistent with the firm's operating and cash flow characteristics, servicing the debt in a prompt and orderly fashion, and obtaining maximum use and support from the debt while minimizing its cost. Short-term financing is available from a variety of sources, including the firm's suppliers, its employees, the government, various financial institutions, and investors. Table 11.3 briefly summarizes the key information on each of the major sources discussed in this chapter. Spontaneous credit results from the normal operations of the firm, whereas nonspontaneous credit repre-

TABLE 11.3
Sources of Short-Term Financing

Type of Financing	Source	Cost and Conditions	Characteristics
SPONTANEOUS SOURCES			
Accounts payable	Suppliers of goods and services	No explicit cost except when cash discount is offered for early payment	Credit extended on open account for 30 to 90 days; largest source of short-term financing
Accruals	Employees, government, and other suppliers of services.	Free	Results from fact that wages, taxes, and other services are paid at points in time after the service has been rendered; hard to manipulate this source of financing
UNSECURED BANK LOANS			
Single-payment note	Commercial banks	Prime plus 0 to 4% risk premium, fixed or floating rate	Single-payment note used to meet a funds shortage expected to last only a short period of time
Lines of credit	Commercial banks	Prime plus 0 to 4% risk premium, fixed or floating rate; 10 to 20% compensating balance required	Prearranged borrowing limit under which funds will be lent to allow the borrower to meet seasonal needs; with a commitment fee, lender guarantees availability of funds to borrower
NONSPONTANEOUS SOURCES			
Secured financing Pledging accounts receivable	Commercial banks and commercial finance companies	2 to 5% above prime plus up to 3% in fees; advance 50 to 90% of collateral value	Selected accounts receivable used as collateral; borrower is trusted to remit to lender on collection of pledged accounts; done on a nonnotification basis
Inventory collateral Floating liens	Commercial banks and commercial finance companies	3 to 5% above prime; advance less than 50% of collateral value	Loan against inventory in general, made when firm has stable inventory of a variety of inexpensive items

Type	Source	Cost	Characteristics
	...tive financing subsidiaries, commercial banks, and commercial finance companies	prime; advance 80 to 100% of cost of collateral	...Loan against collateral that is relatively expensive and can be identified by serial number; collateral remains in possession of borrower, who is trusted to remit proceeds to lender upon sale (often called "floor planning")
Warehouse receipt loans	Commercial banks and commercial finance companies	3 to 5% above prime plus a 1 to 3% warehouse fee; advance 75 to 90% of collateral value	Inventory used as collateral and placed under control of lender; third party (a warehouse company) acts as agent for lender and issues a warehouse receipt held by lender
Factoring accounts receivable	Factors, commercial finance companies, and commercial banks	1 to 3% discount from face value of factored accounts; interest on advances of 2 to 4% above prime; interest on surplus balances left with factor of about .5% per month	Selected accounts sold—generally without recourse—at a discount, with all credit risks; factor makes advances against accounts sold but not yet scheduled for remittance to seller; factor also pays interest on surplus balances; typically done on a notification basis
Commercial paper financing	Other businesses, commercial banks, individuals, insurance companies, and other financial institutions	1 to 3% below prime	Unsecured short-term promissory note issued by financially sound companies; may be placed directly or sold through commercial paper houses
Eurodollar loans	Loans from foreign banks with characteristics similar to large domestic dollar loans. Access to the market is typically limited to larger better-known firms.	1 to 2% above IBOR or the U.S. prime rate. Typically these are variable interest rate loans.	Many are short-term unsecured loans; medium-term loans are also made. Very large loans are typically syndicated to spread the risk.

sents direct loans that are obtained through negotiation with banks and other financial institutions. The two major forms of spontaneous credit are accounts payable and accruals. There is no explicit cost to accounts payable, but there is an implicit cost associated with foregoing any cash discounts. Accruals are liabilities that represent benefits such as wages and taxes that have been received but not yet paid for.

Nonspontaneous financing is used to finance seasonal needs and can be obtained from domestic as well as foreign banks, commercial finance companies, factors, suppliers of major capital goods, and money market investors. Major financing vehicles include unsecured and secured bank loans and lines of credit, factoring, commercial paper, and Eurodollar loans. The two major types of collateral for secured short-term loans are accounts receivable and inventory. In contrast to a single-payment note, a line of credit conveniently provides the borrower with debt financing on a "when-needed" basis. Although all forms of nonspontaneous credit carry explicit interest charges, a line of credit may be subject to a commitment fee, which is a charge for guaranteeing the availability of the money. Another "cost" common with bank loans is a compensating balance requirement, which requires the borrower to maintain a minimum demand deposit with the bank and may result in increasing the effective cost of the credit.

Actively managing a firm's current liabilities involves determining the amount as well as type of financing, and the source and timing of its repayment. Using interest rate futures to hedge interest rate risk is gaining in popularity; the idea is to lock in the prevailing (lower) rate with interest rate futures when interest rates are expected to increase. The management of accounts payable involves decisions with regard to whether or not the firm should take a cash discount, and whether or not it should stretch its payables. To make a factoring decision, the benefits of reduced administrative and bad debt expenses and improved cash flow must be weighed against the costs of the cash discounts, the opportunity cost of the reserve, and the interest charges on advances.

QUESTIONS

11.1. Briefly discuss some of the advantages and disadvantages of short-term credit.

11.2. List and briefly discuss the major suppliers of short-term credit; are these financing sources equally effective in meeting both temporary and permanent working capital needs? Explain.

11.3. Explain the effects inflation has had on the cost of short-term financing. Do you suppose this has had any bearing on the profitability and value of firms? What about the firm's exposure to risk? Finally, what (if any) impact has inflation had on the debt management functions of the firm? Explain.

11.4. Contrast spontaneous with nonspontaneous forms of financing:
  a. Which is the more expensive form of financing?
  b. Note some specific types of spontaneous and nonspontaneous financing.

11.5. The Evergreen Company is facing a serious cash flow problem; specifically, its customers are beginning to slow down their payments at a time when the company is expanding its inventory in anticipation of increased seasonal demand. Discuss each of the following remedial actions, and note the impact each is likely to have on obtaining the needed financing:
  a. Persuade suppliers to use seasonal datings on upcoming inventory purchases.
  b. Forego cash discounts on accounts payable.
  c. Increase the firm's line of credit at the bank.
  d. Factor the receivables with one of the local commercial finance companies.

11.6. For each of the following forms of short-term financing, indicate a type of company (or industry) that would be a major user of such financing, and the probable reason(s) for its use:
  a. Accounts payable as the single most important type of financing.
  b. A flooring line.
  c. Factored accounts receivable.
  d. Commercial paper.

11.7. Discuss the type and amount of managerial discretion inherent in each of the following forms of credit:
  a. Accounts payable.
  b. Accrued wages.
  c. An unsecured bank loan that carries a 30 percent compensating balance requirement.
  d. An unsecured line of credit.
  e. A single-payment note secured by a "jumbo" CD.

11.8. The Malone Distributing Company is evaluating several loan proposals; note the impact, if any, each of the following would have on the effective cost of financing:
  a. Interest is computed using the discount method rather than on the basis of simple interest.
  b. One of the banks requires a compensating balance well above the amount usually carried on deposit by Malone.
  c. Another bank has a compensating balance requirement that is about equal to, or slightly less than, the amount usually carried on deposit by Malone.
  d. Several lenders require a service charge (to be paid at the time the loan is taken out) for setting up the loan and covering the administrative costs associated with collateral.

    e. A commitment fee would have to be paid if the financing is taken out as a line of credit.

    f. Some lenders propose fixed rate loans, and others propose floating interest rates at prime plus .5 to 1.5 percent.

11.9. Why is it important to define the amount and type of financing required as well as the source and timing of repayment when financing packages are being set up?

    a. Note especially the impact of such decisions on continuity of operations, corporate profitability, and risk.

    b. Briefly discuss how debt managers would go about defining the amount and type of financing required.

    c. Explain how debt managers would define the source and timing of repayment.

11.10. Explain how interest rate futures hedging can be used to improve debt timing and reduce attendant exposure to interest rate risk. Why should an expected rise in interest rates be a vital condition for using such hedges? Explain.

11.11. Given that commercial paper rates are frequently less than prime lending rates, why would a firm that has the option choose to borrow money from a bank rather than issue commercial paper? In a similar vein, why would a firm forego the cash discount on trade credit if the money could be raised through a bank loan or line of credit? Explain.

PROBLEMS

11.1. *FOREGOING CASH DISCOUNTS.* Jacobson Tool is considering four possible suppliers of steel. Except for differences in credit terms, their products and services are undifferentiated. The credit terms offered by each supplier are given below.

Supplier	Credit Terms[a]
A	2/10 net 30
B	1/10 net 55
C	3/20 net 70
D	4/10 net 60

[a]Credit period begins at the end of month in all cases.

    a. Calculate the cost of foregoing the cash discount from each supplier.

    b. Assuming that Jacobson Tool needs money and can borrow from its bank at 15 percent, looking at each supplier independently, would Jacobson be wise in taking or foregoing the cash discount if it always pays on the last day of the credit period?

    c. If Jacobson Tool knows it must forego cash discounts since it desperately needs money, from which of the four possible suppliers would you recommend the purchase be made? Explain why.

d.   If Jacobson already has sufficient short-term financing (that is, it will take the cash discount), from which supplier would you recommend the purchase be made? Why?

e.   Compare and contrast your recommendations and findings in (b), (c), and (d) above. What role does the cost of foregoing the cash discount play in the accounts payable decision process?

11.2.   *MANAGING ACCRUALS.* When Bill took over as senior vice-president of finance at Dealer's Distribution Centers, one of his first acts was to change the firm's payday from twice a month (the 15th and the 30th) to just once a month (the 30th). Actually, to minimize any hardships on employees, he instituted the change slowly over a 6-month time period, but this aspect can be ignored in the problem. Dealer's Distribution is a leading importer and distributor of Japanese cars, trucks, specialized motor vehicles, and parts; it has a monthly payroll of about $2.5 million. If the company has a 15 percent opportunity cost, what annual returns, if any, did the firm realize by this move?

11.3.   *FIXED VERSUS FLOATING RATES.*   The Alpha Management Group is a leading firm in one of the major service industries and as a result is considered to be a prime grade borrower. Because of its stature, Alpha is able to borrow at either fixed or floating rates of interest. Alpha's chief financial officer has a policy of trying to formulate interest rate expectations when deciding whether to use a fixed or floating rate. She recently completed her prime rate forecast for the next 12 months; her estimates are as follows:

Period	Prime Rate
1st quarter	13.00%
2nd quarter	13.60
3rd quarter	13.70
4th quarter	13.75

a.   If the company can borrow at prime when it uses a floating rate, what would be the maximum fixed rate Alpha should be willing to pay for a 12-month, single-payment loan? Explain.

b.   What if the financial officer was uncertain about her forecasts (she has only 50 percent confidence in the numbers)? How would this affect your answer?

c.   Briefly outline a strategy you would recommend that Alpha adopt when deciding whether to borrow under fixed or floating rates.

11.4.   *THE COST OF MONEY.*   The financial manager at Bartelow Manufacturing is in the process of evaluating the cost of its short-term financing. The company uses a number of different types of lending arrangements. Find the effective rate of interest for each of the four arrangements below:

a.   It has an $80,000 single-payment note outstanding for 6 months; interest (at 12 percent) was charged on a discount basis.

b.   It has a line of credit for a full year; the line was for $500,000, and the firm had average daily loans outstanding against the line of about $200,000. The bank charged 11 percent simple interest on actual loan use.

c.   It has a monthly instalment loan outstanding taken out for the purpose of buying several special-duty trucks. It is a 3-year, $50,000 loan, and interest is charged on the declining balance at the rate of 13 percent.

d.   It has taken out a 1-year, single-payment loan from a competing bank, and because the company has no demand deposits with the bank, it has to meet a 20 percent compensating balance requirement as part of the condition of the loan. The loan is for $250,000, and interest is charged at the simple interest rate of prime plus 1.5 points (prime is assumed to be 11 percent for the first 4 months of the loan, 11.5 percent for the next 2 months, 12 percent for the next 5 months, and finally 13.5 percent for the last month of the loan).

11.5.   *ALTERNATIVE FINANCING VEHICLES.*   Bud Rose Supplies is a small construction supply company. Murry Weed, the owner, manager, and chief financial officer, recently learned that the company will be facing a tight cash flow situation for the next several months. The company usually runs about $3 million per year in sales, but because of high interest rates and a slump in the economy, revenues and cash flow are expected to drop off substantially. Weed has decided that the best thing to do is to meet the cash flow bind by building up current liabilities. He feels he has three options:

Option 1.   Start passing up cash discounts and instead make payments on trade credit on the net due dates—all the company's suppliers extend credit terms of 1½/10 net 30.

Option 2.   Start stretching payables beyond the net due dates by making payments 15 days late.

Option 3.   Take out a 6-month loan at the bank—the company will need a minimum of $200,000, and a loan can be obtained at 14 percent (simple) interest, with a compensating balance requirement of 25 percent. (Because of the company's present cash flow situation, it is expected the firm's normal checking account balance will drop to about $10,000.)

Which arrangement should Weed choose? Why? In addition to cost, are there any other factors that should be considered in this decision? Explain.

11.6. *PLEDGING OR FACTORING RECEIVABLES.*   Continental Manufacturing is considering obtaining funds through advances against receivables. Total credit sales are $12 million, terms are net 30 days, and payment is made (on average) in 30 days. City State Bank will advance funds under a pledging arrangement for 18 percent annual interest; 80 percent of credit sales will be accepted as collateral. Friendly Finance, in contrast, offers factoring on a nonrecourse basis for a 1.5 percent factoring commission (charged on a discount basis), with interest of 1.5 percent per month on average advances (for 15 days), and requiring a 20 percent hold-back reserve. Under this plan, the firm would factor all accounts and close its credit and collections department, freeing up $600,000 per year, which has a 16 percent opportunity cost.

a. What is the effective interest rate and the average amount of funds made available under pledging and under factoring?

b. What other effects must be considered in choosing either of these plans?

c. Which plan do you recommend, and why?

d. Would your answer in (c) change if Continental planned to use the factor only for this one deal? Explain.

11.7. *USING INTEREST RATE FUTURES.*   Assume it is October 8, and Homeway Finance has just announced it is planning a $3 million, 90-day debt issue at the end of the year (use a 360-day year). Unfortunately, rates have been rising rapidly lately, and the treasurer of Homeway feels very strongly that the rise will probably continue for the rest of the year and possibly into the first quarter of next year. The treasurer's office has prepared forecasts which show prime short-term rates moving to 13.5 percent by year-end from their current level of 12 percent. As a result, it has been decided to use interest rate futures (90-day commercial paper contracts) to lock in the prevailing 12 percent rate.

a. Set up an interest rate futures hedge that will provide protection against perceived interest rate risk. Set up the numbers to show that from a net cost perspective, the company will be indifferent between issuing the debt today at 12 percent, or setting up the hedge and issuing the debt at year-end, at the higher rate of 13.5 percent.

b. Using the hedge you set up above, show what happens to comparative net costs if the company only needs to borrow the money for 30 days.

c. Rework (a), assuming the firm needs to borrow the money for 6 months.

d. Repeat the hedging net cost computations for (a), (b), and (c), assuming interest rates actually fall by 1.5 percent by year-end. Explain the cause of the results you obtained.

SELECTED REFERENCES

Bacon, Peter W., and Richard E. Williams. "Interest Rate Futures: New Tool for the Financial Manager." *Financial Management* 5 (spring 1976), pp. 32–38.

Baxter, Nevin D. *The Commercial Paper Market.* Princeton, N.J.: Princeton University Press, 1964.

———, and Harold T. Shapiro. "Compensating Balance Requirements: The Results of a Survey." *Journal of Finance* 19 (September 1964), pp. 483–496.

Berger, Paul D., and William K. Harper. "Determination of an Optimal Revolving Credit Agreement." *Journal of Financial and Quantitative Analysis* 8 (June 1973), pp. 491–498.

Bonen, Thomas K., and Patricia Brown Kolber. "Hedging Can Reduce Corporate Rate Imbalance." *Financial Executive* 51 (February 1983), pp. 20–30.

Bowlin, Oswald D., and John D. Martin. "Extrapolations of Yields over the Short Run: Forecast or Folly?" *Journal of Monetary Economics* 1 (1975), pp. 275–288.

Brosky, John J. *The Implicit Cost of Trade Credit and Theory of Optimal Terms of Sale.* New York: Credit Research Foundation, 1969.

Crane, Dwight B., and William L. White. "Who Benefits from a Floating Prime Rate?" *Harvard Business Review* 50 (January–February 1972), pp. 121–129.

Denonn, Lester E. "The Security Agreement." *Journal of Commercial Bank Lending* 50 (February 1968), pp. 32–40.

Folks, William R., Jr. "The Analysis of Short-Term Cross-Border Financing Decisions." *Financial Management* 5 (autumn 1976), pp. 19–27.

Handorf, William C. "Flexible Debt Financing." *Financial Management* 3 (summer 1974), pp. 17–23.

Hayes, Douglas A. *Bank Lending Policies: Domestic and International.* Ann Arbor, Mich.: University of Michigan Press, 1971.

MacPhee, William A. *Short-Term Business Borrowing: Sources, Terms and Techniques.* Homewood, Il: Dow Jones-Irwin, 1984.

Nadiri, M. I. "The Determinants of Trade Credit in the U.S. Total Manufacturing Sector." *Econometrics* 37 (July 1969), pp. 408–423.

Nadler, Paul S. "Compensating Balances and the Prime at Twilight." *Harvard Business Review* 50 (January–February 1972), pp. 112–120.

Powell, John R. P., and Roger C. Vergin. "A Heuristic Model for Planning Corporate Financing." *Financial Management* 4 (summer 1975), pp. 13–20.

Prell, Michael J. "How Well Do the Experts Forecast Interest Rates?" Federal Reserve Bank of Kansas City, *Monthly Review*, September–October 1973.

Quarles, J. Carson. "The Floating Lien." *Journal of Commercial Bank Lending* 53 (November 1970), pp. 51–58.

Quill, Gerald D., John C. Cresci, and Bruce D. Shuter. "Some Considerations about Secured Lending." *Journal of Commercial Bank Lending* 57 (April 1977), pp. 41–56.

Roberts, Gordon S., and Jerry A. Viscione. "Captive Finance Subsidiaries: The Manager's View." *Financial Management* 10 (spring 1981), pp. 36–42.

Robichek, Alexander A., D. Teichrow, and J. M. Jones. "Optimal Short-Term Financing Decisions." *Management Science* 12 (September 1965), pp. 1–36.

Rogers, Robert W. "Warehouse Receipts and Their Use in Financing." *Bulletin of the Robert Morris Associates* 46 (April 1964), pp. 317–327.

Schadrack, Frederick C., Jr. "Demand and Supply in the Commercial Paper Market." *Journal of Finance* 25 (September 1970), pp. 837–852.

Schwartz, Robert A. "An Economic Analysis of Trade Credit." *Journal of Financial and Quantitative Analysis* 9 (September 1974), pp. 643–658.

Shay, Robert P., and Carl C. Green. "Banks Move into High-Risk Commercial Financing." *Harvard Business Review* 46 (November–December 1968), pp. 149–153, 156–161.

Silvers, J. B. "Liquidity, Risk and Duration Patterns in Corporate Financing." *Financial Management* 5 (August 1976), pp. 54–64.

Stone, Bernell K. "The Cost of Bank Loans." *Journal of Financial and Quantitative Analysis* 7 (December 1972), pp. 2077–2086.

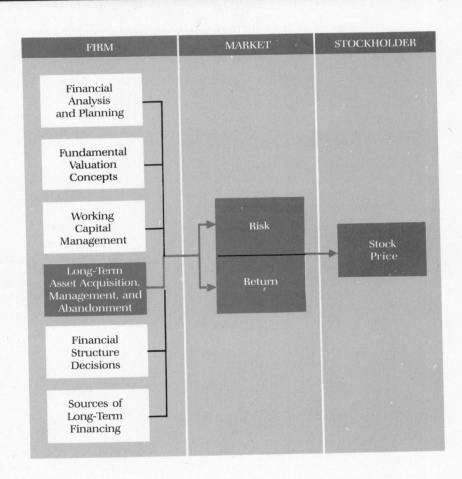

FIRM	MARKET	STOCKHOLDER

Financial Analysis and Planning

Fundamental Valuation Concepts

Working Capital Management

Long-Term Asset Acquisition, Management, and Abandonment

Financial Structure Decisions

Sources of Long-Term Financing

Risk

Return

Stock Price

PART FIVE

LONG-TERM ASSET ACQUISITION, MANAGEMENT, AND ABANDONMENT

This part of the book includes five chapters concerned with decisions surrounding the acquisition, management, and abandonment of long-term, or capital, assets. Unlike current assets, these resources are employed in the production of goods and services and are ordinarily used for many years. Because they are costly and significantly impact the long run, companies often employ large staffs to evaluate and make recommendations on proposed capital expenditures. The plan for these expenditures is called the capital budget. The process of determining how much to spend, and which assets to acquire or abandon, is called capital budgeting. In Chapter 12 the basic concepts of capital budgeting, along with methods for developing the necessary incremental cash flow data are presented. Techniques for evaluating proposed capital expenditures are examined in Chapter 13, and the impact of risk is considered in Chapter 14. The analysis of external growth through mergers and acquisitions, another capital budgeting decision, is the topic of Chapter 15. Finally, Chapter 16 is devoted to considering when the firm should abandon, divest, or possibly liquidate an asset or division. Part Five emphasizes the relationship between capital budgeting decisions and the goal of shareholder wealth maximization.

12

Capital Budgeting and Cash Flow Fundamentals

The financial manager is continually confronted with a wide variety of investment alternatives that must be analyzed to select those that make the greatest contribution to shareholder wealth. This process is called capital budgeting. It involves making capital expenditures—outlays which are expected to provide cash inflows over a number of years. Examples include alternatives such as buying new tire-making equipment or a computer, building a new distribution center, expanding an oil refinery, replacing a fleet of delivery trucks, or undertaking a new research and development (R&D) program. Capital budgeting concepts consider the magnitude, timing, and risks associated with the expected cash outflows and inflows. These same concepts can be applied to many other decisions within the firm including lease versus purchase, mergers, bond refunding, and the divestiture of plants or divisions. Emphasis in this chapter is given to the development of the relevant cash flows required to perform capital expenditure analyses. The first section describes the basic categories of capital expenditures and the structure and goals of capital budgeting. In addition, some procedural aspects of capital budgeting are briefly considered. In the second section, the steps involved in determining the relevant cash flows are described. The final section includes examples of cash flow determination—both for individual alternatives and on an incremental basis—and discusses other issues related to cash flow determination.

The Capital Budgeting Process

Historically, total plant and equipment expenditures by firms are very large. Figure 12.1(a) shows, during the 11-year period from 1972 through 1983, total capital expenditures for new plant and equipment rose from $99 billion to $247 billion. Likewise, as shown in Figure 12.1(b), during all but one of these years, firms made capital expenditures that exceeded their estimated internal cash flows from operations. Clearly, during the period shown, firms made capital expenditures using internally generated cash flows but they also invested substantial amounts of externally raised funds.

For a given firm the amounts involved in different proposals vary widely, from relatively inexpensive proposals to those that involve huge amounts of capital. Since the analysis of these proposals is not costless, the same depth of analysis, or approval process, is not required for all projects. The smaller the expenditure, the less formal the analysis and the further down in the organization the decision will be made. Related to the size of the proposal is its purpose: Is the project designed to reduce costs, increase revenues, or both? Cost reduction proposals usually provide more certainty about estimated cash flows than revenue expansion projects. Further, when a new project may replace an existing one, the analysis must focus on the *incremental cash flows*. That is, the cash flows associated with the existing project must be subtracted from those associated with the new project. Only by doing so will the analysis focus on the relevant incremental cash flows. Also, since firms consider

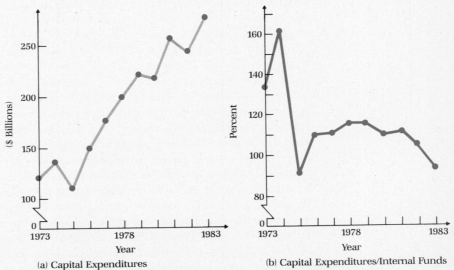

(a) Capital Expenditures   (b) Capital Expenditures/Internal Funds

Figure 12.1   Capital Expenditures on New Plant and Equipment.

Source: Flow of Funds Accounts, Board of Governors of the Federal Reserve System, selected issues.

many capital expenditure proposals simultaneously, the possibility of interrelationships among various projects must be recognized. As we will see, all these considerations can complicate capital expenditure analysis.

Categories of Capital Expenditures

A capital expenditure can be placed into one or more of the following nonexclusive categories: *expansion*, *replacement*, regulatory, miscellaneous, and *abandonment* decisions. Each of these is briefly described in Table 12.1.

Capital budgeting involves the comparison of the expected benefits and the costs of each proposal, taking into account their risks. If the present value of its benefits is greater than the present value of its costs, a project is acceptable (it contributes to shareholder wealth maximization) and therefore should be undertaken by the firm. Our primary focus is on two categories of projects: expansion and replacement. Both types require an outlay of cash followed by a stream of benefits in the form of increased cash inflows or reduced cash outflows. However, the estimation of the cash flows is sometimes more difficult for replacement than for expansion projects. This occurs because replacement projects must be evaluated in terms of their incremental cash flows while expansion projects can be evaluated using aggregate cash flows. However, the costs and benefits associated with an expansion project are often less certain than the savings associated with a project to reduce costs. This is because in the latter case the firm has a better sense of the potential cost savings from past production and cost data. For this reason, the most difficult and uncertain investments for a firm to analyze often concern expansion into a completely new area of operation.

Many of the projects considered by a firm are interrelated since the magnitude of the benefits from one project may depend on whether another is undertaken. Such relationships are described by their degree of dependence, and include both complementary and substitute projects. The nature of dependence is a matter of degree, as the continuum in Figure 12.2 shows. With complementary projects, if one project is undertaken, the cash flows associated with some other project are positively impacted. An example might be the decision of a firm to start producing either washing machines or clothes dryers. By undertaking

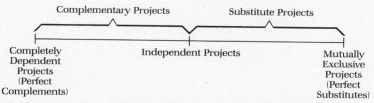

Figure 12.2   Degree of Dependence Among Capital Budgeting Projects.

TABLE 12.1
Capital Expenditure
Categories

Category	Description
Expansion of existing products or markets	Capital budgeting proposals in this category are made to acquire assets to expand production and/or distribution capacity. Generally, financial managers are familiar with the types of assets needed, the costs, and the risks involved in expanding existing facilities.
Expansion into new products or markets	Proposals that involve expansion into new products or markets are categorized separately because of the greater uncertainty involved. A more formal and complicated analysis, often starting with a marketing research study, is required when considering this form of expansion. Any proposed acquisition by the firm is a similar type of decision.
Replacement	Equipment that due to technical or physical obsolescence must be replaced is placed in this category. Generally, replacement decisions are made to achieve increased efficiency or reduced costs.
Regulatory	During the last few years many firms have been forced to make major capital expenditures because of safety or environmental requirements. These have typically been initiated to meet the mandates of the Occupational Safety and Health Administration (OSHA), the Environmental Protection Agency (EPA), or similar agencies. Because this category of expenditures provides no direct benefits to the firm in the form of increased revenues or reduced expenses, the issue becomes one of cost minimization.
Miscellaneous	Projects like office buildings, parking lots, and so on, which are designed to improve the overall comfort and efficiency of the employees but for which it is difficult to estimate specific dollar benefits , are placed in the miscellaneous category. Such projects include R&D projects, ad campaigns, lawsuits under possible antitrust or patent infringement, and the like. These, like those in the regulatory category, are commonly treated as cost minimization projects.
Abandonment	These decisions may involve anything from getting rid of equipment, closing a plant or warehouse, selling a division, or even liquidating the entire firm. Abandonment decisions, which are often overlooked by management, should be systematically analyzed like any other capital budgeting decision.

both projects, the total sales might be higher because families often simultaneously buy both a washer and a dryer. These projects are complementary, but not completely so. Projects that are completely dependent (perfect complements) require that one project must be undertaken only if the other project is also undertaken. All complementary projects, whether completely dependent or not, must be evaluated in light of their potential impact on one another, and should be grouped together in the capital budgeting decision process.

Substitute projects, in contrast, are those where the acceptance of one project reduces the cash flows from another. An example might be a decision by an automobile manufacturer to introduce a new small car. If the new car is expected to take sales from any of the existing cars sold by the manufacturer, the projects are substitutes for each other. Substitute projects must also be grouped together for capital budgeting purposes; otherwise the incremental benefits will be overstated. The extreme case of substitutes (perfect substitutes) is *mutually exclusive projects*. In this case, both projects can accomplish the same task, but only one is needed. An example of mutually exclusive projects might be the consideration of a number of energy saving temperature-control systems for an office building. Acceptance of one rules out the others.

Finally, as also shown in Figure 12.2, independent projects are those for which the benefits of one project are completely unrelated to those of other projects. In *the absense of any budget constraint*, projects that are completely independent can be considered in isolation from all other projects in the capital budgeting decision process.

Structure and Goals of Capital Budgeting

Capital budgeting involves everything from generating and evaluating proposals to selecting and following up on capital projects. In this section we examine the capital budgeting process from identification to postimplementation auditing, and then consider the relationship of this process to the firm's objective of shareholder wealth maximization.

Organizational Aspects. A systematic approach to capital budgeting requires an organizational process that facilitates the gathering and transfer of relevant information so decisions can be made and then monitored. Often organizations using fairly formal and complex systems achieve less than optimal results due to their lack of understanding and/or the inflexibility of the firm's capital budgeting process. One typical failing involves not providing those making the final decision with adequate background information concerning the potential consequences of alternative courses of action.[1] Such a practice results in

---

[1] For an interesting and somewhat critical analysis of this point, see K. Larry Hastie, "One Businessman's View of Capital Budgeting," *Financial Management* 3 (autumn 1974), pp. 36–44.

suboptimal decisions, and hence the goal of shareholder wealth maximization is not achieved.

Figure 12.3 depicts the basic structure of the capital budgeting process. The initial step, and one of the most difficult, involves the search and identification of capital expenditures that are both potentially feasible and in line with the objectives and/or expertise of the firm. Many projects are often suggested, but it requires a highly effective search and identification process to generate potentially rewarding ones compatible with the firm's long-run goals. The next step is the development of benefit and cost estimates, taking into account the varying degrees of risk involved. Obtaining accurate estimates of benefits and costs is time consuming and often viewed as the most difficult part of

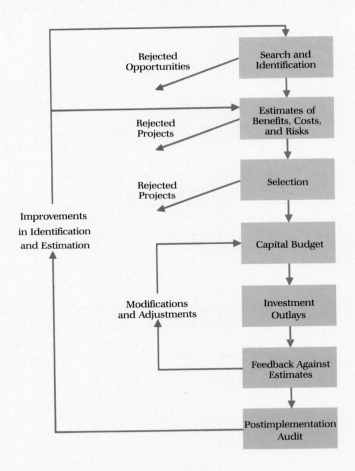

Figure 12.3   The Capital Budgeting Process.

the capital budgeting process.[2] The third step of the capital budgeting process is selection. We consider this phase in detail in Chapters 13 and 14. Once selected, the project is placed in the capital budget. The capital budget is important, because expenditures for major capital projects are often spread out over many years. In addition, there are critical periods within a year when funds for capital expenditures are needed. An effective capital budget schedules and controls the magnitude and timing of such expenditures.

The fifth step is feedback—the actual benefits and costs are compared against those estimated in the capital budget. This phase is important, because all too often the actual figures vary substantially from those estimated. Feedback may overlap with, and occasionally be incorporated into, the final step, which is the *postimplementation audit*. This audit involves a comparison of the actual results of the project to those estimated. Typically some time must pass, such as 2 or 3 years, before a postimplementation audit can be done effectively. Postaudits are difficult to carry out for two reasons: (1) the lack of a responsible group and established procedure to perform the audit, and (2) the need to generate and gather data on actual outcomes. One problem may be the information system employed. With the increased popularity of profit-oriented *responsibility centers*, data are often generated on an "accounting basis," but the relevant data needed for postaudits are cash flows. Some firms do generate the necessary information, but many do not have the capability to do so. Information generated from this phase can be extremely valuable, as it can point to necessary revisions in policies for identifying projects and in procedures for obtaining more accurate estimates of benefits, costs, and risks for future capital budgeting decisions.

Capital Budgeting and Wealth Maximization.   Capital budgeting techniques are based on the economic theory that the firm should take actions up to the point where its marginal benefit equals marginal cost. When applied to capital budgeting, the marginal benefit is measured by the *internal rate of return (IRR)* on an investment, which can be depicted by an *investment opportunities schedule (IOS)*, while the marginal cost is measured by the *marginal cost of capital (MCC)*. A simplified illustration of this concept is presented in Figure 12.4. The level of investment is measured on the horizontal (X) axis, while the investment rate of return and marginal cost of capital are measured on the vertical (Y) axis. In the figure, individual projects are represented by bars; for example, project A has a 17 percent internal rate of return and requires an investment of $3

---

[2]Lawrence J. Gitman and John R. Forrester, Jr., "A Survey of Capital Budgeting Techniques Used by Major U.S. Firms," *Financial Management* 6 (fall 1977), pp. 66–71.

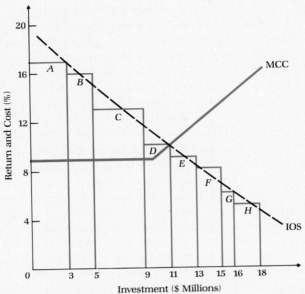

Figure 12.4   Interaction of the Investment and Marginal Cost of Capital Schedules.

million, project B has an IRR of 16 percent and will require $2 million in capital, and so on.

The marginal cost of capital (MCC) curve, on the other hand, depicts the cost to the firm for each additional dollar of financing employed. As seen in Figure 12.4, the MCC curve is constant at 9 percent until the firm has raised about $9.5 million, after which it turns upward. For the firm to operate efficiently and maximize shareholder wealth, all projects that produce a marginal return equal to or greater than the marginal cost should be accepted. So the firm should accept projects A, B, C, and D, which all have a return greater than the corresponding MCC, and reject projects E, F, G, and H. By implementing projects for which the present value of expected benefits is equal to or greater than their cost, the value of the firm will be increased. This increase will result from an increase in the company's anticipated rate of growth, g, which (as we saw in Chapter 7) directly influences the value of the firm's stock. Thus, linkage exists between capital budgeting decisions and the value of the firm. Effective financial managers make decisions consistent with this goal of maximizing shareholder wealth by accepting projects only up to the point where the marginal return (represented by the IOS schedule) is equal to the marginal cost of capital.

Availability of Funds and Capital Rationing   The availability of funds for capital expenditures affects the financial manager's decisions. When funds are unlimited, all independent projects (or groups of projects where the groups are independent) that provide IRRs equal to or greater than the firm's MCC can be accepted.

However, many firms face *capital rationing* to the extent that there are more acceptable projects than the existing budget will permit to be funded. In a recent survey, 52 percent of the firms responding indicated they faced capital rationing.[3] Capital rationing results in the firm accepting projects until the budget is exhausted rather than to the point where the marginal benefit (IRR) equals the marginal cost. In Figure 12.4 for example, if only $5 million were available for funding capital expenditures, only projects A and B could be accepted. The imposition of a capital budgeting constraint results in the firm bypassing profitable opportunities. This constrains the firm's future growth, g, and results in a suboptimal value for the firm. Procedures for evaluating capital budgeting under conditions of capital rationing are considered in Chapter 13 and Appendix 13A.

Abandonment— the Unspecified Alternative?

Although capital budgeting is generally viewed as a selection process, the actual, as opposed to anticipated, economic viability of a project is not known with certainty when it is selected. No matter how effective the selection procedure, future conditions and events will affect the actual project benefits and costs. Managing a capital budget must be viewed as a dynamic process. Because changes in the attractiveness of projects, or even entire divisions, may occur after they are implemented, regular, periodic reappraisals should be undertaken to determine whether the value of continuing with the investment exceeds its abandonment value. Since managing the capital budget often involves rationing capital, firms cannot afford to have funds tied up in investments that are producing less than satisfactory returns.

Consider the example of the Jordan Company, a firm with three divisions. One of the divisions is in the business of growing and marketing lemons and oranges. The California orchard land utilized to grow the lemons and oranges is owned by the company and cost $1 million when acquired 15 years earlier. Because of inflation and the rapid growth of California's population, the land could now be sold for $50 million for residential housing and apartment development. If the value of the lemon and orange division as an ongoing entity is less than $50 million, the Jordan Company would be better off abandoning it and selling the land.[4] The firm would then be acting to maximize shareholder wealth, increase expected growth, and hence increase the market price of the firm's stock.

---

[3]Gitman and Forrester, "A Survey of Capital Budgeting Techniques."
[4]Actually the decision is a little more complicated than this, since it may be more profitable for the firm to hold the land for a few more years and abandon it in the future. Abandonment decisions are considered in Chapter 16.

Developing the Relevant Data: Cash Flow After Taxes

To evaluate capital budgeting alternatives, the after-tax cash flow stream associated with each project (or group of interrelated projects) must be determined.[5] Cash flow refers to cash inflows less cash outflows, or:

Cash flow after tax in year $t = CFAT_t$
$$= \text{cash inflows}_t - \text{cash outflows}_t \quad (12.1)$$

Thus, the *cash flow after tax* in year t for a project equals all cash inflows minus all cash outflows (including taxes) associated with the project in year t. In many years, cash inflows will exceed cash outflows, and the (net) cash flow after tax ($CFAT_t$) will be positive. In other years, most often at the time of initial investment, cash outflows will exceed cash inflows and $CFAT_t$ will be negative.

Why Cash Flows?

In evaluating capital expenditures, we are not interested in the conventional accounting profits and losses from an investment, nor the periods in which revenues and expenses are recognized by accountants. Rather, we are interested in the amount and timing of cash inflows and cash outflows, after taking taxes into account. Net income determined using generally accepted accounting principles typically differs in timing and magnitude from the cash flows. As noted in Chapter 2, discrepancies between the timing of net income and the timing of cash flows occur because accountants use accrual concepts to match costs and associated revenues. Although a variety of net income values can be developed for a project depending on the accounting principles employed, only one set of cash flows is possible (given the depreciation schedule to be employed for tax purposes).

A second and more fundamental reason for preferring CFAT is that cash flow is the theoretically correct measure of economic profit. The financial manager's objective is to maximize shareholder wealth, not earnings per share. This objective is accomplished by maximizing share price which, as noted in Chapter 7, is equal to the present value of all future cash flows accruing to the owners in the form of dividends and/or through liquidation of the stock at some future time. Only when cash flow after tax is considered can the firm assess the impact of a proposed project on the owner's wealth.

---

[5]These are always single projects unless otherwise noted. However, if projects are complements or substitutes, they must be grouped together to determine the relevant cash flows for decision-making purposes. When considering interrelated projects, all the relevant cash flows should be calculated assuming independence, and then the offsetting flows netted out to provide a single net cash flow stream for each year for the entire group of projects.

Depreciation
and Taxes

In Chapter 2 we discussed depreciation[6] and taxes in detail. The primary considerations, as they relate to determining CFAT for capital budgeting purposes, are summarized in Tables 12.2 and 12.3.[7] Financial managers must be aware of the significant and complex impact taxes have on the estimation of relevant cash flows. Reliance on the firm's tax department is essential to ensure that the applicable sections of the Internal Revenue Service Code are properly incorporated in capital expenditure analysis.

Determining
Cash Flow
After Taxes

The cash flow stream employed in capital budgeting decisions has three distinct parts:

1. Original or initial investment (occurs at time t_0)
2. Operating cash flows (occur at times t_1 through t_n)
3. Terminal value (occurs at time t_n)

We noted before that most capital budgeting projects can be broken into two basic categories: expansion and replacement projects. Expansion projects involve those where both revenues and costs are expected to increase as the firm adds to its product line and/or increases its production and distribution facilities. On the other hand, in a replacement situation, the firm is often concerned with generating cost savings from the new investment. As a result, the cash flows associated with the abandoned assets must be netted against the cash flows from the new assets. The relevant cash flows are the incremental cash flows that occur as a result of the proposed capital expenditure. The important comparison when calculating the CFAT figures is between the cash flows expected with the new project and those that will exist without it. Replacement projects always involve incremental cash flows, while expansion situations often do not. We will discuss incremental cash flows further after describing the calculation of basic cash flows.

It should be noted we are considering conventional cash flow streams at this time. By conventional, we simply mean an initial cash outflow occurs at time t_0 followed by a series of positive cash inflows in times t_1 through t_n. Thus, there is only one change in the sign of the cash flow stream—from negative at time t_0 to positive at time t_1. Although this is the

---

[6]Since many firms attempt simultaneously to secure high accounting profits and high near-term cash flows, they frequently use two methods of depreciation: straight line (which often results in higher accounting profits) for reporting income to shareholders, and ACRS depreciation for tax purposes. The difference between the two methods is reconciled by establishing a deferred income tax liability account on the balance sheet. To avoid undue complexity, we ignore this dual depreciation system and concern ourselves only with depreciation for tax purposes.

[7]Since these were covered in Chapter 2, they will not be discussed again. Two examples, later in the chapter, illustrate virtually all of the depreciation and tax aspects of cash flow estimation.

TABLE 12.2
Depreciation and the Accelerated Cost Recovery System (ACRS)

OVERALL CONSIDERATIONS
1. Original cost includes the cost of acquiring, constructing, or modifying assets, including such items as transportation and installation costs.
2. Salvage value is ignored; assets are depreciated to a zero salvage value.
3. Depreciation applies to real and personal property, not land. Real estate improvements are treated somewhat differently.

ACRS GUIDELINES
1. All assets other than real property are grouped into property classes with normal and optional extended recovery periods as follows:

Property Class	Normal Recovery Period	Optional Extended Recovery Periods
Autos, light-duty trucks, research and experimental equipment, certain special tools	3 yr	5 or 12 yr
All other machinery and equipment	5 yr	12 or 25 yr
Certain public utility property, railroad tank cars, residential manufactured homes	10 yr	25 or 35 yr
All other public utility property	15 yr	35 or 45 yr

2. The property classes apply to both new and used assets.
3. Depreciation may be based on straight line over the normal or optional extended recovery periods, or via specific accelerated percentages.
4. The accelerated depreciation percentages by recovery year for assets other than real property using the normal recovery periods under ACRS are:

Recovery Year	Percentage by Recovery Year			
	3 Year	5 Year	10 Year	15 Year
1	25	15	8	5
2	38	22	14	10
3	37	21	12	9
4		21	10	8
5		21	10	7
6			10	7
7–10			9	6
11–15				6

5. A slightly different procedure exists for real property.
6. The first-year depreciation percentages are lower because of the standard use of a "half-year convention" procedure.
7. The half-year convention rule also applies when straight-line depreciation is employed. A 5-year asset depreciated via straight line would have the following depreciation percentage pattern:

Recovery Year	Percentage by Recovery Year
1	10
2–5	20
6	10

This refinement is ignored.

TABLE 12.3
Corporate Taxes and
the Investment
Tax Credit

MARGINAL TAX RATES

1. The tax on income in excess of $100,000 is 46 percent except when income is between $1,000,000 and $1,405,000. For simplicity, a 40 percent marginal tax rate is employed throughout.
2. The maximum tax rate on long-term capital gains is 28 percent. This rate is employed throughout.

TAX CONSEQUENCES WHEN BUSINESS ASSETS ARE SOLD

1. If the asset is held longer than 6 months, the gain will be long term and subject to long-term capital gains tax. (For assets held less than 6 months, all gains are taxed as ordinary income.)
2. Tax consequences:

    Asset sold at price equal to depreciated book value—no tax consequences.

    Asset sold at price greater than depreciated book value but less than original cost—gain taxed at marginal ordinary tax rate.

    Asset sold at price greater than original cost—(1) gain between depreciated book value and original cost taxed at marginal ordinary tax rate; and (2) gain above original cost taxed at marginal capital gains rate.

    Asset sold at less than depreciated book value—tax loss (depreciated book value minus sale price) is deducted from ordinary income and provides a tax savings at the marginal ordinary rate.
3. Treatment for real property, such as buildings, is somewhat different. This refinement is ignored.

INVESTMENT TAX CREDIT (ITC)

1. Applies to cost of equipment and machinery (but not buildings) placed in service during the year.
2. Applies to purchase price of equipment and machinery, and to transportation and installation costs *if* these related costs are capitalized.
3. Amount of ITC depends on normal recovery period specified in the accelerated cost recovery system (ACRS). Three-year assets qualify for a 4 percent ITC, while 5-, 10-, and 15-year assets qualify for an 8 percent ITC.[a]
4. Taking the ITC does not reduce the original cost of the asset for depreciation purposes.[a]
5. ITC results in a direct reduction in the firm's tax liability in the year the asset is purchased.
6. The ITC may be carried back 3 years or forward 15 years and is subject to recapture on assets sold before the normal recovery period is reached. These refinements are ignored.
7. The amount of the ITC taken in a year is limited to the first $25,000 of tax liability plus 85 percent of the excess. This refinement is ignored.
8. The ITC on used property is limited to $125,000 per year and is scheduled to increase to $150,000 beginning after 1987. This refinement is ignored.

[a]Under the Tax Equity and Fiscal Responsibility Act of 1982 firms may elect to take an ITC of 6 percent (for 3-year assets) or 10 percent (for all others). However, if this option is chosen, the depreciable base of the asset is reduced by one-half of the ITC taken. For simplicity we employ 4 percent and 8 percent throughout with the depreciable base remaining unchanged.

typical pattern, it is not the only pattern of cash flows that may occur. Some consequences of other cash flow patterns are discussed in Chapter 13. However, determination of basic cash flows requires the same procedures, no matter when inflows and outflows occur.

Initial Investment.   The *initial investment*, $CFAT_0$, includes all the net cash outflows incurred to implement a proposed capital project. For simplicity, we assume these occur at the present, t_0, although they could be spread out over a longer period of time.[8] Components of the initial investment commonly include:

- Cost of equipment and facilities purchased
- All costs related to purchases (transportation, legal fees, training, spare parts, installation, and so on)
- Land purchased
- Patents and processes purchased
- Additional net working capital required
- Tax liability on the sale of replaced assets[9]
- Recapture of investment tax credit for replaced assets[10]

minus

- Investment tax credit
- Funds realized from the sale of replaced assets[11]
- Tax benefits arising from the sale of replaced assets[12]

The first two items (equipment and facilities purchased, and all other costs related to the purchases) provide the original cost of the asset for depreciation purposes. Land or patents and processes purchased are also included as part of the cash outflow necessary to place certain projects into service. Additional net working capital is often required when revenue expansion projects are considered. For example, if a firm expands its permanent level of operations, it will typically require more cash, inventories, and accounts receivable (due to the anticipated increase in sales). Also, accounts payable, accruals and other spontaneous short-term financing will probably increase, but usually less than current assets, thereby resulting in an increase in net working capital. This incremental net working capital must be considered an initial cash outflow associated with the project. Finally, the tax liability (at t_0) on the

---

[8]If initial cash outflows are spread out over a number of years, they simply show up in the proper year with a negative sign to indicate the outflow. Any cash inflows expected in the same period would then be netted against the outflow to determine the net cash inflow or outflow for the period. In addition, all cash flows for a particular year are assumed to occur at the end of the year. In reality, inflows and outflows are spread out over the year. On certain large and unique projects some firms are known to estimate cash flows on a monthly basis.

[9]Applicable only for replacement projects in which the replaced asset is sold for more than its book value for tax purposes.

[10]Applicable in replacement stiuations where the credit initially taken on the replaced asset was not fully earned.

[11]Applicable only for replacement projects.

[12]Applicable only for replacement projects in which the asset replaced was sold for less than its book value for tax purposes.

sale of replaced assets must be considered. In the case where the asset to be replaced is sold (or can be expected to sell) for more than the depreciated book value for tax purposes, the additional taxes due must be considered part of the cash outlay associated with the proposed replacement. In addition, part of the investment tax credit taken may have to be recaptured (or repaid to the government) if assets are sold before their normal recovery period has expired.

The total cash outflow calculated above must be reduced by certain inflows to determine the (net) initial investment. First, the investment tax credit, if applicable, must be treated as a cash inflow. The ITC applies to the original purchase price of the new asset. If the related costs of transportation, installation, and so on are capitalized and depreciated, the ITC also applies to them. In a replacement situation, funds received from the sale of replaced assets are treated as a cash inflow associated with the new project. If the replaced asset was sold for less than its depreciated book value for tax purposes, the associated tax savings must also be treated as a cash inflow.

Operating Cash Flows.   The items needed to derive the relevant *operating cash flow* stream are the following:

- Cash inflows from expanded operations (or reduced cash outflows from cost saving projects)

    minus

- Cash outflows, including taxes

This relationship can be formalized in a simplified format for a revenue expansion project using the *cash flows before taxes (CFBT)* as:

$$\text{Operating } CFAT_t = CFBT_t (1 - T) + Dep_t(T) \qquad (12.2)$$

where $CFBT_t$ = cash flow before tax in year t = cash inflows$_t$ − cash outflows$_t$ (excluding taxes$_t$)
T = marginal corporate tax rate
Dep_t = depreciation charged for tax purposes in year t

An example will help to explain how the operating cash flow is derived for a revenue expansion project. Consider a project expected to last 10 years, and which for each year has expected cash inflows of $11,000 and cash outflows of $4,000. Depreciation on a straight-line basis is $500 for each of the 10 years, and the marginal tax rate is 40 percent. The annual cash flow before tax (CFBT) in this case is equal to $7,000 ($11,000 − $4,000), while the operating cash flow *after* taxes but *before* the depreciation tax shield is equal to $4,200 [$CFBT$ $(1 - T) = \$7,000 \times (1 - .40)$]. The $4,200 represents the cash flows that would result if depreciation were not deductible for tax purposes. To find the depreciation tax shield, the annual depreciation ($500) is multiplied by the marginal tax rate of 40 percent [$Dep_t(T) = \$500 \times .40 = \$200$].

Adding the depreciation tax shield to the operating cash flow after taxes and before depreciation yields the relevant $CFAT_t$ of $4,400 ($4,200 + $200). The depreciation tax shield exists because depreciation is a tax-deductible expense but not a cash flow item—it represents a noncash charge. Because depreciation is allowed for tax purposes, the taxes paid by the firm are less than they otherwise would be. Although there are other ways to calculate operating cash flows,[13] this method is particularly useful because it is simple, and it highlights the tax subsidy profitable firms receive due to the tax treatment of depreciation.

When a replacement project is being considered, the calculation of operating cash flows is essentially the same, except that incremental cash inflows and outflows must always be determined to show the net change resulting from the use of a new asset in place of an existing asset. Thus, the incremental (represented by Δ) operating cash flow stream for a replacement decision is:

$$\Delta \text{ Operating } CFAT_t = \Delta CFBT_t(1 - T) + \Delta Dep_t(T) \qquad (12.3)$$

In the next section, a detailed example will help clarify the calculation of the incremental operating CFAT stream. In both revenue expansion and replacement situations, we generally assume the firm is profitable. Obviously, if the firm is not profitable, and hence does not pay any corporate income taxes, it receives no depreciation tax subsidy.

Terminal Value.   The *terminal value* is the cash flow associated with the project when it reaches the end of its economic life. The items

---

[13]Operating CFAT can also be calculated as:

Operating $CFAT_t = PAT_t + Dep_t$

where PAT_t = profit after tax = cash inflows$_t$ − cash expenses$_t$
− depreciation$_t$ − income taxes$_t$

Dep_t = depreciation charged for tax purposes in year t

or

Operating $CFAT_t = CFBT_t - \text{Taxes}_t$

where   Taxes$_t$ = income taxes paid in year t

Using the same example and data, profit before taxes is equal to $CFBT_t - Dep_t = \$11,000 - \$4,000 - \$500 = \$6,500$. Taxes = $\$6,500 \times .40 = \$2,600$; hence, PAT_t = profit before taxes − Taxes$_t$ = $\$6,500 - \$2,600 = \$3,900$. Using the method where operating $CFAT_t = PAT_t + Dep_t$, the operating cash flows are equal to $3,900 + $500 = $4,400, the same result achieved earlier. Likewise, employing the approach when operating $CFAT_t = CFBT_t - \text{Taxes}_t$, we have $7,000 − $2,600, or $4,400 again.

included in the CFAT for the expected terminal value of a project are the following:

- Funds realized from sale of assets
- Recovery of net working capital
- Tax benefits arising from sale of assets[14]
- Tax benefits associated with costs of dismantling or disposing of assets

minus

- Costs of dismantling or disposing of assets
- Tax liability arising from sale of assets[15]

Clearly funds expected to be realized from the sale of assets upon termination are part of the terminal CFAT. Since any increase in net working capital required by the project was treated as part of the initial investment, the recovery of net working capital at the termination of the project is treated as a terminal cash inflow. Tax effects resulting from the sale of an asset at termination for more or less than its depreciated book value or prior to earning the full ITC must also be considered. In addition, any costs associated with dismantling or selling assets must be treated as a terminal cash outflow.

Examples of Determining Cash Flows and Other Issues

At this point we have described the procedures for determining the relevant CFAT streams for both revenue expansion and replacement projects. Now we will present examples of both kinds of projects; in the next chapter, we will see how these CFAT figures are used to assess the acceptability of capital expenditure proposals. This section concludes with discussions of how inflation and cost minimization should be incorporated into CFAT estimates.

A Revenue Expansion Project

Royal Delta Company is considering an investment in a new machine that is expected to expand sales and associated revenues. The purchase price of the machine is $45,000, freight and installation costs are $500, and the increase in net working capital (because of increased inventory and accounts receivable) will be $6,000. Because freight and installation costs are low, they will be treated as a current expense instead of being capitalized and depreciated. The 8 percent investment tax credit is available since the machine has a 5-year normal recovery period. The project is expected to generate additional cash inflows of $30,000 per year, and additional operating cash outflows are expected to be $10,000

---

[14]Applies when the asset is sold for less than its book value.
[15]Applies when the asset is sold for more than its book value, or prior to earning the full investment tax credit.

INITIAL INVESTMENT AT $t = 0$		
Purchase price		$45,000
+ Freight and installation		500
+ Increase in net working capital		6,000
− Investment tax credit (8% × $45,000)		− 3,600
= Initial investment	$CFAT_0 =$	$47,900

OPERATING CASH FLOWS IN YEARS 1-5

Year, t	Cash Inflow$_t$ (1)	Cash Outflow$_t$ (2)	$CFBT_t\ (1-T)$ $[(1)-(2)]\ (1-T)$ (3)	Depreciation Tax Shield $[Dep_t\ (T)]$ (4)	$CFAT_t$ $[CFBT_t\ (1-T)$ $+\ Dep_t\ (T)]$ $[(3)+(4)]$ (5)
1	$30,000	$10,000	$12,000	$2,700[a]	$14,700
2	30,000	13,000	10,200	3,960	14,160
3	30,000	16,000	8,400	3,780	12,180
4	30,000	19,000	6,600	3,780	10,380
5	30,000	22,000	4,800	3,780	8,580

TERMINAL CASH FLOW IN YEAR 5

Recovery of net working capital	$6,000

[a]Depreciation tax shield for year 1 equals 15 percent of $45,000 times the tax rate of .40, or (.15 × $45,000)(.40) = $2,700; for year 2 it is (.22 × $45,000)(.40) = $3,960, and so on.

in the first year, increasing by $3,000 per year as the machine wears out. Depreciation will be based on the 5-year ACRS normal recovery percentages given in Table 12.2 applied to the $45,000 cost of the machine. The marginal tax rate on ordinary income is 40 percent, and the firm expects the machine to have a market value equal to its book value of zero at the end of 5 years. Given these estimated cash flows, the relevant CFAT stream can be derived as illustrated in Table 12.4.

As the table shows, the initial investment is $47,900 followed by operating CFATs in years 1 through 5 of $14,700, $14,160, $12,180, $10,380, and $8,580, respectively, and an additional terminal cash flow in year 5 of $6,000 (which is added to the fifth-year operating cash flow). Thus, complete CFAT stream for Royal Delta's expansion project is as follows:

t	0	1	2	3	4	5
$CFAT_t$	−$47,900	$14,700	$14,160	$12,180	$10,380	$14,580

A Replacement Project

The next example, Massey Electronics, Inc., is more complicated, since Massey is considering replacing an existing machine with a new more energy efficient one. The existing machine was purchased 2 years ago for $30,000, is being depreciated under ACRS over its 5-year normal recovery

TABLE 12.5
Determining the
Incremental ΔCFBT
Stream for Massey
Electronics
Replacement Project

Year, t	New Machine			Existing Machine			ΔCFBT, [(3) − (6)] (7)
	Cash Inflow, (1)	Cash Outflow, (2)	CFBT, [(1) − (2)] (3)	Cash Inflow, (4)	Cash Outflow, (5)	CFBT, [(4) − (5)] (6)	
1	$25,000	−$9,000	$16,000	$25,000	−$15,000	$10,000	$6,000
2	25,000	− 9,000	16,000	25,000	− 15,000	10,000	6,000
3	25,000	− 9,000	16,000	25,000	− 15,000	10,000	6,000
4	25,000	− 9,000	16,000	25,000	− 15,000	10,000	6,000
5	25,000	− 9,000	16,000	25,000	− 15,000	10,000	6,000

TABLE 12.6
Determining the
Incremental
Depreciation for
Massey Electronics
Replacement Project

Year, t	Depreciation, New Machine (1)	Depreciation, Existing Machine (2)	ΔDepreciation, [(1) − (2)] (3)
1	$ 8,250[a]	$6,300[b]	$ 1,950
2	12,100	6,300	5,800
3	11,550	6,300	5,250
4	11,550	0	11,550
5	11,550	0	11,550

[a]Depreciation in year 1 equals .15 × $55,000 = $8,250; in year 2 it equals .22 × $55,000 = $12,100; and in years 3–5 it is .21 × $55,000 = $11,550.

[b]Two years of depreciation have already been taken. Hence, the depreciation for each of the 3 remaining years is .21 × $30,000 = $6,300 per year.

period, and has a useful remaining economic life of 5 years.[16] Because of inflation and increased demand, it is anticipated that the existing machine can be sold at the present time ($t = 0$) for $35,000. The new machine has a purchase price of $55,000 and will be depreciated using ACRS over its 5-year normal recovery period. Both machines have an estimated terminal value of zero in 5 years, which will be equal to their depreciated book values. Cash inflows are expected to be $25,000 per year with either the existing or the new machine; however, the cash outflows of $15,000 per year with the old machine are expected to drop to $9,000 per year with the new machine. The marginal tax rate of the firm is 40 percent on ordinary income, and 28 percent on long-term capital gains. The investment tax credit of 8 percent is applicable for the new machine. Any recovery of the ITC on the existing machine will be ignored.

The first step in the process is to determine the ΔCFBT for each year, as illustrated in Table 12.5. Next the incremental depreciation is calculated, as shown in Table 12.6. Because of differences in the remaining

[16]For simplicity, the remaining useful economic life of the existing machine is assumed to be equal to the initial economic life of the new machine. A description of procedures for evaluating projects with unequal lives is included in Chapter 13.

TABLE 12.7
Determining the
Incremental ΔCFAT
Stream for Massey
Electronics
Replacement Project

ΔINITIAL INVESTMENT AT $t = 0$

Purchase price	$55,000
+ Tax at ordinary rate on sale of existing machine[a]	4,440
+ Tax at long-term capital gains rate on sale of existing machine[b]	1,400
− Investment tax credit on new machine ($0.08 \times \$55,000$)	− 4,400
− Proceeds from sale of existing machine	− 35,000
= Δ Initial investment $\Delta CFAT_0 =$	$21,440

ΔOPERATING CASH FLOWS IN YEARS 1–5

Year, t	$\Delta CFBT_t$ (1)	$[\Delta CFBT_t (1-T)]$ $[(1)(1-T)]$ (2)	ΔDepreciation Tax Shield $[\Delta Dep_t(T)]$ (3)	$\Delta CFAT_t$ $[\Delta CFBT_t(1-T) + \Delta Dep_t(T)]$ $[(2)+(3)]$ (4)
1	$6,000	$3,600	$ 780[c]	$4,380
2	6,000	3,600	2,320	5,920
3	6,000	3,600	2,100	5,700
4	6,000	3,600	4,620	8,220
5	6,000	3,600	4,620	8,220

ΔTERMINAL CASH FLOW IN YEAR 5

None	$ 0

[a]The depreciated book value of the old machine is $30,000 − (.15 + .22) \$30,000 = \$30,000 − \$11,100 = \$18,900$. The ordinary tax due to selling it for more than the original purchase price is $0.40 \times (\$30,000 − \$18,900) = \$4,440$.

[b]The long-term capital gains tax due to selling it for $5,000 more than it originally cost is, $.28 \times (\$35,000 − \$30,000) = \$1,400$.

[c]The Δdepreciation tax shield for year 1 equals the Δdepreciation of $1,950 (from Table 12.6) times the tax rate of .40 = $780; for year 2 it equals $5,800 \times .40 = \$2,320$, and so on.

normal recovery periods for the old and new machines (3 years versus 5 years), the incremental depreciation ranges from $1,950 in year 1 to $11,550 in years 4 and 5. Given the estimated cash inflows and outflows, along with the $\Delta CFBT_t$ and ΔDep_t, as computed above, we can determine the complete $\Delta CFAT_t$ stream in Table 12.7. As seen, the incremental initial investment, $\Delta CFAT_0$, is $21,440, while the ΔCFATs in years 1 through 5 are $4,380, $5,920, $5,700, $8,220, and $8,220, respectively. Since there are no incremental terminal cash flows, the complete ΔCFAT stream is:

t	0	1	2	3	4	5
ΔCFAT$_t$	−$21,440	$4,380	$5,920	$5,700	$8,220	$8,220

Incremental
Cash Flows
and the Proper
Alternatives

The proper CFAT stream to use when evaluating a proposed capital expenditure is the stream that would not have otherwise occurred. In effect, any cash flow that already exists must be ignored in the analysis; for example, general administrative or overhead expenditures should not be charged to a new project for capital budgeting purposes unless these expenditures are expected to change as the result of implementing the project.

A Look at Incremental Cash Flows.   Consider a situation in which Evans Instruments, a producer and marketer of hand-held calculators, is investigating the possibility of bringing out a special business calculator. The estimated incremental CFAT stream over the 5-year life of the business calculator is shown in Table 12.8. Note that the total CFAT stream severely overstates the benefits from this project since the firm will suffer a loss in sales on its existing calculators as some customers who would normally buy other Evans calculators will now buy the new business calculator. Accordingly, the relevant CFAT stream is the net or incremental stream that takes into account the anticipated reduction in cash flows from the firm's existing calculators. Failure to consider this cash flow reduction overstates the CFAT stream for the new business calculator, making it appear profitable when in fact its production and sale may not be in the best interest of the firm's owners.

Generating Proper Alternatives.   Every capital expenditure analysis involves the comparison of two or more alternatives. In the simplest case, consider a single independent project, such as the expansion project for Royal Delta discussed previously. The two alternatives facing Royal Delta were (1) acceptance of the project, or (2) rejection. The relevant CFAT stream to employ in this case might be called a total cash flow stream since it compares the costs and benefits from accepting the project versus those (which are zero) from rejecting it.

In a more complicated situation, consider the nature of the cash flow stream if there are two mutually exclusive projects, A and B. Three alternatives exist: acceptance of A, acceptance of B, or rejection of both. Typically, in this situation the cash flow stream is calculated for (1) A compared to doing nothing, and (2) B compared to doing nothing. Both streams are total cash flow streams since the CFATs for the two projects are not directly compared against each other—both are compared against the common status quo (do nothing) base. Hence, the cash flow stream for project A might involve an initial outflow of $750 followed by

TABLE 12.8 Determining Evans Instruments Incremental CFAT Stream ($ thousands)				t			
	0	**1**	**2**	**3**	**4**	**5**	
Total CFAT stream	−$10.0	$5.5	$5.5	$5.5	$4.5	$4.0	
Less: Loss of cash flow from reduced sales of existing products		4.0	3.5	3.0	2.5	2.5	
Incremental CFAT stream	−$10.0	$1.5	$2.0	$2.5	$2.0	$1.5	

TABLE 12.9   Comparison of Total and Incremental CFAT Streams, Projects A and B

	0	1	2	3	4	5	6	$\sum_{t=1}^{6} CFAT_t$	Total Cash Inflows (t_1 to t_6) Minus Initial Outlay at t_0
Total CFAT stream, project B	−$900	$150	$150	$150	$150	$150	$150	$900	$ 0
Total CFAT stream, project A	− 750	100	100	100	100	100	100	600	− 150
Incremental CFAT stream, project B − project A	−$150	$ 50	$ 50	$ 50	$ 50	$ 50	$ 50	$300	+$150

inflows of $100 in each of the next 6 years. Project B might require an initial investment of $900 and expected cash inflows of $150 for each of the next 6 years. Both CFAT streams are total cash flow streams and, as Table 12.9 indicates, in both cases the sum of the positive cash flows in years 1 through 6 is less than or equal to their initial investment. Thus, even without discounting the cash flows to be received after the initial investment, both projects require a larger outflow than the sum of their nondiscounted cash inflows. So both projects, when viewed in terms of their total cash flows, appear to be undesirable since their initial investments are larger than or equal to the sum of their anticipated cash inflows.

Now, however, consider the incremental CFAT stream if project B is considered as a replacement for project A (Table 12.9). In this case the incremental CFAT stream, B − A, provides the relevant cash flows for use in evaluating project B as a replacement for project A. Since A's cash flows are subtracted from B's, project A is the base, and the cash flows of project B are compared to those of project A. The incremental stream B − A provides a set of CFATs that look more promising; the initial cash outlay is $150, and the sum of the cash inflows is $300. Unfortunately, a decision to implement a proposal based on such incremental cash flows would be incorrect. What is wrong with the incremental CFAT stream, B − A? *Because the use of incremental cash flows ignores the total CFAT streams*, almost any alternative (like project B in our example) can be made to appear worthwhile if it is compared to a sufficiently bad alternative. In the example, both projects A and B appear undesirable when viewed independently; but when B is compared to A, it appears to be acceptable. The use of incremental CFATs without examination of the total cash flows implies that one or both of the projects has a desirable set of total CFATs. Great care must therefore be employed to make sure that such is the case when using incremental CFAT streams.

Consider the question once faced by railroads in the United States.

Should old coal-burning locomotives used on a particular passenger line be replaced with newer and more efficient diesel locomotives? If the revenues were not expected to be affected by the choice of locomotive, the logical basis of comparison would be to use the incremental CFAT stream associated with buying the new diesel locomotives versus keeping the old coal burners. On this basis, the investment in the new diesel might appear to be quite profitable due to its lower operating expenses. But suppose, using the old coal burners, the cash inflows from the passenger line were $3 million less than the associated cash outflows. The purchase of the diesel engines may appear desirable on an incremental cash flow basis, but on a total cash flow basis it might still result in cash inflows of $1 million less than the associated cash outflows. If there was no possibility of eliminating the passenger train, the decision to purchase the diesel locomotives might be wise. If, however, the passenger line could be eliminated, the purchase of the diesels could not be justified. The lesson should be clear: When using incremental cash flows, all alternatives must be considered, including the alternative of completely abandoning the project.

Other Issues in Estimating Cash Flows

Two other important topics need to be considered when estimating the relevant CFAT streams. The first is the impact of inflation on the cash flow estimates, and the second concerns cash flow estimates for cost minimization projects.

Inflation.   In estimating cash flows, it is important to consider anticipated inflation. There has often been a tendency to assume that price levels remain unchanged throughout a project's life. Given the inflation/disinflation cycle experienced in recent times, this omission may seriously under- or overstate the relevant cash flow streams. Consider a project that has cash inflows and outflows (in today's dollar) as estimated in Table 12.10. The firm has a marginal tax rate of 40 percent, and depreciation on a $40,000 base is calculated using ACRS over a 3-year normal recovery period. Without considering anticipated inflation, the CFATs in years 1 to 3 are estimated to be $28,000, $27,080, and $17,920.

Suppose, however, that inflation is expected to influence cash inflows at a constant annual rate of 10 percent, and cash outflows at a constant annual rate of 13 percent per year. The revised CFAT figures in Table 12.10 indicate the new CFATs are $30,040, $30,485, and $19,876. In practice the analysis is even more complicated, since anticipated inflation cannot be assumed to be constant over time. This example illustrates the importance of taking anticipated inflation/disinflation into account when estimating CFAT figures. Since anticipated inflation is generally

TABLE 12.10
The Impact of
Anticipated Inflation
on CFAT Streams

			t	
NO INFLATION ASSUMED		1	2	3
Expected cash inflow$_t$		$60,000	$60,000	$50,000
− Expected cash outflow$_t$		20,000	25,000	30,000
= $CFBT_t$		$40,000	$35,000	$20,000
$CFBT_t (1 - T)$, operating cash flow before depreciation		$24,000	$21,000	$12,000
+ $Dep_t (T)^a$		4,000	6,080	5,920
= $CFAT_t$		$28,000	$27,080	$17,920
INFLATION AT 10 PERCENT FOR INFLOWS AND 13 PERCENT FOR OUTFLOWS				
Expected cash inflow$_t$		$66,000	$72,600^b	$66,550^c
− Expected cash outflow$_t$		22,600	31,925^d	43,290^d
= $CFBT_t$		$43,400	$40,675	$23,260
$CFBT_t (1 - T)$, operating cash flow before depreciation		$26,040	$24,405	$13,956
+ $Dep_t (T)^a$		4,000	6,080	5,920
= $CFAT_t$		$30,040	$30,485	$19,876

^{a}Depreciation under the ACRS method (Table 12.2) is:

Year	Amount
1	$.25 \times $40,000 = $10,000$
2	$.38 \times 40,000 = 15,200$
3	$.37 \times 40,000 = 14,800$

Multiplying the depreciation figures times the tax rate, T, yields the depreciation tax shield, $Dep_t (T)$. Thus, $10,000 (.40) = $4,000, $15,200 (.40) = $6,080, and $14,800 (.40) = $5,920.
^{b}$60,000 \times FVIF_{10\%, 2 yr} = $60,000 \times 1.210 = $72,600$.
^{c}$50,000 \times FVIF_{10\%, 3 yr} = $50,000 \times 1.331 = $66,550$.
^{d}Calculated in the same manner as the expected cash inflows, except using expected cash outflows and 13 percent FVIF factors.

embodied in the firm's marginal cost of capital (MCC), ignoring it in the CFAT stream results in a biased capital expenditure analysis.[17]

Cost Minimization.   Often a firm encounters a project that does not have any directly measurable cash inflows. An example might be something as modest as a new parking lot for employees or repainting the inside of a cafeteria. It might also be the kind of major project faced by many firms that were required to make substantial expenditures to comply with Federal Environmental Protection Agency regulations. Conceptually, there is nothing different about regulatory or other *cost*

---

[17]Inflation can be treated by adding an estimate of inflation to the CFAT stream, as illustrated, or by adjusting the required rate of return. However, since the firm's MCC as typically calculated already embodies an adjustment for inflation, it seems preferable to adjust the cash flows. See James C. Van Horne, "A Note on Biases in Capital Budgeting Introduced by Inflation," *Journal of Financial and Quantitative Analysis* 6 (January 1971), pp. 653–658; and M. Chapman Findlay III and Alan W. Frankle, "Capital Budgeting Procedures under Inflation: Cooley, Roenfeldt and Chew vs. Findlay and Frankle," *Financial Management* 6 (autumn 1976), pp. 83–90.

minimization projects except that there are no cash inflows. The same concepts discussed previously can be employed to estimate the relevant cash outflows. Once the cash outflows associated with such projects are estimated, the concepts discussed in Chapter 13 can be employed to determine the least costly alternative. Financial managers often fail to apply capital budgeting techniques to noncash inflow generating, regulatory, or other mandated projects; but by avoiding a formal capital budgeting analysis, they risk accepting projects that do not minimize expected cash outflows.

SUMMARY

Proper analysis of capital expenditures is necessary in order for the firm to achieve its goal of maximizing shareholder wealth. Probably the most difficult aspect of capital budgeting is the search and identification stage. It is extremely important that capital expenditure decisions made by the firm be consistent with its strategic and long-run objectives. Otherwise, the expected benefits from the expenditures will not be forthcoming.

Estimating the relevant cash flows is another crucial step in the capital budgeting process. Cash flows must be accurately estimated for the proper time periods. Taxes, inflation, and the impact of government regulation are major considerations when estimating cash flows. In addition, it is the *incremental* cash inflows and cash outflows that are important. Calculation of total, instead of incremental, cash flows often results in overstated benefits or understated costs, leading to acceptance of projects that should be rejected.

Proper evaluation of long-term investment proposals is crucial to the firm's well-being; successful investment in capital assets will allow the firm to prosper. A very important part of this process is the estimation of the relevant cash flow after tax (CFAT) streams. While throughout this text cash outflow and inflow estimates are given, in practice, accurate estimation of these cash flows is extremely difficult. Unfortunately, as yet there are few guidelines beyond those given in this chapter for arriving at accurate estimates of the cash inflows and cash outflows. More than anything else, estimation of cash flows requires both experience and hard work.

QUESTIONS

12.1. Why is it important to distinguish between revenue expansion, replacement, and cost minimization projects when preparing estimates of cash flow streams?

12.2. Suppose a firm is considering a large number of capital budgeting projects. Explain why:
   a. All complementary or substitute projects must be grouped together.
   b. Mutually exclusive projects are perfect substitutes.
   c. Independent projects are analyzed separately.

12.3. Explain why project identification, estimation of the relevant CFATs, and postimplementation audits are important yet difficult steps in the capital budgeting process.

12.4. Explain:
- **a.** Why it is in the best interest of the owners for capital budgeting projects to be accepted as long as their marginal benefits are greater than or equal to their marginal costs.
- **b.** The relationship in terms of the firm's goal of wealth maximization.
- **c.** Why capital rationing results in suboptimal decisions.

12.5. Why are cash flows employed in evaluating investment projects rather than accounting earnings?

12.6. Depreciation does not represent a cash outflow to the firm, and only cash inflows and outflows are relevant for calculating CFATs. However, depreciation charges play an important role in the calculation of the operating CFAT. Explain this paradox.

12.7. Evaluate the following statement made by a trucking executive: "This route is our most competitive one. The only way we can earn a reasonable profit on it is by using fully depreciated equipment."

12.8. What four tax situations may result from the sale of an asset that is being replaced? Explain the net cash flow considering both the sale of an asset and the tax consequences associated with it.

12.9. Klein Concrete is preparing cash flow estimates for an expansion of its plant. During this phase, several events occur that may impact the estimates already made. Evaluate the impact of each event (separately) on the three distinct parts of the CFAT stream (initial investment, operating cash flows, and terminal cash flows):
- **a.** The investment tax credit is increased from 10 to 15 percent.
- **b.** Congress lowers the ordinary tax rate.
- **c.** Labor unions receive new wage contracts that will increase labor costs.
- **d.** The IRS has determined that the normal recovery period (under the ACRS method) for certain assets used in the plant was too short and has lengthened it. (The change applies only to new assets.)
- **e.** It is realized that the plant expansion will require additional administrative and supervisory personnel, and thus an increase in overhead.

12.10. Differentiate between incremental and total cash flows. Explain why incremental cash flows should be used for replacement projects; is it possible that they may lead to incorrect decisions in such situations? How can this problem be resolved? Are incremental cash flows also applicable to expansion-type projects? Explain.

12.11. Explain:

    a. Why inflation/disinflation should be taken into account when estimating the appropriate CFAT stream.

    b. What values are relevant in cost minimization situations.

PROBLEMS

12.1. *TAX CONSEQUENCES FROM THE SALE OF AN ASSET.* A company purchased a machine 2 years ago for $150,000. It is being depreciated using the ACRS percentages over its 5-year normal recovery period. The firm has a 40 percent marginal tax rate on ordinary income, and a 28 percent long-term capital gains tax rate. The ITC is not in effect. What is the cash flow to the firm from the sale of the machine if it sells the machine for:

    a. $175,000.

    b. $125,000.

    c. $94,500.

    d. $50,000.

12.2. *EXPANSION OPERATING CFAT STREAM.* High Plains Western Stores is contemplating opening a new retail outlet. Cash inflows are expected to be $1,250,000 per year, and cash outflows are forecasted to be $650,000 per year for the foreseeable future. Depreciation is expected to be $250,000 per year, and the firm is in a 40 percent marginal tax bracket. Determine the operating cash flows after taxes.

12.3. *INITIAL AND OPERATING CFATS.* The Southern Valve Company is considering the construction of a new building to allow it to expand the number of valves it produces. The following information related to the initial outlay and first-year operating flows has been gathered:

Land for new building	$ 50,000
Expected sales	400,000
Equipment to be purchased	200,000
Transportation expense for equipment	10,000
Selling and administrative expenses directly associated with new products	20,000
Increase in inventories	40,000
Cost of constructing building	150,000
Increase in accounts receivable	50,000
Decrease in sales of other products (net cash flow)	40,000
Installation expenses on equipment	30,000

Investment tax credit	20,000
Cost of manufacturing valves (including $30,000 of depreciation)	180,000
Increase in current liabilities	30,000

Calculate the initial and first-year operating CFATs, assuming a marginal tax rate of 40 percent on ordinary income.

12.4. *EXPANSION CFAT STREAM: STRAIGHT-LINE DEPRECIATION.* O'Brien Cleaners is investigating opening a self-service dry cleaning shop. It presently owns the building and land, new equipment would cost $160,000, and installation costs are estimated to be $20,000. (All installation costs are capitalized and therefore eligible for depreciation and the ITC.) The firm's net working capital is expected to increase by $3,000. The shop is expected to generate cash inflows of $50,000, $70,000, $80,000, $75,000, and $75,000 over its 5-year life. Cash outflows are estimated at $10,000 for the first year, and will increase by 6 percent per year thereafter. It is anticipated that the dry cleaning units will require periodic additional maintenance of $15,000 and $20,000, which will be expensed at the end of the second and fourth years, respectively. The firm uses straight-line depreciation with no salvage value, the marginal tax rate is 40 percent on ordinary income, and the ITC of 8 percent is in effect. The estimated terminal value is zero. Determine the CFAT stream.

12.5. *REPLACEMENT CFAT STREAM: STRAIGHT-LINE DEPRECIATION.* Bailey Publishing is trying to decide if it should replace some of its older printing equipment. The present (2-year-old) equipment originally cost $90,000 and is being depreciated via straight-line depreciation over its 5-year normal recovery period to a salvage value of zero for tax purposes. While it only has 3 years remaining before it is fully depreciated for taxes, its useful economic life is 5 years. The new equipment is expected to produce cash operating cost savings of $18,000 per year during its 5-year life. If the new equipment is purchased, the older equipment can be sold today for $55,000. The cost of the new equipment is $100,000, and it will be depreciated via straight-line depreciation over its normal recovery period to a salvage value of zero. The marginal tax rate on ordinary income is 40 percent, and the 8 percent ITC is applicable. Neither machine has any terminal value at the end of year 5. (*Note:* Ignore recapture of the ITC on the old equipment.) Determine the relevant CFAT stream.

12.6. *EXPANSION CFAT STREAM: DIFFERENT DEPRECIATION METHODS.* Cartar Employment Agency is considering the purchase of a new automated filing system. The equipment has an installed cost of $450,000 and its salvage value at the end of 5 years is estimated to be zero. The system is expected to save $110,000 per year. The firm is subject to a 40 percent tax rate on ordinary income, and the ITC is not in effect. Derive the relevant depreciation schedules and CFAT stream if Carter employs the following:

a. Straight-line depreciation over the 5-year normal recovery period.

b. Accelerated cost recovery system (ACRS) depreciation over the 5-year normal recovery period.

12.7. *REPLACEMENT CFAT STREAM: DIFFERENT DEPRECIATION METHODS.* Seal-Best is contemplating replacing one of its 2-year-old bottling machines with a newer and more efficient model. The old machine originally cost $400,000 and has a remaining useful economic life of 5 years. It is being depreciated via the ACRS method over its original 5-year normal recovery period. The firm does not expect to realize any return from scrapping the machine in 5 more years (the estimated terminal value is zero), but if it is sold now, Seal-Best would receive $250,000.

The new machine has a purchase price of $400,000, a normal recovery period of 5 years under ACRS, and estimated salvage and terminal values of zero. The 8 percent ITC is in effect for the new machine, and the firm will have to increase net working capital by $10,000. (Ignore recapture of any ITC.) The new machine is expected to economize on electric power usage, labor and repair costs, and also to reduce defective bottles; in total, an annual saving of $60,000 will be realized. The marginal corporate tax rate on ordinary income is 40 percent and 28 percent on long-term capital gains. What is the relevant CFAT stream if:

a. Straight-line depreciation using the 5-year normal recovery period is employed on the new machine.

b. The accelerated cost recovery system (ACRS) depreciation method is employed on the new machine using a 5-year normal recovery period.

12.8. *EXPANSION CFAT STREAM: ACRS DEPRECIATION.* The Sawyer Chemical Company is considering a new process for making phosphoric acid, which it uses to make fertilizer. The new equipment will have an installed cost of $270,000. Total annual savings plus proceeds from the sale of excess acid (from overcapacity) are estimated to amount to $150,000 per year. Operating expenses are estimated to be $50,000 per year. The equipment has an estimated economic life of 6 years, and Sawyer has an effective tax rate on ordinary income of 40 percent. The 8 percent ITC is applicable. Although the economic life is 6 years, Sawyer will depreciate the equipment using the accelerated cost recovery system (ACRS) method over its 5-year normal recovery period. What is the depreciation and the relevant CFAT stream for the 6-year economic life of the equipment?

12.9.   *REPLACEMENT CFAT STREAM: ACRS DEPRECIATION.*   Ace Brick is examining replacing its existing kilns with new ones. Since the existing kilns were purchased before the ACRS method went into effect, they are being depreciated from a current book value of $120,000 over their remaining life of 5 years; they can be currently sold for $70,000. If they are kept for 5 more years, their estimated terminal value at that time will be zero. The new kilns would require an outlay of $630,000, have a 5-year life, and an estimated terminal value in 5 years of zero. The firm estimates the differential CFBT to be $180,000 per year, and it will use the accelerated cost recovery system (ACRS) depreciation method over the 5-year normal recovery period on the new kilns. The marginal tax rate on ordinary income is 40 percent, and the ITC is not applicable. Determine the relevant incremental CFAT stream for Ace Brick.

12.10.   *REPLACEMENT CFAT STREAM: NONIDENTICAL UNITS.*   Executive Air Lines is considering replacing its fleet of eight two-engine piston planes with four new luxury jets. One jet plane can replace two of the present planes. The piston planes have a book value of zero, but can be used for 6 more years if properly maintained.

The four new planes will cost $192,000,000 in total, have a 6-year economic life, and estimated salvage and terminal values of zero. The firm estimates the CFBT will be $15,000,000 per plane with the jets, whereas it is $2,000,000 per plane on the existing aircraft. The 8 percent ITC is in effect for the new jets, and the marginal tax rate on ordinary income is 40 percent and 28 percent on long-term capital gains. What is the replacement CFAT stream if:

a.   Straight-line depreciation over the 5-year normal recovery period is used on the new planes, and the present salvage value (at t_0) of the old planes is zero.

b.   Straight-line depreciation over the 5-year normal recovery period is used on the new planes, and the present salvage value (t_0) of each old plane is $5,000,000. (Round depreciation and taxes to the nearest whole dollar.)

12.11.   *INFLATION.*   Capital Investment Company is considering acquiring the assets of a small division of another firm for cash. The division's assets will cost Capital $40,000 (all of this can be depreciated). Cash inflows are expected to be $80,000 per year, and cash outflows will be $65,000 per year. The terminal value after the 5-year life of the project is estimated to be zero; the marginal tax rate on ordinary income is 40 percent, and the ITC does not apply. Capital employs ACRS depreciation over the assets' 5-year normal recovery period.
a.   Calculate the relevant CFAT stream.
b.   Upon further evaluation, Capital finds no adjustments were made for anticipated inflation. Data for the first year are okay, but after that the cash inflows are expected to grow at 5 percent per year, while the cash outflows are expected to grow at 7 percent per year. Recalculate the CFAT stream, taking into account the anticipated effects of inflation.

12.12.   *COST MINIMIZATION.*   New England Utility is evaluating the construction of a new coal-powered plant or a nuclear plant. Both plants will be depreciated over a 15-year normal recovery period under ACRS. The coal-powered plant will cost $56.25 million and requires annual net cash outlays of $15 million for the first 5 years of operation. After that (due to the company's coal contract), net cash outlays will increase to $20 million per year. The nuclear plant will cost $112.5 million to construct, and net cash outlays will be $12 million for each of the next 15 years. The 8 percent ITC is applicable, and the marginal income tax rate is 40 percent on ordinary income. Determine the relevant CFAT stream for each plant.

SELECTED REFERENCES

Bierman, Harold, Jr., and Seymour Smidt. *The Capital Budgeting Decision,* 5th ed. New York: Macmillan, 1980.

Blank, Leland T., and Donald R. Smith. "A Comparative Analysis of the Accelerated Cost Recovery System as Enacted by The 1981 Economic Recovery Tax Act." *Engineering Economist* 28 (Fall 1982), pp. 1–30.

Bodenhorn, Diran. "A Cash-Flow Concept of Profit." *Journal of Finance* 19 (March 1964), pp. 16–31.

Bussey, Lynn E. *The Economic Analysis of Industrial Projects.* Englewood Cliffs, N.J.: Prentice-Hall, 1978.

Clark, John J., Thomas J. Hindelang, and Robert E. Pritchard. *Capital Budgeting: Planning and Control of Capital Expenditures,* 2nd ed. Englewood Cliffs, N.J.: Prentice-Hall, 1984.

Cooley, Philip L., Rodney L. Roenfeldt, and It-Keong Chew. "Capital Budgeting Procedures under Inflation." *Financial Management* 4 (winter 1975), pp. 18–27.

Federal Tax Course. New York: Commerce Clearing House, annual.

Findlay, M. Chapman III, and Alan W. Frankle. "Capital Budgeting Procedures under Inflation: Cooley, Roenfeldt and Chew vs. Findlay and Frankle." *Financial Management* 6 (autumn 1976), pp. 83–90.

Gitman, Lawrence J., and John R. Forrester, Jr. "A Survey of Capital Budgeting Techniques Used by Major U.S. Firms." *Financial Management* 6 (fall 1977), pp. 66–71.

Hastie, K. Larry. "One Businessman's View of Capital Budgeting." *Financial Management* 3 (autumn 1974), pp. 36–44.

McCarty, Daniel E., and William R. McDaniel. "A Note on Expensing Versus Depreciating Under the Accelerated Cost Recovery System: Comment." *Financial Management* 12 (summer 1983), pp. 37–39.

Meyers, Stephen L. "Avoiding Depreciation Influences on Investment Decisions." *Financial Management* 1 (winter 1972), pp. 17–24.

Petty, J. William, David F. Scott, Jr., and Monroe M. Bird. "The Capital Expenditure Decision-Making Process of Large Corporations." *Engineering Economist* 20 (spring 1975), pp. 159–172.

Pinches, George E. "Myopia, Capital Budgeting and Decision Making," *Financial Management* 11 (autumn 1982), pp. 6–19.

Quirin, G. David, and John C. Wiginton. *Analyzing Capital Expenditures: Private and Public Perspectives.* Homewood, Ill.: Irwin, 1981.

Schall, Lawrence D., Gary L. Sundem, and William R. Geijsbeek, Jr. "Survey and Analysis of Capital Budgeting Methods." *Journal of Finance* 33 (March 1978), pp. 281–287.

Schnell, James S., and Roy S. Nicolosi. "Capital Expenditure Feedback: Project Reappraisal." *Engineering Economist* 19 (summer 1974), pp. 253–261.

Van Horne, James C. "A Note on Biases in Capital Budgeting Introduced by Inflation." *Journal of Financial and Quantitative Analysis* 6 (January 1971), pp. 653–658.

Vancil, Richard F., and Peter Lorange. "Strategic Planning in Diversified Companies." *Harvard Business Review* 53 (January–February 1975), pp. 81–90.

Weaver, James B. "Organizing and Maintaining a Capital Expenditure Program." *Engineering Economist* 20 (fall 1974), pp. 1–35.

13

Evaluation of Long-Term Investment Opportunities

Long-term investments are of major importance to firms and hence to financial managers. International Business Machines, for example, almost doubled its manufacturing space during the 1970s. During the more recent 1980–1982 period, IBM spent almost $7 billion for capital expenditures. Clearly IBM, as well as other firms, must use appropriate capital budgeting techniques to ensure that the best investment decisions are made. In this chapter we will examine the various capital expenditure evaluation procedures and discuss how firms actually use them. At this point, we assume that any investment decisions made by the firm will not alter its existing risk exposure. In essence this means that the projects accepted have the same degree of risk as the firm as a whole. (Techniques for incorporating risk into capital budgeting decisions are discussed in the next chapter.) Also, the firm's marginal cost of capital, or risk-adjusted discount rate (to be discussed in Chapter 17), is assumed to be given.

We will begin by examining techniques not considering present value—the average rate of return and the payback period. Then we will discuss the three main discounted present-value techniques used in capital budgeting: net present value, profitability index, and internal rate of return. After considering the strengths and weaknesses of these approaches, the chapter examines two other important considerations —unequal lives and capital rationing. In the last section capital budgeting in practice is described.

TABLE 13.1	INITIAL INVESTMENT	Project A $60,000		Project B $70,000	
Capital Expenditure Data for Ohio Valley Industries	Year, t	PAT_t	$CFAT_t$	PAT_t	$CFAT_t$
	1	$10,000	$20,000	$25,000	$48,000
	2	10,000	20,000	15,000	20,000
	3	10,000	20,000	5,000	17,000
	4	10,000	20,000	3,000	10,000
	5	10,000	20,000	2,000	5,000
	Average	$10,000	$20,000	$10,000	$20,000

Techniques Not Considering Present Value

There are two basic techniques for assessing the acceptability of capital expenditure proposals without considering present value. One is to calculate the average rate of return; the other is the payback period. We will look at both, using Ohio Valley Industries as our example. We assume that Ohio Valley Industries is currently considering two mutually exclusive capital expenditure proposals: project A, which requires an initial investment of $60,000; and project B, which requires an initial investment of $70,000. The profit after tax (PAT) and relevant after-tax cash flow (CFAT) streams associated with each project are presented in Table 13.1.

Average Rate of Return

This measure is sometimes called the accounting rate of return; its most common definition is

$$\text{Average rate of return} = \frac{\text{average profit after taxes}}{\text{average investment}}$$

$$ARR = \frac{\sum_{t=1}^{n} (PAT_t)/n}{(\text{initial investment} + \text{estimated accounting salvage value})/2} \quad (13.1)$$

Table 13.1 shows that average profit after taxes for both projects is $10,000; the average investment for project A is $30,000 and for B it is $35,000.[1]

Dividing profit after taxes by the average investment results in *average rates of return* of

$$\text{Project A:} \frac{\$10,000}{\$30,000} = 33.33\%$$

$$\text{Project B:} \frac{\$10,000}{\$35,000} = 28.57\%$$

---

[1]The average investment can be found by dividing the difference in the beginning and ending values by 2. For project A this is ($60,000 − 0) ÷ 2 = $30,000; for B it is ($70,000 − 0) ÷ 2 = $35,000. Some firms employ cash flows in the numerator of Equation 13.1 instead of accounting profit.

These results indicate project A is preferable to B, since it has a higher rate of return. The percentages can be interpreted as the annual accounting rate of return expected on the average investment.

The benefit from using the average rate of return is ease of calculation; however, it suffers from two major weaknesses. The first is its use of accounting instead of cash flow data. Cash flows, not accounting profits, are the correct theoretical measure of economic profit. In addition, the average rate of return ignores the timing of cash flows and the time value of fnoney. Because of these weaknesses, this method is inappropriate for effective decision making.[2]

Payback Period

The *payback period* is the amount of time, typically noted in years, required to recover the initial investment; in effect, payback represents the length of time it takes for an investment to pay for itself. Payback occurs when the cumulative net cash inflows minus the initial cash investment equals zero:

Payback = number of years to recover initial investment

$$\text{Payback} = \left[CFAT_0 - \sum_{t=1}^{?} CFAT_t \right] = 0 \qquad (13.2)$$

For instance, in the case of project A, $60,000 must be recovered. After 1 year, $20,000 will be recovered; after 2 years, a total of $40,000 will be recovered; and the entire $60,000 will be recovered by year 3. Thus, the payback period for project A is 3 years. In the case of an annuity like project A, the payback period can be found by dividing the initial investment by the annual CFAT.

Since project B generates an uneven stream of cash inflows, the calculation of the payback period is not quite as clear-cut. In year 1 the firm will recover $48,000 of its $70,000 initial investment. At the end of year 2, $68,000 ($48,000 from year 1 plus $20,000 from year 2) will be recovered. At the end of year 3, $85,000 ($68,000 from years 1 and 2, plus the $17,000 from year 3) will be recovered. Since the amount received by the end of year 3 is more than the initial investment of $70,000, the payback period is somewhere between the second and third year. Because only $2,000 ($70,000 − $68,000) must be recovered during year 3, the payback period for project B is 2.12 years [2 years + ($2,000 ÷

---

[2]Under some simplified conditions (revenue expansion, no terminal value, equal annual cash flows, and no taxes), it is possible to derive the relationship between the average rate of return and the internal rate of return (discussed later in the chapter). See Marshall Sarnat and Haim Levy, "The Relationship of Rules of Thumb to the Internal Rate of Return: A Restatement and Generalization," *Journal of Finance* 24 (June 1969), pp. 479–489. This article also examines the reciprocal of the payback period and its relationship to the internal rate of return.

$17,000)]. Based on the payback criterion, project B would be preferred to project A, since B has a shorter payback period.[3]

The payback period is a better measure of project acceptability than the average rate of return, since it considers CFATs instead of accounting profit. In addition, payback period gives some implicit consideration to the timing of cash flows and therefore the time value of money. Many firms use the payback period as a supplement to present-value-based decision criteria because it can be helpful in assessing the liquidity of an investment and is viewed as a crude measure of risk.[4] Thus, a short payback project has greater liquidity since it provides rapid cash returns. Also, projects with short paybacks may be less risky since near term cash flows are often known with greater certainty than cash flows due many years in the future. However, it has several disadvantages. First, this approach fails to fully take account of the time value of money; by measuring how quickly the firm recovers its initial investment, it only implicitly considers the timing of the cash flows. A second weakness is its failure to recognize cash flows that occur after the payback period. Finally, no matter what else payback does, it does *not* provide a measure of the profitability of the proposed capital expenditure.

Present-Value Techniques

Present-value-based capital budgeting techniques provide measures of profitability and at the same time give explicit consideration to the time value of money. They support maximization of shareholder wealth by providing financial managers with decision-making information completely consistent with this objective. Typically, they employ the firm's marginal cost of capital (MCC) as the minimum required rate of return, although as illustrated in Chapter 14, risk-adjusted discount rates may also be employed. The required rate of return is the minimum that must be earned on a project to leave the firm's market value (the owners' wealth) unchanged. The three most popular present-value capital budgeting techniques are net present value, profitability index, and internal rate of return.

---

[3]This method of finding fractional payback periods implicitly assumes that cash inflows from the project are received at a constant rate throughout the year.

[4]Decisions based on the payback period can be made consistent with the net present value approach discussed later in the chapter. This consistency, which would have to be developed under firm-specific conditions (depreciation policies, taxes, and so forth) allows the two approaches to be operationally equivalent. A firm could state minimum capital budgeting criteria in terms of payback periods for simplicity, while ensuring that the accept-reject decisions made would contribute to the goal of maximizing shareholder wealth. See Wilbur G. Lewellen, Howard P. Lanser, and John J. McConnell, "Payback Substitutes for Discounted Cash Flow," *Financial Management* 2 (summer 1973), pp. 17–23. Some firms also use a discounted payback period, which gives partial recognition to the magnitude and timing of the cash inflows; however, it still ignores any cash flows received after the discounted payback period.

TABLE 13.2
Calculation of NPVs for
Ohio Valley Industries
Capital Expenditure
Alternatives

Project A		Project B			
		Year, t	Cash Inflows (1)	$PVIF_{15\%, t \, yr}$ (2)	Present Value [(1) × (2)] (3)
Annual inflow	$20,000	1	$48,000	.870	$41,760
× $PVIFA_{15\%, 5 \, yr}$	3.352	2	20,000	.756	15,120
= Present value of cash inflows	$67,040	3	17,000	.658	11,186
− Initial investment	60,000	4	10,000	.572	5,720
= Net present value	$ 7,040	5	5,000	.497	2,485
		Present value of cash inflows			$76,271
		− Initial investment			70,000
		= Net present value			$ 6,271

Net Present Value

Net present value (NPV) is one of the most commonly used capital budgeting techniques; it is found as follows:

Net present value = present value of cash inflows − initial investment[5]

$$NPV = \sum_{t=1}^{n} \frac{CFAT_t}{(1 + k)^t} - CFAT_0 \qquad (13.3)$$

where k is the required rate of return, or marginal cost of capital (MCC). The NPV is measured in dollars, and the criterion used with this approach is this: *If NPV ≥ 0, accept the project; otherwise , reject it*. If the NPV is greater than or equal to zero, the firm will earn a return greater than or equal to its required return. The NPV approach can be illustrated using the Ohio Valley Industries data presented in Table 13.1. If the firm has a 15 percent MCC, the net present values for projects A and B can be calculated as in Table 13.2. The results show that the net present values for these projects are $7,040 and $6,271, respectively. Both projects are acceptable, since their NPVs are greater than zero. If the projects were being ranked, project A would be considered superior to B because it has a higher net present value.

There are, however, two primary difficulties associated with the NPV approach. First, it is not as easily understood as some other capital budgeting decision criteria. Most executives intuitively understand the concept of a rate of return or payback, but many find it difficult to develop an intuitive "feel" for NPV. The second difficulty is in choosing the appropriate required rate of return to use in discounting the cash

[5]For computational simplicity, it is assumed all initial cash outflows occur at time zero. If they are spread out over time, the cash outflows (after netting them against any possible cash inflows) occurring after time zero must be discounted to t_0 like any other cash flows.

flows. These difficulties should not be viewed as serious drawbacks, however; for the NPV method is both theoretically sound and logically consistent with the goal of shareholder wealth maximization.

Profitability Index

The *profitability index (PI)* is sometimes called the *benefit-cost ratio,* especially when it is employed in the public (government or not-for-profit) sector. It is similar to the NPV approach except that the PI is a relative measure that shows the present value of cash inflows per dollar initially invested, while the NPV gives the absolute dollar difference between the present value of the cash inflows and the initial investment. The profitability index is defined as:[6]

$$\text{Profitability index} = \frac{\text{present value of cash inflows}}{\text{initial investment}}$$

$$PI = \frac{\sum_{t=1}^{n} \frac{CFAT_t}{(1 + k)^t}}{CFAT_0} \tag{13.4}$$

The decision criterion with PI is as follows: *If PI ≥ 1, accept the project; otherwise, reject it.* A PI greater than or equal to 1 is equivalent to a net present value that is greater than or equal to zero. Therefore, the NPV and PI approaches give the same solution to "accept-reject" decisions.

Profitability indexes for Ohio Valley Industries can be determined using the present values calculated in Table 13.2. The PIs for projects A and B are 1.12 ($67,040 ÷ $60,000) and 1.09 ($76,271 ÷ $70,000), respectively. Since both ratios are greater than 1, both projects are acceptable. Ranking the projects on the basis of their PIs indicates project A is preferable to B, since A returns $1.12 present value for each dollar initially invested, while B returns only $1.09. This particular ranking is the same as that obtained using NPVs; however, conflicting rankings are possible. PI is useful when the firm is faced with single-period capital rationing situations (discussed later in the chapter); except in such situations, the NPV approach is generally a better decision technique than PI. Also, the PI, like NPV, suffers from lack of understanding to the extent that financial managers often have no intuitive feel for PI values.

Internal Rate of Return

The internal rate of return (IRR) is another widely used technique for evaluating proposed capital expenditures. It is defined as the rate of discount that causes the NPV to equal zero by equating the present value of the cash inflows with the initial investment. The internal rate of return is that rate for which:

---

[6]If investment outlays occur over several years, the denominator in Equation 13.4 will be the present value of these outlays.

NPV = 0, or present value of cash inflows = initial investment

$$IRR = \text{NPV of zero, or} \sum_{t=1}^{n} \frac{CFAT_t}{(1 + IRR)^t} = CFAT_0 \qquad (13.5)$$

where IRR is the internal rate of return that will make the present value of the cash inflows exactly equal to the initial investment. The "accept-reject" criterion with IRR is as follows: *If IRR ≥ MCC, accept the project; otherwise, reject it.* The firm's marginal cost of capital is the "hurdle rate" that the IRR must meet or exceed. This indicates the firm is earning an amount greater than or equal to its required return, and, therefore, assures that the market value of the firm will either increase or at least stay the same.

Calculating the IRR for a single lump sum or an annuity is considerably easier than calculating it for an uneven stream of cash inflows.

For Lump Sums.   Finding the IRR for a lump sum involves these steps:

Step 1.   Divide the initial investment by the lump sum cash inflow to determine a PVIF factor.

Step 2.   Use Table A.3 and find the factor (in the appropriate time period row) closest to the present-value interest factor calculated in step 1. The rate of return associated with this factor is the IRR to the nearest 1 percent. Interpolation can be employed for greater accuracy.

To illustrate, consider a 4-year project with an initial investment of $5000 and a single cash inflow of $8100 at time $t = 4$. The calculated present-value factor is 0.617 ($5000 ÷ $8100). In Table A.3, the closest 4-year PVIF factor is 13 percent. By interpolation, the IRR is found to be 12.83 percent.[7]

For Annuities.   Finding the IRR for an annuity involves these steps:

Step 1.   Divide the initial investment by the constant cash inflow to determine a PVIFA factor.

Step 2.   Use Table A.4 to find the factor (in the appropriate time period row) closest to the calculated present-value interest factor for an annuity. The rate of return associated with this factor is the IRR to the nearest 1 percent; interpolation can be employed for greater accuracy.

These steps can be illustrated by applying them to Ohio Valley Industries project A, whose CFATs were given in Table 13.1. The present-value annuity factor for the annuity in project A is 3.000 ($60,000 ÷

---

[7]$IRR = 12\% + \dfrac{0.636 - 0.617}{0.636 - 0.613} = 12\% + \dfrac{0.019}{0.023} = 12.83\%$

$20,000). According to Table A.4, the 5-year present-value interest factor closest to 3.000 is 2.991 (for 20 percent). Therefore, the IRR for project A, to the nearest 1 percent, is 20 percent—or by interpolation, 19.87 percent.[8] Since Ohio Valley Industries has a 15 percent MCC, the project is acceptable.

For an Uneven Stream of Cash Inflows. Calculating the IRR for an uneven stream of cash inflows is more difficult and can be more time-consuming. Basically, it involves a logical search process, or hit-and-miss, as it is more commonly known. One way to simplify the process is to use a "simulated annuity" as a starting point. The steps necessary for calculating an IRR for an uneven stream of cash inflows are the following:

Step 1.   Calculate the average annual CFAT to arrive at a "simulated annuity."

Step 2.   Divide the "simulated annuity" into the initial investment to get a PVIFA factor.

Step 3.   Using Table A.4, find the factor closest to the calculated PVIFA factor (from step 2); this is the approximate IRR for the project. The result will be a *rough* approximation of the IRR based on the assumption that the uneven stream of CFATs is converted to be an annuity.

Step 4.   Subjectively adjust the simulated annuity-based IRR obtained in step 3 up or down, as necessary, by comparing the pattern of average CFATs (calculated in step 1) to the actual stream of cash inflows. If the actual CFAT stream has higher cash inflows in the earlier years, adjust the IRR upward a few percentage points. If the early year actual CFATs are low, reduce the simulated annuity-based IRR a few percentage points.

Step 5.   Using the discount rate estimated in step 4, calculate the net present value of the project. Be sure to use the present-value interest factor (PVIF) in Table A.3 employing the discount rate determined in step 4.

Step 6.   If the resulting NPV is greater than zero, raise the discount rate; if the resulting NPV is less than zero, lower the discount rate. *It is often helpful to make a fairly substantial increase or decrease in the discount rate to bracket the actual IRR as soon as possible.*

Step 7.   Calculate another NPV using the new discount rate. Repeat step 6. Stop once two consecutive discount rates that cause the NPV to be positive and then negative, respectively, have been found. Whichever of these two rates causes the NPV to be closest to zero is the IRR to the nearest 1 percent. Interpolation can be employed for greater accuracy.[9]

---

[8]$IRR = 19\% + \dfrac{3.058 - 3.000}{3.058 - 2.991} = 19\% + \dfrac{0.058}{0.067} = 19.87\%$

[9]Many calculators have IRR functions that solve unequal cash flow problems. Instead of two consecutive discount rates, a quicker (but less accurate) approach is to use a wider set of discount rates to obtain a positive and negative NPV. See footnote 10.

In the previous steps, the use of subjective estimates was suggested. A subjective feel for the amount of adjustment needed in the estimated IRR cannot be taught; but as you work a number of problems, you will develop the ability to make adjustments. Another point is that steps 1 to 4 can be skipped. The advantage of these steps is that they should provide a more accurate first estimate of the project's IRR than simply guessing.

These steps can be illustrated for Ohio Valley Industries' project B. By summing the cash inflows and dividing by the number of years in the life of the project, a simulated annuity of $20,000 results ($100,000 ÷ 5). Dividing the initial investment of $70,000 by the computed simulated annuity of $20,000 yields a calculated PVIFA factor of 3.50, which is closest to a 13 percent discount rate. Since the CFATs in the early years are greater than $20,000, an increase in the initial estimated IRR to 16 or 17 percent might be warranted. By trial and error, the NPV at 20 percent is found to be $537, while it is −$504 at 21 percent. Since 20 and 21 percent are consecutive discount rates that give positive and negative net present values, the trial-and-error process can be terminated; by interpolation the IRR is found to be equal to 20.52 percent.[10] Project B is acceptable, since its IRR (of about 20.5 percent) is greater than Ohio Valley Industries' 15 percent MCC. This is the same conclusion reached using the NPV and PI approaches. Thus, it should be clear that *in any accept-reject situation, all three present-value-based criteria will always provide the same accept/reject decision*. However, as you may have noted, the IRR method suggests project B is preferable (since B's IRR of 20.52 percent is greater than the 19.87 percent for A), while both the NPV and PI approaches suggest project A is preferable to B. The reasons for this conflict in rankings will be examined shortly.

The IRR method has some serious shortcomings, which we will examine in the next section; however, it has one clear advantage in practice over the NPV and PI methods. Financial managers tend to understand the concept of a rate of return much more readily than they understand the NPV or PI approaches. They may not understand the formal definition of an internal rate of return, but they understand its general meaning. This explains, in large part, why the IRR method is so

---

[10]$IRR = 20\% + \dfrac{\$537 - \$0}{\$537 - (-\$504)} = 20\% + \dfrac{\$537}{\$1,041} = 20.52\%$. What happens if we use a wider set of discount rates, say 16 percent and 25 percent? At 16 percent the NPV is $5033; it is $4356 at 25 percent. The approximate IRR is:

$$IRR = 16\% + \left[\dfrac{\$5033 - \$0}{\$5033 - (-\$4356)}\right]\left[25\% - 16\%\right]$$
$$= 16\% + (.5361)(9\%) = 20.82\%$$

This approach, although quicker than using two consecutive discount rates where the NPV is positive and then negative, is less accurate as seen by the approximate IRR of 20.82% versus the more accurate IRR of 20.52% determined previously.

widely used in business, even though it is theoretically inferior to either the NPV or the PI techniques.

Which Is Best—NPV, IRR, or PI?

As long as there is only a single project to evaluate, or the projects are independent, all three present-value-based approaches provide consistent decisions. However, when choices have to be made between mutually exclusive projects, or when the firm faces capital rationing, the alternative projects must be ranked, and under these conditions the three present-value-based methods may provide inconsistent rankings. The NPV approach is theoretically the best procedure and the most appropriate when there are no constraints on available capital. Where capital rationing exists for a single period, the PI approach is often easier to use; however, even then it is often necessary to use NPV.

Conflicts Between NPV and IRR

There are two basic conditions in which the NPV and IRR methods may give different rankings: (1) if there are size disparity effects (the initial investment for one project is substantially larger than that of the other project); and (2) if there are time disparity effects (the timing of cash inflows for the two projects differs, with one having much higher CFATs in the early years while the other has higher CFATs in later years). Although these conditions lead to conflicts in rankings, the basic cause of the conflict is that both the NPV and IRR methods have different implicit assumptions concerning the rate at which intermediate cash inflows generated by the projects are reinvested. The NPV approach implicitly assumes that intermediate cash inflows over the life of the project can be reinvested at a rate equal to the firm's marginal cost of capital; the IRR method, in contrast, assumes that intermediate cash inflows can be reinvested at a rate equal to the IRR for that particular project.

Size Disparity.   Consider two mutually exclusive projects, D and E. Table 13.3 gives the characteristics for the two projects; note that they

TABLE 13.3
Characteristics of Two
Projects (D and E) with
a Size Disparity

Characteristic	Year	Project	
		D	E
Initial investment	0	$110,000	$10,000
CFAT	1	50,000	5,050
	2	50,000	5,050
	3	50,000	5,050
NPV		$6,100	$1,726
IRR		17.28%	24.03%
PI		1.06	1.17
Marginal cost of capital (MCC), $k = 14\%$			

differ in their initial investment, with project D having an initial investment of $110,000, while project E requires an investment of only $10,000.

The projects can be compared graphically by constructing *net present value profiles* that depict the net present values for the projects at various discount rates. For projects D and E the NPVs at various discount rates are as follows:

	NPV	
Discount Rate (%)	D	E
0	$40,000	$5,150
5	26,150	3,751
10	14,350	2,559
15	4,150	1,529
20	− 4,700	635
25	−12,400	− 142

These NPVs are used to graph the net present value profiles in Figure 13.1. Table 13.3 and Figure 13.1 show that if we invoke the IRR rule, project E with an IRR of 24.03 percent is preferable to project D, which has a 17.28 percent return. However, by the NPV rule, project D should be preferred over E, since the former's NPV (employing a 14 percent MCC) is larger.

Although the basic condition is one of size disparity, the cause of the conflict is that the IRR method implicitly assumes intermediate cash

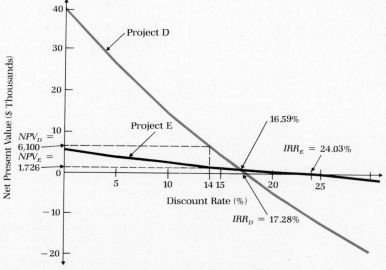

Figure 13.1   Net Present Value Profiles for Projects D and E.

inflows for project E ($5050 for years 1 and 2) can be reinvested at a rate equal to 24.03 percent until year 3; likewise, the IRR method assumes that project D's intermediate cash inflows ($50,000 for years 1 and 2) can be reinvested at a rate equal to 17.28 percent until year 3. In contrast, the NPV method assumes that intermediate cash inflows for both projects are reinvested at the same rate: at the firm's MCC of 14 percent. As Figure 13.1 shows, the NPV profiles for the projects intersect at 16.59 percent. Thus, project D is preferred to project E if the marginal cost of capital is below 16.59 percent, and vice versa. In the absence of capital rationing, project D, which is the largest and has the highest NPV, is the preferred investment; it contributes most toward maximizing the value of the firm. In ranking projects, the NPV method always selects those that maximize the value of the firm; the IRR approach may lead to incorrect ranking decisions.[11]

Time Disparity.   Because the NPV approach takes differences in the size of the projects into account while the IRR approach does not, this might suggest that both methods will rank projects in the same order if the initial investments are equal. This is not the case; even if two projects have the same initial investments, they may be ranked differently depending on the timing of the cash inflows. Consider projects F and G, both of which require an initial investment of $93,000. However, project F has cash inflows of $20,000 in the first year and $110,000 in the second

---

[11]An approach sometimes used in practice is to compute an IRR with an *explicit* reinvestment rate assumption. For both projects D and E, IRRs can be calculated assuming the intermediate cash inflows are reinvested at the firm's marginal cost of capital of 14 percent. This "explicit reinvestment IRR" can be computed as follows:

Project D

1. $50,000 $(FVIFA_{14\%,\ 3\ yr})$ = $50,000 (3.440) = $172,000 at $t = 3$.

2. $PVIF_{?\%,\ 3\ yr} = \dfrac{\$110,000}{\$172,000}$ = 0.640. Looking in the PVIF table across the 3-year row, the PVIF factor for 16 percent and 3 years is .641. Thus the IRR for project E, assuming an explicit reinvestment rate of 14 percent, is just over 16 percent.

Project E

1. $5,050 $(FVIFA_{14\%,\ 3\ yr})$ = $5,050 (3.440) = $17,372 at $t = 3$.

2. $PVIF_{?\%,\ 3\ yr} = \dfrac{\$10,000}{\$17,372}$ = .576. Looking in the PVIF table, the IRR for project D assuming an explicit reinvestment rate of 14 percent is slightly over 20 percent.

In comparing these two IRRs calculated with an explicit 14 percent reinvestment rate, project E is still preferred to project D—the same conclusion reached with the regular IRRs and exactly opposite to the ranking provided by the NPV criterion. Thus, incorporation of an explicit reinvestment rate assumption for the IRR criterion does not overcome the ranking problem associated with size disparities between projects.

Characteristic	Year	Project	
		F	G
Initial investment	0	$ 93,000	$ 93,000
CFAT	1	20,000	100,000
	2	110,000	19,000
NPV		$ 14,340	$ 12,528
IRR		20.00%	23.95%
PI		1.15	1.13
Marginal cost of capital (MCC), $k = 11\%$			

year, while project G has cash inflows of $100,000 in year 1 and $19,000 in year 2. Table 13.4 indicates project G would be accepted based on the IRR criterion, since its IRR of 23.95 percent is larger than project F's, which is 20.00 percent. Using the NPV rule and an 11 percent MCC, project F would be accepted, since its NPV is larger than project G's.

Although the basic condition is one of differences in the timing of the cash flows, the cause of the conflict is again the fact that the IRR method implicitly assumes intermediate cash inflows can be reinvested at a rate equal to the IRR on the project, while the NPV rule assumes these same cash inflows can be reinvested at the firm's MCC. In general, it is the failure of the IRR method to properly evaluate the alternative uses of funds that causes time disparity problems. This can occur even if the projects have the same initial investments and the same time horizons, as long as they do not have identical CFAT streams.[12] Because the NPV method assumes reinvestment at the MCC, it is the preferred approach for either size or time disparity problems.

Multiple Internal Rates of Return

In addition to the differences in rankings that may occur between the IRR and NPV methods, the IRR suffers from another serious problem—multiple rates of return may occur if the sign of the cash flow stream changes more than once. Consider an oil firm that is trying to decide whether or not to install a new high-speed pump on a well that is

---

[12]If we calculate the IRRs using an explicit reinvestment rate (see footnote 11) of 11 percent, the explicit reinvestment IRRs are as follows:

$$\text{IRR}_F \text{ (explicit 11\% reinvestment rate)} = 19.21\%$$

$$\text{IRR}_G \text{ (explicit 11\% reinvestment rate)} = 18.22\%$$

Note that the ranking of these explicit reinvestment rate IRRs is different from the IRRs in Table 13.4; the explicit reinvestment rate IRRs now rank project F as more desirable than project G, which is the same ranking provided by the NPV criterion. Thus, in contrast to size disparity problems, which are not "solved" by making an explicit reinvestment rate assumption, introducing explicit reinvestment rates into the IRR method overcomes problems due to time disparity.

already in production.[13] The cash flows on the new pump, the existing pump, and the incremental CFATs are given in Table 13.5. (Since this is a replacement decision, the focus is on the incremental CFATs.) The new pump will have an installed cost of $57,148. During its first year of operation it will produce $151,435 more oil than the pump currently in place; however, during the second year, the new pump produces $100,000 less oil because the well has been depleted. The question is this: Should the investment in the new pump be made?

Figure 13.2 shows the net present value profile of the incremental project for different discount rates. If the firm's MCC is 15 percent, the NPV method would reject the project because it has a negative NPV (−$999.55). Using the IRR approach, the project is found to have *two* different IRRs, 25 percent and 40 percent.[14] If the firm's required rate of

---

[13]This problem was first considered in detail by James H. Lorie and Leonard J. Savage, "Three Problems in Rationing Capital," *Journal of Business* 28 (October 1955), pp. 227–239.

[14]Mathematically, the multiple IRR problem is a result of Descartes' rule of signs, which implies that every time the sign of the CFAT stream changes, there may be another possible root to the solution. In the pump problem there are two changes of signs (from − at $t = 0$ to + at $t = 1$, and then back to − at $t = 2$). The IRR is the rate that causes the discounted cash inflows, to equal the initial investment, so the NPV equals zero. Solving for the IRR we have:

$$-CFAT_0 + \frac{CFAT_1}{(1 + IRR)^1} + \frac{CFAT_2}{(1 + IRR)^2} = 0$$

$$-\$57,148 + \frac{\$151,435}{(1 + IRR)^1} + \frac{-\$100,000}{(1 + IRR)^2} = 0$$

$$\frac{-\$57,148(1 + IRR)^2 + \$151,435(1 + IRR)^1 - \$100,000}{(1 + IRR)^2} = 0$$

Multiplying both sides by $-(1 + IRR)^2$ we have

$$\$57,148(1 + IRR)^2 - \$151,435(1 + IRR)^1 + \$100,000 = 0$$

This is a quadratic equation with up to two real roots. It has the general form

$$ax^2 + bx + c = 0$$

and can be solved using the quadratic formula

$$x = \frac{-b \pm \sqrt{b^2 - 4ac}}{2a}$$

For the pump example, the roots are as follows:

$$(1 + IRR) = x = \frac{\$151,435 \pm \sqrt{(\$151,435)^2 - 4(\$57,148)(\$100,000)}}{2(\$57,148)}$$

$$(1 + IRR) = \frac{\$151,435 \pm \$8,565}{\$114,296}$$

$$1 + IRR = 1.40 \text{ or } 1.25$$
$$IRR = .40 \text{ or } .25$$
$$IRR = 40\% \text{ or } 25\%$$

This problem is examined in considerably more detail in Lynn E. Bussey, *The Economic Analysis of Industrial Projects* (Englewood Cliffs, N.J.: Prentice-Hall, 1978), pp. 218–237.

TABLE 13.5
Incremental CFATs,
NPVs, and IRRs

Characteristics	Year	New Pump (1)	Existing Pump (2)	Incremental CFATs [(1) − (2)] (3)
Initial investment	0	$ 57,148	0	$ 57,148
CFAT	1	171,435	$ 20,000	151,435
	2	50,000	150,000	− 100,000
NPV		$129,800.45	$130,800	−$ 999.55
IRR		226.76%	Not applicable	25% or 40%
Marginal cost of capital (MCC), $k = 15\%$				

return was between 25 and 40 percent, the project would be accepted. While mathematically the two answers of 25 and 40 percent are accurate, they are incorrect in a capital budgeting sense; we have already determined that the NPV for the pump project is negative.

When multiple internal rates of return occur, the IRR criterion is not reliable and the net present value approach should be employed. Thus, the two reasons why the net present value criterion is theoretically preferable as a decision criterion are because it always ranks mutually exclusive projects correctly, and because each project has a unique NPV, while multiple (and incorrect) IRRs may exist.

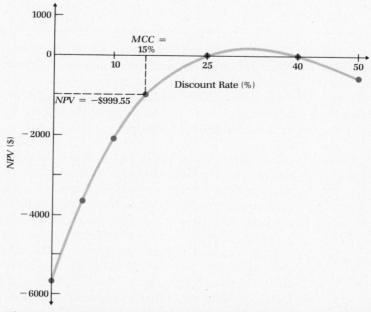

Figure 13.2   Net Present Value Profile of Oil Well Pump with Multiple Internal Rates of Return.

Conflicts
Between NPV
and PI

Because NPV and PI involve the same basic information, they often rank projects in the same order. However, in some situations it is also possible to get a conflict in rankings. Let us reconsider projects D and E (Table 13.3). Recall that they differed in the size of their initial investment. With an MCC of 14 percent, project D had an NPV of $6,100 and a PI of 1.06; project E had an NPV of $1,726 and a PI of 1.17. With the NPV criterion, project D should be accepted; the PI method, however, indicates project E is preferable. Why?

A conflict in rankings between NPV and PI occurs *only* when the initial investments of the two proposals are different. Since the NPV method nets the initial investment with the present value of the future CFATs, while PI divides the present value of future CFATs by the initial investment, projects with different initial investments (a size disparity) may have different rankings. Because of the prevalence of different initial investments, the PI approach must be employed with caution, since it may produce improper rankings for mutually exclusive projects. In the absence of capital rationing, to be discussed subsequently, the NPV rule is preferable since it always ranks projects in the correct order.

Under all situations the NPV approach provides the correct accept-reject decisions and ranks projects properly. Both the IRR and PI approaches, however, will always make the correct accept-reject decision but may rank mutually exclusive projects incorrectly. Because of its theoretical soundness and its ability to provide a correct ranking of project desirability, therefore, the NPV is considered the best decision criterion.

Other
Important
Considerations
in Capital
Budgeting

Now that we understand the capital budgeting decision criteria, two other important topics can be addressed. First, we will consider how the decision is made if two or more mutually exclusive projects have unequal lives. Then we will consider the topic of capital rationing; that is, not being able to fund all acceptable projects. Both topics are important for effective decision making.

Projects with
Unequal Lives

Many capital budgeting decisions involve choosing between two or more projects having different lives. *As long as the projects are independent, the possible impact of unequal lives does not need to be considered.* When the projects are mutually exclusive, however, the impact of different lives must be considered. The decision faced by the Davis Company represents just such a situation. The firm is attempting to choose between two plastic molding equipment systems. The first system (system I) is semi-automatic, requires an initial investment of $160,000, and produces CFATs of $80,000 per year for 3 years, at the end of which it will have no terminal value and must be replaced. The second system (system J) is fully automatic and requires an initial investment of $210,000. Because it is completely automated, system J will last longer. It produces annual

CFATs of $64,000 for each of 6 years, at the end of which it will have no terminal value and will need to be replaced. The firm's marginal cost of capital is 16 percent. Should Davis choose system I or J?

To answer that question, your immediate reaction might be to calculate the NPV of both projects and choose the one with the highest NPV. The NPVs are as follows:

$$NPV_I = \$80,000 \ (PVIFA_{16\%, 3yr}) - \$160,000$$
$$= \$80,000 \ (2.246) - \$160,000$$
$$= \$179,680 - \$160,000 = \$19,680$$

$$NPV_J = \$64,000 \ (PVIFA_{16\%, 6yr}) - \$210,000$$
$$= \$64,000 \ (3.685) - \$210,000$$
$$= \$235,840 - 210,000 = \$25,840$$

These NPVs indicate that system J should be selected. However, the analysis is incomplete, since we did not consider the differing lives of the two mutually exclusive projects. An incorrect decision may have been made. If we choose system I, an opportunity exists to make another similar investment in 3 more years. If we choose system J, we do not have to make a second investment. To properly compare them, we must consider the NPVs of both projects for the same number of years.

Least Common Life.   One approach to equalizing project lives is to find the *least common life;* that is, to repeat each project in order to find some time when both terminate in the same year. For systems I and J, the least common life is 6 years. The NPV for system J of $25,840 is correct, since it was initially computed for a 6-year period. For system I, however, we must calculate a new NPV assuming that Davis invests in system I both at time 0 and time 3. The new 6-year CFAT stream for system I is:

t	0	1	2	3	4	5	6
CFAT 1st system	−$160,000	+$80,000	+$80,000	+ $80,000			
CFAT 2nd system				−$160,000	+$80,000	+$80,000	+$80,000
Combined CFAT	−$160,000	+$80,000	+$80,000	− $80,000	+$80,000	+$80,000	+$80,000

We can find the net present value of this CFAT stream directly,[15] or use

---

[15]Solving for the NPV of system I with the 6-year common life cycle yields:

$$NPV_{I, 6 \, yr} = -\$160,000 + \$80,000(PVIFA_{16\%, 2 \, yr}) - \$80,000(PVIF_{16\%, 3 \, yr})$$
$$+ \$80,000(PVIFA_{16\%, 6 \, yr} - PVIFA_{16\%, 3 \, yr})$$
$$= -\$160,000 + \$80,000 \ (1.605) - 80,000(.641) + 80,000$$
$$(3.685 - 2.246)$$
$$= -\$160,000 + \$128,400 - \$51,280 + \$115,120$$
$$= \$32,240$$

This value, aside from a rounding error of $54.88 due to using PVIF and PVIFA tables with only three significant digits, is equal to $32,294.88.

the knowledge already gained that the NPV of system I for its original 3-year life is \$19,680. Using the latter approach, the 6-year NPV for system I is:

$$NPV_I \text{ for 6 years} = NPV_I \text{ for second system I } (PVIF_{16\%, 3\,yr}) + NPV_I \text{ for first system I}$$
$$= \$19,680 \; (PVIF_{16\%, 3\,yr}) + \$19,680$$
$$= \$19,680 \; (.641) + \$19,680$$
$$= \$12,614.88 + \$19,680 = \$32,294.88$$

This NPV of \$32,294.88 can now be compared with NPV_J. Since NPV_J is equal to \$25,840, Davis will maximize shareholder wealth by selecting system I and replacing it in 3 years with another system I.

The least common life for the two projects considered by Davis Company was 6 years. In some situations, it becomes much more difficult to carry out the calculations over the projects' least common life cycle. For example, if one of the projects had a 7-year life while the other had an 11-year life, the least common life for the two is 77 years! For that reason it is often preferable to use an alternative approach for equalizing project lives.

Annualized Net Present Value.   Another approach for making unequal-lived projects comparable is to calculate an annualized net present value. The *annualized NPV* approach converts a project's NPV into a yearly net present value, assuming the project is replicated over and over again to infinity.[16] The annualized net present value (ANPV) is:

$$ANPV = \frac{NPV_n}{PVIFA_{k,n}} \qquad (13.6)$$

where NPV_n = the project's *NPV* over its initial life, n
   $PVIFA_{k,n}$ = a present-value interest factor for an annuity based on the firm's marginal cost of capital (or required rate of return), k, for the number of years in the project's initial expected life

For the Davis Company's systems I and J, the net present values over

---

[16]This approach is sometimes referred to as the equivalent annual annuity method. A related approach converts the project's NPV over some n-period life to an infinitely replicated NPV, so that

$$NPV_{n,\,\infty} = NPV_n \left[\frac{(1 + k)^n}{(1 + k)^n - 1} \right]$$

This procedure, in essence, converts the NPV_n to a perpetuity, while the annualized NPV method determines the constant annual receipt in a perpetuity.

their initial 3- and 6-year lives, respectively, were $19,680 and $25,840. Employing Equation 13.6, the annualized NPV's are as follows:

$$ANPV_I = \frac{\$19,680}{PVIFA_{16\%,3\,yr}} = \frac{\$19,680}{2.246} = \$8,762.24$$

$$ANPV_J = \frac{\$25,840}{PVIFA_{16\%,6\,yr}} = \frac{\$25,840}{3.685} = \$7,012.21$$

System I, in effect, has an annualized NPV of $8,762.24, while system J has an annualized NPV of $7,012.21. Since Davis is interested in the project with the highest NPV, system I would be selected.

By selecting system I, Davis will make exactly the same decision as it did when it used the least common life approach for comparing unequal-lived projects. However, one problem with both approaches is that they assume future costs and technology will be constant. That is, neither method provides any means for incorporating increases or decreases in both revenues and expenses in the future, nor do they allow for changing technology and the impact it might have on future replications of the same, or somewhat different, projects.

Unequal Lives in Practice.   In times of rapid inflation or changing technology, it is often inappropriate to assume that future costs and technology will be constant. Consider what would happen to the Davis Company's decision if the purchase price of the semi-automatic system (system I) was expected to increase by $15,000 in 3 years and the CFATs starting in year 4 were expected to decrease by $5,000 per year, reducing the CFATs for the 3-year life of the second system I to $75,000 per year. The original CFAT stream for system I over its 6-year common life, assuming constant costs and technology, was as follows:

t	(Initial Investment) 0	1	2	3	4	5	6
Combined CFAT	−$160,000	+$80,000	+$80,000	−$80,000	+$80,000	+$80,000	+$80,000

The new CFAT stream reflecting changes in the cash flows when system I is replaced in 3 years is as follows:

t	(Initial Investment) 0	1	2	3	4	5	6
CFAT 1st system	−$160,000	+$80,000	+$80,000	+$80,000			
CFAT 2nd system				−$175,000	+$75,000	+$75,000	+$75,000
Combined CFAT	−$160,000	+$80,000	+$80,000	− $95,000	+$75,000	+$75,000	+$75,000

The 6-year common life NPV for system I is now:

NPV_I for 6 years $= NPV_I$ for second system $I(PVIF_{16\%,3\,yr}) + NPV_I$ for first
           system I
           $= [\$75,000\ (PVIFA_{16\%,3\,yr}) - \$175,000]\ (PVIF_{16\%,3\,yr}) + \$19,680$
           $= [\$75,000\ (2.246) - \$175,000]\ (.641) + \$19,680$
           $= (\$168,450 - 175,000)\ (.641) + \$19,680$
           $= -\$4,198.55 + \$19,680 = \$15,481.45$

After taking into account the increased costs associated with system I (when it is replaced in 3 years), the 6-year common life NPV_I of $15,481.45 is now less than NPV_J of $25,840, which also has a 6-year life. Given the anticipated change in costs for system I, our decision has been reversed; system J should now be selected.

In practice, the approach to employ with nonconstant costs or technology is to enumerate all the changes in costs and technology and adjust the cash flows accordingly, or impose some common life that takes into account anticipated major changes in technology and costs. The first approach involves a thorough analysis of anticipated initial investments, cash flows, and possible changes in the tax consequences associated with the projects under consideration. Alternatively, a common life assumption may have to be imposed. If the Davis Company imposed a 4-year common life assumption, the choice could be made between the alternative systems based on their respective NPVs over this 4-year period.[17] Additional cash flow information relative to their market value if sold at the end of 4 years would have to be estimated. As before, the firm will then calculate NPVs for the projects and choose the system that maximizes the firm's NPV over the imposed 4-year common life of the two systems. However it is done, financial managers must equalize the lives of different projects and deal with expected future costs and technologies when evaluating mutually exclusive investment opportunities.

Capital Rationing: The Single-Period Case

Capital rationing means the firm may not be able to invest in all acceptable projects because of inadequate funding. In effect, there are more profitable projects than there are funds to invest in them. Such constraints are prevalent in many firms, particularly those that have a policy of financing all capital expenditures internally, or an internally imposed constraint on the amount of debt they will issue. Another example of capital rationing results when divisions of large firms are

---

[17]Any common life could be assumed; there is no need for it to correspond to the economic life of either of the two projects. If Davis Company felt 4 years was a reasonable planning horizon, then 4 years would become the life imposed on both projects for evaluation purposes.

allowed to make capital expenditures only up to a specified budget ceiling. By foregoing investment opportunities that return more than the required rate of return, these firms are foregoing opportunities to enhance the market price of their stock. If capital is rationed the investment policy is, by definition, less than optimal.

In a one-period capital rationing environment, what set of projects should be selected? Since the firm is still trying (to the extent possible) to maximize shareholder wealth, it should invest in that group of projects which collectively has the largest net present value. But this group of projects must be selected without violating the budget constraint. Two approaches permit the firm to arrive at the proper group of projects— the first uses the profitability index (PI) method; the second uses NPV.

With the PI method, the steps are the following:

Step 1. Calculate the PI for all projects. Do not eliminate any projects, even apparently less acceptable mutually exclusive ones. The initial investment for each project must also be specified.[18]

Step 2. Accept projects in descending order, based on PIs, as long as the PIs are ≥ 1.0. If *all* funds specified by the budget constraint are fully expended, the process is complete.

Step 3. If all funds are not fully expended (the next acceptable PI-ranked project causes the budget constraint to be exceeded), a modification of step 2 is necessary. This modification looks at alternative combinations of projects. A weighted PI can then be computed for all feasible combinations of projects by summing the weighted (by investment per project ÷ budget constraint) average of their individual PIs. (Feasible combinations are those that do not contain two or more mutually exclusive projects.) If the complete budget amount is not expended for any set of projects, the remaining unspent funds are given a PI of 1.0 and included in the weighted PI calculation.

Step 4. Accept that group of projects from the feasible combinations that has the largest weighted PI given the one-period budget constraint.

With NPV, the steps are the following:

Step 1. Calculate the NPV for all projects. Do not eliminate any projects, even apparently less acceptable mutually exclusive ones. In addition, determine the initial investment for each project.

Step 2. Evaluate all possible feasible combinations of projects by summing

---

[18]Throughout this section it is assumed that the entire investment for a project occurs at time $t = 0$. Modifications employing a multiperiod capital rationing approach like those considered in Appendix 13A are necessary if the initial investment extends beyond a single time period.

TABLE 13.6
Available Capital
Expenditure Projects
for Packer Products

Project	Initial Investment	PI	NPV
A	$120,000	1.56	$ 67,200
B_1	150,000	1.53	79,500
B_2	300,000	1.37	111,000
C_1	125,000	1.17	21,250
C_2	100,000	1.18	18,000

their individual NPVs; however, the sum of the initial investments, $\sum_{i=1}^{n} CFAT_{0,i}$, must be less than or equal to the budget constraint.

Step 3. Accept that group of projects from the feasible combinations which has the highest total net present value.

To illustrate, consider the situation faced by Packer Products, Inc., which has five possible projects, A, B_1, B_2, C_1, and C_2, as shown in Table 13.6. Note that projects B_1 and B_2 are mutually exclusive, as are projects C_1 and C_2, and that Packer has a one-period maximum capital budget of $400,000. If Packer attempted to select projects simply by taking those with the highest individual PIs, it would take project A with a PI of 1.56, project B_1 with a PI of 1.53, and since B_2 is not available (because it competes with B_1), project C_2 with a PI of 1.18. Alternatively, if Packer selected projects on the basis of the ranked individual NPVs, it would first take project B_2, with an NPV of $111,000. The only other project it could take (and stay within the budget constraint) would be C_2, with an NPV of $18,000. Unfortunately, neither group is correct, since these projects do not maximize the firm's NPV given the options available.

To determine the proper group of projects, it is necessary to consider all feasible two- and three-project combinations. The group of projects selected by looking solely at the individual PIs, A, B_1, and C_2, has a total NPV of $164,700. The group selected by looking simply at individual NPVs was B_2 and C_2, which has a total NPV of $129,000. In Table 13.7, weighted PIs and total NPVs over all combinations of projects are presented. An examination indicates Packer should undertake projects A, B_1, and C_1, which have a total NPV of $167,950. Note that this combination of projects is selected by either weighted PI or total NPV. Also, since C_1 is in the proper group of projects to select given the budget constraint, we see why apparently inferior, mutually exclusive projects cannot be eliminated from consideration. Only the combination of projects A, B_1, and C_1 is consistent with the firm's objective of shareholder wealth maximization, given its one-period capital rationing constraint.

Although financial theory suggests capital rationing should not exist, in practice many (and perhaps most) firms appear to face this situation.[19]

---

[19]For an extensive discussion, see H. Martin Weingartner, "Capital Rationing: n Authors in Search of a Plot," *Journal of Finance* 32 (December 1977), pp. 1403–1431.

Combination	Initial Investment	Weighted PI[a]	Total NPV
A, B$_1$, C$_1$	$395,000	1.420	$167,950
A, B$_1$, C$_2$	370,000	1.412	164,700
A, B$_1$	270,000	1.367	146,700
A, C$_1$	245,000	1.221	88,450
A, C$_2$	220,000	1.213	85,200
B$_1$, C$_1$	275,000	1.252	100,750
B$_1$, C$_2$	250,000	1.244	97,500
B$_2$, C$_2$	400,000	1.322	129,000

[a]The calculation for the combination A, B$_1$, C$_1$ (with $5,000 remaining unspent, which is invested in a project with a PI = 1.0) is as follows:

$$\text{Weighted PI} = (\$120,000/\$400,000)(1.56) + (\$150,000/\$400,000)(1.53) +$$
$$(\$125,000/\$400,000)(1.17) + (\$5,000/\$400,000)(1.0)$$
$$= (0.3)(1.56) + (0.375)(1.53) + (0.3125)(1.17) + (0.0125)(1.00)$$
$$= 0.4680 + 0.57375 + 0.365625 + 0.0125 \approx 1.420$$

The other weighted PIs are calculated in a similar manner.

A fixed one-period constraint is artificial; in practice, there is often some flexibility in the capital budget. In addition, the cost of some investment projects may be spread over a number of years. With a multiperiod analysis, less profitable projects can be postponed to a subsequent period when the capital budget will permit investment. In addition, a one-period analysis does not take into account the intermediate cash flows generated by a project. Projects that provide relatively large cash inflows in the early years might be accepted if these intermediate cash flows could be used to finance subsequent projects. Thus, use of multiperiod capital rationing techniques, as described in Appendix 13A, may be necessary.

Capital Budgeting in Practice

In this section we address two very important questions. Do firms actually employ the more sophisticated (present-value-based) capital budgeting techniques suggested by theory? And do they employ multiple criteria when making capital budgeting decisions? As we will see, there still appears to be some difference between what is suggested by theory and what is done in actual business practice.

Do Firms Employ Present-Value-Based Methods?

Present-value-based capital budgeting techniques have been generally available and recommended since the 1950s. Evidence indicates they are being more widely employed as time passes. In a study of 184 large firms, the IRR or NPV approach was employed by 57 percent in 1970, up considerably from the 38 percent and 19 percent of the firms that employed the same techniques in 1964 and 1959, respectively.[20] Although these survey results suggest increasing use of present-value-based

---

[20]Thomas Klammer, "Empirical Evidence of the Adoption of Sophisticated Capital Budgeting Techniques," *Journal of Business* 45 (July 1972), pp. 387–397.

techniques, they undoubtedly overstate their use, since smaller and less capital-intensive firms were excluded. The results tend to be corroborated by two other recent studies. In one case, 86 percent of the companies used some type of present-value-based approach to capital budgeting.[21] However, the respondents again were generally large, stable firms. Another source reports that 31 of 33 large firms attending a capital budgeting seminar employed the NPV, PI, or IRR method.[22] So it appears the use of present-value-based capital budgeting techniques is fairly widespread, particularly for large, relatively capital-intensive firms.

The same pattern does not appear to exist for medium and small firms; a 1972 survey of small manufacturing firms found that the payback method was used by 51 percent of these firms, that 30 percent used some variation of the average rate of return, and that only 10 percent used one of the present-value-based techniques.[23] For all firms, large or small, survey results indicate the most commonly employed present-value-based capital budgeting decision criterion is the internal rate of return.

The reasons for not using present-value-based techniques are not fully known, but they appear to be lack of understanding of why these techniques are in the best interests of the firm's shareholders, the belief that it is too difficult to accurately estimate cash flows more than a few years into the future, a preference for short payback projects on the part of risk-conscious financial managers with strong liquidity preferences, or concern about possible adverse short-term effects on reported accounting earnings from accepting projects based on discounted cash flow.[24] As long as these feelings persist, some firms will continue to employ other (less appropriate) techniques.

Do Firms Employ Multiple Decision Criteria?

Not only do some firms employ capital budgeting decision criteria other than those based on present value, many firms employ two or more separate decision criteria for making capital expenditure decisions. In a recent study, 93 of 112 respondent firms indicated they employed a secondary capital budgeting selection technique when making decisions.[25] In another case, 86 percent of the responding firms used at least

[21]Lawrence D. Schall, Gary L. Sundem, and William R. Geijsbeek, Jr., "Survey and Analysis of Capital Budgeting Methods," *Journal of Finance* 33 (March 1978), pp. 281–287.

[22]Eugene F. Brigham, "Hurdle Rates for Screening Capital Expenditure Proposals," *Financial Management* 4 (autumn 1975), pp. 17–26.

[23]Otha L. Gray, Monroe M. Bird, and David F. Scott, Jr., "Investing and Financing Behavior of Small Manufacturing Firms," *MSU Business Topics* 20 (summer 1972), pp. 29–38.

[24]For a discussion of some of these issues, see Eugene M. Lerner and Alfred Rappaport, "Limit DCF in Capital Budgeting," *Harvard Business Review* 46 (September–October 1968), pp. 133–138; and Thomas R. Dyckman and James C. Kinard, "The Discounted Cash Flow Investment Decision Model with Accounting Income Constraints," *Decision Sciences* 4 (July 1973), pp. 301–313.

[25]Lawrence J. Gitman and John R. Forrester, Jr., "A Survey of Capital Budgeting Techniques Used by Major U.S. Firms," *Financial Management* 6 (fall 1977), pp. 66–71.

two selection criteria when making capital budgeting decisions.[26] These findings indicate that the use of multiple decision criteria in practice is widespread.[27]

If the multiple decision criteria employed by a firm always agree in selecting or rejecting projects, then the practice is harmless. If the criteria sometimes produce disagreement and decisions not consistent with the goal of maximizing shareholder wealth are made, the resulting capital budget will not contain the proper combination of projects. One of the more prevalant practices appears to be using the payback period in conjunction with another method, such as NPV.

Consider what might happen given the information contained in Table 13.8 for the Garden Shoe Company. Using a maximum payback period of 4 years, Garden would find project B with a payback of 5 years unacceptable, even though it has an NPV of $50,000. Using the NPV approach alone, the firm would have a capital budget consisting of projects A, B, D, and E, with a total initial investment of $325,000 and a

TABLE 13.8
Capital Budgeting
Projects Selected by
Garden Shoe Company

Available Projects			
Project	Initial Investment	NPV	Payback Period (years)
A	$ 50,000	$10,000	2.8
B	140,000	50,000	5.0
C	75,000	− 5,000	2.5
D	100,000	20,000	3.0
E	35,000	15,000	3.5
Capital Budget Selections Using NPV			
Project	Initial Investment		NPV
A	$ 50,000		$10,000
B	140,000		50,000
D	100,000		20,000
E	35,000		15,000
Total	$325,000		$95,000
Capital Budget Selections Using NPV and Payback			
Project	Initial Investment		NPV
A	$ 50,000		$10,000
D	100,000		20,000
E	35,000		15,000
Total	$185,000		$45,000

[26]Schall, Sundem, and Geijsbeek, "Survey and Analysis of Capital Budgeting Methods."
[27]For various approaches to maximizing the capital budget given multiple decision criteria employing mathematical programming, see Sang M. Lee and A. J. Lerro, "Capital Budgeting for Multiple Objectives," *Financial Management* 3 (spring 1974), pp. 58–66; and Jerome S. Osteryoung, *Capital Budgeting: Long-Term Asset Selection*, 2d ed. (Columbus: Grid Publishing, 1979), chap. 11.

total NPV of $95,000. However, since Garden Shoe requires that projects meet both the NPV and payback criteria, the budget consists of projects A, D, and E, with an initial investment and total NPV of $185,000 and $45,000, respectively. Shareholder wealth is *not* maximized by employing both criteria, since total NPV is $50,000 less ($95,000 − $45,000) than it would be if only NPV were employed. In addition, the capital budget is reduced from $325,000 to $185,000 by the joint use of both criteria.

SUMMARY

The average rate of return and the payback period are nondiscounted flow techniques sometimes used for making capital expenditure decisions. However, if the goal of the firm is to maximize shareholder wealth, a present-value-based technique (NPV, PI or IRR) must be employed in capital budgeting. In accept-reject situations where there is only one project, or where projects are independent, all three present-value-based techniques result in the same decision. The internal rate of return, while widely used in practice, has two potential drawbacks. First, it may have more than one value when inflows and outflows switch more than once over the life of the project. Second, it may not rank mutually exclusive projects correctly. The PI method may also rank projects incorrectly if a size disparity exists. The NPV approach does not suffer from the problems faced by either the IRR or PI. For this reason NPV can be safely used in any capital expenditure decision. When mutually exclusive projects have unequal lives, adjustments must be made to compare the projects over equal-length time periods, or incorrect decisions may be made. In one-period capital rationing cases, the use of a weighted PI or NPV approach over all feasible combinations of projects results in the proper set of projects.

Present-value-based techniques are widely employed in practice, particularly by relatively large, capital-intensive firms, although many firms still employ the average rate of return or payback period as well. The use of multiple criteria often results in decisions that are not in the long-run interest of the firm's shareholders. Given the dynamic nature of our economy, and the extensive capital expenditure plans of many firms, a full understanding of capital budgeting procedures is essential for effective financial management.

QUESTIONS

13.1. The average rate of return and payback period techniques are widely used in practice. What are their drawbacks, and why are they used so frequently in view of these drawbacks?

13.2. Explain what net present value measures. How does this criterion correspond to the firm's goal of wealth maximization?

13.3. Why is the NPV of a long-term project with a high percentage of its cash flows expected in distant future years more sensitive to changes in the marginal cost of capital than the NPV of a short-term project?

13.4. What are the decision criteria for the NPV, PI, and IRR methods? Show how the three are equivalent. Why is an NPV of 0 the same as a PI of 1.0, and how do both relate to the IRR?

13.5. The NPV and IRR techniques may rank projects differently when mutually exclusive projects are considered. Explain the following:

  a. Which technique ranks the projects in their proper order? Why?

  b. What conditions lead to differences in rankings, and what is the basic cause of the conflicting rankings?

13.6. Under what conditions will the NPV and PI techniques rank projects differently? What is there about the PI technique that causes this difference in ranking?

13.7. Suppose a capital budgeting project has two internal rates of return, 20 and 40 percent.

  a. Under what conditions can multiple internal rates of return arise?

  b. Graph the net present value profile showing the relationship of the two IRRs to NPV. (*Hint:* There is more than one graph that satisfies this requirement!)

  c. If the firm's MCC is 15 percent, can we safely accept the project since both IRRs are above the MCC? Explain why or why not.

13.8. Why does the NPV method, when improperly applied, tend to give incorrect choices among unequal-lived projects? How can we correct for this?

13.9. With one-period capital rationing, either the PI or NPV method may be applied. Explain why both techniques—when properly employed—select the optimal group of projects, given the capital constraint.

13.10. Explain the fallacy of using multiple decision criteria such as payback and NPV to make capital budgeting decisions. What is the result of such an approach?

PROBLEMS

13.1. *CAPITAL BUDGETING CALCULATIONS AND DIFFERENT RANKINGS.* Morris Metal Company is attempting to select the best of three mutually exclusive proposals for increasing its aluminum extrusion capacity. The initial investment and CFATs associated with each proposal are given below.

Cash Flow	Proposal		
	A	B	C
Initial investment, year 0	$60,000	$100,000	$110,000
CFAT, years 1 to 5	$20,000	$ 31,500	$ 32,500

The firm employs ACRS depreciation over each assets' 5-year normal recovery period.

a. Calculate the average rate of return for each proposal.

b. Calculate the payback period for each proposal.

c. Calculate the NPV of each proposal, assuming the firm has a required rate of return of 13 percent.

d. Calculate the PI of each proposal.

e. Calculate the IRR for each proposal.

f. In light of the firm's required rate of return, which proposal would you recommend and why?

13.2. *EXPANSION—ACRS DEPRECIATION.* Columbus Advertising is considering two alternative computer systems. System A will require an initial investment of $1,600,000 and has yearly operating outflows of $50,000. System B will require an initial investment of $1,000,000 and has yearly operating outflows of $125,000. The economic life of each computer system is 7 years; however, both will be depreciated under ACRS over their 5-year normal recovery period. Regardless of the system chosen, Columbus estimates the anticipated cash inflows to be $400,000 per year. The firm's marginal ordinary tax rate is 40 percent and the 8 percent ITC applies to both systems.

a. Which system should the firm select if its MCC is 15 percent?

b. Does your decision in (a) change if the MCC is only 10 percent?

13.3. *EXPANSION—ACRS AND STRAIGHT-LINE DEPRECIATION.* Robertson Milling must choose between two grain-conveying systems. The initial investment in system P is $960,000, yearly operating cash outflows equal $40,000, and estimated operating cash inflows are $250,000. System Q costs $570,000, and has estimated operating cash inflows of $250,000, but operating cash outflows are expected to be $80,000 per year. The normal recovery period for each system is 5 years, and the 8 percent ITC is in effect. Robertson's marginal ordinary tax rate is 40 percent.

a. If Robertson employs ACRS depreciation for both systems, which system should the firm select if its MCC is 16 percent?

b. If the MCC for Robertson Milling is only 10 percent, does your decision in (a) change?

c. If Robertson had used straight-line depreciation for both systems, what would the NPVs be for both 16 percent and 10 percent MCC? How does the use of ACRS affect the NPVs?

13.4. *REPLACEMENT.* Thornton Nursery installed a new furnace 5 years ago for $9,620. A salesman has recently recommended replacing the furnace with a new heat pump. The estimated annual fuel savings would be $2,400 per year. The cost of the heat pump is $13,000 installed, but the old furnace can be sold today for $2,000. The old furnace had an original estimated usable life of 13 years, straight-line depreciation was employed, and it had a zero estimated salvage value. Since it was purchased before ACRS depreciation was allowable, it is being depreciated over its original 13-year life. The new heat pump has an estimated economic life of 8 years, the 8 percent ITC is in effect, straight-line depreciation will be employed (over its 5-year normal recovery period), and the marginal tax rate on ordinary income for Thornton is 40 percent. There is no recapture of the ITC on the old furnace. Should Thornton replace the furnace if the appropriate risk-adjusted discount rate is 18 percent?

13.5. *REPLACEMENT—NPV AND IRR.* Southern Textile Company is considering the replacement of an existing machine. The new machine costs $1,200,000 and requires installation costs of $150,000. (The installation costs on the new machine will be capitalized, not written off as an initial expense. Depreciation will be taken on the sum of the original cost of the machine plus installation costs.) The existing machine has been depreciated to zero, but can be sold now for $220,000. Over its 5-year normal recovery period, the new machine should reduce operating cash outflows by $400,000 per year. The firm has a 14 percent MCC and a 40 percent marginal tax rate on ordinary income. The new machine will be depreciated on a straight-line basis with no salvage value. The 8 percent ITC is in effect and applies to the original purchase price plus the installation costs. There is no recovery of the ITC on the existing machine.
   a. Develop the relevant CFAT data.
   b. Determine the NPV of the proposal.
   c. Determine the IRR for the proposal.
   d. Make a recommendation to accept or reject the new machine and justify your answer.
   e. What is the highest MCC the firm could have and still accept the project?

13.6. *REPLACEMENT—ACRS DEPRECIATION.* Thompson Toy Company is contemplating the replacement of one of its plastic molding machines. The new machine costs $1,400,000, has a 10-year economic life, and is expected to save $250,000 in operating expenses each year. It will be depreciated under ACRS over its 5-year normal recovery period. The old machine cost $950,000, has a 10-year economic life remaining, but is being depreciated for tax purposes with the 5-year ACRS method. It was purchased 2 years ago, so there are still 3 years of depreciation remaining on the existing machine. The incremental initial investment is $998,000, but the incremental operating cash inflows have yet to be calculated. The firm's MCC is 14 percent, and the marginal tax rate on ordinary income is 40 percent. Should Thompson replace its old machine?

13.7. **SIZE DISPARITY.** Harding Shipping Systems is evaluating two mutually exclusive projects that have the following cash flows:

Cash Flow	Project	
	X	Y
Initial investment, year 0	$80,000	$25,000
CFAT, years 1–4	28,021	10,212

a. Calculate the NPV of each project, assuming the MCC is 9 percent.
b. Calculate the IRR for each project.
c. Explain why the two projects are ranked differently by the two criteria.
d. Graph the NPV profiles for the two projects given the following NPVs, which have been calculated:

Discount Rate	NPV$_X$	NPV$_Y$
0%	$32,084	$15,848
10	8,827	7,372
20	− 7,454	1,439
30	− 19,306	− 2,880

Based on your graph, approximately where does the profile of project X intersect with the profile of project Y?

13.8. **TIME DISPARITY.** Florida Citrus Growers, Inc., is considering two mutually exclusive investments. Project A requires an initial investment of $15,000 and will produce a CFAT stream as follows: year 1, zero; year 2, zero; year 3, $1,000; year 4, $5,000; and year 5, $24,000. Project B also requires an initial investment of $15,000, and is expected to produce CFATs of $5,000 per year for 5 years.

a. If the risk-adjusted discount rate is 8 percent, which project should Florida Citrus accept?

b. Now assume the risk-adjusted discount rate increases to 14 percent. What project do you now recommend?

c. Complete the table below and then use the data to graph the NPV profile. (Round to the nearest dollar.)

Discount Rate	NPV_A	NPV_B
0%	$15,000	$10,000
8	—	—
11	—	—
14	—	—
16	− 175	1,370
20	− 2,363	− 45

d. What is the economic logic that explains why A is preferred at a lower discount rate while B is preferred at a higher MCC? Why does A's NPV profile decline more rapidly than B's?

13.9. *MULTIPLE INTERNAL RATES OF RETURN.*   Construction of a nuclear power plant requiring an initial investment of $48 million at time $t = 0$ is being considered. The revenues are expected to be $156 million in year 1, but in year 2 the nuclear waste must be removed. The net CFAT *outflow* in year 2 is $120 million. No other cash flows are anticipated.

a. Calculate the IRRs for the nuclear power plant.

b. Fill in the table below and graph the power plant's net present value profile.

Discount Rate	NPV ($ Millions)
0%	−$12.000
25	—
50	2.772
75	1.836
100	—
125	− 2.496

c. Should the plant be built if the firm's MCC is 15 percent? 30 percent?

d. What are some other situations in which multiple internal rates of return might occur?

13.10. *UNEQUAL LIVES.*   Information Associates, Inc. is considering the purchase of a new small-scale word processing system. System

P costs $8,000 and has CFATs of $5,200 for each of 2 years, at which time its market value will be zero and the system will have to be replaced. System Q costs $15,000, has a 6-year life, and produces CFATs of $4,000 per year. Its estimated market value at the end of 6 years is also zero. Information Associates estimates that the appropriate risk-adjusted discount rate is 12 percent. There is no ITC.

a. Calculate the NPV of each system, disregarding the differences in lives. Which system appears preferable?

b. Equalize the lives of the two systems by: (1) replacing system P twice to make its life equal to that of system Q; and (2) using the annualized NPV approach.

c. Do your answers agree in terms of which system is preferable? Are the assumptions necessary for use of the annualized NPV approach reasonable for this type of equipment?

13.11. *UNEQUAL LIVES—COST MINIMIZATION USING ANNUALIZED NPV.* The city of Atlanta is considering replacing its fleet of garbage trucks. Each Easyload truck costs $75,000, has operating expenses (negative cash flows) of $7,000 per year, and an estimated market value of $8,000 at the end of its 7-year life. Each Dumpster truck costs $60,000, has operating expenses of $8,500 per year, and an estimated market value of $7,000 at the end of its 5-year life. The city of Atlanta uses a discount rate of 9 percent. Both garbage trucks have the same capacity. Whichever option is chosen, the city is likely to replace the trucks with essentially the same truck indefinitely. (Since this is a tax-exempt situation, neither the ITC nor the depreciation tax shield need to be considered.)

a. Determine the relevant CFAT stream and NPV (which will be negative) for each truck.

b. Using the annualized NPV approach, determine which truck Atlanta should purchase if its objective is to minimize cost.

13.12. *UNEQUAL LIVES—NONCONSTANT COSTS.* New York Marketing Associates is evaluating a new packaging process that can use semiautomated or fully automated equipment. The semiautomated equipment can be purchased for $15,000, has a 4-year life, and has CFATs of $7,000 per year for years 1 through 4. When the semiautomated equipment is replaced in 4 years, similar equipment will have increased in price by 10 percent (from $15,000), while the CFATs for years 5 to 8 are estimated to be only 93 percent of those for years 1 through 4. In 8 years, when the semiautomated equipment is replaced again, it is estimated that the cost of similar equipment will have increased by 25 percent (from $15,000) and the CFATs for years 9 to 12 will be only 85 percent of those in years 1 through 4. There will be no terminal value for any of the semiautomated equipment.

The automated equipment can be purchased for $27,000, has a 6-year life, and CFATs of $8,500 per year for the first 6 years. When it is replaced with similar equipment in 6 years, the automated equipment will cost 20 percent more, while the CFATs for years 7 through 12 will be only 90 percent of those in years 1 through 6. The terminal value is zero. New York Marketing Associates' MCC is 13 percent, and the 8 percent ITC is in effect. Which equipment should be purchased?

13.13. **CAPITAL RATIONING.**   A firm must select the optimal group from the available independent projects given below. Their capital budget is $1,000,000.

Project	Initial Investment	NPV
A	$300,000	$ 84,000
B	100,000	25,000
C	500,000	70,000
D	100,000	50,000
E	800,000	160,000

  a.   Calculate the PIs associated with each project.

  b.   Select the optimal group of projects, employing both the weighted PI and aggregate NPV approaches.

13.14. **INFLATION.** Hastings Food Company is considering a project that requires an initial investment of $40,000 and has a 5-year normal recovery period and economic life. The expected cash inflows are $90,000 per year, and the cash outflows are expected to be $74,000 per year. Hastings' marginal tax rate on ordinary income is 40 percent and its MCC is 12 percent. There is no expected salvage value or ITC.

  a.   If Hastings uses straight-line depreciation over the asset's 5-year normal recovery period, what is the NPV of the proposed investment? Should the investment be accepted?

  b.   On investigation, you discover no adjustments have been made for inflation. The cash receipts are expected to increase 5 percent per year *after* the first year, and the cash expenses will increase at 9 percent per year (also after the first year). In addition, Hastings has decided to use ACRS depreciation over the asset's 5-year normal recovery period. Recalculate the NPV of the project in light of this information. Should the investment be accepted?

SELECTED REFERENCES

Bacon, Peter W. "The Evaluation of Mutually Exclusive Investments." *Financial Management* 6 (summer 1977), pp. 55–58.

Baldwin, Carliss Y. "Optimal Sequential Investment When Capital is Not Readily Reversible." *Journal of Finance* 37 (June 1982), pp. 763–782.

Bernhard, Richard H., and Carl J. Norstrøm. "A Further Note on Unrecovered Investment, Uniqueness of the Internal Rate, and the Question of Project Acceptability." *Journal of Financial and Quantitative Analysis* 15 (June 1980), pp. 421–423.

Bradley, Stephen P., and Sherwood C. Frey, Jr. "Equivalent Mathematical Programming Models of Pure Capital Rationing." *Journal of Financial and Quantitative Analysis* 13 (June 1978), pp. 345–362.

Brenner, Menachem, and Itzhak Venezia. "The Effects of Inflation and Taxes on Growth Investments and Replacement Policies." *Journal of Finance* 38 (December 1983), pp. 1519–1528.

Brigham, Eugene F. "Hurdle Rates for Screening Capital Expenditure Proposals." *Financial Management* 4 (autumn 1975), pp. 17–26.

Bussey, Lynn E. *The Economic Analysis of Industrial Projects.* Englewood Cliffs, N.J.: Prentice-Hall, 1978.

Chambers, Donald R., Robert S. Harris, and John J. Pringle. "Treatment of Financing Mix in Analyzing Investment Opportunities." *Financial Management* 11 (summer 1982), pp. 24–41.

Cooper, Ian, and Julian R. Franks. "The Interaction of Financing and Investment Decisions When the Firm Has Unused Tax Credits." *Journal of Finance* 38 (May 1983), pp. 571–583.

Doenges, R. Conrad. "The Reinvestment Problem in Practical Perspective." *Financial Management* 1 (spring 1972), pp. 85–91.

Dorfman, Robert. "The Meaning of Internal Rates of Return." *Journal of Finance* 36 (December 1981), pp. 1011–1021.

Durand, David. "Comprehensiveness in Capital Budgeting." *Financial Management* 10 (winter 1981), pp. 7–13.

Dyckman, Thomas R., and James C. Kinard. "The Discounted Cash Flow Investment Decision Model with Accounting Income Constraints." *Decision Sciences* 4 (July 1973), pp. 301–313.

Ederington, Louis H., and William R. Henry. "On Costs of Capital in Programming Approaches to Capital Budgeting." *Journal of Financial and Quantitative Analysis* 14 (December 1979), pp. 1049–1057.

Emery, Gary W. "Some Guidelines for Evaluating Capital Investment Alternatives with Unequal Lives." *Financial Management* 11 (spring 1982), 14–19.

Gitman, Lawrence J., and John R. Forrester, Jr. "A Survey of Capital Budgeting Techniques Used by Major U.S. Firms." *Financial Management* 6 (fall 1977), pp. 66–71.

Gordon, Lawrence A., and George E. Pinches. *Improving Capital Budgeting: A Decision Support System Approach.* Reading, Mass.: Addison-Wesley, 1984.

Gray, Otha L., Monroe M. Bird, and David F. Scott, Jr. "Investing and Financing Behavior of Small Manufacturing Firms." *MSU Business Topics* 20 (summer 1972), pp. 29–38.

Herbst, Anthony. "The Unique, Real Internal Rate of Return: Caveat Emptor." *Journal of Financial and Quantitative Analysis* 13 (June 1978), pp. 363–370.

Hoskins, Colin G., and Glen A. Mumey. "Payback: A Maligned Method of Asset Ranking?" *Engineering Economist* 25 (winter 1980), pp. 53–65.

Ignizio, James P. "An Approach to the Capital Budgeting Problem with Multiple Objectives." *Engineering Economist* 21 (summer 1976), pp. 259–272.

Joy, O. Maurice, and R. Corwin Grube. "Cash Flows That Require Negative Discount Rates." *Engineering Economist* 26 (winter 1981), pp. 154–158.

Kim, Suk H. "An Empirical Study on the Relationship Between Capital Budgeting Practices and Earnings Performance." *Engineering Economist* 27 (spring 1982), pp. 185–196.

Klammer, Thomas. "The Association of Capital Budgeting Techniques with Firm Performance." *Accounting Review* 48 (April 1973), pp. 353–364.

———. "Empirical Evidence of the Adoption of Sophisticated Capital Budgeting Techniques." *Journal of Business* 45 (July 1972), pp. 387–397.

Lee, Sang M., and A. J. Lerro. "Capital Budgeting for Multiple Objectives." *Financial Management* 3 (spring 1974), pp. 58–66.

Lerner, Eugene M., and Alfred Rappaport. "Limit DCF in Capital Budgeting." *Harvard Business Review* 46 (September–October 1968), pp. 133–138.

Lewellen, Wilbur G., Howard P. Lanser, and John J. McConnell. "Payback Substitutes for Discounted Cash Flow." *Financial Management* 2 (summer 1973), pp. 17–23.

Lohmann, Jack R., E. W. Foster, and D. J. Layman. "A Comparative Analysis of the Effects of ACRS on Replacement Economy Decisions." *Engineering Economist* 27 (summer 1982), pp. 247–260.

Lorie, James H., and Leonard J. Savage. "Three Problems in Rationing Capital." *Journal of Business* 28 (October 1955), pp. 227–239.

Meyer, Richard L. "A Note on Capital Budgeting Techniques and the Reinvestment Rate." *Journal of Finance* 34 (December 1979), pp. 1251–1254.

Oblak, David J., and Roy Helm, Jr. "Survey and Analysis of Capital Budgeting Methods Used by Multinationals." *Financial Management* 9 (winter 1980), pp. 37–41.

Osteryoung, Jerome S. *Capital Budgeting: Long-Term Asset Selection*, 2d ed. Columbus: Grid Publishing, 1979.

Pratt, John W., and John S. Hammond III. "Evaluating and Comparing Projects: Simple Detection of False Alarms." *Journal of Finance* 34 (December 1979), pp. 1231–1242.

Rappaport, Alfred, and Robert A. Taggart, Jr. "Evaluation of Capital Expenditure Proposals Under Inflation." *Financial Management* 11 (spring 1982), pp. 5–13.

Sarnat, Marshall, and Haim Levy. "The Relationship of Rules of Thumb to the Internal Rate of Return: A Restatement and Generalization." *Journal of Finance* 24 (June 1969), pp. 479–489.

Schall, Lawrence D., Gary L. Sundem, and William R. Geijsbeek, Jr. "Survey and Analysis of Capital Budgeting Methods." *Journal of Finance* 33 (March 1978), pp. 281–287.

Schwab, Bernhard, and Peter Lusztig. "A Comparative Analysis of the Net Present Value and Benefit-Cost Ratio as Measures of the Economic Desirability of Investments." *Journal of Finance* 24 (June 1969), pp. 507–516.

Smidt, Seymour. "A Bayesian Analysis of Project Selection and Post Audit Evaluation." *Journal of Finance* 34 (June 1979), pp. 675–688.

Statman, Meir. "The Persistence of the Payback Method: A Principal-Agent Perspective." *Engineering Economist* 27 (winter 1981), pp. 95–100.

Stephen, Frank. "On Deriving the Internal Rate of Return from the Accountant's Rate of Return." *Journal of Business Finance and Accounting* 3 (summer 1976), pp. 147–150.

Weingartner, H. Martin. "Capital Budgeting of Interrelated Projects: Survey and Synthesis." *Management Science* 12 (March 1966), pp. 485–516.

———. "Capital Rationing: *n* Authors in Search of a Plot." *Journal of Finance* 32 (December 1977), pp. 1403–1431.

Appendix 13A

Capital Rationing: The Multiperiod Case

Mathematical programming techniques can be employed to allocate capital under conditions of multiperiod capital rationing, assuming certainty of the cash flows.[1] If it is possible to undertake fractions of projects, the problem may be formulated using linear programming; otherwise, integer programming should be employed.

Mathematical Programming

The basic linear programming approach to multiperiod capital rationing problems may be expressed as follows:

$$\text{Maximize} \quad \sum_{j=1}^{n} b_j X_j \tag{13A.1}$$

$$\text{Subject to} \quad \sum_{j=1}^{n} C_{tj} X_j \leq C_t$$

$$0 \leq X_j \leq 1$$

where b_j is the net present value of investment proposal j, X_j is an amount (of a project) between 0 and 1, C_{tj} is the investment required in period t for proposal j, and C_t is the budget constraint in period t. The model is set up to maximize total net present value over all projects, given the budget constraints in each period.

To illustrate the application of linear programming, consider the problem originally formulated by Lorie and Savage, shown in Table 13A.1.[2] The nine projects all require investment in each of the two time

---

[1]This section presupposes some familiarity with mathematical programming techniques.

[2]For more information on the specific example employed, see James H. Lorie and Leonard J. Savage, "Three Problems in Rationing Capital," *Journal of Business* 28 (October 1955), pp. 227–239; or H. Martin Weingartner, *Mathematical Programming and the Analysis of Capital Budgeting Problems* (Englewood Cliffs, N.J.: Prentice-Hall, 1963).

Project (j)	b_j	Period 1 Investment (C_{1j})	Period 2 Investment (C_{2j})
1	$14	$12	$ 3
2	17	54	7
3	17	6	6
4	15	6	2
5	40	30	35
6	12	6	6
7	14	48	4
8	10	36	3
9	12	18	3

periods, and cash flows cannot be transferred between the time periods. In addition, the projects are divisible and the capital budget is fixed at $50 in period 1 and $20 in period 2. The problem is to find the set of projects that maximizes total NPV while satisfying the budget constraints. If the projects are independent of one another, the model can be expressed this way:

$$\text{Maximize } NPV = 14\, X_1 + 17\, X_2 + \cdots + 10\, X_8 + 12\, X_9$$

subject to the budget constraints

$$12\, X_1 + 54\, X_2 + \cdots + 36\, X_8 + 18\, X_9 \leq 50$$
$$3\, X_1 + 7\, X_2 + \cdots + 3\, X_8 + 3\, X_9 \leq 20$$
$$0 \leq X_j \leq 1 \ (j = 1, \cdots, 9)$$

This problem can be solved by adding slack variables (S_1 and S_2) to convert the inequalities to equalities.

The solution is shown in Table 13A.2. Projects 1, 3, 4, and 9 are accepted, and projects 6 and 7 are fractionally accepted into the optimal solution, which has an NPV of $70.27. The whole solution is not shown, but two other items should be noted. First, the cash constraints of $50 in period 1 and $20 in period 2 are binding, as shown by the fact that the value of each of the slack variables is zero (they are completely employed). Second, the dual variables (W_1 and W_2) represent the shadow prices on budget constraints. Analysis of W_1 indicates total NPV could be increased by $0.136 if the budget in period 1 were increased from $50 to $51; W_2 indicates NPV could be increased by $1.864 if the budget in period 2 were increased from $20 to $21. These figures represent the opportunity cost of funds to the firm, and indicate that the budget constraint for period 2 is more critical.

In this problem, the capital projects were assumed to be divisible so that part of a project could be undertaken. Most capital budgeting projects are *not* divisible; they are either accepted in total or they are rejected. To deal with this situation, zero-one integer programming can

TABLE 13A.2
Solution for the
Two-Period Capital
Budgeting Constraint
Problem

Project	Solution
1	$X_1 = 1.0$
2	$X_2 = 0$
3	$X_3 = 1.0$
4	$X_4 = 1.0$
5	$X_5 = 0$
6	$X_6 = 0.970$
7	$X_7 = 0.045$
8	$X_8 = 0$
9	$X_9 = 1.0$

$\text{NPV} = 1.0(14) + 1.0(17) + 1.0(15) + 0.970(12) + 0.045(14) + 1.0(12) = \$70.27$

Slack in budget constraints:

$$S_1 = 0$$
$$S_2 = 0$$

Dual variables for budget constraints:

$$W_1 = 0.136$$
$$W_2 = 1.864$$

be employed. For the Lorie-Savage problem, the optimal solution with integer programming is to accept projects 1, 3, 4, 6, and 9, which results in a total NPV of $70. Once the firm is constrained to taking only whole projects, all of project 6 is taken, while project 7 is dropped from the solution. These linear or integer programming approaches may be modified to take into account mutually exclusive projects and to handle staff, financial, and other constraints. With these modifications, programming techniques might prove to be practical for dealing with multiperiod capital rationing.[3]

The Marginal Cost of Capital and Wealth Maximization

The cost to the firm of a budget constraint can be regarded as the opportunity foregone on the next most profitable investment after the budget constraint becomes binding. In our example, it would be the foregone opportunity associated with one of the projects with a positive NPV that could not be accepted (projects 2, 5, 7, 8). Although all cash flows are discounted at the MCC, we cannot accept all projects with positive NPVs, since acceptance is determined by the budget constraint. The MCC sets the lower limit; we would generally not want to accept any proposals yielding less than the MCC. However, we may reject projects that provide positive NPVs. Under capital rationing, the appropriate

[3]See Dwight F. Rychel, "Capital Budgeting with Mixed Integer Linear Programming: An Application," *Financial Management* 6 (winter 1977), pp. 11–19.

opportunity cost to use in finding the NPVs of projects cannot be determined until the optimal set of projects is found. This opportunity cost is determined simultaneously with the optimal set of investment projects and will, in general, be higher than the firm's MCC.[4]

Limitations of Mathematical Programming

The primary difficulty of the mathematical programming approach to multiperiod capital rationing is that it assumes all future investment opportunities are known with certainty. In reality, the generation of investment opportunities is an ongoing process very dependent on new developments both internal and external to the firm. Budget constraints for other than the earliest years are not known because they are contingent on new projects that may be developed over the next few years. Another problem is that the programming approaches also assume future cash flows are known with certainty.

Although many mathematical programming techniques are available, their use in practical capital budgeting applications has been rather slow to spread.[5] This is due in large part to the lack of realism associated with the treatment of uncertainty, which is often an unfortunate by-product of these approaches. At the present stage of development, more work is required before mathematical programming approaches to capital budgeting become widely applied in practice.

[4]See Willard T. Carleton, "Linear Programming and Capital Budgeting Models: A New Interpretation." *Journal of Finance* 24 (December 1969), pp. 825–833; Edwin J. Elton, "Capital Rationing and External Discount Rates," *Journal of Finance* 25 (June 1970), pp. 573–584; and R. M. Burton and W. W. Damon, "On the Existence of a Cost of Capital under Pure Capital Rationing," *Journal of Finance* 29 (September 1974), pp. 1165–1173.

[5]See, for example R. Byrne, A. Charnes, W. W. Cooper, and K. Kortinek, "A Chance-Constrained Programming Approach to Capital Budgeting," *Journal of Financial and Quantitative Analysis* 2 (December 1967), pp. 339–364; F. S. Hillier, *The Evaluation of Risky Interrelated Investments* (Amsterdam: North-Holland Publishing Co., 1969); and Howard E. Thompson, "Mathematical Programming, The Capital Asset Pricing Model and Capital Budgeting of Interrelated Projects," *Journal of Finance* 31 (March 1976), pp. 125–132.

14

Risk Analysis and Capital Budgeting

We found from our study of valuation that a positive relationship should exist between risk and return; other things being equal, the greater the risk or uncertainty of an investment, the more we should expect in the way of returns. Thus far in our discussion of capital budgeting, we have ignored the question of risk altogether. We were able to do this by assuming that the exposure to risk was basically the same for all projects under consideration and as such, risk was not an issue in the decision-making process. Clearly, this assumption rarely holds in practice; instead, the level of potential risk exposure usually does vary across proposals and therefore should be systematically considered, along with return, by financial managers. For as we saw in Chapter 7, *both* risk and return affect the value of an investment and ultimately the value of the firm. This chapter considers the risk dimension of capital projects and shows how it can be evaluated in a capital budgeting framework. After reviewing the conceptual dimensions of risk, we will see how risk-adjusted discount rates and probability distributions can be used by financial managers to measure and assess project risk.[1] Throughout the discussion, we will consider the impact of risk analysis on capital budgeting decisions, including decision making in a portfolio context and the practical dimensions of risk analysis.

The Conceptual Dimensions of Risk

Most financial managers understand intuitively that some capital budgeting projects are more risky than others. Therefore, in order to compensate for increased riskiness, financial managers will follow one

---

[1]Because many of the statistical techniques used in this chapter are derived from the material presented in Chapter 6, the reader may find it helpful to refer back to some of the basic concepts and mechanics developed there.

of two general options—they will either increase the discount rate, k, or alter the estimates of expected cash flows. However, in both theory and practice the decision is more complicated than this solution would suggest, for we simply do not know how to measure risk with precision and in a manner that puts the techniques and criteria together so that they can be conveniently incorporated into the capital budgeting process. To understand some of the problems, we need to examine the two separate types of risk, identified in Chapter 6, that are relevant to capital budgeting: (1) nondiversifiable (market) risk, or beta; and (2) total risk.

Nondiversifiable Risk

In Chapter 6, when examining the relationship between expected risk and return via the capital asset pricing model (CAPM), we concluded that when investors hold diversified portfolios, the total risk of individual securities can be split into two components, so that:

Total security risk = nondiversifiable (market) risk + diversifiable (non-market) risk

Nondiversifiable (or market) risk, as measured by beta, results from factors that affect the stock market as a whole and cannot be diversified away; nonmarket risk, however, is a firm-specific risk that can be eliminated by holding a diversified portfolio. We showed in Chapter 6, therefore, that since investors generally diversify, beta is the relevant measure of risk.

This same framework has implications for the measurement of risk as it relates to capital budgeting. That is, we could state an essentially equivalent expression and define total *asset* risk as follows:

Total asset risk = nondiversifiable risk + diversifiable risk

Total asset risk can be thought of as a function of the variability (variance or standard deviation) of the expected future cash flows accruing to an asset or capital project. If the CAPM, when applied to individual firms, is accurate, then it follows that we are not interested in total asset risk; rather, we are interested in a project's nondiversifiable (or market) risk, as measured by beta. That is, to the extent that the firm is simply a portfolio of assets and capital projects, it is clear that portfolio diversification and firm diversification are perfect substitutes. As a result, the contribution of a new capital project to the variance of the firm's total returns can be ignored, since diversifiable nonmarket risk is eliminated as portfolios are constructed. Thus, under CAPM, the relevant measure of risk for a proposed project is market risk, as measured by the project's beta (β) coefficient. The major implication of CAPM for capital budgeting is that each project should be evaluated solely in terms of expected return and risk as determined by the individual project's beta.[2] Note that CAPM adjusts for risk by adjusting the required rate of return, k, in the investment valuation model.

If the beta coefficient for new projects could be determined, each individual project could have a different required rate of return, such that:

$$k_{project} = R_F + \beta_{project} \times (k_M - R_F) \tag{14.1}$$

where $k_{project}$ = the project's required or expected rate of return
R_F = the risk-free rate of interest
$\beta_{project}$ = the project's nondiversifiable (market) risk, or beta coefficient
k_M = the required or expected returns on the market portfolio

Thus, for an all-equity financed firm,[3] the relevant risk measure for each project is its beta. This relationship between project return and market-determined risk is shown in Figure 14.1; the security market line (SML) depicted there describes the market-determined relationship between risk and return. If the CAPM approach was actually being used, all capital budgeting projects with expected returns lying on or above the SML should be accepted, and those lying below it should be rejected (the rationale for this course of action was developed in Chapter 6).

In this context, the goal of the firm is to search for investment opportunities lying above the SML, as shown in Figure 14.1. If product markets were perfect we would not expect to find such investment opportunities, since they would all lie along or below the SML. However, since product markets are less than perfect (due to such things as constraints on resource allocation, monopolistic power, barriers to entry, and so on), it may indeed be possible to find projects with expected returns above the security market line. The successful firm is one that is able to identify and exploit such opportunities.

---

[2]See, for example, Donald L. Tuttle and Robert H. Litzenberger, "Leverage, Diversification and Capital Market Effects on a Risk-Adjusted Capital Budgeting Framework," *Journal of Finance* 23 (June 1968), pp. 427–443; Robert S. Hamada, "Portfolio Analysis, Market Equilibrium and Corporation Finance," *Journal of Finance* 24 (March 1969), pp. 13–31; and Mark E. Rubinstein, "A Mean-Variance Synthesis of Corporate Financial Theory," *Journal of Finance* 28 (March 1973), pp. 167–182. For a demonstration of the equivalence of these and other formulations, see Lemma W. Senbet and Howard E. Thompson, "The Equivalence of Alternative Mean-Variance Capital Budgeting Models," *Journal of Finance* 33 (May 1978), pp. 395–401. While the capital asset pricing model is a single-period model, its use in multiperiod capital budgeting decisions has been investigated by Marcus C. Bogue and Richard Roll, "Capital Budgeting of Risky Projects with 'Imperfect' Markets for Physical Capital," *Journal of Finance* 29 (May 1974), pp. 601–613.

[3]When the firm employs both debt and equity financing, two adjustments are required. First, betas must reflect only business risk, so appropriate adjustments must be made for financial leverage (or financial risk). Second, the discount rate employed must reflect the costs (or required returns) associated with both debt and equity. These topics are discussed in detail in Chapter 17.

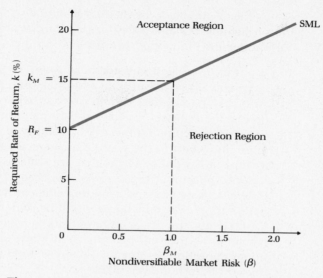

Figure 14.1 The Capital Asset Pricing Model (CAPM) Approach to Capital Budgeting for an All-Equity Firm.

Although beta provides a convenient means of conceptualizing risk, it has not found much application in practice—particularly as it relates to determining required rates of return for individual projects. But as we will see in Chapter 17, it has gained some favor as a means of estimating divisional costs of capital, which at least represents a compromise between (1) using a firmwide cost of capital with no adjustment for risk, and (2) using a series of individual project, risk-adjusted discount rates. To understand why CAPM is not more widely used with individual projects, we need to consider total risk and some of the practical considerations associated with using the model.

Total Risk and Practical Considerations

Total risk is the variability of the expected cash flows accruing to an asset. Consider a firm that is evaluating a major new project which requires an initial outlay of $50 million; the project has a 50 percent probability of generating discounted cash inflows of $120 million and a 50 percent chance of ending up with discounted cash inflows of a negative $10 million (which would cause such severe cash flow problems that the firm may be forced into bankruptcy). Although the expected NPV is a positive $5 million,[4] total risk, as represented by the high probability of bankruptcy, is clearly excessive. In such a case, risk as measured by beta may not be a reasonable estimate of the amount of risk exposure actually faced by the firm.

---

[4]$NPV = [(.50 \times \$120 \text{ million}) + (.50 \times (-\$10 \text{ million})] - \$50 \text{ million}$
$= (\$60 \text{ million} - \$5 \text{ million}) - \$50 \text{ million}$
$= \$55 \text{ million} - \$50 \text{ million} = \$5 \text{ million}$

In general, total risk (as measured by the variability of cash flows or the probability of bankruptcy) appears to be a more appropriate measure under the following conditions:

1. When undiversified investors, firms, and/or financial managers are more concerned about total asset risk than nondiversifiable risk.
2. With less than perfect capital markets, where investor diversification is not a perfect, costless substitute for corporate diversification. Under such circumstances, stability of cash flows is often more important to the firm's managers, workers, customers, suppliers, and creditors. Firms that are suffering low profits and reduced output, or even worse, are close to bankruptcy, have difficulty attracting and retaining efficient managers and workers. Both suppliers and customers will be reluctant to depend on the firm. Finally, the firm will have trouble raising debt or equity capital except at very high costs. All these situations suggest that, under conditions of financial distress, total asset risk is more relevant than nondiversifiable risk.

In addition to situations where total risk appears to be more appropriate than nondiversifiable market risk, certain theoretical and practical considerations impede the application of CAPM to the assessment of individual projects:

1. Fama[5] has demonstrated that in order to use the CAPM for capital budgeting purposes, there can be no uncertainties surrounding the future risk-free rate (R_F), the market price of risk, or the systematic relationship between proportional changes in the project's expected cash flows and the market return (k_M). Thus, expected cash flows are the only parameter whose value can be uncertain through time. Further, Myers and Turnbull[6] demonstrated that if the expected cash flows in time t do not provide the best estimate for cash flows in time $t + 1$, the project's beta will depend on the life of the project and the growth rate of the cash flows. When these factors are considered, it appears that the use of individual project rates of return based on beta, or market risk, has some serious theoretical problems.
2. The measurement of beta for an individual capital project is even more difficult than determining a security beta (as described in Chapter 6).

Thus, because of situations in which total risk appears to be more

---

[5]The market price of risk, λ, is equal to $[E\ (k_M)\ -\ R_F)/\sigma_{\bar{R}M}^2]$. See Eugene F. Fama, "Risk-Adjusted Discount Rates and Capital Budgeting Under Uncertainty," *Journal of Financial Economics* 5 (August 1977), pp. 3–24.

[6]Stewart C. Myers and Stuart M. Turnbull, "Capital Budgeting and the Capital Asset Pricing Model: Good News and Bad News," *Journal of Finance* 32 (May 1977), pp. 321–333.

appropriate than market risk, and because of certain problems associated with employing the CAPM for individual assets, very few firms in practice use CAPM to assess capital expenditures.

Dealing with Risk

Dealing with project risk in practice usually involves the use of a *total risk approach*. One way of doing this is to evaluate the riskiness of a project via the expected cash flows of the proposed investment. That is, the adjustment for risk is accomplished through cash flow probability distributions. (Another procedure for dealing with risk via a project's cash flows is the certainty equivalent method. Although possessing desirable conceptual attributes, certainty equivalents have not enjoyed much acceptance in practice. For a brief discussion of this technique, see Appendix 14A.) Alternatively, a total risk approach can also be taken by adjusting the discount rate or required rate of return based on the project's perceived exposure to risk.

In the material that follows, the focus is on total risk approaches to dealing with risk in capital budgeting. We begin by looking at the use of risk-adjusted discount rates; then we examine the probability distribution approach. Throughout most of this discussion, we will consider the question of risk from an individual project perspective—we will review techniques that can be used by financial managers to measure the risk (and expected return) of each capital proposal. Then, we look briefly at risk assessment from a portfolio perspective. We will show how, in a conceptual framework at least, different combinations of capital projects can affect the firm's exposure to risk.

The whole issue of risk analysis in capital budgeting is an unsettled one that can best be described as involving not only considerable debate, but also continued development in both theory and practice. We explore several approaches to risk analysis that reflect not only the current thinking in this area, but the state of the art as well. Though perhaps not perfect, the approaches and techniques we present can readily be applied in practice to assess exposure to risk.

Risk-Adjusted Discount Rates (RADRs)

Of the several ways to evaluate total project risk, perhaps the most widely used procedure is the risk-adjusted discount rate (RADR). As we will see, its popularity in practice is an outgrowth of its intuitive appeal as well as its procedural simplicity. The RADR method is based on the premise that the riskiness of a proposal may be captured by adjusting the discount rate (used in NPV or PI), or the required rate of return (used as the cutoff rate with IRR). Using the net present value procedure as a basis of discussion, recall from Chapter 13 that we defined NPV as:

$$NPV = \sum_{t=0}^{n} \frac{CFAT_t}{(1 + k)^t} \qquad (14.2)$$

Very simply, the RADR procedure accounts for perceived risk in a capital project by adjusting the denominator in Equation 14.2—by redefining k as an appropriate risk-adjusted discount rate. More specifically, with NPV we would use the following equation:

$$NPV = \sum_{t=0}^{n} \frac{CFAT_t}{(1 + RADR)^t}$$

(14.3)

The RADR in Equation 14.3 is to a large extent project-specific and is defined by assessing the perceived riskiness of the project's cash flows: the higher the perceived risk, the higher the risk-adjusted discount rate. The procedure simply involves substituting the appropriate RADR for the firm's marginal cost of capital (MCC). The only change involved in using a risk-adjusted discount rate is to recognize formally that individual projects may differ in riskiness from the "average" riskiness of the firm. In cases where the projects are more risky than the average project undertaken by the firm, the appropriate RADR would be greater than the firm's marginal cost of capital; if a project is less risky, the discount rate is less than the firm's MCC.

To demonstrate the use of the RADR method, assume that a particular capital expenditure proposal is expected to generate the following cash flows:

t	$CFAT_t$
0	− $42,000
1	15,000
2	20,000
3	25,000

Assume also that although the firm normally employs a cost of capital of 15 percent ($k = 15\%$), management feels that in this case a 20 percent discount rate would be more appropriate. The higher rate is felt to be justified on the grounds of the project's higher risk exposure. Using the 20 percent RADR, the NPV of this proposal is:

$$
\begin{aligned}
NPV &= CFAT_1 \ (PVIF_{20\%, 1 \text{ yr}}) + CFAT_2 \ (PVIF_{20\%, 2 \text{ yr}}) + CFAT_3 \ (PVIF_{20\%, 3 \text{ yr}}) - CFAT_0 \\
&= \$15,000 \ (.833) + \$20,000 \ (.694) + \$25,000 \ (.579) - \$42,000 \\
&= \$12,495 + \$13,880 + \$14,475 - \$42,000 \\
&= -\$1,150
\end{aligned}
$$

In this case the project would be rejected, since it has an NPV of less than zero; it fails to provide a satisfactory rate of return, given its perceived exposure to risk.[7] The negative NPV, in effect, results from the higher return requirements that accompany the project's higher risk exposure. Note that if the project had less risk such that the normal cost of capital ($k = 15\%$) could be used, it would have a lower required return and therefore a positive NPV. It should be obvious that except for the rather simple adjustment to the discount rate, the procedure follows the standard NPV methodology whereby a project is considered acceptable as long as its NPV ≥ 0.

From a managerial perspective, the RADR technique is attractive because it is relatively simple to use, and because of its seemingly logical approach to risk analysis: It makes sense to increase the required return for projects that possess higher levels of risk. Moreover, not only is it intuitively appealing, but it is compatible with standard capital market theory. However, one aspect of this procedure that warrants careful consideration is the fact that the RADR method equates discounting for time with discounting for risk. Since the risk-adjusted discount rate employed in Equation 14.3 embodies both a risk-free rate, which adjusts for the timing of cash flows, and a risk premium, it implicitly assumes that cash flows further in the future are more risky than near-term cash flows. In fact, risk is assumed to increase exponentially as a function of time when the RADR method is employed. Although in many business applications risk may indeed increase over time, this condition is not universal. And even if risk does increase over time, it may not increase exponentially. Thus, financial managers using the RADR method may unwittingly penalize long-term investment projects when they are not, in fact, more risky than shorter-term projects. (For more discussion of how the use of RADR can lead to increasing risk over time, see Appendix 14A.)

Calculating Risk-Adjusted Discount Rates

In addition to developing cash flow information, potential risk exposure must be carefully assessed and an appropriate RADR assigned to each project. Because risk-adjusted discount rates simultaneously adjust for the timing of cash flows and their riskiness, the assigned RADRs should be based on *both* the time value of money and the risk perceptions of the firm's financial managers. A number of approaches are used in practice to estimate the appropriate discount rate. We now look briefly at three

---

[7]The RADR method of risk analysis can also be easily adapted to the PI and IRR procedures. For example, redefining k in the PI model as a RADR, and using the example denoted above, the PI of the proposal (with a RADR of 20 percent) would be: ($12,495 + $13,880 + $14,475)/$42,000 = $40,850/$42,000 = 0.97; clearly, with a PI less than 1.0, the project is unacceptable. Likewise, if IRR had been used to assess the project, we would have found that the proposal offers an IRR of 18.4 percent, which would also lead to rejection of the project, because this is less than the RADR-defined required rate of return (20 percent).

ways of determining the RADR: (1) project categorization, (2) project-specific rates, and (3) use of the capital asset pricing model.

Project Categorization.   Probably the most widely used approach to determining RADRs is to divide corporate projects into a number of different categories on the basis of perceived riskiness, and assign each category a distinct RADR. Then, when proposals are being evaluated, management need only determine the type of project under consideration and refer to the appropriate project category to find the RADR. For example, projects can be categorized according to whether they deal with expansion (of product lines, facilities) or replacement (of worn-out equipment, for technological reasons, etc.). Alternatively, separate RADRs can be assigned to different operating divisions of the company.

Whichever method is used, the standard practice is to adjust the firm's MCC to account for the differential risk of specific project categories in relation to the "average" riskiness for all capital projects undertaken by the firm. An example of project categorization is provided in Table 14.1; these rates, of course, are periodically reassessed and subject to change from time to time. Categorizing projects in this way automatically defines the discount rate to use in present-value evaluation models. For example, according to Table 14.1 if a project involves expanding into an entirely new product line, it would fall into the Expansion/Category III group. As a result, a discount rate of 30 percent would be used when computing the project's NPV or PI, or as the cutoff rate with IRR.

Project-Specific Rates.   Rather than developing general categories of project riskiness, some firms employ a system that results in RADRs being assigned on a project-by-project basis. Usually this involves some type of scheme whereby each proposed capital project is judged on several different points, such as product compatibility, cash flow variability, payback period, and perceived strategic significance. Scores are assigned by various managers for each of the several aspects of the project; then total scores are computed, and a project risk category is determined on the basis of the totals. Table 14.2 on p. 578 provides a scoring system actually used by a major NYSE firm; note that projects are assigned to one of five risk categories, each with its own RADR. An obvious advantage of this approach is that each project can be assessed individually, but an equally obvious weakness is that the system does allow for considerable manipulation by project managers.

Using CAPM.   In some cases, it may be possible to use the capital asset pricing model as a way to assess project risk and assign an appropriate

TABLE 14.1
Risk-Adjusted Discount
Rates for Different
Categories of Capital
Projects (MCC = 15%)

Capital Expenditure Group	Adjustment	Risk-Adjusted Discount Rate (RADR)
EXPANSION		
Category I. New facilities and equipment that will produce products very similar to existing products	MCC + 2%	17%
Category II. New facilities and equipment that will produce products having a complementary relationship to existing products	MCC + 7%	22%
Category III. New plants or equipment to produce products unrelated to existing products	MCC + 15%	30%
REPLACEMENT		
Category I. New facilities and equipment to replace essentially similar older facilities and equipment	MCC − 3%	12%
Category II. New facilities and equipment that possess more advanced technology than existing older facilities and equipment	MCC	15%
Category III. New facilities and equipment to replace and modernize existing facilities and equipment.	MCC + 9%	24%

RADR. In fact, as we saw earlier, if CAPM is valid, then nondiversifiable market risk is the relevant measure of project risk. This is precisely what the use of CAPM accomplishes. In effect, it provides a beta for each capital project or division of the company. The major drawback of this approach, however, is that project betas are (given today's state of the art) difficult to obtain. For example, in order to employ the CAPM approach, market-based rates of return for projects must be estimated in order to derive project betas; failing this, if a publicly traded firm can be identified that derives all or a major portion of its revenues from a product line similar to the proposed project, such a firm's beta may be employed as a substitute. Such betas would then provide the basis for determining different RADRs. Alternatively, the CAPM approach could be employed to estimate divisional costs of capital, which could then be used to determine a structure of division-specific RADRs (the use of CAPM to estimate divisional costs of capital will be discussed in detail in Chapter 17).

TABLE 14.2
A System for Assigning Project-Specific RADRs

Relevant Factors	Product Line and Market Considerations					Points
	Within Current Product Lines and Markets	New Product Line within Existing Markets/ Existing Product Line within New Markets		New Product Line and New Market		
		Weak Competition	Strong Competition	Weak Competition	Strong Competition	
Market acceptance; probability of success	1	3	5	8	15	
Strategic compatibility (Synergism of markets, products, and management)	Excellent 1	Good 3	Moderate 5	Fair 8	Poor 15	
Payback	1 year 1	1 1/2 years 4	2 years 7	2 1/2 years 10	3 years or more 20	
Investment risk	Excellent 1	Good 5	Moderate 8	Fair 20	Poor 30	
					Total	

Risk Category	Total Points	Assigned RADR
1 Low	0–8	12%
2 Normal	9–15	15
3 Moderate	16–25	18
4 Above average	26–29	24
5 High	30+	30

Using Probability Distributions to Measure Risk

In the RADR approach to project risk analysis, we adjusted the denominator of Equation 14.2 to account for risk. Another way to measure risk is to alter the numerator of the same equation—that is, to develop a measure of risk via the cash flow of the project. Up to now, we've used single-point estimates of the project's future cash flow, $CFAT_t$. An alternative, and one that provides the capability of developing a cash-flow-based measure of risk, is to derive expected cash flows from probability distributions. The material that follows will examine the use of probability distributions to assess expected risk and return. After reviewing basic concepts, including determination of the mean and standard deviation of a probability distribution, we will demonstrate how expected return, project variability, and project risk can be defined and used in capital budgeting decisions.

Expected Cash Flows

The annual cash flow (CFAT) obtained from a capital project is to a large degree dependent on how well the economy and the industry perform and how well the company takes advantage of the opportunities presented to it. For example, other things being equal, if the economy is in a boom period, it is likely that most new projects can also be expected to do well, since a vigorous economy creates a favorable climate for investment success. Unfortunately, it is difficult to estimate the state of the economy and other important market and company characteristics with much consistent precision. Financial managers can cope with this situation in one of two ways: (1) use single-point estimates that hopefully will turn out to be close to the actual results; or (2) use probability distributions that embody a full range of possible outcomes. The latter approach is preferable, as it not only recognizes the uncertain nature of future cash flows, but also provides management with a viable measure of investment risk.

The basic starting point in this approach is to develop a cash flow probability distribution for each year over the economic life of a project. In practice, this is done by estimating the impact on CFAT that accrues from different scenarios about the economy, the market, and other relevant factors. Such an evaluation ultimately results in a number of possible CFAT outcomes for each year, along with their respective probabilities of occurrence. Table 14.3 provides a series of probability distributions for a hypothetical investment project. Note that because the $40,000 cash outflow is known with certainty, there is no need to develop a probability distribution for it. Thereafter, however, each year has its own probability distribution; for example, in year 1, there is a 40 percent chance that the cash flow will amount to $25,000 and a 60 percent chance that the CFAT will be $15,000.

For any given distribution, each probability of occurrence is associated with a particular "state" or "event." For example, in year 1, there is a

40 percent chance that the state of the economy will be strong and therefore that the CFAT from the project will be higher than if the state of the economy is weak—which has a 60 percent chance of occurring. Clearly, there is still considerable uncertainty as to what the exact cash flow will be, since we still do not know exactly which state of the economy will occur. A measure that conveniently captures the various states of a given distribution and the associated probabilities/outcomes is the mean, or expected value. More specifically, the mean cash flow for any year t, $\overline{CFAT}_t$, is found as follows:

$$\overline{CFAT}_t = \sum_{i=1}^{n_t} CFAT_{ti}\, Pr_{ti} \tag{14.4}$$

where Pr_{ti} = the probability associated with the ith outcome in year t
$CFAT_{ti}$ = the ith CFAT outcome in year t
n = the number of possible outcomes in year t

From the cash flow distributions provided in Table 14.3, we can see that the mean cash flow for year 1 will be:

$$\overline{CFAT}_1 = (\$25,000)\,(0.4) + (\$15,000)\,(0.6)$$
$$= \$10,000 + \$9,000 = \$19,000$$

Likewise, for year 2, it will be

$$\overline{CFAT}_2 = (\$30,000)\,(0.2) + (\$20,000)\,(0.6) + (\$10,000)\,(0.2)$$
$$= \$6,000 + \$12,000 + \$2,000 = \$20,000$$

And finally, using Equation 14.4, $\overline{CFAT}_3$ will amount to $25,000. Thus, from the information in Table 14.3, the relevant expected cash flow stream is as follows:

Year, t	0	1	2	3
$\overline{CFAT}_t$	$40,000	$19,000	$20,000	$25,000

This cash flow stream can now be used to measure project profitability.

TABLE 14.3
Estimated CFAT
Probability
Distributions

Cash Outflow in Year 0 (Probability, CFAT)	Cash Inflows		
	Distribution For Year 1 (Probability, CFAT)	Distribution for Year 2 (Probability, CFAT)	Distribution for Year 3 (Probability, CFAT)
1.0 $40,000	0.4 $25,000	0.2 $30,000	0.3 $35,000
	0.6 $15,000	0.6 $20,000	0.4 $25,000
		0.2 $10,000	0.3 $15,000

Note, however, that while the $\overline{CFAT}$ stream takes into account different expected states and outcomes, it does not directly account for the risk or uncertainty associated with the cash flows, unless we assume that financial managers have linear utility functions (that they are risk-neutral). This topic is beyond the scope of the present discussion, but the assumption of a linear wealth utility function does not appear to be appropriate. We must conclude, therefore, that use of expected cash flow values does not by itself account for the risk embedded in a project, except under very restrictive circumstances.[8]

Then how can financial managers assess risk when probability distributions are being used? One way is to use risk-adjusted discount rates; another approach (and the one we look at here) is to assess the variability of the CFAT distribution—to use the standard deviation of the distribution. The standard deviation provides a measure of variability within each cash flow distribution; more specifically, it shows the amount of dispersion around the mean cash flow, $\overline{CFAT}_t$. As we will see below, once project variability is defined, we can derive a measure of the amount of riskiness embedded in a capital project.

The process begins by determining a standard deviation (σ_t) for each $\overline{CFAT}_t$, which is done as follows:

$$\sigma_t = \sqrt{\sum_{i=1}^{n} (CFAT_{ti} - \overline{CFAT}_t)^2 \, Pr_{ti}} \tag{14.5}$$

where the variables are as defined above.

Using once again the cash flow information from Table 14.3, along with the respective $\overline{CFAT}_t$s, we see that the σ for year 1 is:

$$\sigma_1 = \sqrt{(\$25,000 - \$19,000)^2 \, (0.4) + (\$15,000 - \$19,000)^2 \, (0.6)}$$

$$= \sqrt{\$14,400,000 + \$9,600,000}$$

$$= \$4,900$$

Repeating the application of Equation 14.5 to the second and third year cash flows will yield the following:

$$\sigma_2 = \$6,325$$
$$\sigma_3 = \$7,746$$

---

[8]See Thomas E. Copeland and J. Fred Weston, *Financial Theory and Corporate Policy* (Reading, Mass.: Addison-Wesley, 1979), chap. 4; or David P. Baron, "On the Utility Theoretic Foundation of Mean-Variance Analysis," *Journal of Finance* 32 (December 1977), pp. 1683–1698.

The financial decision maker now has annual cash flow statistics, $\overline{CFAT_t}$ and σ_t, that can be used to determine the project's expected return, its dispersion[9], and ultimately its exposure to risk.

Measure of Expected Return

The mean cash flows computed above are used to measure project profitability; all the techniques defined in Chapter 13 (NPV, PI, and IRR) can be used for such purposes. For instance, consider the basic NPV model which was defined in Chapter 13 and again in Equation 14.2 as:

$$NPV = \sum_{t=0}^{n} \frac{CFAT_t}{(1 + k)^t}$$

The cash flow in this case is a single-point estimate; all we need do to alter the equation so that it will accommodate mean cash flows is to redefine the numerator as follows:

$$\overline{NPV} = \sum_{t=0}^{n} \frac{\overline{CFAT_t}}{(1 + k)^t} \tag{14.6}$$

where $\overline{NPV}$ = expected NPV

One problem that must be resolved when using Equation 14.6 is specification of the appropriate discount rate, k. Unfortunately, there is no general agreement as to just what the appropriate discount rate should be. On one hand, it is argued that the risk-free rate (R_F) should be employed; others maintain that the firm's MCC (or some variation thereof, such as a divisional cost of capital) is more appropriate. To the extent that $R_F <$ the firm's MCC, it follows that, other things being equal, use of R_F will both enhance the acceptability of a project (its NPV) and reduce the project's measure of risk.

These are clearly serious, and potentially misleading, side effects of using R_F in the project evaluation process, though they are nonexistent so long as all the cash flows used in the present-value models are known with certainty. For a basic assumption underlying the use of R_F is that the CFATs are, in fact, known with perfect certainty—that they represent certainty equivalent values. Whenever this is not the case (and it seldom is), it would be more appropriate to specify the MCC as the discount rate. That is, even when probability distributions are used to derive expected cash flows, the cash flows employed in the project evaluation process

---

[9]This approach was first suggested by Frederick S. Hillier, "The Derivation of Probabilistic Information for the Evaluation of Risky Investments," *Management Science* 9 (April 1963), pp. 443–457. Throughout this section, we assume the CFAT distributions are normally distributed or, lacking that, the central limit theorem holds. Even when the distribution is not normal, we can often make reasonably strong probability statements by using Tchebycheff's inequality.

are still not known with perfect certainty, and therefore are not certainty equivalents. So long as a significant element of uncertainty remains in the cash flow forecasts, then MCC is the appropriate discount rate. Because of the underlying nature of the cash flows used in the capital budgeting process, *we support the use of MCC and employ it thoughout the the discussion that follows.*

Using the firm's normal MCC (a discount rate, k, of 15 percent) and substituting the expected cash flow stream derived from Table 14.3 into Equation 14.6, the expected NPV of the project is found to be:

$$
\begin{aligned}
\overline{NPV} &= \overline{CFAT}_1 \ (PVIF_{15\%, \ 1 \ yr}) + \overline{CFAT}_2 \ (PVIF_{15\%, \ 2 \ yr}) \\
&\quad + \overline{CFAT}_3 \ (PVIF_{15\%, \ 3 \ yr}) - CFAT_0 \\
&= \$19{,}000 \ (.870) + \$20{,}000 \ (.756) + \$25{,}000 \ (.658) - \$40{,}000 \\
&= \$16{,}530 + \$15{,}120 + \$16{,}450 - \$40{,}000 \\
&= \$8{,}100
\end{aligned}
$$

Note that, giving due consideration to the various future states which can occur, along with their associated probabilities and cash flow results, the project is expected to generate a positive NPV and therefore should be considered acceptable—at least as far as project return is concerned. Although only NPV is used to illustrate risk and return analysis, it should be clear that PI and IRR could also have been employed. There are however, some modest, albeit important, procedural modifications that must be made when PI and IRR are used with the probability distribution approach. (See Appendix 14B for a detailed discussion of these alterations.)

Project Variability   Earlier, a standard deviation (σ_i) for the cash flow in each year of the life of the project was computed. Given that management wants to find the variability of the whole project, such annual measures of dispersion are inadequate; rather, to find total project variability, the annual standard deviations must be combined into a single measure of the standard deviation around the expected NPV. The procedure for determining project variability depends on the nature of the project cash flows. In the material that follows, we look at how a single measure of variability is obtained from cash flows that are dependent (perfectly correlated) and from flows that are completely independent; later, we show how conditional probability distributions can be used to find project variability when dealing with cash flows that are interdependent but not perfectly correlated.

Perfectly Dependent Cash Flows.   Some capital projects have cash flows that are dependent; that is, the successive cash flows are perfectly correlated so that the CFAT outcome in the first year will determine all subsequent flows. Put another way, the cash flow outcome in year t is dependent on the outcome in the preceding year $(t - 1)$. Because of the intense impact a single year can have on the project as a whole, project variability is the greatest with proposals that have dependent cash flows. When year-to-year cash flows are assumed to be perfectly correlated, the standard deviation of the total project (σ) can be found as follows:

$$\sigma = \sum_{t=0}^{n} \frac{\sigma_t}{(1 + k)^t} \qquad (14.7)$$

As can be seen, Equation 14.7 simply involves finding the sum of the present values of the annual standard deviation measures, σ_t.

To see how it works, consider the $40,000 proposal developed above and assume that its cash flows are perfectly dependent; recall that the project has these annual σ_t measures:

$$\sigma_1 = \$4,900$$
$$\sigma_2 = \$6,325$$
$$\sigma_3 = \$7,746$$

Given the firm's MCC (k is 15 percent), the project will have an overall standard deviation of:

$$\sigma = \sigma_1 \, (PVIF_{15\%,1\,\mathrm{yr}}) + \sigma_2 \, (PVIF_{15\%,2\,\mathrm{yr}}) + \sigma_3 \, (PVIF_{15\%,3\,\mathrm{yr}})$$
$$= \$4,900 \, (.870) + \$6,325 \, (.756) + \$7,746 \, (.658)$$
$$= \$14,142$$

Thus, the project as a whole has a σ of $14,142, which will later be used to derive an operational measure of risk.

Independent Cash Flows.   Rather than being perfectly dependent, the cash flows of some projects are completely independent. Under such conditions, the successive cash flows over the life of the project are not related in any systematic manner—in effect, there is a random relationship among the CFATs so that what occurs in one year will in no way affect the outcome in the following year. With independence, the variability of the cash flows over the project's life is reduced and hence, other things being equal, project variability (σ) will be considerably less for these projects than for those with dependent cash flows. In the case of independent cash flows, the project's overall variability can be computed as follows:

$$\sigma = \sqrt{\sum_{t=1}^{n} \frac{\sigma_t^2}{(1 + k)^{2t}}} \qquad (14.8)$$

where all variables are as defined earlier. However, note in this case that the discount factor is raised to the $2t$ power (i.e., use present-value interest factors for periods 2, 4, 6, and so on). Also observe that it is the variance (σ_t^2)—which is simply the annual standard deviation (σ_t) squared—that is used in Equation 14.8.

Assume that the same $40,000 proposal we looked at above has completely independent cash flows. We can use Equation 14.8 to find the project's variability. Using $k = 15$ percent and given the same σ_t values $(\sigma_1 = \$4,900; \sigma_2 = \$6,325;$ and $\sigma_3 = \$7,746)$, the project would have a σ of:

$$
\begin{aligned}
\sigma &= \sqrt{\sigma_1^2 \, (PVIF_{15\%,\,2\,yr}) + \sigma_2^2 \, (PVIF_{15\%,\,4\,yr}) + \sigma_3^2 \, (PVIF_{15\%,\,6\,yr})} \\
&= \sqrt{(\$4,900)^2 \, (.756) + (\$6,325)^2 \, (.572) + (\$7,746)^2 \, (.432)} \\
&= \sqrt{\$18,151,560 + \$22,883,218 + \$25,920,223} \\
&= \sqrt{66,955,001} = \$8,183
\end{aligned}
$$

As noted above, when the cash flows are independent, project variability is less than that which results when the cash flows are dependent ($8,183 vs. $14,142). This is especially significant when it is understood that the only thing we changed was our assumption of the type of cash flow involved (all other variables—the economic life of the project, annual measures of dispersion (σ_t), discount rate, and so on—remained unchanged).

Interdependent Cash Flows. Two assumptions concerning the serial correlation among cash flows have been presented above. Unfortunately, in practice the successive CFATs for most projects cannot be so conveniently described as being either completely dependent or completely independent. If this is the case, how can we develop a viable measure of project variability? Three possibilities exist. One would be to compute σ measures under the assumptions of both perfectly correlated and completely independent CFAT streams, and then subjectively determine an appropriately weighted average.[10] For example, if management determined in the illustrated project above that the CFAT stream is "more

---

[10]Hillier has shown that if some of the expected cash flows are perfectly correlated while others are independent, the project's standard deviation is:

$$
\sigma = \sum_{t=1}^{n} \frac{\sigma_{yt}^2}{(1+k)^{2t}} + \sum_{z=1}^{m} \left(\sum_{t=1}^{n} \left[\frac{\sigma_{zt}}{(1+k)^t} \right] \right)^2
$$

where σ_{yt}^2 = the variance for stream y of a completely independent CFAT in period t

σ_{zt} = the standard deviation for stream z of a perfectly correlated CFAT in period t

See Hillier, "The Derivation of Probabilistic Information for the Evaluation of Risky Investments." This model was subsequently expanded by B. Wagle, "A Statistical Analysis of Risk in Capital Investment Projects," *Operational Research Quarterly* 18 (March 1967), pp. 13–33.

independent than dependent," appropriate weights could be assigned to each σ and a weighted average computed as follows:

$$\overline{\sigma} = W_I \, \sigma_I + W_D \, \sigma_D \tag{14.9}$$

where $\overline{\sigma}$ = weighted average project variability
   W_I = weight assigned to independent CFAT
   W_D = weight assigned to dependent CFAT
       (*Note:* $W_I + W_D = 1.0$)
   σ_I = total project variability with independent CFAT stream
   σ_D = total project variability with dependent cash flows

Suppose, in our example, that a 60–40 weighting scheme is deemed appropriate; using Equation 14.9, the project's overall variability $(\overline{\sigma})$ would be

$$\begin{aligned}
\overline{\sigma} &= .60 \, (\$8,183) + .40 \, (\$14,142) \\
&= \$4,910 + \$5,657 \\
&= \$10,567
\end{aligned}$$

This is admittedly a crude approach to measuring project variability, but given the current state of the art, it does work quite well in a large number of cases. Like any measure of project variability, the value of $\overline{\sigma}$ ($10,567) can now be used to derive an operational measure of project risk.

A second approach to dealing with interdependent cash flows is to use simulation to specify a probability distribution for the project as a whole; this procedure will be discussed later in the chapter. The final procedure is to use *conditional probabilities* as a way to specify the perceived relationship among successive (sequential) CFAT probability distributions; such a technique enables the decision maker to build into the model the amount of auto correlation between yearly cash flows.[11] Under this approach, the cash flow from one year to the next is related to the outcome in the preceding year. But unlike completely dependent cash flows, a range of outcomes is possible, since we are dealing with moderately (as opposed to perfectly) correlated CFATs.

Adaptation of this procedure to risk analysis starts with the development of successive CFAT probability distributions. A probability distribution is specified for the first year in the cash flow stream, followed by a

---

[11]See Frederick S. Hillier, *The Evaluation of Risky Interrelated Investments* (Amsterdam: North Holland, 1969), pp. 93–94; Lynn E. Bussey and G. T. Stevens, Jr., "Formulating Correlated Cash Flow Streams," *Engineering Economist* 18 (fall 1972), pp. 1–30; Charles P. Bonini, "Comment on Formulating Correlated Cash Flow Steams," *Engineering Economist* 20 (spring 1975), pp. 209–214; and Roger P. Bey and J. Clayton Singleton, "Autocorrelated Cash Flows and the Selection of a Portfolio of Capital Assets," *Decision Science* 19 (October 1978), pp. 640–657.

separate probability distribution in year 2 for *each outcome* in year 1; the process continues over the economic life of the project. These series of probability distributions are then combined into a single *joint probability distribution*, which is subsequently used to derive measures of project return and variability. An example of the process is provided in Table 14.4; it shows the cash flows and probability distribution associated with a capital investment proposal that will cost $120,000 (in t_0), and is expected to have an economic life of 3 years. Note that each successive probability distribution is developed from the outcome that occurs in the preceding year; thus, even though there are only 3 years in this project, there are 14 possible outcomes and associated joint probabilities.

It can be seen in Table 14.4 that even though CFAT data are used with the probability distributions for years 0 to 3, the joint probability distribution is specified in terms of NPVs. Each net present value—ranging from $112,970 to a negative $30,950—is computed as a separate outcome in itself. For example, using a 15 percent discount rate, the first NPV figure was found to be:

$$NPV_1 = \$75,000 \ (.870) + \$100,000 \ (.756) + \$140,000 \ (.658) - \$120,000$$
$$= \$65,250 + \$75,600 + \$92,120 - \$120,000$$
$$= \$112,970$$

In a similar fashion, NPV_9 was found to be:

$$NPV_9 = \$40,000 \ (.870) + \$80,000 \ (.756) + \$80,000 \ (.658) - \$120,000$$
$$= \$34,800 + \$60,480 + \$52,640 - \$120,000$$
$$= \$27,920$$

The process would be repeated for other "branches" in the joint probability distribution. The joint probability associated with each NPV_i is simply the product of all the relevant conditional probabilities. Thus, for NPV_1, the joint probability is:

$$P_1 = (.60) \ (.70) \ (.60) = .252$$

The project's expected return and its variability is found directly from the joint probability distribution. More specifically, the expected NPV for the project defined in Table 14.4 can be calculated as:

$$\overline{NPV} = \sum_{i=1}^{n} NPV_i \, Pr_i \qquad (14.10)$$

where NPV_i = the net present value associated with the ith set of CFATs

Pr_i = the joint probability of outcome i occurring

TABLE 14.4

A Conditional Probability Approach to Risk Analysis

Initial Cash Outflow—$CFAT_0$ (Pr_0)	Cash Flow Probability Distribution, Year 1 $CFAT_1$ (Pr_1)	Cash Flow Probability Distributions, Year 2 $CFAT_2$ (Pr_2/Pr_1)	Cash Flow Probability Distributions, Year 3 $CFAT_3$ ($Pr_3/Pr_{2,1}$)	i	NPV Joint Probability Distribution NPV_i (Joint Pr_i)
−$120,000	$75,000 (.60)	$100,000 (.70)	$140,000 (.60)	1.	$112,970 (.252)
			$110,000 (.30)	2.	$ 93,230 (.126)
			$ 75,000 (.10)	3.	$ 70,200 (.042)
		$ 60,000 (.30)	$ 90,000 (.40)	4.	$ 49,830 (.072)
			$ 70,000 (.40)	5.	$ 36,670 (.072)
			$ 40,000 (.20)	6.	$ 16,930 (.036)
	$40,000 (.40)	$ 80,000 (.20)	$100,000 (.30)	7.	$ 41,080 (.024)
			$ 90,000 (.40)	8.	$ 34,500 (.032)
			$ 80,000 (.30)	9.	$ 27,920 (.024)
		$ 70,000 (.40)	$ 90,000 (.70)	10.	$ 26,940 (.112)
			$ 50,000 (.30)	11.	$ 620 (.048)
		$ 50,000 (.40)	$ 75,000 (.10)	12.	$ 1,950 (.016)
			$ 50,000 (.30)	13.	−$ 14,500 (.048)
			$ 25,000 (.60)	14.	−$ 30,950 (.096)

Note: A 15 percent discount rate is used in the NPV calculations.

Substituting the information from the joint probability distribution, we have:

$$\overline{NPV} = NPV_1\ (Pr_1) + NPV_2\ (Pr_2) + \cdots + NPV_{14}\ (Pr_{14})$$
$$= \$112{,}970\ (.252) + \$93{,}230\ (.126) + \$70{,}200\ (.042) + \$49{,}830\ (.072) +$$
$$\cdots + \$1{,}950\ (.016) - \$14{,}500\ (.048) - \$30{,}950\ (.096)$$
$$= \$28{,}468 + \$11{,}747 + \$2948 + \cdots + \$31 - \$696 - \$2971$$
$$= \$52{,}171$$

Thus, from a return perspective, the project would be considered acceptable, since it promises to generate an NPV (with $k = 15$ percent) of more than $52,000.

In a similar fashion, project variability (σ) is found as:

$$\sigma = \sqrt{\sum_{i=1}^{n} (NPV_i - \overline{NPV})^2\ (Pr_i)} \tag{14.11}$$

Note that in this case it is not necessary to compute a standard deviation for each year of the project (σ_t); rather, the required data are obtained directly from the NPV joint probability distribution. Thus, using a computational procedure like the one spelled out in Chapter 6 (see Table 6.2), and applying it to the data in Table 14.4, we find the standard deviation for the total project (σ) to be $48,610. This measure of project variability is comparable to that obtained from Equations 14.7 and 14.8, which are used when the annual cash flows are dependent and independent, respectively.

Measures of Project Risk   So far, we have used the probability distribution approach to generate a measure of expected return and a measure of project variability; still lacking is an operational measure of the project risk. However, once project variability has been obtained, we will see that it is rather easy to derive such a measure. This is usually done in one of two ways: (1) by computing a coefficient of variation; or (2) by determining the proposal's probability of success. We will examine both procedures by using the examples developed above; also, as we have done so far, we will couch our discussion in terms of NPV.

Coefficient of Variation.   As noted in Chapter 6, the coefficient of variation (CV) is simply a measure of relative risk that relates project risk to project return:

$$CV = \frac{\sigma}{\overline{NPV}} \tag{14.12}$$

Other things being equal, the greater the CV, the greater the amount of risk exposure. To see how the CV approach works, consider once again the $40,000 project examined earlier. If we felt the cash flows of the project were perfectly dependent, it would have σ of $14,142, and $\overline{NPV}$ of $8,100; using this information in Equation 14.12 results in a CV of:

$$CV = \$14{,}142/\$8{,}100 = 1.75$$

In contrast, for completely independent CFATs, the CV would be:

$$CV = \$8{,}183/\$8{,}100 = 1.01$$

Finally, for the $120,000 proposal (with the moderately correlated cash flows), the CV is:

$$CV = \$48{,}610/\$52{,}171 = 0.93$$

Such information, along with the project's measure of profitability (its $\overline{NPV}$), will provide management with viable measures of risk and return that can be used to assess the relative appeal of competing capital projects. For instance, if the information above actually pertained to three distinct projects, the financial manager would have the following array of risk and return data on which to base a decision:

Project	Return ($\overline{NPV}$)	Risk (CV)
I	$ 8,100	1.75
II	8,100	1.01
III	52,171	0.93

In this case, project II would clearly be preferable to project I, since it provides the same return with less risk, while project III would be preferable to project II, since it offers both higher return and less risk.

Probability of Success.   If the probability distributions are normal (or at least approximately so), the probability of a project having an NPV equal to or greater than zero can readily be determined. Under this approach, the financial manager uses the probability of success as the vehicle through which to assess the risk of capital budgeting proposals. To find the probability of success, we must standardize the distribution and use the table in Appendix A.5 to determine the relevant probability of occurrence. Technically, the equation for standardizing a distribution is:

$$Z = \frac{x - \mu}{\sigma} \tag{14.13}$$

where Z = the standardized variable, or Z value
        x = the outcome of interest
        μ = the mean of the probability distribution
        σ = the standard deviation of the probability distribution

Since we want to find the probability that the expected NPV of a project will actually end up equal to or greater than zero (that the project will turn out to provide the desired rate of return), we can redefine the variables in Equation 14.13 and in so doing, simplify the equation as follows:

$$Z = \frac{0 - \overline{NPV}}{\sigma} = \frac{\overline{NPV}}{\sigma} \tag{14.14}$$

where $\overline{NPV}$ must be greater than zero

We can obtain the probability of success of a project through Equation 14.14, which is basically little more than the reciprocal of Equation 14.12. To see how this works, let us return to the $120,000, 3-year project with the moderately correlated cash flows described in Table 14.4. We have already generated the required input data ($\overline{NPV}$ and σ); all that is left is to compute Z and then use Appendix A.5 to determine the probability of occurrence. Thus:

$$Z = \$52,171/\$48,610 = 1.07$$

Referring to Appendix A.5, it can be seen that a Z value of 1.07 is associated with a probability of occurrence of .3577; that is, given the mean and standard deviation of a normally distributed function, the area between the mean NPV of $52,171 and an NPV of zero is 35.77 percent. Now, since the distribution is symmetrical, we can find the probability of success by adding the computed value of 35.77 percent to 50 percent:

$$\begin{array}{l} \text{Probability} \\ \text{of success} \end{array} = .5000 + \begin{array}{l} \text{value obtained from Table A.5} \\ \text{(for computed } Z \text{ value)} \end{array} \tag{14.15}$$

$$= .5000 + .3577 = .8577 = 85.77\%$$

Other things being equal, the higher the probability of success, the more desirable the project.

Note that there is a better than 85 percent chance that this project will provide an NPV equal to or greater than zero—that the project will turn out to be sufficiently profitable. This can be seen graphically in Figure 14.2. With respect to the project under evaluation, the firm's management will be able to base its decision on the fact that it has an expected

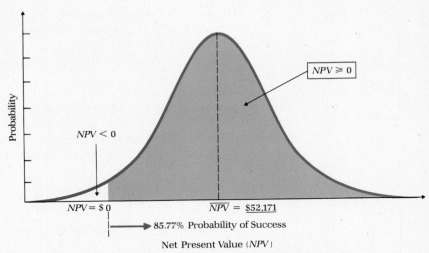

Figure 14.2   Probability Distribution of Net Present Values.

NPV of $52,171 *and* a probability of success of 85.77 percent. Such risk-return information can be used to assess this project relative to others competing for the firm's limited capital resources. In this way, the company's capital budgeting decisions are based, as they should be, on both expected return behavior and exposure to risk. In the long run, this approach will be far superior to basing decisions solely on the level of expected project return as measured by $\overline{NVP}$, $\overline{PI}$, or $\overline{IRR}$.

Decision Making in a Portfolio Context	Until now, we have been concerned with risk analysis for a single capital project. When numerous projects are involved, decision making revolves around different portfolios of capital assets, and as such, risk assessment may differ from that which we have discussed so far because of the impact of diversification. In essence, the decision comes down to selecting from among competing *portfolios of capital projects*. Since a separate risk-return profile can be computed for each portfolio, the selection process is basically an attempt to maximize returns from a given level of risk, or minimize risk at a given level of return. In Chapter 6 and Appendix 6A, diversification with securities was considered; the same concepts also apply to the firm, which conceptually can be viewed as a portfolio of capital assets.[12]

But there are some fundamental differences between securities and

---

[12]James C. Van Horne, "Capital Budgeting Decisions Involving Combinations of Risky Investments," *Management Science* 13 (October 1966), pp. 84–92; and Haim Levy and Marshall Sarnat, "The Portfolio Analysis of Multiperiod Capital Investment Under Conditions of Risk," *Engineering Economist* 18 (fall 1970), pp. 1–19.

capital assets that make diversification within the firm more "lumpy" than for securities. For one thing, capital assets are usually not easily divisible—either the entire project is taken, or it is rejected. Likewise, acquisition and disinvestment costs and opportunities are typically much more important than with securities. Finally, there is a problem of mutual inclusion and/or dependence that is present with capital assets, but not with securities.

Nonetheless, so long as total asset risk, as opposed to nondiversifiable market risk, is important, diversification of assets may be of value to financial managers. Accordingly, in the material that follows, we will demonstrate how capital budgeting decisions can be made in a portfolio context. We do this not so much for its application to everyday situations, but rather as a conceptual way to view this important dimension of the decision. For although the procedure may lack current widespread applicability, the concept does warrant consideration within the decision-making process. Though we may not be able to evaluate it formally, the potential impact of diversification should at least be considered when capital proposals are being selected for implementation.[13]

Basing capital investment decisions on the risk-return behavior of alternative portfolios of capital assets involves finding the expected return and variability for each possible *portfolio*, where each portfolio is made up of the firm's existing assets, plus one or more of the capital proposals currently under consideration (and which, up to now, have been judged individually as acceptable projects). For example, assume that four projects (I, II, III, and IV) have passed the initial screening via the risk-return analysis of individual projects as defined above. Along with the firm's existing portfolio of assets (E), the following portfolios can be constructed:

Portfolio	Asset-Project Combinations
A	E, I
B	E, II
C	E, III
D	E, IV
E	Existing firm (E)
F	E, I, II
G	E, I, III
H	E, I, IV
I	E, II, III
J	E, II, IV
K	E, III, IV

---

[13]The concept of firm diversification and its possible benefits remains controversial and the subject of considerable debate.

Portfolio	Asset-Project Combinations
L	E, I, II, III
M	E, I, II, IV
N	E, I, III, IV
O	E, II, III, IV
P	E, I, II, III, IV

A measure of portfolio return and risk must be computed for each of these 16 portfolios.

For the case of n different capital projects, the expected return on a portfolio $(\overline{P})$ can be found as:

$$\overline{P} = \sum_{i=1}^{n} \overline{NPV}_i \qquad (14.16)$$

where $\overline{NPV}_i$ = the expected NPV on the ith capital project (as computed earlier)

n = the number of capital projects in the portfolio, where one of the projects is the firm's existing portfolio of assets

Similarly, the standard deviation for the portfolio is found as:

$$\sigma_p = \sqrt{\sum_{i=1}^{n} \sum_{j=1}^{n} \rho_{ij} \sigma_i \sigma_j} \qquad (14.17)$$

where σ_p = the standard deviation on a portfolio of n capital projects

ρ_{ij} = the correlation coefficient between $\overline{NPV}$s of the ith and jth projects

σ_i, σ_j = the standard deviation of the ith and jth projects (computed above as σ)

n = the number of capital projects

For a two-asset portfolio, made up of assets A and B, Equation 14.17 reduces to:

$$\sigma_p = \sqrt{\sigma_A{}^2 + 2\rho_{AB}\sigma_A\sigma_B + \sigma_B{}^2} \qquad (14.18)$$

Equation 14.17 suggests that a portfolio's standard deviation depends on the individual standard deviations about the projects' NPVs *and* the amount of correlation between various capital projects. Thus, it is possible to alter portfolio risk simply by altering the composition of the capital projects included in a given portfolio. For example, assume two of the four capital projects denoted previously have the following characteristics:

Project I	Project II
$\overline{NPV} = \$100$	$\overline{NPV} = \$150$
$\sigma_I = \$\ 70$	$\sigma_{II} = \$120$

$$\rho_{I,II} = 0.5$$

Based on this information, the expected return on a portfolio made up of these two assets is:

$$\overline{P} = \$100 + \$150 = \$250$$

Likewise, according to Equation 14.18, the portfolio's standard deviation is:

$$\sigma_p = \sqrt{(\$70)^2 + 2(.5)(\$70)(\$120) + (\$120)^2}$$
$$= \sqrt{\$4900 + \$8400 + \$14,400}$$
$$= \$166.43$$

Calculating the coefficient of variation for the two projects and for the two-asset portfolio, we have:

$$CV_I = \$70/\$100 = 0.70$$
$$CV_{II} = \$120/\$150 = 0.80$$
$$CV_{I,II} = \$166.43/\$250 = 0.67$$

Clearly, the portfolio has less risk than either of the projects individually. Because the correlation between projects I and II is less than 1.0, risk exposure has been reduced by creating a portfolio of capital projects.

When we view the firm as a portfolio of capital assets, the importance of the degree of correlation between new and existing projects becomes obvious. Just as with securities, the correlation coefficient may be positive, zero, or negative, and range between +1.0 and −1.0. In practice, most correlations between capital projects tend to be positive, but less than 1.0. The lack of negative correlations happens because most capital investments interact positively with the state of the economy. Likewise, projects in the same line of business tend to exhibit substantially higher correlations than those in unrelated divisions or lines of business. The important point is that as long as the correlation is less than 1.0, there are benefits to diversification in the form of either higher expected returns with the same level of risk, or constant expected returns with a lower level of risk. With these concepts in mind, let us see how individual capital expenditure proposals are selected within a portfolio context.

Continuing our illustration of the four proposals, expected return $(\overline{P})$ and risk (σ_p) measures would be computed for each of the 16 portfolios (or combinations of projects). The portfolio NPVs and standard deviations are plotted in Figure 14.3. Each point, except the portfolio of existing

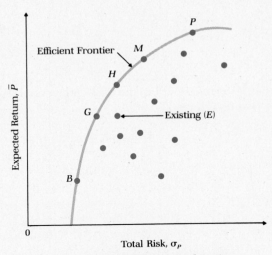

Figure 14.3   Portfolios of Capital Projects.

assets (E), represents the expected return and total risk from combining the firm's existing assets with one or more new capital budgeting proposals. Certain of these combinations (B, G, H, M, and P) dominate the others in the sense that they provide the lowest risk for a given expected return, or the highest expected return per unit of risk. Only those combinations of assets that dominate (that are on the efficient frontier) should be considered by the firm. When we compare the feasible alternatives, it is clear that the firm should at least move to portfolio G or H, since either is an improvement over the existing firm, E. Portfolio G generates the same return as the existing firm but with less risk, while portfolio H provides more return with the same level of risk. This means that if management decides to select portfolio H, it would do so by implementing all the capital projects included in that portfolio. In our illustration, proposals I and IV would be implemented, since portfolio H is made up of the firm's existing assets plus capital projects I and IV. If the firm's financial managers wanted to consider changing the firm's basic risk-return posture, they might also consider the other efficient portfolios—B, M, or P.

Some Practical Dimensions of Risk Analysis

Conversations with business executives and the results of numerous surveys provide an indication of the variety of approaches taken by firms in an attempt to deal with risk. The results of one study, for example, indicated that 71 percent of the responding firms considered risk and uncertainty "in some manner."[14] The most frequent method employed was to increase the discount rate (use the RADR method); the next two

[14]Lawrence J. Gitman and John R. Forrester, Jr., "A Survey of Capital Budgeting Techniques Used by Major U.S. Firms," *Financial Management* 6 (fall 1977), pp. 66–71.

most frequently mentioned procedures involved taking the expected values of cash flows, or subjectively adjusting the discount rates. In addition, some firms also employed sensitivity analysis, computer-based simulation techniques, or risk models based on probability distributions. These results are supported by the findings from another survey, which indicated that 40 percent of the responding firms formally dealt with risk at the project level, 4 percent did not assess risk at all, and the remaining 56 percent attempted to assess risk subjectively.[15] Of the 40 percent that formally dealt with risk, the probability distribution approach was the most widely employed method, followed by sensitivity analysis; there were even 3 percent of the respondents who indicated that they employed techniques related to the use of beta coefficients.

It seems noteworthy that according to the two studies cited above, anywhere from 71 to 96 percent of the sample firms either formally or informally dealt with the question of project risk exposure. Clearly, risk analysis is being conducted in practice. Risk-adjusted discount rates and probability distribution approaches are being used, but so are other techniques. For the most part, these other techniques are being employed as a way to deal with some of the practical aspects or limitations of risk analysis. Two of these procedures are sensitivity analysis and computer-based simulation. We now look briefly at both approaches to risk evaluation, and then address an increasingly important practical consideration—the multinational dimensions of risk analysis.

Sensitivity Analysis

A good capital budgeting procedure should encourage financial managers to pose the question: "What will happen to final project profitability under different assumptions about the level of the CFAT stream, expected life of the project, and so on?" One simple but often effective way to provide such insight involves the use of *sensitivity analysis*, which provides information regarding the responsiveness of capital budgeting results to variable estimation errors. In order to employ sensitivity analysis, the project's return (say, its NPV) is calculated from a given set of assumptions about economic life, CFAT, salvage value, and so on. Then the project's NPV is computed again, but this time one of the key input variables (such as estimated cash revenues) is changed, while all other variables remain constant. If project return changes substantially with the given change in the input variable, the variable under examination is important to the capital budgeting decision. As such, more time or money may need to be spent to determine if the assumptions underlying that variable are realistic. Note that sensitivity analysis does not quantify risk; rather, it locates factors that are potentially the most risk-sensitive.

---

[15]Lawrence D. Schall, Gary L. Sundem, and William R. Geijsbeek, Jr., "Survey and Analysis of Capital Budgeting Methods," *Journal of Finance* 33 (March 1978), pp. 281–287. The percentages were calculated from the survey results listed in the appendix to this article.

To illustrate the application of sensitivity analysis, consider the data presented in Table 14.5, which is for a revenue expansion project being considered by Thompson Shipping. The initial CFAT is $-$50,000, followed by a constant CFAT stream of $16,010 for each of 4 years, with an additional CFAT of $9,990 in year 4 due to the estimated terminal value of the project; assume the firm uses a 10 percent cost of capital. The data presented in the table represent the most likely outcomes and hence, provide the *base case* for the project. Now we begin systematically to change the estimated input values (either by a specific percentage or some relevant dollar amount) to determine how sensitive the NPV is to changes in the assumptions underlying the data.

Each variable is changed by employing values both above and below the base case, calculating the new NPVs, and then plotting them against the variable in question. Figure 14.4 shows sensitivity graphs for two of the input variables: cash revenues and terminal value (there are, of course, other input variables, such as cash expenses and project life). The slopes show how sensitive the project's NPV is to changes in the input variables; the steeper the slope, the more sensitive NPV is to changes in the given variable. Put another way, other things being equal,

TABLE 14.5
Base Case Data for a Proposed Capital Project, Thompson Shipping

INITIAL INVESTMENT ($t = 0$):

$$(CFAT_0) = \$50,000$$

OPERATING CASH FLOWS IN YEARS 1–4:

Year, t	Cash Revenues$_t$ (1)	Cash Expenses$_t$ (2)	$CFBT_t(1 - T)$ $[(1) - (2)(1 - T)]$ (3)	Depreciation Tax Shield $[Dep_t (T)]$ (4)	$CFAT_t$ $[CFBT_t (1 - T) +$ Dep $(T)]$ (5)
1	$29,500	$11,150	$11,010	$5,000[a]	$16,010
2	29,500	11,150	11,010	5,000	16,010
3	29,500	11,150	11,010	5,000	16,010
4	29,500	11,150	11,010	5,000	16,010

TERMINAL CASH FLOW IN YEAR 4:

Year	Estimated Selling Price$_4$ (1)	Book Value$_4$ (2)	Taxable Income$_4$ (3)	Tax$_4$ $[(3) \times T]$ (4)	$CFAT_4$ (1) − (4) (5)
4	$16,650	0	$16,650	$6,660	$9,990

PROJECT'S BASE NPV:

$$NPV = \$16,010 \ (PVIFA_{10\%, \, 4 \, yr}) + \$9,990 \ (PVIF_{10\%, \, 4 \, yr}) - \$50,000$$
$$= \$16,010 \ (3.170) + \$9,990 \ (.683) - \$50,000$$
$$= \$50,752 + \$6,823 - \$50,000 = \$7,575$$

[a]As allowed by ACRS, depreciation is taken on a straight-line basis; depreciation tax shield equals the depreciation per year of $12,500 times the tax rate (T) of 0.40 = $5,000.

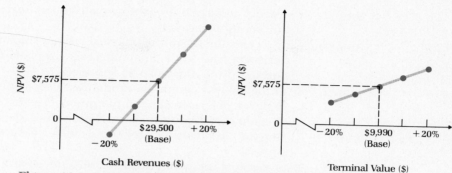

Figure 14.4   Sensitivity Graphs, Thompson Shipping.

the steeper the slope of the sensitivity line, the greater the amount of risk exposure. From Figure 14.4, it is clear that cash revenues are far more important to the final outcome than terminal value. Knowing this, management might want to carefully assess cash revenue projections to determine the kind of risk exposure the firm has in the project. If just a slight drop in revenues will lead to a negative NPV, and if the likelihood of that occurring appears great, the firm may decide to forego or delay the investment. Thus sensitivity analysis provides valuable insights into project risk, and enables management to systematically bring the question of risk into the capital budgeting decision.

Computer Simulation

Although the complete probability distribution method described earlier in the chapter has obvious appeal as far as its ability to capture a project's potential exposure to risk, one of its big drawbacks is the amount of time that must be spent on grinding out the many required computations. Fortunately, computer simulation techniques have been developed, in part, to reduce such computational requirements. A *computer simulation* provides a convenient means of incorporating the interactions of a number of key variables into the analysis of project risk. In essence, a simulation model is little more than a collection of equations and probability distributions that describe the important variables in the decision.[16] To construct a simulation of project profitability, the following steps are necessary:

Step 1.   List all the basic variables that affect the outcome.

---

[16]This approach first gained prominence due to David B. Hertz, "Risk Analysis in Capital Investment," *Harvard Business Review* 42 (January–February 1964), pp. 95–106. See also Lynn E. Bussey and G. T. Stevens, Jr., "Net Present Value from Complex Cash Flow Streams by Simulation," *AIIE Transactions* 3 (March 1971), pp. 81–89; and Lawrence Kryzanowski, Peter Lusztig, and Bernhard Schwab, "Monte Carlo Simulation and Capital Expenditure Decisions—A Case Study," *Engineering Economist* 18 (fall 1972), pp. 31–48.

Step 2. Construct a discrete probability distribution for each variable that is subject to uncertainty.

Step 3. State in equation form the financial relationships that connect the basic variables to the final outcome; correlations between variables and over time must also be specified.

Step 4. With the aid of a computer, randomly select a specific value for each basic variable according to the probability this value has of actually occurring in the future; given these values, use the equation from step 3 to calculate NPV (or some other measure of return) for the project.

Step 5. Repeat step 4 many times (500 to 1000 times) and accumulate the outcomes as a frequency distribution of returns (NPVs).

Consider the situation faced by Sturgeon Construction, whose management has to make a decision regarding whether or not to expand the firm's capability to serve the oil industry in the Rocky Mountains. To serve that industry, Sturgeon Construction will have to make sizable outlays for new equipment and associated materials. Once the equipment is in place, Sturgeon can serve a number of oil companies. To simplify the situation, Sturgeon decided to treat the entire decision as one large capital budgeting problem. Based on considerable analysis of the situation, management was able to identify four variables which it felt would have substantial influence on the desirability of the expansion project: (1) initial investment; (2) annual cash revenues; (3) annual cash expenses; and (4) project life.[17] Sturgeon decided to employ the NPV approach, and to use a discount rate of 12 percent.

The computer will now randomly select specific values for each of the variables, according to the chances of their occurring, and calculate the resulting NPV. For example, assume the computer selects:

Initial outlay	$3,600,000
Cash revenues	$2,000,000 per year
Cash expenses	$1,000,000 per year
Project life	9 years

Given this information, and assuming annual depreciation of $300,000 along with a marginal tax rate of 40 percent, the after-tax cash flows are found to be $720,000 per year, and the NPV is as follows:

$$NPV = CFAT_t (PVIFA_{12\%,\ 9\ yr}) - \text{initial outlay}$$
$$= \$720,000\ (5.328) - \$3,600,000$$
$$= \$3,836,160 - \$3,600,000$$
$$= \$236,160$$

---

[17]These four variables are only a sample of the different factors that affect project cash flows. In addition, other operating considerations—such as marginal tax rates, depreciation rates, and book profit or loss from disposition of facilities—are programmed into the simulation model and automatically used as the situation dictates.

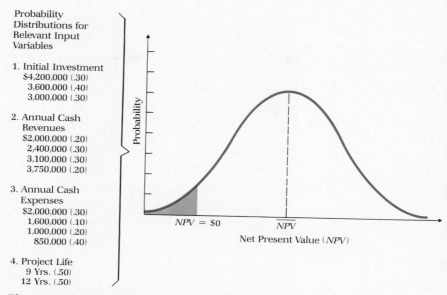

Probability
Distributions for
Relevant Input
Variables

1. Initial Investment
   $4,200,000 (.30)
   3,600,000 (.40)
   3,000,000 (.30)

2. Annual Cash
   Revenues
   $2,000,000 (.20)
   2,400,000 (.30)
   3,100,000 (.30)
   3,750,000 (.20)

3. Annual Cash
   Expenses
   $2,000,000 (.30)
   1,600,000 (.10)
   1,000,000 (.20)
   850,000 (.40)

4. Project Life
   9 Yrs. (.50)
   12 Yrs. (.50)

Figure 14.5   Simulation Approach to Risk Analysis, Sturgeon Construction.

The same sequence would be repeated literally hundreds of times, with other values of the four variables being generated on a random basis according to their probability of occurrence. The result would be a relative frequency distribution of NPVs, as depicted in Figure 14.5. This frequency distribution—like the joint probability distribution developed for projects with interdependent cash flows—then yields (via a computer printout) measures of estimated project profitability and project variability, as well as desired measures of risk. The computer simulation thus provides output that enables management to assess the return and risk characteristics of a proposed expenditure within the capital budget decision-making process. The significant advantage of simulation is the tremendous flexibility it allows in terms of considering the many variables that in practice influence the potential desirability of capital expenditure projects.

MULTINATIONAL DIMENSIONS

Capital Budgeting for Foreign Projects

Foreign capital projects can be analyzed using basically the same techniques as described in this and the previous chapters, but a number of complexities must be introduced. These include the proper perspective to use when evaluating capital expenditure proposals, the impact of foreign exchange and political risks on project profitability, and the strategic implications of the decision.

Profitability: Project and Parent Perspectives.   In analyzing foreign projects, it is necessary to distinguish between the rate of return from the project's perspective and from the parent's perspective. These will differ because of the way in which a project is financed, funds are repatriated, taxes are assessed, foreign exchange rates are levied, and political risks arise. Rate of return from the parent's perspective depends on the size and timing of the CFATs repatriated from the project, the exchange rate at the time of repatriation, and the tax liabilities incurred because of repatriation. One key variable is the way in which the project was originally financed, since most of the funds repatriated are in the form of dividends, loan amortization, license fees, and other purely financial cash flows.

Mixing financial cash flows with operating CFATs violates the normal capital budgeting practice of considering the financing decision as separate from the investment decision. Nevertheless, in the case of foreign projects, we must consider the financial cash flows to the parent because it is only from repatriated funds that dividends can be paid, debt repaid, and taxes paid. Shareholder wealth is not maximized if a foreign project has a highly positive NPV in local currency terms but the funds are blocked in the host country, or if repatriated funds lose their value due to devaluation.

Foreign Exchange Risk.   A project's cash flows may be affected by a change in foreign exchange rates. Local-currency net cash flows are likely to be larger or smaller than expected depending on the effect of exchange rate changes. For example, a local currency devaluation could make the foreign project more competitive in export markets and also more competitive against imports in its home market. On the other hand, the realized higher level of local-currency net cash flow would be worth less in parent currency terms when repatriated. The higher level of cash flow from operations might or might not offset the devaluation effect.

Political Risk.   A possibility exists that the host country may in the future impose foreign exchange controls which effectively block the repatriation of funds. This usually occurs when the host country is experiencing severe balance of payments problems and a shortage of foreign currency reserves. In addition to blocked funds, there is always the possibility that the host country might expropriate the project. Political risk is usually factored into capital budgeting by simulating the project's cash flows under various assumptions about when and how political intervention might occur. The project may still have an acceptable NPV, despite blocked funds or eventual expropriation. This is because, as a practical matter, few firms would even consider investment if political danger is imminent. Political risk is usually more of a threat to cash flows expected in the distant future.

Strategic Considerations.   Many foreign projects are undertaken for strategic reasons, rather than on a pure rate of return basis. For example, a project might be undertaken in a foreign country to preempt that market from competitors. Gaining worldwide market share may be a key determinant for securing competitive economies of scale. Thus, the benefits of a particular foreign project may be reflected in part in the firm's cash flows elsewhere in the world. These differential cash flows must be included in calculating the foreign project's NPV for capital budgeting purposes. Many firms lump all risks together by requiring a higher rate of return on foreign projects than on comparable domestic projects. This practice has the unfortunate effect of ignoring the actual amounts and timing of potential foreign project risks. A better solution is to adjust the foreign project's cash flows for all known foreign risks. Once this is done, the foreign project can be analyzed for business and financial risk like any domestic project.

SUMMARY

Effective risk analysis is a difficult yet extremely important part of the capital budgeting decision process. Many approaches are available, but a key element of risk analysis in practice is to have a systematic procedure to ensure that adequate information is provided to decision makers and that risk is considered directly. In one form or another, risk analysis is practiced by a growing number of firms. Essentially, management has two alternatives: it can deal with risk via the denominator (discount rate) of the basic valuation equation, or via the numerator (expected cash flow).

From a theoretical perspective, the riskiness of capital projects should be assessed within the framework of the capital asset pricing model. However, except for its use in calculating divisional costs of capital, several "real world" obstacles prevent widespread use of the model. The risk-adjusted discount rate (RADR) is the most widely used procedure for assessing project risk. It involves adjusting the discount rate (k) as the way to accommodate the element of risk within a capital budgeting decision—the greater the perceived risk of the project, the higher the discount rate used in present-value valuation models. An alternative procedure, and one that provides the capability of developing a cash-flow-based measure of risk, is to derive expected cash flows from probability distributions. Using this technique, an expected return and measure of project variability, and ultimately project risk, can be obtained. Two measures of project risk are available through this procedure (coefficient of varation and probability of success), although the amount of project variability, and therefore risk exposure, is heavily influenced by the nature of the correlation between cash flows. In addition to the RADR and probability distribution methods, other techniques have been developed to deal with the practicalities of risk analysis; notable among these approaches have been sensitivity analysis and computer-based simulation.

QUESTIONS

14.1. Define the following terms and phrases:
   a. Probability distribution.
   b. Expected net present value.
   c. Risk-adjusted discount rate.
   d. Project variability.
   e. Conditional probabilities.
   f. Coefficient of variation.
   g. Probability of success.
   h. Portfolio effects on capital projects.
   i. Sensitivity analysis.
   j. Simulation techniques.

14.2. An analyst who believes that total asset risk is the relevant measure of risk states: "Since corporations are not portfolios of securities, it is obvious that nondiversifiable market risk is not an appropriate measure of the risk investors are concerned with." Comment on this statement.

14.3. The capital asset pricing model suggests that the discount rate for a project should be:

$$k_{\text{project}} = R_F + \beta_{\text{project}}\,(k_M - R_F)$$

   a. Explain what each of the variables in this equation mean.
   b. What are the implications of this model for capital budgeting decisions?
   c. What major problems exist that limit the usefulness of this approach in capital budgeting?

14.4. The use of probability distributions of CFATs leads to the development of probability distributions of NPVs. Explain the following:
   a. Why the σ assuming independent year-to-year cash flows is smaller than the σ under the assumption of perfectly correlated, year-to-year cash flows?
   b. How the probability of the NPV being equal to or greater than a certain value can be determined.

14.5. Conditional probabilities and simulation appear to be practical ways to incorporate risk analysis into capital budgeting. What are the main problems with these approaches?

14.6. When considering the firm as a portfolio of assets, explain:

a. What benefits can be derived from diversification, and why.

b. Why most capital expenditure projects exhibit positive correlation with each other.

c. Why these benefits are unimportant if the capital asset pricing model is valid.

14.7. Explain why sensitivity analysis does not quantify risk, but rather locates factors that are potentially risk-sensitive. Is there any relationship between sensitivity analysis and simulation?

PROBLEMS

14.1. *EXPECTED CFATs.* Paradise Valley Industries must decide whether or not to open an exclusive vacation resort off the coast of Mexico. CFATs are expected to be $750,000 per year for each of 20 years. The initial cost of the project is estimated to total $3,000,000, and the firm's MCC is 10 percent. Terminal value is zero; the investment tax credit does not apply.

a. Find the NPV of the project. Should the resort be built?

b. Patricia Dee, the CEO, now learns that there exists the possibility of a hurricane hitting the island periodically within the next 20 years. What is the NPV of the project if the hurricane hits immediately after it is opened, causing a total loss (CFATs per year = 0 for years 1–20)?

c. Alternatively, the following probabilities and associated yearly CFATs have been estimated:

Condition	Probability	CFATs Per Year
No hurricane	.3	$750,000
Hurricane: mild damage	.1	300,000
Hurricane: severe damage	.2	200,000
Hurricane: total loss	.4	0

(1) Use probability theory to find the expected net present value. Should the resort be built?

(2) Which decision—that obtained in (a) or (c)—is best, and why?

14.2. *RISK-ADJUSTED DISCOUNT RATES AND PROBABILITY DISTRIBUTIONS.* Ontario Chemical is considering two mutually exclusive investment projects. The planning division does not believe it can estimate the degree of correlation or independence in successive cash flows, and consequently believes the following probability distribution of annual CFATs to be relevant for each of the projects over their 6-year lives.

Project A		Project B	
Pr	CFAT	Pr	CFAT
.1	$20,000	.2	$10,000
.7	30,000	.5	15,000
.2	45,000	.3	25,000

Project A requires an initial outlay of $100,000, while project B requires an investment of $50,000. There is no terminal value or investment tax credit.

a. Calculate the expected CFAT, the standard deviation, and the coefficient of variation for each project's expected cash inflows. (*Hint*: Don't worry about independence or correlation in the cash flows. Employ the CFAT figures above only as a way to calculate the mean, standard deviation, and coefficient of variation.) Which project is riskier? Why?

b. Assume each project's risk is different from that of the firm as a whole. Ontario Chemical has devised the following formula for estimating an appropriate RADR:

$$RADR = R_F + 18 \; CV$$

where $RADR$ = the risk-adjusted discount rate for the project
R_F = the risk-free rate, which is 8%
CV = the coefficient of variation for the project

What is the NPV for projects A and B? (Round the discount rates to the nearest whole number.) Which project should be selected?

14.3. *CAPM, CALCULATION OF BETA, AND RISK-ADJUSTED DISCOUNT RATES.* Byron's Supermarkets is evaluating the proposed purchase of Holland Meat Packing, a privately held firm. As financial manager of Byron's, you have concluded the capital asset pricing model is the appropriate approach to use in determining the risk-adjusted discount rate for this capital investment proposal. Fortunately, a publicly held firm similar to Holland Meat Packing exists; you have decided to use this company's returns as a benchmark for Holland's risk. The historical returns on the similar company (k_j) and the market (k_M) are as follows:

Year	Annual Returns on Similar Companies (k_j)	Annual Returns on the Market (k_M)
1	7%	5%
2	12	15
3	3	0
4	14	10
5	19	20

The risk-free rate is 7 percent, the initial outlay is $175,000, the investment tax credit is not in effect, and the expected CFAT stream is $20,000 per year for years 1–4 and $30,000 per year for years 5–10.

a. Calculate β (*hint*: see Chapter 7 for the calculation of beta) and determine the appropriate risk-adjusted discount rate to employ in evaluating the purchase of Holland. (Round the discount rate to the nearest whole number.)

b. Calculate the NPV. Should Byron's proceed with the acquisition?

14.4. **PROBABILITY DISTRIBUTIONS: CORRELATED CFATs.** San Antonio Steel has developed the following discrete probability distributions of CFATs for a particular capital project:

	Year 1		Year 2		Year 3
Pr	CFAT	Pr	CFAT	Pr	CFAT
.1	$100	.2	$300	.1	S 500
.2	200	.4	400	.3	600
.3	300	.3	500	.3	700
.4	400	.1	600	.3	1000

Assume the probability distributions of CFATs are perfectly correlated over time, the initial cost of the project is $1000, the investment tax credit is not in effect, and the appropriate discount rate is 10 percent.

a. Determine the mean and standard deviation of the yearly CFATs.

b. What is the expected $\overline{\text{NPV}}$ of the project being considered by San Antonio?

c. If the total distribution is approximately normal and continuous, what is the probability that the NPV will be greater than zero?

    d.   If, instead of being perfectly correlated, the successive CFATs are perfectly independent, what is the project's $\overline{NPV}$ and probability of success?

14.5. ***PROBABILITY DISTRIBUTIONS: INDEPENDENT AND CORRELATED CFATs.*** The Carolina Manufacturing Company is considering an investment in a new project that requires an outlay of $1050 with cash flows over the 3-year life of the project as follows:

Year 1		Year 2		Year 3	
Pr	CFAT	Pr	CFAT	Pr	CFAT
.10	$700	.10	$700	.20	$1100
.20	600	.30	600	.50	1000
.40	500	.40	500	.20	700
.30	300	.20	400	.10	300

The appropriate discount rate is 11 percent; ignore the ITC.
    a.   Calculate the expected $\overline{CFAT_t}$ and the standard deviation for each of the three periods.
    b.   What is the expected $\overline{NPV}$ of the project?
    c.   If the successive cash flows are perfectly independent, what is the project's variability (σ)?
    d.   If the successive cash flows are perfectly correlated, what is the project's standard deviation (σ)? Compare this answer with the one obtained in (c). Why the difference?
    e.   What is the probability that the NPV will be greater than zero if: (1) perfect independence is assumed; and (2) perfect correlation is assumed?
    f.   Assuming the project's CFATs are independent, should the investment be accepted or rejected? Explain your answer.

14.6. ***CONDITIONAL PROBABILITY.*** Suntide Canning is considering buying land, irrigating it, and harvesting a new hybrid lemon-orange. Their best estimate of $CFAT_0$ is $-\$700$, the required rate of return is 13 percent, and the CFATs and associated probabilities for the 2-year project are provided on the next page.
    a.   Use NPV to determine a joint probability distribution for this investment.
    b.   Find the project's $\overline{NPV}$.
    c.   Find the project's σ.
    d.   Find the project's probability of success.
    e.   Should this be considered an acceptable investment proposal? Why?

Year 1		Year 2	
Initial Probability Pr_1	$CFAT_1$	Conditional Probability $Pr_{2/1}$	$CFAT_2$
.20	$600	.30	$1000
		.40	800
		.30	600
.30	400	.50	900
		.50	500
.30	200	.50	700
		.50	500
.20	0	.30	500
		.40	300
		.30	100

14.7. *CAPITAL RATIONING AND RISK ANALYSIS.* Huron Industries is faced with several possible capital expenditure projects, along with a one-period capital rationing constraint of $300,000. The following $CFAT_0$s, $\overline{NPV}$s and σs exist (assume all distributions are normal and the projects are independent of each other).

Project	$CFAT_0$	$\overline{NPV}$	σ
A	$100,000	$25,000	$14,000
B	50,000	15,000	15,000
C	100,000	30,000	20,000
D	150,000	25,000	11,000
E	50,000	10,000	5,000

a. Calculate the appropriate profitability indexes and (ignoring risk or σ), determine the most appropriate set of projects, given the budget constraint.

b. Calculate the probability that each project will have an NPV ≥ 0. Which projects would you select if you wanted to minimize risk?

c. Calculate the coefficient of variation for each project. By comparing these and the probability of the NPV ≥ 0, what can we say about the relationship between these two measures of risk?

d. Based on everything, which set of projects do you believe should be chosen? Why?

14.8. *CAPITAL BUDGETING DECISIONS IN A PORTFOLIO CONTEXT.* Westside Bakery has one product line—breads. It is considering adding cakes and pies. Ignoring any complementary or substitution effects, the expected $\overline{NPV}$ and standard deviation for each project are as follows:

Item	NPV	σ
Breads	$200	$80
Cakes	100	50
Pies	50	10

Cakes and breads, or pies and breads, are complementary goods, since market tests show that customers purchasing cakes or pies often purchase bread as well. Cakes and pies, however, are known to be substitute goods. Correlation coefficients between the expected $\overline{NPV}$s are as follows:

Item	Breads	Cakes	Pies
Breads	1.00	—	—
Cakes	.40	1.00	—
Pies	.50	− .80	1.00

a. If the addition of cakes (with the expected $\overline{NPV}$ and standard deviation given above of $100 and $50) increases the $\overline{NPV}$ of breads to $250 (but does not influence its standard deviation of $80), compute the portfolio mean and standard deviation for the two-product company. Based on these results, should Westside offer cakes to its customers?

b. If pies are also added, the $\overline{NPV}$ of breads will increase to $300 (with a σ of $80), but the $\overline{NPV}$ of cakes will decrease to $75 (with a σ of $50). The $\overline{NPV}$ and standard deviation of the pies are $50 and $10 respectively. Should pies, cakes, and breads be sold?

14.9. *SELECTING PORTFOLIOS OF PROJECTS.* Miller Hardware, a regional chain, is considering a number of capital expenditures. Based on all the acceptable projects, management has been able to put together these combinations (portfolios) of projects (see next page):

a. Plot the portfolios and determine which ones dominate.

b. Without making any calculations, which portfolio do you believe should be selected? Why? What does this say about your risk-return preferences?

Project Portfolio	NPV (Millions)	σ (Millions)
Existing	$275	$250
A	250	140
B	260	200
C	130	70
D	375	300
E	190	150
F	330	190
G	55	50

    c. Calculate the coefficient of variation for each portfolio. Would you change the decision reached in (b) on the basis of this new information? Why or why not?

14.10. *SENSITIVITY ANALYSIS.* Dateline Financial Industries has recently completed the evaluation of a new project that requires an outlay of $100,000 and will last for 10 years, with no terminal value. Dateline estimates the CFATs will be $20,000 per year, the appropriate MCC for this project is 10 percent, and there is no ITC.

    a. What is the NPV of the project?

    b. After calculating the NPV, Dateline's finance committee became concerned about the reasonableness of the estimates employed in (a). Accordingly, they requested further information based on the following assumptions:

        (1) The initial outlay is either 120 percent or 80 percent of the original estimate. (For simplicity, assume this does not influence depreciation per year or the yearly CFATs of $20,000.)

        (2) The annual CFATs are either 120 percent or 80 percent of the original estimate.

        (3) The MCC is low and should be 120 percent of the original estimates, or it is high and should be only 80 percent of the original.

        (4) The life of the project may be as short as 8 years or as long as 12 years. (For simplicity, assume this does not influence depreciation per year or the yearly CFATs of $20,000.)

Determine the project's NPV under *all* these conditions and prepare sensitivity graphs; indicate which of the four variables has the greatest impact on NPV, and which has the least effect. Briefly explain how such information would be used in a capital budgeting decision.

SELECTED REFERENCES

Ang, James S., and Wilbur G. Lewellen. "Risk Adjustment in Capital Investment Project Evaluations."*Financial Management* 11 (summer 1982), pp. 5–14.

Ashton, D. J., and D. R. Atkins. "Interactions in Corporate Financing and Investment Decisions—Implications for Capital Budgeting: A Further Comment." *Journal of Finance* 33 (December 1978), pp. 1447–1453.

Baum, Sanford, Robert C. Carlson, and James V. Jucker. "Some Problems in Applying the Continuous Portfolio Selection Model to the Discrete Capital Budgeting Problem." *Journal of Financial and Quantitative Analysis* 13 (June 1978), pp. 333–344.

Baron, David P. "On the Utility Theoretic Foundation of Mean-Variance Analysis." *Journal of Finance* 32 (December 1977), pp. 1683–1698.

Bar-Yosef, Sasson, and Roger Mesnick. 'On Some Definitional Problems with the Method of Certainty Equivalents." *Journal of Finance* 32 (December 1977), pp. 1729–1737.

Bey, Roger P., and R. Burr Porter. "An Evaluation of Capital Budgeting Portfolio Models Using Simulated Data." *Engineering Economist* 23 (fall 1977), pp. 41–65.

———, and J. Clayton Singleton. "Auto Correlated Cash Flows and the Selection of a Portfolio of Capital Assets." *Decision Science* 19 (October 1978), pp. 640–657.

Bogue, Marcus C., and Richard Roll. "Capital Budgeting of Risky Projects with Imperfect Markets for Physical Capital." *Journal of Finance* 29 (May 1974), pp. 601–613.

Bonini, Charles P. "Comment on Formulating Correlated Cash Flow Streams." *Engineering Economist* 20 (spring 1975), pp. 209–214.

Book, L. D. "Correct Procedures for the Evaluation of Risky Cash Outflows." *Journal of Financial and Quantitative Analysis* 17 (June 1982), pp. 287–300.

Booth, Laurence D. "Correct Procedures for the Evaluation of Risky Cash Outflows." *Journal of Financial and Quantitative Analysis* 17 (June 1982), pp. 287–300.

Bower, Richard S., and Jeffrey M. Jenks. "Divisional Screening Rates." *Financial Management* 4 (autumn 1975), pp. 42–49.

Bussey, Lynn E., and G. T. Stevens, Jr. "Formulating Correlated Cash Flow Streams." *Engineering Economist* 18 (fall 1972), pp. 1–30.

———, and ———. "Net Present Value From Complex Cash Flow Streams by Simulation." *AIIE Transactions* 3 (March 1971), pp. 81–89.

Copeland, Thomas E., and J. Fred Weston. *Financial Theory and Corporate Policy.* Reading, Mass.: Addison-Wesley, 1979, chap. 4.

Fama, Eugene F. "Risk-Adjusted Discount Rates and Capital Budgeting Under Uncertainty." *Journal of Financial Economics* 5 (August 1977), pp. 3–24.

Gehr, Adam K. "Risk-Adjusted Capital Budgeting Using Arbitrage. " *Financial Management* 10 (winter 1981), pp. 14–19.

Gitman, Lawrence J. "Capturing Risk Exposure in the Evaluation of Capital Budgeting Projects." *Engineering Economist* 22 (summer 1977), pp. 261–276.

———, and John R. Forrester, Jr. "A Survey of Capital Budgeting Techniques Used by Major U.S. Firms," *Financial Management* 6 (fall 1977), pp. 66–71.

Graver, Robert R. "Investment Policy Implications of the Capital Asset Pricing Model." *Journal of Finance* 36 (March 1981), pp. 127–141.

Hamada, Robert S. "Portfolio Analysis, Market Equilibrium and Corporation Finance." *Journal of Finance* 24 (March 1969), pp. 13–31.

Hertz, David B. "Risk Analysis in Capital Investment." *Harvard Busines Review* 42 (January–February 1964), pp. 95–106.

Hayes, Robert H. "Incorporating Risk Aversion into Risk Analysis." *Engineering Economist* 20 (winter 1975), pp. 99–121.

Hillier, Frederick S. "The Derivation of Probabilistic Information for the Evaluation of Risky Investments." *Management Science* 9 (April 1963), pp. 443–457.

Hong, Hai, and Alfred Rappaport. "Debt Capacity, Optimal Capital Structure, and Capital Budgeting." *Financial Management* 7 (autumn 1978), pp. 7–11.

Hsaio, Frank S. T., and James W. Smith. "An Analytical Approach to Sensitivity Analysis of the Internal Rate of Return Model." *Journal of Finance* 33 (May 1978), pp. 645–649.

Joy, O. Maurice, and Jerry O. Bradley. "A Note on Sensitivity Analysis of Rates of Return." *Journal of Finance* 28 (December 1973), pp. 1255–1261.

Keeley, Robert, and Randolph Westerfield. "A Problem in Probability Distribution Techniques for Capital Budgeting." *Journal of Finance* 27 (June 1972), pp. 703–709.

Lambrix, Robert J., and Surendra S. Singhvi. "How to Set Volume-Sensitive ROI Targets." *Harvard Business Review* 59 (March–April 1981), pp. 174–179.

Lessard, Donald R., and Richard S. Bower. "An Operational Approach to Risk Screening." *Journal of Finance* 28 (May 1973), pp. 321–338.

Levy, Hiam, and Marshall Sarnat. "The Portfolio Analysis of Multiperiod Capital Investment Under Conditions of Risk." *Engineering Economist* 18 (fall 1970), pp. 1–19.

Lewellen, Wilber G., and Michael S. Long. "Simulation Versus Single-Value Estimates in Capital Expenditure Analysis." *Decision Sciences* 3 (October 1972), pp. 19–33.

Lockett, A. Geoffrey, and Anthony E. Gear. "Multistage Capital Budgeting Under Uncertainty." *Journal of Financial and Quantitative Analysis* 10 (March 1975), pp. 21–36.

McBride, R.D. "Finding the Integer Efficient Frontier for Quadratic Capital Budgeting Problems." *Journal of Financial and Quantitative Analysis* 16 (June 1981), pp. 247–253.

Magee, John F. "How to Use Decision Trees in Capital Investment." *Harvard Business Review* 42 (September–October 1964), pp. 79–96.

Martin, John D., and David F. Scott. "Debt Capacity and the Capital Budgeting Decision: A Revisitation." *Financial Management* 9 (spring 1980), pp. 23–26.

Michaud, Richard O. "Risk Policy and Long-Term Investment." *Journal of Financial and Quantitative Analysis* 16 (June 1981), pp. 147–165.

Miller, Edward M. "Uncertainty-Induced Bias in Capital Budgeting." *Financial Management* 7 (autumn 1978), pp. 12–18.

Myers, Stewart C., and Stuart M. Turnbull. "Capital Budgeting and the Capital Asset Pricing Model: Good News and Bad News." *Journal of Finance* 32 (May 1977), pp. 321–333.

Oblak, David J., and Roy J. Helm., Jr. "Survey and Analysis of Capital Budgeting Methods Used by Multinationals." *Financial Management* 9 (winter 1980), pp. 37–41.

Osteryoung, Jerome S., Elton Scott, and Gordon S. Roberts. "Selecting Capital Projects with the Coefficient of Variation." *Financial Management* 6 (summer 1977), pp. 59–64.

Rendleman, Richard J., Jr. "Ranking Errors in CAPM Capital Budgeting Applications." *Financial Management* 7 (winter 1978), pp. 40–44.

Robichek, Alexander A. "Interpreting the Results of Risk Analysis." *Journal of Finance* 30 (December 1975), pp. 1384–1386.

————, and Stewart Myers. "Conceptual Problems with the Use of Risk-Adjusted Discount Rates," *Journal of Finance* 21 (December 1966), pp. 727–730.

Rubinstein, Mark E. "A Mean-Variance Synthesis of Corporate Financial Theory." *Journal of Finance* 28 (March, 1973), pp. 167–182.

Schall, Lawrence D., and Gary L. Sundem. "Capital Budgeting Methods and Risk: A Further Analysis." *Financial Management* 9 (spring 1980), pp. 7–11.

———, and William R. Geijsbeek, Jr. "Survey and Analysis of Capital Budgeting Methods." *Journal of Finance* 33 (March 1978), pp. 281–287.

Senbet, Lemma W., and Howard E. Thompson. "The Equivalence of Alternative Mean-Variance Capital Budgeting Models." *Journal of Finance* 33 (May 1978), pp. 395–401.

Shapiro, Alan C. "Capital Budgeting for the Multinational Corporation." *Financial Management* 7 (summer 1978), pp. 7–16.

Tuttle, Donald L., and Robert H. Litzenberger. "Leverage, Diversification and Capital Market Effects on a Risk-Adjusted Capital Budgeting Framework." *Journal of Finance* 23 (June 1968), pp. 427–443.

Van Horne, James C. "An Application of the CAPM to Divisional Required Returns." *Financial Management* 9 (spring 1980), pp. 14–19.

———, "Capital Budgeting Decisions Involving Combinations of Risky Investments." *Management Science* 13 (October 1966), pp. 84–92.

Wagle, B. "A Statistical Analysis of Risk in Capital Investment Projects." *Operational Research Quarterly* 18 (March 1967), pp. 13–33.

Weston, J. Fred. "Investment Decisions Using the Capital Asset Pricing Model." *Financial Management* 2 (spring 1973), pp. 25–33.

———, and Nai-Ju Chen. "A Note On Cpaital Budgeting and the Three R's." *Financial Management* 9 (spring 1980), pp. 12–13.

Appendix 14A

The Certainty Equivalent Method

Certainty Equivalent Method

The certainty equivalent method of incorporating risk analysis into capital budgeting is based on the belief that risky CFATs should be converted to an amount that is known with complete certainty. The following steps are employed:

Step 1. Determine the mean $\overline{CFAT}$ per period t, $\overline{CFAT}_t$.

Step 2. Analyze the riskiness of the CFATs for each period, using some measure of the CFATs' dispersion and/or other pertinent information.

Step 3. Determine a certainty equivalent factor, α_t, for each $\overline{CFAT}_t$ which reflects the degree of risk as determined by the financial manager. α_t is assumed to range from 0 to 1, with a value of 1 indicating complete certainty and lower values indicating greater uncertainty in the expected $\overline{CFATs}$ per year.[1]

Step 4. Calculate the expected $\overline{NPV}$ using a risk-free rate of interest:

$$\overline{NPV} = \sum_{t=0}^{n} \frac{\alpha_t \, \overline{CFAT}_t}{(1 + R_F)^t} \tag{14A.1}$$

where α_t = the certainty equivalent factor in year t

$\overline{CFAT}_t$ = the mean or expected CFAT in year t

R_F = the risk-free rate of interest

n = the number of time periods

---

[1] If the certainty equivalent coefficient, α_t, is not bounded—$0 \leq \alpha_t \leq 1$—then α_t does not exhibit a unique positive association with risk. See Sasson Bar-Yosef and Roger Mesnick, "On Some Definitional Problems with the Method of Certainty Equivalents," *Journal of Finance* 32 (December 1977), pp. 1729–1737.

Three points need to be made concerning the certainty equivalent method. First, theoretically, this approach is more logical than risk-adjusted discount rates, since it separates the timing of the cash flows from the question of risk. The certainty equivalent approach deals with risk separately, since it explicitly adjusts the numerator of Equation 14A.1 (the risky cash flows) to certain cash flows. Second, the appropriate discount rate to employ with the certainty equivalent method is the risk-free rate, R_F. Finally, implementation is more difficult, since certainty equivalent factors must be determined for each year. While this may not be a big problem for a few years, for long-lived projects of, say, 20 years, the task is much more arduous.

Suppose a firm is evaluating a capital budgeting decision employing the expected cash flow data from Table 14.3. The firm has decided that the relevant certainty equivalent factors are $\alpha_1 = 0.939$, $\alpha_2 = 0.882$, and $\alpha_3 = 0.829$, while the risk-free rate is 8 percent. To calculate the expected NPV, we have:

$$
\begin{aligned}
\overline{NPV} &= (\alpha_1)\ (\overline{CFAT_1})\ (PVIF_{8\%,\,1\,yr}) + (\alpha_2)\ (\overline{CFAT_2})\ (PVIF_{8\%,\,2\,yr}) + (\alpha_3)\ (\overline{CFAT_3}) \\
&\quad (PVIF_{8\%,\,3\,yr}) - \overline{CFAT_0} \\
&= (0.939)\ (\$19,000)\ (0.926) + (0.882)\ (\$20,000)\ (0.857) + (0.829) \\
&\quad (\$25,000)\ (0.794) - \$40,000 \\
&= \$16,520.77 + \$15,117.48 + \$16,455.65 - \$40,000 \\
&= \$8,093.90
\end{aligned}
$$

Since $\overline{NPV}$ is greater than 0, the project should be accepted.

Risk-Adjusted Discount Rates and Implied Certainty Equivalents

The certainty equivalent method separates the timing of the cash flows from their riskiness. This is in sharp contrast to the risk-adjusted discount rate approach, which combines the treatment of risk with the timing aspects, and by implication assumes that risk increases simply as a function of time. To see this, let us examine the present value of an expected $\overline{CFAT}$ in period t using both methods:

$$
\text{Certainty equivalent: } PV = \frac{\alpha_t\ \overline{CFAT_t}}{(1 + R_F)^t} \tag{14A.2}
$$

$$
\text{Risk-adjusted discount rate: } PV = \frac{\overline{CFAT_t}}{(1 + RADR_j)^t} \tag{14A.3}
$$

If both methods are to give the same result, we can set them equal to each other, so:

$$
\frac{\alpha_t\ \overline{CFAT_t}}{(1 + R_F)^t} = \frac{\overline{CFAT_t}}{(1 + RADR)^t} \tag{14A.4}
$$

Since $\overline{CFAT}_t$ is on both sides of Equation 14A.4, it can be cancelled out, and then we can solve for α_t, which produces:

$$(\alpha_t) \, \frac{1}{(1 + R_F)^t} = \frac{1}{(1 + RADR_j)^t}$$

$$(\alpha_t) \, PVIF_{\text{riskless asset}_t} = PVIF_{\text{risky asset}_t}$$

$$\alpha_t = \frac{PVIF_{\text{risky asset}_t}}{PVIF_{\text{riskless asset}_t}} \qquad (14A.5)$$

To illustrate, suppose we are calculating the implied certainty equivalent factor for a cash flow expected 10 years from now, when the risk-free rate is 5 percent while the risky rate is 7 percent. The PVIF factors found in Table A.3 are 0.614 and 0.508 for the risk-free and risky rates, respectively. Therefore, the implied certainty equivalent factor, α_{10}, is:

$$\alpha_{10} = \frac{PVIF_{7\%, \, 10 \, \text{yr}}}{PVIF_{5\%, \, 10 \, \text{yr}}} = \frac{0.508}{0.614} = 0.827$$

This value and the calculation of a number of other implied certainty equivalent factors are presented in Table 14A.1 and graphed in Figure 14A.1. In examining the table, note that the implied certainty equivalent factors (columns 5, 6, and 7) decrease both as a function of time and as a function of the differential between the risk-free and the risky discount rates. In other words, a given α_t necessary to equate the RADR method and the certainty equivalent method is a function of *both* time and risk.

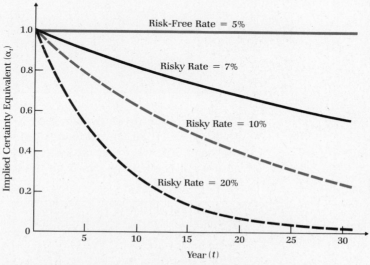

Figure 14A.1   Implied Certainty Equivalents (α_t) over Time from Using Risk-Adjusted Discount Rates.

TABLE 14A.1
Implied Certainty
Equivalent Factors (α_t)
Necessary to Equate
Selected Risk-Adjusted
Discount Rates (RADR)
with Their Certainty
Equivalents over Time
(Risk-Free Rate, 5
Percent)

| | Discount Rates | | | | Implied Certainty Equivalent Factors (α_t) | | |
| | Risk-Free | Risky | | | | | |
t	$PVIF_{5\%,t}$ (1)	$PVIF_{7\%,t}$ (2)	$PVIF_{10\%,t}$ (3)	$PVIF_{20\%,t}$ (4)	7% [(2)÷(1)] (5)	10% [(3)÷(1)] (6)	20% [(4)÷(1)] (7)
0	1.000	1.000	1.000	1.000	1.000	1.000	1.000
1	0.952	0.935	0.909	0.833	0.982	0.955	0.875
10	0.614	0.508	0.386	0.162	0.827	0.629	0.264
20	0.377	0.258	0.149	0.026	0.684	0.395	0.069
30	0.231	0.131	0.057	0.004	0.567	0.247	0.017

PROBLEMS

14A.1. *CERTAINTY EQUIVALENTS.* Marshall Oil is contemplating a capital expenditure project whose projected cash flows are as follows:

Year	State of the Economy	$CFAT_t$ ($ Millions)	Probability
0	Any state	−16.0	1.0
1	Good	6.5	0.1
	Average	6.0	0.8
	Bad	5.5	0.1
2	Good	7.1	0.15
	Average	6.5	0.7
	Bad	5.9	0.15
3	Good	6.2	0.2
	Average	5.5	0.5
	Bad	5.2	0.3
4	Good	6.5	0.3
	Average	5.6	0.4
	Bad	4.7	0.3
5	Good	6.4	0.2
	Average	5.3	0.4
	Bad	4.2	0.4

To derive certainty equivalent factors for a capital expenditure analysis, Marshall Oil calculates the coefficient of variation, of the cash inflows for each year t, CV_t, and assigns certainty equivalent coefficients based on the following schedule:

CV_t	α_t
0.00 to 0.0099	1.00
0.01 to 0.039	0.85
0.04 to 0.059	0.70
0.06 to 0.099	0.55
0.10 to 0.139	0.40
Greater than 0.139	0.25

a. Calculate the mean, standard deviation, and coefficient of variation of CFATs for each year. Determine the appropriate certainty equivalent coefficients from the schedule above.

b. Assuming the risk-free rate is 6 percent, use $\overline{NPV}$ to determine if Marshall Oil should undertake the project?

14A.2. ***RISK-ADJUSTED DISCOUNT RATES AND IMPLIED CERTAINTY EQUIVALENTS.*** Southern California Construction Company usually employs the risk-adjusted discount rate method for evaluating proposed capital expenditures. At the present time, Southern California Construction is considering the purchase of some road graders. The equipment would require an outlay of $75,000 and produce CFATs of $20,000 per year for each of 5 years. It is estimated that the equipment will have an after-tax terminal value of $15,000 at the end of 5 years. The risk-free rate is 7 percent, and the project's specific risk premium is 8 percent. The investment tax credit does not apply.

a. Using the risk-adjusted discount rate method, should the project be accepted?

b. In conversations with other financial executives, the financial manager of Southern California Construction has learned that the risk-adjusted discount rate and the certainty equivalent methods can give the same answers to an NPV problem. However, the financial manager does not know how to establish the proper certainty equivalent factors, α_t, that will produce the same NPV using that approach.

(1) Determine the appropriate yearly certainty equivalent factors for the project which are equivalent to the use of a 15 percent risk-adjusted discount rate. (Carry your calculations to five decimal places for greater accuracy.)

(2) Calculate the NPV using the certainty equivalent factors obtained above. Does this figure agree (except for a rounding error) with the NPV calculated using the RADR method?

c. Evaluate the certainty equivalent factors found in b(1), and explain why the use of RADR is often criticized for adjusting for *both* time and risk, rather than risk alone.

Appendix 14B

Risk Analysis with PI and IRR Techniques

Throughout this chapter, the discussion of risk analysis has been couched in terms of NPV; yet in practice, other capital budgeting techniques can be, and often are, used to evaluate such expenditures. In particular, rather than NPV, financial managers can assess capital expenditure proposals by computing a profitability index (PI), or an internal rate of return (IRR). Using either of these techniques causes no special problems when the risk-adjusted discount rate (RADR) is employed for risk analysis purposes: Simply redefine k (or MCC) as the required RADR, and proceed along the lines spelled out in Equations 13.4 and 13.5. When the probability distribution approach is used, however, several procedural modifications must be introduced to accommodate the PI and IRR techniques. In this appendix we will briefly discuss and illustrate how PI and IRR can be used when risk analysis is conducted via probability distributions.

The Profitability Index and Probability Distributions

When using the profitability index, the first step in the evaluation process is the same as that for NPV—compute the expected cash flows for each year $(\overline{CFAT_t})$ and the respective standard deviations (σ_t). To do this, a CFAT probability distribution must be developed for each year of the project's life. Assume this has already been done and that management is currently evaluating a project with cash flow distributions as defined in Table 14.3. As we showed earlier, this proposal has mean cash flows and annual variability of:

Year, t	$CFAT_t$	σ_t
0	$-\$40,000$	—
1	19,000	\$4,900
2	20,000	6,325
3	25,000	7,746

Using this information, it is a simple matter to find the project's expected PI; that is:

$$\overline{PI} = \frac{\sum_{t=1}^{n} \dfrac{\overline{CFAT_t}}{(1 + k)^t}}{CFAT_0} \tag{14B.1}$$

where all the terms are as previously defined. This is the standard PI equation, except that we have specified the numerator as a mean (expected) cash flow rather than a single-point estimate. Using a 15 percent discount rate (k), we see this project has a profitability index of:

$$\overline{PI} = \frac{\overline{CFAT_1}\,(PVIF_{15\%,\,1\,yr}) + \overline{CFAT_2}\,(PVIF_{15\%,\,2\,yr}) + \overline{CFAT_3}\,(PVIF_{15\%,\,3\,yr})}{CFAT_0}$$

$$= \frac{\$19,000\,(.870) + \$20,000\,(.756) + \$25,000\,(.658)}{\$40,000}$$

$$= \frac{\$48,100}{\$40,000} = 1.2025$$

To measure overall project variability (σ) under conditions of dependent and independent cash flows, the simplest approach is to follow the procedures used with NPV. That is, determine σ for perfectly dependent and/or independent cash flows, as in Equations 14.7 and 14.8. With the project in question, this was found to be:

Dependent cash flows: $\sigma = \$14,140$

Independent cash flows: $\sigma = \$8,180$

Now, since PI is a relative measure of profitability, we define the amount of project variability for PI-evaluated projects as follows:

$$\sigma_{PI} = \frac{\sigma}{CFAT_0} \tag{14B.2}$$

When the cash flows are perfectly dependent, project variability, σ_{PI}, in our example is as follows:

$$\sigma_{PI} = \$14,140/\$40,000 = .3535$$

For completely independent cash flows:

$$\sigma_{PI} = \$8,180/\$40,000 = .2045$$

These values of project variability can now be used to find the coefficient of variation or probability of success. The coefficient of variation can be found as follows:

$$CV = \frac{\sigma_{PI}}{\overline{PI} - 1.00} \tag{14B.3}$$

Continuing our example, we have:

$$\text{Dependent cash flows: } CV = \frac{.3535}{1.2025 - 1.00} = 1.75$$

$$\text{Independent cash flows: } CV = \frac{.2045}{1.2025 - 1.00} = 1.01$$

Recall that these are identical to the CVs derived when NPV was used for project evaluation.[1]

In a similar fashion, we can find the project's probability of success; that is, since a PI of 1.0 is equal to an NPV of 0, the computed Z value is:

$$Z = \frac{\overline{PI} - 1.00}{\sigma_{PI}} \tag{14B.4}$$

For our hypothetical project, and assuming the cash flows are perfectly dependent, the computed Z value is:

$$Z = \frac{1.2025 - 1.00}{.3535}$$
$$= .2025/.3535 = .5728$$

Looking in Appendix Table A.5, it is found that the probability associated with a computed Z value of .5728 is 21.57 percent (for a one-sided distribution); therefore, the probability of success in our example is:

$$.5000 + .2157 = .7157 = 71.57\%$$

---

[1]The PI in Equation 14B.3 is reduced by the value of 1.00 in order to obtain a standardized profitability index that is comparable to an NPV of zero; a similar approach is used later in this appendix with IRR. In effect, the adjustments provide standardized accept/reject criteria across all three present-value-based evaluation models.

Of course, this too would correspond to the probability of success that would exist with the NPV procedure.

When cash flows are interdependent (moderately correlated), the mechanics are basically the same as demonstrated with NPV. That is, a conditional probability/joint probability decision tree (like that illustrated in Table 14.4) is used to find measures of risk and return; the only variation is that each branch of the decision tree is computed in terms of PI. This yields a PI joint probability distribution (as shown in Table 14B.1), which is then used to compute $\overline{PI}$ and σ_{PI}. For example, using a 15 percent discount rate and Equations 14B.1 and 14B.2, we find that the project has a $\overline{PI}$ of 1.4348 and a σ_{PI} of .4051. Likewise, from 14B.3, we see that the project has a CV of:

$$CV = \frac{.4051}{1.4348 - 1.00} = .93$$

and, from Equation 14B.4, a probability of success of:

$$Z = \frac{1.4348 - 1.00}{.4051} = 1.07$$

Probability of success $= .5005 + .3577 = 85.77\%$

Again, these values are *identical* to those derived with NPV. Therefore it is clear that the determination of expected return and project risk via a

		PI Joint Probability Distribution	
Branch (i) (from Table 14.4)		PI_i	Jt. Prob.
1		1.9414	.252
2		1.7769	.126
3		1.5850	.042
4		1.4153	.072
5		1.3056	.072
6		1.1411	.036
7		1.3423	.024
8		1.2875	.032
9		1.2327	.024
10		1.2245	.112
11		1.0052	.048
12		1.0163	.016
13		0.8792	.048
14		0.7421	.096

TABLE 14B.1
A Joint Probability Distribution of Profitability Indexes

profitability index corresponds very closely to that used with net present value; in fact, many, but not all, of the steps are identical.

The Internal Rate of Return and Probability Distributions

When dealing with interdependent (moderately correlated) cash flows, finding the project's expected IRR and variability is accomplished in the same way as with NPV and PI. That is, based on a conditional probability decision tree, a separate internal rate of return is computed for each "branch" so that an IRR joint probability distribution can be created, like the one illustrated in Table 14B.2. The expected internal rate of return ($\overline{IRR}$) for the proposal is determined directly from this conditional probability distribution, as is a measure of the project's variability (σ_{IRR}); for example, the \$120,000, 3-year project depicted in Table 14B.2 has an $\overline{IRR}$ of 36.49 percent and a σ_{IRR} of 20.52 percent. From this information, and given the firm's required rate of return (k), the project's coefficient of variation can be found as follows:

$$CV = \frac{\sigma_{IRR}}{\overline{IRR} - k} \qquad (14B.5)$$

$$= \frac{.2052}{.3649 - .1500} = .96$$

Likewise, given a NPV = 0 (or a PI = 1.0) is equivalent to an IRR = k, the proposal's probability of success is derived from the following Z value:

$$Z = \frac{\overline{IRR} - k}{\sigma_{IRR}} \qquad (14B.6)$$

$$Z = \frac{.3649 - .1500}{.2052} = 1.05$$

Probability of success = .5000 + .3531 = 85.31%

Note that when IRR is used as the basis of evaluation, there is slight variation in the CV and probability of success measures in relation to the values found with NPV and PI. That is, the CV comes out fractionally higher (while the computed Z value is fractionally lower) than that reported with NPV or PI. Such results occur because, other things being equal, a distribution of IRRs will be more skewed to the left than a comparable distribution of, say, NPVs. As a result, the mean IRR is lower and the σ_{IRR} is higher than they would otherwise be.[2] However, in most cases, this bias is insignificant, and given the uncertainty embedded in

---

[2] For an explanation of the inherent bias in IRR distributions, see Robert Keeley and Randolph Westerfield, "A Problem in Probability Distribution Techniques for Capital Budgeting," *Journal of Finance* 27 (June 1972), pp. 703–709; and Alexander A. Robichek, "Interpreting the Results of Risk Analysis," *Journal of Finance* 30 (December 1975), pp. 1384–1386.

TABLE 14B.2
A Joint Probability
Distribution of
Internal Rates of
Return

Branch (i) (from Table 14.4)	IRR Joint Probability Distribution	
	IRR_i	Jt. Prob.$_i$
1	60.08%	.252
2	54.68	.126
3	47.63	.042
4	38.06	.072
5	33.04	.072
6	24.30	.036
7	31.84	.024
8	29.52	.032
9	27.08	.024
10	26.41	.112
11	15.28	.048
12	15.86	.016
13	7.82	.048
14	− 2.24	.096

the forecasted cash flows to begin with, should not be a cause for concern.

The same bias is also present when using IRR to evaluate capital projects that have perfectly dependent or completely independent cash flows. Several approaches can be used with such cash flows, but perhaps the most straightforward procedure is to employ a decision tree (construct a joint probability distribution) to derive both $\overline{IRR}$ and σ_{IRR}. Using this approach, the number of "branches" in the joint probability distribution will depend on whether the cash flow is dependent or independent. In the former case, the number of branches will be defined by the number of possible outcomes in the first year, since once we know the first-year results, the second and subsequent years' cash flows are supposedly known with perfect certainty (they have conditional probabilities of 1.0). Thus, the highest or best outcome in the second and subsequent years will be associated with just one outcome in the first year: the highest or best result. The same is true for the next-to-best outcome, and so on.

With independent cash flows, any outcome is possible in any year—more specifically, any outcome in year n can be associated with any outcome in year $n - 1$, and so forth. As a result, the number of "branches" is defined by the following factorial: number of outcomes possible in year 1 $\times$ number of outcomes possible in year 2 $\times \cdots \times$ number of outcomes possible in year n. For example, with the $40,000, 3-year capital project specified in Table 14.3, there are two outcomes denoted in the probability distribution for year 1 and three each for the distributions in years 2 and 3, so there will be 18 "branches" ($2 \times 3 \times 3$) of possible IRR outcomes in the joint probability distribution.

We can use a project whose cash flows are assumed to be perfectly independent to illustrate this process. Table 14.3 provides the CFAT probability distributions of such a project. From this information, we can construct an 18-branch IRR joint probability distribution, with IRRs ranging from a high of 50.75 percent (for branch 1) to a low of 0 percent (for branch 18). Using this distribution, we find an expected IRR of 25.92 percent and a σ_{IRR} of 11.24 percent, which is comparable to the σ measure obtained from Equation 14.8. Now, employing Equations 14B.5 and 14B.6, it is a simple task to find the project's coefficient of variation and probability of success, respectively. That is:

$$CV = \frac{.1124}{.2592 - .1500} = 1.03$$

$$\text{and} \quad Z = \frac{.2592 - .1500}{.1124} = .97$$

Probability of success = $.5000 + .3340 = 83.40\%$

Once again, it is clear that there is a slight but insignificant bias in these risk measures in relation to those we found with NPV and PI. With a few relatively modest procedural modifications, it is possible to use IRR, as well the profitability index, to evaluate the risk-return characteristics of proposed capital expenditure projects.

PROBLEMS

14B.1. *PROBABILITY DISTRIBUTIONS: INDEPENDENT CFATs.* San Antonio Steel has determined the following discrete probability distributions of CFATs for a particular capital project:

Year 1		Year 2		Year 3	
Pr	CFAT	Pr	CFAT	Pr	CFAT
.1	$100	.2	$300	.1	$ 500
.2	200	.4	400	.3	600
.3	300	.3	500	.3	700
.4	400	.1	600	.3	1000

Assume the CFATs are completely independent, the initial cost of the project is $1000, the investment tax credit is not in effect, and the appropriate discount rate is 10 percent.
  a. Determine the mean and standard deviation of the yearly CFATs.
  b. What is the expected $\overline{PI}$ of the project?
  c. If the total distribution is approximately normal and con-

tinuous, what is the probability that the PI will be greater than 1.0?

d. Instead of PI, use the project's internal rate of return to assess its risk and return. Compute the proposal's expected $\overline{IRR}$ and σ_{IRR}. Given this information, find the project's probability of success.

14B.2. **PROBABILITY DISTRIBUTIONS: INDEPENDENT AND CORRELATED CFATs.** Carolina Manufacturing is considering an investment in a new project that requires an initial outlay of $1050, and that provides cash flows over the 3-year life of the project as follows:

Year 1		Year 2		Year 3	
Pr	CFAT	Pr	CFAT	Pr	CFAT
.10	$700	.10	$700	.20	$1100
.20	600	.30	600	.50	1000
.40	500	.40	500	.20	700
.30	300	.20	400	.10	300

The appropriate discount rate is 11 percent; ignore ITC.

a. Calculate $\overline{CFAT}_t$ and the standard deviation σ_t, for each of the 3 years.

b. What is the $\overline{PI}$ of the project?

c. If the successive cash flows are perfectly independent, what is the project's standard deviation (σ_{PI})?

d. If the successive cash flows are perfectly correlated, what is the project's standard deviation (σ_{PI})?

e. Find the project's coefficient of variation (CV) given that cash flows are (1) completely dependent, and (2) perfectly independent.

f. What is the probability that the PI will be greater than 1.0 if (1) perfect correlation is assumed, and (2) perfect independence is assumed?

14B.3. **CONDITIONAL PROBABILITY.** Suntide Canning is considering buying land, irrigating it, and harvesting a new hybrid lemon-orange. Their best estimate of $CFAT_0$ is $-$700, the required rate of return is 13 percent, and the CFATs and associated probabilities for the 2-year project are provided on the next page.

a. Use IRR to determine a joint probability distribution for this investment.

b. Find the project's expected IRR.

Year 1		Year 2	
Initial Probability Pr_1	CFAT($)	Conditional Probability $Pr_{2/1}$	CFAT($)
.20	800	.30	1000
		.40	800
		.30	600
.30	600	.50	900
		.50	500
.30	500	.50	700
		.50	500
.20	400	.30	500
		.40	400
		.30	300

c. Find the project's σ_{IRR}.
d. Find the project's probability of success.
e. Would you consider this an acceptable investment proposal? Why?

15

Evaluation of External Growth: Mergers and Acquisitions

A firm can achieve growth and diversification through either internal or external expansion. External growth refers to expansion resulting from the acquisition of another firm, or division of a firm. The term *merger* is employed to describe the general process by which one firm acquires the assets of another firm. In this chapter, we take the point of view of the financial manager of firm X who is analyzing the possible purchase of firm Y. Since the firm's objective is to maximize the wealth of its shareholders, a merger should be pursued only if it assists in achieving this goal. A merger decision is an investment decision in which we want to find the maximum price to pay for a firm or some of its assets. As such, it represents another (special) application of the capital budgeting concept. In merger analysis, the dollar amounts involved are usually quite large and expertise may be required in activities quite different from those typically considered by the firm's financial manager. For these reasons, prediction errors may be substantial. Here we will examine how to value both cash and stock financed mergers, as well as some of the administrative considerations and strategies, such as leveraged buyouts, associated with mergers. We begin by looking at the merger record in the United States and then examine some of the reasons for merging.

Mergers and Acquisitions

The Merger Record

As Table 15.1 shows, the number of mergers in the United States has averaged over 1400 per year for the 1967–1982 period. During some years, particularly when economic and stock market conditions were buoyant (like 1968 and 1969), there have been over 1700 mergers per year. Alternatively, in 1975 there were fewer than 1000. During the merger

TABLE 15.1

Number of Mergers in the United States 1967–1982

Year	Number of Mergers
1967	1354
1968	1829
1969	1712
1970	1318
1971	1269
1972	1263
1973	1064
1974	1088
1975	859
1976	1058
1977	1139
1978	1346
1979	1420
1980	1404
1981	2231
1982	2182
Average per year	1408

SOURCE: *Mergers & Acquisitions*, various issues.

wave of the mid- and late sixties, many of the acquisitions were by conglomerates. The multibillion-dollar firms that grew out of that wave include Gulf & Western, Litton, Tenneco, Transamerica, and ITT (International Telephone and Telegraph). Since then, many other firms have also employed mergers as part of their total growth strategy. This trend continues as evidenced by the increasing merger activity in recent years.

Some of the mergers have involved smaller firms, but in many cases large firms have acquired other sizable firms. As Table 15.2 shows, there were 10 acquisitions during 1980, 1981, and 1982 valued at over $2.0 billion each. Included was the largest acquisition of all time—du Pont's

TABLE 15.2

Major Mergers, 1980, 1981, and 1982

Acquiring Firm	Acquired Firm	Value (in Millions)
E. I. du Pont (1981)	Conoco, Inc.	$6,820
U.S. Steel Corporation (1982)	Marathon Oil	6,150
Connecticut General Corporation (1982)	INA Corporation	4,300
Occidental Petroleum (1982)	Cities Service Company	4,202
Norfolk & Western Railway (1982)	Southern Railway	2,900
Elf Aquitaine (1981)	Texasgulf, Inc.	2,800
Freeport Minerals (1981)	McMoRan Oil & Gas	2,540
Kraft, Inc. (1980)	Dart, Inc.	2,500
Kuwait Petroleum (1981)	Santa Fe International	2,500
Sun Company (1980)	Texas Pacific Oil	2,300

SOURCE: *Mergers & Acquisitions*, various issues.

purchase of Conoco for almost $7 billion! The sheer size of the acquisitions, and their importance to the purchaser's future financial performance make merger analysis a crucial capital budgeting topic. Clearly, poorly thought out acquisitions can plague a firm for many years to come, while successful acquisitions can result in significant returns to the acquiring firm's shareholders.

Reasons for Merging From our discussion of valuation in Chapter 7, we know a stock's value is given by:

$$P_0 = \sum_{t=1}^{\infty} \frac{D_t}{(1 + k_s)^t} \tag{15.1}$$

where P_0 is the price of the stock at time $t = 0$, D_t is the dividend expected at the end of year t, and k_s is the required rate of return on the stock given its risk. Mergers that provide financial benefits must result in a combined firm with a higher valuation than the simple sum of the respective premerger market values of the firms. The basic conditions for wealth-maximizing external growth from merging are the following:

1. An increase in the level of expected cash flows and dividends.
2. A reduction in risk and therefore the required rate of return, k_s.
3. If the target (or acquired) firm is undervalued.
4. If the acquiring firm is overvalued and able to finance the merger with its own common stock.

Conditions 3 and 4 may exist occasionally, but their widespread occurrence would indicate that the financial market is inefficient in valuing one or both of the firms. Available empirical evidence does not suggest much inefficiency exists, so we focus on the first two factors, increased cash flows and dividends or reduced risk, as the primary benefits to be realized from successful mergers. In what follows, we examine the major benefits often expected due to a merger. As we will see, some of the reasons often cited for merging do not appear to produce these benefits. As such, some mergers do not appear to be in the current shareholders' best interests.

Economies of Scale and Operating Economies. *Economies of scale* involve "indivisibilities" that can provide increasing returns if spread over a larger number of units of production. In a manufacturing operation with sizable production runs, the use of large automated equipment may lead to lower per unit costs than the use of smaller manual equipment. Similarly, there may be economies of scale in terms of raising capital, in establishing a research and development facility, or in setting up a marketing or distribution system. A related idea pertains to the *operating economies* which may be achieved through merging.

These economies could take the form of eliminating or consolidating duplicate production, marketing, financial, or personnel facilities. Operating economies are most obvious in cases of horizontal integration, which results from combining firms involved in the same stage of the acquisition-production-distribution cycle. Another type of operating economy might be achieved through vertical integration. Combining firms at different stages in the acquisition-production-distribution cycle may result in greater efficiency. Still another type of operating economy might be the elimination of inefficient management in the acquired firm.

The anticipated benefits of economies of scale or operating economies are often referred to as *synergism*; the merged firm has a value greater than the sum of its parts, i.e., $2 + 2 = 5$. Although various reasons have been suggested as to why firms benefit from mergers, there is contradictory evidence concerning whether the shareholders of the acquiring firms benefit, or whether synergism exists. At the same time, there is widespread and persuasive evidence that acquiring firms pay a premium (over the prevailing market price) to the shareholders of the target firm.[1] With this premium, the acquiring firm is paying more than the acquisition is worth as an independent operation. If firms are operating to maximize shareholder wealth, one way these premiums can be justified is if synergism exists and the acquisition provides incremental (or excess) risk-adjusted expected returns. Observation of the performance of merged firms and often the subsequent divestiture of previously acquired firms suggests the anticipated economies attributed to merging have often been overstated.

Diversification and Debt Capacity. In an efficient market, ignoring bankruptcy and agency costs and mergers undertaken specifically for tax purposes (both of which are considered subsequently), is there any benefit from merging simply in terms of the diversification effects? Lewellen[2] suggested that joining two firms whose earnings streams were less than perfectly correlated reduces the risk of default, thereby increasing the debt capacity of the combined firm. Debt capacity is enhanced because the dispersion about the mean of the two streams of cash flows is reduced; there is less risk, and hence the probability of

---

[1]For a careful and thoughtful review of the available evidence, see Dennis C. Mueller, "The Effects of Conglomerate Mergers," *Journal of Banking and Finance* 1 (December 1977), pp. 315–347. Also see Gershon Mandelker, "Risk and Return: The Case of Merging Firms," *Journal of Financial Economics* 1 (December 1974), pp. 303–335; Robert A. Haugen and Terence C. Langetieg, "An Empirical Test for Synergism in Merger," *Journal of Finance* 30 (September 1975), pp. 1003–1014; and Paul J. Halpern, "Empirical Estimates of the Amount and Distribution of Gains to Companies in Mergers," *Journal of Business* 46 (October 1973), pp. 554–575.

[2]Wilbur G. Lewellen, "A Pure Financial Rationale for the Conglomerate Merger," *Journal of Finance* 26 (May 1971), pp. 521–537.

paying principal and interest in full and on time is enhanced. However, this type of action has a co-insurance effect that influences the respective wealth positions of both bondholders and shareholders.[3] The bondholders receive more protection than they had before, since the shareholders of both firms now have to back the claims of the other firm's bondholders. The shareholders position is weakened, however, because the overall liabilities have increased.

The net effect is a wealth transfer from shareholders to bondholders, but it leaves the total value of the combined firm exactly equal to the sum of the values of the two previously independent firms. There are ways to realign the wealth of the various classes of security holders,[4] but the important conclusion is that in an efficient market, *diversification itself is not a reason for merging*. If the market is not totally efficient and/or the capital asset pricing model (CAPM) is not completely valid, total risk (instead of beta risk) is important. In this situation, there may be diversification benefits from merging. The whole subject, however, is still a matter of debate among financial theorists.

Bankruptcy and Agency Costs.   Once we recognize the existence of bankruptcy and agency costs, is it possible to raise the combined value of firms by merging? *Bankruptcy costs* are direct costs such as trustee fees, legal fees, and other costs of reorganization or bankruptcy that are deducted before investors are paid, plus indirect costs such as the opportunity cost of funds being tied up during bankruptcy proceedings, losses in asset values due to forced capital structure changes, lost profits created by decreased sales in anticipation of bankruptcy, disruptions in production during bankruptcy, lost investment opportunities due to their lives being longer than the expected life of the firm, and so on. Agency costs arise in firms because the principals (the shareholders) want to ensure that the agents (the firm's management) make decisions that are in their best interests. To accomplish this, appropriate incentives such as stock options and bonuses are provided, or the performance of the agent can be monitored. Monitoring costs consist of bonding the

---

[3]Robert C. Higgins and Lawrence D. Schall, "Corporate Bankruptcy and Conglomerate Merger," *Journal of Finance* 30 (March 1975), pp. 93–114; Dan Galai and Ronald W. Masulis, "The Option Pricing Model and the Risk Factor of Stock," *Journal of Financial Economics* 3 (January–March 1976), pp. 53–82; and James H. Scott, Jr., "On the Theory of Conglomerate Mergers," *Journal of Finance* 32 (September 1977), pp. 1235–1250.

[4]In a test of this, E. Han Kim and John J. McConnell, "Corporate Mergers and the Co-Insurance of Corporate Debt," *Journal of Finance* 32 (May 1977), pp. 349–368, found no evidence of abnormal returns to the bondholders of merging firms, but they did observe that postmerger financial leverage increased. They concluded: (1) the co-insurance effect did exist, and (2) the wealth transfer to bondholders that would have occurred was negated by the increased use of debt financing. See also Paul Asquith and E. Han Kim. "The Impact of Merger Bids on the Participating Firm's Security Holders." *Journal of Finance* 37 (December 1982), pp. 1209–1228.

agent, systematic reviews of managerial and financial performance, bond covenants, and so on.[5] These incentive and monitoring activities involve costs that are the inevitable result of the separation of corporate ownership and management. Regardless of how they are incurred, the agency costs of monitoring are ultimately borne by the shareholders; their presence causes the firm's value to be less than the present value of its expected cash inflows.

While the exact interrelationships between bankruptcy costs, agency costs, risk reduction, and mergers are only beginning to be understood, it appears there may be economic gains from merging when bankruptcy and agency costs are considered. These gains arise from the reduced probability of bankruptcy, which leads to lower bankruptcy and/or agency costs. Other things being equal, these reduced costs mean the combined worth of the firms may exceed the sum of their premerger values.

Taxes.   Taxes may provide clear economic incentives for merging in three situations. The first is the sale of firms with accumulated tax losses. Although a business purpose must be demonstrated, a firm with tax losses can be acquired via a merger, with the result that the tax loss shelters the positive earnings of the acquiring firm. A business loss can be carried back 3 years or forward 15 years; however, if the losses have been extensive, the target firm may not be able to realize the associated tax benefits. By merging a firm suffering losses into a profitable one, the losses produce an immediate tax benefit for the acquiring firm. Second, when the growth of a firm has slowed so that earnings retention cannot be justified to the Internal Revenue Service, a firm may be better off selling out. Rather than paying out future cash inflows as dividends subject to ordinary income tax, these may be capitalized in a sale to another firm. Not only is the lower capital gains tax applicable, but the taxes are postponed until the securities received (assuming the merger was a tax-free transaction) are sold. Finally, there are tax effects associated with the inheritance tax. As owners become older, they may find it advantageous to sell because of the uncertainty associated with the value to be placed on the firm in connection with estate taxes. Alternatively, a sale may be necessary to provide the liquidity required for the payment of estate taxes. All these tax-related reasons suggest there are often direct economic benefits from merging.

Earnings Per Share Effect.   Mergers can generate short-run increases

---

[5]Michael C. Jensen and William H. Meckling, "Theory of the Firm: Managerial Behavior, Agency Costs and Ownership Structure," *Journal of Financial Economics* 3 (October 1976), pp. 305–360; and Clifford W. Smith, Jr., and Jerold B. Warner, "On Financial Contracting: An Analysis of Bond Covenants," *Journal of Financial Economics* 7 (June 1979), pp. 117–161.

TABLE 15.3
Effects of a Merger on
Earnings Per Share

A. BEFORE MERGER

Financial Data	Rapid Growth Products, Inc.	American Steel Corporation
Earnings per share (EPS)	$1.00	$1.00
Market price per share	16.00	8.00
Price/earnings (P/E) ratio	16 times	8 times
Number of shares of common stock outstanding	200,000	300,000
Total earnings	$200,000	$300,000
Total market value	$3,200,000	$2,400,000

B. AFTER MERGER

Exchange ratio (based on respective premerger market prices per share)— $8 ÷ $16 = 0.50. Hence, a half-share of Rapid Growth Products, Inc., stock will be exchanged for each share of American Steel Corporation common stock.

Total market value	$3,200,000 + $2,400,000 = $5,600,000
Total earnings	$200,000 + $300,000 = $500,000
Total number of shares of common stock outstanding	200,000 + 1/2(300,000) = 350,000 shares
Earnings per share (EPS)	$500,000/350,000 = $1.4286≈$1.43 per share
Price/earnings ratio (P/E)	$16/$1.43 = 11.19 times
Market price per share	$5,600,00/350,000 = $16 per share

Assumptions: Merger benefit is zero, so total market value is simply the sum of the values of the two premerger firms. Both firms are all equity financed.

in earnings per share whether or not economic benefits result.[6] To see this spurious benefit, consider the example in Table 15.3. Rapid Growth Products, Inc. is a small firm, but because of its image it is expected to grow rapidly and therefore commands a price/earnings (P/E) ratio of 16 times current earnings. American Steel Corporation, on the other hand, is a mature firm that has no expected future growth in earnings; it commands a P/E ratio of 8 times. Ignoring any potential premium, we assume Rapid Growth Products arranges to buy American Steel through an exchange of stock, with the exchange ratio being based on the respective premerger market prices. An *exchange ratio* is the number of shares the acquiring firm gives for each of the acquired firm's shares. Employing the premerger prices of $16 per share for Rapid Growth (firm X) and $8 per share for American Steel (firm Y) the *market price exchange ratio is $P_Y/P_X = 0.50$ ($8 ÷ $16); hence American Steel's shareholders will receive a half-share of Rapid Growth stock for each share of American Steel stock owned.

---

[6]In order to reduce some of these spurious benefits, the Accounting Principles Board (APB) Opinions No. 16, *Business Combinations,* and 17, *Intangible Assets,* were enacted in 1970. Until that time firms could often choose to have the merger accounted for as either a "purchase" or a "pooling of interests." They obviously chose the accounting method that resulted in the highest earnings per share. However, even with these changes the earnings per share growth illusion is still available to firms.

As shown in part B of Table 15.3, the merger provides an immediate increase in earnings per share (EPS) from $1.00 to $1.43 for Rapid Growth, even though no value or increase in total earnings was created. This occurred simply because of the difference in the premerger P/E ratios commanded by the two firms. The opportunities for financial manipulation should be obvious. By increasing its reported earnings per share, Rapid Growth may create the illusion of real growth from what is actually "phantom" growth. If investors believe in this phantom growth, they may commit an even bigger mistake by pricing the stock at the premerger P/E ratio of Rapid Growth—16 times earnings. If this happens, contrary to the data presented in the table, the market price per share will increase from $16 to $22.88 ($1.43 per share $\times$ 16 P/E), and the total market value of the combined firm increases from $5,600,000 to $8,008,000 ($22.88 per share $\times$ 350,000 shares).

Exactly this type of consideration was behind much of the wheeler-dealer conglomerate merger activity in the sixties and early seventies. Unfortunately, if the merger string is broken—for example, because of economic conditions or a challenge by the Department of Justice or the Federal Trade Commission—the bubble bursts, and earnings growth and total market value plummet. Spurious benefits in the sense of increased earnings per share may be created by merging. However, these are not real benefits, since in the long run neither total earnings nor total market values of the premerger firms have been increased; in short, no economic benefits have occurred because of the merger.

Managerial-Based Considerations. Empire building, growth for the sake of growth, and possible managerial (as opposed to shareholder) gains from mergers have also been cited as possible reasons for some mergers. Mueller[7] believes one possible explanation for mergers is that managers stand to gain from insider information. Since much of the risk arising from a merger falls to the shareholders, access to insider information may provide managers an opportunity to share disproportionately in the gains while avoiding some of the risks. Whether these beliefs explain much of the observed merger activity is conjecture at this point; however, there are no clear gains from growth itself, or from the increased concentration often brought about by mergers. Hence, the lack of any direct economic benefits tied to growth or managerial objectives suggests these are not adequate reasons for successful mergers.

Potential Economic Benefits: A Synthesis. Mergers that may produce economic benefits are those where there are demonstrated synergistic

---

[7]Mueller, "The Effects of Conglomerate Mergers," pp. 315–347.

effects, a reduction in bankruptcy and/or agency costs, or significant tax benefits. Although the benefits of diversification itself are not completely clear, there do not appear to be any lasting economic benefits (in terms of increased cash flows or reduced risks) from short-run earnings per share effects or strictly managerial-based considerations. Our review suggests mergers are not a panacea. A well-thought-out merger plan can, in some instances, help a firm achieve its longer-term strategic growth objectives. However, there is no reason automatically to prefer external growth by merging to internal growth or to the return of excess cash to the firm's shareholders. This is particularly true when all the costs, including the wide array of administrative skills which are not costless, are considered. Only by accurately evaluating all the costs as well as the anticipated benefits will financial managers be in a position to assess the real impact of proposed acquisitions.

A Capital Budgeting Approach To Merger Evaluation

Merger analysis requires the same conceptual approach as any other capital budgeting decision. The objective is to determine an appropriate acquisition price the acquiring firm, firm X, should be willing to pay. If the merger target, firm Y, is a publicly traded firm, the minimum acquisition price is usually set by its premerger market value. However, acquiring firms generally have to pay a premium over the target's existing market value. The capital budgeting approach requires financial managers to calculate a *maximum acquisition price (MAP)* consistent with their objective of yielding an acceptable net present value (NPV). Since they are seeking a positive NPV, the maximum acquisition price (MAP) firm X should pay is the price for which NPV equals zero. Acquisition prices between the price for which NPV = O and the premerger market value of the target will yield a positive NPV for the acquiring firm.[8] This maximum acquisition price can be calculated directly for mergers financed with cash; for stock-financed mergers, it is easier to calculate the *net advantage to merging (NAM)*. We will now look at how the cash flows, investment horizon, and discount rate are established. Then the capital budgeting procedures used to evaluate either cash or stock-financed mergers are presented.

Cash Flows, Investment Horizon, and the Discount Rate

The benefits from a merger are measured in terms of expected incremental after tax-cash flows (CFATs), which must be expressed on a basis consistent with those for investment proposals generated internally. The relevant operating cash flows for any expenditure proposal are given by:

$$CFAT_t = CFBT_t\,(1\,-\,T)\,+\,Dep_t\,(T) \tag{15.2}$$

---

[8]This, of course, assumes that the value established by the capital budgeting approach is greater than the premerger market value of the target.

where $CFBT_t$ = cash inflow$_t$ − cash outflow$_t$
T = the marginal corporate tax rate
Dep_t = the proposal's depreciation in year t

If increased cash inflows are expected to result from the merger, they must be incorporated into the expected CFAT. Likewise, any expected tax benefits (such as tax shields due to losses) must be included in deriving the expected CFATs. In addition, to represent the incremental cash flows due to the merger accurately, any additional investment by the acquiring firm subsequent to the merger in terms of improving facilities, increases in net working capital, and so on are also taken into account. Finally, it is important to isolate from the CFATs any capital structure impacts that result from the merger. Thus, cash flows associated with interest payments, dividends, and so on should *not* be included when determining the relevant CFAT figures.[9]

The typical capital budgeting project has an investment horizon that coincides with the expected life of the asset. In merger analysis the investment horizon is generally expected to be infinite. However, the assumption of an infinite horizon has little practical appeal. One way to overcome this problem is to limit the investment horizon to a finite number of years, perhaps 5 or 10. A less conservative and somewhat more realistic approach is to estimate the expected CFATs for a finite number of years and then assume the CFATs will not grow at all or will increase at a constant rate thereafter. The latter approach is used here.

Unless the merger is expected to change the acquiring firm's risk complexion, the discount rate used in merger analysis should not differ from that used for any other capital budgeting analysis, given the risks involved. Only if the merger will change the firm's perceived business risk, or its target capital structure, is it necessary to adjust the discount rate.

Determining the Maximum Acquisition Price for Cash-Financed Mergers

When one firm acquires another for cash,[10] it may purchase only the target firm's assets, or it may purchase both its assets and liabilities. The maximum acquisition price (MAP) *when only the assets are purchased* can be determined by:

---

[9]While it is tempting to include the costs of financing, remember that (consistent with the earlier discussion on estimating cash flows for capital budgeting purposes) the entire costs of financing are "captured" in the discount rate, or risk-adjusted required rate of return, employed for the project. To explicitly include financing costs when estimating the CFATs would result in double counting and incorrectly lower the desirability of the proposed acquisition.

[10]A merger can be considered "cash-financed" when it is financed with internally generated funds, debt, or preferred stock. But, when the cash was obtained by an earlier sale of common stock in the capital markets, the merger should be considered a common stock-financed merger.

$$MAP = \sum_{t=0}^{n} \frac{CFAT_t}{(1 + k)^t} \tag{15.3}$$

where $CFAT_t$ = the expected net after-tax cash flows from the target firm in year t

         k = the appropriate after-tax discount rate

On the other hand, the maximum acquisition price *when both the assets and liabilities of the target firm are purchased* is determined by:

$$MAP = \sum_{t=0}^{n} \frac{CFAT_t}{(1 + k)^t} - B_0 \tag{15.4}$$

where B_0 is the *current market value* of firm Y's liabilities transferred in the merger, and all other symbols are as defined before. If both assets and liabilities are purchased, as in Equation 15.4, the market value of Y's liabilities are subtracted, since the acquiring firm has to assume these liabilities. Market rather than book values are appropriate, since they represent the value of the liabilities at the time of the acquisition.[11]

To illustrate, consider Modern Metals, Inc., which is interested in acquiring Atlantic Oxidizing's assets and liabilities. The present market value of Atlantic's common stock is $1.4 million ($14 per share × 100,000 shares of common stock); this obviously establishes the minimum acquisition price that would be acceptable to the owners of Atlantic Oxidizing. To establish the maximum acquisition price (MAP), Modern Metals uses the capital budgeting approach summarized by Equation 15.4. Table 15.4 presents Modern Metal's estimates of the cash flows to be received from Atlantic Oxidizing for the next 10 years. After 10 years, Modern Metals estimates that Atlantic's future cash flows will grow at 7 percent per year to infinity. In addition, Modern Metals estimates an appropriate discount rate of 15 percent, and it uses a 40 percent tax rate on ordinary income. The current market value of Modern Metal's liabilities has been estimated to be $300,000.

After estimating the expected cash flows in Table 15.4, the maximum acquisition price can be determined. In part A of Table 15.5, the present value of Atlantic's expected cash inflows for the next 10 years, discounted at 15 percent, is determined. This is $1,018,940. Then, in part B the maximum acquisition price is found. This process begins by calculating the discounted present value of the cash flows from year 11 to infinity, which is $1,228,950. Then this amount is added to the present value of

---

[11]Note that when the purchasing firm acquires liabilities as well as assets, it may temporarily move away from its current, or target, capital structure. After the acquisition, the firm may then readjust its capital structure. The decision to change a firm's capital structure, which is discussed in Chapter 18, should be considered separately from the acquisition decision.

TABLE 15.4
Calculation of the
Expected Cash Flows
in Years 1 to 10 for
Atlantic Oxidizing
Made by Modern
Metals, Inc.
(Thousands of Dollars)

Year (t)	Cash Inflow$_t$ (1)	Cash Outflow$_t$ (2)	CFBT$_t$ [(1) − (2)] (3)	CFBT$_t$ × (1 − T) (4)	Dep$_t$ (5)	Dep$_t$ (T) (6)	CFAT$_t$ [(4) + (6)] (7)
1	$400	$300	$100	$ 60	$160	$ 64	$124
2	470	340	130	78	180	72	150
3	540	400	140	84	200	80	164
4	600	430	170	102	210	84	186
5	660	480	180	108	230	92	200
6	710	500	210	126	260	104	230
7	750	520	230	138	300	120	258
8	830	560	270	162	340	136	298
9	900	590	310	186	400	160	346
10	950	630	320	192	450	180	372

the expected cash inflows for the first 10 years. From the sum of these two discounted cash flows, Atlantic's existing liabilities of $300,000 are subtracted, resulting in a MAP of $1,947,890.

If Modern Metals pays more than this amount, it is not maximizing its existing shareholders wealth. An obvious bargaining zone exists between this MAP of $1,947,890 and Atlantic's current market value of $1,400,000. Modern Metals will probably attempt to keep the merger terms close to the $1.4 million level, while Atlantic will strive to achieve a substantial premium over its existing market value. Based on the MAP of $1,947,890 and the 100,000 shares of Atlantic Oxidizing's outstanding common stock, Modern Metals could offer up to $19.48 ($1,947,890 ÷ 100,000 shares) per share, or a premium of up to $5.48 for each of Atlantic's shares. Where the final merger terms will be set depends, of course, on the relative bargaining positions of the two firms.

Determining the Net Advantage to Merging for Stock-Financed Mergers

Cash may be employed in financing mergers, but a large proportion of all mergers are financed with common stock. The use of stock is often favored by the shareholders of the target firm for tax reasons (discussed later in the chapter). Likewise, the acquiring firm may favor the use of common stock instead of cash to increase its equity base and conserve cash.

Unlike the straightforward approach to determining the maximum acquisition price when cash is employed, using common stock (or common stock equivalents such as convertible bonds, convertible preferred stock, or warrants) to acquire another company creates additional problems. Some would contend that the initial common stock outlay should be valued at its equivalent cash value (the current market value of the acquiring firms' shares issued in the merger), but this approach can lead to erroneous decisions. The reason is that the benefits generated by the merger must now be shared by both firm X's and firm Y's shareholders; when cash is employed, only the acquiring firm's (X's) shareholders receive all of the postmerger benefits.

A. PRESENT VALUE OF EXPECTED CASH FLOWS FOR THE NEXT 10 YEARS

Year (t)	$CFAT_t$	$PVIF_{15\%,\ t\ yr}$	Present Value$_t$
1	$124	.870	$ 107.88
2	150	.756	113.40
3	164	.658	107.91
4	186	.572	106.39
5	200	.497	99.40
6	230	.432	99.36
7	258	.376	97.01
8	298	.327	97.45
9	346	.284	98.26
10	372	.247	91.88

Present value of expected cash inflows $(t_1$ to $t_{10}) = $1,018.94$

B. CALCULATION OF THE MAXIMUM ACQUISITION PRICE (MAP)

$$\text{MAP} = \begin{array}{c}\text{present value of}\\ \text{expected cash}\\ \text{flows for next 10}\\ \text{years}\end{array} + \begin{array}{c}\text{present value of expected}\\ \text{cash flows from year 11 to}\\ \text{infinity}^a\end{array} - \begin{array}{c}\text{current market}\\ \text{value of existing}\\ \text{liabilities}\end{array}$$

$$= \$1,018.94 + \left[\frac{(\$372)(1.07)}{(.15 - .07)}(PVIF_{15\%,10yr})\right] - \$300$$

$$= \$1,018.94 + \left[\frac{\$398.04}{.08}(.247)\right] - \$300$$

$$= \$1,018.94 + [(\$4,975.5)(.247)] - \$300$$

$$= \$1,018.94 + \$1,228.95 - \$300$$

$$= \$1,947.89$$

^{a}The constant growth formula presented in Chapter 7 is

$$P_0 = \frac{D_1}{k_s - g}$$

where P_0 = the price of the stock at time t_0
D_1 = the cash dividend the shareholder expects at the end of year 1
k_s = the expected or required rate of return on the stock
g = the constant expected growth rate in cash dividends

For our purposes, this formula has been modified to $V_{10} = \frac{CFAT_{11}}{k - g}$. Once the value in year 10, V_{10}, is determined (based on all cash flows subsequent to year 10), it is then discounted to the present (via $PVIF_{15\%,10yr}$) just like all other cash inflows expected from the proposed merger.

When cash is employed, the owners of the target company (Y) receive cash and did not share in the future benefits and cash flows of the merged companies, since they relinquish their ownership position. When stock is employed, both sets of shareholders participate (based on their respective ownership in the merged firm) in future benefits and cash flows. For this reason, the necessary calculations are more complicated. In addition, when stock is employed, the *acquiring firm typically assumes both the assets and the liabilities of the target firm.*

To evaluate a merger when stock is employed, the net advantage to merging (NAM) is calculated according to the following procedure:

Step 1. Estimate the expected CFATs for the acquiring firm X *without the merger* over the relevant time period.

Step 2. Employing firm X's required rate of return, determine the discounted present value of its expected future cash flows, S_X, if it does not undertake the merger.[12]

Step 3. Determine the combined expected CFATs from both firm X and firm Y if the merger takes place (over the same time period employed in step 1). Note that the CFATs have to include any anticipated incremental (or synergistic) benefits arising from the merger, as well as any additional investment that firm X anticipates making in firm Y in the future.

Step 4. Employing the combined firm's required rate of return, determine the discounted present value, NPV_C, of the combined firm's expected future cash flows. The required rate of return employed may differ from that of firm X before the merger if the merger changes investor risk-return expectations.

Step 5. Determine firm X's (the acquiring firm's) ownership position (OP) in the combined firm employing:

$$\text{Firm X's percentage ownership in the combined firm} = OP = \left[\frac{n_X}{n_X + \dfrac{(P_Y \times n_Y)}{P_X}} \right] \quad (15.5)$$

where n_X = the number of outstanding shares of common stock of firm X (the acquiring firm) prior to the merger
   n_Y = the number of outstanding shares of common stock of firm Y (the target firm) prior to the merger
   P_X = the premerger market price per share of firm X
   P_Y = the market price per share offered for each share of firm Y. (This is the *offered* price, not Y's premerger market price per share.)

Step 6. Determine the value of the combined firm, S_C, by subtracting the current market value of firm Y's debt, B_0, from the net present value calculated in step 4:

$$S_C = NPV_C - B_0 \quad (15.6)$$

Step 7. Calculate the net advantage to merging to firm X, NAM_X, as follows:

$$NAM_X = S_C \ (OP) - S_X \quad (15.7)$$

---

[12]This value should be approximately equal to the current market value of firm X's outstanding common stock if the market is efficient. Accordingly, the total market value of firm X's stock can be employed instead of discounting its expected CFATs.

where *OP* is the ownership percentage determined in step 5. The first term on the right side of Equation 15.7 represents the portion of the combined firm that will be "owned" by firm X's current shareholders. If that value is greater than the current worth of their holdings, S_X, the net advantage to merging is positive and the merger will take place; otherwise firm X will not acquire firm Y.

To illustrate merger analysis when common stock is used to acquire a company, the previous example of Modern Metals, Inc., and Atlantic Oxidizing will be continued. The necessary steps follow:

Step 1.   Estimation of the CFATs Modern Metals expects without the merger. For simplicity, the company assumed a 3 percent compound growth rate after year 10. These CFATs are shown in column 1 of Table 15.6.

Step 2.   Employing the required rate of return of 15 percent, the discounted present value of the expected cash flows without the merger for Modern Metals are found to be $2,763,388 (column 3 of Table 15.6).

Step 3.   Estimation of the combined CFATs if the merger is undertaken. In order to accomplish this, Atlantic's CFATs (from Tables 15.4 and 15.5) are shown in column 4 of Table 15.6. These are added to Modern Metals' to show the combined CFATs in column 5 of Table 15.6. Note that Modern Metals' cash flows are expected to grow at a 3 percent compound rate after year 10 while Atlantic's are expected to grow at 7 percent. Modern Metals estimates the *combined* growth rate is 5 percent; it is this growth rate that leads to the value of $9,030,000 for the beyond year 10 cash flows at the bottom of column 5.

Step 4.   Employing the combined firm's required rate of return, which is also 15 percent in this case, the present value of the combined firm's CFATs is found to be $4,978,135.

Step 5.   Determination of Modern Metals existing shareholders proportional interest in the combined firm. To do this, Modern Metals must determine a tentative price they are willing to pay for Atlantic Oxidizing. After an extensive analysis of the prospects of Atlantic Oxidizing, its position in the industry, and the problems anticipated in integrating Atlantic into Modern Metals, Modern Metals has decided $20 per share (a $6 premium over the market price of $14) appears appropriate. Modern Metals presently has 200,000 shares of stock outstanding with a market price of $15 per share, while Atlantic has 100,000 shares of stock outstanding at $14 per share. Thus, the ownership position (OP), employing Equation 15.5, is:

$$\frac{200,000}{200,000 + \frac{(\$20)\,(100,000)}{\$15}} = 0.60$$

TABLE 15.6
Determination of the Net Advantage To Merging if Modern Metals Acquires Atlantic Oxidizing With Stock ($ Thousands)

Year	Modern's Estimated CFATs Without the Merger (1)	PVIF at 15% (2)	Present Value of Modern's CFATs [(1) × (2)] (3)	Atlantic's Estimated CFATs After the Merger (4)	Combined CFATs After the Merger [(1) + (4)] (5)	Present Value of Combined CFATs [(2) × (5)] (6)
1	$ 272	.870	$ 236.640	$124	$ 396	$ 344.520
2	284	.756	214.704	150	434	328.104
3	304	.658	200.032	164	468	307.944
4	330	.572	188.760	186	516	295.152
5	351	.497	174.447	200	551	273.847
6	376	.432	162.432	230	606	261.792
7	413	.376	155.288	258	671	252.296
8	440	.327	143.880	298	738	241.326
9	465	.284	132.060	346	811	230.324
10	488	.247	120.536	372	860	212.420
Beyond 10	$4,188.7[a]	.247	1,034.609	n.a.[b]	9,030[c]	2,230.410
			$S_X = $2,763.388		NPV_C	$4,978.135

Less: Current market value of firm Y's debt, B_0 300.000

Value of the combined firm, S_C $4,678.135

Times: Ownership percentage, OP   × .60

    $2,806.881

Less: Value of firm X without the merger, S_X 2,763.388

Net advantage of merging to firm X, NAM_X $ 43.493

[a] $V_{10} \text{ (Modern Metals)} = \dfrac{CFAT_{10}\,(1 + g)}{k - g} = \dfrac{\$488(1.03)}{.15 - .03}$

[b] Not applicable.

[c] $V_{10} \text{ (Combined)} = \dfrac{CFAT_{10}\,(1 + g)}{k - g} = \dfrac{\$860(1.05)}{.15 - .05}$

Based on the $20 offering price for each share of Atlantic Oxidizing, Modern Metals' current shareholders will own 60.0 percent of the combined firm.

Step 6. By subtracting the current market value of Atlantic's debt of $300,000, the value of the combined firm, S_C of $4,678,135 is found.

Step 7. The net advantage to merging of $43,493 presented at the bottom of column 6 of Table 15.6 indicates that the acquisition of Atlantic Oxidizing for stock valued at $20 per share will enhance the wealth of Modern Metals current shareholders.

It is evident Modern Metals should acquire Atlantic Oxidizing if it can do so for $20 per share or less.[13] This value is greater than the maximum acquisition price of $19.48 per share determined earlier if the merger were financed with cash. Why is this so? The key distinction between cash and stock as a means of financing mergers is that if cash is used, the ultimate payoff to firm X's shareholders does not depend on sharing future benefits since the target firm's shareholders do not have any continuing stock ownership in the combined firm. Thus, the cost can be measured without any reference to the shared future benefits. If stock is offered, however, the ultimate cost of the merger depends on benefits that must be shared by the shareholders of both the firms.

The relevant considerations for stock-financed mergers are (1) the respective ownership position of the shareholders of the combined firm, and (2) the benefit experienced by the acquiring firm's existing shareholders. An important variable that influences the combined CFATs is the duration and rate of growth expected in the respective CFAT streams. Complications with stock-financed mergers become more pronounced when other types of securities (such as convertible bonds, convertible preferred stock, or warrants) are used to finance the merger. However, all these financing packages may be evaluated by employing the same basic approach and analyzing the proportionate ownership the acquiring firm's shareholders expect to receive after the merger is consummated.

Merger Analysis and Earnings Per Share

A frequently employed but less appropriate approach to merger analysis emphasizes the impact of the merger on the acquiring firm's present and future earnings per share. As we saw earlier in the chapter, there are no

---

[13]Analysis indicates Modern Metals can actually pay slightly more than $20.80 per share in stock for Atlantic Oxidizing and still be willing to undertake the merger. For an example of sensitivity analysis of various factors such as sales growth and return on sales as they affect the possible ownership exchange ratios of stock-financed mergers, see Alfred Rappaport, "Financial Analysis for Mergers and Acquisitions," *Mergers & Acquisitions* 10 (winter 1976), pp. 18–36. For an alternative approach to determining the respective market values, see Richard C. Stapleton, "The Acquisition Decision as a Capital Budgeting Problem," *Journal of Business Finance and Accounting* 2 (summer 1975), pp. 187–201.

Financial Data	Diversified, Inc.	Specialty Electronics	Home Building Materials
Total earnings	$100,000	$20,000	$64,000
Number of shares of common stock outstanding	10,000	5,000	8,000
EPS	$10	$4	$8
Market value of stock			
Per share	$150	$80	$96
Total	$1,500,000	$400,000	$768,000
P/E ratio	15 times	20 times	12 times
Expected future earnings growth per year (estimated by Diversified, Inc.)	6%	15%	1%

economic benefits as such, attached to increasing earnings per share. If the EPS approach is employed, the expected total earnings of the combined firms, including those due to synergistic effects or because of tax considerations, must be estimated. The postmerger earnings per share for the combined firm are equal to:

$$EPS_X = CE \div \left[n_X + \frac{(P_Y \times n_Y)}{P_X} \right] \tag{15.8}$$

where CE = the combined postmerger earnings, and the other variables are as defined in Equation 15.5 To illustrate this approach, look at Diversified, Inc., which is considering two different merger candidates—Specialty Electronics and Home Building Materials. Premerger financial data are presented in Table 15.7.[14]

If Diversified and either of the two candidate firms agree to a stock-financed merger based on their respective premerger market prices, the immediate postmerger EPSs for the combined firm are as follows:

$$EPS \text{ (if Specialty is acquired)} = [\$100,000 + \$20,000] \div \left[10,000 + \frac{\$80 \times 5,000}{\$150} \right]$$
$$= \$120,000 \div 12,666.67 = \$9.47$$

$$EPS \text{ (if Home Building is acquired)} = [\$100,000 + \$64,000] \div \left[10,000 + \frac{\$96 \times 8,000}{\$150} \right]$$
$$= \$164,000 \div 15,120 = \$10.85$$

Thus, the immediate impact on the postmerger EPS of Diversified is to decrease it from $10 to $9.47 if Specialty Electronics is acquired or to increase it to $10.85 if Home Building Materials is acquired.

[14]For simplicity, all three firms are financed solely with common stock and no synergistic or tax effects that would increase postmerger earnings are present.

Earnings Growth and Postmerger EPS

To focus on the immediate impact on EPS is, however, overly simplistic, since it ignores future growth. If future growth is ignored, firms would never merge if they expected an immediate dilution in EPS, as in the case of Diversified's proposed acquisition of Specialty Electronics. In Table 15.8 and Figure 15.1, the expected future earnings per share for the next 5 years are estimated, based on a 6 percent growth rate for Diversified without the merger, and 15 and 1 percent growth rates for Specialty Electronics and Home Building Materials, respectively, if acquired by Diversified.

While Diversifed suffers an immediate reduction in EPS if it acquires Specialty Electronics, the higher anticipated growth rate of Specialty's earnings results in an increase in expected EPS for Diversified (as opposed to not merging) after the third year. The initial dilution in EPS is followed by a subsequent increase in EPS. The greater the period of the expected dilution, the less desirable Diversified will consider the proposed merger to be. Likewise, the initial benefit to Diversified in terms of increased postmerger EPS from merging with Home Building Materials results in dilution after year 4. These two examples serve to illustrate an important fact: The duration and rate of expected future growth in

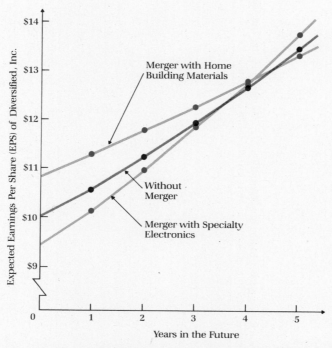

Figure 15.1 Expected Earning Per Share for Diversified, Inc., With and Without the Mergers.

TABLE 15.8
Expected Earnings Per Share for Diversified, Inc., Alone and After the Merger
with Either Specialty Electronic or Home Building Materials

| | Earnings of Diversified, Inc. | | | | | | | |
| | Expected Without Merger | | Merger with Specialty Electronics | | | Merger with Home Building Materials | | |
Year	Diversified's Earnings @ 6% Growth (1)	EPS [(1) ÷ 10,000] (2)	Specialty's Earnings @ 15% Growth (3)	Combined Earnings [(1) + (3)] (4)	EPS [(4) ÷ 12,667] (5)	Home Building's Earnings @ 1% Growth (6)	Combined Earnings [(1) + (6)] (7)	EPS [(7) ÷ 15,120] (8)
1	$106,000	$10.60	$23,000	$129,000	$10.18	$64,640	$170,640	$11.29
2	112,360	11.24	26,450	138,810	10.96	65,286	177,646	11.75
3	119,102	11.91	30,418	149,520	11.80	65,939	185,041	12.24
4	126,248	12.62	34,980	161,228	12.73	66,599	192,847	12.75
5	133,823	13.38	40,227	174,050	13.74	67,265	201,088	13.30

Note: The total number of shares outstanding are 10,000 for Diversified, Inc., without the merger, and 12,667 or 15,120 if it merges with either Specialty Electronics or Home Building Materials.

earnings must be taken into consideration when evaluating potential merger candidates via the EPS approach.

Superiority of the Capital Budgeting Approach

In considering the capital budgeting versus EPS approach to merger analysis, it is immediately obvious that substantial differences exist. By focusing on cash flows, risk, and the timing of the CFATs, the capital budgeting approach is consistent with the financial manager's goal of maximizing shareholder wealth. The EPS approach, in contrast, relies solely on accounting data, does not consider the risk or timing of cash flows, and views the situation only in terms of the "cosmetic" effect of the proposed merger on the resulting EPS of the combined firm.

It is the market value of the combined firm, not its EPS, that is important in any proposed merger. An EPS approach may be extended to consider valuation consequences by examining the current price/earnings (P/E) ratios of the two firms and estimating the anticipated ratio for the combined firm after the merger. Applying the price/earnings valuation approach presented in Chapter 7 by multiplying the anticipated postmerger P/E ratio by the estimated EPS for the combined firms, an estimate of the market value of the combined firm results. Although this extension can be made, the more direct capital budgeting approach is both theoretically superior and less likely to lead managers astray. Hence, the EPS analysis should be discarded, or if used, treated as a supplement to the capital budgeting approach.

Administrative Considerations and Strategies for Mergers

Now that we know how to evaluate potential merger targets, our attention can shift to some of the other important aspects of mergers that financial managers must consider. These include leveraged buyouts, tender offers, defensive tactics, tax considerations, and accounting aspects.

Leveraged Buyouts

A *leveraged buyout* involves the purchase of a company or some of its assets with a large amount of debt and very little equity.[15] The acquirers may be firms, private investment syndicates, or the managers or owners of a division of the selling firm.[16] The initial debt-to-equity ratio may reach as high as 10 to 1. Leveraged buyouts are put together by using the

---

[15]This section is based in part on Nicholas Wallner, "Leveraged Buyouts: A Review of the State of the Art, Parts 1 and 2," *Mergers & Acquisitions* 14 (fall 1979), pp. 4–13, and 14 (winter 1980), pp. 16–26.

[16]The Employee Retirement Income Security Act (ERISA) of 1974 brought significant changes in Employees Stock Ownership Trusts (ESOTs) that greatly facilitate the transfer of corporate ownership to employees by providing some significant tax advantages. First is the 1 percent investment tax credit for corporations that establish an ESOT. Second is the fact that the target firm's earnings are reduced by the cash value of its stock contribution to an ESOT. This means that employees can acquire their firm with tax-free dollars totaling up to 15 percent of the payroll. The tax-sheltered status of the earnings stream makes the use of ESOTs appealing to some lenders in affecting a leveraged buyout.

target firm's assets as collateral and its cash flow stream to amortize the debt. The purchase price is typically at or near net asset value, with a P/E ratio of between 5 and 10 times earnings. Because of the need to rely on future cash flows to service the debt incurred in the leveraged buyout, the firms acquired are usually in manufacturing or distribution and are characterized by having little or no debt, a lot of pledgeable (and preferably liquid) assets, a long record of stable cash flows, low capital intensity, relatively slow sales growth, and a low level of technology.

From the standpoint of the buyers or investors in a leveraged buyout, a crucial element of analysis involves projection of expected cash flows after taxes for the buyout period, typically 5 to 7 years. Employing straightforward capital budgeting techniques, the CFATs must be estimated *after taking specific account of the amount and timing of the interest and principal payments necessary to service the debt.* (Since the focus is on the returns to the equity investors, the specific financing-associated CFATs must be considered in a leveraged buyout. This is the only place in the text that CFATs are calculated after including the specific financing costs.) These CFATs are then discounted at the equity investors' required rate of return, which is generally 20 to 25 percent. Sensitivity analysis is often helpful in assessing the firm's ability to service debt under different circumstances. Because of the number of parties involved, a determination of the CFATs and NPV is almost essential before all the investors agree to the specific provisions of the financing employed in a leveraged buyout.

An analysis of a leveraged buyout may be helpful. In 1971 International Telephone and Telegraph wanted to divest itself of Syracuse China, a restaurant china manufacturer. The firm had sales of $16 million but showed no profits. A purchase price of $7.7 million in cash was agreed upon, with the financing arranged as follows. A major insurance company provided $5 million in long-term debt at 9.5 percent interest and got a 20 percent equity ownership (an equity kicker) for $5,000. The management of Syracuse China then put up 8 percent of the purchase price in cash in exchange for 25 percent of the equity, while the investment bankers received approximately 9.5 percent of the equity in exchange for $35,000. The rest of the cash and equity ownership was shared by another insurance company and a private investor.

In 1972 Syracuse made an acquisition, and in January 1973, 260,000 shares of Syracuse China common were sold to the public at $10 per share. Five years later, the firm was sold to Canadian Pacific for $21 million. The major lender (who supplied $5 million in debt and $5,000 in equity) received a $4 million return on its equity kicker, while the investment bankers netted $2 million on their original cash investment of $35,000. Other original equity investors shared proportionately, while the public shareholders received $27 per share for stock they had bought for $10 a share in 1973. The risks are large, and some leveraged buyouts ultimately fail, but the potential rewards suggest that leveraged buyouts will remain attractive for the foreseeable future.

Tender Offers

The actual merger price is generally determined by negotiation. If the negotiations are confined to the managements and boards of directors of the firms involved, the specific merger price and terms depend on the bargaining ability and strength of the participants. However, the acquiring firm can make its appeal directly to the shareholders of the target firm through a *tender offer*, an offer to purchase shares of stock of the target firm at a fixed price per share from any shareholder who elects to "tender" or sell shares. The offer is normally set at a minimum of 20 percent above the existing premerger price as an incentive to shareholders of the target firm.[17] Acquiring firms often skip negotiations entirely and go directly to a tender offer when they anticipate a less than enthusiastic reception from the management of the target firm.

The tender is solicited through media advertising, from institutional investors, or by direct mail to shareholders of record (if time and conditions warrant). The primary advantage of a cash tender offer from the acquiring firm's standpoint is the speed with which it can be initiated. The only legal requirements are the following: (1) Under the Williams amendment to the Exchange Act, the acquiring firm must identify the parties involved, the source and amount of funds to be used in the offer, and the persons or firms retained to assist in the offer; and (2) there is a 15-day waiting period under Federal Trade Commission regulations.[18] After this, the tender period (which normally lasts from 10 to 14 days) can be initiated. Speed is often essential, especially if the acquiring firm is engaged in a "surprise" tender offer. Although the acquiring firm may not gain majority ownership by a tender offer, acquisition of 20 to 40 percent of the outstanding common stock generally provides it with effective control of the target firm.

---

[17]See Raymond S. Troubh, "Purchased Affection: A Primer on Cash Tender Offers," *Harvard Business Review* 54 (July–August 1976), pp. 79–91. Peter Dodd and Richard Ruback, "Tender Offers and Stockholder Returns," *Journal of Financial Economics* 5 (December 1977), pp. 351–373, and Donald R. Kummer and J. Ronald Hoffmeister, "Valuation Consequences of Cash Tender Offers," *Journal of Finance* 33 (May 1978), pp. 505–516, provide evidence of large positive abnormal returns for shareholders of the target firms and very small positive abnormal returns for the shareholders of the acquiring firms.

[18]Effective September 5, 1978, all proposed business combinations must be registered with the Federal Trade Commission (FTC) if one firm has assets or sales of $100 million or more and the second firm has assets or sales of $10 million or more; *and* (a) if the acquisition exceeds $15 million in value or (b), if 15 percent of the stock or assets of the target firm have an asset value of $10 million or more. Both the acquiring firm and the target firm must register. The minimum waiting period before the transaction can be consummated is 30 days unless it is a tender offer, in which case the waiting period is 15 days. An additional 20 day (10 days for a tender offer) waiting period may be required. See Robert M. Goolrick, "The End of the Midnight Merger: An Overview of the New FTC Premerger Notice Rules," *Business Lawyer* 34 (November 1978), pp. 63–71.

Defensive Tactics

From the standpoint of the target firm, a number of defensive tactics can be employed if it does not want to be acquired through an unfriendly tender offer. Among them are the following:

1. Maintaining the financial affairs of the business in such a way as to avoid becoming a potential takeover candidate. This means using assets effectively, maintaining profitability and a reasonable cash dividend policy, avoiding an excess buildup of cash, and also avoiding excess unused debt capacity.

2. Ensuring through the corporate charter and bylaws that there are effective impediments to ward off a potential acquiring firm. These might take the form of a staggered term for the board of directors and the requirement of, say, 80 percent approval of the common shareholders for a merger. In addition, the state of domicile should also be considered, since it may be important. A number of states have laws that restrict takeovers.

3. Setting up various legal defenses. These might include the possibility of an antitrust suit if the two firms are competitors. Shareholders of the target firm may be encouraged to seek a stockholders' injunction against the takeover because of misrepresentation of the value offered. Finally, steps should be taken to delay as long as possible in providing a shareholder list to the potential acquiring firm.

4. Prearranging a publicity campaign including media advertising and letters to shareholders to stress the positive aspects of keeping the firm a separate entity.

5. Preparing to buy up its own shares to shrink the stock available for tender; or, if all else fails, to seek a "friendly" or "defensive" takeover by another firm (often called a "white knight") under more favorable circumstances.

Ultimately, the most effective takeover protection relies on a combination of financial and legal actions that should be considered long before a firm becomes engaged in a takeover fight.

Seller Tax Considerations

The legal form of a merger has important tax consequences. The Internal Revenue Service has specified that in a tax-free combination, the seller does not usually realize a taxable gain or loss and the precombination tax basis of the assets carries over to the surviving corporation. In general, three forms of business reorganization qualify for tax-free status.

1. Type A. Any statutory merger or consolidation undertaken for a business purpose under which the shareholders of the target firm receive a continuing equity interest in the surviving firm. The continuity of interest test is assumed to be met if the target shareholders receive voting or nonvoting stock of the acquiring

firm equal to at least 50 percent of the value of the formally outstanding stock of the target firm.

2. **Type B.** Any acquisition of 80 percent or more of all classes of stock of the target firm in a single transaction (or series of transactions occurring over a short period of time) in exchange for voting stock of the acquiring firm.

3. **Type C.** Any acquisition of substantially all the assets of the target in exchange for voting stock of the acquiring firm.

A type A reorganization is the only tax-free merger in which payment can be made in nonvoting stock and in which a substantial portion of the payment can also be made in cash or debt securities. Both types B and C require the use of only voting common stock of the acquiring firm.

All other mergers are taxable transactions in which the owners of the target firm realize a taxable gain or loss equal to the difference between the fair market value of the cash or securities received and the tax basis of the stock or assets surrendered.[19] Obviously, where controlling investors in target firms stand to realize large long-term capital gains (and consequently pay the appropriate taxes on these capital gains) if a taxable transaction is initiated, they often support a nontaxable transaction.

Accounting Treatment of Mergers

During the 1960s firms had considerable leeway in terms of whether to account for a merger as a "pooling of interests" or a "purchase." This changed in 1970, when a new set of rules was adopted by the accounting profession.[20] If a merger plan meets the following basic conditions, it must be accounted for as a pooling of interests:

1. The acquiring firm issues only common stock with rights identical to the majority of voting common stock outstanding, and in exchange for substantially all the voting common stock of the target firm. Substantially, in this case, means 90 percent or more.

2. Each of the firms must have been independent or autonomous for at least 2 years prior to the pooling; independent means having no more than 10 percent ownership of the other firm's common stock.

3. The combination must be consummated in a single transaction or in accordance with a specific plan within 1 year after the plan is initiated. There can be no contingent payments based on the future performance of the target firm.

4. The acquiring firm must not later retire or reacquire common stock issued in connection with the merger or dispose of a significant portion of the assets of the combined firms for at least 2 years.

---

[19]Recently hybrid acquisitions have developed. See Norman R. Melefsky, "The Hybrid Acquisition: A New Tax Concept in Acquisition Planning," *Mergers & Acquisitions* 15 (fall 1980), pp. 23–27.

[20]See footnote 6.

TABLE 15.9
Balance Sheet
Treatment of a Pooling
of Interests Versus a
Purchase
($ Thousands)

	Before Merger		Eastern Lodgings Inc., After Merger	
	Eastern Lodgings Inc.	Harbor Island Inn	Pooling of Interests	Purchase
Net tangible assets	$2,300	$300	$2,600	$2,900
Goodwill	0	0	0	150
Total assets	$2,300	$300	$2,600	$3,050
Debt	$ 800	$100	$ 900	$ 900
Net worth	1,500	200	1,700	2,150
Total liabilities and net worth	$2,300	$300	$2,600	$3,050

All mergers that do not meet the pooling of interests conditions must be accounted for as a purchase. With a purchase, the target firm is treated as an investment by the acquiring firm. If the acquiring firm pays a premium above the fair market value of the target firm's assets, this premium must be reflected as goodwill on the acquiring firm's balance sheet; as such it must be amortized for accounting purposes over a period not to exceed 40 years. Reported earnings are reduced by the amount of this amortization when the purchase method is employed. In addition, this amortization of goodwill is not deductible for tax purposes.

In contrast to the purchase method, when pooling of interests is employed the balance sheets of the two firms are simply added together on an account-by-account basis. To illustrate the differences between the pooling of interests and purchase accounting treatment, consider Eastern Lodgings, Inc., a motel chain that is planning to acquire all the common stock of Harbor Island Inn for $750,000 in stock.[21] At the time of the merger, the accounting book value of Harbor Island's assets was $300,000 and their estimated fair market value was $600,000. As shown in Table 15.9, under the pooling of interests method, the respective asset, liability, and net worth accounts are simply added together. Under the purchase method, the assets of Harbor Island are reevaluated to their fair market value of $600,000, with the remaining $150,000 (the difference between the value of the stock exchanged and the fair market value of Harbor Islands assets, $750,000 − $600,000) being reflected as goodwill to be amortized over a period not exceeding 40 years.

[21]For purposes of illustration we assume that Eastern Lodgings can employ either accounting method while the rest of the conditions attached to the merger remain unchanged. In reality, this option is not available and the only way to consider the two alternative accounting treatments is to change some of the merger conditions.

SUMMARY

Evaluation of external growth through merger requires a capital budgeting approach. If the merger is cash-financed, the maximum acquisition price (MAP) the acquiring firm can afford to pay is easily determined using present value techniques. Alternatively, if the merger is stock-financed, the net advantage to merging (NAM) is calculated. In both cases it is necessary to estimate the future CFATs accruing from the acquisition and then discount them at the appropriate discount rate, given the risk involved. This approach provides financial managers with the knowledge necessary to ensure that the acquiring firm (1) is benefited by the merger, and (2) does not pay too much for the acquisition.

One effect of merging may be an increase in the acquiring firm's reported earnings per share; however, this is not a sufficient condition for merging. The primary benefits appear to be from economies of scale or operating economies (synergistic effects), a reduction in bankruptcy and/or agency costs, and tax consequences. Financial managers must be especially careful of cosmetic EPS effects. Merging for short-run EPS effects alone does not contribute to the firm's long-run goal of shareholder wealth maximization.

Merger analysis in practice becomes complicated because of the numerous financing methods and strategies that can be used to effect the transaction. In addition, leveraged buyouts, tender offers, and tax and accounting considerations are important. However, these complications should not distract the financial manager from considering and evaluating mergers in a manner similar to any other capital expenditure. By doing so, an acquiring firm can avoid overpaying for the target firm. Such action is important since overpaying results in a reduction in the acquiring firm's shareholders' wealth.

QUESTIONS

15.1. Evaluate the various reasons cited for merging and indicate whether they result in financial benefits to the shareholders of the acquiring firm.

15.2. Would the book value of a firm's assets be the absolute minimum price to be paid for the firm? Why? Is there any value that would qualify as the absolute minimum?

15.3. Empirical evidence indicates the existence of sizable premiums being paid for target firms resulting in excess risk-adjusted returns for their shareholders, but there is little or no evidence of excess risk-adjusted returns for shareholders of the acquiring firm. Discuss this in terms of the economic consequences for the two groups of shareholders. Does this imply anything about the long-run prospects for the merger benefiting the acquiring firm?

15.4. Explain why a different analytical approach to merger evaluation is needed when stock (or stock-based securities) is employed as the method of payment instead of cash (or straight debt or preferred stock).

15.5. Why should the earnings per share approach to merger evaluation be discarded or employed only as a supplement to the capital budgeting approach?

15.6. Based on rulings of the New York Stock Exchange and the SEC, firms must disclose that they have entered into merger negotiations as soon as they start such discussions. Obviously, many of these discussions are later abandoned. Why do you suppose such rules were put into effect? Are there any negative aspects of such rules?

15.7. Leveraged buyouts generally involve firms or divisions of firms that have certain characteristics. Identify these characteristics and relate them to the means of financing.

15.8. Some individuals have recently expressed concern about the extensive use of tender offers and argue that they are "unfair." Recently the FTC was empowered to require a premerger notification and a minimum 15-day waiting period before a tender can become effective. Discuss the strengths and weaknesses of this new requirement.

15.9. Distinguish between "pooling of interests" versus "purchase" accounting treatments of a merger. Under what conditions would an acquiring firm favor the purchase treatment?

PROBLEMS

15.1. *MAXIMUM ACQUISITION PRICE FOR CASH-FINANCED MERGER.* Southern Forest Industries is evaluating the possible acquisition of one of two lumber firms located in the Pacific Northwest. If Southern acquires one firm it will be precluded from acquiring the other firm; so they are mutually exclusive. The relevant information for the two target firms (as estimated by Southern) is as follows:

| Year | Spencer Lumber ($ Millions) | | |
	Postmerger CFATs (Before Capital Expenses and Working Capital)	Needed After-Tax Capital Expenses	Additional Working Capital
1	$1.00	$0.20	$0.10
2	1.20	0.30	—
3	1.40	0.40	—
4	1.55	0.40	0.10
5	1.65	0.40	—
6	1.70	0.40	—
Beyond 6	$1.75 in perpetuity	$0.40 in perpetuity	—

	Far Western Wood ($ Millions)		
Year	Postmerger CFATs (Before Capital Expenses and Working Capital)	Needed After-Tax Capital Expenses	Additional Working Capital
1	$2.50	$0.5	$0.1
2	2.75	1.0	0.1
3	3.05	1.0	0.1
4	3.50	1.5	0.1
5	4.00	1.5	0.1
6	4.80	1.5	0.1
7	5.80	1.0	0.1
8	7.00	1.0	0.1
Beyond 8	7% growth in perpetuity (for CFATs, capital expenses, and working capital)		

Southern Forest Industries' marginal cost of capital is 13 percent. Its MCC will remain at 13 percent if Spencer Lumber is acquired. However, because of the substantial debt that will have to be issued if Far Western Wood is acquired, Southern estimates its MCC will increase to 16 percent (which is appropriate for evaluating Far Western). Southern will not purchase the liabilities of either firm.

a. Calculate the relevant CFATs Southern should use in evaluating the proposed acquisitions.
b. What is the maximum acquisition price (MAP) Southern can afford to pay to acquire either Spencer or Far Western?
c. If Southern Forest Industries can buy Spencer for $7 million in cash or Far Western for $31.5 million in cash, which alternative (if either) should it choose? Why?

15.2. *MAXIMUM ACQUISITION PRICE FOR CASH-FINANCED MERGER: WITH VERSUS WITHOUT LIABILITIES PURCHASED.* AgCorp, Inc., a food processing company, is negotiating to purchase Texas Tom's, which is a division of Century Electronics. At this point it is not clear whether only the assets of Texas Tom's will be purchased, or both assets and liabilities. AgCorp estimates Texas Tom's CFATs are shown at the top of p. 658.

AgCorp's required rate of return for the merger is 15 percent.
a. Determine the maximum acquisition price if the liabilities are not purchased.
b. What is the maximum acquisition price if AgCorp also has to

Year	CFATs (Thousands)
1	$200
2	205
3	230
4	290
5	330
6	361
7	400
8	441
Beyond 8	5% growth in perpetuity

purchase $900,000 (market value) of Texas Tom's existing liabilities?

15.3. *COMMON-STOCK-FINANCED ACQUISITIONS.* Texas Transmission is seeking merger candidates operating outside its primary business activity, the transmission of natural gas. Two possible candidates have been identified. The first, Sweetwater Petroleum, would increase the overall risk of Texas Transmission, requiring a MCC of 16 percent for the combined firm. The acquisition of National Tobacco would result in a combined MCC of 13 percent.

	CFATs (in $ Millions)		
Year	Texas Transmission (Without Merger)	Sweetwater Petroleum (Postmerger)	National Tobacco (Postmerger)
1	$175	$105	$39
2	189	121	42
3	204	140	45
4	221	160	48
5	239	185	51
6	258	211	55
7	278	243	59
Beyond 7	8% growth in perpetuity	n.a.	n.a.
Number of shares of common stock outstanding	800,000	500,000	400,000
Current market price per share	$100	$128	$20
Current market value of liabilities to be assumed	—	$60 million	$20 million

Texas Transmission's current MCC is 14 percent. The mergers, if undertaken, will involve common stock. The postmerger growth rate in CFATs beyond year 7 will be 9 percent in perpetuity if Sweetwater Petroleum is acquired and 8 percent in perpetuity if National Tobacco is acquired. Texas Transmission has estimated CFATs (in millions) and financial data as given in the second table on p. 658.

a. Is the merger in Texas Transmission's best interest if it offers $140 in stock for each share of Sweetwater Petroleum?

b. What is the maximum Texas Transmission can offer (in stock) for Sweetwater Petroleum?

c. Is the merger in Texas Transmission's best interest if it offers $28 in stock for each share of National Tobacco?

d. What is the maximum Texas Transmission can offer (in stock) for National Tobacco?

e. After calculating the maximum Texas Transmission can pay (in parts b and d), you are informed that the sellers each want a premium of between 30 and 40 percent over their current market price. Is it likely that either acquisition will be made? Explain.

15.4. *MERGER TERMS: CASH VERSUS STOCK.* Delaware Industries is considering the acquisition of Chicago Coil, a maker of refrigeration equipment. During the premerger discussion, this question came up: Should cash or stock be employed to finance the acquisition? From the standpoint of Chicago Coil's shareholders, it will be a taxable transaction if cash is employed, whereas it will be tax-exempt if stock is employed; hence some of their shareholders might be willing to accept a "lower" stock-financed offer as opposed to a "higher" cash offer. Delaware Industries has estimated the following CFAT streams (in thousands):

Year	Delaware Industries (Without Merger)	Chicago Coil (Postmerger)
1	$ 700	$300
2	770	325
3	850	350
4	930	380
5	1,025	410
6	1,130	440
After 6	6% growth in perpetuity	4% growth in perpetuity (if cash financed)

Chicago Coil currently has $500,000 in liabilities that will have to be assumed by Delaware Industries. Delaware's MCC of 15 percent is the appropriate discount rate; it has 200,000 shares of stock outstanding and its current market price per share is $40. Chicago Coil has 50,000 shares of stock outstanding.

a. If cash is employed, determine the maximum acquisition price Delaware Industries can pay: (1) in total, and (2) on a per-share basis.

b. Now consider the use of stock instead of cash. Is it in Delaware's best interest to acquire Chicago Coil with stock if it values Chicago at: (1) $45 per share, or (2) $48 per share? (*Note:* Assume the combined firm's annual growth rate in CFATs will be 5.45 percent per year after year 6 in perpetuity. Also, carry Delaware's percentage ownership in the combined firm to four places.)

c. Explain why Delaware can pay more in cash than if it employs common stock in the acquisition.

d. From both Delaware's and Chicago Coil's standpoints, which form of financing do you think is more appropriate? Why?

15.5. *COMBINED CASH- AND STOCK-FINANCED ACQUISITION.* Engle Electronics is interested in the purchase of Scott and Sons Stereo and TV, a retail outlet for high-quality television, radio, and stereo equipment. The merger is expected to provide synergistic benefits. Engle's MCC of 12 percent will remain unchanged for the combined firms. In addition, the combined firm's postmerger annual growth rate is estimated to be 4 percent per year in perpetuity. Engle has estimated the following pertinent data:

| Year | CFATs (Millions) | | |
	Engle (Without Merger)	Scott & Sons (Without Merger)	Synergistic Effect (ΔCFATs Due to Merger)
1	$360	$200	$68
2	383	290	26
3	416	305	75
4	435	412	60
5	471	524	75
Beyond 5	5% growth in perpetuity	n.a.	0%
Number of shares of common stock outstanding	750,000	450,000	
Current market price per share	$30	$40	
Current market value of liabilities to be assumed	—	$20 million	

Should Engle merge if:

a. Scott and Sons stock is valued at $48 per share and the transaction is entirely stock-financed?

b. In addition to the stock financing in (a), Engle must pay Scott and Sons $22.5 million dollars in cash?

15.6. *EPS ANALYSIS.* Jackson Milk is evaluating two possible acquisition candidates—Tidelands Dairy Products and Sea Breeze Ice. The relevant financial data are as follows:

	Jackson Milk	Tidelands Dairy Products	Sea Breeze Ice
Current EPS	$5	$2	$3
Expected growth per year in EPS	10%	18%	4%
Number of shares of common stock outstanding	8 million	2 million	3 million
Market price per share	$50	$30	$15

There are no synergistic benefits. Jackson Milk is concerned about the impact on EPS both immediately and for the next 5 years; hence a graph of its EPS without and with either of the proposed mergers is necessary. In the discussions, Tidelands demands payment of a 20 percent premium over its current market price per share, while Sea Breeze demands payment of a 10 percent premium.

a. Calculate and plot Jackson's EPS without the merger for the next 5 years.

b. Determine the market price exchange ratio for Jackson and Tidelands; then calculate and plot the EPS from the combined firm for each of the next 5 years.

c. Determine the market price exchange ratio for Jackson and Sea Breeze; then calculate and plot the EPS from the combined firm for each of the next 5 years.

d. If Jackson is not willing to suffer any dilution in EPS by the time 5 years are up, should either merger be made? Why?

e. Discuss the general impact of premiums required by the merger candidate on the merger performance of the combined firm. What is the impact of premiums on the attractiveness of the merger to the acquiring firm?

15.7. *EPS VERSUS STOCK-FINANCED.* Stevenson Laboratories is evaluating the possible acquisition of Jones Piano and Organ. Stevenson's MCC is estimated to be 16 percent before the proposed merger; the combined firms MCC is also estimated to be 16 percent. In addition, the combined firm's growth rate in CFATs beyond year 5 is estimated to be 3 percent per year in perpetuity. Relevant data pertaining to both companies are as follows:

	CFATs (Thousands)	
Year	Stevenson Laboratories (Without Merger)	Jones Piano and Organ (Postmerger)
1	$518	$206
2	592	255
3	667	296
4	735	444
5	794	458
Beyond 5	4% growth in perpetuity	n.a.
Current EPS	$1	$10
EPS growth per year	5%	3%
Number of shares of common stock outstanding	100,000	40,000
Current market price per share	$30	$24
Current market value of liabilities to be assumed	—	$60,000

If Jones requires a premium of 50 percent over its current market price per share, evaluate the proposed merger employing the:

a. Stock-financed net advantage to merging (NAM) method. Should Jones be acquired?

b. EPS method. Should Jones be acquired?

c. Which method is best and why? What recommendations would you offer Stevenson? Explain?

15.8. *LEVERAGED BUYOUT.* Phyllis Nobel, a wealthy investor, is considering the purchase of Arrow Machine Tool Company via a leveraged buyout. Phyllis would have to put up $1 million in equity funds, on which she demands a 20 percent return (ignoring her personal taxes). To evaluate the desirability of the possible buyout, Phyllis employs a net-present-value approach based on the following equation:

$$NPV \text{ (to Phyllis Nobel)} = \sum_{t=0}^{a} \frac{CFAT_t}{(1 + k_s)^t} + \frac{AV_a}{(1 + k_s)^a} - B_0$$

where AV_a is the abandonment value at the end of year a, and $B_0 =$ the market value of existing liabilities that *will not* be paid off via the CFATs. If the NPV is greater than $1 million, Phyllis will consider the project acceptable. Arrow will require some additional capital investments in the next 5 years. Hence, Phyllis prepared the following table to determine the cash flows available to service the debt during each of the next 5 years:

Year	CFAT with No Additional Capital Expenditures (Thousands)	−	Additional Capital Expenditures (Thousands)	+	Tax Shield from Additional Depreciation (Thousands)	=	CFAT to Service Debt and Equity (Thousands)
1	$500	−	$ 50	+	$ 6	=	$456
2	525	−	100	+	8	=	433
3	550	−	75	+	12	=	487
4	560	−	75	+	12	=	497
5	570	−	75	+	12	=	507

A bank has agreed to lend $1.2 million for the buyout at 14 percent amortized over 5 years annually. The partially completed amortization schedule is as follows:

Year	Beginning Balance	Payment	Repayment of Principal	Interest	Ending Balance
1	$1,200,000	$349,549	$181,549	$168,000	$1,018,451
2	1,018,451	349,549	206,966	—	811,485
3	—	349,549	—	113,608	—
4	—	349,549	—	—	—
5	—	349,491	—	—	0

Phyllis Nobel has established the following format for use in completing her analysis:

Year	CFAT to Service Debt and Equity	−	Payment on Loan	+	Tax Subsidy on Loan Interest ($T = .40$)	=	CFAT to Equity Owner
1	$456,000	−	$349,549	+	$67,200[a]	=	$173,651
2	433,000	−	—	+	—	=	—
3	487,000	−	—	+	—	=	—
4	497,000	−	—	+	—	=	—
5	507,000	−	—	+	—	=	—

[a] $67,200 = $168,000 × .40.

Phyllis estimates Arrow will have an abandonment value (AV_a) of $4,640,000 at the end of 5 years, but liabilities of $1,200,000 will also exist at that time. (Thus, $B_0 = $1,200,000$.)

a. Complete the loan amortization schedule.

b. Complete the table to calculate the CFAT that will result for the equity owner, Phyllis Nobel.

c. Calculate the NPV of the leverage buyout using a discount rate of 20 percent. Should Phyllis acquire Arrow Machine Tool?

SELECTED REFERENCES

Ashton, D. J., and D. R. Atkins. "A Partial Theory of Takeover Bids." *Journal of Finance* 39 (March 1984), pp. 167–183.

Asquith, Paul, and E. Han Kim. "The Impact of Merger Bids on the Participating Firms' Security Holders." *Journal of Finance* 37 (December 1982), pp. 1209–1228.

Baron, David P. "Tender Offers and Management Resistance," *Journal of Finance* 38 (May 1983), pp. 331–343.

Bernstein, Peter W. "Who Buys Corporate Losers." *Fortune* 103 (January 26, 1981), pp. 60–62ff.

Bradley, Michael. "Interfirm Tender Offers and the Market for Corporate Control." *Journal of Business* 53 (October 1980), pp. 345–376.

Dodd, Peter. "Merger Proposals, Management Discretion and Stockholder Wealth." *Journal of Financial Economics* 8 (June 1980), pp. 105–137.

————, and Richard Ruback. "Tender Offers and Stockholder Returns." *Journal of Financial Economics* 5 (December 1977), pp. 351–373.

Eger, Carol Ellen. "An Empirical Examination of the Redistribution Effect in Pure Exchange Mergers." *Journal of Financial and Quantitative Analysis* 18 (December 1983), pp. 547–572.

Galai, Dan, and Ronald W. Masulis. "The Option Pricing Model and the Risk Factor of Stock." *Journal of Financial Economics* 3 (January–March 1976), pp. 53–82.

Goolrick, Robert M. "The End of the Midnight Merger: An Overview of the New FTC Premerger Notice Rules." *Business Lawyer* 34 (November 1978), pp. 63–71.

Halpern, Paul J. "Empirical Estimates of the Amount and Distribution of Gains to Companies in Mergers." *Journal of Business* 46 (October 1973), pp. 554–575.

————. "Corporate Acquisitions: A Theory of Special Cases? A Review of Event Studies Applied to Acquisitions." *Journal of Finance* 38 (May 1983), pp. 297–317.

Haugen, Robert A., and Terence C. Langetieg. "An Empirical Test for Synergism in Merger." *Journal of Finance* 30 (September 1975), pp. 1003–1014.

Higgins, Robert C., and Lawrence D. Schall. "Corporate Bankruptcy and Conglomerate Merger." *Journal of Finance* 30 (March 1975), pp. 93–114.

Hochman, Stephen A., and Oscar D. Folger. "Deflecting Takeovers: Charter and By-Law Techniques." *Business Lawyer* 34 (January 1979), pp. 537–559.

Jensen, Michael C., and William H. Meckling. "Theory of the Firm: Managerial Behavior, Agency Costs and Ownership Structure." *Journal of Financial Economics* 3 (October 1976), pp. 305–360.

Joehnk, Michael D., and James F. Nielsen. "The Effects of Conglomerate Merger Activity on Systematic Risk." *Journal of Financial and Quantitative Analysis* 9 (March 1974), pp. 215–225.

Kim, E. Han, and John J. McConnell. "Corporate Mergers and the Co-Insurance of Corporate Debt." *Journal of Finance* 32 (May 1977), pp. 349–368.

Kummer, Donald R., and J. Ronald Hoffmeister. "Valuation Consequences of Cash Tender Offers." *Journal of Finance* 33 (May 1978), pp. 505–516.

Langetieg, Terence C. "An Application of a Three-Factor Performance Index to Measure Stockholder Gains from Merger." *Journal of Financial Economics* 6 (December 1978), pp. 365–384.

Lewellen, Wilbur G. "A Pure Financial Rationale for the Conglomerate Merger." *Journal of Finance* 26 (May 1971), pp. 521–537.

———, and Michael G. Ferri. "Strategies for the Merger Game: Management and the Market." *Financial Management* 12 (December 1983), pp. 25–35.

Mandelker, Gershon. "Risk and Return: The Case of Merging Firms." *Journal of Financial Economics* 1 (December 1974), pp. 303–335.

Melefsky, Norman R. "The Hybrid Acquisition: A New Tax Concept in Acquisition Planning." *Mergers & Acquisitions* 15 (fall 1980), pp. 23–27.

Mueller, Dennis C. "The Effects of Conglomerate Mergers." *Journal of Banking and Finance* 1 (December 1977), pp. 315–347.

Rappaport, Alfred. "Capital Budgeting Approach to an Exchange-of-Shares Acquisition." *Mergers & Acquisitions* 10 (fall 1975), pp. 27–29.

———. "Financial Analysis for Mergers and Acquisitions." *Mergers & Acquisitions* 10 (winter 1976), pp. 18–36.

———. "Strategic Analysis for More Profitable Acquisitions." *Harvard Business Review* 57 (July–August 1979), pp. 99–110.

Rosenbloom, Arthur H., and Alex W. Howard. "'Bootstrap' Acquisitions and How to Value Them." *Mergers & Acquisitions* 11 (winter 1977), pp. 18–26.

Ruback, Richard S. "The Cities Service Takeover: A Case Study." *Journal of Finance* 38 (May 1983), pp. 319–330.

Salter, Malcolm S., and Wolf A. Weinhold. "Diversification via Acquisition: Creating Value." *Harvard Business Review* 56 (July–August 1978), pp. 166–176.

Scott, James H., Jr. "On the Theory of Conglomerate Mergers." *Journal of Finance* 32 (September 1977), pp. 1235–1250.

Shrives, Ronald E., and Donald L. Stevens. "Bankruptcy Avoidance as a Motive for Merger." *Journal of Financial and Quantitative Analysis* 14 (September 1979), pp. 501–515.

Smith, Clifford W., Jr., and Jerold B. Warner. "On Financial Contracting: An Analysis of Bond Covenants." *Journal of Financial Economics* 7 (June 1979), pp. 117–161.

Stapleton, Richard C. "The Acquisition Decision as a Capital Budgeting Problem." *Journal of Business Finance and Accounting* 2 (summer 1975), pp. 187–202.

Troubh, Raymond S. "Purchased Affection: A Primer on Cash Tender Offers." *Harvard Business Review* 54 (July–August 1976), pp. 79–91.

Wallner, Nicholas. "Leveraged Buyouts: A Review of the State of the Art, Parts 1 and 2." *Mergers & Acquisitions* 14 (fall 1979), pp. 4–13, and 14 (winter 1980), pp. 16–26.

Wansley, James W., Rodney L. Roenfeldt, and Philip L. Cooley. "Abnormal Returns from Merger Profiles," *Journal of Financial and Quantitative Analysis* 18 (June 1983), pp. 149–162.

16

Abandonment, Divestiture, and Failure

The long-term capital budgeting decisions we have considered up to now have all focused on the acquisition of assets. But the capital budgeting process is much broader; it also involves consideration of when to abandon a project, to divest some of the firm's assets, or even to liquidate the entire firm. Capital budgeting techniques employing present-value-based models are applicable in all these situations. The projects themselves may be very small, or as large as International Paper's recent sale of its Canadian operations to Canadian Pacific for $910 million. To understand abandonment problems, we begin by examining simple abandonment rules. Next the question of divestiture—selling off part of the firm's operations, is considered. Finally, we look at failure, including the decision whether to liquidate or reorganize. All these decisions, as we will see, are capital budgeting decisions.

The Abandonment Decision

Knowing when to abandon a project is as important, from the standpoint of maximizing shareholder wealth, as knowing when to undertake a new project. If a machine has become unproductive and obsolete, it may be fairly obvious that it should be abandoned. A somewhat more difficult decision arises, however, if a firm acquired another firm a few years earlier and is now asking the question, "Is that acquisition continuing to make a positive contribution to our goal of shareholder wealth maximization?" Or the firm may have decided to reposition its funds into some new assets or operations. Again, managers must know how to make abandonment decisions. The basic criterion employed in all abandonment decisions is to compare the net benefits to be received from keeping the assets to the net benefits received from selling them. The firm then selects the alternative with the greatest net benefit.

Robichek and Van Horne[1] first emphasized the importance of abandonment values and proposed that a project be abandoned in the first year its abandonment value exceeds the present value of the remaining after-tax cash flow stream (discounted at the appropriate discount rate) associated with continued operation of the project. However, it has been shown there may be an even greater advantage to abandonment in some subsequent period.[2] Thus it may be necessary to consider all possible abandonment opportunities, in addition to the first year in which the abandonment value exceeds the present value of continued operation. While the Robichek-Van Horne analysis was concerned with the question of whether the firm should abandon, the broader questions are the following: Should the firm abandon? If so, when is the proper time to abandon?

The Basic Abandonment Rule

To calculate the net benefits of keeping versus abandoning a project, it is helpful to start with the case of an asset that is already owned. The question is whether to keep it or abandon it. This approach is also applicable for considering independent new capital budgeting projects when the firm wants to simultaneously determine the optimal time for abandonment. The abandonment rule and the steps for keep-abandon decisions are as follows:[3]

Let $CFAT_t$ = expected operating cash flow after taxes in year t
k = the required rate of return
n = expected economic life of the project
AV_a = expected after-tax abandonment value at the end of year a

Step 1.   Set $a = 1$ where a is equal to a specific time interval (years) in the future.

Step 2.   Compute the NPV of the project, given abandonment at the end of year a, NPV_a where

$$NPV_a = \sum_{t=1}^{a} \frac{CFAT_t}{(1 + k)^t} + \frac{AV_a}{(1 + k)^a} \tag{16.1}$$

---

[1]Alexander A. Robichek and James C. Van Horne, "Abandonment Value and Capital Budgeting," *Journal of Finance* 22 (December 1967), pp. 577–589.

[2]Edward A. Dyl and Hugh W. Long, "Abandonment Value and Capital Budgeting: Comment," *Journal of Finance* 24 (March 1969), pp. 88–95; and Robicheck and Van Horne, "Abandonment Value and Capital Budgeting: Reply," *Journal of Finance* 24 (March 1969), pp. 96–97.

[3]O. Maurice Joy, "Abandonment Values and Abandonment Decisions: A Clarification," *Journal of Finance* 31 (September 1976), pp. 1225–1228.

This step requires an estimation of the net benefits associated with keeping the asset and, as specified by AV_a, abandoning it at some time in the future. With the subscript a set equal to 1, we would calculate the net present value associated with keeping the asset for one more year and then abandoning it.

Step 3.   Compare the net benefits associated with keeping the project, as evidenced by NPV_a, versus the net benefits arising from selling it immediately, as shown by AV_0. If $NPV_a > AV_0$, keep the project and reevaluate it in year a. (In year a the analysis is undertaken again starting with step 1.) If $NPV_a < AV_0$, go to step 4.

Step 4.   Repeat steps 2 and 3 for $a = 2, 3, \ldots, n$ until either $NPV_a > AV_0$ for some time a (keep the project and reevaluate starting with step 1 in year a), or $NPV_a < AV_0$ for all a (abandon the project now). This last step increases the subscript a and calculates the net benefits associated with keeping the asset for 2 years and then abandoning, for 3 years and then abandoning, and so on. If the NPV associated with keeping the asset is never greater than its current abandonment value, the firm should abandon the asset immediately.

The keep-abandon decision for currently owned assets requires no action concerning the optimal time at which assets should be abandoned. Rather, the decision to keep the asset requires only one instance where the present value of continuing to hold it exceeds the current abandonment value, AV_0. If the firm finds a single instance when it is better off keeping the asset, no further analysis is required until the specific point is reached (time a) when $NPV_a > AV_0$; at this point the abandonment decision must be reconsidered.

The abandonment process initially may appear complicated; an example should help to clarify the concepts. Consider Royal Electric, which is evaluating whether to keep or abandon an industrial robot. The robot is expected to last 7 more years and has cash flows after tax and expected after-tax abandonment values as specified in Table 16.1. The required discount rate for this decision is equal to the firm's marginal

TABLE 16.1 Royal Electric's Estimated CFATs and Abandonment Values from Continued Use of the Industrial Robot	Year (t)	Estimated $CFAT_t$	Estimated After-Tax Abandonment Value at the End of Year a (AV_a)
	0	—	$5400
	1	$1000	5000
	2	1300	4600
	3	1300	4300
	4	1300	3500
	5	1400	2500
	6	1400	1500
	7	1400	400

I.   ALTERNATIVE: OPERATE 1 MORE YEAR AND THEN ABANDON

$$NPV_a = \sum_{t=1}^{a} \frac{CFAT_t}{(1 + k)^t} + \frac{AV_a}{(1 + k)^a}$$

$$NPV_1 = \$1000 \ (PVIF_{15\%, \ 1 \ yr}) + \$5000 \ (PVIF_{15\%, \ 1 \ yr})$$
$$= \$6000 \ (.870) = \$5220$$

Decision: Since AV_0 of \$5400 is > \$5220, proceed to evaluate at year 2.

II.   ALTERNATIVE: OPERATE 2 MORE YEARS AND THEN ABANDON

$$NPV_2 = \$1000 \ (.870) + (\$1300 + \$4600) \ (.756)$$
$$= \$870 + \$4460.40 = \$5330.40$$

Decision: Since AV_0 of \$5400 is > \$5330.40, proceed to evaluate at year 3.

III.   ALTERNATIVE: OPERATE 3 MORE YEARS AND THEN ABANDON

$$NPV_3 = \$1000 \ (.870) + \$1300 \ (.756) + (\$1300 + \$4300) \ (.658)$$
$$= \$870 + \$982.80 + \$3684.80 = \$5537.60$$

Decision: Since AV_0 of \$5400 is < \$5537.60, continue to operate and reevaluate possible abandonment in 3 more years.

cost of capital (MCC) of 15 percent. The current abandonment value, AV_0, of the robot is \$5400.

To determine whether to abandon immediately, the calculations shown in Table 16.2 are required. Since the current abandonment value of \$5400 is greater than the NPV_1 of \$5220 (part I of Table 16.2) from employing the robot 1 more year, the tentative decision is to abandon. However, before that decision can be finalized, the possibilities of using the robot for additional years must be evaluated. By looking at years 2 and 3 (parts II and III of Table 16.2), we see that NPV_3 is greater than AV_0. Since the net present value of keeping the robot exceeds its abandonment value, Royal Electric should keep the robot for 3 more years and then reevaluate its decision. In essence, there is economic justification for keeping the robot—it still is an appropriate use of the company's resources. In 3 years, the same analysis will be repeated.[4] If in the current analysis (at $t = 0$) Royal had not found *any* NPV from operating the robot that was greater than its current abandonment value, the decision would be to abandon immediately.

---

[4]In 3 years, if the estimated CFATs and AVs do not change from those in Table 16.1, the abandonment value of \$4300 is greater than the NPV from operating the robot over any number of additional years into the future. Hence, the decision would be for Royal Electric to abandon the robot at that time.

When we discussed capital budgeting decisions in Chapter 13, we did not explicitly consider how to decide when assets already owned should be abandoned. Instead, we simply assumed they would be held to the end of their useful economic lives as estimated (at t_0) when they were acquired. However, the approach described above can also be employed during the initial acquistion of an asset to determine if the asset should continue to be held until the end of its estimated useful economic life. This approach provides the mechanism by which firms can periodically assess all current resource commitments to see if they continue to pass the test of maximizing shareholder wealth.

Some Special Situations

The foregoing analysis is applicable to keep-abandon decisions for assets already held, as well as for determining the optimal abandonment period when independent new projects are being considered, but it does not apply in other situations. If the firm is considering whether to invest in one of a group of new mutually exclusive projects, or is faced with capital rationing and wants to determine the optimal abandonment period associated with the proposed investments, a more exhaustive procedure is required. In this case it is necessary to perform the abandonment analysis over the full planning horizon to determine which projects dominate. Thus, an exhaustive search will be required, based on the following steps:

Step 1.   Compute NPV_a for $a = 1, 2, . . ., n$ for each project. This step requires NPVs to be calculated for all projects for all possible planning horizons. Suppose there are three mutually exclusive new projects being considered, each with a 10-year economic life. To make this decision, the firm would have to calculate 30 (three projects × 10 years each) different NPVs to determine the optimal abandonment period (which might be less than the projects' 10-year economic lives).

Step 2.   Select the maximum NPV_a for each project, and then choose that project with the largest positive maximum NPV_a. This step involves first the selection of the optimal abandonment period for *each* project, after which their maximum individual NPVs are compared to select the best project from the group of mutually exclusive alternatives.

This procedure vastly complicates the abandonment analysis, but in certain situations it is necessary to resort to this approach instead of the simpler one presented earlier. Likewise, uncertainty can also be incorporated, if needed.[5]

[5]See, for example, Anthony F. Herbst, "An Algorithm for Systematic Economic Analysis of Abandonment Value in Capital Budgeting," *Engineering Economist* 22 (fall 1976), pp. 63–71; and Charles P. Bonini, "Capital Investment Under Uncertainty with Abandonment Options," *Journal of Financial and Quantitative Analysis* 12 (March 1977), pp. 39–54.

A word of caution concerning abandonment problems: Capital budgeting projects must be monitored, and the possibility of abandonment must always be considered as an option. However, it is often extremely difficult to estimate the total cash flows associated with abandoning large capital projects that may involve closing down or selling off a product line or division. Such changes may result in tax implications, managerial reassignment, work force and/or labor union considerations, impact on the community or society, and other major factors. The process can entail very long lead times that substantially modify the simple, straightforward procedures we have described. And many executives find it more difficult because of emotional ties and/or ego involvement to consider abandoning assets, projects, or divisions. These difficulties make it all the more important for financial managers to be well versed in how to evaluate abandonment and divestiture decisions.

Divestiture Decisions

Divestiture involves the selling off of a chunk of the firm's assets, such as a division or subsidiary. Since such decisions are a form of abandonment, they can be analyzed in a similar manner. All potential divestiture decisions must be consistent with the firm's objective of shareholder wealth maximization—that is, firms should divest the division or subsidiary if selling can net the firm greater benefits than retaining the division. This involves a comparison of the divestiture proceeds versus the discounted present value of the expected cash flows from continuing to operate the division. The decision criteria differ slightly depending upon whether (1) the liabilities associated with the division are sold,[6] or (2) the associated liabilities are not sold.

If the *associated liabilities are sold,* the decision criterion is to divest as long as:

Net after-tax divestiture proceeds	>	NPV of future cash flows till abandonment	+	Present value of the future abandonment	−	Current market value of debt

$$NP > \sum_{t=1}^{a} \frac{CFAT_t}{(1 + k)^t} + \frac{AV_a}{(1 + k)^a} - B_0 \qquad (16.2)$$

where NP = net proceeds after tax realized from divesting or abandoning the division now

$CFAT_t$ = the expected after-tax cash flows in year t from continued operation of the division

AV_a = the expected after-tax abandonment value at the end of year a

[6]Note that when the liabilities are sold, the firm may temporarily move away from its target capital structure. However, when the gross proceeds are reinvested, the firm should return to its original capital structure.

k = the required rate of return for the division

B_0 = the current market value of the division's current liabilities and allocated long-term debt[7]

The following steps, similar to those employed in the abandonment analysis, should be used for divestiture decisions:

Step 1.   Set $a = 1$, where a is equal to a specific time interval (years) in the future.

Step 2.   Compute the NPV of the divestiture, given it takes place of the end of year a, NPV_a, (the right-hand side of Equation 16.2) where

$$NPV_a = \sum_{t=1}^{a} \frac{CFAT_t}{(1 + k)^t} + \frac{AV_a}{(1 + k)^a} - B_0$$

Step 3.   If $NPV_a > NP$; keep the division and reevaluate in year a; if $NPV_a < NP$, go to step 4.

Step 4.   Repeat steps 2 and 3 for $a = 2, 3, \ldots, n$ until $NPV_a > NP$ for some a (keep the division and reevaluate starting with step 1 in year a), or $NPV_a < NP$ for all a (divest the division now).

If the *associated liabilities are kept* by the divesting firm, the decision criterion is to divest as long as:

Gross after-tax divestiture proceeds	Current market − value of debt	NPV of future cash > flows till abandonment	Present value of + the future abandonment	Current market − value of debt
GP −	B_0	$> \displaystyle\sum_{t=1}^{a} \frac{CFAT_t}{(1 + k)^t} +$	$\dfrac{AV_a}{(1 + k)^a}$	$- B_0$ (16.3)

In the former case, the purchaser assumes the responsibility for the division's debts, while in the latter case the divesting firm retains the responsibility for servicing its debts. When the liabilities are kept by the selling firm, the divestiture decision is made following the same four-step procedure described when the liabilities are sold, except that NPV_a is calculated ignoring the liabilities, and the gross proceeds after tax, GP,

---

[7]Since the market value of the current debt is employed, it is already in present value form and does *not* have to be discounted. The net divestiture proceeds, NP, in Equation 16.2 are expressed after the value of the division's debt at time t_0 has been deducted. It is this net amount the selling firm would realize from selling both the division's assets and associated liabilities. For consistency the current-market value of the division's debt must also be subtracted from the right-hand side of the equation.

Year (t)	Estimated $CFAT_t$	Estimated After-Tax Abandonment Value at the End of Year a (AV_a)
1	$10.0	$52.0
2	10.2	53.0
3	10.4	53.0
4	10.6	53.0

are employed instead of the net proceeds. Thus Equation 16.3 can be modified to obtain Equation 16.4 where:

$$GP > \sum_{t=1}^{a} \frac{CFAT_t}{(1 + k)^t} + \frac{AV_a}{(1 + k)^a} \qquad (16.4)$$

Notice that the proceeds received from the sale will be smaller when the liabilities are sold (Equation 16.2) *than when they are kept* (Equation 16.4).

To illustrate the divestiture decision, consider Gulf Enterprises, which is evaluating whether to sell off its steel shipping container division. Gulf Enterprises has received an offer of $60 million after taxes for the division, given it retains the division's current liabilities and allocated long-term debt, which is equal to $20 million. Gulf Enterprises estimates the container division's risk is slightly less than the firm's overall risk, so a discount rate of 14 percent is appropriate. After extensive analysis, the CFATs and abandonment values shown in Table 16.3 have been estimated for the next 4 years.

To determine whether to divest the steel container division for $60 million or to continue to operate it, the calculations presented in Table 16.4 are necessary. Since the gross proceeds, GP, of $60 million is greater than the expected NPV of operating the division for only 1 more year (part I of Table 16.4), the tentative decision is to divest. However, the possibility of operating the division for additional years must also be evaluated. By looking consecutively at years 2, 3, and 4 (parts II, III, and IV of Table 16.4), we see that Gulf Enterprises should operate the container division for at least 4 more years rather than divest now, since NPV_4, of $61.285 million is greater than the gross proceeds of $60 million. If Gulf Enterprises does not find any operating period for which NPV_a is greater than GP, it should divest the division now. However, since NPV_4 is greater than the gross proceeds, Gulf should retain the division and reconsider divestiture in 4 more years.[8]

---

[8]Our approach has focused on a comparison of the gross proceeds (less debt, if applicable) versus the NPV of continuing to operate the division. Note, however, that the interrelationship between divisions might be important. Thus, the firm might conclude the aggregate value of a portfolio of divisions is more than the simple sum of their independent values. In such a case, these synergistic effects must be taken into account in estimating the CFATs to determine whether to retain or divest a division.

TABLE 16.4
Calculations for Gulf
Enterprises'
Divestiture Decision
(in Millions of Dollars)

I. ALTERNATIVE: OPERATE 1 MORE YEAR AND THEN DIVEST

$$NPV_a = \sum_{t=1}^{a} \frac{CFAT_t}{(1+k)^t} + \frac{AV_a}{(1+k)^a}$$

$$NPV_1 = \$10 \, (PVIF_{14\%, \, 1 \, yr}) + \$52 \, (PVIF_{14\%, \, 1 \, yr})$$
$$= \$62 \, (.877) = \$54.374$$

Decision: Since *GP* of $60 million is > $54.374 million, proceed to evaluate at
year 2.

II. ALTERNATIVE: OPERATE 2 MORE YEARS AND THEN DIVEST

$$NPV_2 = \$10 \, (.877) + (\$10.2 + \$53) \, (.769)$$
$$= \$8.77 + \$48.6008 = \$57.3708$$

Decision: Since *GP* of $60 million is > $57.3708 million, proceed to evaluate at
year 3.

III. ALTERNATIVE: OPERATE 3 MORE YEARS AND THEN DIVEST

$$NPV_3 = \$10 \, (.877) + \$10.2 \, (.769) + (\$10.4 + \$53) \, (.675)$$
$$= \$8.77 + \$7.8438 + \$42.795 = \$59.4088$$

Decision: Since *GP* of $60 million is > $59.4088 million, proceed to evaluate at
year 4.

IV. ALTERNATIVE: OPERATE 4 MORE YEARS AND THEN DIVEST

$$NPV_4 = \$10 \, (.877) + \$10.2 \, (.769) + \$10.4 \, (.675) + (\$10.6 + \$53) \, (.592)$$
$$= \$8.77 + \$7.8438 + \$7.02 + \$37.6512 = \$61.285$$

Decision: Since *GP* of $60 million is < $61.285 million, continue to operate the
container division and reevaluate possible divestiture in 4 more years.

In practice, additional considerations also influence the divestiture
decision. An important complicating factor may be the form of payment
for the division to be divested. If common stock (or other equity-based
securities) is used, the capital abandonment approach to divestiture
decisions must be modified to account for any expected future changes
in the market value of the stock to be received. Legal, tax, and accounting
considerations may also be important, particularly if they have a
significant impact on the expected proceeds to be realized from the
divestiture. Finally, any significant delays before the divestiture can be
effected are also important.

Just as many firms use mergers to enhance the wealth of the
shareholders, more and more firms are recognizing that divesting
unwanted divisions may also contribute to this goal. By divesting, firms

can concentrate on fewer activities in order to maximize their value. The process by which Texaco cut back substantially on its gasoline retail marketing is just one example of the growing awareness of the importance of properly formulated divestiture decisions. Firms like Texaco are stressing shareholder wealth maximization instead of "marketing in all 50 states" or other goals that are incompatible with the long-run goal of the firm.

Business Failure

Thus far we have considered the abandonment of a single asset and the divestiture of a whole division. However, it is also possible for firms to fail altogether. A firm is considered to be technically insolvent if it is unable to pay its liabilities as they come due. On the other hand a firm is *bankrupt* if its liabilities exceed its assets. Failure, as we use the term here, includes the entire range of possibilities between these two extremes.

The Failure Record

Business failure is widespread, as Table 16.5 shows. During the 1970–1982 period, between 6,619 and 16,794 firms failed each year. The failure rate has been between 24 and 81 firms per 10,000 concerns during this time period. One interesting trend is the increase in the size of average current liabilities per failure between 1970 and 1982. This is due to both inflation and to the rising number of larger bankruptcies.

Table 16.6 indicates the fifteen largest U.S. bankruptcies of all time. Some of these firms underwent successful reorganization, like Penn Central, but many were dismantled during the bankruptcy procedure.

TABLE 16.5
Failure Rates in the United States, 1970–1982

Year	Number of Failures	Annual Failure Rate Per 10,000 Concerns	Current Liabilities (Thousands)	Average Current Liabilities Per Failure (Thousands)
1970	10,748	44	$1,887,754	$175.6
1971	10,326	42	1,916,927	185.6
1972	9,566	38	2,000,244	209.1
1973	9,345	36	2,298,606	246.0
1974	9,915	38	3,053,137	307.9
1975	11,432	43	4,380,170	383.1
1976	9,628	35	3,011,271	312.8
1977	7,919	28	3,095,317	390.9
1978	6,619	24	2,656,006	401.3
1979	7,564	28	2,667,362	352.6
1980	11,742	42	4,635,080	394.7
1981	16,794	61	6,955,180	414.1
1982 (six months)	11,752	82[a]	7,574,643	644.5

[a]Estimated.

SOURCE: Dun & Bradstreet Corp. and *Dun's Statistical Review: Quarterly Failure Report,* various issues.

Firm	Total Liabilities (in Millions of Dollars)	Bankruptcy Petition Date
Penn Central Transportation	$3,300	June 1970
Wickes	2,000	April 1982
Itel	1,700	January 1981
Braniff Airlines	1,100	May 1982
W. T. Grant	1,000	October 1975
Seatrain Lines	785	February 1981
Continental Mortgage Investors	607	March 1976
United Merchants & Manufacturing	552	July 1977
AM International	510	April 1982
Saxon Industries	461	April 1982
Commonwealth Oil Refining	421	March 1978
W. Judd Kassuba	420	December 1973
Erie Lackawanna Railroad	404	June 1972
White Motor	399	September 1980
Investors Funding	379	October 1974

[a]Excluding commercial banks.

SOURCE: Joseph W. Duncan, The Dun & Bradstreet Corporation, House Committee on Small Business, June 23, 1982.

Other firms, like Wickes and Braniff Airlines, are still attempting to regain profitability instead of liquidating. Tables 16.5 and 16.6 actually understate the financial problems of many firms, because they fail to take into account the numerous mergers, with or without government intervention, that have occurred in recent years. For example, the Federal Home Loan Bank system has assisted in arranging the absorption of many troubled savings and loans in recent years. Chrysler and Lockheed both received government loan guarantees, while numerous airlines (such as Pan American and National, or Texas Air and Continental) have merged in an attempt to improve their competitive position and/or avert possible failure.

The Prediction of Financial Distress

Although the causes of business failures are numerous, most are attributable directly or indirectly to managerial incompetence. Usually, fatal financial problems result from the cumulative effects of a number of bad decisions or unlucky events. Several studies have shown that the signs of failure are evident up to 1, 2, or 3 years before the event. In one of the first attempts to use financial data to predict failure, Beaver employed a number of different financial ratios to see if there were significant differences between healthy firms and firms that were going to fail.[9] The "best" ratio was the cash flow-to-total debt ratio, shown in Figure 16.1. The average cash flow-to-total debt ratio was lower for failed firms than for nonfailed firms up to 5 years before failure. Not only was it

[9]See William H. Beaver, "Financial Ratios as Predictors of Failure," *Empirical Research in Accounting: Selected Studies*, supplement to *Journal of Accounting Research* 4 (1966), pp. 71–111.

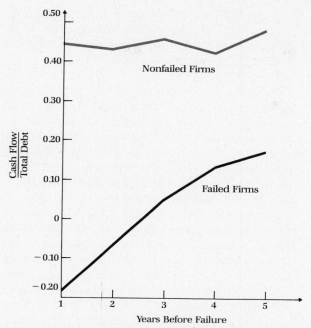

Figure 16.1   Comparison of Average Cash Flow-to-Total Debt Ratio for Failed and Nonfailed Firms.

lower, but it also deteriorated markedly as failure approached. Other ratios that showed similar trends were net income-to-total assets, total debt-to-total assets, and working capital-to-total debt.

Using discriminant analysis (discussed in Appendix 10A), Altman developed the following model, which simultaneously employs five financial ratios to discriminate potentially bankrupt firms from non-bankrupt firms:[10]

$$Z = .012X_1 + .014X_2 + .033X_3 + .006X_4 + .010X_5 \qquad (16.5)$$

where Z = the calculated discriminant value

         X_1 = net working capital (current assets − current liabilities)/ total assets

---

[10]See Edward I. Altman, "Financial Ratios, Discriminant Analysis and the Prediction of Corporate Bankruptcy," *Journal of Finance* 23 (September 1968), pp. 589–609. When computing the Z score for a firm, the ratios are expressed in absolute percentage terms; e.g., a net working capital-to-total assets ratio of 0.10 or 10 percent is expressed as 10.0 and a sales-to-total assets ratio of 2.5 or 250 percent is expressed as 250.0. In Altman's original article, the last variable, X_5, was not expressed in absolute percentage terms; we have modified it for consistency.

X_2 = retained earnings/total assets
X_3 = earnings before interest and taxes (EBIT)/total assets
X_4 = market value of common stock/book value of debt
X_5 = sales/total assets

Employing such financial data, a Z score is calculated for each firm and compared to a cutoff value of 2.675. Firms with scores below 2.675 are classified as failure candidates. In testing this model, Altman correctly classified 95 percent of the firms examined using data from 1 year before the failure. Even 2 years before failure, the model was able to correctly classify 72 percent of the firms examined.[11]

To see how this type of financial model might be used, let us see if it can predict the potential bankruptcy of W. T. Grant, which filed for bankruptcy in October 1975. Typical of many retailers, W. T. Grant had a fiscal year that ended on January 31. Table 16.7 shows the financial data for W. T. Grant for the 5 years preceding their bankruptcy application. Using Equation 16.5, its Z score for each of the 5 years prior to bankruptcy proceedings are calculated. These scores declined from 3.582 to 3.154 to 2.850 in the years 1971 through 1973, although they were still above the cutoff point of 2.675. In 1974, the value was 2.413; in 1975, it dropped to 1.260. Both were below the cutoff point. Clearly, there was ample evidence from published financial reports to indicate that W. T. Grant was going to fail.[12]

Models similar to this one encounter some problems, however, when they are used to predict the possibility of financial distress. First, they always misclassify some firms—that is, some firms that actually fail are predicted to remain solvent, while other firms that continue to remain solvent are predicted to fail. Likewise, over time, the coefficients of the models need to be updated, and certain variables may need to be added or deleted. However, even with these problems, models of this type have become an important tool for regulators in monitoring the financial well-being of banks, savings and loans, railroads, utilities, and insurance companies. In addition, an increasing number of investment bankers and security analysts use an updated version of the financial distress

---

[11]There is some question about the predictive ability of bankruptcy models. See, for example, R. Charles Moyer, "Forecasting Financial Failure: A Re-Examination," *Financial Management* 6 (spring 1977), pp. 11–17; and James A. Ohlson, "Financial Ratios and the Probabilistic Prediction of Bankruptcy," *Journal of Accounting Research* 18 (spring 1980), pp. 109–131.

[12]For studies in other industries, see Edward I. Altman, "Predicting Railroad Bankruptcies in America," *Bell Journal of Economics and Management Science* 4 (spring 1973), pp. 184–211; George E. Pinches and James S. Trieschmann, "The Efficiency of Alternative Models for Solvency Surveillance in the Insurance Industry," *Journal of Risk and Insurance* 41 (December 1974), pp. 563–577; and Joseph T. Sinkey, "A Multivariate Statistical Analysis of the Characteristics of Problem Banks," *Journal of Finance* 30 (March 1975), pp. 21–36.

TABLE 16.7

Prediction of Failure Using Altman's Model for *W. T. Grant*

A. FINANCIAL DATA FOR 5 YEARS PRECEDING BANKRUPTCY APPLICATION (IN ABSOLUTE PERCENTAGE TERMS)

Year[a]	X_1 Net Working Capital/ Total Assets	X_2 Retained Earnings/ Total Assets	X_3 EBIT/ Total Assets	X_4 Market Value of Common Stock/ Book Value of Debt	X_5 Sales/ Total Assets
1971	32.3	28.5	11.3	143.9	155.9
1972	37.6	25.9	8.3	101.3	145.9
1973	31.2	23.5	7.6	68.7	148.4
1974	32.9	19.8	4.8	17.2	147.9
1975	16.2	3.5	−19.3	3.5	163.2

B. CALCULATION OF Z VALUE

$$Z = .012X_1 + .014X_2 + .033X_3 + .006X_4 + .010X_5$$

1971 $Z = (.012)(32.3) + (.014)(28.5) + (.033)(11.3) + (.006)(143.9) + (.010)(155.9)$
$= 0.3876 + 0.3990 + 0.3729 + 0.8634 + 1.5590$
$= 3.582$ (Classify as nonbankrupt)

1972 $Z = (.012)(37.6) + (.014)(25.9) + (.033)(8.3) + (.006)(101.3) + (.010)(145.9)$
$= 3.154$ (Classify as nonbankrupt)

1973 $Z = (.012)(31.2) + (.014)(23.5) + (.033)(7.6) + (.006)(68.7) + (.010)(148.4)$
$= 2.850$ (Classify as nonbankrupt)

1974 $Z = (.012)(32.9) + (.014)(19.8) + (.033)(4.8) + (.006)(17.2) + (.010)(147.9)$
$= 2.413$ (Classify as potentially bankrupt)

1975 $Z = (.012)(16.2) + (.014)(3.5) + (.033)(−19.3) + (.006)(3.5) + (.010)(163.2)$
$= 1.260$ (Classify as potentially bankrupt)

[a]For fiscal year ending January 31.

model described here.[13] Early warning allows firms to consider taking corrective action, such as instituting better financial controls, replacing management, divestiture or abandonment of certain divisions, or even selling out to another firm—action which may save the firm from having to formally consider liquidation.

Voluntary Settlements, Bankruptcy, and Liquidation-Reorganization Decisions

When a firm becomes technically insolvent or fails, there are two ways to resolve the problem: (1) through a voluntary (or out-of-court) settlement, or (2) through legal bankruptcy proceedings leading to liquidation or reorganization.

Voluntary Settlement

The best time to deal with financial difficulties is generally before they become serious enough to force the firm into formal bankruptcy proceedings. However, when all else fails, firms typically have to deal directly with creditors. The three basic types of voluntary settlement are extension, composition, and assignment.

An *extension* involves nothing more than the postponement of payment of the claims held by one or more creditors. For example, a trade creditor might agree to convert the credit obtained into longer-term, interest-bearing notes. An extension is probably most appropriate when the debtor suffers primarily from a short-term liquidity problem; during the extension, the debtor can attempt to correct the imbalance between cash inflows and outflows in order to build up needed liquid reserves.

If the debtor's problems are more severe, a *composition*—that is, the pro rata settlement of the creditors' claims in cash or promissory notes, may be necessary. In a composition, all creditors agree to accept a stated percentage (less than 100 percent) of their claim as full satisfaction. In return for the concessions granted by either an extension or composition, creditors usually demand additional safeguards. These might include forming a creditors' committee to oversee the financial affairs of the debtor, placing restrictions on the sale of assets or stock, and requiring the firm's owners to put up additional collateral. Finally, if neither extension nor composition is feasible, an *assignment*, or voluntary out-of-court liquidation, may be required. An assignment saves the court costs associated with bankruptcy and can be employed when all parties (both creditors and shareholders) agree on the terms of the liquidation.

---

[13]See Edward I. Altman, Robert G. Halderman, and P. Narayanan, "Zeta Analysis: A New Model to Identify Bankruptcy Risk of Corporations," *Journal of Banking and Finance* 1 (June 1977), pp. 29–54; and "The Economic Case Against Federal Bailouts—and Who May Need Them," *Business Week*, March 24, 1980, pp. 104–107.

Bankruptcy Proceedings

If a voluntary settlement cannot be arranged, the only alternative left may be bankruptcy. Most legal procedures undertaken in conjunction with failing firms are covered by the Bankruptcy Reform Act of 1978, which became effective October 1, 1979. It provides for either liquidation or reorganization of a firm, and contains provisions substantially different from those of the Bankruptcy Act of 1898, as amended by the Chandler Act of 1938. Principal among the changes are the following:

1. The establishment of a network of bankruptcy courts with jurisdiction over all matters involving bankruptcy.
2. Elimination of the requirement under the previous act that the debtor commit one of six acts of bankruptcy before involuntary procedures can be initiated. Under the new act, involuntary proceedings can be initiated by three creditors upon petition.
3. Elimination of filings under Chapter X, XI, or occasionally XII for reorganization; now all filings are covered by the more general and streamlined Chapter 11.
4. Replacement of the previous rule of absolute priority with the "best interests" or relative priority test. Under the new act, senior creditors may have to wait for payment in order to increase the chances of providing some value to junior creditors and stockholders. In reorganization, even if creditors receive less than full payment, the owners may retain a portion of their ownership interest as long as the creditors receive more than they would upon liquidation.

If the firm is reorganized, substantially more flexibility exists under the new law. A reorganization plan is a contract between the debtor and creditors. In recent years, some significant reorganizations have been effected. The largest was that of Penn Central, which filed for bankruptcy in 1970, was reorganized, and after reorganization has once again resumed business minus virtually all its transportation activities. Penn Central Corporation is still enjoying the tax-loss carryforwards from the reorganization of Penn Central Transportation; however, its main activities are in energy, real estate, manufacturing, and leisure services, not railroads. It also undertook a number of mergers to generate sufficient earnings to take advantage of its tax-loss carryforwards. Thus, reorganization can result in the successful restructuring of firms that otherwise would be forced to liquidate.

The Liquidation-Reorganization Decision

Financial managers, or the courts if the firm has filed for protection under the Bankruptcy Reform Act, may have to decide whether it is better for a firm to continue to operate or to liquidate. The liquidation decision is a pressing one when a firm is insolvent or approaching insolvency, but this is not the only circumstance for which the firm may choose to terminate its business. In recent years, a number of healthy firms have liquidated because they were worth more "dead" than "alive."

Any liquidation decision can be approached in the same manner as abandonment or divestiture decisions. The question becomes one of determining the benefits if the firm liquidates versus the benefits that would accrue if the firm continues to operate. If the firm is a profitable, ongoing concern but is contemplating voluntary liquidation, Equation 16.4 can be employed, except that any costs of liquidation, L_c, must also be subtracted from the gross after-tax proceeds (the left-hand side of Equation 16.4).[14] With this one minor change, the voluntary liquidation of a firm is seen to be no more than another type of divestiture decision. However, if the firm is insolvent, the analysis becomes a little more complicated, since the major emphasis is on satisfying, to the extent possible, the firm's creditors.[15] The point of view shifts from maximizing shareholder wealth to providing creditors with the highest returns—or more realistically, with the least losses. The question then becomes this: Will the creditors recover a greater portion of their claims through liquidation than through reorganization? In insolvency, a firm should be liquidated if:[16]

Gross after-tax liquidation proceeds	−	Current market value of debt	−	Liqui- dation costs	>	NPV of future cash flows till abandonment	+	Present value of the future abandon- ment	−	Current market value of debt	−	Reorga- nization costs

$$GP \quad - \quad B_0 \quad - \quad L_c \quad > \quad \sum_{t=1}^{a} \frac{CFAT_t}{(1 + k)^t} \quad + \quad \frac{AV_a}{(1 + k)^a} \quad - \quad B_0 \quad - \quad R_c \qquad (16.6)$$

where GP = gross proceeds after tax realized from liquidating the firm now

B_0 = the current market value of the firm's current liabilities and long-term debt

L_c = the costs incurred if the firm liquidates

$CFAT_t$ = the expected after-tax cash flows in year t from continued operation of the firm

AV_a = expected after-tax abandonment value at the end of year a[17]

---

[14]The current market value of the firm's debt, B_0, will show up on both sides of this modification of Equation 16.4; therefore it can be ignored.

[15]Under the new bankruptcy code, however, shareholders may be entitled to a certain percentage of the liquidation proceeds. A joint approach to "satisfy" both creditors and shareholders may be required. We assume, for simplicity, that the creditors hold the dominant position when an involuntary liquidation is being contemplated.

[16]Gross proceeds less debt and liquidation costs is assumed to be negative, since the firm is legally bankrupt. The right-hand side of Equation 16.6 may be positive or negative. The creditors will choose the alternative that minimizes their loss.

[17]Given the liquidation versus reorganization situation, creditors may not want to contemplate any future abandonment or liquidation values. In such cases AV_a will be zero, and the decision to liquidate or reorganize will hinge on the other variables in Equation 16.6.

k = the required rate of return for the firm. (Note this rate must now reflect the returns required by both creditors and shareholders, since it is creditors who will have, in all probability, a major stake in the firm if it is reorganized. In addition, k will also increase because of the risk associated with reorganizing a firm.)

R_c = the costs incurred if the firm is reorganized

The thrust of Equation 16.6 is to evaluate the alternatives of liquidating immediately versus operating the firm for 1, 2, $\cdots$, a years in the future, at which time its operations will be terminated. Notice that the current market value of the firm's debt, B_0, shows up on both sides of the equation. In reality creditors may have to settle for less than 100 percent of their claims if the firm is liquidated. In that case B_0 on the left-hand side of the equation would be replaced by the amount the creditors agreed to accept.

To illustrate the liquidation decision when a firm is insolvent, consider Tennessee Motor Homes, which because of the rapid rise in gasoline prices, experienced a sales decline of 80 percent. Tennessee Motor Homes filed for bankruptcy. The question now is this: Should the firm be liquidated, or should it be reorganized? The bankruptcy trustee estimates that $21 million can be received after taxes from immediate liquidation of the firm; a foreign automobile manufacturer would buy the plant. Tennessee Motor Homes' current and long-term liabilities are $29 million and liquidation costs are estimated to be $1 million; hence, creditors in total would suffer a loss in liquidation of $9 million ($21 million − $29 million − $1 million). Because of the high risks involved in motor home manufacturing, the trustee estimates that a risk-adjusted discount rate of 20 percent is appropriate. Reorganization costs plus the expected CFATs and abandonment values shown in Table 16.8 have been estimated for the next 5 years; the trustee is unwilling to project them any further into the future.

To determine whether to liquidate Tennessee Motor Homes for a $9

Year (t)	Estimated $CFAT_t$	Estimated After-Tax Abandonment Value at the End of Year a ($AV_{\hat{a}}$)
1	$7	$16
2	6	14
3	6	12
4	6	10
5	6	8
Reorganization costs = $2		

million loss to the creditors or to continue to operate it, the calculations presented in Table 16.9 are necessary. As long as the left-hand side of Equation 16.6 results in a smaller loss than the right-hand side, the creditors are better off if the firm liquidates immediately instead of continuing to operate. Since this is true if the firm operates 1 more year (part I of Table 16.9), the creditors are better off if the firm is liquidated instead of operating for another year. By evaluating the options of operating the firm for 2, 3, 4, or 5 years (parts II, III, IV, and V of Table 16.9), we see that the outcome is always the same: the creditors are best served by the immediate liquidation of Tennessee Motor Homes. Any further operation of the firm results in an expected loss to the creditors in excess of $9 million.

In practice, liquidation decisions are complicated dramatically because of the difficulties encountered in estimating the CFAT stream and discount rate to employ. Also, the price the firm's assets will command in liquidation is difficult to predict unless they can be sold in some established secondary market. There are also questions about management's desire to continue operating the firm and the importance to the community of retaining the firm as a source of employment and taxes. But even though all these complicating factors exist, the basic decision follows from a consideration of the losses suffered by liquidating immediately versus those expected to be suffered by continued operation after reorganization.

SUMMARY

Capital abandonment decisions apply the same basic concepts discussed previously for evaluating capital expenditure proposals and/or mergers. However, the focus of abandonment decisions is on answering these questions: (1) Should we abandon? (2) When is the optimal time to abandon?

The essence of the process is to compare the current after-tax abandonment value of the asset, division, or firm with the sum of the discounted cash flows and future after-tax abandonment values resulting from continued operations. If the asset's risk is equal to the firm's overall risk, the firm's MCC is employed as the discount rate; otherwise an appropriate risk-adjusted discount rate is required. If the immediate abandonment value is greater than the NPV from continuing to operate over all feasible periods, the decision is to abandon. Otherwise, the asset should be retained and the abandonment question reconsidered in the future.

Business failure increased dramatically in the early 1980s. When firms face failure, they can sell out to another firm, seek a voluntary agreement with their creditors, or file for protection under the revised bankruptcy code. Firms should voluntarily liquidate when the net proceeds from the liquidation are greater than the present value of the cash flows resulting from continuing to operate. If the firm has filed for bankruptcy protec-

TABLE 16.9
Calculations for Tennessee Motor Homes' Liquidation Decision (in Millions of Dollars)

I. ALTERNATIVE: OPERATE 1 MORE YEAR AND THEN ABANDON

$$GP - B_0 - L_c \overset{?}{>} \sum_{t=1}^{a} \frac{CFAT_t}{(1+k)^t} + \frac{AV_a}{(1+k)^a} - B_0 - R_c$$

$$\$21 - \$29 - \$1 \overset{?}{>} \$7 \, (PVIF_{20\%,\,1\,yr}) + \$16 \, (PVIF_{20\%,\,1\,yr}) - \$29 - \$2$$

$$- \$9 \overset{?}{>} \$23 \,(.833) - \$29 - \$2$$

$$- \$9 \overset{?}{>} \$19.159 - \$29 - \$2$$

$$- \$9 \overset{?}{>} -\$11.841$$

Decision: Since the loss from liquidation is less than the loss with reorganization, proceed to evaluate the decision at year 2.

II. ALTERNATIVE: OPERATE 2 MORE YEARS AND THEN ABANDON

$$\$21 - \$29 - \$1 \overset{?}{>} \$7 \,(.833) + \$20 \,(.694) - \$29 - \$2$$

$$- \$9 \overset{?}{>} \$5.831 + \$13.880 - \$29 - \$2$$

$$- \$9 \overset{?}{>} -\$11.289$$

Decision: Since the loss from liquidation is less than the loss with reorganization, proceed to evaluate the decision at year 3.

III. ALTERNATIVE: OPERATE 3 MORE YEARS AND THEN ABANDON

$$\$21 - \$29 - \$1 \overset{?}{>} \$7 \,(.833) + \$6 \,(.694) + \$18 \,(.579) - \$29 - \$2$$

$$- \$9 \overset{?}{>} \$5.831 + \$4.164 + \$10.422 - \$29 - \$2$$

$$- \$9 \overset{?}{>} -\$10.583$$

Decision: Since the loss from liquidation is less than the loss with reorganization, proceed to evaluate the decision at year 4.

IV. ALTERNATIVE: OPERATE 4 MORE YEARS AND THEN ABANDON

$$\$21 - \$29 - \$1 \overset{?}{>} \$7 \,(.833) + \$6 \,(.694) + \$6 \,(.579) + \$16 \,(.482) - \$29 - \$2$$

$$- \$9 \overset{?}{>} \$5.831 + \$4.164 + \$3.474 + \$7.712 - \$29 - \$2$$

$$- \$9 \overset{?}{>} -\$9.819$$

Decision: Since the loss from liquidation is less than the loss with reorganization, proceed to evaluate the decision at year 5.

V. ALTERNATIVE: OPERATE 5 MORE YEARS AND THEN ABANDON

$$\$21 - \$29 - \$1 \overset{?}{>} \$7 \,(.833) + \$6 \,(.694) + \$6 \,(.579) + \$6 \,(.482) + \$14 \,(.402) - \$29 - \$2$$

$$- \$9 \overset{?}{>} \$5.831 + \$4.164 + \$3.474 + \$2.892 + \$5.628 - \$29 - \$2$$

$$- \$9 \overset{?}{>} -\$9.011$$

Decision: Since the loss from liquidation is less than the loss with reorganization, the trustee should proceed with the liquidation of Tennessee Motor Homes. In none of the next 5 years can the firm expect to generate sufficient cash flows to warrant continued operation.

tion, the procedure becomes more complicated since the creditors assume the dominant position. However, the basic decision is similar and involves determining if the firm and its creditors are financially better off liquidating or reorganizing the firm.

Effective procedures for considering abandonment decisions are becoming much more important. Numerous examples exist of firms selling off divisions or other large units of their operations. In addition, large-scale failures such as Wickes and Braniff have become more prevalent. Financial managers who understand the abandonment process are in a better position to make acquisition and disinvestment decisions that are consistent with the firm's long-run objective of shareholder wealth maximization.

QUESTIONS

16.1. Explain the process required to evaluate whether currently owned assets should be retained or abandoned.

   a. If you elect to retain the assets, when should the abandonment question be reconsidered?

   b. Does the same procedure hold for the accept-abandon decision for new, independent capital budgeting projects? Why or why not?

   c. What about new, mutually exclusive capital budgeting projects or projects under capital rationing? Is another process required in these cases? Why or why not?

16.2. Divestiture decisions are treated essentially like abandonment decisions, except for: (1) disposition of the division's current liabilities and allocated long-term debt, and (2) the possible effects of stock (or something else other than cash) being received. Explain the adjustments that might be needed.

16.3. In recent years, firms like Chrysler and Lockheed have been saved from bankruptcy by federal assistance. Some propose that the government should become the "lender of last resort" and rescue insolvent corporations by guaranteeing loans and pumping in cash needed to prevent bankruptcy. Others argue that the possibility of bankruptcy is a necessary incentive for efficiency, and that subsidizing inefficient companies merely creates perverse incentives for them to produce a lot of unwanted products. Discuss the pros and cons of government intervention.

16.4. "Statistical models cannot be relied upon to predict failure; only knowledgeable analysts can do this." Comment on this statement.

16.5. What are the major reforms brought about by the Bankruptcy Reform Act of 1978?

16.6. After a firm files for bankruptcy, explain why the financial manager's or trustee's objective shifts from maximizing shareholder wealth to maximizing the return to the firm's creditors. How does this situation differ from that of the possible liquidation of the firm if it is still a going concern?

16.7. Explain the role that liquidation costs and reorganization costs play in the process of making liquidation-reorganization decisions.

16.1. *WHEN TO ABANDON.* Minneapolis Property, Inc., owns 160 acres of Georgia farmland. Yearly estimated CFATs from raising cotton are $125,000 in year 1, $175,000 in year 2, negative ($-$) $160,000 in year 3, and $130,000 in year 4. A local real estate agent has offered $500,000 to buy the farmland to be used as a site for a new shopping mall. Due to inflation, the abandonment value of the land will increase at a rate of 11 percent per year from AV_0 of $500,000. When should Minneapolis Property abandon the farmland if the appropriate risk-adjusted discount rate is 10 percent? (*Note:* Since Minneapolis wants to determine when to abandon, you should calculate four different NPVs—one for each of the options available.)

16.2. *ABANDONMENT.* Erie Mills is faced with the decision of whether to abandon one or both of two older plants—the Plattsburgh Mill and the Scranton Mill.

The Plattsburgh Mill has a current depreciated book value of mill and equipment of $5 million, a remaining depreciable (and economic) life of 10 years, and the company (years ago before the ACRS method became available) set up the depreciation schedule employing straight-line depreciation to an estimated salvage value of zero. The marginal corporate tax rate is 40 percent, and Erie's MCC is 14 percent. The plant can be (1) sold now for $8 million, or (2) operated for the next 10 years, at which time management estimates it can be sold for $2 million. If it is operated, the cash revenues are estimated to be $4 million per year for each of the 10 years, while the cash expenses are estimated to be $2.2 million per year for the first 5 years and $2.8 million per year for the last 5 years.

The Scranton Mill has a depreciated book value of zero and must be abandoned within 4 years to make way for an urban renewal project. Erie Mills can abandon the mill now or any time during the next 4 years. If it is abandoned now (t_0), the mill and associated land can be leased for 4 years at $750,000 per year. (This option is available *only* if Erie abandons now; there are no lease revenues if the mill is abandoned in 1, 2, or 3 years.) Thus, $AV_0 = \$750,000\ (1 - T)\ (PVIFA_{14\%,\ 4\ yr})$. If Scranton Mill continues to operate, the following cash receipts and cash expenses are expected:

Year (t)	Cash Receipts$_t$	Cash Expenses$_t$
1	$4.0 million	$2.0 million
2	2.5	2.0
3	2.5	2.0
4	2.0	2.0

a. Should the Plattsburgh Mill be abandoned now or be operated for the next 10 years? (*Hint:* Remember the tax consequences of selling now or after 10 years.)

b. Should the Scranton Mill be abandoned now, after 1 year, after 2 years, after 3 years, or after 4 years?

16.3. *ABANDONMENT AND CHANGING CONDITIONS.* Southern Forest Products has the opportunity to lease and acquire the rights to harvest and sell the pine trees on a parcel of land. The land would have to be leased for 15 years and the firm would have to pay $80,000 now ($t_0$) for the right to lease. The pine trees are mature, and some cutting of trees will be done during each year to provide a positive CFAT (over and above the yearly lease payments and other expenses). The productive life of the pine trees is as follows:

Time Period (Years)	Expected CFAT Per Year
1–5	$11,000
6–10	9,000
11–15	8,000

Southern believes that mass cutting should be done at the end of 5, 10, or 15 years. (Since the land will be developed for a housing project in 15 years, assume that Southern will not replant trees once they are harvested.) Trees harvested in mass at the end of 5, 10, or 15 years have expected CFATs of $80,000 at the end of 5 years, $140,000 at the end of 10 years, and $250,000 at the end of 15 years. Southern's MCC is 12 percent.

a. Determine the NPV of each of the three alternatives. Should Southern lease the land? Should it plan to do the mass cutting 5, 10, or 15 years from now?

b. Assume Southern leased the land, and it is now 10 years later. Southern recognizes that a glut of mature trees exists.

If Southern sells now, it will receive only $75,000 after tax. However, if it keeps the trees, the expected CFAT for the next 5 years (years 11–15) drops from $8,000 to $7,000 per year. In addition, the selling price in 5 more years is expected to remain depressed and will be only $125,000 instead of $250,000. Should Southern cut now or wait five more years?

16.4. *DIVESTITURE: SELL ASSETS AND LIABILITIES.*   Memphis Records and Tapes has three divisions: gospel, classical, and country and western. The popularity of classical music has diminished in the local market. Memphis is considering a tentative offer of $550,000 after tax from a foreign record producer to buy the assets and liabilities of the classical records division. Current liabilities and allocated long-term debt are $700,000 for the division. The appropriate risk-adjusted discount rate is 19 percent. Based on the following estimated future cash flows and abandonment values, should Memphis divest the classical division?

Year (t)	$CFAT_t$	After-Tax AV_a
1	$228,000	$1,240,000
2	214,000	1,130,000
3	206,000	1,090,000
4	183,000	980,000

16.5. *DIVESTITURE: SELL ASSETS.*   Pittsburgh Steel Works has been experiencing considerable difficulty maintaining adequate profitability from its flat products division due to intense foreign competition. Recently it received a tentative offer from the management and employees of the division to buy *only* the assets of the flat products division. Under the terms offered, Pittsburgh would realize gross proceeds of $46 million after taxes; the flat products division's current liabilities and allocated long-term debt is $15 million. Pittsburgh's marginal cost of capital is 13 percent; however, because of the risk involved, it believes the appropriate discount rate is 15 percent. The estimated future cash flows and abandonment values are as follows:

Year (t)	$CFAT_t$	After-Tax AV_a
1	$5.0 million	$30 million
2	5.4	28
3	5.6	27
4	5.0	26
5	5.0	26

Should Pittsburgh attempt to finalize the terms and divest the flat products division? (*Note:* Make the decision using only the data for the 5 years given, since Pittsburgh is unwilling to project any further into the future.)

16.6. *DIVESTITURE AND ACQUISITION NEGOTIATIONS.* Certified Chemicals is contemplating the sale of its rayon division to Big E Oil & Chemical. Certified's managers estimate that if they keep the rayon division, its CFAT next year ($t = 1$) will be \$200,000, and unless significant capital expenditures are made, this amount will decline by 4 percent per year in perpetuity. Certified is unwilling to make any more capital investments in the rayon division; hence, it is considering divesting it.

Big E Oil & Chemical made the following estimates of the expected cash flows associated with the rayon division if it is purchased via a cash acquisition:

Year (t)	Capital Expenditures$_t$	$CFBT_t$	Depreciation$_t$
1	\$300,000	\$280,000	\$140,000
2	500,000	335,000	150,000
3	300,000	420,000	180,000
4	190,000	500,000	180,000
5	190,000	560,000	180,000
Annually, after 5 years	190,000	585,000	180,000

The rayon division's risk is equal to the average corporate risk for either Certified or Big E Oil & Chemical. Big E's MCC cost is 14 percent, and its marginal tax rate is 40 percent. Certified's MCC is 13 percent.

a. Calculate the minimum price at which Certified should sell the rayon division. (*Hint:* Since the estimated CFATs decline in perpetuity and there are no abandonment values, there is only one minimum selling price.)

b. Calculate the CFAT stream if Big E Oil & Chemical acquires the rayon division.

c. If *only* the assets are acquired, what is the maximum cash acquisition price Big E should pay for the rayon division?

d. Is an agreement possible between Certified and Big E? Why or why not?

16.7. *BANKRUPTCY PREDICTION.* Massachusetts Investors, Inc., manages the pension funds for more than 20 large firms. In order to assist both the equity and the fixed-income investment departments, Massachusetts closely monitors the financial health of many firms through the Z score approach, employing

$$Z = .012X_1 + .014X_2 + .033X_3 + .006X_4 + .010X_5$$

where a score of less than 2.675 indicates a high probability of bankruptcy.

Based on the ratios given below, calculate the Z scores for each firm for the past 5 years. (*Note:* Ratios are expressed in absolute percentage terms for use in the Z equation.)

MEAT PACKERS, INC.	X_1 Net Working Capital/ Total Assets	X_2 Retained Earnings/ Total Assets	X_3 EBIT/ Total Assets	X_4 Market Value of Common Stock/ Book Value of Debt	X_5 Sales/ Total Assets
$t-5$	13.4	9.6	7.4	47.8	1,130.9
$t-4$	8.3	7.0	6.8	32.4	852.9
$t-3$	6.7	7.0	10.1	14.2	675.2
$t-2$	5.0	10.3	13.3	10.6	744.2
$t-1$	−59.3	−38.5	−58.7	3.1	1,070.5
ALPHA PRODUCTS, INC.					
$t-5$	19.5	4.0	7.2	180.0	200.0
$t-4$	23.2	− 0.8	4.0	147.6	200.0
$t-3$	17.6	− 7.0	− 5.8	143.2	166.0
$t-2$	1.6	−30.1	−20.7	74.2	150.0
$t-1$	− 6.1	−62.6	−31.8	40.1	150.0

a.   Which firm appears to face financial difficulties based on its Z score?

b.   Does the other firm appear to face financial difficulty even though its Z score does not predict possible bankruptcy?

16.8.   *VOLUNTARY LIQUIDATION.*   Collins Industries is a miniconglomerate operating as a holding company, with three separate divisions all acquired during the conglomerate merger wave of the late 1960s. Collins has common stock outstanding, but does not have its own debt; all liabilities are direct obligations of its divisions. Collins' total market value at the current time is $20 million, an amount that its financial managers think is substantially below what it is "worth." Recently, Collins investigated the possibility of selling off the divisions and liquidating. The relevant financial data (in millions of dollars) are as follows:

Year (t)	Carpet Division		Insulation Division		Truck Leasing Division	
	$CFAT_t$	After-Tax AV_a	$CFAT_t$	After-Tax AV_a	$CFAT_t$	After-Tax AV_a
1	$1	$30	$2	$16	$3.0	$7.5
2	1	29	2	18	2.5	7.0
3	1	28	3	20	2.0	6.0
4	1	27	4	24	2.0	5.0
5	1	26	6	27	1.5	4.0
6	1	25	8	30	1.5	4.0
Current gross after-tax liquidation value (before subtracting debt)		$30		$10		$17
Less: Divisional debt		$15		$5		$12
Equals: Benefits from liquidation		$15		$5		$5

Because of uncertainties about the future, Collins is unwilling to project outcomes beyond 6 years. The divisions cannot be sold off separately; they must all be kept and operated or all sold. Collins' MCC is 18 percent.

a. Given the benefits from liquidation and the current market value of the firm's common stock, should Collins consider liquidating?

b. If it decides to consider liquidation, would it be better off liquidating now or waiting until some future year (which year)?

16.9. *LIQUIDATION OR REORGANIZATION.* Rotary Motor Company, due to significant underestimation of the difficulties involved in perfecting its rotary motors, has suffered financial losses and filed for protection under the bankruptcy laws.

The trustee estimates that the liquidation proceeds, after costs have been deducted, will be $550,000; alternatively, the firm can be reorganized without any infusion of additional funds, with the following expected cash flows and abandonment values:

Year (t)	$CFAT_t$	After-Tax AV_a
1	$ 50,000	$500,000
2	75,000	525,000
3	100,000	550,000
4	100,000	550,000
5	100,000	550,000

The trustee is unwilling to project beyond 5 years. The market value of the outstanding liabilities is $100,000, and the trustee estimates the appropriate discount rate to be 16 percent. Should the trustee recommend liquidation or reorganization of Rotary Motor?

16.10.   *LIQUIDATION OR REORGANIZATION: ADDITIONAL FUNDS.* Enterprise Printing Company is experiencing financial difficulties. Liquidation proceeds (AV_0) are $200,000, and liquidation costs are estimated to be $50,000. However, one of the owners is convinced that the firm's problems can be solved with the infusion of additional funds in the amount of $550,000. After reviewing the situation, the trustee agrees to consider reorganization and provides the following estimates:

Year (t)	$CFAT_t$	After-Tax AV_a
1	$ 50,000	$ 550,000
2	150,000	700,000
3	200,000	800,000
4	250,000	900,000
5	300,000	1,000,000

The trustee is unwilling to project beyond 5 years. The additional $200,000 would be supplied by the firm's present creditors in exchange for half of the firm's common stock. However, there is additional risk involved, resulting in an applicable risk-adjusted discount rate of 20 percent. The market value of the outstanding liabilities is $300,000. From the creditors' standpoint, would they be better off investing the additional $550,000, or should they support liquidation of the firm?

SELECTED REFERENCES

Aharony, Joseph, Charles P. Jones, and Itzhak Swary. "An Analysis of Risk and Return Characteristics of Corporate Bankruptcy Using Capital Market Data." *Journal of Finance* 35 (September 1980), pp. 1001–1016.

Alberts, William W., and James M. McTaggart. "The Divestiture Decision: An Introduction." *Mergers & Acquisitions* 14 (fall 1979), pp. 18–30.

Altman, Edward I. "Financial Ratios, Discriminant Analysis and the Prediction of Corporate Bankruptcy." *Journal of Finance* 23 (September 1968), pp. 589–609.

———. "Predicting Railroad Bankruptcies in America." *Bell Journal of Economics and Management Science* 4 (spring 1973), pp. 184–211.

———, Robert G. Halderman, and P. Narayanan. "Zeta Analysis: A New Model to Identify Bankruptcy Risk of Corporations." *Journal of Banking and Finance* 1 (June 1977), pp. 29–54.

Baldwin, Carliss Y., and Scott P. Mason. "The Resolution of Claims in Financial Distress: The Case of Massey Ferguson." *Journal of Finance* 38 (May 1983), pp. 505–516.

Beaver, William H. "Financial Ratios as Predictors of Failure." *Empirical Research in Accounting: Selected Studies,* supplement to *Journal of Accounting Research* 4 (1966), pp. 71–111.

Bonini, Charles P. "Capital Investment Under Uncertainty with Abandonment Options." *Journal of Financial and Quantitative Analysis* 12 (March 1977), pp. 39–54.

Clark, Truman A., and Mark I. Weinstein. "The Behavior of the Common Stock of Bankrupt Firms." *Journal of Finance* 38 (May 1983), pp. 489–504.

Collins, Robert A. "An Empirical Comparison of Bankruptcy Prediction Models." *Financial Management* 9 (summer 1980), pp. 52–57.

Dambolena, Ismael G., and Sarkis J. Khoury. "Ratio Stability and Corporate Failure." *Journal of Finance* 35 (September 1980), pp. 1017–1025.

Dyl, Edward A., and Hugh W. Long. "Abandonment Value and Capital Budgeting: Comment." *Journal of Finance* 24 (March 1969), pp. 88–95.

"The Economic Case Against Federal Bailouts—and Who May Need Them." *Business Week,* March 24, 1980, pp. 104–107.

Gordon, Myron J. "Towards a Theory of Financial Distress." *Journal of Finance* 26 (May 1971), pp. 347–356.

Herbst, Anthony F. "An Algorithm for Systematic Economic Analysis of Abandonment Value in Capital Budgeting." *Engineering Economist* 22 (fall 1976), pp. 63–71.

Hite, Gailen L., and James E. Owens. "Security Price Reactions Around Corporate Spin-Off Announcements." *Journal of Financial Economics* 12 (December 1983), pp. 409–436.

Howe, Keith M., and George M. McCabe. "On Optimal Asset Abandonment and Replacement." *Journal of Financial and Quantitative Analysis* 18 (September 1983), pp. 295-305.

Joy, O. Maurice. "Abandonment Values and Abandonment Decisions: A Clarification." *Journal of Finance* 31 (September 1976), pp. 1225–1228.

Largay, James A. III, and Clyde P. Stickney. "Cash Flows, Ratio Analysis and the W. T. Grant Company Bankruptcy." *Financial Analysts Journal* 36 (July–August 1980), pp. 51–54.

Miles, James A., and James D. Rosenfeld. "The Effect of Voluntary Spin-Off Announcements on Shareholder Wealth." *Journal of Finance* 38 (December 1983), pp. 1597–1606.

Moyer, R. Charles. "Forecasting Financial Failure: A Re-Examination." *Financial Management* 6 (spring 1977), pp. 11–17.

Ohlson, James A. "Financial Ratios and the Probabilistic Prediction of Bankruptcy." *Journal of Accounting Research* 18 (spring 1980), pp. 109–131.

Pinches, George E., and James S. Trieschmann. "The Efficiency of Alternative Models for Solvency Surveillance in the Insurance Industry." *Journal of Risk and Insurance* 41 (December 1974), pp. 563–577.

Robicheck, Alexander A., and James C. Van Horne. "Abandonment Value and Capital Budgeting." *Journal of Finance* 22 (December 1967), pp. 577–589.

———, and ———. "Abandonment Value and Capital Budgeting: Reply." *Journal of Finance* 24 (March 1969), pp. 96–97.

Schipper, Katherine, and Abbie Smith. "Effects of Recontracting on Shareholder Wealth." *Journal of Financial Economics* 12 (December 1983), pp. 437–467.

Sinkey, Joseph T. "A Multivariate Statistical Analysis of the Characteristics of Problem Banks." *Journal of Finance* 30 (March 1975), pp. 21–36.

White, Michelle J. "Bankruptcy Costs and the New Bankruptcy Code." *Journal of Finance* 38 (May 1983), pp. 477–488.

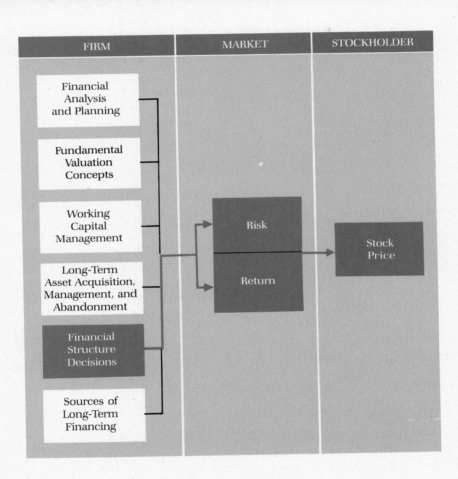

FIRM	MARKET	STOCKHOLDER

Financial Analysis and Planning

Fundamental Valuation Concepts

Working Capital Management

Long-Term Asset Acquisition, Management, and Abandonment

Financial Structure Decisions

Sources of Long-Term Financing

Risk

Return

Stock Price

PART SIX

FINANCIAL STRUCTURE DECISIONS

In Part Six we continue the discussion on how financial managers make long-term decisions. Unlike the preceding part, which dealt with the firm's capital budgeting process, Part Six investigates the concept and calculation of the firm's marginal cost of capital (MCC), and the related and equally important considerations of capital structure and dividend policy. Effective decisions in these areas are important as they contribute to maximizing the value of the firm and minimizing its MCC (or appropriate risk-adjusted discount rate). Chapter 17 examines the cost of capital, including the marginal cost of capital schedule and divisional costs of capital. In Appendix 17A the explicit costs of term loans, convertibles, and leases are considered. Chapter 18 and Appendix 18A examine the target or optimal capital structure; in Chapter 19 we consider the firm's cash dividend policy and internal financing decisions. Effective decision making in all these areas is necessary to achieve the goal of maximizing shareholder wealth.

17

The Cost
of Capital

Many executives, when asked about their cost of funds, respond by defining it as an accounting-based concept, such as return on total assets. This approach, unfortunately, is incorrect. It is based on historical information, whereas it is the future that matters. And accounting data, as we know, bear little or no relationship to cash flows or the after-tax cost of financing to the firm. The financial manager's attention, therefore, should be on developing a future-oriented marginal cost of capital that takes into account expected financing costs and the firm's proposed financing mix. It is the marginal cost of capital (MCC)—or, stated more simply, its cost of funds—that brings the investment and financing decisions of the firm together. To understand this important tool, we begin by considering the cost of capital concept, the cost of specific sources of capital, and how these costs should be estimated. Next we examine the marginal cost of capital schedule, including its multinational dimensions. The chapter concludes with a discussion of divisional costs of capital or screening rates that are widely employed in practice.

The Marginal Cost of Capital Concept

The marginal cost of capital is the correct measure of a firm's financing costs and is fundamental to effective capital budgeting. In addition, other financial decisions—such as those related to working capital—also require specification of the firm's marginal cost of capital. The *marginal cost* of any item is the cost of the last unit of that item. As a firm tries to attract more and more capital at any specific time, the cost of each dollar will, at some point, rise. Thus, the *marginal cost of capital (MCC)* is the cost of obtaining the last dollar of new capital.

We use a future-oriented marginal cost for two reasons. First, use of any rate lower than the marginal cost of capital, such as an average cost, would result in acceptance of projects that will tend to lower the future value of the firm (or the value of its common stock); so using any rate lower than the firm's MCC works against the concept of shareholder wealth maximization. Second, past costs of financing have no direct bearing on the actual costs of financing new projects; in other words, it is the expected increase in future cash flows (and dividends) that contributes to the increased value of the firm. For future projects to cause an increase in the firm's cash flows and dividends, the last-added project—that is, the one accepted with the lowest rate of return—must produce a return at least equal to the cost of the last-acquired increment of capital. Otherwise the future value of the firm will decrease.

Why a Weighted Cost of Capital?

In discussing the cost of capital, there is often a tendency to equate MCC with the direct cost of financing a specific project. Suppose a firm's before-tax cost of debt is estimated to be 15 percent, and it has decided to finance a major plant expansion with debt. The argument could be made that the appropriate cost of capital is the after-tax cost of debt which, with a 40 percent marginal tax rate, is 9 percent [$15\% \times (1 - .40)$]. But this approach views the firm at only one point in time, rather than as an ongoing concern. The ability of the firm to finance this particular plant expansion at 9 percent is a function of both past and potential future investment and financing decisions of the firm. If the firm employs debt for this expansion, the next major capital budgeting project might have to be financed entirely with equity, and at a 20 percent after-tax cost. If both projects were equally risky and each had a 16 percent internal rate of return, one would be accepted while the second would be rejected.

To avoid this problem, we generally separate the investment decision from the financing decision. Thus, the firm should be viewed as an ongoing concern, and the MCC calculated as a weighted average based upon the mix and costs of the various types of funds the firm intends to use over the foreseeable future. In this chapter, we assume the firm is operating at its target capital structure and ignore the question of the appropriate mix of funds for the firm (this issue is considered in Chapter 18 and Appendix 18A). In other words we assume the firm's *financial risk*, as evidenced by its capital structure, does not change as a result of accepting any new capital expenditure projects.[1] When we discuss divisional costs of capital, however, allowances for differences in financial risk between divisions will be considered.

---

[1]This assumption, which is of great importance, is often glossed over. If the acceptance of a particular project causes a permanent change in the firm's capital structure, the approach described in this chapter has to be modified. Another assumption implicitly made is that the firm's dividend policy is constant and set in a manner that maximizes the value of the firm. The question of dividend relevance is considered in Chapter 19.

The Assumption of Equal Riskiness for Proposed Capital Expenditure Projects

Business risk is related to the sensitivity of the firm's revenue stream to changing economic factors and the response of the firm's cash flows to changes in sales. When the MCC is used to evaluate investment alternatives, it is implicitly assumed that the acceptance of any single project does not affect the firm's business risk. Alternatively, the projects under consideration are viewed as having approximately the same amount of risk as the firm as a whole. If a firm accepts a major project that is considerably more risky than its current portfolio of assets, the suppliers of funds may become concerned about the firm's business risk (in terms of wider fluctuations in future cash flows), and the firm's MCC may increase. In such a situation, long-term lenders would charge a higher interest rate and common stockholders would require increased returns to compensate them for the additional uncertainty of receiving future cash dividends. By assuming that the business risk of the firm does not change, we also assume that the firm's overall asset mix remains essentially unchanged as new capital expenditure projects are accepted.

In Chapter 6 using the capital asset pricing model (CAPM), we showed that the required rate of return consisted of the risk-free rate plus a risk premium: $k_s = R_F + r$. Here we divide the risk premium, r, into two components—r_{bp} (a business or operating risk premium) and r_{fp} (a financial risk premium). Thus, the required rate of return on equity for a firm, k_s, is:

$$k_s = R_F + r_{bp} + r_{fp} \tag{17.1}$$

The risk-free rate, R_F, is a function of general economic conditions, both domestic and international anticipated inflation, Federal Reserve policy, and the like. The business risk premium is a function of the nature of the firm's industry, its degree of operating leverage, its diversification, the riskiness of the capital expenditure proposals accepted, and so on. Financial risk depends upon the degree of financial leverage (or the capital structure) employed by the firm. As general economic conditions influence the risk-free rate, the firm's MCC will change even if business and financial risk remain constant. This is why firms must recalculate their MCC periodically, even if there have been no perceived changes in their business or financial risk.

Calculating the Cost of Specific Sources of Capital

Each source of capital has an *explicit* after-tax cost—namely, the current cost to the firm of raising funds from that particular source. This cost is stated in percentage terms. Our concern is with the long-term sources of funds, since they supply the permanent financing of the firm.[2] The basic sources, therefore, are bonds, preferred stock, common stock, and internally generated funds not paid out to the firm's stockholders. In addition, a number of other sources are sometimes used to raise capital, including term loans, convertibles, and leases. (The explicit costs of the latter sources are examined in Appendix 17A.)

Once we have a measure of the specific costs, we will use this information, as demonstrated later in the chapter, to compute the firm's weighted marginal cost of capital—its MCC. Although the calculations indicate that precise costs of the different capital sources can be determined, financial managers should realize that the MCC is merely an *approximation* due to the numerous assumptions and forecasts that underlie the calculations.

Cost of Debt (Long-Term Bonds), k_i

The explicit cost of debt can be determined by solving for the discount rate which equates the net proceeds of the debt issue with the present value of the scheduled interest plus principal payments, and then adjusting the cost obtained for taxes.[3] Specifically, the after-tax cost of debt, k_i, is equal to:

$$k_i = k_b (1 - T) \qquad (17.2)$$

where k_b is the before-tax cost of debt to the firm and T is the firm's marginal tax rate.[4] The before-tax cost, k_b, can be determined by using

---

[2] One troubling problem that is often ignored is the cost of short-term financing from payables and accruals. If the amount of short-term financing is negligible, it can be ignored; if the amount is material, it must be considered. The approach we employ, and the one implicitly or explicitly employed by most firms, is simply to ignore these short-term payables and accruals, since they are *netted out* against short-term uses of funds such as investments in accounts receivable and inventory. In Chapter 12 when we derived the initial cash outlay for capital budgeting purposes, we were concerned only with the *incremental* amount of net working capital (the difference between current assets and current liabilities) required by the proposed project. We were operating on the assumption that the costs of short-term, spontaneously generated funds could be ignored. An alternative approach is to bring the gross investment in short-term assets into the capital budgeting process and then also consider short-term, spontaneously generated funds when determining the firm's MCC.

[3] The return on a bond when viewed by a purchaser—not an issuer—is called the *yield to maturity* since it represents the investor's expected return from purchasing the bond and holding it to maturity. Our concern is the viewpoint of the issuer, so we emphasize the *cost to maturity*. The cost to maturity will be more than the yield to maturity if there are underwriting and flotation costs.

[4] Fred D. Arditti and Haim Levy, "The Weighted Average Cost of Capital As a Cutoff Rate: A Critical Analysis of the Classical Textbook Weighted Average," *Financial Management* 6 (fall 1977), pp. 24–34, argue that the explicit cost of debt should not be adjusted for taxes. Their reasoning is that the tax advantage of debt has already been reflected in the cost of equity capital, due to the fact that dividends are higher than they would be without the tax advantage. See also Kenneth J. Boudreaux and Hugh W. Long, "The Weighted Average Cost of Capital As a Cutoff Rate: A Further Analysis," *Financial Management* 8 (summer 1979), pp. 7–14; John R. Ezzell and R. Burr Porter, "Correct Specification of the Cost of Capital and Net Present Value," *Financial Management* 8 (summer 1979), pp. 15–17; and Moshe Ben-Horim, "Comment on 'The Weighted Average Cost of Capital As a Cutoff Rate,'" *Financial Management* 8 (summer 1979), pp. 18–21.

the techniques discussed in Chapter 7, or it can be supplied by the firm's investment banker when a new bond is sold.

To illustrate the approach, consider King Industries, Inc., which is contemplating selling $10 million of 25-year, 12 percent bonds, each with a par (or maturity) value of $1000. Since similar risk and maturity bonds are yielding more than 12 percent, the firm must sell the bonds at a discount of $15 (the selling price is $985). The investment banking house underwriting the bond receives a fee of 2 percent of the par value of the bond (2% × $1000 = $20); as such, the net proceeds to King Industries are $965 ($985 − $20).[5] First, the before-tax cost of debt, k_b, to King Industries must be determined; it is calculated as follows:[6]

$$\text{At 12\% } B_0 = \$120 \ (PVIFA_{12\%,\ 25\ yr}) + \$1000 \ (PVIF_{12\%,\ 25\ yr})$$
$$= \$120 \ (7.843) + \$1000 \ (.059)$$
$$= \$941.16 + \$59.00 = \$1000.16 \approx \$1000$$

$$\text{At 13\% } B_0 = \$120 \ (PVIFA_{13\%,\ 25\ yr}) + \$1000 \ (PVIFA_{13\%,\ 25\ yr})$$
$$= \$120 \ (7.330) + \$1000 \ (.047)$$
$$= \$879.60 + \$47.00 = \$926.60$$

Since the actual proceeds are $965, interpolation is employed to find the specific before-tax cost to maturity, which is:

$$k_b = 12\% + \frac{\$1000 - \$965}{\$1000 - \$926.60} = 12\% + \frac{\$35.00}{\$73.40} = 12.48\%$$

Now with a marginal tax rate, T, of 40 percent, we can find the after-tax cost:

$$k_i = 12.48\% \ (1 - .40) = 7.49\%$$

The marginal after-tax cost of new debt is therefore 7.49 percent. To put the costs of debt and equity on a comparable basis, we adjust the before-tax cost of debt to take into account the preferential tax treatment

---

[5]An investment banker "underwrites" a bond issue by buying it at a discount from the issuer and selling it on behalf of the issuer. The discount compensates the underwriter for acting as a middleman.

[6]The before-tax cost to maturity can be approximated by:

$$k_b = \frac{I + (M - B_0)/n}{(M + B_0)/2}$$

where I = the annual interest payment in dollars
  M = the par or maturity value of the bond (usually $1000)
  B_0 = the net proceeds from the sale of the bond
  n = the term of the bond in years

This is an approximation, since it does not consider compounding effects. For King Industries' bonds, the approximation yields $k_b = 12.36\%$.

of debt.[7] (Note that we are not interested in any existing or outstanding debt since these funds have already been used by the firm.) Debt generally has the lowest explicit cost of any source of capital available to the firm. This is partly because of the tax deductibility of interest payments. It also has a low cost compared to other sources because, from the investors' standpoint, judicious debt usage is the safest financing the firm can employ. Debt holders are paid before suppliers of any other long-term capital sources, and debt has a prior claim on the firm's assets in the event of liquidation. Because there is less risk in holding debt, investors will accept a lower required return on this form of financing.

Cost of Preferred Stock, k_{ps}

Preferred stock represents ownership in the firm, even though the preferred stockholders have accepted a prior but fixed claim on earnings. Unlike interest payments on debt, however, preferred dividends are not tax deductible. They are paid out of after-tax earnings. Therefore, a dollar paid in preferred dividends is exactly equal to a dollar in after-tax cash outflows to the firm. For noncallable preferred stock,[8] the after-tax cost, k_{ps}, is found by:

$$k_{ps} = \frac{D_{ps}}{P_0 (1 - f)}$$ (17.3)

where D_{ps} is the annual cash dividend, P_0 is the sale price before flotation costs, and f is the percentage flotation costs.

For example, King Industries, Inc., is contemplating the issuance of $2.5 million of $100 par 11.5 percent preferred stock that is expected to be sold at $100 per share, less 3 percent of the offering price for underwriting fees. The dollar amount of the annual dividend is $11.50 (11.5% of $100), and the net proceeds are $97 [$100 × (1 − .03)]. The after-tax cost is:

$$k_{ps} = \frac{\$11.50}{\$97} = 11.86\%$$

In comparison to King Industries' previously calculated 7.49 percent, cost of debt, the cost of preferred stock is higher. This is due primarily to the fact that preferred dividends are not tax deductible.

---

[7]This calculation presumes that the firm is profitable; the tax rate is zero for a firm with a loss. Therefore, for an unprofitable firm the explicit cost of debt, k_i, is equal to k_b.

[8]If the preferred stock is callable, its cost is determined in exactly the same way as the *before-tax* cost of debt, with the call date treated as the maturity date.

Cost of New Common Stock, k_e

The cost of new common stock financing is conceptually similar to the cost of debt, but the actual measurement process is far more complicated. Firms issuing debt create a legally enforceable promise to pay specific amounts at regular intervals, but a similar promise is not made when common stock is issued. Future dividends or returns are subject to considerable uncertainty. Consequently, estimating the magnitude and risk of future returns is important in any assessment of the explicit cost of new common stock financing.

Two basic approaches for estimating the cost of new common stock financing are available—the common stock valuation approach and the capital asset pricing model (CAPM). Neither approach requires adjustment for corporate taxes since dividends paid to common stockholders come from after-tax earnings.

The Valuation Approach. The dividend valuation approach (discussed in detail in Chapter 7) expresses the current market price of common stock as the present value of expected dividends, discounted at the investors' required rate of return, so that:

$$P_0 = \frac{D_1}{(1 + k_s)} + \frac{D_2}{(1 + k_s)^2} + \cdots + \frac{D_\infty}{(1 + k_s)^\infty}$$ (17.4)

where P_0 = the current market price of the stock
D_t = the dividend the shareholder expects to receive at the end of year t
k_s = the common stockholders' expected or required rate of return

If the dividends are expected to grow at a constant percentage rate over time, Equation 17.4 reduces to:

$$P_0 = \frac{D_1}{k_s - g}$$ (17.5)

where g is the constant expected annual growth rate in cash dividends. We can solve to obtain the investors' required return on common equity, which is:

$$k_s = \frac{D_1}{P_0} + g$$ (17.6)

Thus, investors expect to obtain a dividend yield, D_1/P_0, and a capital gain, g, for a total return of k_s. The after-tax explicit cost of new common stock, k_e, is determined by adjusting Equation 17.6 for flotation costs; thus k_e is measured as:

$$k_e = \frac{D_1}{P_0\,(1-f)} + g \tag{17.7}$$

where f is the percentage flotation cost incurred in selling the issue. The flotation costs include both the underpricing (from the current market price) that is necessary to induce investors to purchase the stock and underwriting fees. The only difference between the cost of new common stock, k_e, and internally generated funds, k_s, discussed subsequently, is the flotation cost, f, which is incurred with the former, but not with the latter.

Estimation of the Growth Rate.   For all growth situations, the most important element in determining the cost of new common stock is the growth rate, g, in dividends perceived by investors. Because expected growth in dividends is not directly observable, it must be estimated. At least three approaches may be employed to estimate the expected growth rate.

Method 1: Projection of Historical Dividend Growth.   If past growth rates in dividends have been reasonably stable and it is felt investors are projecting a continuation of past trends, g might be based on the firm's historical growth rate in dividends.[9]

Method 2: Security Analysts' Forecasts.   If a firm's past growth has been abnormally high or low, or if either firm-specific or general economic conditions have changed, investors will in all probability not be extrapolating past growth rates into the future. In this case, estimates of security analysts, who regularly make earnings and dividend growth projections, may be employed to estimate g.

Method 3: Reinvested Earnings.   A third possible approach is to estimate the anticipated growth as being equal to the product of the firm's retention rate ($1 -$ dividend payout ratio) times its projected return on equity (ROE), or

$$g = (1 - \text{dividend payout ratio})\,(\text{ROE}) \tag{17.8}$$

---

[9]In practice, the historical, or expected, growth rate in earnings is often employed instead of dividends. This is done to ensure that the cash dividend decision, which is discussed in Chapter 19 and results from the discretionary action of the firm's directors, does not unduly influence estimates of future growth rates.

The logic behind this calculation is that the firm can grow only if it reinvests earnings in the company. Ignoring external financing opportunities, such an approach seems reasonable.

In practice, it is best to employ a number of different procedures, since the cost of equity capital is of critical importance. Also, note that if the growth rate is expected to change, the cost of equity capital cannot be determined by assuming a constant rate of growth, g. In such a case, it is necessary to use the variable dividend growth valuation model described in Chapter 7. Estimating the growth rate is the most difficult step in calculating the cost of new common stock using the valuation approach. Experience in estimating the cost of equity capital suggests that both careful analysis and judgment are required.

Assume King Industries is using the valuation approach to estimate its cost of new common stock. The prevailing market price of its stock is $80 per share, and the firm expects to pay a dividend, D_1, of $4.75 at the end of the coming year. King estimates new common stock would have to be priced at $78 per share and that the underwriter fees will be 6.73 percent of the offering price (6.73% × $78 = $5.25). Because of the stability of King's growth over the past few years and its policy of maintaining a fixed dividend payout ratio, the rate of growth in dividends can be estimated from the dividends paid over the last 6 years, which are as follows:

1984	$4.40
1983	4.00
1982	3.75
1981	3.60
1980	3.25
1979	2.86

The compound growth rate in future dividends suggested by the past dividends is 9 percent.[10] The net proceeds per share to King will be equal to the offering price of $78 per share minus the underwriting expenses of $5.25. Substituting D_1 = $4.75, net proceeds of $72.75, and g = 9% into Equation 17.7 results in an after-tax explicit cost of new common stock of:

$$k_e = \frac{\$4.75}{\$72.75} + .09 = .0653 + .09 = .1553 = 15.53\%$$

The 15.53 percent represents the return required by common shareholders for investing in King Industries. As such, it represents King's estimated after-tax cost of new common stock.

---

[10]By dividing the earliest dividend by the most recent one, a present-value interest factor for $1 of 0.650 ($2.86 ÷ $4.40) is obtained. Although six dividends are shown, they reflect only 5 years of growth. Looking across Table A.3 for present-value interest factors for 5 years, the factor closest to 0.650 occurs at 9 percent.

The Capital Asset Pricing Model (CAPM) Approach.   The second approach for estimating the cost of new common stock involves the capital asset pricing model (first presented in Chapter 6), which describes the relationship between the investor's required rate of . return and the nondiversifiable (or market) risk of the firm, as reflected by its beta coefficient, β. To use this approach, the following steps are required:

Step 1.   Estimate the risk-free rate, R_F, which is set equal to the rate on 90-day U.S. Treasury bills, unless there have been, or are expected to be, substantial changes in this rate.

Step 2.   Estimate the firm's beta coefficient, β, using the techniques described in Chapter 6 or security analysts' estimates.

Step 3.   Estimate the expected return on the market, k_M. This may be estimated directly, or can be based on estimates provided by security analysts.[11]

Step 4.   Estimate the required rate of return on the firm's stock before underpricing and underwriting fees, employing the following equation:

$$k_s = R_F + \beta \times (k_M - R_F) \tag{17.9}$$

Step 5.   Adjust the required rate of return determined in step 4 for the underpricing and flotation costs associated with the issuance of new common stock.[12]

To illustrate this approach, assume King Industries also decided to use the CAPM to estimate its cost of new common stock. From information provided by its investment banker, along with the firm's own analysts, we see that R_F = 10 percent, the firm's beta is 0.80, k_M = 16 percent, and underpricing and flotation costs cause the net proceeds to equal only 90.94 percent ($72.75/$80) of the current market price of the

[11]The expected rate of return on the market cannot be measured directly. However, one way of estimating what it might be is to add three components: (1) the real rate of growth expected in the economy; (2) an adjustment for anticipated inflation in the next year; and (3) a risk premium for the riskiness of the market portfolio. The real rate of growth in the economy can be estimated from past data provided by the U.S. government, and the expected rate of inflation can be estimated from data provided by the government or investment advisors. Often the expected return on U.S. government securities provides a basis for estimating inflation. The risk premium for the market portfolio is often estimated as the difference between expected returns on bonds and on common stocks. Although this estimate of the risk premium is not precise, by using historical data it could be forecasted to be in the neighborhood of 4 to 5 percent. For information on historical and forecasted rates of return, see Roger G. Ibbotson and Rex O. Sinquefield. *Stocks, Bonds, Bills, and Inflation: The Past and the Future*, 1982 edition. (Charlottesville, VA: Financial Analysts Research Foundation, 1982).

[12]It should be noted that there is no generally agreed upon method to adjust for underpricing and flotation costs when the CAPM approach is employed. As an *approximation*, the required rate of return calculated using Equation 17.9 is divided by the percent of the current market price the firm will realize from the sale of new common stock.

stock. Substituting into Equation 17.9, the cost of external equity before considering underpricing and flotation costs is:

$$k_s = 10.00\% + .80 \times (16.00\% - 10.00\%) = 10.00\% + 4.80\% = 14.80\%$$

Adjusting for underpricing and flotation costs yields the following estimate of the cost of new common stock:

$$k_e = \frac{k_s}{\text{net proceeds to firm (\%)}} = 14.80\%/.9094 = 16.27\% \quad (17.10)$$

We estimated the cost of new common stock for King to be 15.53 percent using the valuation approach and 16.27 percent with the CAPM approach. Although it is unlikely the two approaches will ever provide exactly the same estimates, the results are generally close enough to give financial managers a reasonable estimate of the cost of new common stock. The two figures could be averaged to provide a cost of new common stock of 15.90 percent [(15.53% + 16.27%)/2 = 15.90%]; however, because of the assumptions that underlie both estimates, an "eyeball" figure of 16 percent is employed as the approximate cost of new common stock.

Cost of Internally Generated Funds, k_s

For most firms, a large portion of new financing is derived from internally generated funds. A number of complex issues related to this topic require attention before we consider the mechanics of computing the cost. The most important issues are these: (1) What are internally generated funds? and (2) Are internally generated funds costless?

What Are Internally Generated Funds?   By *internally generated funds* we mean that part of current cash flows not paid out in dividends, but rather retained for reinvestment. Given the differences in accounting treatment for financial reporting versus tax reporting, and the differences between accounting flows and cash flows, the item "to retained earnings" determined from the income statement is taken as a "rough" proxy for the net new internal funds available. Financial managers will often have internal data which provide a more accurate estimate of the amount of these funds.

Is depreciation a source of funds? In the statement of changes in financial position, depreciation is shown as a major source of funds. For financing capital budgeting projects, should depreciation be considered a source of internally generated funds, or should it be ignored? The answer is it should be ignored, since we are interested in *net* increases in assets (expansion projects and the incremental aspects of replacement projects) in an economic sense. Theoretically, depreciation is assumed to provide just enough funds to replace worn-out equipment each year.

In other words, cash outflows used to replace equipment each year are assumed to be exactly equal to the cash inflows generated through depreciation. Since the two cancel each other out and depreciation-generated funds are used for replacement investments, they are not available for net new investment by the firm.[13] Thus, a rough proxy for a net new internally generated funds is the amount of incremental retained earnings per period, as reflected on the income statement.[14]

Are Internally Generated Funds Costless?   On a cursory examination, it might appear that internally generated funds are costless, since they are generated by the ongoing activities of the firm. This is false logic: The earnings retained by the firm are not owned by the firm—they are owned by the shareholders. In addition, there is an opportunity cost involved; that is, internally generated funds should earn at least as much as shareholders themselves could earn in alternative investments of comparable risk. When a firm retains cash flows, it is *preemptively* deciding that present shareholders will reinvest in the firm instead of in another firm or asset. Because of this preemptive decision, the firm must recognize the existence of an opportunity cost associated with the reinvestment of internally generated funds.

Determining the Cost of Internally Generated Funds.   Two basic approaches are suggested for determining the cost of internally generated funds—the after-tax return required by investors and the "external yield" criterion from the firm's viewpoint. For reasons to be specified

---

[13]To understand this idea, it is necessary to remember that financial theory is based on the economic concepts of income and depreciation. Economic income per period from an asset (ignoring taxes, and so on) is equal to the cash flow from that asset minus economic depreciation, which is equal to the difference in the present value of the cash flow stream computed at the beginning of the period and the present value of the remaining cash flow stream computed at the end of the period. Continued reinvestment of an amount equal to the economic depreciation per year in the existing assets is necessary to maintain the economic value of these assets. Failure to make these reinvestments results in a loss of value; reinvestment of an amount equal to the per-year economic depreciation is necessary *before* we consider the investment of funds in any new assets. The implicit assumption contained in most textbook discussions of the magnitude of internal funds is that accounting depreciation is equal to economic depreciation. The realism of this assumption is of course open to debate.

[14]If we choose to view the capital expenditure decision as being concerned with *gross* capital expenditures, including those investments necessary to maintain currently owned assets at their revenue-generating capacity, depreciation would be viewed as a source of funds. In this case, the cost of these "depreciation-generated" funds must be specified. It should be viewed as being equal to the weighted marginal cost of capital for the firm before new common stock is employed. The rationale is that the firm could, if it desired, distribute the "depreciation-generated" funds to those who enabled the firm to purchase the assets—to creditors and stockholders. If the funds are distributed, the distribution must be to investors in proportion to their contribution to the capital structure; otherwise, the capital structure will change. Hence, the cost of "depreciation-generated" funds is equal to the MCC (excluding new common stock) of the firm.

shortly we favor the external yield criterion, which states that the cost of internally generated funds, k_s, is equal to the cost of new common stock, k_e, without adjustment for underpricing and flotation costs.

After-Tax Returns Required by Investors.   Viewing the cost of internally generated funds as the after-tax return required by investors means taking into account the ordinary and long-term capital gains tax provisions that affect the after-tax returns available to investors. Before consideration of taxes, the return required by equity investors for investing in the firm is equal to k_s, which is an equilibrium rate that considers both dividend income and capital appreciation. Once personal taxes on both dividends and long-term capital gains or losses are considered, the after-tax return realized to investors is equal to:

$$\text{After-tax return} = k_s \left[\frac{(1 - T_p)}{(1 - T_g)} \right] \tag{17.11}$$

where T_p is the personal ordinary income tax rate and T_g is the personal long-term capital gains tax rate.

There are two problems with this approach. First, most firms' shareholders have many different ordinary income and long-term capital gains tax rates. To employ this approach, firms must estimate the "average" ordinary and long-term capital gains tax rates applying to all shareholders. Given differences in tax rates among shareholders, it is impossible to determine a minimum yield by which *all* shareholders are better off if the firm reinvests its cash flows instead of paying cash dividends.[15] Second, this approach ignores the firm's alternative investment opportunities.

External Yield Criterion.   The second approach to determining the cost of internally generated funds is based on the *external yield criterion*. The premise underlying this approach is that the firm should evaluate buying the stock of similar-risk firms and consider this the cost of the best alternative investment the firm foregoes as its opportunity cost. This opportunity cost of internally generated funds is determined independent of the personal tax consequences of the firm's shareholders. Therefore, if firms cannot invest their internally generated funds at a rate equal to or greater than k_s as defined in Equations 17.6 or 17.9, they should pay them out to their shareholders. Thus, the cost of internally generated funds is *less* than the cost of new common stock, primarily because of underpricing and flotation cost savings. For King Industries,

---

[15]See Wilbur G. Lewellen, *The Cost of Capital* (Dubuque, Iowa: Kendall/Hunt, 1976); and Timothy J. Nantell and C. Robert Carlson, "The Cost of Retained Earnings," in *Issues in Managerial Finance*, eds. Eugene F. Brigham and Ramon E. Johnson (Hinsdale, Ill.: Dryden Press, 1976), pp. 340–347.

k_s based on the valuation approach is equal to 14.94 percent [($4.75/$80) + .09 = .0594 + .09]; it is 14.80 percent when the CAPM approach is used [10% + .80 × (16% − 10%)]. Hence, the opportunity cost of internally generated funds to King of approximately 14.9 percent is less than its 16 percent approximate cost of new common stock financing.

It is no accident the cost of common equity capital is higher than the cost of debt or preferred stock. Part of the reason is that dividend payments are not deductible, while interest payments on debt are deductible. Also, except for flotation costs, the explicit costs of capital represent the "market's" required rate of return for the various types of funds supplied to the firm. From the standpoint of investors, common stock is the riskiest financial instrument issued by the firm. Investors will buy it and/or continue to hold it only if they are compensated for the increased risk exposure with a higher rate of return. For these reasons, both internally generated funds and new common stock have higher specific costs to the firm than do other sources of capital.

Calculating the Firm's MCC

Now that the costs of specific sources of long-term capital have been calculated, they can be combined with the firm's target capital structure to determine the firm's weighted marginal cost of capital (MCC). We look first at how to choose the appropriate weights and then at the calculation of a single MCC for a given financing increment.

Market Value Weights

In the next chapter we will examine in detail the effects of financial leverage on the costs of debt and equity, and the market value of the firm, and we show that the optimal mix of financing is the one that maximizes the value of the firm. Rational, wealth-maximizing firms use this optimal mix as their target capital structure. They base this structure on the market value of their debt, preferred stock, and common equity, not on its accounting or book value.[16] The market values of a firm's financing instruments (bonds, preferred stock, and common stock) are generally different from the book values shown on the firm's balance sheet. Since the market values measure their current economic worth and also form the basis for estimating future costs of financing, they are the only relevant data.

One way to approach weighting is to view the firm as having to re-create its capital structure as it raises additional funds. This can be

---

[16]This point has been made by many writers, including Franco Modigliani and Merton H. Miller, "Corporate Income Taxes and the Cost of Capital: A Correction," *American Economic Review* 53 (June 1963), pp. 433–443; Timothy J. Nantell and C. Robert Carlson, "The Cost of Capital As a Weighted Average," *Journal of Finance* 30 (December 1975), pp. 1343–1355; and William Beranek, "The Weighted Average Cost of Capital and Shareholder Wealth Maximization," *Journal of Financial and Quantitative Analysis* 12 (March 1977), pp. 17–31.

done by answering the following question: what would it take for the firm to re-create its capital structure (in part or in total) as it raises incremental funds? Over the long term, the firm raises funds in the market-based proportions specified by its target capital structure and based on the current market prices of the securities. These weights and prices are all based on *current market values*—hence market values are the appropriate values to use when estimating the firm's marginal cost of capital.

To illustrate the differences between book value and market value weights, consider King Industries, as shown in Table 17.1. Based on book values taken from the firm's balance sheet, the capital structure weights would appear to be 40 percent long-term debt, 10 percent preferred stock, and 50 percent common stock equity. However, as Table 17.1 also shows, the market value weights (based on current market prices of the firm's debt and preferred and common stock)[17] indicate how the firm actually is valued in the marketplace, and how it intends to raise long-term funds. The market-value-based proportions are the following: long-term debt, 20 percent; preferred stock, 5 percent; common equity, 75 percent.[18] For most firms, the market value of common stock equity is greater than book value. Thus, the use of book value weights underestimates the firm's reliance on common equity (particularly internally generated funds) in relation to debt and/or preferred stock. It is this misstating of the economic value of the firm that causes book value weights generally to understate the weighted marginal cost of capital.

The MCC for a Single Financing Increment

To determine a firm's weighted MCC, we use the previously determined after-tax costs of financing for the specific sources, and their appropriate market value weights, W. The MCC, k, is calculated as follows:

$$k = W_b k_b + W_{ps} k_{ps} + W_s k_s + W_e k_e \qquad (17.12)$$

where W_b, W_{ps}, W_s, and W_e are the market-value-determined proportions of debt, preferred stock, internally generated funds, and new common

---

[17]The current prices of the firm's existing long-term debt, preferred stock, and common stock are generally available for most medium- and large-size publicly owned firms. The specific market price of common stock to use is often difficult to determine. Should it be the price as of a specific day, an average of high and low prices over a specific period of time, or what? Recognizing that market values fluctuate over time and that the firm's capital structure generally fluctuates within a few percentage points of its target, our preference is to use an "average" market price based on the last few months of historical prices, adjusted for any expected and/or foreseen changes in the next few months. When one considers all the estimates necessary to derive the cost of equity capital, the specification of the "exact" market price is probably not critical.

[18]We assume the firm intends to maintain its target capital structure in approximately the existing market value proportions. If a change in target capital structure is planned, the new capital structure proportions should be employed.

TABLE 17.1
Book and Market Value Weights for King Industries' Capital Structure

	Book Value			Market Value (Target Capital Structure)		
Source of Capitol	Book Value	Proportion of Long-Term Capital		Source of Capital	Market Value	Proportion of Long-Term Capital
Long-term debt	$20,000,000	.40		Long-term debt	$19,000,000[a]	.20
Preferred stock	5,000,000	.10		Preferred stock	4,750,000[b]	.05
Common equity				Common equity	71,250,000[c]	.75
Common stock	$15,000,000					
Internally generated (retained earnings)	10,000,000					
	25,000,000	.50				
Totals	$50,000,000	1.00			$95,000,000	1.00

[a]Market value of debt is $19 million, which is 95 percent of the book value.
[b]Market value of preferred stock is $4.75 million, which is also 95 percent of book value.
[c]Average market price of common stock is $80 per share, and 890,625 shares are outstanding; $80 × 890,625 = $71,250,000.

TABLE 17.2

Marginal Cost of Capital (MCC) for a Single $30 Million Financing Increment: King Industries, Inc.

Source of Capital	Market Value[a] (1)	Market Value Proportion (2)	Explicit Cost (3)	Weighted Cost [(2) × (3)] (4)
Long-term debt	$19,000,000	.20	7.49%	1.498%
Preferred stock	4,750,000	.05	11.86	0.593
Common equity	71,250,000	.75	14.90	11.175
Totals	$95,000,000	1.00		13.266%

[a]From Table 17.1.

stock, respectively, and k_i, k_{ps}, k_s, and k_e are the associated costs, as noted earlier.

This idea can now be illustrated for King Industries, Inc., for a single level of anticipated new financing—$30 million. King has estimated that its internally generated equity funds will be $22.5 million for the coming period; this is 75 percent of the $30 million in long-term funds to be raised. Like most firms, King employs internally generated common equity before it resorts to issuing new common stock. This 75 percent is in line with King's target capital structure proportions of 20 percent debt, 5 percent preferred stock, and 75 percent common equity. The other $7.5 million will have to be raised by issuing $6 million in debt (20% × $30 million) and $1.5 million in preferred stock (5% × $30 million). We can now use Equation 17.12 to compute the firm's MCC. That is, given the financing proportions and the previously calculated explicit marginal costs of 7.49 percent for long-term debt, 11.86 percent for preferred stock, and 14.90 percent for internally generated equity, we see in Table 17.2 the MCC for King Industries for this financing increment is 13.266 percent.[19]

Two points should be mentioned before we turn to the MCC schedule. First, for many firms, the calculation of a single weighted MCC may be sufficient at any specific point in time. Often, due to internal or external constraints (real or imposed), firms develop a capital expenditure plan that requires a specific dollar amount of funds. In spite of the fact that this approach may place a rationing constraint on the capital budgeting process, many firms are known to operate in this manner. For these firms, the calculation of a single weighted MCC, which is constant over the relevant financing range, is sufficient. In practice, most firms use a single, firm-wide MCC calculated as we have described above, or divisional costs of capital that reflect differences in risk among various divisions of the firm.

The second point is that many firms do not differentiate between the

[19]For computational completeness, the MCC estimates are carried out to three decimal places. Because of the estimates that go into deriving them, such precision is not necessary in practice.

cost of internally generated common equity and the cost of new common stock. Instead, a single cost, k_s, is calculated and applied to all anticipated common equity financing. This practice is appropriate as long as the firm is large and the amount of new common stock financing is relatively small. For smaller firms, or for those going public for the first time, the costs associated with new common stock financing are often significantly higher than those associated with the use of internally generated funds. In these cases, separate costs of common equity should be employed.

The Marginal Cost of Capital Schedule

As the firm increases its volume of financing *at any one point in time*, it becomes more risky to the marketplace that supplies its capital. To understand this, consider a firm that is contemplating a 10 percent increase in size versus a 100 percent increase. Increasing its size by 100 percent generally exposes the firm to substantially more risk, since there is a limit to how fast a firm can grow and still maintain efficiency and effectiveness. Because the suppliers of capital view the firm as being more risky at the point in time when it seeks larger and larger amounts of funds, they require a higher return. This in turn increases the firm's marginal cost of capital as it attempts to raise more and more funds at any given point in time.

A graph or schedule relating the firm's cost of capital to different dollar amounts of new financing is called the *marginal cost of capital schedule*. It is based on the notion that as more funds are raised at any point in time, the increased risk causes the cost of the various sources of funds to rise. For simplicity, we view the specific costs of financing to be constant until they reach their breaking points. At a breaking point, the suppliers of the given form of financing require an increased return, so the firm's MCC increases at each breaking point.

Calculating the MCC Schedule

To calculate its MCC schedule, a firm must first determine the explicit cost of each source of financing at various levels of *total* new financing. To do this, the following steps are necessary:

Step 1. The cost of each source of financing for various levels of use is determined through an analysis of current market conditions. In addition, the firm's target capital structure must be specified.

Step 2. Using the target capital structure proportions of debt, preferred stock, and common equity, the levels of total new financing at which the cost of the financing components change is determined. The levels of total financing at which the component costs increase, the *breaking points*, are calculated as:

$$BP_i = \frac{TF_i}{W_i} \tag{17.13}$$

where BP_i = breaking point for financing source i
   TF_i = total financing from source i at the breaking point
   W_i = target capital structure proportion for financing
    source i

Step 3. Once the breaking points have been determined, a new weighted marginal cost of capital (employing Equation 17.12) is computed between breaking points over the range of total new financing. First, the MCC for a level of financing up to the first breaking point is found. Then, another MCC for the financing between the first and second breaking points is found, and so on. It is important to recognize that for each range of new financing between breaking points, certain capital costs increase, causing the MCC schedule to rise.

Step 4. Once the MCC for each range has been determined, a schedule of the results is prepared. The schedule, which is commonly presented as a graph, provides the financial manager with a valuable tool for choosing those capital expenditure projects that best contribute toward maximizing shareholder wealth.

Using King Industries, Inc., as an example will help us understand how the MCC schedule is determined. We will follow the four-step process.

Step 1. King's target capital structure (Table 17.1) consists of 20 percent long-term debt, 5 percent preferred stock, and 75 percent common equity. Based on current financial market conditions and relying on its investment bankers, King estimated the explicit costs of its three capital sources over various ranges of new financing. This information, presented in Table 17.3, indicates that as more financing is secured from each of the capital sources (at any given point in time), the explicit costs rise. Note the firm will employ internally generated common equity before issuing new common stock to save additional common equity.

Step 2. Using the target capital structure proportions given in column 1 of Table 17.3 and the financing ranges given in column 2, the breaking points for each source of capital are calculated in column 3 of Table 17.4. To calculate the breaking points, Equation 17.13 is employed as follows. For long-term debt, the first $10 million has an explicit cost of 7.49 percent; dividing $10 million by the target capital structure proportion of 20 percent indicates that $50 million ($10 million/.20) of total new financing can be raised before the explicit cost of long-term debt increases from 7.49 to 8.60 percent. Likewise, the explicit cost of the first $2.5 million of preferred stock is 11.86 percent. Based on the target capital structure proportion of 5 percent for preferred stock, the explicit cost of preferred stock will not change until $50 million ($2.5 million/.05) in total new

TABLE 17.3
Data for Calculating
the Marginal Cost of
Capital Schedule for
King Industries, Inc.

Source of Capital	Market Value (Target Capital Structure) Proportion[a] (1)	Range of New Financing[b] ($ Millions) (2)	Explicit Cost[c] (3)
Long-term debt	.20	$0–$10	7.49%
		$10–$30	8.60
		Greater than $30	11.00
Preferred stock	.05	$0–$2.5	11.86
		Greater than $2.5	13.80
Common equity[d]	.75	$0–$22.5	14.90
		$22.5–$75	16.00
		Greater than $75	20.00

[a]From Table 17.1.

[b]These ranges are for the corresponding sources of capital. *They do not represent levels of total new financing.*

[c]The following explicit costs, 7.49 percent (long-term debt), 11.86 percent (preferred stock), 14.90 percent (internally generated common equity) and 16.00 percent (new common stock) are the costs calculated earlier in the chapter. The rest of the explicit costs were provided by the firm's investment bankers.

[d]King Industries expects to generate $22.5 million internally after paying cash dividends. Thus, the first increment of common equity is generated internally; additional common equity financing will come from the issuance of new common stock.

financing has been secured. This process is repeated for all points at which the cost of a financing component changes; breaking points in total new financing of $30 million, $50 million, $100 million, and $150 million result for King Industries.

Step 3.   Based on the breaking points computed in step 2, we have the following "ranges of total new financing": $0 to $30 million, $30 to $50 million, and so on. A weighted marginal cost of capital must now be computed for *each* of these five ranges. Starting with the $0 to $30 million range, we see in Table 17.5 that the weighted marginal cost of capital is 13.266 percent. Note we used the same procedure for computing the MCC as shown in Table 17.2. For the second financing range, $30 to $50 million, the explicit costs of long-term debt and preferred stock remain the same. However, the explicit cost of common equity increases to 16.0 percent, since new common stock (instead of internally generated funds) must be issued. The MCC for the second financing range is 14.091 percent. Similar calculations for the next three financing ranges are shown in Table 17.5 on p. 720.

Step 4.   Once the marginal cost of capital for each of the five financing ranges has been determined, the MCC schedule can be prepared, as in Figure 17.1 on p. 721. There could, of course, be still more breaking points in the MCC schedule as explicit costs of various sources of

TABLE 17.4
Breaking Points and Total New Financing Ranges for King Industries' Capital Sources
(In Millions of Dollars)

Source of Capital	Explicit Cost[a] (1)	Range of New Financing, by Source (2)	Breaking Point[b] (3)	Range of Total New Financing[c] (4)
Long-term debt	7.49%	$0–$10	$\frac{\$10}{.20} = \$50$	$0–$50
	8.60	$10–$30	$\frac{\$30}{.20} = \$150$	$50–$150
	11.00	Greater than $30	—	Greater than $150
Preferred stock	11.86	$0–$2.5	$\frac{\$2.5}{.05} = \$50$	$0–$50
	13.80	Greater than $2.5	—	Greater than $50
Common equity	14.90	$0–$22.5	$\frac{\$22.5}{.75} = \$30$	$0–$30
	16.00	$22.5–$75	$\frac{\$75}{.75} = \$100$	$30–$100
	20.00	Greater than $75	—	Greater than $100

[a]From Table 17.3
[b]Breaking points were calculated by dividing the upper limit of the financing ranges by the appropriate target capital structure proportion from column 1 of Table 17.3. The breaking points are calculated using Equation 17.13.
[c]Using the breaking point calculated in column 3, the range of total new financing corresponding to each source-specific new financing range given in column 2 is determined.

TABLE 17.5
Calculation of the Marginal Cost of Capital Schedule for King Industries, Inc.

Range	Range of Total Financing ($ Millions)	Source of Capital (1)	Market Value (Target Capital Structure) Proportion (2)	Explicit Cost[a] (3)	Weighted Marginal Cost [(2) × (3)] (4)
1	$0–$30	Debt	.20	7.49%	1.498%
		Preferred	.05	11.86	.593
		Common	.75	14.90	11.175
		Weighted MCC for first range[b]			13.266%
2	$30–$50	Debt	.20	7.49%	1.498%
		Preferred	.05	11.86	.593
		Common	.75	16.00	12.000
		Weighted MCC for second range			14.091%
3	$50–$100	Debt	.20	8.60%	1.720%
		Preferred	.05	13.80	.690
		Common	.75	16.00	12.000
		Weighted MCC for third range			14.410%
4	$100–$150	Debt	.20	8.60%	1.720%
		Preferred	.05	13.80	.690
		Common	.75	20.00	15.000
		Weighted MCC for fourth range			17.410%
5	Greater than $150	Debt	.20	11.00%	2.200%
		Preferred	.05	13.80	.690
		Common	.75	20.00	15.000
		Weighted MCC for fifth range			17.890%

[a]The costs for each range of total new financing are obtained from a comparison of columns 1 and 4 of Table 17.4.
[b]This MCC is the same as that calculated in Table 17.2.

capital increase. At the limit, one can think of an MCC schedule with so many breaking points that it rises as a smoothed, continuous function beyond some given level of total new financing.

Combining the Marginal Cost of Capital and Investment Opportunities Schedules

The MCC schedule is employed to find the appropriate discount rate for use in determining net present values (NPVs) and profitability indexes (PIs), or the hurdle rate for use with the internal rate of return (IRR). To determine the appropriate discount rate, financial managers need to determine the investment opportunities schedule (IOS) of proposed capital budgeting projects, as shown in Table 17.6 on p. 722. For example, project A requires an initial investment of $15 million, has cash inflows of $5,237,430 for each of 5 years, and has an internal rate of return of 22 percent; project F has an internal rate of return of 14 percent, requires an

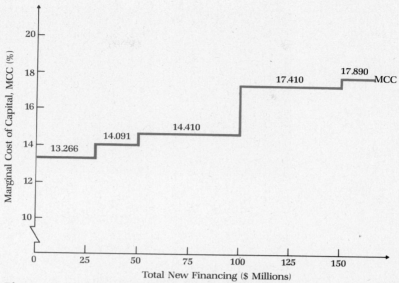

Figure 17.1 Marginal Cost of Capital (MCC) Schedule for King Industries, Inc.

initial investment of $40 million, and has cash inflows of $7,668,712 for each of 10 years, and so on.[20]

[20]For simplicity, the projects are assumed to be independent, the cash inflows are constant, and there is no capital rationing. The internal rate of return is employed in deriving the investment opportunities schedule (IOS) because of ease of comparison and graphic explanation. An alternative approach is to calculate net present values at various discount rates, such as the MCCs estimated for the various financing ranges. With the MCCs of 14.091, 14.410, and 17.410, the following NPVs result:

Project	Cumulative New Financing ($ Million)	Marginal Costs of Capital		
		14.091% ($30 to $50 Million)	14.410% ($50 to $100 Million)	17.410% ($100 to $150 Million)
A	$ 15	$2,941,266	$2,804,752	$1,599,651
B	20	724,971	687,779	356,740
C	40	3,685,054	3,413,325	1,086,175
D	70	3,908,029	3,440,124	− 488,388
E	95	384,271	249,157	− 963,763
F	135	− 140,767	− 631,018	− 4,800,821
G	145	− 731,639	− 802,162	− 1,424,710
H	165	− 2,706,212	− 2,856,001	− 4,167,773

(*Note:* These calculations were made using more detailed present-value interest factor tables than those contained in Appendix A.) An analysis of this schedule of net present values leads to the selection of projects A, B, C, D, and E—the same result we obtained using the IRR approach.

TABLE 17.6
Potential Capital
Budgeting Projects
Available to King
Industries, Inc. The
Investment
Opportunities
Schedule (IOS)

Project	Annual Cash Inflows (CFATs)	Project Life (Years)	Internal Rate of Return (%)	Initial Investment, $CFAT_0$ ($ Millions)	Cumulative New Investment ($ Millions)
A	$ 5,237,430	5	22%	$15	$ 15
B	1,968,504	4	21	5	20
C	4,804,228	9	19	20	40
D	6,014,435	12	17	30	70
E	10,950,504	3	15	25	95
F	7,668,712	10	14	40	135
G	2,705,628	5	11	10	145
H	4,458,315	6	9	20	165

Using the data developed in Table 17.6, King Industries' IOS schedule is shown in Figure 17.2. The figure also reproduces King's MCC schedule from Figure 17.1. Combining the IOS and MCC schedules allows King to determine its appropriate marginal cost of capital to use for decision-making purposes. Given the IOS and MCC schedules plotted in Figure 17.2, King should accept five new projects (A, B, C, D, and E), since their rates of return are in excess of the MCC required to finance them. Projects F, G, and H should be rejected, since acceptance diminishes the value of the firm.[21] Therefore, King's capital budget should be $95 million.

One additional point deserves attention. Financial managers must recognize that raising funds is "lumpy," and that strict target capital structure proportions cannot always be maintained. However, most firms strive to maintain roughly proportional financing over time. Deviations may occur, and may last as long as 2 or 3 years, but they are considered only temporary fluctuations. It is in this broad sense that financial managers calculate and use an MCC schedule.

---

[21]One question often raised is this: "What happens if the MCC cuts through one of the projects?" For example, suppose project E required an outlay of $40 million, instead of $25 million. In this case, the MCC schedule would cut right through the project. Should we accept project E in this case? If a partial investment of only $30 million ($100 million −$70 million) could be made, this should be our course of action. Otherwise, the answer is determined by finding the average cost of funds needed to finance project E and comparing it to E's IRR of 15 percent. Project E would require $30 million of funds costing 14.410 percent and $10 million costing 17.410 percent. Based on these respective weights ($30 million or 75% at 14.410% and $10 million or 25% at 17.410%), the cost of funds to finance project E would be 15.16 percent (.75×14.410%=10.8075% plus .25×17.410%= 4.3525%). Since this cost is greater than project E's IRR of 15 percent, the project should be rejected.

Another problem involves the issue of why we do not take project F first, since then it would be accepted because its IRR of 14 percent would be more than the 13.266 percent cost of funds. We do not do this because we are interested in *maximizing the excess of returns over costs, or the total area above the MCC schedule but below the IOS schedule.* To accomplish this, we accept those projects with the highest returns first.

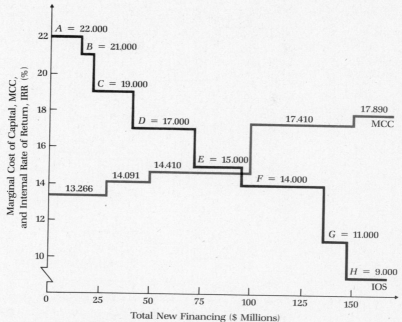

Figure 17.2 Combining King Industries, Inc., Marginal Cost of Capital (MCC) and Investment Opportunities (IOS) Schedules to Determine the Appropriate Discount Rate.

MULTINATIONAL DIMENSIONS

Cost of Capital

If we assume King Industries, Inc. is a large multinational firm, Figure 17.2 can be modified to take into account international financing opportunities. Multinational firms have access to the huge Eurocurrency markets and to the local money markets in which affiliates are located. We will see in Part Seven that such firms also have access to the Eurobond market, as well as to foreign equity markets. This added availability of capital should lower their MCC schedules compared to those of purely domestic firms.[22]

Given King's IOS schedule which, of course, includes potential projects abroad, it should have a lower MCC and a larger number of acceptable capital budgeting projects. This lower MCC schedule would appear as the broken line (labeled MCC') in Figure 17.3. It crosses the IOS schedule at a point below project F, which would now be accepted. According to Table 17.6, project F requires an initial

---

[22]In addition to increased availability of capital, other international factors can lower a firm's MCC. A discussion of them is beyond the scope of this book, but they are covered in international financial management texts such as David K. Eiteman and Arthur I. Stonehill, *Multinational Business Finance*, 3d ed. (Reading, Mass.: Addison-Wesley, 1982).

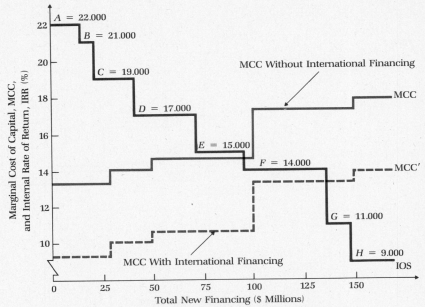

Figure 17.3 MCC and IOS Schedules for King Industries, Inc., with International Financing.

investment of $40 million. Therefore, the optimal capital budget would increase from its original level of $95 million to a new level of $135 million. The MCC for the firm at its optimal capital budget falls from 14.410 percent to 13.6 percent when access to international capital markets is considered.

The market value or target capital structure proportions remain unchanged from those shown in Table 17.1, but the range of new financing possibilities is increased for each source of capital. For example, by tapping the Eurobond market, King is appealing to a whole new group of foreign investors. Their required rate of return will differ from that of American investors because of differences in perceived foreign exchange, political, and tax factors. In some cases, these factors would mitigate against foreign investors purchasing U.S. dollar-denominated long-term debt securities. However, under some conditions, foreign investors will purchase many such issues. The same reasoning applies to other long-term financing instruments once access to international markets is assured. Thus, the international MCC schedule in Figure 17.3 is shown to be lower than its domestic counterpart at all levels.

Dynamic
Considerations

Conditions change over time, so financial managers must be prepared to reestimate the firm's cost of capital at least every year. Even if the firm's business and financial risk are constant over time, capital costs may change in response to changing economic conditions.

Consider the possible consequences if the risk-free rate changes as the anticipated rate of inflation drops. The impact of a decrease in R_F will cause the explicit cost of debt, preferred stock, and common equity to decline. The impact on common equity costs is shown in Figure 17.4(a), which illustrates how a 2 percent decrease in anticipated inflation causes the security market line, SML, to shift downward, resulting in a decreased cost of common equity funds. The amount of the cost reduction will be 2 percent regardless of the level of nondiversifiable risk, β. However, this may not be the only consequence of a decrease in anticipated inflation. If decreased inflation causes investors to also become less risk-averse, the slope of the SML will decline, leading to a reduced risk premium. This relationship, in addition to the shift in the risk-free rate, is shown in Figure 17.4(b).

The decrease in risk aversion in Figure 17.4(b) causes the average firm's (with $\beta = \beta_M = 1.0$) cost of common equity to decline by an additional 2 percent. Firms with nondiversifiable risk above or below $\beta_M = 1.0$ will experience larger or smaller decreases in common equity costs. In addition, there might be secondary influences causing *relative* shifts in the cost of common equity versus debt or preferred stock. Hence, dynamic considerations resulting from fiscal, monetary, or

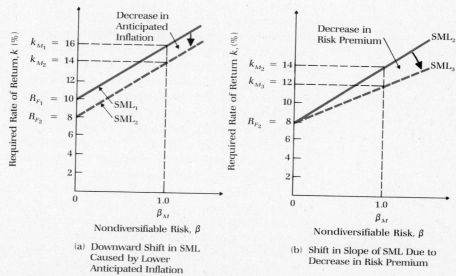

Figure 17.4   Possible Shifts in Security Market Line (SML) due to Decreases in Anticipated Inflation and Risk Aversion.

worldwide actions influencing supply and demand conditions in the financial markets may therefore cause changes in a firm's MCC, even if its business and financial risk remain constant.

Equally important, a firm's business risk may change over time because of growth in the size of the firm or because of a change in the investment opportunities undertaken by the firm. Such a change in business risk will cause changes in the explicit costs of funds, even if the firm's target capital structure does not change. Finally, long-run changes in capital market conditions may cause pronounced changes in the relative costs of various types of funds. This will cause the firm to reevaluate and possibly change its target capital structure. To make the transition from one target capital structure to another, the firm will rely primarily on one specific type of financing. For example, it may finance with debt until the desired target capital structure is achieved. During the transition period, financial managers should estimate the MCC using the new target capital structure proportions.

Divisional Costs of Capital

Because of the vast differences in business and financial risk among various lines of business, and because of the growth of conglomerates and other diversified firms, many companies have begun to use risk-adjusted divisional costs of capital. By division we mean some subunit of the firm, whether it is an actual division, a subsidiary, a project, or a line of business. If the capital expenditure projects undertaken by the division are essentially similar with respect to risk (but differ in general risk level from projects of other divisions), the use of *divisional screening rates*, which are the division-specific MCCs should be used. Those divisions with greater risk than that of the firm as a whole will have higher MCCs, whereas those with below-average risk will have lower costs of capital than the firm-wide MCC.

The concepts discussed earlier in the chapter apply as well to divisional screening rates; that is, we must concern ourselves with the appropriate target capital structure for each division, and then calculate the explicit costs for each source of financing. The explicit costs of debt and preferred stock could be adjusted from those for the firm as a whole, but typically they are not. However, the cost of common equity, which reflects economic conditions and the exposure to business risk for a firm with no debt or preferred stock must be determined for each division. In calculating divisional costs of capital, the important elements are the division's target capital structure (reflecting primarily financial risk) and its cost of equity capital (reflecting primarily business risk).

The target capital structure for each division will be based on the judgment of the firm's financial managers, and also on the advice of its investment bankers. For example, regulated firms such as electric or natural gas utilities often use substantial amounts of debt financing due to the predictable nature of their cash flows. Machinery and equipment manufacturers and others in cyclical industries tend to use substantially less debt, given the wide variability in their cash flows over the business cycle.

Once the target capital structure is determined, the division's cost of common equity capital must be estimated. This may be accomplished by using the capital asset pricing model approach discussed earlier. What we attempt to do is identify firms with publicly traded common stock that are engaged solely in the same business as the division. This obviously involves careful consideration of the products or services produced by the division. For some divisions, this matching can only be approximated.

After the appropriate firms are identified, their betas are obtained and the required return on common equity for the division in question is estimated.[23] When obtaining betas from other publicly traded firms, note that if a firm has debt or preferred stock outstanding, the betas reflect both the company's line of business (business risk) and its long-term capital structure (financial risk). If the publicly traded firms' capital structures differ significantly from the target capital structure for the division, adjustments will have to be made in the betas.[24] After the division's cost of common equity is determined, it is combined with the costs of other sources of long-term financing to determine the division's weighted marginal cost of capital.

Let us again use King Industries, Inc., as an example. King's firm-wide target capital structure was 20 percent debt, 5 percent preferred stock, and 75 percent common equity financing. Recall from Table 17.5 that the explicit financing costs for the first financing increment were $k_i = 7.49\%$, $k_{ps} = 11.86\%$, and $k_s = 14.90\%$. Based on this information, King's first-increment, firm-wide MCC was estimated to be 13.266 percent. Assume now that King Industries has both a natural gas pipeline subsidiary and a heavy duty machinery division. After receiving input from its investment banker and undertaking a careful analysis of firms

---

[23]In calculating the division's cost of common equity, underpricing and flotation costs are ignored.

[24]The relationship between the levered beta, β_L, and an unlevered beta, β_U, is

$$\beta_U = \beta_L \left(\frac{S_L}{S_U} \right)$$

where β_U = the firm's unlevered market beta
   β_L = the firm's levered market beta based on the firm's existing capital structure
   S_L = the market value of the firm's equity
   S_U = the estimated market value of the firm's equity if unlevered

See Robert S. Hamada, "The Effect of the Firm's Capital Structure on the Systematic Risk of Common Stocks," *Journal of Finance* 27 (May 1972), pp. 435–452; and Richard S. Bower and Jeffrey M. Jenks, "Divisional Screening Rates," *Financial Management* 4 (autumn 1975), pp. 42–49. For notational simplicity the subscript L for the levered firm's beta is ignored.

similar to each of the two divisions, King's financial managers determined that the appropriate divisional target capital structure weights (W_i) were as follows:

Sources of Capital	Target Capital Structure Weights	
	Natural Gas Division	Machinery Division
Long-term debt	.40	.20
Preferred stock	.20	0
Common equity	.40	.80
Totals	1.00	1.00

For each division, three publicly traded firms with similar product lines and capital structures were found. Based on data from these firms, and assuming $R_F = 10\%$ and $k_M = 16\%$, the natural gas division's cost of common equity was estimated to be 13.60 percent, and the machinery division's cost was estimated to be 19 percent (Table 17.7). Finally, the respective divisional weighted MCCs were calculated as shown in Table 17.8. The natural gas division, which has a low degree of business risk and uses large amounts of debt and preferred stock in its capital structure, has an MCC of 10.808 percent. The machinery division, due to its high degree of business risk and relatively lower usage of debt, has a MCC of 16.698 percent.

Once the divisional MCCs have been determined, capital should be allocated throughout the firm on a risk-adjusted basis. The higher the risk of the division, the higher its risk-adjusted MCC. Too often in multidivisional firms a single discount rate is employed for capital expenditure analysis. An order comes from top management stating that "all projects must return at least 15 percent in order to be accepted." The

	TABLE 17.7	Division	Publicly Traded Firm	Beta (β)

TABLE 17.7
Divisional Costs of Equity Capital for King Industries, Inc., Based on Other Publicly Traded Firms

Division	Publicly Traded Firm	Beta (β)
NATURAL GAS	A	.75
	B	.50
	C	.55
	Average for product line =	.60
$k_{s(natural\ gas)} = 10\% + .60 \times (16\% - 10\%) = 13.60\%$		
MACHINERY	D	1.70
	E	1.60
	F	1.20
	Average for product line =	1.50
$k_{s(machinery)} = 10\% + 1.50 \times (16\% - 10\%) = 19.00\%$		

TABLE 17.8
Divisional Weighted
Marginal Costs of
Capital for King
Industries, Inc.

TABLE 17.8
Divisional Weighted Marginal Costs of Capital for King Industries, Inc.

Source of Capital	Target Capital Structure (1)	Explicit Cost (2)	Weighted Cost [(1) × (2)] (3)
NATURAL GAS			
Long-term debt	.40	7.49%	2.996%
Preferred stock	.20	11.86	2.372
Common equity	.40	13.60	5.440
Totals	1.00	MCC =	10.808%
MACHINERY			
Long-term debt	.20	7.49%	1.498%
Preferred stock	0	11.86	0
Common equity	.80	19.00	15.200
Totals	1.00	MCC =	16.698%

problem with this approach is that certain relatively safe divisions may have to reject projects that actually provide a return greater than the division's risk-adjusted MCC. Likewise, relatively risky divisions may end up accepting projects that would be rejected if appropriate divisional MCCs were employed. Thus, the use of a firm-wide MCC when divisional risk differs substantially makes low-risk divisions too conservative in project generation and acceptance, and high-risk divisions too aggressive. Clearly such results are inconsistent with the goal of shareholder wealth maximization.

SUMMARY

Financial managers recognize that accurate estimation of the firm's marginal cost of capital (MCC) is essential for effective capital expenditure decision making. The primary determinants of the firm's MCC are its business risk, as determined by its mix of assets and its financial risk, as evidenced by its target capital structure. The MCC is future-oriented in that the relevant factors it considers are (1) the market-based proportions of capital the firm intends to raise in the future, and (2) the future annual cost of the capital raised from each of these various sources. Any other data, particularly historical or accounting, are irrelevant. Finally, it is the marginal cost, or the cost of the last unit of capital to be raised, that is important.

Once the target capital structure and the explicit costs of various financing sources have been determined, the firm's MCC can be calculated. For firms with fixed capital budgets, it is often sufficient to calculate a single MCC over the expected financing range. However, a fuller understanding is possible if the firm's entire marginal cost of capital schedule is developed. Once established, the firm's MCC (and its intersection with the IOS schedule) determines the appropriate cost of capital for use in capital budgeting decision making. If the target capital structure changes, or if new capital expenditures alter the firm's business risk, the MCC must be revised. In addition, since economic and financial conditions change, firms must recalculate their MCC every year or so.

In recent years, many firms have begun to employ risk-adjusted divisional costs of capital. This approach, which employs the same basic concepts used to calculate a firm-wide MCC, stimulates divisional efficiency by allocating funds to divisions on the basis of their risk-adjusted MCCs. Without the use of such an approach, firms encourage safe divisions to bypass wealth-maximizing opportunities and stimulate more risky divisions to undertake projects that are expected to provide lower returns than the division's risk-adjusted MCC.

QUESTIONS

17.1 Define the following, using equations in addition to verbal definitions:
a. k_i.
b. k_{ps}.
c. k_e.
d. k_s.
e. k.

17.2 Explain in detail the implications for calculating a firm's MCC of two fundamental assumptions—that both business risk and financial risk are constant and hence can be ignored.

17.3 Explain why:
a. The explicit cost of debt is generally considered to be the cheapest source of long-term funds available to the firm.
b. The explicit cost of preferred stock is greater than the cost of debt, but less than the cost of common equity.
c. The cost of new common stock is greater than the cost of internally generated funds.
d. The cost of internally generated funds is not zero.

17.4 The following formulas are often employed to estimate the explicit cost of internally generated funds:

$$k_s = D_1/P_0 + g$$
$$k_s = R_F + \beta \times (k_M - R_F)$$

Explain the implications of both formulas. Under what circumstances would you expect the formulas to provide (a) similar answers, or (b) different answers?

17.5 Market value (or target capital structure) weights, instead of book value weights, should be employed when estimating the marginal cost of capital. Why is this so? What would be the "typical" effect on the marginal cost of capital if book value weights were employed? Why? What type of mistake would the use of book value weights typically cause financial managers to make?

17.6   Answer the following:

a.   What does the marginal cost of capital schedule represent?

b.   How and why is the MCC schedule employed in conjunction with the firm's investment opportunities schedule (IOS), to determine the appropriate discount rate for use in capital budgeting?

17.7   What effect does having access to international financial markets have on the MCC? Why does this occur? Under what conditions would a firm's international MCC schedule lie above (instead of below) the solid MCC schedule in Figure 17.3? What steps should financial managers take in such a case?

17.8   Assume a firm is financed with only two sources of capital—debt and internally generated funds—and that the firm's capital structure will not change. How would each of the following actions affect (increase, decrease or no change) the firm's cost of debt, k_b, its cost of internally generated funds, k_s, and its MCC? (Assume other things are held constant. Note that several of the actions probably have no single correct answer, depending on (1) the explicit or implicit assumptions made, and (2) the counteracting nature of some of the influences.)

Action	Effect on		
	k_i	k_s	MCC
a. The corporate tax rate is increased.	____	____	____
b. Inflation is expected to decrease.	____	____	____
c. The flotation costs of issuing new securities increase.	____	____	____
d. Investors become less risk averse.	____	____	____
e. Standard & Poor's raises its rating of the firm's bonds because it considers the bonds less risky than previously.	____	____	____
f. The Federal Reserve tightens credit.	____	____	____
g. The firm expands into a new market area that is more risky than the previous market area.	____	____	____

h. The stock market rallies substantially due to favorable economic prospects. The firm's price also rises. _____ _____ _____

i. Due to "excessive profits," an excess profits tax is imposed on the firm. _____ _____ _____

j. The firm merges with another whose earnings are countercyclical to its own. _____ _____ _____

17.9 Explain the following:
a. How divisional costs of capital should be estimated.
b. What kind of care must be taken if betas from publicly traded firms similar to the division under examination are employed.
c. What kinds of incorrect capital budgeting decisions are made when a firm employs a single, firm-wide MCC disregarding the fact that its divisions have significantly different risk-adjusted MCCs.

PROBLEMS

17.1 *EXPLICIT COST OF DEBT.* Calculate the after-tax cost to the firm for each of the $1000 par value bonds described below assuming annual interest payments and a 40 percent marginal corporate tax rate:

Bond	Life	Selling Price (Before Underwriting Fee)	Underwriting Fee	Coupon Rate
A	25 yr	$1000	$25	10%
B	20	975	15	9
C	10	1040	20	12
D	25	960	60	13
E	30	1050	50	11

17.2 *EXPLICIT COST OF PREFERRED STOCK.* Nancy's Oil Services, Inc., has decided to employ $100 par preferred stock to raise additional capital. Find the explicit cost if:
a. The stock sells for $105 per share, flotation costs are 3 percent of par, and the annual dividend is $9 per share.
b. The stock has an annual dividend of 11 percent per share, flotation costs of $4 per share, and sells for $99 per share.
c. The flotation costs are $2.50 per share, the stock sells for par, and it pays an annual dividend of $10 per share.

17.3 *EXPLICIT COSTS OF COMMON EQUITY: VALUATION APPROACH.* Scientific Products, Inc., has to estimate its costs of internally generated funds and new common stock equity. Employing the valuation approach, what are these costs in the following situations?

a. Present market price, P_0, is $90 per share, new common stock can be sold for $73 per share less $3 per share flotation costs, the current dividend, D_0, is $4 per share, and the expected growth rate, g, in dividends is 10 percent per year.

b. The flotation costs and underpricing will be 20 percent of the current market price, P_0, of $100 per share, current dividends, D_0, are $5 per share, and the expected dividend growth rate, g, is 8 percent per year.

c. The current market price, P_0, is $60 per share, flotation costs are 10 percent of the current market price, underpricing is $5 per share, current dividends, D_0, are $4.75 per share, and there is no growth expected in per share dividends.

d. The past dividend yield, D_0/P_0, is 6 percent, current market price is $70 per share, the expected growth rate in dividends is 11 percent per year, and underpricing and flotation costs are estimated to be $7 per share.

17.4. *EXPLICIT COSTS OF COMMON EQUITY: VALUATION APPROACH CALCULATING GROWTH RATE.*   Ed Lynch has been asked by his boss to calculate the costs of internally generated funds and new common stock for two proposed acquisitions the firm is considering. After consulting with the firm's investment bankers, Lynch concludes that the past dividend pattern of each of the firms is expected to continue for the foreseeable future. Based on the valuation approach, what are the estimated explicit costs of internally generated funds and new common stock for each of the firms?

Battery Storage Corporation		Property Management Associates	
Year	Dividend	Year	Dividend
1984	$1.57	1984	$1.96
1983	1.50	1983	1.75
1982	1.40	1982	1.60
1981	1.35	1981	1.45
1980	1.29	1980	1.30
		1979	1.16
Present market price, $20 Underpricing and flotation costs, $2 per share		Present market price, $80 Underpricing and flotation costs, $15 per share	

17.5 *EXPLICIT COSTS OF COMMON EQUITY: CAPM APPROACH.* Mississippi Printing Services, Inc., uses the CAPM approach to estimate its cost of internally generated funds and new common stock. What are these costs under the following conditions?

a. The estimated risk-free rate, (R_F), and market return (k_M), are 7 and 14 percent, respectively; the investment bankers estimate nondiversifiable risk (β) to be .95, and underpricing and flotation costs will result in net proceeds to the firm equal to 95 percent of the current market price of the common stock.

b. R_F is 8 percent, k_M is 12 percent, the standard deviation of the market returns is 2 percent, the standard deviation of Mississippi's returns is 4 percent, and the correlation between the expected return for the market and the expected return for the firm is .70. Underpricing and flotation costs will cause net proceeds to equal 90 percent of the market price of the stock.

c. The risk-free rate is 7 percent, the correlation between the expected return for the market and the expected return for the firm is .80, the standard deviation of the firm's expected return is 1.64 percent, underpricing and flotation costs will result in net proceeds equal to 94 percent of the current market price, and the expected return on the market is as follows:

Pr	k_M
.2	9%
.3	11
.3	13
.2	15

d. R_F is 9 percent, k_M is 15 percent, the correlation between the expected return for the market and the expected return for the firm is .50, the standard deviation of the expected return on the market is 1.25 percent, underpricing will cause net proceeds to equal 80 percent of the current market price, and the expected return on the firm's stock is given by the following probability distribution:

Pr	k_s
.25	14%
.25	20
.25	22
.25	28

17.6. *EXPLICIT COSTS OF COMMON EQUITY: CAPM APPROACH CALCULAT-
ING MARKET RISK FROM HISTORICAL DATA.* Kathie Hartman has
been asked by her boss to calculate the costs of internally
generated funds and new common stock for two proposed
acquisitions. Based on information she recently acquired from
working with the firm's investment bankers (shown in the
following table), Hartman has decided to use the CAPM, employing past return data for the two firms as well as the market. The
risk-free rate is expected to be 9 percent. What are the explicit
costs of internally generated funds and new common stock for
both firms?

| Year | Return | | |
	Whiz Discount Stores, Inc.	Apex Forecasting Company	Market (k_M)
1984	12%	28%	18%
1983	8	8	7
1982	17	18	16
1981	16	25	19
1980	12	6	10
Net proceeds (as a percent of current market price) due to underpricing and flotation costs	93%	90%	

17.7. *BOOK VALUE VERSUS MARKET VALUE WEIGHTS.* Grimms Publishing Company has the following book value balance sheet:

Current Assets	$300,000	Current liabilities and accruals	$150,000
Fixed assets (net)	650,000	Long-term debt	400,000
		Common stock (30,000 shares at $2 par)	60,000
		Retained earnings	340,000
Total assets	$950,000	Total liabilities and net worth	$950,000

The firm's marginal tax rate is 40 percent and the current
long-term debt carries a coupon interest rate of 6 percent. (The
current debt is a perpetuity; it has no maturity date.) New debt

can be issued with a before-tax cost to the firm of 12 percent. New internally generated funds are estimated to cost 14 percent, and the cost of new common stock is 16 percent. Based on market value considerations, the firm estimates it can finance half of its common equity needs with internally generated funds; the other half will have to be raised by issuing new common stock. The current and anticipated price of the common stock is $60 per share.

a. Book value weights?

b. Market value weights?

17.8. *MARGINAL COST OF CAPITAL: NO BREAKING POINT.* Jefferson Cement Company requires $15 million to fund the current year's projects. Jefferson will finance part of the projects with $9 million in internally generated funds. The firm's common stock is currently priced at $120 per share. Dividends of $5 per share at t_0 are expected to grow at a rate of 11 percent per year. Another part will be funded with the proceeds (at $96 per share) from an issue of 9375 shares of 10 percent, $100 par value preferred stock that will be privately placed. The remainder will be financed with debt. Five thousand (5000) 10-year, $1000 par value bonds with a coupon rate of 15 percent will be issued to net the firm $1050 each, less 3 percent of the par value for underwriting fees. Since the firm operates within its relevant financing range, costs of the required funds will remain constant.

a. Determine the explicit costs of: (1) debt, (2) preferred stock, and (3) internally generated funds.

b. What is Jefferson's target capital structure (based on the financing mix used)?

c. Calculate the firm's weighted marginal cost of capital.

17.9. *MARGINAL COST OF CAPITAL SCHEDULE: ONE BREAKING POINT.* Investor's Utilities, Inc., has a target capital structure that consists of 50 percent long-term debt, 10 percent preferred stock, and 40 percent common equity (internally generated funds or new common stock). The firm's marginal tax rate is 40 percent, and it expects to raise $30 million in new capital this year. New funds can be acquired as follows: *Debt:* Any amount of 20-year, $1000 par value bonds having a 12 percent coupon rate can be sold to net the firm $980 per bond. *Preferred Stock:* 10 percent preferred stock, $100 par value, can be sold in any amount, with proceeds to the firm being $95 per share. *Common Equity:* The current market price of the common stock is $50 per share, the past dividend yield, D_0/P_0, is 6 percent, and the expected rate of growth in dividends is 7 percent per year. New common stock can be sold to net the firm $42 per share. Internally generated funds available are expected to total $10 million.

a.   Calculate the explicit cost for each source of financing.
b.   What is the breaking point in new total financing associated with the exhaustion of internally generated funds?
c.   Determine the weighted MCC for each of the two MCC schedule segments.

17.10   *MARGINAL COST OF CAPITAL SCHEDULE.*   Basic Metals, Inc., projects a target capital structure consisting of 40 percent long-term debt and 60 percent common equity (internally generated funds and/or new common stock). The first $10 million in new bonds will have a coupon rate of 11 percent, and any additional bonds will carry a 13 percent coupon rate. In either case, the new proceeds to Basic Metals is equal to the par value of the bonds.

The common stock is currently selling for $60 per share, and the dividend payment during 1985, D_1, is expected to be $3 per share. Its dividend payments, which have approximated 60 percent of earnings for the past 5 years, have been:

1984	$2.83
1983	2.65
1982	2.50
1981	2.35
1980	2.24

Earnings during 1985 are expected to be $15 million; $18 million in new common stock can be sold to net the firm proceeds of $55 per share; any additional common stock will net the firm $45 per share. The firm's marginal tax rate is 40 percent.

a.   What are the explicit costs of debt and common equity for Basic Metals?
b.   At what dollar amounts of total new capital will breaks in the MCC schedule occur? (There are three breaks—one where internally generated funds are used up, a second when the cost of debt rises, and the third when the per share net proceeds from the sale of common stock decrease.)
c.   Calculate the four weighted MCC figures.
d.   Assume Basic Metals has the following investment opportunities: (1) It can invest up to $12 million at a 13 percent rate of return. (2) Another $10 million can be invested at an 11.4 percent return. (3) $14 million more can be invested at 10.2 percent, after which future investments will return the firm

9.5 percent. Determine Basic Metals optimal capital budget and the appropriate MCC.

17.11. *MCC AND IOS: REVIEW OF CAPITAL BUDGETING CALCULATIONS.* Diversified Food Processors, Inc., has compiled the following data on its three sources of financing:

Source of Capital	Range of New Financing ($ Millions)	Explicit Cost
Long-term debt	$0–$10	7%
	$10 and above	8.5
Preferred stock	$0–$8	9%
	$8 and above	10
Common equity	$0–$6	13%
	$6–$20	15
	$20 and above	17

Diversified employs a target capital structure consisting of 40 percent long-term debt, 20 percent preferred stock, and 40 percent common equity. The firm has asked you to develop its MCC and IOS schedules. The following prospective investments are available (assume they are independent):

Capital expenditure proposal	Description
I	Develop new plastic products capability. Cost, $15 million; expected life, 8 years; expected CFAT, $3,342,751 per year.
II	Replace its existing data processing equipment. Cost, $8 million; expected life, 5 years; expected CFAT, $2,110,261 per year.
III	Install pollution control equipment. Cost, $10 million; expected life, 4 years; expected CFAT, $3,019,324 per year.
IV	Expand and update its fleet of transport trucks. Cost, $13 million; expected life, 6 years; expected CFAT, $3,038,619 per year plus $1,000,000 additional in the sixth year.

V   Build a new plant to manufacture agri-
cultural fertilizer. Cost, $8 million; ex-
pected life, 10 years; expected CFAT,
$1,533,708 per year.

VI   Invest in a joint venture pilot plant to
test the feasibility of a new coal gasifica-
tion process. Cost, $6 million; expected
life, 3 years; expected CFAT, nothing
until the end of the third year, at which
time it is $7,352,941.

a. Calculate the breaking points in the MCC schedule. (There
are four breaking points—one where the cost of debt
increases, another where the cost of preferred stock increases, and two when the cost of common equity increases).

b. Calculate the weighted marginal cost of capital for each
segment of the MCC schedule.

c. Graph the MCC schedule.

d. Calculate the IRRs for the six capital expenditure proposals.

e. Which capital expenditures should Diversified implement?
What is the appropriate MCC for the firm?

17.12. *DIVISIONAL COST OF CAPITAL.* Furniture Imports, Inc., is interested in determining a marginal cost of capital for each of its
two divisions, Home Furnishings and Apartment Rentals. The
firm's financial manager has identified two publicly traded firms
that are very similar to the divisions in terms of product line
and capital structure. The two firms, along with the relevant
data, are as follows:

Firm	Beta	Corresponding Division
Grandview Furnishings Company	.90	Home Furnishings
Securance Rentals, Inc.	1.40	Apartment Rentals

The estimated return on the market, k_M, is 14 percent, and the
Treasury Bill rate (an estimate of R_F) is 8 percent. Home
Furnishings' capital structure is 35 percent debt and 65 percent
equity. Apartment Rentals, which is slightly more risky, has a
capital structure of 40 percent debt and 60 percent equity.
Furniture Imports' before-tax cost of debt, k_b, is 10 percent, and
the marginal tax rate is 40 percent. Use the CAPM approach to

determine the cost of equity capital for each division. What is the marginal cost of capital for each division?

17.13. *DIVISIONAL COST OF CAPITAL: EXPANSION.* National Stores, Inc., is interested in building separate warehouses for its two divisions at a cost of $700,000 each. Estimated cash flows after tax for each warehouse are $110,000 per year for 20 years. National has determined that Stylehouse, Inc., traded on the New York Stock Exchange, is very similar to its sportswear division. Recreational Products, also traded on the New York exchange, is similar to its sporting goods division. Stylehouse has a beta of 1.8 and a capital structure containing 50 percent debt and 50 percent equity. Recreational Products is a less risky firm and thus has a lower beta of .75; its capital structure is 30 percent debt and 70 percent equity. National has decided that the appropriate amount of debt for each of its divisions is equal to the debt of the similar publicly traded firm. Also, National's before-tax cost of debt, k_b, is 18 percent and the marginal tax rate is 40 percent. If the return on the market k_M is 18 percent, and the risk-free rate, R_F is 6 percent:

a. Find the weighted marginal cost of capital for each division and round to the nearest whole percent.

b. Should the sportswear division build the warehouse?

c. Should the sporting goods division build the warehouse?

d. Why is the project accepted by one division and not by the other?

SELECTED REFERENCES

Agmon, Tamir, and Donald R. Lessard, "Investor Recognition of Corporate International Diversification." *Journal of Finance* 32 (September 1977), pp. 1049–1055.

Alberts, W. W., and S. H. Archer. "Some Evidence of the Effect of Company Size on the Cost of Equity Capital." *Journal of Financial and Quantitative Analysis* 8 (March 1973), pp. 229–245.

Arditti, Fred D., and Haim Levy. "The Weighted Average Cost of Capital As a Cutoff Rate: A Critical Analysis of the Classical Textbook Weighted Average." *Financial Managment* 6 (fall 1977), pp. 24–34.

———, and Milford S. Tysseland. "Three Ways to Present the Marginal Cost of Capital." *Financial Management* 2, (summer 1973), pp. 63–67.

Ben-Horim, Moshe. "Comment on 'The Weighted Average Cost of Capital As a Cutoff Rate'." *Financial Management* 8 (summer 1979), pp. 18–21.

Beranek, William. "The Weighted Average Cost of Capital and Shareholder Wealth Maximization." *Journal of Financial and Quantitative Analysis* 12 (March 1977), pp. 17–31.

Bierman, Harold Jr., and Jerome E. Hass. "Investment Cut-off Rates and Dividend Policy." *Financial Management* 12 (December 1983), pp. 19–24.

Boquist, John A., and William T. Moore. "Estimating the Systematic Risk of an Industry Segment: A Mathematical Programming Approach." *Financial Management* 12 (December 1983), pp. 11–19.

Boudreaux, Kenneth J., and Hugh W. Long. "The Weighted Average Cost of Capital

As a Cutoff Rate: A Further Analysis." *Financial Management* 8 (summer 1979), pp. 7–14.

Bower, Richard S., and Jeffrey M. Jenks. "Divisional Screening Rates." *Financial Management* 4 (autumn 1975), pp. 42–49.

Chen, Andrew. "Recent Developments in the Cost of Debt Capital." *Journal of Finance* 33 (June 1978), pp. 863–883.

Cordes, Joseph J., and Steven M. Sheffrin. "Estimating the Tax Advantage of Corporate Debt." *Journal of Finance* 38 (March 1983), pp. 95–105.

Eiteman, David K., and Arthur I. Stonehill. *Multinational Business Finance*, 3d ed. Reading, Mass.: Addison Wesley, 1982.

Elliott, J. Walter. "The Cost of Capital and U.S. Capital Investment: A Test of Alternative Concepts." *Journal of Finance* 35 (September 1980), pp. 981–999.

Ezzell, John R., and R. Burr Porter. "Correct Specification of the Cost of Capital and Net Present Value." *Financial Management* 8 (summer 1979), pp. 15–17.

———, and ———. "Flotation Costs and the Weighted Average Cost of Capital." *Journal of Financial and Quantitative Analysis* 11 (September 1976), pp. 403–414.

Fuller, Russell J., and Halbert S. Kerr. "Estimating the Divisional Cost of Capital: An Analysis of the Pure-Play Technique." *Journal of Finance* 36 (December 1981), pp. 997–1009.

Gitman, Lawrence J., and Vincent A. Mercurio. "Cost of Capital Techniques Used by Major U.S. Firms: Survey and Analysis of Fortune's 1000." *Financial Management* 11 (winter 1982), pp. 21–29.

Gordon, Myron J., and Lawrence I. Gould. "The Cost of Equity Capital: A Reconsideration." *Journal of Finance* 33 (June 1978), pp. 849–861.

Gup, Benton E., and Samuel W. Norwood III. "Divisional Cost of Capital: A Practical Approach," *Financial Management* 11 (spring 1982), pp. 20–24.

Haley, Charles W., and Lawrence D. Schall. "Problems with the Concept of the Cost of Capital." *Journal of Financial and Quantitative Analysis* 13 (December 1978), pp. 847–870.

Hamada, Robert S. "The Effect of the Firm's Capital Structure on the Systematic Risk of Common Stocks." *Journal of Finance* 27 (May 1972), pp. 435–452.

Hughes, John S., Dennis E. Logue, and Richard J. Sweeney. "Corporate International Diversification and Market Assigned Measures of Risk and Diversification," *Journal of Financial and Quantitative Analysis* 10 (November 1975), pp. 627–637.

Ibbotson, Roger G., and Rex O. Sinquefield. *Stocks, Bonds, Bills, and Inflation: The Past and the Future.* (1983 ed.) Charlottesville, Va.: Financial Analysts Research Foundation, 1983.

Jarrett, Jeffrey E. "Estimating the Cost of Capital for a Division of a Firm, and the Allocation Problem in Accounting." *Journal of Business Finance and Accounting* 5 (spring 1978), pp. 39–48.

Lessard, Donald R. "World, Country, and Industry Relationships in Equity Returns; Implications for Risk Reduction Through International Diversification." *Financial Analysts Journal* 32 (January–February 1976), pp. 32–38.

Lewellen, Wilbur G. *The Cost of Capital.* Dubuque, Iowa: Kendall/Hunt, 1976.

Litzenberger, Robert H., and O. Maurice Joy. "Decentralized Capital Budgeting Decisions and Shareholder Wealth Maximization." *Journal of Finance* 30 (September 1975), pp. 993–1002.

———, Krishna Ramaswamy, and Howard Sosin. "On the CAPM Approach to the Estimation of a Public Utility's Cost of Equity Capital." *Journal of Finance* 35 (May 1980), pp. 369–383.

Miles, James A., and John R. Ezzell. "The Weighted Average Cost of Capital, Perfect Capital Markets, and Project Life: A Clarification." *Journal of Financial and Quantitative Analysis* 15 (September 1980), pp. 719–730.

Modigliani, Franco, and Merton H. Miller. "Corporate Income Taxes and the Cost of Capital: A Correction." *American Economic Review* 53 (June 1963), pp. 433–443.

Nantell, Timothy J., and C. Robert Carlson. "The Cost of Capital As a Weighted Average." *Journal of Finance* 30 (December 1975), pp. 1343–1355.

——, and ——. "The Cost of Retained Earnings." In *Issues in Managerial Finance*, eds. Eugene F. Brigham and Ramon E. Johnson. Hinsdale, Ill.: Dryden Press, 1976.

Petry, Glenn H. "Empirical Evidence of the Cost of Capital Weights." *Financial Management* 4 (winter 1975), pp. 58–65.

Shapiro, Alan C. "Financial Structure and Cost of Capital in the Multinational Corporation." *Journal of Financial and Quantitative Analysis* 13 (June 1978), pp. 211–226.

Shiller, Robert J., and Franco Modigliani. "Coupon and Tax Effects on New and Seasoned Bond Yields and the Measurement of the Cost of Debt Capital." *Journal of Financial Economics* 7 (September 1979), pp. 297–318.

Solnite, Bruno H. "Testing International Asset Pricing: Some Pessimistic Views." *Journal of Finance* 32 (May 1977), pp. 503–512.

Stanley, Marjorie T. "Capital Structure and Cost of Capital for the Multinational Firm." *Journal of International Business Studies* 12 (spring–summer 1981), pp. 103–120.

Thompson, Howard. "Estimating the Cost of Equity Capital for Electric Utilities: 1958–1976." *Bell Journal of Economics* 10 (autumn 1979), pp. 619–635.

Van Horne, James C. "An Application of the CAPM to Divisional Required Returns." *Financial Management* 9 (spring 1980), pp. 14–19.

Appendix 17A

Cost of Term Loans, Convertibles, and Leases

Firms employ many other sources of long-term financing in addition to debt, preferred stock, and common equity. Among these other sources are term loans, convertible securities, and leases. Legal and other features of each of these sources of financing will be discussed in later chapters; only their explicit costs are considered here. These costs, along with their respective market value weights, are used in determining the firm's marginal cost of capital employing Equation 17.12.

Term Loans   *Term loans* are intermediate-term (1- to 10-year) borrowing arrangements usually negotiated directly between the borrowing firm and a financial institution, such as a bank, insurance company, or pension fund. Term loans are generally amortized so that equal dollar payments are made over the life of the loan, but with varying amounts of each payment going toward principal and interest. The after-tax cost of term loans is determined by solving for k_b so that:

$$M(1 - f) = \sum_{t=1}^{n} \frac{B_t + I_t(1 - T)}{(1 + k_i)^t} \tag{17A.1}$$

where $M(1 - f)$ = net proceeds received from the loan

$\quad\quad M$ = the maturity value of the loan

$\quad\quad f$ = percentage flotation (or placement) costs

$\quad\quad n$ = maturity of the loan, in years

$\quad\quad B_t$ = principal repayment in the tth year

$\quad\quad I_t$ = interest payment in the tth year

$$T = \text{firm's marginal tax rate}$$
$$k_i = \text{after-tax cost of the loan}$$

Consider the after-tax cost for a firm in the 40 percent tax bracket that enters into a $100,000 term loan at 11 percent with placement costs of 1.5 percent of the amount borrowed. In Table 17A.1 the schedule of after-tax principal and interest payments for the firm (the numerator in Equation 17A.1) are presented, assuming a single payment is made annually over the 5-year life of the loan. The net proceeds to the firm equal $98,500 ($100,000 − (.015 × $100,000) = $100,000 − $1,500). The after-tax cost of the term loan is determined by substituting the net proceeds and the after-tax cash flows (from Table 17A.1) into Equation 17A.1 and solving for k_b, such that:

$$\$98,500 = \frac{\$22,657.03}{(1 + k_i)^1} + \frac{\$23,363.54}{(1 + k_i)^2} + \frac{\$24,147.77}{(1 + k_i)^3} + \frac{\$25,018.25}{(1 + k_i)^4} + \frac{\$25,984.50}{(1 + k_i)^5}$$

By interpolation, the after-tax cost of the term loan is seen to be equal to 7.15 percent.[1]

Convertible Securities

Convertible securities are bonds or preferred stock issued by the firm that may be converted into shares of common stock of the issuing firm.[2]

---

[1]The calculations are as follows:

At 7 percent:

$$M (1 - f) = \$22,657.03 \, (PVIF_{7\%, 1 \, yr}) + \$23,363.54 \, (PVIF_{7\%, 2 \, yr}) + \$24,147.77$$
$$(PVIF_{7\%, 3 \, yr}) + \$25,018.25 \, (PVIF_{7\%, 4 \, yr}) + \$25,984.50 \, (PVIF_{7\%, 5 \, yr})$$
$$= \$22,657.03 \, (.935) + \$23,363.54 \, (.873) + \$24,147.77 \, (.816)$$
$$+ \$25,018.25 \, (.763) + \$25,984.50 \, (.713)$$
$$= \$21,184.32 + \$20,396.37 + \$19,704.58 + \$19,088.92 + \$18,526.95$$
$$= \$98,901.14$$

At 8 percent:

$$M(1 - f) = \$22,657.03 \, (.926) + \$23,363.54 \, (.857) + \$24,147.77 \, (.794) + \$25,018.25$$
$$(.735) + \$25,984.50 \, (.681)$$
$$= \$20,980.41 + \$20,022.55 + \$19,173.33 + \$18,388.41 + \$17,695.44$$
$$= \$96,260.14$$

Since the actual proceeds, $M (1 - f)$, are $98,500, we must interpolate to find the specific before-tax cost of the term loan:

$$k_i = 7\% + \frac{\$98,901.14 - \$98,500}{\$98,901.14 - \$96,260.14} = 7\% + \frac{\$401.14}{\$2,641.00} = 7.15\%$$

[2]The valuation of convertible securities and other contingent claims is a complex process that may also be approached with the option pricing model (see Appendix 23A).

TABLE 17A.1
Term Loan
Amortization Schedule
and After-Tax Cash
Flow to the Firm[a]

Year	Payment	Repayment of Principal	Interest	After-Tax Cash Flow Per Year to Firm[b]
1	$ 27,057.03	$ 16,057.03	$11,000.00	$ 22,657.03
2	27,057.03	17,823.30	9,233.73	23,363.54
3	27,057.03	19,783.87	7,273.16	24,147.77
4	27,057.03	21,960.09	5,096.94	25,018.25
5	27,057.03	24,375.71	2,681.32	25,984.50
	$135,285.15	$100,000.00	$35,285.15	$121,171.09

[a]The calculations necessary to derive the yearly payment, repayment of principal, and interest are presented in Chapter 21.

[b]This equals $B_t + (1 - T) I_t$. For year 1, $22,657.03 = $16,057.03 + (1 - .40) ($11,000) = $16,057.03 + $6,600, and so on.

Because of the dual nature of convertibles, which combine both the fixed-return aspect of bonds or preferreds and the possibility of common equity returns, a firm can usually sell convertible securities at a lower coupon rate than nonconvertible bonds or preferred stocks of comparable quality. The techniques for determining the cost of convertible preferred stock is exactly the same as for convertible debentures, except that no tax adjustment is required on preferreds. Because calculating the cost of convertible debentures is more complex and also because they are more widely used in practice, we illustrate its calculation below.

The after-tax cost of convertible debentures, k_c, if the firm expects the convertibles to be converted is:

$$M (1 - f) = \sum_{t=1}^{n} \frac{I_t (1 - T)}{(1 + k_c)^t} + \frac{P_0 (1 + g)^n \times R}{(1 + k_c)^n} \qquad (17A.2)$$

However, if the firm does *not* expect the debentures to be converted, the after-tax cost, k_i, is:

$$M (1 - f) = \sum_{t=1}^{n} \frac{I_t (1 - T)}{(1 + k_i)^t} + \frac{M}{(1 + k_i)^n} \qquad (17A.3)$$

where $M (1 - f)$ = net proceeds received from the convertible debenture
M = the par or maturity value, typically $1000
f = percentage flotation costs
n = number of years to expected conversion (Equation 17A.2) or the number of years to maturity (Equation 17A.3)[3]

---

[3]If the firm intends to call the debentures in a specific number of years, to force conversion or to retire them if the market price of the common stock has not risen sufficiently for conversion, n becomes the number of years until call.

I_t = interest payment in the tth year

T = firm's marginal tax rate

P_0 = initial market price of the firm's common stock

g = constant expected growth rate in dividends and common stock market price

R = conversion ratio, or number of shares of common stock received upon conversion

k_c = after-tax cost of convertible debentures if converted

k_i = after-tax cost of convertible debentures if not converted

Typically, when firms issue convertible securities they expect that part or all of them will be converted; hence, Equation 17A.2 is appropriate. However, if the firm does not anticipate that the market price of its common stock will increase sufficiently to make conversion attractive, the cost of convertibles is calculated in exactly the same fashion as for nonconvertibles bonds illustrated in the chapter.

Suppose a firm is planning to issue 20-year convertible debentures with a $1000 par value and flotation costs of 4 percent of par per bond. The coupon rate is 12 percent, the firm is in the 40 percent marginal tax bracket, and it plans to force conversion into common stock in 10 years. The present price of the firm's common stock, P_0, is $70 per share, the expected growth rate in dividends and market price is 9 percent per year, and the debenture can be converted into 10 shares of the firm's common stock. Employing Equation 17A.2, the after-tax cost of the convertible is found to equal 11.71 percent.[4] Alternatively, if the firm does not expect the market price of its common stock to increase sufficiently for conversion over the 20-year life bond (because of low growth or zero growth in dividends and the market price of the common stock), the

---

[4]At 11 percent:

$$M (1 - f) = \$72 \, (PVIFA_{11\%, \, 10 \, yr}) + \$70 \, (FVIF_{9\%, \, 10 \, yr}) \, 10 \, (PVIF_{11\%, \, 10 \, yr})$$
$$= \$72 \, (5.889) + \$70 \, (2.367) \, 10 \, (.352)$$
$$= \$424.01 + \$583.23 = \$1007.24$$

At 12 percent:

$$M (1 - f) = \$72 \, (5.650) + \$70 \, (2.367) \, 10 \, (.322)$$
$$= \$406.80 + \$533.52 = \$940.32$$

Since the proceeds, $M (1 - f)$ are $960, interpolation is employed to find the after-tax cost:

$$k_c = 11\% + \frac{\$1007.24 - \$960.00}{\$1007.24 - \$940.32} = 11\% + \frac{\$47.24}{\$66.92} = 11.71\%$$

after-tax cost, k_i, is found (using Equation 17A.3) to equal 7.61 percent.[5]

Leasing

Leasing of assets has become widespread. If firms employ leasing as a significant form of long-term financing, the after-tax cost of leasing to the firm must be determined. In order to calculate this cost, we consider the initial cost of the asset, the lease payments net of any tax consequences, and the depreciation tax shield that would have been available if the asset had been purchased.[6] The cost of the lease includes not only the lease payments themselves, but the depreciation tax deduction forgone by leasing instead of purchasing the asset. This latter item is an opportunity cost that is forgone when the asset is leased. The after-tax cost of leasing, k_l, is found by:

$$CLA_0 - LP_0 (1 - T) = \sum_{t=1}^{n-1} \frac{LP_t (1 - T)}{(1 + k_l)^t} + \sum_{t=1}^{n} \frac{Dep_t (T)}{(1 + k_l)^t} \qquad (17A.4)$$

where CLA_0 = cost of the leased asset
  LP_0 = lease payment at time $t = 0$
  T = firm's marginal tax rate
  n = term of the lease in years
  LP_t = lease payment at beginning of the tth period
  Dep_t = depreciation in tth period if the asset was owned
  k_l = after-tax cost of leasing

Suppose a firm decided to lease an asset that costs $100,000 and the investment tax credit (ITC) is not available. The lease payments are $32,000 per year for 5 years, payable in advance; the corporate tax rate is 40 percent; and annual straight-line depreciation (if the asset were

---

[5]At 7 percent:

$$M (1 - f) = \$72 \ (PVIFA_{7\%, \ 20 \ yr}) + \$1000 \ (PVIF_{7\%, \ 20 \ yr})$$
$$= \$72 \ (10.594) + \$1000 \ (.258)$$
$$= \$762.77 + \$258 = \$1020.77$$

At 8 percent:

$$M (1 - f) = \$72 \ (9.818) + \$1000 \ (.215)$$
$$= \$706.90 + \$215 = \$921.90$$

By interpolation, the after-tax cost is:

$$k_i = 7\% + \frac{\$1020.77 - \$960.00}{\$1020.77 - \$921.90} = 7\% + \frac{\$60.77}{\$98.87} = 7.61\%$$

[6]For simplicity we ignore such items as the investment tax credit (if retained by the lessee) or accelerated depreciation. These items, which are considered in Chapter 22, can be incorporated into the analysis without major adjustment to the approach employed.

owned) would be $20,000. The after-tax cost of leasing the asset, taking into account both the lease payments and the forgone depreciation tax shield, is 15.48 percent.[7]

17A.1. *EXPLICIT COST OF TERM LOANS.* What is the after-tax cost of a 4-year 9 percent term loan in the amount of $20,000, where there are issue-related expenses of $1,000? The tax rate is 40 percent.

17A.2. *COST OF CONVERTIBLE DEBENTURES.* Mayflower Instruments is planning to issue some 12 percent coupon rate, $1,000 par, convertible debentures at a price to net the firm $960 per debenture. It plans to retire the bonds in 5 years by forcing conversion, or by calling them.

a.   If the conversion ratio is 20, the current market price of the firm's common stock is $40, and dividends are expected to grow at 15 percent per year, what is the cost to Mayflower if conversion is forced (in 5 years)?

b.   Alternatively, the common stock price may not rise, and in fact may decline. If there is no call premium, what is the after-tax cost to Mayflower of calling in 5 years if their marginal corporate tax rate is 40 percent?

17A.3. *COST OF CONVERTIBLE PREFERRED STOCK.* Sunflower Inc. will issue $60 par, 10 percent dividend, convertible preferred stock to net the firm $51. Each share of stock is convertible into two shares of common stock. The current market price of the firm's common stock is $25, the growth rate in cash dividends is conservatively estimated at 6 percent per year, and the firm's marginal corporate tax rate is 40 percent. If the firm forces

---

[7]$100,000 $-$ $32,000 (1 $-$ .40) = $32,000 (1 $-$ .40) $(PVIFA_{?\%,4\ yr})$ + $20,000 (.40)

$$(PVIFA_{?\%,\ 5\ yr})$$

$100,000 $-$ $80,000 = $19,200 $(PVIFA_{?\%,\ 4\ yr})$ + $8,000 $(PVIFA_{?\%,\ 5\ yr})$

At 15%   = $19,200 (2.855) + $8,000 (3.352)
           = $54,816 + $26,816 = $81,632

At 16%   = $19,200 (2.798) + $8,000 (3.274)
           = $53,721.60 + $26,192 = $79,913.60

By interpolation

$$k_l = 15\% + \frac{\$81,632 - \$80,800}{\$81,632 - \$79,913.60} = 15\% + \frac{\$832}{\$1,718.40} = 15.48\%$$

conversion, it will be in 9 years. What is the after-tax cost to Sunflower if events occur as projected and conversion is forced in 9 years?

17A.4. *EXPLICIT COST OF LEASING.* A $700,000 price of equipment is needed by Waynes Auto Parts. The asset's normal recovery period (for depreciation) is 5 years, and straight-line depreciation will be used if the asset is leased. The ITC is not applicable. The lease payments are $200,000 per year for 5 years payable in advance, and the firm's marginal corporate tax rate is 40 percent. What is the after-tax cost of the machinery if it is leased?

18

Target Capital Structure

Firms in some industries tend to use substantial amounts of fixed-cost, long-term financing, while those in other industries use very little. For example, public utility firms typically issue large amounts of debt and preferred stock to finance the construction of power plants. This financing often amounts to 50 percent or more of the utilities' capital structure. However, other firms, such as those in the rapidly growing microcomputer industry, rely heavily on internally generated funds and new common stock financing. How can we account for these large differences? How do firms arrive at their appropriate, or target, capital structure? To answer these questions, we examine the impact that the use of debt financing, as opposed to equity financing, has on the marginal cost of capital and total value of the firm. We begin by examining the theoretical aspects of capital structure decisions and then discuss the notion of a target capital structure. The next section presents practical guidelines that can be used in developing the firm's target capital structure and monitoring it over time. The final section describes the multinational dimensions of capital structure.

Theory of the Optimum Capital Structure

To examine the impact of financial leverage on the total market value of the firm, V, and its marginal cost of capital, MCC or k, we will hold the firm's business risk and total size constant. Thus, our primary concern is with financial risk (or financial leverage) and its impact on the firm. Unless business risk is held constant, it is impossible to isolate the impact of financial risk. Likewise, the total size of the firm is held constant so we can focus on the impact that changes in long-term debt financing—that is, the percentage of the funds provided by debt as

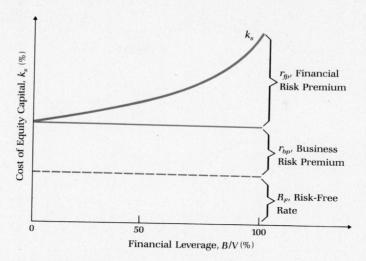

Figure 18.1 Relationship Between Cost of Equity Capital, Business Risk, Financial Risk, and Financial Leverage.

opposed to common equity—has on the firm. Our concern is with how the total value of the firm, V, and its cost of capital, MCC, change as the firm's *financial leverage*, measured by the ratio of the market value of debt to the firm's total market value, changes.

The Traditional Approach

The traditional approach asserts that there is an optimal capital structure and that the firm can increase its total value through the judicious use of long-term debt.[1] Let us focus initially on the cost of equity capital, k_s. In Chapter 6, k_s was defined as being equal to the risk-free rate plus a risk premium, so $k_s = R_F + r$. This risk premium, as shown in Chapter 17, can also be depicted as:

$$k_s = R_F + r_{bp} + r_{fp} \qquad (18.1)$$

where r_{bp} is the business risk premium and r_{fp} is the premium for financial risk.

Figure 18.1 illustrates the underlying position of the traditional approach and shows how the cost of equity capital is related to financial risk, as measured by the degree of financial leverage. Note that the amount of business risk is constant, since all we are doing is changing the financial risk by shifting the percentage of funds being supplied by

---

[1]Ezra Solomon, *The Theory of Financial Management* (New York: Columbia University Press, 1963), chap. 8.

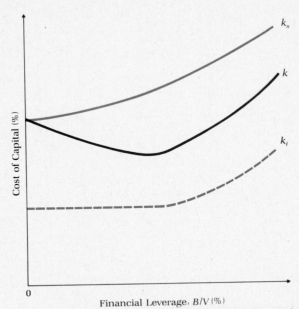

Figure 18.2   The Traditional Approach to the Optimal Capital Structure.

debt versus equity as we move across the graph. As more financial leverage is employed by substituting debt for equity, equity investors view the firm as having more financial risk; hence, they demand a higher return in compensation for the increased risk. This action increases the firm's cost of equity capital, which eventually becomes so expensive that, for all practical purposes, it is no longer a viable financing alternative.

Given the existence of corporate taxes, we already know that the after-tax cost of debt, k_i, is cheaper than the cost of equity. Thus, as firms begin to add debt to their capital structure, the marginal cost of capital declines because the use of a larger proportion of "cheap" debt funds more than offsets the higher cost of equity funds (see Figure 18.2). As the firm continues to add more debt to its capital structure, the after-tax cost of debt eventually begins to increase. The cost of equity capital, k_s, also continues to increase as investors view the firm as becoming more risky. Note that the marginal cost of capital function, k, simply represents a series of weighted marginal costs of capital for different degrees of financial leverage. Each of these weighted marginal costs of capital along line k are computed in exactly the same manner as described in Chapter 17. Increases in the costs of both debt and equity eventually cause the firm's marginal cost of capital to increase. The traditional position on financial leverage is that the firm's cost of capital is a U-shaped function of financial leverage, although the exact shape of the curve is subject to considerable debate.[2] Traditionalists argue that the cost of capital is *not* independent of the firm's capital structure; instead, the judicious use of debt reduces the cost of capital and hence maximizes the value of the firm.

The optimal capital structure for a specific firm will vary, depending upon the amount of business risk involved in its operations and the attitude of the capital market toward this uncertainty. This attitude, in turn, is a composite of the expectations of lenders and investors about the firm's product markets and prices, the degree to which costs are fixed or variable, the liquidity and marketability of the firm's assets, and lenders' and investors' general assessment of the quality of the firm's management. Insofar as these elements are related to the firm's line of business, and the view lenders and investors have toward firms in that industry, a firm's capital structure is likely to resemble that of other firms in the same industry. Interindustry differences, however, may be significant. Because of this, firms in different industry groups may have significantly different capital structures.

The Modigliani-Miller Approach

The traditional approach to the influence of capital structure on the firm's cost of capital and value is in sharp contrast to the original *Modigliani-Miller (MM) position*.[3] In the absence of corporate taxes and in a world of perfect markets and rational investors, MM argued that two identical companies—two sets of assets offering *earnings before interest and taxes (EBIT)* of the same size and quality—must have the same market value regardless of differences in capital structures. They argue that even though debt is cheaper than equity, the use of cheaper debt funds is *exactly* offset by the increased cost of equity capital (which arises from higher risk exposure), with the result that the firm's marginal cost of capital does not change with the addition of more debt. This condition is shown in Figure 18.3(a).

Once the presence of corporate taxes is acknowledged, MM's position[4] is that the cost of capital will decrease because of the tax shield provided by the deductibility of interest on the firm's debt. While the cost of equity capital continues to increase linearly with increased financial leverage, the firm's marginal cost of capital decreases with additional financial

---

[2]It is often suggested that instead of being U-shaped, the relationship between the cost of capital and the firm's capital structure is pan-shaped. Firms incur higher capital costs when they use either very small or very large amounts of debt. Within these extremes, however, k is viewed as being relatively independent of the firm's capital structure. If the pan-shaped concept is valid, any change in the firm's capital structure that leaves the firm on the bottom part of the pan will not affect its marginal cost of capital.

[3]Franco Modigliani and Merton H. Miller, "The Cost of Capital, Corporation Finance and the Theory of Investment," *American Economic Review* 48 (June 1958), pp. 261–297.

[4]Franco Modigliani and Merton H. Miller, "Corporate Income Taxes and the Cost of Capital: A Correction," *American Economic Review* 53 (June 1963), pp. 433–443.

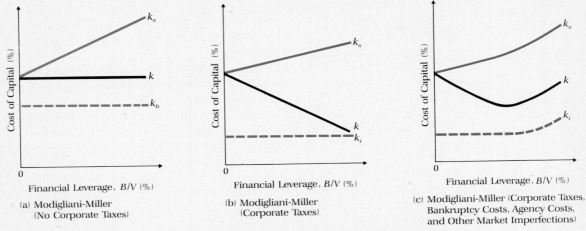

Figure 18.3   Modigliani-Miller Approach to the Optimal Capital Structure.

leverage. As Figure 18.3(b) shows, the extreme position is that the firm would be better off if it financed virtually its entire needs with debt. By doing so, the cost of capital is minimized and the value of the firm is maximized.

The Modigliani-Miller position has created substantial debate in both the academic and business communities since its introduction. However, some solid arguments have been presented in support of the existence of optimal, or target, capital structures for individual firms. As Appendix 18A shows in detail, three factors support the existence of an optimal capital structure, even if the basic MM ideas are accepted: bankruptcy costs, agency costs, and market imperfections. The result of incorporating these costs and imperfections into the MM position, as shown in Figure 18.3(c), suggests the existence of an optimal capital structure.

Debt Capacity   In an attempt to integrate theory and practice to explain why firms have target capital structures, one logical possibility is the idea of an "appropriate" debt capacity for the firm. Donaldson[5] defined *debt capacity* as the point where the probability of trouble becomes unacceptably high, but he provided no definition of the meaning of trouble. More recently, Myers[6] presented an analysis of why firms have corporate debt policies, based on the argument that since most firms are going concerns, their

---

[5]Gordon Donaldson, "New Framework for Corporate Debt Policy," *Harvard Business Review* 40 (March–April 1962), pp. 117–131.

[6]Stewart C. Myers, "Determinants of Corporate Borrowing," *Journal of Financial Economics* 5 (November 1977), pp. 147–175.

value reflects an expectation of continued future investment by the firm. However, this investment is discretionary since the amount invested depends on the net present values of opportunities that arise in the future. *Thus, part of the value of the firm is accounted for by the present value of options to make future investments.*

When firms have risky debt outstanding they may pass up profitable investments—opportunities that could make a positive net contribution to the market value of the firm. This may occur when the debt matures before an investment option is to be exercised, so that the firm does not take advantage of all wealth-maximizing investment opportunities. Issuing risky debt may reduce the present market value of the firm by inducing a suboptimal investment strategy in the future. Given the existence of corporate taxes, firms will trade off the tax advantage of debt financing against a suboptimal future investment strategy. This approach suggests firms may have rational limits to their debt capacity and that this limit is a function of the maturity of their debt relative to the point in time at which the investment options can be exercised.

In a somewhat different vein, Turnbull[7] argues that debt capacity exists because of limits on the credit that lenders are willing to supply. In equilibrium, and assuming there are costs associated with bankruptcy, lenders will require a specified minimum rate of return to compensate them for the risk of default and its associated costs. Although this rate of return can be increased up to a point, eventually lenders reach a position where it is rational to limit the amount of credit they extend to a firm. The existence of a maximum credit line provides a natural definition of debt capacity. Turnbull's analysis implies that a firm's ability to alter its capital structure may be restricted if the optimal capital structure calls for a greater amount of debt than lenders are willing to extend; in addition, the value of investment projects to the firm may also depend on how they affect its debt capacity.[8]

The Current View   The concept of debt capacity, in addition to the implications that arise once the impact of bankruptcy costs, agency costs, and other market imperfections are included in the MM position, all suggest, as does the traditional theory, that firms *can* reduce their cost of capital by the judicious use of debt. Thus, although considerable controversy and uncertainty still exist, most executives and academicians agree that the capital structure decision is important because it has a direct bearing on

---

[7]Stuart M. Turnbull, "Debt Capacity," *Journal of Finance* 34 (September 1979), pp. 931–940.

[8]Turnbull also observes that the firm's debt capacity limit always occurs at a higher debt to total value level than its optimal capital structure. This result, while not completely generalizable, suggests the very tentative and incomplete nature of our understanding of the relationship among a firm's capital structure, its minimum cost of capital, and the maximum value of the firm once corporate taxes, bankruptcy costs, agency costs, and other market imperfections are introduced.

TABLE 18.1
Financial Statements for Michigan Foods, Inc.

Balance Sheet		
Debt	$	0
Common stock (1,000,000		
shares at $2 per share)		2,000,000
Total assets $2,000,000 Total stockholders' equity		$ 2,000,000

Income Statement		
Sales		$18,000,000
Less: Fixed operating costs	$4,000,000	
Less: Variable operating costs		
(50% of sales)	9,000,000	13,000,000
Earnings before interest		$ 5,000,000
and taxes (EBIT)		
Less: Interest		—
Earnings before taxes (EBT)		$ 5,000,000
Less: Income taxes (40%)		2,000,000
Earnings after taxes (EAT)		$ 3,000,000

the firm's cost of capital, as well as on the total value of the firm. In light of this general agreement, we call the appropriate capital structure for the firm its *target capital structure.* This target is what the firm strives for over time, although at any given instant it may be above (too much debt) or below (too much equity) its target.

Target Capital Structure: Risk and Return

To investigate the target capital structure concept further, and to see how a firm's total market value and marginal cost of capital are affected by financial leverage, consider Michigan Foods, Inc., whose abbreviated balance sheet and income statement are presented in Table 18.1. At the present time the firm has a capital structure composed entirely of common stock. Michigan Foods pays all its earnings out in the form of cash dividends. As indicated in Table 18.1, the book value of Michigan Foods' assets and stockholders' equity is $2 million; but, as we know, book value is not indicative of a firm's market value, and it is market value that the financial manager attempts to maximize.

The Impact of Financial Leverage on Total Value and Cost of Capital

To determine the impact of financial leverage on the firm's total value, we will change Michigan Foods' capital structure while holding other factors constant. For simplicity, we assume the firm is not expected to grow; hence, earnings before interest and taxes (EBIT) remain at $5 million per year.[9] After discussion with its investment bankers, Michigan

---

[9]For simplicity, we assume the firm has no accruals, capitalized leases, paid-in capital, retained earnings, and so on. Capital structure concepts can be illustrated, but with more difficulty, if such items are included. Also for simplicity, costs are classified as either fixed or variable, and the firm's marginal tax rate is 40 percent.

learns that the first $6 million in debt issued will have a before-tax cost, k_b, of 12 percent. As more debt is issued, the firm is viewed by investors as becoming more risky—so the before-tax cost of all its debt increases. Estimates of the cost of debt are given in Table 18.2. Further discussion with the investment bankers indicates that as the firm continues to substitute debt for equity, it becomes more risky in the stockholders' eyes. The reason for the increased risk is that Michigan Foods is placing a fixed-payment obligation (to its bondholders) between EBIT and the after-tax earnings which accrue to the stockholders. This increased risk results in an increase in nondiversifiable (or beta) risk, which as Table 18.2 shows, results in a higher required return, or cost of equity capital, to the firm.

In our example, let us assume the firm adjusts its capital structure by issuing debt and using the proceeds to buy back common stock. Since EBIT does not change, we can assess how the capital structure decision influences the overall value of a firm, V, and its cost of capital, k. The total market value of the firm is equal to the value of debt, B, plus the value of the stock, S, so:

$$V = B + S \tag{18.2}$$

For simplicity, the market value of the debt is assumed to be equal to its par value. The market value of the stock is found by dividing earnings after taxes by the equity capitalization rate:[10]

$$S = \frac{(EBIT - I)(1 - T)}{k_s} \tag{18.3}$$

where $EBIT$ = expected earnings before interest and taxes

---

[10]The market value, P_0, of a nongrowth stock is:

$$P_0 = \frac{D_0}{k_s}$$

where D_0 are the dividends per share to be received at time $t = 0$, and k_s is the required rate of return. Since all earnings are being paid out as dividends, this equation can be written as:

$$P_0 = \frac{EPS_0}{k_s}$$

Multiplying both sides by the number of shares, N, produces:

$$P_0 \times N = \frac{EPS_0 \times N}{k_s}$$

and since $P_0 \times N$ equals the total stock value of the firm, S, and $EPS_0 \times N$ equals the total earnings available for common stockholders, $[EPS_0 \times N = (EBIT - I)(1 - T)]$, this is equal to Equation 18.3.

Market Value of Debt ($ Millions)	Interest Rate on All Debt, $k_b{}^a$	Estimated Stock Beta, $\beta_j{}^a$	Required Return or Cost of Equity, $k_s{}^b$
$ 0	— %	1.10	14.4%
3	12.0	1.25	15.0
6	12.0	1.35	15.4
9	13.0	1.45	15.8
12	14.0	1.60	16.4
15	16.0	1.80	17.2
18	18.0	2.10	18.4
21	20.0	2.75	21.0

[a] As estimated by Michigan Foods on the advice of its investment bankers.
[b] $k_s = R_F + \beta(k_M - R_F)$. The firm's investment bankers estimate R_F at 10 percent and k_M at 14 percent.

I = expected annual interest payments
T = firm's marginal tax rate
k_s = required return, or cost of equity capital

An examination of Table 18.3 indicates that the market value of Michigan Foods, with no debt in its capital structure, is $20.833 million. As the firm substitutes debt for equity, its total market value increases until $12 million in debt is employed. Above $12 million, the increase in the respective costs of both debt and equity, due to greater and greater risk (as perceived by lenders and investors), causes the total value of the firm to decrease.

Note that the $12 million of debt results not only in the maximum value of Michigan Foods, but also in the minimum cost of capital for the firm:

$$k = k_i \left(\frac{B}{V}\right)(1 - T) + k_s \left(\frac{S}{V}\right) \tag{18.4}$$

where k_i is the firm's after-tax cost of debt, $k_i = k_b(1 - T)$, and all the symbols are as earlier defined. When there is no debt, the cost of capital is equal to the cost of equity capital, k_s. The initial use of cheaper debt funds results in a *decrease* in the firm's cost of capital, which reaches its minimum when $12 million of debt is employed. Beyond that point, the use of additional debt results in higher and higher costs of both debt, k_i, and equity, k_s, to the firm. Hence, Michigan Foods can increase the total value of the firm and reduce its cost of capital by the judicious use of debt financing. This relationship is graphed in Figure 18.4 on p. 760, which shows that the value of the firm is a mirror image of its cost of capital—the value of the firm can indeed be increased as the firm's cost of capital decreases. Note also that the new market price per share with $12

TABLE 18.3
Market Value and Cost of Capital for Michigan Foods, Inc.

Market Value of Debt, B ($ Millions)[a]	Market Value of Stock, S ($ Millions)[b]	Market Value of Firm, V ($ Millions)[c]	Financial Leverage, B/V	Before-Tax Cost of Debt, k_b[a]	Cost of Equity, k_s[a]	Cost of Capital, k[d]
S 0	S20.833	S20.833	0%	0%	14.4%	14.40%
3	18.560	21.560	13.91	12.0	15.0	13.92
6	16.675	22.675	26.46	12.0	15.4	13.23
9	14.544	23.544	38.23	13.0	15.8	12.74
12	12.146	24.146	49.70	14.0	16.4	12.42
15	9.070	24.070	62.32	16.0	17.2	12.46
18	5.739	23.739	75.82	18.0	18.4	12.64
21	2.286	23.286	90.18	20.0	21.0	12.88

[a]From Table 18.2.
[b]The market value of the stock, S, was found by using Equation 18.3.
[c]Total market value found by using Equation 18.2.
[d]Cost of capital was found by using Equation 18.4.

million in debt is $24.15 ($12.146 million ÷ 503,023 shares of stock).[11] In Table 18.4, p. 761, we see that the market price of the common stock is maximized at $12 million of debt, the same point at which the total value of the firm was maximized and the cost of capital minimized. Hence, maximization of the value of the firm, maximization of market price per share, P_0, and minimization of the marginal cost of capital are accomplished simultaneously when a firm achieves its target capital structure.

Further Analysis of Financial Leverage: Risk and Return

Up to now we have talked about how the firm's total value and MCC change as its degree of financial leverage changes. However, risk also changes as firms vary their financial leverage. Instead of using a single level of EBIT, consider what happens if Michigan Foods expected EBIT can take on any of three values—$2 million, $5 million, or $8 million, with probability of 0.20, 0.60, and 0.20, respectively. As shown in Table 18.5, when Michigan Foods has zero debt, its expected earnings per share (representing expected return) is $3.00. Risk can be examined by

---

[11]Another way to think about this is that as the firm engages in the recapitalization, investors react to or anticipate the results. Since the recapitalization will result in a change in the total value of the firm, by buying and/or selling investors will drive the market value of the firm up or down from the $20.833 million at the zero debt level. This price change occurs *before* the proceeds of the debt issue are available to buy back the necessary common stock. The following sequence would occur when the firm moves from zero to $12 million in debt. First, the firm announces the recapitalization and the stock market reacts, resulting in a new value of the firm of $24.146 million. Second, since there are still 1 million shares of stock outstanding, the market price per share is $24.146 ($24.146 million divided by 1 million shares.) Third, the firm uses the $12 million to buy back shares of stock at $24.146 per share, resulting in 496,977 shares being repurchased by the firm. Fourth, the market price per share of the shares of common stock *not* purchased is unaffected and remains at $24.146. For simplicity, we assume all these steps occur instantaneously.

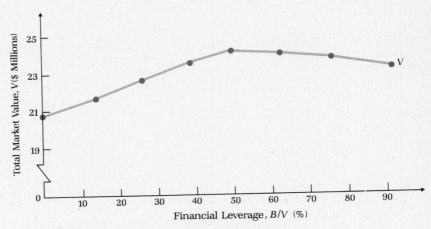

(a) Total Market Value Versus Financial Leverage

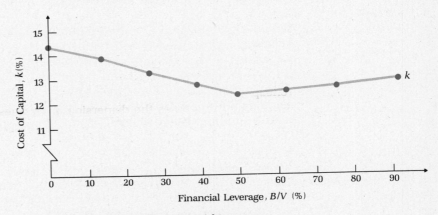

(b) Cost of Capital Versus Financial Leverage

Figure 18.4   Total Market Value, V, and Cost of Capital, k, for Different Amounts of Financial Leverage for Michigan Foods, Inc.

considering the standard deviation and coefficient of variation of the expected EPS. For Michigan Foods with zero debt in their capital structure, the standard deviation is $1.14 while the coefficient of variation is 0.38.

Consider what happens if Michigan Foods shifts its capital structure to include $12 million of debt. As shown in Table 18.5, p. 762, the firm's expected EPS increases from $3.00 to $3.96. However, risk also increases with the addition of the debt as shown by the standard deviation of $2.26 and coefficient of variation of .57, both of which are substantially higher than they were with zero debt. When Michigan Foods moves from zero debt to $12 million in debt, both risk and expected return increase.

TABLE 18.4
Market Price Per Share for Michigan Foods, Inc.

Market Value of Debt, B ($ Millions)[a] (1)	Market Value of Equity, S ($ Millions)[a] (2)	Market Value of Firm, V ($ Millions)[a] [(1) + (2)] (3)	Market Value of Equity to Market Value of the Firm, S/V [(2) ÷ (3)] (4)	Original Number of Shares of Common Stock, N (5)	Number of Shares of Common Stock After Substituting Debt for Equity [(4) × (5)] (6)	Market Price Per Share, P_0 [(2) ÷ (6)] (7)
$ 0	$20.833	$20.833	100.0000%	1,000,000	1,000,000	$20.83
3	18.560	21.560	86.0853	1,000,000	860,853	21.56
6	16.675	22.675	73.5391	1,000,000	735,391	22.68
9	14.544	23.544	61.7737	1,000,000	617,737	23.54
12	12.146	24.146	50.3023	1,000,000	503,023	24.15
15	9.070	24.070	37.6818	1,000,000	376,818	24.07
18	5.739	23.739	24.1754	1,000,000	241,754	23.74
21	2.286	23.286	9.8171	1,000,000	98,171	23.29

[a]From Table 18.3.

These relationships among the firm's capital structure, its expected EPS, and the risk associated with the expected earnings are examined further in Table 18.6, p. 763, and Figure 18.5, p. 764. As shown, the use of "cheap" debt funds results in an increase in expected EPS, while at the same time it increases the dispersion or riskiness of these earnings. As investors perceive the increased riskiness of the firm's earnings, the nondiversifiable (or beta) risk increases, leading to an increase in the investors' required return. This increased risk also influences lenders, who increase the interest rate required before they will lend to Michigan Foods, which causes the after-tax cost of debt to increase. The use of increased financial leverage by the firm, therefore, clearly involves a risk-return tradeoff: Higher leverage increases expected EPS, but it also increases the firm's risk resulting in higher returns being demanded by lenders and investors. This result is consistent with our discussion of the theoretical relationship between the cost of specific capital components and capital structure, which leads firms to establish target capital structures.

Practical Aspects of Capital Structure Decisions

Now that we have demonstrated the importance of a target capital structure for the firm, what practical guidelines can we supply? As we will see, although a number of tools exist, they do not always provide nice, neat answers. The capital structure question in practice is another decision that requires experience and a good deal of judgment. However, the following concepts and tools should help in making this decision.

TABLE 18.5
Expected EPS, Standard Deviation of EPS, and Coefficient of Variation of EPS for Three States of the Economy, for Michigan Foods, Inc. (In Millions of Dollars, Except Per Share Figures)

	State of Economy		
	Weak	Normal	Strong
Probability	0.2	0.6	0.2
Sales	$12.000	$18.000	$24.000
Less: Fixed costs	4.000	4.000	4.000
Less: Variable costs (50% of sales)	6.000	9.000	12.000
Total costs (except interest)	$10.000	$13.000	$16.000
Earnings before interest and taxes (EBIT)	$ 2.000	$ 5.000	$ 8.000
ZERO DEBT			
Less: Interest	$ 0.000	$ 0.000	$ 0.000
Earnings before taxes (EBT)	$ 2.000	$ 5.000	$ 8.000
Less: Taxes (40%)[a]	(0.800)	(2.000)	(3.200)
Earnings after taxes (EAT)	$ 1.200	$ 3.000	$ 4.800
Earnings per share on 1 million shares[b]	$ 1.20	$ 3.00	$ 4.80

Expected earnings per share, $\overline{\text{EPS}}$ = $3.00
Standard deviation, σ_{EPS} = $1.14
Coefficient of variation, CV_{EPS} =   .38

$12 MILLION OF DEBT			
Less: Interest (0.14 × $12,000,000)	$ 1.680	$ 1.680	$ 1.680
Earnings before taxes (EBT)	$ 0.320	$ 3.320	$ 6.320
Less: Taxes (40%)[a]	0.128	1.328	2.528
Earnings after taxes (EAT)	$ 0.192	$ 1.992	$ 3.792
Earnings per share on 503,023 shares[b]	$ 0.38	$ 3.96	$ 7.54

Expected earnings per share, $\overline{\text{EPS}}$ = $3.96
Standard deviation, σ_{EPS} = $2.26
Coefficient of variation, CV_{EPS} =   .57

[a]Although not shown here, a tax credit on losses is assumed at $15, $18, and $21 million of debt.
[b]Number of shares of stock from column 6, Table 18.4.

Flexibility and Timing   Raising funds is not a one-time decision; rather, it involves an ongoing sequence of events that extends over time. If future outcomes were known with certainty, or if the firm were not growing, raising capital would be relatively simple. But this is not the case for most firms. The financial manager must consider both the present circumstances facing the firm and its future capital needs when raising funds.

Such planning provides the flexibility financial managers need in order to make capital structure decisions consistent with the firm's target capital structure goals. If today's financing decision reduces the number of future options open to the firm—and in particular if it increases the firm's dependence on less reliable sources of capital—that action reduces management's flexibility. When a firm borrows funds, it

TABLE 18.6
Expected EPS,
Standard Deviation of
EPS, and Coefficient of
Variation of EPS, for
Michigan Foods, Inc.

Market Value of Debt, B ($ Millions) (1)	Expected Earnings Per Share, EPS (2)	Standard Deviation, σ_{EPS}[a] (3)	Coefficient of Variation, CV_{EPS}[a] [(3) ÷ (2)] (4)
$ 0	$3.00	$ 1.14	.38
3	3.23	1.32	.41
6	3.49	1.55	.44
9	3.72	1.84	.49
12	3.96	2.26	.57
15	4.14	3.02	.73
18	4.37	4.71	1.08
21	4.89	11.59	2.37

[a]Values for zero and $12 million in debt were taken from Table 18.5. The other values were calculated in exactly the same manner as indicated in Table 18.5.

commits a portion of its future cash flows to pay interest and repay principal.[12] Lenders assess the firms ability to meet interest and/or principal payments when evaluating a borrowing request. Ultimately, lenders become reluctant to supply additional credit unless the borrower's equity base and cash flow increase; obviously, as lender reluctancy increases, the firm becomes more dependent on the external equity market for capital. In addition, both the bond and the stock markets are unstable and may, at certain points in time, become very unattractive for raising capital. So its limited debt capacity and the volatile nature of the long-term capital markets are important factors for a firm to consider when raising capital.

Equally important, and closely related to flexibility, is the question of timing. Ideally, financial managers would like to issue debt when interest costs are low and equity when stock prices are high. In recent years, however, these conditions have seldom existed. This has caused firms to reduce capital expenditures or finance at substantially higher costs than expected. The timing aspect of raising capital suggests why many firms that employ a target capital structure are concerned with maintaining it only within a few percentage points over a period of 1, 2, or more years. In addition, since raising funds is "lumpy," firms are also willing to maintain only approximate capital structure proportions. By "lumpy" we are referring to the need (because of financing costs, and so on) for a bond or stock issue to be of sufficient size. Although a firm may

---

[12]Although this discussion concerns debt, any form of fixed-payment obligation entered into by the firm must be considered. For example, leasing causes the firm to "use up" part of its debt capacity and must be taken into account. Recognition of the importance of leasing to capital structure decisions was largely responsible for the issuance of FASB No. 13 (Accounting for Leases) by the Financial Accounting Standards Board. It requires firms to capitalize lease obligations under certain conditions, and to restate both the asset and liability side of the balance sheet to reflect these lease obligations.

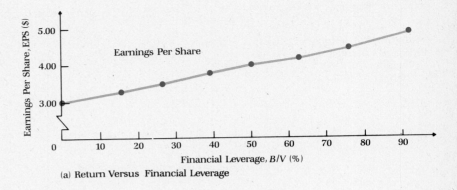

(a) Return Versus Financial Leverage

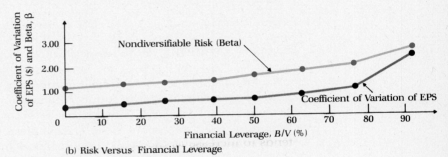

(b) Risk Versus Financial Leverage

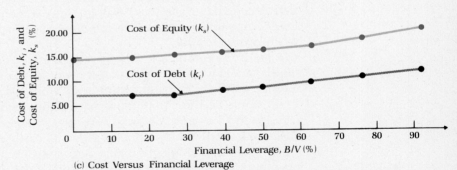

(c) Cost Versus Financial Leverage

Figure 18.5 Return (Earnings Per Share), Risk (Coefficient of Variation and Beta), and Costs (k_i and k_s) for Michigan Foods, Inc., as the Amount of Financial Leverage Increases.

need only $5 million, it may find, because of the relative size of the issue and current capital market conditions, that a $10 million issue is more appropriate. This will cause the firm's actual capital structure to deviate from its target structure. Effective financial managers understand this and try to balance risk and return when raising capital over time.

External Financial Standards

Also important in practice are the external standards of performance that are imposed on corporate capital structures. As Table 18.7 shows, the use of debt tends to vary substantially among industries.[13] Both retailers and aircraft manufacturers, for example, make very heavy use of debt, whereas drug manufacturers use substantially less. In addition, chemical, petroleum, and steel, all capital-intensive industries, use more long-term debt than the other industries examined. Table 18.7 also shows that small manufacturers use relatively large amounts of current debt (primarily trade credit) to finance their operations, whereas large manufacturers (with assets over $1 billion) have about equal amounts of current and long-term liabilities in their capital structures.

The presence of lender-imposed standards reinforces the tendency of financial mangers to compare their firm's financial structure with those of other firms or with industry averages. The standards may be established by bankers, by investment advisors working with the firm on new financing, or for large firms issuing debt to the public, by bond-rating agencies. Bond ratings published by Moody's or Standard & Poor's, attempt to estimate the relative safety of bond issues over the foreseeable future. Bond ratings are important, since the before-tax interest rate tends to vary inversely with the rating assigned. Although the interest rate may be 11 percent for the highest-rated bond (a triple-A rating), it tends to increase as the bond rating is lowered. A firm's bond rating is thus a matter of major concern to financial managers.

Many factors influence bond ratings. Table 18.8 indicates the financial leverage, coverage, and size differences among rating groups for both industrial and public utility firms. Betas, by rating group, are also included for the industrials. An examination of this table suggests that larger firms, with lower degrees of financial leverage and higher coverage ratios, tend to have higher bond ratings. In addition, Table 18.8 also shows an inverse relationship between nondiversifiable (or beta) risk and a firm's bond ratings. Firms with low beta values, which are generally larger firms with relatively stable earnings, tend to have higher bond ratings and hence a lower cost of debt.

Leverage and Earnings Per Share: EBIT-EPS Analysis

Financial leverage involves the use of funds obtained at a fixed cost in the hope of increasing the return to common stockholders. In addition to lender-imposed standards, the target capital structure decision requires a qualitative balancing of the increase in expected income from using debt, leases, or preferred stock against the increased risks from greater income variability, the increased chance of bankruptcy, and

---

[13]Although the values in Table 18.7 are book values, the use of market values would indicate somewhat similar patterns.

TABLE 18.7
Sources of Financing as a Percentage of Total Assets, 1982

	Percentage of Total Assets[a]			
Industry	Current Liabilities	Long-Term Debt	Total Liabilities	Equity
Retail trade	28.5%	29.4%	57.9%	42.1%
Total manufacturing	25.5	25.6	51.1	48.9
Assets under $5 million	35.3	19.1	54.4	45.6
Assets over $1 billion	24.3	26.4	50.7	49.3
Selected manufacturing industries				
Aircraft	54.3	13.2	67.5	32.5
Chemicals	21.8	26.9	48.7	51.3
Drugs	22.8	19.2	42.0	58.0
Food	26.2	24.3	50.5	49.5
Petroleum	17.7	31.1	48.8	51.2
Steel	22.2	42.3	64.5	35.5

[a] The percentages given are based upon book values.
SOURCE: Federal Trade Commission, *Quarterly Financial Report for Manufacturing, Mining and Trade Corporations,* Third Quarter, 1983.

TABLE 18.8
Financial Leverage, Coverage, Size, and Common Stock Beta for Moody's Bond-Rating Groupings

	Aaa	Aa	A	Baa	Ba	B
Financial leverage						
Industrial[a]	—%	9%	16%	15%	15%	21%
Public utility[b]	49	52	53	54	—	—
Coverage						
Industrial[c]	—×	13.7×	4.0×	3.6×	3.2×	5.1×
Public utility[d]	4.2	3.8	3.4	2.9	—	—
Size ($ millions)						
Industrial—issue size	$ —	$ 74	$ 45	$ 19	$23	$18
Public utility—total assets	1,900	1,304	1,082	1,418	—	—
Beta—industrial	.59	.67	.82	1.05	1.16	1.43

[a] Long-term debt/total assets.
[b] Long-term debt/invested capital.
[c] (Net income + interest)/interest.
[d] Earnings before interest and taxes/fixed charges.
SOURCES: George E. Pinches and Kent A. Mingo, "A Multivariate Analysis of Industrial Bond Ratings," *Journal of Finance* 28 (March 1973), pp. 1–18; Carl J. Schwendiman and George E. Pinches, "An Analysis of Alternative Measures of Investment Risk," *Journal of Finance* 30 (March 1975), pp. 193–200; and George E. Pinches, J. Clay Singleton, and Ali Jahankhani, "Fixed Coverage as a Determinant of Electric Utility Bond Ratings," *Financial Management* 7 (summer 1978), pp. 45–55.

reduced flexibility. One useful approach is to examine the impact increased financial leverage will have on expected EPS.

Consider Home Motion Pictures, Inc.; as Table 18.9 on p. 768 shows, its current capital structure consists of $10 million of 9 percent coupon-rate long-term debt, no preferred stock, and $75 million of common equity at market value. Home is interested in raising $15 million in additional financing, and based on the advice of its investment bankers, it decided to raise the entire $15 million from one source. Note that Home's financing is "lumpy," so the firm may temporarily deviate from its target capital structure. As shown in Table 18.9, Home's investment bankers identified three options: selling 300,000 shares of common stock at $50 per share net to the firm; issuing $15 million of 12 percent coupon-rate long-term debt; or selling $15 million of preferred stock with a dividend rate of 10 percent.

EBIT-EPS Charts.   To conduct an *EBIT-EPS analysis*, as illustrated in Figure 18.6 on p. 769, we need two data points for each of the three financing plans. The first point is the EPS expected for some level of EBIT, say $16 million from Table 18.10, p. 768. At this level of EBIT, the EPS is $6.97, $7.98, and $7.56, respectively, for the common stock, debt, and preferred stock financing plans. We plot these EPS figures at the $16 million EBIT mark. The second point could be at any other level of EBIT; our preference is to employ that EBIT necessary to cover all fixed financing costs for a particular plan. It is then plotted on the horizontal, or EBIT, axis. For the common stock alternative there is $0.9 million in interest payments (from the existing debt) that must be met. Hence, the necessary EBIT so that Home's EPS is exactly equal to zero is $0.9 million. For the debt financing plan, we must have an EBIT of $2.7 million to cover interest charges; so $2.7 million becomes the EBIT axis intercept. The preferred stock alternative is more complicated, since we must have $0.9 million to cover the existing interest and enough additional EBIT so that after paying taxes at the rate of 40 percent, $1.5 million is left to pay the preferred dividends. The proper amount of EBIT needed to pay the preferred dividends is determined by dividing annual preferred dividends of $1.5 million by 1 minus the tax rate ($1.5 million/0.6); thus, $2.5 million is needed to cover the preferred dividends, plus $0.9 million to cover the existing interest, for a total of $3.4 million. This is the EBIT axis intercept for the preferred stock financing plan.

This EBIT-EPS chart greatly simplifies and enriches the interpretation of the impact of alternative financing plans on the firm's EPS. In Figure 18.6, we see that at levels of EBIT above $8.7 million, the debt financing alternative provides higher EPS than common stock financing. Likewise, above EBIT levels of $11.73 million, the preferred stock plan provides EPS higher than those under the common stock plan. The range of earnings chart provides graphic evidence of the potential benefits and risks associated with the use of debt or preferred stock. Note that it is always the *top* line of the graph that is preferable: We would maximize EPS with common stock financing up to $8.7 million in earnings before interest and taxes, after which debt financing is superior, since it provides a

TABLE 18.9

Home Motion Pictures' Capital Structure at Current Market Value, and After Three Alternative Financing Plans (In Millions of Dollars and Shares)

	Market Value Capital Structure							
	Current		After Common Stock Financing		After Debt Financing		After Preferred Stock Financing	
	$	%	$	%	$	%	$	%
SOURCE OF CAPITAL								
Long-term debt	$10	11.8%	$ 10	10%	$ 25	25%	$ 10	10%
Preferred stock	0	—	0	—	0	—	15	15
Common equity	75	88.2	90	90	75	75	75	75
Total capital	$85	100%	$100	100%	$100	100%	$100	100%
OTHER INFORMATION								
Annual interest	$0.90		$0.90		$2.70		$0.90	
Annual preferred dividend	0		0		0		$1.50	
Number of shares of common stock outstanding	1.00		1.30		1.00		1.00	

TABLE 18.10

Home Motion Pictures, Inc.'s, Earnings Per Share (In Millions of Dollars or Shares, Except EPS Values)

	Financing Plan		
	Common Stock	Debt	Preferred Stock
EBIT	$16.00	$16.00	$16.00
Less: Interest	0.90	2.70	0.90
Earnings before taxes (EBT)	$15.10	$13.30	$15.10
Less: Taxes (40%)	6.04	5.32	6.04
Earnings after taxes (EAT)	$ 9.06	$ 7.98	$ 9.06
Less: Preferred dividends	—	—	1.50
Earnings available for common stockholders	$ 9.06	$ 7.98	$ 7.56
Number of shares of common stock outstanding	1.30	1.00	1.00
Earnings per share (EPS)	$ 6.97	$ 7.98	$ 7.56

larger EPS. The issue thus becomes this: "What are the firm's chances of equaling or exceeding the $8.7 million EBIT level?"

Indifference Points. An "indifference point" can be determined where the level of EPS from the two plans is equal; we can do this by finding that level of EBIT which provides the same EPS for two alternative

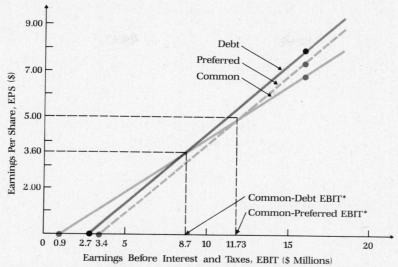

Figure 18.6   EBIT-EPS Chart for Three Different Financing Plans for Home Motion Pictures, Inc.

financing plans, such as common stock versus debt or common stock versus preferred stock. The following equation is used to compute the indifference point:

$$\frac{(EBIT^* - I_1)\,(1 - T) - D_{PS_1}}{N_1} = \frac{(EBIT^* - I_2)\,(1 - T) - D_{PS_2}}{N_2} \quad (18.5)$$

where $EBIT^*$ = the unknown indifference point in $EBIT$

   I_1, I_2 = the annual interest charges under the two alternative financing plans

   T = the firm's marginal tax rate

   D_{PS_1}, D_{PS_2} = annual preferred dividends on an after-tax basis for the two plans

   N_1, N_2 = the number of shares of common stock outstanding under the two plans

For the common stock versus debt alternative, the indifference point is found by:

$$\frac{(EBIT^* - 0.9)\,(1 - .4)}{1.3} = \frac{(EBIT^* - 2.7)\,(1 - .4)}{1.0}$$

Rearranging and solving for *EBIT*, we have:

$$1.0 \ (EBIT^* - 0.9) \ (.6) = 1.3 \ (EBIT^* - 2.7) \ (.6)$$
$$0.6 \ EBIT^* - 0.54 = 0.78 \ EBIT^* - 2.106$$
$$0.18 \ EBIT^* = 1.566$$
$$EBIT^* = \$8.7 \text{ million}$$

Likewise, for the common versus preferred stock alternative, the indifference point is found by:

$$\frac{(EBIT^* - 0.9) \ (1 - .4)}{1.3} = \frac{(EBIT^* - 0.9) \ (1 - .4) - 1.5}{1.0}$$
$$1.0 \ (EBIT^* - 0.9) \ (.06) = 1.3 \ [(EBIT^* - 0.9) \ (.6) - 1.5]$$
$$0.6 \ EBIT^* - 0.54 = 1.3 \ [0.6 \ EBIT^* - 0.54 - 1.5]$$
$$0.6 \ EBIT - 0.54 = 0.78 \ EBIT^* - 2.652$$
$$0.18 \ EBIT^* = 2.112$$
$$EBIT^* = \$11.73 \text{ million}$$

There is no indifference point between the debt and preferred stock financing alternatives. Since interest is tax-deductible while preferred dividends are paid out of after-tax earnings, for *any* level of EBIT, the EPS will *always* be greater with debt than with preferred stock.[14]

An Assessment of EBIT-EPS Analysis.   In addition to increasing EPS, financial leverage also increases the variability in EPS. Firms must attempt to assess the impact of the increased financial risk on their cost of equity capital and hence on the total market value of the firm. To illustrate this let us continue with the Home Motion Pictures example where they had EBIT of $16 million. Assume Home's cost of equity capital was 12 percent before the financing and it paid all its earnings out in the form of dividends. If equity investors do not change their assessment of Home after the financing and if common stock financing is employed, the market price for Home's stock will be $58.08:

$$P_0 = \frac{D_1}{k_s} = \frac{EPS_1}{k_s} = \$6.97 \div 0.12 = \$58.08$$

---

[14]Anytime the number of shares of common stock is the same under alternative financing plans (such as debt versus preferred stock), there will be no indifference point. One plan always dominates the other at any level of EBIT. Given the relative after-tax costs, debt always provides cheaper financing as long as the firm is profitable. For this reason most firms do not use much preferred stock for financing. One exception is the public utility industry, where many regulatory authorities encourage the use of preferred stock financing to maintain a "balanced" capital structure. Because of the regulated nature of their returns, public utility firms are generally able to pass these higher costs of financing on to consumers in the form of higher utility bills.

However, as illustrated in Table 18.11, a vast number of possible market prices can result, depending on which financing plan is employed and how investors assess Home's expected risk and return. If equity investors believe debt financing has substantially increased the firm's risk and they now require a 15 percent return, the market value of common stock will be only $53.20 per share ($7.98 ÷ 0.15). The information in Table 18.11 serves to reinforce the point made elsewhere that *maximization of EPS is not the same as wealth maximization.* Although financial leverage may increase EPS, financial managers must weigh the increased risks and returns, and consider how they will affect the firm's value as assessed by its stockholders.

Two other aspects of the EBIT-EPS chart deserve mention. First, the chart is a static concept measure at a given point in time; it is appropriate only within certain limited EBIT levels. We would be reluctant to estimate what Home's EPS would be if its EBIT under "normal" conditions increased to $40 million. Obviously, other factors might also change dramatically, and they would need to be taken into account. Second, the chart implies that firms will use the cheapest source of financing, but it does not provide a direct means of considering how that financing influences the firm's target capital structure. The chart may provide financial managers with a reasonable indication of the impact of alternative financing plans on the firm's EPS, but it does *not* deal directly with risk analysis, flexibility, and wealth maximization.[15]

Financial Leverage, Risk, and Cash Flow

Coverage Ratios. Among the ways to gain insight into debt capacity, and a technique frequently employed by lenders, is the use of coverage ratios similar to that presented in Chapter 3. One of the most comprehensive coverage ratios is the times burden covered, which includes interest payments, lease obligations, preferred dividends, and repayment of principal or sinking fund payments, so that:

$$\text{Times burden covered} = \frac{EBIT + LP}{I + LP + \dfrac{D_{PS} + SF}{1 - T}} \tag{18.6}$$

where $EBIT$ = earnings before interest and taxes
LP = annual lease payments
I = annual interest on debt
D_{PS} = annual preferred dividends

---

[15]See U. E. Reinhardt, "Break-Even Analysis for Lockheed's Tri Star: An Application of Financial Theory," *Journal of Finance* 28 (September 1973), pp. 821–838; and Richard D. Gritta, "The Effect of Financial Leverage on Air Carrier Earnings: A Break-Even Analysis," *Financial Management* 8 (summer 1979), pp. 53–60.

	Common Stock Plan	Debt Plan	Preferred Stock Plan
EPS[a]	$ 6.97	$ 7.98	$ 7.56
Equity capitalization rates, k_s	Market Price Per Share[b]		
11%	$63.36	$72.55	$68.73
12	58.08	66.50	63.00
13	53.62	61.38	58.15
14	49.79	57.00	54.00
15	46.47	53.20	50.40

[a]From Table 18.10.

[b]Obtained by $P_0 = \dfrac{D_1}{k_s} = \dfrac{EPS_1}{k_s}$; for example, $6.97 \div 0.11 = 63.36$. The rest of the figures were calculated in a similar manner.

SF = annual sinking fund payments or repayment of principal on debt

T = firm's marginal tax rate

Assuming that Home's EBIT is $16 million, that its lease payments are $0.2 million per year, and that both the existing and proposed bond issues require sinking fund payments of $0.5 million per year, their times burden covered ratios are as follows:

Common Stock Financing	Debt Financing	Preferred Stock Financing
8.38×	3.55×	3.65×

There are no precise rules of thumb specifying appropriate coverages ratios; however, they are often compared by the firm to itself over time, with other firms in the same industry, or with some industry standard. Obviously, Home has a far higher coverage ratio with common stock financing than under either the debt or preferred stock financing alternatives.

The Flow of Funds.   A logical extension of coverage ratios is to examine all funds flowing through a firm. By funds, we mean any form of payment, whether it is cash, an increase in trade credit, or a new loan. During a recession, declining levels of EBIT may produce low coverage ratios that suggest an increased risk of bankruptcy. However, during the same period the firm may be able to reduce its variable costs, and its investment in accounts receivable and inventories. If these reductions are large enough, the firm may still be in a good position to meet its financial obligations, even though coverage ratios have declined.

To examine the impact of financial leverage in a funds flow context, we use a format very similar to the cash budget developed in Chapter 4. We have prepared such a statement for Home Motion Pictures, Inc., if it accepts the debt financing plan, for a downturn in economic activity lasting three quarters with an upturn occurring in the fourth quarter.[16] The firm is assumed to have a beginning cash balance of $1.5 million. As Table 18.12 shows, during the first three quarters revenues will decline, causing net funds from operations to drop to a low of $5.6 million in the second quarter. As economic activity turns down, Home reduces its accounts receivable and inventories. At the same time, its use of accounts payable as a means of financing will be restricted. In estimating funds flow, Home decided that new investments could be cut back in the second quarter without adverse long-term consequences, and that both fixed operating expenses and promotion expenses could be reduced. Beginning in the second quarter, Home begins to experience some cash constraints; by the third quarter, it needs $1.5 million more in funds than will be available. Note that the cash deficit occurs in the third quarter, while the lowest level of net funds from operations occurs in the second quarter. This is primarily because working capital provides cash during the first two quarters and consumes it during the last two.

With these data, financial managers at Home Motion Pictures are now in a position to evaluate possible cash needs during a downturn in economic activity. If they can reduce the outflow of cash more, or stretch out payables, further modifications can be made to the analysis presented in Table 18.12. In addition, they should determine whether or not new investments can be postponed by a quarter or two, or if other sources of financing are available. These might include unused lines of bank credit, or new debt or equity issues. By undertaking such an analysis, Home's financial managers are in a much better position to judge whether or not the use of additional debt is feasible.

Other Techniques. In addition to the funds flow analysis, other techniques can be used to determine the impact of financial leverage on the firm's cash flow position. Among these are the following:

1. *Inventory of resources.* This inventory identifies the sources of readily available funds, such as unused lines of credit, additional bank loans, reduced cash outflows, and so on, that financial managers have at their disposal if cash needs become severe.[17]
2. *Sensitivity analysis and planning models.* Many firms have constructed corporate planning models to examine the effects of numerous factors on the future prospects of the firm.[18] By employ-

---

[16]For greater reality, we assume a dividend payout ratio of 25 percent.

[17]See Gordon Donaldson, "Strategy for Financial Emergencies," *Harvard Business Review* 47 (November–December 1969), pp. 67–79.

[18]See Willard T. Carleton, Charles L. Dick, Jr., and David H. Downes, "Financial Policy Models: Theory and Practice," *Journal of Financial and Quantitative Analysis* 8 (December 1973), pp. 691–709; Jack Clark Francis and Dexter R. Rowell, "A Simultaneous Equation Model of the Firm for Financial Analysis and Planning," *Financial Management* 7 (spring 1978), pp. 29–44; Stewart C. Myers and Gerald A. Pogue, "A Programming Approach to Corporate Financial Management," *Journal of Finance* 29 (May 1974), pp. 579–599; and Roy L. Crum, Darwin D. Klingman, and Lee A. Tavis, "Implementation of Large-Scale Financial Planning Models: Solution Efficient Transformations," *Journal of Financial and Quantitative Analysis* 14 (March 1979), pp. 137–152.

TABLE 18.12
Analysis of Funds Flow During an Economic Downturn with a Debt Financing Plan: Home Motion Pictures, Inc. (In Millions of Dollars)

Funds Flow	Quarter			
	1	2	3	4
Funds from operating revenues	$12.000	$10.000	$11.000	$16.000
− Variable operating expenses (40%)	4.800	4.000	4.400	6.400
− Taxes	0.900	0.400	0.650	1.700
= Net funds from operations	$ 6.300	$ 5.600	$ 5.950	$ 7.900
Increase (decrease) in current assets and liabilities exclusive of cash				
Accounts receivable	(0.900)	(0.300)	0.000	0.500
Inventories	(0.600)	(0.300)	(0.100)	0.300
Accounts payable	(0.100)	(0.200)	0.300	0.400
+ Net funds from working capital	$ 1.400	$ 0.400	$(0.200)	$(0.400)
Nonoperating expenses				
New investment	2.000	1.250	2.000	2.000
Fixed operating expenses	3.500	3.250	3.250	3.250
Promotion expenses	0.700	0.500	0.500	0.650
− Funds consumed by nonoperating expenses	$6.200	$5.000	$5.750	$5.900
= Net funds available to meet financial burdens	$1.500	$1.000	$ 0	$1.600
Financial burdens				
Legal burdens				
Interest payments	$0.675	$0.675	$0.675	$0.675
Lease payments	0.050	0.050	0.050	0.050
Sinking fund payments	0.250	0.250	0.250	0.250
Policy burdens				
Common stock cash dividends	0.525	0.525	0.525	0.525
− Total financial burdens	$1.500	$1.500	$1.500	$1.500
= Net increase (decrease) in cash	$ 0	$(0.500)	$(1.500)	$0.100
Beginning cash	$1.500	$ 1.500	$1.000	$(0.500)
+ Net increase (decrease) in cash	0	(0.500)	(1.500)	0.100
= Ending cash	$1.500	$ 1.000	$(0.500)	$(0.400)
− Minimum cash	1.000	1.000	1.000	1.000
= Surplus (deficit) cash	0.500	0	(1.500)	(1.400)

ing these models and changing the assumptions, a sensitivity analysis can be conducted to assess the potential severity of future cash needs.

Advances continue to be made in providing financial managers with information concerning the potential impact of alternative decisions on the value of the firm. However, managers will have to continue making qualitative decisions about risk-return tradeoffs in attempting to position

TABLE 18.13
Debt Ratios in Selected
Industries and
Countries, 1979–1980

	Auto-mobiles	Chem-icals	Elec-trical	Foods	Iron and Steel	Non-Ferrous Metals	Paper	Tex-tiles
Benelux	61.8	60.0	50.8	64.3	66.2	41.4	63.2	54.2
France	67.3	72.1	72.5	77.7	74.1	66.3	74.4	73.9
West Germany	57.1	56.2	66.4	48.8	51.6	67.8	69.8	65.0
Italy	21.7	67.7	79.2	83.4	90.2	86.1	77.4	77.7
Japan	71.3	81.2	65.7	76.3	87.5	88.2	76.6	77.6
Sweden	75.2	67.5	76.9	62.8	69.3	56.1	55.5	59.7
United Kingdom	72.8	49.8	59.9	55.3	50.7	56.7	55.9	50.7
United States	58.0	54.7	53.6	55.4	54.3	57.6	58.2	47.5

SOURCE: J. Markham Collins and William S. Sekely, "The Relationship of Headquarters Country and Industry Classification to Financial Structure," *Financial Management* 12 (Autumn 1983), p. 48.

the firm at the appropriate target capital structure. The numerous approaches we have discussed can provide a framework for assessing the risks and returns involved. If managers err in practice, it is that many have a tendency to be too conservative in their approach to the target capital structure decision by retaining an excessive reserve of borrowing power. Perhaps the best advice in practice is for the firm to: " . . . issue debt up to the point where the financial manager begins to lose some sleep. If he loses a great deal of sleep, the firm has probably gone too far. If he sleeps well, the firm hasn't gone far enough."[19]

MULTINATIONAL DIMENSIONS

Capital Structure

Although industry, size, and lender-imposed guidelines help to explain differences in target capital structures within the United States, these structures are also influenced by a particular country's institutional, cultural, and historical development. Indeed, country norms for target capital structures vary far more dramatically than do differences among individual firms or industries within a single country. As Table 18.13 shows, there are large differences in capital structures within the same industry in different countries.[20] Notice the consistently higher leverage ratios in France and Japan compared to their United States counterparts in each industry. Determinants of

[19]Stewart C. Myers, ed., *Modern Developments in Financial Management* (New York: Praeger, 1976), p. 127.

[20]Like those in Table 18.7, these figures are in book value terms, but the use of market values would indicate somewhat similar patterns.

target capital structures for firms outside the United States are more influenced by lender guidelines. Since the long-term debt and equity markets are not nearly as developed or efficient outside the United States, with the possible exception of the United Kingdom, industrial firms are more dependent on their bankers for financing. In fact, the availability of capital is primarily a function of the firm's internal generation of funds, plus the amount of short- and medium-term debt banks are willing to lend. This tendency, along with the rapid growth experienced in many countries, has caused these firms to have relatively high debt ratios.

The willingness of foreign bankers to support high debt ratios in client firms is influenced by several institutional factors that differ from those found in the United States. One important difference is that a number of countries permit commercial banks to own shares of common stock in individual firms. For example, banks in both Germany and Japan often combine their lending activities with investing in the common stock of client firms. Another important institutional factor in some countries is the rather close cooperation among government, banks, and industry. This is particularly true in Japan, where the phenomenon has been called "Japan, Inc." by frustrated U.S. competitors. This support is important. In bad times, for instance, support for a beleaguered firm might include its bank extending loan maturities and maybe even reducing or deferring interest payments, suppliers extending more liberal credit terms, and other firms providing management or technical expertise. Given this system of close cooperation and support, the risk of the firm defaulting on debt is considerably reduced, even though its debt ratio appears high by United States standards.

SUMMARY

Determination of the firm's target capital structure is one of the most important long-term decisions financial managers face. Both the traditional approach and the MM approach, taking into account corporate taxes, bankruptcy costs, agency costs, and other market imperfections, suggest the existence of target capital structures. The firm's target capital structure results from a tradeoff between risk and return that occurs when financial leverage is employed. Thus, higher leverage leads to increases in expected EPS, but it also increases the firm's risk. If properly maintained over time, the target capital structure (1) balances risk and return, (2) maximizes the market value of the firm, and (3) minimizes its marginal cost of capital. Utilization of any other capital structure is inconsistent with the goal of shareholder wealth maximization.

In practice, a number of techniques can aid in determining the target capital structure. Primary among these are externally imposed standards, EBIT-EPS analysis, coverage ratios, and the flow of funds analysis. The primary thrust of all of these techniques centers on assessing the risk-return tradeoff resulting from the use of fixed payment long-term financing. Debt, preferred stock, and leases are fixed payment long-term financing since they must be paid before anything accrues to the benefit of the firms common stockholders. Effective financial managers assess these tradeoffs while recognizing that raising capital is not a one-time decision. Flexibility must be maintained while the firm's actual capital structure fluctuates around its target capital structure over time.

QUESTIONS

18.1. Compare the traditional theory of capital structure and the Modigliani-Miller approach both with and without corporate taxes, and also when corporate taxes, bankruptcy costs, agency costs, and other imperfections are introduced. What is the impact on the firm's marginal cost of capital and its market value?

18.2. Explain how consideration of "debt capacity" suggests the existence of a target capital structure.

18.3. What is the relationship between nondiversifiable (or beta) risk and financial leverage?

18.4. Explain in detail how the target capital structure relates to: (1) the value of the firm, (2) the cost of capital, and (3) the firm's common stock market price.

18.5. Financial leverage has two effects on the firm's EPS. Explain what they are and why they occur.

18.6. What is the expected benefit from using financial leverage? What are the risks involved? Why doesn't maximization of EPS automatically lead to maximization of share price and hence to maximization of shareholder wealth?

18.7. Explain how financial managers use the following to provide information for the target capital structure decision:
   a. External financial standards.
   b. EBIT-EPS chart.
   c. Coverage ratios.
   d. Funds flow analysis.

18.8. Explain how to determine the indifference point when two financing plans are analyzed using the EBIT-EPS approach. When won't there be an indifference point between alternative financing plans?

18.9. What differences in other countries often cause debt ratios to be higher than in the United States?

PROBLEMS

18.1. *SUBSTITUTING DEBT FOR COMMON STOCK.* Latin American Wholesalers, Inc., has no debt outstanding, is not expected to grow, and has a current financial status of:

EBIT = $345,000

Earnings available for common
   stockholders = $207,000

Current number of shares
   outstanding   = 200,000

Cost of equity, k_s, = 10%

S/V = 100%

$B = 0$

Current EPS = $1.035

Tax rate, T, = 40%

The firm is considering the sale of $500,000 of long-term debt at par with a coupon rate of 11 percent and simultaneously repurchasing $500,000 of its common stock. If it sells the bonds, the cost of equity capital, k_s, will increase to 12 percent to reflect the increased risk. The firm pays out all its earnings in the form of dividends.

a. Find the current market price per share, P_0, and the overall value of the firm, V.

b. If Latin American Wholesalers recapitalizes itself, as noted above, what will be the new earnings available for common stockholders, value of the stock, S, total value of the firm, V, ratio of S to V, new number of shares of common stock outstanding, new earnings per share, EPS, and new market price per share, P_0? (Assume the market value of the debt, B, is equal to its par value.)

c. What has happened to the EPS and market price under the two situations (i.e., current and proposed)? Does maximization of EPS lead to maximization of the market price per share? Why not?

d. What can we say about the use of $500,000 in debt in relation to the firm's optimal or target capital structure?

18.2. *TARGET CAPITAL STRUCTURE.*   Pacific Hydroelectric Power currently has $20 million of 12 percent (coupon-rate) debt outstanding, EBIT of $14 million, and its cost of equity capital, k_s, is 11 percent. Because of a decrease in long-term interest rates and because it is not at its target capital structure, Pacific Hydroelectric has decided to call its existing $20 million bond issue and issue a new $40 million or $60 million bond issue. (The bonds will be called at par, so $20 million is required.) In either case, Pacific will use the proceeds beyond the $20 million necessary to refund the existing bond issue to buy back currently outstanding shares of common stock. The $40 million bond issue can be sold at par with a coupon rate, k_b, of 10 percent; the cost of equity capital is expected to remain at 11 percent if this option is chosen. If the $60 million bond issue is employed, it can also be sold at par, k_b is 11 percent, and because of increased risk the estimated cost of equity, k_s, is expected to increase to 12 percent. The corporate tax rate is 40 percent. All earnings are paid out as dividends.

a. What is the total value of the firm currently if the $20 million in bonds are worth 110 percent of par?

b. What will be the total value of Pacific Hydroelectric if the $40 million or the $60 million bond issue is sold? (Assume the market value of the bonds is equal to par.)

c. If Pacific's financial managers want to maximize shareholder wealth, which proposed action should they take? Why?

18.3. *TARGET CAPITAL STRUCTURE, VALUE OF FIRM, AND COST OF CAPITAL: CAPM.* Williams Equipment, which has no debt outstanding, has the following current financial condition:

Sales	$100,000,000
Less: Operating costs	80,000,000
EBIT	$ 20,000,000
Less: Taxes (40%)	8,000,000
Earnings available for common stockholders	$ 12,000,000
Shares of common stock outstanding (number)	2,000,000
EPS	$ 6.00

The firm's nondiversifiable risk, β, is .60, the expected return on the market, k_M, is 12 percent, and the expected risk-free rate, R_F, is 7 percent. The management of Williams has decided its target capital structure probably should include some debt; however, it does not know how much debt should be issued, with the proceeds being used to repurchase common stock. Based on conversations with its investment bankers, Williams estimates that the following amounts of debt could be issued, with the specified costs of debt, k_b, and nondiversifiable risk, β:

Amount of Debt Issued	Before-Tax Cost of Debt, k_b	Nondiversifiable Risk, β
$50,000,000	12%	.80
80,000,000	14	1.20

(The debt is issued at par, and the market value of the debt is equal to par.)

a. Based on the $12 million in earnings available for common stockholders (with no debt) and the current beta of .60, calculate the current value of the firm ($S = V$).

b. Based on the two alternative amounts of debt available, calculate the EBIT, earnings available for common stockholders, value of the stock, S, and total value of the firm, V, if the firm issues debt and uses the proceeds to buy back common stock. (*Hint:* $k_s = 11\%$ when $B = \$50,000,000$.) Graph the resulting total market values versus the firm's B/V ratio. At what capital structure, B/V, is the firm's value maximized?

c. For the current condition and the two possible levels of debt financing, calculate the firm's marginal cost of capital, k. Graph the resulting costs of capital versus the firm's B/V ratio. Does the minimum cost of capital occur at the same B/V ratio where the value of the firm, V, is maximized in (b)?

18.4. *TARGET CAPITAL STRUCTURE: EXPECTED RETURN AND RISK OF EPS.* Precision Engineers has a marginal corporate tax rate of 40 percent and estimates its revenues and expenses are as follows, based on the state of the economy (figures in millions of dollars):

| | State of Economy | | |
	Weak	Normal	Strong
Probability	0.25	0.50	0.25
Sales	$90	$100	$110
Fixed operating costs	40	40	40
Variable operating costs (40% of sales)	36	40	44
Total operating costs (except interest)	$76	$ 80	$ 84
EBIT	$14	$ 20	$ 26

a. If Precision employs debt of $0, $30 million, and $60 million, with a pre-tax cost, k_b, of 0, 10 percent, and 15 percent, respectively, calculate the expected earnings per share, *EPS*, standard deviation of EPS, σ, and coefficient of variation, *CV*, of EPS for the following capital structures: (1) zero debt with 2 million shares of common stock outstanding; (2) $30 million debt with 1.5 million shares of common stock outstanding; and (3) $60 million debt with 0.5 million shares of common stock outstanding. (*Hint:* σ is $1.6971 when $B = \$30$ million.)

b. Based on these values, what effect does the use of more debt have on the firm's beta and cost of equity capital? Are these values consistent with the behavior of the before-tax cost of debt, k_b? Why or why not?

c. *Optional:* If the probability distribution of expected EPS is assumed to be continuous and normal, what is the probability that Precision's EPS will be (1) less than $4 per share, or (2) between $5 and $10 per share, for each of the three possible capital structures?

18.5. ***ALTERNATIVE FINANCING PLANS: EXPANSION IN SALES AND OPERA-TING COSTS.*** Auburn Plastics plans to raise $2 million to meet present and future financing needs. It is confronted with the following alternatives: (1) sell common stock at $50 per share; (2) sell 8 percent preferred stock at its $50 par value; or (3) issue 9.5 percent debentures at their $1,000 par value. Assume there are no issuance costs. Auburn expects both its sales and operating costs to increase by 20 percent after the additional funds are obtained.

Balance Sheet		Income Statement	
Total assets	$4,500,000	Sales	$11,000,000
		Less: Operating costs	9,700,000
Current liabilities	$ 600,000	EBIT	$ 1,300,000
Common stock ($10 par)	1,500,000	Less: Interest (on	
Retained earnings	2,400,000	current liabilities)	50,000
Total liabilities and			
stockholders' equity	$4,500,000	EBT	$ 1,250,000
		Less: Taxes (.40)	500,000
		EAT	$ 750,000

  a. Determine the current EPS of Auburn Plastics.
  b. What is the EPS under each of the three alternative financing plans if sales and operating costs both increase immediately by 20 percent?
  c. Restate the balance sheet after implementing the new financing in each of the plans.

18.6. ***ALTERNATIVE FINANCING PLANS: MEAN AND DISPERSION OF EARN-INGS PER SHARE.*** Bernard Labs is expanding its manufacturing capability for generic drugs. It plans to raise the needed $500,000 by issuing either 20,000 shares of common stock, or bonds (at par) with a 12 percent coupon rate. Its present income statement is:

Sales	$2,000,000
Less: Operating costs	1,500,000
EBIT	$ 500,000
Less: Interest	50,000
EBT	$ 450,000
Less: Taxes (.40)	180,000
EAT	$ 270,000

Earnings per share on the currently outstanding 100,000 shares are therefore $2.70. After the new financing, Bernard's financial managers estimate the EBIT will be $500,000, $700,000, or $1,000,000, with probabilities of 0.4, 0.5, and 0.1, respectively.

a. Determine the EPS for each level of EBIT for the two financing plans.

b. What is the expected EPS, its standard deviation, and the coefficient of variation of EPS for each plan?

c. Which plan should Bernard Labs choose? Why? What other factors should be considered?

18.7. **EBIT-EPS CHART, INDIFFERENCE POINT, AND TOTAL VALUE: COMMON STOCK AND DEBT.** Outboard Marine is an all-equity-financed firm, with the following financial statements:

Balance Sheet		Income Statement	
Total assets	$1,000,000	Sales	$2,500,000
		Less: Operating costs	2,100,000
Common stock ($5 par)	$ 250,000	EBIT = EBT	
Retained earnings	750,000	(16% of sales)	$ 400,000
Total stockholders' equity	$1,000,000	Less: Taxes (.40)	160,000
		EAT	$ 240,000

Outboard Marine is planning to raise $400,000 through the sale of common stock at $50 per share or the issuance of debt with a 10 percent coupon rate. The current price/earnings ratio is 11, this P/E is expected to continue if the stock plan is used. If the debt plan is implemented, the P/E ratio is expected to decrease to 10 due to the increased risk. Once the expansion is completed, sales are expected to increase to $3 million while EBIT should continue to be the same percent of sales.

a. Determine the number of shares of stock currently outstanding and Outboard Marine's present EPS.

b. Plot the EBIT-EPS chart when sales are $3 million for the (1) common stock, and (2) debt financing alternatives. *Estimate* the indifference point (without calculating it).

c. Calculate the indifference point, using Equation 18.5. How close was your graphic estimate in (b)?

d. Estimate the total value, V, of Outboard Marine under the two alternative plans using the appropriate price/earnings, P/E, multiples.

e. Based on your analysis, which plan should the firm choose? Why?

18.8. EBIT-EPS CHART, INDIFFERENCE POINT, AND TOTAL VALUE: COMMON STOCK, PREFERRED STOCK, AND DEBT. Standard International currently has 150,000 shares of common stock outstanding, with a market price of $50 per share. It also has $2 million in 9 percent coupon-rate bonds outstanding. Standard is considering a $3 million expansion program that it will finance with (1) all common stock that can be sold to net the firm $40 per share; (2) preferred stock sold at par, with an 8 percent dividend rate; (3) debentures sold at par, with a 9 percent coupon rate; or (4) a combination of half common stock at $40 per share and half 9 percent coupon-rate debentures (sold at par). The firm is in the 40 percent marginal tax bracket and estimates with a probability of .5 that EBIT will be $1 million, and with a probability of .5 that EBIT will be $2 million.

   a. Calculate the EPS for each level of EBIT for all four plans. Also, calculate the mean or expected EPS for each financing plan.

   b. Draw an EBIT-EPS chart showing the four possible financing plans. From the chart, *estimate* the indifference points between all common stock and each of the other three plans.

   c. Calculate the exact indifference points, using Equation 18.5. Why is the indifference point between the common stock and debt financing plans the same as the indifference point between the common stock plan and the combination common stock and debt financing plan?

   d. The cost of equity capital, k_s, is 10 percent if common stock financing is employed, 10.5 percent if the combination plan is employed, and 11 percent if either the preferred stock or debt financing plans are employed. What is the total value of Standard International under each of the four alternative plans, using the mean or expected EPS calculated in (a)? Assume all earnings are paid out as dividends, so that $P_0 = EPS/k_s$.

   e. Which of the plans should Standard International select? Why?

18.9 INDIFFERENCE POINT AND TIMES BURDEN COVERED. The Buffalo Paper Company, which is in the 40 percent marginal tax bracket, needs to expand its assets by $3 million. The financing for this expansion will come from one of three sources: (1) common stock issued at $30 per share (100,000 shares); (2) preferred stock with a 10 percent dividend rate; (3) long-term debt with a 13 percent coupon rate. Interest on the existing long-term debt is $100,000, and there are 500,000 shares of common stock currently outstanding. The financial managers of Buffalo Paper estimate that the following states of the economy and EBIT are likely after the expansion:

State of the Economy	EBIT
Weak	$2,100,000
Normal	4,100,000
Strong	6,100,000

a. Calculate the exact indifference points for the common stock and preferred stock plans, and the common stock and debt plans, using Equation 18.5. Why is there no indifference point between the preferred stock and debt plans?

b. The existing debt for Buffalo Paper has a sinking fund requirement of $150,000 per year. The new debt will also have a $150,000 per year sinking fund requirement. Using the times burden covered formula (Equation 18.6), calculate the coverage in the three states of the economy for all three financing plans. Which plan provides the best coverage? Why?

SELECTED REFERENCES

Agmon, T., A. R. Ofer, and A. Tamir. "Variable Rate Debt Instruments and Corporate Debt Policy." *Journal of Finance* 36 (March 1981), pp. 113–125.

Aivazian, Varouj A., and Jeffrey L. Callen. "Corporate Leverage and Growth: The Game-Theoretic Issues." *Journal of Financial Economics* 8 (December 1980), pp. 379–399.

Ang, James S., Jess H. Chua, and John J. McConnell. "The Administrative Costs of Corporate Bankruptcy: A Note." *Journal of Finance* 37 (March 1982), pp. 219–226.

Arditti, Fred D., and John M. Pinkerton. "The Valuation and Cost of Capital of the Levered Firm with Growth Opportunities." *Journal of Finance* 33 (March 1978), pp. 65–73.

Carleton, Willard T., Charles L. Dick, Jr., and David H. Downes. "Financial Policy Models: Theory and Practice." *Journal of Financial and Quantitative Analysis* 8 (December 1973), pp. 691–709.

Castanios, Richard. "Bankruptcy Risk and Optimal Capital Structure." *Journal of Finance* 38 (December 1983), pp. 1617–1635.

Collins, J. Markham, and William S. Sekely. "The Relationship of Headquarters Country and Industry Classification to Financial Structure." *Financial Management* 12 (autumn 1983), pp. 45–51.

Crum, Roy L., Darwin D. Klingman, and Lee A. Tavis. "Implementation of Large-Scale Financial Planning Models: Solution Efficient Transformations." *Journal of Financial and Quantitative Analysis* 14 (March 1979), pp. 137–152.

DeAngelo, Harry, and Ronald W. Masulis. "Optimal Capital Structure Under Corporate and Personal Taxation." *Journal of Financial Economics* 8 (March 1980), pp. 3–29.

Donaldson, Gordon. "New Framework for Corporate Debt Policy." *Harvard Business Review* 40 (March–April 1962), pp. 117–131.

————, "Strategy for Financial Emergencies," *Harvard Business Review* 47 (November–December 1969), pp. 67–79.

Eiteman, David K., and Arthur I. Stonehill. *Multinational Business Finance*, 3d ed. Reading, Mass.: Addison-Wesley, 1982.

Ferri, Michael G., and Wesley H. Jones. "Determinants of Financial Structure: A New Methodological Approach." *Journal of Finance* 34 (June 1979), pp. 631–644.

Francis, Jack Clark, and Dexter R. Rowell. "A Simultaneous Equation Model of the Firm for Financial Analysis and Planning." *Financial Management* 7 (spring 1978), pp. 29–44.

Franks, J. R., and J. J. Pringle. "Debt Financing, Corporate Financial Intermediaries and Firm Valuation." *Journal of Finance* 37 (June 1982), pp. 751–761.

Gordon, Myron, and Clarence C. Y. Kwan. "Debt Maturity, Default Risk, and Capital Structure." *Journal of Banking and Finance* 3 (December 1979), pp. 313–329.

Gritta, Richard D. "The Effect of Financial Leverage on Air Carrier Earnings: A Break-Even Analysis." *Financial Management* 8 (summer 1979), pp. 53–60.

Harris, John M., Jr., Rodney L. Roenfeldt, and Philip L. Cooley. "Evidence of Financial Leverage Clienteles." *Journal of Finance* 38 (September 1983), pp. 1125–1132.

Haugen, Robert A., and Dean W. Wichern. "The Intricate Relationship Between Financial Leverage and the Stability of Stock Prices." *Journal of Finance* 30 (December 1975), pp. 1283–1292.

Hite, Gailen L. "Leverage, Output Effects, and the M-M Theorems." *Journal of Financial Economics* 4 (March 1977), pp. 177–202.

Kim, E. Han, Wilbur G. Lewellen, and John J. McConnell. "Financial Leverage Clienteles: Theory and Evidence." *Journal of Financial Economics* 7 (March 1979), pp. 83–109.

Kornbluth, Jonathan S. H., and Joseph D. Vinso. "Capital Structure and the Financing of the Multinational Corporation: A Fractional Multiobjective Approach." *Journal of Financial and Quantitative Analysis* 17 (June 1982), pp. 147–178.

Marsh, Paul. "The Choice Between Equity and Debt: An Empirical Study." *Journal of Finance* 37 (March 1982), pp. 121–144.

Masulis, Ronald W. "The Effects of Capital Structure Change on Security Prices: A Study of Exchange Offers." *Journal of Financial Economics* 8 (June 1980), pp. 139–178.

————. "The Impact of Capital Structure Change on Firm Value: Some Estimates." *Journal of Finance* 38 (March 1983), pp. 107–126.

Merton, Robert C. "On the Pricing of Contingent Claims and the Modigliani-Miller Theorem." *Journal of Financial Economics* 5 (November 1977), pp. 241–249.

Modigliani, Franco, and Merton H. Miller. "The Cost of Capital, Corporation Finance and the Theory of Investment." *American Economic Review* 48 (June 1958), pp. 261–297.

————, and ————. "Corporate Income Taxes and the Cost of Capital: A Correction." *American Economic Review* 53 (June 1963), pp. 433–443.

Myers, Stewart C. "Determinants of Corporate Borrowing." *Journal of Financial Economics* 5 (November 1977), pp. 147–176.

———— (ed.). *Modern Developments in Financial Management*. New York: Preager, 1976.

————, and Gerald A. Pogue. "A Programming Approach to Corporate Financial Management." *Journal of Finance* 29 (May 1974), pp. 579–599.

Peterson, Pamela P., and Gary A. Benesh. "A Reexamination of the Empirical

Relationship Between Investment and Financing Decisions." *Journal of Financial and Quantitative Analysis* 18 (December 1983), pp. 439–453.

Phillips, Paul D., John C. Groth, and R. Malcolm Richards. "Financing the Alaskan Project: The Experience at Sohio." *Financial Management* 8 (autumn 1979), pp. 7–16.

Pinches, George E., and Kent A. Mingo. "A Multivariate Analysis of Industrial Bond Ratings." *Journal of Finance* 28 (March 1973), pp. 1–18.

———, J. Clay Singleton, and Ali Jahankhani. "Fixed Coverage as a Determinant of Electric Utility Bond Ratings." *Financial Management* 7 (summer 1978), pp. 45–55.

Reinhardt, U. E. "Break-Even Analysis for Lockheed's Tri Star: An Application of Financial Theory." *Journal of Finance* 28 (September 1973), pp. 821–838.

Ross, Stephen A. "The Determination of Financial Structure: The Incentive-Signalling Approach." *Bell Journal of Economics* 8 (spring 1977), pp. 23–40.

Schwindiman, Carl J., and George E. Pinches. "An Analysis of Alternative Measures of Investment Risk." *Journal of Finance* 30 (March 1975), pp. 193–200.

Scott, David F., Jr., and Dana J. Johnson. "Financing Policies and Practices in Large Corporations." *Financial Management* 11 (summer 1982), pp. 51–59.

Scott, James H. "A Theory of Optimal Capital Structure." *Bell Journal of Economics* 7 (spring 1976), pp. 33–54.

Seitz, Neil. "Shareholder Goals, Firm Goals and Firm Financing Decisions." *Financial Management* 11 (autumn 1982), pp. 20–26.

Shalit, Sol S. "On the Mathematics of Financial Leverage." *Financial Management* 4 (spring 1975), pp. 57–66.

Solomon, Ezra. *The Theory of Financial Management.* New York: Columbia University Press, 1963.

Stanley, Marjorie T. "Capital Structure and Cost of Capital for the Multinational Firm." *Journal of International Business Studies* 12 (spring–summer 1981), pp. 103–120.

Stonehill, Arthur, Theo Beekhuisen, Richard Wright, Lee Rimmers, Norman Toy, Antonio Parés, Alan Shapiro, Douglas Egan, and Thomas Bates. "Financial Goals and Debt Ratio Determinants: A Survey of Practice in Five Countries." *Financial Management* 4 (autumn 1975), pp. 27–41.

Taggart, Robert A., Jr. "A Model of Corporate Financing Decisions." *Journal of Finance* 32 (December 1977), pp. 1467–1484.

———. "Taxes and Corporate Capital Structure in an Incomplete Market." *Journal of Finance* 35 (June 1980), pp. 645–659.

Turnbull, Stuart M. "Debt Capacity." *Journal of Finance* 34 (September 1979), pp. 931–940.

Appendix 18A

Capital Structure Theory

In the chapter we briefly discussed the Modigliani-Miller proposition that in the absence of taxes, the firm's marginal cost of capital and its overall value are independent of its capital structure. However, once taxes, bankruptcy costs, agency costs, and other market imperfections were introduced, we concluded that the firm's cost of capital and total value are, in fact, related to the capital structure employed. This appendix reviews the major theoretical developments surrounding the Modigliani-Miller position.

The Net Income (NI) and Net Operating Income (NOI) Approaches

Assumptions and Definitions

A capital market equilibrium approach is assumed such that:

1. Two types of capital are employed, long-term debt and common stock.
2. The firm's total assets are fixed, but its capital structure can be changed immediately by selling debt to repurchase common stock, or vice versa.
3. The net operating income (NOI or EBIT) is not expected to grow.[1]
4. All earnings of the firm are paid out in the form of cash dividends.
5. There is no corporate income tax.
6. The firm is expected to continue indefinitely.

In addition to these assumptions, the following symbols are employed:

---

[1] The same basic conclusions arrived at in this appendix can be reached in the growth situation. See Franco Modigliani and Merton H. Miller, "The Cost of Capital, Corporation Finance and the Theory of Investment: Reply," *American Economic Review* 49 (September 1959), pp. 655–669; Merton H. Miller and Franco Modigliani, "Dividend Policy, Growth, and the Valuation of Shares," *Journal of Business* 34 (October 1961), pp. 411–433; and Miller and Modigliani, "Some Estimates of the Cost of Capital to the Electric Utility Industry, 1954–57," *American Economic Review* 56 (June 1966), pp. 333–391.

B = total market value of the debt
S = total market value of the stock (equity)
V = total market value of the firm $= B + S$
NOI = net operating income = earnings before interest and taxes (EBIT)
I = total dollars of annual interest
k_b = cost of debt capital before taxes (risk-free cost of debt)
k_s = cost of equity capital
k = marginal cost of capital

Given these assumptions, the firm's cost of debt is:

$$k_b = \frac{I}{B} \qquad (18A.1)$$

while its cost of equity is:

$$k_s = \frac{NOI - I}{S} \qquad (18A.2)$$

The cost of capital to the firm is equal to the weighted average of the debt and equity costs where:

$$k = k_b \left(\frac{B}{V}\right) + k_s \left(\frac{S}{V}\right) \qquad (18A.3)$$

The total value of the firm is equal to the combined values of debt and equity, or:

$$V = B + S = \frac{I}{k_b} + \frac{NOI - I}{k_s} \qquad (18A.4)$$

These definitions and equations are not controversial—they are used in all discussions of capital structure theory. Our concern is with what happens to k_b, k_s, and k when the firm's capital structure (as denoted by the ratio of B/V) changes. Two extreme positions, the net income and net operating income approaches, have been identified to reflect the impact of changes in the firm's capital structure on the valuation of its earnings, and hence its marginal cost of capital and total value.[2]

---

[2]David Durand, "Cost of Debt and Equity Funds for Business: Trends and Problems of Measurement," *Conference on Research on Business Finance* (New York: National Bureau of Economic Research, 1952), pp. 215–247; reprinted in *The Theory of Business Finance*, 2d ed., eds. Stephen H. Archer and Charles A. D'Ambrosio (New York: Macmillan, 1976), pp. 420–452.

The Net Income
(NI) Approach

The fundamental difference between the two approaches relates to what happens to the cost of equity and consequently to the market value of the stock and the total value of the firm as the firm employs more debt in its capital structure. Under the NI approach, the costs of both debt and equity capital are constant regardless of the amount of debt employed. Since both the cost of debt and equity are assumed constant, and because debt is cheaper than equity, as the firm adds more "cheap" debt to its capital structure, its cost of capital declines. At the same time that k declines, the overall value of the firm increases.

To illustrate the NI approach, assume a firm has NOI of $1,200, k_b is 8 percent, and k_s is 12 percent. If the firm has $2,250 of debt, the value of the common stock is:

$$S = \frac{NOI - I}{k_s} = \frac{\$1,200 - \$180}{.12} = \frac{\$1,020}{.12} = \$8,500$$

Since the debt is valued at $2,250, the total value of the firm is:

$$V = B + S = \$2,250 + \$8,500 = \$10,750$$

while its cost of capital is:

$$k = k_b \left(\frac{B}{V}\right) + k_s \left(\frac{S}{V}\right)$$

$$= 8\% \left(\frac{\$\ 2,250}{\$10,750}\right) + 12\% \left(\frac{\$\ 8,500}{\$10,750}\right) = 11.163\% \simeq 11.16\%$$

Alternatively, the cost of capital can be found by:

$$k = \frac{NOI}{V} = \frac{\$\ 1,200}{\$10,750} = 11.163\% \simeq 11.16\% \qquad (18A.5)$$

Consider what happens if the firm increases its debt from $2,250 to $6,000 and uses the proceeds to repurchase common stock. The new value of common equity is:

$$S = \frac{\$1,200 - \$480}{.12} = \frac{\$720}{.12} = \$6,000$$

The total value of the firm is:

$$V = \$6,000 + \$6,000 = \$12,000$$

while the firm's cost of capital is:

$$k = 8\% \left(\frac{\$\ 6{,}000}{\$12{,}000}\right) + 12\% \left(\frac{\$\ 6{,}000}{\$12{,}000}\right) = 10\%$$

or, alternatively,

$$k = \frac{\$\ 1{,}200}{\$12{,}000} = 10\%$$

Under the NI approach, the firm is able to lower its cost of capital as the amount of financial leverage increases. Table 18A.1 indicates the values of V and k for various other capital structure proportions.

Graphically, the effects on the firm's cost of capital and its total market value are shown in Figure 18A.1. If k_b and k_s are constant, as is assumed in the NI approach, then as the proportion of cheaper debt funds in the capital structure increases, the cost of capital decreases. Thus, under the NI approach the firm can lower its cost of capital and raise its total market value through the addition of debt capital. Critical to this approach is the implied assumption that the firm does not become more risky in the eyes of creditors and investors as more debt is added to its capital structure.

The Net Operating Income (NOI) Approach   The NOI approach differs from the NI approach in that the total value of the firm is found by capitalizing the firm's NOI at an appropriate capitalization rate, which is the firm's cost of capital. Consider the example used before, where the cost of debt, k_b, is 8 percent and NOI is $1,200; but now the cost of capital is assumed to be constant at 10 percent. The total value of the firm is found by capitalizing NOI by k, so that:

$$V = \frac{NOI}{k} = \frac{\$1{,}200}{.10} = \$12{,}000$$

TABLE 18A.1
Net Income Approach: Effect of Capital Structure on Total Market Value and Cost of Capital

Variable	Financial Leverage (B/V)				
	0%	20.93%	50.00%	81.82%	100.00%
Value of debt, B	$ 0	$ 2,250	$ 6,000	$11,250	$15,000
Value of equity, S	10,000	8,500	6,000	2,500	0
Total value, V	$10,000	$10,750	$12,000	$13,750	$15,000
Cost of debt, k_b	8.00%	8.00%	8.00%	8.00%	8.00%
Cost of equity, k_s	12.00	12.00	12.00	12.00	12.00
Cost of capital, k	12.00	11.16	10.00	8.73	8.00

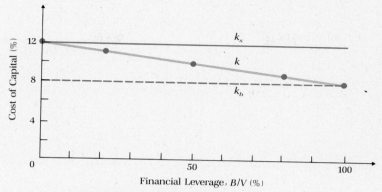

(a) Cost of Capital Versus Financial Leverage

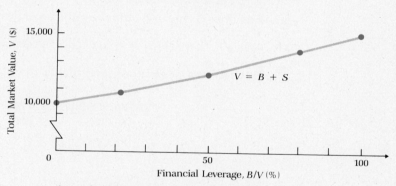

(b) Total Market Value Versus Financial Leverage

Figure 18A.1   Cost of Capital and Total Market Value Under the Net Income Approach.

With \$2,250 in debt, the equity value is a residual that is determined by subtracting the debt from the total value of the firm:

$$S = V - B = \$12,000 - \$2,250 = \$9,750$$

The implied cost of equity is then determined by:

$$k_s = \frac{NOI - I}{S} = \frac{\$1,200 - \$180}{\$9,750} = \frac{\$1,020}{\$9,750} = 10.462\% \simeq 10.46\%$$

The firm's cost of capital, which was initially assumed to be 10 percent, is just the weighted average of the costs of debt and equity:

$$k = 8\% \left(\frac{\$\ 2,250}{\$12,000}\right) + 10.46\% \left(\frac{\$\ 9,750}{\$12,000}\right) = 10\%$$

TABLE 18A.2
Net Operating Income Approach: Effect of Capital Structure on Total
Market Value and Cost of Equity

Variable	Financial Leverage (B/V)				
	0%	18.75%	50.00%	90.00%	99.00%
Value of debt, B	$ 0	$ 2,250	$ 6,000	$10,800	$11,880
Value of equity, S	12,000	9,750	6,000	1,200	120
Total value, V	$12,000	$12,000	$12,000	$12,000	$12,000
Cost of debt, k_b	8.00%	8.00%	8.00%	8.00%	8.00%
Cost of equity, k_s	10.00	10.46	12.00	28.00	208.00
Cost of capital, k	10.00	10.00	10.00	10.00	10.00

If the firm increases its debt to $6,000 and uses the proceeds to repurchase common stock, the overall value of the firm remains constant, as does its cost of capital, so the stock value is:

$$S = V - B = \$12{,}000 - \$6{,}000 = \$6{,}000$$

The implied cost of equity is now higher than before, where:

$$k_s = \frac{\$1{,}200 - \$480}{\$6{,}000} = \frac{\$\ 720}{\$6{,}000} = 12\%$$

while the cost of capital is still 10 percent:

$$k = 8\% \left(\frac{\$\ 6{,}000}{\$12{,}000}\right) + 12\% \left(\frac{\$\ 6{,}000}{\$12{,}000}\right) = 10\%$$

Table 18A.2 indicates the values of V, k_s, and k for various other capital structure proportions.

Under the NOI approach, the capital structure selected is a "mere detail" since the value of the firm is independent of the firm's capital structure. If the firm increases its use of financial leverage by employing more debt, this is directly offset by an increase in the cost of equity capital. This relationship, as presented in Figure 18A.2, indicates that as more and more debt is added to the firm's capital structure, the cost of equity capital rapidly rises.[3] According to the NOI approach, the cost of debt has two parts: the explicit cost, which is represented by the interest rate, and an implicit or hidden cost, which results from the increased cost of equity attributable to increases in the degree of financial leverage. At extreme degrees of financial leverage, this hidden cost becomes very

---

[3]In measuring financial leverage, either the debt-to-total value, B/V, or the debt-to-equity, B/S, ratios may be employed. Under the NOI approach, the cost of equity is an exponential function of the firm's B/V ratio, but a linear function of the firm's B/S ratio.

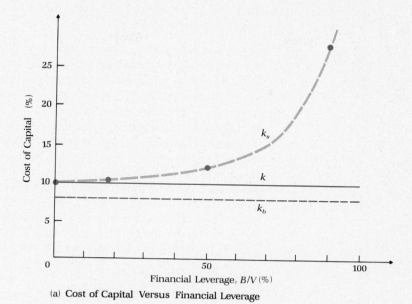

(a) Cost of Capital Versus Financial Leverage

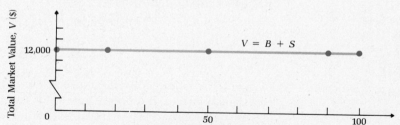

(b) Total Market Value Versus Financial Leverage

Figure 18A.2   Cost of Capital and Total Market Value Under the Net Operating Income Approach.

high; hence, the firm's cost of capital and its total market value are not influenced by the use of additional "cheap" debt funds.

The Modigliani-Miller Position

The net income and net operating income approaches represent extreme cases that were purely definitional in nature until the work of Modigliani and Miller (MM).[4] Their work offered substantial support for the position and conclusions of the NOI approach.

---

[4]Franco Modigliani and Merton H. Miller, "The Cost of Capital, Corporation Finance and the Theory of Investment," *American Economic Review* 48 (June 1958), pp. 261–297.

Assumption and Propositions

The theoretical and behavioral justification for the MM approach rests on the following assumptions:

1. *Perfect capital markets.* Information is costless and readily available to all investors; no transaction costs or government restrictions interfere with capital market transactions; and all securities are infinitely divisible. In addition, both firms and individuals can borrow or lend at the same rate, R_F.
2. *Homogeneous expectations.* All present and prospective investors have identical estimates of the expected value of the probability distribution for each firm's future NOI.
3. *Homogeneous or "equivalent" return classes of firms.* Firms can be classified based on their degree of business risk. Since all firms within a class are equally risky, their expected future earnings are capitalized at the same rate. (This assumption is later relaxed.)
4. *No taxes.* There are no taxes on either corporations or individuals. (This assumption is later relaxed.)

Modigliani and Miller advanced three propositions:

Proposition I.

The total market value, V, of any firm is independent of its capital structure and is determined by capitalizing its expected return $(NOI - I)$ at a rate appropriate for its risk class, k:

$$V = \frac{NOI - I}{k}$$

Proposition II.

The expected cost of equity for a levered stream, k_{sL}, is equal to the capitalization rate of a pure (unlevered) equity stream in the class, k_{sU}, plus a premium for financial risk equal to the difference between k_{sU} and the cost of debt, k_b, times the ratio of debt to equity, B/S:[5]

k_{sL} = return on unlevered equity stream + financial risk premium

$$k_{sL} = k_{sU} + (k_{sU} - k_b) \, B/S \qquad \text{(18A.6)}$$

Proposition III.

The cutoff rate for investment purposes is completely independent of the type of security used to finance the investment.

---

[5]Notice that the MM Proposition II presents a linear relationship between the cost of equity and the firm's financial leverage, as measured by the B/S ratio. As mentioned in note 3, financial leverage can be measured by either the B/V or B/S ratios. We could have calculated the cost of equity under the NOI approach with Equation 18A.6. Thus when debt was $2,250:

$$k_{sL} = k_{sU} + (k_{sU} - k_b) \frac{B}{S}$$

$$k_{sL} = 10\% + (10\% - 8\%) \frac{\$2,250}{\$9,750} = 10.462\% \simeq 10.46\%$$

which is exactly the same result calculated using the relationship, $k_s = (NOI - I)/S$.

Taken together, the MM propositions imply that although debt is less expensive than equity, including more debt in a firm's capital structure does not benefit the firm, since the cost of equity then rises, offsetting any potential gain. Also, the analysis provides economic justification for separating the investment and financing decisions of the firm. The MM analysis follows the NOI approach and indicates that the value of the firm is completely independent of its capital structure. The important difference between the NOI and MM approaches is that MM provided strong theoretical and behavioral support for the absence of an optimal capital structure.

Arbitrage and the MM Propositions

MM argue the total risk of the firm is not altered by changes in its capital structure; hence, the total value of the firm is the same regardless of financial leverage. The support for this hypothesis is the arbitrage process. The term *arbitrage*, as used by MM, refers to the simultaneous buy and sell process investors would enter into if they saw two identical firms selling at different prices because of differences in their capital structures.[6] MM argue that the value of these two firms has to be the same; otherwise investors would profit by selling the shares of the overvalued firm and buying those of the undervalued one.

The essence of their argument is that investors substitute personal leverage for corporate leverage. Consider two firms in the same risk class, one of which is levered (L) and the other unlevered (U). The two firms are identical in all respects except for their capital structures. Thus, *NOI* is $1,200, k_b is 8 percent, and the unlevered firm has an all-equity capital structure, whereas the levered firm has $6,000 in debt outstanding. Initially, let us assume that the NI approach is valid and that the cost of equity, k_s, is 10 percent. Under these conditions, the values of the two firms are:

Unlevered (U) firm:

$$\text{Value of U's stock} = S_U = \frac{NOI - I}{k_s} = \frac{\$1,200 - 0}{.10} = \$12,000$$

$$\text{Value of firm U} = V_U = B_U + S_U = 0 + \$12,000 = \$12,000$$

$$\text{U's cost of capital} = k = \frac{NOI}{V_U} = \frac{\$1,200}{\$12,000} = 10\%$$

Levered (L) firm:

$$\text{Value of L's stock} = S_L = \frac{NOI - I}{k_s} = \frac{\$1,200 - \$480}{.10} = \$7,200$$

$$\text{Value of firm L} = V_L = B_L + S_L = \$6,000 + \$7,200 = \$13,200$$

$$\text{L's cost of capital} = k = \frac{NOI}{V_L} = \frac{\$1,200}{\$13,200} = 9.09\%$$

---

[6]See Franco Modigliani and Merton H. Miller, "Reply to Heins and Sprenkle," *American Economic Review* 59 (September 1969), pp. 592–595; and Modigliani and Miller, "The Cost of Capital, Corporation Finance and the Theory of Investment: Reply."

The total market value of firm L, $13,200, is greater than that of firm U, which is $12,000. MM maintain this situation will not continue, since rational investors can increase their return without increasing their risk by engaging in an arbitrage process.

To illustrate this process, suppose you owned 15 percent of L's stock, so that your investment was $1,080 (15% × $7,200). By substituting personal leverage for corporate leverage, you can increase your return as follows:

Step 1.   Sell your stock in L for $1,080.

Step 2.   Borrow an amount equal to your previous proportional participation in the leverage of firm L. Thus, you borrow an amount equal to $900 (15% × $6,000) at 8 percent interest.

Step 3.   Buy 15 percent of the shares of firm U for $1,800 (15% × $12,000). Note you have money left over since the sum of the funds from steps 1 and 2 is greater than your investment in step 3 by $180 ($1,080 + $900 − $1,800).

Now let us consider what happened to your income:

Old Income (L)	New Income (U)

Stock 10% × $1,080 = $108	Stock 10% × $1,800 = $180
	Less: 8% × $900 on
	        loan 72
	                    $108

Since firm L paid all its earnings out in the form of dividends, your income prior to the arbitrage process was $108. After the arbitrage process your return is still $108, but you have an additional $180 still available for investment; being a rational investor, you will therefore prefer to invest in firm U. In essence, your return has increased while your risk, according to MM, is the same.

As rational investors engage in this process, the effect will be to increase the demand for firm U's shares and reduce the demand for L's shares. These actions will drive the price of firm U's stock up and lower its k_s, while driving the price of L's stock down and raising its k_s. The arbitrage process will continue until there are no further opportunities for investors to profit; at that point, the total values of the two firms and their costs of capital will be the same. Hence, under the assumptions specified and in the absence of taxes, MM present a strong theoretical argument with behavioral justifications which indicates that the value of the firm and its cost of capital are independent of its capital structure.

Given MM's assumptions and the existence of perfect capital markets, their conclusions follow logically. Therefore, to dispute the MM propositions we must examine the assumptions to determine if there are systematic market imperfections that would impede the equilibrium process. After investigating some of the basic assumptions, we introduce corporate taxes. Then we discuss bankruptcy costs, agency costs, personal taxes, and end with a brief review of relevant empirical testing.

Relaxing Some of the Perfect Market Assumptions

Existence of Homogeneous Risk Classes. MM originally introduced the idea of risk classes because at the time of their original study no market equilibrium pricing model (such as the CAPM) existed. However, with the capital asset pricing model nondiversifiable (or beta) risk, β, is the only relevant measure of risk; thus, the cost of equity capital for a levered firm, k_{sL}, is:

$$k_{sL} = k_{sU} + (k_{sU} - k_b) \text{ B/S}$$

which is exactly the same relationship specified by MM as proposition II.[7] Once the CAPM is introduced, the existence of homogeneous risk classes as originally specified by MM is unnecessary.[8]

Substitution of Personal for Corporate Leverage. Implied in the MM analysis is the condition that personal and corporate leverage are perfect substitutes. But because of the existence of limited liability for corporations, increased perceived personal risk from margin calls, and greater inconvenience, investors may not view personal leverage as a perfect substitute for corporate leverage. The arbitrage, however, need not occur in terms of investors actually borrowing at the market rate or using margin; all that is required is that there be sufficient investors who have the ability to adjust their holdings of bonds.[9] In addition, institutions as well as individuals are assumed to engage in this process. So although personal and corporate leverage may not be perfect substitutes, it

---

[7]See Robert S. Hamada, "Portfolio Analysis, Market Equilibrium and Corporation Finance," *Journal of Finance* 24 (March 1969), pp. 13–31; Robert A. Haugen and James L. Pappas, "Equilibrium in the Pricing of Corporate Assets, Risk-Bearing Debt Instruments and the Question of Optimal Capital Structure," *Journal of Financial and Quantitative Analysis* 6 (June 1971), pp. 943–953; and Yutaka Imai and Mark E. Rubinstein, "Comment," and Haugen and Pappas, "Reply," *Journal of Financial and Quantitative Analysis* 7 (September 1971), pp. 2001–2003; 2005–2008.

[8]The MM propositions can be illustrated in the context of the CAPM. See Mark E. Rubinstein, "A Mean-Variance Synthesis of Corporate Financial Theory," *Journal of Finance* 28 (March 1973), pp. 167–181; and Jack Becker, "General Proof of Modigliani-Miller Propositions I and II Using Parameter-Preference Theory," *Journal of Financial and Quantitative Analysis* 13 (March 1978), pp. 65–69.

[9]See David Durand, "The Cost of Capital, Corporation Finance and the Theory of Investment: Comment," *American Economic Review* 49 (September 1959), pp. 639–655; Joseph E. Stiglitz, "A Re-Examination of the Modigliani-Miller Theorem," *American Economic Review* 69 (December 1969), pp. 784–793; and Peter R. Lloyd-Davies, "Optimal Financial Policy in Imperfect Markets," *Journal of Financial and Quantitative Analysis* 10 (September 1975), pp. 457–481.

appears that this difference is not enough, by itself, to invalidate the MM proposition.

Different Costs of Borrowing.   Also implied in the MM analysis is the condition that the cost of borrowing is the same for individuals and corporations. Due to market imperfections however, the effective cost of borrowing may be higher for individual investors than for corporations. But, as just mentioned, the arbitrage process may be carried out simply by investors varying their holdings of bonds.[10] Also, since institutional investors can often borrow on a basis very similar to the corporate rate, the impact of this imperfection does not appear to seriously weaken the MM propositions.

Institutional Restrictions.   The arbitrage process depends on a sufficient number of personal or institutional investors being capable of engaging in the process, or at least being able to restructure their portfolios through the purchase or sale of bonds. Because of restrictions on margin transactions, short sales, and limitations imposed by regulatory authorities on the bonds or stocks acceptable for investment, institutional investors appear to be able only partially to participate in the arbitrage process envisioned by MM.[11] Although the total impact of these restrictions is not clear, it appears they may have some effect on the MM arbitrage process.

The combined impact of these four items suggests that the arbitrage process may not operate as efficiently as MM envisioned. However, it is not clear that the four (separately or jointly) are sufficient to invalidate the MM propositions.

The MM
Propositions
with Corporate
Taxes

Once corporate taxes are introduced, MM's position is that the value of the firm can increase (and k decrease) as new debt is added to its capital structure.[12] In essence, their position is very similar to the NI approach, since firms can increase their total value and reduce their marginal cost of capital by increasing the use of debt.

To examine this, consider the cash flow streams that exist for

---

[10]See Stiglitz, "A Re-Examination of the Modigliani-Miller Theorem; and David P. Baron, "Default Risk, Homemade Leverage, and the Modigliani-Miller Theorem," *American Economic Review* 64 (March 1974), pp. 176–182.

[11]See Durand, "The Cost of Capital, Corporation Finance and the Theory of Investment: Comment"; and David W. Glenn, "Super Premium Security Prices and Optimal Corporate Financing Decisions," *Journal of Finance* 31 (May 1976), pp. 507–524.

[12]Franco Modigliani and Merton H. Miller, "Corporate Income Taxes and the Cost of Capital: A Correction," *American Economic Review* 53 (June 1963), pp. 433–443.

unlevered versus levered firms. For the unlevered firm, the cash flow stream (CF_U) is:

$$CF_U = NOI\,(1 - T) \tag{18A.7}$$

while for the levered firm it is:

$$CF_L = (NOI - k_bB_L)\,(1 - T) + k_bB_L \tag{18A.8}$$

where T is the corporate tax rate. In Equation 18A.8, the first term to the right of the equals sign is the income available to stockholders, and the second term is that available to bondholders; thus, for levered firms, CF_L is the total cash flow available to all investors in the firm.

Since the unlevered firm does not use debt, its total market value is equal to its common stock value. The total value of an unlevered firm is determined by discounting its cash flow after taxes by its cost of equity:

$$V_U = S_U = \frac{NOI\,(1 - T)}{k_{sU}} \tag{18A.9}$$

The situation is more complicated for the levered firm, since part of the firm's cash flow benefits the common stockholders and the rest benefits the bondholders. Rewriting Equation 18A.8 as:

$$CF_L = NOI\,(1 - T) + k_bB_LT \tag{18A.10}$$

the first term on the right of the equals sign is the same cash flow stream that benefits an unlevered firm's stockholders (Equation 18A.7), and the second term represents the tax savings that occur because interest is deductible for tax purposes.

To determine the total market value of the levered firm, both parts of the cash flows given in Equation 18A.10 must be capitalized. Since the first part of the stream is exactly the same as the numerator of Equation 18A.9, it is capitalized at the rate k_{sU}. The second part of the stream is assumed to be risk free and hence should be capitalized at the risk-free cost of debt, k_b. The total value of the levered firm is thus:

$$V_L = \frac{NOI\,(1 - T)}{k_{sU}} + \frac{k_bB_LT}{k_b} = \frac{NOI\,(1 - T)}{k_{sU}} + B_LT \tag{18A.11}$$

However, since the value of an unlevered firm, V_U, is equal to $[NOI\,(1 - T)]/k_{sU}$, Equation 18A.11 can be rewritten as:

$$V_L = V_U + B_LT \tag{18A.12}$$

The value of the levered firm is thus equal to the value of an unlevered firm plus the tax shield provided by the debt, $B_L T$. In the absence of leverage, V_L equals V_U; with corporate taxes, however, it is in the firm's best interest to take advantage of the tax subsidy offered by the government. By increasing its use of debt, a firm can increase its total value and simultaneously reduce its cost of capital.

Rewriting Equation 18A.9, the cost of equity capital for the unlevered firm is thus:

$$k_{sU} = \frac{NOI\ (1 - T)}{S_U} \qquad (18A.13)$$

Obviously, since there is no debt in the unlevered firm's capital structure, its cost of capital is equal to its cost of equity, $k_U = k_{sU}$. For the levered firm, on the other hand, its cost of equity is equal to the after-tax cash flow accruing to the stockholders, divided by the value of the equity:

$$k_{sL} = \frac{(NOI - I)\ (1 - T)}{S_L} \qquad (18A.14)$$

Likewise, the cost of capital for the levered firm, considering income taxes, is a weighted average of its component costs:

$$k_L = k_b \left(\frac{B_L}{V_L}\right) (1 - T) + k_{sL} \left(\frac{S_L}{V_L}\right) \qquad (18A.15)$$

An alternative and equivalent expression for the levered firm's cost of capital is:

$$k_L = k_{sU} \left(1 - \frac{B_L}{V_L} T\right) \qquad (18A.16)$$

Thus, using Equation 18A.16, the cost of capital for a levered firm is equal to the cost of equity capital for an unlevered firm, *reduced* by the tax subsidy provided by the government. With corporate taxes considered, MM's approach indicates that the cost of capital declines steadily as more debt is added to the firm's capital structure.

Consider a firm with *NOI* at \$1200, k_b at 8 percent, k_{sU} at 10 percent, and T at 40 percent. The value of the unlevered firm is thus:

$$V_U = \frac{NOI\ (1 - T)}{k_{sU}} = \frac{\$1,200\ (.6)}{.10} = \$7,200$$

If the firm now changes its capital structure and issues \$4,500 of debt, total firm value is equal to the unlevered equity value plus the tax shield:

$$V_L = V_U + B_L T = \$7{,}200 + (\$4{,}500)\,(.4) = \$9{,}000$$

The value of the levered firm's equity is equal to:

$$S_L = V_L - B_L = \$9{,}000 - \$4{,}500 = \$4{,}500$$

If the before-tax cost of debt is still 8 percent, the cost of equity capital for the levered firm is:

$$k_{sL} = \frac{(NOI - I)\,(1 - T)}{S_L} = \frac{(\$1{,}200 - \$360)\,(.6)}{\$4{,}500} = 11.2\%$$

which is higher than the cost of equity capital of 10 percent for the unlevered firm. Finally, the cost of capital for the levered firm, employing Equation 18A.15 or 18A.16, is:

$$
\begin{aligned}
k_L &= k_b\!\left(\frac{B_L}{V_L}\right)(1 - T) + k_{sL}\!\left(\frac{S_L}{V_L}\right) \\
&= 8\%\left(\frac{\$4{,}500}{\$9{,}000}\right)(.6) + 11.2\%\left(\frac{\$4{,}500}{\$9{,}000}\right) \\
&= 2.4\% + 5.6\% = 8\%
\end{aligned}
$$

or

$$k_L = k_{sU}\!\left(1 - \frac{B_L}{V_L}\,T\right) = 10\%\left[1 - \frac{\$4{,}500}{\$9{,}000}(.4)\right] = 8\%$$

These and other market values and costs of capital are shown in Table 18A.3 and plotted in Figure 18A.3. As we have noted, when corporate taxes are introduced, the MM approach indicates the firm's marginal cost of capital decreases and the total value of the firm increases as more debt is added to the capital structure. Carried to its extreme, this implies that firms should finance entirely (or virtually entirely) with debt.

The Importance of Bankruptcy Costs

Once the existence of corporate taxes is recognized, another immediate possibility must be recognized—increased risk and bankruptcy costs. Risk is attached to the tax savings because of the possibility that tax rates may change in the future, or the possibility that at some future date the firm may have no taxable income against which interest payments on the debt may be offset. It is as yet unclear whether the presence of risky debt can, by itself, lead to the existence of an optimal capital structure.[13]

---

[13]See Michael J. Brennan and Eduardo S. Schwartz, "Corporate Income Taxes, Valuation, and the Problem of Optimal Capital Structure," *Journal of Business* 51 (January 1978), pp, 103–114; and Andrew H. Chen and E. Han Kim, "Theories of Corporate Debt Policy: A Synthesis," *Journal of Finance* 34 (May 1979), pp. 371–384.

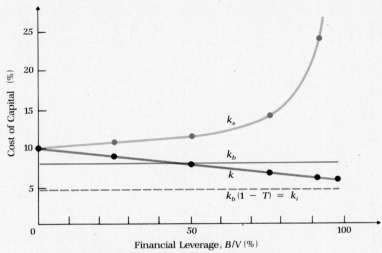

(a) Cost of Capital Versus Financial Leverage

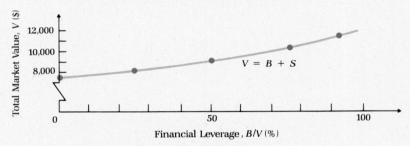

(b) Total Market Value Versus Financial Leverage

Figure 18A.3   Cost of Capital and Total Market Value Under the MM Approach with Corporate Taxes.

TABLE 18A.3
MM Approach with Corporate Taxes: Effect of Capital Structure on Total Market Value, Cost of Equity, and Cost of Capital

	Financial Leverage (B/V)					
Variable	0%	25.00%	50.00%	76.92%	92.11%	97.97%
Value of debt, B	$ 0	$2,000	$4,500	$ 8,000	$10,500	$11,600
Value of equity, S	7,200	6,000	4,500	2,400	900	240
Total value, V	$7,200	$8,000	$9,000	$10,400	$11,400	$11,840
Cost of debt, k_b	8.00%	8.00%	8.00%	8.00%	8.00%	8.00%
Cost of equity, k_s	10.00	10.40	11.20	14.00	24.00	68.00
Cost of capital, k	10.00	9.00	8.00	6.92	6.32	6.08

However, once bankruptcy costs are considered, optimal or target capital structures appear to exist for firms.[14] Bankruptcy costs refer to direct costs such as trustee fees, legal fees, and other costs of reorganization or bankruptcy that are deducted before investors are paid, *plus* indirect costs such as the opportunity cost of funds being tied up during bankruptcy proceedings, lost profits created by decreased sales in anticipation of bankruptcy, disruptions in production during bankruptcy, lost investment opportunities due to their economic lives being longer than the expected life of the firm, and so on.

In the event or anticipation of bankruptcy, security holders as a whole receive less than they would otherwise. Thus, the "dead-weight" losses associated with bankruptcy cause the value of the firm to be less than the discounted present value of the expected cash flows from operations. To the extent that levered firms have a greater probability of bankruptcy, their value will be less than that of unlevered ones. Although the probability of bankruptcy is not a simple linear or exponential function of the firm's financial leverage, our current state of knowledge suggests that: (1) bankruptcy is related somehow to financial leverage; (2) suppliers of capital do pay attention to a firm's degree of financial leverage; and (3) higher-levered firms, other things being equal, are viewed as being more risky than lower-levered firms.

Because the costs per dollar of debt and equity increase as the degree of financial leverage increases, and because the firm recognizes the cost associated with the risk of bankruptcy, it trades off bankruptcy costs against the tax benefits of debt; consequently, there exists an optimal capital structure for the firm. If we let C_l be the average bankruptcy cost per dollar of debt, the total value of the firm, recognizing both the tax advantage associated with debt and bankruptcy costs, can be obtained by modifying Equation 18A.12 so that:[15]

$$V_L = V_U + B_L(T - C_l) \qquad (18A.17)$$

---

[14]See Stewart C. Myers, "Determinants of Corporate Borrowing," *Journal of Financial Economics* 5 (November 1977), pp. 147–176; E. Han Kim, "A Mean-Variance Theory of Optimal Capital Structure and Corporate Debt Capacity," *Journal of Finance* 33 (March 1978), pp. 45–65; Robert A. Haugen and Lemma W. Senbet, "The Insignificance of Bankruptcy Costs to the Theory of Optimal Capital Structure," *Journal of Finance* 33 (May 1978), pp. 383–393; Andrew H. Chen, "Recent Developments in the Cost of Debt Capital," *Journal of Finance* 33 (June 1978), pp. 863–877; and Stuart M. Turnbull, "Debt Capacity," *Journal of Finance* 34 (September 1979); pp. 931–940.

[15]Two difficulties associated with this approach are these: (1) measuring the bankruptcy costs, C_l, per dollar of debt; and (2) the fact that the value of debt, B_L, and the total value, V_L, have to be solved simultaneously. For further discussion on this approach, see Hai Hong and Alfred Rappaport, "Debt Capacity, Optimal Capital Structure, and Capital Budgeting Analysis," *Financial Management* 7 (autumn 1978), pp. 7–11.

TABLE 18A.4

MM Approach with Corporate Taxes and Bankruptcy Costs: Effect on Total Market Value and Cost of Capital

Variable	Financial Leverage (B/V)					
	0%[a]	25.00%	50.00%	76.92%	92.11%	97.97%
Bankruptcy costs per dollar of debt, C_I	0%	10%	15%	25%	30%	35%
Total value, V^b	$7,200	$7,800	$8,325	$8,400	$8,250	$7,780
Cost of capital, k^c	10.00%	9.23%	8.65%	8.57%	8.73%	9.25%

[a]These financial leverage percentages are the same as used in Table 18A.3. At the original debt level of 25 percent, the modified B/V value used in Equation 18A.18 is $2,000/$7,800 = 25.64%. For consistency, the original debt percentages are employed in Tables 18A.4 and 18A.5, and in Figures 18A.4 and 18A.5

[b]Calculated using Equation 18A.17, with bankruptcy costs, C_I, given above, and debt values from Table 18A.3.

[c]Calculated using Equation 18A.18, with debt values from Table 18A.3 and total values as calculated above.

Note: This approach is only approximate, since the use of the debt values from Table 18A.3 is not strictly correct. The debt and equity values should be solved for simultaneously while V_L is being estimated.

Likewise, the cost of capital, including bankruptcy costs, is:

$$k_L = k_{sU} \left[1 - \frac{B_L}{V_L} (T - C_I)\right] \qquad \text{(18A.18)}$$

Table 18A.4 indicates the market value and cost of capital when both tax effects and bankruptcy costs are recognized. The joint effect is illustrated in Figure 18A.4. Thus, the conclusion is that in a world of both corporate taxes and bankruptcy costs, it appears that firms have optimal capital structures, even if all the other tenets of the MM approach hold.

The Importance of Agency Costs

Recently, the importance of agency costs to a firm's optimal capital structure has received attention in the literature.[16] An *agency relationship* is defined as a contract under which one or more principals engage agents to perform some service on their behalf by delegating some decision-making authority to the agent. The costs associated with the agency agreement consist of monitoring expenditures by the principal, bonding expenditures by the agent, and other residual losses that arise because the agent's decisions often are not the decisions that would maximize the wealth of the principal. Given the separation of ownership and control that exists for virtually all corporations, and the use of both external debt and equity, the modern firm is involved in numerous agency relationships. On the one hand, there are monitoring costs associated with the firm's use of equity. If a firm is owned exclusively by a single individual (the owner-manager), he or she will obviously make

---

[16]See Michael C. Jensen and William H. Meckling, "Theory of the Firm: Managerial Behavior, Agency Costs and Ownership Structure," *Journal of Financial Economics* 3 (October 1976), pp. 305–360; and Myers, "Determinants of Corporate Borrowing."

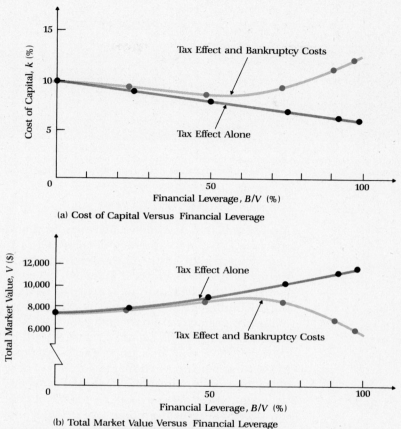

(a) Cost of Capital Versus Financial Leverage

(b) Total Market Value Versus Financial Leverage

Figure 18A.4   Cost of Capital and Total Market Value Under the MM Approach with Corporate Taxes and Bankruptcy Costs.

only those decisions that are wealth-maximizing. However, if some of the ownership rights are sold to new stockholders, obvious conflicts in interest may arise. The new stockholders will have to incur monitoring costs in one form or another to ensure that the co-owner-manager makes decisions that are in the stockholders' best interests. These costs are borne by the firm's stockholders as a reduction in the value of the firm.

Further, there is a problem associated with the issuance of debt. The interests of the owner-manager may lead to investment decisions that are in the stockholders' interests but at the expense of the bondholders' interests. This happens because the set of investments that maximize the firm's total (combined bond and stock) value is not the same as the set of

TABLE 18A.5

MM Approach with Corporate Taxes, Bankruptcy Costs, and Agency Costs: Effect on Total Market Value and Cost of Capital

Variable	Financial Leverage (B/V)					
	0%[a]	25.00%	50.00%	76.92%	92.11%	97.97%
Bankruptcy and agency costs per dollar of debt, C_I	0%	15%	25%	35%	45%	50%
Total value, V[b]	$7,200	$7,700	$7,875	$7,600	$6,675	$6,040
Cost of capital, k[c]	10.00%	9.35%	9.14%	9.47%	10.79%	11.92%

[a]These financial leverage percentages are the same as used in Tables 18A.3 and 18A.4 for consistency in presentation.
[b]Calculated using Equation 18A.17, with bankruptcy and agency costs given above, and debt values from Table 18A.3.
[c]Calculated using Equation 18A.18, with debt values from Table 18A.3, and total values as calculated above.

investments that maximizes share value.[17] Complete protection requires specification of an extremely detailed set of protective covenants and high enforcement costs. All these monitoring costs reduce the value of the firm. Ultimately, however incurred, the costs of monitoring are borne by the stockholders, and they cause the value of the firm to be less than the discounted present value of the expected cash flows from operations.

Agency costs act as an incentive for the firm to balance the amount of debt and equity in its capital structure. With increased agency costs, as the amount of debt in a firm's capital structure increases, there is an incentive for the firm to limit the amount of debt. To illustrate the impact of agency costs, consider Table 18A.5, where C_I now includes both bankruptcy and agency costs per dollar of debt. As Figure 18A.5 shows, the previous tradeoff among taxes, bankruptcy costs, and the cost of capital has to be modified. Agency costs act as another factor increasing the cost of capital and reducing the value of the firm as the degree of financial leverage increases. Thus the optimal capital structure, as shown in Figure 18A.5, occurs at an even lower debt-to-total value ratio for the firm. Agency costs reinforce the conclusion that firms have optimal capital structures.

The Impact of Personal Taxes

The combination of market imperfections, corporate taxes, bankruptcy costs, and agency costs suggest the existence of an optimal capital structure. The presence of taxes on personal income, however, may reduce the advantage associated with debt financing. If the returns to

---

[17]If the capital markets are not perfect, all security holders must protect themselves against capital structure changes that would erode their position. These "me-first" rules ensure that one party cannot gain at the expense of another. See E. Han Kim, John J. McConnell, and Irwin H. Silberman, "Capital Structure Rearrangements and Me-First Rules in an Efficient Capital Market," *Journal of Finance* 32 (June 1977), pp. 789–810; and Eugene F. Fama, "The Effects of a Firm's Investment and Financing Decisions on the Welfare of Its Security Holders," *American Economic Review* 68 (June 1978), pp. 272–284.

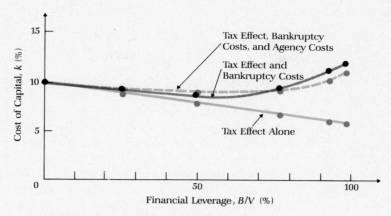

(a) Cost of Capital Versus Financial Leverage

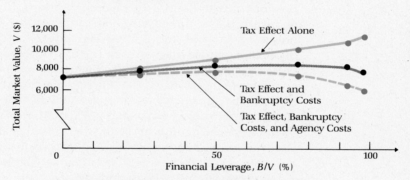

(b) Total Market Value Versus Financial Leverage

Figure 18A.5   Cost of Capital and Total Market Value Under the MM Approach with Taxes, Bankruptcy Costs, and Agency Costs.

investors from purchasing debt instruments are taxed at a higher rate than the returns on common stock, the overall advantage of debt financing *in the economy* (not for a single firm) is reduced. In the MM approach, with corporate taxes (and ignoring bankruptcy and agency costs), the net gain from leverage, G, is the difference between the value of the levered and unlevered firms from Equation 18A.12, or:

$$G = V_L - V_U = B_L T \qquad (18A.19)$$

which shows that the gain from leverage is equal to the debt subsidy, $B_L T$. However, once personal taxes on stocks, T_{pS}, and bonds, T_{pB}, are recognized, the gain from leverage is as follows:[18]

---

[18]Merton H. Miller, "Debt and Taxes," *Journal of Finance* 32 (May 1977), pp. 261–275.

$$G = \left[1 - \frac{(1 - T)\,(1 - T_{pS})}{(1 - T_{pB})}\right]B \tag{18A.20}$$

Note that when the personal tax rates (T_{pS} and T_{pB}) are set equal to zero in Equation 18A.20, the gain from leverage is equal to the earlier gain specified in Equation 18A.19. Likewise, if $T_{pS} = T_{pB}$, Equation 18A.20 is equal to 18A.19, and the gain from leverage is the same as originally specified by MM with corporate taxes. If there are no personal taxes, or if personal taxes on stocks are equal to personal taxes on bonds, we are back to the MM approach with corporate taxes.

What happens, however, if the tax on stocks is less than the tax on bonds?[19] The gain from leverage when personal taxes are considered (Equation 18A.20) is then less than the gain from leverage given by Equation 18A.19. If the personal income tax on stocks is less than the personal tax on bonds, the before-tax return on bonds has to be high enough to offset this disadvantage to investors; otherwise, they would not want to hold the bonds. The impact is that the advantage of deductible interest payments to the firm is, in part, offset by differential personal tax rates; this results in higher interest payments by the firm to compensate investors for the differential personal tax rates.

Taken to its conclusion, the presence of differential personal taxes suggests that there will be an equilibrium level of aggregate corporate debt in the economy; however, there will be no optimal degree of financial leverage for any individual firm. Firms following a no-leverage or low-leverage strategy will find a market among investors in high tax brackets; those opting for a high-leverage strategy will find a natural clientele for their securities among low-bracket or tax-exempt investors. In this sense, it would still be true that the value of the firm, in equilibrium, will be independent of its capital structure.

Empirical Tests

Empirical testing of the MM propositions has encountered some very difficult problems. Among them are the questions of how to: (1) measure expected future growth; (2) deal with a simultaneous change in a firm's capital structure and in its asset structure and possibly risk; and (3) determine a homogeneous group of firms that have the same business risk. Most of the studies have used firms within an "industry" in an attempt to deal with a homogeneous group, but as Boness and Frankfurter[20] indicate, even in an industry like electric utilities, they are not as homogeneous as we would like. So although there has been empirical

---

[19]The effective tax rate on stock appears to be lower than the effective tax rate on bonds because of the $100 dividend exclusion on individual returns and because of the relatively higher capital gains component for common stocks.

[20]A. James Boness and George M. Frankfurter, "Evidence of Non-Homogeneity of Capital Costs Within 'Risk-Classes'", *Journal of Finance* 32 (June 1977), pp. 775–787.

testing of the MM propositions, at this point the evidence is suggestive rather than conclusive.

Modigliani and Miller [21] in their original study found evidence which suggests that the cost of capital is not affected by a firm's capital structure. In a subsequent study,[22] however, they found evidence which suggests that there is a significant value to the tax subsidy firms receive; this indicates there are gains to employing financial leverage. Weston[23] also obtained results consistent with the MM proposition that, with corporate taxes, the cost of capital declines with increased financial leverage. Finally, Hamada[24] found that levered firms had more nondiversifiable or beta risk than unlevered firms. These empirical results suggest the relevance of financial leverage, but fail to provide any indication of where the optimal capital structure exists for individual firms.

PROBLEMS

18A.1.   *NI AND NOI APPROACHES.*   The Ohio Valley Steel Company has net operating income, NOI, of \$5 million and pays a coupon rate of 10 percent on all debt. Assume there are no taxes and all debt is issued at par.

a.   Under the net income, NI, approach, assuming a cost of equity capital, k_s, of 15 percent, compute the value of the firm, V, and the cost of capital [both ways: $k = k_b (B/V) + k_s (S/V)$, and $k = (NOI/V)$] for:

   1.   An all-equity capital structure.
   2.   Debt of \$23 million.
   3.   An all-debt capital structure. (*Hint:* The maximum amount of debt is determined when $k_b \times B = NOI$.)

b.   Under the net operating income, NOI, approach, assuming a cost of capital of 12.5 percent, compute the value of the firm, V, the cost of equity capital, k_s, and the cost of capital based on $k = k_b (B/V) + k_s (S/V)$ for:

   1.   An all-equity capital structure.
   2.   Debt of \$23 million.
   3.   An all-debt capital structure.

c.   Graph k_b, k_s, and k as B/V increases for both the NI approach and the NOI approach.

d.   Why is the capital structure issue important under the NI

---

[21]Modigliani and Miller, "The Cost of Capital, Corporation Finance and the Theory of Investment."

[22]Miller and Modigliani, "Some Estimates of the Cost of Capital to the Electric Utility Industry, 1954–57."

[23]J. Fred Weston, "A Test of Cost of Capital Propositions," *Southern Economic Journal* 30 (October 1963), pp. 105–112.

[24]Robert S. Hamada, "The Effect of the Firm's Capital Structure on the Systematic Risk of Common Stocks," *Journal of Finance* 27 (May 1972), pp. 435–452.

approach and only a "mere detail" under the NOI approach?

18A.2. **MM ARBITRAGE PROCESS.** Gulf Distributors, Inc., and Southeastern Products, Ltd., are in the same risk class and are identical except that Gulf Distributors is levered and Southeastern Products is not. Assume there are no taxes. The values and costs are as follows:

Variable	Gulf Distributors	Southeastern Products
Financial leverage, B/V	25.00%	0%
Market value of debt, B	$ 55,000	$ 0
Market value of equity, S	165,000	200,000
Total value, V,	$220,000	$200,000
Cost of debt, k_b	9.00%	0%
Cost of equity, k_s	11.545	12.00
Cost of capital, k	10.909	12.00

a. An investor owns 20 percent ($33,000) of the common stock of Gulf Distributors. Show the process employed and the amount by which he or she would (via arbitrage) reduce total personal investment while maintaining the same income.
b. According to MM, when will this process terminate?
c. Ignoring taxes, bankruptcy costs, and agency costs, what are some possible reasons why this process may not work as efficiently as MM envision? Do you believe this inefficiency is enough, by itself, to invalidate the MM arguments? Why or why not?

18A.3. **MM PROPOSITION WITH CORPORATE TAXES.** Company U is an unlevered firm with net operating income, NOI, of $2 million, a cost of equity capital of 12.5 percent, and a corporate tax rate of 40 percent.
a. What is the after-tax cash flow, CF_U, and total value, V_U, for the unlevered firm?
b. Company U decides to change its capital structure to become a levered firm, L, by issuing debt and buying back its common stock. The before-tax cost of debt, k_b, is 10 percent. Determine the total market value, V_L, value of the stock, S_L, cost of equity capital, k_{sL}, and cost of capital, using both $k_L = k_b (B_L/V_L) (1 - T) + k_{sL} (S_L/V_L)$, and $k_L = k_{sU} [1 -$

(B_L/V_L) $T]$ for the following amounts of debt issued at par:
1. $1 million.
2. $6 million.
3. $11 million.

c. Plot the after-tax cost of debt, $k_i = k_b (1 - T)$, cost of equity, k_{sL}, and cost of capital, k_L, against the firm's financial leverage, B_L/V_L, for the levered firm.

d. According to MM, where is the firm's optimum capital structure once corporate taxes are introduced, but before considering bankruptcy costs, agency costs, and personal taxes? Does this position have more similarity to the NI or the NOI positions?

18A.4. *MM PROPOSITION WITH CORPORATE TAXES, BANKRUPTCY COSTS, AND AGENCY COSTS.* Bay Area Fisheries at the present time is unlevered, with net operating income, NOI, of $3 million, a total value of $16 million, and a marginal corporate tax rate of 40 percent. In an effort to determine its target capital structure, Bay Area calculated the value of the firm, V, the after-tax cost of debt, k_i, the cost of equity, k_s, and the cost of capital, k, for the three levels of debt shown below:

Amount of Debt ($ Millions)	V ($ Millions)	k_i (%)	k_s (%)	k (%)
$2	$16.80	4.80%	11.51%	10.71%
9	19.60	4.80	12.91	9.18
12	20.80	4.80	13.91	8.66

Note: Debt is issued at par value.

Upon completing the analysis, Bay Area realized it had failed to consider bankruptcy and agency costs, which are as follows:

Amount of Debt ($ Millions)	Bankruptcy and Agency Costs Per Dollar of Debt (%)
$2	10%
9	30
12	50

a. Employing the bankruptcy and agency cost information above, recalculate the value of the firm, V, the after-tax cost of debt, k_i, the cost of equity, k_s, and the cost of capital, k, for each level of debt. (*Hint:* The before-tax cost of debt is 8 percent.)

b. Graph k versus the B/V ratio:

    1. Without bankruptcy and agency costs.

    2. With bankruptcy and agency costs.

    c. Based on your observation of capital markets, do you agree that bankruptcy and agency costs enter into a firm's capital structure decision? Explain.

SELECTED REFERENCES

Alberts, William W., and Gailen L. Hite. "The Modigliani-Miller Leverage Equation Considered in a Product Market Context." *Journal of Financial and Quantitative Analysis* 18 (December 1983), pp. 425–437.

Barnea, Amir, Robert A. Haugen, and Lemma W. Senbet. "An Equilibrium Analysis of Debt Financing Under Costly Tax Arbitrage and Agency Problems." *Journal of Finance* 36 (June 1981), pp. 569–581.

———, ———, and ———. "Market Imperfections, Agency Problems, and Capital Structure: A Review." *Financial Management* 10 (summer 1981), pp. 7–22.

Baron, David P. "Default Risk, Homemade Leverage, and the Modigliani-Miller Theorem." *American Economic Review* 64 (March 1974), pp. 176–182.

Becker, Jack. "General Proof of Modigliani-Miller Propositions I and II Using Parameter-Preference Theory." *Journal of Financial and Quantitative Analysis* 13 (March 1978), pp. 65–69.

Boness, A., James, and George M. Frankfurter. "Evidence of Non-Homogeneity of Capital Costs Within 'Risk-Classes.'" *Journal of Finance* 32 (June 1977), pp. 775–787.

Brennan, Michael J., and Eduardo S. Schwartz. "Corporate Income Taxes, Valuation, and the Problem of Optimal Capital Structure." *Journal of Business* 51 (January 1978), pp. 103–114.

Chance, Don M. "Evidence on a Simplified Model of Systematic Risk." *Financial Management* 11 (autumn 1982), pp. 53–63.

Chen, Andrew H. "Recent Developments in the Cost of Debt Capital." *Journal of Finance* 33 (June 1978), pp. 863–877.

———, and E. Han Kim. "Theories of Corporate Debt Policy: A Synthesis." *Journal of Finance* 34 (May 1979), pp. 371–384.

DeAngelo, Harry, and Ronald W. Masulis. "Optimal Capital Structure Under Corporate and Personal Taxation." *Journal of Financial Economics* 8 (March 1980), pp. 3–29.

Durand, David. "The Cost of Capital, Corporation Finance and the Theory of Investment: Comment." *American Economic Review* 49 (September 1959), pp. 639–655.

———. "Cost of Debt and Equity Funds for Business: Trends and Problems of Measurement." *Conference on Research on Business Finance*. New York: National Bureau of Economic Research, 1952, pp. 215–247. Reprinted in *The Theory of Business Finance*, 2d ed., eds. Stephen H. Archer and Charles A. D'Ambrosio. New York: Macmillan, 1976.

Fama, Eugene F. "The Effects of a Firm's Investment and Financing Decisions on the Welfare of Its Security Holders." *American Economic Review* 68 (June 1978), pp. 272–284.

Flath, David, and Charles R. Knoeber. "Taxes, Failure Costs and Optimal Industry Capital Structure: An Empirical Test." *Journal of Finance* 35 (March 1980), pp. 99–117.

Glenn, David W. "Super Premium Security Prices and Optimal Corporate Financing Decisions." *Journal of Finance* 31 (May 1976), pp. 507–524.

Hamada, Robert S. "The Effect of the Firm's Capital Structure on the Systematic Risk of Common Stocks." *Journal of Finance* 27 (May 1972), pp. 435–452.

————. "Portfolio Analysis, Market Equilibrium and Corporation Finance." *Journal of Finance* 24 (March 1969), pp. 13–31.

Haugen, Robert A., and James L. Pappas. "Equilibrium in the Pricing of Corporate Assets, Risk-Bearing Debt Instruments and the Question of Optimal Capital Structure." *Journal of Financial and Quantitative Analysis* 6 (June 1971), pp. 943–953.

———— and ————. "Reply." *Journal of Financial and Quantitative Analysis* 7 (September 1971), pp. 2005–2008.

————, and Lemma W. Senbet. "The Insignificance of Bankruptcy Costs to the Theory of Optimal Capital Structure." *Journal of Finance* 33 (May 1978), pp. 383–393.

Heinkel, Robert. "A Theory of Capital Structure Relevance Under Imperfect Information." *Journal of Finance* 37 (December 1982), pp. 1141–1150.

Hong, Hai, and Alfred Rappaport. "Debt Capacity, Optimal Capital Structure, and Capital Budgeting Analysis." *Financial Management* 7 (autumn 1978), pp. 7–11.

Imai, Yutaka, and Mark E. Rubinstein. "Comment." *Journal of Financial and Quantitative Analysis* 7 (September 1971), pp. 2001–2003.

Jensen, Michael C., and William H. Meckling. "Theory of the Firm: Managerial Behavior, Agency Costs and Ownership Structure," *Journal of Financial Economics* 3 (October 1976), pp. 305–360.

Kim, E. Han. "A Mean-Variance Theory of Optimal Capital Structure and Corporate Debt Capacity." *Journal of Finance* 33 (March 1978), pp. 45–65.

————. "Miller's Equilibrium, Shareholder Leverage Clienteles, and Optimal Capital Structure." *Journal of Finance* 37 (May 1982), pp. 301–319.

————, John J. McConnell, and Irwin H. Silberman. "Capital Structure Rearrangements and Me-First Rules in an Efficient Capital Market." *Journal of Finance* 32 (June 1977), pp. 789–810.

Lloyd-Davies, Peter R. "Optimal Financial Policy in Imperfect Markets." *Journal of Financial and Quantitative Analysis* 10 (September 1975), pp. 457–481.

Merton, Robert C. "On the Pricing of Contingent Claims and the Modigliani-Miller Theorem." *Journal of Financial Economics* 5 (November 1977), pp. 241–249.

Miller, Merton H. "Debt and Taxes." *Journal of Finance* 32 (May 1977), pp. 261–275.

————, and Franco Modigliani. "Dividend Policy, Growth and the Valuation of Shares." *Journal of Business* 34 (October 1961), pp. 411–433.

————, and ————. "Some Estimates of the Cost of Capital to the Electric Utility Industry, 1954–57." *American Economic Review* 56 (June 1966), pp. 333–391.

Modigliani, Franco. "Debt, Dividend Policy, Taxes, Inflation and Market Valuation." *Journal of Finance* 37 (May 1982), pp. 255–273.

————, and Merton H. Miller. "The Cost of Capital, Corporation Finance and the Theory of Investment: Reply." *American Economic Review* 49 (September 1959), pp. 655–669.

————, and ————. "Reply to Heins and Sprenkle." *American Economic Review* 59 (September 1969), pp. 592–595.

Myers, Stewart C. "Determinants of Corporate Borrowing." *Journal of Financial Economics* 5 (November 1977), pp. 147–176.

Rubinstein, Mark E. "A Mean-Variance Synthesis of Corporate Financial Theory." *Journal of Finance* 28 (March 1973), pp. 167–181.

Senbet, Lemma W., and Robert A. Taggart, Jr. "Capital Structure Equilibrium and Market Imperfections and Incompleteness." *Journal of Finance* 39 (March 1984), pp. 93–103.

Stiglitz, Joseph E. "A Re-Examination of the Modigliani-Miller Theorem." *American Economic Review* 59 (December 1969), pp. 784–793.

Taggart, Robert A., Jr. "Taxes and Corporate Capital Structure in an Incomplete Market." *Journal of Finance* 35 (June 1980), pp. 645–659.

Trzcinka, Charles. "The Pricing of Tax-Exempt Bonds and the Miller Hypothesis." *Journal of Finance* 37 (September 1982), pp. 907–923.

Turnbull, Stuart M. "Debt Capacity." *Journal of Finance* 34 (September 1979), pp. 931–940.

Weston, J. Fred. "A Test of Cost of Capital Propositions." *Southern Economic Journal* 30 (October 1963), pp. 105–112.

Yagill, Joe. "On Valuation, Beta, and the Cost of Equity Capital: A Note." *Journal of Financial and Quantitative Analysis* 17 (September 1982), pp. 441–449.

19

Dividend Policy and Internal Financing

The dividend policy adopted by a firm is indicative of how it intends to divide its net income between cash dividends and retained earnings. Both affect the value of the firm and shareholder wealth. On the one hand, the more funds the firm retains and profitably reinvests, the higher will be the expected rate of corporate growth; alternatively, the more dividends the firm distributes, the larger will be the immediate cash flow to the stockholders. The objective of a firm's dividend policy should be to resolve this apparent conflict by finding a dividend payout ratio that balances shareholder needs for current income against the demands of expected future growth in such a way as to maximize the value of the firm. In this chapter we look at dividends and retained earnings, and at the important role dividend policy plays in determining the value of the firm. After reviewing some of the institutional dimensions of corporate dividends, we will examine various theories which argue for and against the relevance of dividends in stock valuation, and then analyze the interrelationships among the investment, financing, and dividend decisions; the final part of the chapter considers some of the institutional and administrative aspects of dividend policy.

Corporate Dividends

On September 10, 1982, the Boeing Company paid to its common stockholders a quarterly dividend of 35 cents per share—the equivalent of an annual dividend rate of $1.40 per share. Boeing has over 96 million shares of common stock outstanding and as a result, it paid out nearly $135 million in dividends during 1982. The company, of course, could have decided to retain the funds rather than pay them out—in which case, they could have been used to finance corporate growth and/or service the principal portion of the company's debt. Dividends are paid from accumulated after-tax earnings, and represent a distribution of corporate profits to shareholders. Unless it is a "return of capital" dividend,[1] any dividends paid are charged against the company's retained earnings account, and if it is a cash dividend, an equal amount is deducted from its cash balance. Corporate earnings that are not distributed to stockholders are retained and considered a source of internally generated financing.

Cash Dividend Policies

Corporations pay dividends in the form of cash and/or, occasionally, by issuing additional shares of stock to their shareholders (the discussion of stock dividends will be deferred to Chapter 20—here we deal only with cash dividends). The dividend payment practices of firms that pay cash dividends tend to fall into one of three general categories: regular dividends, regular plus extra dividends, or fixed payout ratio.

Regular Dividends.   Perhaps the most common type of dividend policy, the *regular dividend* approach is based on maintaining a fixed annual cash dividend rate for several years in a row, increasing it only when future earnings look sufficiently strong to support a new, higher level of dividends. Firms that follow this policy go to almost any extent to avoid missing or decreasing the level of dividends. While stable dividends are the objective of this policy, the amount of per share dividends paid over time usually increases as the firm's profits increase. In essence, dividends are flat for a while; they then move up in step fashion and hold until a new, higher level of sustained earnings is attained. As Figure 19.1 shows, annual earnings may fluctuate under this policy, but dividends remain relatively stable.

Often, a target dividend payout ratio (or a range of payout ratios) will be used to develop a stable dividend policy. The dollar amount of dividends paid, in essence, is linked to an ideal payout ratio, and is held stable until the payout ratio hits, or drops below, a minimum. The dollar amount of dividends paid is then raised to a level compatible with the target payout ratio. Figure 19.1 depicts a company that holds to its annual dividend rate until the payout ratio drops to around 35 percent, at which time, given that management is assured the observed increase in earnings is sustainable, dividends are raised to the point where the payout ratio rises to around 45 to 50 percent. Regardless of how management sets the desired level of dividends, it is clear that firms that adopt a regular dividend policy feel the payment of dividends is an important variable in the stock valuation process.

Regular Plus Extra Dividends.   Some firms will combine regular dividends with the payment of additional dividends whenever earnings are

---

[1]A *return of capital dividend* is a special type of cash dividend (used chiefly by public utilities) that is charged to the capital stock position on the balance sheet and represents a return to stockholders of their original paid-in capital.

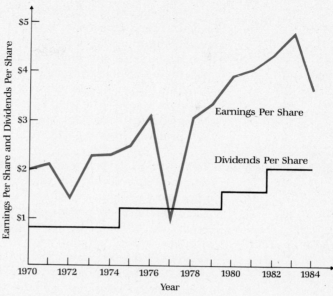

Earnings/Share	$2.00	2.10	1.40	2.25	2.30	2.50	3.10	1.00	3.05	3.40	3.90	4.05	4.35	4.75	3.80
Dividends/Share	$ .75	.75	.75	.75	.75	1.20	1.20	1.20	1.20	1.20	1.50	1.50	2.00	2.00	2.00
Dividend Payout Ratio	38%	36%	54%	33%	33%	48%	39%	120%	39%	35%	38%	37%	46%	42%	53%

Figure 19.1 The Behavior of Earnings and Dividends Under a Stable Dividend Policy.

sufficiently high to warrant it. The additional dividends are usually, but not always, paid in the final quarter of the year and are called *extra dividends* to avoid giving stockholders the impression that a new level of regular dividends is about to be established. Such a practice is often followed by companies that want to project the image of following a regular dividend policy but which experience noticeable fluctuations in earnings and cash flows. Under such conditions, the regular dividends are set at fairly low levels (low enough so that dividends can be maintained even in off years) and then supplemented with extra dividends when profits are high and excess funds are available (and not needed for reinvestment purposes). Companies that follow this policy clearly feel dividends are important, but also recognize the critical role internally generated funds play in financing the long-term growth of the firm.

Fixed Payout Ratio.   A dividend policy that gives the most attention to the firm, and that some would argue gives too little weight to the needs of stockholders, is the *fixed payout ratio*. Under this policy, the company establishes a fixed percentage of earnings that will be paid out each year as dividends; as long as profitable reinvestment opportunities exist, the ratio is generally kept fairly low (20 to 25 percent or less). Given the target payout ratio, the level of dividends paid will obviously fluctuate with variations in earnings. Little attention is given to the dollar amount of dividends since the financing needs of the company are considered paramount. Not surprisingly, the biggest drawback of this policy is instability of dividends, which often leads to erratic market prices for the company's stock. The fixed payout policy is most suited to firms that are experiencing above-average growth rates and funding needs—those that can profitably reinvest earnings.

Dividend Patterns

Table 19.1 provides 20 years of aggregate dividend and retained earnings data and shows that the total amount of cash dividends paid by U.S. corporations has risen, *without interruption*, each year since 1962. Such increases have, on average, outstripped that of inflation. That is, as seen in the lower panel of the table, while consumer prices went up an average of 5.97 percent over the period from 1962 to 1981, annual dividends rose at a compound rate of 8.29 percent. In real terms, dividends have remained remarkably stable and provide further evidence of the seemingly general infatuation of American corporations with the policy of maintaining a regular level of dividends.

The fourth column in Table 19.1 provides average payout ratios. Not surprisingly, it reveals a fair amount of year-to-year instability—due, of course, to the underlying instability of corporate earnings. Ranging from a high of almost 62 percent in 1970 to a low of 36.6 percent in 1979, dividend payout ratios have clearly drifted downward in recent years as the high cost of financing has placed a premium on internally generated funds. Paying out less of their earnings to stockholders obviously enables firms to retain more, and as the last column shows, retained earnings have always been an important source of corporate financing. (Note that in all but 5 of the 20 years, there was more money raised through retained earnings than from all other forms of external long-term financing combined.) It would seem that so long as profitable investment opportunities are available to the firm, there is an incentive for using internally generated funds as a source of financing, especially when the cost of funds is high.

Dividend Theories: Conflicting Views on the Relevance of Dividends in Stock Valuation

From a stock valuation perspective, both the payment of dividends and a high growth rate enhance the value of a firm. Recall from the discussion of common stock valuation in Chapter 7 that the basic stock valuation model was shown as:

$$P_0 = \frac{D_1}{(k_s - g)} \tag{19.1}$$

Other things being equal, it is clear in Equation 19.1 that an increase in the amount of dividends paid will raise D_1 and result in higher stock

TABLE 19.1
Dividends Paid and
Financing Raised by
U.S. Corporations,
1962–1981
(In Billions of Dollars)

Year (1)	Corporate Profits After Tax (2)	Cash Dividends Paid (3)	Dividend Payout Ratio (4)	Earnings Retained (5)	Long-Term Financing Raised Externally[a] (6)	Portion of Long-Term Financing Raised Internally[b] (7)
1981	$150.9	$65.1	43.1%	$85.8	$72.2	54.3%
1980	157.8	58.1	36.8	99.7	62.9	61.3
1979	144.1	52.8	36.6	91.3	51.4	64.0
1978	121.5	47.2	38.8	74.3	47.1	61.2
1977	104.5	42.1	40.3	62.4	53.8	53.7
1976	92.2	35.8	38.8	56.4	53.2	51.5
1975	73.4	32.4	44.1	41.0	53.6	43.3
1974	74.5	31.0	41.6	43.5	38.2	53.2
1973	67.1	27.8	41.4	39.3	31.9	55.2
1972	54.6	24.6	45.1	30.0	40.1	42.8
1971	44.3	23.0	51.9	21.3	45.0	32.1
1970	37.0	22.9	61.9	14.1	38.9	26.6
1969	43.8	22.6	51.6	21.2	26.6	44.4
1968	46.2	21.9	47.4	24.3	21.8	52.7
1967	44.9	20.1	44.8	24.8	24.7	50.1
1966	47.1	19.4	41.2	27.7	18.0	60.6
1965	44.3	19.1	43.1	25.2	15.9	61.3
1964	36.7	17.3	47.1	19.4	13.8	58.4
1963	31.5	15.5	49.2	16.0	12.1	56.9
1962	29.6	14.4	48.6	15.2	10.6	58.9

DIVIDENDS AND INFLATION
Compound Growth Rates

Period	Consumer Prices	Dividends
1976–1981	9.83%	12.71%
1971–1981	8.44	10.97
1966–1981	7.11	8.42
1962–1981	5.97	8.29

[a]External financing includes bonds, preferred stock, and common stock.
[b]Internally generated funds include retained earnings only; does not include depreciation and other capital consumption allowances.
SOURCE: U.S. Department of Commerce, Bureau of Economic Analysis, *Survey of Current Business*, various issues; and Board of Governors of the Federal Reserve System, *Federal Reserve Bulletin*, various issues.

prices. In contrast, an increase in the earnings retention rate will mean that more earnings are being plowed back into the business. They will act to stimulate corporate growth (g) and therefore increase the price of the stock (P_0). Arguments can be advanced either in support of the idea that dividends are irrelevant, or that they are highly relevant to the stock valuation process. The material that follows will examine the theoretical importance of dividend policy. We will first review the "residual theory of dividends," which argues that dividends are passive (or unimportant) in stock valuation, and then look at the arguments which support the relevancy of dividends.

The Residual Theory of Dividends

When we examined capital budgeting and the marginal cost of capital, we showed that a firm's investment opportunities schedule (IOS) must be combined with its cost of capital schedule to determine an appropriate MCC; that is, the firm's capital budget is defined simultaneously with the level of required financing. The *residual theory of dividends* is consistent with this managerial philosophy, since it implies that only "surplus" funds should be distributed to shareholders. The firm, in effect, should pay dividends only if more earnings are available than needed to support the current capital budget; otherwise, the company should retain its earnings so long as it can generate a rate of return on reinvested funds that exceeds the return stockholders can obtain on other investments of comparable risk. Thus, dividend policy is viewed solely as a financing decision, and as such considered irrelevant to shareholder wealth.

To see why the residual theory treats dividend policy as a passive variable, consider the case of Valdez Industries, an all-equity-financed firm with expected earnings of $4 million. Assume Valdez has a marginal cost of capital of 15 percent and presently has the following investment opportunities:

Project	Internal Rate of Return (IRR)	Initial Investment ($CFAT_0$)	Cumulative Investment
A	20%	$800,000	$ 800,000
B	17	600,000	1,400,000
C	15	600,000	2,000,000
D	12	500,000	2,500,000
E	11	800,000	3,300,000

When plotted, these projects result in the investment opportunities schedule shown in Figure 19.2. In the absence of capital rationing, a firm should accept each capital budgeting project that has an internal rate of return equal to or greater than its marginal cost of capital. Based on this decision criterion, Valdez's financial manager should accept those projects whose IRR is equal to or greater than 15 percent—projects A, B, and C. The MCC schedule is also shown in Figure 19.2; note that since the only source of capital is internally generated equity, and since Valdez has $4 million in expected earnings (more than enough to fund any or all of the proposed projects), the MCC curve is constant at 15 percent.[2]

---

[2]The MCC schedule will, of course, curve upward if additional stock is issued as the cost of equity and consequently the marginal cost of capital rises. For simplicity, we used an all-equity firm for analytical purposes; the analysis is similar for firms that employ debt in their capital structure, but one modification should be noted. When a company has a target capital structure, it is presumed that funds will be raised in proportion to the desired debt-equity ratio. For example, with a 60/40 debt-equity ratio, the amount of internally generated funds required to finance a given capital project would equal only 40 percent of the cost ($CFAT_0$). With a 60/40 debt-equity ratio, Valdez could implement projects A, B, and C by employing only $800,000 of retained earnings ($2,000,000 × .40), with the rest being raised through debt.

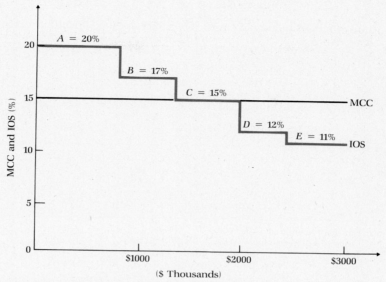

Figure 19.2   Marginal Cost of Capital and Investment Opportunities Schedule for Valdez Industries.

Using the basic stock valuation model shown in Equation 19.1, let us now examine the consequences of accepting one or more of these projects on the dividend payout ratio and total value of Valdez Industries. To do this, we define the dividend expected next year, D_1, as equal to the company's expected earnings (E_1) times its dividend payout ratio (d): $D_1 = E_1 \times d$. Furthermore, for firms that use no external debt or equity financing, we can define the expected growth rate for the firm, g, as equal to 1 minus the dividend payout ratio times the firm's expected return on its equity: $g = (1 - d)(ROE)$. Finally, for an all-equity firm in equilibrium, expected ROE will be equal to the average expected return (IRR) on all its capital budgeting projects. Given these relationships, we can determine the payout ratio and hence the level of capital expenditures that maximizes the value of Valdez Industries.

Table 19.2 gives total market values for Valdez under different capital expenditure, payout ratio and rate of return assumptions. It shows that the firm's value is maximized at $32,258,000 when the dividend payout ratio is 50 percent—which provides exactly the amount of internal financing needed to accept capital projects A, B, and C. If expectations materialize, Valdez should be able to earn approximately 17.6 percent on its reinvested funds. It should be clear, however, that because of the taxes paid on dividends received and other transactions costs, the stockholders would have to generate a rate of return substantially higher than 17.6 percent to realize the same net benefits. Specifically, given that transactions costs incurred by stockholders to reinvest dividends equal 4 percent of the amount of securities purchased, and assuming an investor

TABLE 19.2

The Total Value of Valdez Industries Under Alternative Capital Expenditure Plans and Dividend Payout Ratios

Projects	Earnings Available for Dividends After Accepting Projects ($ Thousands) (1)	Dividend Payout Ratio (d) (2)	Retention Rate $(1 - d)$ (3)	Internal Rate of Return[b] (4)	Growth Rate (IRR × Retention Rate) (5)	Total Value of the Firm[c] ($ Thousands) (6)
A	$3,200	.800[a]	.200	.2000	.0400	$29,091
A and B	2,600	.650	.350	.1871	.0655	30,769
A, B, and C	2,000	.500	.500	.1760	.0880	32,258
A, B, C, and D	1,500	.375	.625	.1648	.1030	31,915
A, B, C, D, and E	700	.175	.825	.1515	.1250	28,000

[a]Based on earnings available of $4,000,000.
[b]That rate of return which equates total benefits to total costs.
[c]Calculated by employing the basic stock valuation model:

$$P_0 = \frac{D_1}{k_s - g}$$

where P_0 = total value of the firm
D_1 = total dividends to be paid (from column 1)
k_s = investor's required rate of return or MCC = 15%
g = expected growth rate (from column 5)

For project A, P_0 = $3,200/(.15 − .04): = $3,200/(.11) = $29,091. The other total market values are derived in a similar manner.

has a marginal tax rate of 36 percent, he or she would have to earn slightly more than 29 percent on the reinvested dividends just to match the payoffs from the 17.6 percent earned by Valdez. That is:

$$RR_s = \frac{IRR_c}{1 - (\text{transaction cost} + \text{investor's marginal tax rate})} \qquad (19.2)$$

$$= \frac{.1760}{1 - (.04 + .36)} = \frac{.1760}{1 - .40} = .2933$$

where RR_s = investor's required return on reinvested dividends
IRR_c = internal rate of return earned by the firm on earnings retained

So long as Valdez's shareholders cannot earn superior returns, they will benefit from management's decision to retain up to $2 million of available earnings.[3]

---

[3]The computations in Equation 19.2 assume, of course, that the stockholder reinvests in firms with dividend and capital gains profiles similar to that of the company that initially paid the dividend and as such, that the ultimate sources of investor payoffs are comparable.

In the case of Valdez, was dividend policy itself a relevant consideration in the decision? No; dividends were simply a passive residual that remained after the firm made its investment decisions and employed whatever portion of internally generated funds were needed to finance the chosen capital projects. The remaining funds—whether 100 percent, zero, or anywhere in between—were considered "surplus" and hence distributed to shareholders in the form of cash dividends. The residual theory of dividends implies that from the shareholders' standpoint, dividends are irrelevant; put another way, shareholders are indifferent between receiving dividends or capital gains. If dividends are irrelevant, then the investment and financing decisions of the firm are paramount (as they affect the value of the firm and shareholder wealth), and the matter of the size and stability of dividends is of secondary concern. As long as the firm has profitable investment opportunities that are equal or superior to those available to shareholders, it follows that the firm should retain the funds as needed.

Miller and Modigliani[4] have presented the most comprehensive formal argument for dividends being irrelevant. They assert that, given the investment decisions of the firm (and in a world of certainty, no taxes, or other market imperfections), the wealth of shareholders is unaffected by the distribution of dividends and therefore the value of the firm is not influenced by its dividend policy. They argue that the value of the firm is determined solely by the earning power of the company's assets (or its investment policy) and that the manner in which the earnings stream is split between dividends and internally retained (and reinvested) funds does not affect this value. In essence, MM show through a series of mathematical expressions that share price behavior will compensate for any excesses or deficiencies in the level of dividends paid in such a way that the net result will be identical returns to the stockholder, regardless of how earnings are distributed.

Thus, it is not the firm's dividend policy that is important; rather, the value of the firm is influenced only by its expected future earnings stream. Fischer Black and Myron Scholes also studied dividend policy by using the capital asset pricing model to empirically relate a stock's market behavior to its dividend payout ratio. They found that stocks with high payout ratios did not provide returns that were significantly different from those with low payouts. As a result, they concluded that such evidence tended to be consistent with the idea that dividend policy does not matter.[5] If dividend policy is irrelevant, what does this imply about the basic valuation model, which states that the price of a share of stock is equal to the present value of expected future dividends? The

---

[4]Merton H. Miller and Franco Modigliani, "Dividend Policy, Growth, and the Valuation of Shares," *Journal of Business* 34 (October 1961), pp. 411–433.

[5]Fischer Black and Myron Scholes, "The Effects of Dividend Yield and Dividend Policy on Common Stock Prices and Returns," *Journal of Financial Economics* 2 (May 1974), pp. 1–22.

answer is that dividend policy affects only the timing of the expected dividends, not their present value. The irrelevance position maintains that the present value of expected future dividends will remain unchanged, even though dividend policy may change the timing of payments. Thus, dividends (including liquidating dividends) may be paid or not: postponement or acceleration is a matter of indifference to stockholders.

The Relevance of Dividends

The size and consistency of corporate dividend payments can be treated as passive decision variables if, in fact, dividends are irrelevant. But if dividend policy is relevant, it follows that dividends can actively influence the value of the firm and shareholder wealth. In such a case, there is reason for management to concern itself with the development and implementation of a dividend policy. In this section, we examine some of the arguments in support of the position that dividends are relevant to stock valuation and that dividend policy is an active decision variable. It is argued here that investors will *not* be indifferent about receiving dividends so long as uncertainty, differential tax rates, and market imperfections exist.

Resolving Investor Uncertainty. This school of thought maintains that most investors would prefer to receive a cash dividend today as opposed to some time in the future, since "a bird in the hand is worth two in the bush." Current dividend payments, it is argued, reduce investor uncertainty and, other things being equal, increase the market price of a share of stock. Reduced risk exposure means a lower required rate of return (k_s), and according to the basic stock valuation model, a higher value for the firm's stock. The dividend relevance school's leading proponent, Myron J. Gordon, suggests that stockholders do have a preference for current dividends—that, in fact, there is a direct relationship between the dividend policy of a firm and its market value. Gordon argues that investors are generally risk-averse and therefore attach less risk to current as opposed to future dividends or capital gains.[6]

Although this argument seems intuitively logical, it has elicited several thought-provoking counterarguments. In one case it was shown that if a firm follows a rational capital expenditure policy and accepts all projects with an IRR equal to or greater than the firm's MCC, then higher dividends, other things being equal, will force the firm to acquire more external capital to compensate for the higher payout ratio. In a world of

---

[6]Myron J. Gordon, "Optimal Investment and Financing Policy," *Journal of Finance* 18 (May 1963), pp. 264–272; and Gordon, "The Savings, Investment and Valuation of a Corporation," *Review of Economics and Statistics* 40 (February 1962), pp. 37–51.

rational investors, even with uncertainty, the value of a share of stock will adjust to the firm's current payout ratio and its expected future dividend stream only so long as the firm's investment policy is unaffected by any changes in its dividend policy.[7] That is, if the firm still accepts all capital expenditures for which the IRR is greater than the firm's MCC, the value of the firm is not affected by its dividend payout ratio. Only if the firm acts in a manner to make its investment and dividend decisions interdependent will the dividend payout ratio influence its value. Others have suggested that if shareholders want a cash income stream which differs from that offered by the firm, they can achieve it by periodically liquidating some shares or by reinvesting the dividend proceeds.[8] Since (in perfect markets with no taxes) these "homemade" dividends are perfect substitutes for corporate dividends, a firm's dividend policy is not a thing of value for investors. Whether or not dividends resolve investor uncertainty and therefore affect stock valuation depends in large part on whether the firm can do something for investors that they cannot do for themselves. Clearly, the dividend policies of many firms seem to intimate that they feel they can do just that.

Information Content.   Another argument for the relevance of dividends is based on the premise that the mere payment of dividends imparts certain information to shareholders. Known as the *information content of dividends theory*, this idea implies that dividends have an impact on share prices because they communicate information to investors about the firm's profitability. An increase in the dividend rate, for example, says favorable things about the future outlook of the company. It has been suggested that implicit in the MM dividend irrelevance argument is the assumption that the market knows a company's expected return stream exactly, and discounts this stream to determine the value of the firm. Advocates of information content argue that what is really valued in the marketplace is the perceived return stream. If this is the case, then changes in dividend policy will alter the market's perception about the firm and therefore affect the valuation process. Tests for an information content effect have uncovered some short-run impact on share prices due to changes in dividend policy, though little long-lasting effect was found.[9]

If investors truly attribute unambiguous information content to dividend policy, it would seem that any dramatic and/or erratic changes

---

[7]Michael Brennan, "A Note on Dividend Irrelevance and the Gordon Valuation Model," *Journal of Finance* 26 (December 1971), pp. 1115–1121.

[8]Robert C. Higgins, "Dividend Policy and Increasing Discount Rates: A Clarification," *Journal of Financial and Quantitative Analysis* 7 (June 1972), pp. 1757–1762.

[9]R. Richardson Pettit, "Dividend Announcements, Security Performance, and Capital Market Efficiency, " *Journal of Finance* 27 (December 1972), pp. 993–1007; and Ross Watts, "The Information Content of Dividends," *Journal of Business* 46 (April 1973), pp. 191–211.

in a firm's dividend rate or payout ratio will heighten investor uncertainty and influence stock prices. It is reasonable to conclude, therefore, that regardless of the dividend policy chosen, the practice of stability is recommendable. Major dividend changes are likely to be perceived as containing substantial information and hence should be made only after careful consideration of the consequences.

Clientele Effects.   There are many reasons why particular investors may prefer one payout policy to another. The market is so diverse that while some investors actively pursue firms with high dividend rates, others couldn't care less about them. The *clientele effect*, as originally discussed by Miller and Modigliani[10], suggests that if investors have preferences for different dividend policies, they will be attracted to firms that have policies consistent with their objectives. Likewise, firms will find it advantageous to adjust their dividend policies to the needs of their target investors. Clientele effect proponents argue that every firm has an implied, if not formal, dividend payment pattern which attracts stockholders whose preferences with respect to the payment and stability of dividends correspond to those of the firm. Any attempt on the part of the firm to abruptly alter its dividend payment pattern will lead to price changes (some of which may be severe), as investors alter their holdings to compensate for the changes. There is some empirical evidence that a clientele effect does exist, though its magnitude is not felt to be large.[11] The existence of even relatively small effects, however, may in part explain a firm's reluctance to alter established patterns.

Tax Effects.   A key premise of the irrelevance argument is that investors are indifferent as to whether they receive their return in dividend income or share price appreciation. In the absence of personal taxes, this premise is reasonable. However, once differential personal tax rates are considered, there may well be a preference for long-term capital gains, since they are taxed at lower rates than cash dividends. Moreover, the tax on capital gains is deferred until an investor actually disposes of the stock. Thus, once personal taxes are considered, it follows that for a given level of risk, investors will require a higher total return on a security the larger the proportion of its return attributable to dividends, since dividends are subject to a higher tax rate than long-term capital gains.[12] This implies that not only are stock prices influenced by

[10]Miller and Modigliani, "Dividend Policy, Growth, and the Valuation of Shares," p. 429.

[11]Edwin J. Elton and Martin J. Gruber, "Marginal Stockholder Tax Rates and the Clientele Effect," *Review of Economics and Statistics* 52 (February 1970), pp. 68–74; R. Richardson Pettit, "Taxes, Transactions Costs and the Clientele Effects of Dividends," *Journal of Financial Economics* 5 (December 1977), pp. 419–436; and Wilbur G. Lewellen, Kenneth L. Stanley, Ronald C. Lease, and Gary G. Schlarbaum, "Some Direct Evidence of the Dividend Clientele Phenomenon," *Journal of Finance* 33 (December 1978), pp. 1385–1399.

[12]Michael J. Brennan, "Taxes, Market Valuation and Corporate Financial Policy," *National Tax Journal* 23 (December 1970), pp. 417–427.

dividends, they are influenced in a negative way—high dividends actually hurt stock prices.

This proposition also has important theoretical and empirical implications for the capital asset pricing model because it suggests that dividend payout should be included as a second factor in explaining the equilibrium rate of return on securities. In attempting to empirically test a version of the CAPM that contained a dividend influence, Litzenberger and Ramaswamy[13] concluded that dividends were highly significant. Specifically, they found that as cash dividends increased, investors raised their before-tax returns by bidding down the price of the stock. In essence, investors sought more preferentially taxed capital gains as the way to maintain a desired after-tax rate of return. Such findings suggest a definite relationship between dividend policy and expected returns, and provide evidence that the differential tax on dividends and capital gains creates a preference for capital gains.[14]

Other Market Imperfections.   Many other market imperfections exist, but we will concentrate on two: (1) flotation costs, and (2) other legal or institutional factors that cause markets to be less than perfectly efficient.

The dividend irrelevance position is based on the idea that firms can issue or repurchase securities at will, and at no cost, to undertake desired capital expenditures, and use whatever dividend payout policy they feel is worthwhile. However, equity flotation costs incurred by firms cause them to favor the retention of earnings. For every dollar paid out in the form of cash dividends, the existence of flotation costs means that the firm has to issue more than a dollar's worth of new financing. Also, financing is "lumpy," in the sense that small issues are more difficult and more expensive to market than larger ones. Such factors will, of course, cause firms to prefer retention of earnings.

Institutional restrictions may also inhibit the perfect market dividend process. First, the tax treatment of dividends received by firms (85 percent of the cash dividends received are tax free) creates a demand for current dividends. Also, some institutional investors are restricted by law to investing only in stocks that appear on "approved lists." Since a common standard for admission to an approved list is the duration of cash dividends paid by the firm, these investors are forced to favor shares of dividend-paying firms. Many trusts, estates, and endowment funds have restrictions governing the liquidation of principal and the distribution of the income earned. Also, the income beneficiaries are

---

[13]Robert H. Litzenberger and Krishna Ramaswamy, "The Effect of Personal Taxes and Dividends on Capital Asset Prices," *Journal of Financial Economics* 7 (June 1979), pp. 163–195.

[14]Other studies have been conducted to show that even in the face of differential tax rates, dividend policy is still irrelevant; however, these studies continue to rely on major theoretical assumptions. See, for example, Merton H. Miller and Myron S. Scholes, "Dividends and Taxes," *Journal of Financial Economics* 6 (December 1978), pp. 333–364.

often different from the principal beneficiaries, so to the extent that current income is needed by the income beneficiaries, there is clearly an institutionally derived preference for high dividend-paying stocks. All these factors create demand for dividend-paying stocks.

It is obvious from the preceding review that no clear-cut consensus exists with respect to the relevance of dividend policy. On the one hand, theory plainly demonstrates that in the absence of taxes, transaction costs, and other market imperfections, a firm's dividend policy has no effect on its value. Once taxes are introduced, however, we see that the firm can maximize shareholder wealth by paying no cash dividends, so long as the personal tax rate on dividend income is higher than the rate on capital gains. Moreover, because of vastly different tax circumstances and a variety of other market imperfections, there is the possibility that a clientele effect may exist, wherein shareholders choose the firm with the dividend payout policy they prefer. At this point, the empirical evidence is contradictory concerning whether dividend policy has any effect on the value of the firm. But so long as it does, or so long as there is the remotest chance that it does, it follows that dividend policy is a decision variable which should be taken seriously by financial management. Accordingly, an underlying assumption in the rest of this chapter is that in the real world of taxes and uncertainty, dividends *do* matter.

Impact of Investment and Financing Decisions on Dividend Policy

We will look now at the practical dimensions of dividend policy. In particular, we will deal with several considerations that have an important bearing on dividend policy in action, including the impact of investment and financing decisions on corporate dividend policy, and the effect of a financing constraint on dividend decisions. We begin by examining the important interrelationships that exist among a firm's investment, financing, and dividend decisions.

Investment, Financing, and Dividend Decisions

We saw in Chapter 18 the importance of a target capital structure to the long-run well-being of a firm, and we have seen in this chapter that dividend policy affects not only the level of dividends paid, but also the amount of internally generated equity capital left to reinvest in the company. Thus, for a firm with a target capital structure, current investment plans can, and indeed will, affect dividend payout. To appreciate the interrelationship between investment, financing, and dividend decisions, consider the case of Kentucky Furniture. The company, which has total capital of $100 million, expects to generate after-tax earnings of $20 million; in addition, it has a target capital structure of 30 percent debt and 70 percent equity, a target payout ratio of 40 percent, and $20 million in profitable investment opportunities it would like to undertake. Given these financial variables (and assuming there are no other constraints), Kentucky Furniture can meet its investment objectives and still maintain its financing and dividend targets if the firm is willing (and able) to issue more stock. That is, to undertake the $20 million investment program, Kentucky Furniture can raise only $12 million internally and still meet the 40 percent dividend payout ratio—$20 million × (1 − .4). Now, given the company's desired capital structure, Kentucky Furniture could issue $6 million in new debt and $2 million in additional equity (new common stock) while maintaining the desired debt-equity ratio. The details of this situation are summarized in Table 19.3, which shows that given the firm's cash flow requirements and *the fact that it can issue additional equity*, all three of the financial variables (investment opportunities, target capital structure, and dividend payout) can be accommodated.

The Effect of a Financing Constraint

But what happens to the interrelationship between investment, financing, and dividend decisions if a constraint is placed on the firm and it finds itself reluctant or unable to sell additional common stock? A firm might find itself unable or unwilling to issue new common stock if (1) it is small and has great difficulty raising equity capital externally; (2) the firm's financial manager feels the stock is undervalued; (3) the issuance costs associated with new equity issues are excessive; or (4) management fears excessive dilution in earnings per share. For whatever reason, many firms are reluctant to issue new equity capital via public offerings. Over the last two decades, nonfinancial firms have raised substantially less than 10 percent of their total funds through new common stock; and when public utility firms are excluded, the figures drop below 5 percent. To see the effect of such a constraint (no new stock issues), let us continue the example of Kentucky Furniture. As Table 19.4, p. 831, shows, Kentucky now has three options. (I) It can forego some of its investment opportunities and implement only $17.1 million in new capital projects; (II) it can lower its dividend payout ratio to 30 percent of earnings; or (III) it can increase its debt ratio to 31.7 percent of total capital.

From theory, we know that the firm should not pass up wealth-maximizing investment opportunities. So Kentucky Furniture should make every effort to undertake the whole $20 million investment program (which would effectively eliminate option I as a viable alternative). Second, we know that once taxes and other costs are considered, a firm's capital structure will have a bearing on its MCC. In the case of Kentucky Furniture, a small change in its target capital structure (from 30 to 31.7 percent debt) would probably not affect its MCC; however, over time, the firm's financial leverage could change substantially, causing it to move away from its target capital structure. Such behavior, of course, would mean that the firm is suboptimizing and hence not maximizing shareholder wealth.

Since both the investment and financing decisions (options I and III in Table 19.4) are active policy variables influencing the value of the firm, let us consider the dividend decision. Earlier in this chapter, we established

TABLE 19.3
Investments,
Dividends, and Capital
Structure: Kentucky
Furniture
(In Millions of Dollars)

BEFORE NEW INVESTMENTS		
Debt	$ 30	(30%)
Equity	70	(70%)
Total capital	$100	
AFTER NEW INVESTMENTS		
Investment opportunities (projects with NPV ≥ 0)		$20
Financed with internally generated funds	$ 12	
Financed with external funds	8	
Total funds raised	$ 20	
DIVIDENDS PAID (target payout ratio = 40%)		$8
Earnings	$ 20	
Less: earnings retained	<12>	
Dividends paid	$ 8	
Dividend payout ratio (8/20): 40%		
CAPITAL STRUCTURE (target = 30% debt)		30/70
Total funds required	$ 20	
Less: earnings retained	<12>	
External financing required	$ 8	
External financing		
New debt issue	$ 6	
New stock issue	2	
Total external financing	$ 8	
Capital structure after financing		
Existing debt	$ 30	
New debt	6	
Total Debt	$ 36	
Existing equity	$ 70	
New retained earnings	12	
New stock	2	
Total equity	$ 84	
Total Capital	$120	
Debt/total capital ratio (36/120): 30%		

(1) that there is contradictory evidence concerning whether a firm's dividend policy directly influences the value of its common stock; and (2) that changes in a firm's dividend policy are viewed as signals of anticipated profitability. Because of the purported information content of dividends, and because of tradition in the financial marketplace, most firms are reluctant to change (lower) the level of per share dividends paid. In fact, the observed actions of financial decision makers indicate that they do not view dividend policy as a short-run passive residual. Rather, most firms behave as though dividends do matter. The feeling is that the level of payout should not be altered abruptly. So although Kentucky Furniture could reduce dividends to $6 million (see option II),

TABLE 19.4
Alternative
Investments,
Dividends, and Capital
Structures with No
New External Equity:
Kentucky Furniture
(In Millions of Dollars)

	Options		
	I	II	III
	Reduce Capital Investments	Lower Dividend Payout Ratio	Alter Capital Structure
BEFORE NEW INVESTMENTS			
Debt	$ 30.0	$ 30.0	$ 30.0
Equity	70.0	70.0	70.0
Total capital	$100.0	$100.0	$100.0
AFTER NEW INVESTMENTS			
Investment opportunities (projects with NPV $\geq 0 = \$20$)			
Financed with internally generated funds	$ 12.0	$ 14.0	$ 12.0
Financed with external funds	5.1	6.0	8.0
Total funds raised	$ 17.1	$ 20.0	$ 20.0
DIVIDENDS PAID (target payout ratio = 40%)			
Earnings	$ 20.0	$ 20.0	$ 20.0
Less: Earnings retained	<12.0>	<14.0>	<12.0>
Dividends paid	$ 8.0	$ 6.0	$ 8.0
Dividend payout ratio	40%	30%	40%
CAPITAL STRUCTURE (target = 30% debt)			
Total funds required	$ 17.1	$ 20.0	$ 20.0
Less: Earnings retained	<12.0>	<14.0>	<12.0>
External financing required	$ 5.1	$ 6.0	$ 8.0
External financing			
New debt issue	$ 5.1	$ 6.0	$ 8.0
New stock issue	—	—	—
Total external financing	$ 5.1	$ 6.0	$ 8.0
Capital structure after financing			
Existing debt	$ 30.0	$ 30.0	$ 30.0
New debt	5.1	6.0	8.0
Total debt	$ 35.1	$ 36.0	$ 38.0
Existing equity	$ 70.0	$ 70.0	$ 70.0
New retained earnings	12.0	14.0	12.0
New stock	—	—	—
Total equity	$ 82.0	$ 84.0	$ 82.0
Total capital	$117.1	$120.0	$120.0
Debt/total capital ratio	30%	30%	31.7%

it is more likely that the capital structure, or possibly even the investment program, will be changed to suit the financing constraint facing the firm. Yet of the options available, the best choice, and the one closest to that suggested by financial theory, is to treat the dividend decision as a long-run residual subject to short-run constraints. In order to do this, the firm will have to develop a long-run (5-year) target dividend payout ratio, given: (1) its anticipated investment needs, (2) the firm's target capital structure ratio, and (3) any plans for issuing new common stock. Based on these considerations, the ratio of anticipated net residual funds to anticipated total earnings will then become the firm's long-run target payout ratio.

The long-run target payout ratio is expressed in terms of *percentages*. In the short run, however, the variability to be avoided is in the *dollars per share* paid out by the firm. The firm sets the dollar amount of dividends per share at a level that is consistent with the average target payout ratio over the planning horizon. As earnings fluctuate from period to period, the percentage paid out will also fluctuate; in some years it will be above (or below) the target. At the same time, the firm strives to maintain total dollars paid out at a constant amount and increases it only when a proven higher level of earnings has been achieved and there is great likelihood the firm will be able to maintain the new, higher level of dividends. Firms that treat dividends as a long-run residual usually try to set dividends per share at such a level that they will not have to be reduced (except perhaps under the most severe conditions). Empirical investigations have uncovered evidence that many firms try to behave in this manner, and that once a long-run dividend payout target has been set, not even unusually heavy capital expenditure requirements have much effect on modifying the firm's dividend policy.[15]

Institutional and Administrative Aspects of Dividend Policy

Once a long-term target payout ratio has been established, financial management is then in a position to spell out the details of the firm's policy and carry it out in the face of short-run corporate and market developments. The actual execution of dividend policy is influenced by a number of factors, all of which affect in one way or another the final dividend decisions of the firm.

Factors Influencing the Dividend Decision

The corporate, institutional, and legal factors that influence the dividend decisions of a firm include the growth and profitability of the firm, its liquidity position, the cost and availability of alternative forms of financing, concerns about the managerial control of the firm, the existence of external (largely legal) restrictions, and the impact of inflation on cash flow.

---

[15]See, for example, John Lintner, "Distribution of Incomes of Corporations Among Dividends, Retained Earnings, and Taxes," *American Economic Review* 46 (May 1956), pp. 97–113; John A. Brittain, *Corporate Dividend Policy* (Washington, D.C.: The Brookings Institution, 1966); and Eugene F. Fama and Harvey Babiak, "Dividend Policy: An Empirical Analysis," *Journal of the American Statistical Association* (December 1968), pp. 1132–1161.

Growth and Profitability. The amount of growth a firm can sustain and its profitability are related to its dividend decisions, so long as the firm (because of managerially imposed or external market constraints) cannot issue additional common stock. To see that this relationship exists, consider the model developed by Higgins.[16] He relates the *sustainable growth* (g^*) in sales to the firm's dividend policy, capital structure, and profitability, such that:

$$g^* = \frac{p(1-d)(1+L)}{t - p(1-d)(1+L)} \qquad (19.3)$$

where g^* = sustainable growth in sales
       p = after-tax profit margin on new and existing sales
       d = target dividend payout ratio
       L = target total debt to total equity ratio
       t = ratio of total assets to net sales, applicable to new and existing sales

For example, assume a firm had a profit margin (p) of 5.5 percent, a target dividend payout ratio (d) of 33 percent, and target capital structure ratio (L) of 88 percent. If it required \$73 of assets to support \$100 of sales, then according to the Higgins model, the firm's maximum sustainable growth in sales (g^*) would be 10.5 percent:

$$g^* = \frac{(.055)(.67)(1.88)}{.73 - (.055)(.67)(1.88)} = .105$$

However, consider the interdependency that exists if, for example, the firm's profit margin is only 5 percent instead of 5.5 percent. As shown in Table 19.5, the drop in the firm's profitability causes its sustainable growth to decrease to 9.44 percent, unless there is a decrease in the dividend payout ratio or an increase in its financial leverage, or unless the firm increases its turnover and is able to generate more sales per dollar of assets employed. Similar interrelations exist if any of the other policy variables in the Higgins model are changed. We can see from this why firms with strong growth prospects maintain low target payout ratios. In essence, firms that experience above-average growth rates are expected to have low dividend payout ratios since, in line with the residual theory of dividends, a greater number of profitable investment opportunities should result (other things being equal) in a greater need for earnings retention. *This interrelationship among the firm's growth, its profitability, and its investment, financing, and dividend decisions cannot be overemphasized.*

---

[16]Robert C. Higgins, "How Much Growth Can a Firm Afford?" *Financial Management* 6 (fall 1977), pp. 7–16.

TABLE 19.5
Impact of Changes in
Profit Margin on
Sustainable Growth,
Dividend Payout Ratio,
Capital Structure, and
Ratio of Assets to Sales

If $p = 5\%$, then $g^* = 9.44\%$

$$g^* = \frac{(.05)(.67)(1.88)}{.73 - (.05)(.67)(1.88)}$$
$$= .0944, \text{ or } 9.44\%$$

If $p = 5\%$ and $g^* = 10.5\%$, then:

Dividend payout $(d) = 26\%$

$$.105 = \frac{(.05)(x)(1.88)}{.73 - (.05)(x)(1.88)}$$
$$x = .74 = 1 - d$$
$$d = 0.26, \text{ or } 26\%$$

Capital structure $(L) = 107\%$

$$.105 = \frac{(.05)(.67)(x)}{.73 - (.05)(.67)(x)}$$
$$x = 2.07 = 1 + L$$
$$L = 1.07, \text{ or } 107\%$$

Ratio of total assets to
sales $(t) = 66\%$

$$.105 = \frac{(.05)(.67)(1.88)}{x - (.05)(.67)(1.88)}$$
$$x = .66 = t = 66\%$$

Liquidity. The liquidity position of a firm is often an important consideration in dividend decisions. Since dividends represent a cash outflow, it follows that the better the cash position and overall liquidity of the firm, the greater is the firm's ability to pay (and maintain) a cash dividend. A growing, profitable firm may not be liquid, since it needs funds for new capital expenditures and to build up its permanent working capital position. Likewise, firms in cyclical industries may experience times when they lack liquidity due to general economic conditions. Hence, the degree of liquidity is a variable of concern when a firm's dividend policy is being assessed.

Cost and Availability of Alternative Forms of Financing. The ability of a firm to raise money externally will have a direct bearing on the level of dividends paid to stockholders. Clearly, a company that has easy access to the capital markets, and that can conveniently and economically raise funds in a number of alternative ways, will have greater latitude in setting dividend policy than a firm that has to rely heavily on earnings retention as a source of financing. In essence, the key question is whether or not a firm can (if the need arises) finance its dividend payments externally. Those that can are likely to set higher dividend levels than those that cannot.

Two aspects that tend to work against this approach to dividend payments are the cost of financing and issue expenses. Financing dividends externally may have merit so long as the cost of financing is relatively low. However, when interest rates rise, especially as they did in 1981, the idea of financing dividends begins to lose its appeal. Moreover, issue expenses and other flotation costs will lower desired payout ratios, since they raise the cost of financing. This is particularly true when the amount of external financing involved is fairly small, for flotation costs are inversely related to the size of the issue and tend to rise rapidly as the size of an issue declines.

Managerial Control.   In some cases, control of the firm may be a factor to consider when establishing dividend policy. Suppose a fairly substantial proportion of the firm is owned by a controlling group, and the remainder of the stock is publicly held. Under these circumstances, the higher the payout ratio, the more likely that a subsequent issue of common stock may be needed to finance capital expenditures. Those in control might prefer to minimize the likelihood of an offering of common stock to avoid any dilution in their ownership position. Hence, they would prefer a low payout policy. On the other hand, a firm may establish a relatively high dividend payout ratio (if it believes that is what shareholders desire) as a way to keep the firm from being acquired in a merger or acquisition.

External Restrictions.   The protective covenants in a bond indenture or loan agreement often include a restriction on the payment of cash dividends. This restriction is imposed by the lender(s) to preserve the firm's ability to service its debt. Similar in intent are the *capital impairment laws* that exist in most states. Such statutes limit or preclude the payment of cash dividends from original paid-in capital—that is, from anything other than retained earnings, as reported on the firm's balance sheet.

IRS penalties on undue retention of earnings, in contrast, will tend to cause an increase in the payout ratio, as firms try to do what they can to avoid the penalty. The purpose of this provision is to keep a firm from accumulating excess capital which, if distributed, would be taxed as ordinary income; put another way, by retaining excessive earnings in the firm, the owner-managers may be able to convert ordinary income into preferentially taxed long-term capital gains. Certainly, the IRS will not hesitate to use the resources at its disposal to get its point across, and in this case, the defendant (the firm) is guilty until proven innocent. That is, the company must prove that the retention of earnings was not a tax sham but rather was in the best interest of the company and used to finance its long-term growth and prosperity.

Inflation.   Finally, inflation must be taken into account when a firm establishes its dividend policy. On the one hand, investors would like to receive larger cash dividends because of inflation. But from the firm's viewpoint, inflation causes it to have to invest substantially more to replace existing equipment, finance new capital expenditures, and meet permanent working capital needs. Thus, in inflationary times, there may be a tendency to hold down cash dividends. We showed earlier in this chapter that dividends (in the aggregate) have kept pace with the rate of inflation, suggesting that perhaps management does feel some pressure to maintain a healthy level of dividends. However, we also showed that dividend payout ratios have clearly drifted downward over recent periods of high inflation which, in itself, would point to a preference on the part of management to use retained earnings to meet the ever-increasing reinvestment needs of the firm.

Administrative
Details
of a Dividend
Distribution

Generally speaking, corporations pay dividends quarterly and a period of about 6 to 8 weeks will elapse between the time a dividend is declared and the time it is finally paid to shareholders. The actual decision to pay a dividend is made by the company's board of directors after a briefing by key financial executives on the firm's liquidity position, its current and prospective earnings, its capital investment plans, and so forth (in essence, the same decision variables and factors we have noted above). When the board declares a dividend, it will issue a statement to the press indicating the decision, along with the pertinent payment dates. Typical of the statements released to the financial media would be the following one made by Amalgamated Products: "On May 10, the directors of Amalgamated Products met and declared a regular dividend of 80 cents a share, payable to holders of record on June 17, payment to be made on June 30, 1984." In this instance, the dividend *declaration date* was May 10.

Once the board decides to declare a dividend, the actual mechanics of the distribution are straightforward and follow a well-established pattern of events; this sequence is briefly described below:

1. *Date of record.* This is the date on which the investor must be a registered shareholder of the company to be entitled to receive the just-declared dividend; such stockholders are referred to as *holders of record.* In the case of Amalgamated Products, June 17 would be the date of record; on this date, the firm (or more than likely, a transfer agent, such as a bank, employed expressly to maintain stockholder records) closes the stock transfer books and prepares a list of stockholders. All stockholders who appear on the list as of the close of business on the date of record will receive the dividends that have just been declared.

2. *Ex-dividend date.* Because of the time needed to make bookkeeping entries, the stock market-brokerage industry has adopted a procedure whereby the right to a just-declared dividend remains with a stock when it is traded up to four business days prior to the date of record. In our example, the ex-dividend date is June 13. Investors who buy the stock on, say, June 14 will not be entitled to the dividends; instead, the seller of the stock will receive the dividends.

3. *Payment date.* Amalgamated Products (or its disbursing agent) will actually mail the dividend checks to its shareholders on the payment date, June 30, and by so doing complete the dividend distribution process.

Automatic Dividend Reinvestment Plans

In recent years, a growing number of firms have established *automatic dividend reinvestment plans (ADRs)* whereby shareholders can have their cash dividends automatically reinvested in additional shares of company stock. In essence, the stockholder takes his or her cash dividend in the form of additional shares of stock. Stockholders like ADRs because they offer a convenient way to plow their money back into the company at a considerable savings in brokerage commissions; and in some cases (with qualified utility plans) up to $1,500 in reinvested dividends can be exempted (deferred) from federal income tax.[17] The popularity of ADRs is perhaps best evidenced by the fact that today about a thousand companies (including many of the country's blue chip corporations) offer dividend reinvestment programs.

There are two types of ADR plans: one consists of the purchase of *outstanding stock,* and the other involves the purchase of *newly issued stock.* In the case of outstanding stock, a bank, acting as a trustee, will purchase shares of the company's stock in the open market. The shareholder is charged a small management fee, but little or no brokerage fees are levied. When the stock is newly issued, the firm sells the stock directly to the shareholders, with no charges involved. In fact, such shares are often issued at a discount from current market prices. Corporations like this kind of ADR program, because not only does it provide a valuable and highly regarded service to shareholders, it also offers an inexpensive way of raising equity capital. Indeed, for some companies, new-issue ADR plans are a significant source of financing. In 1979, for example, AT&T raised nearly $1 billion through its dividend reinvestment program.

The use of an ADR plan provides the corporation with an additional benefit: It reduces the immediate cash outflow that would otherwise result from the payment of dividends. The experience of a number of firms that have active ADR plans is summarized in Table 19.6. For these firms, dividend payout ratios without ADR plans averaged 63.1 percent; with ADR funds plowed back, these firms actually paid out only 50.9 percent of their earnings in the form of cash dividends. The use of ADR

---

[17]Unfortunately, except for qualified utility reinvestment programs, a major disadvantage of ADRs to shareholders is that the reinvested dividends are viewed as cash dividends by the IRS (even though they are never physically received) and are therefore subject to ordinary income tax. For a more thorough discussion of ADR plans, see Richard H. Pettway and R. Phil Malone, "Automatic Dividend Reinvestment Plans of Nonfinancial Corporations," *Financial Management* 2 (winter 1973), pp. 11–18. Note also that unless changed by Congress, the utility dividend reinvestment exemption is scheduled to expire on January 1, 1986.

TABLE 19.6
Dividend Payout Ratios
Without and With
Automatic Dividend
Reinvestment Plans

Company	Declared (Without ADR)	Actual (With ADR)
Allied Chemical	45.6%	35.7%
American Electric Power	96.1	78.1
American Telephone & Telegraph	63.1	45.3
Bankers Trust	41.5	34.9
Commonwealth Edison	88.1	67.4
Illinois Power	81.4	69.0
NICOR	63.8	45.6
Pullman	40.7	36.8
Standard Brands	50.2	43.4
Texasgulf	70.6	51.1
Union Carbide	41.3	35.2
Universal Foods	74.4	68.0
Average	*63.1%*	*50.9%*

SOURCE: *Business Week*, August 27, 1979, p. 105.

plans enabled the companies to retain more funds, thereby lessening their dependence on issuing other securities; in addition, firms that employed new-issue ADR schemes were able to increase their equity bases.

SUMMARY

To establish a dividend policy, financial decision makers must determine whether the policy chosen influences the value of the firm. In terms of the basic stock valuation model, it is obvious that a firm's dividend policy affects the timing of future cash dividends. The question, however, is whether the firm's dividend policy influences the required rate of return or, by implication, the firm's expected growth rate in such a manner that the value of the firm and hence the firm's MCC are affected. If dividend policy is relevant, then it influences the value of the firm; otherwise, the firm's dividend policy is irrelevant.

Under the residual theory of dividends, a firm should accept all profitable investment opportunities and then pay out any remaining funds in the form of cash dividends. This position leads directly to the irrelevance of dividends argument, which stresses that in the absence of uncertainty, taxes, and other market imperfections, a shareholder is indifferent between dividends and capital gains. The essence of the argument is (1) that the value of the firm is determined by its investments, and (2) that shareholders can create homemade dividends as efficiently as the firm can, thereby making dividend policy a mere detail. Once personal taxes are introduced, however, the firm can maximize shareholder wealth by paying no cash dividends as long as the capital gains tax rate is less than the ordinary tax rate. Although different dividend clienteles exist, it is unclear at present whether they have much of an effect on the value of the firm. In contrast, the information content of dividends, especially the message imparted by an abrupt change in dividend policy, was found to have a greater impact on firm valuation because it tended to provide new information to shareholders about the perceived future cash flows of the company.

In practice, the firm's investment, financing, and dividend decisions are interdependent when there is a constraint (however imposed) on the issuance of common equity. As a practical matter, therefore, firms should treat the dividend decision as a long-run residual, subject to short-run constraints. Under this approach, the target dividend payout is determined by the ratio of anticipated net residual funds (after taking into account new capital expenditures) to total anticipated earnings over a long time period. Other factors to consider when establishing the firm's dividend policy are its interrelationship with growth and profitability, liquidity, the cost and availability of alternative forms of financing, managerial control, external restrictions, and inflation.

QUESTIONS

19.1. Note the accounting entries that would be made and the impact on a firm's cash flow that would result from the following dividend schemes:
   a. Fixed payout ratio.
   b. Automatic dividend reinvestment program.

19.2. Most firms are reluctant to cut their dividend rate. What does this reluctance suggest about a firm's payment pattern over time and the time series behavior of its dividend payout ratio?

19.3. Explain how, in theory, the residual theory of dividends leads to the proposition that dividends are irrelevant. Be sure to specify: (1) why investors are indifferent, and (2) why homemade dividends are important.

19.4. Is the clientele effect consistent with dividend irrelevance? Explain.

19.5. Can differential tax rates (ordinary income versus long-term capital gains) affect a firm's dividend policy? Explain. Based on your observations, do firms actually behave in such a fashion?

19.6. Under what conditions are the investment, financing, and dividend decisions of a firm interrelated? Explain how these variables are related to a firm's sustainable growth.

19.7. Explain why the firm should treat the dividend decision as a long-run residual, subject to short-run constraints.
   a. List and briefly discuss the constraints and factors that should be taken into consideration when establishing a dividend policy.
   b. Does this imply that dividend policy is relevant or irrelevant to the value of the firm?

19.8. Distinguish between declaration date, date of record, ex-dividend date, and payment date. Are the same procedures employed for cash dividends and ADR plans?

19.9. Explain the most likely effect that each of the following could have on the dividend decisions of the firm:

a. A severely reduced net cash flow.

b. A high level of profitability, coupled with high growth demands.

c. An elimination of the double taxation on dividends (dividends received would be tax-free). Assume, for simplicity, that long-term capital gains are subject to a maximum 25 percent tax rate.

d. A steep rise in interest rates.

19.10. Describe the two basic types of automatic dividend reinvestment plans, and explain why the use of ADRs might prove mutually beneficial to both the firm and its shareholders.

PROBLEMS

19.1. *EFFECTS OF DIVIDEND POLICY ON LEVEL OF DIVIDENDS.* A firm has had the following earnings per share over the past 10 years:

Year	Earnings Per Share	Year	Earnings Per Share
1984	$4.00	1979	$ 2.40
1983	3.80	1978	1.20
1982	3.20	1977	1.80
1981	2.80	1976	−0.50
1980	3.20	1975	0.25

a. If the firm's dividend policy was based on a constant payout ratio of 40 percent for all years with positive earnings and a zero payout otherwise, determine the annual dividend for each year.

b. If the firm had a dividend payout of $1 per share, increasing by $.10 per share whenever the payout fell below 50 percent for 2 consecutive years, what annual dividend would the firm pay each year?

c. Determine the annual cash dividends for each year given the firm's policy to pay annual dividends of $.50 per share except when earnings per share exceeded $3, in which case an extra dividend equal to 80 percent of earnings beyond $3 would be paid.

d. Discuss the pros and cons of each dividend policy described in (a) through (c).

19.2. *INVESTMENT OPPORTUNITIES, MARGINAL COST OF CAPITAL, AND DIVIDEND POLICY.* The Eastern Land Company has traditionally followed a policy of paying out approximately half its earnings in the form of cash dividends. However, Sharon Black, a new addition to the finance staff, has convinced the firm that it should consider treating the dividend decision as a residual. In planning for next year's capital expenditures, Eastern Land has three projects under consideration:

Project	Initial Investment $CFAT_0$ (\$ Millions)	IRR (%)
A	\$ 5	16%
B	9	14
C	10	12

Sharon has put together the following information to determine the firm's MCC:

- Total internally generated funds (earnings) = \$20.8 million.
- Target dividend payout ratio = 50%.
- Number of shares of common stock outstanding = 4 million.
- Target debt/total capital ratio = 20%.
- Current market price per share = \$40.
- Expected annual growth rate in earnings and dividends = 6%.
- Net proceeds per share from additional common stock = \$33.33.
- Cost of new debt (before tax) = 12%.
- Effective tax rate = 40%.

a. Calculate the dividends per share that would be paid if Eastern Land maintains its target payout ratio. Next, using the firm's target capital structure proportions, calculate the marginal cost of capital both above and below the point where internally generated funds are exhausted. (*Hint*: Refer to Chapter 17 if you have difficulty calculating the firm's MCC.)

b. Graph Eastern Land's MCC and IOS schedules. Which capital expenditure projects should Eastern accept?

c. Following Sharon Black's suggestion of a residual dividend policy, Eastern Land has decided to investigate whether or not changing the dividend payout ratio will allow it to increase capital expenditures. Calculate the amount of additional internally generated funds that would be needed to undertake all three projects. Regraph the firm's MCC and IOS schedules. Should Eastern Land now accept all three projects? Explain.

19.3. *DIVIDEND PAYOUT, GROWTH, AND VALUE OF THE FIRM.* Superior Farm Products, Inc., is considering four new capital expenditure projects:

Project	Initial Investment $CFAT_0$ (S Millions)	IRR (%)
A	S3.0	14%
B	1.5	18
C	1.0	11
D	2.0	16

Superior's MCC is 14 percent, and its expected earnings are $10 million.

a. Rank the projects and then determine the cumulative initial investment required for the first, second, and so on capital projects, the corresponding dividend payout ratios, and the firm's retention rate at each level of expenditure.

b. What is the expected growth rate of the firm after accepting the various combinations of projects? (*Hint*: Use $g = (1 - d)(ROE)$.)

c. Determine the total value of the firm after accepting the first, second, and so on capital projects. Where is the total value of the firm maximized? Would the same investment decision be made if it were based on the firm's MCC? Explain.

19.4. *ALTERNATIVE DIVIDEND POLICIES.* The Camron Refractory Company has forecast its internally generated funds and capital expenditure requirements for the next 5 years as follows (in millions of dollars):

Year	Internally Generated Funds	Capital Expenditures
1	$3	S2
2	2	2
3	2	2
4	2	1
5	1	2

The firm currently has 1 million shares of common stock outstanding and pays a dividend of $1 per share. Assume new common stock can be sold at $20 per share. Given this information, determine dividends per share for each year and the amount of external financing required if dividend policy is treated as a residual. Now, compute the amount of external financing needed if the present level of dividends per share is maintained. Under what conditions would you encourage management to adopt a residual dividend policy? One of maintaining an established level of dividends? Under which policy are the total dividends paid out maximized? Under which policy is total external financing minimized?

19.5. *INTERRELATIONSHIP OF INVESTMENT, FINANCING, AND DIVIDEND DECISIONS.* The Morton Walters Company has an opportunity to make some major capital investments this year; the investments require $100 million. The firm is presently operating at its target capital structure and dividend payout ratios. The market value of the firm's debt is $180 million, and the equity is worth $220 million. Current earnings are $60 million, the firm has 7 million shares of stock outstanding, and it pays dividends of $3 per share.

    a. Determine Walters' target capital structure and dividend payout ratios. If Walters undertakes all the new capital investment proposals while maintaining its target capital structure and dividend payout ratios, how much new external equity capital will it have to raise?

    b. What alternatives are available if Walters is unwilling (or unable) to issue new common stock? What happens to the level of capital investments undertaken, the target capital structure, and the target dividend payout ratio under each alternative? Which policy, or combination of policies, would you recommend? Why?

19.6. *SUSTAINABLE GROWTH, PROFITABILITY, AND LEVERAGE.* Kambles Department Stores has become concerned about their profitability and rate of growth in sales. Kambles is operating at its target dividend payout ratio and desired ratio of debt to total equity. Abbreviated financial statements for Kambles are as follows:

Income Statement ($ Millions)		Balance Sheet—Righthand Side ($ Millions)	
Sales	$200.00	Total debt	$ 65.88
Cost of goods sold	146.67	Total equity	94.12
Other expenses	40.00	Total debt and	
Earnings before taxes	13.33	owners' equity	$160.00
Taxes (40%)	5.33		
Earnings after tax	$ 8.00		
Dividends paid	$ 2.00		

a. Using the formula $g^* = \dfrac{p(1-d)(1+L)}{t - p(1-d)(1+L)}$, determine Kambles' sustainable growth rate in sales.

b. What changes could be made in any of the model variables if Kambles desires to achieve: (1) an 8 percent sustainable growth rate, or (2) a 12 percent sustainable growth rate?

c. Is the dividend policy change, with the 12 percent sustainable growth rate (above), an acceptable option? If yes, what does this imply about the ability to use dividend policy to change the expected growth rate of the firm?

19.7. *EFFECTS OF CASH DIVIDENDS AND ADR PLANS ON THE BALANCE SHEET.* Keystone Copper Mines, Inc., has just declared a quarterly cash dividend of $.30 per share. The present (condensed) balance sheet—prepared before the payment of dividends—is given in the table below.

Assets		Liabilities and Owners' Equity	
Cash	$ 30,000,000	Debt	$ 50,000,000
Other assets	95,000,000	Common stock (40 million shares authorized; 20 million shares outstanding, $1 par)	20,000,000
		Additional paid-in capital	10,000,000
		Retained earnings	45,000,000
Total	$125,000,000	Total	$125,000,000

a. Construct a pro forma balance sheet that shows the effects of the cash dividend on asset and equity accounts.

b. Assume Keystone's stock is selling for $10 per share, and that the company offers its shareholders an automatic dividend reinvestment plan (i.e., stockholders enrolled in the plan can obtain *new* shares, at a 10 percent discount from the current market price, in place of their cash dividends). Suppose holders of 8 million shares participate in the firm's ADR plan; construct another pro forma balance sheet to show the effects of the cash dividend/ADR plan on the firm's asset and equity accounts. What impact did the ADR plan have on the firm?

SELECTED REFERENCES

Aharony, J., and I. Swary. "Quarterly Dividend and Earnings Announcements and Stockholders' Returns: An Empirical Analysis." *Journal of Finance* 35 (March 1980), pp. 1–12.

Baker, H. K., and W. H. Seippel. "New Look at Dividend Reinvestment Plans." *M.S.U. Business Topics* (summer 1980), pp. 39–42.

Black, F., and M. Scholes. "The Effects of Dividend Yield and Dividend Policy on Common Stock Prices and Returns." *Journal of Financial Economics* 2 (May 1974), pp. 1–22.

Brennan, Michael. "A Note on Dividend Irrelevance and the Gordon Valuation Model." *Journal of Finance* 26 (December 1971), pp. 1115–1121.

———. "Taxes, Market Valuation and Corporate Financial Policy." *National Tax Journal* 23 (December 1970), pp. 417–427.

Brittain, John A. *Corporate Dividend Policy* (Washington, D.C.: The Brookings Institution, 1966).

DeAngelo, H., and R. W. Masulis. "Leverage and Dividend Irrelevancy Under Corporate and Personal Taxation." *Journal of Finance* 35 (May 1980), pp. 453–467.

Elton, Edwin J., and Martin J. Gruber. "Marginal Stockholder Tax Rates and the Clientele Effect." *Review of Economics and Statistics* 52 (February 1970), pp. 69–74.

Fama, E., L. Fisher, M. Jensen, and R. Roll. "The Adjustment of Stock Prices to New Information." *International Economic Review* (February 1969), pp. 1–21.

———, and Harvey Babiak. "Dividend Policy: An Empirical Analysis." *Journal of the American Statistical Association* (December 1968), pp. 1132–1161.

Gordon, Myron J. "Optimal Investment and Financing Policy." *Journal of Finance* 18 (May 1963), pp. 264–272.

———. "The Savings, Investment and Valuation of a Corporation." *Review of Economics and Statistics* 40 (February 1962), pp. 37–51.

Higgins, Robert C. "How Much Growth Can a Firm Afford?" *Financial Management* 6 (fall 1977), pp. 7–16.

———. "Dividend Policy and Increasing Discount Rates: A Clarification." *Journal of Financial and Quantitative Analysis* 7 (June 1972), pp. 1757–1762.

Lewellen, Wilbur G., Kenneth L. Stanley, Ronald C. Lease, and Gary G. Schlarbaum. "Some Direct Evidence of the Dividend Clientele Phenomenon." *Journal of Finance* 33 (December 1978), pp. 1385–1399.

Lintner, John. "Distribution of Incomes of Corporations Among Dividends, Retained Earnings, and Taxes." *American Economic Review* 46 (May 1956), pp. 97–113.

Litzenberger, R. H., and J. C. Van Horne. "Elimination of the Double Taxation of Dividends and Corporate Financial Policy." *Journal of Finance* 33 (June 1978), pp. 737–750.

———, and Krishna Ramaswamy. "Dividends, Short Selling Restrictions, Tax-Induced Investor Clienteles and Market Equilibrium." *Journal of Finance* 35 (May 1980), pp. 469–485.

———, and ———. "The Effect of Personal Taxes and Dividends on Capital Asset Prices." *Journal of Financial Economics* 7 (June 1979), pp. 163–195.

Long, John B., Jr. "The Market Valuation of Cash Dividends: A Case to Consider." *Journal of Financial Economics* 6 (June–September 1978), pp. 235–264.

Mehta, Dileep R. "The Impact of Outstanding Convertible Bonds on Corporate Dividend Policy." *Journal of Finance* 31 (May 1976), pp. 489–506.

Michel, A. "Industry Influence on Dividend Policy." *Financial Management* 8 (autumn 1979), pp. 22–26.

Miller, Merton H., and Franco Modigliani. "Dividend Policy, Growth, and the Valuation of Shares." *Journal of Business* 34 (October 1961), pp. 411–433.

———, and Myron S. Scholes. "Dividends and Taxes." *Journal of Financial Economics* 6 (December 1978), pp. 333–364.

Pettit, R. Richardson. "Dividend Announcements, Security Performance, and Capital Market Efficiency." *Journal of Finance* 27 (December 1972), pp. 993–1007.

―――. "The Impact of Dividend and Earnings Announcements: A Reconciliation." *Journal of Business* 49 (January 1976), pp. 86–96.

―――. "Taxes, Transactions Costs and the Clientele Effects of Dividends." *Journal of Financial Economics* 5 (December 1977), pp. 419–436.

Pettway, Richard H., and R. Phil Malone. "Automatic Dividend Reinvestment Plans of Nonfinancial Corporations." *Financial Management* 2 (winter 1973), pp. 11–18.

Schnabel, Jacques A. "The Stable Dividend Hypothesis." *Journal of Business Research* 9 (March 1981), pp. 13–27.

Soter, D. S. "Dividend Controversy—What It Means for Corporate Policy." *Financial Executive* (May 1979), pp. 38–43.

Watts, Ross. "The Information Content of Dividends." *Journal of Business* 46 (April 1973), pp. 191–211.

Wittebort, Suzanne. "Do Investors Really Care About Dividends?" *Institutional Investor* (March 1981), pp. 213–219.

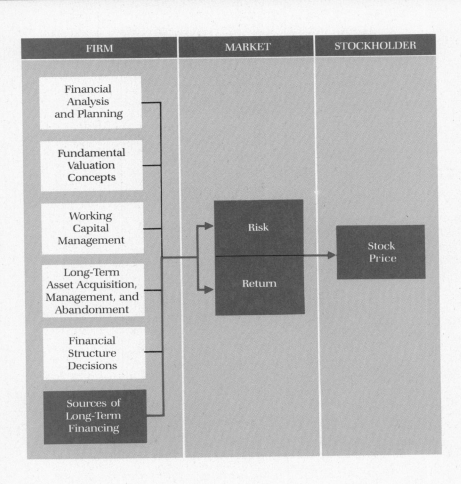

PART SEVEN

SOURCES
OF LONG-TERM
FINANCING

The material in the previous part dealt with the conceptual and theoretical aspects of financial structure decisions. This part of the text contains four chapters that focus on the various financing vehicles that can be used to construct efficient capital structures. In Chapter 20, we look at raising funds externally through common stock financing. The chapter starts off with a brief review of the role and importance of investment banking, and then considers the use of common stock and the important managerial dimensions that accompany such financing. In Chapter 21, long-term debt (term loans and bonds) and preferred stock financing are discussed. These are basically fixed-payment securities that provide the firm with financial leverage. Finally, in the last two chapters, we deal with nontraditional and hybrid forms of financing. In particular, Chapter 22 considers leasing, which in the past two decades has become a major source of financing. In Chapter 23, we look at convertibles, warrants, and options—financing vehicles that provide their holders (the investors) with the option to convert to, acquire, or sell the common stock of a company.

20

Raising Funds Externally: Investment Banking and Common Stock Financing

In 1983, American corporations raised $100 billion by issuing various types of securities to the general public. Billions more were obtained by issuing securities through private placements, and by securing directly negotiated term loans. Such financing is used, along with internally generated funds, to meet the capital and operating needs of the firm, and in general to support corporate growth. This chapter is the first of four dealing with various sources of long-term corporate financing; each builds on the material developed in Part Six and addresses implementation rather than policy issues. In this chapter we deal with the use of common stock. Although equity financing is linked with the dividend decision, we will assume that the question of internally generated funds has been resolved; our attention at this point can, therefore, center on the acquisition and servicing of common stock financing. Because we are dealing with external forms of financing, we begin with a brief review of the role and purpose of investment banking; this is followed by a description of the key characteristics and uses of common stocks and then a discussion of the managerial dimensions of common stock financing.

Investment Banking

Common stocks, as well as other kinds of corporate securities, are initially issued to the public in the primary market and then subsequently traded in the secondary markets. The primary market is the only one in which the issuing corporation actually receives money from the

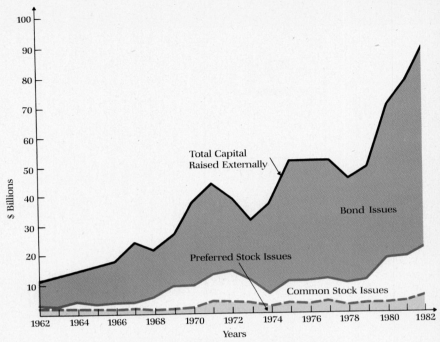

Figure 20.1 Composition and Volume of Corporate Securities.
Issued 1962–1982.

Source: Securities and Exchange Commission, *Monthly Statistical Review*, various issues; and "Corporate Financing Directory," *Investment Dealers' Digest*, various issues.

transaction, since the firm is usually not a party to transactions in the secondary market.[1] Some companies—particularly the smaller, younger ones—do not issue stock to the general public; instead, the shares are held by a small, select group (usually various family members and/or key management personnel). These are privately owned, "closely held," corporations, and there is no real primary or secondary market for their shares.[2] In contrast, the shares of publicly held corporations are owned by a large number of investors, the vast majority of whom are in no way actively or directly involved with the operations of the firm.

Corporate
Financing
Patterns

Figure 20.1 shows the pattern of corporate security financing over the time period 1962 through 1982, and gives an idea of the extent to which firms have used alternative sources of external capital. The overwhelming dominance of bonds as a corporate financing vehicle is clear. During

[1] As we will see later in this chapter, firms can repurchase their shares in the secondary market, at which time they become a direct party to the transaction, much like any institutional or individual investor.

[2] Not all closely held (privately owned) corporations are small; some closely held firms include well-known companies like United Parcel, Mars Candy, Johnson Wax, Hallmark Cards, and Amway Products. For a brief look at other large, privately owned corporations, see "Private Lives," *Forbes*, June 23, 1980, pp. 114–116.

the decade of the seventies, bonds accounted for over 75 percent of net new money raised by corporations. The preference for bond financing can be attributed to their relatively low after-tax cost and the flexibility they offer financial managers; also, in inflationary times, they enable borrowers to repay debt with deflated dollars. The least popular form of financing is preferred stock: Given current tax statutes, it is viewed as a very expensive form of financing since preferreds carry yields that are closely linked to bond returns, but their dividends are paid from after-tax cash flows.

Companies can be expected to shift to greater or lesser reliance on one form of financing or another in response to imbalances in target capital structure ratios and as relative costs of funds change. In the aggregate, however, the volume of financial assets issued tends to vary with the level of economic activity. Specifically, financing requirements are usually the greatest just when the business cycle begins to turn down; the decline in sales that accompanies a drop in economic activity leads to reduced earnings retention at a time when ongoing capital expenditure programs remain high. This increases the size of financial needs and forces greater reliance on external funding sources. On the other hand, requirements are normally lowest when the economy is pulling out of a recession; at this point companies are operating well below capacity, and even a small increase in sales will produce a sharp improvement in the level of profits and internally generated funds.

Investment Banker Functions	Much of the capital firms secure externally is raised with the help of investment bankers. *Investment bankers* offer a variety of services, but their main contribution to corporate finance is providing efficient, low-cost access to the capital markets. Since most companies make only occasional trips to the capital markets, they tend to rely on investment banking firms for the knowhow, contacts, and sales organization necessary to package and distribute new security issues to potential investors. The extent of investment banker involvement in raising corporate capital is evident in Table 20.1, which lists the annual volume of domestic security offerings handled by underwriting firms over the 5-year period ending 1982. For example, investment bankers participated in over 1,400 public issues and another 573 private placements in 1982 alone.

Investment bankers perform several important functions in their capacity as underwriters, including (1) the dissemination of financial advice and counsel (known as the "origination" function), (2) underwriting (the risk-bearing function), and (3) the final distribution of securities (the marketing-resale function). The underwriting process begins with financial advice and counsel. The originating house provides information and makes recommendations to the company on such matters as issue timing, pricing, issue characteristics, and other aspects that are designed to yield the best terms for the issue. Acting in an advisory capacity, the investment banker analyzes the firm's financial position,

TABLE 20.1
Volume of Investment-
Banker-Assisted
Corporate Securities
Issued, 1977–1982
(In Billions of Dollars)

	Year				
	1982	1981	1980	1979	1978
PUBLICLY ISSUED SECURITIES					
Common stock	$16.5	$15.0	$12.8	$ 5.5	$ 5.3
Preferred stock	5.3	1.7	3.2	2.0	1.4
Corporate bonds	57.2	47.0	38.8	24.0	20.0
Total	$79.0	$63.7	$54.8	$31.5	$26.7
PRIVATE PLACEMENTS	$11.3	$18.3	$15.6	$21.4	$21.5
Total all securities	$90.3	$82.0	$70.4	$52.9	$48.2
Number of public issues	1418	1475	1234	694	655
Number of privately placed issues	573	1047	1016	1277	1324

SOURCE: "Corporate Financing Directory," *Investment Dealers' Digest*; and "Directory of Private Placements," *Investment Dealers' Digest*, various issues.

the purpose of the issue, and the disposition of the funds to make sure that the firm and its proposed issue are financially sound. The underwriter also prepares the prospectus and other sales documents, secures a credit rating, establishes a tentative sales date, and may even conduct presale market tests to determine demand levels for the issue at tentative reoffering prices.

A principal function of investment bankers is their willingness to assume the risk in a new issue by underwriting it. It is at this stage that the investment banker actually buys the securities from the issuing corporation; the investment banker, not the corporation, then assumes the risk of being able to place the issue with the investing public. The corporate issuer receives what is known as the "net proceeds" from the issue, and for all practical purposes is out of the picture. Since the investment banker actually owns the securities, if the market deteriorates, the underwriting house will have to either reduce the "reissue" price to investors, or face a sizable inventory of unsold securities. Due to the size of many new issues, *purchase syndicates* (made up of two or more investment banking firms) are often formed to lessen the risk of loss to any single underwriter. Each underwriter in the syndicate is responsible for a given portion of the issue; generally, the originating house will retain the major position and other firms, brought in via syndication, assume the remainder.

Finally, the issue moves to the distribution stage, which involves formally placing it on the market and in the hands of investors. Like the underwriting function, the distribution function is conducted quickly, since time is of the essence at this point. A *selling group* is formed to expedite the marketing and distribution of the new issue; it may be made up of as many as 40 to 50 investment banking firms, or more. Figure 20.2 contains an announcement of a new stock issue and shows the number of investment bankers involved in the distribution of a new issue to the public. Note that for this $73.6 million stock issue, there is a lead underwriter (it is Morgan Stanley and its name appears at the top of the list) and another 9 large investment banking firms in the selling group. Once an issue has been offered for sale, the purchase syndicate will attempt to stabilize the market price so that the entire issue can be sold at the initial reoffering price. This activity, referred to as *price pegging*, is legal as long as the intent is disclosed in the registration statement filed with the SEC. Price pegging is in the best interest of both the issuer and the underwriting syndicate to the extent that it reduces underwriter risk and thereby lowers the cost to the issuer.[3]

Since 1982, companies have been provided with an effective alternative to using underwriters to publicly issue new securities. This procedure is known as *shelf registration* and was authorized by the SEC to expedite filing procedures for companies offering securities. Basically, shelf registration allows a company to file a single document summarizing its long-term financing plans; such a registration document then "remains on the shelf" for a period of 2 years, during which time the company can enter the market any time it deems suitable without delay, additional paperwork, or the services of an investment banker. Best of all, if the amount of debt or equity listed in the registration document isn't sold in the first offering, the company can jump into the market when the next "window" appears and repeat the process until the volume on the shelf registration has been reached or the 2-year period expires. While shelf registration may be a viable procedure for a number of issuers, investment bankers are still used in the vast majority of cases (and even by many firms that use shelf registration). Accordingly, we continue our discussion of investment bankers and examine several types of underwriter arrangements.

Types of Underwriter Arrangements and Security Offerings

Securities can be issued in a variety of ways. If an investment banker is used, the securities can be issued under one of several underwriter arrangements: they can be formally underwritten or issued on a best efforts basis, in which case the investment banker assumes no underwriting risk. And if the issue is underwritten, it can be sold via competitive bidding or on a negotiated basis. A cash offering can be used if the issue is to be sold to the general public; alternatively, when the

---

[3]For a more complete discussion of investment banking, syndication, and underwriter functions, see I. W. Burnham, "The Securities Industry: Financing Corporate America," *Financial Executive*, (March 1976), pp. 26–31; Irwin Friend et al., *Investment Banking and the New Issues Market*, (New York: World, 1967); and Samuel L. Hayes III, "Investment Banking: Power Structures in Flux," *Harvard Business Review* 49 (March–April 1971), pp. 136–152.

1,100,000 Shares

Walt Disney Productions

Common Stock
(no par value)

Price $66⅞ a Share

MORGAN STANLEY & CO.
Incorporated

BLYTH EASTMAN PAINE WEBBER   **GOLDMAN, SACHS & CO.**   **KIDDER, PEABODY & CO.**
Incorporated   *Incorporated*

LEHMAN BROTHERS KUHN LOEB   **MERRILL LYNCH WHITE WELD CAPITAL MARKETS GROUP**
Incorporated   *Merrill Lynch, Pierce, Fenner & Smith Incorporated*

SHEARSON/AMERICAN EXPRESS INC.   **SMITH BARNEY, HARRIS UPHAM & CO.**
Incorporated

WERTHEIM & CO., INC.   **DEAN WITTER REYNOLDS INC.**

January 28, 1983

Figure 20.2   An Announcement of a New Stock Issue.
Source: Morgan Stanley & Co. Incorporated.

offering involves a new issue of common stock, a privileged subscription (or rights offering) can be used if management wants (or has) to first offer the new issue to existing stockholders. Finally, rather than going public, the security can be privately placed.

Underwritten or Best Efforts.   When a security is *underwritten*, the investment banker (or purchase syndicate) actually buys the entire issue from the issuing corporation and accepts the risk of having to resell the securities to the public. When common stocks are sold via a rights offering, the new issue is usually underwritten by using a *standby agreement*. Basically, in a rights offering (which we discuss in more detail below), the existing shareholders are given rights that enable them to purchase the new common stock on favorable terms for a specified period of time. Shareholders can sell these rights, exercise them, or let them expire. A firm can guarantee the success of a rights offering by having an investment banker "stand by" to underwrite the unsold portion of the issue. If an issue is undersubscribed, the investment banker is obligated to step in and purchase the unsold portion at a predetermined subscription price.

Occasionally, a new security offering may be so risky that investment bankers will be unwilling to underwrite it. Under such conditions, the issue can be sold through an underwriter on a *best efforts* basis. The investment banker provides origination services and assists in distributing the issue, but the banker's only commitment is to do its best to sell as many of the securities as it can at the established offering price. The issuing firm bears the risk of an undersubscribed issue. Other things being equal, best efforts is the least costly way of issuing securities, but it is also the most risky. While best efforts offerings are used most frequently by small, unseasoned companies, the rights offerings of large, well-established companies are sometimes handled on a best efforts basis if management feels that the prospects for oversubscription are highly likely. These firms would use the best efforts procedure as a way to minimize underwriter costs.[4] Because of the obvious risk involved, however, most large firms that use this procedure also have backup financing in case the issue is not fully subscribed.

Competitive and Negotiated Underwritings.   A public offering of a new issue can be handled through an investment banker in one of two ways. It can be issued through competitive bidding or on a negotiated basis. A *competitive bidding arrangement* is a public auction in which a new issue is sold to the underwriter who submits the highest bid to the

---

[4]For an analysis (from the corporation's perspective) of a best efforts offering versus an underwritten issue, see Gershon Mandelker and Artur Ravic, "Investment Banking: An Economic Analysis of Optimal Underwriting Contracts," *Journal of Finance* 32 (June 1977), pp. 683–694.

issuer. When securities are sold through competitive bidding, the issuing company simply invites bids from investment bankers. The investment banking firm (or syndicate) that bids the highest price for the security wins the issue. It then purchases the security from the company and resells it at a higher price to investors. The winning competitive bidder provides the risk-bearing and distribution functions, but not origination services; rather, in a competitive bid arrangement, the issuing firm sets the terms of the issue itself, or more than likely, employs a financial advisor to do so.

A *negotiated sale*, in contrast, is a contractual arrangement between an underwriter and the issuing firm whereby the underwriter is given the exclusive right to design, underwrite, and distribute the new security. The investment banker performs all underwriter functions, from origination through distribution of the issue. Unlike competitive bidding, the amount of underwriter compensation in a negotiated sale is subject to direct negotiation between issuer and underwriter. The vast majority of publicly offered corporate securities are sold through negotiated underwriting arrangements—for example, around 85 percent of bonds and preferred stock were issued this way in 1981, and so was over 97 percent of common stock.[5]

On the surface, such statistics suggest that negotiated arrangements should be the least costly from the firm's point of view. However, except perhaps during times of unstable market conditions, studies have found that the competitive procedure generally results in the lowest cost to the issuer.[6] Some of this lower cost can be attributed to the fact that there are no origination services in competitive underwritings. A more persuasive argument, however, uses the negotiated arrangement's lack of competition to explain why it is more costly. The argument is that the negotiated underwriter, because of the exclusive contractual position, enjoys monopoly power not available to competitive bidders, and as a result is in a position to extract a spread which exceeds that possible under competitive bidding and/or to set resale prices above required equilibrium levels. Why, then, are corporations such persistent users of negotiated underwriter arrangements? The only rational answer is that firms apparently feel the added services offered by negotiated underwritings are worth the added cost. In addition, negotiated underwriters are useful in bringing to the market issues that would otherwise have difficulty being

---

[5]In addition, all privileged subscriptions—rights offerings handled through underwriters—and all securities issued on a best efforts basis are set up as negotiated deals.

[6]See, for example, U.S. Securities and Exchange Commission, *Cost of Flotation of Corporate Securities 1951–1955, 1957* (Washington, D.C.: U.S. Government Printing Office, 1957); E. A. Dyl and M. D. Joehnk, "Competitive vs. Negotiated Underwriting of Public Utility Debt," *Bell Journal of Economics* 7 (autumn 1976), pp. 680–689; L. H. Ederington, "Negotiated vs. Competitive Underwriting of Corporate Bonds," *Journal of Finance* 31 (March 1976), pp. 17–28; and G. D. Tallman, D. F. Rush, and R. W. Melicher, "Competitive vs. Negotiated Underwriting Costs of Regulated Industries," *Financial Management* 3 (summer 1974), pp. 49–55.

placed—examples include issues that are new to the market, those that have a very low credit rating, and those that are unusual (complex) in structure or large in size.

Cash Offering or Privileged Subscription.   Publicly issued securities are sold as general cash offerings or as privileged subscriptions. New issues are sold to investors at large (to the general investing public) in a *cash offering*; nearly all bonds and preferred stocks are sold by general cash offering, and so are a large number of common stocks (companies that "go public" for the first time usually issue their stock via a cash offering). In contrast, a *privileged subscription* or (*rights offering*) is used with a new issue of common stock when the firm wants or has to restrict the offering to existing stockholders. Some firms are required through "preemptive right provisions" to issue new shares of stock in this way. In a privileged subscription, each stockholder is issued one right for each share of stock he or she holds; the *right* represents an option to buy a certain number of new shares (usually a fraction) at a stipulated subscription price. The actual number of rights required to buy a single share of the new stock will be a function of the number of new shares being issued. For example, if a company has 10 million shares outstanding and intends to issue 1 million new shares, 10 rights will be required to buy a single share of new stock. Generally speaking, the use of rights offerings to raise equity capital is cheaper than a public cash offering.

Private Placements.   A *private placement* differs from a public issue in that the new issue is placed directly with a single or small group of institutional investors (perhaps as few as two or three institutional investors will buy a whole issue). Such issues are not underwritten; rather, investment bankers are used as *finders*, whereby they arrange for the direct placement of the issue with an institution or group of institutions. In addition to acting as a finder, investment bankers also provide advice and counsel. Although once the almost-exclusive preserve of small- to medium-sized, high-risk firms hunting capital in amounts ranging from $500,000 to $5 million, the private placement market has matured to the point that it is now also used by the largest and most creditworthy corporations seeking amounts that often run into the hundreds of millions of dollars.

Issuing a security via public distribution generally involves a considerable amount of time and money, whereas private placements are less difficult, less time-consuming, and less expensive. A major reason for this is the fact that privately placed issues are exempt from SEC registration—indeed, the private placement procedure itself was originally instituted as a way to avoid the onerous registration requirements created by the Securities Act of 1933. One study estimated that, depending on the size of the issue, a private placement has administrative and underwriting costs that are one-fourth to one-half those of a public issue.[7] Unfortunately, such cost savings are often more than offset by a differential in the cost of funds that was found, in a study by Hays et al, to amount to an average of about 50 basis points (or one-half of one percent).[8] Such a cost differential can add up: 50 basis points on a $25 million, 20-year term bond translates into added interest costs of $2.5 million over the life of the issue. Some of this spread can be attributable to the smaller size of the average privately placed issue and/or to the near-monopolistic position of investors. But it is also likely that a major portion of the differential is explained by the greater marketability risk assumed by private placement investors—there is no established secondary market for such issues. In spite of the higher net cost to the issuing firm, private placements continue to be popular not only with small- to medium-sized companies that are experiencing high growth rates and the corresponding need for capital, but also with firms that seek fast placement and confidentiality, the ability to tailor the terms of the issue, and the ability to put together complex and highly sophisticated deals. In such cases, the benefits of a private placement may outweigh the higher costs.

Flotation Costs | The cost of issuing securities is composed of (1) registration and general administrative expenses, and (2) underwriter or investment banker compensation. The first type of cost is made up of such things as printing expenses, legal and accounting fees, registration fees, and other miscellaneous expenses incurred in the flotation of a new issue. Several studies have examined these expenses and found them to range from around 5 percent on $1 million issues to about four-tenths of 1 percent on $50 million issues.[9] Although the absolute amount will decline with smaller issues[10], most of these costs are essentially fixed, so there are definite economies of scale that can be enjoyed with larger issues.

The second cost, *underwriter spread*, represents the compensation to investment bankers for services rendered. It too varies according to the size of the issue. A recent study of common stock flotation costs indicated that underwriter compensation ranged from about 10.5 percent on small ($2 million) issues to as low as 3.8 percent for issues in the

[7]A. B. Cohan, *Yields on Corporate Debt Directly Placed* (New York: National Bureau of Economic Research, 1967), p. 127.

[8]P. Hays, M. Joehnk, and R. Melicher, "Differential Determinants of Risk Premiums in the Public and Private Corporate Bond Markets," *Journal of Financial Research* (fall 1979), pp. 143–152.

[9]C. W. Smith, "Alternative Methods for Raising Capital: Rights Versus Underwritten Offerings," *Journal of Financial Economics* 7 (November 1977), pp. 273–307; and R. Hillstrom and R. King (eds.), *1960–69: A Decade of Corporate and International Finance* (New York: Investment Dealers' Digest, 1970).

[10]For example, the registration and general administrative fees for a $10 million issue will approximate $70,000, yet the same expenses for a much larger $50 million issue will be only slightly more, around $100,000.

$100–$500 million range.[11] Another study used regression analysis to examine the underwriting cost function and found a significant fixed element in underwriter pricing systems, confirming substantial economies of scale for larger issues.[12]

Underwriter spread is also a function of the type of issue being marketed; for example, bonds generally have the lowest spread, followed by preferred stock, with common stock being the most expensive. Typical underwriter compensation is given in the following table, which shows the spreads for three comparably sized issues—a bond, a preferred stock, and a common stock—that were all brought to the market by public utility firms within a two-week period in mid-March 1980:

	Bond	Preferred Stock	Common Stock
Issuer	Kansas Gas & Electric	Illinois Power	Kansas City Power & Light
Size of issue	$30.0 million	$36.0 million	$27.8 million
Underwriters spread	0.8%	1.1%	5.3%
Underwriter compensation[a]	$ 240,000	$ 396,000	$ 1,473,400
Proceeds to issuer[b]	$29,760,000	$35,604,000	$26,326,600

[a]Underwriter compensation = size of issue × underwriter's spread.
[b]Proceeds to issuer = size of issue − underwriter compensation.
SOURCE: *Institutional Investor*, May 1980, pp. 217–218.

Although the securities were comparable, the amount of underwriter compensation clearly varied according to the type of issue being marketed. Note also that actual underwriter compensation depends on the amount of the spread and the size of the issue,[13] and that the *proceeds to the issuer* represents the net amount the issuer will realize after underwriter compensation has been deducted. Of course, since registration and general administrative expenses must also be deducted from the proceeds, the amount actually realized by the issuer will be somewhat less than that shown above.

As might be expected, compensation to investment bankers is considerably less for best efforts arrangements, since the security is not underwritten. Registration and other administrative expenses are about

---

[11]Smith, "Alternative Methods for Raising Capital."
[12]Dyl and Joehnk, "Competitive vs. Negotiated Underwriting of Public Utility Debt."
[13]As an example of how underwriter spread is disbursed to various investment banker participants, consider a negotiated underwritten cash offering: about 10 to 20 percent of the underwriter spread in this case goes to the originating investment banker, 30 to 40 percent to the purchase syndicate, and the remainder (40 to 60 percent) is commission to the selling group.

the same, but banker compensation is made up only of charges for providing financial advice and selling commissions. Underwriter compensation in standby agreements is also a bit different. It consists of two parts: a flat "standby" fee, and an additional "take-up" fee. The flat fee portion represents normal charges for the financial counsel provided, and for assisting in the distribution of the rights. The take-up fee is paid for each unsubscribed share of stock that the underwriter has to buy and represents compensation for assuming the risk-bearing function.

Characteristics and Use of Common Stock Financing

As we saw above, investment bankers play an important role in the stock financing activities of a firm, and are a vital link in channeling equity funds to the corporation. However, there is more to the management of common stock than periodically issuing new shares. Accordingly, we now direct our attention to common stock financing and examine some of the dimensions of this important managerial function.

The owners of a corporation are the common stockholders who invest their money in the firm on the basis of their expectations of future returns. Common stockholders hold a residual ownership position in the firm, since they own whatever is left after all other claims on income and assets have been satisfied. Excluding preferred stock, the equity of a corporation is made up of the common stock it has issued over time and the earnings it has retained. Also known as "net worth" or "book value," stockholders' equity can increase internally (as when the firm generates and retains a profit) or externally (as when the company issues new stock). The question of internally generated funds and the important role dividend policy plays therein was addressed in detail in the preceding chapter. In contrast to internally generated funds, firms engage in new stock issues only on an infrequent and irregular basis. Thus, much of management's time is taken up with "servicing" outstanding shares, rather than planning and developing new issues. We now direct our attention to a discussion of common stocks as a financing vehicle: their issue characteristics and their role as a form of financing.

Common Stock Features

Each share of common stock represents a prorated, undivided interest in the net assets and earnings of a company. Most firms have only one class of common stock outstanding, but in some cases special classes of common, known as *classified stock*, are created to meet special needs. When a company has classified stock outstanding, it is customary to designate one type of stock as class A, and the second as class B, and so on. Although the various classifications have no standard meanings, they usually denote either different voting rights and/or different dividend obligations on the part of the firm. A variation of this concept is used by some public utility firms, which reinvest all or a large portion of dividend income into additional shares of the company for class A (capital gains) stock, and pay out regular cash dividends to the class B (income) stock.

The Rights of Stockholders. Common stockholders acquire certain rights when they buy shares in a company. They are entitled, for example, to the periodic receipt of information about the financial affairs of the corporation; in addition they have the right to share the residual assets of the corporation on dissolution. The two most important attributes of share ownership, however, involve income and control. Common stockholders are residual owners and provide risk capital to the firm. As such, they are entitled to a prorated share of undivided earnings and dividends paid. So long as the firm prospers and grows, there is no limit to the returns (dividends and/or capital appreciation) a stockholder can earn. The return on stockholders' capital is, to a large extent, a function of the decisions and actions of management. That is, the financial and other managerial decisions of the company affect the level and volatility of net earnings, which in turn have an influence on the price behavior of the stock[14] and on the level of dividends paid out each year to stockholders.

The link between stockholder returns and the actions of management leads to the matter of control. Technically, the common stockholders are the owners of the corporation, and as such they have ultimate control over its affairs. In practice, however, this control is limited to the right to vote, either in person or by proxy, in the election of directors and in a number of other matters (like the decision to enter into a merger, to hire a new auditing firm, or to change the amount of authorized common stock). Some issues of common stock provide shareholders with "preemptive rights," which allow stockholders to maintain their proportionate ownership position in the corporation when new shares of common are issued. Preemptive rights, in effect, enable existing shareholders to maintain their voting control and to protect themselves against dilution of earnings.

Control of the company is exerted through the voting rights of the common stockholders. Unless there is classified common stock outstanding, each share of stock entitles the holder to cast one vote. In the election of directors, a stockholder's vote can be cast in different ways. If the corporation's articles specify a majority voting system, each director is voted on separately and stockholders cast one vote for each share they own. If cumulative voting is permitted, the directors are voted on jointly and the stockholders can, if they wish, cast all their votes for just one candidate (the number of votes cast being a product of the number of directors to be elected and the number of shares owned). Cumulative

---

[14]For a discussion of the effects of earnings per share on share price behavior in an efficient market, see James H. Lorie and Mary T. Hamilton, *The Stock Market: Theories and Evidence* 2d ed. (Homewood, Ill.: Irwin, 1982), chaps. 5, 6.

voting provides minority stockholders with an opportunity to elect at least some of the directors, and in so doing to obtain representation on the board.

Except in special situations, an absolute majority position is defined as 50 percent plus one. It is sometimes possible in large corporations, however, for an individual or small group to exercise operating control with a much smaller portion of the stock—often with as little as 10 to 20 percent of the voting stock, or even less. Such control is possible because the block of votes controlled by the individual or group simply dominates all others. As a result, the person or group exercises considerable influence over the affairs of the corporation. The question of control has become an important issue in management and finance in recent years. Certainly, the frequency of proxy fights has increased substantially, as have attempts by one corporation to take over another by purchasing a majority of the outstanding stock. Managers who do not have majority control of the firm's stock are very much concerned about takeovers, and many of them are attempting to get stockholder approval for changes in the corporate charter that would make takeovers much more difficult. Some companies, for instance, have tried to get their stockholders to require a 75 percent affirmative vote to approve pending mergers.

Accounting Treatment.   The corporate charter states the number of shares of common stock a firm is authorized to issue. However, not all authorized shares are outstanding; since it is time-consuming and sometimes difficult to amend a charter to authorize additional shares, firms generally authorize more shares than they plan to issue in the foreseeable future. Having shares that are authorized but unissued gives management flexibility in granting stock options, negotiating mergers, or distributing stock dividends. Common stock may be sold with or without *par value*, a relatively useless value arbitrarily placed on some stocks. It has absolutely no relation to a stock's book or market values. Par value, as a rule, is generally set quite low, since in many states the firm's owners can be held liable for an amount equal to the difference between the par value and the price paid for the stock if the price paid for the stock is less than par value. A low par value may also be advantageous in states where certain types of corporate taxes are levied on the par value of the stock. Firms often issue *no par stock*, in which case they may simply assign the stock an arbitrary value for accounting purposes, or place the stock on the books at the price at which it was actually sold. In the absence of state statutes, the placement of a par value on a stock is done more out of tradition than anything else. There are no managerial, market, or cost motivations to using par versus no par stock; only the accounting treatment differs.

The normal accounting treatment of the common stock portion of the firm's balance sheet is as follows:

STOCKHOLDER'S EQUITY	
Common stock, $5 par value; 1,000,000 shares authorized, 590,000 shares issued (less 12,000 shares in Treasury—see below)	$ 2,950,000
Paid-in capital in excess of par value	6,342,500
Retained earnings	11,615,625
Total	$20,908,125
Less: Treasury stock (12,000 shares at cost)	$ 670,500
Total stockholders' equity	$20,237,625

As this illustration demonstrates, the stockholders' equity, or net worth, section of the balance sheet reflects the accumulated investment of the corporation's stockholders at historical cost. This section represents the book or residual value of the corporation, and is equal to the difference between total assets and total liabilities.

The common stock account shows the par or stated value of the common shares issued. Typically, shares are issued at a price in excess of their par (or stated) value, in which case the excess is recorded in the "paid-in capital in excess of par value" account. In addition, the value of any capital received by the company that did not involve issuing shares, such as donated assets, is included in this account. Retained earnings represent the cumulative earnings of the company, less any dividends paid. This account also includes the cumulative affects of any special credits and charges, such as prior period adjustments not included in the income statement. *Treasury stock* is a company's own stock that has been issued and subsequently reacquired, but not yet formally retired; it is shown on the balance sheet as a deduction, at cost, from capital. Such stock do not have voting privileges and do not enter into earnings per share computations.[15] Treasury stock can subsequently be used by the corporation for purposes of mergers and acquisitions, to meet employee stock option plans, or as a way to pay stock dividends.

Using Common Stock as a Form of Financing

Over the decade of the seventies, American corporations raised $77.8 billion in common stock financing. The annual volume of new stock issues ranged from a low of $4 billion in 1974 to a high of $10.7 billion in 1972, and in 1982, such financing hit $16.5 billion. The volume and pattern of common stock financing is influenced by a variety of forces, some internal and some exogenous to the firm. In the material that follows we will briefly review some of these variables, starting with the advantages and disadvantages of this form of financing.

---

[15]For a more detailed discussion of the accounting treatment of equity capital, see David F. Hawkins, *Corporate Financial Reporting: Text and Cases*, rev. ed. (Homewood, Ill.: Irwin, 1977), chap. 22.

Advantages and Disadvantages.   The basic advantage of common stock stems from the fact that it is a source of financing which places a minimum of constraints on the firm: Dividends do not have to be paid on common stock (there are no fixed charges on common stock), and their nonpayment does not jeopardize the position of other security holders. The fact that common stock has no maturity, thereby eliminating any future repayment obligation, also enhances the desirability of common stock financing. Another advantage of common stock over other forms of long-term funds is its ability to increase the firm's borrowing power. The more common stock the firm sells, the larger the firm's equity base, and therefore (other things being equal), the more easily and cheaply additional long-term debt financing can be obtained.

Unfortunately, there are some disadvantages to common stock financing, the most obvious of which include potential dilution of voting power and earnings. The sale of common stock extends voting rights and control to other investors, and it is for this reason that common stock financing is often avoided by small or new firms, whose owner-managers may be reluctant to share control with outsiders. And unless a rights offering is used, common stock financing gives more owners the right to share in income, which in turn produces dilution of earnings. Another disadvantage is the high cost of common stock; as we saw in Chapter 17, common equity is normally the most expensive form of long-term financing. This is because dividends are not tax deductible and common stock is a riskier security than either debt or preferred stock. Finally, as a rule, common stock also has high flotation costs.

Factors That Influence the Decision to Use Common Stock Financing. The decision to issue common stock depends on a number of variables, including comparative costs, market conditions, risk, and control. The financing needs of the company are obviously important; for example, the decision to float a new issue of common stock may be in order when the level of attractive (sufficiently profitable) investment opportunities exceeds the amount of internally generated funds and/or the amount that can economically be raised through debt and other forms of capital. Because of the high cost of equity capital, firms customarily look to other sources before deciding to issue stock. Such reluctance, however, tends to lessen as market conditions improve, for studies have shown, not surprisingly, that stocks are more likely to be issued following a significant rise in share prices.[16] Higher prices mean that fewer shares have to be issued, and therefore that the financing will have a less detrimental impact on the cost of capital.

---

[16]See R. A. Taggart, "A Model of Corporate Financing Decisions," *Journal of Finance* 32 (December 1977), pp. 1467–1484. This is just what occurred in the strong market of 1983, when nearly $40 billion of common stock was issued.

If we take as given that comparative costs and market conditions are favorable, we can now shift to the question of risk and control. Among the important elements in assessing the extent of risk exposure likely to occur with new stock financing are the firm's financial structure and its market risk (or level of beta). The new financing, of course, should be compatible with the firm's target capital structure; failure in this regard can lead to unnecessary increases in the firm's marginal cost of capital. The stock's beta should also be assessed before and after the proposed issue to see the impact the new issue is likely to have. Other things being equal, stock financing would be viewed as desirable so long as it results in lowering the security's beta. This would reduce the firm's market risk and have a positive effect on the value of the firm. Finally, the matter of managerial control has to be resolved. If the stock is already widely held, then there is probably little or no concern about control; if the shares are closely held, then the issue of control may cause problems and act as a deterrent to the use of common stock financing.

Managerial Dimensions of Common Stock Financing

From a strictly administrative perspective, the management of common stock revolves around two broad activities: (1) issuing new stock and (2) servicing outstanding stock. The former is an eposodic type of activity, whereas the latter, especially for widely traded, publicly held stock, is a recurring activity that requires the ongoing attention of financial management.

Issuing Stock

Several important activities fall under the broad category of issuing stock; these include the decision to go public, the decision to list a company's stock, and the decision to issue additional shares of stock.

Going Public.   One of the early decisions management must make in the area of common stock financing is whether to go public or to remain a private, closely held corporation. Going public is an important (and often traumatic) corporate decision. From the owner's and/or founder's perspective, it involves sharing the company and its earnings with others, and meeting a variety of regulatory obligations with respect to periodic financial disclosure. Often, firms go public to avoid potentially nasty probate problems, or when the founder is nearing retirement and none of the obvious successors is a close family member. In a strictly corporate context, the chief reasons for going public are to raise new capital funds and to open up new channels of capital to the firm—in effect, to provide the immediate and future capital to meet continued growth and capital funding needs.

There are two ways a firm can go public: through an initial public offering, or through a secondary distribution. The number of initial public offerings (or IPOs for short) tends to vary directly with the strength of the stock market—the incidence increases with bull markets and decreases with market slumps. The major beneficiary of an *initial public offering* is the company. The original owners retain all or most of their shares (and usually absolute control of the firm), so the money is raised by issuing additional shares of corporate stock. A *secondary distribution*, in contrast, is a procedure whereby the original owners can dispose of all or a major portion of their holdings. Except for gaining wider access to capital markets, the firm itself receives no direct benefits from such an offering; rather, total net proceeds go to the original owners, who are the sellers in the transaction.

The Decision to List.   As a company expands, the advantages of listing its stock tend to increase as well. Corporate growth and trading activity become so large that the needs of the firm are best served on one of the listed exchanges. In the past, most firms went from the OTC to the American Stock Exchange or one of the regional exchanges; the ultimate goal, of course, was to become listed on the NYSE. With the advent of NASDAQ, however, many firms have chosen to stay on the OTC for a longer period of time; the reason for this is the greater price continuity, trading activity, and visibility provided by the NASDAQ system.

The decision to list carries with it enhanced prestige and an even greater access to capital market funds; often, trading activity also picks up as share liquidity increases. The net result is that management may be able to lower the firm's cost of capital; that is, the risk-return character of the stock may be altered in such a way so as to reduce the stockholders' required rate of return. Studies on the value of listing have turned in mixed results. For example, Ying et al. found that listing led to a net increase in share prices and therefore had a desirable affect on the cost of equity to the firm; in contrast, a more recent study by Fabozzi was unable to generate results to support the contention that listing reduces the cost of equity capital. Instead, Fabozzi suggests that management will have to point to benefits other than reduced equity costs to justify listing.[17]

The decision to list the company's common stock is made by management as the company grows, establishes an earnings record, and expands the number of shares outstanding. A firm becomes listed by simply filing an application for listing and meeting the minimum requirements established by the exchange in question. As an example, to be eligible for listing on the NYSE (which has the most stringent requirements), a firm must have at least 2000 shareholders that own 100

---

[17]Louis K. W. Ying, Wilbur G. Lewellen, Gary G. Schlarbaum, and Ronald C. Lease, "Stock Exchange Listing and Securities Returns," *Journal of Financial and Quantitative Analysis* 12 (September 1977), pp. 415–432; and Frank J. Fabozzi, "Does Listing on the AMEX Increase the Value of Equity?" *Financial Management* 10 (spring 1981), pp. 43–50.

shares or more; have a minimum of 1 million shares outstanding that are publicly held; have a demonstrated earning power of $2.5 million (before taxes); have net tangible assets of $16 million; and have publicly traded shares with a minimum market value of between $8 and $16 million, depending on market conditions.

Subsequent Stock Issues. Another important decision, and one that can reoccur a number of times over the life of a firm, pertains to issuing additional shares of new common stock. When a company is faced with a decision to sell additional stock, it must decide early in the process whether the issue will be offered directly (i.e., issued without the use of an investment banker), be fully underwritten, or distributed on a best efforts basis; if it is to be underwritten, the firm must further decide whether the offering should be handled on a negotiated or competitive basis. To gain an understanding of the elements that go into the decision to issue additional shares of common, consider the case of a company that decides to issue stock through a rights offering.

Establishing the Subscription Price. Once the decision to issue stock (via a rights offering) has been made, attention can shift to the most important element in the offering: establishing a subscription price for the new issue. Of course, other matters have to be addressed (like determining the number of rights needed to buy one new share of stock), but these can be handled routinely once the subscription price has been set. The subscription price must be set below the current market price, but the extent of the discount is a function of the sensitivity of the market to a price change, the degree of dilution in ownership and earnings, and the size of the offering itself. The biggest problem at this point is to arrive at a subscription price that will be sufficiently attractive to existing and potential stockholders to result in a fully or oversubscribed offering, while at the same time avoiding such a low price that existing stockholders suffer an unnecessary amount of dilution in earnings per share. The dilution problem comes from the fact that although the new shares will become part of the capital structure immediately, the returns on the capital raised will be delayed until the projects can be implemented, and profits and cash flow reach their full potential. The net result is that immediately following the distribution of the new shares, the earnings per share of the firm, and its share price, will drop in proportion to the size of the new issue. For example, if a company had $40 million in net profit after taxes and 10 million shares outstanding, net earnings per share would be:

$$\text{EPS} = \text{net profit after tax/number of shares outstanding}$$
$$= \$40 \text{ million/10 million} = \$4 \text{ per share}$$

If the stock were selling at 12 times earnings, its market price would be:

$$\text{Price} = \text{EPS} \times \text{price/earnings multiple}$$
$$= \$40 \times 12 = \$48$$

Now look at what happens when the company issues an additional 1 million shares of common stock. Since net profits do not change immediately, earnings per share will drop:

$$\text{EPS} = \$40 \text{ million/11 million shares} = \$3.64$$

At a multiple of 12, the price also drops, to 43 5/8.

The same principle is at work when the firm establishes the subscription price in a rights offering. To understand how the subscription price might be set, let us continue our example, but in this case assume the firm knows only that it needs to raise about $40 million in new equity capital (for simplicity, ignore underwriter spread and other flotation costs). If the company could issue the stock at its present market price of $48 per share, it would have to issue 833,333 shares to raise the $40 million. Such an action would of course cause some dilution; to be exact, EPS would fall to $40 million/10,833,333 = $3.69. At a multiple of 12, the price would drop to $3.69 × 12 = $44.28. Under these conditions, it should be clear that the company cannot issue the new stock at $48 per share, nor can it raise $40 million by issuing 833,333 shares at $44.28 (833,333 × $44.28 = $36.9 million). But it does provide a perspective on a subscription price. Assume that a further 10 percent price concession is necessary to enhance the prospects of a successful offering. Rounded to the nearest dollar, the net result would be a subscription price of $40 per share: $44.28 × .90 = $39.85 ≈ $40.

Given this subscription price, it is now possible to determine the number of rights required to purchase a single share of stock. Since the amount of funds to be raised is known, we can find the total number of shares that must be sold by dividing the amount of capital to be raised by the subscription price. Then, dividing the total number of shares outstanding by the total number of new shares to be sold, the number of rights required to purchase a single share of stock can be determined. In our example, the firm would have to issue 1 million new shares of stock, and 10 rights would be required to buy one new share at a subscription price of $40. If the market and the multiple remain unchanged, this new issue will probably be successful, because its subscription price will be well below the new (post-issue) diluted price. That is, after the issue, the stock's EPS and price should be: $40 million/11 million shares = $3.64 × 12 = $43.68. In fact, given no change in the price/earnings multiple, the maximum subscription price that could be established in this case would be $44 per share. At this price, the fully diluted (post-issue) price of the stock will just equal the subscription price. To raise $40 million at $44 per share, the company will have to issue 909,000 new shares of stock; as a result, the new fully diluted (post-issue) price of the stock will be: $40,000,000/10,909,000 = $3.67 × 12 = $44. A higher subscription price would lead to a post-issue price *less* than the price asked for the new issue, which investors would likely find unattractive. It is logical for underwriters to want to establish as *low* a subscription price as possible to reduce their risk in a standby agreement (it is easier to sell low-price stock and have a fully subscribed or oversubscribed issue), but it is clearly in the firm's best interest to have the price set as *high* as possible to reduce the number of shares issued and thereby reduce dilution and unfavorable stockholder reactions.

Issuing Rights.   In a rights offering, the board of directors sets a date of record, which is the last date on which the recipient of a right must be the legal owner as indicated on the company's stock ledger. Due to the lag in bookkeeping procedures, stocks are sold ex-rights (without rights) for four business days prior to the date of record. Prior to this date, the stock is sold cum rights (or "rights-on"), which means the purchaser of the stock will receive the rights. The issuing firm sends rights to holders of record, each of them receiving one right for each share of stock they hold. Rights are transferable, and many are traded actively on the various stock exchanges (even for the very short period of time that they exist).

The Value of a Right.   Theoretically, the value of a right should be the same whether the stock is selling with rights or ex-rights; however, the market value of rights may differ from their theoretical value. Once a rights offering has been declared, shares will trade for a while with rights-on. Equation 20.1 is used to find the theoretical value of a right when the stock is trading with rights-on, R_o:

$$R_o = \frac{M_o - S}{N + 1} \tag{20.1}$$

where R_o = theoretical value of a right when stock is selling rights-on
   M_o = market value of the stock with rights-on
   S = subscription price of the stock
   N = number of rights needed to purchase a share of stock

For example, in our illustration, recall that it takes 10 rights to buy 1 new share of stock and that a stockholder would have to surrender 10 rights plus $40 to receive 1 of the newly issued shares. To find the theoretical value of the rights we can use Equation 20.1, and given that the shares are trading rights-on at $48 per share, we see that the theoretical value of 1 right is:

$$R_o = \frac{\$48 - \$40}{10 + 1} = \frac{\$8}{11} = \$.73$$

In contrast, when the stock is trading ex-rights, its share price of the stock should be expected to drop by an amount equal to the value of a right. That is, the market value of a stock trading ex-rights, M_e, is:

$$M_e = M_o - R_o \qquad (20.2)$$

According to this equation, the stock in our example should trade at an ex-rights price of:

$$M_e = \$48.00 - \$.73 = \$47.27.$$

Given this information, the value of a right when the stock is trading ex-rights, R_e, can be found according to Equation 20.3:

$$R_e = \frac{M_e - S}{N} \qquad (20.3)$$

Continuing our example, we can see that the theoretical value of a right is the same regardless of whether it is selling rights-on or ex-rights. That is, using Equation 20.3, and the information provided above, we see that the value of a right when the stock is selling ex-rights is:

$$R_e = \frac{\$47.27 - \$40.00}{10} = \$.73$$

Servicing Stock Once the stock has been publicly issued, management's attention shifts to the routine administration and servicing of the outstanding shares. Several dimensions of this task are important, including implementation of dividend policy, the question of stock dividends and stock splits, and share repurchase decisions.[18] The cash dividend decision is one of the most important ongoing decisions of the firm and has a dramatic effect on the corporate financial structure. Considerable attention was devoted

---

[18]Maintaining a sound financial public relations program is also a vital part of the servicing function, especially for larger firms. With respect to this activity, suffice it to say that stockholders must be informed of important corporate developments and kept abreast of a variety of financial matters. One of the most important activities in this regard is the preparation and dissemination of the annual stockholders' report, and to a lesser extent the quarterly reports. Dividend announcements, the undertaking of major investment programs, and other important developments require well-placed press releases to ensure wide distribution and full impact. The benefits of a well-run financial public relations program are well-informed investors, security analysts, brokerage firms, and underwriting houses, all of which (if the firm has an appealing "story" to tell) may enhance the market price of the stock and therefore reduce the firm's cost of equity capital.

to cash dividends in Chapter 19, so they will not be discussed here. Rather, our attention will now be directed toward stock dividends, stock splits, and share repurchases.

Stock Dividends.   Most companies that pay dividends do so in the form of cash dividends. However, stock dividends are used occasionally by some firms either as a replacement for, or a supplement to, the payment of cash dividends. A *stock dividend* is simply a disbursement of additional shares of stock to the firm's shareholders—for example, in a 10 percent stock dividend, investors would receive 1 share of stock for every 10 shares held.

Accounting for Stock Dividends.   From an accounting perspective, a stock dividend involves nothing more than a bookkeeping transfer from retained earnings to the common stock and paid-in capital accounts. It results in a restructuring of the firm's equity capital. The amount transferred from retained earnings depends on the market value of the company's stock at the time the stock dividend is disbursed. The amount transferred is determined as follows:

$$\text{Amount transferred} = \left(\begin{array}{c}\text{shares}\\\text{outstanding}\end{array}\right)\left(\begin{array}{c}\text{market}\\\text{price of stock}\end{array}\right)\left(\begin{array}{c}\text{size of}\\\text{stock dividend}\end{array}\right)$$

For example, consider the case of Medical Technology, Inc., which has 400,000 shares of ($2 par value) common stock outstanding; it is trading at $20 per share, and the company has declared a 5 percent stock dividend. The amount transferred from retained earnings would be:

$$\text{Amount transferred} = (400,000)\ (\$20)\ (.05) = \$400,000$$

Some of this $400,000 will be credited to the common stock account and the balance to paid-in capital. Since there are 400,000 shares outstanding, a 5 percent stock dividend will result in the issuance of 20,000 new shares of stock—400,000 × .05. The stock carries a par value of $2, so $40,000 will be allocated to the common stock account (20,000 new shares × $2 par value), and the balance ($360,000) to paid-in capital. Table 20.2 summarizes the stockholders' equity position of Medical Technology before and after the stock dividend; it also contrasts the impact of a stock dividend with that of a cash dividend. As can be seen, total stockholders' equity is unchanged with a stock dividend, although the book value of the capital structure does decline with the payment of cash dividends. The reason for this is that in the latter case, the stockholder is receiving something of value (cash), while with a stock dividend, the shareholder receives nothing he or she does not already own.

TABLE 20.2
Effects of Stock (and
Cash) Dividends on
Stockholders' Equity:
Medical Technology,
Inc.

Stockholders' Equity Accounts	Before Dividend	After Stock Dividend	After Comparable Cash Dividend
Common stock ($2 par)	$ 800,000	$ 840,000	$ 800,000
Paid-in capital	1,000,000	1,360,000	1,000,000
Retained earnings	3,200,000	2,800,000	2,800,000
Total stockholders' equity	$5,000,000	$5,000,000	$4,600,000
Number of shares of common stock outstanding	400,000	420,000	400,000

Economic Considerations. From an economic standpoint, neither the firm nor its stockholders are better or worse off after a stock dividend, unless there is an increase in the dividend payout ratio and/or the stock's P/E ratio increases. In fact, it has been shown empirically[19] that the value of a company's stock tends to rise after a stock dividend when it is accompanied by an increase in cash dividends, but to fall after stock dividends that are not accompanied by rising cash dividends. Ignoring changes in dividend payout and/or P/E ratios, we can further examine the 5 percent stock dividend declared by Medical Technology to see why stockholders should be indifferent about such dividends. Recall that the firm initially had 400,000 shares of common outstanding. As shown in Table 20.3, it also has $1 million in total earnings, pays $400,000 in cash dividends, and based on a P/E ratio of 8 times earnings, has a total market value of $8 million. After a 5 percent stock dividend, the number of shares of common stock outstanding increases by 20,000 to 420,000 shares; however, since nothing of value was created, the firm's total earnings remain at $1,000,000, while earnings per share decrease because of the additional shares of common outstanding. Now, if total cash dividends paid by Medical Technology remain the same (at $400,000), dividends per share will obviously drop; even more important, note in Table 20.3 that the total value of the firm will stay at $8 million. Likewise, as shown in the bottom half of the table, an individual investor who owned 100 shares of stock before the dividend is no better off after the stock dividend. Even though the number of shares owned by the investor has increased to 105, earnings per share, dividends per share, and market value per share have all declined—leaving the investor in exactly the same position after the stock dividend as before.

Now consider the possibility that the firm increases the total amount of cash dividends it pays out. If Medical Technology continues to pay out $1 per share after the 5 percent stock dividend, it will pay out a total of

[19]C. A. Barker, "Evaluation of Stock Dividends," *Harvard Business Review* 36 (July–August 1958), pp. 99–114; and Eugene Fama, Lawrence Fisher, Michael Jensen, and Richard Roll, "The Adjustment of Stock Prices to New Information," *International Economic Review* 10 (February 1969), pp. 1–21.

TABLE 20.3
Earnings, Dividends, and Total Valuation Before and After a 5 Percent Stock Dividend: Medical Technology, Inc.

	Before Dividend		After 5 Percent Stock Dividend	
	Total	Per Share	Total	Per Share[a]
THE FIRM				
Shares	400,000	—	420,000	—
Earnings	$1,000,000	$2.50	$1,000,000	$2.3810
Dividends	$400,000	$1.00	$400,000	$.9524
Dividend payout	40%	—	40%	—
P/E ratio	8×	—	8×	—
Total market value (or price)	$8,000,000	$20.00	$8,000,000	$19.0476

An Individual Owning 100 Shares Before and 105 Shares After Stock Dividend

	Before (100 shares)		After (105 shares)	
Claim on earnings	100 shares × $2.50 =	$250	105 shares × $2.3810 =	$250
Dividends	100 shares × $1.00 =	$100	105 shares × $.9524 =	$100
Value of stock	100 shares × $20.00 = $2,000		105 shares × $19.0476 = $2,000	

[a]Additional decimal places carried for accuracy.

$420,000. In effect, all the firm has done is increase its dividend payout ratio from 40 to 42 percent ($420,000/$1,000,000). Is the shareholder better off in terms of the cash received? Yes, but the reason is because of the increased dividend payout ratio—not the stock dividend. This adjustment could have been accomplished just as easily, and with less expense, simply by raising the cash dividend from $1.00 to $1.05 per share ($420,000/400,000 shares).

Does the firm's P/E ratio stay the same or change as a result of the stock dividend? Many financial managers seem to believe the market folklore which suggests that stocks have an "optimal" or "popular" trading range at which there is greater demand and hence a higher P/E ratio for the firm's stock. There is, however, no empirical evidence to suggest that, after adjusting for differences in risk, a stock's P/E ratio is influenced by its trading range. Therefore, there is no reason to believe that a firm can influence its P/E ratio simply by declaring a stock dividend. Why then do firms continue to use stock dividends? The reasons appear to be threefold: (1) to project an image of growth and, hopefully, create a favorable impression on current or prospective shareholders; (2) to attempt to "fool" shareholders when cash must be conserved by "paying out earnings in the form of stock rather than cash;" and (3) to provide more protection for shareholders in the event of financial difficulty by capitalizing some of the retained earnings into common stock and/or additional paid-in capital. On the negative side, stock dividends are much more expensive to administer than cash dividends.

Stock Splits.   Stock splits have an effect on a firm's share price similar to that of stock dividends; in fact, for all practical purposes stock splits and stock dividends are similar from an economic standpoint and differ only from an accounting perspective. When a company splits its stock, the number of shares outstanding is increased through a proportional reduction in the par (or stated) value of the common stock. The firm merely announces its intention to increase the number of shares outstanding by exchanging a specified number of new shares for each outstanding share of stock. For example, in a 2 for 1 stock split, 2 new shares of stock are exchanged for each old share.[20] A stock split increases the number of shares outstanding but does not change the shareholder's proportional interest in the company, so it does not represent any economic value to investors. The accounting treatment of a stock split can be seen by referring to Table 20.4. In this case, the company has just executed a 2 for 1 stock split. As seen, the only entries are (1) a reduction (by half) in the par value of the shares, and (2) an increase (doubling) in the number of shares authorized and outstanding. Note that the dollar value of all three equity accounts remains unchanged.

One possible motive for a stock split is an increase in the breadth of the market for the firm's common stock. Another is to reduce the price per share so that the stock is priced in a more popular trading range. In fact, *Accounting Research Bulletin* No. 43 describes a stock split as an action that "is prompted mainly by a desire to increase the number of outstanding shares for the purpose of effecting a reduction in the unit market price and, thereby, of obtaining wider distribution and improved marketability of the shares."[21] Even so, a stock split (like a stock dividend) has no economic benefit unless (1) the firm's dividend payout ratio increases, and/or (2) the firm's P/E ratio increases. There is no evidence to suggest that broadening the market for a firm's common stock has any impact on its price. Rather, empirical studies have shown consistently that stock prices tend to fall after a stock split by the proportional increase in the number of shares outstanding, except when accompanied by a change in the dividend payout ratio. When accompanied by an *increase* in cash dividends, the price falls less than proportionally; when accompanied by a *decrease* in the dividend payout ratio, the price falls more than proportionally.

Share Repurchase.   In recent years, a growing number of firms have been repurchasing a portion of their own outstanding common stock.

---

[20]Sometimes *a reverse stock split* is declared; such splits reduce the number of shares outstanding and increase the price of the stock by exchanging less than one share of new stock for each outstanding share. For example, in a 1 for 2 split, one new share of stock is exchanged for two old shares. Reverse splits are used to enhance the trading appeal of the stock by boosting the price to a supposedly more respectable range.

[21]Hawkins, *Corporate Financial Reporting*, p. 651.

TABLE 20.4
Stockholders' Equity
Position Before and
After a 2 for 1 Stock
Split

BEFORE STOCK SPLIT	
Common stock, $5 par value	
5,000,000 shares authorized, 4,000,000 outstanding	$20,000,000
Additional paid-in capital	18,484,000
Retained earnings	42,445,000
Total stockholders' equity	$80,929,000
AFTER 2 FOR 1 STOCK SPLIT	
Common stock, $2.50 par value	
10,000,000 shares authorized, 8,000,000 outstanding	$20,000,000
Additional paid-in capital	18,484,000
Retained earnings	42,445,000
Total stockholders' equity	$80,929,000

Table 20.5 gives an idea of the proportions share repurchases can attain; it lists some of the largest transactions in the 1978–1980 period. Many reasons have been suggested for this phenomenon, but here we consider repurchases in terms of their impact as a dividend decision, a financing decision, and an investment decision. Firms can repurchase their own stock in one of three ways: through a tender offer made directly to stockholders, through a series of open market transactions, or by repurchasing a large block of stock from a single individual or institutional investor. Regardless of how it is carried out, we will see that stock repurchases make sense only when (1) shareholders prefer capital gains

TABLE 20.5
Some Large Share
Repurchases,
1978–1980[a]

Company	Dollar Value of Shares Repurchased ($ Millions)	Number of Shares Repurchased (Millions)
IBM	$438.6	1.7
Standard Oil (Indiana)	389.1	5.1
Marriott	308.6	13.6
Ashland Oil (1979)	294.3	7.0
Ashland Oil (1978)	235.0	5.0
Reliance Group (1978)	220.0	6.6
Sears, Roebuck	217.5	10.0
Travelers	154.8	4.4
Georgia-Pacific	139.5	4.5
NCR	137.1	2.0
Reliance Group (1980)	120.0	2.0
Phillips Petroleum	112.5	2.3
Weyerhaeuser	112.0	3.5
Standard Oil (Ohio)	104.6	1.7
Texaco	100.1	3.0

[a]First six months of 1980 only.
SOURCE: *Institutional Investor*, August 1980, p. 155.

to ordinary income, or (2) this is the most expedient way to maintain or adjust the firm's target capital structure.[22]

Share repurchase can be viewed as a dividend decision to the extent that a company can accomplish the same basic objective of a cash dividend by repurchasing shares of the firm's stock. In the absence of personal taxes (or differential tax rates on ordinary income and long-term capital gains), shareholders should be indifferent between cash dividends and stock repurchases. With repurchases, fewer shares remain outstanding, and consequently earnings per share increase. As a result, the market price of the stock should increase and provide capital gains from the share repurchase in an amount exactly equal to the cash dividends that would otherwise have been received.

To see how this can occur, consider the situation presented in Table 20.6. Before the repurchase, the firm was planning to distribute dividends of $2.25 per share. If investors receive the cash dividend, the value of the stock will equal $77.25—the value of the stock ex-dividend ($75 per share), plus the expected dividend of $2.25. However, instead of paying the cash dividend, suppose the firm elects to repurchase shares of its own stock at $77.25 per share. As shown in the lower part of the table, this will involve the retirement of 29,126 shares of stock. Since total earnings will remain at $5 million, the firm's earnings per share increases to $5.15. With the price/earnings multiple at 15, the market price of the stock will increase from $75 to $77.25—exactly the amount of the expected cash dividend. Thus, if investors are indifferent between ordinary income and capital gains, then the value of the firm ($75 million) is not affected by the manner in which funds are returned to stockholders. However, if a firm's shareholders, because of differences in ordinary income versus long-term capital gains tax rates, prefer capital gains, then the shareholders' position is improved by repurchasing stock in lieu of paying cash dividends.[23]

---

[22]For a more complete discussion of share repurchases, see Samuel S. Stewart, Jr., "Should a Corporation Repurchase Its Own Stock?" *Journal of Finance* 31 (June 1976), pp. 911–921; Ronald W. Masulis, "Stock Repurchase by Tender Offer: An Analysis of the Causes of Common Stock Price Changes," *Journal of Finance* 35 (May 1980), pp. 305–319; and Suzanne Wittebort, "The New Boom in Stock Repurchases," *Institutional Investor* 14 (August 1980), pp. 153–158.

[23]As long as the stock is held for the required time period, the share price increase resulting from repurchasing common stock is subject to long-term capital gains taxes, whereas cash dividends are subject to the ordinary income tax rate. If shareholders manufacture "homemade" dividends by selling off sufficient stock to match the cash dividend that otherwise would have been received, the proceeds realized are not totally subject to capital gains taxes. Only the excess of the price realized over and above the original cost of the stock is subject to taxation (at the capital gains rate). Thus, for tax reasons, shareholders are usually better off with share repurchases than cash dividends as long as the capital gains tax rate is below the ordinary tax rate. On the other hand, if the IRS can establish that the repurchases were strictly for the avoidance of taxes on dividends, penalties may be levied under the excess earnings accumulation provision of the IRS code. Cases have been brought against privately held firms under this provision, but no known action against publicly owned firms has been upheld.

TABLE 20.6
Effect of Share
Repurchase on the
Value of the Firm

BEFORE SHARE REPURCHASE (CASH DIVIDEND PAID)	
Net income after taxes	$ 5,000,000
Number of shares of common stock outstanding	1,000,000
Earnings per share ($5,000,000 ÷ 1,000,000)	$5.00
Price/earnings ratio	15×
Market price per share, ex-dividend ($5.00 × 15)	$75.00
Dividend payout ratio	45%
Dividends per share	$2.25
Total cash dividends paid out	$2,250,000
Total market value of the firm ($75 × 1,000,000)	$75,000,000
AFTER SHARE REPURCHASE (NO CASH DIVIDEND PAID)	
Shares of common stock repurchased ($2,250,000 ÷ $77.25)	29,126
Shares outstanding after repurchase (1,000,000 − 29,126)	970,874
Earnings per share ($5,000,000 ÷ 970,874)	$5.15
Market price per share ($5.15 × 15)	$77.25
Total market value of the firm ($77.25 × 970,874)	≈$75,000,000

Share repurchase is often categorized as a financing decision since it can be an effective way for the firm to maintain or shift its target capital structure. Because of proposed tax-free mergers and acquisitions,[24] outstanding stock options, pension or retirement plans, and the possible conversion of convertible securities or warrants, firms may find themselves issuing more common stock than they want and thereby deviating from their target capital structure. In such a case, stock repurchases may be an effective means of controlling the issuance of additional common stock so that the firm does not drift too far from its target capital structure. On the other hand, a firm may wish to dramatically increase the proportion of debt in its capital structure without raising new capital. In this case, as before, stock repurchases may offer an easy way to bring about this repositioning. Finally, some firms buy back common stock to shrink their equity base, thereby making it more difficult for them to be acquired by another firm.

We can also view share repurchase as an investment decision, in which case the repurchase is appropriate only if it yields a return greater than the firm's marginal cost of capital. Employing a straightforward capital budgeting approach, the initial outlay in a share repurchase is equal to the market price of the firm's stock (P_0), while the expected cash inflows (or savings) are equal to the annual per share dividends (D_t) that would otherwise be paid on the repurchased stock. We can evaluate this investment decision by computing the expected IRR on the transaction and comparing it to the firm's MCC, which for an all-equity firm is equal

---

[24]The SEC has recently taken action that limits the use of repurchased stock for tax-free mergers. Any stock repurchased within the 2 years immediately prior to the merger is considered to be "tainted" and may not be used if the merger is to be treated as a tax-free exchange (to the shareholders of the target firm).

to k_s. Finding the investment's NPV and setting it equal to zero yields the following expression:

$$P_0 = \sum_{t=1}^{\infty} \frac{D_t}{(1 + r)^t} \tag{20.4}$$

where P_0 = stock's market price per share
D_t = annual per share dividends expected in year t
r = internal rate of return when NPV = 0

Comparing Equation 20.4 with our general valuation formula

$$P_0 = \sum_{t=1}^{\infty} \frac{D_t}{(1 + k_s)^t}$$

we see that the internal rate of return (r) on the repurchase transaction must equal the MCC (k_s) if P_0 is the firm's equilibrium share price. Based on this analysis, we see that repurchase is acceptable as an investment only so long as the firm's shares are selling below their equilibrium value—in other words, only if the shares are "undervalued." For only in this case can the IRR on the repurchase transaction exceed the firm's MCC. However, the only way a firm can sell below its equilibrium value (for any extended period of time) is for the financial market to be inefficient in terms of its assessment of the value of the firm. In recent years, many financial managers have stated that their firm's stocks were undervalued; however, there is no evidence to support this belief. Hence, while share repurchase may be defensible as a dividend decision (for shareholders who prefer capital gains to ordinary income) or as a financing decision (as a way to alter a firm's target capital structure), we can conclude that it generally cannot be justified as an investment decision.

SUMMARY

Common stocks, as well as other types of securities, are issued and traded in a well-organized network of capital markets. Companies often issue securities by using the services of an investment banking firm. These firms provide financial advice, assist in pricing and packaging the issue, and distribute the securities to the final investor in an efficient and economical manner. A variety of underwriter arrangements is available, depending on the needs of the firm; they include negotiated arrangements, competitive offerings, standby agreements, and offerings made on a best efforts basis. Sometimes, the decision to use one type of underwriter arrangement or another is dictated by statute or regulatory mandates. At other times, the decision is based on the services offered and/or the underwriter functions performed. Investment bankers are used in public offerings, rights offerings, and often in private placements, where they act as "finders."

The common stockholders are the residual owners of the company. They subordinate their claims to those of other parties, but in return they obtain certain rights, the most important of which are the right to control the company and the right to an unlimited claim on the residual earnings of the firm. The basic advantage of common stock financing stems from the fact that it offers a source of financing which places a minimum of constraints on the firm. Common stock financing also allows the firm to enhance its borrowing power. The disadvantages of common stock include the potential dilution of voting power and earnings, and the high cost of this form of financing. Generally speaking, firms will use common stock financing as long as it has a favorable or neutral effect on cost of funds, risk exposure, and control.

The managerial aspects of common stock financing include the issuing and servicing of these securities. Questions of whether or not to go public or to list stock, as well as rights offerings, are included within the issuing function. So long as the original owners are willing to share the control and earnings of the firm with others, the decision to go public can open up new channels of capital to the firm. The decision to list carries with it enhanced prestige, but it is still unclear whether or not listing is truly a thing of value. Servicing common stock includes such activities as developing a dividend policy, evaluating the merits of stock dividends and stock splits, and implementing stock repurchase programs. Neither a stock dividend nor a stock split has any economic benefit unless it is accompanied by an increase in the dividend payout and/or price/earnings multiple. Likewise, stock repurchases usually make sense only as dividend or financing decisions.

QUESTIONS

20.1. Assume you are the treasurer of a large corporation, and that your firm is contemplating a new issue of common stock. Listed below are several ways of using the services of an investment banker. Briefly discuss the pros and cons of each arrangement.

   a. A negotiated arrangement to issue the stock via a rights offering on a standby basis.

   b. A competitive underwriting arrangement to issue the stock publicly.

   c. Using rights to issue the stock on a best efforts basis.

20.2. Explain what is meant by the private placement of a security issue. What securities typically would be considered likely candidates for private placement?

20.3. What is an underwriter's spread, and how is it determined? Are there other costs of issuing securities that must be absorbed by the issuing firm?

20.4. What are the key advantages and disadvantages of using common stock to raise capital?

20.5. Explain the concept of dilution.

    a. Note how it can affect voting rights as well as EPS.

    b. Show how dilution can adversely affect shareholder wealth.

    c. Why does the subscription price of a new issue play such an important role in determining the level of dilution?

20.6. What is the difference between the number of shares of common stock authorized and the number of shares outstanding? Why are firms likely to authorize more shares than they initially intend to issue?

    a. Note the effect treasury stock has on the stockholders' equity account.

    b. Why might a firm issue classified common stock?

20.7. Explain the mechanics of a rights offering. How is the subscription price on a right determined? How does the firm decide on the number of rights to issue?

20.8. Is a stock split something of value to a shareholder? Is it something of value to the company? Explain. Is a stock dividend something of value to a shareholder? To the company? Explain.

20.9. Briefly discuss the impact on the firm's cash flow, stockholders' equity, and shareholder wealth from each of the following corporate actions:

    a. Declaring a 10 percent stock dividend.

    b. Splitting the company's stock 2 for 1.

    c. Instituting a share repurchase program to retire 10 percent of the company's stock.

20.10. Why would a company buy back its own stock? Show how a share repurchase program can be viewed as a financing decision.

20.11. Shareholders should, in theory, be indifferent between cash dividends and the repurchase of common stock. Why, in practice, do you think shareholders may prefer one over the other?

PROBLEMS

20.1. *UNDERWRITER COSTS.* The Mid-States Packing Company wants to sell some common stock to raise capital for plant expansion. The company has consulted its investment banking firm and has been advised that 250,000 shares can probably be sold for $40 per share. The deal would be fully underwritten and handled on a negotiated basis; because of the considerable risk involved, the underwriter has proposed a 7¼ percent underwriter spread, covering all advising, underwriting, and selling costs. Mid-States also estimates that registration, legal, printing and other miscellaneous administrative costs will amount to another $300,000.

    a. What will be the total underwriter compensation in this transaction?

    b. What will be the net proceeds to the issuer?

c. Mid-States estimates it will need $9 million for plant expansion; will that amount be available after all costs have been deducted?

20.2. *STOCKHOLDERS' EQUITY.* Note the changes to a firm's balance sheet that would occur from the following transactions:
a. A company sells 200,000 shares of $3 par common for $13 per share.
b. A company sells 200,000 shares of no par common for $13 per share.
c. A company repurchases 200,000 shares of its own $3 par common for $13 per share.

20.3. *ESTABLISHING THE SUBSCRIPTION PRICE OF A NEW ISSUE.* The New Jersey Box Car Company (NJBC) is currently trying to put together a new issue of common stock. The treasurer, John Maffeo, wants to do some preliminary work before contacting the firm's investment banker. In the course of his analysis, Maffeo has become concerned about the potential dilution that will result from the new issue and has decided to take a closer look. NJBC feels it will need $10 million to finance proposed capital projects (ignore underwriter compensation and other costs of issuing the securities). The company's latest after-tax earnings were $18 million (this is expected to increase significantly when the new projects become fully operational, several years from now), and it has 4.5 million shares of stock outstanding.
a. Given that the stock can hold its current price/earnings multiple of 15, how many shares of stock would have to be issued (using the latest market price of the stock) to raise $10 million? What will happen to EPS and the market price of the stock when the additional shares are issued?
b. How much would be raised if the number of new shares (computed above) can be sold at the new market price (also computed above)? How does this figure compare to the $10 million NJBC needs to raise? What accounts for the difference?
c. Given the *new* market price computed in (a), how many shares would have to be issued if Maffeo felt that the subscription price of the new issue would require a further 5 percent price concession to assure a successful offering? What would happen to EPS and market price?
d. What is probably the maximum subscription price NJBC can set on its new issue?

20.4. *RIGHTS OFFERING.* Montana Iron Mines wants to raise $1 million in common stock financing by using a rights offering. The company has 500,000 shares of common stock outstanding, which have recently been trading at around $28 per share. The firm believes that if the subscription price is set at $25, the shares will be fully subscribed.

a. Determine the number of new shares the firm must sell to raise the desired amount of capital.

b. How many rights will be required to buy a new share of stock?

c. What is the theoretical value of a right if the current market price is $27 and the subscription price is $25? Answer for both rights-on and ex-rights situations.

d. Lois Lane is vice-president of finance at Montana Iron Mines, and owns 35,000 shares of the company's common stock. If she exercises her rights, how many new shares can she purchase? Using her rights, how much would it cost her to buy the new shares? How much could she get if she sold her rights when the shares were trading ex-rights?

e. If the date of record for the new issue is Monday, March 15, on what days would the stock sell (1) rights-on and (2) ex-rights?

20.5. **EFFECTS OF STOCK DIVIDENDS AND STOCK SPLITS ON THE BALANCE SHEET.** Keystone Copper Mines has just declared a 3 for 2 stock split; at the same time, it has decided to keep its quarterly cash dividend at $.30 per share. The current market value of the stock is $10 per share. The present (condensed) balance sheet, before the stock split or the cash dividend, is given below:

Assets		Liabilities and Owners' Equity	
Cash	$ 30,000,000	Debt	$ 50,000,000
Other assets	95,000,000	Common stock (40 million shares authorized; 20 million shares outstanding, $1 par)	20,000,000
		Additional paid-in capital	10,000,000
		Retained earnings	45,000,000
Total	$125,000,000	Total	$125,000,000

a. Construct a pro forma balance sheet that shows the effects of both the stock split and the cash dividend on the firm's asset and equity accounts. How much would the firm have paid out in cash dividends had it not split its stock 3 for 2?

b. Assume that instead of a 3 for 2 stock split and a 30-cent cash dividend, Keystone declared a 50 percent stock dividend; prepare a pro forma balance sheet to show the effects of the stock dividend on the firm's asset and equity accounts.

c. Repeat (b) assuming the company also kept its regular cash dividend rate at 30 cents per share.

20.6. **STOCK DIVIDENDS.** Computer Software has the following common stock equity accounts:

Common stock ($4 par)	$ 800,000
Additional paid-in capital	300,000
Retained earnings	1,000,000
Total common equity	$2,100,000

Determine what Computer Software's common equity accounts will look like if the firm's common stock is selling for $30 per share and it declares a 15 percent stock dividend. Other things being equal, what would be the stock's new price per share?

20.7. **STOCK DIVIDENDS FROM THE INVESTOR'S VIEWPOINT.** Arizona Paper Products declared a 20 percent stock dividend on August 10, payable to shareholders of record on September 8. The market price of the stock (before the stock dividend) was $60 per share. You own 125 shares of the stock.

a. When is the ex-dividend day? (*Hint:* See Chapter 19.)

b. If you sold the stock on August 30, what price would you receive, other things being equal?

c. How many shares would you own after the ex-dividend date?

d. At what price should the stock sell on September 7, other things being equal?

e. What will be the total value of your holdings before and after the stock dividend, other things being equal?

20.8. **SHARE REPURCHASE AND TAX RATES.** Lone Star Concrete is owned by several wealthy Texans who are all in the 50 percent marginal tax bracket. The firm is expected to have $5 million in earnings this year and has plans to pay out $1.50 per share on its 2 million shares of common stock. The stock has recently traded (among current shareholders) at $51.50 per share, which represents the typical ($50) market price of the stock plus the anticipated ($1.50) cash dividend. Instead of paying a cash dividend, the owners have been discussing the possibility of a repurchase at $51.50 per share.

a. How much stock should be repurchased if this option is selected?

b. What will the new market price per share be after the repurchase? Ignoring taxes, which option should be selected?

c. Once taxes are considered, should the owners prefer one action to the other? Explain. What factors might preclude the firm from selecting the option preferred by its owners?

20.9. *STOCK REPURCHASE AT DIFFERENT PRICES.*   Leeway Instruments has earnings of $8 million and a dividend policy of paying out 80 percent of its earnings. The firm has 800,000 shares of common stock outstanding and is currently selling at $128 per share, of which $8 is due to an anticipated cash dividend. Bill Walker, who owns 40,000 shares, has expressed great displeasure with Leeway's financial and managerial policies. The chief financial officer of Leeway has approached Walker with the prospect of selling his shares back to the firm. What is the effect of the repurchase on the remaining shareholders if the repurchase is effected at (carry to four decimal places for accuracy):

a. $125 per share?

b. $128 per share?

c. $135 per share?

SELECTED REFERENCES

Angermueller, Hans H., and Michael A. Taylor. "Commercial vs. Investment Bankers." *Harvard Business Review* 55 (September–October 1977), pp. 132–144.

Austin, D. V., and T. J. Scampini. "Senior Debt Securities Revisited." *The Bankers Magazine*, November–December 1980, pp. 73–82.

Baker, H. Kent, and Patricia L. Gallagher. "Management's View of Stock Splits." *Financial Management* 9 (summer 1980), pp. 73–77.

Barker, C. A. "Evaluation of Stock Dividends." *Harvard Business Review* 36 (July–August 1958), pp. 99–114.

Baron, David P. "A Model of the Demand for Investment Banking and Advising and Distribution Services for New Issues." *Journal of Finance* 37 (September 1982), pp. 955–976.

Bear, Robert M., and Anthony J. Curley. "Unseasoned Equity and Financing." *Journal of Financial and Quantitative Analysis* 10 (June 1975), pp. 311–325.

Block, S., and M. Stanley. "Financial Characteristics and Price Movement Patterns of Companies Approaching the Unseasoned Securities Market in the Late 1970's." *Financial Management* 9 (winter 1980), pp. 30–36.

Burnham, I. W. "The Securities Industry: Financing Corporate America." *Financial Executive* (March 1976), pp. 26–31.

Cohan, A. B. *Yields on Corporate Debt Directly Placed.* New York: National Bureau of Economic Research, 1967.

Copeland, T. "Liquidity Changes Following Stock Splits." *Journal of Finance* 34 (March 1979), pp. 115–141.

Dielman, Terry, Timothy J. Nantell, and Roger L. Wright. "Price Effects of Stock Repurchasing: A Random Coefficient Regression Approach." *Journal of Financial and Quantitative Analysis* 15 (March 1980), pp. 175–189.

Dyl, E. A., and M. D. Joehnk. "Competitive vs. Negotiated Underwriting of Public Utility Debt." *Bell Journal of Economics* 7 (autumn 1976), pp. 680–689.

Ederington, L. H. "Negotiated vs. Competitive Underwriting of Corporate Bonds." *Journal of Finance* 31 (March 1976), pp. 17–28.

Fabozzi, Frank J. "Does Listing on the AMEX Increase the Value of Equity?" *Financial Management* 10 (spring 1981), pp. 43–50.

Fama, Eugene, Lawrence Fisher, Michael Jensen, and Richard Roll. "The Adjustment of Stock Prices to New Information." *International Economic Review* 10 (February 1969), pp. 1–21.

Feinberg, P. "New-Issues War of Nerves." *Institutional Investor* 14 (December 1980), pp. 47–50.

Friend, Irwin, et al. *Investment Banking and the New Issues Market.* New York: World, 1967.

Fruhan, William E., Jr. "Lessons from Levitz: Creating Share Value." *Financial Analysts Journal* 36 (March–April 1980), pp. 25–32, 34–40, 42–45.

Gup, B. E. "Financial Consequences of Corporate Growth." *Journal of Finance* 35 (December 1980), pp. 1257–1265.

Hansen, Robert S., and John M. Pinkerton. "Direct Equity Financing: A Resolution of a Paradox." *Journal of Finance* 37 (June 1982), pp. 651–665.

Hawkins, David F. *Corporate Financial Reporting: Text and Cases*, rev. ed. Homewood, Ill.: Irwin, 1977.

Hayes, Samuel L. III. "Investment Banking: Power Structures in Flux." *Harvard Business Review* 49 (March–April 1971), pp. 136–152

——— "The Transformation of Investment Banking." *Harvard Business Review* 57 (January–February 1979), pp. 153–170.

Hays, P., M. Joehnk, and R. Melicher. "Differential Determinants of Risk Premiums in the Public and Private Corporate Bond Markets." *Journal of Financial Research* 2 (fall 1979), pp. 143–152.

Hillstrom, R., and R. King, eds. *1960–69: A Decade of Corporate and International Finance* New York: Investment Dealer's Digest, 1970.

Ibbotson, R. R. "Price Performance of Common Stock New Issues." *Journal of Financial Economics* 3 (September 1975), pp. 235–272.

Joehnk, Michael, and David Kidwell. "Comparative Costs of Competitive and Negotiated Underwritings in the State and Local Bond Markets." *Journal of Finance* 34 (June 1979), pp. 725–731.

Johnson, Keith, T. Gregory Morton, and M. Chapman Findlay III. "An Empirical Analysis of the Flotation Cost of Corporate Securities 1971–72." *Journal of Finance* 30 (June 1975), pp. 1129–1133.

———, ———, and ———. "An Analysis of the Flotation Cost of Utility Bonds." *Journal of Financial Research* 2 (fall 1979), pp. 133–142.

Logue, Dennis E., and Robert A. Jarrow. "Negotiation vs. Competitive Bidding in the sale of Securities by Public Utilities." *Financial Management* 7 (autumn 1978), pp. 31–39.

Lorie, James H., and Mary T. Hamilton. *The Stock Market: Theories and Evidence*, 2d ed. Homewood, Ill.: Irwin, 1982.

Mandelker, Gershon, and Artur Ravic. "Investment Banking: An Economic Analysis of Optimal Underwriting Contracts." *Journal of Finance* 32 (June 1977), pp. 683–694.

Masulis, Ronald W. "Stock Repurchase by Tender Offer: An Analysis of the Causes of Common Stock Price Changes." *Journal of Finance* 35 (May 1980), pp. 305–319.

Millar, James A., and Bruce D. Fielitz. "Stock Split and Stock Dividend Decisions." *Financial Management* 2 (winter 1973), pp. 35–45.

Osborn, Neil. "The Furor Over Shelf Registrations." *Institutional Investor* 16 (June 1982), pp. 61–71.

Parker, George, and Daniel Cooperman. "Competitive Bidding in the Underwriting of Public Utility Securities." *Journal of Financial and Quantitative Analysis* 13 (December 1978), pp. 885–902.

Smith, C. W. "Alternative Methods for Raising Capital: Rights Versus Underwritten Offerings." *Journal of Financial Economics* 7 (November 1977), pp. 273–307.

Sorensen, Eric H. "The Impact of Underwriting Method and Bidder Competition upon Corporate Bond Interest Cost." *Journal of Finance* 34 (September 1979), pp. 863–869.

Stewart, Samuel S., Jr. "Should a Corporation Repurchase Its Own Stock?" *Journal of Finance* 31 (June 1976), pp. 911–921.

Stoll, Hans R. "The Supply of Dealer Services in Securities Markets." *Journal of Finance* 33 (September 1978), pp. 1133–1151.

Taggart, R. A. "A Model of Corporate Financing Decisions." *Journal of Finance* 32 (December 1977), pp. 1467–1484.

Tallman, G. D., D. F. Rush, and R. W. Melicher. "Competitive vs. Negotiated Underwriting Costs of Regulated Industries." *Financial Management* 3 (summer 1974), pp. 49–55.

U.S. Securities and Exchange Commission. *Cost of Flotation of Corporate Securities, 1951–1955, 1957.* Washington, D.C.: U.S. Government Printing Office, 1957.

White, R. W., and P. A. Lusztig. "The Price Effects of Rights Offerings." *Journal of Financial and Quantitative Analysis* 15 (March 1980), pp. 25–40.

Wittebort, Suzanne. "The New Boom in Stock Repurchases." *Institutional Investor* 14 (August 1980), pp. 153–158.

Ying, Louis, Wilbur G. Lewellen, Gary G. Schlarbaum, and Ronald C. Lease. "Stock Exchange Listings and Securities Returns." *Journal of Financial and Quantitative Analysis* 12 (September 1977), pp. 415–432.

21

Financing
with Long-Term Debt
and Preferred Stock

Long-term debt and other types of fixed-income securities are important sources of capital to American business firms, regardless of their size or form. They enable companies to use varying amounts of financial leverage and have an important bearing on the marginal cost of capital. A company can choose from a wide array of fixed-income financing vehicles: It can use term loans, or one of the many different kinds of publicly or privately placed bonds, or it can even issue preferred stock (which, though it is equity, is considered a fixed-income security because the dividend rate is (usually) set for the life of the issue). Each of these financial instruments places different demands on the firm, and each has a different role to play in a firm's capital structure. Earlier, we noted how fixed-income securities affect the cost of capital and the optimum capital structure. Building on this theoretical base, the discussion in this chapter is centered on the institutional and administrative dimensions of term loans, bonds, and preferred stock. We begin with an overview of long-term debt as a form of corporate financing; then we look at term loans and bonds, including some of the managerial aspects of debt financing. The chapter ends with a brief discussion of preferred stock.

Long-Term Debt as a Financing Vehicle

Generally speaking, long-term debt is used to minimize the cost of financing and to reduce the company's overall cost of capital; this is possible, as we saw in Chapter 17, because interest charges on debt are treated as tax-deductible expenses. Long-term debt is a multipurpose

TABLE 21.1
Capitalization Rates of
U.S. Corporations,
1960–1980
(As a Percentage of
Total Financial
Structure)

	1960	1965	1970	1975	1980
Current liabilities	8.5%	9.5%	10.8%	11.5%	15.3%
Long-term debt	27.5	29.8	34.0	36.0	35.1
Total corporate debt	36.0	39.3	44.8	47.5	50.4
Stockholders' equity	64.0	60.7	55.2	52.5	49.6
Total capitalization	100.0%	100.0%	100.0%	100.0%	100.0%
Debt-equity ratio[a]	.43	.49	.62	.69	.71

[a]Long-term debt/total stockholders' equity.

SOURCE: Federal Trade Commission, *Quarterly Financial Report: Manufacturing, Mining, and Trade Corporations* (Washington, D.C.: U.S. Government Printing Office, various issues).

vehicle that can be used to finance major acquisitions, improve the firm's working capital position, finance major capital expenditures, and implement capital restructuring programs. Most firms use long-term debt to one extent or another; in fact, as the comparative data on corporate financial structures in Table 21.1 show, the relative extent of use has increased substantially over the past two decades. Some of the growth in total corporate debt was obviously due to a growing use of short-term debt, but comparative debt-equity ratios indicate that significant changes have taken place in capital structures as well.[1] By 1980, the average corporation was carrying about 71 cents in long-term debt for every dollar of equity, compared to only 43 cents in 1960.

There are a number of advantages to using long-term debt as a form of corporate financing. Perhaps the most notable is its low after-tax cost. As such, when judiciously used, long-term debt financing can have desirable effects on the marginal cost of capital. Moreover, except for variable-rate debt, the cost of financing is fixed for the life of the issue. Still another advantage is the deferred repayment provision; this enables a firm to employ more of its funds internally for investment purposes, and places less demand on the company's cash flow (at least in the short run). A final advantage of long-term debt financing is that the owners do not have to share their control of the company with others.

There are also several disadvantages, the major one being the increased risk the firm and its stockholders must bear. Because debt

[1]A special type of long-term debt financing that is growing in popularity with multimillion-dollar capital projects is *project financing*: a procedure whereby a major capital project (such as an oil pipeline, a steel mill, or factory) is set up and financed as an entity separate and distinct from the company. As such, the project, *not* the company, undertakes the financing. Although the company will invest some equity in the project, it is usually quite small, so the amount of debt financing is correspondingly large. In addition, this debt financing is not based on the credit worthiness of the company but on the earning capacity of the project itself. Since this project is distinct from the company, the debt financing does *not* appear on the balance sheet of the sponsoring firm (thus, project financing is a form of "off-balance sheet" financing). For more discussion of project financing, see James C. T. Mao, "Project Financing: Funding the Future," *Financial Executive* 50 (August 1982), pp. 23–28.

involves fixed charges, there is an increased risk that if earnings do fluctuate, or drop below a certain level, the firm may be unable to meet its fixed cost obligations. What is more, financing with debt adds financial leverage to the firm, which magnifies earnings fluctuations; and earnings instability not only affects the cost of debt financing, but as we noted in Chapter 18, can also have a detrimental impact on the cost of equity. Another disadvantage is that because debt generally has a specified maturity date or sinking fund provision, the financial officer must make provision for eventual repayment of the principal. Finally, long-term debt financing often involves provisions that constrain the firm's operations, and limit the investment, financing, and dividend decisions of the financial manager.

Term Loans

A *term loan* represents a type of long-term debt that is obtained from such sources as commercial banks, equipment manufacturers, and insurance companies. Used to some extent by nearly every type of business, term loans are especially important to small firms that lack access to the public capital markets. Companies like term loans because of their competitive rates, and because the debt can be raised quickly and conveniently. Formal procedures are minimized, and the key provisions of the debt can generally be worked out more quickly and with more flexibility than a public issue. The term to maturity on most term loans ranges from a minimum of about 3 years to a maximum of 7 to 10 years, though longer maturities are possible. Most term loans are retired through systematic *amortization payments* made over the life of the obligation. Usually, these take the form of equal monthly instalments, although other payment periods (such as quarterly or annual) are also used, and a number of term loans carry *balloon payments* (a lump-sum payment at maturity that is much larger than normal). In fact, there is no absolute requirement that term loans be amortized in equal instalments; rather, management can choose, with the lender's approval, to structure the repayment schedule so that it will be compatible with the expected future cash flows of the firm. Obviously, if equal debt service requirements are likely to cause a problem for the firm, it would be in the best interest of both the lender and the borrower to use an uneven payment schedule.

The vast majority of term loans are made on a secured basis. Typically, the collateral takes the form of machinery and equipment and is secured with a chattel mortgage or a conditional sales contract. Because of the extended period of time involved, it is customary for lenders to use loan agreements when making term loans. The loan agreement spells out the terms of the loan and sets up certain conditions the borrower is expected to meet. The amount, maturity, and interest rate on the loan; payment dates; collateral; and the action to be taken in the event of default are all items normally specified in loan agreements. The purpose of such a document is, of course, to protect the lender for the period of the loan. Should the operating results and financial condition of the borrower begin to deteriorate, or should the borrower fail to live up to the conditions of the loan, the loan agreement is the legal document that spells out the recourse of the lender.

Use of Term Loans

Most term loans are made for the purpose of equipment financing. This type of loan enables the firm to acquire high-priced assets by paying for them systematically over time. The financing usually requires a minimum down payment that represents the firm's equity position in the equipment. Term debt is also used to finance the *fixed* working capital needs of the firm. Occasionally, a company will face a problem in the fixed portion of its working capital position that can best be taken care of over a period of say, 3 to 5 years. This might be the case, for example, with a permanent buildup in inventory that accompanies a significant increase in the level of operations. Under such conditions, it may be difficult to free the cash from inventory to service short-term financing. As a result, a term loan may be a more appropriate financing vehicle. Sometimes term loans will be used as interim financing. This is especially common when long-term borrowing rates are high; under these conditions, many firms that need capital will simply shorten the maturities on their loans and try to ride out the period of high interest rates. Most of these loans are not amortized, since the intent is to refinance the interim loan at maturity, hopefully at a lower long-term rate. Finally, term loans can be used for refinancing, as a way to alter the firm's financial structure. Such refinancing is done to change maturities or to lower interest costs.

Servicing Term Debt

Term loans are normally paid off over time through a predetermined series of amortization payments, such payments being made up of both principal and interest. A variety of factors can combine to influence the actual cost of money for a given loan, the most important of which include the basic cost of money, the loan's term to maturity, the size of the credit, and the financial riskiness of the borrower. The interest charged on term loans is responsive to economic conditions and will vary with the cost of long-term money in the capital market. A summary of commercial bank term loan activity in early 1982 is provided in Table 21.2. It shows that the cost of money tends to decline with larger loans, and that term loans are commonly set up with floating interest rates, where the rate charged on the loan is pegged to the prevailing prime rate.

Instalment Payments.   The size of an instalment payment is important because it can have a direct bearing on the amount of strain placed on

TABLE 21.2
Member Bank Term
Loans to Commercial
and Industrial
Customers
(Week of May 3–8,
1982)

	Size of Loan Categories			
	Less Than $100,000	$100,000 to $500,000	$500,000 to $1,000,000	Over $1,000,000
Average size of loan	$13,919	$265,557	$672,316	$5,119,004
Average maturity (in months)	29.9	50.1	43.3	51.8
Average interest rate	18.80%	17.59%	17.29%	16.69%
Percentage of loans with floating rates	38.6%	45.9%	83.5%	77.7%

SOURCE: Board of Governors of the Federal Reserve System, *Federal Reserve Bulletin*, October 1982.

the firm's future cash flow. The size of the equal-instalment payments necessary to amortize a given loan can readily be determined according to the following equation:

$$\text{Instalment payments} = \frac{\text{size of loan}}{PVIFA_{k,n}} \tag{21.1}$$

where $PVIFA_{k,n}$ equals the present-value interest factor of an annuity, as obtained from Appendix Table A-4. Equation 21.1 is simply a variation of the basic present-value model that solves for the size of the future cash flows. To illustrate, consider a firm that wants to borrow $250,000 for 5 years. The loan is to be paid off in 5 annual instalments, and it is estimated that the loan will carry a 10 percent rate of interest. Given this information, we can compute the size of the instalment payments as follows:

$$\text{Instalment payments} = \frac{\$250,000}{3.791} = \$65,945.66$$

In this case, five annual instalments of $65,945.66 will retire the principal portion of the loan ($250,000) and provide the lender with a 10 percent return on investment.[2] This can be seen in Table 21.3, which shows each annual payment broken down by its principal and interest components. If management feels, in the example above, that payments of nearly $66,000 a year are likely to be more than the firm's cash flow can afford, then it can seek lower or uneven payments and/or a longer maturity as a way of bringing the amortization payments into line with the company's expected debt service capacity.

---

[2]Although the illustration above uses annual instalment periods, the same procedure would be used for shorter intervals. If semiannual payments were required, the PVIFA should be for 5% and 10 payments (rather than 10 percent and 5 instalments), and the size of such payments would amount to $250,000/7.722 = $32,375.03.

TABLE 21.3
The Principal and
Interest Components
of Term Loan
Amortization
Payments
(Figures Based on a
$250,000, 5-Year, 10
Percent Loan
Amortized with Equal
Annual Instalments of
$65,945.66)

Year	Principal Balance Outstanding During Year[a]	Interest on Loan (10%)	Amount of Annual Payment Credited to Principal Reduction ($65,945.66 − Interest)
1	$250,000.00	$25,000.00	$ 40,945.66
2	209,054.34	20,905.43	45,040.23
3	164,014.11	16,401.41	49,544.25
4	114,469.86	11,446.99	54,498.67
5	59,971.19	5,997.12	59,971.19[b]
Total		$79,752.95	$250,000.00

[a]Principal balance declines each year by the amount of the preceding year's payment credited to principal.
[b]Due to rounding, the calculated value of the final principal reduction of $59,948.54 would not fully repay the loan; therefore the actual remaining principal repayment of $59,971.19 has been included here.

Balloon Payments.   Whenever balloon payments are used, the procedure for finding the size of instalment payments must be modified slightly. In particular, the following procedure would apply:

Step 1. Given the size of the balloon payment, find the present value of that balloon payment by using a present-value interest factor for a single cash flow ($PVIF_{k,n}$) for the stipulated interest rate (k) and term to maturity (n) on the loan.

Step 2. Subtract the present value of the balloon payment from the principal amount of the loan to determine the amount of the loan that must be amortized from equal instalment payments.

Step 3. Use Equation 21.1 to find the size of the instalment payments necessary to amortize the *remaining balance* of the loan, using a $PVIFA_{k,n}$ for the stated interest rate and $n - 1$ payments.

To show how this works, let us return to the $250,000 loan above. In this case, however, we assume that the borrowing firm wants a balloon of $100,000 as its final payment. The problem is to find the size of the four remaining payments necessary to retire the loan. We can use the steps above to solve this problem:

1. Present value of balloon payment: $100,000 × .621 = $62,100.
2. Balance to be amortized: $250,000 − $62,100 = $187,900.
3. Annual instalment payments: $187,900 ÷ 3.170 = $59,274.45.

The firm can make four annual payments of $59,274.45 and a final balloon payment of $100,000 to repay this 10 percent loan over 5 years.

Bonds   In a single month, American firms will raise billions of dollars in the corporate bond market. April 1981 was typical: During this period 37 bonds, valued at nearly $4.2 billion, were publicly issued; among the issues were a $300 million obligation by Cities Service, a $400 million Sun Company bond, and $250 million in Pacific Gas and Electric bonds. As these numbers suggest, bond financing is an important source of corporate capital. In fact, by year-end 1981, there was nearly $490 billion of such corporate debt outstanding. A *bond* is simply legal evidence of long-term debt incurred by a company; it is essentially a promissory note that formally sets out the conditions of the loan, and that specifies the cost of borrowing the money and when the principal will be repaid. The material that follows examines the institutional and managerial dimensions of corporate bonds, including financing costs, types of corporate bonds, issue characteristics, bond ratings, and the use of Eurobonds. We begin with a general review of corporate bond financing.

Corporate Bond Financing Activity: An Overview

In contrast to term loans, a bond normally carries a much longer maturity. Most bonds are issued with 15- to 30-year maturities, though even longer due dates are not unheard of. The maturity on a bond indicates when the debt is to be repaid, but as we will see below, this is somewhat of a misnomer because corporate bonds usually carry sinking fund provisions which require that all or a portion of the bond be retired prior to maturity. Most bonds are also fairly large, as evidenced by the fact that in 1982, the average publicly issued bond had a principal (or par) value of some $90 million; in fact, issues of $500 million or more are not out of the ordinary.[3] The stated interest rate on a bond is the percentage of the bond's principal value that will be paid annually (usually in two semi-annual instalments) and is known as the *coupon*, or *nominal rate*. It defines the cost of funds to the firm and is influenced not only by economic conditions, but by issue characteristics as well.

Bonds are the single most important source of external corporate capital and are issued by all types of companies, from industrial concerns to banks and public utilities. The amount of funds raised annually through this financing vehicle is given in Table 21.4, which summarizes the level of corporate bond activity over 23 years, 1960 through 1982. It shows that corporations issued well over half a trillion dollars in bonds over this period, as the level of such obligations issued each year rose from a low of slightly more than $8 billion in 1960 to a record $54.9 billion in 1982. Note also that since the mid-1970s, annual new issue activity has been in the neighborhood of, or exceeded, the $50 billion mark with regularity.[4]

---

[3]At the time of this writing, the largest public offering in corporate history was a $1 billion issue by IBM that came out in two parts on October 5, 1979. For an interesting behind-the-scenes look at the activity surrounding this issue, and some of the problems that arose, see Walter Guzzardi, Jr., "The Bomb I.B.M. Dropped on Wall Street," *Fortune*, November 19, 1979, pp. 52–56.

[4]For an excellent historical review of the public bond market, see Sidney Homer, "The Historical Evolution of Today's Bond Market," *Journal of Portfolio Management* 1 (spring 1975), pp. 6–11.

TABLE 21.4
New Corporate Bond
Issues, 1960–1982
(In Billions of Dollars)

Year	Amount Issued	Year	Amount Issued
1982	$54.9	1970	$30.3
1981	47.0	1969	26.7
1980	48.8	1968	22.0
1979	48.5	1967	24.8
1978	45.1	1966	18.1
1977	51.3	1965	16.0
1976	52.5	1964	14.0
1975	49.9	1963	12.2
1974	36.9	1962	10.7
1973	21.2	1961	13.2
1972	27.8	1960	8.1
1971	31.0		

SOURCES: Board of Governors of the Federal Reserve System, *Federal Reserve Bulletin*, various issues; and "Corporate Financing Directory," *Investment Dealers' Digest*, various issues.

Cost of Bond Financing

Figure 21.1 provides a look at the time series behavior of bond interest rates through 1982; the Standard & Poor's composite AA corporate bond rate is used as representative of the complex structure of corporate bond yields. Figure 21.1 shows the initial surge in interest rates that took place in the latter part of the 1960s. Except for occasional ups and downs, the sharp increases in rates held for most of the 1970s until 1979, when rates rose to record-breaking levels. By the decade's end, *average* AA bond rates had moved up to nearly 11 percent, and by the first half of 1982, were nearing the 15 percent mark. In fact, many investment-quality obligations were being issued at that time with coupons in the 16 to 18 percent range.

The cost of funds to issuers depends on a number of economic and firm-specific variables. For example, issue characteristics like risk of default, term to maturity, coupon, and indenture provisions (such as call feature and sinking fund) can all affect the cost of borrowing. The reason is that such variables enter the present-value-based bond valuation models used by investors, and since they have a bearing on an investor's risk exposure, they affect the required rate of return (discount rate) used in the valuation process. (Refer back to Chapter 7 for a review of the principles of bond valuation.) Clearly, the higher the required rate of return demanded by lenders and investors, the greater the cost of funds to issuers. However, to the extent that management can affect the issue characteristics a bond possesses, it should be equally clear that management decisions can have at least a modest impact on the cost of borrowing.

Another important variable affecting the cost of bond financing is the behavior of consumer prices. Inflation has exacted a heavy toll on the cost of bond financing, especially since the latter part of the 1960s. To a

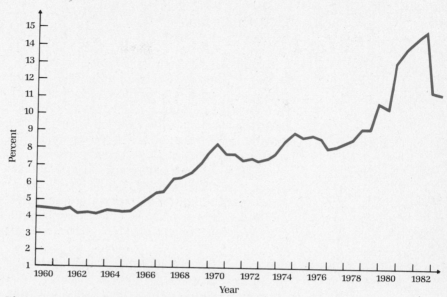

Figure 21.1   Corporate Bond Rates, 1960–1982 (S & P Composite AA Yields).

large extent, the high and unstable interest rates that have prevailed over the recent past are a reflection of the equally high and unstable rates of inflation this country had been experiencing. Perceived and anticipated inflation is embedded in new issue bond yields and has been a major cause of the wide swings in market interest rates. Indeed, because inflation has such a heavy impact on bond interest rates, it is of prime concern to corporate issuers, especially in terms of issue timing and term to maturity.

Types of Corporate Bonds

Bonds are classified according to whether or not they are secured by pledges of specific assets. Senior securities are secured bonds backed by real assets (plant and equipment, rolling stock) or financial assets, like stocks and bonds; first and second mortgage bonds, equipment trust certificates, and collateral trust bonds all have specific assets pledged against them as collateral and are therefore all examples of secured debt. If the issuer defaults on a secured bond, the collateral can be used to (fully or partially) satisfy bondholder claims. The junior securities of the firm are the unsecured issues, whose only collateral is the good faith and credit of the issuer. A firm's unsecured debt would include its debentures, subordinated debentures, convertible debentures, and income bonds. Many firms, even the most creditworthy, have both secured and unsecured debt outstanding. Other things being equal, secured debt is likely to have a slightly lower financing cost because it has a prior claim on income and provides investors with greater protection in case of default.[5]

In addition to secured and unsecured bonds, there are several types of special feature issues; these include variable-rate notes, bonds with early redemption options, deep-discount new issues, bonds with contingent takedown options, and corporate-related municipal bonds (industrial development and pollution control bonds). These obligations are usually issued as unsecured debt. Table 21.5, pp. 900–901, provides a brief description and some unique characteristics of the various types of secured, unsecured, and special feature bonds. Clearly, management has many financing options. Some issues, like variable-rate notes and deep-discount bonds, can have a dramatic effect on the cost of funds to the issuer; others place significant constraints on the use of the firm's resources and therefore reduce managerial discretion.

Issue Characteristics

A bond can be issued with a variety of different characteristics. Some bonds are secured and others are not; most have fixed coupon rates, but some have coupons that float; and some (like equipment trust certificates) are issued with a series of maturities rather than a single maturity date. These features and others like them are important, since they can have an impact on the cost of borrowing. There are also a number of other issue characteristics of which a financial manager should be aware, including the bond indenture, the trustee, closed- and open-end mortgage clauses, after-acquired clauses, sinking fund provisions, call features, and call price. Table 21.6, pp. 902–903, provides a short description and briefly notes the purpose of each of these; later we will see how some of these issue characteristics play an important part in the debt management process, and how they can affect the cost of funds to the issuer.

Bond Ratings

Most corporate bonds are rated by the two major rating agencies, Moody's and Standard & Poor's; the exceptions are bonds considered too small to rate, privately placed bonds, debt issued by newly organized companies(those with less than 5 years of operating history), and certain industry categories (for example, as a matter of policy, the rating agencies do not rate the bonds of some financial institutions). Ratings provide a measure of the relative riskiness of a bond. The key concern in the rating process is the ability of the firm to service principal and

---

[5]Although a slight yield spread may exist, Hickman shows that the collateral of an obligation, or the lack of it, does not become important until the issue actually approaches default; see W. Braddock Hickman, *Corporate Bond Quality and Investor Experience* (Princeton, N.J.: Princeton University Press, 1958).

interest requirements in a prompt and timely fashion. Agency ratings capture a bond's risk of default (or the business and financial risk embedded in an issue); they are not intended to be a measure of a bond's market (or systematic) risk.

Prior to the SEC registration of a new bond issue, the chief financial officer of a corporation will often meet with one of the rating agencies in order to get an indication of what the rating might be if the firm were to proceed with the offering. Although the details of the actual credit analysis conducted by the rating agency depend on the issuer, there are several major factors that enter into most rating processes. These include an analysis of the issue's indenture provisions, an in-depth study of the firm's earning power, a look at the firm's liquidity and its management, a study of the firm's debt ratios, and an in-depth exploration of its leverage/coverage ratio to determine how well it can service both its existing debt and any new bonds being contemplated or proposed. A fee that usually ranges from $500 to $15,000 is charged for rating each corporate bond, and is paid by the issuer or by the underwriter of the securities being rated.[6]

The agencies assign letter ratings indicating what they believe to be the risk of default, or overall quality, of an obligation. These ratings range from the triple A to C or D, with Moody's having 9 grades and Standard & Poor's having 12. Table 21.7, p. 904, summarizes these and provides a brief description of each. Except for slight variations in designations, the meaning and interpretation of the ratings is basically the same. The top four ratings are the *investment-grade* class; bonds in this group, which include high- and medium-grade securities, are considered to be of high quality and are the most actively traded. The next group contains the *speculative issues*, and includes the BB (or Ba) and B obligations. The C and D categories are made up of poor quality and income obligations, many of which are *trading flat* (meaning they are in arrears with regard to interest payments), or are in outright default.

There is normally an inverse relationship between the rating of a bond and its interest rate, or cost of funds—high-quality bonds can be expected to have lower yields than lower-quality bonds. Table 21.8, p. 905, provides a summary of average yields and yield spreads; it shows that a change in rating can have a large impact on the cost of funds to the issuer. Note that these spreads vary as interest rates change, and that in periods of high yields, the spread can become especially large. Although bond ratings are largely a function of the operating results and financial

---

[6]For an in-depth examination of the corporate rating process, see *Standard & Poor's Rating Guide* (New York: McGraw-Hill, 1979), chaps. 1–17; and George E Pinches and Kent A. Mingo, "A Multivariate Analysis of Industrial Bonds Ratings," *Journal of Finance* 28 (March 1973), pp. 201–206.

TABLE 21.5
Types of Corporate Bonds

Type of Bond	Description
First mortgage bonds	A form of secured debt collateralized with a first lien on real property or buildings; normally, the market value of the property is greater than the principal amount of the mortgage bond being issued. These bonds are generally considered the most senior form of corporate debt.
Second mortgage bonds	A bond that gives holders a secondary claim on assets already secured by a first mortgage; because of their less secure position, they normally carry a higher interest rate than first mortgage bonds. Second mortgages tend to be issued against seasoned (or older) plant and property that has undergone significant appreciation in value.
Equipment trust certificates	A form of secured debt widely used by railroads, airlines, and other transportation firms as a way to finance rolling stock. The certificates are backed by a specific piece of equipment, like a railroad car or jet plane; they are usually issued on a serial basis (the bond is divided into parts, each with its own maturity date).
Collateral trust bonds	A bond secured with financial assets, like the stock and bonds of companies other than the issuer; the value of the collateral generally must be 25 to 30 percent greater than the par value of the bond it supports.
Debentures	A form of unsecured debt that has a claim only on the firm's earnings, and not its assets; debentures generally have a higher cost than secured debt, but are popular because of the managerial flexibility they provide.
Subordinated debentures	An unsecured bond whose claim on income and assets is ranked behind all other types of unsecured debt; some issuers view subordinated debentures as an equity surrogate.
Convertible debentures	A bond that is convertible, at the option of the holder, into a certain number of shares of the issuing firm's common stock (convertible securities are examined in detail in Chapter 23).
Income bonds	An unsecured bond on which interest need be paid only when earnings are sufficiently large; income bonds are used primarily by weak firms undergoing reorganization. Unpaid interest generally must be paid prior to the payment of dividends to preferred or common stockholders. For obvious reasons, the coupon rate on income bonds is generally quite high.
Variable rate notes	Notes that do *not* have fixed coupons; rather, the coupon "floats" so that every six months it is reset at, or a certain amount above, a stipulated money or capital market rate. The notes are usually redeemable at par, at the holder's option, every six months. Their use tends to increase as market rates move up; when rates are high, firms use "floaters" as a way to avoid being locked into high interest rates for the long haul. The major risk to the issuing corporation is that it will end up paying out more in interest if rates drift up, rather than down, over the life of the issue.
Bonds with early redemption (put) options	Bonds similar to variable rate notes, except that they are normally issued with fixed coupons. In effect the early redemption option enables the holder to sell the bond back to the issuer at a stipulated price (or yield)—that is, to redeem the issue prior to maturity. To the extent that the holder has the right to sell a financial asset at a set price at a set point(s) in time, the early redemption feature is often viewed as a "put" option. Hence, these bonds are also known as "put

TABLE 21.5
Types of Corporate Bonds
continued

Type of Bond	Description
	bonds." The early redemption provision is usually deferred for several years after date of issue, and then it may allow the bondholder to exercise the option every six months (every coupon date), or on only a limited number of specified dates (say, at two or three times over a 5- to 10-year period). The big advantage is that these bonds lower the cost of funds to issuers, since they reduce the price risk exposure of investors.
Original issue deep discount (and zero coupon) bonds	Deep discount bonds are issued with very low (or zero) coupons; as a result, they are sold at a price well below par value, even though they are redeemable at maturity at full face value. For example, in April 1981, at a time when comparably rated bonds were being sold with coupons of more than 15.5 percent, Alcoa issued a 30-year, 7.5 percent bond at a price of 48.36 percent of par (for a $1000 bond, that translates into a price of $483.60) to provide a yield to investors of 14.70 percent. These bonds are appealing to issuers for two reasons: first, they can be sold at much lower yields than conventional bonds (the interest savings often amounts to a full percentage point or more); and second, the issuer can take a tax deduction for the annual amortization of the discount, even though no cash payout is involved (the actual repayment of principal will not occur until maturity).
Bonds with contingent takedown options	Bonds similar to bonds with warrants attached (see Chapter 23) to the extent that the contingent takedown option (CTO) enables the holder to buy one of the issuing company's bonds, with a stated coupon and at a stipulated price, any time over the life of the option. The CTO is attached to a bond and is sold to the public as a "unit" (usually, one CTO attached to every $1000 par value bond). Shortly after issue, the option is usually detachable from the bond, at which time they trade separately. A CTO will have an intrinsic value to investors so long as the underlying bond issue specified in the takedown option is going up in price and its market value exceeds the price at which the issue can be purchased by exercising the CTO. To the firm, bonds with contingent takedown options will reduce the cost of financing and at the same time provide a potential source of additional future funding.
Municipals—industrial development bonds (IDB) and pollution control bonds (PCB)	A way of indirectly raising capital in the tax-exempt municipal market. The corporation is not the issuer of such bonds; they are issued by industrial development or pollution control authorities created by cities, counties, and other municipalities; the bonds are issued as revenue bonds by a municipal authority for the benefit of a specific company, which uses the funds to build or acquire various types of fixed assets. The corporation is a part of the issue to the extent that it enters into a contractual agreement with the political subdivision whereby it agrees, as a part of a lease or some other financing package, to meet certain lease or debt service requirements over the life of the obligation. The major attraction of these municipal issues is the substantial reduction in financing costs (as a rule, municipal rates are about one-third less than comparable corporate yields). The proceeds from IDB's are used to finance the construction of plants, warehouses, and other facilities that will encourage industrial development (and employment) in a community or region. The proceeds from pollution control bonds are used to finance the construction of mandated pollution control devices at plants and public utility generating facilities. Federal legislation limits the size of industrial development bonds to $10 million, though there is no size limit on PCBs.

TABLE 21.6
Bond Issue Characteristics

Bond Feature or Provision	Description and Purpose
Bond indenture	A legal document stating the conditions under which a bond has been issued; spells out both the rights of bondholders and the duties of the issuing corporation. Also included in the indenture are certain restrictions, such as constraints on working capital, limitations on the liquidation and acquisition of fixed assets, and constraints on subsequent borrowing activity.
Trustee	An individual or institution representing the interests of the bondholders. A trustee makes sure the issuer lives up to the provisions of the indenture, and if the issuer defaults or fails to fulfill its contractual obligations, takes the specified action on behalf of the bondholders. A trustee normally participates in the creation of the indenture, making sure that all the necessary legal protections have been provided for in the agreement.
Closed-end mortgage clause	A provision common in first mortgage bond indentures that prohibits additional borrowing on collateralized property; the firm cannot issue second mortgage bonds on property secured with a closed-end first mortgage.
Open-end mortgage clause	A provision that permits the issuance of additional bonds under the same mortgage contract; provides the issuer with financing flexibility while protecting creditors by placing restrictions on the amount of additional borrowing that can occur.
After-acquired clause	A clause which provides that all property acquired by the firm after the first mortgage has been filed will be added to the property already pledged as security for the first mortgage; enhances the claim of current mortgage holders by automatically giving them a lien on any additional property acquired by the company.
Sinking fund provision	A provision that specifies how a bond will be paid off over time; in many respects, sinking fund payments on bonds are much like the instalment or amortization payments on term debt. They are beneficial in two ways: First, they reduce default risk by providing for the orderly retirement of the bonds; second, they help provide liquidity to the secondary market. The net effect of reduced default and market risk is a reduced cost of borrowing to the firm. There are several types of sinking fund provisions. Utility issuers often employ provisions that actually give them the right to use periodic sinking funds to reduce the amount of debt outstanding or to increase the capital asset base of the firm. This is known as an *improvement fund* and requires an annual sinking fund of at least 1 percent of the total amount of bonds the issuer has outstanding. The standard sinking fund provision requires the firm to retire a predetermined amount of bonds each year; in addition, an option may be included to enable the firm to retire more than the mandated amount if the cash flow can support it. This optional extra can amount to as much as 150 percent of the required annual sinking fund, and lets the firm speed up the retirement of debt. Sinking fund requirements generally begin 1 to 5 years after date of issue, and continue annually thereafter until all or most of the issue is paid off; any amount not repaid by maturity would then be retired with a single balloon payment. In most cases, the firm is given the right to handle the sinking fund by calling the stipulated amount for redemption or buying the required amount of bonds in the open market.

TABLE 21.6
Bond Issue Characteristics

Bond Feature or Provision	Description and Purpose
Call feature	A feature that spells out whether or not, and under what conditions, the issue can be prematurely retired for purposes other than meeting sinking fund provisions. There are three types of call provisions: (1) a bond can be *freely callable*, which means the issuer can retire the bond at any time; (2) it can be *noncallable*, in which case the issuer would be prohibited from retiring the bond prior to maturity; or (3) the bond could carry a *deferred call feature*, which stipulates that the obligation cannot be called for a certain length of time after the date of issue, after which it becomes freely callable. Generally, the greater the call protection, the lower the cost of funds to the issuer. Noncallable bonds will be least costly to the firm, followed by deferred callable issues, with freely callable obligations being the most expensive. Call features are used most often to replace an outstanding issue with one that carries a lower coupon (refunding). Some bonds are callable but not refundable; that is, the call provision may prohibit the retirement of an issue from the proceeds of a lower coupon bond, but not prohibit the firm from prematurely retiring the issue for any other reason. Thus, if the firm has excess cash, the issue could carry a nonrefunding provision, but still be retired prior to maturity through the call feature.
Call price	A price (or series of prices) for all sinking fund bonds, and for all bonds with freely callable or deferred call provisions; stipulates the price the company must pay to the bondholder to initiate premature retirement of the debt. For call or refunding provisions, the call price in the first year the issue is callable is usually established at a *call premium* of approximately one year's interest above the par value of the issue (for example, a 10 percent bond would have an initial call price of $1100); this initial price would then decline each year so that it would drop to par (or slightly above) just before maturity. The call price for a sinking fund involves a much smaller call premium (usually no more than 1 to 2 percent above par) and is far less costly to the firm.

condition of the firm, it is obviously in the firm's best interest to work for as high a rating as possible. For example, according to Table 21.8, from 1965 through 1982, the difference between double and single A-rated corporate bonds averaged 25 basis points, or one-quarter of one percentage point. Using this average spread and ignoring sinking fund requirements, an improvement of one rating category on a $50 million, 30-year issue will result in interest savings of nearly $3.8 million over the life of the obligation. Agency ratings are also important because they can affect the marketability of an issue and the firm's ability to raise bond funds; this is so because most corporate bonds are purchased by institutional investors, many of which cannot invest in low-rated (or speculative-grade) bonds.

Moody's	Standard & Poor's	Interpretation
HIGH GRADE		
Aaa	AAA	The highest rating assigned to a debt instrument, indicating an extremely strong capacity to pay principal and interest. Bonds in this category are often called "gilt edge" securities.
Aa	AA	High-quality bonds by all standards, with strong capacity to pay principal and interest. These bonds are rated lower primarily because the margins of protection are not as strong as for Aaa and AAA.
MEDIUM GRADE		
A	A	These bonds possess many favorable investment attributes, but elements may be present that suggest a susceptibility to impairment given adverse economic changes.
Baa	BBB	Bonds regarded as having adequate capacity to pay principal and interest, but lacking certain protective elements in the event of adverse economic conditions that could lead to a weakened capacity for payment.
SPECULATIVE		
Ba	BB	Bonds regarded as having only moderate protection of principal and interest payments during both good and bad times. Bonds that generally lack the characteristics of other desirable investments. Assurance of interest and principal payments over any long period of time may be small.
B	B	
DEFAULT		
Caa	CCC	Poor-quality issues that may be in default or in danger of default.
Ca	CC	Highly speculative issues that are often in default or possess other marked shortcomings.
C		The lowest rating assigned by Moody's. These issues can be regarded as extremely poor in investment quality.
	C	Rating given to income bonds on which no interest is being paid.
	DDD DD D	Issues in default with principal and/or interest payments in arrears (actual rating indicates relative salvage value).

Note: In addition to the standard rating categories denoted above, Moody's uses numerical modifiers (1, 2, or 3) on bonds rated A to B, while S & P uses plus (+) or minus (−) signs on the same rating classes to show relative standing within a major rating category.

SOURCES: Adapted from Moody's Investor Service and Standard & Poor's NYSE Reports.

TABLE 21.8
Effects of Agency
Ratings on
Comparative Bond
Yields
(Average S & P
Composite Yields)

Year	AAA	AA	A	BBB
1965	4.47%	4.55%	4.67%	4.85%
1966	5.13	5.22	5.33	5.71
1967	5.53	5.66	5.80	6.21
1968	6.05	6.31	6.53	6.93
1969	6.93	7.16	7.40	7.84
1970	7.84	8.21	8.56	9.13
1971	7.38	7.65	8.02	8.66
1972	7.26	7.51	7.66	8.24
1973	7.55	7.71	7.87	8.40
1974	8.25	8.56	8.65	9.37
1975	8.64	8.89	9.30	10.11
1976	8.43	8.75	9.09	9.75
1977	8.02	8.24	8.49	8.97
1978	8.73	8.92	9.12	9.45
1979	9.63	9.94	10.20	10.69
1980	11.87	12.37	12.71	13.40
1981	13.90	14.32	14.60	15.49
1982	13.32	13.73	14.19	15.45

AVERAGE YIELD SPREADS

AAA–AA	27 basis points[a]
AA–A	25 basis points
A–BBB	58 basis points
AAA–A	52 basis points
AA–BBB	83 basis points
AAA–BBB	110 basis points

[a]1 basis point = 1/100 of 1 percent.

MULTINATIONAL
DIMENSIONS

Eurobonds

A *Eurobond* is simply a bond that is sold in a country (or countries) other than the one in whose currency the issue is denonimated—thus, an American corporation would issue dollar-denominated bonds in the European markets. The Eurobond market is used mostly by large multinational companies and government organizations; in fact, in 1980, U.S. multinational firms accounted for about $4.1 billion of the $23.9 billion in new Eurobonds issued. Eurobonds are usually issued as debentures or with convertible features, and are underwritten and sold by international syndicates composed of the world's leading commercial banks and investment banking houses. Most Eurobonds have sinking funds, call features, and other traits similar to their domestic counterparts. However, one unique feature of these issues is that most are issued in bearer form (rather than registered) to shield the investor's identity from government officials —a characteristic important to many international investors.

For large multinational firms, Eurobonds offer several special advantages:

1. Although many foreign countries maintain tight control over access to their capital markets when issues are denominated in domestic currencies, access to these markets for securities denominated in foreign currencies is often relatively easy.

2. Disclosure requirements in the Eurobond market are much more lenient than those required by the SEC to register bonds for sale in the United States.

3. Eurobonds are usually issued by subsidiaries of multinational firms located in tax havens, such as the Netherlands Antilles, where no withholding taxes are required on interest payments to foreigners; since foreign investors hold Eurobonds in bearer form, one must assume some of them are able to avoid paying taxes on interest earnings to any government, a feature that obviously contributes to the demand for such issues.

The borrowing rates on Eurobonds closely follow the behavior of interest rates in the country in which they are denominated. As is true of short-term Eurocurrency interest rates, long-term interest rates vary considerably from currency to currency. However, once again this is somewhat illusory, because foreign exchange rates will act to balance effective borrowing costs. Recent comparative long-term interest rates, unadjusted for exchange rate changes, are shown in Figure 21.2; note that the long-term rates on dollars are not nearly as far out of line with other currencies as is the case with short-term rates. Although the main denomination of Eurobonds has historically been dollars, U.S. firms have been only modest borrowers in the Eurobond market, accounting for only about 15 to 20 percent of the new issue activity. The lack of heavy use by American firms is probably due to the fact that access to the domestic bond market is relatively wide open; in addition, domestic American firms are not able to take advantage of the disclosure and tax benefits of Eurobonds. They already must be in compliance with SEC disclosure requirements, and the tax haven breaks are not that important to U.S. institutional investors like pension funds and insurance companies, which are already in very low, or zero, tax brackets.

Debt Management: Issue Costs and Bond Refunding

Decisions about the use of debt generally revolve around matters of financial leverage and the cost of capital. Unless the firm is already excessively leveraged, financial managers can use debt as a way to increase returns to stockholders. Two leverage ratios are particularly important to the firm: one is the debt-equity ratio, which shows the

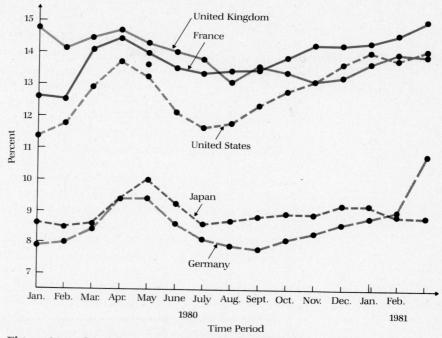

Figure 21.2   Long-Term Rates Interest in the United States and Other Countries.

Source: OECD, *Financial Market Trends*, March 1981, p. 92.

relative amount of debt the firm is using, and the other is the coverage ratio, which measures the firm's ability to service its debt. These ratios are closely monitored by lenders, rating agencies, institutional investors, and other bond market participants.

In addition to using debt to achieve a desired impact on leverage, financial managers are also concerned with minimizing the effective cost of debt financing. We noted in Chapter 18 that the use of debt is influenced to a large extent by capital structure considerations; financial structure is also important in defining the size of an issue, as is the cost and availability of funds from alternative sources of financing.[7] Such considerations not withstanding, two aspects of debt management are particularly important to achieving a minimum cost of financing: One is to structure the bond and its indenture to achieve the most efficient and cost-effective financing package, and the other is to consider restructuring outstanding debt (via refunding operations) as a way to realize interest savings. Here we will examine the various elements of debt

[7]For an excellent discussion of the issue size decision, see E. A. Dyl and W. Sawaya, "The Bond Issue Size Decision Revisited," *Financial Management* 8 (winter 1979), pp. 60–67.

administration that can have a pronounced effect on the cost of financing.

Controlling Cost of Funds at Time of Issue

When a firm comes to market with a new issue, it is only after a number of important decisions have already been made, many with input from the firm's investment banker and financial advisor. To begin with, an estimate of the firm's financing requirements must be made; as we saw in Chapter 4, much of this is done through the preparation of short- and long-term financial plans. Assuming that an evaluation and analysis of the company's capital structure suggests that funds can best be raised in the form of long-term debt, management's attention then shifts to developing a cost-effective financing package. The idea is to structure the bond and its indenture in such a way that the issue will be appealing to investors, and yet meet the financing needs of the firm in the least expensive way.

An issue's indenture is important because a number of the indenture provisions (such as an issue's call feature) can have a subtle, but nonetheless important, impact on the cost of financing. For example, issuing a bond with a deferred call provision, rather than making it freely callable, can reduce the coupon on an issue (and therefore the net interest cost to the issuer) by 15 to 20 basis points (or more) depending on the prevailing level of interest rates. The value of the call privilege to the issuer is a function of the firm being able to refund the bond in question with a lower-cost issue; theoretically, it is equal to the present value of future interest savings, less the cost of calling and refunding. Clearly, the greater the probability that rates will fall over the life of the call deferment period of an issue, the greater the chance that a deferred call provision will have a positive value.[8] Thus, when interest rates are high and likely to fall, the call feature will be highly valued. By using a deferred or noncallable provision in periods of high interest rates, financial managers can obtain a significant interest savings, but only at the cost of foregoing the opportunity of refunding the issue when and if rates decline. In general, if the firm thinks the prospects are good for a near-term decline in rates (and greater cost savings are available by issuing a freely callable obligation, and refunding it when rates do drop, than the savings available from using a deferred call issue), its financial managers should give serious consideration to using the freely callable provision.

Several other aspects of a bond package are just as important as an issue's call feature and perhaps more so. These include issue timing and the bond repayment–sinking fund provisions.

---

[8]See, for example, Gordon Pye, "The Value of the Call Option on a Bond," *Journal of Political Economy* 74 (April 1966), pp. 200–205; and Frank C. Jen and James E. Wert, "The Deferred Call Provision and Corporate Bond Yields," *Journal of Financial and Quantitative Analysis* 3 (June 1968), pp. 157–169.

Issue Timing: Hedging with Financial Futures.   The matter of issue timing is important because it plays a significant role in defining the yield (i.e., cost) of an issue. Reports of firms that save half a percentage point or more by issuing a bond two weeks earlier (or later) than planned are not uncommon, especially when the market is highly unstable. Unfortunately, it is equally common to read of firms that had to carry the added interest burden of half a percentage point or more because they issued a bond a couple of weeks too early or too late. The fact is that interest rates, even over the short term, are difficult to project. Studies have shown that the behavior of interest rates is not unlike that of common stock prices to the extent that they are a product of a highly efficient market and therefore difficult to predict with consistent precision.[9] Because of the considerable uncertainty in trying to project the future behavior of market yields, a growing number of financial managers are turning to *interest rate hedging* as a way to deal with the timing question. This can be done by using interest rate futures to lock in a given cost of funds to the issuer. (See Appendix 21A for a detailed explanation of interest rate futures contracts and their use in hedging strategies.)

Interest rate futures provide an excellent vehicle for hedging against near-term movements in long-term interest rates. For example, a firm planning a bond issue could short-sell GNMA futures contracts to hedge against the risk of long-term rates moving up during presale activities. A simple strategy is to use a *naive hedge*, in which the amount of GNMA futures shorted is equal to the par value of the pending bond issue. Thus, if the company is planning to issue a $25 million bond, it would short 250 GNMA futures contracts (each GNMA contract is for delivery of $100,000 of the underlying security). To see how this works, assume corporate bond rates are presently at 10 percent, and for simplicity assume that GNMA futures are also trading at a price to yield 10 percent. Because management expects market rates to rise to 11.5 percent by the date of issue, the firm decides to use a financial futures hedge to reduce or eliminate the cost of being left with a higher coupon. Table 21.9 shows what happens if interest rates on both corporate bonds and GNMA futures contracts do rise as expected by the issue date; note that in this case, we make the heroic assumption, strictly for simplicity, that the rates on corporate bonds and GNMA futures will rise by the same amount, from 10 to 11.5 percent. As can be seen, the profit from the interest rate hedge is used to reduce the principal amount of the bond issue. As such, even though the company has to issue the bond with the

---

[9]See, for example, Michael J. Prell, "How Well Do the Experts Forecast Interest Rates," *Federal Reserve Bank of Kansas City, Monthly Review*, October 1973, pp. 3–13; and O. D. Bowlin and J. Martin, "Extrapolations of Yields over the Short Run: Forecast or Folly?" *Journal of Monetary Economics* 1 (1975), pp. 275–288.

TABLE 21.9

Using Financial
Futures to Hedge on a
Forthcoming Bond
Issue

CONDITION:
Company plans to raise $25 million by issuing a 20-year bond several months from now; rates are presently 10%, but expected to rise to 11.5% by the date of issue.

ACTION TAKEN NOW TO INITIATE THE HEDGE
Sell 250 GNMA futures contracts
at a yield of 10% at 86 $^{12}/_{32}$
(.86375 × $25,000,000) $21,593,750

POSITION WHEN HEDGE IS COVERED
Buy 250 GNMA futures contracts
at a yield of 11.5% at 77 $^{30}/_{32}$ (.779375 × $25,000,000) $19,484,375
   NET PROFIT TO FIRM $ 2,109,375

FUNDS REQUIRED FROM BOND ISSUE
Size of issue planned $25,000,000
Less: Net profit to the firm from
  financial futures hedge (per above)   (2,109,375)
   REVISED ISSUE SIZE $22,890,625

EFFECTIVE COST OF FINANCING[a]
Issuing a $22.9 million, 20-year,
  11.5% bond, rather than a $25
  million issue, results in
  an effective cost of   10.39%

[a]The effective cost of financing is defined in the appendix to this chapter.

higher 11.5 percent coupon, it is able to issue a smaller amount ($22.9 million instead of $25 million without the hedge) and in this way reduce the total effective cost of financing to only 10.39 percent.[10]

The hedge will not eliminate the higher coupon; rather, the proceeds from it will offset all, or a major portion, of the higher interest cost that accompanies a rise in rates. On the other hand, if market rates do not move against the issuer but instead remain stable, the only costs to the firm are commissions and other transaction costs. In fact, the worst thing that can happen is for market rates to undergo a sizable decline— for when rates drop, not only will the firm have to absorb the commission and transaction costs, but it also will realize a loss on the futures contracts that will eat up all or most of the interest savings which would otherwise occur by being able to issue the bond at a lower coupon. Hedging with financial interest rate futures, therefore, is not without its risks. For one thing, issuer expectations may be wrong and market rates may, in fact, not move against the firm—in which case the hedge would

---

[10]Alternatively, and perhaps what is done more commonly in practice, the profits from the hedge could be used to offset the higher interest charges. That is, the bond is issued at the same size as planned, and the profits from the financial futures hedge are used to reduce the early interest payments on the obligation. (*Note*: First-year interest requirements on a $25 million, 11.5 percent issue equal $2.9 million.) The net effect of this action is still the same—to keep the effective cost of financing down to around 10.39 percent.

produce only commissions and/or opportunity costs. In addition, because it is so difficult to obtain identical coupons and maturities for both the corporate issue and the financial future being used as the hedging vehicle, differences in price behavior are likely to make the hedge itself less than perfect. Finally, and perhaps most important, even though their time-series behavior is generally highly correlated, there is no reason to expect the yields on corporate bonds and futures contracts to move together; price movements in the two securities can differ substantially over time, and the hedge can end up performing below expectations.[11]

Bond Repayment: Sinking Fund Provisions.   The cost of financing to the firm is also influenced by the way the bond is to be repaid. Bonds are issued either with a single balloon payment at maturity or with a *sinking fund provision*, which provides for systematic retirement of the principal over time. The issuer can meet sinking fund provisions by making a cash payment to a trustee who in turn calls the required number of bonds by lot; or by purchasing the required amount of bonds in the open market and delivering them to the trustee. The latter procedure would be used when the firm's bonds are trading at a discount, for so long as the price is less than par, it is obviously less costly to do it this way than to call the bonds for redemption. In essence, the open market purchase of discount bonds enables the issuer to repay the debt with an amount less than that which was borrowed. However, even when interest rates have risen sharply, it is not always possible to buy bonds for sinking fund purposes at prices well below par. Sometimes, a company is forced to deal with an *accumulated issue*; these are bonds in which all, or nearly all, of the issue has been accumulated by one or two institutional investors. Such bondholders are in a monopolistic position; they can unilaterally set sinking fund purchase prices at or near par, even though the issue should be trading in the open market at a deep discount. In fact, the deep discounts of sinking fund bonds make them appealing to institutional investors who are in a position to accumulate such bonds and in so doing earn above-average returns on their investments.[12]

Although the use of a sinking fund is influenced in large part by industry standards and market pressures, a firm need not employ one if it is willing to absorb the higher initial coupon cost that generally accompanies non-sinking-fund issues. Generally, the yield on sinking

[11]For a more extensive discussion of hedging, see Appendix 21A and Richard W. McEnally and Michael L. Rice, "Hedging Possibilities in the Flotation of Debt Securities," *Financial Management* 8 (winter 1979), pp. 12–18; and Peter Bacon and Richard Williams, "Interest Rate Futures: New Tool for the Financial Manager," *Financial Management* 5 (spring 1976), pp. 32–38.

[12]For an interesting discussion of accumulated sinking fund bonds (from both the issuer and investor perspectives), see Andrew Kalotay, "On the Management of Sinking Funds," *Financial Management* 10 (summer 1981), pp. 34–40.

fund bonds, and therefore the cost of funds to the issuer, averages about 15 basis points less than that for comparable issues without such provisions.[13] Even though a sinking fund lowers the interest cost to the issuer, the non-sinking-fund provision enables the issuer to use the loan proceeds for a longer period of time. This means there is an opportunity cost to the sinking fund feature, which can be used, along with the interest savings that accrue from such issues, to assess the desirability of issuing bonds with sinking fund provisions.

The opportunity cost of a sinking fund feature can be captured by assuming that all sinking fund payments are financed with a series of new debt issues over time. That is, if a firm issuing sinking fund bonds is to have the full amount of financing available over the life of the bond, it must replace the funds expended on sinking fund payments with new debt. In addition, each new debt issue will involve issuance and underwriter costs, which become a part of the opportunity cost; and the interest differential for the new financing must also be included. Actually, the interest differential will be a concern only if market rates are expected to undergo substantial change. For if the cost of financing the new debt is assumed to remain unchanged from present levels, the interest differential portion of the model equals zero, and this variable can be effectively ignored in the computations. In contrast, an expected increase in refinancing rates will be detrimental to the value of a sinking fund provision, whereas a decrease in rates will add to the appeal of this feature.

The relative attractiveness of a sinking fund can be assessed by comparing the present value of interest savings on sinking fund issues with the present value of issuing new debt to replace the sinking fund payments, as specified by the following decision model:

$$PV(SF) = \begin{bmatrix} \text{present value of} \\ \text{interest savings on} \\ \text{the sinking fund issue} \end{bmatrix} - \begin{bmatrix} \text{present value of the} \\ \text{opportunity cost of} \\ \text{issuing new debt to} \\ \text{service the sinking} \\ \text{fund provision} \end{bmatrix}$$

$$PV(SF) = \sum_{t=1}^{m} \frac{(i_n - i_s)B}{(1 + i_s)^t} - \sum_{t=f}^{m-1} \frac{(F \times S_t) + (\Delta i \times S_t)}{(1 + i_s)^t} \qquad (21.2)$$

where m = bond maturity
  i_n = interest rate on non-sinking-fund issue
  i_s = interest rate on sinking fund issue
  B = size of bond issue

---

[13]See E. A. Dyl and M. D. Joehnk, "Sinking Funds and the Cost of Corporate Debt," *Journal of Finance* 34 (September 1979), pp. 887–894.

f = year in which first sinking fund payment will be made
F = flotation, underwriting, and other issuance costs
S_t = periodic sinking fund payment
Δi = expected *average* change in refinancing rates on new debt issues

Note that because the cost on sinking fund bonds (i_s) is the lowest rate at which the firm can obtain funds, it is used as the measure of the time value of money.[14] Clearly, so long as $PV(SF)$ is positive, it follows that the interest savings on a sinking fund bond are greater than the opportunity cost associated with financing such payments over time, and therefore the sinking fund issue should be employed.[15]

To see how Equation 21.2 works, assume that a firm is evaluating the desirability of issuing one of two comparable 20-year, $60 million bonds. One has a sinking fund that begins in the sixth year and requires straight-line amortization of the principal by maturity (it carries a coupon rate of 9 percent) and the other is a non-sinking-fund issue that carries a coupon rate of 9.15 percent. In this case, we will assume the issuance costs (made up of underwriter compensation, SEC fees, legal and accounting costs, and the like) equal 1 percent of the amount of debt being issued; for simplicity, we will also assume that financing costs, and therefore the cost of financing sinking fund payments, remain unchanged over time (i.e., that $\Delta i = 0\%$). Given that sinking fund payments occur over a 15-year period (from years 6 to 20), it follows that annual sinking fund payments (S_t) are $60 million/15 = $4 million per year. Using a 9 percent discount rate, we see that $PV(SF)$ is positive and therefore that the sinking fund bond should be selected:

$$
\begin{aligned}
PV(SF) &= [(9.15\% - 9.00\%)\,(\$60{,}000{,}000) \times 9.129] - \{[(1.0\% \times \$4{,}000{,}000) \\
&\quad + (0\% \times \$4{,}000{,}000)] \times 5.060\,\} \\
&= (\$90{,}000 \times 9.129) - (\$40{,}000 \times 5.060) \\
&= \$821{,}610 - \$202{,}400 \\
&= \$619{,}210
\end{aligned}
$$

Note that the opportunity cost present-value interest factor (of 5.060) represents the $PVIFA_{k,n}$ for periods f to $m - 1$ (years 6 to 19). For a 9 percent discount rate, we have $8.950 - 3.890 = 5.060$.

We assumed the cost of financing the sinking fund payments would remain unchanged, so that $\Delta i = 0\%$; but what happens to $PV(SF)$ if rates go up instead by an average of, say, 2 percent ($\Delta i = 2\%$)? In this case, by substituting a value of 2 percent for Δi, we see that the opportunity cost

---

[14]Because this and similar financing decisions are viewed as essentially risk-free investment projects, using the lowest cost of financing as the present-value discount rate is generally viewed as an acceptable opportunity cost for the firm.

[15]This decision model was adopted from one developed by Dyl and Joehnk, in "Sinking Funds and the Cost of Corporate Debt."

component of the model increases to \$607,200 and $PV(SF)$ drops to \$214,410—an amount that still indicates the use of a sinking fund feature is economically justified. In fact, given that we know the value of $PV(SF)$ when $\Delta i = 0\%$, we can solve the following simple equation to find out how far refinancing rates must rise before $PV(SF) = \$0$, and the sinking fund provision becomes unattractive:

$$\Delta i = \frac{PV(SF)^*}{(PVIFA_{k,n}{}^*)\,(S_t)} \qquad (21.3)$$

where $PV(SF)^*$ = present value of Equation 21.2 with $\Delta i = 0\%$
$PVIFA_{k,n}{}^*$ = present-value interest factor for an annuity for periods f to $m - 1$, from Equation 21.2

Continuing with our example and solving Equation 21.3 for Δi, we see that:

$$\Delta i = \frac{\$619,210}{(5.060)(\$4,000,000)} = .0306$$

Thus, if the level of average interest rates is expected to rise less than 3.06 percentage points, a sinking fund bond remains the superior financing vehicle.

Financial managers can assess the likelihood of such a change occurring and use that insight to put together the most cost-efficient bond package. So long as the chance is quite small that rates will actually go up by the amount indicated by Δi in Equation 21.3, and so long as sinking fund payments are not expected to place an unusually heavy strain on the company's cash flow, the firm's planned financing should include a sinking fund feature.

The Refunding Decision

Deciding whether or not to refund a bond is an important part of a debt administration program. If interest rates decline during the term of an outstanding obligation, the issuer can often realize substantial interest savings by retiring the existing bond and replacing it with one bearing a lower interest cost. Reducing interest expense is only one (albeit the primary) motive for bond refunding; other reasons include the elimination of restrictive indenture provisions and the reorganization or consolidation of outstanding debt. The restructuring of outstanding debt via bond refunding is a financial tactic that can affect not only corporate profitability, but also the amount of financial risk to which the firm is exposed. Refunding, in effect, can yield cost savings and at the same time reduce risk of default by lowering debt service requirements.

A company's capital structure should be continually monitored for issues that may be candidates for refunding. This can be done fairly easily by tracking a bond's *crossover refunding rate*. Ignoring transaction costs and bond discounts or premiums, every bond has a crossover refunding rate that represents the market rate which would have to be obtained on the refunding issue to justify refunding. This rate is computed as follows:

$$\text{Crossover refunding rate} = \frac{\text{annual coupon payment}}{\text{current call price on the issue}} \qquad (21.4)$$

For example, a 10 percent bond would have annual coupon payments of $100 and most likely an initial call price of around $1100; its crossover refunding rate would be $100/$1100 = .0909. In this case, market interest rates must fall to 9.09 percent before the bond can even be considered for possible refunding.

Once a refunding candidate has been identified, the economic justification for actually executing a proposed refunding operation must be determined. The decision to refund can be evaluated by using a standard present-value-based benefit-cost model. Other things being equal, refunding would be advisable so long as the present value of the cash savings from refunding (the benefits) exceeds the costs. There are two basic parts to a corporate refunding decision: the net cash outflow that occurs at the time the refunding takes place, and the annual net cash benefits that occur over time. The initial cash outflow contains four elements: the cost of calling the old bonds (COB_0), less the net proceeds from the new issue (PNB_0), plus the expense of issuing the new bonds (BIE_0), less the tax savings from writing off the old bonds (TS_0). The initial cash outflow (C_0) may therefore be defined as follows:

$$C_0 = COB_0 - PNB_0 + BIE_0 - TS_0 \qquad (21.5)$$

The benefits from a refunding operation are the after-tax interest savings that result from replacing the old bond with the new, lower-cost issue. Because these interest savings occur annually over the remaining life of the refunded issue, they must be converted to a present-value basis. Having determined the stream of annual after-tax interest savings, the benefits of refunding (B_t) can be stated as:

$$B_t = \sum_{t=1}^{m} \frac{IS_t}{(1 + i)^t} \qquad (21.6)$$

where
m = remaining term to maturity of the refunded issue
IS_t = periodic after-tax interest savings
i = interest rate on the refunding issue

One issue that remains the topic of considerable debate is specification of the appropriate discount rate to use in defining the benefits of refunding.[16] Most writers agree that the traditional cost of capital is inappropriate for refunding purposes. Rather, the current borrowing rate is generally considered the relevant discount rate, since the stream of cash flows in Equation 21.6 falls into the same risk category as the principal and interest payments on existing debt. In effect, this is the same discount rate used in the market valuation process to price debt securities. Still, one question remains: whether to use the before- or the after-tax rate. Lewellen and Emery[17] show that it really does not make any difference which rate is used, so long as the conditions surrounding the refunding are properly defined in the cash flow. If the firm's leverage is to be altered by issuing a refunding bond that is, say, larger than the principal remaining on the refunded issue, the additional debt burden should be added to the cash flow and a before-tax cost used as the appropriate discount rate. In contrast, so long as the company is executing a "pure refunding" operation by replacing old debt with a new issue that is identical in all respects but coupon,[18] the firm's financial leverage position will not be altered. In this case, the after-tax cost of the new funds to the issuer is the correct discount rate. Since our discussion presumes a pure refunding situation, we will use an after-tax rate in our cash flow model.

Given the costs and benefits as described in Equations 21.5 and 21.6, the present value of the refunding operation (PVR) is simply:

$$PVR = B_t - C_0 \tag{21.7}$$

$$= \sum_{t=1}^{m} \frac{IS_t}{(1 + i)^t} - C_0$$

Clearly, so long as PVR is positive, refunding should be given serious consideration. Before we move to an illustration, a few tax-related points should be mentioned. In particular, several aspects of the costs and benefits warrant further explanation; these include bond discounts and premiums, call premiums, and flotation costs.

When a bond is sold at a price different from its par value, the firm is required to amortize the discount (price < par) or premium (price > par) over the life of the issue. The amortized discount is treated as a tax-deductible *expense*, while the amortized premium is treated as pre-tax *income*. For refunding purposes, if a bond is retired prior to

---

[16]For an excellent discussion of some of the problems surrounding the bond refunding decision, see A. R. Ofer and R. A. Taggart, "Bond Refunding: A Clarifying Analysis," *Journal of Finance* 32 (March 1977), pp. 21–30.

[17]Wilbur G. Lewellen and Douglas R. Emery, "On the Matter of Parity Among Financial Obligations," *Journal of Finance* 35 (March 1980), pp. 97–111.

[18]This assumes that the refunding and refunded bonds are the same size, and that any maturity differences are neutralized by using the maturity of the old bond as the relevant horizon for measuring cash flow benefits.

maturity, any unamortized discount or premium is written off at the time of refunding; writing off the unamortized discount results in a tax shield, since this noncash expense reduces corporate profitability and therefore reduces the tax liability of the firm. (Just the opposite occurs with unamortized premium.) The *call premium* of a bond is the amount by which the call price exceeds the par value of the issue at the time the bond is called. It is paid by the issuer to the bondholder to buy back the bonds prior to maturity, and is an out-of-pocket expenditure that is also treated as a tax-deductible expense in the year of the call. Finally, *flotation costs* are those expenses incurred in the process of issuing a bond; such expenses are amortized over the life of an issue. The annual writeoff is therefore a noncash, tax-deductible expense. If a bond is retired prior to maturity, any unamortized portion of this cost is deducted at the time of refunding. We will see in the illustration below how these costs and their related tax treatments play an important role in defining the benefits and costs of a refunding operation.

To illustrate the mechanics of the refunding decision model, consider the following hypothetical example: Lynnwood Industries has a $50 million bond issue outstanding; the bond has 25 years remaining to maturity and carries a coupon of 12.5 percent. Because the deferred call provision on the issue has elapsed and management feels it can issue a new bond at a cost of 10 percent, the chief financial officer of Lynnwood decides to look into the possibility of refunding the outstanding issue and replacing it with a 25-year, 10 percent bond. The outstanding bonds have a call price of 112.5 ($1125), which includes a call premium of 1 year's interest. The bonds initially netted proceeds of only $48.5 million, due to a discount of $30 per bond; the flotation costs were $450,000 and were incurred when the bond was issued 5 years ago (the bond was initially issued as a 30-year obligation). Lynnwood intends to issue $50 million worth of 10 percent, 25-year bonds and use the net proceeds from this issue to retire the old bonds.[19] The firm has been advised by its investment banker that it should be able to sell the new bonds at a price net to the issuer of 99.5; in addition, other flotation costs are estimated to be $600,000. Lynnwood has a marginal tax rate of 40 percent, and given the 10 percent cost of financing for the refunding issue, management will use an after-tax present value discount rate of 6 percent [.10 × (1 − .4) = .06]. Finally, the firm expects a 60-day (2-month) lag between the time the new issue is sold and the old bonds are called. This lag will result in a period of overlapping interest, during which time interest must be paid on both the old and the new bonds.

---

[19]To maintain a condition of pure refunding, and for simplicity, we use a term to maturity on the refunding issue equal to the number of years remaining on the old bonds; where inequalities exist, the usual procedure is to measure differential cash flow benefits only up to the maturity date of the old bonds. However, if either or both issues called for sinking fund payments, the net cash benefits would have to be adjusted to accommodate total debt service requirements (interest and principal payments).

Cost of calling old bonds $(1.125 \times \$50,000,000)$		$56,250,000
Less: Net proceeds from new issue $(.995 \times \$50,000,000)$		49,750,000
		$ 6,500,000
Plus: Flotation costs on new bonds		600,000
Interest on old bonds during overlap period		
$(.125 \times 2/12 \times \$50,000,000)$		1,041,667
Cash Outflow Before Tax Shields		$ 8,141,667
Less tax savings:		
Call premium $(.125 \times \$50,000,000 \times .40)$	$2,500,000	
Overlapping interest $(\$1,041,667 \times .40)$	416,667	
Unamortized discount on old bonds		
$(\$1,500,000 \times 25/30 \times .40)^a$	500,000	
Unamortized issue cost on old bonds		
$(\$450,000 \times 25/30 \times .40)$	150,000	$ 3,566,667
INITIAL CASH OUTFLOW (C_0)		$ 4,575,000

^{a}Discount on old bonds $= \$50,000,000 -$ initial net proceeds to issuer of $48,500,000 =$ $1,500,000; since the first 5 years (of a total of 30) have been amortized, 25 years are left and the unamortized balance is therefore 25/30.

The initial cash outflow of the refunding operation is shown in detail in Table 21.10. Note that it contains the elements defined in Equation 21.5: the cost of calling the old bond, less the net proceeds from the new issue, less issue expenses, and the tax effects of writing off the unamortized discount and issue expenses on the old bonds. In the case of Lynnwood Industries, we see that the initial cash outflow for this particular refunding operation will amount to $4,575,000.

The question before management is whether or not there will be sufficient benefits to recover such a large cash outflow. This, of course, is a function of the present value of the annual benefits the refunding is expected to generate. Table 21.11 provides the annual cash benefits that will result if the refunding is undertaken. The benefits of refunding are the annual after-tax interest savings that accrue to the firm with the lower-coupon refunding issue; in this particular case, the annual after-tax cash inflow amounts to $737,600 per year. Using a 6 percent after-tax discount rate, these benefits can be put on a present-value basis, and the present value of the refunding operation, PVR, can then be determined according to equation 21.7:

$$PVR = \$737,600 \, (12.783) - \$4,575,000$$
$$= \$9,428,741 - \$4,575,000$$
$$= \$4,853,741$$

Thus, even though the refunding will require an initial cash outflow of nearly $4.6 million, the present value of the annual cash benefits will

TABLE 21.11
Determining the
Annual Cash Benefits
of a Refunding
Operation: Lynnwood
Industries

OLD BOND		
Annual interest (.125 × $50,000,000)	$6,250,000	
Less tax savings:		
Interest ($6,250,000 × .40)	(2,500,000)	
Amortization of discount		
[($1,500,000 ÷ 30) × .40]	(20,000)	
Amortization of flotation costs		
[($450,000 ÷ 30) × .40]	(6,000)	
Annual Cash Outflow (Old)		$3,724,000
LESS: NEW BOND		
Annual interest (.10 × $50,000,000)	$5,000,000	
Less tax savings:		
Interest ($5,000,000 × .40)	(2,000,000)	
Amortization of discount		
[($250,000 ÷ 25) × .40][a]	(4,000)	
Amortization of flotation costs		
[($600,000 ÷ 25) × .40]	(9,600)	
Annual Cash Outflow (New)		2,986,400
ANNUAL CASH BENEFITS (IS_t)		$ 737,600

[a]Discount on new bonds = (1 − net selling price of .995) × $50,000,000 = .005 × $50,000,000 = $250,000.

equal more than $9.4 million and as a result, *PVR* will amount to a substantial $4.8 million. Since *PVR* is positive, the proposed refunding plan should be given serious consideration.[20]

Of course, a positive *PVR* alone is insufficient reason for undertaking a refunding operation. Although a *PVR* > 0 means that the refunding operation under consideration is worthwhile and economically justifiable, the timing may not be right. For if interest rates are declining, and the decline is expected to continue, management may prefer to delay the refunding operation until rates fall even more. Such a course of action will result in even greater interest savings to the issuer (and an even higher *PVR*). Because much of the input to the refunding model is already known or highly predictable, the determination of *PVR* is mostly mechanical; not so with the decision of when to refund, which is largely a function of expectations of future interest rate behavior. As we noted earlier, the efficient nature of interest rate movements makes such predictions extremely uncertain. In determining whether or not to proceed with a refunding, the financial manager should, of course, consider the possibility of a further decline in interest rates. Other things being equal, the more uncertain such expectations are, the less desirable it is to postpone the refunding. Complex dynamic programming models have been developed in an attempt to deal with the timing of refunding

[20]For a discussion of how bonds are refunded in the municipal market, see E. A. Dyl and M. D. Joehnk, "Refunding Tax Exempt Bonds," *Financial Management* 5 (summer 1976), pp. 59–66.

decisions; unfortunately, these models have not enjoyed widespread practical application due to their complexity and the fact that their solutions rely heavily on uncertain input in the form of interest rate expectations.[21]

Preferred Stock

Having examined term loans and bonds, we now look at another type of fixed-income financing vehicle: preferred stock. Firms generally do not issue large quantities of preferred stock. For example, in 1982, $5.3 billion of preferred stock was issued, accounting for only 6.7 percent of publicly issued corporate securities. As a result, a typical company's ratio of preferred to common stock outstanding is normally quite low. Preferred stock is considered to be a hybrid form of security because it possesses the features of both common stocks and corporate bonds. Preferred is like common to the extent that preferreds pay dividends and such dividends may be passed when corporate earnings fall below certain levels. Moreover, preferreds are a form of equity ownership and are issued without stated maturity dates. Preferreds are like bonds because they provide investors with prior claims on income and assets, and the level of current income is usually fixed for the life of the issue. Many preferred stocks also carry call features and sinking fund provisions, and a firm can have two or more issues of preferred outstanding at any point in time. Most important, because these securities usually trade on the basis of the yield they offer to investors,[22] they are viewed in the marketplace as *fixed-income obligations*. As such, preferred stocks can be used to alter the financial leverage of the firm.

Issue Characteristics

The contractual agreement of a preferred stock specifies the rights and privileges of preferred stockholders. The most important of these deals with level of annual dividends, preferred claim on income, voting rights, and claim on assets. The issuing firm agrees to pay stockholders a fixed level of quarterly dividends, with such dividends taking priority over common stock dividends. The firm, however, is under no legally binding obligation to make the preferred dividend payments; if conditions deteriorate, these dividends may be passed (of course, the company cannot miss dividends on preferreds and still pay them to common stockholders, as this would violate the stock's preferential claim on income). Normally, even though they hold an ownership position in the

---

[21]See, for example, Harold Bierman, "The Bond Refunding Decision as a Markov Process," *Management Science* 12 (August 1966), pp. 545–551; and H. Martin Weingartner, "Optimal Timing of Bond Refunding," *Management Science* 13 (March 1967); pp. 511–524.

[22]Because most preferred dividends are fixed (they are, in effect, a perpetuity), the value—or price—of a high-grade preferred stock is found (as noted in Chapter 7) by relating the issue's fixed dividend income to the prevailing market yield of comparably rated preferreds; that is, the market price of a preferred equals annual dividend income divided by market yield. In a similar fashion, we can see that the cost of preferred stock financing to the firm equals annual dividend income divided by market price of preferred.

TABLE 21.12
Preferred Stock Issue Characteristics

Preferred Stock Features and Provisions	Description
Cumulative provision	Nearly all preferreds are issued on a cumulative basis, which means any preferred dividends passed must be made up in full before dividends can be restored to common stockholders. As long as dividends on preferreds remain in arrears, a corporation will not be able to make dividend payments to common stockholders. If the preferred is not cumulative, passed dividends do not accumulate. Other things being equal, a cumulative provision is generally highly valued by investors and as a result carries a lower cost to the firm.
Participation provision	Ocasionally, a preferred is sold as a participating issue, meaning that preferred stockholders enjoy additional dividends if payouts to common stockholders exceed a certain amount. This type of preferred not only specifies the annual dividend it will pay, but also sets a maximum common stock dividend level as well; once that maximum has been met, the provision is triggered, and any additional dividends to common stockholders must be shared on a specified basis (perhaps 50/50) with preferred stockholders. From the firm's perspective, a participation provision is unattractive: not only does it place an added burden on the cost of financing, but it also handicaps the firm's dividend-paying powers.
Call feature	As with bonds, call features give the firm the right to call the preferred in for retirement. The call option on a preferred is typically deferred for 5 to 10 years, after which the preferred can be retired for refunding or refinancing at a call price usually somewhat higher than the original offering price. A call provision is attractive to an issuer, since it enables the firm to eliminate costly fixed-payment commitments, though it generally results in a more costly form of financing.
Sinking fund provision	A provision that enables the firm to systematically pay off all or part of a preferred stock issue over time; in effect, it places an implied but unspecified maturity date on an issue that otherwise has no maturity. A typical sinking fund provision might require the firm to retire 75 percent of the issue over a 10-year period by retiring 7.5 percent per year. Because sinking fund preferreds result in the systematic amortization of all or part of the issue, they reduce the stockholders' risk of default and are therefore generally less costly than non-sinking-fund preferreds.
Adjustable (or floating) rates	Although most preferreds carry dividend rates that remain fixed for the life of the issue, some are issued with floating dividend rates. Known as adjustable (or floating) rate preferreds, the dividends on these issues are adjusted quarterly in line with yields on specific Treasury issues, although a minimum and maximum dividend rate is usually established as a safeguard.

firm, preferred stockholders have no voting rights so long as the company remains healthy. If the firm finds it necessary to pass one or more consecutive quarterly preferred dividends, then the preferred stockholders are usually given the right to elect a certain number of corporate directors so that their views may be represented on the board. If matters should continue to deteriorate to the point that the firm undergoes liquidation, the holders of preferred stock are given a prior claim on assets. These preferred claims, which are limited to the par or stated value of the preferred stock, must be filled before those of the common stockholders.

Preferred stocks can carry a number of different features. Among the more important special features are cumulative and participating provisions, the call feature, and the sinking fund provision. These features, along with adjustable (or floating) rate preferreds, are identified and briefly discussed in Table 21.12, p. 921.

Advantages and Disadvantages

There are several advantages and disadvantages of preferred stock financing. Among the more significant advantages of this financing vehicle is the fact that it enables the firm to increase its leverage. Since preferred stock obligates the firm to a specified level of dividends, its presence in the capital structure helps to increase the firm's financial leverage. However, although preferred stock provides added leverage in much the same way as a bond, it differs from a bond in that the issuer can pass a dividend payment without suffering the consequences that occur when an interest payment is missed.

In addition, non-sinking-fund preferreds offer a cash flow advantage over bonds to the extent that preferreds are free from periodic amortization payments and therefore have lower cash flow demands than comparable amounts of debt. To illustrate, consider the figures below:

	Bonds			Preferreds
Year	Principal	After-Tax Interest[a]	Total Cash Outflow	Total Cash Outflow to Dividends
1	$100,000	$60,000	$160,000	$95,000
2	100,000	54,000	154,000	95,000
3	100,000	48,000	148,000	95,000
4	100,000	42,000	142,000	95,000
5	100,000	36,000	136,000	95,000
6	100,000	30,000	130,000	95,000
7	100,000	24,000	124,000	95,000
8	100,000	18,000	118,000	95,000
9	100,000	12,000	112,000	95,000
10	100,000	6,000	106,000	95,000

[a]Using a 40% tax rate, after-tax cost of interest equals interest expense times $(1 - .40)$.

Here we compare the after tax principal and interest requirements on a $1 million, 10 percent 10-year bond (its principal is amortized on a straight-line basis) with the after-tax dividend requirement on $1 million worth of 9.5 percent preferred stock (as we will see, preferreds generally carry before-tax yields that are slightly less than those of comparably rated bonds.) Although an obvious (and at times substantial) preferred stock cash flow advantage exists as long as the bond is outstanding, it should be clear that this advantage is short-lived and eventually disappears, as, unlike a bond, the cash flow requirement on a preferred continues indefinitely.

The two major disadvantages to using preferred stock as a financing vehicle include the seniority of the preferred stockholder's claims and its after-tax cost. Adding preferred stock to the firm's capital structure creates additional claims prior to those of the common stockholders, and if after-tax earnings are unstable, the firm's ability to pay at least token dividends to its common stockholders may be seriously impaired. The net result could be an increase in the firm's cost of equity and a decline in the value of the firm. In addition, the after-tax cost of preferred stock financing is higher than the cost of debt financing because interest on debt is tax deductible, whereas preferred dividends must be paid from after-tax earnings. Compared to bonds, the use of preferred stock burdens the issuer with a fixed financing cost, but without the benefit of the tax deductibility of interest payments.

Financing with Preferreds

Preferred stock first came into widespread use in this country with the financing of America's railroads, when it was used as a way to "sweeten" deals. The popularity of preferreds began to decline, however, with the introduction of corporate income taxes; and as corporate tax rates rose to higher and higher levels, the financing appeal of preferreds almost disappeared. Because preferred dividends are not considered a tax-deductible expense, the rate of return required on preferred financing is much higher than the stated dividend rate. For example, a firm with a 40 percent tax rate must earn a 14.2 percent pretax return to generate the funds necessary to service an 8.5 percent preferred dividend rate— $.085/(1 - .40) = .142$. Not surprisingly, as market yields on preferreds began to move to higher levels, the number of sufficiently attractive corporate investment opportunities diminished to the point where few deals could provide the type of payoff required. Primarily because of its high cost, the use of preferred stock as a financing vehicle is largely confined to public utility firms, to companies involved in mergers and acquisitions, and to unseasoned corporate issuers. However, under the proper circumstances, preferreds may also be useful to firms with volatile sales and earnings, as well as to those companies with high debt ratios.

Generally speaking, preferred stocks are considered to be riskier than bonds because their claims are subordinated to those of bondholders in the event of liquidation, and because bondholders are more likely to continue to receive income during hard times. This should rationally result in a higher after-tax return on preferred stocks, and it does. However, from a pretax yield perspective, the general tendency in the marketplace is for preferreds to yield returns slightly less than those of comparably rated bonds. Such behavior is evident in Figure 21.3, which traces the yields on average high-grade preferred stocks against the yields on high-grade corporate bonds. The reason for such yield spread behavior is that 85 percent of the dividends received by one corporation from another are exempt from corporate income tax. Thus, if a company were to issue bonds and preferred stocks on the same date, we would expect the preferreds to carry a dividend yield less than the interest rate on the bonds. If the bonds carry a coupon of, say, 9.5 percent, the preferreds might well be priced to yield around 9 percent. Yet on an after-tax basis, the preferred yield to a corporate investor will be greater than the after-tax return on the bonds. For a company with a .40 percent tax rate, the after-tax return on the bonds would be $9.5(1 - .40) = 9.5(.60) = 5.70\%$. The after-tax yield on the preferreds to the same company would be $9.0(.85) + 9.0(.15)(1 - .40) = 8.46\%$.

Most firms that have a choice will select some form of debt when considering financing with a vehicle other than common stock. Still, the use of preferreds as a financing vehicle may sometimes be justified by

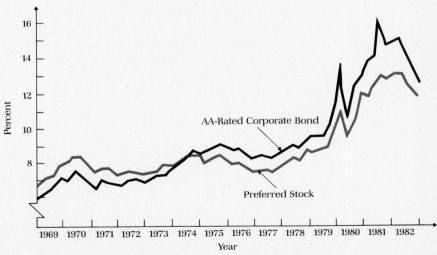

Figure 21.3 Average High-Grade Preferred Stock Yields Versus Average Market Yields on AA-Rated Corporate Bonds.

Source: S & P's *Trade & Securities Statistics*, 1981. Standard & Poor's Corporation.

conditions that fall between those that favor the use of common stock and those that favor the use of debt. For example, if sales and profits are subject to wide fluctuation, the use of debt (with its fixed charges) may be unduly risky, and preferred stock may offer an attractive compromise. The use of preferreds may also be strongly favored if the firm already has a high debt ratio. Gordon Donaldson, in a classic article,[23] argues strongly that when a company has utilized its debt capacity, it may be able to obtain further amounts of reasonably priced, fixed-cost financing by using preferred stock. To the extent that a firm has a preferred stock capacity *in addition* to its debt capacity, Donaldson maintains that under these circumstances (and given that the company's debt capacity has been exhausted), using preferred stock may have a more favorable effect on returns to common stockholders than the use of some other form of equity, such as retained earnings.

SUMMARY

Term loans, bonds, and preferred stock are three principal sources of external financing. Term loans are a form of intermediate-term debt obtained directly through negotiations with a lender; they generally have maturities that fall within the 3- to 7-year range. They are especially popular as a form of equipment financing, but are also widely used to meet other intermediate-term needs. Term loans are typically amortized through monthly, quarterly, semiannual, or annual instalment payments. Some loans provide for balloon payments at maturity; others require that equal amortization payments be made to retire the full amount of the loan.

Bonds are long-term financial assets that carry a formal promise to pay interest and principal at specified future dates; they are issued by large, publicly traded corporations and generally in very large amounts. Each bond is issued under the provisions of a bond indenture which, very much like a loan agreement, sets the conditions of the debt as well as the allowable actions and restrictions placed on the borrowing firm. Bonds can be issued as secured or unsecured debt, and some are issued with floating coupons; they also can carry a variety of sinking fund and call features. Most corporate bonds are assigned ratings by Moody's and Standard & Poor's; such ratings are meant to be indicative of the overall quality of an issue. Bonds provide an effective way of reducing a firm's cost of capital and increasing returns to stockholders. To obtain the maximum benefits, however, the firm must minimize the cost of this form of financing. This involves packaging the obligation effectively at the time of issue, and seeing to it that outstanding issues are serviced in a

---

[23]Gordon Donaldson, "In Defense of Preferred Stock," *Harvard Business Review* 40 (July–August 1962), pp. 123–136.

prompt and timely fashion. Timing is also an important matter, and the use of interest rate hedges during unstable markets can be a viable financial tactic. Once the issues are outstanding, consideration should also be given to the possibility of restructuring the debt through refunding.

Preferred stocks are another form of fixed-income security and can be used to alter a firm's financial leverage. Preferred stockholders are given preference over common stockholders with respect to the distribution of both income and assets. Though preferred stock is a form of equity, it is also similar to debt in many respects. Preferred stock financing enables the firm to achieve financial leverage but avoid the risk of default associated with debt financing; in addition, its use as a financing vehicle will not affect ownership control.

QUESTIONS

21.1. After careful deliberation, C&I Construction Supplies has decided to proceed with a major long-term financing package; the chief financial officer of C&I feels that the firm will need to raise about $5 million to finance current expansion plans. The company can obtain the needed capital through a term loan or by publicly issuing a bond.
  a. Briefly explain the key characteristics of each of these financing vehicles; what are the advantages and disadvantages of each?
  b. Which procedure would you recommend? Fully explain your answer.

21.2. How are most term loans paid off? What are balloon payments, and how do they differ from normal loan payments?

21.3. Contrast a bond indenture with a term loan agreement. What role does a trustee play in a bond indenture?

21.4. Contrast the following types of bonds:
  a. First mortgage bond and equipment trust certificate.
  b. Secured bond and subordinated debenture.
  c. Income bond and variable-rate note.

21.5. What are bond ratings, and what are they supposed to show? Explain the rating process. Cite two reasons why a bond's rating is important to the issuing firm.

21.6. Briefly note how each of the following will affect the cost of bond financing to the firm:
  a. The company's rating drops from A to Baa.
  b. The bond is issued on a noncallable rather than freely callable basis.
  c. The debt is issued without sinking fund provisions.
  d. The rate of inflation is expected to shoot up and remain high for the foreseeable future.

21.7. The treasurer of a major Southeastern manufacturing firm has just started putting together a large bond issue. Her analysis suggests that the company will have to borrow about $25 million. The details are currently being worked out, and she anticipates that the issue will be brought to the market in about 3 months. This lag has her concerned since interest rates have been moving up at a rapid clip lately.

    a. Explain how an interest rate futures hedge could be helpful in this situation. How would the firm benefit?

    b. What are the major costs and risks the firm would face if it employs such a hedge?

21.8. Briefly explain how sinking funds can affect both the cost of financing and the firm's cash flow. What are the managerial implications?

21.9. What is the difference between a bond premium and a call premium? Do they have the same effect on corporate income? How are they treated for tax purposes?

21.10. Why would a company refund an outstanding bond issue? Under what conditions would refunding be a desirable course of action? How could interest rate expectations affect the refunding decision?

21.11. What are the advantages of raising funds through preferred stock? Are there any disadvantages to preferred stock as a source of financing?

21.12. What is cumulative, participating preferred stock? Do preferreds ever carry call or sinking fund provisions? If so, what effect do these provisions have on the cost of funds to the issuer?

21.13. Why is preferred stock so expensive? In view of its high after-tax cost, why is preferred stock used at all?

PROBLEMS

21.1. *TERM LOAN PAYMENTS.* Wally Christopher is the treasurer of a major Hollywood record company, and is presently working up a request for a term loan. He feels the company will need $4 million and wants to take out a 3-year loan. Although the bank views the record company as an excellent credit customer, loan rates are nonetheless high—the bank has informed Christopher that the current rate on 3-year loans is 16 percent.

    a. How large will the instalment payments have to be if the company wants to amortize the loan through equal annual payments?

    b. How large will the payments be if they are made on a quarterly basis?

    c. Contrast the total amount of interest paid (over the three-year period) with annual payments against the amount that would be paid with quarterly installments. How do you explain the difference?

> d. How large will the annual payments be if a $2,000,000 balloon payment is used?

21.2 **THE COST OF FIXED COUPONS VERSUS FLOATERS.** Terry T. J. Patrick is president of Precision Machine Co., manufacturers and distributors of soft drink dispensers. Patrick feels that to maintain the company's rate of growth, it will need to issue a $5 million, 10-year note. The firm's investment bankers report that the note can be issued with a fixed coupon of 12 percent, or with a variable-rate pegged at 1.5 percent above prevailing U.S. Treasury note rates. In both cases, interest will be paid annually, and the coupon on the floating rate note will also be adjusted annually. Straight-line sinking funds will be required for both issues and will commence at the end of the first year.

   a. Complete the comparative interest and cash flow table below:

Year	Prevailing U.S. Treasury Note Rate	Variable Rate Note				Fixed Coupon Bond		
		Bond Coupon	Interest Cost	Sinking Fund	Total Cash Flow	Interest Cost	Sinking Fund	Total Cash Flow
1	11.5%	%	$	$	$	$	$	$
2	13.0							
3	10.0							
4	9.0							
5	9.0							
6	7.5							
7	7.5							
8	7.5							
9	8.5							
10	8.5							

   b. Which alternative would you recommend? Why?
   c. Discuss the risks in your recommendation.

21.3. **IMPACT OF INTEREST SAVINGS.** The chief financial officer of a well-known company is putting together a new bond issue. She has been advised that the following actions will reduce the cost of funds to the firm: (1) The use of a first mortgage bond rather than a debenture will reduce the coupon by 10 basis points; (2) the use of a 10-year call deferment in place of a freely callable provision will lead to a savings of 5 basis points. Assuming the CFO is thinking of issuing a $30 million, 25-year sinking fund bond ($1 million sinking fund payments would begin at the end of the *sixth* year), how much interest could be saved over the life of the issue by making it a mortgage bond with a 10-year call deferment period? Comment on your answer.

21.4.   *COMPARATIVE INTEREST COSTS.* Assume a company can issue long-term bonds at a base rate of 8 percent. Also assume the final coupon rate can be influenced by altering the issue's characteristics and its indenture provisions as follows: (1) Issuing a mortgage bond rather than a debenture will result in an improvement in the assigned agency rating and a reduction in interest costs of 20 basis points; (2) Because of the shape of the yield curve, the use of a 15-year note rather than a 25-year bond can result in an interest savings of 30 basis points; (3) Putting a 5-year deferred call provision on the bond instead of a freely callable provision should reduce interest by 10 basis points; (4) Using a sinking fund will reduce the rate by 15 basis points. Given this information, determine which bond, from each pair below, offers the lowest effective interest cost to the issuer:

a.   A 25-year freely callable, non-sinking-fund debenture *or* a 25-year deferred call first mortgage bond with standard sinking fund provisions.

b.   A 15-year freely callable, non-sinking-fund debenture *or* a 25-year deferred call mortgage bond with no sinking fund requirements.

c.   A 25-year freely callable sinking fund mortgage bond *or* a 15-year freely callable debenture with no sinking fund requirements.

21.5.   *DEEP DISCOUNT BONDS.* Lois Charlene Weaver is the chief financial officer of Maffeo Metals. Recently, she has been working closely with the company's investment banking firm, trying to put the finishing touches on a pending $250 million, 20-year deep discount bond issue. Even though the current market rate for comparably rated bonds is 16 percent, Weaver wants the new Maffeo (non-sinking-fund) issue to carry a 5 percent coupon. The investment banking firm feels such an issue can be sold at a cost to the firm of 15.5 percent. (For this problem, ignore all flotation and underwriter costs.)

a.   At what price will the company be able to sell this 5 percent, 20-year bond if it has to provide a yield to investors of 15.5 percent? (Refer to the bond valuation material in Chapter 7 if you have trouble with this problem.)

b.   Given that the bond discount is to be amortized on a straight-line basis, determine the amount of the annual bond discount amortization charge. If Maffeo has a 40 percent marginal tax rate, what effect will this amortization charge have on the firm's after-tax cash flow?

c. Excluding the eventual repayment of the principal, what is the total annual *after-tax* cash outflow required to service this bond (include both interest charges and amortization of bond discount)? How does this compare to the annual after-tax cash outflow required to service the interest payments on a 16 percent, non-sinking fund bond sold at par?

d. Rework (a), (b), and (c) assuming the company can issue the bond with a coupon of zero. Keep everything else the same, including the issue's yield of 15.5 percent.

21.6. *INTEREST RATE HEDGING.* A company expects to issue $10 million in long-term debt in about 6 months; the funds will be used to finance a major expansion project. The firm is concerned, however, that interest rates may move up significantly between now and the date of issue. Such a course of action could prove costly to the firm in terms of added interest expense. To counter this possibility, the company decides to set up an interest rate hedge. It does this by short-selling 100 GNMA futures contracts at a price of 99 16/32. Six months later, interest rates have indeed risen by two percentage points; as a result, rather than issuing the 20-year bonds with an 8 percent coupon, the company is going to have to issue the debt at 10 percent. Fortunately, the company has made a profit on its interest rate hedge to cover at least part of the added interest cost. Specifically, the firm can cover its short hedge by buying back the GNMA contracts at 84 8/32.

a. What is the total amount of profit the company stands to make by short-selling 100 GNMA futures contracts?

b. Given that the profit from the interest rate hedge is used to reduce the size of the new issue, what is the effective cost of financing to the company? (Use annual discounting.)

c. Show how the company was able to raise the required $10 million.

21.7. *SINKING FUND OR NON-SINKING FUND.* The chief financial officer of Floyd's Brewery is putting together a new bond issue. The company is about to issue a 20-year, $25 million bond, and the CFO has been advised by the company's investment bankers that a sinking fund provision should result in a 20-basis-point reduction in interest costs. It is felt that a non-sinking-fund bond will require a 10.7 percent coupon versus a 10.5 percent coupon on a sinking fund issue (the sinking funds would begin in the eleventh year and amount to $2.5 million per year to amortize the issue fully by maturity). Flotation and other issuance costs are estimated at 2 percent of the amount of debt being issued, and future interest rates are expected to drift upward an average of 1.5 percentage points. Giving full consideration to the interest savings and opportunity cost of a sinking fund feature, should the company issue a sinking fund or non-sinking-fund bond?

21.8.   *BOND REFUNDING.*   Tom Lasnicka is the treasurer and chief financial officer of a large electrical equipment manufacturing firm. He is presently evaluating the possibility of refunding one of the company's bonds. The company has a $50 million bond outstanding, and Lasnicka is considering replacing it with a new $50 million issue; the outstanding bond is now freely callable, and since rates have dropped sharply in recent months, Lasnicka feels a refunding operation could result in substantial interest savings to the company. The old bonds have 20 years remaining to maturity and the refunding bond would be issued with the same maturity; the company has a 40 percent marginal tax rate, did not use sinking funds on the old bonds, and does not anticipate using a sinking fund provision on the new bonds. Here is some additional information about the old and refunding bonds. *Old bonds.* Issued 5 years ago, they carry a 10 percent coupon. They were issued at 99¼, and the firm also incurrred $400,000 in issuance costs; the securities are presently callable at a call premium of one year's interest. *Refunding bonds.* The new bonds would carry an 8 percent coupon and could be issued at par; flotation costs would amount to $600,000 and there would be 3 months of overlapping interest. Should the bonds be refunded? What if the chances are good that rates could continue to drop by another 50 basis points over the near term?

21.9.   *SERVICING INTEREST AND DIVIDENDS.*   Fred Penn and Associates had earnings before interest and taxes of $850,000 last year. The company has a marginal tax rate of 35 percent and had the following capital structure:

Long-term debt (8.5% interest)	$1,500,000
Preferred stock (25,000 shares of $6 preferreds outstanding)	1,500,000
Total common stock equity (200,000 shares authorized and outstanding; latest annual dividends = $1 per share)	2,500,000
Total	$5,500,000

a. What was the firm's net profit after taxes?

b. How much profit was left after preferred dividends were paid? How about after common stock dividends were paid?

c. What pretax rate of return must Fred Penn and Associates earn on its debt capital to generate enough funds to service the interest payments on its long-term debt? What pretax rate of return must the firm earn on its preferred stock capital to have enough funds (after taxes) to pay preferred stock dividends? How do you account for the difference?

21.10. *COST OF PREFERRED FINANCING.* The Geo. Joch Shipping Company needs to raise $5 million in new capital. It has two options: It can raise the money (1) by issuing 8 percent long-term debt, or (2) by issuing 100,000 shares of 7.5 percent preferred stock. Both issues would carry sinking fund provisions and be amortized over time at much the same rate.

a. What are the annual interest charges on the debt? What will annual dividend payments be on the preferred? Which is cheaper?

b. Assume the company has a 40 percent marginal tax rate; determine the after-tax cost of the debt to the firm and the after-tax cost of the preferred.

c. Joch Shipping hopes to generate a 15 percent pretax rate of return from the $5 million in new capital; how much money would be left after taxes and after interest (or dividend) payments and after taxes under each alternative? Which procedure would you recommend, and why?

SELECTED REFERENCES

Agman, T., A. R. Ofer, and A. Tamir. "Variable Rate Debt Instruments and Corporate Debt Policy." *Journal of Finance* (March 1981), pp. 113–125.

Alexander, Gordon J. "Applying the Market Model to Long-Term Corporate Bonds." *Journal of Financial and Quantitative Analysis* 15 (December 1980), pp. 1063–1080.

Bacon, Peter, and Richard Williams. "Interest Rate Futures: New Tool for the Financial Manager." *Financial Management* 5 (spring 1976), pp. 32–38.

Bierman, Harold. "The Bond Refunding Decision as a Markov Process." *Management Science* 12 (August 1966), pp. 545–551.

Bierwag, G. O. "Immunization, Duration, and the Term Structure." *Journal of Financial and Quantitative Analysis* 12 (December 1977), pp. 701–742.

Bildersee, John S. "Some Aspects of the Performance of Non-Convertible Preferred Stocks." *Journal of Finance* 28 (December 1973), pp. 1187–1201.

Black, Fischer, and John C. Cox. "Valuing Corporate Securities: Some Effects of Bond Indenture Provisions." *Journal of Finance* 31 (May 1976), pp. 351–367.

Bodie, Z., and R. A. Taggart, Jr. "Future Investment Opportunities and the Value of the Call Provision on a Bond." *Journal of Finance* 33 (September 1978), pp. 1187–1200.

Bowlin, O. D. and J. Martin. "Extrapolations of Yields over the Short Run: Forecast or Folly?" *Journal of Monetary Economics* 1 (1975), pp. 275–288.

Bullington, Robert A. "How Corporate Debt Issues Are Rated." *Financial Executive* (September 1974), pp. 28–37.

Caks, John. "The Coupon Effect on Yield to Maturity." *Journal of Finance* 32 (March 1977), pp. 103–115.

Donaldson, Gordon. "In Defense of Preferred Stock." *Harvard Business Review* 40 (July–August 1962), pp. 123–136.

Draper, Dennis W. "Financial Futures for Hedging Long-Term Debt." *Harvard Business Review* 61 (March-April 1983), pp. 172–176.

Dyl, E. A., and M. D. Joehnk. "Sinking Funds and the Cost of Corporate Debt." *Journal of Finance* 34 (September 1979), pp. 887–894.

———, and ———. "Refunding Tax Exempt Bonds." *Financial Management* 5 (summer 1976), pp. 59–66.

———, and W. Sawaya. "The Bond Issue Size Decision Revisited." *Financial Management* 8 (winter 1979), pp. 60–67.

Elsaid, Hussein H. "The Function of Preferred Stock in the Corporate Financial Plan." *Financial Analysts Journal* 25 (July–August 1969), pp. 112–117.

Ferri, Michael G. "The Interest Elasticity of Corporate Bond Supply: An Expectational Model." *Journal of Economics and Business* 31 (winter 1979), pp. 126–133.

Fisher, Donald E., and Glenn A. Wilt, Jr. "Non-Convertible Preferred Stock as a Financing Instrument, 1950–1965." *Journal of Finance* 23 (September 1968), pp. 611–624.

Franks, J. R. "Debt Financing, Corporate Financial Intermediaries and Firm Valuation." *Journal of Finance* (June 1982), pp. 751–761.

Gay, Gerald D., and Robert W. Kolb. "The Management of Interest Rate Risk." *Journal of Portfolio Management* 9 (winter 1983), pp. 65–70.

Guzzardi, Walter, Jr. "The Bomb IBM Dropped on Wall Street." *Fortune* (November 19, 1979), pp. 52–57.

Harris, R. S. "Refunding of Discounted Debt: An Adjusted Present Value Analysis." *Financial Management* 9 (winter 1980), pp. 7–12.

Hickman, W. Braddock. *Corporate Bond Quality and Investor Experience* (Princeton, N.J.: Princeton University Press, 1958).

Homer, Sidney. "The Historical Evolution of Today's Bond Market." *Journal of Portfolio Management* 1 (spring 1975), pp. 6–11.

Jahankhani, Ali, and George E. Pinches. "Duration and the Nonstationarity of Systematic Risk for Bonds." *Journal of Financial Research* 5 (summer 1982), pp. 151–160.

Jen, Frank C., and James E. Wert. "The Deferred Call Provision and Corporate Bond Yields." *Journal of Financial and Quantitative Analysis* 3 (June 1968), pp. 157–169.

Johnson, Rodney, and Richard Klein. "Corporate Motives in Repurchase of Discounted Bonds." *Financial Management* 3 (autumn 1974), pp. 44–49.

Kalotay, Andrew. "On the Management of Sinking Funds." *Financial Management* 10 (summer 1981), pp. 34–40.

Laber, G. "Implications of Discount Rates and Financing Assumptions for Bond Refunding Decisions." *Financial Management* 8 (spring 1979), pp. 7–12.

Lewellen, Wilbur G., and Douglas R. Emery. "On the Matter of Parity Among Financial Obligations." *Journal of Finance* 35 (March 1980), pp. 97–111.

Mao, James C. T. "Project Financing: Funding the Future." *Financial Executive* 50 (August 1982), pp. 23–28.

Marshall, William, and Jess B. Yawitz. "Optimal Terms of the Call Provision on a Corporate Bond." *Journal of Financial Research* 3 (summer 1980), pp. 203–211.

McEnally, Richard W., and Michael L. Rice. "Hedging Possibilities in the Flotation of Debt Securities." *Financial Management* 8 (winter 1979), pp. 12–18.

McInish, T. H., and D. J. Puglisi. "Ex-Dividend Behavior of Preferred Stocks." *Review of Business and Economic Research* 16 (fall 1980), pp. 81–90.

Morris, James R. "A Model for Corporate Debt Maturity Decisions." *Journal of Financial and Quantitative Analysis* 11 (September 1976), pp. 339–358.

———. "On Corporate Debt Maturity Strategies." *Journal of Finance* 31 (March 1976), pp. 29–37.

Ofer, A. R., and R. A. Taggart. "Bond Refunding: A Clarifying Analysis." *Journal of Finance* 32 (March 1977), pp. 21–30.

Pinches, George E. "Financing with Convertible Preferred Stock, 1960–1967." *Journal of Finance* 25 (March 1970), pp. 53–63.

———, and Kent Mingo. "A Multivariate Analysis of Industrial Bond Ratings." *Journal of Finance* 28 (March 1973), pp. 1–18.

———, and ———. "The Role of Subordination and Industrial Bond Ratings." *Journal of Finance* 30 (March 1975), pp. 201–206.

———, and J. Clay Singleton. "The Adjustment of Stock Prices to Bond Rating Changes." *Journal of Finance* 33 (March 1978), pp. 29–44.

Piper, Thomas R., and W. A. Weinhold." How Much Debt is Right for Your Company?" *Harvard Business Review* 60 (July-August 1982), pp. 106–113.

Pogue, Thomas F., and Robert M. Soldofsky. "What's in a Bond Rating?" *Journal of Financial and Quantitative Analysis* 4 (June 1969), pp. 201–208.

Prell, Michael J. "How Well Do the Experts Forecast Interest Rates." Federal Reserve Bank of Kansas City. *Monthly Review* (October 1973), pp. 3–13.

Pye. Gordon. "The Value of the Call Option on a Bond." *Journal of Political Economy* 74 (April 1966), pp. 200–205.

Racette, George A., and Wilbur G. Lewellen. "Corporate Debt Coupon Rate Strategies." *National Tax Journal* 29 (June 1976), pp. 165–178.

Rendleman, Richard J., Jr. "The Effects of Default Risk on the Firm's Investment and Financing Decisions." *Financial Management* 7 (spring 1978), pp. 45–53.

Reilly, Frank K., and Michael D. Joehnk. "The Association Between Market-Determined Risk Measures for Bonds and Bond Ratings." *Journal of Finance* 31 (December 1976), pp. 1387–1403.

Riener, K. D. "Financial Structure Effects of Bond Refunding." *Financial Management* 9 (summer 1980), pp. 18–23.

Standard & Poor's Rating Guide (New York: McGraw-Hill, 1979).

Steinberg, John S., and Larry R. Arnold. "An Interactive Approach for Optimizing Debt Repayment Schedules." *Journal of Financial Research* (summer 1981), pp. 137–146.

Stevenson, Richard A. "Retirement of Non-Callable Preferred Stock." *Journal of Finance* 25 (December 1970), pp. 1143–1152.

Van Horne, J. C. "Called Bonds: How Does the Investor Fare?" *Journal of Portfolio Management* 6 (summer 1980), pp. 58–61.

Weingartner, H. Martin. "Optimal Timing of Bond Refunding." *Management Science* 13 (March 1967), pp. 511–524.

Weinstein, Mark I. "The Seasoning Process of New Corporate Bond Issues." *Journal of Finance* 13 (December 1978), pp. 1343–1354.

Yawitz, Jess B., and James A. Anderson. "The Effect of Bond Refunding on Shareholder Wealth." *Journal of Finance* 32 (December 1977), pp. 1738–1746.

Ziese, Charles H., and Roger K. Taylor. "Advance Refunding: A Practitioner's Perspective." *Financial Management* 6 (summer 1977), pp. 73–76.

Appendix 21A

Hedging Financial Strategies with Interest Rate Futures

A *financial futures contract* is simply a commodities contract written on a certain type of financial instrument. Companies use financial futures as a hedging vehicle, and like any hedge strategy, the financial future is intended to reduce risk—in this case, to reduce the risk of holding or selling a certain type of financial asset or instrument. Financial futures were developed in response to the economic turmoil the United States experienced beginning in the early part of the 1970s. The dollar became unstable on the world market and caused serious problems for multinational firms; closer to home, interest rates behaved in a volatile manner, which caused severe difficulties for corporate treasurers, financial institutions, and money managers in general. All these parties needed a way to protect themselves from the ravages of wide fluctuations in the value of the dollar and in interest rates, and so a market for financial futures was born. Trading in foreign currencies began in May 1972; a few years later, trading was expanded to include futures contracts on debt securities, and in 1982, stock index futures were introduced.

There are three basic types of financial futures: currency futures, stock index futures, and interest rate futures. Trading in currency futures is conducted in eight foreign currencies (such as the British pound, German mark, Swiss franc, and Japanese yen); these futures are used primarily by multinational firms seeking to protect themselves in certain types of international transactions. Stock index futures are available on several popular stock market indexes—including the S&P 500, the NYSE Composite Index, and the Value Line Stock Index; they enable portfolio managers to protect their stock holdings against adverse swings in market prices. Interest rate futures are written on several short- and long-term debt securities (like Treasury bills, CDs, GNMA pass-through certificates, and Treasury bonds), and are used by nonfinancial corporations to reduce the risk in certain types of investment and financing activities.[1] As we will see, interest rate futures can be used to hedge a firm's short-term investment portfolio, as well as its short- and long-term borrowing activities.

The Nature of Interest Rate Futures Trading

Interest rate futures contracts are actively traded on several of the major commodities exchanges. Interest rate futures contracts control large amounts of the underlying financial instrument and are issued with a variety of delivery months (the delivery month is equivalent to an expiration date and defines the life of the contract). Contracts can be purchased (or sold) with lives as short as 3 months or less, or as long as 2 to 3 years—the choice of delivery month is a function of how long the financial manager wants to set up the hedge. The amount of debt securities underlying each contract varies with the type of interest rate future and ranges from a minimum of $100,000 to a maximum of $3 million. This amount is important, since it indicates the number of contracts that would have to be bought (or sold) in a given situation. For example, if a manager wants to hedge a $10 million loan by using GNMA contracts, he or she would have to take a position in 100 contracts; that is, since each contract is written on $100,000 in GNMA bonds, it would take 100 contracts to cover the $10 million loan.[2]

The value of an interest rate contract responds to changes in interest rates exactly like that of the underlying debt security: when rates go up, the value of an interest rate futures contract goes down, and vice versa. The contract quote system, however, reflects the market value of the contract, not the behavior of interest rates. Thus, when rates go down, the quoted price (and therefore the market value) of an interest rate futures contract goes up. Interest rate contracts are quoted in two ways. For the short-term issues (T-bills and CDs), an index price system is used in which the yield on the contract is subtracted from an index of 100. Thus, when the yield on the underlying security is, say, 5.25 percent, the futures contract would be quoted at 94.75. The following equation would then be used to find the actual market value of a $1,000,000 contract:

---

[1] The material in this appendix will be devoted solely to the use of interest rate futures, and we will limit our discussion to the needs of a typical *nonfinancial* institution or corporation.

[2] We assume throughout that the firm creates a futures hedge with an equal (1-to-1) ratio between the amount of futures contracts bought or sold and the amount of financial transactions the firm is trying to protect. Of course, in practice this ratio can vary, in which case the amount of protection obtained would increase or decrease, depending on the ratio used.

$$\text{Market value} = \$1{,}000{,}000 - \left(\frac{Y \times M \times \$10{,}000}{360}\right) \qquad (21A.1)$$

where Y = yield on the underlying security
          M = maturity (in days) of the underlying security

For example, the value of a 90-day T-bill futures contract quoted at 94.75 to yield 5.25 percent is:

$$\text{Market value} = \$1{,}000{,}000 - \left(\frac{5.25 \times 90 \times \$10{,}000}{360}\right) = \$986{,}875$$

A handy shortcut for tracking the behavior of short-term futures contracts is to remember that, regardless of the length of the contract, the market value will change by $25 for every one basis-point change in the quoted index. For example, if the index goes up by 50 basis points (from 94.75 to 95.25), the value of the contract will rise by: 50 × $25 = $1,250.

The long-term contracts (GNMA issues and Treasury bonds) are quoted in 32s and priced at a percentage of the par value of the underlying debt instrument. Therefore, a quote of, say, 89-30 translates into 89-30/32, which when 32 is divided into 30, equates to 89.9375 percent of par. Applying this figure to the $100,000 par value of the underlying security yields a contract market value of .899375 × $100,000 = $89,937.50. Again, a shortcut is available to track the market behavior of these contracts. Every 1/32 change in the quote (on a $100,000 contract) is worth $31.25, so that if the quote on a GNMA contract goes down 8/32, from 89-30 to 89-22, its value will fall: 8 × $31.25 = $250. Table 21A.1 provides a summary of selected issue characteristics, along with an illustration of both kinds of quotation systems.

All trading is subject to normal transaction costs, which include round-trip commissions of approximately $70 to $250. for each contract traded, although lower negotiated commissions are generally available for large-volume transactions. What is more, all trading is done on margin. That is, only a small fraction of the total value of the contract has to be deposited at the time of the initial purchase (or sale). The size of the required margin deposit is specified as a dollar amount per contract; it varies according to the type of contract and, in some cases, the exchange on which the contract is traded. In all cases, however, margin requirements are kept very low; for example, the initial margin on a 90-day T-bill contract is only $3,000, even though the par value of the underlying Treasury bills is $1,000,000. There are two types of margin requirements. The first is the initial margin deposit, which specifies the amount of capital that must be deposited at the time of the buy (or sell) transaction. The second is the maintenance margin deposit; it is slightly less than the initial deposit (for example, $2,000 on a 90-day T-bill contract), and establishes the minimum amount of margin that must be kept at all times. Buying a contract is referred to as taking a long position; selling

TABLE 21A.1

Features of the Principal Types of Interest Rate Futures Contracts

ISSUE CHARACTERISTICS				
Contract	Par Value of Underlying Security	Dollar Value of Change in Price	Initial Margin Requirement[a]	Typical Round-Trip Commission[a]
Short-term issues:				
90-day T-bill	$1,000,000	1 basis point = $25	$3,000	$70
90-day bank CD	1,000,000	1 basis point = $25	3,000	70
Long-term issues:				
GNMA bonds	100,000	1/32=$31.25	3,000	70
T-bonds	100,000	1/32=$31.25	3,000	70
T-notes	100,000	1/32=$31.25	3,000	70

QUOTE SYSTEM

Interest rate futures quoted on index price system:
TREASURY BILLS (IMM)—$1 mil.; pts. of 100%

	Open	High	Low	Settle	Chg.	Discount Settle	Discount Chg.	Open Interest	
June	90.77	90.80	90.70	90.79	+.06	9.21	−.06	9,413	
Sept	90.67	90.72	90.61	90.71	+.04	9.29	−.04	9,629	
Dec	90.70	90.72	90.63	90.70	+.03	9.30	−.03	9,604	
Mar80	90.75	90.76	90.67	90.75	+.02	9.25	−.02	8,845	
June	90.82	90.82	90.75	90.81	+.02	9.19	−.02	7,921	
Sept	90.77	90.83	90.77	(90.82)	....	(9.18)	.....	4,762	100−discount of 9.18
Dec	90.84	90.84	90.76	90.82	....	9.18	.....	3,243	= quote of 90.82
Mar	90.82	90.84	90.80	90.83	−.01	9.17	+.01	798	

　　Est vol 7,075; vol Wed 6,661; open int 54,215, +672

Interest rate futures quoted in 32s:
GNMA 8% (CBT)—$100,000 prncpl; pts., 32nds of 100%

	Open	High	Low	Settle	Chg.	Yield Settle	Yield Chg.	Open Interest	
June	87–22	87–26	87–21	87–24	+1	9.773	−.005	8,566	
Sept	87–26	87–30	87–25	87–28	+1	9.753	−.005	6,444	
Dec	87–30	87–31	87–28	87–31	+2	9.738	−.010	8,643	
Mr80	87–29	88–00	87–29	87–31	+2	9.738	−.010	8,624	
June	87–26	87–28	87–26	87–27	+2	9.758	−.010	8,853	
Sept	87–23	87–24	87–22	87–24	+1	9.773	−.005	8,368	
Dec	87–19	87–22	87–19	(87–22)	....	9.784	.....	6,107	87–22=87 22/32
Mr81	87–17	87–19	87–17	87–19	+1	9.799	−.005	3,780	= 87.6875% of par
June	87–13	87–14	87–13	87–14	−1	9.824	+.005	1,856	
Sept	87–12	87–12	97–12	87–12	−1	9.834	+.005	473	
Dec	87–10	87–10	87–10	87–10	....	9.845	.....	271	

　　Est vol 1,500; vol Wed 2,652; open int 61,985, + 149

[a]Margin requirements and commissions as quoted by major brokerage firm, July 1982.

one is called a short position.[3] If prices should go up, the investor who is short may have to post additional margin, while the investor who has a long position can request that the gain be credited to a cash or money fund account, or maintained with the broker as surplus margin. In the futures markets, accounts are closed out at the end of each trading day, a process called "mark-to-the-market." Traders are not allowed to accumulate losses if the market has moved against them (if their margin falls below the maintenance level); rather, they must be brought back up to required levels that very day.

Developing Trading Strategies

Depending upon the type of position the hedging company wants to protect, it can execute a buy (long) hedge, or a sell (short) hedge. In a buy hedge, a firm would go long (buy futures contracts) in anticipation of a decline in interest rates. The hedging firm is trying to protect itself against an expected drop in rates by capturing the benefits (profits) that accompany such a fall. For example, if a firm knows that it will be making a major addition to its marketable securities portfolio in, say, the next 60 to 90 days, and if it anticipates a sharp drop in security yields in the interim, it could use a buy hedge to lock in the high yields now available on money market securities. In a sell hedge, a firm would go short (sell futures contracts) in anticipation of a rise in interest rates. As demonstrated in the chapter, sell hedges are used to capture the profits from a rise in interest rates, enabling the firm to lock in the prevailing lower cost of financing (a short seller makes money when rates go up and the value or price of a debt security drops). Sell hedges are used almost exclusively as part of the hedging firm's financing activities. Several interest rate futures hedging strategies have been developed with regard to both short-term and long-term financial transactions; each of these strategies involves the application of buy and sell hedge positions to a given set of financial circumstances.

Short-Term Hedging Strategies

A company can use futures hedging to reduce the risk of (1) managing its short-term investments portfolio, and (2) carrying out its short-term financing activities. The former situation would involve a buy hedge and the latter a sell. Hedging short-term financial transactions is usually done with 90-day T-bills or CD futures. To illustrate a typical short-term hedge, consider the case in which the firm anticipates making a large investment in a marketable security, but fears money market rates are about to drop sharply. Assume the company knows that in 3 months'

---

[3]Both long and short positions are closed out by simply executing offsetting transactions; the short position, for example, would be covered (terminated) by buying an equal number of the contracts. As a matter of interest, less than 1 percent of all futures trades are settled by actual delivery of the underlying commodity.

time it will have $12 million to invest in short-term Treasury bills; assume further that although current T-bill rates are at 12.5 percent, all indications are that bill rates should decline to about 10 percent over the course of the next 3 months. Management therefore decides to use a financial futures hedge as a way to lock in the high yields that currently exist. It does this by buying twelve 90-day T-bill futures contracts. Now if rates do go down, then the hedge will be able to capture the profits that accompany a fall in yields, which can then be used to (totally or partially) offset the loss in investor return.

Table 21A.2 summarizes the situation. Observe that if rates for both Treasury bills and T-bill futures do drop by 2.5 points, the profit from the futures transaction amounts to $75,000 and offsets exactly the loss in return that comes from earning 10 rather than 12.5 percent from a 90-day T-bill investment. Unfortunately, note in the second panel of Table 21A.2 that should market rates rise (rather than fall), the hedging firm would miss the added profits altogether, since the futures hedge locks in the return at or near the rate that existed when the hedge was established. The identical profit and loss figures were obtained because (1) the interest rates on both the Treasury bill and the T-bill future changed by the same amount; and (2) the futures contract had the same maturity as that on the investment vehicle itself. The lower two sections of Table 21A.2 show what happens when these conditions are not met. In particular, when rates behave as expected, *additional* profit is earned when the yield drops more on the futures contract, and when the futures contract has a longer maturity than the investment horizon. Because the hedging firm has an ownership position in the futures contracts, these conditions will *always* hold for buy hedges; just the opposite, of course, would hold for sell hedges.

The other basic type of short-term hedge involves creating a sell hedge as a way to protect against a future rise in rates when a firm is planning to issue short-term debt. For example, if management has plans to issue a large amount of commercial paper in, say, 60 days, but is concerned that short-term borrowing rates will be higher by then, it can short-sell interest rate futures as a way to lock in the lower borrowing rate that exists today. (This strategy was illustrated in Chapter 11.)

Long-Term Hedging Strategies   Since nonfinancial corporations are usually not in the business of making long-term investments in securities, the principal application of a futures hedge for long-term financial transactions is to protect the future sale of a bond issue (or, what amounts to the same thing, the future placement of a term loan). In such cases, sell hedges are set up using Treasury bond or GNMA futures contracts to protect the firm against the possibility of an increase in market rates. The firm wants to keep the cost of financing down by locking in the prevailing market rate. The idea is to capture a profit from the short hedge, which can then be

HEDGE IS CREATED AND RATES FALL TO 10%

September 1: *Buy* 12 90-day T-bill futures contracts yielding 12.5%, valued at $968,750 each $11,625,000

December 1: *Sell* 12 90-day T-bill futures contracts yielding 10.0%, valued at $975,000 each 11,700,000

  Profit from futures trades .... $ 75,000

Also on December 1:

Invest $12,000,000 in 90-day Treasury bills at a yield of 10.0% and earn a total return over the 90 days of[a] $300,000

Versus: Total 90-day return if $12,000,000 investment could have been made at a yield of 12.5% 375,000

  Loss in return .... $ 75,000

    Net profit (or loss) 0

HEDGE IS CREATED AND RATES RISE TO 14%

September 1: Buy futures contracts, as above $11,625,000

December 1: Sell contracts when they yield 14.0% and are valued at $965,000 each 11,580,000

  Loss on futures trades .... $ 45,000

Also on December 1:

Invest $12,000,000 for 90 days at 14% and earn .... $ 420,000

Versus: Total 90-day return at a yield of 12.5% 375,000

  Added return .... $ 45,000

    Net profit (or loss) 0

HEDGE IS CREATED AND RATES FALL, BUT BY DIFFERENT AMOUNTS

Condition: T-bill futures rate falls by 250 basis points (from 12.5% to 10%), while actual market rates on Treasury bills fall only 200 basis points (from 12.5% to 10.5%).

September 1: Buy futures contracts, as above $11,625,000

December 1: Sell contracts at yield of 10% 11,700,000

  Profit from futures trades .... $ 75,000

Also on December 1:

Invest $12,000,000 at 10.5% for 90 days and earn .... $ 315,000

Versus: Total return at yield of 12.5% 375,000

  Loss in return .... $ 60,000

    Net profit (or loss) .... $ 15,000

HEDGE IS CREATED BUT MATURITIES DIFFER

Condition: 90-day futures contract is used to hedge a 60-day investment position (both issues undergo a 250-basis-point drop in yield)

September 1: Buy 12 90-day futures contracts at 12.5% yield, as above $11,625,000

December 1: Sell contracts at 10% yield, as above 11,700,000

  Profit from futures trades .... $ 75,000

Also on December 1:

Invest $12,000,000 for 60 days at a yield of 10% and earn .... $ 200,000

Versus: Total 60-day return at 12.5% yield 250,000

  Loss in return .... $ 50,000

    Net profit (or loss) .... $ 25,000

[a] $.10 \times \$12,000,000 \times 90/360 = \$300,000$

used to reduce the amount of bonds that will have to be issued at the new (higher) rate of interest.[4] The technique, which was illustrated in the main body of this chapter, will enable the firm to keep its effective cost of financing down to a rate approximating that which existed when the hedge was set up.

The effective cost of financing produced by this kind of futures hedge can be determined by solving for the discount rate, i, in the following equation:

$$A_o = \sum_{t=1}^{n} \frac{A_R C_R}{(1 + i)^t} + \frac{A_R}{(1 + i)^n} \qquad (21A.2)$$

where A_o = original amount of debt the company intended to raise (in the absence of the futures hedge)

A_R = revised (actual) amount of debt raised, where $A_R = A_o$ less the profit earned from the futures hedge

C_R = actual coupon rate on debt

This is simply a variation of the standard bond valuation model described in Chapter 7 (and of course semiannual, rather than annual, compounding can be used if greater precision is desired).

| PROBLEMS |

21A.1.   *PRICING FINANCIAL FUTURES.*   Find the market value of the following interest rate futures contracts: (1) A 90-day CD quoted at 86.15. (2) A long-term Treasury bond quoted at 86-15. How much price behavior (change in market value) will occur in these futures contracts if:

   a.   The CD future moves to a yield of 12 percent?

   b.   The Treasury bond future moves to a quote of 82-00?

21A.2.   *HEDGING WITH FINANCIAL FUTURES.*   The chief financial officer of Hallman Manufacturing has just announced that the company will need to issue a $40 million, 15-year bond within the next three to four months. After exhaustive study, the CFO feels that with the way interest rates are behaving, the market rate for

---

[4]The same conditions noted with short-term hedges must also exist with this long-term strategy in order to obtain a perfect hedge—for example, the interest rates on the futures contract and cash financial instrument must move by the same amount. Should one or more of these conditions not exist, the hedging firm will fail to realize an effective cost of financing that equals the rate which existed when the hedge was created. Depending on the comparative terms and actual yield spread behavior, the effective cost could end up higher than the benchmark rate, or it could be lower. For a discussion of some of the sources and problems that can occur with futures hedges, see Richard W. McEnally and Michael L. Rice, "Hedging Possibilities in the Flotation of Debt Securities," *Financial Management* 8 (winter 1979), pp. 12–18.

15-year bonds will probably move from its present level of 10 percent to as high as 12.5 percent by the time the new issue can be brought to market. Management would like to set up an interest rate futures hedge to protect the firm against the risk of a substantial rise in interest rates; the CFO turns to you for help.

a. Is the firm going to have to set up a buy hedge or a sell hedge? Explain.

b. Assume a decision has been made to use long-term T-bond futures contracts as the hedging device. How many futures contracts will the firm have to buy (or sell) to set up the hedge, given that it wants the amount of underlying securities in the futures contracts to equal the size of the loan ($40 million)?

c. Assume that T-bond futures contracts are presently selling at 87-10 (to yield 9.85 percent), and they are expected to move to a price of 77-30 (to yield 11.5 percent) by the time the new issue is to be brought to the market. Ignoring transaction costs, how much profit does the firm stand to make from the futures hedge if the price of the T-bond futures behaves as expected?

d. Given that the profit from the futures hedge will be used to reduce the size of the planned bond issue, find the effective cost of financing to the firm (use annual compounding). How does this compare with the 12.5 percent the firm would have had to pay if it had not used the hedge? What savings in annual interest *and* in total interest (over the 15-year life of the bond) will occur as a result of being able to issue the smaller bond? (Assume the bond is a non-sinking-fund issue that will be paid off in full at maturity.)

e. What could the firm do to get the effective cost of financing (with the hedge) closer to the 10 percent rate that existed at the time the company announced the new issue?

22

Leasing

Leasing allows a firm to acquire the use of an asset without having to purchase it. In a leasing arrangement, the firm agrees to make a series of payments to the party that owns the asset in exchange for its use—that is, the company obtains the services of the leased asset, but not the title to it. The firm is the lessee in such an arrangement and has physical possession of the asset; the lessor is the party that owns the asset and holds the title. Just about any type of real property or physical asset can be obtained through leasing, from equipment and rolling stock to warehouses and complete manufacturing plants. Conceptually, leasing is quite similar to borrowing, in that a lease obligates the company to a series of fixed payments. In this chapter we look at leasing as a financing vehicle, and at the institutional and managerial dimensions of this form of financing. After reviewing the basic types of leases and other administrative aspects of leasing, we will examine the procedure for setting lease rates. The final portion of the chapter presents a lease evaluation model for use in assessing the economic desirability of leasing an asset as opposed to purchasing it.

Forms of Lease Financing

Over the past two decades, leasing has become a major source of financing to business and is today a multibillion-dollar industry. Leasing is used as a financing vehicle by small companies as well as by giant corporations, by blue chip firms and by firms that rank much lower on the quality scale, and by firms in virtually every industry category. Some leasing is done by individuals and other nonbusiness users, but most observers agree that the vast majority of leases involve financing for business purposes. Leasing ranks with bonds and common stock equity as a source of capital and well ahead of convertible security and preferred stock financing. Basically, there are two types of leases a firm can enter into: one is an operating lease and the other is a finance lease.

As we will see, there are substantial differences between the two forms, especially with respect to length of lease and services provided. Here we devote special attention to finance leases since this form of leasing is our primary concern in this chapter.

Operating Leases

An *operating lease* is a short-term contractual agreement whereby the lessee agrees to make periodic payments to the lessor to obtain the use of an asset; these are also known as service leases because they provide for the servicing as well as the financing of a leased piece of equipment. Small computer equipment, office machines, automobiles, and trucks are some of the primary types of equipment involved in operating leases. These leases require that the lessor maintain and service the equipment, and very often that the lessor pay any insurance premiums and property taxes on the leased asset; such costs are, of course, built into the lease payments. In addition, operating leases generally are not fully amortized. That is, the length of time and amount of the payments required under the lease contract are not sufficient for the lessor to recover the full cost of the equipment. Since the period of the lease agreement is substantially shorter than the life of the equipment, the lessor expects to recover the full cost (plus a reasonable profit) through subsequent leases and/or disposal of the equipment. In some instances, the contract gives the lessee the option to purchase the leased asset. Frequently, operating (or service) leases contain a cancellation clause giving the lessee the right to cancel the lease and return the equipment before the expiration of the lease period. This may be an important consideration from the lessee's perspective, as it provides the opportunity to return an asset if it is no longer needed or becomes technically obsolete. Being able to shift the risk of technical obsolescence to the lessor is a primary reason for using a service lease, and explains in part why a company would be willing to pay the generally very costly rates associated with operating lease agreements. A recent survey by the American Association of Equipment Lessors indicated that the original cost of equipment leased under operating leases exceeded $4.1 billion.

Finance Leases

A *finance lease* is a "true" lease as recognized by the Internal Revenue Service that (1) normally does not provide for any maintenance or service, (2) is not cancellable without a penalty, and (3) is fully or close to fully amortized from lease payments over the life of the lease. In a finance lease, the period of the lease is typically longer than in an operating lease, and the lessee acquires almost all the economic benefits and risks of the leased property as well as the responsibility for all service, insurance, and taxes. There are three main types of finance leases: the direct acquisition of an asset under a lease, a sale-leaseback arrangement, and leveraged leasing.

Direct Leasing. The most common form of a finance lease is the *direct lease*. It is a straightforward lease whereby the lessee obtains the use of an asset it did not previously have by entering into a finance lease agreement with the lessor. Typically, the lessee selects the equipment it requires and negotiates the lease price and delivery terms with the lessor. Most direct finance leases are obtained from one of four major types of lessors: (1) manufacturers (especially those that produce expensive capital goods); (2) the leasing divisions of major financial institutions (primarily commercial banks, investment bankers, and commercial finance companies); (3) independent leasing companies; and (4) investors (particularly those who participate in publicly and privately placed limited partnership deals). In every case except that in which the manufacturer does the leasing, the vendor sells the asset to the lessor, and the lessor in turn leases it to the lessee.[1] Since the lessor receives the return after or net of any maintenance, insurance, and property tax expenses, this type of lease is often called a *net lease*.[2] The American Association of Lessors estimated that assets with an original cost of more than $26 billion are covered by direct leases.

Sale-Leaseback. In a *sale-leaseback* arrangement, a firm owning land, buildings, or equipment will sell the property or equipment to a lessor and simultaneously execute an agreement to lease the property or equipment back for a specific period of time under specific terms. The company that used to own the assets becomes the lessee. This technique is used primarily by firms that need to raise capital and yet want to retain the economic use of the asset.[3] The lessee, of course, gives up title to the asset, along with any expected residual or salvage value; however, as is the case in many sale-leaseback arrangements, the company is often given the option to repurchase the property at the end of the lease period. Lessors who engage in sale-leaseback agreements include insurance companies, independent leasing companies, pension funds, and other institutional investors.

Leveraged Leasing. Over the last 20 years, a special form of leasing has been developed in conjunction with assets that require large capital

---

[1]Note that if a manufacturer acts as the lessor, the investment tax credit and depreciation are less than if the company sold the asset to another firm which acted as the lessor; this is primarily because the manufacturer cannot capitalize the estimated profits from the sale. See Jack E. Gaumnitz and Allen Ford, "The Lease or Sell Decision," *Financial Management* 7 (winter 1978), pp. 69–74.

[2]Under a net lease the lessee makes these payments and may also agree to make up any deficiency between the actual residual (or salvage) value at the end of the lease and the salvage amount the lessee guaranteed to the lessor.

[3]For more discussion on sale-leaseback agreements, see E. Han Kim, Wilbur G. Lewellen, and John J. McConnell, "Sale-and-Leaseback Agreements and Enterprise Valuation," *Journal of Financial and Quantitative Analysis* 13 (December 1978), pp. 871–883.

outlays. This type of leasing, called *leveraged leasing*, differs from the arrangements noted above because three parties are directly involved in the lease: (1) the lessee, (2) the lessor or equity participant, and (3) the lender. From the standpoint of the lessee, there is no difference between a leveraged lease and any other kind of finance lease arrangement. However, the role of the lessor is changed; this party supplies only a portion, say 20 percent, of the funds needed to purchase the asset (hence the name *equity participant*). The remaining amount, 80 percent in this case, is provided by one or more long-term lenders. The loan is taken out, usually on a nonrecourse basis, by the lessor, and is secured by a first mortgage on the equipment or facilities and by an assignment of the lease payments. A trust agreement is set up that provides for a trustee to hold title to the asset for the benefit of the lessor. Lease payments are sent directly to the trustee, where principal and interest requirements on the loan are deducted (and forwarded to the lender) before any money is sent to the lessor. Occasionally, the debt service requirement will be greater than some of the lease payment, for a short period of time, in which case the lessor will have to make up the difference. All of these, however, are complications for the lessor; they in no way affect the conduct or evaluation of the lease from the lessee's perspective. Over $17.1 billion of equipment is estimated to be leased under leveraged lease agreements.

Administrative Dimensions of Leasing

Firms use leasing because it is a convenient and oftentimes cost-effective form of financing. In fact, cost-effectiveness should be the single most important reason for using a lease; for so long as leasing is economically competitive and is compatible with the firm's capital structure, its use will contribute to the long-run value of the firm and shareholder wealth maximization. If we ignore the benefits of ownership (like the investment tax credit and depreciation), leasing companies can offer quoted lease rates that are below conventional loan rates. This is done by building the benefits of ownership into the lease rates and passing a portion of them back to the lessee in the form of reduced quoted rates. However, when the lessee considers the benefits of ownership (as they should), the effective lease rate goes up substantially and is not nearly as attractive (to the lessee) as the quoted rate. The final cost may not be less than that of conventional loan rates, but when the added services and/or risk transfers are factored in, the effective cost becomes far more competitive.

In addition to the economics of leasing,[4] the basic advantages and disadvantages of leasing as well as certain administrative factors must be considered, including (1) the tax treatment of the lease payment, (2)

---

[4]The economic analysis of leasing is, of course, of paramount importance in assessing the desirability of a lease and will be considered separately later in the chapter.

accounting for leases, and (3) the expected provisions and costs attached to leasing.

The convenience and cost of leasing are often regarded as advantages of leasing. Another advantage is that it supposedly enables firms to increase their credit availability (this assumes, of course, that leasing has less impact on debt capacity than borrowing). The point may have merit from a practical perspective to the extent that leasing provides firms with a means of obtaining equipment and facilities financing without accessing traditional capital markets. It also allows firms to conserve cash and working capital since nearly 100 percent financing can be obtained with leasing. Except for the first payment (which is made at the start of the lease), there are no large down payment requirements. In fact, a tight cash position is often one of the more important reasons for entering into a lease. The chance to transfer the risk of obsolescence to the lessor is also an important advantage. The cost of leasing will obviously increase as the amount of perceived risk increases, but many firms, especially those facing high exposure to obsolescence, view the cost as worthwhile. Other advantages include being able to shift the burden of equipment disposal to the lessor, and being able to avoid restrictive loan covenants.

Leasing also has several noteworthy disadvantages. Perhaps the most obvious is the loss of an ownership position in the assets. These include the right to claim the investment tax credit and depreciation charges, and to retain an equity position in the residual value of the equipment. However, through effective negotiation with the lessor, most of these benefits can be reclaimed through a reduced lease rate. One disadvantage common to nearly all leases that do not have repurchase options is that the lessee gives up potential appreciation in the residual value of the leased asset. This may be a substantial source of profit to the lessor, especially in inflationary periods, but it represents a potentially significant opportunity cost to the lessee. Finally, leasing may raise the fixed payment obligations of the lessee above the level associated with purchasing, thereby placing a greater burden on the firm's cash flow.

Tax Treatment

The tax treatment of leases has undergone some change in recent years. Prior to 1981 the Internal Revenue Service operated under strict rules about what constituted a lease for tax purposes. The Economic Recovery Tax Act of 1981 did away with most of these rules and substituted a very lenient definition of what constituted a lease for tax purposes. This change lead to the development of what were called safe-harbor leases. These were not, in fact, true leases; rather they provided a means for encouraging economic recovery by allowing unprofitable firms to sell their unusable investment tax credit or depreciation benefits to profitable firms. However, with the passage of the Tax Equity and Fiscal Responsibility Act (TEFRA) of 1982, safe-harbor leasing was abolished.[5]

To qualify as a true or finance lease under TEFRA, the following conditions apply:

1. The lessor must hold title to the property and expect a pretax profit from leasing it.
2. The lessor must be a corporation, partnership, or grantor trust.[6]
3. The lessor and the lessee must agree the transaction is a lease, the length of the lease must meet conditions established by the IRS, and the lessee must state that it is "designated lease property" on its income tax return.
4. The lease must be entered into within 90 days after the property is placed in service.
5. The lessee may have an option to repurchase the property, but the price must be equal to or greater than 10 percent of the original purchase price.
6. "Limited use" property, such as smokestacks or a piece of equipment integral to some larger process, can be leased.

The tax treatment of a lease transaction is of critical importance to financial managers.[7] In fact, the existence of differential corporate tax rates between lessors and lessees is generally regarded as the single most important reason for the substantial boom in leasing that has occurred over the past couple of decades.

Under the assumption that capital markets are perfect (no transactions costs, costless and readily available information, no bankruptcy costs, and no taxes), it can be shown that firms would be indifferent between leasing or purchasing an asset.[8] However, once any differential tax status between lessors and lessees is introduced, this indifference quickly disappears. Other things being equal, firms with low margin-

---

[5]Safe-harbor leasing was repealed after December 31, 1983. In addition, it was severely restricted for property placed into service after July 1, 1982. Special transitional rules apply to commercial passenger aircraft, automobile manufacturing property, steel production property, certain turbines and boilers for cooperatives, and mass-commuting vehicles.

[6]To be specific, the lessor must be either (1) a corporation (other than a personal holding company or what is called a Sub-chapter S corporation); (2) a partnership where all partners are defined as in (1); or (3) a grantor trust where the grantor and all the beneficiaries are qualified corporate entities as defined in (1) or (2).

[7]Because of the complex nature of the tax treatment for leases (and because the regulations are subject to frequent changes), it is advisable to obtain expert advice from a tax accountant or lawyer when setting up major lease deals.

[8]See, for example, Merton H. Miller and Charles W. Upton, "Leasing, Buying, and the Cost of Capital Services," *Journal of Finance* 31 (June 1976), pp. 761–786; Wilbur G. Lewellen, Michael L. Long, and John J. McConnell, "Asset Leasing in Competitive Capital Markets," *Journal of Finance* 31 (June 1976), pp. 787–798; and James C. Van Horne, "The Cost of Leasing with Capital Market Imperfections," *Engineering Economist* 23 (fall 1977), pp. 1–12.

al tax rates will find it advantageous to lease assets more frequently than firms with higher marginal tax rates. This is because companies with low marginal tax rates can take greater advantage of the subsidies by passing them on to another, more profitable, firm (the lessor). Leasing firms have thus tended to become specialized entities designed to take full advantage of the tax subsidies that other firms (the lessees) are unable to completely utilize. When the leasing company also happens to be owned by the firm that manufactures the equipment, still another benefit exists due to the deferral of taxes on the manufacturing profit that the manufacturer gains by leasing the asset rather than selling it.

Accounting for Leases

What constitutes a finance or true lease for tax purposes is not the same as a *capital lease* for accounting purposes. A capital lease exists and must be recognized in the lessee's balance sheet when one or more of the following conditions are met:

1. The lease transfers title of the asset to the lessee by the end of the lease period.
2. The lease contains an option giving the lessee the right to purchase the asset at a price below its fair market value.
3. The lease period is equal to or greater than 75 percent of the estimated economic life of the asset.
4. At the beginning of the lease, the present value of the minimum lease payments equals or exceeds 90 percent of the fair value of the leased property to the lessor (minus any investment tax credit realized by the lessor).[9]

Prior to 1976 firms did not have to report the existence of leases on their financial statements. Thus, they obtained "off balance sheet" financing since neither the leased assets nor the liabilities arising because of the lease appeared on the lessee's balance sheet. However, now they have to capitalize certain leases. This is intended to provide a more complete and accurate statement of the assets and liabilities of the firm that uses leasing.[10] In particular, if the capital leasing criteria are met, both the asset and the corresponding liability must be recorded by the lessee at the present value of the stream of rental payments. The leases must be broken out for reporting purposes only on the liability side of the balance sheet. This is done by taking all future payments the company is required to make under capital lease obligations and

---

[9]FASB Statement 13, *Accounting for Leases* (Stamford, Conn.: Financial Accounting Standards Board, 1976). At the present time the FASB is reevaluating their financial reporting requirements for leases.

[10]For an excellent discussion of lease capitalization and its potential impact on reported accounting figures, see Sidney Davidson and Roman Weil, "Lease Capitalization and Inflation Accounting," *Financial Analysts Journal* 31 (November–December 1975), pp. 22–29.

discounting them back to their present value; the current portion (lease payments due over the next 12 months) of this present-value amount is then listed as a current liability, and the balance as a long-term obligation.

On the asset side, the amount of capital leases must be included as part of the firm's fixed assets (property, plant, and equipment), but does not have to be broken out for reporting purposes. To arrive at a "net fixed asset" value of a lease, the total (gross) amount of the lease obligation is "depreciated" at a present-value rate compatible with the amortization of the lease obligation on the liability side. In order to avoid these reporting requirements, many leases are presently being written that do not meet the capital lease requirements. For these and other operating leases, the lessee is required to provide only a list of the future lease payments, and such information can be reported in the footnotes rather than the body of the balance sheet.

Terms and Costs of Leases

Although leases are widely used as a form of financing, there is a conspicuous lack of empirical data on the terms and costs of leasing. However, a recent study that analyzed 50 leases does shed some light on the subject.[11] The leases varied from very small ($9,000) to large ($8 million) and were written over the 7-year period from 1973 through 1980; none of the leases were operating leases, and in each case the lessee was responsible for maintenance, taxes, and insurance. Table 22.1 summarizes the key features of these leases and reveals that all asset categories required some prepayment; that the average life of a lease was 7.56 years; and that the investment tax credit was retained by the lessor in 70 percent of the cases.

The study used internal rate of return techniques to estimate the cost of leasing to the lessee. The researchers calculated that the average before-tax cost was almost 21 percent. Assuming that all the firms were in the 46 percent tax bracket, they found that the apparent after-tax cost dropped to 14 percent, while it was 17.9 percent if the tax rate was 20 percent. When any of these rates are compared to the after-tax cost of debt estimated to exist at the time the leases were written (such costs averaged about 8 percent), the leases were judged to be a fairly expensive form of financing.[12] The reasons offered for the high cost of leasing were the following: (1) firms that lease assets are more prone to failure, thus requiring lessors to demand a higher risk premium; (2) considerable

---

[11]Peggy J. Crawford, Charles P. Harper, and John J. McConnell, "Further Evidence on the Terms of Financial Leases," *Financial Management* 10 (autumn 1981), pp. 7–14.

[12]Ivar W. Sorensen and Ramon E. Johnson, "Equipment Financial Leasing Practices and Costs: An Empirical Study," *Financial Management* 6 (spring 1977), pp. 33–40; and Vincent J. McGugan and Richard E. Caves, "Integration and Competition in the Equipment Leasing Industry," *Journal of Business* 47 (July 1974), pp. 382–396, also found above-average costs for lease financing.

TABLE 22.1
Characteristics of Selected Leases

Characteristics	Asset Category								
	Computers and Processors	Construction	Aircraft	Railroad	Marine Equipment	Manufacturing	Hospital	Office	Total
Number of contracts	22	2	5	4	3	4	3	7	50
Mean cash outlay	$623,000	$29,000	$763,000	$5,820,000	$853,000	$411,000	$257,000	$86,000	$929,000
Mean pre-payment (as a % of outlay)	4.32%	8.00%	3.40%	2.00%	1.00%	3.25%	3.67%	6.00%	4.10%
Mean maturity (in years)	6.09	6.50	7.00	14.25	12.33	8.00	5.00	7.86	7.56
ITC retained by lessor (% of contracts)	82%	0%	20%	100%	100%	75%	67%	57%	70%

SOURCE: Peggy J. Crawford, Charles P. Harper, and John J. McConnell, "Further Evidence on the Terms of Financial Leases," *Financial Management* 10 (autumn 1981), p. 9.

imperfections exist in the leasing market; or (3) there are fundamental and not completely understood differences between lease contracts and debt contracts. The only conclusion one can draw at this point is that the available evidence indicates lease financing is apparently more expensive than debt financing.

Setting the Lease Rate

Knowing how lease rates are set is important to the lessee because it enables the firm's financial managers to compare the effective costs of competitive bids, and provides a basis for knowledgeable bargaining in lease negotiations. There are three major benefits that go along with owning an asset rather than leasing it: (1) the investment tax credit, (2) a tax shield (reduction) due to depreciation, and (3) salvage value. Not all the benefits will necessarily be present in all leases—for example, the equipment may have an expected salvage value of zero.

When a lessee gives up ownership of an asset in order to lease it, some or all of these benefits are passed to the lessor. However, knowledgeable lessees can capture a part of the benefits of ownership through the lease payments by negotiating with the leasing company to have the lease rate set low enough to reflect the benefits that passed from the lessee to the lessor. Thus, at the minimum, it would seem that the financial managers of the lessee firm should ascertain which benefits are included in the lease rate and what impact any missing benefits have on the cost of the lease. Throughout this discussion on setting lease rates, we will take the perspective of the lessor, but we do so only to provide the lessee firm with insight on the cost of any leased asset.

Like any firm, the lessor sets lease rates that will provide a satisfactory (risk-adjusted) rate of return. With finance leases, the cash flows associated with maintenance, insurance, and property taxes can be ignored; the leasing company needs to be concerned only with the cost of financing. In setting the lease rate, the leasing company will want to quote a figure that will not only be competitive (attractive to the lessee), but also be sufficiently generous to result in a satisfactory rate of return to the lessor. This can be done with a straightforward present-value procedure that relates the present value of the benefits of owning the equipment to the original cost of the equipment. In setting this lease rate, the lessor's required rate of return and its marginal tax rate play a crucial role, since the lessor must set the rate at a level that provides the firm's required after-tax return.

The Basic Steps

To set a lease rate, the lessor uses the following five-step procedure.

Step 1. Determine the cash flow benefits accruing to the lessor from ownership. These benefits are the investment tax credit, the tax shield due to the depreciation (which is equal to the annual depreciation deduction times the lessor's marginal tax rate), and any salvage value (on an after-tax basis).

Step 2. Compute the present value of the cash flow from the ownership benefits, employing the lessor's after-tax required rate of return. (Since all cash flows are on an after-tax basis, it follows that the lessor's after-tax discount rate is appropriate for all calculations.) The present value of the ownership benefits is thus equal to:

$$\text{Present value of ownership benefits} = ITC + \sum_{t=1}^{n} \frac{Dep_t \, (T)}{[1+k(1-T)]^n} + \frac{SV_n}{[1+k(1-T)]^n} \tag{22.1}$$

where ITC = investment tax credit on the asset[13]
Dep_t = depreciation taken for tax purposes by the lessor in the tth year
k = lessor's after-tax required rate of return
T = lessor's marginal tax rate
SV_n = estimated after-tax salvage value of the asset in year n

---

[13]Under the Tax Equity and Fiscal Responsibility Act of 1982, lessors can claim only 20 percent of the investment tax credit in the year the asset is placed in service. The remainder is evenly spread over the next 4 years. For simplicity we ignore this complication.

Step 3. Determine the net amount that must be recovered from the lease payments by subtracting the after-tax ownership benefits (step 2) from the cost of the leased asset, CLA_0. Thus, the net amount to be recovered is given by:

$$\text{Net amount to be recovered} = CLA_0 - \text{present value of} \atop \text{ownership benefits} \quad (22.2)$$

Step 4. Determine the after-tax lease payment, ATLP necessary for the lessor to recoup the "net amount to be recovered" (from step 3), based on the lessor's after-tax required rate of return. The after-tax lease payment is obtained by solving for ATLP in the following equation:

$$\text{Net amount to be recovered} = ATLP(1.00) + \frac{ATLP}{[1+k(1-T)]^{n-1}} \quad (22.3)$$

As is customary, the lease payments in Equation 22.3 are assumed to be made in advance (at the beginning of each year). The first lease payment takes place at t_0 and the last payment occurs at t_{n-1} (or, what amounts to the same thing, at the end of the next-to-the-last year).[14]

Step 5. Calculate the before-tax lease payment, LP, which will be the lessor's quoted rate, by adjusting the after-tax lease payment as follows:

$$LP = \frac{ATLP}{1 - \text{lessor's marginal tax rate}} \quad (22.4)$$

This last step is necessary, since all the calculations in the first four steps were based on the lessor's after-tax cash flows and required rate of return. The quoted lease rate, LP, however, must be on a before-tax basis.

An Illustration To illustrate this procedure in action, consider the case of Allied Leasing Company. It has been asked to write a 5-year lease on equipment that costs $1.4 million and has an estimated salvage value of zero. The firm feels it needs a 15 percent before-tax return on the lease; the marginal tax rate is 40 percent; the 8 percent ITC applies; and Allied Leasing will depreciate the equipment over its 5-year normal recovery period via the ACRS method. To calculate Allied's lease rate, which will provide the 15 percent (before-tax) return, the five-step procedure just developed will be employed (see Table 22.2):

Steps 1 and 2. The depreciation tax shield and ITC are presented in Table 22.2 and then discounted at the after-tax rate of 9 percent [15% × (1 − .40)

---

[14]This same basic procedure can also be employed in setting monthly, as opposed to yearly, lease rates.

TABLE 22.2
Setting Lease Rates for
Allied Leasing

STEPS 1 AND 2. OWNERSHIP BENEFITS AND THEIR PRESENT VALUE

Time Period	ITC	Depreciation Tax Shield[a]	Salvage[b]	Cash Flow Ownership Benefit	Present Value of Ownership Benefits[c]
0	$112,000	$ —		$112,000	$112,000
1		84,000		84,000	77,028
2		123,200		123,200	103,734
3		117,600		117,600	90,787
4		117,600		117,600	83,261
5		117,600	0	117,600	76,440

Present value of cash flow ownership benefits = $543,250

STEP 3. NET AMOUNT TO BE RECOVERED

$$\$1,400,000 - \$543,250 = \$856,750$$

STEP 4. SIZE OF ANNUAL AFTER-TAX LEASE PAYMENT (ATLP)

$$\$856,750 = ATLP\,(1.000) + ATLP\,(PVIFA_{9\%,\ 4\ yr})$$
$$\$856,750 = ATLP\,(1.000) + ATLP\,(3.240)$$
$$\$856,750 = 4.240\ ATLP$$
$$ATLP = \$202,064$$

STEP 5. BEFORE-TAX LEASE PAYMENT (LP) QUOTED BY LESSOR TO LESSEE

$$LP = \frac{\$202,064}{1 - .40} = \frac{\$202,064}{.60} = \$336,773$$

[a]Depreciation in year 1 is 15% × $1,400,000 = $210,000. The tax shield is $210,000 (.40) = $84,000. For year 2, the depreciation is $308,000 (22% × $1,400,000) and the depreciation tax shield is $123,200 ($308,000 × .40), and so on.

[b]If there were any salvage value, it would be included here after adjusting for any tax effects.

[c]Given Allied's 15 percent desired rate of return and a 40 percent marginal tax rate, the appropriate after-tax discount rate is: 15% (1 − T) = 15% (1 − .40) = 15% (.60) = 9%.

= 15% × (.60) = 9%]. The present value of the cash flows from owning the asset equals $543,250.

Step 3.   By subtracting the present value of the ownership benefits from the cost of the asset (of $1,400,000), the net amount to be recovered is determined to be $856,750. Note that this amount must be recovered from the lease payments themselves.

Step 4.   The after-tax annual lease payments, ATLP, assuming five lease payments made in advance, is found to be $202,064 based on Allied Leasing's 9 percent after-tax required return.

Step 5.   Adjusting the after-tax lease payment for Allied's 40 percent marginal tax rate, we find that Allied Leasing will quote a lease payment of $336,773 for 5 years, payable each year in advance. By quoting this rate, Allied can achieve its desired before-tax rate of return of 15 percent on the equipment.

Given knowledge of how lease rates are set, the lessee should be in a better position to determine the appropriateness of any lessor offering. Other things being equal, the following actions on the part of the lessor will result in higher lease rates:

1. Using straight-line instead of ACRS depreciation.
2. Estimating no, or a low, salvage value.
3. Increasing the required rate of return.
4. Moving into a lower marginal tax bracket.

Lessees might be especially interested in attempting to determine the lessor's expected or required rate of return and the estimated salvage value employed. By examining the potential impact of these factors on the lease rate, lessees can place themselves in a better bargaining position for lease negotiations.

Evaluation of Finance Leases

The evaluation of finance leases is relatively straightforward so long as certain fundamental considerations are kept in mind throughout the analysis. In particular, three assumptions are necessary: (1) that the firm is at its appropriate target capital structure (and that leasing is compatible with this capital structure); (2) that the asset under consideration is generally as risky as the typical asset employed by the firm; and (3) that finance leases are economically equivalent to debt to the extent that leasing uses up debt capacity in exactly the same manner that debt financing does. This last point is an important one. The purpose of this assumption is to neutralize the financial risk differential between a lease and a loan in order to compare the financial instruments involved in a lease or buy decision. Franks and Hodges illustrate how a lease is equivalent to debt by demonstrating that the financial burden associated with a lease (the fixed stream of rental payments) is the amount of debt service capacity displaced by the lease (which they define as the size of the loan that could have been obtained and repaid with the cash flows consumed by the lease).[15] Thus, when evaluating a lease, we implicitly assume that the borrowing alternative being considered (on the buy-and-borrow side of the decision) has the same future cash flow requirements as the lease and therefore the same degree of risk exposure.

With these conditions satisfied, we can proceed to develop an evaluation model that can be used by financial managers to assess the economic desirability of a finance lease. Basically, the decision revolves around the question of whether it would be better to lease or to buy. The value of the firm and shareholder wealth will be maximized so long as

---

[15]Julian R. Franks and Stewart D. Hodges, "Valuation of Financial Lease Contracts: A Note," *Journal of Finance* 33 (May 1978), pp. 657–669.

management selects the alternative that keeps both the real and the opportunity costs of financing at a minimum and below the level of the expected return from the asset under consideration. The lease evaluation model we develop and demonstrate below is based on the same economic principle. Before we look at this model, however, we will consider how lease evaluation is related to basic capital budgeting decisions.

Leasing and the Capital Budgeting Decision

When a firm is evaluating a capital budgeting decision, it will employ the company's marginal cost of capital (MCC) or some risk-adjusted discount rate to calculate the net present value (NPV) of the proposed investment, as demonstrated in Chapters 13 and 14. The firm will accept the project so long as it has an NPV equal to or greater than zero. Exactly the same type of analysis is required when the firm is considering whether or not to lease an asset. However, when leasing is a real possibility, standard capital budgeting procedures must be supplemented by further calculations to see if the firm should lease or buy the asset. In most cases, when a firm evaluates a capital project, the implicit assumption is that the asset under consideration will be purchased; this, of course, is not necessarily the case when there is a real chance that the asset can be leased. In such cases, the underlying cash flows will be altered, and as a result the possibility of a lease must be evaluated along with the profitability of the capital project.[16] Thus, when leasing is involved, capital budgeting becomes a two-tiered decision: the first part of the decision pertains to the profitability of the asset, and the second to the method of financing the asset. In fact, even if the NPV on an asset is negative, it may still be in the firm's best interest to acquire the use of the asset through a lease, so long as the lease terms are especially favorable. Hence, an NPV of −$400 on an asset, if purchased, may be offset by the present-value benefits of leasing if the net advantage of leasing (NAL) is greater than $400.

When the present-value benefits of leasing are superior to those of purchasing an asset, the net advantage of leasing (NAL) will be positive. As we will see below, when used in a lease evaluation context, a positive NAL implies that leasing is more desirable than purchasing an asset. In such cases, the positive NAL figure should be subtracted from the amount of the capital outlay when traditional capital budgeting analysis (NPV) is undertaken. Failure to do so will lead to an understatement of the asset's NPV, which in turn may lead not only to incorrect accept-reject decisions, but also to improper ranking and project selection

---

[16]For an excellent discussion of this concept, and a more detailed explanation of why the capital budgeting–leasing decision should be made simultaneously, see Kerry Cooper and Robert H. Strawser, "Evaluation of Capital Investment Projects Involving Asset Leases," *Financial Management* 4 (spring 1975), pp. 44–49.

when capital rationing conditions exist. If NAL is negative, purchasing is preferable to leasing, in which case standard capital budgeting analysis alone is sufficient to determine whether or not the asset should be purchased—that is, whether or not the investment should be made. Thus, only in those situations where NAL is positive should the capital budgeting–lease evaluation decisions be made simultaneously. The possible interactions between NAL and NPV are summarized in Table 22.3. The appendix to this chapter demonstrates the simultaneous NPV-NAL decision in detail. Because our primary concern is with leasing, we will concentrate on the lease evaluation decision and the determination of NAL. Throughout the balance of this chapter, we will simply assume that if NAL is positive, financial managers will use a system similar to that described in Appendix 22A to deal with the capital budgeting dimension of the decision.

| | A finance lease is evaluated from the lessee's perspective on the basis of |
| The Lease | the after-tax cash flows and opportunity costs incurred by leasing rather |

The Lease
Evaluation
Model

A finance lease is evaluated from the lessee's perspective on the basis of the after-tax cash flows and opportunity costs incurred by leasing rather than buying the equipment or asset in question. A major item in this analysis is the periodic lease payment, LP; in fact, in most finance leases, this is the only differential out-of-pocket cost incurred by the lessee. Granted that in finance leases the lessee is generally responsible for maintenance, insurance, and other operating expenses, but the firm would also be responsible for these same expenses if the asset were to be purchased. Therefore, in the absence of any incremental operating costs, we can ignore such expenses when evaluating leases.[17] In addition to lease payments, there are the opportunity costs that arise as a result of losing the benefits of ownership. These benefits will exist with the purchase of the equipment, but not when the asset is leased; they therefore qualify as incremental cash flow items and are included in the lease evaluation model as opportunity costs incurred when the asset is leased. As noted above, the benefits of ownership include the investment tax credit, depreciation, and salvage value.

Depreciation is included in the analysis because it is a tax-deductible noncash expenditure and therefore provides a tax shield to the owner-

---

[17]If there are any incremental operating costs, O_t, associated with owning rather than leasing the asset, they can be incorporated in the lease evaluation model to be presented in Equation 22.5 as follows:

$$NAL = CLA_0 - \left[ITC + LP_0(1 - T) + \sum_{t=1}^{n-1} \frac{LP_t(1 - T)}{(1 + k_i)^t} + \sum_{t=1}^{n} \frac{Dep_t (T)}{(1 + k_i)^t} + \frac{SV_n}{(1 + k_i)^n} - \sum_{t=1}^{n} \frac{O_t(1 - T)}{(1 + k)^t} \right]$$

where k = the firm's marginal cost of capital. The cost of capital, MCC, is used to discount the operating costs, O_t, to their present value because of the operating nature of the cash flow and the amount of differential risk imbedded in these forecasted values (*note*: all other variables are discounted at k_i, the firm's after-tax borrowing rate). As can be seen, the net affect of including O_t in Equation 22.5 is to increase the appeal of leasing—these are costs that can be avoided if the asset is leased rather than purchased.

TABLE 22.3
Relationship Between
Net Present Value and
Net Advantage of
Leasing for Asset
Investment and
Financing Decisions

Situation	Investment and Financing Decision
NET ADVANTAGE OF LEASING IS POSITIVE (+)	
Net present value positive (+)	Acquire use of asset by leasing
Net present value negative (−)	
Absolute value of NAL less than absolute value of NPV	Do not acquire or lease asset
Absolute value of NAL greater than absolute value of NPV	Acquire use of asset by leasing
NET ADVANTAGE OF LEASING IS NEGATIVE (−)	
Net present value positive (+)	Acquire asset by purchasing
Net present value negative (−)	Do not acquire asset

lessor. We can find the depreciation tax subsidy lost by the lessee simply by multiplying the annual depreciation charge, Dep_t, by the lessee's marginal tax rate, T; the depreciation tax shield used in the lease evaluation model is therefore:

$$Dep_t\,(T)$$

The investment tax credit, ITC, is assumed to occur at the beginning of the first year of the lease period (at t_0).[18] In contrast, the salvage value SV_n, is the expected amount, *net* of any taxes, that will be realized from the sale of the equipment or leased asset at the end of the lease period (in year $t = n$); thus, SV_n must be placed on a present-value basis. Likewise, we can find the after-tax cost of the lease payments to the firm as follows:

$$LP_t(1 - T)$$

These items are the relevant incremental cash flows that, when compared to the cost of the leased asset, CLA_0, determine the net advantage of leasing, NAL. More precisely, the net advantage of leasing is found according to the following lease evaluation model:[19]

$$NAL = CLA_0 - \left[ITC + LP_0\,(1 - T) + \sum_{t=1}^{n-1} \frac{LP_t(1 - T)}{(1 + k_i)^t} + \sum_{t=1}^{n} \frac{Dep_t(T)}{(1 + k_i)^t} + \frac{SV_n}{(1 + k_i)^n} \right] \quad (22.5)$$

---

[18]If the investment tax credit is passed from the lessor to the lessee (and assuming the ITC is the same whether the asset is leased or purchased), it has no effect on the net advantage to leasing (NAL), and the ITC variable in Equation 22.5 takes on a value of zero.

[19]Equation 22.5 is similar, though not identical, to the models developed by Stewart C. Myers, David A. Dill, and Alberto J. Bautista, "Valuation of Financial Lease Contracts," *Journal of Finance* 31 (June 1976), pp. 799–819; and Franks and Hodges, "Valuation of Financial Lease Contracts: A Note." Our treatment of depreciation differs, however, since both of them show the depreciation tax shield occurring at t_0, just like the first lease payment. The difference will, of course, have an affect on NAL, with our more realistic treatment resulting in lower present-value lease costs and therefore a slight bias in favor of leasing.

where CLA_0 = cost of the leased asset if purchased
   ITC = investment tax credit
   LP_0 = first lease payment (in advance)
   T = firm's marginal tax rate
   LP_t = subsequent yearly lease payments (for years 1 through $n - 1$)
   n = number of years for which the asset is leased
   Dep_t = depreciation of the asset in year t
   SV_n = after-tax salvage value
   k_i = firm's after-tax cost of borrowing

This model simply finds the present value of the lease payments and the foregone opportunity costs associated with owning the equipment (the part of Equation 22.5 in brackets) and subtracts it from the cost of the leased asset. Clearly, so long as the cost of leasing is less than the cost of buying, NAL will be positive, indicating that leasing is the preferred course of action.[20]

Note in Equation 22.5 that the first lease payment, LP_0, is shown to occur at t_0, or at the beginning of the first year of the lease period. This is customary practice in the leasing industry. As a result, the remaining lease payments, LP_t, are shown to run from the end of the first year ($t = 1$) to the end of the next-to-last year of the lease period ($t = n - 1$). Of course, only these latter lease payments are put on a present-value basis. In contrast, the depreciation tax shield in Equation 22.5 is taken at the

---

[20]To understand Equation 22.5 it is important to recognize that it is simply the result of looking at the incremental cash flows that occur if the asset is purchased, versus those that occur if the asset is leased. Thus, the following cash flow streams exist:

Cash flow if leased = $CFBT_t(1 - T) - LP_t(1 - T)$
Cash flow if purchased = $-CLA_0 + ITC + CFBT_t (1 - T) + Dep_t(T) + SV_n$

By subtracting the purchase cash flows from the lease cash flows, we find the incremental cash flows due to leasing or:

Incremental cash flows due to leasing = cash flows if leased − cash flows if purchased
   = $CFBT_t(1 - T) - LP_t(1 - T) - [-CLA_0 + ITC + CFBT_t(1 - T) + Dep_t(T) + SV_n]$
   = $CFBT_t(1 - T) - LP_t(1 - T) + CLA_0 - ITC - CFBT_t(1 - T) - Dep_t(T) - SV_n$

Since the two $CFBT_t(1 - T)$ terms cancel each other out, by rearranging we have:

   = $CLA_0 - ITC - LP_t(1 - T) - Dep_t(T) - SV_n$
   = $CLA_0 - [ITC + LP_t(1 - T) + Dep_t(T) + SV_n]$

In Equation 22.5 the lease payment term LP_t has been broken into two separate components—LP_0 which occurs at t_0 and does not have to be discounted, and the rest of the lease payments from $t = 1$ to $n - 1$, which have to be discounted. Viewed in this framework, the NAL approach to lease evaluation is similar to the replacement capital budgeting decision examined in Chapter 13, which also looked at incremental cash flows.

end of each year, from $t = 1$ to n. This is consistent with standard capital budgeting procedures and assumes that the depreciation can be obtained only after the asset in question has been held or used over the course of the year.[21]

The Appropriate Discount Rate.   As noted earlier, in order to compare the lease alternative with the purchase alternative, it is necessary to neutralize risk by ensuring that the debt capacity implied by the purchase alternative is the same as the debt capacity used if the asset is leased.[22] This is accomplished by establishing an equivalent borrowing amount that, in terms of the net cash flows in each future period, is exactly the same as the after-tax lease payments. To ensure this comparability in debt capacity, the implied loan repayment in each period (interest after tax plus repayment of principal) must be equal to the sum of the corresponding after-tax lease payment and depreciation tax saving [that is, $LP_t (1 - T) + Dep_t (T)$]. Given such a stream of implied repayments, it follows that the size of the equivalent loan is simply the present value of this stream of repayments discounted at the firm's borrowing rate.

Because the risk is neutralized in such a situation, the question of whether to lease or not becomes a pure financing decision; in this context, the question is not whether to lease or buy, but whether to lease or borrow, so we can use the firm's borrowing rate as a proxy for the buy-and-borrow alternative. However, because the government's tax subsidy on interest means that the cost of borrowing to the firm is net of taxes, the appropriate discount rate to use in the lease evaluation model is the after-tax borrowing rate of the firm.[23] Thus, we define k_i in

---

[21]We have assumed the number of years (or length) of the lease is equal to its normal recovery period as specified under ACRS. In many instances this will not be true; the lease might be for a shorter or a longer period of time. In such a case n will not be the same for the lease payment, LP, as it is for the depreciation, Dep.

[22]This point was first made by Richard S. Bower, "Issues in Lease Financing," *Financial Management* 2 (winter 1973), pp. 25–34. See also Myers, Dill, and Bautista, "Valuation of Financial Lease Contracts;" Franks and Hodges, "Valuation of Financial Lease Contracts: A Note"; and Haim Levy and Marshall Sarnat, "Leasing, Borrowing, and Financial Risk," *Financial Management* 8 (winter 1979), pp. 47–54. Both Franks and Hodges, and Levy and Sarnat provide examples that show how to specify the principal and interest payments per year on the implied equivalent borrowing necessary to neutralize the risk differential between the lease and purchase alternatives.

[23]Not only is this after-tax discount rate compatible with the Franks and Hodges treatment, but Lewellen and Emery show that it is identical to the Myers, Dill, and Bautista model when interest benefits are removed (though MDB use a pretax rate in their model, exactly the same results are obtained with an after-tax borrowing rate if their model excludes foregone interest tax benefits); see Wilbur G. Lewellen and Douglas R. Emery, "On the Matter of Parity among Financial Obligations," *Journal of Finance* 35 (March 1980), pp. 97–111.

Equation 22.5 as the after-tax cost of debt to the firm: $k_i = k_b (1 - T)$, where k_b = the lessee's before-tax borrowing rate.[24]

An Illustration. To demonstrate the use of Equation 22.5, let us consider once again the 5-year lease offered by Allied Leasing. Assume the managers of National Products want to evaluate the economic desirability of entering into the lease. (They have already evaluated the equipment from a capital budgeting perspective and found it to be a highly acceptable investment project; now they want to find out whether the equipment should be leased or bought.) Given the lease rate determined in Table 22.2 (lease payments of $336,773 per year for years t_0 through t_4) and assuming that National Products uses the ACRS depreciation method over the equipment's 5-year normal recovery period, a zero salvage value, a before-tax borrowing rate of 13.33 percent, an ITC of 8 percent, and a 40 percent marginal tax rate, we can determine the NAL of this lease proposal. Note that the after-tax cost of borrowing is 8 percent [13.33% × (1 − .40) = 13.33% × .60 = 7.998% ≈ 8%]. Using Equation 22.5, the NAL is found as follows:

NAL = cost of leased asset − [investment tax credit + first lease payment (in t_0) + present value of remaining lease payments (in years t_1 through t_4) + present value of depreciation tax shield (in years t_1 through t_5)]

= $1,400,000 − [$112,000 + $336,773 (1 − .40) + $336,773 (1 − .40) $PVIFA_{8\%, 4 \text{ yr}}$ + present value at 8% of depreciation tax shield]

= $1,400,000 − [$112,000 + $202,064 + $202,064 (3.312) + present value of depreciation tax shield]

The present value of the depreciation tax shield is as follows:

---

[24]Note in Equation 22.5 that the after-tax borrowing rate is used to discount SV_n to its present value. Although there is no complete agreement on the subject, it is generally felt that because of risk differentials between the certainty of the salvage value cash flow versus the nature of the cash flows in the remainder of the model (all of which are defined with a high degree of accuracy), the firm's marginal cost of capital should be employed as the discount rate in such present-value computations. Our decision to use the firm's after-tax borrowing rate is based on the desire for simplicity and the fact that any differences are likely to be minor. That is, because the after-tax borrowing rate will be less than the firm's MCC, the present value (of SV_n) will be greater when the borrowing rate is used, but since salvage value generally occurs so far in the future, the impact on NAL will be insignificant. Dyl and Joehnk, in a paper dealing with municipal leases, provide a simple yet effective way of evaluating the amount of risk imbedded in the estimated salvage value of a leased asset. They show that such risk is a function of the probability that the actual salvage value will change enough to reverse the sign of the computed NAL; implicitly, therefore, it would seem that salvage value has a minimal effect on the risk of leasing, since it follows that, because the central element in risk evaluation is the present value of a distant cash flow, the magnitude of the change in SV_n required to reverse NAL is generally very large. As a result, the probability of such an event occurring is quite small. See Edward A. Dyl and Michael D. Joehnk, "Leasing as a Municipal Finance Alternative," *Public Administration Review* 38 (November–December 1978), pp. 560–561.

Year	Dep_t	$Dep_t(T)$	Present Value (at $k_i = 8\%$)
1	$210,000	$ 84,000	$ 77,784
2	308,000	123,200	105,582
3	294,000	117,600	93,374
4	294,000	117,600	86,436
5	294,000	117,600	80,086
		$\sum_{t=1}^{n} \dfrac{Dep_t(T)}{(1+k_i)^t} =$	$443,262

Substituting this value (of $443,262) into the equation above, we have:

$$NAL = \$1,400,000 - [\$112,000 + \$202,064 + \$669,236 + \$443,262]$$
$$= \$1,400,000 - \$1,426,562 = -\$26,562$$

Since the NAL is negative, National Products should not acquire the use of the assets by leasing. However, since the project's NPV is positive, the assets should be purchased.

Finding the Effective Cost of a Lease.   Rather than solving Equation 22.5 for the NAL, it is also possible to use a variation of this model to find the effective rate on a lease (or cost to the lessee). This is done by using an internal rate of return approach to solve for the after-tax cost of the lease, k_l. To do this, it is necessary to restate Equation 22.5 as follows:

$$CLA_0 - ITC - LP_0(1 - T) = \sum_{t=1}^{n-1} \frac{LP_t(1 - T)}{(1 + k_l)^t} + \sum_{t=1}^{n} \frac{Dep_t(T)}{(1 + k_l)^t} + \frac{SV_n}{(1 + k_l)^n} \quad (22.6)$$

The effective percentage cost of a lease can now be found by solving for the value of k_l, which equates the discounted present value of the righthand side of the equation with the current costs on the lefthand side of the equation.[25]

To demonstrate, consider the same lease as described previously. The net amount of the current costs involved in this situation were as follows:

$$CLA_0 - ITC - LP_0(1 - T) = \$1,400,000 - \$112,000 - \$336,773 (1 - .40)$$
$$= \$1,085,936$$

This provides a figure for the lefthand side of Equation 22.6, and it is

---

[25]Equation 22.6 is the same equation presented in Appendix 17A (Equation 17A.4) to find the cost of a lease for cost of capital purposes, except that Equation 22.6 includes both the ITC and SV_n which, for simplicity, were omitted in Equation 17A.4.

what the discounted present value of the righthand side of the equation must equal. Finding this present value can greatly be simplified by combining the after-tax lease payments, the depreciation tax shield, and the after-tax salvage value (if any) into a single cash flow stream, as shown below:

Year	$LP_t (1 - T)$	$Dep_t(T)$	Future Cash Flow
1	$202,064	S 84,000	$286,064
2	202,064	123,200	325,264
3	202,064	117,600	319,664
4	202,064	117,600	319,664
5	—	117,600	117,600

Using the future cash flow column, we have to find the discount rate or internal rate of return, which discounts this stream to a present value of $1,085,936. Through a series of present-value calculations, the effective cost of this lease to National Products is found to be 9 percent. This rate can then be compared to the firm's after-tax cost of borrowing to determine whether the asset should be leased or purchased. In particular, if the computed effective cost of the lease is greater than the after-tax cost of borrowing, the asset should not be leased. In our illustration, it is clear that National Products should not lease the equipment, since the effective cost of 9 percent is well above the company's after-tax cost of borrowing of 8 percent.[26]

General Factors Favoring Purchasing

Many factors influence the decision to lease or to purchase, but in general anything that tends to make the cost of leasing higher will have the effect of reducing the NAL and hence the benefits to the firm from leasing. These basic effects are summarized in Table 22.4. As noted earlier, it is in the lessee's interest to recapture some of these benefits by negotiating with the lessor to include as many of the benefits of ownership as possible in the quoted lease rate. To do this, lessees must understand both the rate-setting process discussed above and the proper procedure for evaluating whether they should acquire the use of the assets by purchasing or by leasing them.

---

[26]Careful observation shows that this after-tax cost to National Products is the same as the after-tax required rate of return to the lessor, Allied Leasing, as noted earlier in the chapter. This occurrence is no accident, since all the assumptions regarding the ITC, depreciation schedule to employ, tax rate, and so on are exactly the same. Thus, if both the lessor and the lessee face exactly the same conditions, the after-tax required rate of return to the lessor must equal the after-tax cost to the lessee. However, if the tax rates differ between the lessor and the lessee, the after-tax cost to the lessee is not the same as the after-tax return required by the lessor.

1. Lower cost of the leased asset, CLA_0
2. An investment tax credit, ITC, that cannot be retained by the lessee if the asset is leased
3. Higher lease payments, LP_0 and LP_1 through LP_{n-1}
4. Higher tax rate, T[a]
5. Lower after-tax cost of equivalent debt financing, k_i
6. ACRS depreciation[b]
7. Higher salvage value
8. No incremental operating expenses if purchased[c]

[a]Of course, a change in the tax rate also affects the firm's MCC and consequently the NPV of the project.

[b]If straight-line depreciation is employed in the National Products example, the present value of the depreciation tax shield is $447,216, which makes the NAL −$30,516. This result appears contradictory, since straight-line depreciation should favor leasing. However, the result is due to a simplifying assumption used throughout the book. That is, when straight-line depreciation is used under the new tax code, a half-year convention is imposed in the first year, thus stretching the depreciation over six periods (for a 5-year asset), so that the following depreciation percentages apply: year 1, 10 percent; years 2–5, 20 percent; and year 6, 10 percent. The simplification we have employed throughout the book is that the depreciation percentages for a 5-year asset depreciated via straight line are 20 percent per year. If the half-year convention had been employed, thus stretching depreciation over 6 years, the present value of the depreciation tax shield is $430,640, which makes the NAL −$13,940. Thus ACRS depreciation (which resulted in an NAL of −$26,562) does favor purchasing as opposed to leasing.

[c]See note 17.

Leasing in Action: The Anaconda Deal

In one of the larger leases consummated to date, Anaconda agreed to lease a new aluminum reduction mill from a consortium of five banks and one commercial finance company.[27] The mill cost $110.7 million, and Anaconda agreed to make 40 semiannual payments over a 20-year period; the first 21 payments were $3,985,034 each, and the last 19 were $5,460,278 each. The lessors obtained the mill's future salvage value (in 1993) and the use of the investment tax credit of $7,749,000. Since the agreement provided for a finance lease, Anaconda was responsible for all operating cash flows, including maintenance, taxes, and insurance. Because of the expropriation of its Chilean mines, Anaconda had a tax loss of nearly $360 million, so the plant's investment tax credit and depreciation tax shield were of no immediate value to the company.

Employing the NAL procedure just described, the net advantage to the lessors has been estimated to be $3.03 million.[28] The advantage of the

[27]This was a leveraged lease because $72 million was raised through debt obtained from three insurance companies, who had a chattel mortgage on the mill and a first claim on the lease payments. However, they had no claims against the lessors if Anaconda defaulted and the principal and interest due could not be recovered.

[28]The analysis from the lessor's viewpoint is just the same as from the lessee's except that all the signs are reversed. The depreciation method employed in the Anaconda deal was the optimal one under the then existing class life Asset Depreciation Range (ADR) system, with an 11-year depreciable life. The lessor's residual value was estimated to be $10,896,000.

TABLE 22.5
Value of the Lease to
Anaconda with
Different Tax
Commencement Dates

TABLE 22.5
Value of the Lease to
Anaconda with
Different Tax
Commencement Dates

Number of Years Before Anaconda Resumes Payment of Taxes	Value (NAL) of the Lease ($ Millions)
0	−$ 3.03
1	− 2.67
2	− 1.93
3	− 0.90
4	0.38
5	1.85
6	5.70
7	13.07
8	23.64
9	27.94
10	31.17
15	35.56
20	30.31

SOURCE: Julian R. Franks and Stewart D. Hodges, "Valuation of Financial Lease Contracts: A Note," *Journal of Finance* 33 (May 1978), pp. 667

lease to Anaconda is a function of the length of time before Anaconda expected to resume paying taxes. As shown in Table 22.5, if Anaconda paid taxes immediately, the NAL would be a negative $3.03 million. However, because of its tax loss, Anaconda faced a substantial period before it could take advantage of the depreciation tax shield (and it would have lost the benefit of the investment tax credit entirely). So long as Anaconda didn't resume paying taxes before the fourth year, leasing of the mill would be preferable to purchasing it. And if the non-tax-paying period is 10 years, the NAL is $31.17 million—an impressive sum. Overall, it appears that Anaconda probably benefited by leasing the mill instead of purchasing it. Although not widely recognized or incorporated into the lease versus purchase decision until recently, the differential effective tax rates of the lessor and the lessee appear to be a critical factor in determining whether a firm should lease an asset. Since Anaconda could not use the investment tax credit and depreciation tax shield in the near future, it was able to pass them on to a group of lessors who could take advantage of these benefits. But in passing the benefits on, Anaconda appears to have negotiated lease terms favorable to its goal of maximizing shareholder wealth.

SUMMARY

In the past two decades, more and more firms have acquired the use of assets by leasing instead of purchasing them. Operating (or service) leases are short-term leases that are not fully amortized over the expected life of the asset. The rationale for operating leases is often the transfer of the risk of obsolescence from lessee to lessor. Finance leases are generally longer-lived leases by which the lessee acquires almost all the economic benefits and risks associated with the leased asset. Firms may acquire the use of assets through direct leases, sale and leaseback agreements, or leveraged leases; the analysis of any of these is the same from the lessee's standpoint. One of the most important elements to consider when leasing is the quoted lease rate—the size of the annual (or periodic) lease payments. The lease rate will have an obvious effect on the cost of leasing, so knowing how lease rates are set is important because it enables the lessee to compare alternative lease rates, and it provides a basis for effective negotiations with a lessor.

To evaluate leases, two decisions are required. First, the capital budgeting decision of whether the asset should be acquired is necessary; in addition, the financing decision of whether to lease or purchase must be made. Especially favorable lease terms may result in the decision to acquire the use of an asset even if the NPV from the capital budgeting analysis is negative. Hence, simultaneous consideration of both the investment and the financing decision is essential for correct decision making when evaluating leases. To make the lease or purchase decision properly, it is necessary to neutralize the risk differential between leasing an asset, and purchasing it with an equivalent amount of debt. This can be handled in a simple, practical way by using the after-tax cost of borrowing as the appropriate discount rate in the lease evaluation model.

A lease is evaluated by comparing the real and opportunity costs of leasing with the cost of purchasing an asset or piece of equipment. So long as the net advantage of leasing (NAL) is positive, leasing is the preferred method of financing. A number of variables affect the desirability of leasing, but perhaps the most important is the existence of differential tax rates; such differences in lessor and lessee tax rates enables both parties to maximize their benefits. Other things being equal, firms with low effective tax rates or those with substantial tax losses will generally find leasing highly advantageous. The major benefits of ownership include the investment tax credit, the depreciation tax shield, and the estimated salvage value. These should be considered, one way or another, when the lease rate is being set and when the lessee is evaluating the economic desirability of leasing.

QUESTIONS

22.1. Differentiate an operating lease from a finance lease in terms of:
   a. General nature, length, and estimated residual value.
   b. Payment of maintenance, insurance, and property taxes.

22.2. Associated Fast Foods, Inc., owns and operates a chain of fast food outlets in 15 states along the Atlantic seaboard. The company has been growing fairly rapidly over the past 3½ years, adding an average of one new restaurant a month. Such growth has placed a strain on the firm's debt capacity and has led to some minor debt service problems; as a result, the financial managers of Associated Fast Foods are thinking about using lease financing as a way to continue to expand the number of outlets (so far, none of the outlets are leased; all are owned by the company).

   a. Explain how leasing can be helpful to Associated Fast Foods under the present circumstances.

   b. Do you think it will improve the debt service position of the company? Explain.

   c. Would Associated Fast Foods be better off using leveraged leasing rather than straight finance leases?

   d. Explain how a substantial tax rate differential between lessor and lessee could improve the appeal of leasing to Associated Fast Foods.

22.3. In recent years, many firms have constructed physical facilities, such as manufacturing plants, retail stores, and restaurants, and then entered into an immediate sale and leaseback agreement. Explain fully what advantages there are to both lessee and lessor from this arrangement.

22.4. Explain the IRS requirements for leasing under the Tax Equity and Fiscal Responsibility Act of 1982. How do they differ from the accounting requirements established in FASB Statement 13? What effect do you believe these differences have on financial managers?

22.5. What legal and/or economic factors provide the incentives for leasing? Is it possible to use leasing as a way to obtain "off balance sheet" financing? Are there any real advantages to "off balance sheet" financing?

22.6. The evaluation of leasing requires the simultaneous consideration of both the investment and financing decisions. Explain why this is so. What type of error might be made if only the financing decision were considered?

22.7. In order to compare the lease and purchase alternatives correctly, it is necessary to ensure that the risk, in terms of cash flows and use of debt capacity, be the same between the lease and the implied loan.

   a. How, in simple, straightforward terms, would you explain this to your boss so that the proper decision could be made?

   b. Why is it appropriate to use the after-tax cost of the implied loan as the discount rate in the evaluation process?

22.8. Identify the three benefits of ownership and note why they are so important to the leasing decision. Then explain how they are used in lease rate setting and in evaluating the economic desirability of a lease.

22.9. Explain how the "cost" of leasing can be calculated using the basic NAL equation as a starting point. How is this cost then employed to make the lease or buy decision?

22.10. Other things being equal, explain how the following events will affect the evaluation of a lease (the calculation of the NAL). Assume that the NPV remains positive, but the following events occur before the lease or purchase decision is final.

    a. Congress passes new legislation that allows firms to employ more rapid depreciation than presently available.

    b. The investment tax credit is repealed.

    c. The company finds the estimated residual value has increased substantially due to rising land and building prices.

    d. Congress lowers the corporate tax rate.

PROBLEMS

22.1. *SETTING LEASE RATES.* Massachusetts Leasing is in the process of establishing lease rates for a number of different prospective leases. In setting lease rates, Massachusetts Leasing adjusts its required rate of return depending on the perceived risk associated with the lease; all lease payments are due in advance, and straight-line depreciation over the 5-year normal recovery period is used for all leases. Given that Massachusetts Leasing has a marginal tax rate of 40 percent, determine the annual payments required for each of the following leases:

    a. An asset requiring a cash outlay of $500,000 that will be leased over its 5-year life. There is no estimated salvage value, the ITC of 8 percent is in effect, and the required before-tax rate of return is 16.67 percent.

    b. Rework (a) given everything is the same except that there is an estimated *before-tax* salvage value of $80,000. [*Note:* Under the new tax code the asset will be depreciated to zero for tax purposes and *then* taxes will be paid on the gain realized when the asset is sold. Hence, the depreciation per year does not change from that determined in (a).]

    c. An oil drilling platform requiring a cash outlay of $20 million will be leased over a 5-year period. The platform will be depreciated to zero, the 8 percent ITC is in effect and the before-tax required rate of return is 20 percent.

    d. Rework (c) given everything is the same except that the lease is for 8 years instead of 5. (*Note:* The platform will still be depreciated over 5 years.)

22.2. *SETTING LEASE RATES: ACRS DEPRECIATION.* Remco Leasing Enterprises, which has a 40 percent marginal tax rate, is determining lease rates for a number of different pieces of equipment. It uses the ACRS depreciation method and varies its required rate of return depending on the perceived risk of the asset. Determine the following lease rates:

    a. A fleet of trucks costing $120,000 in total, which will be depreciated over their 3-year normal recovery period. The ITC (at 4 percent) is applicable, there is no salvage value, and the before-tax required rate of return is 15 percent.

b.   Rework (a) given everything is the same except that there is an estimated *before-tax* salvage value of $25,000. [*Note:* Under the new tax code the trucks will be depreciated to zero for tax purposes and *then* taxes will be paid on the gain realized when the asset is sold. Hence, the depreciation per year does not change from that determined in (a).]

c.   A computer requiring a cash outlay of $5 million, which has a 5-year normal recovery period. The 8 percent ITC is in effect, there is no salvage value, and the before-tax required rate of return is 18.33 percent.

d.   Rework (c) given everything is the same except that the lease is for 7 years instead of 5. (*Note:* The computer will still be depreciated over 5 years.)

22.3.   *LEASE EVALUATION.*   Greenman Manufacturing is thinking about leasing a piece of used equipment; the equipment is still in good shape and should be usable for another 5 years. Even though the equipment is used, it qualifies for the 8 percent ITC. The asset has an estimated salvage value of zero, straight-line depreciation will be employed over its 5-year normal recovery period if purchased, the firms marginal tax rate is 40 percent, and the before-tax borrowing rate is 16.67 percent. The equipment will cost $500,000; but it can be leased for $115,000 per year (payable at the beginning of the year for 5 years).

a.   Should Greenman Manufacturing lease or purchase the equipment (assume the NPV is highly positive)?

b.   Rework the problem using semiannual lease payments of $60,000 (payable at the beginning of each 6-month period). (*Note:* Continue to use annual depreciation.)

22.4.   *LEASE EVALUATION: ACRS DEPRECIATION.*   Cherrywood Furniture has decided to replace the equipment at one of its older lumber mills. The NPV on the new equipment is $101,400. Now Cherrywood has to decide whether to lease or purchase the new equipment, which requires an initial outlay of $2,100,000 and has a normal recovery period of 5 years, at which time the salvage value is expected to be zero. The accelerated cost recovery system depreciation is employed, the 8 percent ITC is in effect, and the firm's marginal tax rate is 40 percent. If the firm leases the equipment, the annual lease payments, payable at the beginning of each of the 5 years, will be $500,000. If the firm purchases the equipment, the before-tax cost of borrowing is 15 percent. Should Cherrywood lease or purchase the equipment?

22.5. *EFFECTIVE COST OF A LEASE.* Omaha Beef Processors, Inc., is considering the acquisition of several new assets. In all cases, the NPVs on the assets are substantial. As a result, the question now facing management is whether to lease or purchase the assets. Assume in each case that straight-line depreciation will be used, that there is no salvage value, that the assets qualify for the 8 percent or 4 percent ITC as appropriate, that the term of the lease is the same as the life of the asset, and that all lease payments are made at the beginning of the year. The following assets are being evaluated:

- *Asset A:* costs $400,000, has a 5-year life, and can be leased for $100,000 per year.
- *Asset B:* costs $500,000, has a 5-year life, and can be leased for $110,000 per year.
- *Asset C:* costs $810,000, has a 3-year life, and can be leased for $275,000 per year.

Using Equation 22.6, find the effective cost for each of these leases. If Omaha Beef has a 40 percent marginal tax rate and a before-tax cost of borrowing of 13.33 percent, should it lease any of these assets? If so, which one(s)?

22.6. *COST OF LEASING: ACRS DEPRECIATION.* San Diego Marine Supplies is investigating whether to lease or purchase some additional trucks. Their cost is $80,000, the ITC is 4 percent, ACRS depreciation over the 3-year normal recovery period will be employed, and there is no estimated salvage value for the trucks. The lease period would be for 3 years, payable in advance, and the yearly lease payment is $40,000 per year. Finally, San Diego Marine's tax rate is 40 percent, and its after-tax equivalent loan rate is 10 percent.

  a. Calculate the percentage cost of leasing the trucks. Should San Diego lease or purchase its trucks?

  b. What happens to the percentage cost of leasing and the decision if the lease payments drop $32,000 per year?

22.7. *IMPACT OF BENEFITS OF OWNERSHIP ON LEASE DECISION.* C&T Industries is evaluating a major equipment acquisition. The chief financial officer of C&T wants to evaluate the possibility of leasing the equipment, which costs $1.4 million, has a 5-year normal recovery period, and will be depreciated (on a straight-line basis) to a salvage value of zero. The equipment qualifies for the 8 percent ITC, the firm is in the 40 percent tax bracket, and its after-tax cost of borrowing is 10 percent. Lasnickle Leasing has agreed to lease the equipment to C&T for a period of 5 years at an annual lease rate of $340,000 payable at the beginning of each year. The project has a highly positive NPV.

a. Should C&T Industries lease the equipment?

b. Rework the problem if C&T negotiates with Lasnickle to receive the ITC even if the asset is leased. [*Note:* Since C&T has the ITC whether it leases or purchases the asset, the ITC term drops out of the NAL in Equation 22.5. Explain the differences in the NAL in relation to (a).]

c. Rework the problem, starting from (a), if C&T estimates that before-tax scrap proceeds would be $140,000 in year 5 if the asset is purchased. (*Note:* Under the new tax code law, the asset will still be depreciated to zero and then taxes will be paid when the asset is sold.) Explain the differences in the NAL in relation to (a).

d. Rework the problem, starting from (a), if C&T estimates that it will incur $20,000 in additional operating and maintenance expenses before taxes per year if the asset is purchased (but not if leased) and if its MCC is 17 percent. (*Note:* The operating expenses, as explained in note 17, cause leasing to be more favorable.)

22.8. *TAX RATES AND THE LEASE DECISION.* Dominion Airways needs four planes to stay in business. The planes cost $3 million each, have an expected useful life and normal recovery period of 5 years, and no expected salvage value. The planes are eligible for the 8 percent ITC, straight-line depreciation will be used if they are purchased, and the firm's before-tax cost of debt is 15 percent. If the planes are leased, the lease payments will be $3 million (in total) each year, payable at the beginning of each of the 5 years. Should Dominion lease the planes if:

a. Its marginal tax rate is 40 percent?

b. Its marginal tax rate is 20 percent? (*Note:* The firm's new marginal tax rate changes the discount rate employed.)

c. What if the firm's marginal tax rate is zero? (*Note:* This influences the discount rate, the ability of the firm to use the ITC, and the after-tax cost and benefits of the lease payments and the depreciation tax shield.)

22.9. *REQUIRED RATE OF RETURN AND COST OF LEASING.* George Scotty is the financial manager of Oklahoma Crude and is presently negotiating the terms of a possible lease with Kidwell Leasing. The leased equipment will cost $2.5 million, have a 5-year normal recovery period, and be depreciated to zero via the ACRS method. The equipment is eligible for the 8 percent ITC, and both parties agree that the estimated salvage value (after taxes are paid) in year 5 will be $500,000. Kidwell Leasing is in the 40 percent tax bracket and wants to earn a 20 percent before-tax return on the lease. It proposes to set up a 5-year lease for Oklahoma Crude, with annual lease payments being made at the beginning of the year. All benefits of ownership would be kept by Kidwell. Oklahoma Crude is an independent oil exploration and drilling company, and because of a variety of tax incentives offered to small independent oil producers, the firm's marginal tax rate is only 20 percent. Its before-tax cost of borrowing is 18 percent.

a. Find the lease rate that Kidwell will quote to Oklahoma Crude.

b. Find the effective after-tax cost of the lease to Oklahoma Crude.

c. How do you explain the difference between the after-tax required return to Kidwell and the effective after-tax cost to Oklahoma Crude?

d. Should Oklahoma Crude enter into the lease?

SELECTED REFERENCES

Anderson, Paul F., and John D. Martin. "Lease vs. Purchase Decisions: A Survey of Current Practice." *Financial Management* 6 (spring 1977), pp. 41–47.

Athanasopoulos, Peter J., and Peter W. Bacon. "The Evaluation of Leveraged Leases." *Financial Management* 9 (spring 1980), pp. 76–80.

Bower, Richard S. "Issues in Lease Financing." *Financial Management* 2 (winter 1973), pp. 25–34.

———, and George S. Oldfield, Jr. "Of Lessees, Lessors, and Discount Rates, and Whether Pigs Have Wings," *Journal of Business Research* 9 (March 1981), pp. 29–38.

Brealey, R. A., and C. M. Young. "Debt, Taxes and Leasing—A Note." *Journal of Finance* 35 (December 1980), pp. 1245–1250.

Capettini, Robert, and Howard Toole, "Designing Leveraged Leases: A Mixed Integer Linear Programming Approach." *Financial Management* 10 (autumn 1981), pp. 15–23.

Cooper, Kerry, and Robert H. Strawser. "Evaluation of Capital Investment Projects Involving Asset Leases." *Financial Management* 4 (spring 1975), pp. 44–49.

Copeland, Thomas E., and J. Fred Weston. "A Note on the Evaluation of Cancellable Operating Leases." *Financial Management* 11 (summer 1982), pp. 60–67.

Crawford, Peggy J., Charles P. Harper, and John J. McConnell. "Further Evidence on the Terms of Financial Leases." *Financial Management* 10 (autumn 1981), pp. 7–14.

Davidson, Sidney, and Roman Weil. "Lease Capitalization and Inflation Accounting." *Financial Analysts Journal* 31 (November–December 1975), pp. 22–29.

Dyl, Edward A., and Michael D. Joehnk. "Leasing as a Municipal Finance

Alternative." *Public Administration Review* 38 (November–December 1978), pp. 560–561.

Flath, David. "The Economics of Short-Term Leasing." *Economic Inquiry* 18 (April 1980), pp. 247–259.

Franks, Julian R., and Stewart D. Hodges. "Valuation of Financial Lease Contracts: A Note." *Journal of Finance* 33 (May 1978), pp. 657–669.

Gaumnitz, Jack E., and Allen Ford. "The Lease or Sell Decision." *Financial Management* 7 (winter 1978), pp. 69–74.

Gordon, Myron J. "A General Solution to the Buy or Lease Decision: A Pedagogical Note." *Journal of Finance* 29 (March 1974), pp. 245–250.

Grimlund, Richard D., and Robert Capettini. "A Note on the Evaluation of Leveraged Leases and Other Investments." *Financial Management* 11 (summer 1982), pp. 68–72.

Gritta, Richard D. "The Impact of Lease Capitalization." *Financial Analysts Journal* 30 (March–April 1974), pp. 47–52.

Hull, John C. "The Bargaining Positions of the Parties to a Lease Agreement." *Financial Management* 11 (autumn 1982), pp. 71–79.

Idol, Charles R. "A Note on Specifying Debt Displacement and Tax Shield Borrowing Opportunities in Financial Lease Valuation Models." *Financial Management* 9 (summer 1980), pp. 24–29.

Johnson, Robert W., and Wilbur G. Lewellen. "Analysis of the Lease-or-Buy Decision." *Journal of Finance* 27 (September 1972), pp. 815–823.

Kim, E. Han, Wilbur G. Lewellen, and John J. McConnell. "Sale-and-Leaseback Agreements and Enterprise Valuation." *Journal of Financial and Quantitative Analysis* 13 (December 1978), pp. 871–883.

Klein, Benjamin, Robert G. Crawford, and Armen A. Alchian. "Vertical Integration, Appropriate Rents, and the Competitive Contracting Process." *Journal of Law and Economics* 21 (October 1978), pp. 297–326.

Levy, Haim, and Yoram Landskroner. "Lease Financing: Cost Versus Liquidity." *Engineering Economist* 27 (fall 1981), pp. 59–69.

———, and Marshall Sarnat. "Leasing, Borrowing and Financial Risk." *Financial Management* 8 (winter 1979), pp. 47–54.

Lewellen, Wilbur G., and Douglas R. Emery. "On the Matter of Parity Among Financial Obligations." *Journal of Finance* 35 (March 1980), pp. 97–111.

———, Michael L. Long, and John J. McConnell. "Asset Leasing in Competitive Capital Markets." *Journal of Finance* 31 (June 1976), pp. 787–798.

Long, Michael S. "Leasing and the Cost of Capital." *Journal of Financial and Quantitative Analysis* 12 (November 1977), pp. 579–598.

McConnell, John J., and James S. Schallheion. "Valuation of Asset Leasing Contracts." *Journal of Financial Economics* 12 (August 1983), pp. 237–261.

McGugan, Vincent J., and Richard E. Caves. "Integration and Competition in the Equipment Leasing Industry." *Journal of Business* 47 (July 1974), pp. 382–396.

Miller, Merton H., and Charles W. Upton. "Leasing, Buying, and the Cost of Capital Services." *Journal of Finance* 31 (June 1976), pp. 761–786.

Myers, Stewart C., David A. Dill, and Alberto J. Bautista. "Valuation of Financial Lease Contracts." *Journal of Finance* 31 (June 1976), pp. 799–819.

O'Brien, Thomas J., and Bennie H. Nunnally, Jr. "A 1982 Survey of Corporate Leasing Analysis. "*Financial Management* 12 (summer 1983), pp. 30–36.

Ofer, Aharon R. "The Evaluation of the Lease Versus Purchase Alternatives." *Financial Management* 5 (summer 1976), pp. 67–74.

Perg, Wayne F. "Leveraged Leasing: The Problem of Changing Leverage." *Financial Management* 7 (autumn 1978), pp. 47–51.

Schachner, Leopold. "The New Accounting for Leases." *Financial Executive* 46 (February 1978), pp. 40–47.

Smith, Bruce D. "Accelerated Debt Repayment in Leveraged Leases." *Financial Management* 11 (summer 1982), pp. 73–80.

Sorensen, Ivar W., and Ramon E. Johnson. "Equipment Financial Leasing Practices and Costs: An Empirical Study." *Financial Management* 6 (spring 1977), pp. 33–40.

Van Horne, James C. "The Cost of Leasing with Capital Market Imperfections." *Engineering Economist* 23 (fall 1977), pp. 1–12.

Appendix 22A

Simultaneous Capital Budgeting–Lease Evaluation Decisions

Most of the time, when a proposed capital project is under evaluation, the financial manager will obtain a measure of its expected profitability (via some present-value technique like NPV) and use such information as the basis for the investment decision (these procedures were discussed in Chapters 12, 13, 14, 15 and 16). However, whenever there is a strong possibility of leasing, the lease evaluation question itself should become part of the capital budgeting decision. This has to be done because the benefits of leasing may contribute to the NPV of the project. The lease is evaluated by using the lease evaluation model discussed in the chapter (Equation 22.5). If the NAL is positive, leasing is preferred to purchasing the asset, and the NAL value should be subtracted from the purchase price of the asset in question before the traditional capital budgeting process is undertaken. In practice, the whole procedure usually begins with the capital budgeting decision and the computation of NPV; then for any project that has a serious chance of implementation (regardless of whether NPV is positive or not), NAL is determined for those assets that would probably be leased if attractive terms could be arranged; finally, for those leases that result in positive NALs, the NPV of the project is adjusted as follows: Adjusted $NPV = NPV + NAL$. The NPV is adjusted to reflect the fact that the asset will be leased rather than purchased (as is assumed in standard NPV computations). The adjusted net present value is then used to rank the project for the purpose of deciding which capital projects to implement. If the NAL is negative, leasing is ignored, and the capital budgeting decision is made on the basis of the unadjusted NPV alone.

To demonstrate the impact of leasing on the capital budgeting decision, consider Troy Industries, which is contemplating the acquisi-

TABLE 22A.1
The Capital Budgeting Evaluation of an Asset That Can Be Leased

GIVEN:

Initial cost, CLA_0, = \$5000

Normal recovery period = 5 years

Estimated salvage value = \$0

Investment tax credit, ITC, = 0%

Straight-line depreciation;
  Dep_t = \$1000 per year

Lease payment, LP_t, = \$1100 per year

$CFBT_t$ = \$1800 per year

MCC = 14%

Tax rate = 40%

After-tax cost of debt = 6%

Length of lease = 5 years

ANALYSIS OF THE INVESTMENT DECISION (COMPUTE NPV)

$$NPV = -CLA_0 + [CFBT_t(1 - T) + Dep_t(T)](PVIFA_{14\%, 5\,yr})$$
$$= -\$5000 + [\$1800(.60) + \$1000(.40)](3.433)$$
$$= -\$5000 + (\$1480)(3.433)$$
$$= -\$5000 + \$5080.84 = \$80.84$$

LEASE VERSUS PURCHASE ANALYSIS (COMPUTE NAL)

$$NAL = CLA_0 - [LP_0(1 - T) + LP_t(1 - T)(PVIFA_{6\%\,4\,yr}) + Dep_t(T)(PVIFA_{6\%, 5\,yr})]$$
$$= \$5000 - [\$1100(1 - .40) + \$1100(1 - .40)(3.465) + \$1000(.40)(4.212)]$$
$$= \$5000 - [\$660 + \$660(3.465) + \$400(4.212)]$$
$$= \$5000 - (\$660 + \$2287 + \$1685) = \$368$$

ADJUSTED NET PRESENT VALUE ANALYSIS TAKING INTO ACCOUNT THE DECISION TO LEASE (COMPUTE ADJUSTED NPV)

$$\text{Adjusted } NPV = NPV + NAL$$
$$= \$80.84 + \$368.00 = \$448.84$$

tion of a new grinding machine at a cost of \$5000; the machine can be purchased or leased. As shown in Table 22A.1, there is no salvage value or ITC, and straight-line depreciation will be employed over its 5-year normal recovery period. The cash flow for capital budgeting purposes, $CFBT_t$, is estimated to be \$1800 per year, the firm's marginal tax rate is 40 percent, the lease payments, LP_t, will be \$1100 per year (commencing in t_0 and running through t_4), the firm's MCC is 14 percent and the after-tax cost of debt, k_i, is 6 percent. Table 22A.1 shows the steps involved in analyzing this project; note the evaluation starts with the calculation of the project's NPV, which is a positive \$80.84. Hence, the new grinder should be acquired; the question now is should it be leased or purchased? Employing Equation 22.5, the net advantage of leasing (NAL) is found to be \$368. Since NAL is positive, the firm maximizes shareholder wealth by leasing rather than purchasing the grinder. As such, NPV must be adjusted to reflect the fact that the machine will be leased. This is done at the bottom of Table 22A.1, which shows an adjusted NPV of \$448.84. Clearly, because the asset will be leased rather than purchased, its profitability has improved substantially, and by using the adjusted NPV, the proposal has much greater appeal from a capital budgeting perspective and may even move up a notch or two in the ranking of proposed capital projects.

In this example, the NPV of the original analysis was positive, indicating that the asset should be acquired. However, consider the situation if the $CFBT_t$ had been only \$1700 per year instead of \$1800. Recalculating the NPV yields:

$$NPV = -\$5000 + [\$1700(.60) + \$1000(.40)] \,(3.433)$$
$$= -\$5000 + (\$1420) \,(3.433)$$
$$= -\$5000 + \$4874.86 = -\$125.14$$

Does the negative NPV mean the grinder should be rejected? No, that decision (when leasing is available) cannot be made until after the NAL analysis is also considered. Favorable lease terms may make the acquisition feasible, even though it would not be undertaken if the asset had to be purchased. For Troy Industries, adjustment of the NPV figure, taking into account the leasing of the asset, yields an adjusted NPV of:

$$\text{Adjusted } NPV = NPV + NAL$$
$$= -\$125.14 + \$368.00 = \$242.86$$

The favorable lease terms more than offset the initial negative NPV and lead to the final conclusion that the grinder should be acquired by leasing. This simultaneous approach is crucial in the lease versus buy decision in order to ensure that both the financing and investment decisions are considered. Favorable leasing terms can make the acquisition of an asset feasible when it otherwise would be rejected.

Occasionally a firm must evaluate the acquisition of an asset that is only available if it is leased. In such a situation, the financing and the investment decisions are made concurrently. The previous NPV-NAL procedure is inappropriate for evaluating whether the use of the asset should be acquired. Although no approach is entirely without problems, in the case where an asset can only be leased, the best procedure is to evaluate the project based on its investment merits alone. The first step would be to determine the present value of the benefits expected from the project, ignoring the lease payments associated with the lease financing. Thus, the after-tax cash flow $[CFBT_t \,(1 - T)]$ would be calculated and discounted at the firm's marginal cost of capital, MCC. Then, the cost of the lease would be determined and placed on a present-value basis by multiplying the after-tax lease payments $[LP_t \,(1 - T)]$ by the appropriate after-tax borrowing rate. If the present value of the benefits is greater than the present value of the lease payments, the asset should be acquired by leasing; otherwise, the firm should reject the project.

PROBLEMS

22A.1. *SIMULTANEOUS CAPITAL BUDGETING–LEASE EVALUATION DECISIONS.* Time Saver Inc., operates a chain of grocery convenience stores in the Northeast. To improve its distribution efficiency, the firm is contemplating modernization of its warehouse facilities and replacement of its equipment. In a separate analysis, it has already decided that the warehouse should be modernized. Now it is considering whether the existing equipment—trucks, forklifts, and the like—should be replaced. The equipment has a useful life and normal recovery period of 5 years, requires an initial outlay of $4.5 million, the ITC of 8 percent is in effect, and straight-line depreciation will be employed to depreciate the equipment to a salvage value of zero. Time Saver's marginal tax rate is 40 percent, and the estimated cash flows before taxes, $CFBT_t$, for capital budgeting purposes are $1.5 million for each of 5 years. The firm's marginal cost of capital is 15 percent. Two methods of financing the equipment exist. It can be purchased, or it can be leased at $1 million per year, with the lease payments to occur at the beginning of each year. The firm's before-tax cost of borrowing is 16.67 percent.

a. Compute the NPV of the capital budgeting decision. Should the equipment be replaced?

b. Irrespective of your answer to (a), find the NAL of leasing the equipment.

c. If the NAL in (b) is positive, compute the adjusted NPV of the project.

d. Explain why both the investment and the financing decisions have to be considered before a firm can decide whether to lease or buy the assets.

22A.2. *ASSET THAT CAN ONLY BE LEASED.*   Gulf Shipping is considering leasing dock facilities on the Mississippi River near New Orleans from the Lower Mississippi Port Authority. Gulf Shipping would use the facilities for 5 years. To use the dock facilities, Gulf would be required to spend $150,000 immediately to put equipment in a building; after 5 years the equipment becomes the property of the Lower Mississippi Port Authority. The CFATs (*note:* these are after-tax cash flows) expected are $100,000 in year 1, $200,000 in year 2, and $300,000 in each of years 3, 4, and 5. The Port Authority requires lease payments of $230,000 per year payable at the beginning of the year. Gulf estimates the implied after-tax cost of comparable leases to be 10 percent. Gulf Shipping's marginal cost of capial is 18 percent, and its marginal tax rate is 40 percent. Should Gulf Shipping undertake the project and lease the dock facilities, or should it reject the project?

23

Convertibles, Warrants, and Options

Unlike the financing vehicles examined in previous chapters, the securities we examine in this chapter are unique in that they provide holders with the option to convert to, acquire, or sell shares of common stock in a specified company. That is, a *convertible*—initially issued as a bond or preferred stock—permits the holder to convert the security into shares of the issuing firm's common stock (at no cost to the investor). A *warrant*, in contrast, is generally attached to a bond issue and enables the holder to acquire the issuing firm's common stock (or in some cases, bonds) at a special price. Finally, there are two types of stock options: a *put*, which gives the holder the right to sell 100 shares of a stipulated stock at a specified price over a set period of time; and a *call*, which gives the holder the right to buy the stock under the same conditions. Convertible securities and warrants are issued by firms as a way to raise capital. This is not the case with options: they are not issued by the corporations on whose shares of stock the option is written, but instead are created by investors. Convertible securities and warrants are not used as extensively as other forms of financing (except, perhaps, for preferred stock); even so, they do increase the financing alternatives of the firm, and provide the financial manager with additional ways of raising long-term capital. We will examine the key characteristics of convertible securities and warrants, and consider the costs and risks associated with using them as a source of funds. In addition, listed stock options and the implications they hold for financial management will be briefly considered—with an extensive discussion of the option pricing model provided in Appendix 23A.

Convertible Securities

Convertible securities are hybrid forms of financing that combine features of both debt and equity; they are used predominantly by low- and medium-quality firms as a way to raise capital. In 1980, there were

212 securities issued with conversion or warrant features. They had a total par value of some $6.3 billion, and most of them were convertibles. Of the total amount, $5.4 billion (116 issues) were convertible securities, and the balance ($900 million and 96 issues) were securities with warrants attached. Largely because of the tax subsidy available on debt, most convertible securities are issued as bonds (generally as debentures), though some are issued as preferreds. In 1980, for example, new convertible bond issues dominated new convertible preferreds by a ratio of better than 3 to 1. Although convertible preferreds enjoyed rather widespread use in financing mergers from 1960 through 1968, subsequent changes in tax and accounting treatment no longer encourage their use.[1] Regardless of the type, convertible securities carry a provision that allows the holder, within a stipulated time period, to convert the issue into a certain number of shares of the issuing corporation's common stock. Generally, there is little or no cash involved at the time of conversion, since the investor merely trades in the convertible security for shares of the company's stock. The firm raises no new capital at the time of conversion, even though the conversion will affect the number of shares of common stock outstanding, the debt-equity ratio, and other leverage measures.

Issue Characteristics

The key element of any convertible issue is its *conversion privilege*, which stipulates the conditions and specific nature of the conversion feature. To begin with, it states exactly when the issue can be converted. Generally, there will be an initial waiting period of 6 months to perhaps 3 to 5 years after the date of issue, during which time the security cannot be converted; then the conversion period begins and the issue can be converted. Although the conversion period typically extends for the rest of the life of the issue, it may exist for only a certain number of years.[2] This is done to provide the issuing firm with more control over its capital structure. If an issue has not been converted by the end of its conversion

---

[1]See George E. Pinches, "Financing with Convertible Preferred Stock, 1960–1967," *Journal of Finance* 25 (March 1970), pp. 53–63; Ronald W. Melicher, "Financing with Convertible Preferred Stock: Comment," *Journal of Finance* 26 (March 1971), pp. 144–147; Jerry J. Weygandt, "A Comment on Financing with Convertible Preferred Stock, 1960–1967," *Journal of Finance* 26 (March 1971), pp. 148–149; and George E. Pinches, "Financing with Convertible Preferred Stock, 1960–1967: Reply," *Journal of Finance* 26 (March 1971), pp. 150–151.

[2]James E. Walter and Agustin V. Que, "The Valuation of Convertible Bonds," *Journal of Finance* 28 (June 1973), pp. 713–732, indicated that 31.5 percent of 108 convertible bonds they examined had conversion privileges that expired prior to maturity; with two exceptions the length of these conversion privileges was 10 years. Similarly Pinches, "Financing with Convertible Preferred Stock, 1960–1967," found that 59 out of 335 convertible preferred stocks issued between 1960 and 1967 had limited conversion period privileges. An examination of the convertible bonds listed in *Moody's Bond Record* suggests that the vast majority of convertible bonds outstanding have conversion privileges that extend over the entire life of the bond.

period, it reverts to a straight debt issue (with no conversion privileges) for the remainder of its term to maturity.

Perhaps the most important provision of a convertible security is its conversion ratio, which stipulates the number of shares of common stock into which the security can be converted. That is, conversion ratio is found as:

$$\text{Conversion ratio} = \frac{\text{par value of the convertible security}}{\text{conversion price}} \qquad (23.1)$$

In Equation 23.1, conversion price is the stated "price" per share at which the stock will be delivered upon conversion, and as such, represents the effective price that will be paid for the shares. (Conversion ratio and conversion price are obviously interrelated—for example, a $1000 convertible bond with a conversion ratio of 20 means that the stock carries a conversion price of $50; either one can be found, given the other.) One noteworthy difference between a convertible bond and a convertible preferred is that while the conversion ratio on a bond generally involves large numbers of common stock (such as 15, 20, or 30 shares), the conversion ratio of a preferred is usually very small, often being less than 1 share of stock and seldom exceeding more than 3 or 4 shares.

The conversion ratio normally is fixed over the conversion period, although some convertibles are issued with conversion ratios that decrease over the conversion period to reflect an expected steadily increasing value for the equity. As a rule the conversion ratio is also adjusted for stock splits and significant stock dividends. When the ratio includes fractional shares of common (as it often does), the conversion privilege will specify how any fractional shares are to be handled: Either the investor can put up the additional funds necessary to purchase another full share of the stock at the stated conversion price, or the issuing firm pays the investor the cash equivalent of the fractional share. Table 23.1 lists selected issue characteristics for a number of actively traded convertible bonds and preferreds, and a variety of conversion privileges. Except for these privileges, convertible securities normally carry the same types of provisions (call features, sinking funds, and the like) as other debt and preferred stock issues.

Valuation
of Convertible
Securities

The market value of a convertible debenture is a function of both the bond and the stock dimensions of the issue. (For convenience, we will deal only with convertible bonds; however, it should be clear that the same concepts, with appropriate modifications, can be applied to the valuation of convertible preferreds.) Convertibles will trade much like their underlying common stock whenever the market price of the stock approximates or exceeds the stated conversion price. In sharp contrast, when the price of the common is depressed, so that it is trading well

TABLE 23.1
Selected Issue Characteristics of
Some Actively Traded Convertible Securities[a]

Issuer	Year Issued	Coupon Rate	Maturity	Conversion Price	Conversion Ratio	Conversion Period	Current Price of Common	Current Price of Convertible
CONVERTIBLE BONDS								
A. G. Edwards	1981	10 1/2%	2006	$25.00	40.00	Until 2006	$23	102
Pittston International	1978	9.20	2004	50.00	20.00	Until 2004	29 1/2	84 1/4
RCA	1967	4 1/2	1992	59.00	16.95	Until 1992	21 1/8	53 1/2
Santa Fe Industries	1968	6 1/4	1998	10.67	93.72	Until 1998	25 1/2	233 1/2
Southern Bankcorp	1981	10	1996	13.00	76.92	Until 1996	11	102
Pfizer	1972	4	1997	47.50	21.05	Until 1997	48	101 1/4
CONVERTIBLE PREFERRED STOCKS								
Am. Tel. & Tel. (par = $50)	1971	$4.00	NA	$47.62	1.05	Life of preferred	$55 1/2	57 5/8
Atlantic Richfield (par = $70)	1969	2.80	NA	29.17	2.40	Life of preferred	48 1/2	114 1/2
Bristol-Myers (par = $50)	1968	2.00	NA	47.17	1.06	Life of preferred	50 1/2	53 1/2
Ingersol Rand (par = $47.50)	1969	2.35	NA	79.17	0.60	Life of preferred	59 1/4	36 1/2
Travelers (par = $50)	1966	2.00	NA	45.45	1.10	Life of preferred	43 5/8	41 1/2
Western Union (par = $100)	1966	4.60	NA	47.17	2.12	Life of preferred	22 1/4	47 1/2

[a]As of July 24, 1981. For the convertible bonds, the price is a percentage of par; a price of 233 1/2 is equivalent to $2335.
SOURCES: *Moody's Bond Record; Moody's Industrial Manual; Moody's Transportation Manual; Moody's Public Utility Manual; Moody's Bank and Finance Manual; Standard & Poor's Stock Guide; Standard and Poor's Bond Guide;* and *The Wall Street Journal,* various issues.

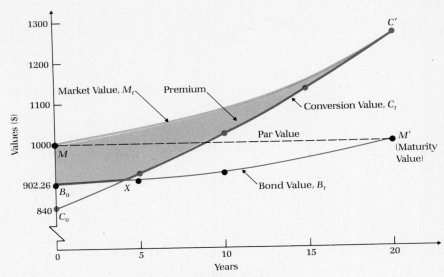

Figure 23.1   A Model Of Convertible Bond Valuation.

Note: Values based on Memorial Steel's 7 percent, 20-year convertible bond, where straight bonds yield 8 percent.

below the conversion price, the convertible will lose its ties to the underlying common and begin to trade as a bond, in accordance with prevailing market yields on comparable (nonconvertible) debt issues. The value of a convertible, therefore, hinges on expected interest income from the bond portion of the issue, as well as anticipated capital appreciation in the convertible security itself, which derives ultimately from the expected price behavior of the underlying stock.

The expected return on the bond portion of a convertible is a function of the coupon rate on the issue and the price paid for the bond. Expected capital appreciation, on the other hand, is not so simple. It depends on (1) the relationship between the stock price at time of issue and the conversion price, and (2) the expected growth rate in the price of the stock. In order to understand the various stock-bond relationships of a convertible issue, consider Figure 23.1, which provides a graphic description of a new convertible bond being considered by the Memorial Steel Corporation.[3] To simplify the analysis we initially assume that (1)

---

[3]This model is based on Eugene F. Brigham, "An Analysis of Convertible Debentures: Theory and Some Empirical Evidence," *Journal of Finance* 21 (March 1966), pp. 35–54. An alternative approach to valuing contingent claim securities, such as convertible bonds, employs the option pricing model; see Appendix 23A, and Michael J. Brennan and Eduardo S. Schwartz, "Convertible Bonds: Valuation and Optimal Strategies for Call and Converting," *Journal of Finance* 32 (December 1977), pp. 1699–1715; or Jonathan E. Ingersoll, Jr., "A Contingent-Claim Valuation of Convertible Securities," *Journal of Financial Economics* 4 (May 1977), pp. 289–322.

the bond market is stable and interest rates do not change over the life of the bond; (2) Memorial Steel's common stock price is expected to grow at a constant compound rate of 2 percent per year;[4] and (3) the bond has a fixed conversion ratio of 20, no sinking fund requirements, and the firm does not plan to call the bond prior to maturity. The par value of Memorial's convertible, M, is $1000, which is also the anticipated initial price of the bond.[5]

Bond Value.   Every convertible debenture has a floor below which the price of the issue will not fall. This price floor is defined by the issue's *bond value*, which indicates the price at which the bond would trade if it were nonconvertible and priced at or near prevailing market yields for comparable straight debt issues (in essence, this is the price at which the convertible would trade when the market price of the underlying stock is very low). We assume that Memorial's convertible bond will be issued with a coupon of 7 percent, even though the firm's investment bankers have indicated that comparably rated nonconvertible issues would carry a coupon of 8 percent. The straight bond value is determined in the same manner as the value of any nonconvertible bond; that is, according to the present value of the annuity of interest payments, plus the present value of the bond at maturity. As described in Chapter 7, the value of a bond, B_t, is detemined by:

$$B_t = \sum_{t=1}^{n} \frac{I_n}{(1 + k_i)^t} + \frac{M}{(1 + k_i)^n} \tag{23.2}$$

where I = amount of interest paid each year (annual interest payments are assumed for simplicity)

M = par or maturity value

k_i = appropriate rate of return on a straight bond

n = number of years until the bond matures

Since comparable-quality nonconvertible bonds carry an 8 percent coupon, the initial value (B_0) of Memorial's convertibles, based solely on their straight bond value, is:

$$B_0 = \sum_{t=1}^{20} \frac{\$70}{(1.08)^t} + \frac{\$1000}{(1.08)^{20}}$$

$$= \$70 \, (PVIFA_{8\%, \, 20 \, yr}) + \$1000 \, (PVIF_{8\%, \, 20 \, yr})$$

$$= \$70 \, (9.818) + \$1000 \, (.215)$$

$$= \$687.26 + \$215.00 = \$902.26$$

---

[4]The expected growth rate of 2 percent per year was specified purposefully low to maintain the graphic appearance of Figure 23.1; as discussed later in this chapter, firms with very low expected growth rates normally do not find convertible financing particularly attractive.

[5]For simplicity, we ignore flotation costs until we consider the cost of capital to the issuing firm.

Repeating Equation 23.2 for different years to maturity allows us to graph the convertible's bond value, as depicted by line B_0XM' in Figure 23.1.

Conversion Value.   *Conversion value* is an indication of what a convertible should trade for if it were priced to sell on the basis of its stock value; it denotes the market value that would be received upon conversion. To find conversion value, simply multiply the conversion ratio by the current market price of the underlying stock. For example, if Memorial's common stock is trading at $42 per share at the time the convertible is issued, then (with a conversion ratio of 20) the original conversion value of this convertible security is: $20 \times 42 = \$840$; this is designated at C_0 in Figure 23.1. To estimate the expected behavior of conversion value at any time in the future, we can use the constant growth model for valuing common stocks, originally presented in Chapter 7. That is, given that the stock price is expected to grow at a constant rate, g, it follows that the expected conversion value, C_t, of a convertible security can be determined as:

$$C_t = P_0 (1 + g)^t R \tag{23.3}$$

where P_0 = initial price of the common stock
g = expected rate of growth in the price of the stock—note that $(1 + g)^t$ is the future-value interest factor, $FVIF_{g,t}$ for g percent rate of return in year t
R = conversion ratio

The expected conversion value for Memorial Steel's convertible bond over time is traced by line C_0XC' in Figure 23.1. For example, 5 years hence ($t = 5$), the conversion value will be:

$$\begin{aligned} C_5 &= P_0 \, (FVIF_{2\%,\,5\,yr})R \\ &= \$42 \, (1.104) \, 20 \\ &= \$927.36 \end{aligned}$$

Expected conversion values can be found for any other year employing Equation 23.2; note that by year 20, it grows to $1248.24.

Price Premiums.   A convertible security will never sell below its value as a straight bond for long—if it did, bond investors would quickly start buying up the convertible and drive its market price back up to the bond value floor (line B_0XM' in Figure 23.1). Similarly, a convertible will not sell below its conversion value (line C_0XC'). If it did, arbitragers would buy the bond and convert it in order to purchase the common stock at a "bargain price," thus driving its price back up to conversion value. The lines B_0XM' and C_0XC', therefore, serve as floors below which the price of the convertible cannot fall. Since the higher of the two floors dominates (a

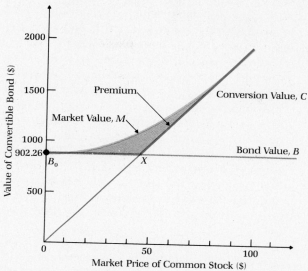

Figure 23.2 Relationship Among Straight Bond Value, Conversion Value, and Premium.

Note: Values based on Memorial Steel's 7 percent, 20-year convertible bond, where straight bonds yield 8 percent.

convertible will always sell at the higher of its bond or conversion values), the bond line B_0XM' forms an effective *market floor* for the convertible. However, a convertible security will typically sell at a premium over its theoretical market floor; that is, as seen in Figure 23.1, the market price, M_t, of a convertible is such that M_t usually exceeds both B_t and C_t (see line MC'). The actual size of the price premium depends on the relationship between the issue's conversion value, C_t, and its bond value, B_t. For, other things being equal, when bond value and conversion value are close to each other—regardless of which is greater—the premium is generally high; when the bond value and conversion value are far apart, the premium is low.

Figure 23.2 indicates the relationship, as of the issue date, between the straight bond value and conversion value for Memorial Steel's convertible bonds.[6] The market floor is given by the horizontal line beginning at $902.26, extending to point X, and continuing upward to the right along

---

[6]The assumptions underlying Figure 23.2 are slightly different from those embodied in Figure 23.1. In the earlier figure, the *expected* relationship over the entire life of the bond was presented; in Figure 23.2 the situation as of a *specific point in time* is considered. Thus, the straight bond value is fixed at $902.26. Likewise, growth (g) in the common stock price is ignored; however, the common stock price is *allowed to change* to examine the impact of possible changes in the market price of the firm's common stock on both the conversion value and premium of the convertible security.

the conversion value line, C. Let us first examine the behavior of the conversion premium when the market floor is equal to the bond value of the security. This is depicted in Figure 23.2 as the horizontal bold line running between the two points B_0 and X. With the market price of the common stock at $42 per share, the conversion value of $840 is reasonably close to the straight bond value of $902.26; therfore, the conversion premium is relatively high. It is high because of the potential upside returns that would accompany an increase in the market price of the firm's common stock (as indicated by the conversion value line.) However, consider what happens if the market price of the stock suddenly drops to $25 per share. At this price, the conversion value is $500, well below the straight debt value of the security. Thus, since the potential value of the conversion feature (that is, the stock dimension of the convertible security) is worth very little, the premium is likewise very low.

Now if the market price of Memorial's stock increases to $47 per share, then the conversion value of $940 exceeds the bond value; the market floor is now defined by the conversion value of the issue. We are now on the bold line XC at a point just above X. In this case, conversion and bond values are still close and the conversion premium remains relatively high, due to both the upside potential that remains in the conversion feature and the limited downside risk provided by the nearness of the convertible's bond floor. Finally, consider the situation that occurs if the market price of Memorial's stock increases to $80 per share. At this price, the conversion value of $1600 is well above the bond value of $902.26. The premium, therefore, is relatively small (almost nonexistent) because of the substantial downside risk that now exists. If the stock price should retreat, the convertible has a long way to fall before it hits its bond floor.[7]

The principal reason for the price premium over both the conversion value and straight debt value is the unusual appeal of a convertible as both a bond and a stock. It offers the holder downside protection, together with the opportunity to participate in upward movements in the price of the underlying common stock. Thus, the distribution of possible returns is favorably skewed to the right. Because of the skewed nature of the distribution of possible outcomes, the convertible security should have more value, the greater the volatility in the market price for the firm's common stock. To the extent that investors have limited downside risk plus unlimited upside potential, it follows that the wider the probability distribution of possible common stock prices, the higher the expected rate of return on the convertible. The actual market

---

[7]Although we assume (for simplicity) that the firm does not intend to call before maturity, in practice most companies do not plan to leave their convertibles outstanding to maturity. In fact, as conversion values increase, the possibility of the firm calling the bond increases as well, which also contributes to a smaller conversion premium—new and potential investors obviously are not willing to pay a high premium if there is a good chance they will lose it all when the bond is called.

behavior of convertible securities, however, has not quite lived up to these conceptual expectations, particularly with regard to its downside risk protection. Our discussion up to now has assumed that interest rates do not change over the life of the issue. Unfortunately, in reality, market interest rates have not only risen sharply since the late 1960s, but they have become highly volatile as well. Hence, the bond floor that is intended to limit downside risk has become unstable and to some extent unreliable. This dramatic shift in market interest rates, along with low stock prices, explains why many convertibles were trading at half their par values in the late 1970s and early 1980s. While the limited downside risk idea appears initially attractive, evidence suggests that the bond value contributes less to the worth of a convertible security than is generally believed.[8]

Financing Strategies

Because a convertible security is a bond (or preferred stock) with features of a common stock, it must be packaged at the time of issue in a manner that makes it attractive to potential investors while maximizing the value of the firm to existing shareholders. This tradeoff is admittedly difficult to achieve, because the features that make a convertible security attractive to potential investors are the same ones that are potentially detrimental to existing shareholders. Here we will examine some of the managerial dimensions of convertible securities, including aspects of issue packaging, the matter of issue timing, and corporate conversion policy.

Packaging Convertible Securities. Surveys of corporate motives for using convertible bonds have indicated that the majority of issuing firms regard convertible issues as a way of raising deferred equity capital at an attractive price; only a small number look on them as a means of selling low-cost debt.[9] Yet to consider convertible bonds as an "either-or" situation is not altogether correct. For evidence suggests that the realized rates of return on convertible securities are higher than the realized returns on the issuing firm's bonds.[10] Similarly, the beta or market risk of convertible bonds is generally less than or equal to the beta risk of the issuing firm's common stock.[11]

---

[8]See Walter and Que, "The Valuation of Convertible Bonds."

[9]See James C. Pilcher, *Raising Capital with Convertible Securities* (Ann Arbor: University of Michigan, 1955); and Brigham, "An Analysis of Convertible Debentures: Theory and Some Empirical Evidence."

[10]See Robert M. Soldofsky, "Yield-Risk Performance of Convertible Securities," *Financial Analysts Journal* 27 (March–April 1971): pp. 61–65, 79.

[11]A. W. Frankle and C. A. Hawkins, "Beta Coefficients for Convertible Bonds," *Journal of Finance* 30 (March 1975): pp. 207–210, indicate that the convertible bond beta will always be less than the beta on the underlying common stock except, perhaps, when the conversion value is so low that the option value is nonexistent. Walter and Que, "The Valuation of Convertible Bonds," in investigating betas for 13 convertible bonds and their associated common stocks, found that the beta values for 12 of the 13 common stocks surpassed their convertible bond counterparts.

Two features that are important in designing a convertible security are the issue's bond value and its conversion value. Although not a perfect tradeoff, one would expect that, other things being equal, a lower bond coupon would be accompanied by a reduced conversion price. As a practical matter, because convertibles are treated as deferred equity by most issuing companies, the incentive is for management to set the conversion price as high as possible to reduce future earnings dilution when the securities are converted. As we will see below, the benefit of this tactic is that the higher the conversion price on the underlying common stock, the fewer the number of shares that must be issued by the firm on conversion. But if the conversion price is set too far above the prevailing market price of the stock, the convertible security will have to be sold as a fixed-income obligation with a yield commensurate with what the firm would pay on a straight debt issue. For this reason, there are practical limits on how high the conversion price can be set; generally, most convertibles are issued at price premiums of about 10 to 20 percent over the issue's underlying conversion value. That is, the common stock carries a conversion price that is 10 to 20 percent above the market price of the stock at the time the convertible is issued. If the common stock is trading in the market at $50 per share, a 20 percent conversion premium would result in a conversion price of $60. In exchange for a reasonably priced conversion premium, the issuing company will be able to obtain a coupon on the bond portion of the issue that is 1 to 3 percentage points below comparably rated nonconvertible bond yields; and at times, the yield differential may be even greater. For example, a company could issue a convertible bond with a coupon of, say, 10 percent at a time when it should be paying 12 to 15 percent for straight debt obligations. The payoff to the company for having to use a conversion price that may be less than desired is a bond coupon rate well below that of the market.

Creditors in general do not like to see convertible bonds issued with a claim on income and assets equal to their own, so virtually all convertible bonds are subordinated. In addition, most convertible bonds issued in recent years have been unsecured. As such, convertible bonds are typically issued as subordinated convertible debentures. With regard to issue characteristics, most convertibles have fixed conversion prices,[12] and conversion periods that extend for the full life of the issue (or for a minimum of at least 15 years). This is done to maximize the deferred equity appeal of the conversion privilege. Also, virtually all convertibles

---

[12]As noted earlier in the chapter, most convertibles have a provision protecting the convertible against stock splits and stock dividends; in addition, there is generally a clause in the indenture that adjusts the conversion price for the sale of new common stock at prices below the conversion price. The typical provision states that if common stock is sold at a price below the stated conversion price, the conversion price must be lowered to the price at which the stock was issued.

TABLE 23.2
Earnings Per Share
for Memorial Steel
Before and After
Conversion[a]

	Convertible Debenture Outstanding	After Conversion
Earnings before interest and taxes (EBIT)	$14,000,000	$14,000,000
Less: Interest (0.07 × $15,000,000)	1,050,000	0
Earnings before taxes (EBT)	$12,950,000	$14,000,000
Less: Taxes (40%)	5,180,000	5,600,000
Earning after taxes (EAT or NI)	$ 7,770,000	$ 8,400,000
Number of common shares outstanding	2,000,000	2,300,000
Earnings per share (EPS)	$3.89	$3.65

[a]Figures based on Memorial Steel's 7 percent, 20-year convertible bond.

are issued as freely callable obligations, though a few do have deferred call provisions.

When a convertible issue is being considered by a firm, the present shareholders tend to recognize the potential dilution in their position before the actual conversion takes place. To illustrate this effect, consider once again the 7 percent, $15 million convertible debenture being considered by Memorial Steel; with a conversion price of $50, there will be 300,000 new shares issued if full conversion takes place ($15 million/$50 = 300,000 shares). Given that the firm's current earnings before interest and taxes (EBIT) are $14 million, that there is no other debt outstanding, that the firm presently has 2 million shares of common stock outstanding, and that its marginal tax rate is 40 percent, we can determine the company's earnings per share before and after conversion, as shown in Table 23.2. Note that earnings per share of $3.89 drops to $3.65 after conversion takes place. Conversion has a favorable effect to the extent that it reduces (in this case, eliminates) interest expense and therefore increases earnings; however, conversion also increases the number of shares outstanding. As a result, the net effect on the firm's EPS in unfavorable.[13]

Although potential dilution clearly does exist, the use of a convertible issue may still be attractive. As a form of deferred equity financing, the use of a convertible will result in less dilution, both now and in the future compared to what would occur if the company decides to go directly with a new common stock. Consider, for example, what would

---

[13]Based on actions by the Accounting Principles Board (Earnings Per Share, *Opinion No. 15*, 1969), firms with convertibles or warrants outstanding must report earnings per share in two ways: (1) *primary* earnings per share, based on the present number of outstanding shares of common stock; and (2) *fully diluted* earnings per share, which shows what they would be if all convertibles and warrants had been converted or exercised prior to the reporting date. For firms with large amounts of these securities outstanding, the differences can be substantial. The purpose of this requirement is to give investors a more accurate picture of the potential dilution inherent in convertible security or warrant financing.

have happened to Memorial Steel if it had employed direct common stock financing rather than the convertible issue as the way to raise the needed $15 million in capital. In this case, by selling the common stock at $42 per share, the firm would have had to issue 357,143 shares instead of the 300,000 shares issued when the convertible issue is fully converted —and the higher number of shares would have had to be issued immediately, rather than deferred to sometime in the future. With an EBIT of $14 million, the immediate impact on EPS would have been to reduce it even further to $3.56 ($14 million $\times$ (1 − .40)/2.357 million shares = $3.56). By using the convertible debenture with the conversion price set above the current market price of the firm's common stock, the firm can: (1) keep current EPS from falling from $3.89 to $3.56, and (2) reduce the number of additional shares of common stock that will ultimately be issued. This strategy is more favorable than direct common stock financing, but it may be less favorable than straight debt. In fact, compared to straight debt, critics of convertible financing maintain that it is an inefficient form of financing, and that the same results could be achieved if the company were to issue short-term debt, followed by a public offering of common stock.[14]

Issue Timing.   As a form of deferred equity, the timing of a convertible issue depends on current market conditions for the firm's common stock and the firm's growth prospects. When the price of the firm's common stock is depressed, it may be wise to avoid convertible financing. For if the price of the common is low, the firm will incur an incremental amount of dilution that would not otherwise occur with higher share prices. In essence, so long as conversion price is directly related to the prevailing market price of the company's stock, it follows that (other things being equal) reduced market prices lead to higher levels of dilution. Also, firms with promising growth prospects should be able to use convertible securities at an interest rate lower than what the company would have to pay on a straight debt issue, since the conversion feature makes the issue more attractive. And as we saw above, the greater the value of the conversion feature, the lower the yield on the issue. Even though yields in the bond market affect the interest rate the convertible must carry, market conditions normally play a secondary role in timing a convertible issue. Again, this is because convertibles are viewed principally as deferred equity, so minimizing potential dilution will have a greater positive effect on shareholder wealth than reducing the coupon rate by a point or two. Obviously, other things being equal, it

---

[14]W. G. Lewellen and G. A. Racette, "Convertible Debt Financing," *Journal of Financial and Quantitative Analysis* 8 (December 1973): pp. 777–792.

is better to issue in a strong bond market than a weak one, but not at the cost of passing up higher stock prices.[15]

Conversion Policy.   Firms usually issue convertible securities with the expectation that they will be converted into common stock within a certain length of time. Conversion may occur voluntarily by the investor, or it may be forced by the issuer. Voluntary conversion could occur if the dividend rate on the underlying stock rose to the point where the total current income from dividends (dividends per share × conversion ratio) exceeded the annual interest income from the convertible.[16] Another reason for voluntary conversion is if the conversion privilege is about to expire and the common stock is selling above its conversion price. An obvious trading profit will be lost in this situation if the security is not converted.

Forcing Conversion.   In contrast to voluntary conversion, the firm can take the initiative and force conversion by exercising its call provision. Although it is in the firm's best interest to call the convertible as soon as its market price is above its call price,[17] in fact the market price usually has to be substantially higher than the call price to ensure that investors will convert rather than accept the cash value of the call price. Most firms will not call an issue, assuming they are attempting to force conversion, unless the market price is at least 20 percent higher than the call price.[18] For example, if the call price on Memorial Steel's convertibles is 107 (107 percent of par, or $1070), the market price of the common would have to rise to $64.20 before the firm would feel safe in calling the issue ($64.20 × 20 shares = $1284/$1070 = a premium over call price of 20%). In fact, market evidence confirms such behavior; empirical results suggest that forced conversions usually follow a period of abnormal

---

[15]Appendix 17A provides a thorough discussion of how to determine the cost of capital on convertible securities; not surprisingly, such cost of capital computations are also based on both the bond and the stock features of the issue.

[16]For example, ignoring conversion premium, if an investor holds a 7 percent bond that is convertible into 20 shares of the firm's stock, the common would have to be paying dividends of $3.50 per share to provide the same current income as the bond: $3.50 × 20 = annual dividend income of $70. When the dividend rate exceeds $3.50 per share, in the absence of conversion premium, the stocks will provide a higher current income than the convertible bond, and voluntary conversion will hold merit. In essence, investors will be able to improve return by converting, since not only will they be able to get the same equity play from the stock, but they will earn higher current income as well.

[17]See Brennan and Schwartz, "Convertible Bonds: Valuation and Optimal Strategies for Call and Conversion," and Ingersoll, "An Examination of Corporate Call Policies on Convertible Securities," *Journal of Finance* 32 (May 1977), pp. 463–478. Ingersoll, in examing 179 convertibles called during the 1968–1975 period, concluded that all but nine of the firms waited too long in calling their convertibles.

[18]Ingersoll maintains that the optimum time to call a convertible is when conversion value exceeds call price by 13 percent or less.

price appreciation in the company's stock; then, after the conversion is completed, stock prices tend to drop off sharply.[19] When the call is announced, investors have three choices: (1) convert into the common, (2) sell the convertible at its market value to someone who wants to convert, or (3) receive in cash the call price of the bond.[20] Bondholders typically have up to a month to decide. If the conversion value of the convertible security declines to (or near) its call price, and bondholders accept that price, the company may be faced with a large outflow of cash instead of more equity. Firms can hedge against this possibility by using an underwriter when calling a convertible security; under the usual arrangement, the underwriter arranges to buy any unconverted securities and convert them.

Stimulating Conversion.   Other means are available to the firm to "stimulate" rather than "force" conversion. This could be done, for example, by establishing a stepped-up conversion price at set intervals in the future. As an illustration, if Memorial Steel had a $50 conversion price for the first 5 years, followed by a $60 conversion price for the next 5 years, the number of shares available upon conversion would drop from 20 to 16.67. Hence, immediately before the first 5-year period expires, investors might be encouraged to convert if the stock is trading in the, say, $55 to $60 range. Other ways to stimulate conversion are through raising the cash dividends on the firm's common stock and/or establishing a limited conversion period. Each of these steps will encourage conversion under the proper conditions; invariably, however, some investors will not convert. Consequently, calling the issue is the only way of ensuring virtually complete conversion.

Overhanging Issues.   If the market price of the firm's common stock does not reach a level significantly above the stated conversion price, the issue will not be converted and is thus considered to be "overhanging." Potential investors and lenders do not like the uncertainty of an overhanging issue. (Will the issue remain out to maturity as debt, or will it be converted to equity and lead to dilution in the firm's EPS?) Such an issue reduces the firm's future financing flexibility by making it difficult to sell additional convertible securities; in fact, it may even hinder the ability of the firm to issue straight debt or common stock. Of course, the firm could call the issue for refunding, but this could be costly if prevailing market rates have risen well above the coupon rate on the

---

[19]See Gordon Alexander and Roger Stover, "The Effect of Forced Conversions on Common Stock Prices," *Financial Management* 9 (spring 1980), pp. 39–45.

[20]For a discussion of ways to notify bondholders of the call and assure that a high percent convert, see Alexander B. Miller, "How to Call Your Convertibles," *Harvard Business Review* 49 (May–June 1971), pp. 66–70.

convertible. The risk of an overhanging issue, therefore, may offset (at least in part) the advantages associated with using convertible securities for meeting the capital needs of the firm. Because raising capital is not a one-time operation, financial managers should consider in advance the possibility of an overhanging issue, and establish contingency plans that spell out how the firm would deal with this situation.

Warrants

A *warrant* is an option issued by a corporation that enables investors to buy a specified number of shares of the company's stock at a stated price during a designated time period (warrants can occasionally be used to purchase preferred stock or even bonds,[21] but common stock is the principal redemption vehicle). The issuing firm realizes a capital inflow at the time the warrants are issued and also when they are exercised. Warrants have no voting rights, they pay no dividends (or interest), and they offer no claim on the assets or income of the company. Most warrants are issued as "sweeteners" to bond issues—that is, as a way to make the bond more attractive to potential investors, warrants will sometimes be attached to a new issue, thereby giving investors a debt obligation with an equity kicker. In addition, warrants have been used successfully in mergers, as compensation to employees, and as compensation to underwriters and venture capitalists. With a few notable exceptions, warrant financing is used primarily by low- and medium-quality firms. Warrants are nearly always detachable, though they are sometimes (albeit, very rarely) nondetachable. A detachable warrant may be separated from the bond and traded by itself. In many cases, the detachable provision is deferred for a certain (usually fairly short) period of time after the date of issue; detachable warrants may be listed on the NYSE or AMEX, or traded in the OTC market.

Issue Characteristics

A warrant has three features of particular interest to both corporate management and investors; these are the warrant's exchange ratio, exercise price, and expiration date. The *exchange ratio* specifies the number of shares of common stock that may be purchased, at the special exercise price, in exchange for each warrant; it is similar in many respects to the conversion ratio on convertible securities, except that additional cash is required for an investor to exercise a warrant, whereas none is needed for conversion. Most warrants have an exchange ratio of 1.0 (one share of stock can be purchased in exchange for each warrant). The ratio sometimes exceeds 1.0, but rarely is it more than 3 or 4. The

---

[21]For example, in November 1981, Manufacturers Hanover issued a bond with two warrants attached, each warrant entitling the holder to purchase one Zero Coupon bond at a price equal to 36.854 percent of par. For purposes of simplicity, we confine our discussion of warrants to those that can be used to buy shares of the issuing firm's *common stock*.

exercise price is the stated price the warrant holder will have to pay to acquire the stock; it is the price per share paid to the firm when the warrant is used to buy the stock. Note that, as we will show below, once a warrant is exercised, it ceases to exist since the warrant is replaced (exchanged) for a new share (or shares) of common stock. Usually the exercise price is fixed, but some warrants may provide for an exercise price that increases as it nears its expiration date. In addition, the exercise price will automatically be adjusted for stock splits and major stock dividends. The *expiration date* specifies the deadline for exercising the warrant. Most warrants have maturity (or expiration) dates that cover a minimum of 5 to 10 years from the date of issue. Occasionally, they have no expiration date at all—these are known as *perpetual warrants*.

Valuation of Warrants

Unlike convertible securities, warrants have no value independent of the common stock of the firm. This is because the sole value of a warrant is derived from its option feature. The theoretical minimum value of a warrant is equal to the difference in its exchange value and its exercise value. Exchange value is the product of the warrant's exchange ratio and the market price of the common stock; exercise value is equal to the exchange ratio times the exercise price; that is:

$$V_w = RP - RX \qquad (23.4)$$
$$= R(P - X)$$

where V_w = theoretical minimum value of a warrant
        R = exchange ratio
        P = price of the common stock
        X = exercise price

For example, consider warrants issued by Frontier Airlines. Assume the market price of the common is $12.50, the exercise price is $11.37, and the exchange ratio is 1.0. Thus, they have a theoretical minimum value of:

$$V_w = 1.0(\$12.50 - 11.37)$$
$$= \$1.13$$

Obviously, if $P < X$, then $V_w = 0$, since a warrant cannot have a negative value, even in a theoretical sense.

The theoretical minimum value denotes the lowest value at which the warrant should sell. If for some reason the market price of the warrant drops below this minimum value, arbitragers would quickly eliminate the difference by buying the warrants, exercising them, and selling the common stock. As a practical matter, warrants generally command a premium over the theoretical minimum value. The premium (in dollars) is simply the difference between the market price on the warrant and its theoretical value, V_W.

Price Premiums.   The primary reason a warrant almost always sells for more than its theoretical minimum value is the leverage such securities offer investors. Leverage arises from being able to participate in the price appreciation of the common stock, but with a capital investment much smaller than the amount that would be required if the stocks were purchased directly. To understand the concept of leverage, consider once again the case of Memorial Steel. This time, assume that Memorial is considering the sale of $15 million worth of subordinated debentures with warrants attached. The debenture will carry an interest rate of 7.50 percent; comparable quality straight-debt obligations could be issued with an 8 percent coupon, but Memorial is able to obtain the lower rate because of the warrants that will be attached to the bond. Thus, bonds with warrants attached have the same type of effect on coupon rates as convertible issues (though perhaps not to the same magnitude). One warrant will be attached to each debenture and will allow the holder to purchase three shares of the company's common at $50 per share for the next 5 years; the warrants are detachable immediately after issue. If the market price of Memorial Steel's common stock is presently $42 per share, an equity investor would have to spend $4200 to purchase 100 shares of the firm's stock. However, if the investor used the $4200 to purchase the company's warrants, and if they were priced as indicated in Table 23.3, then the warrants would be trading at $7 each (when the stock is trading at $42), and the investor could have purchased 600 Memorial Steel warrants.

To see the difference in potential return, assume the price of the common stock increases to $80 per share. For the investor who owns

TABLE 23.3 Relationship Between Common Stock Price, Theoretical Value, Market Value, and Price Premium[a]	Common Stock Price	Theoretical Minimum Value of Warrant	Market Value of Warrant	Dollar Premium on Warrant
	$ 20	$ 0	$ 1	$ 1
	30	0	3	3
	40	0	5	5
	42	0	7	7
	50	0	15	15
	60	30	42	12
	70	60	69	9
	80	90	96	6
	90	120	123	3
	100	150	151	1

[a]Figures based on Memorial Steel's warrants.

stock, the return is 90.48 percent. However, consider the potential return to the investor who purchased Memorial Steel warrants. At a stock price of $80, we assume in Table 23.3 (which accounts for both theoretical value and expected price premium) that the market price of the warrants will be $96; in this case the return from investing in Memorial Steel's warrants is 1,271.43 percent [($96 − $7)/$7 × 100 = 1,271.43%)]. Put another way, while the value of 100 shares of stock moves from $4,200 to $8,000 (a profit of $3,800), the value of the 600 warrants would move from the same investment base of $4,200 to $57,600 (generating a profit of $53,400). By investing in the warrants instead of the firm's common stock, the investor can buy a greater number of warrants than shares of common stock, and as the stock moves up in price, earn a substantially improved return on invested capital. Of course, leverage works both ways; the percentage change can be almost as pronounced on the negative side. There is downside protection, however, since it is unlikely that the price of the warrant will fall to zero (see Table 23.3). In fact, for the market price of the warrant to fall to zero, there would have to be no probability at all that the market price of the stock would exceed the exercise price during the option period.

A Graphic Framework.   The functional relationship between the market value of a warrant and the value of the associated common stock is shown in Figure 23.3; the data for Memorial Steel are used for illustrative purposes. The theoretical minimum value is represented by the bold line that runs horizontally from $0 to $50, and then angles upward to the right; the market value of the warrant is represented by the dashed line.

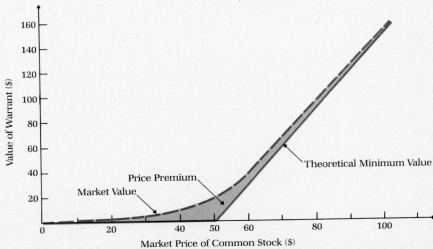

Figure 23.3   Relation Between Theoretical and Market Values of a Warrant.
Note: Values based on Memorial Steel's warrants.

When the market price of Memorial's stock is low in relation to the exercise price of the warrant, the market value of the warrant is just slightly above its theoretical minimum value. But as the price of the common starts to rise and approach the exercise price, the warrant premium increases. In fact, as Figure 23.3 shows, premium can generally be expected to peak out at a market share price that approximates exercise price. As the stock price increases beyond the exercise price, the premium decreases. There are two reasons for the decrease in the premium. First, leverage potential decreases as the price of the common increases. An investor who buys Memorial common at $60 and sells at $80 has a potential return of around 33 percent; the investor who purchases the warrant when the common is $60 and sells when the stock is $80 obtains a return of over 128 percent [from Table 23.3: ($96 − $42)/$42 × 100 = 128.57%]. While there are still leverage gains from investing in the warrant as opposed to the common stock, it is clear that they are substantially smaller than in the earlier example (where the initial price of the stock was $42). The second reason for declining premium is that the loss potential increases as the warrant moves to higher and higher prices. Clearly, the price of the warrant has a longer way to fall when its theoretical value is $90 or $100 than when it is $9 or $10.

Like convertible securities, the skewed distribution of possible outcomes (see Figure 23.3) means that warrants have more value the greater the volatility in the market price for the firm's common stock. Investors have some limit on their risk, plus unlimited profit potential. The wider the probability distribution of possible common stock prices, the higher the expected rate of return on the warrant. In addition, it should be obvious that the longer the expiration period on the warrant, the more likely the market price of the firm's common stock will, at some time, exceed the exercise price specified in the warrant. Hence, price premiums will be higher the greater the volatility in the firm's common stock and the longer the period of time during which the warrant may be exercised.[22]

Financing with Warrants

Firms will encounter many of the same tradeoffs and considerations when using warrants as a financing vehicle as they will using convertible securities. A notable difference is that because the equity portion of the financing is much less with warrants, the bond market plays a more

---

[22]Warrants can be valued employing concepts based on the option pricing model discussed in Appendix 23A. See, for example, Eduardo S. Schwartz, "The Valuation of Warrants: Implementing a New Approach," *Journal of Financial Economics* 4 (January 1977), pp. 79–93. Empirical work on warrant prices is contained in: John P. Shelton, "The Relation of the Price of a Warrant to the Price of Its Associated Stock," *Financial Analysts Journal* 23 (May–June and July–August 1967), pp. 141–151, 88–99; and David F. Rush and Ronald W. Melicher, "An Empirical Examination of Factors Which Influence Warrant Prices," *Journal of Finance* 29 (December 1974), pp. 1449–1466.

important role in issue timing. For example, whereas a single ($1000) convertible bond may involve the potential issuance of 20 to 30 shares of stock upon conversion, that same issue as a bond with warrants attached may involve the potential issuance of only 1 or 2 shares of stock. Even so, the exercise price stipulated on the warrant is important, and has traditionally been set at 10 to 20 percent above the prevailing price of the stock at the time the bond-warrant unit is issued. It is obviously to the advantage of the issuing firm to set the exercise price as high as possible, but the market acts to limit the price to a reasonable level. As with convertibles, a tradeoff exists between the coupon rate (or cost of funds) on the bond and the exercise price on the warrant. If the exercise price is set too high, investors will ignore the warrant portion of the issue and price the bond as a straight debt obligation. In this case, the issuing firm will not be able to obtain a lower coupon on the bond. In fact, in the case of bonds with warrants attached, the issuing firm probably has more to gain by setting a liberal (low) exercise price in exchange for a more favorable coupon rate, since not only will the issue involve a relatively small amount of stock, but the interest cost savings to the firm will continue on the bonds long after most warrants are exercised or expire.

Also, prospective warrant purchasers would like to invest in warrants that have a perpetual or very long life, while the firm (and its shareholders) would prefer to issue warrants with relatively short lives. Consider, for example, the combination warrant and debt financing undertaken by American Telephone and Telegraph in April 1970.[23] Warrants were issued to subscribe to 31.4 million shares of stock at an exercise price of $52 per share up to March 15, 1975. In part because of the short life on the warrants, the market price of AT&T's stock exceeded the exercise price only a few times during the exchange period. As a result, only about 3 million shares of stock (approximately 10 percent of the issue) were ever purchased. Clearly, in this case the short exchange period played a part in preventing investors from receiving much in the way of benefits from the warrants.[24] In contrast to convertible securities, firms cannot force warrants to be exercised. Consequently, most firms perfer to use warrants with short to intermediate lives. In addition, some companies like to use an accelerated exercise price to stimulate holders to exercise their warrants.

---

[23]Until the AT&T issue, the New York Stock Exchange had a policy against listing warrants because they were viewed as being speculative securities. When AT&T issued its warrants, the Exchange changed its policy; since then, warrants for a number of other firms have been listed on the NYSE.

[24]Some writers argue that the AT&T situation is not all that unusual, since investors generally do tend to overvalue warrants when they are issued; as such, warrant financing benefits the firm's current shareholders at the expense of the warrant buyers. See, for example, Bernell K. Stone, "Warrant Financing," *Journal of Financial and Quantitative Analysis* 11 (March 1976), pp. 143–153.

Effects on EPS. Using bonds with warrants attached will have an impact on both reported earnings per share (EPS) and the corporate capital structure. To illustrate this point, let us compare Memorial Steel's convertible debentures to its issue of bonds with attached warrants. The 7 percent convertibles will be issued at par and can be converted into 20 shares of common stock (per $1000 debenture); the 7.5 percent bonds can also be issued at par, but each ($1000) bond will carry one detachable warrant giving the holder the right to purchase 3 shares of common at $50 per share. As with the earlier examples, $15 million of financing will be raised and the expected earnings before interest and taxes are $14 million. Table 23.4 shows the earnings per share before and after the warrants are exercised. There is some dilution with the warrants (EPS dropped from $3.86 to $3.78), but it is substantially less than when the convertible debentures are employed (EPS fell to $3.65 in Table 23.2). Less dilution occurs with the warrants because a maximum of only 45,000 new shares of common stock will be issued, as opposed to the 300,000 new shares of common that will be issued with the convertible debentures.

Effects on Capital Structure. Memorial Steel's capital structure will also be affected by the type of financing used (see Table 23.5). Using the convertible issue to raise $15 million means that upon conversion, 300,000 new shares of common stock will be issued. But because the capital structure is merely recapitalized (debt is replaced with equity), total capitalization stays at $55 million. However, in the case of the bonds with warrants attached, we see that the debt remains outstanding after the warrants are exercised. Also, when they are exercised, the firm will receive an additional $2.25 million in new money, since the warrant holders will have to pay $50 per share for the new stock (45,000 shares × $50 = $2.25 million). Consequently, the firm receives $2.25 million in new equity capital, and total capitalization increases to $57.25 million. Also, the comparative debt-equity ratios show that the firm's leverage position

	Bonds with Warrants	
	Before Exercise	After Exercise
Earnings before interest and taxes (EBIT)	$14,000,000	$14,000,000
Less: Interest (0.075 × $15,000,000)	1,125,000	1,125,000
Earnings before taxes (EBT)	$12,875,000	$12,875,000
Less: Taxes (40%)	5,150,000	5,150,000
Earnings after taxes (EAT or NI)	$ 7,725,000	$ 7,725,000
Number of shares of common stock	2,000,000	2,045,000
Earnings per share (EPS)	$3.86	$3.78

TABLE 23.4
Earnings Per Share for Memorial Steel Before and After Exercise of Warrants

TABLE 23.5

Capital Structure of Memorial Steel with Convertible Debenture Financing and Bonds with Warrants Attached

	Before Financing	Convertible Debenture[a]		Bonds with Warrants[b]	
		Before Conversion	After Conversion	Before Exercise	After Exercise
Debentures	$ 0	$15,000,000	$ 0	$15,000,000	$15,000,000
Common stock ($10 par value)	20,000,000	20,000,000	23,000,000	20,000,000	20,450,000
Capital surplus	0	0	12,000,000	0	1,800,000
Retained earnings	20,000,000	20,000,000	20,000,000	20,000,000	20,000,000
Total stockholders' equity	$40,000,000	$40,000,000	$55,000,000	$40,000,000	$42,250,000
Total capitalization	$40,000,000	$55,000,000	$55,000,000	$55,000,000	$57,250,000
Debt-equity ratio	0	0.38	0	0.38	0.36

[a] $15 million issue of 7% debentures convertible into common stock at $50 per share.

[b] $15 million issue of 7½% debentures with one warrant attached giving the holder the right to purchase 3 shares of common stock at $50 per share.

is altered considerably more with the convertibles than with the bond-warrant financing, and will remain so until the debt (the debenture issued with the warrants) is repaid.

Options

An *options contract* is a negotiable security that gives the holder the right to buy or sell 100 shares of common stock at a specified price for a specified period of time, normally 9 months or less.[25] A *call* is an option to buy; a *put* is an option to sell. Puts and calls are unique because they are not issued by the corporation on whose stock the options are written. Rather, they are created by investors (known as "writers" or "makers") who, for a fee, sell to other investors the right to buy or sell shares of stock at a fixed price and for a set period of time. The seller makes money from the fee he collects (if the price of the stock does not move against him), whereas the buyer makes money, depending upon whether it is a put or a call, if the price of the stock drops below (put) or

[25] In addition to stock options, puts and calls are also available on other securities-investment vehicles; for example, in late 1983, there were *interest rate* options (puts and calls on Treasury bills, notes and bonds), *foreign currency* options (options on British pounds, Swiss francs, German marks, Canadian dollars, and Japanese yen), *stock index* options (options on market and industry indexes, like the NYSE Index and computer technology stocks), and even options on *futures* (puts and calls on Treasury bond, gold, sugar, and the S & P Stock Index futures contracts). Chiefly because of the relevancy they hold for managerial finance, we confine our discussion to put and call options on specific common stocks.

rises above (call) the exercise price on the option. (In essence, the seller is betting that the buyer's price expectations are wrong.) The company that issued the underlying stock is *not* a party to the transaction; it receives nothing when the options are issued, and it has no obligation when and if the options are exercised. Put and call options are the liability of the option writers, not the company on whose stock the option is written. Since stock options are not a liability of the company, it follows that when an option is exercised, the number of common shares outstanding is unchanged.

Although stock options have attracted considerable recognition in the investment community, they have received only scant attention in the financial management literature—probably because they are not a corporate obligation in the normal sense of the word. However, several recent studies that examined the impact of options trading on the firm yielded results which indicate that: (1) option trading decreases the price volatility of a firm's common shares; and (2) the presence of option trading activity increases the trading volume of the underlying firm's common shares.[26] These findings suggest that firms may benefit from having options traded on their common stock because of the increased liquidity provided for the firm's common shares. Perhaps the most significant contribution of the options concept to corporate finance has to do with the recent development of a far-reaching theoretical model known as the option pricing model (or OPM for short). This highly complex mathematical model is being used in a theoretical context as a way to price risky assets, and its growing body of followers believe that, much like the capital asset pricing model, the OPM may someday have wide application in the valuation of corporate assets and obligations (Appendix 23A provides additional information on stock options and the option pricing model.)

SUMMARY

Convertible securities and warrants are contingent claim securities often employed by low- and medium-quality firms as a way to raise capital. Selling subordinated convertible debentures (or convertible preferred stock) provides an immediate infusion of capital into the firm; however, no additional capital is received when conversion takes place. Because of limited downside risk and unlimited upside potential, convertible bonds normally sell at a premium above their theoretical value. The use of

---

[26]See CBOE, *Analysis of Volume and Price Patterns in Stocks Underlying CBOE Options from December 30, 1974 to April 30, 1975*, (Chicago: July 1975); CBOE, *Analysis of Volume and Price Patterns in Stocks Underlying CBOE Options from December 31, 1975 to January 16, 1976*, (Chicago: February 1976); Samuel L. Hayes, III, and Michael E. Tennenbaum, "The Impact of Listed Options on the Underlying Shares," *Financial Management* 8 (winter 1979), pp. 72–76; and Dennis T. Officer and Gary L. Trennepohl, "Price Behavior of Corporate Equities Near Option Expiration Dates," *Financial Management* 10 (summer 1981), pp. 75–80.

convertibles will result in higher current earnings per share (EPS) than if common stock had been employed directly; in fact, even after conversion, EPS will be higher because fewer shares of common stock will be issued with the convertible security. However, convertibles may be less attractive than straight debt financing in terms of shareholder wealth maximization. Firms can force conversion by calling the convertibles, something that is often done when the market price of the common has risen well above the conversion price. When the firm cannot force conversion, an overhanging issue is said to exist; this is an unfavorable condition, as it may limit the future financing flexibility of the firm.

Warrants are usually issued along with debentures as a type of "sweetener"; their value depends solely on the behavior of the firm's common stock. Warrants generally trade at a market value above their theoretical minimum value because of the leverage embodied in the security. Like convertibles securities, warrants are appropriate for low- and medium-quality firms with good growth prospects. However, unlike convertibles, firms cannot force warrants to be exercised; only the expiration date specifies with certainty how long warrants will remain outstanding. Stock options represent still another kind of financial asset. However, in contrast to convertibles and warrants, stock options are securities that are the liability of the option writer, not the firm. They benefit the firm only to the extent that option trading may lead to decreased price volatility and increased trading activity (liquidity) for the firm's common stock.

QUESTIONS

23.1. Biotronics Feedback Systems is a "hi-tech" company involved in the application of scientific technology to high-speed information systems. It went public several years ago and since then has raised capital through privately placed debt issues; the company has shown very little profit so far and as a result, its equity position, is made up almost solely of its original stock issue. However, Biotronics has made some significant technological breakthroughs, and so things are beginning to look up. But to make the breakthroughs commercially feasible will require more capital. In general terms, give several reasons why Biotronics should consider the use of a subordinated convertible debenture as a way to meet its present financing needs. What arguments can you make against the use of a convertible? Would a bond with warrants attached be a better form of financing? Explain.

23.2. Using Figure 23.1, explain why convertible bonds are expected to trade at a premium over both their straight debt and conversion values. What assumptions underlie Figure 23.1? What happens if we relax these assumptions?

23.3. Why do the premiums for convertible securities decrease the further away the conversion value is from the bond value, and those for warrants decrease the further the market price of the common stock is away from the exercise price?

23.4. Why is the distribution of possible outcomes skewed to the right for both convertible securities and warrants? Why would investors in both convertible securities and warrants prefer, other things being equal, to invest in securities whose underlying common stock has high price volatility?

23.5. Why is it inappropriate to view convertible debt as either (1) deferred equity or (2) low-cost debt? How should it be viewed?

23.6. A firm is designing a 9 percent, 20-year convertible debenture and is considering the following alternative provisions:

a. A conversion period of 5 years versus 15 years.

b. A fixed conversion price versus a stepped-up conversion price.

c. An initial conversion premium of 10 percent versus one of 20 percent.

d. Callable from the outset versus a 10-year deferred call provision.

e. No call premium versus a call premium that declines by $2 per year.

f. No sinking fund requirement versus a sinking fund that begins in year 10 and retires one-tenth of the original issue for each of the next 10 years.

From the standpoint of the issuing firm, which provisions would you prefer? Why? From the standpoint of a potential investor, which provisions would you prefer? Why? Is there *any* agreement between the preferences of the issuing firm and the prospective investor on the provisions?

23.7. Why is the anticipated growth of the firm's earnings (and dividends) so important in determining whether a firm should employ convertible securities? What happens at the time of initial offering if investors do not perceive much possible growth? What problems may the firm face in the future if the anticipated growth is not forthcoming?

23.8. Under what conditions will investors voluntarily convert a convertible security? How can conversion be forced?

23.9. Explain the similarities and differences from the firm's standpoint of convertible debentures versus subordinated debentures with warrants attached as methods of financing. Comment on the following:

a. Amount, timing, and certainty of capital raised.

b. Potential dilution.

c. Impact on the firm's capital structure.

d. Impact on the firm's earnings per share.

23.10. What are the two basic types of options? From a managerial perspective, are these securities a liability of the firm on whose shares they are written? What, if any, benefits can the existence of options (on the firm's shares) have for the firm or its owners? Explain.

PROBLEMS

23.1. *CONVERSION PREMIUM AND BOND VALUES.* A firm pays dividends of $3 per share, has a dividend payout ratio of 75 percent, and a price/earnings ratio of 20 times. The firm is in need of additional financing and has decided to sell a $20 million, 11 percent, 20-year convertible debenture, with a conversion ratio of 10 (the par value of each bond is $1000):

a. What is the firm's earnings per share?

b. What is the market price of the common stock?

c. What conversion price will the convertible issue carry?

d. What is the percentage conversion premium (over the conversion value) at the time of issue?

e. If 80 percent of the debentures are ultimately converted, how many shares of common stock will be issued?

f. If comparable straight bonds are yielding 12 percent, what is the initial bond value of the convertible?

23.2. *EFFECTIVE MARKET FLOOR FOR CONVERTIBLES.* Nine years ago Pennsylvania Products issued a 5 percent, 25-year convertible debenture at par. At that time the market rate of interest on comparable-quality straight bonds was 6 percent. The bonds were convertible into common stock at a conversion price of $125 per share; the common was then selling for $100.

a. What was the bond value floor for the Pennsylvania Products convertibles when they were issued? What was their conversion value at the time of issue? In dollars, what was the size of the premium over the security's straight debt or conversion values (whichever was greater) at the issue date?

b. What was the expected bond value of the convertibles in 9 years? (Assume the market rate of interest on comparable-quality straight debt was expected to remain at 6 percent.)

c. Subsequently, the common stock was split 2 for 1 (the conversion price was adjusted) and currently sells at $36 per share. Comparable-quality straight bonds of similar maturity (16 years) currently have a market interest rate of 10 percent.

   1. What is the present conversion value of the convertible?

   2. What is the present bond value of the convertible?

   3. What happened to the market floor protection suggested in (a)?

23.3. *VALUATION: RETURNS TO INVESTORS FROM CONVERTIBLE SECURITIES.* Ohio Electric is planning to raise $50 million by selling convertible debentures at par (ignore any flotation costs). The stock is currently selling at $50 per share ($P_0$), and the price of the stock is expected to grow at a constant rate (g) of 6 percent per year for the foreseeable future. The 20-year convertible debenture will carry a 6 percent coupon, while comparable-quality straight debt currently is being issued at 8 percent. The conversion price is $55.55, so that each debenture may be converted into 18 shares of common stock. In the past, Ohio Electric has forced conversion when the market price of the stock exceeds the conversion price by 15 percent.

a. Employing the constant growth model, find the conversion value of the convertible security in 4 years ($t = 4$).

b. What will the bond value of the convertible issue be in 4 years if nonconvertible rates hold at 8 percent? What will it be if straight debt rates rise to 12 percent by the fourth year?

c. What price must the convertible reach if conversion is to occur? Given there is no conversion premium, how high will the price of the stock have to go before conversion is triggered? In what year can investors expect Ohio Electric to force conversion?

23.4. *COMPARATIVE COST OF FINANCING.*   Fantasyland, Inc., operates a string of amusement parks across the United States. It has decided to issue $35 million in convertible debentures as a way to raise long-term capital needed for further expansion. The current stock price (P_0) is $65 per share, while the expected growth rate (g) is 9 percent per year for the foreseeable future. In discussions with its investment bankers, two possible combinations were suggested:

Convertible Debenture A

- Conversion price = $76.92 ($R$ = 13 shares of common stock)
- Coupon interest rate, I, = 10%
- Issue price (and maturity value), M, = $1000
- Term to maturity = 15 years

Convertible Debenture B

- Conversion price = $90.90 ($R$ = 11 shares of common stock)
- Coupon interest rate, I, = 11%
- Issue price (and maturity value), M, = $1000
- Term to maturity = 15 years

In either case, the bonds will not be called unless the conversion value, C_t, exceeds $1200. Fantasyland has a 40 percent marginal tax rate (ignore flotation costs).

a. Ignoring conversion premium, in what year is the conversion of debenture A likely to take place? In what year will debenture B probably be converted?

b. Given the company currently pays an annual dividend (D_0) of $6 per share and it too is expected to grow at 9 percent per year, find the after-tax cost of servicing debenture A versus debenture B over the full 15-year life of the issues (use the years to conversion you computed above to determine when the issues go from debt to equity). Based on these comparative cost of financing figures, which convertible issue would you choose?

c. Using the cost of capital formula for convertible securities from Appendix 17A—use Equation 17A.2—find the after-tax cost of the two convertibles (use the same years to conversion as above and keep flotation costs at $f = 0$). Based on these comparative costs, which convertible issue (A or B) would you choose? Does your answer change from (b)? Explain.

23.5. *VALUATION AND COST OF FINANCING.*   Hawaiian Turf, Ltd., plans to issue an 8 percent, 10-year convertible bond at par:

a. Comparable-quality straight debt with a similar maturity is selling at a market rate of 10 percent. Determine the bond value of H. T.'s convertible at times t_0, t_3, and t_6. Use these three points plus the maturity value (at time t_{10}) to graph the straight debt value of the convertible.

b. At time t_0 the conversion value of the bond is $800, since the initial stock price is $40 and the conversion ratio is 20. The price of the stock is expected to grow at a rate of 7 percent per year. Calculate the expected conversion value at t_3, t_6, and t_{10}. Graph the conversion value, C_t, on the graph constructed in (a).

c. What is the minimum price the convertible can sell for in years 0, 3, and 6 if: (1) the market interest rate does not change, and (2) the anticipated growth in the stock price is realized?

d. To estimate the expected market price of the convertible, draw a curve between the issue price of $1000 and the conversion price in year 10 on the graph you constructed in (a) and (b). If the firm plans to call the convertible when the conversion value (common stock value) is 120 percent of par value, in what year do you anticipate the call will take place? What is the approximate market value in the year you estimate the convertible will be called?

e. Using the cost of capital formulas from Appendix 17A (Equations 17A.2 and 17A.3), find the expected costs given the convertible debentures are issued at par, flotation costs are 5 percent of par, the firm's marginal tax rate is 40 percent, and:
   1. The company does not plan to call the debentures until year 10. (*Hint:* Try 9 percent.)
   2. It calls the debentures in the year you estimated in (d).
   What does your answer to these cost of capital problems suggest in terms of call strategy?

23.6. *THEORETICAL VALUE OF A WARRANT.* The following information is available for six warrants:

Warrant	Exchange Ratio	Market Price of Common Stock	Exercise Price
A	1	$ 5	$25
B	1	15	25
C	1	25	25
D	1	35	25
E	1	45	25
F	1	55	25

a. Compute the theoretical minimum value of each of the warrants.
b. Prepare a graph with the theoretical value of the warrant on the vertical axis and the market price of the stock on the horizontal. Plot the theoretical minimum values computed in (a).
c. Given the market values of the warrants below, plot and fit a curve to them on the graph constructed in (b).

Warrant	Market Value
A	$ 1
B	4
C	8
D	15
E	23
F	31

d. Explain the relationship between the theoretical value of a warrant and its actual market price.

23.7. *ALTERNATIVE FINANCING: CONVERTIBLES VERSUS WARRANTS.* Parish Cement is preparing to issue $10 million in new 20-year bonds. The bonds will be convertible, or they will be issued with warrants attached. The convertible debentures would be issued with 9 percent coupons and a conversion price of $50, while a bond with warrants would carry an 11 percent coupon and a detachable warrant giving the holder the right to purchase 2 shares of stock at $50 each. In either case, the bonds can be issued at par (ignore flotation costs). The company's balance sheet and income statement is presented below:

Parish Cement Company—Abbreviated Balance Sheet

Current assets	$10,000,000	Current liabilities	5,000,000
Fixed assets	20,000,000	Common stock ($10 par)	5,000,000
Total assets	30,000,000	Retained earnings	20,000,000
		Total debt & equity	30,000,000

Parish Cement Company—Abbreviated Income Statement

Gross profit (EBIT)	$4,500,000
Interest (on current liabilities)	200,000
Earnings before taxes (EBT)	$4,300,000
Taxes (40 percent)	1,720,000
Earnings after tax (EAT)	$2,580,000
Number of shares of common stock	500,000
Earnings per share	$5.16

a. Show the capital structure of the firm if it issues the convertible debentures; do likewise for the bonds with warrants.

b. Given the EBIT figure, what will earnings per share be under the two plans?

c. What would the market price of the common stock be under the two plans, given a P/E ratio of 15 times earnings?

d. In five years, EBIT is expected to be $8 million; all the convertible debentures are expected to be converted (or all the warrants exercised). Determine the alternative capital structure for Parish Cement in 5 years under the two options (assume current liabilities remain at $5 million but that retained earnings are $30 million). What differences exist (aside from increased retained earnings) from the capital structures shown in (a)?

e. If EBIT is expected to be $8 million in 5 years and interest on current liabilities is expected to remain at $200,000, what will earnings per share be in 5 years under the two alternatives? Why does the ordering differ from that found in (b)?

f. Given the EPS values you computed in (e), what will the common stock be priced at if the P/E ratio is 16 times earnings for both plans?

SELECTED REFERENCES

Alexander, Gordon J., and Roger D. Stover. "The Effect of Forced Conversion on Common Stock Prices." *Financial Managment* 9 (spring 1980), pp. 39–45.

———, and ———. "Pricing in the New Issue Convertible Debt Market." *Financial Management* 6 (fall 1977), pp. 35–39.

———, ———, and David B. Kuhnau. "Market Timing Strategies in Convertible Debt Financing." *Journal of Finance* 34 (March 1979), pp. 143–155.

Bierman, Harold J., Jr. "The Cost of Warrants." *Journal of Financial and Quantitative Analysis* 8 (June 1973), pp. 494–504.

Brennan, Michael J., and Eduardo S. Schwartz. "Convertible Bonds: Valuation and Optimal Strategies for Call and Conversion." *Journal of Finance* 32 (December 1977), pp. 1699–1716.

Brigham, Eugene F. "An Analysis of Convertible Debentures: Theory and Some Empirical Evidence." *Journal of Finance* 21 (March 1966), pp. 35–54.

Courtadon, Georges. "A More Accurate Finite Difference Approximation for the Valuation of Options." *Journal of Financial and Quantitative Analysis* 17 (December 1982), pp. 697–703.

Cox, John C., Stephen A. Ross, and Mark Rubinstein. "Option Pricing: A Simplified Approach." *Journal of Financial Economics* 6 (September 1979), pp. 229–263.

Dawson, Steven M. "Timing Interest Payments for Convertible Bonds." *Financial Management* 3 (summer 1974), pp. 14–16.

Frank, Werner G., and Charles O. Kroncke. "Classifying Conversions of Convertible Debentures over Four Years." *Financial Management* 3 (summer 1974), pp. 33–42.

Frankle, A. W., and C. A. Hawkins. "Beta Coefficients for Convertible Bonds." *Journal of Finance* 30 (March 1975), pp. 207–210.

Greenebaum, M. "Climate Is Right for Convertibles." *Fortune*, October 6, 1980, pp. 107–108.

Hayes, Samuel L. III, and Michael E. Tennenbaum. "The Impact of Listed Options on the Underlying Shares." *Financial Management* 8 (winter 1979), pp. 72–76.

Hsia, Chi-Cheng. "Optimal Debt of a Firm: An Option Pricing Approach." *Journal of Financial Research* 4 (fall 1981), pp. 221–231.

———, and Henry B. Reiling. "Sophisticated Financing Tool: The Warrant." *Harvard Business Review* 47 (January–February 1969), pp. 137–150.

Ingersoll, Jonathan. "An Examination of Corporate Call Policies on Convertible Securities." *Journal of Finance* 32 (May 1977), pp. 463–478.

———. "A Contingent Claim Valuation of Convertible Securities." *Journal of Financial Economics* 4 (May 1977), pp. 289–322.

Jennings, Edward H. "An Estimate of Convertible Bond Premiums." *Journal of Financial and Quantitative Analysis* 9 (January 1974), pp. 33–56.

Lewellen, W. G., and G. A. Racette. "Convertible Debt Financing." *Journal of Financial and Quantitative Analysis* 8 (December 1973), pp. 777–792.

Liebowitz, Martin L. "Convertible Securities." *Financial Analysts Journal* 30 (November–December 1974), pp. 57–67.

MacBeth, James D., and Larry J. Melville. "An Empirical Examination of the Black-Scholes Call Option Pricing Model." *Journal of Finance* 34 (December 1979), pp. 1173–1186.

Margrabe, William. "The Value of an Option to Exchange One Asset for Another." *Journal of Finance* 33 (March 1978), pp. 177–198.

Melicher, Ronald W. "Financing with Convertible Preferred Stock: Comment." *Journal of Finance* 26 (March 1971), pp. 144–147.

———, and J. R. Hoffmeister. "Issuing Convertible Bonds." *Financial Executive*, June 1980, pp. 20–23.

Miller, Alexander B. "How to Call Your Convertibles." *Harvard Business Review* 49 (May–June 1971), pp. 66–70.

Murray, Roger F. "A New Role for Options." *Journal of Financial and Quantitative Analysis* 14 (November 1979), pp. 895–899.

Officer, Dennis T., and Gary T. Trennepohl. "Price Behavior of Corporate Equities Near Option Expiration Dates." *Financial Management* 10 (summer 1981), pp. 75–80.

Pilcher, James C. *Raising Capital with Convertible Securities* (Ann Arbor: University of Michigan Press, 1955).

Pinches, George E. "Financing with Convertible Preferred Stock, 1960–1967." *Journal of Finance* 25 (March 1970), pp. 53–63.

———. Financing with Convertible Preferred Stock, 1960–1967: Reply." *Journal of Finance* 26 (March 1971), pp. 150–151.

Rao, Ramesh K. S. "Modern Option Pricing Models: A Dichotomous Classification." *Journal of Financial Research* 4 (spring 1981), pp. 33–44.

Rush, David F., and Ronald W. Melicher. "An Empirical Examination of Factors Which Influence Warrant Prices." *Journal of Finance* 29 (December 1974), pp. 1449–1466.

Schwartz, Eduardo S. "The Valuation of Warrants: Implementing a New Approach." *Journal of Financial Economics* 4 (January 1977), pp. 79–94.

Sears, Stephen R., and Gary L. Trennepohl. "Measuring Portfolio Risk in Options." *Journal of Financial and Quantitative Analysis* 17 (September 1982), pp. 391–409.

Shelton, John P. "The Relation of the Price of a Warrant to the Price of Its Associated Stock." *Financial Analysts Journal* 23 (May–June 1967), pp. 143–151, and (July–August 1967): pp. 88–99.

Soldofsky, Robert M. "Yield-Risk Performance of Convertible Securities." *Financial Analysts Journal* 27 (March–April 1971), pp. 61–65, 79.

Sprecher, C. Ronald. "A Note on Financing Mergers with Convertible Preferred Stock." *Journal of Finance* 26 (June 1971), pp. 683–686.

Sterk, William Edward. "Option Pricing: Dividends and the In-and-Out-of-the-Money-Bias." *Financial Management* 12 (winter 1983), pp. 47–53.

Stone, Bernell K. "Warrant Financing." *Journal of Financial and Quantitative Analysis* 11 (March 1976), pp. 143–154.

Turov, Daniel. "Dividend Paying Stocks and Their Warrants." *Financial Analysts Journal* 29 (March–April 1973), pp. 76–78.

Walter, James E., and Agustin V. Que. "The Valuation of Convertible Bonds." *Journal of Finance* 28 (June 1973), pp. 713–732.

Weygandt, Jerry J. "A Comment on Financing with Convertible Preferred Stock, 1960–1967." *Journal of Finance* 26 (March 1971), pp. 148–149.

Appendix 23A

The Option
Pricing Model

Valuation, whether based on the traditional dividend capitalization approach introduced in Chapter 6 or the capital asset pricing model (CAPM) approach of Chapter 7, has been addressed in the absolute sense of trying to determine the specific value of a stock (or asset) based on its expected cash flow stream, and its risk to investors, who are assumed to hold diversified portfolios. In this appendix, our focus is different; instead of being concerned about valuation in an absolute sense, we are concerned about the valuation of financial instruments in relation to the value of the common stock of the company involved. Although originally an outgrowth of valuing stock options, or option contracts, the option pricing model (OPM) can be employed to value any contingent claim. Since a great many financial claims are contingent, the model has important implications for financial theory and practice.

Factors That Affect Option Prices

Options give the holder the right to buy or sell a security at a specified price during a designated time period. To keep the discussion simple, the following terminology is employed:

- *Call option*. An option that gives the owner the right to *purchase* a given number of shares of stock at a specified price during a given time period. Call options are all we consider in this appendix.
- *Put option*. An option that gives the holder the right to *sell* a given number of shares of a security at a specified price during a given time period.[1]

---

[1]For information on puts, see Michael Parkinson, "Option Pricing: The American Puts," *Journal of Business* 50 (January 1977), pp. 21–36.

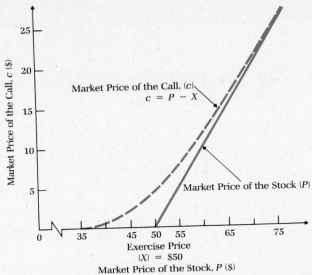

Figure 23A.1   Relation Between Call Price and Market Price of the Underlying Common Stock.

- *European option.* An option that can be exercised only on its maturity date and on which there are no cash dividends paid on the underlying common stock.[2] European options are all we consider in this appendix.
- *American option.* An option that can be exercised at any time up to and including maturity date.[3]
- *The exercise or striking price.* That price specified in the option at which the underlying stock can be bought or sold.

Basically, there are three factors that are important in determining the market price (c) of options.[4] They are the stock price (P), the exercise price (X), and the termination or maturity date (T). Obviously, the higher

---

[2]The effect of dividends on the valuation of European options is considered later in the appendix.

[3]It can be demonstrated that for non-dividend-paying stocks it is always advantageous to delay exercising an option until the latest possible date, its maturity. See Robert C. Merton, "The Rational Theory of Option Pricing," *Bell Journal of Economics and Management Science* 4 (spring 1973), pp. 141–183; and Clifford W. Smith, Jr., "Option Pricing: A Review," *Journal of Financial Economics* 3 (January–March 1976), pp. 3–51.

[4]The Chicago Board Options Exchange (CBOE) was established on April 26, 1973, when trading began in 16 call stock options. Since then a number of other exchanges have started trading in both put and call options. The unique features that led to trading of options were (1) the establishment of standard termination dates and exercise prices, (2) creation of a central, regulated marketplace, (3) introduction of a Clearing Corporation to guarantee every option, and (4) development of an organized secondary market.

the value of the underlying stock, the greater the value of the option written on it. This is seen in Figure 23A.1, which shows the normal relationship between the price of an option and the value of the underlying stock. Note that an option has a positive value even when the stock price is less than its exercise price.[5] In fact, as long as investors believe there is a chance the price of the stock will exceed the exercise (or striking) price on or before the maturity date of the option, the option will be valuable. As a rule, the lower the exercise price on the option, the greater the market value of the call—other things being equal. Thus, options are more valuable when the exercise price is $50 rather than $60. The third factor that influences the market price of calls is the length of time to maturity. That is, as the length of the option maturity is extended, the market price of the call increases as well. The reason is that with more time to maturity, there is a greater chance that the stock price will climb above the exercise price.

In addition to the stock price, exercise price, and time to maturity, two other important, but less obvious, factors also affect an option's value. These are the instantaneous variance (measured over a short interval) of the rate of return of the common stock (σ^2) and the risk-free rate (R_F). The holder of a call option prefers more variance in the rate of return of the stock to less variance because the greater the variance, the greater the probability that the stock price will exceed the exercise price. Remember that the call option is a *contingent claim*—it is valuable to the option holder only under the condition that the stock price exceeds the exercise price at termination date. Thus, there is an important difference between the value of options and the value of the underlying stock. If we hold the stock, the entire probability distribution of outcomes is of concern; and if we are risk-averse, we prefer low-variance to high-variance stocks. However, if we hold an option, we receive payoffs only from the right tail of the distribution; thus the contingent claim feature of options means that high variance in rate of return is desirable.

The final factor that influences the value of an option is the risk-free rate, R_F. By combining the purchase of the underlying stock with a short position in the stock's call option it can be shown that it is possible to create a risk-free hedge position.[6] Thus, as the risk-free rate of return increases (or decreases), the rate of return on the option also increases (decreases).

The preceding description implies that five factors are important in determining the market value (c) of a European call option: the price of the common stock, P; the exercise price stated on the option, X; the time

---

[5]An option for which the market price of the stock exceeds its exercise price is called an "in the money" option. Similarly, an "out of the money" option has an exercise price above the market price for the stock.

[6]This point is discussed further in the next section.

to maturity of the option, T; the instantaneous variance of the rate of return of the stock, σ^2; and the risk-free rate, R_F. Before we move on to consider the option pricing model, it is appropriate to note one other feature of call options. At the expiration or terminal date of the option, its value is given by:

$$c = MAX(P - X, 0) \qquad (23A.1)$$

where all symbols are as previously defined, and MAX is the maximum of the value $P - X$ or zero, whichever is greater. The quantity $P - X$ is simply the difference between the market price of the common stock on the termination date and the exercise price specified in the option. At maturity, if the market price is greater than the exercise price, the value of the option, c, is equal to $P - X$. Otherwise it is equal to zero, because the value of the option cannot be negative. With this background, we can now formally consider the option pricing model.

The Valuation of European Call Options

To derive the option pricing model, Black and Scholes[7] employ the following assumptions:

1. Capital markets are frictionless, with no transactions costs or taxes; options and stocks are infinitely divisible; and information is simultaneously and costlessly available to all individuals.
2. No imperfections exist in selling an option or short selling a stock.
3. The short-term interest rate (R_F) is known and constant throughout the length of the contract.[8]
4. Both stock trading and stock prices are continuous[9]; the instantaneous variance of the rate of return, therefore, is constant over the life of the option contract.
5. The stock pays no dividends.[10]
6. The option can be exercised only at the terminal date of the contract.

---

[7]The seminal work on options is by Fischer Black and Myron Scholes, "The Pricing of Options and Corporate Liabilities," *Journal of Political Economy* 81 (May–June 1973), pp. 637–654.

[8]This assumption has been relaxed by Robert C. Merton, "The Theory of Rational Option Pricing," *Bell Journal of Economics and Management Science* 4 (spring 1973), pp. 141–183.

[9]John C. Cox and Stephen A. Ross, "The Valuation of Options for Alternative Stochastic Processes," *Journal of Financial Economics* 4 (January–March 1976), pp. 637–659, modify the model to allow for noncontinuous trading. If the stock price is continuous, it means there are no jumps in the price.

[10]For the valuation of call options on dividend-paying stocks, see Richard Roll, "An Analytic Valuation Formula for Unprotected American Call Options with Known Dividends," *Journal of Financial Economics* 5 (November 1977), pp. 251–258; Eduardo S. Schwartz, "The Valuation of Warrants; Implementing a New Approach," *Journal of Financial Economics* 4 (January 1977), pp. 79–93; and Robert Geske, "The Pricing of Options with Stochastic Dividend Yield," *Journal of Finance* 33 (May 1978), pp. 617–625.

Given these assumptions, the equilibrium value of a call option can be determined by:

$$c = P \times N(\text{dist. 1}) - Xe^{-R_F\,(T)} \times N(\text{dist. 2}) \qquad (23A.2)$$

where c = current price or value of the option
 P = current price of the stock
 e = 2.71828
 X = call option's exercise price
 R_F = continuously compounded risk-free rate
 T = time remaining before expiration of the option (in years, for example, 90 days = 0.25)
 $N(\text{dist.}_i)$ = value of the cumulative normal density function for distribution i

$$\text{Dist. 1} = \frac{ln(P/X) + (R_F + \tfrac{1}{2}\sigma^2)T}{\sigma\sqrt{T}} \qquad (23A.3)$$

$$\text{Dist. 2} = \text{Dist. 1} - \sigma\sqrt{T} \qquad (23A.4)$$

where ln = natural logarithm
 σ^2 = annualized variance of the rate of return on the stock[11]

Although Equation 23A.2 appears formidable, almost all the required data are readily observable. The only variable that is not directly observable, and hence must be estimated, is the volatility of the price changes (σ^2) of the underlying common stock. If we knew that the future outcomes were $N(\text{dist. 1}) = N(\text{dist. 2}) = 1.0$, then Equation 23A.2 reduces to:

$$c = P - Xe^{-R_F\,T} \qquad (23A.5)$$

Equation 23A.5 says nothing more than the theoretical value of an option under conditions of certainty is the current price of the stock minus the present value of the exercise price continuously discounted back from the expiration date. A specific example will help us understand the application of Equations 23A.2 through 23A.4, which is the slightly more complex version of the OPM when uncertainty is considered.[12] Suppose

---

[11]All variables in the OPM must be estimated over a consistent time dimension. If T is defined in years (90 days = .25), the σ^2 should be on an annual basis. If some interval other than a year is used to estimate σ^2, the estimate must be annualized.

[12]The stock market price can be found in the financial quotation page of a current newspaper, while the exercise price and time are specified for the option. The risk-free rate can be estimated from rates on short term U.S. Treasury bills, while the variance could be approximated from the daily prices of the stock for the last three months. This is only an approximation, but it serves to illustrate the calculations. We assume the stock does not pay any cash dividends.

the current market price of the stock is $55, the exercise price is $50, the risk-free rate is 6 percent, the option matures in 3 months, and the instantaneous variance is .20. To determine the expected option price, it is necessary to solve for dist. 1 (Equation 23A.3) and dist. 2 (Equation 23A.4), and then to solve for c, the expected option value (Equation 23A.2). We begin by solving for dist. 1, where:[13]

$$\text{Dist. 1} = \frac{\ln(55/50) + [.06 + (.20/2)]\ .25}{\sqrt{.20} \times \sqrt{.25}}$$

$$= \frac{.0953 + .04}{.2236}$$

$$= \frac{.1353}{.2236} = .6051$$

Dist. 2 can be found using Equation 23A.4 so that:

$$\text{Dist. 2} = .6051 - \sqrt{.20} \times \sqrt{.25}$$

$$= .6051 - .2236 = .3815$$

Substituting into Equation 23A.2, we have:

$$c = P \times N(.6051) - Xe^{-R_F\ (T)} \times N(.3815)$$

$$= \$55 \times N(.6051) - \$50e^{-.06 \times .25} \times N(.3815)$$

To solve for the expected option value, c, we must calculate the value of the cumulative distribution function specified by $N(.6051)$ and $N(.3815)$. For dist. 1, with a value of .6051, we use Appendix Table A.5 and find the value to be .2274.[14] Since we need the cumulative distribution, we add the total area under the lefthand tail of the distribution, which is .5000. Thus, the cumulative probability associated with $N(.6051)$ is .7274. Using the same procedure, we find that for dist. 2, $N(.3815)$ has a cumulative probability of .6486. Substituting these values for $N(.6051)$ and $N(.3815)$, we now have:

$$c = \$55(.7274) - \$50e^{-.06 \times .25}\ (.6486)$$

---

[13]The natural logarithm of (55/50) can be found by using a table of natural logarithms. Many hand-held calculators also have natural logarithms.

[14]Employing linear interpolation, the approximate value can be determined to be

$$.2257 + \frac{.6051 - .6000}{.6100 - .6000}\ (.2291 - .2257) = .2257 + .0017 = .2274$$

[15]Many hand-held calculators also have functions for evaluating natural antilogarithms.

Stock Price (P)	Dist. 1	N(dist. 1)	Dist. 2	N(dist. 2)	Call Price (c)
$35	−1.4166	.0783	−1.6402	.0505	$ .25
45	−.2925	.3849	−.5162	.3028	2.41
55	.6051	.7274	.3815	.6486	8.06
65	1.3524	.9119	1.1288	.8705	16.39
75	1.9924	.9768	1.7688	.9615	25.90

[a]Assumptions: Exercise price (X) = $50; time to maturity (T) = 3 months = 0.25 years; risk-free rate (R_F) = .06; instantaneous variance (σ^2) = .20.

The evaluation of the term $e^{-.06 \times .25}$ involves continuous compounding as described in Appendix 5A.[15] The value of $e^{-.06 \times .25}$ is .9851. Substituting this value into the call option valuation formula, we have:

$$c = \$55(.7274) - \$50(.9851)(.6486)$$

$$= \$40.01 - \$31.95 = \$8.06$$

Thus, when the underlying stock is trading at $50, the expected value of this 3-month call option is $8.06. The value of this call option for various other possible stock prices is calculated in Table 23A.1. The relationship is also plotted in Figure 23A.1. Note that the call option has little value until the stock price (P) rises to a point where it is near the exercise price $(X = \$50)$. When stock prices are well below the exercise price, the option is "out of the money," and the call option is not worth much. When the stock price is above the exercise price, the option is "in the money." The higher the market price, the greater the value of the option and the more likely it is to be exercised.[16] Finally, we should note that the Black-Scholes option pricing model implies the following relationships (holding other things constant) for any given exercise price, X:

1. The higher the market price of the common stock, P, the higher the call price, c.
2. The longer the time to maturity, T, the higher the call price, c.
3. The higher the risk-free rate, R_F, the higher its call price, c.
4. The larger the instantaneous variance of the underlying common stock, σ^2, the higher the call price, c.

These relationships are the same as those we presented on an intuitive basis above.

The market value of the call option, c, given by solving Equation 23A.2, is the equilibrium value of the option. In addition, $N(\text{dist. 1})$ tells us the

---

[16]The upper value of the call option reaches $P - Xe^{-R_F T}$ at the limit for very high stock prices.

appropriate hedge ratio (of shares of stock to options) to use to maintain a fully hedged position. In our example, this ratio is .7274. This means that the movement in the stock price will be accompanied by a .7274 movement in the option price. To maintain the risk-free hedge position, an investor should purchase .7274 shares of stock for each call option written. With these proportions, price movements of the two financial assets will offset each other. If the actual market value of the option is greater or less than the value of c of $8.06 given by solving Equation 23A.2, investors can establish this riskless hedged position and earn a return in excess of the short-term or risk-free interest rate. As arbitragers enter the market, the excess return will eventually be driven out, and the market price of the option will equal that given by the Black-Scholes model.

Three further points should be noted. First, it is necessary continuously to adjust the short position in options for changes in the stock price and in the time to maturity if the riskless hedge position is to be maintained. In the real world, with transaction costs, it is not possible to continuously adjust the short position; however, the risk that will appear as a result of modest changes in the price of underlying common stock or the passage of time will be small. In practical terms, it is possible to maintain a hedge position that is approximately risk-free. Second, it should be stressed again that the major unobservable input to the option pricing model is the instantaneous variance (σ^2) of the underlying stock's return. Caution is needed if the stock's past price volatility is used as an estimate of expected future volatility.[17]

Finally, the entire discussion up until now has assumed that the underlying common stock does not pay any cash dividends. However, the presence of cash dividends tends, other things being equal, to lower the value of the option. In effect a cash dividend respesents the partial liquidation of the firm to which shareholders, but not option holders, are entitled. With an American option, the presence of cash dividends may influence when the option is exercised.[18] One approach to adjust for the presence of cash dividends is to treat all future dividends up to the expiration date of the option as if they had been paid. The present value of these dividends is subtracted from the current value (P) of the firm's common stock. The option pricing formula (Equation 23A.2) is then based on this adjusted market price of the common stock.[19]

---

[17]For some approaches to estimating or determining the implied variance of the stock price ratio, see Henry A. Latane and Richard J. Rendleman, Jr., "Standard Deviations of Stock Price Ratios Implied in Option Prices," *Journal of Finance* 31 (May 1976), pp. 369–381; Richard Schmalensee and Robert R. Trippi, "Common Stock Volatility Expectations Implied by Option Premia," *Journal of Finance* 33 (March 1978), pp. 129–147; and James D. MacBeth and Larry J. Merville, "An Empirical Examination of the Black-Scholes Call Option Pricing Model," *Journal of Finance* 34 (December 1979), pp. 1173–1186.

[18]See Schwartz, "The Valuation of Warrants: Implementing a New Approach."

[19]See William F. Sharpe, *Investments* 2nd ed. (Englewood Cliffs, N.J.: Prentice-Hall, 1981), pp. 446–447; and Roll, "An Analytic Valuation Formation for Unprotected American Call Options with Known Dividends."

Although the presence of cash dividends complicates the analysis, the basic relationships implied by the Black-Scholes option pricing model still hold, but not as precisely as in the absence of cash dividends. For some options, the expiration date is relatively near and the cash dividends paid on the underlying common stock before the option expires are not material. In these circumstances, it may not be worthwhile to make the dividend adjustment. This is particularly true when the ex-dividend date is some time away.[20]

Empirical Tests of the OPM

Empirical testing of the Black-Scholes model is being undertaken by many researchers. Based on recent test results by Black and Scholes, Galai, and MacBeth and Melville,[21] the following tentative conclusions can be reached:

1. Using ex post hedge returns, trading strategies (in the absence of transaction costs) based on the model earn significant excess returns. However, once transactions costs are introduced, the excess returns vanish.

2. The results appear to be fairly constant with respect to changes in the risk-free rate or the instantaneous variance of the underlying stock's returns.

3. The results are somewhat sensitive to the influence of cash dividends. Trading in options of common stock paying high cash dividends yielded lower profits than trading in options written on low-dividend stocks. This, of course, results because the option pricing model assumes no cash dividends.

4. There is conflicting evidence on whether the model overprices or underprices options. Black[22] and Merton[23] suggest that the option pricing model generally underprices "out of the money" options. However, MacBeth and Melville come to exactly opposite conclusions: They find that the OPM overprices deep "out of the money" options and underprices deep "in the money" options. They suggest that this conflicting empirical evidence may be the result of a nonstationary variance.

Taken together, the studies suggest that the Black-Scholes model predicts options prices very well. Substantial additional theoretical and

---

[20]For a discussion of cash dividends and ex-dividend dates, see Chapter 19.

[21]Black and Scholes, "The Pricing of Options and Corporate Liabilities"; Dan Galai, "Tests of Market Efficiency of the Chicago Board Options Exchange," *Journal of Business* 50 (April 1977), pp. 167–197; and MacBeth and Melville, "An Empirical Examination of the Black-Scholes Call Option Pricing Model."

[22]Fischer Black, "Fact and Fantasy in the Use of Options," *Financial Analysts Journal* 31 (July–August 1975), pp. 36–41, 61–72.

[23]Robert C. Merton, "Option Pricing When Underlying Stock Returns Are Discontinuous," *Journal of Financial Economics* 3 (January–March 1976), pp. 125–144.

empirical research is needed, but the available evidence indicates that the OPM provides reasonable and generally consistent results. But although it has important implications for pricing options, our major interest in the model is its broad application, which allows it to be used to evaluate any contingent claim.

Implications of the Option Pricing Model for Managerial Finance

The option pricing model has many important potential applications beyond valuing call options. With suitable modifications, the model can be applied to the valuation of a wide variety of financial instruments, such as warrants, convertible and subordinated debt, and contracts.[24] It can also be employed to derive an alternative approach to analyzing the risk (or term) structure of interest rates.[25] Of equal or perhaps greater importance is that the option pricing model may be used to value the equity portion of a levered firm. To illustrate, consider the following example where, for simplicity, we assume: (1) the firm issues pure discount bonds[26] with a provision that no cash dividends may be paid until after the bond matures; (2) there are no transactions costs or corporate taxes; (3) there is a known risk-free rate of interest; and (4) there are homogeneous expectations about the process that describe the value of the firm's assets. Given these assumptions, we can envision a simple firm that issues only one bond issue secured by the assets of the firm.

The value of the shareholders' position in this situation can be shown to be equal to the discounted value of the bonds and a call option. For if, when the bond matures, the value of the firm, V, exceeds the fair value of the bond, B, then the shareholders will exercise their option and pay off the bond issue and retain any excess. If, however, the value of the firm is less than the face of the bond, the shareholders will default on the debt by failing to exercise their option. Hence, at maturity, the shareholder's wealth, W_0, is:

$$W_0 = MAX\ [0, V - B] \tag{23A.6}$$

This, of course, is a European call option, and the form of Equation 23A.6 is exactly the same as that of Equation 23A.1 for valuing an option. We

---

[24]See, for example, Smith, "Option Pricing: A Review"; Fischer Black and John C. Cox, "Valuing Corporate Securities: Some Effects of Bond Indenture Provisions," *Journal of Finance* 31 (May 1976), pp. 351–367; Michael J. Brennan and Eduardo S. Schwartz, "Savings Bonds, Retractable Bonds and Callable Bonds," *Journal of Financial Economics* 5 (August 1977), pp. 67–88; and Schwartz, "The Valuation of Warrants: Implementing a New Approach."

[25]Robert C. Merton, "On the Pricing of Corporate Debt: The Risk Structure of Interest Rates," *Journal of Finance* 29 (May 1974), pp. 449–470.

[26]Pure discount bonds pay interest only at maturity.

can use the Black-Scholes formula to value Equation 23A.6. The bondholders' wealth is equal to MIN [V,B]. By suitable modification of this approach, the model can be applied to many financial decisions, including dividend policy, optimal capital structure questions, acquisitions and divestitures, and conglomerate mergers.[27] At this point in time, we are just beginning to understand the implications of the approach for analyzing many of these questions.

Finally, the option pricing approach may allow the development of more appropriate methods of making capital budgeting decisions under uncertainty. Although the time-state preference capital budgeting approach has been known, it has always appeared too general for practical application. Not only does the expected cash inflow (CFAT) have to be estimated for each state of the economy (weak, normal, strong) for each time period, but state "prices" must also be known or estimated. Based on the option pricing model approach, Banz and Miller[28] provide specific estimates of the state "prices" for each period in the future contingent on the present state of the economy. This is accomplished by using an option pricing model approach to estimate prices of future cash payoffs contingent on the rate of return realized on the market portfolio. By multiplying each contingent cash flow by its corresponding state "price" and summing, the present certainty equivalent value of a stream of cash flows is obtained. Following the procedures outlined in Chapters 13 and 14, financial decision makers would then accept the investments that maximize their net present values.

PROBLEMS

23A.1. *OPTION PRICING MODEL.* The common stock of Longhorn Farm Industries is currently selling for $30, and a call option on this stock sells for $1. The call option matures in 3 months, the current risk-free rate is 7 percent, the firm pays no cash dividends, and the exercise price of the call option is $35. After careful study, you conclude that an instantaneous variance of the rate of return for the next 3 months of .5 is appropriate.
   a. Using the Black-Scholes option pricing model, is the option overvalued or undervalued?
   b. If you believe your results, what should you do?

23A.2. *OPTION PRICING MODEL: CHANGES IN INPUT DATA.* What is the value of a call option on National Medical Supply if the exercise price is $20, the maturity is 6 months, the stock price is $24, the instantaneous variance of the rate of return is .40 and the

---

[27]Dan Galai and Ronald W. Masulis, "The Option Pricing Model and the Risk Factor of Stock," *Journal of Financial Economics* 3 (January–March 1976), pp. 53–82.

[28]See Rolf W. Banz and Merton H. Miller, "Prices for State-Contingent Claims: Some Estimates and Applications," *Journal of Business* 51 (October 1978), pp. 653–672.

risk-free rate is 6 percent? Holding everything else constant, but changing one variable at a time, calculate what happens to the option price if the following occurs (explain why the change occurs).

a. The length of time to expiration is 1 year.
b. The risk-free rate is 8 percent.
c. The variance is .64.
d. The exercise price is $15.

23A.3. *OPTION PRICING MODEL APPLIED TO VALUE A FIRM.* The Walnut Grove Furniture Company has a current market value of $20,000,000; the face value (not the market value) of the firm's outstanding debt is $8,000,000. The debt matures in 10 years, and interest on the debt is paid only at that time. The risk-free rate is 7 percent, and the instantaneous variance of the firm's rate of return on assets is .30. Employing the Black-Scholes option pricing model, determine the market value of Walnut Creek Furniture's stock *(S)* and debt *(D)*. *(Hint:* the current market value of the firm is *P*, and the face value of the debt = $8,000,000 = *X.)* After determining the market value of Walnut Grove Furniture, assume the risk-free rate, due to unanticipated inflation, rises to 11 percent.

1. What happens to the respective market values of the stock *(S)* and bonds *(D)* of Walnut Grove Furniture, given this unanticipated inflation?

2. Independent of (a), the firm has decided to undertake less risky projects in the future, with the consequence that the instantaneous variance of the rate of return is expected to drop to .10. What is the effect of a reduction in riskiness on the respective value of the stock *(S)* and the bonds *(D)*? Does this suggest that investment actions may be viewed differently by a firm's bondholders and shareholders? Explain.

SELECTED REFERENCES

Banz, Rolf W., and Merton H. Miller. "Prices for State-Contingent Claims: Some Estimates and Applications." *Journal of Business* 51 (October 1978), pp. 653–672.

Black, Fisher. "Fact and Fantasy in the Use of Options." *Financial Analysts Journal* 31 (July–August 1975), pp. 36–41, 61–72.

———, and John C. Cox. "Valuing Corporate Securities: Some Effects of Bond Indenture Provisions." *Journal of Finance* 31 (May 1976), pp. 351–367.

———, and Myron Scholes. "The Pricing of Options and Corporate Liabilities." *Journal of Political Economy* 81 (May–June 1973), pp. 637–654.

Cox, John C., and Stephen A. Ross. "The Valuation of Options for Alternative Stochastic Processes." *Journal of Financial Economics* 3 (January–March 1976), pp. 637–659.

Galai, Dan. "Tests of Market Efficiency of the Chicago Board Options Exchange." *Journal of Business* 50 (April 1977), pp. 167–197.

————, and R. W. Masulis. "The Option Pricing Model and the Risk Factor of Stock." *Journal of Financial Economics* 3 (January–March 1976), pp. 53–82.

Geske, Robert. "The Pricing of Options with Stochastic Dividend Yields." *Journal of Finance* 33 (May 1978), pp. 617–625.

Latané, Henry A., and Richard J. Rendleman, Jr. "Standard Deviations of Stock Price Ratios Implied in Option Prices." *Journal of Finance* 31 (May 1976), pp. 369–381.

MacBeth, James D., and Larry J. Melville. "An Empirical Examination of the Black-Scholes Call Option Pricing Model." *Journal of Finance* 34 (December 1979), pp. 1173–1186.

Merton, Robert C. "Option Pricing When Underlying Stock Returns Are Discontinuous." *Journal of Financial Economics* 3 (January–March 1976), pp. 125–144.

————. "On the Pricing of Corporate Debt: The Risk Structure of Interest Rates." *Journal of Finance* 29 (May 1974), pp. 449–470.

————. "The Rational Theory of Option Pricing." *Bell Journal of Economics and Management Science* 4 (spring 1973), pp. 143–183.

Parkinson, Michael. "Option Pricing: The American Puts." *Journal of Business* 50 (January 1977), pp. 21–36.

Roenfeldt, Rodney L., Philip L. Cooley, and Michael J. Gombola. "Market Performance of Options on the Chicago Board Options Exchange." *Journal of Business Research* 7 (1979), pp. 95–107.

Roll, Richard. "An Analytic Valuation Formulation for Unprotected American Call Options with Known Dividends." *Journal of Financial Economics* 5 (November 1977), pp. 251–258.

Schmalensee, Richard, and Robert R. Trippi. "Common Stock Volatility Expectations Implied by Option Premia." *Journal of Finance* 33 (March 1978), pp. 129–147.

Sharpe, William F. *Investments*, 2nd ed. (Englewood Cliffs, N.J.: Prentice-Hall, 1981).

Smith, Clifford W., Jr. "Option Pricing: A Review." *Journal of Financial Economics* 3 (January–March 1976), pp. 3–52.

Schwartz, Eduardo S. "The Valuation of Warrants: Implementing a New Approach." *Journal of Financial Economics* 4 (January 1977), pp. 79–93.

Trennepohl, Gary. "A Comparison of Listed Option Premiums and Black and Scholes Model Prices: 1973–1979." *Journal of Financial Research* 3 (spring 1981), pp. 11–20.

Appendix A

Financial Tables

TABLE A.1

Future-Value Interest Factors for One Dollar Compounded at k Percent for n Periods:

$FVIF_{kn} = (1 + k)^n$

Period	1%	2%	3%	4%	5%	6%	7%	8%	9%	10%
1	1.010	1.020	1.030	1.040	1.050	1.060	1.070	1.080	1.090	1.100
2	1.020	1.040	1.061	1.082	1.102	1.124	1.145	1.166	1.188	1.210
3	1.030	1.061	1.093	1.125	1.158	1.191	1.225	1.260	1.295	1.331
4	1.041	1.082	1.126	1.170	1.216	1.262	1.311	1.360	1.412	1.464
5	1.051	1.104	1.159	1.217	1.276	1.338	1.403	1.469	1.539	1.611
6	1.062	1.126	1.194	1.265	1.340	1.419	1.501	1.587	1.677	1.772
7	1.072	1.149	1.230	1.316	1.407	1.504	1.606	1.714	1.828	1.949
8	1.083	1.172	1.267	1.369	1.477	1.594	1.718	1.851	1.993	2.144
9	1.094	1.195	1.305	1.423	1.551	1.689	1.838	1.999	2.172	2.358
10	1.105	1.219	1.344	1.480	1.629	1.791	1.967	2.159	2.367	2.594
11	1.116	1.243	1.384	1.539	1.710	1.898	2.105	2.332	2.580	2.853
12	1.127	1.268	1.426	1.601	1.796	2.012	2.252	2.518	2.813	3.138
13	1.138	1.294	1.469	1.665	1.886	2.133	2.410	2.720	3.066	3.452
14	1.149	1.319	1.513	1.732	1.980	2.261	2.579	2.937	3.342	3.797
15	1.161	1.346	1.558	1.801	2.079	2.397	2.759	3.172	3.642	4.177
16	1.173	1.373	1.605	1.873	2.183	2.540	2.952	3.426	3.970	4.595
17	1.184	1.400	1.653	1.948	2.292	2.693	3.159	3.700	4.328	5.054
18	1.196	1.428	1.702	2.026	2.407	2.854	3.380	3.996	4.717	5.560
19	1.208	1.457	1.753	2.107	2.527	3.026	3.616	4.316	5.142	6.116
20	1.220	1.486	1.806	2.191	2.653	3.207	3.870	4.661	5.604	6.727
21	1.232	1.516	1.860	2.279	2.786	3.399	4.140	5.034	6.109	7.400
22	1.245	1.546	1.916	2.370	2.925	3.603	4.430	5.436	6.658	8.140
23	1.257	1.577	1.974	2.465	3.071	3.820	4.740	5.871	7.258	8.954
24	1.270	1.608	2.033	2.563	3.225	4.049	5.072	6.341	7.911	9.850
25	1.282	1.641	2.094	2.666	3.386	4.292	5.427	6.848	8.623	10.834
30	1.348	1.811	2.427	3.243	4.322	5.743	7.612	10.062	13.267	17.449
35	1.417	2.000	2.814	3.946	5.516	7.686	10.676	14.785	20.413	28.102
40	1.489	2.208	3.262	4.801	7.040	10.285	14.974	21.724	31.408	45.258
45	1.565	2.438	3.781	5.841	8.985	13.764	21.002	31.920	48.325	72.888
50	1.645	2.691	4.384	7.106	11.467	18.419	29.456	46.900	74.354	117.386

continued

TABLE A.1

Future-Value Interest Factors for One Dollar Compounded at k Percent for n Periods:

$FVIF_{kn} = (1 + k)^n$

Period	11%	12%	13%	14%	15%	16%	17%	18%	19%	20%
1	1.110	1.120	1.130	1.140	1.150	1.160	1.170	1.180	1.190	1.200
2	1.232	1.254	1.277	1.300	1.322	1.346	1.369	1.392	1.416	1.440
3	1.368	1.405	1.443	1.482	1.521	1.561	1.602	1.643	1.685	1.728
4	1.518	1.574	1.630	1.689	1.749	1.811	1.874	1.939	2.005	2.074
5	1.685	1.762	1.842	1.925	2.011	2.100	2.192	2.288	2.386	2.488
6	1.870	1.974	2.082	2.195	2.313	2.436	2.565	2.700	2.840	2.986
7	2.076	2.211	2.353	2.502	2.660	2.826	3.001	3.185	3.379	3.583
8	2.305	2.476	2.658	2.853	3.059	3.278	3.511	3.759	4.021	4.300
9	2.558	2.773	3.004	3.252	3.518	3.803	4.108	4.435	4.785	5.160
10	2.839	3.106	3.395	3.707	4.046	4.411	4.807	5.234	5.695	6.192
11	3.152	3.479	3.836	4.226	4.652	5.117	5.624	6.176	6.777	7.430
12	3.498	3.896	4.334	4.818	5.350	5.936	6.580	7.288	8.064	8.916
13	3.883	4.363	4.898	5.492	6.153	6.886	7.699	8.599	9.596	10.699
14	4.310	4.887	5.535	6.261	7.076	7.987	9.007	10.147	11.420	12.839
15	4.785	5.474	6.254	7.138	8.137	9.265	10.539	11.974	13.589	15.407
16	5.311	6.130	7.067	8.137	9.358	10.748	12.330	14.129	16.171	18.488
17	5.895	6.866	7.986	9.276	10.761	12.468	14.426	16.672	19.244	22.186
18	6.543	7.690	9.024	10.575	12.375	14.462	16.879	19.673	22.900	26.623
19	7.263	8.613	10.197	12.055	14.232	16.776	19.748	23.214	27.251	31.948
20	8.062	9.646	11.523	13.743	16.366	19.461	23.105	27.393	32.429	38.337
21	8.949	10.804	13.021	15.667	18.821	22.574	27.033	32.323	38.591	46.005
22	9.933	12.100	14.713	17.861	21.644	26.186	31.629	38.141	45.923	55.205
23	11.026	13.552	16.626	20.361	24.891	30.376	37.005	45.007	54.648	66.247
24	12.239	15.178	18.788	23.212	28.625	35.236	43.296	53.108	65.031	79.496
25	13.585	17.000	21.230	26.461	32.918	40.874	50.656	62.667	77.387	95.395
30	22.892	29.960	39.115	50.949	66.210	85.849	111.061	143.367	184.672	237.373
35	38.574	52.799	72.066	98.097	133.172	180.311	243.495	327.988	440.691	590.657
40	64.999	93.049	132.776	188.876	267.856	378.715	533.846	750.353	1051.642	1469.740
45	109.527	163.985	244.629	363.662	538.752	795.429	1170.425	1716.619	2509.583	3657.176
50	184.559	288.996	450.711	700.197	1083.619	1670.669	2566.080	3927.189	5988.730	9100.191

continued

TABLE A.1

Future-Value Interest Factors for One Dollar Compounded at k Percent for n Periods:

$$FVIF_{k,n} = (1 + k)^n$$

Period	21%	22%	23%	24%	25%	26%	27%	28%	29%	30%
1	1.210	1.220	1.230	1.240	1.250	1.260	1.270	1.280	1.290	1.300
2	1.464	1.488	1.513	1.538	1.562	1.588	1.613	1.638	1.664	1.690
3	1.772	1.816	1.861	1.907	1.953	2.000	2.048	2.097	2.147	2.197
4	2.144	2.215	2.289	2.364	2.441	2.520	2.601	2.684	2.769	2.856
5	2.594	2.703	2.815	2.932	3.052	3.176	3.304	3.436	3.572	3.713
6	3.138	3.297	3.463	3.635	3.815	4.001	4.196	4.398	4.608	4.827
7	3.797	4.023	4.259	4.508	4.768	5.042	5.329	5.629	5.945	6.275
8	4.595	4.908	5.239	5.589	5.960	6.353	6.767	7.206	7.669	8.157
9	5.560	5.987	6.444	6.931	7.451	8.004	8.595	9.223	9.893	10.604
10	6.727	7.305	7.926	8.594	9.313	10.086	10.915	11.806	12.761	13.786
11	8.140	8.912	9.749	10.657	11.642	12.708	13.862	15.112	16.462	17.921
12	9.850	10.872	11.991	13.215	14.552	16.012	17.605	19.343	21.236	23.298
13	11.918	13.264	14.749	16.386	18.190	20.175	22.359	24.759	27.395	30.287
14	14.421	16.182	18.141	20.319	22.737	25.420	28.395	31.691	35.339	39.373
15	17.449	19.742	22.314	25.195	28.422	32.030	36.062	40.565	45.587	51.185
16	21.113	24.085	27.446	31.242	35.527	40.357	45.799	51.923	58.808	66.541
17	25.547	29.384	33.758	38.740	44.409	50.850	58.165	66.461	75.862	86.503
18	30.912	35.848	41.523	48.038	55.511	64.071	73.869	85.070	97.862	112.454
19	37.404	43.735	51.073	59.567	69.389	80.730	93.813	108.890	126.242	146.190
20	45.258	53.357	62.820	73.863	86.736	101.720	119.143	139.379	162.852	190.047
21	54.762	65.095	77.268	91.591	108.420	128.167	151.312	178.405	210.079	247.061
22	66.262	79.416	95.040	113.572	135.525	161.490	192.165	228.358	271.002	321.178
23	80.178	96.887	116.899	140.829	169.407	203.477	244.050	292.298	349.592	417.531
24	97.015	118.203	143.786	174.628	211.758	256.381	309.943	374.141	450.974	542.791
25	117.388	144.207	176.857	216.539	264.698	323.040	393.628	478.901	581.756	705.627
30	304.471	389.748	497.904	634.810	807.793	1025.904	1300.477	1645.488	2078.208	2619.936
35	789.716	1053.370	1401.749	1861.020	2465.189	3258.053	4296.547	5653.840	7423.988	9727.598
40	2048.309	2846.941	3946.340	5455.797	7523.156	10346.879	14195.051	19426.418	26520.723	36117.754
45	5312.758	7694.418	11110.121	15994.316	22958.844	32859.457	46697.973	66748.500	94739.937	134102.187
50	13779.844	20795.680	31278.301	46889.207	70064.812	104354.562	154942.687	229345.875	338440.000	497910.125

continued

Future-Value Interest Factors for One Dollar Compounded at k Percent for n Periods:

$$FVIF_{k,n} = (1 + k)^n$$

Period	31%	32%	33%	34%	35%	36%	37%	38%	39%	40%
1	1.310	1.320	1.330	1.340	1.350	1.360	1.370	1.380	1.390	1.400
2	1.716	1.742	1.769	1.796	1.822	1.850	1.877	1.904	1.932	1.960
3	2.248	2.300	2.353	2.406	2.460	2.515	2.571	2.628	2.686	2.744
4	2.945	3.036	3.129	3.224	3.321	3.421	3.523	3.627	3.733	3.842
5	3.858	4.007	4.162	4.320	4.484	4.653	4.826	5.005	5.189	5.378
6	5.054	5.290	5.535	5.789	6.053	6.328	6.612	6.907	7.213	7.530
7	6.621	6.983	7.361	7.758	8.172	8.605	9.058	9.531	10.025	10.541
8	8.673	9.217	9.791	10.395	11.032	11.703	12.410	13.153	13.935	14.758
9	11.362	12.166	13.022	13.930	14.894	15.917	17.001	18.151	19.370	20.661
10	14.884	16.060	17.319	18.666	20.106	21.646	23.292	25.049	26.924	28.925
11	19.498	21.199	23.034	25.012	27.144	29.439	31.910	34.567	37.425	40.495
12	25.542	27.982	30.635	33.516	36.644	40.037	43.716	47.703	52.020	56.694
13	33.460	36.937	40.745	44.912	49.469	54.451	59.892	65.830	72.308	79.371
14	43.832	48.756	54.190	60.181	66.784	74.053	82.051	90.845	100.509	111.119
15	57.420	64.358	72.073	80.643	90.158	100.712	112.410	125.366	139.707	155.567
16	75.220	84.953	95.857	108.061	121.713	136.968	154.002	173.005	194.192	217.793
17	98.539	112.138	127.490	144.802	164.312	186.277	210.983	238.747	269.927	304.911
18	129.086	148.022	169.561	194.035	221.822	253.337	289.046	329.471	375.198	426.875
19	169.102	195.389	225.517	260.006	299.459	344.537	395.993	454.669	521.525	597.625
20	221.523	257.913	299.937	348.408	404.270	468.571	542.511	627.443	724.919	836.674
21	290.196	340.446	398.916	466.867	545.764	637.256	743.240	865.871	1007.637	1171.343
22	380.156	449.388	530.558	625.601	736.781	866.668	1018.238	1194.900	1400.615	1639.878
23	498.004	593.192	705.642	838.305	994.653	1178.668	1394.986	1648.961	1946.854	2295.829
24	652.385	783.013	938.504	1123.328	1342.781	1602.988	1911.129	2275.564	2706.125	3214.158
25	854.623	1033.577	1248.210	1505.258	1812.754	2180.063	2618.245	3140.275	3761.511	4499.816
30	3297.081	4142.008	5194.516	6503.285	8128.426	10142.914	12636.086	15716.703	19517.969	24201.043
35	12719.918	16598.906	21617.363	28096.695	36448.051	47190.727	60983.836	78660.188	101276.125	130158.687
40	49072.621	66519.313	89962.188	121388.437	163433.875	219558.625	294317.937	393684.687	525508.312	700022.688

continued

TABLE A.1

Future-Value Interest Factors for One Dollar Compounded at k Percent for n Periods:

$FVIF_{k,n} = (1 + k)^n$

Period	41%	42%	43%	44%	45%	46%	47%	48%	49%	50%
1	1.410	1.420	1.430	1.440	1.450	1.460	1.470	1.480	1.490	1.500
2	1.988	2.016	2.045	2.074	2.102	2.132	2.161	2.190	2.220	2.250
3	2.803	2.863	2.924	2.986	3.049	3.112	3.177	3.242	3.308	3.375
4	3.953	4.066	4.182	4.300	4.421	4.544	4.669	4.798	4.929	5.063
5	5.573	5.774	5.980	6.192	6.410	6.634	6.864	7.101	7.344	7.594
6	7.858	8.198	8.551	8.916	9.294	9.685	10.090	10.509	10.943	11.391
7	11.080	11.642	12.228	12.839	13.476	14.141	14.833	15.554	16.304	17.086
8	15.623	16.531	17.486	18.488	19.541	20.645	21.804	23.019	24.293	25.629
9	22.028	23.474	25.005	26.623	28.334	30.142	32.052	34.069	36.197	38.443
10	31.059	33.333	35.757	38.337	41.085	44.007	47.116	50.421	53.934	57.665
11	43.793	47.333	51.132	55.206	59.573	64.251	69.261	74.624	80.361	86.498
12	61.749	67.213	73.119	79.496	86.380	93.806	101.813	110.443	119.738	129.746
13	87.066	95.443	104.560	114.475	125.251	136.956	149.665	163.456	178.410	194.620
14	122.763	135.529	149.521	164.843	181.614	199.956	220.008	241.914	265.831	291.929
15	173.095	192.451	213.814	237.374	263.341	291.936	323.411	358.033	396.098	437.894
16	244.064	273.280	305.754	341.819	381.844	426.226	475.414	529.888	590.170	656.841
17	344.130	388.057	437.228	492.219	553.674	622.289	698.859	784.234	879.354	985.261
18	485.224	551.041	625.235	708.794	802.826	908.541	1027.321	1160.666	1310.236	1477.892
19	684.165	782.478	894.086	1020.663	1164.098	1326.469	1510.161	1717.785	1952.252	2216.838
20	964.673	1111.118	1278.543	1469.754	1687.942	1936.642	2219.936	2542.321	2908.854	3325.257
21	1360.188	1577.786	1828.315	2116.445	2447.515	2827.496	3263.304	3762.633	4334.188	4987.883
22	1917.865	2240.455	2614.489	3047.679	3548.896	4128.137	4797.051	5568.691	6457.941	7481.824
23	2704.188	3181.443	3738.717	4388.656	5145.898	6027.078	7051.660	8241.664	9622.324	11222.738
24	3812.905	4517.641	5346.355	6319.656	7461.547	8799.523	10365.934	12197.656	14337.258	16834.109
25	5376.191	6415.047	7645.289	9100.305	10819.242	12847.297	15237.914	18052.516	21362.508	25251.164
30	29961.941	37037.383	45716.496	56346.535	69348.375	85226.375	104594.938	128187.438	156885.438	191751.000

TABLE A.2

Future-Value Interest Factors for a One-Dollar Annuity Compounded at k Percent for n Periods:

$$FVIFA_{kn} = \sum_{t=1}^{n} (1 + k)^{t-1} \text{ or } \frac{(1 + k)^n - 1}{k}$$

Period	1%	2%	3%	4%	5%	6%	7%	8%	9%	10%
1	1.000	1.000	1.000	1.000	1.000	1.000	1.000	1.000	1.000	1.000
2	2.010	2.020	2.030	2.040	2.050	2.060	2.070	2.080	2.090	2.100
3	3.030	3.060	3.091	3.122	3.152	3.184	3.215	3.246	3.278	3.310
4	4.060	4.122	4.184	4.246	4.310	4.375	4.440	4.506	4.573	4.641
5	5.101	5.204	5.309	5.416	5.526	5.637	5.751	5.867	5.985	6.105
6	6.152	6.308	6.468	6.633	6.802	6.975	7.153	7.336	7.523	7.716
7	7.214	7.434	7.562	7.898	8.142	8.394	8.654	8.923	9.200	9.487
8	8.286	8.583	8.892	9.214	9.549	9.897	10.260	10.637	11.028	11.436
9	9.368	9.755	10.159	10.583	11.027	11.491	11.978	12.488	13.021	13.579
10	10.462	10.950	11.464	12.006	12.578	13.181	13.816	14.487	15.193	15.937
11	11.567	12.169	12.808	13.486	14.207	14.972	15.784	16.645	17.560	18.531
12	12.682	13.412	14.192	15.026	15.917	16.870	17.888	18.977	20.141	21.384
13	13.809	14.680	15.618	16.627	17.713	18.882	20.141	21.495	22.953	24.523
14	14.947	15.974	17.086	18.292	19.598	21.015	22.550	24.215	26.019	27.975
15	16.097	17.293	18.599	20.023	21.578	23.276	25.129	27.152	29.361	31.772
16	17.258	18.639	20.157	21.824	23.657	25.672	27.888	30.324	33.003	35.949
17	18.430	20.012	21.761	23.697	25.840	28.213	30.840	33.750	36.973	40.544
18	19.614	21.412	23.414	25.645	28.132	30.905	33.999	37.450	41.301	45.599
19	20.811	22.840	25.117	27.671	30.539	33.760	37.379	41.446	46.018	51.158
20	22.019	24.297	26.870	29.778	33.066	36.785	40.995	45.762	51.159	57.274
21	23.239	25.783	28.676	31.969	35.719	39.992	44.865	50.422	56.764	64.002
22	24.471	27.299	30.536	34.248	38.505	43.392	49.005	55.456	62.872	71.402
23	25.716	28.845	32.452	36.618	41.430	46.995	53.435	60.893	69.531	79.542
24	26.973	30.421	34.426	39.082	44.501	50.815	58.176	66.764	76.789	88.496
25	28.243	32.030	36.459	41.645	47.726	54.864	63.248	73.105	84.699	98.346
30	34.784	40.567	47.575	56.084	66.438	79.057	94.459	113.282	136.305	164.491
35	41.659	49.994	60.461	73.651	90.318	111.432	138.234	172.314	215.705	271.018
40	48.885	60.401	75.400	95.024	120.797	154.758	199.630	259.052	337.872	442.580
45	56.479	71.891	92.718	121.027	159.695	212.737	285.741	386.497	525.840	718.881
50	64.461	84.577	112.794	152.664	209.341	290.325	406.516	573.756	815.051	1163.865

continued

TABLE A.2

Future-Value Interest Factors for a One-Dollar Annuity Compounded at k Percent for n Periods:

$$FVIFA_{kn} = \sum_{t=1}^{n} (1+k)^{t-1} \text{ or } \frac{(1+k)^n - 1}{k}$$

Period	11%	12%	13%	14%	15%	16%	17%	18%	19%	20%
1	1.000	1.000	1.000	1.000	1.000	1.000	1.000	1.000	1.000	1.000
2	2.110	2.120	2.130	2.140	2.150	2.160	2.170	2.180	2.190	2.200
3	3.342	3.374	3.407	3.440	3.472	3.506	3.539	3.572	3.606	3.640
4	4.710	4.779	4.850	4.921	4.993	5.066	5.141	5.215	5.291	5.368
5	6.228	6.353	6.480	6.610	6.742	6.877	7.014	7.154	7.297	7.442
6	7.913	8.115	8.323	8.535	8.754	8.977	9.207	9.442	9.683	9.930
7	9.783	10.089	10.405	10.730	11.067	11.414	11.772	12.141	12.523	12.916
8	11.859	12.300	12.757	13.233	13.727	14.240	14.773	15.327	15.902	16.499
9	14.164	14.776	15.416	16.085	16.786	17.518	18.285	19.086	19.923	20.799
10	16.722	17.549	18.420	19.337	20.304	21.321	22.393	23.521	24.709	25.959
11	19.561	20.655	21.814	23.044	24.349	25.733	27.200	28.755	30.403	32.150
12	22.713	24.133	25.650	27.271	29.001	30.850	32.824	34.931	37.180	39.580
13	26.211	28.029	29.984	32.088	34.352	36.786	39.404	42.218	45.244	48.496
14	30.095	32.392	34.882	37.581	40.504	43.672	47.102	50.818	54.841	59.196
15	34.405	37.280	40.417	43.842	47.580	51.659	56.109	60.965	66.260	72.035
16	39.190	42.753	46.671	50.980	55.717	60.925	66.648	72.938	79.850	87.442
17	44.500	48.883	53.738	59.117	65.075	71.673	78.978	87.067	96.021	105.930
18	50.396	55.749	61.724	68.393	75.836	84.140	93.404	103.739	115.265	128.116
19	56.939	63.439	70.748	78.968	88.211	98.603	110.283	123.412	138.165	154.739
20	64.202	72.052	80.946	91.024	102.443	115.379	130.031	146.626	165.417	186.687
21	72.264	81.698	92.468	104.767	118.809	134.840	153.136	174.019	197.846	225.024
22	81.213	92.502	105.489	120.434	137.630	157.414	180.169	206.342	236.436	271.028
23	91.147	104.602	120.203	138.295	159.274	183.600	211.798	244.483	282.359	326.234
24	102.173	118.154	136.829	158.656	184.166	213.976	248.803	289.490	337.007	392.480
25	114.412	133.333	155.616	181.867	212.790	249.212	292.099	342.598	402.038	471.976
30	199.018	241.330	293.192	356.778	434.738	530.306	647.423	790.932	966.698	1181.865
35	341.583	431.658	546.663	693.552	881.152	1120.699	1426.448	1816.607	2314.173	2948.294
40	581.812	767.080	1013.667	1341.979	1779.048	2360.724	3134.412	4163.094	5529.711	7343.715
45	986.613	1358.208	1874.086	2590.464	3585.031	4965.191	6879.008	9531.258	13203.105	18280.914
50	1668.723	2399.975	3459.344	4994.301	7217.488	10435.449	15088.805	21812.273	31514.492	45496.094

continued

TABLE A.2
Future-Value Interest Factors for a One-Dollar Annuity Compounded at k Percent for n Periods:

$$FVIFA_{k,n} = \sum_{t=1}^{n} (1+k)^{t-1} \text{ or } \frac{(1+k)^n - 1}{k}$$

Period	21%	22%	23%	24%	25%	26%	27%	28%	29%	30%
1	1.000	1.000	1.000	1.000	1.000	1.000	1.000	1.000	1.000	1.000
2	2.210	2.220	2.230	2.240	2.250	2.260	2.270	2.280	2.290	2.300
3	3.674	3.708	3.743	3.778	3.813	3.848	3.883	3.918	3.954	3.990
4	5.446	5.524	5.604	5.684	5.766	5.848	5.931	6.016	6.101	6.187
5	7.589	7.740	7.893	8.048	8.207	8.368	8.533	8.700	8.870	9.043
6	10.183	10.442	10.708	10.980	11.259	11.544	11.837	12.136	12.442	12.756
7	13.321	13.740	14.171	14.615	15.073	15.546	16.032	16.534	17.051	17.583
8	17.119	17.762	18.430	19.123	19.842	20.588	21.361	22.163	22.995	23.858
9	21.714	22.670	23.669	24.712	25.802	26.940	28.129	29.369	30.664	32.015
10	27.274	28.657	30.113	31.643	33.253	34.945	36.723	38.592	40.556	42.619
11	34.001	35.962	38.039	40.238	42.566	45.030	47.639	50.398	53.318	56.405
12	42.141	44.873	47.787	50.895	54.208	57.738	61.501	65.510	69.780	74.326
13	51.991	55.745	59.778	64.109	68.760	73.750	79.106	84.853	91.016	97.624
14	63.909	69.009	74.528	80.496	86.949	93.925	101.465	109.611	118.411	127.912
15	78.330	85.191	92.669	100.815	109.687	119.346	129.860	141.302	153.750	167.285
16	95.779	104.933	114.983	126.010	138.109	151.375	165.922	181.867	199.337	218.470
17	116.892	129.019	142.428	157.252	173.636	191.733	211.721	233.790	258.145	285.011
18	142.439	158.403	176.187	195.993	218.045	242.583	269.885	300.250	334.006	371.514
19	173.351	194.251	217.710	244.031	273.556	306.654	343.754	385.321	431.868	483.968
20	210.755	237.986	268.783	303.598	342.945	387.384	437.568	494.210	558.110	630.157
21	256.013	291.343	331.603	377.461	429.681	489.104	556.710	633.589	720.962	820.204
22	310.775	356.438	408.871	469.052	538.101	617.270	708.022	811.993	931.040	1067.265
23	377.038	435.854	503.911	582.624	673.626	778.760	900.187	1040.351	1202.042	1388.443
24	457.215	532.741	620.810	723.453	843.032	982.237	1144.237	1332.649	1551.634	1805.975
25	554.230	650.944	764.596	898.082	1054.791	1238.617	1454.180	1706.790	2002.608	2348.765
30	1445.111	1767.044	2160.459	2640.881	3227.172	3941.953	4812.891	5873.172	7162.785	8729.805
35	3755.814	4783.520	6090.227	7750.094	9856.746	12527.160	15909.480	20188.742	25596.512	32422.090
40	9749.141	12936.141	17153.691	22728.367	30088.621	39791.957	52570.707	69376.562	91447.375	120389.375
45	25294.223	34970.230	48300.660	66638.937	91831.312	126378.937	173692.875	238384.312	326686.375	447005.062

continued

TABLE A.2

Future-Value Interest Factors for a One-Dollar Annuity Compounded at k Percent for n Periods:

$$FVIFA_{k,n} = \sum_{t=1}^{n}(1+k)^{t-1} \text{ or } \frac{(1+k)^n - 1}{k}$$

Period	31%	32%	33%	34%	35%	36%	37%	38%	39%	40%
1	1.000	1.000	1.000	1.000	1.000	1.000	1.000	1.000	1.000	1.000
2	2.310	2.320	2.330	2.340	2.350	2.360	2.370	2.380	2.390	2.400
3	4.026	4.062	4.099	4.136	4.172	4.210	4.247	4.284	4.322	4.360
4	6.274	6.362	6.452	6.542	6.633	6.725	6.818	6.912	7.008	7.104
5	9.219	9.398	9.581	9.766	9.954	10.146	10.341	10.539	10.741	10.946
6	13.077	13.406	13.742	14.086	14.438	14.799	15.167	15.544	15.930	16.324
7	18.131	18.696	19.277	19.876	20.492	21.126	21.779	22.451	23.142	23.853
8	24.752	25.678	26.638	27.633	28.664	29.732	30.837	31.982	33.167	34.395
9	33.425	34.895	36.429	38.028	39.696	41.435	43.247	45.135	47.103	49.152
10	44.786	47.062	49.451	51.958	54.590	57.351	60.248	63.287	66.473	69.813
11	59.670	63.121	66.769	70.624	74.696	78.998	83.540	88.335	93.397	98.739
12	79.167	84.320	89.803	95.636	101.840	108.437	115.450	122.903	130.822	139.234
13	104.709	112.302	120.438	129.152	138.484	148.474	159.166	170.606	182.842	195.928
14	138.169	149.239	161.183	174.063	187.953	202.925	219.058	236.435	255.151	275.299
15	182.001	197.996	215.373	234.245	254.737	276.978	301.109	327.281	355.659	386.418
16	239.421	262.354	287.446	314.888	344.895	377.690	413.520	452.647	495.366	541.985
17	314.642	347.307	383.303	422.949	466.608	514.658	567.521	625.652	689.558	759.778
18	413.180	459.445	510.792	567.751	630.920	700.935	778.504	864.399	959.485	1064.689
19	542.266	607.467	680.354	761.786	852.741	954.271	1067.551	1193.870	1334.683	1491.563
20	711.368	802.856	905.870	1021.792	1152.200	1298.809	1463.544	1648.539	1856.208	2089.188
21	932.891	1060.769	1205.807	1370.201	1556.470	1767.380	2006.055	2275.982	2581.128	2925.862
22	1223.087	1401.215	1604.724	1837.068	2102.234	2404.636	2749.294	3141.852	3588.765	4097.203
23	1603.243	1850.603	2135.282	2462.669	2839.014	3271.304	3767.532	4336.710	4989.379	5737.078
24	2101.247	2443.795	2840.924	3300.974	3833.667	4449.969	5162.516	5985.710	6936.230	8032.906
25	2753.631	3226.808	3779.428	4424.301	5176.445	6052.957	7073.645	8261.273	9642.352	11247.062
30	10632.543	12940.672	15737.945	19124.434	23221.258	28172.016	34148.906	41357.227	50043.625	60500.207
35	41028.887	51868.563	65504.199	82634.625	104134.500	131082.625	164818.438	206998.375	259680.313	325394.688

continued

Future-Value Interest Factors for a One-Dollar Annuity Compounded at k Percent for n Periods:

$$FVIFA_{k,n} = \sum_{t=1}^{n} (1 + k)^{t-1} \text{ or } \frac{(1 + k)^n - 1}{k}$$

Period	41%	42%	43%	44%	45%	46%	47%	48%	49%	50%
1	1.000	1.000	1.000	1.000	1.000	1.000	1.000	1.000	1.000	1.000
2	2.410	2.420	2.430	2.440	2.450	2.460	2.470	2.480	2.490	2.500
3	4.398	4.436	4.475	4.514	4.552	4.592	4.631	4.670	4.710	4.750
4	7.201	7.300	7.399	7.500	7.601	7.704	7.807	7.912	8.018	8.125
5	11.154	11.366	11.581	11.799	12.022	12.247	12.477	12.710	12.947	13.188
6	16.727	17.139	17.560	17.991	18.431	18.881	19.341	19.811	20.291	20.781
7	24.585	25.337	26.111	26.907	27.725	28.567	29.431	30.320	31.233	32.172
8	35.665	36.979	38.339	39.746	41.202	42.707	44.264	45.874	47.538	49.258
9	51.287	53.510	55.825	58.235	60.743	63.352	66.068	68.893	71.831	74.887
10	73.315	76.985	80.830	84.858	89.077	93.494	98.120	102.961	108.028	113.330
11	104.374	110.318	116.586	123.195	130.161	137.502	145.236	153.383	161.962	170.995
12	148.168	157.651	167.719	178.401	189.734	201.752	214.497	228.007	242.323	257.493
13	209.916	224.865	240.837	257.897	276.114	295.558	316.310	338.449	362.062	387.239
14	296.982	320.308	345.397	372.372	401.365	432.514	465.975	501.905	540.471	581.858
15	419.744	455.837	494.918	537.215	582.980	632.470	685.983	743.819	806.302	873.788
16	592.839	648.288	708.732	774.589	846.321	924.406	1009.394	1101.852	1202.390	1311.681
17	836.903	921.568	1014.486	1116.408	1228.165	1350.631	1484.809	1631.740	1792.560	1968.522
18	1181.034	1309.625	1451.714	1608.626	1781.838	1972.920	2183.667	2415.974	2671.914	2953.783
19	1666.257	1860.666	2076.949	2317.421	2584.665	2881.461	3210.989	3576.640	3982.150	4431.672
20	2350.422	2643.144	2971.035	3338.084	3748.763	4207.926	4721.148	5294.422	5934.402	6648.508
21	3315.095	3754.262	4249.574	4807.836	5436.703	6144.566	6941.082	7836.742	8843.254	9973.762
22	4675.281	5332.047	6077.887	6924.281	7884.215	8972.059	10204.383	11599.375	13177.441	14961.645
23	6593.145	7572.500	8692.375	9971.957	11433.109	13100.195	15001.434	17168.066	19635.383	22443.469
24	9297.332	10753.941	12431.090	14360.613	16579.008	19127.273	22053.094	25409.730	29257.707	33666.207
25	13110.234	15271.582	17777.445	20680.270	24040.555	27926.797	32419.027	37607.387	43594.965	50500.316
30	73075.500	88181.938	106315.250	128058.125	154105.313	185273.000	222540.625	267055.375	320172.750	383500.000

TABLE A.3
Present-Value Interest Factors for One Dollar Discounted at k Percent for n Periods:

$$PVIF_{k,n} = \frac{1}{(1 + k)^n}$$

Period	1%	2%	3%	4%	5%	6%	7%	8%	9%	10%
1	.990	.980	.971	.962	.952	.943	.935	.926	.917	.909
2	.980	.961	.943	.925	.907	.890	.873	.857	.842	.826
3	.971	.942	.915	.889	.864	.840	.816	.794	.772	.751
4	.961	.924	.888	.855	.823	.792	.763	.735	.708	.683
5	.951	.906	.863	.822	.784	.747	.713	.681	.650	.621
6	.942	.888	.837	.790	.746	.705	.666	.630	.596	.564
7	.933	.871	.813	.760	.711	.665	.623	.583	.547	.513
8	.923	.853	.789	.731	.677	.627	.582	.540	.502	.467
9	.914	.837	.766	.703	.645	.592	.544	.500	.460	.424
10	.905	.820	.744	.676	.614	.558	.508	.463	.422	.386
11	.896	.804	.722	.650	.585	.527	.475	.429	.388	.350
12	.887	.789	.701	.625	.557	.497	.444	.397	.356	.319
13	.879	.773	.681	.601	.530	.469	.415	.368	.326	.290
14	.870	.758	.661	.577	.505	.442	.388	.340	.299	.263
15	.861	.743	.642	.555	.481	.417	.362	.315	.275	.239
16	.853	.728	.623	.534	.458	.394	.339	.292	.252	.218
17	.844	.714	.605	.513	.436	.371	.317	.270	.231	.198
18	.836	.700	.587	.494	.416	.350	.296	.250	.212	.180
19	.828	.686	.570	.475	.396	.331	.277	.232	1.94	.164
20	.820	.673	.554	.456	.377	.312	.258	.215	.178	.149
21	.811	.660	.538	.439	.359	.294	.242	.199	.164	.135
22	.803	.647	.522	.422	.342	.278	.226	.184	.150	.123
23	.795	.634	.507	.406	.326	.262	.211	.170	.138	.112
24	.788	.622	.492	.390	.310	.247	.197	.158	.126	.102
25	.780	.610	.478	.375	.295	.233	.184	1.46	.116	.092
30	.742	.552	.412	.308	.231	.174	.131	.099	.075	.057
35	.706	.500	.355	.253	.181	.130	.094	.068	.049	.036
40	.672	.453	.307	.208	.142	.097	.067	.046	.032	.022
45	.639	.410	.264	.171	.111	.073	.048	.031	.021	.014
50	.608	.372	.228	.141	.087	.054	.034	.021	.013	.009

continued

TABLE A.3

Present-Value Interest Factors for One Dollar Discounted at k percent for n Periods:

$$PVIF_{k,n} = \frac{1}{(1 + k)^n}$$

Period	11%	12%	13%	14%	15%	16%	17%	18%	19%	20%
1	.901	.893	.885	.877	.870	.862	.855	.847	.840	.833
2	.812	.797	.783	.769	.756	.743	.731	.718	.706	.694
3	.731	.712	.693	.675	.658	.641	.624	.609	.593	.579
4	.659	.636	.613	.592	.572	.552	.534	.516	.499	.482
5	.593	.567	.543	.519	.497	.476	.456	.437	.419	.402
6	.535	.507	.480	.456	.432	.410	.390	.370	.352	.335
7	.482	.452	.425	.400	.376	.354	.333	.314	.296	.279
8	.434	.404	.376	.351	.327	.305	.285	.266	.249	.233
9	.391	.361	.333	.308	.284	.263	.243	.225	.209	.194
10	.352	.322	.295	.270	.247	.227	.208	.191	.176	.162
11	.317	.287	.261	.237	.215	.195	.178	.162	.148	.135
12	.286	.257	.231	.208	.187	.168	.152	.137	.124	.112
13	.258	.229	.204	.182	.163	.145	.130	.116	.104	.093
14	.232	.205	.181	.160	.141	.125	.111	.099	.088	.078
15	.209	.183	.160	.140	.123	.108	.095	.084	.074	.065
16	.188	.163	.141	.123	.107	.093	.081	.071	.062	.054
17	.170	.146	.125	.108	.093	.080	.069	.060	.052	.045
18	.153	.130	.111	.095	.081	.069	.059	.051	.044	.038
19	.138	.116	.098	.083	.070	.060	.051	.043	.037	.031
20	.124	.104	.087	.073	.061	.051	.043	.037	.031	.026
21	.112	.093	.077	.064	.053	.044	.037	.031	.026	.022
22	.101	.083	.068	.056	.046	.038	.032	.026	.022	.018
23	.091	.074	.060	.049	.040	.033	.027	.022	.018	.015
24	.082	.066	.053	.043	.035	.028	.023	.019	.015	.013
25	.074	.059	.047	.038	.030	.024	.020	.016	.013	.010
30	.044	.033	.026	.020	.015	.012	.009	.007	.005	.004
35	.026	.019	.014	.010	.008	.006	.004	.003	.002	.002
40	.015	.011	.008	.005	.004	.003	.002	.001	.001	.001
45	.009	.006	.004	.003	.002	.001	.001	.001	a	a
50	.005	.003	.002	.001	.001	.001	a	a	a	a

[a]PVIF is zero to three decimal places.

continued

TABLE A.3
Present-Value Interest Factors for One Dollar Discounted at k Percent for n Periods:

$$PVIF_{k,n} = \frac{1}{(1 + k)^n}$$

Period	21%	22%	23%	24%	25%	26%	27%	28%	29%	30%
1	.826	.820	.813	.806	.800	.794	.787	.781	.775	.769
2	.683	.672	.661	.650	.640	.630	.620	.610	.601	.592
3	.564	.551	.537	.524	.512	.500	.488	.477	.466	.455
4	.467	.451	.437	.423	.410	.397	.384	.373	.361	.350
5	.386	.370	.355	.341	.328	.315	.303	.291	.280	.269
6	.319	.303	.289	.275	.262	.250	.238	.227	.217	.207
7	.263	.249	.235	.222	.210	.198	.188	.178	.168	.159
8	.218	.204	.191	.179	.168	.157	.148	.139	.130	.123
9	.180	.167	.155	.144	.134	.125	.116	.108	.101	.094
10	.149	.137	.126	.116	1.07	.099	.092	.085	.078	.073
11	.123	.112	.103	.094	.086	.079	.072	.066	.061	.056
12	.102	.092	.083	.076	.069	.062	.057	.052	.047	.043
13	.084	.075	.068	.061	.055	.050	.045	.040	.037	.033
14	.069	.062	.055	.049	.044	.039	.035	.032	.028	.025
15	.057	.051	.045	.040	.035	.031	.028	.025	.022	.020
16	.047	.042	.036	.032	.028	.025	.022	.019	.017	.015
17	.039	.034	.030	.026	.023	.020	.017	.015	.013	.012
18	.032	.028	.024	.021	.018	.016	.014	.012	.010	.009
19	.027	.023	.020	.017	.014	.012	.011	.009	.008	.007
20	.022	.019	.016	.014	.012	.010	.008	.007	.006	.005
21	.018	.015	.013	.011	.009	.008	.007	.006	.005	.004
22	.015	.013	.011	.009	.007	.006	.005	.004	.004	.003
23	.012	.010	.009	.007	.006	.005	.004	.003	.003	.002
24	.010	.008	.007	.006	.005	.004	.003	.003	.002	.002
25	.009	.007	.006	.005	.004	.003	.003	.002	.002	.001
30	.003	.003	.002	.002	.001	.001	.001	.001	a	a
35	.001	.001	.001	.001	a	a	a	a	a	a
40	a	a	a	a	a	a	a	a	a	a
45	a	a	a	a	a	a	a	a	a	a
50	a	a	a	a	a	a	a	a	a	a

[a]PVIF is zero to three decimal places.

continued

TABLE A.3

Present-Value Interest Factors for One Dollar Discounted at k Percent for n Periods:

$$PVIF_{k,n} = \frac{1}{(1 + k)^n}$$

Period	31%	32%	33%	34%	35%	36%	37%	38%	39%	40%
1	.763	.758	.752	.746	.741	.735	.730	.725	.719	.714
2	.583	.574	.565	.557	.549	.541	.533	.525	.518	.510
3	.445	.435	.425	.416	.406	.398	.389	.381	.372	.364
4	.340	.329	.320	.310	.301	.292	.284	.276	.268	.260
5	.259	.250	.240	.231	.223	.215	.207	.200	.193	.186
6	.198	.189	.181	.173	.165	.158	.151	.145	.139	.133
7	.151	.143	.136	.129	.122	.116	.110	.105	.100	.095
8	.115	.108	.102	.096	.091	.085	.081	.076	.072	.068
9	.088	.082	.077	.072	.067	.063	.059	.055	.052	.048
10	.067	.062	.058	.054	.050	.046	.043	.040	.037	.035
11	.051	.047	.043	.040	.037	.034	.031	.029	.027	.025
12	.039	.036	.033	.030	.027	.025	.023	.021	.019	.018
13	.030	.027	.025	.022	.020	.018	.017	.015	.014	.013
14	.023	.021	.018	.017	.015	.014	.012	.011	.010	.009
15	.017	.016	.014	.012	.011	.010	.009	.008	.007	.006
16	.013	.012	.010	.009	.008	.007	.006	.006	.005	.005
17	.010	.009	.008	.007	.006	.005	.005	.004	.004	.003
18	.008	.007	.006	.005	.005	.004	.003	.003	.003	.002
19	.006	.005	.004	.004	.003	.003	.003	.002	.002	.002
20	.005	.004	.003	.003	.002	.002	.002	.002	.001	.001
21	.003	.003	.003	.002	.002	.002	.001	.001	.001	.001
22	.003	.002	.002	.002	.001	.001	.001	.001	.001	.001
23	.002	.002	.001	.001	.001	.001	.001	.001	.001	a
24	.002	.001	.001	.001	.001	.001	.001	a	a	a
25	.001	.001	.001	.001	.001	a	a	a	a	a
30	a	a	a	a	a	a	a	a	a	a
35	a	a	a	a	a	a	a	a	a	a
40	a	a	a	a	a	a	a	a	a	a
45	a	a	a	a	a	a	a	a	a	a
50	a	a	a	a	a	a	a	a	a	a

[a]PVIF is zero to three decimal places.

continued

Present-Value Interest Factors for One Dollar Discounted at *k* Percent for *n* Periods:

$$PVIF_{k,n} = \frac{1}{(1 + k)^n}$$

Period	41%	42%	43%	44%	45%	46%	47%	48%	49%	50%
1	.709	.704	.699	.694	.690	.685	.680	.676	.671	.667
2	.503	.496	.489	.482	.476	.469	.463	.457	.450	.444
3	.357	.349	.342	.335	.328	.321	.315	.308	.302	.296
4	.253	.246	.239	.233	.226	.220	.214	.208	.203	.198
5	.179	.173	.167	.162	.156	.151	.146	.141	.136	.132
6	.127	.122	.117	.112	.108	.103	.099	.095	.091	.088
7	.090	.086	.082	.078	.074	.071	.067	.064	.061	.059
8	.064	.060	.057	.054	.051	.048	.046	.043	.041	.039
9	.045	.043	.040	.038	.035	.033	.031	.029	.028	.026
10	.032	.030	.028	.026	.024	.023	.021	.020	.019	.017
11	.023	.021	.020	.018	.017	.016	.014	.013	.012	.012
12	.016	.015	.014	.013	.012	.011	.010	.009	.008	.008
13	.011	.010	.010	.009	.008	.007	.007	.006	.006	.005
14	.008	.007	.007	.006	.006	.005	.005	.004	.004	.003
15	.006	.005	.005	.004	.004	.003	.003	.003	.003	.002
16	.004	.004	.003	.003	.003	.002	.002	.002	.002	.002
17	.003	.003	.002	.002	.002	.002	.001	.001	.001	.001
18	.002	.002	.002	.001	.001	.001	.001	.001	.001	.001
19	.001	.001	.001	.001	.001	.001	.001	.001	.001	a
20	.001	.001	.001	.001	.001	.001	a	a	a	a
21	.001	.001	.001	a	a	a	a	a	a	a
22	.001	a	a	a	a	a	a	a	a	a
23	a	a	a	a	a	a	a	a	a	a
24	a	a	a	a	a	a	a	a	a	a
25	a	a	a	a	a	a	a	a	a	a
30	a	a	a	a	a	a	a	a	a	a
35	a	a	a	a	a	a	a	a	a	a
40	a	a	a	a	a	a	a	a	a	a
45	a	a	a	a	a	a	a	a	a	a
50	a	a	a	a	a	a	a	a	a	a

[a]PVIF is zero to three decimal places.

TABLE A.4

Present-Value Interest Factors for a One-Dollar Annuity Discounted at k Percent for n Periods:

$$PVIFA_{k,n} = \sum_{t=1}^{n} \frac{1}{(1+k)^t} \text{ or } \frac{1 - \dfrac{1}{(1+k)^n}}{k}$$

Period	1%	2%	3%	4%	5%	6%	7%	8%	9%	10%
1	.990	.980	.971	.962	.952	.943	.935	.926	.917	.909
2	1.970	1.942	1.913	1.886	1.859	1.833	1.808	1.783	1.759	1.736
3	2.941	2.884	2.829	2.775	2.723	2.673	2.624	2.577	2.531	2.487
4	3.902	3.808	3.717	3.630	3.546	3.465	3.387	3.312	3.240	3.170
5	4.853	4.713	4.580	4.452	4.329	4.212	4.100	3.993	3.890	3.791
6	5.795	5.601	5.417	5.242	5.076	4.917	4.767	4.623	4.486	4.355
7	6.728	6.472	6.230	6.002	5.786	5.582	5.389	5.206	5.033	4.868
8	7.652	7.326	7.020	6.733	6.463	6.210	5.971	5.747	5.535	5.335
9	8.566	8.162	7.786	7.435	7.108	6.802	6.515	6.247	5.995	5.759
10	9.471	8.983	8.530	8.111	7.722	7.360	7.024	6.710	6.418	6.145
11	10.368	9.787	9.253	8.760	8.306	7.887	7.499	7.139	6.805	6.495
12	11.255	10.575	9.954	9.385	8.863	8.384	7.943	7.536	7.161	6.814
13	12.134	11.348	10.635	9.986	9.394	8.853	8.358	7.904	7.487	7.013
14	13.004	12.106	11.296	10.563	9.899	9.295	8.745	8.244	7.786	7.367
15	13.865	12.849	11.938	11.118	10.380	9.712	9.108	8.560	8.061	7.606
16	14.718	13.578	12.561	11.652	10.838	10.106	9.447	8.851	8.313	7.824
17	15.562	14.292	13.166	12.166	11.274	10.477	9.763	9.122	8.544	8.022
18	16.398	14.992	13.754	12.659	11.690	10.828	10.059	9.372	8.756	8.201
19	17.226	15.679	14.324	13.134	12.085	11.158	10.336	9.604	8.950	8.365
20	18.046	16.352	14.878	13.590	12.462	11.470	10.594	9.818	9.129	8.514
21	18.857	17.011	15.415	14.029	12.821	11.764	10.836	10.017	9.292	8.649
22	19.661	17.658	15.937	14.451	13.163	12.042	11.061	10.201	9.442	8.772
23	20.456	18.292	16.444	14.857	13.489	12.303	11.272	10.371	9.580	8.883
24	21.244	18.914	16.936	15.247	13.799	12.550	11.469	10.529	9.707	8.985
25	22.023	19.524	17.413	15.622	14.094	12.783	11.654	10.675	9.823	9.077
30	25.808	22.396	19.601	17.292	15.373	13.765	12.409	11.258	10.274	9.427
35	29.409	24.999	21.487	18.665	16.374	14.498	12.948	11.655	10.567	9.644
40	32.835	27.356	23.115	19.793	17.159	15.046	13.332	11.925	10.757	9.779
45	36.095	29.490	24.519	20.720	17.774	15.456	13.606	12.108	10.881	9.863
50	39.196	31.424	25.730	21.482	18.256	15.762	13.801	12.233	10.962	9.915

continued

TABLE A.4

Present-Value Interest Factors for a One-Dollar Annuity Discounted at k Percent for n Periods:

$$PVIFA_{k,n} = \sum_{t=1}^{n} \frac{1}{(1+k)^t} \text{ or } \frac{1 - \dfrac{1}{(1+k)^n}}{k}$$

Period	11%	12%	13%	14%	15%	16%	17%	18%	19%	20%
1	.901	.893	.885	.877	.870	.862	.855	.847	.840	.833
2	1.713	1.690	1.668	1.647	1.626	1.605	1.585	1.566	1.547	1.528
3	2.444	2.402	2.361	2.322	2.283	2.246	2.210	2.174	2.140	2.106
4	3.102	3.037	2.974	2.914	2.855	2.798	2.743	2.690	2.639	2.589
5	3.696	3.605	3.517	3.433	3.352	3.274	3.199	3.127	3.058	2.991
6	4.231	4.111	3.998	3.889	3.784	3.685	3.589	3.498	3.410	3.326
7	4.712	4.564	4.423	4.288	4.160	4.039	3.922	3.812	3.706	3.605
8	5.146	4.968	4.799	4.639	4.487	4.344	4.207	4.078	3.954	3.837
9	5.537	5.328	5.132	4.946	4.772	4.607	4.451	4.303	4.163	4.031
10	5.889	5.650	5.426	5.216	5.019	4.833	4.659	4.494	4.339	4.192
11	6.207	5.938	5.687	5.453	5.234	5.029	4.836	4.656	4.486	4.327
12	6.492	6.194	5.918	5.660	5.421	5.197	4.988	4.793	4.611	4.439
13	6.750	6.424	6.122	5.842	5.583	5.342	5.118	4.910	4.715	4.533
14	6.982	6.628	6.302	6.002	5.724	5.468	5.229	5.008	4.802	4.611
15	7.191	6.811	6.462	6.142	5.847	5.575	5.324	5.092	4.876	4.675
16	7.379	6.974	6.604	6.265	5.954	5.668	5.405	5.162	4.938	4.730
17	7.549	7.120	6.729	6.373	6.047	5.749	5.475	5.222	4.990	4.775
18	7.702	7.250	6.840	6.467	6.128	5.818	5.534	5.273	5.033	4.812
19	7.839	7.366	6.938	6.550	6.198	5.877	5.584	5.316	5.070	4.843
20	7.963	7.469	7.025	6.623	6.259	5.929	5.628	5.353	5.101	4.870
21	8.075	7.562	7.102	6.687	6.312	5.973	5.665	5.384	5.127	4.891
22	8.176	7.645	7.170	6.743	6.359	6.011	5.696	5.410	5.149	4.909
23	8.266	7.718	7.230	6.792	6.399	6.044	5.723	5.432	5.167	4.925
24	8.348	7.784	7.283	6.835	6.434	6.073	5.746	5.451	5.182	4.937
25	8.422	7.843	7.330	6.873	6.464	6.097	5.766	5.467	5.195	4.948
30	8.694	8.055	7.496	7.003	6.566	6.177	5.829	5.517	5.235	4.979
35	8.855	8.176	7.586	7.070	6.617	6.215	5.858	5.539	5.251	4.992
40	8.951	8.244	7.634	7.105	6.642	6.233	5.871	5.548	5.258	4.997
45	9.008	8.283	7.661	7.123	6.654	6.242	5.877	5.552	5.261	4.999
50	9.042	8.304	7.675	7.133	6.661	6.246	5.880	5.554	5.262	4.999

continued

TABLE A.4

Present-Value Interest Factors for a One-Dollar Annuity Discounted at k Percent for n Periods:

$$PVIFA_{k,n} = \sum_{t=1}^{n} \frac{1}{(1 + k)^t} \text{ or } \frac{1 - \dfrac{1}{(1 + k)^n}}{k}$$

Period	21%	22%	23%	24%	25%	26%	27%	28%	29%	30%
1	.826	.820	.813	.806	.800	.794	.787	.781	.775	.769
2	1.509	1.492	1.474	1.457	1.440	1.424	1.407	1.392	1.376	1.361
3	2.074	2.042	2.011	1.981	1.952	1.923	1.896	1.868	1.842	1.816
4	2.540	2.494	2.448	2.404	2.362	2.320	2.280	2.241	2.203	2.166
5	2.926	2.864	2.803	2.745	2.689	2.635	2.583	2.532	2.483	2.436
6	3.245	3.167	3.092	3.020	2.951	2.885	2.821	2.759	2.700	2.643
7	3.508	3.416	3.327	3.242	3.161	3.083	3.009	2.937	2.868	2.802
8	3.726	3.619	3.518	3.421	3.329	3.241	3.156	3.076	2.999	2.925
9	3.905	3.786	3.673	3.566	3.463	3.366	3.273	3.184	3.100	3.019
10	4.054	3.923	3.799	3.682	3.570	3.465	3.364	3.269	3.178	3.092
11	4.177	4.035	3.902	3.776	3.656	3.544	3.437	3.335	3.239	3.147
12	4.278	4.127	3.985	3.851	3.725	3.606	3.493	3.387	3.286	3.190
13	4.362	4.203	4.053	3.912	3.780	3.656	3.538	3.427	3.322	3.223
14	4.432	4.265	4.108	3.962	3.824	3.695	3.573	3.459	3.351	3.249
15	4.489	4.315	4.153	4.001	3.859	3.726	3.601	3.483	3.373	3.268
16	4.536	4.357	4.189	4.033	3.887	3.751	3.623	3.503	3.390	3.283
17	4.576	4.391	4.219	4.059	3.910	3.771	3.640	3.518	3.403	3.295
18	4.608	4.419	4.243	4.080	3.928	3.786	3.654	3.529	3.413	3.304
19	4.635	4.442	4.263	4.097	3.942	3.799	3.664	3.539	3.421	3.311
20	4.657	4.460	4.279	4.110	3.954	3.808	3.673	3.546	3.427	3.316
21	4.675	4.476	4.292	4.121	3.963	3.816	3.679	3.551	3.432	3.320
22	4.690	4.488	4.302	4.130	3.970	3.822	3.684	3.556	3.436	3.323
23	4.703	4.499	4.311	4.137	3.976	3.827	3.689	3.559	3.438	3.325
24	4.713	4.507	4.318	4.143	3.981	3.831	3.692	3.562	3.441	3.327
25	4.721	4.514	4.323	4.147	3.985	3.834	3.694	3.564	3.442	3.329
30	4.746	4.534	4.339	4.160	3.995	3.842	3.701	3.569	3.447	3.332
35	4.756	4.541	4.345	4.164	3.998	3.845	3.703	3.571	3.448	3.333
40	4.760	4.544	4.347	4.166	3.999	3.846	3.703	3.571	3.448	3.333
45	4.761	4.545	4.347	4.166	4.000	3.846	3.704	3.571	3.448	3.333
50	4.762	4.545	4.348	4.167	4.000	3.846	3.704	3.571	3.448	3.333

continued

TABLE A.4

Present-Value Interest Factors for a One-Dollar Annuity Discounted at k Percent for n Periods:

$$PVIFA_{k,n} = \sum_{t=1}^{n} \frac{1}{(1 + k)^t} \text{ or } \frac{1 - \dfrac{1}{(1 + k)^n}}{k}$$

Period	31%	32%	33%	34%	35%	36%	37%	38%	39%	40%
1	.763	.758	.752	.746	.741	.735	.730	.725	.719	.714
2	1.346	1.331	1.317	1.303	1.289	1.276	1.263	1.250	1.237	1.224
3	1.791	1.766	1.742	1.719	1.696	1.673	1.652	1.630	1.609	1.589
4	2.130	2.096	2.062	2.029	1.997	1.966	1.935	1.906	1.877	1.849
5	2.390	2.345	2.302	2.260	2.220	2.181	2.143	2.106	2.070	2.035
6	2.588	2.534	2.483	2.433	2.385	2.339	2.294	2.251	2.209	2.168
7	2.739	2.677	2.619	2.562	2.508	2.455	2.404	2.355	2.308	2.263
8	2.854	2.786	2.721	2.658	2.598	2.540	2.485	2.432	2.380	2.331
9	2.942	2.868	2.798	2.730	2.665	2.603	2.544	2.487	2.432	2.379
10	3.009	2.930	2.855	2.784	2.715	2.649	2.587	2.527	2.469	2.414
11	3.060	2.978	2.899	2.824	2.752	2.683	2.618	2.555	2.496	2.438
12	3.100	3.013	2.931	2.853	2.779	2.708	2.641	2.576	2.515	2.456
13	3.129	3.040	2.956	2.876	2.799	2.727	2.658	2.592	2.529	2.469
14	3.152	3.061	2.974	2.892	2.814	2.740	2.670	2.603	2.539	2.478
15	3.170	3.076	2.988	2.905	2.825	2.750	2.679	2.611	2.546	2.484
16	3.183	3.088	2.999	2.914	2.834	2.757	2.685	2.616	2.551	2.489
17	3.193	3.097	3.007	2.921	2.840	2.763	2.690	2.621	2.555	2.492
18	3.201	3.104	3.012	2.926	2.844	2.767	2.693	2.624	2.557	2.494
19	3.207	3.109	3.017	2.930	2.848	2.770	2.696	2.626	2.559	2.496
20	3.211	3.113	3.020	2.933	2.850	2.772	2.698	2.627	2.561	2.497
21	3.215	3.116	3.023	2.935	2.852	2.773	2.699	2.629	2.562	2.498
22	3.217	3.118	3.025	2.936	2.853	2.775	2.700	2.629	2.562	2.498
23	3.219	3.120	3.026	2.938	2.854	2.775	2.701	2.630	2.563	2.499
24	3.221	3.121	3.027	2.939	2.855	2.776	2.701	2.630	2.563	2.499
25	3.222	3.122	3.028	2.939	2.856	2.776	2.702	2.631	2.563	2.499
30	3.225	3.124	3.030	2.941	2.857	2.777	2.702	2.631	2.564	2.500
35	3.226	3.125	3.030	2.941	2.857	2.778	2.703	2.632	2.564	2.500
40	3.226	3.125	3.030	2.941	2.857	2.778	2.703	2.632	2.564	2.500
45	3.226	3.125	3.030	2.941	2.857	2.778	2.703	2.632	2.564	2.500
50	3.226	3.125	3.030	2.941	2.857	2.778	2.703	2.632	2.564	2.500

continued

TABLE A.4

Present-Value Interest Factors for a One-Dollar Annuity Discounted at k Percent for n Periods:

$$PVIFA_{k,n} = \sum_{t=1}^{n} \frac{1}{(1+k)^t} \text{ or } \frac{1 - \frac{1}{(1+k)^n}}{k}$$

Period	41%	42%	43%	44%	45%	46%	47%	48%	49%	50%
1	.709	.704	.699	.694	.690	.685	.680	.676	.671	.667
2	1.212	1.200	1.188	1.177	1.165	1.154	1.143	1.132	1.122	1.111
3	1.569	1.549	1.530	1.512	1.493	1.475	1.458	1.441	1.424	1.407
4	1.822	1.795	1.769	1.744	1.720	1.695	1.672	1.649	1.627	1.605
5	2.001	1.969	1.937	1.906	1.876	1.846	1.818	1.790	1.763	1.737
6	2.129	2.091	2.054	2.018	1.983	1.949	1.917	1.885	1.854	1.824
7	2.219	2.176	2.135	2.096	2.057	2.020	1.984	1.949	1.916	1.883
8	2.283	2.237	2.193	2.150	2.109	2.069	2.030	1.993	1.957	1.922
9	2.328	2.280	2.233	2.187	2.144	2.102	2.061	2.022	1.984	1.948
10	2.360	2.310	2.261	2.213	2.168	2.125	2.083	2.042	2.003	1.965
11	2.383	2.331	2.280	2.232	2.185	2.140	2.097	2.055	2.015	1.977
12	2.400	2.346	2.294	2.244	2.196	2.151	2.107	2.064	2.024	1.985
13	2.411	2.356	2.303	2.253	2.204	2.158	2.113	2.071	2.029	1.990
14	2.419	2.363	2.310	2.259	2.210	2.163	2.118	2.075	2.033	1.993
15	2.425	2.369	2.315	2.263	2.214	2.166	2.121	2.078	2.036	1.995
16	2.429	2.372	2.318	2.266	2.216	2.169	2.123	2.079	2.037	1.997
17	2.432	2.375	2.320	2.268	2.218	2.170	2.125	2.081	2.038	1.998
18	2.434	2.377	2.322	2.270	2.219	2.172	2.126	2.082	2.039	1.999
19	2.435	2.378	2.323	2.270	2.220	2.172	2.126	2.082	2.040	1.999
20	2.436	2.379	2.324	2.271	2.221	2.173	2.127	2.083	2.040	1.999
21	2.437	2.379	2.324	2.272	2.221	2.173	2.127	2.083	2.040	2.000
22	2.438	2.380	2.325	2.272	2.222	2.173	2.127	2.083	2.040	2.000
23	2.438	2.380	2.325	2.272	2.222	2.174	2.127	2.083	2.041	2.000
24	2.438	2.380	2.325	2.272	2.222	2.174	2.127	2.083	2.041	2.000
25	2.439	2.381	2.325	2.272	2.222	2.174	2.128	2.083	2.041	2.000
30	2.439	2.381	2.326	2.273	2.222	2.174	2.128	2.083	2.041	2.000
35	2.439	2.381	2.326	2.273	2.222	2.174	2.128	2.083	2.041	2.000
40	2.439	2.381	2.326	2.273	2.222	2.174	2.128	2.083	2.041	2.000
45	2.439	2.381	2.326	2.273	2.222	2.174	2.128	2.083	2.041	2.000
50	2.439	2.381	2.326	2.273	2.222	2.174	2.128	2.083	2.041	2.000

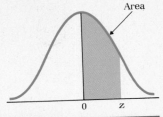

Area

0   z

z	.00	.01	.02	.03	.04	.05	.06	.07	.08	.09
0.0	.0000	.0040	.0080	.0120	.0160	.0199	.0239	.0279	.0319	.0359
0.1	.0398	.0438	.0478	.0517	.0557	.0596	.0636	.0675	.0714	.0753
0.2	.0793	.0832	.0871	.0910	.0948	.0987	.1026	.1064	.1103	.1141
0.3	.1179	.1217	.1255	.1293	.1331	.1368	.1406	.1443	.1480	.1517
0.4	.1554	.1591	.1628	.1664	.1700	.1736	.1772	.1808	.1844	.1879
0.5	.1915	.1950	.1985	.2019	.2054	.2088	.2123	.2157	.2190	.2224
0.6	.2257	.2291	.2324	.2357	.2389	.2422	.2454	.2486	.2517	.2549
0.7	.2580	.2611	.2642	.2673	.2704	.2734	.2764	.2794	.2823	.2852
0.8	.2881	.2910	.2939	.2967	.2995	.3023	.3051	.3078	.3106	.3133
0.9	.3159	.3186	.3212	.3238	.3264	.3289	.3315	.3340	.3365	.3389
1.0	.3413	.3438	.3461	.3485	.3508	.3531	.3554	.3577	.3599	.3621
1.1	.3643	.3665	.3686	.3708	.3729	.3749	.3770	.3790	.3810	.3820
1.2	.3849	.3869	.3888	.3907	.3925	.3944	.3962	.3980	.3997	.4015
1.3	.4032	.4049	.4066	.4082	.4099	.4115	.4131	.4147	.4162	.4177
1.4	.4192	.4207	.4222	.4236	.4251	.4265	.4279	.4292	.4306	.4319
1.5	.4332	.4345	.4357	.4370	.4382	.4394	.4406	.4418	.4429	.4441
1.6	.4452	.4463	.4474	.4484	.4495	.4505	.4515	.4525	.4535	.4545
1.7	.4554	.4564	.4573	.4582	.4591	.4599	.4608	.4616	.4625	.4633
1.8	.4641	.4649	.4656	.4664	.4671	.4678	.4686	.4693	.4699	.4706
1.9	.4713	.4719	.4726	.4732	.4738	.4744	.4750	.4756	.4761	.4767
2.0	.4772	.4778	.4783	.4788	.4793	.4798	.4803	.4808	.4812	.4817
2.1	.4821	.4826	.4830	.4834	.4838	.4842	.4846	.4850	.4854	.4857
2.2	.4861	.4864	.4868	.4871	.4875	.4878	.4881	.4884	.4887	.4890
2.3	.4893	.4896	.4898	.4901	.4904	.4906	.4909	.4911	.4913	.4916
2.4	.4918	.4920	.4922	.4925	.4927	.4929	.4931	.4932	.4934	.4936
2.5	.4938	.4940	.4941	.4943	.4945	.4946	.4948	.4949	.4951	.4952
2.6	.4953	.4955	.4956	.4957	.4959	.4960	.4961	.4962	.4963	.4964
2.7	.4965	.4966	.4967	.4968	.4969	.4970	.4971	.4972	.4973	.4974
2.8	.4974	.4975	.4976	.4977	.4977	.4978	.4979	.4979	.4980	.4981
2.9	.4981	.4982	.4982	.4983	.4984	.4984	.4985	.4985	.4986	.4986
3.0	.4987	.4987	.4987	.4988	.4988	.4989	.4989	.4989	.4990	.4990
3.5	.4998									
4.0	Area is .5000 to four decimal places.									

To find the cumulative area from the left tail to z, the following procedure is employed.

1. z to the left of 0. Cumulative area = .5000 − normal distribution area. For z of 1.10, the cumulative area is .5000 − .3643 = .1357.
2. z to the right of 0. Cumulative area = .5000 + normal distribution area. For z of 1.33, the cumulative area is .5000 + .4082 = .9082.

TABLE A.6
Accelerated Cost
Recovery System
(ACRS) Present-Value
Factors Discounted at
k Percent for n (Either
3, 5, 10 or 15) Periods:
$ACRS_{k,n}$

Discount Rate k (%)	ACRS Life			
	3 Yr	5 Yr	10 Yr	15 Yr
1	.979	.970	.949	.928
2	.959	.941	.902	.864
3	.940	.913	.858	.806
4	.921	.886	.818	.754
5	.902	.861	.780	.707
6	.885	.837	.745	.664
7	.868	.814	.712	.626
8	.851	.791	.682	.590
9	.835	.770	.653	.558
10	.819	.750	.626	.528
11	.804	.730	.601	.501
12	.790	.711	.578	.476
13	.775	.693	.556	.454
14	.761	.676	.535	.432
15	.748	.659	.516	.413
16	.735	.643	.497	.395
17	.722	.628	.480	.378
18	.710	.613	.463	.362
19	.698	.599	.448	.348
20	.686	.585	.433	.334
21	.675	.572	.419	.322
22	.664	.559	.406	.310
23	.653	.547	.394	.299
24	.643	.535	.382	.288
25	.633	.523	.371	.279
26	.623	.512	.360	.269
27	.613	.501	.350	.261
28	.604	.491	.340	.253
29	.595	.481	.331	.245
30	.586	.471	.322	.237
31	.577	.462	.314	.231
32	.568	.453	.306	.224
33	.560	.444	.298	.218
34	.552	.435	.291	.212
35	.544	.427	.283	.206
36	.536	.419	.277	.201
37	.529	.411	.270	.196
38	.521	.404	.264	.191
39	.514	.397	.258	.186
40	.507	.390	.252	.182
41	.500	.383	.247	.177
42	.494	.376	.242	.173
43	.487	.370	.236	.169
44	.481	.363	.231	.166
45	.475	.357	.227	.162
46	.468	.351	.222	.158
47	.462	.346	.218	.155
48	.457	.340	.214	.152
49	.451	.334	.209	.149
50	.445	.329	.205	.146

continued
A-23

The present value of the depreciation on a $20,000, 3-year asset using ACRS can be determined using this table. Assume the discount rate is 15 percent.

ACRS 3-Year Factors	×	PVIF at 15%	=	Discounted Present Value of ACRS
0.25		0.870		0.21750
0.38		0.756		0.28728
0.37		0.658		0.24346
				0.74824 ≈ 0.748.

$ACRS_{k,n}$
factor that
appears in
table

0.748 × $20,000 = $14,960.

Appendix B

Answers to Selected Problems

Chapter 2

2.1 a. (1) $24,000
 (2) $5,000
 (3) $64,000
 b. (1) $39,000
 (2) $20,000
 (3) $54,000

2.4 a. $22,500
 $33,000
 $31,500
 b. Year 1 $105,000
 Year 2 $109,200
 Years 3–5 $108,600

2.5 a. $554,830
 b. $793,170
 c. $1,143,170
 d. $693,170
 e. $443,170

2.6 a. $33,600
 b. $24,160
 $8,960
 $0
 −$3,440

2.10 a. $1,200
 $18,800
 b. $8,000
 $12,000

Chapter 3

3.2 a. Current ratio = 2.36
 Quick ratio = 1.16
 Inventory turnover = 3.99
 Average collection period = 38.35
 Total asset turnover = 1.40
 Debt-equity ratio = 1.30
 Debt service margin = 3.39
 Operating ratio = 86.36%
 Net profit margin = 6.27%
 Return on investment = 8.76%
 Return on equity = 20.19%

3.4 a. Net working capital = $800,000
 Inventory turnover = 7.89
 Debt-equity ratio = .54
 Times interest earned = 6.50
 Net profit margin = 6.6%

Earnings per share = $15.25
Dividend payout ratio = .33
Book value per share = $195.00

3.5 a. ROI (1983) = 8.77%   ROE (1983)
        = 15.84%
        ROI (1984) = 6.06%   ROE (1984)
        = 12.77%

Appendix 3A

3A.2 a. $15,000,000
      c. $10,000,000

Chapter 4

4.2 a. Mean sales volume = $8,985,000
4.3 b. Minimum sales level = $15,023,850
4.4 a. Operating receipts (April)
        = $845,000
        Operating receipts (May)
        = $895,000
        Operating receipts (June)
        = $905,000
      c. Net cash flow (April) = $ 12,250
         Net cash flow (May) = $ 99,750
         Net cash flow (June) = ($249,000)
4.6 Month-end liquidity position:

December	$150,000
January	235,000
February	267,000
March	203,000
.	.
.	.
.	.
September	50,000
October	35,000
November	85,000
December	150,000

4.8 F* = $1,193,750 (or approximately
     $1.2 million)

Appendix to Chapter 4

4A.1 a. $Y_i = 496.55 + (91.31)X_i$
         $R^2 = .9010$

b. $Y_i = 100.17 + (4.43)X_i$
   $R^2 = .6491$

Chapter 5

5.2 a. $10,600
     b. $11,200
     c. $14,050
        $17,620
5.3 a. $14,337
     b. $16,059
5.5 $2,911.02
5.8 a. (1) $2,163
        (2) $21,679
        (3) $136,220
     b. (1) $1,876.20
        (2) $16,775.50
        (3) $101,840.00
5.11 a. $12,934.00
         $14,978.00
         $10,253.75
5.15 $649.20
5.17 a. $26,378.26
         $16,103.06
5.18 a. 11%
         9%
         10%

Chapter 6

6.2 a. 10%
        4%
        11%
     b. σ_A 14.83%
        CV_A 1.483
        σ_B 13.38%
        CV_B 3.345
        σ_C 22.78%
        CV_C 2.071
6.3 a. 11.51%
        8.08%
     b. 57.93%
        27.43%
     c. 37.59%
        60.06%

6.5 a. 5%
             11%
             19%
        b. σ18.03%
             19.97%
             24.98%
             CV 3.606
             1.815
             1.315
        c. 12.62/σ_M
             10.98/σ_M
             19.98/σ_M
6.6 a. Security R   18%
                            19.39%
             Security S   21%
                            31.37%
        b. .31
6.12 a. 13.2%
        b. (1) 15.8%
             (2) 10.6%
        c. (1) 14.2%
             (2) 11.2%
        d. (1) 14.4%
             (2) 11.2%

Appendix 6A
6A.2 a. 12.77%
             20.66%
             15.49%
        b. (1) Y
             (2) X
        c. .536
             3.314
             1.429
6A.4 a. 100% kp = 5%
                   σ_p = 4%
             75% kp = 6.25%
                   σ_p $(p = 1.0)$ = 6.0%
                   σ_p $(p = 0.0)$ = 4.24%
                   σ_p $(p = -1.0)$ = 0.00
             50% kp = 7.5%
                   σ_p $(p = 1.0)$ = 8.0%
                   σ_p $(p = 0.0)$ = 6.32%
                   σ_p $(p = -1.0)$ = 4.00%

25% kp = 8.75%
      σ_p $(p = 1.0)$ = 10.0%
      σ_p $(p = 0.0)$ = 9.06%
      σ_p $(p = -1.0)$ = 8.00%
0% kp = 10%
      σ_p = 12%

Chapter 7
7.3 a. (1) $935.60
                 $999.80 or $1,000
                 $1,070.95
             (2) $826.28
                 $1,000.16 or $1,000
                 $1,229.64
             (3) $762.48
                 $1,000.28 or $1,000
                 $1,393.16
7.4 a. $112.34
             $499.94
             $1,299.04
        b. $112.47
             $499.82
             $1,300.68
7.7 a. $360
        b. $212
7.11 a. $11.44
        b. $17.67
        c. $36.33
        d. $8.33
        e. $6.47
7.12 a. $57.44
        b. $25.34
        c. $30.80
7.13 a. $125,000
        b. $175,000
        c. $169,460
7.17 a. $30
        b. $29.71
        c. $42.85
        d. $37.50
7.20 a. $100
        b. $55.56
        c. $44.44
        d. $125
        e. $83.33

Chapter 8

8.1 a. Current $48,000
              2.82%
          Proposed $74,250
              4.37%

      c. $63,000
              3.23%

8.2 a. Current liability financing $69,850
                                          $70,225
                                          $71,300
          Long-term financing $71,050
                                          $72,175
                                          $75,400
      b. Current liability financing   1.16
                                          $19,000
          Long-term financing   1.75
                                          $60,000

Chapter 9

9.2 Net savings = $225,000
9.5 a. $225,996
      b. $677,988
      c. $296,138
          $888,414
      d. $284,737
          $854,211
9.7 a. 8.75%
      b. 9.75%
      c. 7.50%
      d. 9.167%

Appendix 9A

9A.2 a. $7,292
              $23,403
      b. 5.83%
          7.02%
      c. 5.95%
          7.29%

Chapter 10

10.1 a. $45,000
      b. $38,250
      c. $ 6,885

10.6 Since profits decrease by $1,047.40, they should not discontinue the cash discount.
10.7 Since profits increase by $9,440, relax the collection activities.
10.11 a. 200
      b. 122.22
      c. 33.33

Chapter 11

11.4 a. 12.77%
      b. 11%
      c. 26%
      d. 16.51%
11.5 a. 27.41%
      b. 15.66%
      c. 17.73%
11.6 a. 18%
              19.70%

Chapter 12

12.1 a. $145,800
      b. 112,800
      c.   94,500
      d.   67,800
12.3 −$480,000
          126,000
12.6 a. t_0 −$450,000
              t_1–t_5 $102,000
      b. t_0 −$450,000
          t_1 $93,000
          t_2 $105,600
          t_3–t_5 $103,800
12.8 t_0 −$248,400
      t_1 $76,200
      t_2 $83,760
      t_3–t_5 $82,680
      t_6 $60,000
12.11 a. t_0 −$40,000
              t_1 $11,400
              t_2 $12,520
              t_3–t_5 $12,360
      b. t_0 −$40,000
          t_1 $11,400

t_2 $12,190
t_3 $11,629
t_4 $11,149
t_5 $10,583

Chapter 13

13.3 a. $NPV_P = -\$223,714$
    $NPV_Q = -\$43,825$
    Select Q if one *must* be selected;
    otherwise reject both.
  b. $NPV_P = -\$117,534$
    $NPV_Q = \$33,282$
    Select Q.
  c. 16% $NPV_P = -\$219,224$
    $NPV_Q = -\$41,158$
    10% $NPV_P = -\$114,385$
    $NPV_Q = \$35,152$

13.4 $NPV = -\$476$

13.6 $NPV = -\$22,520$

13.7 a. $NPV_Y = \$10,788$
    $NPV_Y = \$8,087$
  b. $IRR_X = 15\%$
    $IRR_Y = 23\%$

13.11 a. $NPV_{Easyload} = -\$105,855$
    $NPV_{Dumpster} = -\$88,515$
  b. $ANPV_{Easyload} = -\$21,032$
    $ANPV_{Dumpster} = -\$22,754$

13.14 a. $NPV = \$6,144$
  b. $NPV = -\$3,727$

Chapter 14

14.1 c. $\overline{NPV} = \$1,187,225$

14.2 a. For Project A:
    $\overline{CFAT} = \$32,000$
    $\sigma = \$7,141$
    $CV = 0.223$
  b. $\overline{NPV}$ (project A) = $31,552 (using a
    RADR = 12%)

14.4 b. $\overline{NPV} = \$182.62$
  c. Probability of Success = 72.91%
  d. Probability of Success = 84.85%

14.6 b. $\overline{NPV} = \$43.13$
  c. $\sigma = \$333.81$
  d. Probability of Success = 55.17%

14.8 a. $\overline{P} = \$350$
    $\sigma_p = \$110$
    CV (with cakes and breads) = .31

Appendix 14A

14A.1 b. $\overline{NPV} = \$1.85$ million

14A.2 a. With $RADR = 15\%$, $NPV = -\$505$

14A.6 (2) $NPV = -\$486$

Appendix 14B

14A.1 b. $\overline{PI} = 1.18$
  c. Probability of Success = 84.38%

14A.3 b. $\overline{IRR} = 43.08\%$
  c. $\sigma_{IRR} = 24.67\%$
  d. Probability of Success = 88.88%

Chapter 15

15.1 b. $MAP_{Spencer} = \$8.950$
    $MAP_{Far\ Western} = \$32.475$
  c. Acquire Spencer.

15.3 a. $NAM = -\$632.350$
  b. $75.09
  c. $NAM = \$790.673$
  d. $89.69
  e. Acquire National Tobacco.

15.4 a. $MAP = \$2,645.330$
    MAP per share = $52.91
  b. At $45 per share: $NAM = \$37.871$
    At $48 per share: $NAM = -\$93.405$

Chapter 16

16.1 Abandon in year 2 since $NPV_2 = \$767,032$.

16.4 Since net divestiture proceeds of $550,000 are greater than NPV_1 of $533,120, they should divest.

16.7 a. Alpha Products, Inc.
  b. Yes, because three of its ratios become negative at $t = 1$.

16.9 Since the liquidation proceeds of $550,000 are greater than NPV_5 of $427,525, they should liquidate.

Chapter 17

17.1 Bond A: 6.18%
Bond B: 5.68%
Bond C: 7.00%
Bond D: 8.71%
Bond E: 6.60%

17.4 k_e (Battery Storage) $= 14.16\%$
k_s (Battery Storage) $= 13.25\%$
k_e (Property Management) $= 14.35\%$
k_s (Property Management) $= 13.72\%$

17.7 a. 10.75%
b. 14.22%

17.9 a. $k_i = 7.37\%$
$k_{ps} = 10.53\%$
$k_s = 13.42\%$
$k_e = 14.64\%$
b. $25 million
c. $MCC_1 = 10.11\%$
$MCC_2 = 10.59\%$

17.12 $MCC_{Home\ Furnishings} = 10.81\%$
$MCC_{Apartment\ Rentals} = 12.24\%$

Appendix 17A

17A.1 7.62%
17A.4 10.94%

Chapter 18

18.1 a. $V = \$2,070,000$
b. $P_0 = \$9.75$

18.3 a. $k = 10\%$; $V = \$120$
b. $B = \$50$; $V = \$126,363,636$
$B = \$80$; $V = \$120,615,385$

18.6 a.

EBIT	EPS (Stock)	EPS (Bonds)
$ 500,000	$2.25	$2.34
$ 700,000	$3.25	$3.54
$1,000,000	$4.75	$5.34

b.

Plan	EPS	σ	CV
Stock	$3.00	$.75	.25
Bonds	$3.24	$.90	.28

18.8 a.

Plan	EPS
Common	$3.52
Preferred	$3.68
Debt	$4.20
Common/debt	$3.79

c. Estimated cross-over points:
Common versus preferred = $1,380,000
Common versus debt = $990,000
Preferred versus common/debt = $1,640,000

Appendix 18A

18A.1 a. (1) $k = 15\%$
(2) $k = 12.2\%$
(3) $k = 10\%$
b. (1) $k = 12.5\%$
(2) $k = 12.5\%$
(3) $k = 12.5\%$

18.3 a. $CF_U = \$1.2$
$V_U = \$9.6$
b. Debt = $1 million; $k_L = 12\%$
Debt = $6 million; $k_L = 10\%$
Debt = $11 million; $k_L = 8.57\%$

Chapter 19

19.1 b. Dividends:

1975	$1.00
1976	1.00
1977	1.00
1978	1.00
1979	1.00
1980	1.10
1981	1.20
1982	1.30
1983	1.40
1984	1.50

19.3 a.

Project	IRR	Retention Rate
B	18%	15%
D	16	35
A	14	65
C	11	75

c. Total value of firm is maximized with projects B, D, and A ($89,743,590).

19.6 a. $g^* = 6.8\%$
c. $g^* = 9.29\%$

Chapter 20

20.1 a. $725,000
b. $8,975,000
20.3 b. $9,650,000
d. $57.75
20.4 a. 40,000
c. 14.8¢
20.7 b. $60
d. $50
20.8 a. Number of shares repurchased: 58,252

Chapter 21

21.1 a. $1,780,944
b. $426,212
d. $1,693.453
21.3 Total interest saved: $840,000
21.4 a. 7.70% versus 7.25%
c. 7.35% versus 8.00%
21.6 a. Net profit: $1,525,000
b. 8.16%
21.8 PVR = $3,370,215
21.10 a. Debt: $400,000
Preferred: $375,000
b. Cost of Debt: 4.8%
Cost of Preferred: 7.5%
c. Debt: $210,000
Preferred: $75,000

Appendix 21A

21A.2 b. 400
c. $3,750,000
d. 11.06%
Total Interest Savings: $7,031,250

Chapter 22

22.1 a. $LP_t = \$123,262$
b. $LP_t = \$111,348$
c. $LP_t = \$5.215$ million
d. $LP_t = \$3.783$ million

22.4 $NAL = \$13,124$

22.5

Asset	Effective After-Tax Cost of Lease
A	10.49%
B	6.33%
C	3.83%

22.8 a. $NAL = -\$326,400$
b. $NAL = -\$379,200$
c. $NAL = \$435,000$

Appendix 22A

22A.1 a. $NPV = \$83,520$
b. $NAL = \$873,240$
c. Adjusted $NPV = \$956,760$

Chapter 23

23.1 a. $4.00
c. $100.00
d. 25%
e. 160,000 shares
23.3 a. $1,135.80
b. $823.06 (at 8%)
$581.44 (at 12%)
23.4 c. Bond A: 10.25%
Bond B: 9.24%
23.5 a. $B_0 = \$877.60$
$B_3 = \$902.44$
$B_6 = \$936.60$
e. (1) 9.32%
23.7 b. EPS (CV) = $4.08
EPS (wT) = $3.84
e. EPS (CV) = $6.69
EPS (wT) = $7.73

Appendix 23A

23A.2 a. $8.27
b. $6.67
c. $7.45
d. $19.14

Glossary

Numbers in parentheses indicate the chapter in which the term is first discussed in detail.

Abandonment (12)   A capital budgeting decision that involves getting rid of equipment, closing a plant or warehouse, selling a division, or even closing the firm.

ABC System (10)   System in which inventory is segregated into three groups according to the size of the dollar investment. Control of the A items should be the most extensive due to the high-dollar investment involved; B and C items are subject to less sophisticated control procedures.

Accelerated Cost Recovery System (ACRS) (2)   The method for determining depreciation for tax purposes required by the Economic Recovery Tax Act of 1981; includes 3, 5, 10, and 15 normal recovery periods and elective extended periods.

Accounts Payable (11)   A form of credit that results when a firm purchases goods and services from other firms and does not pay for them at once or on delivery.

Accounts Receivable (10)   A short-term investment of funds that results when a firm makes a sale on credit. A current asset.

Accruals (11)   Liabilities for services received by the firm for which payment has not yet been made; the most common items accrued are wages and taxes.

Accrual System (1)   System of accounting in which revenues and expenses are recognized at the time when transactions involving the exchange of goods and services occur, regardless of whether any cash changes hands.

Accumulated Issue (21)   Situation in which all, or nearly all, of a bond issue has been accumulated by one or two institutional investors, who are in a monopolistic position; they can unilaterally set sinking fund purchase prices at or near par even though the issue should be trading in the open market at a deep discount.

Adjustable (or Floating) Rate Preferreds (21)   A type of preferred stock whose cash dividends are adjusted quarterly in line with yields on specific Treasury issues, although a minimum and maximum dividend rate is usually established as a safeguard.

After-Acquired Clause (21)   A clause which provides that all property acquired by the firm after the first mortgage has been filed will be added to the property already pledged as security for the first mortgage; enhances the claim of current mortgage holders by automatically giving them a lien on any additional property acquired by the company.

Agency Costs (1)   Costs to the owners when a firm is managed by others (managers); includes monitoring expenditures to prevent satisficing behavior by managers, any bonding assurances made by managers as agents, and any residual losses that cannot be eliminated through monitoring or bonding.

Agency Relationship (18)   A contract under which one or more principals in a firm engage agents to perform some service on their behalf by delegating some decision-making authority to the agent. *See also Agency Costs.*

Aging Schedule (10)   A method of monitoring accounts receivable that shows the proportion that has been outstanding for a given period of time; a way of controlling turnover and delinquent accounts.

Amortization Payments (5)   *See Loan Amortization Payments.*

Annualized Net Present Value (13)   Technique for evaluating mutually exclusive capital budgeting projects with unequal lives by converting a project's NPV into a yearly net present value, assuming the project is replicated over and over to infinity.

Annuity (5)   A series of equal cash flows that occurs at regular time intervals over a specified number of periods. An ordinary annuity has cash flows occurring at the end of each period, while an annuity due has the cash flows occurring at the beginning of each period.

Arbitrage (18)   The simultaneous buying and selling of two essentially identical securities, or the buying of a security in one market and the simultaneous sale of the same security in another market.

Assignment (16)   Voluntary out-of-court liquidation.

Automatic Dividend Reinvestment Plans (ADRs) (19)   Plan established by a growing number of firms in recent years whereby shareholders can have their cash dividends automatically reinvested in additional shares of the firm's stock at a considerable savings in brokerage fees; in some cases, up to $1500 in reinvested dividends can be exempted (deferred) from federal income tax.

Average Cost Method (10)   A method of accounting for inventory investment in which a weighted cost per unit is computed and used to determine the cost of goods sold.

Average Rate of Return (ARR) (13)   Method for assessing the acceptability of capital expenditure proposals without considering present value; sometimes called the *accounting rate of return.* Calculated by dividing average profit after taxes by average investment.

Average Tax Rate (2)   The rate paid by a firm on its ordinary income; found by dividing its total taxes by its taxable income.

Balance Sheet (3)   A statement of a company's assets, liabilities, and stockholders' equity; a summary of the firm's resources balanced against its debt and ownership positions at a single point in time.

Balloon Payment (5)   A final payment to retire a long-term loan that is considerably larger than earlier payments.

Bankruptcy (16)   A situation in which a firm's liabilities exceed its assets.

Bankruptcy Costs (15)   Direct costs such as trustee fees, legal fees, and other costs of reorganization or bankruptcy that are deducted before investors are paid, plus indirect costs such as the opportunity cost of funds being tied up during bankruptcy proceedings, losses in asset value due to forced capital structure changes, or lost profits created by lower sales in anticipation of bankruptcy.

Baumol Model (9)   A cash management model that uses the inventory approach to maintain appropriate cash balances and assumes certainty about future cash needs.

Benefit-Cost Ratio (13)   *See Profitability Index.*

Best-Efforts (20)   An arrangement whereby an investment banker has *no* obligation to purchase the unsold portion of a new issue of securities—they simply agree to do their best in selling as many securities as possible at the established offering price.

Beta (6)   A measure of nondiversifiable risk that gives an indication of the extent to which the return on a financial asset varies with the market; generally positive but can be negative. The slope of the characteristic line.

Bond (7)   Financial asset that indicates a certain amount of money has been borrowed, and a promise has been made to repay it in the future. Issued by corporations and governmental units.

Bond Indenture (21)   A legal document stating the conditions under which a bond has been issued; spells out both the rights of bondholders and the duties of the issuing corporation.

Bonds with Contingent Takedown Options (21)   Bonds with a contingent takedown option (CTO) that enables the holder to buy one of the issuing company's bonds, with a stated coupon and at a stipulated price, any time over the life of the option.

Bonds with Early Redemption (Put) Options (21)   Bonds similar to variable rate notes, except that they are normally issued with fixed coupons.

Bond Value (23)   The price at which a convertible bond would trade if it were nonconvertible and priced at or near prevailing market yields for comparable straight debt issues.

Breakeven Analysis (3)   Analysis that involves finding the point at which the level of sales will just equal total operating costs; sometimes called cost-volume-profit analysis, it considers the relationships between sales, fixed costs, and variable expenses and is used to evaluate corporate profitability.

Breaking Points (17)   The levels of total financing at which the explicit costs increase. Used in calculating the marginal cost of capital schedule.

Budget Variance Report (4)   A statement that reconciles actual performance with forecasted behavior.

Business Risk (17)   Fluctuations in the firm's revenue stream (EBIT) in response to changing economic factors.

Buy-and-Hold (9)   Investment strategy in which the firm buys securities that carry maturities which closely correspond to the expected cash and investment needs of the firm. The securities are then held until they mature.

Call Feature (21) A feature that spells out whether or not, and under what conditions, a bond or preferred stock can be prematurely retired for purposes other than meeting sinking fund provisions.

Call Option (23) An option that gives the holder the right to buy a stipulated number of securities at a stipulated price for a set period of time.

Call Price (21) A price (or series of prices) for all sinking fund bonds, and for all bonds with freely callable or deferred call provisions; stipulates the price the company must pay to the bondholder to initiate premature retirement of the debt.

Capital Asset Pricing Model (CAPM) (6) A fundamental financial theory specifying the relationship that is expected to hold between rates of return and risk; the required return on any asset is equal to the risk-free rate plus a risk premium:

$$k_j = R_F + \beta_j \times (k_M - R_F)$$

Capital Budgeting (12) Process that involves everything from generating and evaluating proposals to following up on capital projects. The goal of capital budgeting is to select investment alternatives that make the greatest contribution to stockholder wealth.

Capital Gain (2) Difference between sale price and original purchase price when capital assets are sold for more than the original purchase price; may be long term (if the asset is held for more than 1 year) or short term.

Capital Impairment Laws (19) Statutes that limit or preclude the payment of cash dividends from original paid-in capital; dividends may not be paid from (i.e., charged against) anything other than retained earnings, as reported on the firm's balance sheet.

Capital Lease (22) For accounting purposes, a lease that transfers title of the asset to the lessee by the end of the lease period; contains an option giving the lessee the right to purchase the asset at a price below its fair market value; has a lease period equal to or greater than 75 percent of the estimated economic life of the asset; or has a present value of the minimum lease payments at the beginning of the lease that equal or exceed 90 percent of the fair value of the leased property to the lessor. The present value of the future lease payments is recorded as a liability on the balance sheet, with an offsetting entry made to the fixed asset account.

Capital Market (2) Financial market in which long-term debt and equity securities, such as bonds, common stocks, preferred stocks, and convertible issues, are traded.

Capital Market Line (CML) (6) Attainable combinations of portfolios comprised of various proportions of investment in the risk-free rate and the market portfolio of risky assets. The CML represents the market price of risk and describes the tradeoff between the expected rate of return and total risk.

Capital Rationing (12) Situation in which limited funds are available for capital expenditures and there are more acceptable projects than the existing budget will permit funding for.

Cash Breakeven Analysis (3) The evaluation of the breakeven point on a cash, rather than accrual (accounting), basis; calculated because a firm's cash receipts and expenditures are unlikely to correspond with the accounting recognition of income and expenses.

Cash Budget (4)   Summary of estimated cash receipts and expenditures for the firm; usually prepared on a monthly basis to cover a period of 1 year or less.

Cash Cycle (9)   The amount of time that elapses from the point when the firm makes an outlay to purchase raw materials to the point when cash is collected from the sale of the finished goods produced with the raw materials.

Cash Discount (11)   A percentage deduction from the invoiced amount as long as payment is made within the cash discount period; a method of speeding up collection of accounts receivable.

Cash Discount Period (11)   The maximum number of days after the beginning of the credit period that the cash discount can be taken; typically between 5 and 20 days.

Cash Dividend (19)   Return to stockholders paid from net after-tax earnings; a distribution of corporate profits to shareholders.

Cash Flow After Tax (CFAT) (12)   The difference in the expected cash inflows in period t and the expected cash outflows (including taxes) in period t. The operating $CFAT$ is equal to $CFBT_t (1 - T) + Dep_t (T)$ where $CFBT$ equals the cash flow before taxes, Dep equals the depreciation, and T is the firm's marginal corporate tax rate.

Cash Flow Before Tax (CFBT) (12)   The difference in the cash inflows in year t and the cash outflows (excluding taxes) in year t. Used in calculating operating cash flow after taxes.

Cash Flow System (1)   System in which primary attention is given to the timing of the actual receipt of revenues (a cash inflow) and the actual payment of expenses (a cash outflow).

Cash Offering (20)   A procedure used to sell a new issue of securities to the general investing public; the way nearly all bonds and preferred stocks are issued, as well as a large number of common stocks.

Cash Turnover (9)   The number of times each year the firm's cash is actually turned over; cash velocity.

Characteristic Line (6)   Least squares regression line specifying the relationship between returns on an asset (the dependent variable) and the returns on the market (the independent variable). Its slope is beta.

Classified Stock (20)   Special class of common stock created to meet special needs; the stock usually carries different voting rights and/or different cash dividend obligations.

Clientele Effect (19)   A theory which states that if investors have preferences for different cash dividend policies, they will be attracted to firms that have policies consistent with their objectives.

Closed-End Mortgage Clause (21)   A provision common in first mortgage bond indentures that prohibits additional borrowing on collateralized property; the firm cannot issue second mortgage bonds on property secured with a closed-end first mortgage.

Coefficient of Variation (CV) (6)   A relative measure of risk calculated by dividing the standard deviation by its respective expected value.

Collateral (11)   Security for a loan that commonly takes the form of a physical or financial asset, such as accounts receivable, inventory, fixed assets, stocks, bonds, or money market securities.

Collateral Trust Bonds (21)   A bond secured with financial assets, like the stock and bonds of companies other than the issuer; the value of the collateral generally must be 25 to 30 percent greater than the par value of the bond it supports.

Collection Activities (10)   The firm's basis for action when established credit terms are violated.

Collection Float (9)   Float that results from the time delay between when a customer deducts a payment from its checking account and when the vendor actually receives the funds in spendable form.

Commercial Paper (2)   Short-term, unsecured promissory notes issued by commercial finance and industrial firms having high credit ratings; maturities range from 3 days to 270 days, and minimum amounts are usually $100,000.

Commitment Fee (11)   The fee charged for the unused portion of a line of credit; compensation to the bank for making the money available on a when-needed basis.

Compensating Balance (11)   The required minimum balance a firm must maintain in its deposit account at a bank under the terms of a loan.

Competitive Bidding Arrangement (20)   A public auction in which a new issue is sold to the underwriter who submits the highest bid to the issuer; the issuing company invites bids from investment bankers, and the firm or syndicate that bids the highest price for the security wins the issue, purchases the security from the company, and resells it at a higher price to investors.

Composition (16)   A pro rata settlement of creditors' claims against a debtor in cash or promissory notes. The creditors agree to accept less than 100 percent in full payment of their claims.

Compounding (5)   Calculating interest on interest so that at the end of each period, the earnings base (or invested funds) increases according to the rate of return earned on the investment.

Compound Value (5)   *See Future Value.*

Computer Simulation (14)   A technique for capturing a project's potential exposure to risk by incorporating the interactions of a number of key variables into the risk analysis; a simulation model is a collection of equations and probability distributions that describe the important variables in the decision.

Concentration Banking (9)   Technique used to reduce collection float by shortening the mail and transit components through the use of collection center banks that serve given geographic areas, from which funds are transferred by wire to a concentration bank.

Continuous Compounding (Discounting) (5)   Process of compounding (discounting) continually as opposed to using discrete time periods.

Contribution Margin (3)   The percentage of each sales dollar that remains after variable costs have been met, it reflects the extent to which revenues are contributing to fixed costs or profits.

Controlled Disbursing (9)   The strategic use of mailing points and bank accounts to pay a firm's bills in order to lengthen mail and transit floats.

Conversion Privilege (23)   Provision of a convertible issue that stipulates the conditions and specific nature of the conversion feature: exactly when the issue can be converted and the conversion ratio (the number of shares of common stock into which the security can be converted).

Conversion Value (23)   An indication of what a convertible should trade for if it were priced to sell on the basis of its stock value; the market value that would be received upon conversion. Calculated by multiplying the conversion ratio by the current market price of the underlying stock.

Convertible Securities (17)   A bond or preferred stock that permits the holder to convert it into shares of the issuing firm's common stock at no cost to the investor; issued by a firm as a way to raise long-term capital.

Corporation (2)   Form of business organization which is a legal entity given the statutory power of an individual, but owned by stockholders.

Correlation Coefficient (6)   A standardized statistic that describes how much linear co-movement exists between two random variables. Its range is from +1.0 (perfect positive correlation) through zero (no correlation) to −1.0 (perfect negative correlation).

Cost Minimization (12)   Projects for which there are no directly measureable revenues; however, costs and risks still occur. Capital budgeting techniques can be employed; however, the objective is to minimize the discounted present value of the cash outflows.

Coupon (or Nominal) Interest Rate (7)   The stated interest rate on a bond; the percentage of the bond's principal value that will be paid annually; defines the before-tax cost of funds to the firm and is influenced not only by economic conditions, but by issue characteristics as well.

Covered Interest Arbitrage (2)   Foreign exchange transaction technique whereby an investor can make a profit almost without risk provided the forward premium or discount between two currencies does not equal the expected interest rate differential between the two countries.

Credit Analysis (3)   The application of financial analysis to lending situations; used with bonds and other forms of debt to assess the ability of the borrowing firm to service its debt in a prompt and timely fashion.

Credit Period (11)   The length of time that can elapse before payment in full is required for a credit purchase; also known as the *net period*.

Credit Policy (10)   System for managing accounts receivable; includes credit standards, credit terms, and collection activities.

Credit Scoring (10)   Method of categorizing customers desiring credit into risk classes by a quantitative procedure that results in a weighted average of the scores obtained on a variety of key financial and credit characteristics.

Credit Standards (10)   Rules that provide the basis for specifying acceptable levels of credit risk and determining who will receive credit.

Credit Terms (10)   Conditions under which credit will be extended; includes cash discount policies, the length of time for which credit will be extended, and the finance charges when accounts are not paid on time.

Crossover Refunding Rate (21)   The market rate that would have to be obtained on a refunded issue to justify a bond refunding operation; calculated by dividing the annual coupon payment by the current call price on the issue.

Cumulative Provision (21)   A provision that means any cash dividends on preferred stock not paid must be made up in full before cash dividends can be restored to common stockholders.

Date of Record (19)   The date on which the investor must be a registered shareholder of the company to be entitled to receive the just-declared dividend.

Debentures (21)   A form of unsecured debt that has a claim only on the firm's earnings, and not its assets; in case of default, holders are entitled to any of the assets remaining after the claims of all secured creditors have been satisfied.

Debt Capacity (18)   The maximum amount of debt a firm can safely handle; point at which carrying additional debt incurs unacceptably high costs.

Dependent Cash Flows (14)   A type of cash flow stream in which the outcome in 1 year is dependent upon the cash flow results in the preceding year.

Depository Transfer Check (DTC) (9)   An unsigned check drawn on one of the firm's bank accounts and deposited into its account at another bank—typically a concentration or disbursing bank. Used to transfer funds between a firm's accounts at different banks.

Diminishing Marginal Utility (6)   The concept that after some point investors derive less and less incremental utility from each additional increment in total wealth.

Direct (Net) Lease (22)   A finance lease whereby the lessee obtains the use of an asset it did not previously have by entering into a lease agreement with the lessor. Because the lessor receives the return after or net of any maintenance, insurance, and property tax expenses, this lease is also called a net lease.

Direct Send (9)   Technique used to reduce transit float by directly presenting checks for payment to the bank on which they are drawn.

Disbursement Float (9)   Float that results from the time lapse between when a firm deducts a payment from its checking account ledger and when the funds are actually withdrawn from its account.

Discounting (5)   The process used to determine the present value (usually at time t_0) of a future amount of dollars, when discounted at k percent.

Discount Method (11)   Deducting interest from the initial principal rather than paying it at the end of the loan; the effective rate of interest is thereby increased.

Disinflation (1)   A slowing down in the rate of inflation.

Diversifiable Risk (6)   That risk which is unique to the firm and can be diversified away, or mitigated, in a portfolio; also called *nonmarket* or *unsystematic risk*.

Divestiture (16)   The selling off of a part of a firm's assets, such as a division or a subsidiary.

Divisional Screening Rates (17)   Division-specific marginal costs of capital used when capital expenditure projects undertaken by a division are essentially similar with respect to risk, but dissimilar among divisions.

Domestic Tax Neutrality (2)   U.S. government tax principle that one dollar earned domestically is taxed at the same rate as one equivalent dollar earned abroad.

Earnings Before Interest and Taxes (EBIT) (18)   Earnings arising from the firm's operations before the effects of interest costs due to debt financing and corporate income taxes are taken into account.

EBIT-EPS Analysis (18)   Procedure for determining the effect of different long-term financing alternatives on a firm's expected EPS. Can be conducted either graphically or numerically.

Economic Exposure (8)   Foreign exchange risk caused by the possibility that the market value of a firm will be affected by a change in long-run cash flows due to an unexpected change in foreign exchange rates.

Economic Order Quantity (EOQ) Model (10)   A commonly used tool for determining the optimal order quantity for an item of inventory by minimizing the total costs (both ordering and carrying).

$$EOQ = \sqrt{2SO/C}$$

Economies of Scale (15)   "Indivisibles" that can provide increasing returns if spread over a larger number of units of production. Examples include raising capital, research and development expenditures, and large automated machinery and equipment.

Efficient Frontier (6)   The boundary that defines the set of efficient portfolios.

Efficient Portfolio (6)   A portfolio that provides the highest expected return for a given amount of risk, or the lowest risk for a given expected return.

Equipment Trust Certificates (21)   A form of secured debt widely used by railroads, airlines, and other transportation firms as a way to finance rolling stock.

Equity Participant (22)   A lessor who provides only a portion of the funds needed to purchase the asset; the remaining amount is provided by one or more long-term lenders. Occurs when leveraged leasing is employed.

Equivalent Bond Yield (9)   Used to convert a discount rate on a money market security to a rate comparable to a bond.

$$Y = \left[\frac{365 \times d}{360 - (d \times n)} \right] \times 100$$

Eurobond (21)   A bond sold in a country (or countries) other than the one in whose currency the issue is denominated; an American corporation, for example, might issue dollar-denominated bonds in the European market.

Eurodollar Loans (11)   International loans that have most of the characteristics of large domestic dollar loans; they usually carry a variable interest rate that is adjusted every quarter.

Exchange Ratio (15)   The number of shares of common stock the acquiring firm gives for each share of a target firm's common stock in a stock-financed merger.

Ex-Dividend Date (19)   The date up to which the right to a just-declared dividend remains with a stock when it is traded; the ex-dividend date occurs four business days prior to the date of record.

Exercise Price (23)   The stated price the warrant holder will have to pay to acquire the stock; the price per share paid to the firm when the warrant is used to buy the stock.

Expansion Project (12)   Category of capital budgeting that involves the expansion of either existing products and markets, or into new products and markets. The cash flows are typically presented in aggregate (or total) form for decision-making purposes.

Expected Return (7)   The future return one expects to receive from owning a given investment.

Expected Value or Mean (6)   A measure of central tendency calculated as the sum of the possible outcomes times each outcome's individual probability of occurrence. Also known as the *mean*.

Expiration Date (23)   The deadline for exercising a warrant.

Extension (16)   The postponement of payment of a debtor's claims held by one or more creditors.

External Yield Criterion (17)   Approach to determining the cost of internally generated funds that says the (opportunity) cost is equal to the best alternative investment the firm foregoes.

Extra Dividend (19)   Supplemental payment of additional cash dividends whenever earnings are sufficiently high to warrant it; usually paid in the final quarter of the year as a one-time "bonus."

Face (or Par) Value (7)   The value of a bond that must be repaid at maturity, usually $1000.

Factoring (11)   The outright sale of a firm's accounts receivables to another party.

Finance Lease (22)   A "true" lease as recognized by the Internal Revenue Service that (1) normally does not provide for any maintenance or service; (2) is not cancellable without a penalty; and (3) is fully or close to fully amortized from lease payments over the life of the lease.

Financial Leverage (18)   The use of debt, preferred stock, and leases for long-term financing that results in a fixed cost of financing. Financial leverage increases the risk to common shareholders; accordingly, it should also increase their expected returns. It is measured by the ratio of the market value of debt to the firm's total market value.

Financial Ratios (3)   A set of financial relationships dealing with the liquidity, leverage, and profitability of the firm, as derived from annual financial statements; when compared to historical and/or industry standards, they help management assess the financial condition, operating results, and future needs of the firm.

Financial Risk (17)   The risk that arises when a firm employs fixed-cost financing such as debt, preferred stock, or leases. This risk is borne by the common stockholders; accordingly, they demand a higher expected return when financial risk is present.

First-In, First-Out (FIFO) (10)   Method used to account for inventory in which the cost of the earliest inventory purchased is assigned to the cost of goods sold.

First Mortgage Bonds (21)   A form of secured debt collateralized with a first lien on real property or buildings; normally, the market value of the property is greater than the amount of the mortgage bond being issued.

Fisher Effect (2)   Theory that nominal interest rates are equal to the required real rate of return to the investor plus the expected rate of inflation.

Fixed Payout Ratio (19)   Dividend policy under which a company establishes a fixed percentage of earnings that will be paid out each year as cash dividends; dollar amounts therefore vary as earnings vary.

Fixed Percentage Rate Loan (11)   Loan that carries a specific rate which does not change over the life of the loan.

Float (9)   Those funds that have been dispatched by a payor to a payee but which are not yet in a form that can be spent by the payee.

Floating Inventory Lien (11)   A form of inventory loan used when the firm has a fairly stable level of inventory that consists of a diversified group of merchandise, no single item of which has a high dollar value; like floating liens, the percentage advanced is normally less than 50 percent of the book value of the inventory.

Floating Lien (11)   A loan against accounts receivable that covers all the firm's receivables; the percentage advanced against a pledge of accounts receivable under a floating lien is normally less than 50 percent of the book value of the receivables.

Floating Rate Loan (11)   Loan whose initial rate is pegged at or near the bank's prime rate. The initial rate on the loan varies as the prime rate varies.

Flooring Lines (11)   A form of loan in which the inventory remains in the hands of the borrower; the lender files a lien on each item financed and advances as much as 100 percent of the cost of the merchandise. Also known as *trust receipt loans* or *floor planning*.

Flotation Costs (21)   Expenses incurred in the process of issuing a bond which are amortized over the life of the issue.

Flow of Funds Statement (3)   A statement of changes in financial position that summarizes significant investment and financing decisions that have occurred over a given accounting period; integrates the balance sheet with key summary figures from the income statement.

Foreign Exchange Market (2)   The market in which one country's currency is exchanged for another country's currency; an international communications network linking banks, firms, brokers, government agencies, and individuals who need to trade in foreign currencies.

Forward Transaction (2)   Foreign exchange transaction in which the buyer takes possession of the foreign currency at some date in the future, but the rate of exchange is agreed upon now.

Future Value (5)   The amount an investment made today will be worth at some point in the future, given the compound rate of return and the length of time the money is tied up; also known as *compound value*.

Generally Accepted Accounting Principles (GAAP) (2)   A series of statements of acceptable financial accounting practices and procedures set by the Financial Accounting Standards Board (FASB), a division of the American Institute of Certified Public Accountants.

Gordon Model (7)   Constant growth model, based on cash dividends, for valuing common stocks.

$$P_0 = D_1/(k_s - g)$$

Hedging (11)   Taking a position in the futures market as a temporary substitute for the purchase or sale of an actual financial instrument such as a Treasury bill.

Holders of Record (19)   Those stockholders who are entitled to receive a dividend payment from the firm; registered owners as of the date of record.

Holding Period Return (9)   Used with money market securities to determine the percentage return secured over the time period the security was held.

$$\text{HPR} = \left\{ do \pm \left[\frac{|do - ds| \, (n - h)}{h} \right] \right\} \times 100$$

If the discount rate drops (rises) during the holding period, the bracketed term is subtracted (added) to *do*.

Income Bonds (21)   An unsecured bond on which interest need be paid only when earnings are sufficiently large; income bonds are used primarily by weak firms undergoing reorganization.

Income Statement (3)   A financial summary of the operating results of the firm that covers activities over a period of time.

Incremental Cash Flows (12)   The difference between the cash flows associated with an existing project and those associated with a new project.

Independent Cash Flows (14)   The successive cash flows over the life of an asset are not related in any systematic manner; instead, there is a random relationship among the cash flows so that what occurs in 1 year will have no bearing on the outcome in the following year.

Inflation (1)   A condition in which the general price level increases rapidly.

Information Content of Dividends Theory (19)   The theory that cash dividends have an impact on share prices because they communicate additional information to investors about the firm's future profitability.

Initial Investment (12)   All net cash outflows incurred to implement a new capital project.

Initial Public Offering (20)   The first time a company goes public with its common stock; when the shares are issued to the general investing public.

Interdependent Cash Flows (14)   Cash flows that are moderately, as opposed to perfectly, correlated over time; the results in 1 year do have an effect on the outcome in the following year, as described by a conditional probability distribution.

Interest Rate Futures Contract (11)   A commodities contract written on a large quantity of an underlying debt instrument—T-bills, 90-day commercial paper, bank CDs, and so forth.

Interest Rate Hedging (21)   Using interest rate futures to lock in a given cost of funds to the issuer.

Interest Rate Parity (2)   Theory that the forward exchange rate discount or premium between two currencies should be equal but opposite in sign to the difference in national interest rates between the two countries.

Internally Generated Funds (17)   That part of current cash flows not paid out in cash dividends, but rather retained for reinvestment in the business.

Internal Rate of Return (IRR) (12)   The marginal benefit of an action measured by the rate of return on investment. It is the discount rate which causes the NPV to equal zero by equating the present value of the expected cash inflows with the initial outlay at time $t = 0$.

International Fisher Effect (2)   Theory of international transactions which states that the expected change in the spot exchange rate should be equal but in the opposite direction to the differential interest rate between two countries.

Investment Bankers (20)   Firms who offer a variety of services, but whose main contribution to managerial finance is providing efficient, low-cost access to the capital markets.

Investment-Grade Bond (21)   A bond rated by a rating agency as of high quality; there is a high degree of assurance that the principal and interest obligations of the debt will be serviced in a prompt and timely fashion.

Investment Opportunities Schedule (IOS) (12)   A figure which shows the investments available to the firm in rank order and their initial outlay. The investments' internal rate of return is often calculated to show the expected return.

Investment Tax Credit (ITC) (2)   Tax credit allowed firms whenever they acquire certain types of depreciable capital assets; the ITC is applied directly to a firm's tax liability and reduces its taxes on a dollar-for-dollar basis.

Joint Venture (2)   A hybrid organizational form often used to conduct foreign operations or to undertake a project too big or complicated for any one firm; often takes the form of one corporation owned by two or more other corporations.

Last-In, First-Out (LIFO) (10)   Method used to account for inventory in which the costs of the most recently purchased items are assigned to the cost of goods sold.

Leasing (22)   An agreement in which a firm or individual agrees to make a series of payments to the party that owns an asset in exchange for its use; that is, the company or individual obtains the services of the leased asset, but not the title to it.

Least Common Life (13)   Capital budgeting decision technique for mutually exclusive projects with unequal lives; consists of equalizing the lives of the projects by repeating each project in order to find some time when both terminate in the same year.

Leveraged Buyout (15)   The purchase of a company or some of its assets with a large amount of debt and very little equity.

Leveraged Leasing (22)   A special form of leasing developed in conjunction with assets that require large capital outlays; involves three parties: the lessee, the lessor or equity participant, and the lender.

LIBOR (11)   International interest rate much like the prime rate in the United States; the London Interbank Offered Rate.

Line of Credit (11)   An agreement between a commercial bank and a business firm that states the amount of short-term borrowing the bank will make available to the firm over a given period of time. The firm may borrow and repay at will up to the specific amount during this period.

Loan Amortization Payments (5)   Equal periodic installment payments made over time to retire long-term loans, each of which provides the lender with a specified interest return on the unrepaid principal balance and partial recovery of the loan principal.

Lockbox System (9)   Technique used to reduce collection float by having payments mailed to a post office box that is emptied by a bank, which then deposits the funds in the firm's account; funds are wired from each lockbox bank to the firm's concentration bank.

Long-Range Financial Forecast (4)   An extension of the cash budget that deals with expected receipts and expenditures over a longer period in the future—usually 3 to 7 years.

Marginal Cost (17)   The cost of the last unit of an item.

Marginal Cost of Capital (MCC) (12)   The cost of obtaining the last dollar of new capital. It is calculated by multiplying the explicit costs of financing for the sources employed, times their market-value-determined weights given by the firm's (or division's) target capital structure.

Marginal Cost of Capital Schedule (17)   A graph or schedule relating the firm's marginal costs of capital to different dollar amounts of new financing.

Marginal Tax Rate (2)   Rate at which a firm's income above a certain amount is taxed. The marginal rates are 15, 18, 30, 40, and 46 percent.

Marginal Utility (6)   The additional utility an investor receives from a change in wealth; the increase or decrease in total utility for each one-unit change in wealth.

Marketable Securities (2)   Short-term money market instruments that have low default risk, short maturities, and (generally) high marketability.

Market Efficiency (7)   The degree to which stock prices reflect all available information, and investors cannot consistently "beat the market." In an efficient market, many rational investors have access to and react swiftly and in an unbiased fashion to new information; and the current market price is the best estimate of the value of a stock.

Market Price Exchange Ratio (15)   The number of shares of common stock the acquiring firm gives for each of the target firm's shares in a merger; determined by dividing the per share market price of the target firm by the per share market price of the acquiring firm.

Market Value (7)   The consensus price for a security based on the interaction of many buyers and sellers; the price at which transactions take place between marginally satisfied buyers and sellers.

Maximum Acquisition Price (MAP) (15)   A capital budgeting technique for analyzing a cash-financed merger in which the highest price the acquiring firm should pay is calculated.

$$\text{MAP} = \sum_{t=0}^{n} \frac{CFAT_t}{(1 + k)^t} - B_0$$

Merger (15)   The general process by which one firm acquires the assets and sometimes the liabilities of another firm.

Miller and Orr (M&O) Model (9)   A cash management model which assumes that net cash flows fluctuate in a random fashion rather than being certain and constant.

Modigliani-Miller (MM) Position (18)   The position that, in the absence of corporate taxes and with a perfectly efficient capital market, two identical companies—two sets of assets offering earnings before interest and taxes of the same size and quality—must have the same market value, regardless of differences in their capital structures.

Money Market (2)   Financial market in which short-term debt securities (with maturities of 1 year or less) are issued and traded; instruments include U.S. Treasury bills, negotiable certificates of deposit, commercial paper, and banker's acceptances.

Money Spread (Interest-Rate Arbitrage) (9)   An investment strategy used with money market securities; employed whenever the yield differential between two types of money market securities is abnormally wide. The strategy is to short-sell the lower-yielding security and use the proceeds to invest in the higher-yielding security.

Municipals—Industrial Development Bonds (IDB) and Pollution Control Bonds (PCB) (21)   A way of raising capital in the tax-exempt municipal market. Issued by industrial development or pollution control authorities created by cities, counties, and other municipalities. Issued as revenue bonds by a municipal authority for the benefit of a specific company, which uses the funds to build or acquire various types of fixed assets.

Mutually Exclusive Projects (12)   Two or more capital budgeting projects that are perfect substitutes for one another. Acceptance of one precludes the need for the other(s).

Negotiated Sale (20)   A contractual arrangement between an underwriter and the issuing firm whereby the underwriter is given the exclusive right to design, underwrite, and distribute the new security.

Net Advantage to Merging (NAM) (15)   A capital budgeting technique for analysis of a merger opportunity financed with stock rather than cash. It involves comparing the acquiring firm's percentage ownership of the combined firm with the value of the acquiring firm in the absence of the merger.

$$NAM = S_c \ (OP) - S_x$$

Net Lease (22)   *See Direct Lease.*

Net Present Value (NPV) (13)   A capital budgeting selection technique calculated as the present value of the cash inflows discounted at the firm's marginal cost of capital (or some appropriate risk-adjusted discount rate) minus the initial investment. The selection criterion is to accept a project if NPV is greater than or equal to zero; if not, reject.

Net Present Value Profile (13)   Graphic comparison of projects that depict the net present value for the project at various discount rates.

Netting (8)   Technique that allows a firm to net payments between related affiliates which eliminates cash flows and thereby greatly reduces transaction costs by avoiding the foreign exchange market.

Net Working Capital (8)   The difference between a firm's current assets and its current liabilities.

Nondiversifiable Risk (6)   Risk that stems from factors such as inflation, recessions, and interest rates that influence all returns and cannot be eliminated in a diversified portfolio. These factors tend to affect rates of return on all firms simultaneously. Also called *market* or *systematic risk*. Measured by beta.

Nonspontaneous Financing (11)   Short-term financing obtained through direct negotiations with banks and other financial institutions. Unsecured bank loans, secured loans, factoring accounts receivable, commercial paper, and Eurodollar loans are examples of nonspontaneous financing vehicles.

Open-End Mortgage Clause (21)   A provision that permits the issuance of additional bonds under the same mortgage contract; provides the issuer with financing flexibility while protecting creditors by placing restrictions on the amount of additional borrowing that can occur.

Operating Cash Flow (12)   The net cash flow, resulting from cash inflows, cash outflows, depreciation, and taxes, that are expected to occur each year of the project from year 1 to its termination.

Operating Economies (15)   Economies that may result from merging—eliminating or consolidating duplicate production, marketing, financial, and personnel facilities. Most obvious in cases of horizontal integration, but may also be achieved through vertical integration.

Operating Lease (22)   A short-term contractual arrangement whereby the lessee agrees to make periodic payments to the lessor to obtain the use of an asset; also known as a service lease because it provides for the servicing as well as the financing of a leased asset.

Operating Leverage (3)   The use of fixed costs in a firm's cost structure that leads to magnified profits from a given increase in revenue.

Opportunity Cost (5)   The cost of using money for one purpose rather than another; the return foregone by choosing one investment alternative over another.

Option Contract (23)   A negotiable security that gives the holder the right to buy or sell a certain number of securities at a specified price for a specified period of time, normally 9 months or less.

Organized Security Exchanges (2)   Organizations in whose physical premises securities are traded. The key exchanges are the New York Stock Exchange (NYSE) and the American Stock Exchange (AMEX).

Original Issue Discount (and Zero Coupon) Bonds (21)   Deep discount bonds that are issued with very low (or zero) coupons; as a result, they are sold at a price well below par value, even though they are redeemable at maturity at full face value.

Original Purchase Price (2)   Price at which a capital asset later sold by a firm was purchased; used to compute capital gain or loss.

Overdraft System (9)   System in which a bank will automatically lend the firm enough money to cover the amount of an overdraft if the firm's checking account balance is insufficient to cover all checks presented against the account.

Over-the-Counter (OTC) Market (2)   A nationwide network of brokers and dealers who execute transactions in securities that are not listed on one of the organized exchanges; active traders are linked by a telecommunications network, and an automated system provides up-to-date bid and ask prices on several thousand securities.

Par Value (20)   Except for accounting purposes, a relatively useless value placed on the company's stock by a corporation; usually set quite low, since in some states a firm's owners can be held liable for an amount equal to the difference between the par value and the price initially paid for the stock if the price is less than the par value.

Participation Provision (21)   A provision that enables preferred stockholders to enjoy additional cash dividends if payouts to common stockholders exceed a certain amount.

Partnership (2)   Form of business organization consisting of two or more people doing business together, commonly in a service-oriented business such as finance, insurance, or real estate.

Payable-Through Draft (9)   An instrument that is not payable on demand; approval of the issuer is required before the bank will pay the draft. A way of playing the float.

Payback Period (13)   Amount of time, usually given in years, required to recover the initial investment in a capital budgeting project; the length of time it takes for an investment to pay for itself.

Payment Date (19)   The date on which cash dividend checks are actually mailed to shareholders; the completion of the dividend distribution process.

Perpetual Bond (7)   A bond that pays a stated amount of interest periodically (annually or semiannually) over an infinite time horizon; a bond whose par value is never repaid.

Perpetual Warrant (23)   A warrant that has no expiration date.

Perpetuity (5)   An infinite-lived annuity; an annuity that never stops providing its holder with a specified number of dollars per period.

Playing the Float (9)   A way of consciously anticipating the resulting float associated with the payment process; used by firms to stretch out accounts payable.

Pledge of Accounts Receivable (11)   A way of obtaining short-term financing through accounts receivable; creates a secured short-term loan.

Portfolio (6)   A combination or group of assets.

Portfolio Theory (6)   Theory of why investors diversify based on the assumption that all relevant information can be obtained by considering two parameters of distributions: the mean or expected value, and the variance or standard deviation. Also called *Markowitz portfolio theory, two-parameter portfolio theory* and *mean-variance portfolio theory.*

Postimplementation Audit (12)   The final step of the capital budgeting process in which a comparison is made of the actual results of the project and the estimated results; often done after some time has passed, such as 2 or 3 years.

Preauthorized Check (PAC) (9)   A check written for an agreed-upon amount by the firm and drawn on a given customer's checking account at a scheduled future date.

Preferred Dividend Roll (9)   An investment strategy in which the firm actively trades in and out of preferred stocks to collect as many as 8 to 12 cash dividends a year rather than investing in preferreds for the long term. By doing so, they take maximum advantage of the 85 percent tax exemption on cash dividends received from other domestic corporations.

Present Value (5)   The value today of a dollar that will be received at a future date, discounted at some specified discount rate, *k*.

Price Pegging (20)   An activity whereby an underwriter attempts to stabilize the market price of a new security, once it has been offered for sale to the public, so that the entire issue can be sold at the initial reoffering price.

Primary Market (2)   Market in which financial assets are originally sold, with the proceeds going to the issuing firm (or governmental unit).

Private Placement (20)   Placement of a new security issue directly with a single or small group of institutional investors.

Privileged Subscription (20)   An offering of a new stock issue that is offered first to existing stockholders; each stockholder is issued one right for each share of stock held, and the rights enable the stockholder to buy a certain number of the new shares at a stipulated subscription price. Also known as a *rights offering.*

Probability (4)   The chance, or odds, of a single event occurring.

Probability Distribution (4)   A complete description of the possible outcomes of an event and their associated probabilities. The sum of the probabilities is 1.00.

Profit Plan (4)   Forecasted (pro forma) income statements that summarize revenues and costs and reflect the potential impact of cash budgets and long-range financial forecasts on operating results; prepared over both short- and long-term budget horizons.

Profitability Index (PI) (13)   A relative capital budgeting selection measure that shows the present value of cash flows per dollar invested; also called the *benefit-cost ratio*.

Pro Forma Balance Sheet (4)   Forecasted balance sheet that demonstrates the potential effects of budgets and forecasts on the company's asset and financing mix; provides an indication of the resource requirements and financing needs that can be expected at various levels of operations.

Purchase Syndicate (20)   Group formed by two or more investment banking firms for the purpose of underwriting a new issue that would be too much of a risk for any single underwriter to carry; each underwriter in the syndicate is given the responsibility for a portion of the issue, and generally the originating house retains the major position and distributes the remainder among the other members of the syndicate.

Put (23)   An option that gives the holder the right to sell a stipulated number of securities at a stipulated price for a set period of time.

Range (6)   Measure of risk; the difference between the highest and the lowest outcomes.

Ratio Analysis (3)   Study of the relationships that exist among and between various financial accounts at a given point in time and over time.

Realized Return (7)   A return that could have been received by an investor who actually owned the given security during the time period in question.

Receivables Portfolio (10)   A firm's investment in or collection of accounts receivable, each possessing certain risk-return characteristics.

Regular Dividend Policy (19)   Policy of maintaining a fixed annual cash dividend rate for several years in a row and increasing it only when future earnings look sufficiently strong to support a new, higher level of dividends.

Replacement Project (12)   Capital budgeting category where existing equipment is replaced by new equipment due to technical or physical obsolescence. The cash flow stream employed for decision making is typically the incremental (new minus existing) set of cash flows resulting from the replacement.

Required Return (7)   The minimum return an investor would like to receive from an investment; it depends on the level of risk involved and the investor's general disposition toward risk.

Residual Theory of Dividends (19)   A theory which states that only "surplus" funds should be distributed to shareholders after all capital needs have been taken care of; considers cash dividends to be a passive residual and, as such, irrelevant to firm valuation.

Responsibility Center (12)   Subunit within a firm, such as a division or some part of a division, for which accounting profits and costs are broken out so individuals can judge, and be held accountable for, how well they are performing.

Return (6)   The realizable cash flow on an investment earned on behalf of its owner during a specified period of time.

$$\text{Calculated as } (P_t - P_{t-1} + D_t)/P_{t-1}$$

Riding the Yield Curve (9)   An investment strategy that involves taking advantage of yield spreads that exist because of maturity differences; results in substantially increased exposure to risk.

Right (20)   An option to buy a certain number of new shares at a stipulated subscription price.

Rights Offering (20)   *See Privileged Subscription.*

Risk (6)   Situation where we know or can estimate, based on historical data, the probabilities associated with various possible outcomes.

Sale-Leaseback (22)   An arrangement under which a firm owning land, buildings, or equipment will sell the property or equipment to a lessor and simultaneously execute an agreement to lease the property or equipment back for a specific period of time under specific terms; the company that used to own the asset becomes the lessee.

Sales Forecast (4)   Provides a projected level of sales revenues that are expected to be generated over a given period of time in the future; plays an important role in defining levels of production and operating needs.

Seasonal Dating (11)   A technique used by suppliers in seasonal businesses that provides longer credit periods than would normally be extended; the supplier ships goods to the purchaser in advance of the selling season, but does not require payment until after the actual demand for the item is expected.

Secondary Distribution (2)   Financial market transaction involving the sale and redistribution of a large block of stock sometime after it was originally sold by the issuing firm. Except for gaining wider access to capital markets, the firm itself receives no direct benefit from such a sale because total net proceeds go to the original owners as the sellers.

Secondary Market (2)   Financial market in which outstanding securities are traded between individuals and/or institutions.

Second Mortgage Bonds (21)   A bond that gives holders a secondary claim on assets already secured by a first mortgage; because of their less secure position, they normally carry a higher interest rate than first mortgage bonds.

Security Agreements (11)   A way of arranging secured financing in which documents specify the property being pledged and provide the lender with an enforceable claim on the collateral; the documents also specify the other conditions of the loan.

Security Analysis (3)   Deals with the long-term profitability and suitability of equity investments; involves the use of financial analysis to assess the potential risk and return from common stock investments.

Security Market Line (SML) (6)   A graphic version of the CAPM that shows the required returns associated with various degrees of nondiversifiable risk as measured by beta. The slope of the SML reflects the extent to which investors are averse to risk; the steeper the slope, the greater the risk aversion.

Self-Liquidating Loan (11)   Loans made by banks to provide the firm with sufficient financing to meet seasonal needs; it is expected that as receivables and inventories are worked down and converted into cash, the funds needed to retire the loans will automatically be generated.

Selling Group (20)   Group of investment bankers formed to expedite the marketing and distribution of a new issue; may be made up of as many as 40 to 50 investment banking firms, or more.

Sensitivity Analysis (14)   A procedure used to evaluate project profitability by providing information regarding the responsiveness of capital budgeting results to various estimation errors.

Shelf Registration (20)   SEC procedure that allows companies offering securities to file a single document summarizing their total long-term financing plans over a period of up to 2 years; so long as it does not exceed the total amount shown on the shelf registration, the company can enter the market with a new issue at any point during that period without delay, additional paperwork, or the services of an investment banker.

Signature Loan (11)   Unsecured bank loan backed by the full faith and credit of the borrowing firm; often guarantees from the owners will be obtained, especially with smaller firms.

Simple Interest (11)   Commonly used way of calculating interest in which the amount of interest charged is based on the actual amount outstanding on a day-to-day basis. Calculated as the principal times the interest rate times the portion of the year funds are borrowed for.

Single-Payment Note (11)   A loan made when a borrower needs funds for a short period of time, but does not believe the need will recur; one payment, which includes principal and interest, is made at the end of the loan period.

Sinking Fund Provision (21)   Provision that specifies the systematic retirement of the principal amount of a bond over time; can be done by making a cash payment to a trustee that in turn calls the required number of bonds by lot, or by purchasing the required amount of bonds in the open market and delivering them to the trustee.

Sole Proprietorship (2)   A small firm owned by one person; usually operating in the wholesale, retail, or service industry.

Speculative Issue (21)   Rating assigned to bonds that denotes only moderate protection of principal and interest payments during both good and bad times; issues that generally lack the characteristics of other desirable investments.

Spontaneous Financing (11)   Short-term financing that results from the normal operations of the business; accounts payable and accruals are the two major sources.

Spot Transaction (2)   Foreign exchange transaction in which the buyer takes possession of the foreign currency at once.

Standard Deviation (6)   Measure of the average deviation about the expected value or mean. Calculated by taking the square root of the sum of the squared deviations from the mean weighted by their probabilities of each outcome occurring.

Standby Agreement (20)   A method of guaranteeing the success of a rights offering or privileged subscription whereby the investment banker agrees to "stand by" to underwrite the unsold portion of the issue—to guarantee to purchase the unsold portion at a predetermined subscription price.

Stock Dividend (20)   A disbursement of additional shares of stock to the firm's shareholders.

Stone Model (9)   A cash management model that provides flexible control limits which can be adjusted as experience requires; smooths out the transactions associated with cash management by recognizing not only the current status of the firm's cash balance, but also the existence of fairly accurate near-term cash balance forecasts.

Stretching Payables (11)   Delaying the payment of accounts payable beyond their due date. Results in a lower explicit cost for trade credit.

Subordinated Debentures (21)   An unsecured bond whose claim on income and assets is ranked behind all other types of unsecured debt.

Synergism (15)   Anticipated benefits of economies of scale or operating economies; the merged firm has a value greater than the sum of its parts. Often called the $2 + 2 = 5$ effect.

Target Capital Structure (18)   The appropriate capital structure (mixture of debt and equity) for an individual firm that maximizes the value of the firm while minimizing its cost of capital.

Technical Insolvency (8)   A situation in which a firm is unable to pay its liabilities as they come due, even though its assets exceed its liabilities.

Tender Offer (15)   An offer to purchase shares of stock of the target firm from any shareholder who elects to "tender" or sell shares; often set at a minimum of 20 percent above the existing premerger price as an incentive to stockholders of the target firm.

Terminal Value (12)   Cash flows associated with a project when it reaches the end of its economic life at t_n.

Term Loan (17)   Intermediate (3- to 10-year) borrowing arrangements usually negotiated directly between the borrowing firm and a financial institution, normally a bank, insurance company, or pension fund; usually amortized so that equal dollar payments are made over the life of the loan.

Total Risk (6)   The sum of the diversifiable and nondiversifiable risk; measured by the standard deviation.

Trade Credit (11)   A form of spontaneous financing that arises when a firm purchases goods or services from other firms on credit.

Trading Flat (21)   Bonds in arrears with regard to interest payments, or in outright default.

Transaction Exposure (8)   Foreign exchange risk to which a firm is exposed when it must settle outstanding claims or obligations that are denominated in a foreign currency.

Transfer Pricing (8)   Pricing system for goods or services purchased from or sold to related affiliates.

Translation Exposure (8)   Foreign exchange risk to which a firm is subject when some of its assets, liabilities, revenues, or expenses are originally denominated in a foreign currency, and an exchange rate must be chosen to "translate" from the foreign currency to a U.S. dollar equivalent for consolidation into the U.S. parent firm's financial statements.

Treasury Stock (20)　A company's own stock that has been issued and subsequently reacquired, but not yet formally retired.

Trustee (21)　An individual or institution representing the interest of the bondholders.

Unbundling Transfers (8)　Technique to minimize political risk by structuring relationships with foreign affiliates so that repatriation of funds to the parent need not be only in the form of cash dividends.

Uncertainty (6)　Exists where we do not know the probabilities and for which no historical data are available to estimate a probability distribution.

Underwriter Spread (20)　A cost of issuing securities that represents the compensation to investment bankers for services rendered.

Underwritten Issue (20)　A new security issue that is sold in its entirety (by the issuing corporation) to an investment banker or syndicate, which then accepts the risk of having to resell the securities to the public.

Util (6)　The unit of measure for utility.

Utility (6)　A measure of psychic gain or pleasure.

Valuation (7)　The process used to determine the worth or value of an asset; based on the expected future cash flows it will provide over its life and the risks involved.

Variable Rate Notes (21)　Notes that do *not* have fixed coupons; rather, the coupon "floats" so that every 6 months it is reset at, or a certain amount above, a stipulated money or capital market rate.

Warehouse Receipt Loan (11)　A form of inventory financing whereby the lender actually receives control of the pledged collateral. The lender selects the inventory that is acceptable for collateral and hires a warehousing company to take possession. It issues a warehouse receipt which, when forwarded to the bank, causes the bank to advance a specified percentage of the collateral value to the borrower and file a lien on all items listed on the receipt.

Warrant (23)　An option issued by a corporation that enables investors to buy a specified number of shares of the company's stock at a stated price during some designated time period (warrants can occasionally be used to purchase preferred stock or even bonds). Warrants have no voting rights and pay no cash dividends or interest; they offer no claim on the assets or income of the company.

Wire Transfers (9)　Telegraphic communications that, via bookkeeping entries, remove funds from the payor bank and deposit them in an account of the payee bank; a mobilization technique for moving funds into key disbursing accounts.

Yield Curve (9)　Graphic representation of the comparison of the yield to maturity for similar-risk securities having different terms to maturity.

Yield to Maturity (YTM) (7)　The rate investors earn if they buy a bond at a specific price and hold it until maturity; the basis on which bonds generally trade.

Zero-Balance Account (9)　A checking account in which a zero balance is maintained. Each day the firm totals the amount of the checks presented against the account and transfers (from its master account) exactly that amount into the account, reestablishing the final balance at zero.

INDEX